Glencoe

Algebra 1

Integration
Applications
Connections

Solutions Manual

GLENCOE
McGraw-Hill
New York, New York   Columbus, Ohio   Woodland Hills, California   Peoria, Illinois

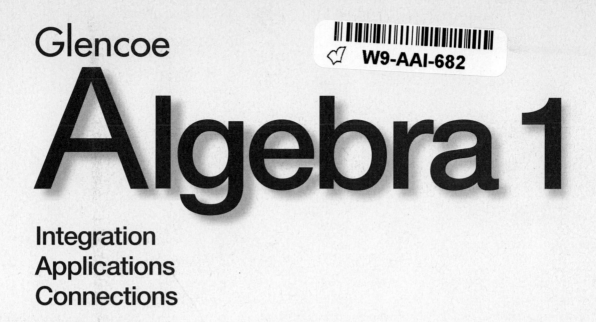

Glencoe/McGraw-Hill
A Division of The ***McGraw-Hill*** *Companies*

Send all inquiries to:
Glencoe/McGraw-Hill
936 Eastwind Drive
Westerville, OH 43081-3374

Algebra I
Solutions Manual

ISBN: 0-02-824869-4

3 4 5 6 7 8 9 10 066 03 02 01 00 99 98

Contents

Chapter 1 Exploring Expressions, Equations, and Functions

1-1 Variables and Expressions

Page 9 Check for Understanding

1. Multiply 15 times 20.
2. Yes; evaluate s^3 where s is the measure of a side.
3. x is used as a factor 7 times
4. Algebraic expressions include variables.
5. Tonya; Sample explanation: The square of any number between 0 and 1 is less than the number; $0.5^2 = 0.25$ and $0.5 > 0.25$.
6. $a^4 \cdot b^2$ **7.** $3y^2 - 6$ **8.** 7 to the fifth power
9. 3 times x squared increased by 4
10. 4^3 **11.** a^7 **12.** $6^2 = 6 \cdot 6 = 36$
13. $2^5 = 2 \cdot 2 \cdot 2 \cdot 2 \cdot 2 = 32$ **14.** πr^2

Pages 9–11 Exercises

15. $k + 20$ **16.** $16p$ **17.** a^7 **18.** $49 + 2x$
19. $\frac{2x^2}{3}$ or $\frac{2}{3}x^2$ **20.** $5m + \frac{n}{2}$ or $5m + \frac{1}{2}n$
21. $b + 8$ **22.** $3w$
23. 4 times m to the fifth power
24. x squared divided by 2
25. c squared plus 23
26. one half the cube of n
27. 2 times 4 times 5 squared
28. 3 times x squared minus 2 times x
29. 8^2 **30.** 10^5 **31.** 4^7 **32.** t^3
33. z^5 **34.** d^{10} **35.** $7^2 = 7 \cdot 7 = 49$
36. $9^2 = 9 \cdot 9 = 81$ **37.** $4^3 = 4 \cdot 4 \cdot 4 = 64$
38. $5^3 = 5 \cdot 5 \cdot 5 = 125$ **39.** $2^4 = 2 \cdot 2 \cdot 2 \cdot 2 = 16$
40. $3^5 = 3 \cdot 3 \cdot 3 \cdot 3 \cdot 3 = 243$
41. $3(55 - w^3)$ **42.** $4(r + s) + 2(r - s)$
43. $a + b + \frac{a}{b}$ **44.** $4s$
45. $y + 10x$ **46.** 5^3; $5 \cdot 5 \cdot 5 = 125$ cubes
47. $4^2 = 4 \cdot 4 = 16$; $24 = 2 \cdot 2 \cdot 2 \cdot 2 = 16$
47a. They are equal; no; no.
47b. no; for example, $2^3 \neq 3^2$
48a. $7x$ **48b.** $3x$ **48c.** $7x - 3x$
49a. $3.5x$ **49b.** $3.5y$ **49c.** $3.5x + 3.5y$
50. $2\ell w + 2\ell h + 2wh$

Page 11 Mathematics and Society

1. See students' work.
2. See students' work.
3. See students' work.

1-2 Patterns and Sequences

Pages 15–16 Check for Understanding

1. When the problem is difficult, you can solve simpler problems and look for a pattern that could help you solve the more difficult problem.
2. Sample answer: 7, 12, 17, 22
3. Either person could be right. You would need to know the fourth term to decide which pattern is correct.

4a. 50 + 2 or 52 pieces **4b.** $y + 2$
5.

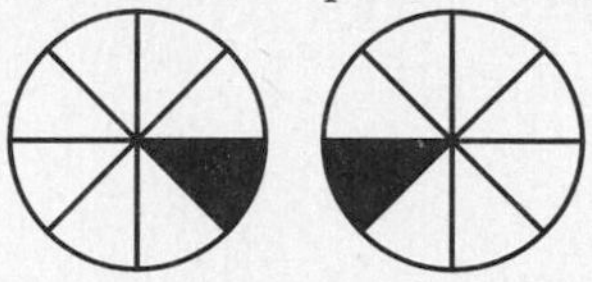

6. $58 - 9 = 49$, $49 - 9 = 40$
7. $(4+1)x + 1 = 5x + 1$, $(5+1)x + 1 = 6x + 1$
8a. 3 units; 4 units; 5 units; 6 units
8b.

5 + 2 or 7 units

8c. 12 units **8d.** $n + 2$ units
9a.

4^1	4^2	4^3	4^4	4^5
4	16	64	256	1024

9b. 6; $4^6 = 4 \cdot 4 \cdot 4 \cdot 4 \cdot 4 \cdot 4 = 4096$
9c. 4; When the exponent is odd, 4 is in the ones place.

Pages 16–18 Exercises

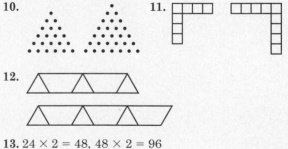

10.

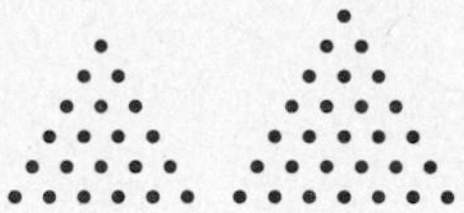

11.

12.

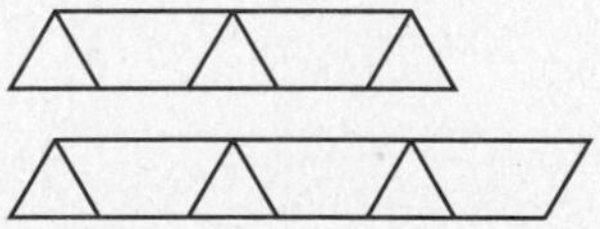

13. $24 \times 2 = 48$, $48 \times 2 = 96$
14. $8.5 + 1.5 = 10$, $10 + 1.5 = 11.5$
15. $5^2 = 25$, $6^2 = 36$
16. $12 - 2 = 10$, $10 + 3 = 13$
17. $a + 7$, $a + 9$ **18.** $x - 4y$, $x - 5y$
19a.

19b. White; even-numbered figures are white.

19c. 12 sides; the shapes come in pairs. Since $19 \div 2 = 9.5$, the 19th figure will be part of the 10th pair. The 10th pair will have 10 + 2 or 12 sides.

20a.

3^1	3^2	3^3	3^4	3^5	3^6
3	9	27	81	243	729

20b. 3, 9, 7, 1, 3, 9, . . . **20c.** 7, 1, 3, 9, 7, 1

20d. 1; 100 is divisible by 4. According to the pattern, all powers with exponents divisible by 4 have 1 in the ones place.

21a. $1 = 1$
$1 + 3 = 4$
$1 + 3 + 5 = 9$
$1 + 3 + 5 + 7 = 16$
$1 + 3 + 5 + 7 + 9 = 25$

21b. The sums are perfect square numbers; that is $1^2, 2^2, 3^2, 4^2, 5^2, \ldots$.

21c. $100^2 = 100 \cdot 100 = 10{,}000$ **21d.** x^2

22a. Replace y with 2 and find $2 \cdot 2$.

22b. 2, 4, 6, 8, 10, 12, 14, 16, 18, 20

22c. even numbers

23a. **i.** 1,999,998 **ii.** 2,999,997 **iii.** 3,999,996 **iv.** 4,999,995

23b. 8,999,991

24a.

10^1	10^2	10^3	10^4	10^5
10	100	1000	10,000	100,000

24b. $10^0 = 1$

25. $3(1) + 1 = 3 + 1 = 4$
$3(2) + 1 = 6 + 1 = 7$
$3(3) + 1 = 9 + 1 = 10$
$3(4) + 1 = 12 + 1 = 13$
$3(5) + 1 = 15 + 1 = 16$
4, 7, 10, 13, 16

26. $5 + 8 = 13$, $8 + 13 = 21$
$13 + 21 = 34$, $21 + 34 = 55$
$34 + 55 = 89$, $55 + 89 = 144$
13, 21, 34, 55, 89, 144

27. The bus departs every 48 minutes, starting at 8:25 A.M.
10:49 + 0:48 = 11:37 A.M.
11:37 + 0:48 = 12:25 P.M.
12:25 + 0:48 = 1:13 P.M.
The earliest Olga can catch the bus is 1:13 P.M.

28a. $5 \cdot 6 = 30$ cans

28b. $6 + 12 + 20 + 30 + 42 + 56 + 72 + 90 = 328$ cans

29a. $3 + 6 + 9 + 12 + 15 + 18 + 21 + 16 = 100$ cards

29b–d. See students' work.

30. $q^2 - 8$ **31.** x cubed divided by 9 **32.** m^9

33. 4^3; $4^3 = 4 \cdot 4 \cdot 4 = 64$ cubes

34. $20{,}000 + 2(12)(x) = 20{,}000 + 24x$

35. $x + \frac{1}{11}x$

1-3 Order of Operations

Page 22 Check for Understanding

1. Multiply 7 and 2.
2. parentheses, brackets, braces, fraction bar; to show what operation should be completed first
3. First, divide 30 by 6, which equals 5. Second, add 5 and 5, which equals 10. Third, square 10, which equals 100. Fourth, multiply 100 times 2, which equals 200.
4. $15 + 3 \cdot 2 = 15 + 6$
$= 21$
5. $5^3 + 3(4^2) = 5^3 + 3(16)$
$= 125 + 3(16)$
$= 125 + 48$
$= 173$
6. $\frac{38 - 12}{2 \cdot 13} = (38 - 12) \div (2 \cdot 13)$
$= 26 \div 26$
$= 1$
7. $12 \div 3 \cdot 5 - 4^2 = 12 \div 3 \cdot 5 - 16$
$= 4 \cdot 5 - 16$
$= 20 - 16$
$= 4$
8. $wx - yz = 12 \cdot 5 - 6 \cdot 4$
$= 60 - 24$
$= 36$
9. $2w + x^2 - yz = 2 \cdot 12 + 5^2 - 6 \cdot 4$
$= 2 \cdot 12 + 25 - 6 \cdot 4$
$= 24 + 25 - 24$
$= 49 - 24$
$= 25$
10. Sample answer: $xz - \frac{w}{y}$
11. $a^2 - a = 1.5^2 - 1.5 = 2.25 - 1.5 = 0.75$; $a^2 - a$ is less
12. $A = l \cdot w$
$= (2t + 1)(t)$
$= (2 \cdot 6 + 1)(6)$
$= (12 + 1)(6)$
$= 13(6)$
$= 78 \text{ in}^2$

Pages 22–24 Exercises

13. $3 + 2 \cdot 3 + 5 = 3 + 6 + 5$
$= 14$
14. $(4 + 5)7 = (9)7$
$= 63$
15. $29 - 3(9 - 4) = 29 - 3(5)$
$= 29 - 15$
$= 14$
16. $50 - (15 + 9) = 50 - 24$
$= 26$
17. $15 \div 3 \cdot 5 - 4^2 = 15 \div 3 \cdot 5 - 16$
$= 5 \cdot 5 - 16$
$= 25 - 16$
$= 9$

18. $$\begin{aligned} 4(11 + 7) - 9 \cdot 8 &= 4(18) - 9 \cdot 8 \\ &= 72 - 72 \\ &= 0 \end{aligned}$$

19. $$\begin{aligned} \frac{(4 + 3)^2 \cdot 5}{(9 + 3)} &= [(4 \cdot 3)^2 \cdot 5] \div (9 + 3) \\ &= (12^2 \cdot 5) \div 12 \\ &= (144 \cdot 5) \div 12 \\ &= 720 \div 12 \\ &= 60 \end{aligned}$$

20. $$\begin{aligned} [7(2) - 4] + [9 + 8\,(4)] &= (14 - 4) + (9 + 32) \\ &= 10 + 41 \\ &= 51 \end{aligned}$$

21. $$\begin{aligned} \frac{6 + 4^2}{3^2(4)} &= (6 + 4^2) \div [3^2\,(4)] \\ &= (6 + 16) \div [9(4)] \\ &= (22) \div 36 \\ &= \frac{22}{36} \\ &= \frac{11}{18} \end{aligned}$$

22. $$\begin{aligned} (5 - 1)^3 + (11 - 2)^2 + (7 - 4)^3 &= 4^3 + 9^2 + 3^3 \\ &= 64 + 81 + 27 \\ &= 172 \end{aligned}$$

23. $$\begin{aligned} \frac{2 \cdot 8^2 - 2^2 \cdot 8}{2 \cdot 8} &= (2 \cdot 8^2 - 2^2 \cdot 8) \div (2 \cdot 8) \\ &= (2 \cdot 64 - 4 \cdot 8) \div 16 \\ &= (128 - 32) \div 16 \\ &= 96 \div 16 \\ &= 6 \end{aligned}$$

24. $$\begin{aligned} 7(0.2 + 0.5) - 0.6 &= 7(0.7) - 0.6 \\ &= 4.9 - 0.6 \\ &= 4.3 \end{aligned}$$

25. $$\begin{aligned} (v + 1)(v^2 - v + 1) &= (5 + 1)(5^2 - 5 + 1) \\ &= 6(25 - 5 + 1) \\ &= 6(20 + 1) \\ &= 6(21) \\ &= 126 \end{aligned}$$

26. $$\begin{aligned} \frac{x^2 - x + 6}{x + 3} &= \frac{3^2 - 3 + 6}{3 + 3} \\ &= (3^2 - 3 + 6) \div (3 + 3) \\ &= (9 - 3 + 6) \div 6 \\ &= (6 + 6) \div 6 \\ &= 12 \div 6 \\ &= 2 \end{aligned}$$

27. $$\begin{aligned} [a + 7(b - 3)]^2 \div 3 &= [7 + 7(5 - 3)]^2 \div 3 \\ &= [7 + 7(2)]^2 \div 3 \\ &= (7 + 14)^2 \div 3 \\ &= (21)^2 \div 3 \\ &= 441 \div 3 \\ &= 147 \end{aligned}$$

28. $$\begin{aligned} v^2 - (x^3 - 4b) &= 5^2 - (3^3 - 4 \cdot 5) \\ &= 5^2 - (27 - 4 \cdot 5) \\ &= 5^2 - (27 - 20) \\ &= 5^2 - 7 \\ &= 25 - 7 \\ &= 18 \end{aligned}$$

29. $$\begin{aligned} (2v)^2 + ab - 3x &= (2 \cdot 5)^2 + 7 \cdot 5 - 3 \cdot 3 \\ &= 10^2 + 7 \cdot 5 - 3 \cdot 3 \\ &= 100 + 7 \cdot 5 - 3 \cdot 3 \\ &= 100 + 35 - 9 \\ &= 135 - 9 \\ &= 126 \end{aligned}$$

30. $$\begin{aligned} \frac{a^2 - b^2}{v^3} &= \frac{7^2 - 5^2}{5^3} \\ &= (7^2 - 5^2) \div (5^3) \\ &= (49 - 25) \div 125 \\ &= 24 \div 125 \\ &= \frac{24}{125} \end{aligned}$$

31. $$\begin{aligned} r^2 + 3s &= 2^2 + 3 \cdot 5 \\ &= 4 + 3 \cdot 5 \\ &= 4 + 15 \\ &= 19 \end{aligned}$$

32. $$\begin{aligned} t(4s + r) &= \tfrac{1}{2}(4 \cdot 5 + 2) \\ &= \tfrac{1}{2}(20 + 2) \\ &= \tfrac{1}{2}(22) \\ &= 11 \end{aligned}$$

33. $$\begin{aligned} (r + s)t^2 &= (2 + 5)\left(\frac{1}{2}\right)^2 \\ &= (7)\left(\frac{1}{2}\right)^2 \\ &= 7\left(\frac{1}{4}\right) \\ &= \frac{7}{4} \end{aligned}$$

34. $$\begin{aligned} r^5 - t &= 2^5 - \tfrac{1}{2} \\ &= 32 - \tfrac{1}{2} \\ &= 31\tfrac{1}{2} \end{aligned}$$

35. $$\begin{aligned} P = a + b + c &= 5 + 6 + 8.5 \\ &= 19.5 \text{ mm} \end{aligned}$$

36. $$\begin{aligned} P = 4c &= 4(8.5) \\ &= 34 \text{ yd} \end{aligned}$$

37. $$\begin{aligned} P = 2(a + b) &= 2(5 + 6) \\ &= 2\,(11) \\ &= 22 \text{ in.} \end{aligned}$$

38. Enter: 5 [X] 2 4 [+] 3 [ENTER] 83

39. Enter: [(] [(] 5 [X] 7 [)] [^] 2 [+] 5 [)] [÷] [(] 9 [X] 3 [^] 2 [−] 7 [)] [ENTER]

16.62162162 or about 16.62

40. Enter: 4.79 [X] .05 [^] 2 [+] .375 [X] 6.34 [^] 3 [ENTER] 95.577014 or about 95.58

41. Enter: 1.35 [STO▸] [X,T,θ] [2nd] [:] 1 [−] 2 [X] [X,T,θ] [+] 3 [X] [X,T,θ] [^] 2 [ENTER]

3.7675 or about 3.77

42a.

x	$\frac{1}{2}$	1	10	50	100
$\frac{2x - 1}{2x}$	0	$\frac{1}{2}$	$\frac{19}{20}$	$\frac{99}{100}$	$\frac{199}{200}$

42b. As the value of x gets larger, the value of the expression approaches 1.

42c. 1

43a. Sample answer: $(4 - 2)5 \div (3 + 2)$

43b. $4 \times 2 \times 5 \times 3 \times 2$

44a. $30(3) + 25(4) + 65(3)$

44b. $90 + 100 + 195 = \$385$

45a. $\frac{1}{3}Bh$

45b. $V = \frac{1}{3}Bh$

$= \frac{1}{3}(4050)(147) = 1350(147)$

$= 198{,}450 \text{ m}^3$

46. $16 \times 2 = 32,\ 32 \times 2 = 64$

47. $12.5 + 3.5 = 16,\ 16 + 3.5 = 19.5$

48. $a^5b^4c^3d^2e,\ a^6b^5c^4d^3e^2f$

49. $525 - 357 = 168$; after 18 days she will have \$171; June 18.

50. h^5 **51.** $t + 3$ **52.** $11^2 = 11 \cdot 11 = 121$

53. 9 more than two times y

1-4 Integration: Statistics Stem-and-Leaf Plots

Pages 28–29 Check for Understanding

1. Answers will vary. Responses should include least and greatest values, frequency in categories, distribution, clusters, and gaps.
2. not beginning an axis at 0, not using uniform spacing on scales, not indicating that the scale does not begin at 0 with a broken line
3. Step 1: Decide on stems.
   Step 2: Place stems and leaves on a chart.
   Step 3: Arrange leaves in numerical order.
4. Sample answer: I can use stem-and-leaf plots to keep a record of my math test scores. From this plot, I can determine my lowest and highest scores. I can also determine the interval where most of my scores fall.
5. stem 12, leaf 2
6. stem 6, leaf 3
7. stem 126, leaf 9
8. 0, 1, 2, 3, 4, 5

9a. 35 tickets sold one day

9b. 31 tickets **9c.** 75 tickets

9d. $31 + 33 + 35 + 45 + 45 + 46 + 47 + 50 + 50 + 51 + 51 + 52 + 53 + 53 + 63 + 64 + 64 + 64 + 71 + 75 = 1043$ tickets

10a.

Stem	Leaf
2	6 6 7 8 9 9
3	0 0 1 1 2 2 3 4 5 6
4	0 1 2 3
5	2 4 6

4|3 = 43

10b. 26 floors **10c.** 56 floors

10d. 9 buildings **10e.** 6 buildings

Pages 29–31 Exercises

11. stem 13, leaf 3
12. stem 4, leaf 5
13. stem 44, leaf 3
14. stem 9, leaf 9
15. stem 111, leaf 3
16. stem 0, leaf 8
17. stem 14, leaf 2
18. stem 1, leaf 0
19. stem 111, leaf 4
20. 9, 11, 12, 13, 27, 39, 43, 44, 48, 50, 77
21. rounded to the nearest hundred: 9, 12, 24, 27, 36, 39, 40
22. 8, 12, 13, 17, 27, 29, 33, 37

23a. Sample answer: Both teens and young adults had similar distribution of responses.

23b. Sample answer: The market research shows that the new game is equally appealing to teens and young adults. Therefore, we should concentrate our marketing efforts toward both teens and young adults.

24a. 6.8 **24b.** 8.0

24c. $16 - 7$ or 9 more **24d.** 5.1

25a.

1980	Stem	1993
4	1	3
6	2	4
8 5 1	3	3 7 7
	4	6
1	5	

3|7 = 3700

25b. 3000 to 3900; 3000 to 3900

25c. Sample answer: Farm sizes seem to be shrinking.

26a.

Stem	Leaf
3	0 0 1 1 1 4 5 6 6 8 9
4	2 2 3 3 4
5	0 1 3 4 4
6	1 5 6 9
7	2
8	0 0 7 8

6|5 = 650

26b. $880 - 300 = 580$ miles **26c.** 11 rivers

27. $3 \cdot 6 - \frac{12}{4} = 18 - \frac{12}{4}$

$= 18 - 3$

$= 15$

28. $9a - 4^2 + b^2 \div 2 = 9 \cdot 3 - 4^2 + 6^2 \div 2$

$= 9 \cdot 3 - 16 + 36 \div 2$

$= 27 - 16 + 18$

$= 11 + 18$

$= 29$

29a. $\frac{s}{5}$ **29b.** $\frac{s}{5} = \frac{10}{5} = 2$ miles; yes

30. $\frac{9+2}{32 \cdot 2} = \frac{11}{64},\ \frac{11+2}{64 \cdot 2} = \frac{13}{128}$

31. 

1-5 Open Sentences

Pages 34–35 Check for Understanding

1. An open sentence cannot be true or false until the variable or variables are replaced. If a sentence has no variables, the sentence is automatically either true or false.
2. An expression is two or more numbers and/or variables with operation symbols. Open sentences have numbers, variables, or expressions connected with a relationship symbol such as =, <, or >.
3. A solution set is a subset of the replacement set that makes the open sentence true.

4. Replace n with 10 and see if the statement is true. Then replace n with each of the other elements in the replacement set. Write a set of the elements from the replacement set that make the open sentence true.

5. See students' work.

6. $7(x^2) - 15 \div 5 = 25$

$7(2^2) - 15 \div 5 \stackrel{?}{=} 25$

$7(4) - 15 \div 5 \stackrel{?}{=} 25$

$28 - 3 \stackrel{?}{=} 25$

$25 = 25$ true

7. $\frac{7a + a}{(9 \cdot 3) - 7} = 4$

$\frac{7 \cdot 5 + 5}{(9 \cdot 3) - 7} \stackrel{?}{=} 4$

$\frac{35 + 5}{27 - 7} \stackrel{?}{=} 4$

$\frac{40}{20} \stackrel{?}{=} 4$

$2 \neq 4$ false

8.

Replace x with:	$3x + 2 > 2$	True or False?
0	$3(0) + 2 \stackrel{?}{>} 2 \rightarrow 2 > 2$	false
1	$3(1) + 2 \stackrel{?}{>} 2 \rightarrow 5 > 2$	true
2	$3(2) + 2 \stackrel{?}{>} 2 \rightarrow 8 > 2$	true

Therefore, the solution set for $3x + 2 > 2$ is $\{1, 2\}$.

9.

Replace y with:	$2y^2 - 1 > 0$	True or False?
1	$2 \cdot 1^2 - 1 \stackrel{?}{>} 0 \rightarrow 1 > 0$	true
3	$2 \cdot 3^2 - 1 \stackrel{?}{>} 0 \rightarrow 17 > 0$	true
5	$2 \cdot 5^2 - 1 \stackrel{?}{>} 0 \rightarrow 49 > 0$	true

Therefore, the solution set for $2y^2 - 1 > 0$ is $\{1, 3, 5\}$.

10. $x - 2 = y$

$6 - 2 = y$

$4 = y$

11. $2x^2 + 3 = y$

$2 \cdot 6^2 + 3 = y$

$2 \cdot 36 + 3 = y$

$72 + 3 = y$

$75 = y$

12a. $g = 15{,}579 + 6220 + 18{,}995$

12b. 40,794 glasses

Pages 35–36 Exercises

13. $a + \frac{3}{4} = \frac{3}{2} + \frac{1}{4}$

$\frac{1}{2} + \frac{3}{4} \stackrel{?}{=} \frac{3}{2} + \frac{1}{4}$

$\frac{2}{4} + \frac{3}{4} \stackrel{?}{=} \frac{6}{4} + \frac{1}{4}$

$\frac{5}{4} \neq \frac{1}{4}$ false

14. $\frac{3 + 15}{x} = \frac{1}{2}x$

$\frac{3 + 15}{6} \stackrel{?}{=} \frac{1}{2}(6)$

$\frac{18}{6} \stackrel{?}{=} 3$

$3 = 3$ true

15. $y^6 = 4^3$

$2^6 \stackrel{?}{=} 4^3$

$64 = 64$ true

16. $3x^2 - 4(5) = 6$

$3 \cdot 3^2 - 4(5) \stackrel{?}{=} 6$

$3 \cdot 9 - 4(5) \stackrel{?}{=} 6$

$27 - 20 \stackrel{?}{=} 6$

$7 \neq 6$ false

17. $\frac{5^2 - 2y}{5^2 - 6} \leq 1$

$\frac{5^2 - 2 \cdot 3}{5^2 - 6} \stackrel{?}{\leq} 1$

$\frac{25 - 2 \cdot 3}{25 - 6} \stackrel{?}{\leq} 1$

$\frac{25 - 6}{19} \stackrel{?}{\leq} 1$

$\frac{19}{19} \stackrel{?}{\leq} 1$

$1 \leq 1$ true

18. $a^5 \div 8 \div a^2 \div a < \frac{1}{2}$

$2^5 \div 8 \div 2^2 \div 2 \stackrel{?}{<} \frac{1}{2}$

$32 \div 8 \div 4 \div 2 \stackrel{?}{<} \frac{1}{2}$

$4 \div 4 \div 2 \stackrel{?}{<} \frac{1}{2}$

$1 \div 2 \stackrel{?}{<} \frac{1}{2}$

$\frac{1}{2} \not< \frac{1}{2}$ false

19.

Replace y with:	$y - 2 < 6$	True or False?
5	$5 - 2 \stackrel{?}{<} 6 \rightarrow 3 < 6$	true
10	$10 - 2 \stackrel{?}{<} 6 \rightarrow 8 \not< 6$	false
15	$15 - 2 \stackrel{?}{<} 6 \rightarrow 13 \not< 6$	false
20	$20 - 2 \stackrel{?}{<} 6 \rightarrow 18 \not< 6$	false

Therefore, the solution set for $y - 2 < 6$ is $\{5\}$.

20.

Replace y with:	$y + 2 > 7$	True or False?
5	$5 + 2 \stackrel{?}{>} 7 \rightarrow 7 \not> 7$	false
10	$10 + 2 \stackrel{?}{>} 7 \rightarrow 12 > 7$	true
15	$15 + 2 \stackrel{?}{>} 7 \rightarrow 17 > 7$	true
20	$20 + 2 \stackrel{?}{>} 7 \rightarrow 22 > 7$	true

Therefore, the solution set for $y + 2 > 7$ is $\{10, 15, 20\}$.

21.

Replace x with:	$8x + 1 < 8$	True or False?
$\frac{1}{2}$	$8 \cdot \frac{1}{2} + 1 \stackrel{?}{<} 8 \rightarrow 5 < 8$	true
$\frac{3}{4}$	$8 \cdot \frac{3}{4} + 1 \stackrel{?}{<} 8 \rightarrow 7 < 8$	true
1	$8 \cdot 1 + 1 \stackrel{?}{<} 8 \rightarrow 9 \not< 8$	false
$\frac{5}{4}$	$8 \cdot \frac{5}{4} + 1 \stackrel{?}{<} 8 \rightarrow 11 \not< 8$	false

Therefore, the solution set for $8x + 1 < 8$ is $\left\{\frac{1}{2}, \frac{3}{4}\right\}$.

22.

Replace x with:	$2x > 1$	True or False?
$\frac{1}{2}$	$2 \cdot \frac{1}{2} \stackrel{?}{>} 1 \rightarrow 1 \not> 1$	false
$\frac{3}{4}$	$2 \cdot \frac{3}{4} \stackrel{?}{>} 1 \rightarrow \frac{3}{2} > 1$	true
1	$2 \cdot 1 \stackrel{?}{>} 1 \rightarrow 2 > 1$	true
$\frac{5}{4}$	$2 \cdot \frac{5}{4} \stackrel{?}{>} 1 \rightarrow \frac{5}{2} > 1$	true

Therefore, the solution set for $2x > 1$ is $\left\{\frac{3}{4}, 1, \frac{5}{4}\right\}$.

23.

Replace y with:	$\frac{y}{5} \geq 2$	True or False?
5	$\frac{5}{5} \overset{?}{\geq} 2 \rightarrow 1 \not\geq 2$	false
10	$\frac{10}{5} \overset{?}{\geq} 2 \rightarrow 2 \geq 2$	true
15	$\frac{15}{5} \overset{?}{\geq} 2 \rightarrow 3 \geq 2$	true
20	$\frac{20}{5} \overset{?}{\geq} 2 \rightarrow 4 \geq 2$	true

Therefore, the solution set for $\frac{y}{5} > 2$ is {10, 15, 20}.

24.

Replace x with:	$3x \leq 4$	True or False?
$\frac{1}{2}$	$3 \cdot \frac{1}{2} \overset{?}{\leq} 4 \rightarrow \frac{3}{2} \leq 4$	true
$\frac{3}{4}$	$3 \cdot \frac{3}{4} \overset{?}{\leq} 4 \rightarrow \frac{9}{4} \leq 4$	true
1	$3 \cdot 1 \overset{?}{\leq} 4 \rightarrow 3 \leq 4$	true
$\frac{5}{4}$	$3 \cdot \frac{5}{4} \overset{?}{\leq} 4 \rightarrow \frac{15}{4} \leq 4$	true

Therefore, the solution set of $3x \leq 4$ is $\left\{\frac{1}{2}, \frac{3}{4}, 1, \frac{5}{4}\right\}$.

25. $y = \frac{14-8}{2}$
$y = \frac{6}{2}$
$y = 3$

26. $4(6) + 3 = a$
$24 + 3 = a$
$27 = a$

27. $\frac{21-3}{12-3} = x$
$\frac{8}{4} = x$
$2 = x$

28. $d = 3\frac{1}{2} \div 2$
$d = \frac{7}{2} \cdot \frac{1}{2}$
$d = \frac{7}{4}$ or $1\frac{3}{4}$

29. $s = 4\frac{1}{2} + \frac{1}{3}$
$s = 4\frac{3}{6} + \frac{2}{6}$
$s = 4\frac{5}{6}$

30. $x = 5^2 - 2^3$
$x = 25 - 8$
$x = 17$

31. Sample answer: $p = 1$ and $q = 2$, $p = 2$ and $q = 10$, $p = 3$ and $q = 8$, $p = 4$ and $q = 20$, and $p = 5$ and $q = 15$

32a. $t = 3(144)$; Texas should have about 3 times their yearly average.

32b. 432 tornados

32c. Sample answer: Write an equation that estimates the number of tornadoes that Oklahoma will have in the next five years; $t = 5(45)$.

33a. $C = \frac{3500 \cdot 4}{14}$

33b. $C = \frac{14{,}000}{14} = 1000$ Calories

34a. $d = (3.36)(1.5)$ **34b.** 5.04 miles

34c. Yes, it can travel 100 ft in $100 \div 2.3$ or 43.5 s

35. 2, 5, 6, 7, 9 **36.** 85 goals

37. $5(13 - 7) - 22 = 5(6) - 22$
$= 30 - 22$
$= 8$

38. $(8 + 2)a + 7 + 2 = 10a + 9$,
$(10 + 2)a + 9 + 2 = 12a + 11$

39. 5 less than x to the fifth power

40. $a + b + c$

Page 36 Self Test

1. $3a + b^2$ **2.** $w^5 - 37$

3. 10:21 + 0:43 = 11:04, 11:04 + 0:04 = 11:08, 11:08 + 0:43 = 11:51, 11:51 + 0:04 = 11:55

4. $5(8 - 3) + 7 \cdot 2 = 5(5) + 7 \cdot 2$
$= 25 + 14$
$= 39$

5. $6(4^3 + 2^2) = 6(64 + 4)$
$= 6(68)$
$= 408$

6. $(9 - 2 \cdot 3)^3 - 27 + 9 \cdot 2 = (9 - 6)^3 - 27 + 9 \cdot 2$
$= 3^3 - 27 + 9 \cdot 2$
$= 27 - 27 + 9 \cdot 2$
$= 27 - 27 + 18$
$= 0 + 18$
$= 18$

7.

Stem	Leaf
4	8
5	4
6	7
7	7
8	5 9

6 | 7 = 67

8.

Stem	Leaf
1	0
2	4 5
3	5 9
4	5
7	5 6

3 | 5 = 350

9.

Replace x with:	$x + 2 > 7$	True or False?
4	$4 + 2 \overset{?}{>} 7 \rightarrow 6 \not> 7$	false
5	$5 + 2 \overset{?}{>} 7 \rightarrow 7 \not> 7$	false
6	$6 + 2 \overset{?}{>} 7 \rightarrow 8 > 7$	true
7	$7 + 2 \overset{?}{>} 7 \rightarrow 9 > 7$	true
8	$8 + 2 \overset{?}{>} 7 \rightarrow 10 > 7$	true

Therefore, the solution set of $x + 2 > 7$ is {6, 7, 8}.

10.

Replace x with:	$9x - 20 = x^2$	True or False?
4	$9 \cdot 4 - 20 \overset{?}{=} 4^2 \rightarrow 16 = 16$	true
5	$9 \cdot 5 - 20 \overset{?}{=} 5^2 \rightarrow 25 = 25$	true
6	$9 \cdot 6 - 20 \overset{?}{=} 6^2 \rightarrow 34 \neq 36$	false
7	$9 \cdot 7 - 20 \overset{?}{=} 7^2 \rightarrow 43 \neq 49$	false
8	$9 \cdot 8 - 20 \overset{?}{=} 8^2 \rightarrow 52 \neq 64$	false

Therefore, the solution set of $9x - 20 = x^2$ is {4, 5}.

1-6 Identity and Equality Properties

Pages 40–41 Check for Understanding

1. two or more things that are exactly alike

2. No; because $a + 1 \neq a$.

3. You cannot divide by 0. **4.** 1

5. Reverse the numerator and the denominator.

6. $\frac{1}{7}$ **7.** $\frac{2}{9}$ **8.** $\frac{1}{c}$

9. c multiplicative property of 0

10. b multiplicative identity property

11. e reflexive property (=)

12. g substitution property (=)

13. d multiplicative inverse property

14. a additive identity property

15. f symmetric property (=)

16. $(14 \cdot \frac{1}{14} + 8 \cdot 0) \cdot 12$

$= (1 + 8 \cdot 0) \cdot 12$	multiplicative inverse
$= (1 + 0) \cdot 12$	multiplicative prop. of 0
$= 1 \cdot 12$	additive identity
$= 12$	multiplicative identity

17. $6(12 - 48 \div 4) + 9 \cdot 1$

$= 6(12 - 12) + 9 \cdot 1$	substitution (=)
$= 6(0) + 9 \cdot 1$	substitution (=)
$= 0 + 9 \cdot 1$	multiplicative property
$= 0 + 9$	multiplicative indentity
$= 9$	additive identity

18. $3 + 5(4 - 2^2) - 1$

$= 3 + 5(4 - 4) - 1$	substitution (=)
$= 3 + 5(0) - 1$	substitution (=)
$= 3 + 0 - 1$	multiplicative prop. of 0
$= 3 - 1$	additive identity
$= 2$	substitution (=)

19a. $4(20) + 7$

19b. $4(20) + 7 = 80 + 7$ substitution (=)
$= 87$ substitution (=)

19c. 87 years

20. $\frac{1}{9}$ **21.** 9 **22.** 4 **23.** $\frac{1}{p}$

24. $\frac{a}{2}$ **25.** $\frac{2}{3}$ **26.** symmetric (=)

27. substitution (=) **28.** substitution (=)

29. multiplicative identity

30. multiplicative inverse

31. multiplicative inverse, multiplicative identity

32. additive identity **33.** symmetric (=)

34. multiplicative property of 0

35. reflexive (=) **36.** transitive (=)

37. $2(3 \cdot 2 - 5) + 3 \cdot \frac{1}{3}$

$= 2(6 - 5) + 3 \cdot \frac{1}{3}$	substitution (=)
$= 2(1) + 3 \cdot \frac{1}{3}$	substitution (=)
$= 2 + 3 \cdot \frac{1}{3}$	multiplicative identity
$= 2 + 1$	multiplicative inverse
$= 3$	substitution (=)

38. $26 \cdot 1 - 6 + 5(12 \div 4 - 3)$

$= 26 \cdot 1 - 6 + 5(3 - 3)$	substitution (=)
$= 26 \cdot 1 - 6 + 5(0)$	substitution (=)
$= 26 - 6 + 5(0)$	multiplicative identity
$= 26 - 6 + 0$	multiplicative prop. of 0
$= 20 + 0$	substitution (=)
$= 20$	additive identity

39. $7(5 \cdot 3^2 - 11 \cdot 4)$

$= 7(5 \cdot 9 - 11 \cdot 4)$	substitution(=)
$= 7(45 - 44)$	substitution (=)
$= 7(1)$	substitution (=)
$= 7$	multiplicative identity

40. $4(16 \div 4^2)$

$= 4(16 \div 16)$	substitution (=)
$= 4(1)$	substitution (=)
$= 4$	multiplicative identity

41. $(15 - 8) \div 7 \cdot 25$

$= 7 \div 7 \cdot 25$	substitution (=)
$= 1 \cdot 25$	substitution (=)
$= 25$	multiplicative identity

42. $(8 \cdot 3 - 19 + 5) + (3^2 + 8 \cdot 4)$

$= (8 \cdot 3 - 19 + 5) + (9 + 8 \cdot 4)$	substitution (=)
$= (24 - 19 + 5) + (9 + 32)$	substitution (=)
$= (10) + (41)$	substitution (=)
$= 51$	substitution (=)

43. $(2^5 - 5^2) + (4^2 - 2^4)$

$= (32 - 25) + (16 - 16)$	substitution
$= (7) + (0)$	substitution
$= 7$	additive identity

44. $8[6^2 - 3(11)] \div 8 \cdot \frac{1}{3}$

$= 8[36 - 3(11)] \div 8 \cdot \frac{1}{3}$	substitution (=)
$= 8(36 - 33) \div 8 \cdot \frac{1}{3}$	substitution (=)
$= 8(3) \div 8 \cdot \frac{1}{3}$	substitution (=)
$= 24 \div 8 \cdot \frac{1}{3}$	substitution (=)
$= 3 \cdot \frac{1}{3}$	substitution (=)
$= 1$	multiplicative inverse

45. $5^3 + 9\left(\frac{1}{3}\right)^2$

$= 125 + 9\left(\frac{1}{9}\right)$	substitution (=)
$= 125 + 1$	multiplicative inverse
$= 126$	substitution (=)

46a. No; a number is never less than itself. Sample example: 4 is *not* less than 4.

46b. No; if one number is less than a second number, then the second number can never be less than the first number. Sample example: 4 is less than 5, but 5 is *not* less than 4.

46c. Yes; if one number is less than a second number and a second number is less than a third number, then the first number will be less than the third number. Sample example: $4 < 5$ and $5 < 6$, so $4 < 6$.

47a. $[21(12 \cdot 2)] + [23(15 \cdot 2)] + [67(10 \cdot 2)]$

47b. $[21(12 \cdot 2)] + [23(15 \cdot 2)] + [67(10 \cdot 2)]$

$= [21(24)] + [23(30)] + [67(20)]$	substitution (=)
$= 504 + 690 + 1340$	substitution (=)
$= 2534$	substitution (=)

47c. $2534 \div 100 = \$25.34$

48a. $0.32 + 0.23(14)$

48b. $0.32 + 0.23(14) = 0.32 + 3.22$ substitution (=)
$= 3.54$ substitution (=)

48c. $3.54

49. $15 \div 3 + 7 < 13$
$5 + 7 < 13$
$12 < 13$ true

50. $m = (18 - 3) \div (3^2 - 2^2)$
$= (15) \div (9 - 4)$
$= 15 \div 5$
$= 3$

51. $(2n^2 + 6) \div 4 \leq 5$
$(2 \cdot 3^2 + 6) \div 4 \overset{?}{\leq} 5$
$(2 \cdot 9 + 6) \div 4 \overset{?}{\leq} 5$
$(18 + 6) \div 4 \overset{?}{\leq} 5$
$24 \div 4 \overset{?}{\leq} 5$
$6 \not\leq 5$ false

52. when there are 2 sets of data

53. See students' work.

54. $5(7-2)-3^2 = 5(5)-3^2$
$= 25-9$
$= 16$

55. $xy-2y = 6\cdot 9 - 2\cdot 9$
$= 54-18$
$= 36$

56. $10+3=13,\ 13+3=16$

57. $12y$

1-7A Modeling Mathematics: The Distributive Property

Page 44

1. 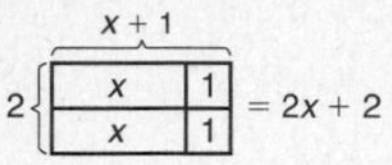

2. 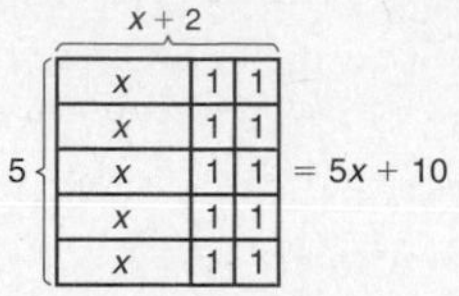

3. 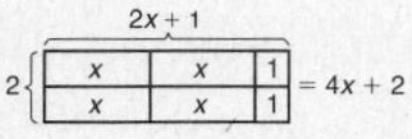

4. 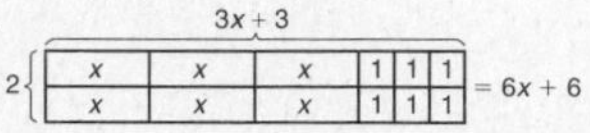

5. false
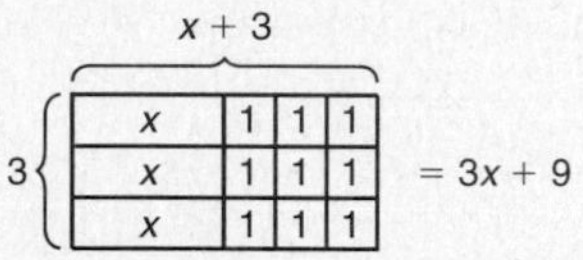

6. true
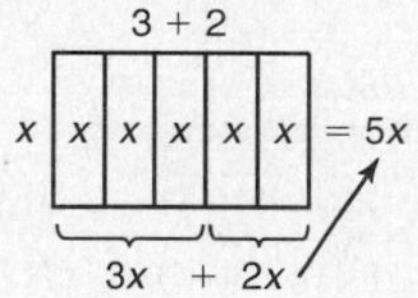

7a. Adita

7b. 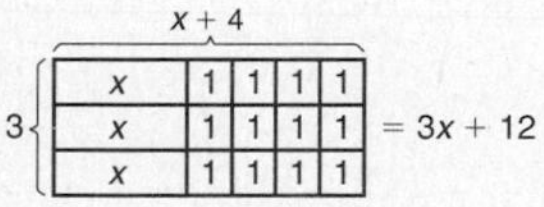

1-7 The Distributive Property

Pages 48–49 Check for Understanding

1. According to the distributive property, $2(a-3) = 2a-6$.
2. Sample answer: $5a+3a+a+2b$
3. Multiply 3 times $2x$ and 3 times 4. Subtract the product of 3 and 4 from the product of 3 and $2x$.
4. 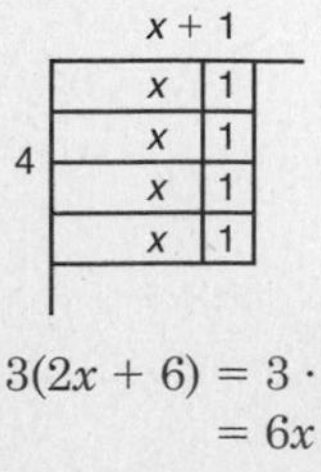

5. b $8\cdot 10 + 8\cdot 4$
6. e $(12)(6)-(3)(6)$
7. a $(4+x)^2$
8. d $2x+10$
9. c $2x-2$

10. $3(2x+6) = 3\cdot 2x + 3\cdot 6$
$= 6x+18$

11. $2(a-b) = 2a-2b$

12. $15\cdot 99 = 15(100-1)$
$= 1500-15$
$= 1485$

13. $28\left(2\frac{1}{7}\right) = 28\left(2+\frac{1}{7}\right)$
$= 56+4$
$= 60$

14. 2.5 **15.** 7 **16.** $\frac{3}{5}$ **17.** $4y^4, y^4$ **18.** $3a^2, 9a^2; 4c, c$

19. $t^2+2t^2+4t = (1+2)t^2+4t$
$= 3t^2+4t$

20. in simplest form

21. $16a^2b+7a^2b+3ab^2 = (16+7)a^2b+3ab^2$
$= 23a^2b+3ab^2$

22. $7p+q-p+\frac{2q}{3} = (7-1)p+\left(1+\frac{2}{3}\right)q$
$= 6p+1\frac{2}{3}q$

23. $5.35(24)+5.35(32);\ 5.35(24+32)$

Pages 49–50 Exercises

24. $2(4+t) = 2\cdot 4 + 2t$
$= 8+2t$

25. $(g-9)5 = g\cdot 5 - 9\cdot 5$
$= 5g-45$

26. $5(x+3) = 5x+5\cdot 3$
$= 5x+15$

27. $8(3m+6) = 8\cdot 3m + 8\cdot 6$
$= 24m+48$

28. $28\left(y-\frac{1}{7}\right) = 28y - 28\cdot\frac{1}{7}$
$= 28y-4$

29. $a(5-b) = 5a-ab$

30. $5\cdot 97 = 5(100-3)$
$= 500-15$
$= 485$

31. $\left(3\frac{1}{17}\right)\times 17 = \left(3+\frac{1}{17}\right)17$
$= 51+1$
$= 52$

32. $16(102) = 16(100+2)$
$= 1600+32$
$= 1632$

33. $24(2.5) = 24(2+0.5)$
$= 48+12$
$= 60$

34. $999\cdot 6 = (1000-1)6$
$= 6000-6$
$= 5994$

35. $3\times 215 = 3(200+15)$
$= 600+45$
$= 645$

36. $15x+18x = (15+18)x$
$= 33x$

37. in simplest form

38. $10n+3n^2+9n^2 = 10n+(3+9)n^2$
$= 10n+12n^2$

39. $5a+7a+10b+5b = (5+7)a+(10+5)b$
$= 12a+15b$

40. $7(3x^2y-4xy^2+xy) = 7\cdot 3x^2y - 7\cdot 4xy^2 + 7xy$
$= 21x^2y-28xy^2+7xy$

41. in simplest form

42. $5(6a+4b-3b) = 5\cdot 6a + 5\cdot 4b - 5\cdot 3b$
$= 30a+20b-15b$
$= 30a+(20-15)b$
$= 30a+5b$

43. $3(x+2y)-2y = 3x+3\cdot 2y - 2y$
$= 3x+6y-2y$
$= 3x+(6-2)y$
$= 3x+4y$

44. $\frac{2}{3}\left(c-\frac{3}{4}\right)+c(1+b) = \frac{2}{3}c - \frac{2}{3}\left(\frac{3}{4}\right)+c+cb$
$= \frac{2}{3}c-\frac{1}{2}+c+cb$
$= \left(\frac{2}{3}+1\right)c-\frac{1}{2}+cb$
$= \frac{5}{3}c-\frac{1}{2}+cb$

45. $a + \frac{a}{5} + \frac{2}{5}a = \left(1 + \frac{1}{5} + \frac{2}{5}\right)a$
$= 1\frac{3}{5}a$

46. $4(3g + 2) + 2(g + 3) = 4 \cdot 3g + 4 \cdot 2 + 2g + 2 \cdot 3$
$= 12g + 8 + 2g + 6$
$= (12 + 2)g + (8 + 6)$
$= 14g + 14$

47. $3(x + y) + 2(x + y) + 4x = 3x + 3y + 2x + 2y + 4x$
$= (3 + 2 + 4)x + (3 + 2)y$
$= 9x + 5y$

48a. yes, if $C \neq 0$

48b. Change the / in the If statement to ∧; only for $C = 1$.

49. No; sample counterexample:
$2 + (4 \cdot 5) \neq (2 + 4)(2 + 5)$

50a. 4(16.15 + 32.45); 4(16.15) + 4(32.45)

50b. $194.40

51a. $2[x + (x + 14)] = 2x + 2(x + 14)$
$= 2x + 2x + 2 \cdot 14$
$= 2x + 2x + 28$
$= (2 + 2)x + 28$
$= 4x + 28$

51b. $4x + 28 = 4(17) + 28$
$= 68 + 28$
$= 96$

51c. $x(x + 14) = 17(17 + 14)$
$- 17(31)$
$= 527 \text{ ft}^2$

52. symmetric (=)

53. multiplicative prop. of 0

54.

Replace x with:	$3x - 5 > 7$	True or False?
2	$3(2) - 5 \overset{?}{>} 7 \to 1 \not> 7$	false
3	$3(3) - 5 \overset{?}{>} 7 \to 4 \not> 7$	false
4	$3(4) - 5 \overset{?}{>} 7 \to 7 \not> 7$	false
5	$3(5) - 5 \overset{?}{>} 7 \to 10 > 7$	true
6	$3(6) - 5 \overset{?}{>} 7 \to 13 > 7$	true

Therefore, the solution set of $3x - 5 > 7$ is {5, 6}.

55a. $d = (1129)(2)$

55b. 2258 ft

56.

Stem	Leaf
2	9
3	6 6 7
4	5 5
5	1 5 8

3 | 7 = 37

57. $\frac{4^2 - 2^3}{24 - 2(10)} = (4^2 - 2^3) \div [24 - 2(10)]$
$= (16 - 8) \div (24 - 20)$
$= 8 \div 4$
$= 2$

58. $(20 + 5)a^{4+1} = 25a^5, (25 + 5)a^{5+1} = 30a^6$

59. 1992 − 12 = 1980, 1980 − 12 = 1968, 1968 − 12 = 1956, 1956 − 12 = 1944, 1944 − 12 = 1932, 1932 − 12 = 1920, 1920 − 12 = 1908; 8 years

60. $2k - 37$

1-8 Commutative and Associative Properties

Page 53 Check for Understanding

1. Answers will vary. Sample answer:
$(2 \cdot 3) \cdot 5 = 2 \cdot (3 \cdot 5)$
$6 \cdot 5 = 2 \cdot 15$
$30 = 30$

2. Use the commulative property of multiplication to rewrite the problem as $5 \cdot 2 \cdot 6.5$. Since $5 \cdot 2 = 10$, the answer 65 can be determined without a calculator or paper and pencil.

3. The commutative properties allow a different *ordering* of numbers while the associative properties allow a different *grouping* of numbers.

4. Division is *not* commutative since the examples have different quotients.

5. See students' work.

6. associative (+)

7. commutative (+)

8. substitution (=)

9. associative (×)

10a.	$ab(a + b) = (ab)a + (ab)b$	distributive prop.
10b.	$= a(ab) + (ab)b$	commutative (×)
10c.	$= (a \cdot a)b + a(b \cdot b)$	associative (×)
10d.	$= a^2b + ab^2$	substitution (=)

11. $4a + 2b + a = 4a + a + 2b$
$= (4 + 1)a + 2b$
$= 5a + 2b$

12. $3p + 2q + 2p + 8q = 3p + 2p + 2q + 8q$
$= (3 + 2)p + (2 + 8)q$
$= 5p + 10q$

13. $3(4x + y) + 2x = 3 \cdot 4x + 3y + 2x$
$= 12x + 3y + 2x$
$= 12x + 2x + 3y$
$= (12 + 2)x + 3y$
$= 14x + 3y$

14. $6(0.4x + 0.2y) + 0.5x = 6 \cdot 0.4x + 6 \cdot 0.2y + 0.5x$
$= 2.4x + 1.2y + 0.5x$
$= 2.4x + 0.5x + 1.2y$
$= (2.4 + 0.5)x + 1.2y$
$= 2.9x + 1.2y$

15. $6z^2 + (7 + z^2 + 6)$	
$= 6z^2 + (z^2 + 7 + 6)$	commutative (+)
$= (6z^2 + z^2) + (7 + 6)$	associative (+)
$= (6 + 1)z^2 + (7 + 6)$	distributive property
$= 7z^2 + 13$	substitution (=)

16. commutative (+)

17. multiplicative identity

18. distributive property

19. associative (×)

20. multiplicative property of zero

21. distributive property

22. substitution (=)

23. commutative (×)

24. associative (+)

25. associative (+)

26a.	$3c + 5(2 + c)$	
	$= 3c + 5(2) + 5c$	distributive property
26b.	$= 3c + 5c + 5(2)$	commutative (+)
26c.	$= (3c + 5c) + 5(2)$	associative (+)
26d.	$= (3 + 5)c + 5(2)$	distributive property
26e.	$= 8c + 10$	substitution (=)

27. $4x + 5y + 6x = 4x + 6x + 3b$
$= (4 + 6)x + 5y$
$= 10x + 5y$

28. $8a + 3b + a = 8a + a + 3b$
$= (8 + 1)a + 3b$
$= 9a + 3b$

29. $5x + 3y + 2x + 7y = 5x + 2x + 3y + 7y$
$= (5 + 2)x + (3 + 7)y$
$= 7x + 10y$

30. $4 + 6(ac + 2b) + 2ac = 4 + 6ac + 6 \cdot 2b + 2ac$
$= 4 + 6ac + 12b + 2ac$
$= 4 + 6ac + 2ac + 12b$
$= 4 + (6 + 2)ac + 12b$
$= 4 + 8ac + 12b$

31. $2(3x + y) + 4x = 2 \cdot 3x + 2y + 4x$
$= 6x + 2y + 4x$
$= 6x + 4x + 2y$
$= (6 + 4)x + 2y$
$= 10x + 2y$

32. $4y^4 + 3y^2 + y^4 = 4y^4 + y^4 + 3y^2$
$= (4 + 1)y^4 + 3y^2$
$= 5y^4 + 3y^2$

33. $16a^2 + 16 + 16a^2 = 16a^2 + 16a^2 + 16$
$= (16 + 16)a^2 + 16$
$= 32a^2 + 16$

34. $3.2(x + y) + 2.3(x + y) + 4x$
$= 3.2x + 3.2y + 2.3x + 2.3y + 4x$
$= 3.2x + 2.3x + 4x + 3.2y + 2.3y$
$= (3.2 + 2.3 + 4)x + (3.2 + 2.3)y$
$= 9.5x + 5.5y$

35. $\frac{1}{4}x + 2x + 2\frac{3}{4}x = \left(\frac{1}{4} + 2 + 2\frac{3}{4}\right)x$
$= 5x$

36. $0.5[3x + 4(3 + 2x)] = 0.5(3x + 4 \cdot 3 + 4 \cdot 2x)$
$= 0.5(3x + 12 + 8x)$
$= 0.5(3x + 8x + 12)$
$= 0.5[(3 + 8)x + 12]$
$= 0.5(11x + 12)$
$= 0.5 \cdot 11x + 0.5 \cdot 12$
$= 5.5x + 6$

37. $\frac{3}{4} + \frac{2}{3}(m + 2n) + m = \frac{3}{4} + \frac{2}{3}m + \frac{2}{3} \cdot 2n + m$
$= \frac{3}{4} + \frac{2}{3}m + \frac{4}{3}n + m$
$= \frac{3}{4} + \frac{2}{3}m + m + \frac{4}{3}n$
$= \frac{3}{4} + \left(\frac{2}{3} + 1\right)m + \frac{4}{3}n$
$= \frac{3}{4} + \frac{5}{3}m + \frac{4}{3}n$

38. $\frac{3}{5}\left(\frac{1}{2}p + 2q\right) + 2p = \frac{3}{5} \cdot \frac{1}{2}p + \frac{3}{5} \cdot 2q + 2p$
$= \frac{3}{10}p + \frac{6}{5}q + 2p$
$= \frac{3}{10}p + 2p + \frac{6}{5}q$
$= \left(\frac{3}{10} + 2\right)p + \frac{6}{5}q$
$= \frac{23}{10}p + \frac{6}{5}q$

39. $2(s + t) - s$

$= 2s + 2t - s$	distributive property
$= 2t + 2s - s$	commutative (+)
$= 2t + (2s - s)$	associative (+)
$= 2t + (2s - 1s)$	multiplicative identity
$= 2t + (2 - 1)s$	distributive property
$= 2t + 1s$	substitution (=)
$= 2t + s$	multiplicative identity

40. $\frac{1}{2}\left(p + 2q\right) + \frac{3}{4}q$

$= \frac{1}{2}p + q + \frac{3}{4}q$	distributive property
$= \frac{1}{2}p + \left(q + \frac{3}{4}q\right)$	associative (+)
$= \frac{1}{2}p + \left(1q + \frac{3}{4}q\right)$	multiplicative identity
$= \frac{1}{2}p + \left(1 + \frac{3}{4}\right)q$	distributive property
$= \frac{1}{2}p + \frac{7}{4}q$	substitution (=)

41.

$5xy + 3xy = (5 + 3)xy$	distributive property
$= 8xy$	substitution (=)

42. $4(a + b) + 2(a + 2b)$

$= 4a + 4b + 2a + 4b$	distributive property
$= 4a + 2a + 4b + 4b$	commutative (+)
$= (4 + 2)a + (4 + 4)b$	distributive property
$= 6a + 8b$	substitution (=)

43. $\frac{1}{100}$; Each denominator and the following numerator represent the number 1. The resulting expression is 1 in the numerator and 100 in the denominator multiplied by numerous 1s. Since 1 is the multiplicative identity, the product is $\frac{1}{100}$.

44. No; answers will vary. Sample answer: $5 - 3 \neq 3 - 5$

45. No; sample example: Let $a = 1$ and $b = 2$; then $1 * 2 = 1 + 2(2)$ or 5 and $2 * 1 = 2 + 2(1)$ or 4.

46a. no

46b. Sample answer: practicing piano and doing homework

46c. Sample answer: putting clothes into the washer and dryer

47a. $G = \frac{(60)^2}{32.2 \times 30} = \frac{3600}{966} = 3.73$

47b. See students' work.

48. $\frac{4}{5}$

49. $100d + 80d + 8d$, $188d$

50. substitution (=)

51. $\frac{3}{2}$

52. $\frac{3k - 3}{7} + 13 < 17$
$\frac{3(8) - 3}{7} + 13 \overset{?}{<} 17$
$\frac{24 - 3}{7} + 13 \overset{?}{<} 17$
$\frac{21}{7} + 13 \overset{?}{<} 17$
$3 + 13 \overset{?}{<} 17$
$16 < 17$ true

53.

Stem	Leaf
10	0 0 0 1 1 1 1 3
9	5 7 7 9 9 9

10|3 = 103

54. $(25 - 4) \div (2^2 - 1^3) = 21 \div (4 - 1)$
$= 21 \div 3$
$= 7$

55. ▼▲

56. $5p^6$

1-9 A Preview of Graphs and Functions

Pages 59–60 Check for Understanding

1. The numbers represent different values. The first number represents the number on the horizontal axis and the second represents the number on the vertical axis.

2. Sample answers: \$3000; \$800

3a. world population in billions of people from 1900 to the year 2000

3b. horizontal axis: time in years; vertical axis: population in billions

3c. Sample answer: (1924, 2); In 1925 the world's population was about 2 billion people. (1950, 2.5): In 1950 the world's population was about 2.5 billion people.

3d. The estimated world population for the year 2000 is 6.2 billion.

3e. Sample answer: The world's population has increased since 1900.

4. Sample answer: Every day, the patient's condition becomes worse.

5a. Graph 3 **5b.** Graph 4 **5c.** Graph 2

5d. Graph 1

6.

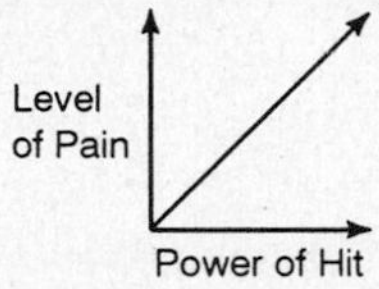

The independent variable is how hard you hit your thumb; the dependent variable is how much it hurts.

7a. False; *A* is the younger player, but *B* runs the mile in less time.

7b. False; *A* made more 3-point shots, but *B* made more 2-point shots.

7c. True; *B* is the older player and *B* made more 2-point shots.

7d. True; *A* is the younger player and *A* made more free-throw shots.

Pages 60–62 Exercises

8. Graph b; The bus gains speed, and then travels at a level speed. Later, it slows to a stop. Then the pattern continues.

9. Graph a; An average person makes no money as a child, then his or her income increases for several years, and finally levels off.

10a. Sample answer: Jorge saved steadily from January to June. In July, he withdrew money to go on vacation. He started saving again in September. Then in November he withdrew money for holiday presents.

10b. The domain includes the months of the year; the range is the amount of money.

11a. Graph 5 **11b.** Graph 3 **11c.** Graph 1

11d. Graph 4 **11e.** Graph 6 **11f.** Graph 2

12.

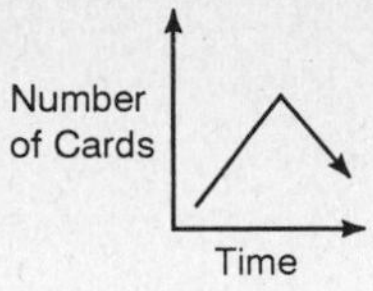

13.

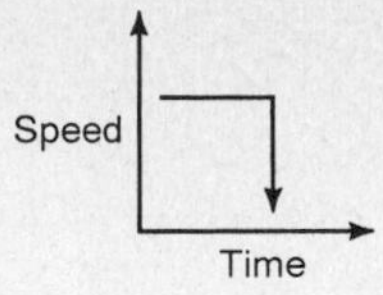

14.

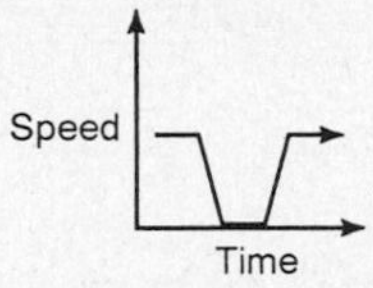

15.

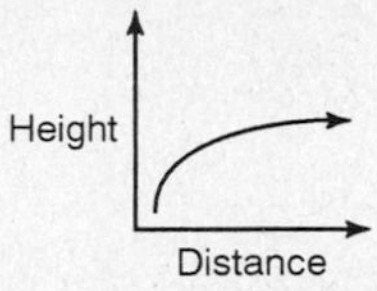

16. See students' work.

17a. independent variable: time in years; dependent variable: millions of dollars

17b. In 1991 the telethon raised 45 million dollars.

17c. Money raised in the telethon decreased, then increased steadily.

17d. The money raised increased.

17e. Answers will vary. See students' work.

18. Sample answer: Rock music was the best seller. Rap music sold better than country music.

19. $5p + 7q + 9 + 4q + 2p = 5p + 2p + 7q + 4q + 9$
$= (5 + 2)p + (7 + 4)q + 9$
$= 7p + 11q + 9$

20. $9a + 14(a + 3) = 9a + 14a + 14 \cdot 3$
$= 9a + 14a + 42$
$= (9 + 14)a + 42$
$= 23a + 42$

21. $14(1) - 27(0) = 14 - 0$
$= 14$

22. $5m + 6^2 = 56$
$5 \cdot 4 + 6^2 \stackrel{?}{=} 56$
$20 + 36 \stackrel{?}{=} 56$
$56 = 56$ true

23. $\frac{1}{3}Bh$

Chapter 1 Highlights

Page 63 Understanding and Using the Vocabulary

1. a additive identity property
2. c multiplicative identity property
3. e multiplicative property of zero
4. d multiplicative inverse property
5. f reflexive property
6. h symmetric property
7. g substitution property
8. i transitive property
9. b distributive property

Chapter 1 Study Guide and Assessment

Pages 64–66 Skills and Concepts

10. $x + 21$ **11.** x^5 **12.** $3x - 8$ **13.** $5x^2$

14. twice a number p squared

15. three times a number m to the fifth power

16. the sum of one half a number x and 2

17. the difference of four times m squared and twice m

18.

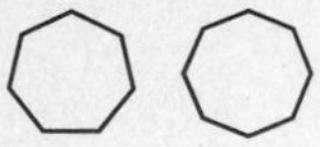

19. $16 \cdot 2 = 32,\ 32 \cdot 2 = 64$ 20. $3 + 5 = 8,\ 5 + 8 = 13$

21. $(3 + 1)x + y = 4x + y,\ (4 + 1)x + y = 5x + y$

22. $10{,}000 \cdot 10 = 100{,}000;\ 100{,}000 \cdot 10 = 1{,}000{,}000$

23. $10 = 10^1,\ 100 = 10^2,\ 1000 = 10^3,\ 10{,}000 = 10^4$

24. $10^9,\ 10^{13}$

25. $\begin{aligned} 3 + 2 \times 4 &= 3 + 8 \\ &= 11 \end{aligned}$

26. $\begin{aligned} (10 - 6) \div 8 &= 4 \div 8 \\ &= \tfrac{1}{2} \end{aligned}$

27. $\begin{aligned} 18 - 4^2 + 7 &= 18 - 16 + 7 \\ &= 2 + 7 \\ &= 9 \end{aligned}$

28. $\begin{aligned} 0.8(0.02 + 0.05) - 0.006 &= 0.8(0.07) - 0.006 \\ &= 0.056 - 0.006 \\ &= 0.05 \end{aligned}$

29. $\begin{aligned} (3 \times 1)^3 - (4 + 6) \div (9.1 + 0.9) &= 3^3 - 10 \div 10 \\ &= 27 - 10 \div 10 \\ &= 27 - 1 \\ &= 26 \end{aligned}$

30. $\begin{aligned} t^2 + 3y &= 3^2 + 3(2) \\ &= 9 + 6 \\ &= 15 \end{aligned}$

31. $\begin{aligned} xty^3 &= (0.1)(3)(2)^3 \\ &= (0.1)(3)(8) \\ &= 2.4 \end{aligned}$

32. $\begin{aligned} ty \div x &= 3 \cdot 2 \div 0.1 \\ &= 6 \div 0.1 \\ &= 60 \end{aligned}$

33. $\begin{aligned} yx + t^2 &= (2)(0.1) + 3^2 \\ &= (2)(0.1) + 9 \\ &= 0.2 + 9 \\ &= 9.2 \end{aligned}$

34.

Stem	Leaf
4	6 9
5	3 6 6 7 8
6	0 0 3 3 4 4 5 6 7 7 7 8
7	0 1 1 2 3 4 7 8 8 9
8	0 1 3 5 8
9	0 0

$7|2 = 72$

35. 90

36. 46

37. No, because some presidents are still alive.

38. 60 – 70

39. $\begin{aligned} x + 13 &= 22 \\ 8 + 13 &\overset{?}{=} 22 \\ 21 &\neq 22 \quad \text{false} \end{aligned}$

40. $\begin{aligned} 2b + 2 &\overset{?}{<} b^3 \\ 2 \cdot 2 + 2 &\overset{?}{<} 2^3 \\ 4 + 2 &\overset{?}{<} 8 \\ 6 &< 8 \quad \text{true} \end{aligned}$

41. $\begin{aligned} (y + 4) \div (y + 2) &\le 2 \\ (2 + 4) \div (2 + 2) &\overset{?}{\le} 2 \\ 6 \div 4 &\overset{?}{\le} 2 \\ \tfrac{3}{2} &\le 2 \quad \text{true} \end{aligned}$

42.

Replace x with:	$3x + 1 \le 13$	True or False?
2	$3 \cdot 2 + 1 \overset{?}{\le} 13 \rightarrow 7 \le 13$	true
4	$3 \cdot 4 + 1 \overset{?}{\le} 13 \rightarrow 13 \le 13$	true
6	$3 \cdot 6 + 1 \overset{?}{\le} 13 \rightarrow 19 \not\le 13$	false
8	$3 \cdot 8 + 1 \overset{?}{\le} 13 \rightarrow 25 \not\le 13$	false

Therefore, the solution set of $3x + 1 \le 13$ is $\{2, 4\}$.

43. $\begin{aligned} y &= 4\tfrac{1}{2} + 3^2 \\ &= 4\tfrac{1}{2} + 9 \\ &= 13\tfrac{1}{2} \end{aligned}$

44. $\begin{aligned} y &= 5[2(4) - 1^3] \\ &= 5[2(4) - 1] \\ &= 5(8 - 1) \\ &= 5(7) \\ &= 35 \end{aligned}$

45. $\frac{1}{3}$ 46. $\frac{1}{y}$ 47. 5

48. multiplicative identity 49. additive identity

50. $\begin{aligned} 2[3 \div (19 - 4^2)] &= 2[3 \div (19 - 16)] && \text{substitution } (=) \\ &= 2(3 \div 3) && \text{substitution } (=) \\ &= 2(1) && \text{substitution } (=) \\ &= 2 && \text{multiplicative identity} \end{aligned}$

51. $2 \cdot 4 + 2 \cdot 7$ 52. $4x + 4$

53. $\begin{aligned} 3\left(\tfrac{1}{3} - p\right) &= 3 \cdot \tfrac{1}{3} - 3p \\ &= 1 - 3p \end{aligned}$

54. $\begin{aligned} 6 \times 103 &= 6\,(100 + 3) \\ &= 600 + 18 \\ &= 618 \end{aligned}$

55. $\begin{aligned} 3 \times 98 &= 3(100 - 2) \\ &= 300 - 6 \\ &= 294 \end{aligned}$

56. $\begin{aligned} 12(1.5) &= 12(1 + 0.5) \\ &= 12 + 6 \\ &= 18 \end{aligned}$

57. $\begin{aligned} 3m + 5m + 12n - 4n &= (3 + 5)m + (12 - 4)n \\ &= 8m + 8n \end{aligned}$

58. $\begin{aligned} 2p(1 + 16r) &= 2p \cdot 1 + 2p \cdot 16r \\ &= 2p + 32pr \end{aligned}$

59. commutative (+) 60. associative (+)

61. commutative (×) 62. associative (×)

63. $\begin{aligned} 2x + 2y + 3x + 3y &= 2x + 3x + 2y + 3y \\ &= (2 + 3)x + (2 + 3)y \\ &= 5x + 5y \end{aligned}$

64. $\begin{aligned} 5(x + y) - 2x &= 5x + 5y - 2x && \text{distributive} \\ &= 5x - 2x + 5y && \text{commutative } (+) \\ &= (5 - 2)x + 5y && \text{distributive} \\ &= 3x + 5y && \text{substitution } (=) \end{aligned}$

65. $\begin{aligned} 2pq + pq &= (2 + 1)pq && \text{distributive} \\ &= 3pq && \text{substitution } (=) \end{aligned}$

66. Graph b 67. Graph c 68. Graph a

Page 66 Applications and Problem Solving

69a. $80s$ 69b. $80(4) = 320$ 69c. $80(8) = 640$

70a. $\begin{aligned} I &= prt \\ &= (100)(0.05)(2) \\ &= \$10 \end{aligned}$

70b. $\begin{aligned} I &= prt \\ &= 200(0.06) \\ &= \$12 \end{aligned}$

$\$200 + \$12 = \$\,212$

71a. $3 + 4 > 5 \rightarrow 7 > 5$ true

$3 + 5 > 4 \rightarrow 8 > 4$ true

$4 + 5 > 3 \rightarrow 9 > 3$ true

71b. $3 + 6 > x$ and $x + 3 > 6$

$9 > x$

$x < 9$ ft and $x > 3$ ft

The minimum length is $x > 3$ ft.

Page 67 Alternative Assesment: Thinking Critically

- No, the distributive property applies to only addition; sample example:

  $\begin{aligned} 2(3 \cdot 4) &\overset{?}{=} (2 \cdot 3)(2 \cdot 4) \\ 2(12) &\overset{?}{=} 6 \cdot 8 \\ 24 &\neq 48 \quad \text{false} \end{aligned}$
- See students' work.

Chapter 2 Exploring Rational Numbers

2-1 Integers and the Number Line

Pages 74–75 Check for Understanding

1. An arrow would be drawn, starting at 0 and going to −4. Starting at −4, an arrow would be drawn to the right 6 units long. The arrow ends at the sum of 2.

2. 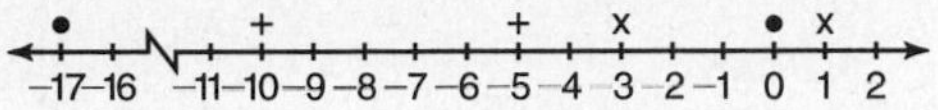

3. 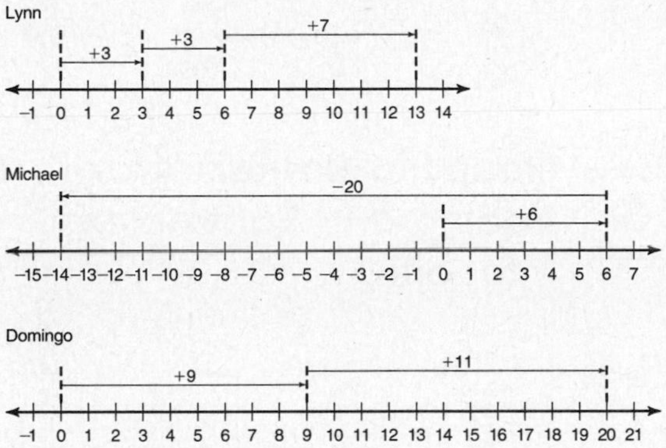

4. See students' work.

5. 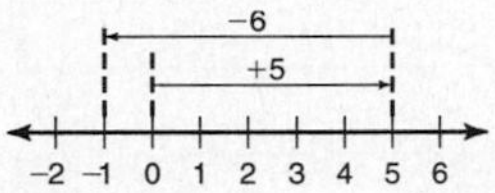

6. {−3, −2, −1}

7. {−1, 0, 1, 2, . . .}

8. 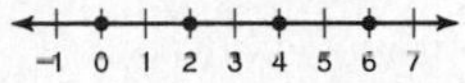

9. 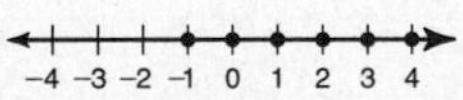

10. 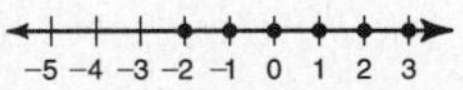

11. $-4 + (-3) = -7$
12. $4 + (-4) = 0$
13. $-8 + 3 = -5$
14. $-7 + (-15) = -22$
15. $5 + (-3) + 7 =$ 9-yard gain

Pages 75–77 Exercises

16. {. . . , −2, −1, 0, 1, 2, 3}
17. {−4, −3, −2, −1}
18. {0, 2, 5, 6, 8}
19. {− 7, − 3}
20. {− 2, −1, 1, 2}
21. {. . ., − 5, − 4, − 3, − 2, − 1, 0}

22. 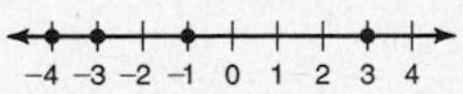

23. 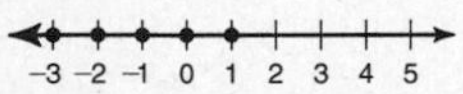

24. 

25. 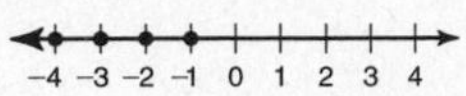

26. 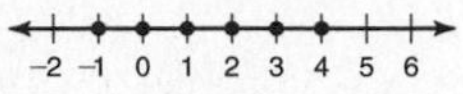

27. 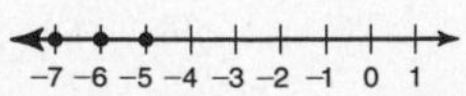

28. 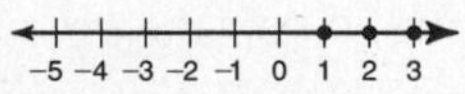

29. 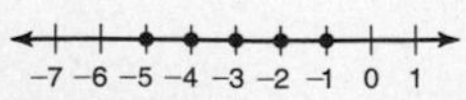

30. 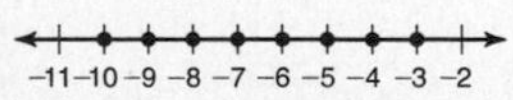

31. 13
32. −13
33. −5
34. −13
35. −12
36. 2
37. 6
38. 0
39. −23
40. See students' work.
41. $-17 + 82 = 65$; 65°F
42a. Hong Kong: $8 - (-5) = 8 + 5 = 13$ hours
10 A.M. + 13 hours = 11:00 P.M. the same day.
42b. Los Angeles: $-8 - (-5) = 8 + 5 = -3$ hours
10 A.M. − 3 hours = 7:00 A.M. the same day.
42c. Rio de Janeiro: $-3 - (-5) = 2$ hours
10 A.M. + 2 hours = 12 noon the same day.
42d. Bombay: $5\frac{1}{2} - (-5) = 5\frac{1}{2} + 5 = 10\frac{1}{2}$ hours
10 A.M. + $10\frac{1}{2}$ hours = 8:30 P.M. the same day.
43a. 4°F
43b. −31°F
43c. −15°F
43d. 9°F
44. See students' work.

45. 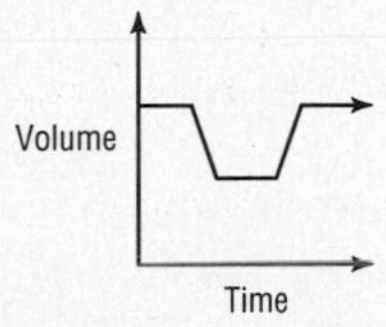

46. b
47. commutative (×)
48. $16a + 21a + 30b - 7b = (16 + 21)a + (30 - 7)b$
$= 37a + 23b$
49. substitution (=)
50. $5(7) + 6 = x$
$35 + 6 = x$
$41 = x$
51. $9(0.4 + 1.2) - 0.5 = 9(1.6) - 0.5$
$= 14.4 - 0.5$
$= 13.9$
52. 9.5 + 1.5 = 11, 11 + 1.5 = 12.5, 12.5 + 1.5 = 14

Page 77 Mathematics and Society

1. 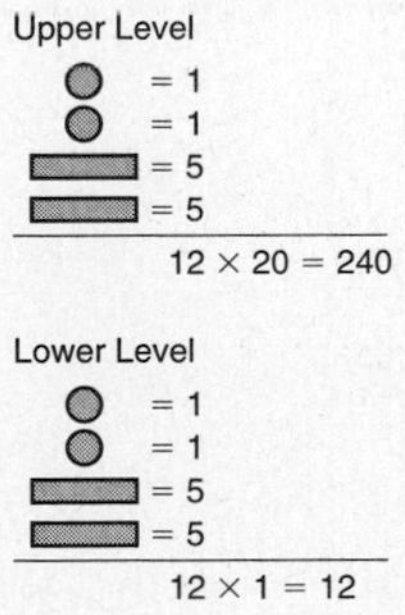

2. See students' work.
3. See students' work.

2-2 Integration: Statistics Line Plots

Page 80 Check for Understanding

1. See students' work.
2. See students' work.
3. See students' work.
4. from 0 to 70

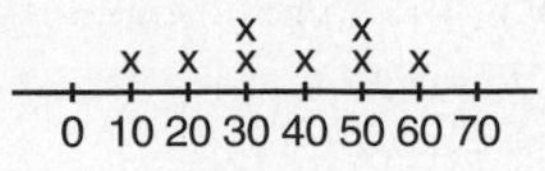

5. from 35 to 80

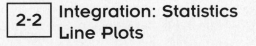

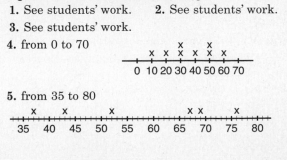

6a.

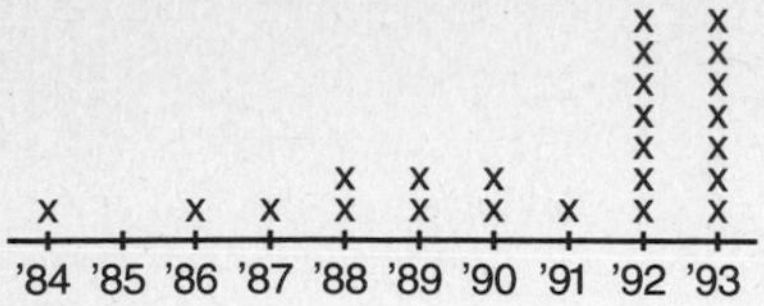

6b. \$1950 to \$ 11,475

6c.

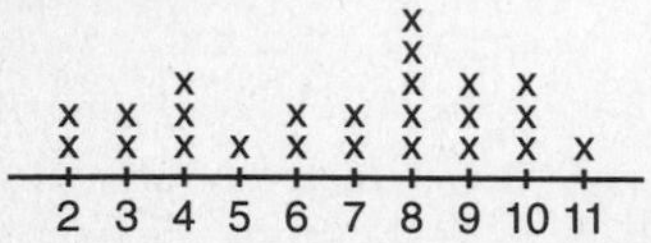

Pages 80–83 Exercises

7a.

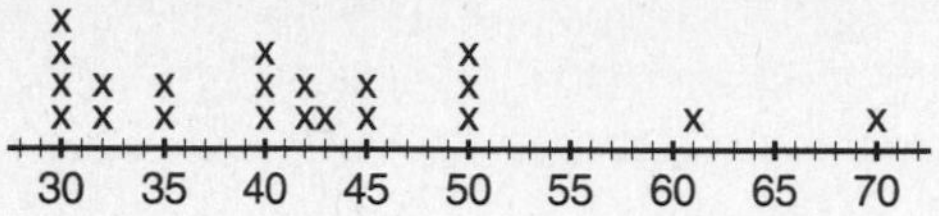

7b. 70 mph; cheetah **7c.** 30 mph

7d. 30 mph **7e.** 12 **7f.** 4

8a. from 1787 to 1959

8b.

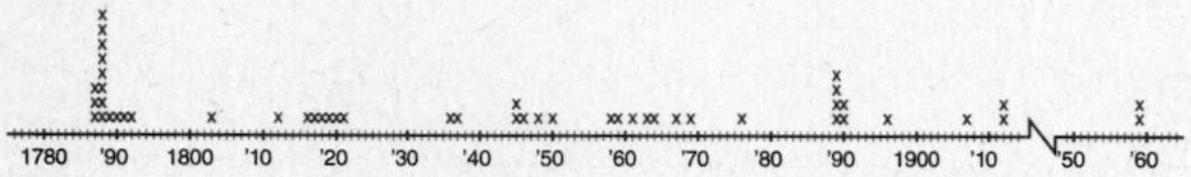

8c. yes, 1788; states ratified constitution and became official United States of America.

9a. from 20 to 75 by 5s

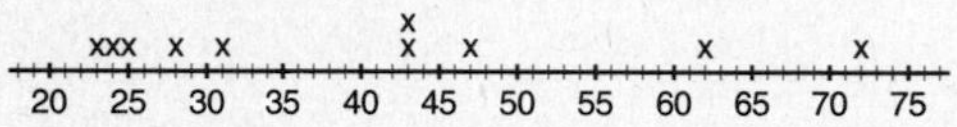

9b. yes, 25 and 42 **9c.** See students' work.

9d. See students' work.

10a.

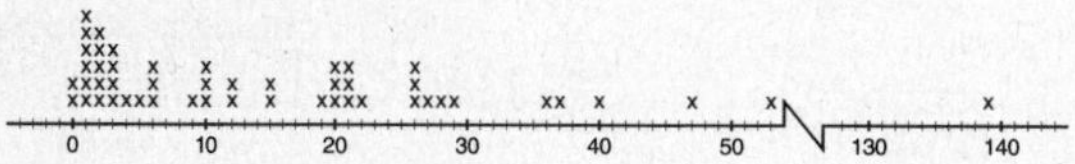

10b. yes; 1, 2, and 3

10c. Texas, because of weather patterns and geographical location.

11a. Ms. Martinez's

11b. No; in Ms. Martinez's class, the hours that the students talked on the phone were close to each other (4 ± 2 hours). In Mr. Thomas' class, the students had a wider range of hours spent talking on the phone. The range was from 0 to 8 hours, with no hours clustered around a certain number.

12a.

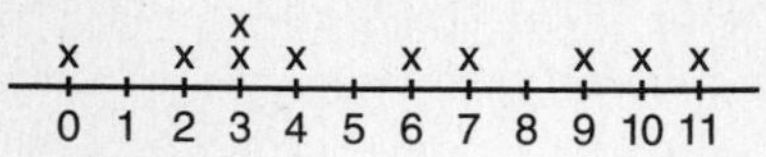

12b. Answers will vary. Sample answer:

1. Did any countries win the same number of gold medals?
2. How many countries won more than three gold medals?
3. How many gold medals did the countries win altogether?

13. Mr. Thomas', $\frac{0+0+1+2+3+4+5+6+7+8}{10} = \frac{36}{10} = 3.6$ hours;

Ms. Martinez's, $\frac{2+2+3+3+3+4+4+5+5+6}{10} = \frac{37}{10} = 3.7$ hours; yes

14.

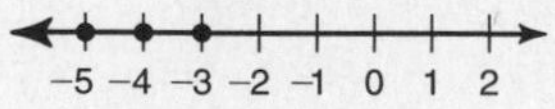

15. associative (×)

16. $15(124) = 15(100 + 24)$
$= 1500 + 360$
$= 1860$

17. $m = \frac{22-8}{7}$
$= \frac{14}{7}$
$= 2$

18. $np + st = 7 \cdot 6 + 4 \cdot 5$
$= 42 + 20$
$= 62$

2-3A Modeling Mathematics: Adding and Subtracting Integers

Page 84

1.

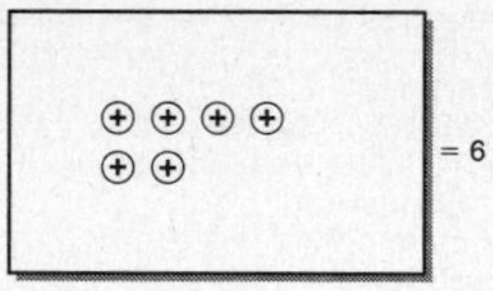

2.

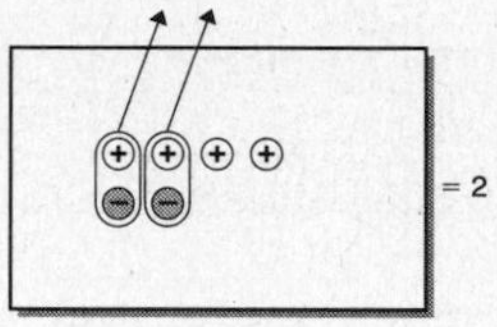

3.

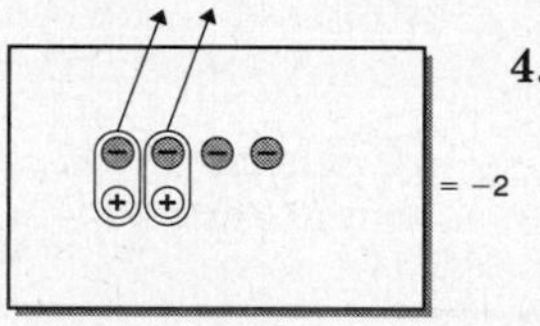

4.

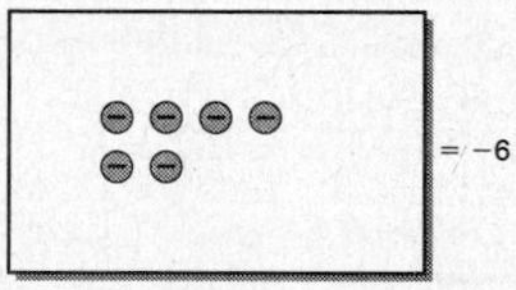

5.

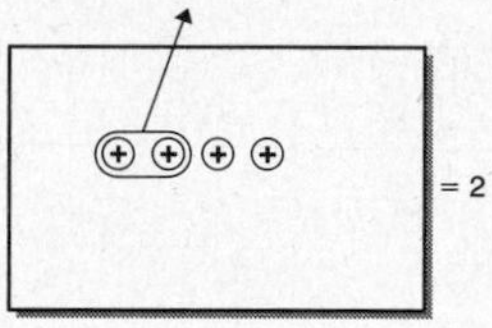

6.

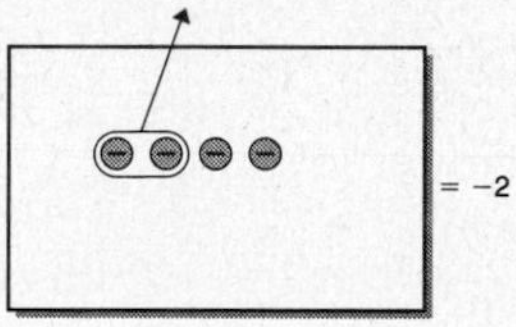

7.

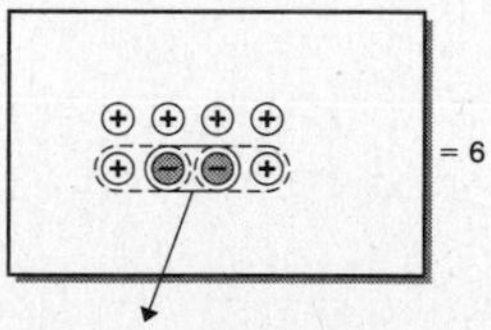

8.

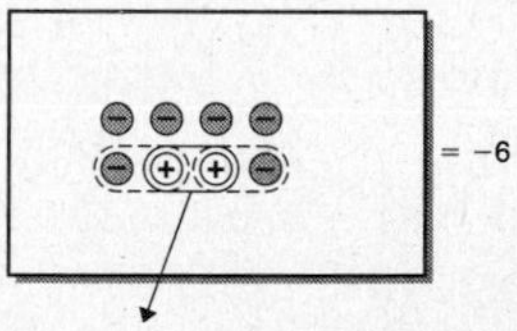

9. false

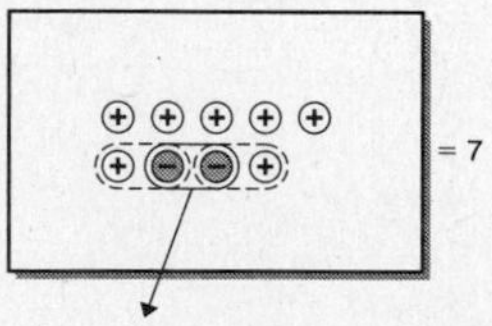

10. true

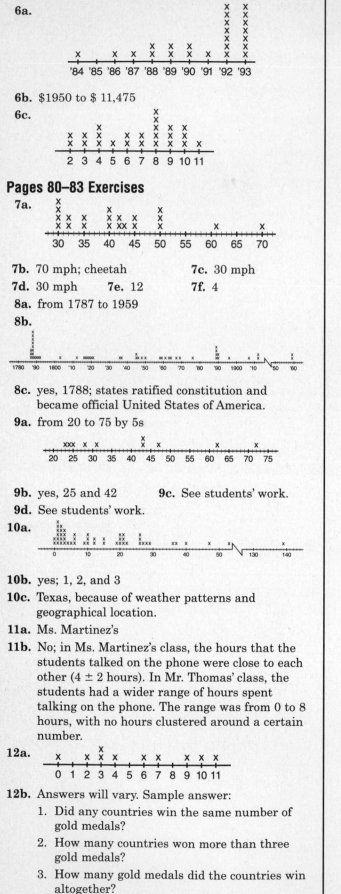

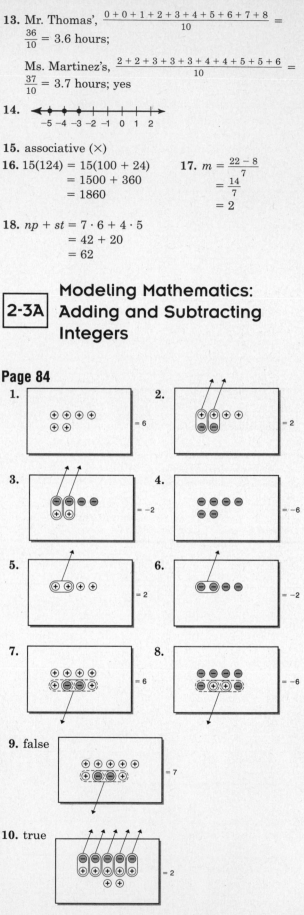

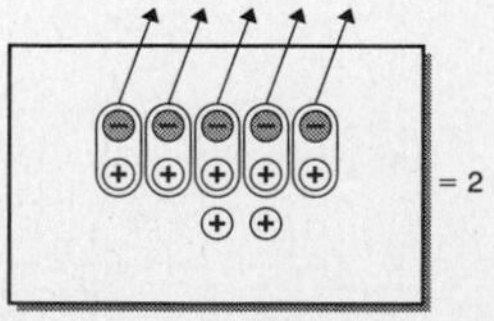

11. true

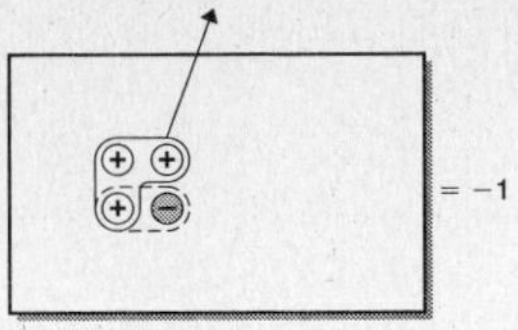

12. false

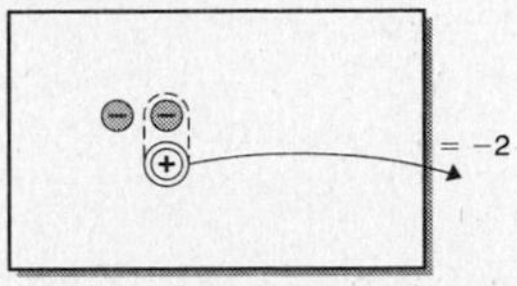

13. Answers should include using the number line.

2-3 Adding and Subtracting Integers

Pages 89–90 Check for Understanding

1. A zero pair of counters has equal amounts of positive and negative counters, therefore there are equal pairs of opposites and they will add to zero, which shows the additive inverse property.

2. Sample answer: −2; Start at zero. The absolute value is two places to the right.

3a. Sample answers: On a number line, start at zero. Move left three spaces to −3. Then move left one space to add −1. The sum is −4.

3b. On a number line, start at zero. Move right five spaces to +5. Then move left seven spaces to add −7. The sum is −2.

3c. On a number line, start at zero. Move right four spaces to +4. Then move nine spaces to the left to subtract 9. The difference is −5.

3d. On a number line, start at zero. Move right six spaces to +6. Subtracting −5 is the same as adding +5. So move right five more spaces to add +5. The sum is 11.

4a. 0 **4b.** 0 **5.** $-3 + 5 = 2$

6. $-9 - (-4) = -5$

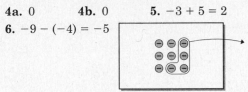

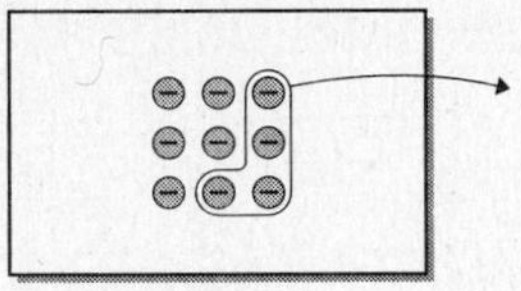

7. −7, 7 **8.** 20, 20 **9.** 0, 0

10. $-12 + (-8) = -20$

11. $-11 - (-7) = -11 + (+7)$
$= -4$

12. $-36 + 15 = -21$

13. $18 - 29 = 18 + (-29)$
$= -11$

14. $|-6 - 4| = |-6 + (-4)|$
$= |-10|$
$= 10$

15. $-|5 - 5| = -|5 + (-5)|$
$= -|0|$
$= 0$

16. $-16y - 5y = -16y + (-5y)$
$= [-16 + (-5)]y$
$= -21y$

17. $32c - (-8c) = 32c + (+8c)$
$= (32 + 8)c$
$= 40c$

18. $-9d + (-6d) = [-9 + (-6)]d$
$= -15d$

19. $y - 7 = 3 - 7$
$= 3 + (-7)$
$= -4$

20. $16 + z = 16 + (-6)$
$= 10$

21. $|8 + x| = |8 + (-5)| = |3| = 3$

22. $\begin{bmatrix} 3 & 2 \\ 5 & 0 \end{bmatrix} + \begin{bmatrix} 4 & -2 \\ -1 & 6 \end{bmatrix} = \begin{bmatrix} 3 + 4 & 2 + (-2) \\ 5 + (-1) & 0 + 64 \end{bmatrix}$
$= \begin{bmatrix} 7 & 0 \\ 4 & 6 \end{bmatrix}$

23. $\begin{bmatrix} 3 & 2 \\ 5 & 0 \end{bmatrix} - \begin{bmatrix} 4 & -2 \\ -1 & 6 \end{bmatrix} = \begin{bmatrix} 3 - 4 & 2 - (-2) \\ 5 - (-1) & 0 - 6 \end{bmatrix}$
$= \begin{bmatrix} -1 & 4 \\ 6 & -6 \end{bmatrix}$

24a. −125°F **24b.** $200 - (-125) = 325$

Pages 90–92 Exercises

25. −12, 12 **26.** 45, 45 **27.** 302, 302

28. 2 **29.** 0 **30.** 23

31. $0 - 32 = 0 + (-32) = -32$

32. $16 - (-23) = 16 + 23 = 39$

33. −16 **34.** −88 **35.** −70

36. $-18 - 4 = -18 + (-4)$
$= -22$

37. $9 - 24 = 9 + (-24)$
$= -15$

38. $-21 - (-24) = -21 + 24$
$= 3$

39. $-13 - (-8) = -13 + 8$
$= -5$

40. $29t - 17t = (29 - 17)t$
$= 12t$

41. $17b - (-23b) = 17b + 23b$
$= (17 + 23)b$
$= 40b$

42. $-6w + (-13w) = [-6 + (-13)]w$
$= -19w$

43. $6p + (-35p) = [6 + (-35)]p$
$= -29p$

44. $54y - 47y = (54 - 47)y$
$= 7y$

45. $-5d + 31d = (-5 + 31)d$
$= 26d$

46. $b + 14 = -4 + 14$
$= 10$

47. $d - 6 = 2 - 6$
$= 2 + (-6)$
$= -4$

48. $15 + p = 15 + (-5)$
$= 10$

49. $d + (-17) = 2 + (-17)$
$= -15$

50. $d + 7 = 2 + 7$
$= 9$

51. $|p| = |-5|$
$= 5$

52. $|6+b| = |6+(-4)|$
$= |2|$
$= 2$

53. $|p-3| = |-5-3|$
$= |-5+(-3)|$
$= |-8|$
$= 8$

54. $-|-22+p| = -|-22+(-5)|$
$= -|-27|$
$= -27$

55. $|-58+(-41)| = |-99|$
$= 99$

56. $|-93| - (-43) = 93 + (+43)$
$= 136$

57. $-|-345-(-286)| = -|-345+(+286)|$
$= -|-59|$
$= -59$

58. $\begin{bmatrix} 3 & 2 \\ 4 & -1 \end{bmatrix} + \begin{bmatrix} 0 & 5 \\ -3 & -4 \end{bmatrix} = \begin{bmatrix} 3+0 & 2+5 \\ 4+(-3) & -1+(-4) \end{bmatrix}$
$= \begin{bmatrix} 3 & 7 \\ 1 & -5 \end{bmatrix}$

59. $\begin{bmatrix} 2 & 4 \\ -1 & 0 \end{bmatrix} + \begin{bmatrix} -2 & -1 \\ 3 & 2 \end{bmatrix} = \begin{bmatrix} 2+(-2) & 4+(-1) \\ -1+3 & 0+2 \end{bmatrix}$
$= \begin{bmatrix} 0 & 3 \\ 2 & 2 \end{bmatrix}$

60. $\begin{bmatrix} 1 & 6 \\ -4 & -5 \end{bmatrix} - \begin{bmatrix} -3 & -6 \\ 2 & -4 \end{bmatrix} = \begin{bmatrix} 1-(-3) & 6-(-6) \\ -4-2 & -5-(-4) \end{bmatrix}$
$= \begin{bmatrix} 1+3 & 6+6 \\ -4+(-2) & -5+4 \end{bmatrix} = \begin{bmatrix} 4 & 12 \\ -6 & -1 \end{bmatrix}$

61. $\begin{bmatrix} 2 & 3 \\ 4 & 2 \\ 5 & -5 \end{bmatrix} - \begin{bmatrix} 6 & 8 \\ 8 & 7 \\ -5 & -2 \end{bmatrix} = \begin{bmatrix} 2-6 & 3-8 \\ 4-8 & 2-7 \\ 5-(-5) & -5-(-2) \end{bmatrix}$
$= \begin{bmatrix} 2+(-6) & 3+(-8) \\ 4+(-8) & 2+(-7) \\ 5+5 & -5+2 \end{bmatrix} = \begin{bmatrix} -4 & -5 \\ -4 & -5 \\ 10 & -3 \end{bmatrix}$

62. $RS + ST = RT$
$RS + 9 = 15$
$RS = 6$
$QR + RS = QS$
$4 + 6 = QS$
$QS = 10$ units

63. $67 - 43 = 67 + (-43)$
$= 24$th floor

64a.

3	4	−1
−2	2	6
5	0	1

64b.

−2	−1	−6
−7	−3	1
0	−5	−4

64c.

−6	−5	−10
−11	−7	−3
−4	−9	−8

65a. Monday

	Sesame	Poppy	Blueberry	Plain
East Store	120	80	64	75
West Store	65	105	77	53

Tuesday

	Sesame	Poppy	Blueberry	Plain
East Store	112	76	56	74
West Store	69	95	82	50

65b. Monday + Tuesday

$\begin{bmatrix} 120 & 80 & 64 & 75 \\ 65 & 105 & 77 & 53 \end{bmatrix} + \begin{bmatrix} 112 & 76 & 56 & 74 \\ 69 & 95 & 82 & 50 \end{bmatrix} =$

	Sesame	Poppy	Blueberry	Plain
East Store	232	156	120	149
West Store	134	200	159	103

65c. Monday − Tuesday

$\begin{bmatrix} 120 & 80 & 64 & 75 \\ 65 & 105 & 77 & 53 \end{bmatrix} - \begin{bmatrix} 112 & 76 & 56 & 74 \\ 69 & 95 & 82 & 50 \end{bmatrix} =$

	Sesame	Poppy	Blueberry	Plain
East Store	8	4	8	1
West Store	−4	10	−5	3

This matrix represents the difference between Monday's and Tuesday's sales in each category.

66a. $65 - 72 = -7$
$74 - 72 = +2$
$69 - 72 = -3$
$71 - 72 = -1$

66b. $-7 + 2 + (-3) + (-1) = -9$

66c. Under par; yes, it is better than par 72.

67a. from 100 to 146

67b.

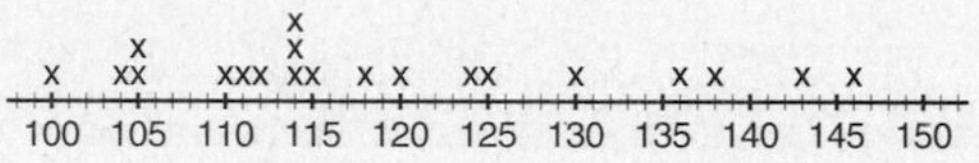

67c. yes; 114

67d. Siberian Elm; American Elm

68. $4 + (-6) = -2$

69.

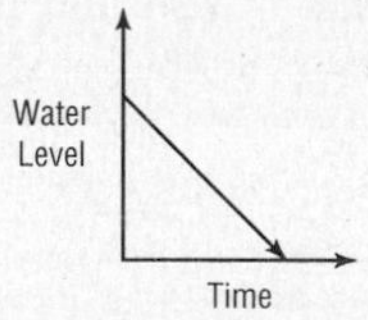

70. commutative (+)

71. $23y^2 + 32y^2 = (23+32)y^2$
$= 55y^2$

72. multiplicative property of 0

73. symmetric (=)

74. $p = 6\frac{1}{4} + \frac{1}{2}$
$= 6\frac{1}{4} + \frac{2}{4}$
$= 6\frac{3}{4}$

75. 14, 20, 29, 34, 37, 38, 43, 59, 64, 74, 84

76. $19 + 5 \cdot 4 = 19 + 20$
$= 39$

77. $16 + 4 = 20$,
$20 + 4 = 24$;
The sixth term is 24.

78. $n + 33$

2-4 Rational numbers

Pages 96–97 Check for Understanding

1. Sample answers: $\frac{1}{2}$, $\frac{10}{3}$, 0.32
2. none

3. One way is to represent these numbers as decimals and then find three decimal values between 0.2 and 0.25, such as 0.21 or 0.24, and then convert these back into fraction form. Another way is to use the calculator to find the mean of the two decimal equivalents. That is one in-between value. Then find the mean of the first decimal and the new value for the second value and the mean of the second decimal and the new value for the third value.

4. A fraction cannot have zero in the denominator because that would make the fraction undefined.

5. Yes; since $\frac{a}{b} < \frac{c}{d}$ then what needs to be shown is that $\frac{a}{b} < \frac{a+c}{b+d} < \frac{c}{d}$. If $\frac{a}{b} < \frac{c}{d}$, then $ad < bc$ and then adding ab to both sides, $ad + ab < bc + ab$. Then $a(d + b) < b(c + a)$ and $\frac{a}{b} < \frac{a+c}{b+d}$. The same method can be used to show the other side also.

6. See students' work. **7.** $-4 < 8$

8. $-5 \ \underline{?}\ 0 - 3$
$-5 < -3$

9. $\frac{5}{14} \ \underline{?}\ \frac{25}{70}$
$5(70) \ \underline{?}\ 14(25)$
$350 = 350$
$\frac{5}{14} = \frac{25}{70}$

10. $\frac{1}{6} = 0.1\overline{6}$, $\frac{1}{2} = 0.5$, $\frac{2}{3} = 0.6$; therefore, $\frac{1}{6} < \frac{1}{2} < \frac{2}{3}$.

11. $\frac{3}{4} = 0.75$, $\frac{7}{8} = 0.875$; therefore, $-0.5 < \frac{3}{4} < \frac{7}{8} < 2.5$.

12. unit cost of 6-ounce can: $1.59 \div 6 = 0.265$; unit cost of 3 3-ounce cans: $2.19 \div 9 = 0.243$; $0.243 < 0.265$; a package of 3 three-ounce cans for $2.19 is a better buy.

13. See students' work.

Pages 97–99 Exercises

14. $-3 < 5$ **15.** $-1 > -4$

16. $-6 - 3 \ \underline{?}\ -9$
$-9 = -9$

17. $5 \ \underline{?}\ 8.4 - 1.5$
$5 < 6.9$

18. $4 \ \underline{?}\ \frac{16}{3}$
$4(3) \ \underline{?}\ 16$
$12 < 16$
$4 < \frac{16}{3}$

19. $\frac{8}{15} \ \underline{?}\ \frac{9}{16}$
$8(16) \ \underline{?}\ 9(15)$
$128 < 135$
$\frac{8}{15} < \frac{9}{16}$

20. $\frac{14}{5} \ \underline{?}\ \frac{25}{13}$
$14(13) \ \underline{?}\ 5(25)$
$182 > 125$
$\frac{14}{5} > \frac{25}{13}$

21. $\frac{4}{3}(6) \ \underline{?}\ 4\left(\frac{3}{2}\right)$
$8 > 6$
$\frac{4}{3}(6) > 4\left(\frac{3}{2}\right)$

22. $\frac{0.4}{3} \ \underline{?}\ \frac{1.2}{8}$
$0.4(8) \ \underline{?}\ 3(1.2)$
$3.2 < 3.6$
$\frac{0.4}{3} < \frac{1.2}{8}$

23. $\frac{6}{7} = 0.86$, $\frac{2}{3} = 0.\overline{6}$, $\frac{3}{8} = 0375$; therefore, $\frac{3}{8} < \frac{2}{3} < \frac{6}{7}$.

24. $-\frac{4}{15} = -0.2\overline{6}$, $-\frac{6}{17} = -0.35$, $-\frac{3}{16} = -0.1875$; therefore, $-\frac{6}{17} < -\frac{4}{15} < -\frac{3}{16}$.

25. $\frac{4}{14} = 0.29$, $\frac{3}{23} = 0.13$, $\frac{8}{42} = 0.19$; therefore, $\frac{3}{23} < \frac{8}{42} < 14$.

26. 6.7, $-\frac{5}{7} = -0.7$, $\frac{6}{13} = 0.46$; therefore, $-\frac{5}{7} < \frac{6}{13} < 6.7$.

27. 0.2, $-\frac{2}{5} = -0.4$, -0.2; therefore, $-\frac{2}{5} < -0.2 < 0.2$.

28. $\frac{4}{5} = 0.8$, $\frac{9}{10} = 0.9$, 0.7; therefore, $0.7 < \frac{4}{5} < \frac{9}{10}$.

29. unit cost for a 16-ounce drink: $0.59 \div 16 = 0.037$; unit cost for a 20-ounce drink: $0.89 \div 20 = 0.045$; $0.037 < 0.045$; the 16-ounce drink for $0.59 is the better buy.

30. unit cost for a 32-ounce bottle of shampoo: $3.59 \div 32 = 0.112$; unit cost for a 64-ounce bottle of shampoo: $6.99 \div 64 = 0.109$; $0.109 < 0.102$; the 64-ounce bottle for $ 6.99 is the better buy.

31. unit cost for a package of 48 paper plates: $2.39 \div 48 = 0.050$; unit cost for a package of 75 paper plates: $3.29 \div 75 = 0.044$; $0.044 < 0.050$; the package of 75 paper plates for $3.29 is the better buy.

32. Sample answer: $\frac{1}{2}$ **33.** Sample answer: $\frac{2}{3}$

34. Sample answer: -1

35. $\frac{1}{4} = \frac{5}{20}$, $\frac{1}{2} = \frac{10}{20}$; sample answer: $\frac{7}{20}$

36. $\frac{1}{3} = \frac{4}{12}$, $\frac{5}{6} = \frac{10}{12}$; sample answer: $\frac{6}{12}$

37. $-0.5 = -\frac{3}{6}$, $\frac{1}{3} = \frac{2}{6}$; sample answer: $\frac{1}{6}$

38. $b - c < 0 \rightarrow b < c$, $a - b > 0 \rightarrow a > b$, and $c - a < 0 \rightarrow c < a$. Therefore, a is the greatest.

39. $\frac{1}{2} - \frac{1}{14} = \frac{7}{14} - \frac{1}{14}$
$= \frac{6}{14}$ or $\frac{3}{7}$
$\frac{3}{7} \div 2 = \frac{3}{7} \cdot \frac{1}{2} = \frac{3}{14}$
$E = \frac{1}{14} + \frac{3}{14} = \frac{4}{14}$ or $\frac{2}{7}$
$G = \frac{1}{2} + \frac{3}{14} = \frac{7}{14} + \frac{3}{14} = \frac{10}{14}$ or $\frac{5}{7}$
$H = \frac{10}{14} + \frac{3}{14} = \frac{13}{14}$

40. $8.2 < 9.8$

41. $0.391 - \left(\frac{1}{64}\right) = 0.391 - 0.016 = 0.375$ inch

42a. $h = 61.412 + 2.317F$
$= 61.412 + 2.317(47.9)$
$= 172.4$ cm

42b. $h = 73.570 + 2.970H$
$= 73.570 + 2.970\ (35.7)$
$= 179.6$ cm

43. $-9, 9$

44.

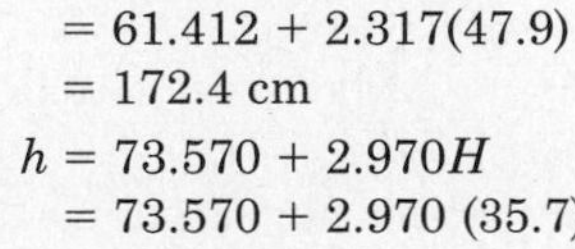

from 130 to 150 by 5s

45.

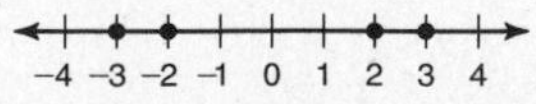

46a. Bryce

46b. Maria **46c.** See students' work.

47. $\frac{2}{5}m + \frac{1}{5}(6n + 3m) + \frac{1}{10}(8n + 15)$

$= \frac{2}{5}m + \frac{1}{5} \cdot 6n + \frac{1}{5} \cdot 3m + \frac{1}{10} \cdot 8n + \frac{1}{10} \cdot 15$

$= \frac{2}{5}m + \frac{6}{5}n + \frac{3}{5}m + \frac{8}{10}n + \frac{15}{10}$

$= \frac{2}{5}m + \frac{3}{5}m + \frac{6}{5}n + \frac{8}{10}n + \frac{15}{10}$

$= \left(\frac{2}{5} + \frac{3}{5}\right)m + \left(\frac{6}{5} + \frac{8}{10}\right)n + \frac{15}{10}$

$= m + 2n + \frac{3}{2}$

48. $27(3) = 81,\ 81(3) = 243,\ 243(3) = 729$

49. two times x squared plus six

Page 99 Self Test

1.

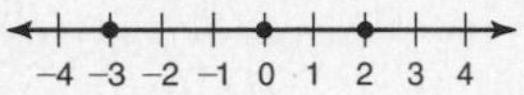

2.

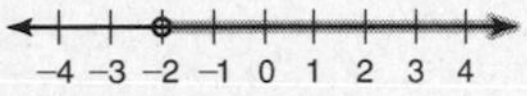

3. -17 **4.** -9 **5.** $23 - (-32) = 23 + 32$
$= 55$

6. $-12 - 4 = -12 + (-4)$
$= -16$

7a.

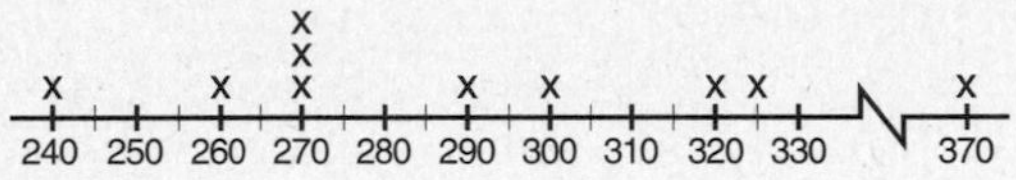

7b. yes; \$270

8. $-7 - 5 \ \underline{?}\ -11$
$-12 < -11$

9. $\frac{7}{16} \ \underline{?}\ \frac{8}{15}$
$7(15) \ \underline{?}\ 8(16)$
$105 < 128$
$\frac{7}{16} < \frac{8}{15}$

10. $\frac{5}{4}(4) \ \underline{?}\ 8\left(\frac{1}{2}\right)$
$5 > 4$
$\frac{5}{4}(4) > 8\left(\frac{1}{2}\right)$

2-5 Adding and Subtracting Rational Numbers

Pages 102–103 Check for Understanding

1. Answers will vary. Sample answer: One method is to add together the numbers of the same sign first and then add the two sums together.

$-2.4 + 5.87 + (-2.87) + 6.5 = [-2.4 + (-2.87)] + (5.87 + 6.5) = (-5.27) + 12.37 = 7.1$

Another method is to subtract the absolute values of the negative numbers from the positive numbers and then add those two differences together.

$-2.4 + 5.87 + (-2.87) + 6.5 = (5.87 - 2.4) + (6.5 - 2.87) = 3.47 + 3.63 = 7.1$

2. See students' work.

3.

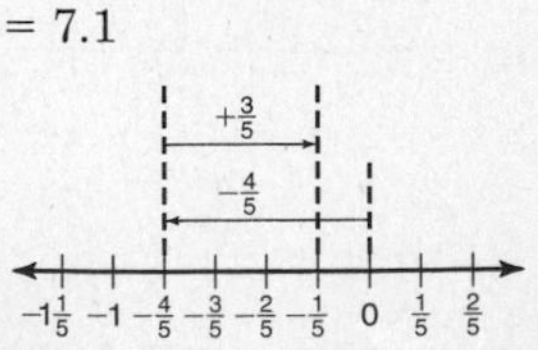

4.

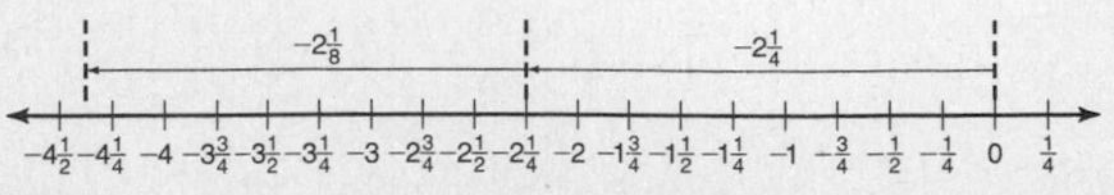

5. $\frac{7}{9} - \frac{8}{9} = \frac{7}{9} + \left(-\frac{8}{9}\right)$
$= -\frac{1}{9}$

6. $-\frac{7}{12} + \frac{5}{6} = -\frac{7}{12} + \frac{10}{12}$
$= \frac{3}{12}$
$= \frac{1}{4}$

7. $-\frac{1}{8} + \left(-\frac{5}{2}\right) = -\frac{1}{8} + \left(-\frac{20}{8}\right)$
$= -\frac{21}{8}$
$= -2\frac{5}{8}$

8. $-69.5 - 82.3 = -69.5 + (-82.3)$
$= -151.8$

9. $4.57 + (-3.69) = 0.88$

10. $-\frac{2}{5} + \frac{3}{15} + \frac{3}{5} = -\frac{2}{5} + \frac{1}{5} + \frac{3}{5}$
$= \frac{2}{5}$

11. $a - (-5) = 0.75 - (-5)$
$= 0.75 + 5$
$= 5.75$

12. $\frac{11}{2} - b = \frac{11}{2} - \left(-\frac{5}{2}\right)$
$= \frac{11}{2} + \frac{5}{2}$
$= \frac{16}{2} = 8$

13a. $2\frac{3}{8} + \left(-\frac{1}{4}\right) + \left(-\frac{3}{8}\right) + \left(2\frac{1}{4}\right) + \left(-3\frac{1}{2}\right)$

$= \left[2\frac{3}{8} + \left(-\frac{3}{8}\right)\right] + \left(-\frac{1}{4} + 2\frac{1}{4}\right) + \left(-3\frac{1}{2}\right)$

$= 2 + 2 + \left(-3\frac{1}{2}\right)$

$= \left(3\frac{2}{2}\right) + \left(-3\frac{1}{2}\right)$

$= +\frac{1}{2}$

13b.

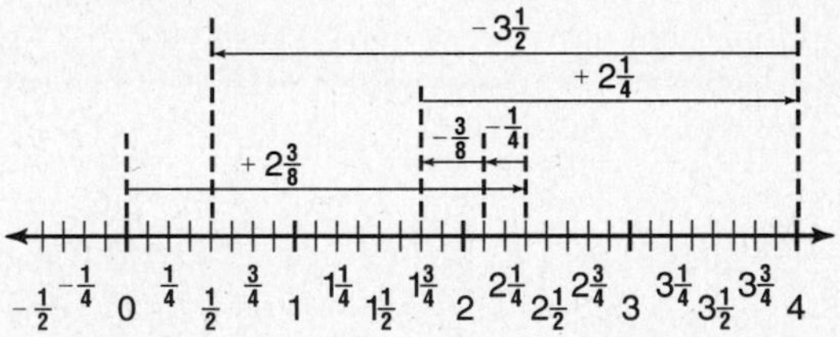

Pages 103–104 Exercises

14. $\frac{5}{8} + \left(-\frac{3}{8}\right) = \frac{2}{8}$
$= \frac{1}{4}$

15. $-\frac{7}{8} - \left(-\frac{3}{16}\right) = -\frac{14}{16} + \frac{3}{16}$
$= -\frac{11}{16}$

16. $-1.6 - 3.8 = -1.6 + (-3.8)$
$= -5.4$

17. $3.2 + (-4.5) = -1.3$

18. $\frac{1}{2} + \left(-\frac{8}{16}\right) = \frac{8}{16} + \left(-\frac{8}{16}\right)$
$= 0$

19. $\frac{2}{3} + \left(-\frac{2}{9}\right) = \frac{6}{9} + \left(-\frac{2}{9}\right)$
$= \frac{4}{9}$

20. $-38.9 + 24.2 = -14.7$

21. $-0.0007 + (-0.2) = -0.2007$

22. $-\frac{3}{7} + \frac{1}{4} = -\frac{12}{28} + \frac{7}{28}$
$= -\frac{5}{28}$

23. $-5\frac{7}{8} - 2\frac{3}{4} = -5\frac{7}{8} + \left(-2\frac{6}{8}\right)$
$= -7\frac{13}{8}$
$= -8\frac{5}{8}$

24. $79.3 - (-14.1) = 79.3 + 14.1$
$= 93.4$

25. $-0.0015 + 0.05 = 0.0485$

26. $-9.16 - (-10.17) = 9.16 + 10.17$
$= 1.01$

27. $-5.6 + (-9.45) + (-7.89) = -22.94$

28. $\frac{1}{4} + 2 + \left(-\frac{3}{4}\right) = 2 + \left[\frac{1}{4} + \left(-\frac{3}{4}\right)\right]$
$= 2 + \left(-\frac{2}{4}\right)$
$= 1\frac{2}{2} + \left(-\frac{1}{2}\right)$
$= 1\frac{1}{2}$

29. $-0.87 + 3.5 + (-7.6) + 2.8$
$= [-0.87 + (-7.6)] + (3.5 + 2.8)$
$= (-8.47) + 6.3$
$= -2.17$

30. $\frac{3}{4} + \left(-\frac{4}{5}\right) + \frac{2}{5} = \frac{15}{20} + \left(-\frac{16}{20}\right) + \frac{8}{20}$
$= \frac{7}{20}$

31. $-4\frac{1}{4} + 6\frac{1}{3} + 2\frac{2}{3} + \left(-3\frac{3}{4}\right)$
$= \left[-4\frac{1}{4} + \left(-3\frac{3}{4}\right)\right] + \left(6\frac{1}{3} + 2\frac{2}{3}\right)$
$= -8 + 9$
$= 1$

32. $-3\frac{1}{3} - b = -3\frac{1}{3} - \frac{1}{2}$
$= -3\frac{2}{6} + \left(-\frac{3}{6}\right)$
$= -3\frac{5}{6}$

33. $r - 2.7 = -0.8 - 2.7$
$= -0.8 + (-2.7)$
$= -3.5$

34. $n - 0.5 = -0.8 - 0.5$
$= -0.8 + (-0.5)$
$= -1.3$

35. $t - (-1.3) = -18 - (-1.3)$
$= -18 + 1.3$
$= -16.7$

36. $\frac{4}{3} - p = \frac{4}{3} - \frac{4}{5}$
$= \frac{20}{15} - \frac{12}{15}$
$= \frac{8}{15}$

37. $-\frac{12}{7} - s = -\frac{12}{7} - \frac{16}{21}$
$= \left(-\frac{36}{21}\right) + \left(-\frac{16}{21}\right)$
$= -\frac{52}{21}$

38. $\begin{bmatrix} 3 & -2 \\ 5 & 6.2 \end{bmatrix} + \begin{bmatrix} 2.4 & 5 \\ -4 & 1 \end{bmatrix} = \begin{bmatrix} 3 + 2.4 & -2 + 5 \\ 5 + (-4) & 6.2 + 1 \end{bmatrix}$
$= \begin{bmatrix} 5.4 & 3 \\ 1 & 7.2 \end{bmatrix}$

39. $\begin{bmatrix} -1.3 & 4.2 \\ 0 & -3.4 \end{bmatrix} - \begin{bmatrix} 2.5 & 4.3 \\ -1.7 & -6.3 \end{bmatrix} =$
$\begin{bmatrix} -1.3 - 2.5 & 4.2 - 4.3 \\ 0 - (-1.7) & -3.4 - (-6.3) \end{bmatrix} = \begin{bmatrix} -3.8 & -0.1 \\ 1.7 & 2.9 \end{bmatrix}$

40. $\begin{bmatrix} \frac{1}{2} & -2 \\ 7 & \frac{1}{4} \end{bmatrix} + \begin{bmatrix} 3 & -5 \\ \frac{2}{3} & 6 \end{bmatrix} = \begin{bmatrix} \frac{1}{2} + 3 & -2 + (-5) \\ 7 + \frac{2}{3} & \frac{1}{4} + 6 \end{bmatrix}$
$= \begin{bmatrix} 3\frac{1}{2} & -7 \\ 7\frac{2}{3} & 6\frac{1}{4} \end{bmatrix}$ or $\begin{bmatrix} \frac{7}{2} & -7 \\ \frac{23}{3} & \frac{25}{4} \end{bmatrix}$

41. $\begin{bmatrix} \frac{1}{2} & 6 \\ 1 & 5 \\ 4 & -7 \end{bmatrix} + \begin{bmatrix} -\frac{1}{4} & 5 \\ -4 & 3 \\ -3\frac{1}{2} & -5 \end{bmatrix} =$

$\begin{bmatrix} \frac{1}{2} + \left(-\frac{1}{4}\right) & 6 + 5 \\ -1 + (-4) & 5 + 3 \\ 4 + \left(-3\frac{1}{2}\right) & -7 + (-5) \end{bmatrix} = \begin{bmatrix} \frac{1}{4} & 11 \\ -5 & 8 \\ \frac{1}{2} & -12 \end{bmatrix}$

42. $\begin{bmatrix} 3.2 & 6.4 & -4.3 \\ 5 & -4 & 0.4 \end{bmatrix} - \begin{bmatrix} 1.4 & 3.7 & 5 \\ -1 & 5 & 0.4 \end{bmatrix} =$

$\begin{bmatrix} 3.2 - 1.4 & 6.4 - 3.7 & -4.3 - 5 \\ 5 - (-1) & -4 - 5 & 0.4 - 0.4 \end{bmatrix} = \begin{bmatrix} 1.8 & 2.7 & -9.3 \\ 6 & -9 & 0 \end{bmatrix}$

43. Answers will vary. Sample answer:
$\begin{bmatrix} 5 & 3 \\ 1 & 7 \end{bmatrix}, \begin{bmatrix} 4 & -3 \\ 1 & 2 \end{bmatrix}, \begin{bmatrix} 9 & 0 \\ 2 & 9 \end{bmatrix}, \begin{bmatrix} 18 & 0 \\ 4 & 18 \end{bmatrix}$

$\begin{bmatrix} 5 & 3 \\ 1 & 7 \end{bmatrix} + \begin{bmatrix} 4 & -3 \\ 1 & 2 \end{bmatrix} = \begin{bmatrix} 9 & 0 \\ 2 & 9 \end{bmatrix} = \begin{bmatrix} 4 & -3 \\ 1 & 2 \end{bmatrix} + \begin{bmatrix} 5 & 3 \\ 1 & 7 \end{bmatrix}$

$\left(\begin{bmatrix} 5 & 3 \\ 1 & 7 \end{bmatrix} + \begin{bmatrix} 4 & -3 \\ 1 & 2 \end{bmatrix}\right) + \begin{bmatrix} 9 & 0 \\ 2 & 9 \end{bmatrix} = \begin{bmatrix} 18 & 0 \\ 4 & 18 \end{bmatrix} = \begin{bmatrix} 5 & 3 \\ 1 & 7 \end{bmatrix} +$
$\left(\begin{bmatrix} 4 & -3 \\ 1 & 2 \end{bmatrix} + \begin{bmatrix} 9 & 0 \\ 2 & 9 \end{bmatrix}\right)$

44. Yes; $\frac{1}{4} + \frac{2}{5} + \frac{1}{2} = \frac{5}{20} + \frac{8}{20} + \frac{10}{20}$
$= \frac{23}{20}$ or $1\frac{3}{20}$ rolls needed
$1\frac{1}{2} - 1\frac{3}{20} = 1\frac{10}{20} - 1\frac{3}{20} = \frac{7}{20}$ of a roll is left over.

45a. $7.89 + 1.12 = 9.01$, $9.01 + 1.12 = 10.13$, $10.13 + 1.12 = 11.25$

45b. $5.65 - 4.53 = 1.12$

45c. $-2 + \frac{3}{4} = -\frac{8}{4} + \frac{3}{4} = -\frac{5}{4}$
$-\frac{5}{4} + \frac{3}{4} = -\frac{2}{4} = -\frac{1}{2}$
$-\frac{1}{2} + \frac{3}{4} = -\frac{2}{4} + \frac{3}{4} = \frac{1}{4}$
$\frac{1}{4} + \frac{3}{4} = \frac{4}{4} = 1;$
The first five terms are $-2, -\frac{5}{4}, -\frac{1}{2}, \frac{1}{4}, 1;$
$-2 - \frac{5}{4} - \frac{1}{2} + \frac{1}{4} + 1 = \left(-\frac{8}{4} - \frac{5}{4} - \frac{2}{4}\right) + \frac{1}{4} + \frac{4}{4} =$
$-\frac{15}{4} + \frac{5}{4} = -\frac{10}{4} = -2\frac{1}{2}$

46. 46 feet 9 in. + $1\frac{3}{4}$ in. + 1 foot $2\frac{1}{2}$ in.
= (46 + 1) feet + $\left(9 + 1\frac{3}{4} + 2\frac{1}{2}\right)$ in.
= 47 feet + $\left(9 + 1\frac{3}{4} + 2\frac{2}{4}\right)$ in.
= 47 feet + $\left(13\frac{1}{4}\right)$ in.
= 48 feet + $1\frac{1}{4}$ in.

47. <

48. $-|-9+2x| = -|-9+2\cdot 7|$
$= -|-9+14|$
$= -|5|$
$= -5$

49a.

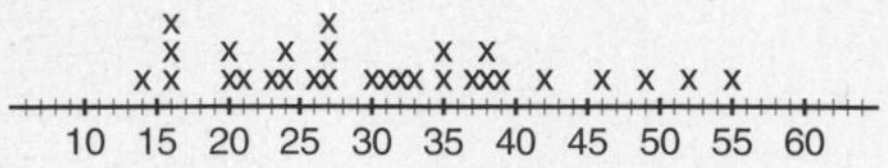

49b. no

50. $3(12) - 3 - 12 - 2 + 12 - 9 - 11$
$= 36 + 12 + [-3 + (-12) + (-2) + (9) + (-11)]$
$= 48 + (-37)$
$= 11$ slices

51. multiplicative property of 0

52. $7[4^3 - 2(4+3)] \div 7 + 2 = 7[64 - 2(7)] \div 7 + 2$
$= 7[64 - 14] \div 7 + 2$
$= 7(50) \div 7 + 2$
$= 350 \div 7 + 2$
$= 50 + 2$
$= 52$

53. $\frac{1}{3}, \frac{1+2}{3\cdot 2} = \frac{3}{6}, \frac{3+2}{6\cdot 2} = \frac{5}{12}, \frac{5+2}{12\cdot 2} = \frac{7}{24}$

54. $8^4 = 8\cdot 8\cdot 8\cdot 8 = 4096$

2-6A Modeling Mathematics: Multiplying Integers

Page 105

1. See students' work; take out two sets of negative counters.

2.

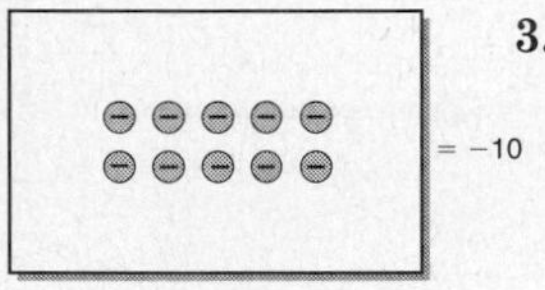

3.

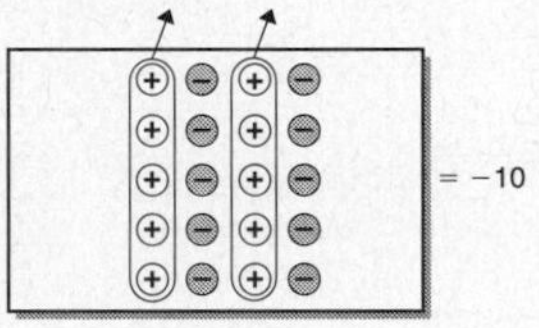

4.

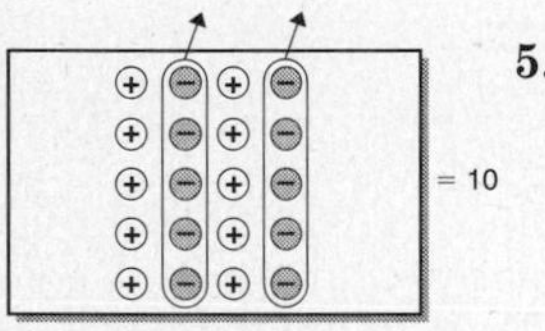

5.

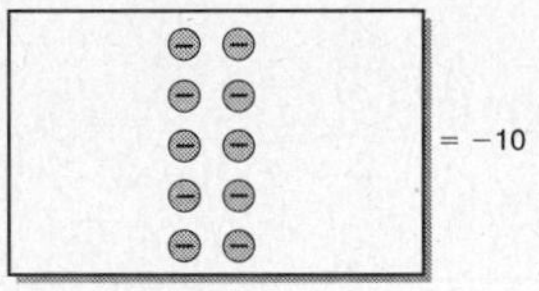

6.

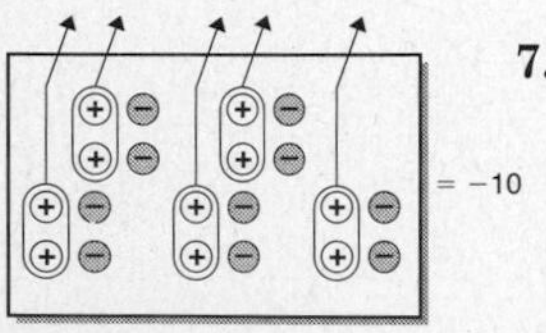

7.

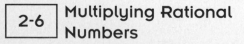

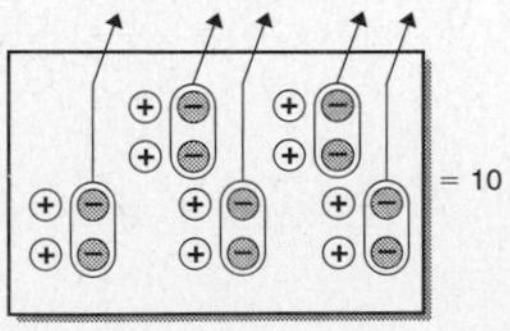

8. The product is the same. The order of multiplication using counters is different.

2-6 Multiplying Rational Numbers

Pages 108–109 Check for Understanding

1a. ab is positive if a and b have the same signs, either both positive or both negative.

1b. ab is negative if a and b have opposite signs, one is negative and the other is positive.

1c. ab is equal to 0 if either a or b is 0, or both a and b are 0.

2a. If a^2 is positive, then a is either negative or positive.

2b. If a^3 is positive, then a is positive.

2c. If a^3 is negative, then a is negative.

3. $a + a^2 = -2 + (-2)^2$
$= -2 + 4$
$= 2$
$2 > -4$; therefore, $a + a^2$ is greater.

4. $2 \times (-3) = -6$

5. -18 6. 32 7. 24 8. $\frac{49}{9}$

9. $\left(-\frac{4}{5}\right)\left(-\frac{1}{5}\right)(-5) = \left(-\frac{4}{5}\right)\left(-\frac{1}{5}\cdot -5\right)$
$= \left(-\frac{4}{5}\right)(1)$
$= -\frac{4}{5}$

10. $-\frac{12}{35}$

11. $3y - 4x = 3\left(-\frac{2}{3}\right) - 4\left(\frac{1}{2}\right)$
$= \left(\frac{3}{1}\right)\left(-\frac{2}{3}\right) - \left(\frac{4}{1}\right)\left(\frac{1}{2}\right)$
$= -2 - 2$
$= -4$

12. $x^2y = \left(\frac{1}{2}\right)^2\left(-\frac{2}{3}\right)$
$= \left(\frac{1}{2}\cdot\frac{1}{2}\right)\left(-\frac{2}{3}\right)$
$= \frac{1}{4}\left(-\frac{2}{3}\right)$
$= -\frac{1}{6}$

13. $5s(-6t) + 2s(-8t) = -30st - 16st$
$= -46st$

14. $6x(-7y) + (-3x)(-5y) = -42xy + 15xy$
$= -27xy$

15. $\begin{bmatrix} 3(-2) & 3(4) \\ 3(-1) & 3(5) \end{bmatrix} = \begin{bmatrix} -6 & 12 \\ -3 & 15 \end{bmatrix}$

16. $\begin{bmatrix} -5(-1) & -5(0) \\ -5(4.5) & -5(8) \\ -5(3.2) & -5(-4) \end{bmatrix} = \begin{bmatrix} 5 & 0 \\ -22.5 & -40 \\ -16 & 20 \end{bmatrix}$

17. $\$0.30(19{,}534.1 - 19{,}438.6) = \$0.30(95.5)$
$= \$28.65$

Pages 109–111 Exercises

18. 78 19. -60 20. 42 21. -1

22. $-\frac{5}{6}\left(-\frac{2}{5}\right) = \frac{1}{3}$ 23. $(-5)\left(-\frac{2}{5}\right) = 2$

24. 360 25. 0.00879 26. 60

27. $\left(\frac{2}{3}\right)\left(\frac{3}{5}\right)(-3) = -\frac{6}{5}$ 28. $\left(-\frac{7}{12}\right)\left(\frac{6}{7}\right)\left(-\frac{3}{4}\right) = \frac{3}{8}$

29. $\frac{6}{11}\left(-\frac{33}{34}\right) = -\frac{9}{17}$ 30. 0.4125 31. 85.7095

32. 0

33. $\left(\frac{3}{5}\right)(5)(-2)\left(-\frac{1}{2}\right) = \left(\frac{3}{5}\right)\left(\frac{5}{1}\right)\left(\frac{-2}{1}\right)\left(-\frac{1}{2}\right)$
$= 3$

34. -24

35. $\left(\frac{2}{11}\right)(-11)(-4)\left(-\frac{3}{4}\right) = \left(\frac{2}{11}\right)\left(\frac{-11}{1}\right)\left(\frac{-4}{1}\right)\left(-\frac{3}{4}\right)$
$= -6$

36. $6m = 6\left(-\frac{2}{3}\right)$
$= \frac{6}{1}\left(-\frac{2}{3}\right)$
$= -4$

37. $nq = \left(\frac{1}{2}\right)\left(2\frac{1}{6}\right)$
$= \left(\frac{1}{2}\right)\left(\frac{13}{6}\right)$
$= \frac{13}{12}$

38. $2m - 3n = 2\left(-\frac{2}{3}\right) - 3\left(\frac{1}{2}\right)$
$= \left(\frac{2}{1}\right)\left(-\frac{2}{3}\right) - \left(\frac{3}{1}\right)\left(\frac{1}{2}\right)$
$= -\frac{4}{3} - \frac{3}{2}$
$= -\frac{8}{6} - \frac{9}{6}$
$= -\frac{17}{6}$

39. $pq - m = \left(-3\frac{3}{4}\right)\left(2\frac{1}{6}\right) - \left(-\frac{2}{3}\right)$
$= \left(-\frac{15}{4}\right)\left(\frac{13}{6}\right) + \frac{2}{3}$
$= -\frac{65}{8} + \frac{2}{3}$
$= -\frac{195}{24} + \frac{16}{24}$
$= -\frac{179}{24}$

40. $m^2\left(-\frac{1}{4}\right) = \left(-\frac{2}{3}\right)^2\left(-\frac{1}{4}\right)$
$= \left[-\frac{2}{3} \cdot \left(-\frac{2}{3}\right)\right]\left(-\frac{1}{4}\right)$
$= \left(\frac{4}{9}\right)\left(-\frac{1}{4}\right)$
$= -\frac{1}{9}$

41. $n^2(q + 2) = \left(\frac{1}{2}\right)^2\left(2\frac{1}{6} + 2\right)$
$= \left(\frac{1}{2} \cdot \frac{1}{2}\right)\left(2\frac{1}{6} + 2\right)$
$= \frac{1}{4}\left(4\frac{1}{6}\right)$
$= \frac{1}{4}\left(\frac{25}{6}\right)$
$= \frac{25}{24}$

42. $6ac - 36ry$ **43.** $-30rt + 4s$

44. $7m(-3n) + 3m(-4n) = -21mn - 12mn$
$= -33mn$

45. $5(2x - x) + 4(x + 3x) = 5 \cdot 2x - 5x + 4x + 4 \cdot 3x$
$= 10x - 5x + 4x + 12x$
$= 21x$

46. $18bc + 63ab$

47. $3.2(5x - y) - 0.3(-1.6x + 7y)$
$= 3.2 \cdot 5x + 3.2(-y) - 0.3(-1.6x) - 0.3 \cdot 7y$
$= 16x - 3.2y + 0.48x - 2.1y$
$= 16x + 0.48x - 3.2y - 2.1y$
$= (16 + 0.48)x + (-3.2 - 2.1)y$
$= 16.48x - 5.3y$

48. $\begin{bmatrix} -7(-1) & -7(8.2) & -7(0) \\ -7(4) & -7(5.6) & -7(-1) \\ -7(3.2) & -7(7) & -7(7) \end{bmatrix}$
$= \begin{bmatrix} 7 & -57.4 & 0 \\ -28 & -39.2 & 7 \\ -22.4 & -49 & -49 \end{bmatrix}$

49. $\begin{bmatrix} \frac{1}{2}(4) & \frac{1}{2}(12) & \frac{1}{2}(6) \\ \frac{1}{2}(5) & \frac{1}{2}(10) & \frac{1}{2}(2) \end{bmatrix} = \begin{bmatrix} 2 & 6 & 3 \\ \frac{5}{2} & 5 & 1 \end{bmatrix}$

50. $\begin{bmatrix} 4(1.3) & 4(-2) & 4(-4) \\ 4(0.5) & 4(-0.3) & 4(5) \\ 4(6.6) & 4(2.1) & 4(-8) \end{bmatrix} = \begin{bmatrix} 5.2 & -8 & -16 \\ 2 & -1.2 & 20 \\ 26.4 & 8.4 & -32 \end{bmatrix}$

51. $\begin{bmatrix} -4(2.25) & -4(-5.67) \\ -4(5.6) & -4(2.5) \\ -4(-7.2) & -4(-2.78) \end{bmatrix} = \begin{bmatrix} -9 & 22.68 \\ -22.4 & -10 \\ 28.8 & 11.12 \end{bmatrix}$

52. $\begin{bmatrix} -8(0.2) & -8(4.5) \\ -8(-1.4) & -8(-3) \\ -8(3) & -8(2.4) \\ -8(-7) & -8(-3.2) \end{bmatrix} = \begin{bmatrix} -1.6 & -36 \\ 11.2 & 24 \\ -24 & -19.2 \\ 56 & 25.6 \end{bmatrix}$

53. $\begin{bmatrix} \frac{2}{3}(9) & \frac{2}{3}(27) & \frac{2}{3}(6) \\ \frac{2}{3}(0) & \frac{2}{3}(3) & \frac{2}{3}(4) \end{bmatrix} = \begin{bmatrix} 6 & 18 & 4 \\ 0 & 2 & \frac{8}{3} \end{bmatrix}$

54. It is positive. **55.** It is negative.

56a. $\frac{1}{3} \cdot \frac{1}{3} = \frac{1}{9}, \frac{1}{9} \cdot \frac{1}{3} = \frac{1}{27}, \frac{1}{27} \cdot \frac{1}{3} = \frac{1}{81}$

56b. $3 \div 9 = \frac{1}{3}$

56c. $-6 \cdot 0.5 = -3, -3 \cdot 0.5 = -1.5, -1.5 \cdot 0.5 = -0.75, -0.75 \cdot 0.5 = -0.375; -6 + (-3) + (-1.5) + (-0.75) + (-0.375) = -11.625$

57a. No; it meets the requirement that no dimensions can be less than 20 feet, but the minumum of 1250 square feet is not met because this yard would have 1216 square feet.

57b. No; it meets the requirement that yards must have a minimum of 1250 square feet because it would have 1330 square feet, but the requirement that no dimension can be less than 20 feet is not met because it has a side of length 19 feet.

57c. Answers will vary. Sample answer: 30 feet

58. $\frac{2}{5}(3) = \frac{6}{5}$ or $1\frac{1}{5}$ feet **59.** -2.2

60. $12 \underline{\ ?\ } 15 - 7$
$12 > 8$

61. $a - 12 = -8 - 12$
$= -20$

62. from 1 to 15 by 1s

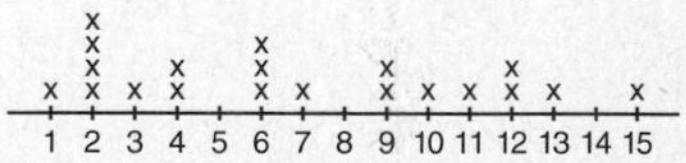

63. -7 **64.** $5(x + y) - z$ or $5(x + y - z)$

65.

Replace y with:	$y + 3 > 8$	True or False?
3	$3 + 3 \overset{?}{>} 8 \rightarrow 6 \not> 8$	false
4	$4 + 3 \overset{?}{>} 8 \rightarrow 7 \not> 8$	false
5	$5 + 3 \overset{?}{>} 8 \rightarrow 8 \not> 8$	false
6	$6 + 3 \overset{?}{>} 8 \rightarrow 9 > 8$	true
7	$7 + 3 \overset{?}{>} 8 \rightarrow 10 > 8$	true

Therefore, the solution set of $y + 3 > 8$ is $\{6, 7\}$.

66a. stem 13 and leaf 2 **66b.** stem 35 and leaf 7

66c. stem 153 and leaf 4

67. $6(4^3 + 2^2) = 6(64 + 4)$
$= 6(68)$
$= 408$

68. 4^3; 64 cubes

2-7 Dividing Rational Numbers

Page 115 Check for Understanding

1. Both multiplying and dividing rational numbers involve multiplication. In division, you multiply by the reciprocal of the second number.
2. multiplying by its reciprocal
3. Sample answer: $x = \frac{1}{2}$
4. Miguel is correct. $-\frac{4}{5} = (-1)\frac{4}{5} = \frac{(-1)4}{5} = \left(\frac{1}{-1}\right)\frac{4}{5} = \frac{4}{-5}$; $\frac{-4}{-5} = \frac{(-1)4}{(-1)5} = \left(\frac{-1}{-1}\right)\left(\frac{4}{5}\right) = (1)\frac{4}{5} = \frac{4}{5} \neq -\frac{4}{5}$
5. -4
6. -7
7. $-\frac{3}{4} \div 8 = -\frac{3}{4} \cdot \frac{1}{8}$
   $= -\frac{3}{32}$
8. $\frac{2}{3} \div 9 = \frac{2}{3} \cdot \frac{1}{9}$
   $= \frac{2}{27}$
9. $\frac{\frac{-5}{6}}{8} = -\frac{5}{6} \div 8$
   $= -\frac{5}{6} \cdot \frac{1}{8} = -\frac{5}{48}$
10. $9s$
11. $-6x$
12. $\frac{6b + 12}{6} = \frac{6b}{6} + \frac{12}{6}$
    $= b + 2$
13. $\$5.6$ million $\div$ $\$168\ \frac{\text{million}}{\text{hr}}$
    $= \frac{\$5.6\text{ million}}{1} \cdot \frac{1\text{ hr}}{\$168\text{ million}}$
    $= \frac{1}{30}$ hr
    $\frac{1\text{ hr}}{30} \cdot \frac{60\text{ minutes}}{1\text{ hr}} = 2$ minutes
    It took about 2 minutes for the goverment to spend the money.

Pages 115–117 Exercises

14. -9
15. 6
16. $-9 \div \left(-\frac{10}{17}\right) = -\frac{9}{1} \cdot -\frac{17}{10}$
    $= \frac{153}{10}$
17. $-\frac{2}{3} \div 12 = -\frac{2}{3} \cdot \frac{1}{12}$
    $= -\frac{2}{36}$
    $= -\frac{1}{18}$
18. $-64 \div (-8) = -64 \cdot \left(-\frac{1}{8}\right)$
    $= \frac{-64}{-8}$
    $= 8$
19. $-\frac{3}{4} \div 12 = -\frac{3}{4} \cdot \frac{1}{12}$
    $= -\frac{3}{48}$
    $= -\frac{1}{16}$
20. $-18 \div 9 = -18 \cdot \frac{1}{9}$
    $= -\frac{18}{9}$
    $= -2$
21. $78 \div (-13) = 78 \cdot \left(-\frac{1}{13}\right)$
    $= -\frac{78}{13}$
    $= -6$
22. $-108 \div (-9) = -108 \cdot \left(-\frac{1}{9}\right)$
    $= \frac{-108}{-9}$
    $= 12$
23. $-\frac{2}{3} \div 8 = -\frac{2}{3} \cdot \frac{1}{8}$
    $= -\frac{2}{24}$
    $= -\frac{1}{12}$
24. $-\frac{1}{3} \div (-4) = -\frac{1}{3} \cdot -\frac{1}{4}$
    $= \frac{1}{12}$
25. $-9 \div \left(-\frac{10}{27}\right) = -9 \cdot \left(-\frac{27}{10}\right)$
    $= \frac{243}{10}$
26. $\frac{\frac{5}{6}}{-10} = \frac{5}{6} \div (-10)$
    $= \frac{5}{6} \cdot \left(-\frac{1}{10}\right)$
    $= -\frac{5}{60}$
    $= -\frac{1}{12}$
27. $-\frac{7}{\frac{3}{5}} = -7 \div \left(\frac{3}{5}\right)$
    $= -\frac{7}{1} \cdot \frac{5}{3}$
    $= -\frac{35}{3}$
28. $\frac{-5}{\frac{2}{7}} = -5 \div \left(\frac{2}{7}\right)$
    $= -\frac{5}{1} \cdot \frac{7}{2}$
    $= -\frac{35}{2}$
29. $-65m$
30. $-9c$
31. $\frac{8r + 24}{8} = \frac{8r}{8} + \frac{24}{8}$
    $= r + 3$
32. $\frac{6a + 24}{6} = \frac{6a}{6} + \frac{24}{6}$
    $= a + 4$
33. $\frac{40a + 50b}{-2} = \frac{40a}{-2} + \frac{50b}{-2}$
    $= -20a - 25b$
34. $\frac{-5x + (-10y)}{-5} = \frac{-5x}{-5} + \frac{(-10y)}{-5}$
    $= x + 2y$
35. $\frac{42c - 18d}{-3} = \frac{42c}{-3} - \frac{18d}{-3}$
    $= -14c + 6d$
36. $\frac{-8f + (-16g)}{8} = \frac{-8f}{8} + \frac{(-16g)}{8}$
    $= -f - 2g$
37. $\frac{-4a + (-16b)}{4} = \frac{-4a}{4} + \frac{(-16b)}{4}$
    $= -a - 4b$
38. $\frac{b}{c} = \frac{-6}{-1.5}$
    $= \frac{-6}{\frac{-3}{2}}$
    $= \frac{-6}{1} \div \frac{-3}{2} = \frac{-6}{1} \cdot \frac{-2}{3} = 4$
39. $b \div a = -6 \div -5$
    $= -\frac{6}{1} \cdot \frac{1}{5}$
    $= -\frac{6}{5}$ or -1.2
40. $(a + b) \div c = [5 + (-6)] \div -1.5$
    $= -1 \div -1.5$
    $= -\frac{1}{1} \div -\frac{3}{2}$
    $= -\frac{1}{1} \cdot -\frac{2}{3}$
    $= \frac{2}{3}$ or $0.\overline{6}$

41. $(a + b + c) \div 3 = [5 + (-6) \div (-1.5)] \div 3$
$= -2.5 \div 3$
$= -\frac{5}{2} \div \frac{3}{1}$
$= -\frac{5}{2} \cdot \frac{1}{3}$
$= -\frac{5}{6}$ or $-0.8\overline{3}$

42. $\frac{c}{a} = -\frac{1.5}{5}$
$= \frac{-\frac{3}{2}}{5}$
$= -\frac{3}{2} \div 5$
$= -\frac{3}{2} \cdot \frac{1}{5}$
$= -\frac{3}{10}$ or -0.3

43. $\frac{ab}{ac} = \frac{5(-6)}{5(-1.5)}$
$= \frac{-30}{-7.5}$
$= -30 \div \frac{-15}{2}$
$= -\frac{30}{1} \cdot -\frac{2}{15}$
$= 4$

44a. You would get an error since you are asking the calculator to divide by 0 and this is undefined.

44b. You will end up with the original number since you reciprocated and the reciprocated again. If n is even, you will get the original number. If n is odd, you will get the reciprocal of the number.

44c. 1; You multiplied a number by its reciprocal, which always results in a product of 1.

45a.

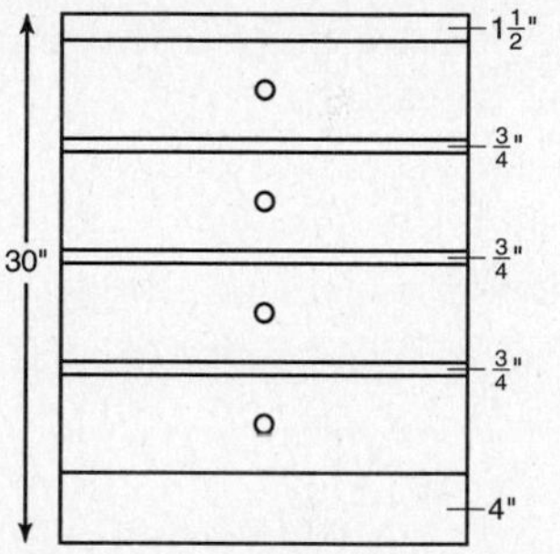

45b. $30 - \left(1\frac{1}{2} + \frac{3}{4} + \frac{3}{4} + \frac{3}{4} + 4\right) = 30 - \left(7\frac{3}{4}\right) = 22\frac{1}{4}$

$22\frac{1}{4} \div 4 = \frac{89}{4} \cdot \frac{1}{4} = \frac{89}{16} = 5\frac{9}{16}$ inches

46. If they buy them each individually, the total cost will be \$113.47 $\left(\frac{1}{5}\text{ off each pair}\right)$. If Sharon buys the two most expensive pairs and LaShondra buys the next two most expensive pairs and then one of them buys the fifth pair by itself, the total cost will be \$110.37 . Therefore, the latter is how they should buy the shoes.

47. $\left(24\frac{1}{4} - 4\right) \div 5 = 20\frac{1}{4} \div 5$
$= \frac{81}{4} \cdot \frac{1}{5}$
$= \frac{81}{20}$
$= 4\frac{1}{20}$ inches

48. $\left(-\frac{1}{5}\right)\left(\frac{3}{2}\right)(-2) = \left(-\frac{1}{5}\right)\left(\frac{3}{2}\right)\left(-\frac{2}{1}\right)$
$= \frac{3}{5}$

49. $\frac{9}{4} + \frac{x}{6} = \frac{9}{4} + \frac{-7}{6}$
$= \frac{27}{12} + \frac{-14}{12}$
$= \frac{13}{12}$

50. $\frac{2}{3} = \frac{16}{24}, \frac{7}{8} = \frac{21}{24}$; Sample answer: $\frac{19}{24}$

51a. $\begin{bmatrix} 1 & 4 \\ 5 & 7 \end{bmatrix} + \begin{bmatrix} -3 & 0 \\ -2 & 5 \end{bmatrix} = \begin{bmatrix} 1 + (-3) & 4 + 0 \\ 5 + (-2) & 7 + 5 \end{bmatrix} = \begin{bmatrix} -2 & 4 \\ 3 & 12 \end{bmatrix}$

51b. $\begin{bmatrix} 1 & 4 \\ 5 & 7 \end{bmatrix} - \begin{bmatrix} -3 & 0 \\ -2 & 5 \end{bmatrix} = \begin{bmatrix} 1 - (-3) & 4 - 0 \\ 5 - (-2) & 7 - 5 \end{bmatrix} = \begin{bmatrix} 4 & 4 \\ 7 & 2 \end{bmatrix}$

52a. $574 - 443 = 131$

52b.

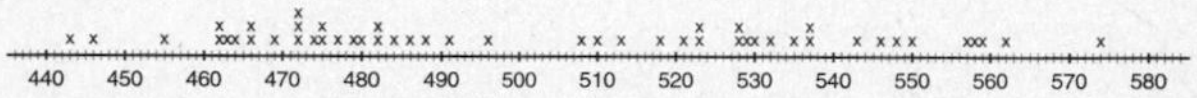

52c. yes, 472

53. $8b + 12(b + 2) = 8b + 12b + 24$
$= 20b + 24$

54. $\frac{5}{4}$

55a.

Stem	Leaf
13	0
15	4
17	2 3
19	4
20	0
22	0 2
24	5
25	1 4
27	9
29	0
30	4 7
33	0
34	6
52	5

13|0 = 13,000

55b. \$13,000 55c. \$52,500 55d. 9

2-8A Modeling Mathematics: Estimating Square Roots

Page 118

1. 4 – 5 2. 21 – 22 3. 13 – 14 4. 14 – 15
5. 1 – 2
6. Begin with a $1 \times n$ rectangle made of blocks, where n is the number being factored. As you form new rectangles with the same blocks, the first factor increases in value while the second factor decreases. When you find the square root, both dimensions are the same.

2-8 Square Roots and Real Numbers

Pages 122–123 Check for Understanding

1. Sample answer:

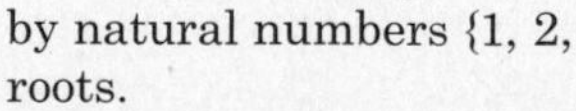

2. The comic is funny because you usually count off by natural numbers {1, 2, 3, 4, . . .} not square roots.
3. Yes; 36 is a perfect square because its square root is the rational number 6; rationals, integers, whole number, natural numbers.

4. 3(3) = 9 and (−3)(−3) = 9. Therefore, 3 and −3 are both square roots of 9.

5. $x \leq 0$

6. Sample answer: A rational number is a number that can be expressed as a common fraction. An irrational number is a number that cannot be expressed as a common fraction.

7. 8 **8.** −6 **9.** 11.05 **10.** ±0.28

11. $\sqrt{x} = \sqrt{256}$
$= 16$

12. $\sqrt{y} = \sqrt{151}$
≈ 12.29

13. Q

14. Q, Z, W, N **15.** Q **16.** I

17.
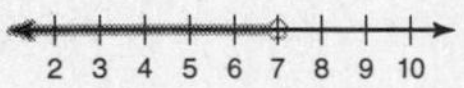

18.
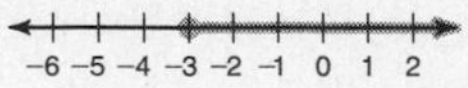

19.
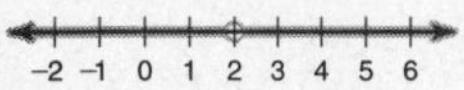

20. $\sqrt{15(135)} = \sqrt{2025}$
$= 45$

Pages 123–125 Exercises

21. 13 **22.** 0.07 **23.** $\frac{2}{3}$ **24.** −17

25. 20.49 **26.** $\frac{5}{8}$ **27.** 15 **28.** ±34.03

29. −25 **30.** 1.4 **31.** $\frac{3}{5}$ **32.** −2.41

33. $\sqrt{x} = \sqrt{87}$
≈ 9.33

34. $\pm\sqrt{t} = \pm\sqrt{529}$
$= \pm 23$

35. $-\sqrt{m} = -\sqrt{2209}$
$= -47$

36. $\sqrt{c + d} = \sqrt{23 + 56}$
$= \sqrt{79}$
≈ 8.89

37. $-\sqrt{np} = -\sqrt{16 \cdot 25}$
$= -\sqrt{400}$
$= -20$

38. $\pm\sqrt{\frac{a}{b}} = \pm\sqrt{\frac{64}{4}}$
$= \pm\sqrt{16}$
$= \pm 4$

39. Z, Q **40.** W, Z, Q **41.** Q **42.** Q **43.** Q

44. N, W, Z, Q **45.**Q **46.** N, W, Z, Q **47.** I

48. Q **49.** Q **50.** N, W, Z, Q

51.
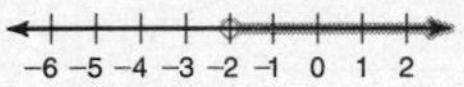

52.
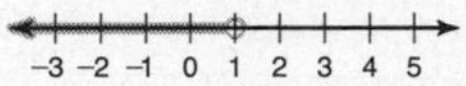

53.
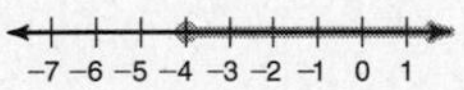

54.
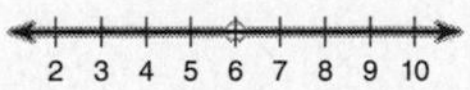

55.
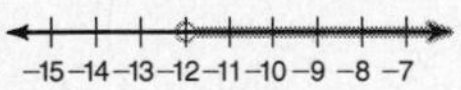

56.
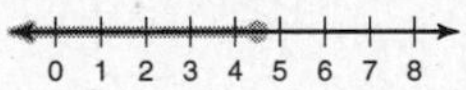

57.
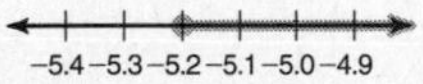

58.
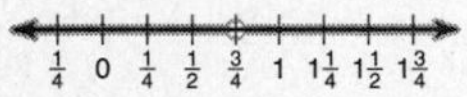

59.
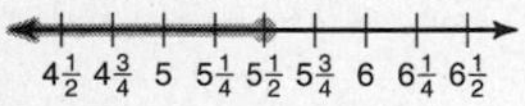

60. $V = \ell \cdot w \cdot h = 100$
$h = \ell \cdot w$
$\ell \cdot w \cdot (\ell \cdot w) = 100$
$(\ell w)^2 = 100$
$\ell w = 10$
$h = 10$
$\ell = w = \sqrt{10} \approx 3.16$ or $\ell = h = 10$ and $w = 1$.
Dimensions are 3.16 cm × 3.16 cm × 10 cm or 10 cm × 10 cm × 1 cm.

61. Yes, it lies between 27 and 28.

62a. $\sqrt{10}$, $\sqrt{11}$, $\sqrt{12}$, $\sqrt{13}$, $\sqrt{14}$, and $\sqrt{15}$

62b. $\sqrt{28}$, $\sqrt{29}$, and $\sqrt{30}$

63. $d = 1.4\sqrt{h}$
$= 1.4\sqrt{1275}$
$\approx$ 50 miles

64. $s = \sqrt{24d}$
$= \sqrt{24 \cdot 40}$
$= \sqrt{960}$
$\approx$ 31 miles per hour

65. $3\frac{7}{50} = 3.14$, $\frac{864}{275} \approx 3.141818182$; Fibonacci

66a. $\frac{2450}{24} \approx 102.08$; 103 or more cases

66b.
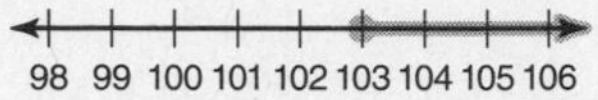

67. $(-3a)(4)\left(\frac{2}{3}\right)\left(\frac{1}{6}a\right) = (-3 \cdot 3)(4)\left(\frac{2}{3}\right)\left(\frac{1}{6} \cdot 3\right)$
$= (-9)(4)\left(\frac{2}{3}\right)\left(\frac{3}{6}\right)$
$= (-36)\left(\frac{1}{3}\right)$
$= -\frac{36}{1} \cdot \frac{1}{3}$
$= -12$

68. $-\frac{5}{12} + \frac{3}{8} = -\frac{10}{24} + \frac{9}{24}$
$= -\frac{1}{24}$

69. unit cost for a 1-pound package of lunch meat:
1.95 ÷ 16 = 0.12
unit cost for a 12-ounce package of lunch meat:
1.80 ÷ 12 = 0.15
0.12 < 0.15; the 1-pound package of lunch meat for $1.95 is the better buy.

70. $-5 - (-6) = -5 + (+6)$
$= 1$

71. from 500 to 520 by 5s.

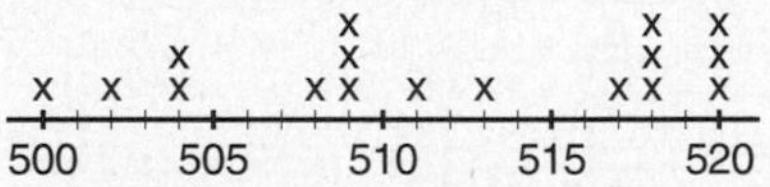

72.
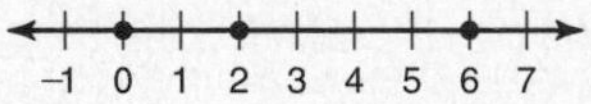

73. Graph b **74.** associative (+)

75a. to the nearest ten thousand

75b. 10 **75c.** $690,000

76. $12(19 - 15) - 3 \cdot 8 = 12(4) - 3 \cdot 8$
$= 48 - 24$
$= 24$

77. 20 + 6 = 26, 26 + 6 = 32 **78.** p^6

2-9 Problem Solving Write Equations and Formulas

Pages 129–130 Check for Understanding

1. Answers will vary. Sample answers: How much does her normal heart rate have to increase to reach her target heart rate? During the entire workout, how much does her heart rate decrease? During the entire workout, how much does her heart rate increase?

2. A formula is a type of an equation that states a rule for the relationship between certain quantities.
3. Answers will vary. Sample answer: If José has a garden with the dimensions of 20 feet by 30 feet, what is the area?
4. See students' work.

5a. 4 points **5b.** 15 questions **5c.** 86

5d. 6 points **5e.** $15 - n$ **5f.** $4n$

6. $2x + 3y = 13$ **7.** $n + 5 \geq 48$

8. $P = 2(a + b)$

9. Let s = average speed; $s = \frac{189}{3} = 63$

10. Let q = number of quarters; $q + (q + 4) + (q + 4 - 7) = 28$

11. The product of a times the sum of y and 1 is b.

12. Answers will vary. Sample answer: Your mother works 8 less than 5 times the number of hours that you work during the summer. How many hours did your mother work if you worked 20 hours this week?

Pages 130–132 Exercises

13a. 640 feet **13b.** $y - 80$

13c. $\ell + \ell + w + w$ or $2\ell + 2w$

13d.
$$2\ell + 2w = 640$$
$$2(y - 80) + 2y = 640$$
$$2y - 160 + 2y = 640$$
$$4y - 160 = 640$$
$$4y = 800$$
$$y = 200 \text{ ft}$$

13e.
$$A = \ell w$$
$$= (200)(200 - 80)$$
$$= (200)(120)$$
$$= 24{,}000 \text{ ft}^2$$

13f. Is there enough space to build the playground as designed?

14. $V = \frac{1}{3}bh$ **15.** $a^2 + b^3 = 25$ **16.** $\frac{x}{y} \geq 18 + 5(x + y)$

17. $x < (a - 4)^2$ **18.** $C = 2\pi r$ **19.** $\frac{7}{8}(a + b + c^2) = 48$

20. Sample answer: t = how many tapes Nicole has. $25 - t$ = how many CDs Nicole has.
$4 + \frac{1}{2}t = 25 - t$ or $4 + 1\frac{1}{2}t = 25$

21. Sample answer:
x = first number
$x + 25$ = second number
$25 + 2x = 106$

22. Sample answer:
$2D$ = Anna's age
D = Dennis' age
$D - 4$ = Curtis' age
$2D + D + D - 4 = 32$

23. Sample answer: y = how much money Hector saves; $y = 7(2)(50)$ or $y = 14(50)$

24. The square of the product of m and n is equal to p.

25. V is equal to the quotient of a times h and three.

26. The quantity of the sum of a and two, divided by five is greater than ten.

27. Sample answer: Three times the number of miles home from school is 36. How many miles away from home is the school?

28. Sample answer: Manny's Suits for Men is having a \$25.00 off sale. If the original cost of a suit is p, find the original cost of the suit if the sale price is \$150.00.

29. Sample answer: The number of hours spent waiting for a doctor in the waiting room is 5 minutes more than 6 times the number of appointments she has. How long would you have to wait for a doctor with d appointments?

30. $a^2 - b^2$

31.
$$ab - 2(2) + d(c + 2) - 2(2) = ab - 4 + cd + 2d - 4$$
$$= ab + cd + 2d - 8$$

32.
$$s^2 + \pi\left(\frac{s}{2}\right)^2 + \pi\left(\frac{s}{2}\right)^2 = s^2 + \pi \cdot \frac{s^2}{4} + \pi \cdot \frac{s^2}{4}$$
$$= s^2 + 2\pi \cdot \frac{s^2}{4}$$
$$= s^2 + \pi \cdot \frac{s^2}{2}$$

33. Sample answer: $4.5 + x + x = 24 + x$
$$x = 19.5$$

34a. What is the area of two 7-inch pizzas and what is the area of one 12-inch pizza?

34b. See students' work.

34c. $A = \pi r^2$

(two 7-inch pizzas)
$A = \pi(3.5)^2$
$A = 12.25\pi$ or
$\approx 38.5 \text{ in}^2$ each
2 pizzas $\approx 77 \text{ in}^2$

(one 12-inch pizza)
$A = \pi(6)^2$
$A = 36\pi$ or
$\approx 113.1 \text{ in}^2$

One 12-inch pizza is the best buy.

34d. If crust were a factor, you would have to take circumference into consideration and figure out how the circumferences compare.

35a. $A = \frac{1}{2}h(a + b)$

35b.
$$A = \frac{1}{2}(7)(20 + 11)$$
$$= \frac{7}{2}(31)$$
$$= 108\frac{1}{2} \text{ ft}^2$$

36a.

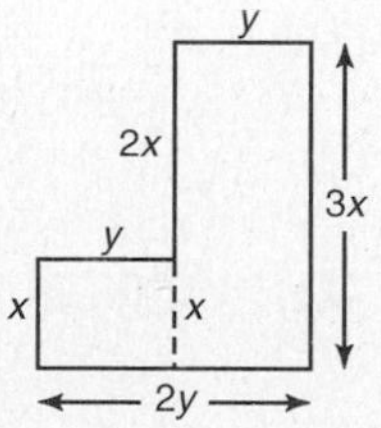

36b.
$$P = x + 2y + 3x + y + 2x + y$$
$$P = (x + 3x + 2x) + (2y + y + y)$$
$$P = 6x + 4y$$

36c. $A = xy + 3xy$ or $A = 4xy$

36d.
$$P = 6(5.5) + 4(4)$$
$$= 33 + 16$$
$$= 49 \text{ cm}$$
$$A = 4(5.5) + 4(4)$$
$$= 88 \text{ cm}^2$$

37. -8 **38.** $-72 \div (-6) = \frac{-72}{1} \cdot -\frac{1}{6} = 12$

39. $\begin{bmatrix} -4(-2) & -4(0.4) \\ -4(-3) & -4(54) \end{bmatrix} = \begin{bmatrix} 8 & -1.6 \\ 12 & -20 \end{bmatrix}$

40. $\frac{1}{3} = \frac{14}{42}, \frac{4}{7} = \frac{24}{42}$; Sample answer: $\frac{20}{42}$

41. $-25, 25$ **42.** c

43.

Replace y with:	$4y + 2 > 9$	True or False?
1	$4(1) + 2 \overset{?}{>} 9 \to 6 \not> 9$	false
2	$4(2) + 2 \overset{?}{>} 9 \to 10 > 9$	true
3	$4(3) + 2 \overset{?}{>} 9 \to 14 > 9$	true
4	$4(4) + 2 \overset{?}{>} 9 \to 18 > 9$	true
5	$4(5) + 2 \overset{?}{>} 9 \to 22 > 9$	true

The solution set for $4y + 2 > 9$ is {2, 3, 4, 5}.

Chapter 2 Highlights

Page 133 Understanding and Using the Vocabulary

1. true **2.** false, additive inverse **3.** true

4. true **5.** false, sample answer: $\frac{\frac{1}{2}}{5}$

6. false, integer or rational number

7. true **8.** false, sample answer: -3

9. true **10.** true

Chapter 2 Study Guide and Assessment

Pages 134–136 Skills and Concepts

11. 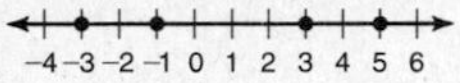

12. 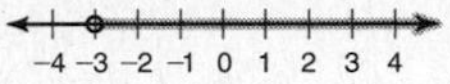

13. 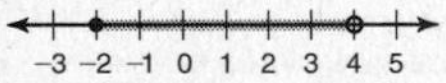

14. 0 **15.** -5 **16.** -20 **17.** -4 **18.** -22 **19.** -5

20. 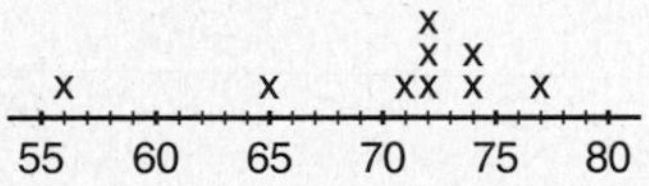

21. 56% **22.** 6 years **23.** 8

24. $14 - 36 = 14 + (-36) = -22$ **25.** -2

26. $18 - (-5) = 18 + 5 = 32$

27. $-7 - (-11) = -7 + 11 = 4$

28. -48 **29.** -5

30. $-54 - (-34) = -54 + 34 = -20$

31. $>$ **32.** $\frac{3}{8} \underline{\ ?\ } \frac{4}{11}$ **33.** $<$

$3(11) \underline{\ ?\ } 8(4)$

$33 > 32$

$\frac{3}{8} > \frac{4}{11}$

34. $\frac{-3.6}{0.6} \underline{\ ?\ } -7$ **36.** Sample answer: 0

$-6 > -7$

$\frac{-3.6}{0.6} > -7$

36. Sample answer: $-\frac{20}{45}$ **37.** $\frac{6}{7} + \left(-\frac{13}{7}\right) = -\frac{7}{7}$
$= -1$

38. 0.0295 **39.** $3.72 - (-8.65) = 3.72 + 8.65$
$= 12.37$

40. $-\frac{4}{3} + \frac{5}{6} + \left(-\frac{7}{3}\right) = -\frac{8}{6} + \frac{5}{6} + \left(-\frac{14}{6}\right)$
$= -\frac{17}{6}$

41. $-4.57 - 8.69 = -4.57 + (-8.69)$
$= -13.26$

42. $-4.5y - 8.1y = -4.5y + (-8.1y)$
$= [-4.5 + (-8.1)]y$
$= -12.6y$

43. -99 **44.** 252 **45.** $\left(\frac{3}{5}\right)\left(-\frac{5}{7}\right) = -\frac{3}{7}$

46. -50.152284 **47.** -90 **48.** $-4\left(\frac{7}{12}\right) = -\frac{4}{1}\left(\frac{7}{12}\right) = -\frac{7}{3}$

49. -9 **50.** $-15 \div \left(\frac{3}{4}\right) = -\frac{15}{1} \cdot \frac{4}{3}$
$= -20$

51. $\frac{\frac{4}{5}}{-7} = \frac{4}{5} \div (-7)$ **52.** $-115x$

$= \frac{4}{5} \cdot -\frac{1}{7}$

$= -\frac{4}{35}$

53. $218 \div (-2) = \frac{218}{1} \cdot -\frac{1}{2}$
$= -109$

54. $-78 \div (-6) = -\frac{78}{1} \cdot -\frac{1}{6}$
$= 13$

55. $\sqrt{y} = \sqrt{196} = 14$

56. $\pm\sqrt{t} = \pm\sqrt{112} \approx \pm 10.58$

57. $-\sqrt{ab} = -\sqrt{36 \cdot 25}$ **58.** $\pm\sqrt{\frac{c}{d}} = \pm\sqrt{\frac{169}{16}}$

$= -\sqrt{900}$ $= \pm\sqrt{10.625}$

$= -30$ $= \pm 3.25$

Page 136 Applications and Problem Solving

59a. 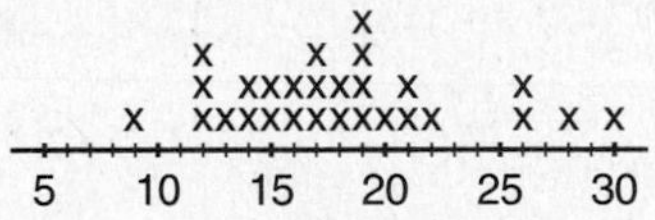

59b. 14 detergents

60. $-432 + (+189) = -243$; 243 meters below the surface

61. unit cost of 0.75 liter of soda:
$0.89 \div 0.75 = 1.19$
unit cost of 1.25 liters of soda:
$1.31 \div 1.25 = 0.95$
$0.95 < 1.19$; The 1.25 liters of soda for \$1.31 is the better buy.

62. $V = \sqrt{4.6 \cdot 1200} = 74.3$ $V = \sqrt{4.6 \cdot 1500} + 83.1$
$V = \sqrt{5.2 \cdot 1200} = 79$ $V = \sqrt{5.2 \cdot 1500} = 88$
4.6 ohms and 1500 watts or 5.2 ohms and 1200 watts

63a. $+\frac{3}{8} + \frac{1}{8} + 0 - \frac{3}{4} + \frac{1}{2} = \frac{3}{8} + \frac{1}{8} + 0 - \frac{6}{8} + \frac{4}{8} = \frac{2}{8}$ or $\frac{1}{4}$

$-\frac{1}{4} + \frac{1}{8} + \frac{1}{8} - \frac{1}{4} + \frac{1}{2} = -\frac{2}{8} + \frac{1}{8} + \frac{1}{8} - \frac{2}{8} + \frac{4}{8} = \frac{2}{8}$ or $\frac{1}{4}$

They both saw a gain of $\frac{1}{4}$ for the week.

63b. CompNet

63c. It changed $-\frac{3}{4}$ from Wednesday to Thursday.

64. Let w = Minal's weight; $w + (w + 8) = 182$.

65. Let n = the number; $3n - 21 = 57$.

66. Let c = Cecile's age now; $3(c - 4) = 42$.

Page 137 Alternative Assessment: Thinking Critically

- Sample answer: Terminating and repeating decimals can be written as fractions.
- Sample answer: If the original number is positive, then the quotient is greater; if the original number is negative, then the product is greater.

Cumulative Review, Chapters 1–2

Pages 138–139

1. $-1 + 2\frac{1}{2} = 1\frac{1}{2}, 1\frac{1}{2} + 2\frac{1}{2} = 4, 4 + 2\frac{1}{2} = 6\frac{1}{2}$; D

2. B. April is mild, with temperatures usually between 60 and 80 degrees.

3. $3t^2 - g(w - t) = 3 \cdot 3^2 - 5(-2 - 3)$
$= 3 \cdot 9 - 5(-5)$
$= 27 + 25$
$= 52$ D

4. Let b = Bill's age now.
$2[(b + s) + (b + 3 + 5)] = 5b$; C

5. $2 + 4 + (-3) + 7 + (-12) = -2$ down; 2 floors from the mailroom. The mailroom is on the third floor. B

6. $5(12) \div 1\frac{1}{2} = 60 \div \frac{3}{2}$
$= \frac{60}{1} \cdot \frac{2}{3}$
$= 40$ pieces D

7. $10a^3 + 7 - 2(2a^3 + a) + 3$
$= 10a^3 + 7 - 2.2a^3 - 2a + 3$
$= 10a^3 + 7 - 4a^3 - 2a + 3$
$= 10a^3 - 4a^3 - 2a + 7 + 3$
$= (10 - 4)a^3 - 2a + (7 + 3)$
$= 6a^3 - 2a + 10$ C

8. A. $4 + 3 \cdot 4 = 4 + 12 = 16$
B. $\frac{75}{3} - 2 = 25 - 2 = 23$
C. $8 \cdot 4 - 8 = 32 - 8 = 24$
D. $(5 + 3) \cdot 7 \div 2 = 8 \cdot 7 \div 2$
$= 56 \div 2$
$= 28$
D

9. $7 + 15 \div 2 + 4(-2)$
$= 7 + 15 \div 2 + (-8)$
$= 7 + 7\frac{1}{2} + (-8)$
$= 6\frac{1}{2}$

10. $y - z < 0 \rightarrow y < z$
$x - y > 0 \rightarrow x > y$
$z - x < 0 \rightarrow z < x$
least to greatest: y, z, x

11.
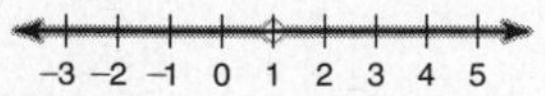

12. $P = z + y + z + y + x$
$= 2z + 2y + x$
$= 2\left(1\frac{1}{2}\right) + 2(3) + 7$
$= 3 + 6 + 7$
$= 16$ ft

13.
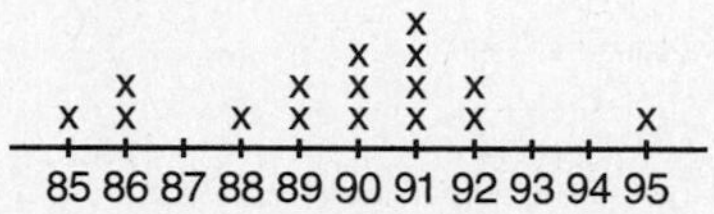

The scores ranged from a low of 85 to a high of 95 with a cluster around the score of 91.

14. Ella $= 5(3)x = 15x$; $15(2) = 30$
Corey $= 2(5)y = 10y$; $10(3) = 30$
Corey, 3; Ella, 2

15. $-a$

16. $9 - 3y$

17. Sample answer: $6 + 1.5 = 7.5$, $7.5 + 1.5 = 9$, $9 + 1.5 = 10.5$, $10.5 + 1.5 = 12$, $12 + 1.5 = 13.5$

18. $-2 - 1$ _?_ $- 2(-1)$
$-2 + (-1)$ _?_ 2
$-3 < 2$

19a. $5.35(20)x + 2(20)x = 350$
$107x + 40x = 350$
$147x = 350$
$x \approx 2.38$
about $2\frac{1}{2}$ weeks, not counting tips

19b. other expenses they have, amount of tips Joia makes

20. No; see students' work.

Chapter 3 Solving Linear Equations

3-1A Modeling Mathematics: Solving One-Step Equations

Page 143

1.
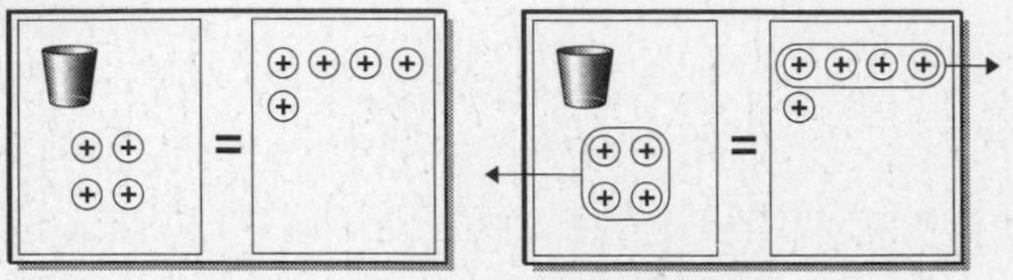

$x + 4 = 5$ $x = 1$

2.
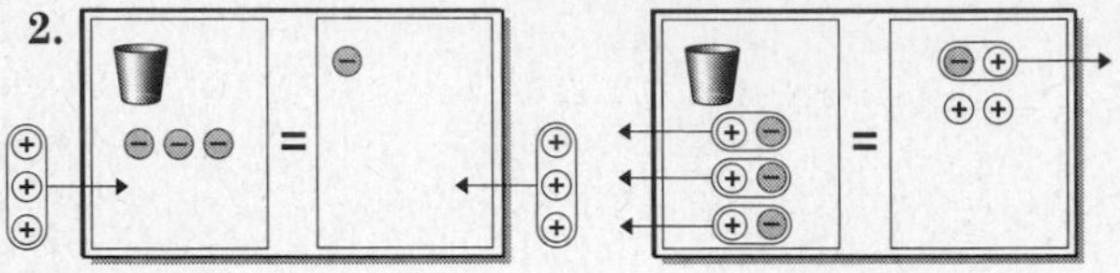

$y + (-3) = -1$ $y = 2$

3.
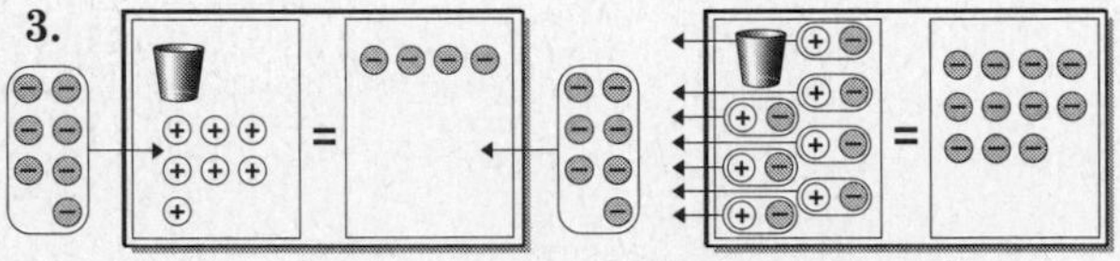

$y + 7 = -4$ $y = -11$

4.
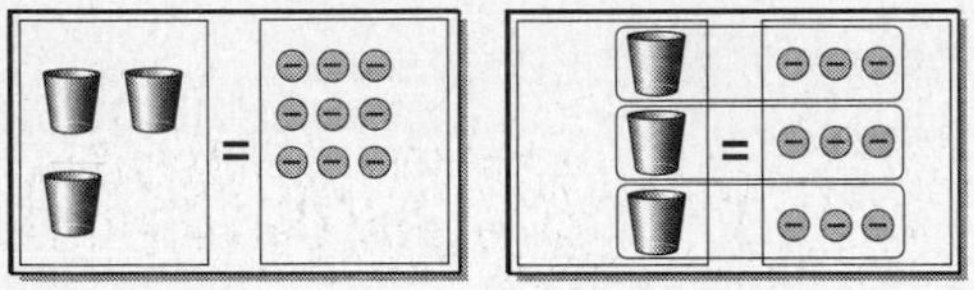

$3z = -9$ $z = -3$

5.
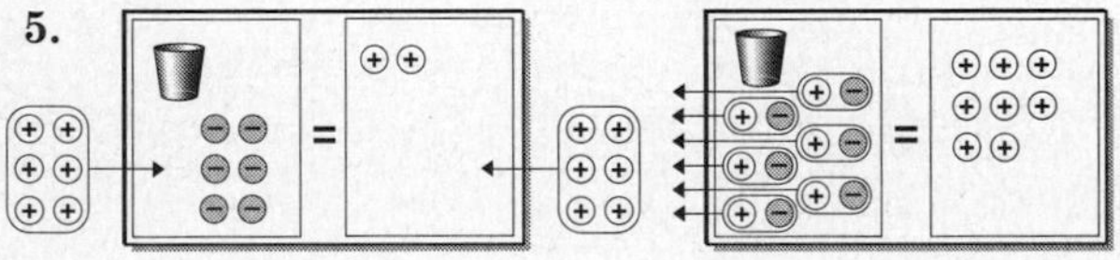

$m + (-6) = 2$ $m = 8$

6.
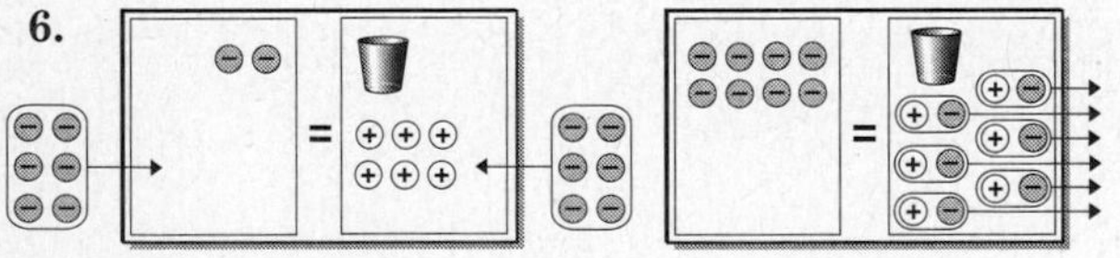

$-2 = x + 6$ $-8 = x$

7.
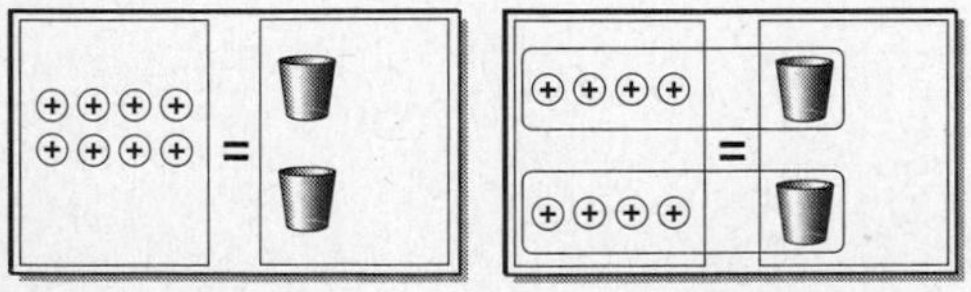

$8 = 2a$ $4 = a$

8.
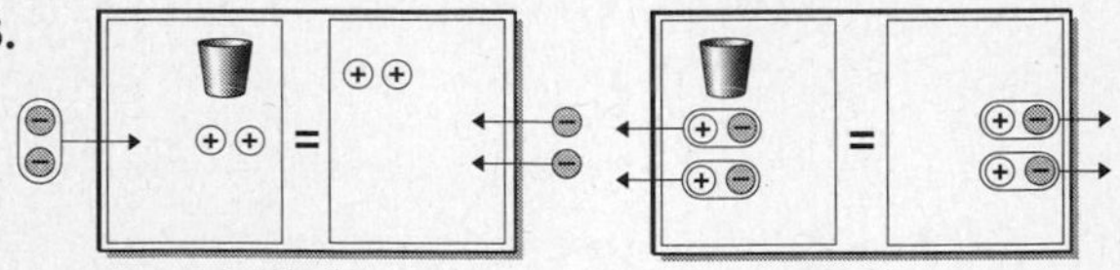

$w + 2 = 2$ $w = 0$

9.
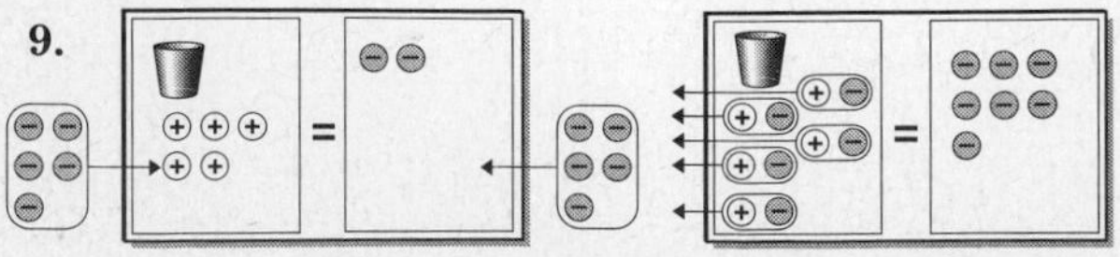

$x + 5 = -2$ $x = -7$

no

10.
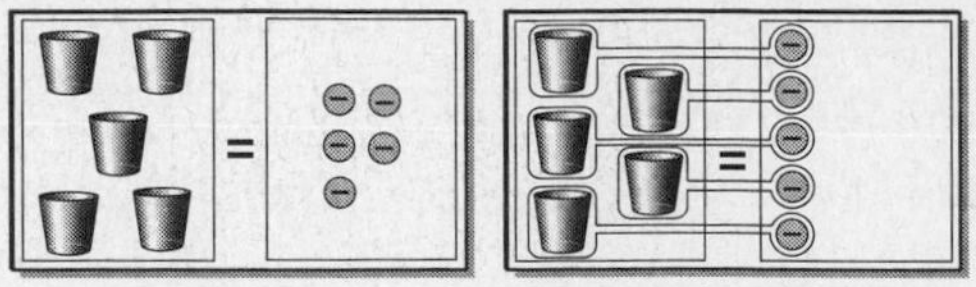

$5b = -5$ $b = -1$

yes

11.
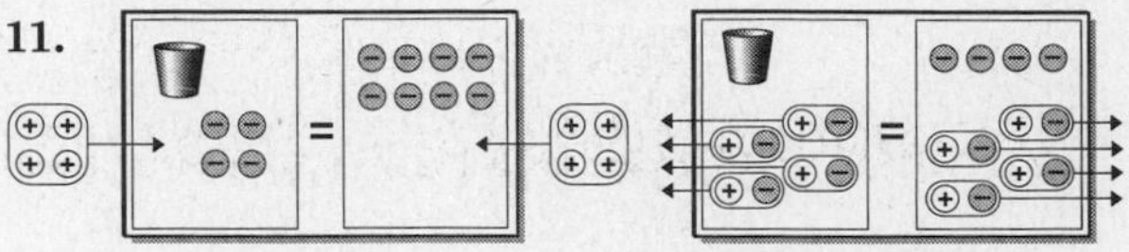

$y + (-4) = -8$ $y = -4$

yes

12. Add 5 negative counters to each side. Group and remove the counters that form zero pairs. The cup will be matched with 13 negative counters. Thus, $m = -13$.

3-1 Solving Equations with Addition and Subtraction

Page 148 Check for Understanding

1. $2.3 - w = 7.8$
$-2.3 + w = -7.8$ *Take the opposite of each term.*
$w - 2.3 = -7.8$
b

2. See students' work.

3. Substitute 4.5 for x in the equation.
$x - 1.2 = 3.3$
$4.5 - 1.2 = 3.3$
$3.3 = 3.3$
The solution is 4.5.

4. $x - 6 = 21$
$x - 6 + 6 = 21 + 6$
$x = 27$
$x + 7 = 27 + 7 = 34$

5.
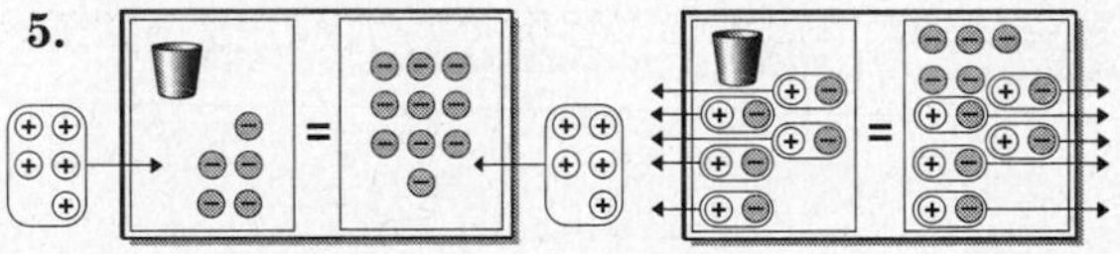

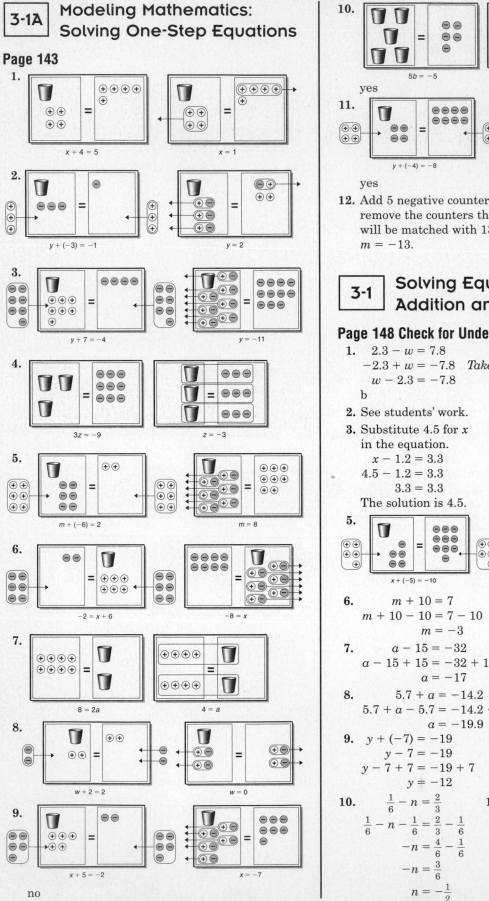

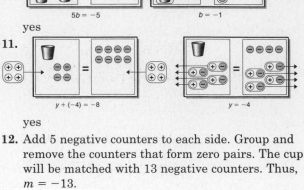

$x + (-5) = -10$ $x = -5$

6. $m + 10 = 7$
$m + 10 - 10 = 7 - 10$
$m = -3$

7. $a - 15 = -32$
$a - 15 + 15 = -32 + 15$
$a = -17$

8. $5.7 + a = -14.2$
$5.7 + a - 5.7 = -14.2 - 5.7$
$a = -19.9$

9. $y + (-7) = -19$
$y - 7 = -19$
$y - 7 + 7 = -19 + 7$
$y = -12$

10. $\frac{1}{6} - n = \frac{2}{3}$
$\frac{1}{6} - n - \frac{1}{6} = \frac{2}{3} - \frac{1}{6}$
$-n = \frac{4}{6} - \frac{1}{6}$
$-n = \frac{3}{6}$
$n = -\frac{1}{2}$

11. $d - (-27) = 13$
$d + 27 = 13$
$d + 27 - 27 = 13 - 27$
$d = -14$

12. Let n = the number.
$$n - 13 = -5$$
$$n - 13 + 13 = -5 + 13$$
$$n = 8$$
The number is 8.

13. Let n = the number.
$$n + (-56) = -82$$
$$n - 56 = -82$$
$$n - 56 + 56 = -82 + 56$$
$$n = -26$$
The number is −26.

Pages 148–149 Exercises

14. $k + 11 = -21$
$$k + 11 - 11 = -21 - 11$$
$$k = -32$$

15. $41 = 32 - r$
$$41 - 32 = 32 - r - 32$$
$$9 = -r$$
$$-9 = r$$

16. $-12 + z = -36$
$$-12 + z + 12 = -36 + 12$$
$$z = -24$$

17. $2.4 = m + 3.7$
$$2.4 - 3.7 = m + 3.7 - 3.7$$
$$-1.3 = m$$

18. $-7 = -16 - k$
$$-7 + 16 = -16 - k + 16$$
$$9 = -k$$
$$-9 = k$$

19. $0 = t + (-1.4)$
$$0 = t - 1.4$$
$$0 + 1.4 = t - 1.4 + 1.4$$
$$1.4 = t$$

20. $r + (-8) = 7$
$$r - 8 = 7$$
$$r - 8 + 8 = 7 + 8$$
$$r = 15$$

21. $h - 26 = -29$
$$h - 26 + 26 = -29 + 26$$
$$h = -3$$

22. $-23 = -19 + n$
$$-23 + 19 = -19 + n + 19$$
$$-4 = n$$

23. $-11 = k + (-5)$
$$-11 = k - 5$$
$$-11 + 5 = k - 5 + 5$$
$$-6 = k$$

24. $r - 6.5 = -9.3$
$$r - 6.5 + 6.5 = -9.3 + 6.5$$
$$r = -2.8$$

25. $t - (-16) = 9$
$$t + 16 = 9$$
$$t + 16 - 16 = 9 - 16$$
$$t = -7$$

26. $-1.43 + w = 0.89$
$$-1.43 + w + 1.43 = 0.89 + 1.43$$
$$w = 2.32$$

27. $m - (-13) = 37$
$$m + 13 = 37$$
$$m + 13 - 13 = 37 - 13$$
$$m = 24$$

28. $-4.1 = m + (-0.5)$
$$-4.1 = m - 0.5$$
$$-4.1 + 0.5 = m - 0.5 + 0.5$$
$$-3.6 = m$$

29. $-\frac{5}{8} + w = \frac{5}{8}$
$$-\frac{5}{8} + w + \frac{5}{8} = \frac{5}{8} + \frac{5}{8}$$
$$w = \frac{10}{8}$$
$$w = \frac{5}{4} \text{ or } 1\frac{1}{4}$$

30. $x - \left(-\frac{5}{6}\right) = \frac{2}{3}$
$$x + \frac{5}{6} = \frac{2}{3}$$
$$x + \frac{5}{6} - \frac{5}{6} = \frac{2}{3} - \frac{5}{6}$$
$$x = \frac{4}{6} - \frac{5}{6}$$
$$x = -\frac{1}{6}$$

31. $g + \left(-\frac{1}{5}\right) = -\frac{3}{10}$
$$g - \frac{1}{5} = -\frac{3}{10}$$
$$g - \frac{1}{5} + \frac{1}{5} = -\frac{3}{10} + \frac{1}{5}$$
$$g = -\frac{3}{10} + \frac{2}{10}$$
$$g = -\frac{1}{10}$$

32. Let n = the number.
$$23 - n = 42$$
$$23 - n - 23 = 42 - 23$$
$$-n = 19$$
$$n = -19$$
The number is −19.

33. Let n = the number.
$$n + 5 = 34$$
$$n + 5 - 5 = 34 - 5$$
$$n = 29$$
The number is 29.

34. Let n = the number
$$n - 45 = -78$$
$$n - 45 + 45 = -78 + 45$$
$$n = -33$$
The number is −33.

35. Let n = the number.
$$n - (-23) = 35$$
$$n + 23 = 35$$
$$n + 23 - 23 = 35 - 23$$
$$n = 12$$
The number is 12.

36. Let n = the number.
$$n + (-45) = 77$$
$$n - 45 = 77$$
$$n - 45 + 45 = 77 + 45$$
$$n = 122$$
The number is 122.

37. Let n = the number.
$$n + (-35) = 98$$
$$n - 35 = 98$$
$$n - 35 + 35 = 98 + 35$$
$$n = 133$$
The number is 133.

38. Yes; a typical answer is $n^2 = 25$; $n = \pm 5$.

39a. Let s = the growth in the number of subscribers.
1. $203{,}600 + s = 19{,}300{,}000$
2. $19{,}300{,}000 - s = 203{,}600$
$$203{,}600 + s = 19{,}300{,}000$$
$$203{,}600 + s - 203{,}600 = 19{,}300{,}000 - 203{,}600$$
$$s = 19{,}096{,}400$$
There were 19,096,400 more subscribers in 1994 than in 1985.

39b. Sample answer: 25 million

40a. Let t = cost of the lipstick in London.
1. $5.94 + 4.89 = t$
2. $t - 5.94 = 4.89$
$$t - 5.94 + 5.94 = 4.89 + 5.94$$
$$t = 10.83$$
The lipstick cost \$10.83 in London.

40b. $5.94 + t = 26.54$
$$5.94 + t - 5.94 = 26.54 - 5.94$$
$$t = 20.60$$
The lipstick cost \$20.60 more in San Paulo than in Los Angeles.

41a. 24 years old

41b. 24 years

41c. $68 + 5 + 5 = 78$ years

41d. $24 + 10 = 34$ years old

41e. 24 years

42. $\sqrt{256} = 16$

43. $65 \div (-13) = -5$

44. $82 - \frac{3}{4}(8) = 82 - \frac{3}{4}\left(\frac{8}{1}\right)$
$= 82 - 6$
$= 76$

45. $-0.23x + (-0.5x) = [-0.23 + (0.5)]x$
$= -0.73x$

46. $6(5a + 3b - 2b) = 6(5a + b)$
$= 6(5a) + 6b$
$= 30a + 6b$

47. $12 \div 4 + 15 \cdot 3 = 3 + 45$
$= 48$

3-2 Solving Equations with Multiplication and Division

Page 152 Check for Understanding

1. Doralina is correct. There is no value for x that would make the statement $0x = 8$ true.
2. Rise is the number of units in a vertical direction, and run is the number of units in a horizontal direction.
3. $12x =$ the number of inches of run
$12(30) = 360$ inches or 30 feet
4.

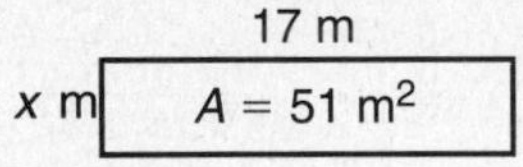

Let $x =$ the width. Then $17x = 51$, and $x = 3$.

5.

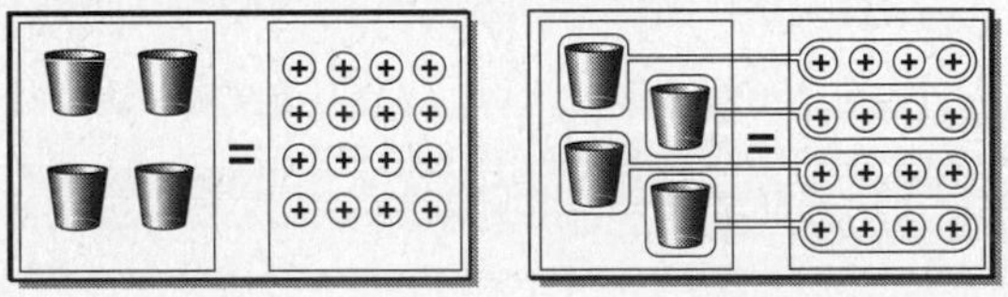

$4x = 16$ $\qquad$ $x = 4$

6. $-8t = 56$
$\frac{-8t}{-8} = \frac{56}{-8}$
$t = -7$

7. $-5s = -85$
$\frac{-5s}{-5} = \frac{-85}{-5}$
$s = 17$

8. $42.51x = 8$
$\frac{42.51x}{42.51} = \frac{8}{42.51}$
$x \approx 0.19$

9. $\frac{k}{8} = 6$
$8\left(\frac{k}{8}\right) = 8(6)$
$k = 48$

10. $-10 = \frac{b}{-7}$
$-7(-10) = -7\left(\frac{b}{-7}\right)$
$70 = b$

11. $-5x = -3\frac{2}{3}$
$-5x = -\frac{11}{3}$
$-\frac{1}{5}(-5)x = -\frac{1}{5}\left(-\frac{11}{3}\right)$
$x = \frac{11}{15}$

12. Let $n =$ the number.
$8n = 216$
$\frac{8n}{8} = \frac{216}{8}$
$n = 27$
The number is 27.

13. Let $n =$ the number.
$-7n = 1.477$
$\frac{-7n}{-7} = \frac{1.477}{-7}$
$n = -0.211$
The number is -0.211.

Pages 153–154 Exercises

14. $-4r = -28$
$\frac{-4r}{-4} = \frac{-28}{-4}$
$r = 7$

15. $5x = -45$
$\frac{5x}{5} = \frac{-45}{5}$
$x = -9$

16. $9x = 40$
$\frac{9x}{9} = \frac{40}{9}$
$x \approx 4.44$ or $4\frac{4}{9}$

17. $-3y = 52$
$\frac{-3y}{-3} = \frac{52}{-3}$
$y \approx -17.33$ or $-17\frac{1}{3}$

18. $3w = -11$
$\frac{3w}{3} = -\frac{11}{3}$
$w \approx -3.67$ or $-3\frac{2}{3}$

19. $434 = -31y$
$\frac{434}{-31} = \frac{-31y}{-31}$
$-14 = y$

20. $1.7b = -39.1$
$\frac{1.7b}{1.7} = \frac{-39.1}{1.7}$
$b = -23$

21. $0.49x = 6.277$
$\frac{0.49x}{0.49} = \frac{6.277}{0.49}$
$x = 12.81$

22. $-5.73c = 97.41$
$\frac{-5.73c}{-5.73} = \frac{97.41}{-5.73}$
$c = -17$

23. $-0.63y = -378$
$\frac{-0.63y}{-0.63} = \frac{-378}{-0.63}$
$y = 600$

24. $11 = \frac{x}{5}$
$5(11) = 5\left(\frac{x}{5}\right)$
$55 = x$

25. $\frac{h}{11} = -25$
$11\left(\frac{h}{11}\right) = 11(-25)$
$h = -275$

26. $\frac{c}{-8} = -14$
$-8\left(\frac{c}{-8}\right) = -8(-14)$
$c = 112$

27. $\frac{2}{5}t = -10$
$\frac{5}{2}\left(\frac{2}{5}\right)t = \frac{5}{2}(-10)$
$t = -\frac{50}{2}$ or -25

28. $-\frac{11}{8}x = 42$
$-\frac{8}{11}\left(-\frac{11}{8}\right)x = \frac{-8}{11}(42)$
$x = \frac{-336}{11}$ or $-30\frac{6}{11}$

29. $-\frac{13}{5}y = -22$
$-\frac{5}{13}\left(-\frac{13}{5}\right)y = -\frac{5}{13}(22)$
$y = \frac{110}{13}$ or $8\frac{6}{13}$

30. $3x = 4\frac{2}{3}$
$3x = \frac{14}{3}$
$\frac{1}{3}(3)x = \frac{1}{3}\left(\frac{14}{3}\right)$
$x = \frac{14}{9}$ or $1\frac{5}{9}$

31. $\left(-4\frac{1}{2}\right)x = 36$
$-\frac{9}{2}x = 36$
$-\frac{2}{9}\left(-\frac{9}{2}\right)x = -\frac{2}{9}(36)$
$x = \frac{-72}{9}$ or -8

32. Let $n =$ the number.
$6n = -96$
$\frac{6n}{6} = \frac{-96}{6}$
$n = -16$
The number is -16.

33. Let $n =$ the number.
$-12n = -156$
$\frac{-12n}{-12} = \frac{-156}{-12}$
$n = 13$
The number is 13.

34. Let $n =$ the number.
$\frac{1}{4}n = -16.325$
$4\left(\frac{1}{4}\right)n = 4(-16.325)$
$n = -65.3$
The number is -65.3.

35. Let $n =$ the number.
$\frac{4}{3}n = 4.82$
$\frac{3}{4}\left(\frac{4}{3}\right)n = \frac{3}{4}(4.82)$
$n = 3.615$
The number is 3.615.

36. Let n = the number.

$$\frac{7}{8}n = 14$$
$$\frac{8}{7}\left(\frac{7}{8}\right)n = \frac{8}{7}(14)$$
$$n = 16$$

The number is 16.

37. $3x = 15$

$$x = 5$$
$$9x = 9 \cdot 5 = 45$$

38. $10y = 46$

$$y = \frac{46}{10}$$
$$5y = 5 \cdot \frac{46}{10}$$
$$= \frac{46}{2} \text{ or } 23$$

39. $2a = -10$

$$a = -5$$
$$-6a = -6 \cdot (-5) = 30$$

40. $12b = -1$

$$b = -\frac{1}{12}$$
$$4b = 4\left(-\frac{1}{12}\right) = -\frac{1}{3}$$

41. $7k - 5 = 4$

$$7k = 9$$
$$k = \frac{9}{7}$$
$$21k - 15 = 21\left(\frac{9}{7}\right) - 15$$
$$= 27 - 15$$
$$= 12$$

42. No; if x is negative, then $-x$ is positive.

43a. Let ℓ = the number of left-handed people.

$$7\ell = 350 \qquad 7\ell = 583$$
$$\frac{7\ell}{7} = \frac{350}{7} \qquad \frac{7\ell}{7} = \frac{583}{7}$$
$$\ell = 50 \text{ people} \qquad \ell = 83 \text{ people}$$

43b. $\frac{p}{7} = 65$

$$7\left(\frac{p}{7}\right) = 7(65)$$
$$p = 455 \text{ people}$$

44. $1\frac{1}{2}t = 19{,}819{,}000$

$$\frac{3}{2}t = 19{,}819{,}000$$
$$\frac{2}{3}\left(\frac{3}{2}t\right) = \frac{2}{3}(19{,}819{,}000)$$
$$t = 13{,}212{,}667$$

45a. Let m = the number of minutes.

$$0.10m = 2.30$$
$$\frac{0.10m}{0.10} = \frac{2.30}{0.10}$$
$$m = 23 \text{ minutes}$$

45b. $0.10(18) = c$

$$\$1.80 = c$$

46. $-11 = a + 8$

$$-11 - 8 = a + 8 - 8$$
$$-19 = a$$

47. Let y = the number of years for a tree to become $33\frac{1}{2}$ feet tall.

$$17 + 1\frac{1}{2}y = 33\frac{1}{2}$$
$$17 + 1\frac{1}{2}y - 17 = 33\frac{1}{2} - 17$$
$$1\frac{1}{2}y = 16\frac{1}{2}$$
$$\frac{2}{3}\left(\frac{3}{2}\right)y = \frac{2}{3}\left(\frac{33}{2}\right)$$
$$y = \frac{66}{6} \text{ or } 11 \text{ years}$$

48. $\left[(2132 \cdot 12) + 2\frac{1}{2}\right] \div \frac{1}{2} = (25{,}586.5)\left(\frac{2}{1}\right)$

$$= 51{,}173 \text{ slices}$$

49. $\frac{1}{2}\left(\frac{1}{2} + \frac{6}{7}\right) = \frac{1}{2}\left(\frac{7}{14} + \frac{12}{14}\right)$

$$= \frac{1}{2}\left(\frac{19}{14}\right)$$
$$= \frac{19}{28}$$

50. 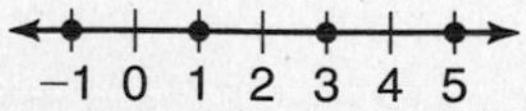

51a. The number of bags increased during the day.

51b. The machine was refilled.

51c. See students' work.

52. $5(3x + 2y - 4y) = 5(3x + 2y)$

$$= 5(3x) + 5(-2y)$$
$$= 15x - 10y$$

53. $a + b^2 + c^2 = 6 + 4^2 + 3^2$

$$= 6 + 16 + 9$$
$$= 31$$

3-3A Modeling Mathematics: Solving Multi-Step Equations

Page 155

1.

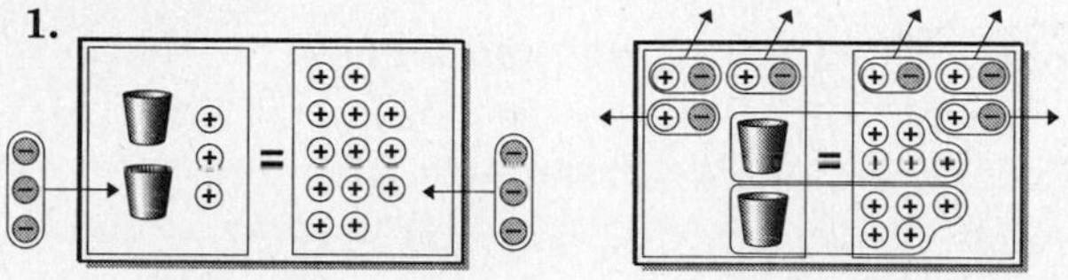

$2x + 3 = 13$ $\qquad$ $x = 5$

2.

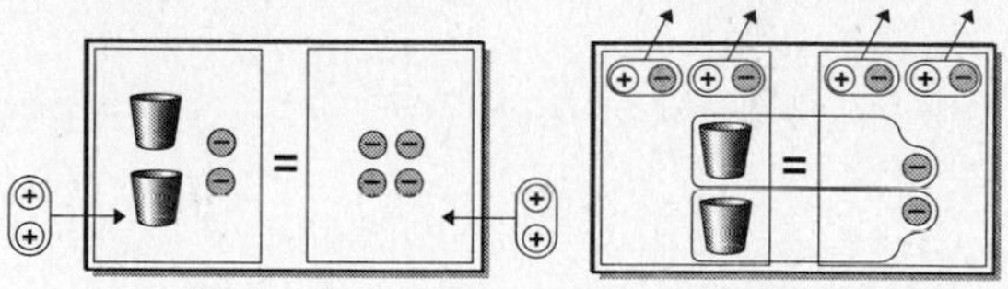

$2y - 2 = -4$ $\qquad$ $y = -1$

3.

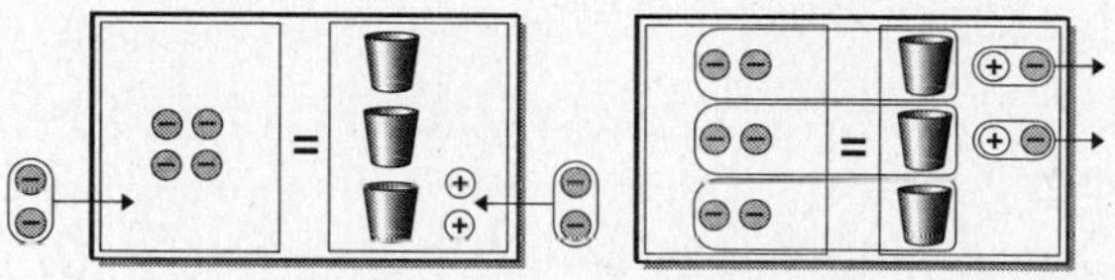

$-4 = 3a + 2$ $\qquad$ $-2 = a$

4.

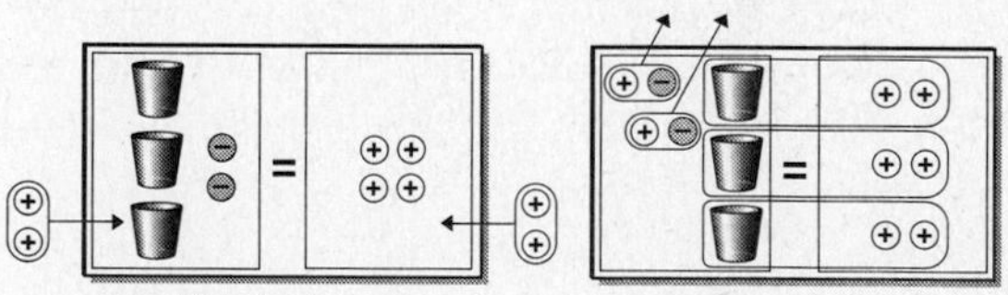

$3m - 2 = 4$ $\qquad$ $m = 2$

5.

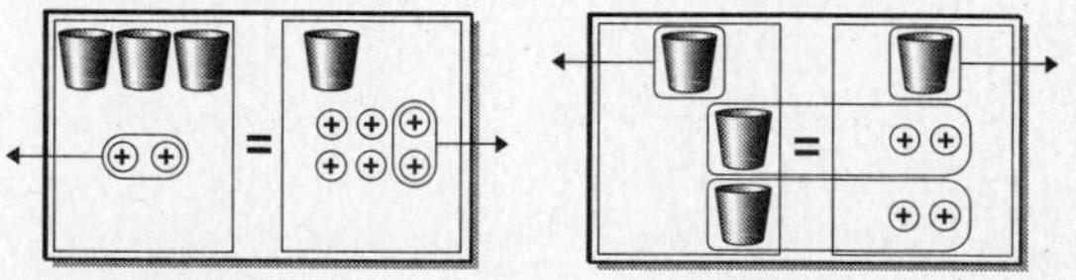

$3x + 2 = x + 6$ $\qquad$ $x = 2$

6.

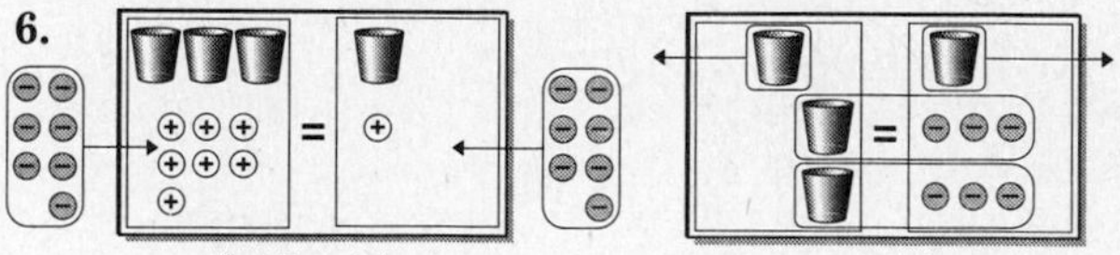

$3x + 7 = x + 1$ $\qquad$ $x = -3$

7.

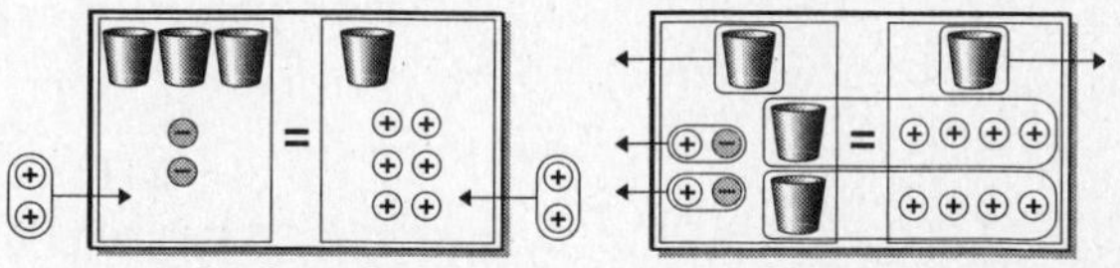

$3x - 2 = x + 6$ $\qquad$ $x = 4$

8.

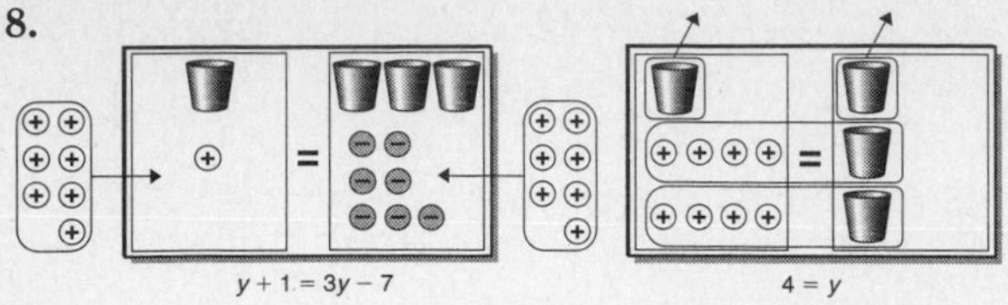

9.

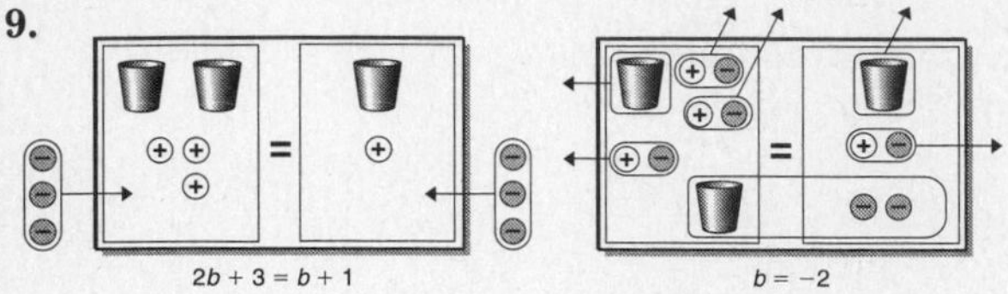

3-3 Solving Multi-Step Equations

Page 159 Check for Understanding

1a. Divide each term by 2.

1b. Fractions would be introduced.

2. Let $2n$ and $2n + 2$ represent consecutive even numbers and let $2n + 1$ and $2n + 3$ represent consecutive odd numbers.

$$2n + 2n + 2 = (2n + 1) + (2n + 3)$$
$$4n + 2 = 4n + 4$$
$$2 = 4$$

Since this is not a true statement, the sum of two consecutive even numbers can never equal the sum of two consecutive odd numbers.

3. Subtract 2; $n - 2$.

4.
$$4x + 3x - 5 = 27$$
$$4(-2) + 3(-2) - 5 \stackrel{?}{=} 27$$
$$-8 + (-6) - 5 \stackrel{?}{=} 27$$
$$-19 \neq 27$$

A solution of -2 does not give a true statement.

5. $-18 - 4 = -22$, $-18 - 2 = -20$; the integers are -22, -20, -18.

6. If $2x + 1 = 5$, then $2x = 4$, and $x = 2$; $3x - 4 = 3(2) - 4 = 6 - 4 = 2$.

7.

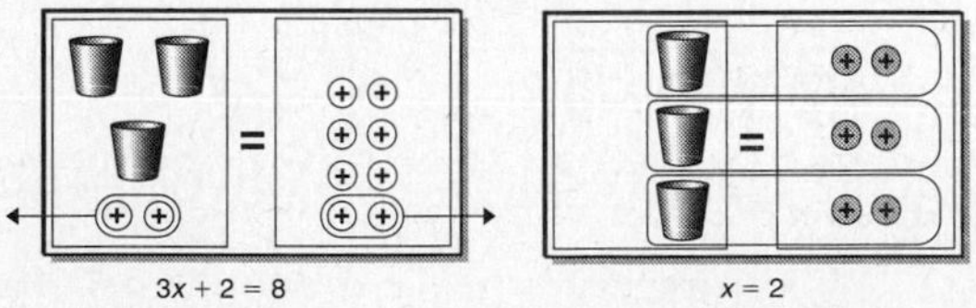

8. Add 5 to each side, then divide each side by 4.
$$4a - 5 = 15$$
$$4a - 5 + 5 = 15 + 5$$
$$4a = 20$$
$$\frac{4a}{4} = \frac{20}{4}$$
$$a = 5$$

9. Subtract 7 from each side, then divide each side by 3.
$$7 + 3c = -11$$
$$7 + 3c - 7 = -11 - 7$$
$$3c = -18$$
$$\frac{3c}{3} = -\frac{18}{3}$$
$$c = -6$$

10. Add 6 to each side, then multiply each side by $\frac{9}{2}$.
$$\frac{2}{9}v - 6 = 14$$
$$\frac{2}{9}v - 6 + 6 = 14 + 6$$
$$\frac{2}{9}v = 20$$
$$\frac{9}{2}\left(\frac{2}{9}\right)v = \frac{9}{2}(20)$$
$$v = \frac{180}{2} \text{ or } 90$$

11. Subtract 3 from each side, then multiply each side by -7.
$$3 - \frac{a}{7} = -2$$
$$3 - \frac{a}{7} - 3 = -2 - 3$$
$$-\frac{a}{7} = -5$$
$$-7\left(-\frac{a}{7}\right) = -7(-5)$$
$$a = 35$$

12. Multiply each side by 7, then add 3 to each side.
$$\frac{x - 3}{7} = -2$$
$$7\left(\frac{x - 3}{7}\right) = 7(-2)$$
$$x - 3 = -14$$
$$x - 3 + 3 = -14 + 3$$
$$x = -11$$

13. Rewrite the numerator as $p + 5$, multiply each side by -2, and then subtract 5.
$$\frac{p - (-5)}{-2} = 6$$
$$\frac{p + 5}{-2} = 6$$
$$-2\left(\frac{p + 5}{-2}\right) = -2(6)$$
$$p + 5 = -12$$
$$p + 5 - 5 = -12 - 5$$
$$p = -17$$

14. Let n = the lesser integer.
Then $n + 1$ = the greater integer.
$$n + (n + 1) = -31$$
$$2n + 1 = -31$$
$$2n + 1 - 1 = -31 - 1$$
$$2n = -32$$
$$\frac{2n}{2} = -\frac{32}{2}$$
$$n = -16$$
$$n + 1 = -16 + 1 = -15$$
The consecutive integers are -16 and -15.

15. Let n = the least odd integer.
Then $n + 2$ = the next greater odd integer, and $n + 4$ = the greatest of the three odd integers.
$$n + (n + 2) + (n + 4) = 21$$
$$3n + 6 = 21$$
$$3n + 6 - 6 = 21 - 6$$
$$3n = 5$$
$$\frac{3n}{3} = \frac{15}{3}$$
$$n = 5$$
$$n + 2 = 5 + 2 \qquad n + 4 = 5 + 4$$
$$n + 2 = 7 \qquad n + 4 = 9$$
The consecutive odd integers are 5, 7, and 9.

16. Let n = the number.

$$\begin{aligned} 29 &= 13 + 4n \\ 29 - 13 &= 13 + 4n - 13 \\ 16 &= 4n \\ \frac{16}{4} &= \frac{4n}{4} \\ 4 &= n \end{aligned}$$

The number is 4.

Pages 160–161 Exercises

17.
$$\begin{aligned} 3x - 2 &= -5 \\ 3x - 2 + 2 &= -5 + 2 \\ 3x &= -3 \\ \frac{3x}{3} &= -\frac{3}{3} \\ x &= -1 \end{aligned}$$

18.
$$\begin{aligned} -4 &= 5n + 6 \\ -4 - 6 &= 5n + 6 - 6 \\ -10 &= 5n \\ \frac{-10}{5} &= \frac{5n}{5} \\ -2 &= n \end{aligned}$$

19.
$$\begin{aligned} 5 - 9w &= 23 \\ 5 - 9w - 5 &= 23 - 5 \\ -9w &= 18 \\ \frac{-9w}{-9} &= \frac{18}{-9} \\ w &= -2 \end{aligned}$$

20.
$$\begin{aligned} 17 &= 7 + 8y \\ 17 - 7 &= 7 + 8y - 7 \\ 10 &= 8y \\ \frac{10}{8} &= \frac{8y}{8} \\ y &= 1.25 \text{ or } 1\tfrac{1}{4} \end{aligned}$$

21.
$$\begin{aligned} -2.5d - 32.7 &= 74.1 \\ -2.5d - 32.7 + 32.7 &= 74.1 + 32.7 \\ -2.5d &= 106.8 \\ \frac{-2.5d}{-2.5} &= \frac{106.8}{-2.5} \\ d &= -42.72 \end{aligned}$$

22.
$$\begin{aligned} 0.2n + 3 &= 8.6 \\ 0.2n + 3 - 3 &= 8.6 - 3 \\ 0.2n &= 5.6 \\ \frac{0.2n}{0.2} &= \frac{5.6}{0.2} \\ n &= 28 \end{aligned}$$

23.
$$\begin{aligned} \tfrac{3}{2}a - 8 &= 11 \\ \tfrac{3}{2}a - 8 + 8 &= 11 + 8 \\ \tfrac{3}{2}a &= 19 \\ \tfrac{2}{3}\left(\tfrac{3}{2}\right)a &= \tfrac{2}{3}(19) \\ a &= \tfrac{38}{3} \text{ or } 12\tfrac{2}{3} \end{aligned}$$

24.
$$\begin{aligned} 5 &= -9 - \tfrac{p}{4} \\ 5 + 9 &= -9 - \tfrac{p}{4} + 9 \\ 14 &= -\tfrac{p}{4} \\ -4(14) &= -4\left(-\tfrac{p}{4}\right) \\ -56 &= p \end{aligned}$$

25.
$$\begin{aligned} 7 &= \tfrac{c}{-3} + 5 \\ 7 - 5 &= \tfrac{c}{-3} + 5 - 5 \\ 2 &= \tfrac{c}{-3} \\ -3(2) &= -3\left(\tfrac{c}{-3}\right) \\ -6 &= c \end{aligned}$$

26.
$$\begin{aligned} \tfrac{m}{-5} + 6 &= 31 \\ \tfrac{m}{-5} + 6 - 6 &= 31 - 6 \\ \tfrac{m}{-5} &= 25 \\ -5\left(\tfrac{m}{-5}\right) &= -5(25) \\ m &= -125 \end{aligned}$$

27.
$$\begin{aligned} \tfrac{g}{8} - 6 &= -12 \\ \tfrac{g}{8} - 6 + 6 &= -12 + 6 \\ \tfrac{g}{8} &= -6 \\ 8\left(\tfrac{g}{8}\right) &= 8(-6) \\ g &= -48 \end{aligned}$$

28.
$$\begin{aligned} 6 &= -12 + \tfrac{h}{-7} \\ 6 + 12 &= -12 + \tfrac{h}{-7} + 12 \\ 18 &= \tfrac{h}{-7} \\ -7(18) &= -7\left(\tfrac{h}{-7}\right) \\ -126 &= h \end{aligned}$$

29.
$$\begin{aligned} \tfrac{b + 4}{-2} &= -17 \\ -2\left(\tfrac{b + 4}{-2}\right) &= -2(-17) \\ b + 4 &= 34 \\ b + 4 - 4 &= 34 - 4 \\ b &= 30 \end{aligned}$$

30.
$$\begin{aligned} \tfrac{z - 7}{5} &= -3 \\ 5\left(\tfrac{z-7}{5}\right) &= 5(-3) \\ z - 7 &= -15 \\ z - 7 + 7 &= -15 + 7 \\ z &= -8 \end{aligned}$$

31.
$$\begin{aligned} -10 &= \tfrac{17 - s}{4} \\ 4(-10) &= 4\left(\tfrac{17 - s}{4}\right) \\ -40 &= 17 - s \\ -40 - 17 &= 17 - s - 17 \\ -57 &= -s \\ 57 &= s \end{aligned}$$

32.
$$\begin{aligned} \tfrac{4t - 5}{-9} &= 7 \\ -9\left(\tfrac{4t - 5}{-9}\right) &= -9(7) \\ 4t - 5 &= -63 \\ 4t - 5 + 5 &= -63 + 5 \\ 4t &= -58 \\ \tfrac{4t}{4} &= -\tfrac{58}{4} \\ t &= -14\tfrac{1}{2} \text{ or } -14.5 \end{aligned}$$

33.
$$\begin{aligned} \tfrac{7n + (-1)}{6} &= 5 \\ 6\left[\tfrac{7n + (-1)}{6}\right] &= 6(5) \\ 7n + (-1) &= 30 \\ 7n - 1 &= 30 \\ 7n - 1 + 1 &= 30 + 1 \\ 7n &= 31 \\ \tfrac{7n}{7} &= \tfrac{31}{7} \\ n &= \tfrac{31}{7} \text{ or } 4\tfrac{3}{7} \end{aligned}$$

34.
$$\begin{aligned} \tfrac{-3j - (-4)}{-6} &= 12 \\ \tfrac{-3j + 4}{-6} &= 12 \\ -6\left(\tfrac{-3j + 4}{-6}\right) &= -6(12) \\ -3j + 4 &= -72 \\ -3j + 4 - 4 &= -72 - 4 \\ -3j &= -76 \\ \tfrac{-3j}{-3} &= \tfrac{-76}{-3} \\ j &= \tfrac{76}{3} \text{ or } 25\tfrac{1}{3} \end{aligned}$$

35. Let n = the number.

$$\begin{aligned} 12 - 2n &= -7 \\ 12 - 2n - 12 &= -7 - 12 \\ -2n &= -19 \\ \tfrac{-2n}{-2} &= \tfrac{-19}{-2} \\ n &= \tfrac{19}{2} \text{ or } 9\tfrac{1}{2} \end{aligned}$$

The number is $9\frac{1}{2}$.

36. Let n = the least integer.
Then $n + 1$ = the next greater integer, and
$n + 2$ = the greatest of the three integers.

$$\begin{aligned} n + (n + 1) + (n + 2) &= -33 \\ 3n + 3 &= -33 \\ 3n + 3 - 3 &= -33 - 3 \\ 3n &= -36 \\ \tfrac{3n}{3} &= \tfrac{-36}{3} \\ n &= -12 \end{aligned}$$

$n + 1 = -12 + 1 \qquad n + 2 = -12 + 2$

$n + 1 = -11 \qquad n + 2 = -10$

The consecutive integers are -12, -11, and -10.

37. Let n = the least integer.
Then $n + 1$ = the next greater integer, and $n + 2$ = the next greater integer, and $n + 3$ = the greatest of the four integers.

$$n + (n + 1) + (n + 2) + (n + 3) = 86$$
$$4n + 6 = 86$$
$$4n + 6 - 6 = 86 - 6$$
$$4n = 80$$
$$\frac{4n}{4} = \frac{80}{4}$$
$$n = 20$$

$n + 1 = 20 + 1$ $\quad n + 2 = 20 + 2$ $\quad n + 3 = 20 + 3$
$n + 1 = 21$ $\quad n + 2 = 22$ $\quad n + 3 = 23$

The consecutive integers are 20, 21, 22, and 23.

38. Let n = the lesser odd integer.
Then $n + 2$ = the greater odd integer.

$$n + (n + 2) = 196 \qquad n + 2 = 97 + 2$$
$$2n + 2 = 196 \qquad = 99$$
$$2n + 2 - 2 = 196 - 2$$
$$2n = 194$$
$$\frac{2n}{2} = \frac{194}{2}$$
$$n = 97$$

The consecutive odd integers are 97 and 99.

39.

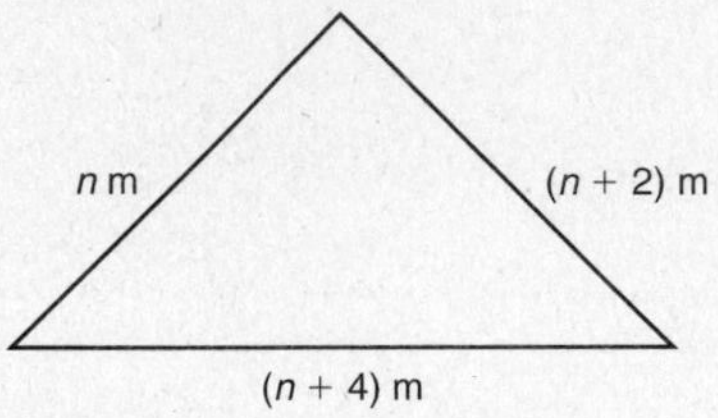

Let n = the least odd integer.
Then $n + 2$ = the next odd integer, and $n + 4$ = the greatest of the three odd integers.

$$n + (n + 2) + (n + 4) = 39$$
$$3n + 6 = 39$$
$$3n + 6 - 6 = 39 - 6$$
$$3n = 33$$
$$\frac{3n}{3} = \frac{33}{3}$$
$$n = 11$$

$n + 2 = 11 + 2$ $\quad n + 4 = 11 + 4$
$n + 2 = 13$ $\quad n + 4 = 15$

The lengths of the sides are 11 m, 13 m, and 15 m.

40.

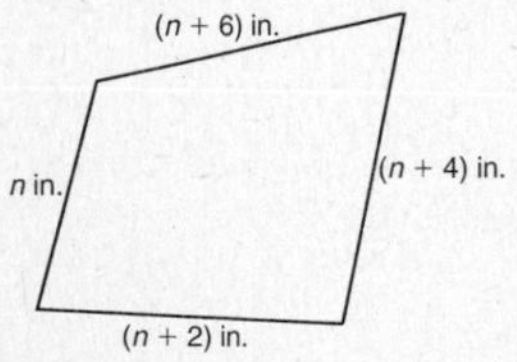

Let n = the least even integer. Then $n + 2$ = the next greater even integer, and $n + 4$ = the the next greater even integer, and $n + 6$ = the greatest of the four even integers.

$$2n + (n + 6) = 120$$
$$3n + 6 = 120$$
$$3n + 6 - 6 = 120 - 6$$
$$3n = 114$$
$$\frac{3n}{3} = \frac{114}{3}$$
$$n = 38$$

$n + 2 = 38 + 2$ $\quad n + 4 = 38 + 4$ $\quad n + 6 = 38 + 6$
$n + 2 = 40$ $\quad n + 4 = 42$ $\quad n + 6 = 44$

The lengths of the sides are 38 in., 40 in., 42 in., and 44 in.

41.
$$0.2x + 3 = 8.6$$
$$0.2x + 3 - 3 = 8.6 - 3$$
$$0.2x = 5.6$$
$$\frac{0.2x}{0.2} = \frac{5.6}{0.2}$$
$$x = 28$$

42.
$$4.91 + 7.2x = 39.4201$$
$$4.91 + 7.2x - 4.91 = 39.4201 - 4.91$$
$$7.2x = 34.5101$$
$$\frac{7.2x}{7.2} = \frac{34.5101}{7.2}$$
$$x = 4.793$$

43.
$$\frac{3 + x}{7} = -5$$
$$7\left(\frac{3 + x}{7}\right) = 7(-5)$$
$$3 + x = -35$$
$$3 + x - 3 = -35 - 3$$
$$x = -38$$

44.
$$\frac{-3n - (-4)}{-6} = -9$$
$$-6\left(\frac{-3n - (-4)}{-6}\right) = -6(-9)$$
$$-3n - (-4) = 54$$
$$-3n + 4 = 54$$
$$-3n + 4 - 4 = 54 - 5$$
$$-3n = 50$$
$$\frac{-3n}{-3} = \frac{50}{-3}$$
$$n = -\frac{50}{3}$$
$$n = -16\tfrac{2}{3} \text{ or } -16.67$$

45. Let $3n - 1$ = the least integer.
Then $(3n - 1) + 2 = 3n + 1$ = the next greater even integer, and $(3n - 1) + 4 = 3n + 3$ = the greatest of the three even integers.
$(3n - 1) + (3n + 1) + (3n + 3)$

46a. Let d = the number of days before the baby weighs 12 pounds.

$$(7.5 \text{ lb})\left(\frac{16 \text{ oz}}{1 \text{ lb}}\right) = 120 \text{ oz}$$
$$(120 - 5) + (d - 5) = 192$$
$$115 + d - 5 = 192$$
$$d + 110 = 192$$
$$d + 110 - 110 = 192 - 110$$
$$d = 82$$

The baby weighs 12 pounds after 82 days.

46b.

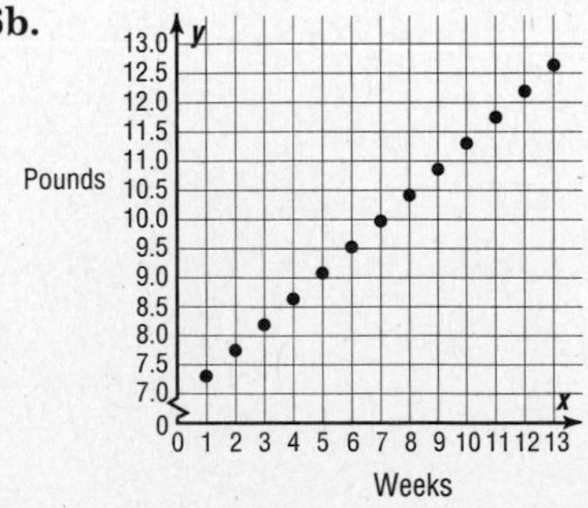

47. Let a = the number of letters in the Hawaiian alphabet.

$$2a + 2 = 26$$
$$2a + 2 - 2 = 26 - 2$$
$$2a = 24$$
$$\frac{2a}{2} = \frac{24}{2}$$
$$a = 12$$

There are 12 letters.

48.

Family	Bags Left	+	Bags Bought	=	Original Number of Bags
Wimberly	0		1 + 1		2
Bright-feather	2		1 + 3		6
Martinez	6		1 + 7		14
Wilson	14		1 + 15		30

Wilson, 1 + 15 or 16 bags; Martinez, 1 + 7 or 8 bags; Brightfeather, 1 + 3 or 4 bags; Wimberly, 1 + 1 or 2 bags.

49a. See students' work.

49b. See students' work.

50. $x + 4 = 15$
$x + 4 - 4 = 15 - 4$
$x = 11$
$x - 2 = 11 - 2 = 9$

51. I

52. $-4x$

53. $4(7) - 3(11) = 28 - 33$
$= -5$

54. substitution (=)

55. $a = \frac{12 + 8}{4}$
$= \frac{20}{4}$
$= 5$

56. $\frac{3}{4}(6) + \frac{1}{3}(12) = \frac{18}{4} + \frac{12}{3}$
$= \frac{9}{2} + 4$
$= \frac{9}{2} + \frac{8}{2}$
$= \frac{17}{2}$ or $8\frac{1}{2}$

Page 161 Self Test

1. $-10 + k = 34$
$-10 + k + 10 = 34 + 10$
$k = 44$

2. $y - 13 = 45$
$y - 13 + 13 = 45 + 13$
$y = 58$

3. $20.4 = 3.4y$
$\frac{20.4}{3.4} = \frac{3.4y}{3.4}$
$6 = y$

4. $-65 = \frac{f}{29}$
$29(-65) = 29\left(\frac{f}{29}\right)$
$-1885 = f$

5. $-3x - 7 = 18$
$-3x - 7 + 7 = 18 + 7$
$-3x = 25$
$\frac{-3x}{-3} = \frac{25}{-3}$
$x = -8\frac{1}{3}$

6. $5 = \frac{m-5}{4}$
$4(5) = 4\left(\frac{m-5}{4}\right)$
$20 = m-5$
$20 + 5 = m-5 + 5$
$25 = m$

7. Let n = the number.
$23 - n = 42$
$23 - n - 23 = 42 - 23$
$-n = 19$
$n = -19$
The number is -19.

8. Let w = the width of the rectangle.
$\ell w = A$
$34w = 68$
$\frac{34w}{34} = \frac{68}{34}$
$w = 2$
The width is 2 cm.

9. Let n = the lesser even integer.
Then $n + 2$ = the greater even integer.
$n + (n + 2) = 126$
$2n + 2 = 126$
$2n + 2 - 2 = 126 - 2$
$2n = 124$
$\frac{2n}{2} = \frac{124}{2}$
$n = 62$
$n + 2 = 62 + 2$
$n + 2 = 64$
The consecutive even integers are 62 and 64.

10. Let p = the price of a movie ticket in 40 years.
$p = 10(5.05) - 3.50$
$= 50.50 - 3.50$
$= 47$
The price of a movie ticket in 40 years will be \$47.

3-4 Integration: Geometry Angles and Triangles

Pages 165–166 Check for Understanding

1a. A compliment is an expression of praise. A comlement is something that completes or fills.

1b. The word *complement* has the mathematical meaning.

2. A supplement is something added to complete something, make up for a deficiency, or extend or strengthen the whole. The supplement of an angle completes a 180° angle, which is a straight line.

3. acute, obtuse, and right, respectively

4. See students' work.

5. The sum of their measures is 90°.

6. none
$180° - 130° = 50°$

7. $90° - 11° = 79°$
$180° - 11° = 169°$

8. $90° - 24° = 66°$
$180° - 24° = 156°$

9. $(90 - 3x)°$
$(180 - 3x)°$

10. $90° - (2x + 40)° = (50 - 2x)°$
$180° - (2x + 40)° = (140 - 2x)°$

11. $90° - (x - 20)° = (110 - x)°$
$180° - (x - 20)° = (200 - x)°$

12. $16 + 42 + x = 180$
$58 + x = 180$
$58 + x - 58 = 180 - 58$
$x = 122°$

13. $50 + 45 + x = 180$
$95 + x = 180$
$95 + x - 95 = 180 - 95$
$x = 85°$

14. Let y = the third angle.
$x + (x + 20) + y = 180$
$(2x + 20) + y = 180$
$(2x + 20) + y - (2x + 20) = 180 - (2x + 20)$
$y = (160 - 2x)°$

15. Let c = the greater measure. Then $c - 38$ = the lesser measure.

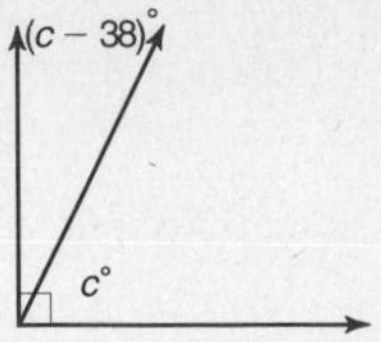

$$(c - 38) + c = 90$$
$$2c - 38 = 90$$
$$2c - 38 + 38 = 90 + 38$$
$$2c = 128$$
$$\frac{2c}{2} = \frac{128}{2}$$
$$c = 64°$$
$$c - 38 = 64 - 38$$
$$c - 38 = 26°$$

The measures are 64° and 26°.

16. $x + (x + 5) + (2x + 3) = 180$

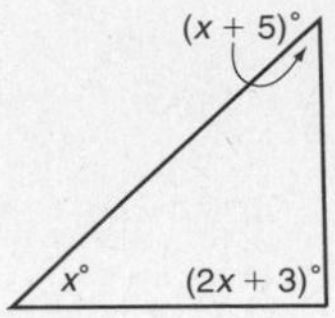

$$4x + 8 = 180$$
$$4x + 8 - 8 = 180 - 8$$
$$4x = 172$$
$$\frac{4x}{4} = \frac{172}{4}$$
$$x = 43°$$

$(x + 5) = 43 + 5$
$= 48°$

$(2x + 3) = 2(43) + 3$
$= 86 + 3 = 89°$

The measures are 43°, 48°, and 89°.

Pages 166–167 Exercises

17. $90° - 42° = 48°$
$180° - 42° = 138°$

18. $90° - 87° = 3°$
$180° - 87° = 93°$

19. none
$180° - 125° = 55°$

20. none
$180° - 90° = 90°$

21. $90° - 21° = 69°$
$180° - 21° = 159°$

22. none
$180° - 174° = 6°$

23. none
$180° - 99° = 81°$

24. $(90 - y)°$
$(180 - y)°$

25. $(90 - 3a)°$
$(180 - 3a)°$

26. $90° - (x + 30)° = (60 - x)°$
$180° - (x + 30)° = (150 - x)°$

27. $90° - (b - 38)° = (128 - b)°$
$180° - (b - 38)° = (218 - b)°$

28. $90° - (90 - z)° = z°$
$180° - (90 - z)° = (90 + z)°$

29.
$$x + 40 + 70 = 180$$
$$x + 110 = 180$$
$$x + 110 - 110 = 180 - 110$$
$$x = 70°$$

30.
$$x + 90 + 30 = 180$$
$$x + 120 = 180$$
$$x + 120 - 120 = 180 - 120$$
$$x = 60°$$

31.
$$x + 63 + 12 = 180$$
$$x + 75 = 180$$
$$x + 75 - 75 = 180 - 75$$
$$x = 105°$$

32.
$$x + 43 + 118 = 180$$
$$x + 161 = 180$$
$$x + 161 - 161 = 180 - 161$$
$$x = 19°$$

33.
$$x + 4 + 38 = 180$$
$$x + 42 = 180$$
$$x + 42 - 42 = 180 - 42$$
$$x = 138°$$

34. Let z = the third angle.
$$x + y + z = 180$$
$$x + y + z - x - y = 180 - x - y$$
$$z = (180 - x - y)° \text{ or } 180 - (x + y)°$$

35. Let x = the third angle.
$$x + p + (p - 10) = 180$$
$$x + 2p - 10 = 180$$
$$x + 2p - 10 - 2p + 10 = 180 - 2p + 10$$
$$x = (190 - 2p)°$$

36. Let x = the third angle.
$$x + c + (2c + 1) = 180$$
$$x + 3c + 1 = 180$$
$$x + 3c + 1 - 3c - 1 = 180 - 3c - 1$$
$$x = (179 - 3c)°$$

37. Let x = the third angle.
$$x + y + 135 - y = 180$$
$$x + 135 = 180$$
$$x + 135 - 135 = 180 - 135$$
$$x = 45°$$

38.

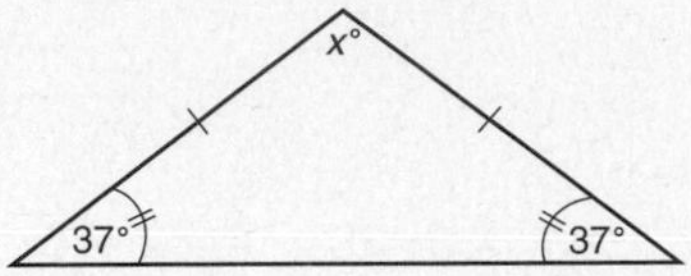

The measure of the other congruent angle is 37°.
Let x = the measure of the vertex angle.
$$37 + 37 + x = 180$$
$$74 + x = 180$$
$$74 + x - 74 = 180 - 74$$
$$x = 106°$$

The vertex angle measures 106°.

39.

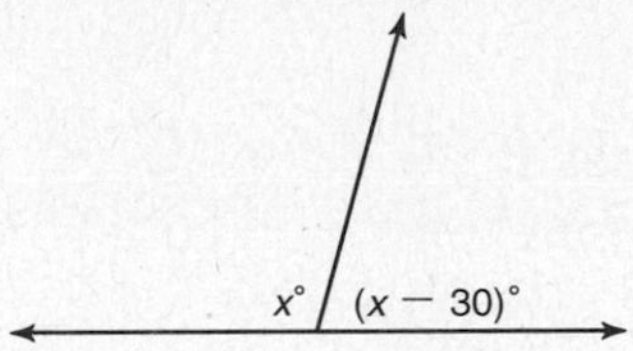

Let x = the greater measure.
Then $x - 30$ = the lesser measure.
$$x + (x - 30) = 180$$
$$2x - 30 = 180$$
$$2x - 30 + 30 = 180 + 30$$
$$2x = 210$$
$$\frac{2x}{2} = \frac{210}{2}$$
$$x = 105°$$
$$x - 30 = 105 - 30 = 75°$$

The measure of the lesser angle is 75°.

40. $53 + 37 + x = 180$

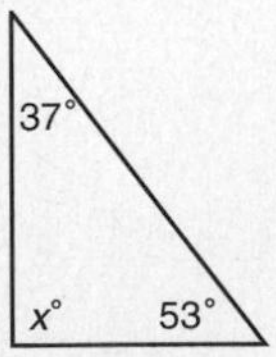

$$90 + x = 180$$
$$90 + x - 90 = 180 - 90$$
$$x = 90°$$

The third angle measures 90°.

41. Let x = the lesser measure. Then $30 + 3x$ = the greater measure.

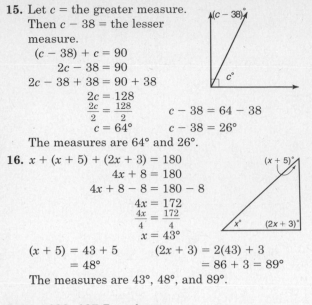

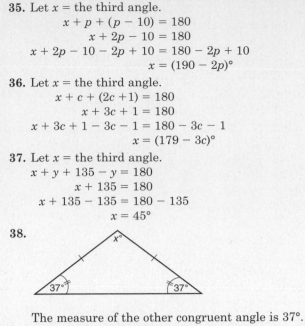

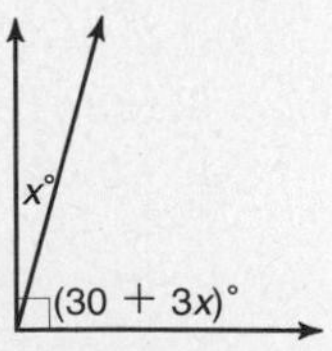

$$x + (30 + 3x) = 90$$
$$4x + 30 = 90$$
$$4x + 30 - 30 = 90 - 30$$
$$4x = 60$$
$$\frac{4x}{4} = \frac{60}{4}$$
$$x = 15°$$
$$30 + 3x = 30 + 3(15)$$
$$= 75°$$

The measures are 15° and 75°.

42.

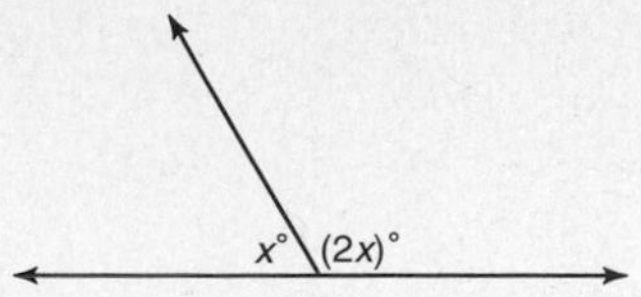

Let x = the lesser measure.
Then $2x$ = the greater measure.

$$x + 2x = 180$$
$$3x = 180$$
$$\frac{3x}{3} = \frac{180}{3}$$
$$x = 60°$$

The lesser measure is 60°.

43.

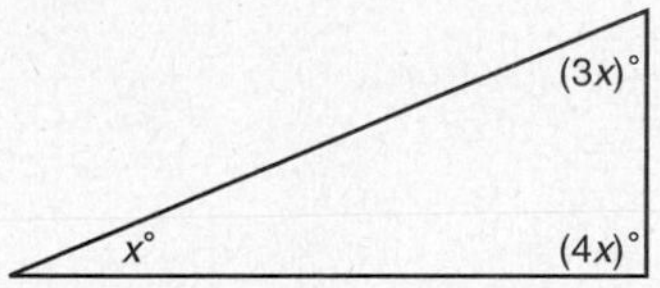

$$x + 3x + 4x = 180$$
$$8x = 180$$
$$\frac{8x}{8} = \frac{180}{8}$$
$$x = 22.5°$$

The measures are 22.5°, 3(22.5°) or 67.5°, and 4(22.5°) or 90°.

44. See students' work.

45. Let x = the third angle.

$$x + 30 + 90 = 180$$
$$x + 120 = 180$$
$$x + 120 - 120 = 180 - 120$$
$$x = 60°$$

46a.
$$x + 3 + 90 = 180$$
$$x + 93 = 180$$
$$x + 93 - 93 = 180 - 93$$
$$x = 87°$$

46b.
$$x + 18 + 90 = 180$$
$$x + 108 = 180$$
$$x + 108 - 108 = 180 - 108$$
$$x = 72°$$

46c. shuttle

47.
$$x + 50 + 90 = 180$$
$$x + 140 = 180$$
$$x + 140 - 140 = 180 - 140$$
$$x = 40°$$

48.
$$4 + 7x = 39$$
$$4 + 7x - 4 = 39 - 4$$
$$7x = 35$$
$$\frac{7x}{7} = \frac{35}{7}$$
$$x = 5$$

49a. Let x = the original price.

$$\frac{1}{4}x = 20$$
$$4\left(\frac{1}{4}x\right) = 4(20)$$
$$x = 80$$

The original price was $80.

49b. $\frac{1}{4}(299) = \$74.75$

50.
$$h + (-13) = -5$$
$$h - 13 = -5$$
$$h - 13 + 13 = -5 + 13$$
$$h = 8$$

51.
$$5(3t - 2t) + 2(4t - 3t) = 5(t) + 2(t)$$
$$= 5t + 2t$$
$$= 7t$$

52.
$$5y + (-12y) + (-21y) = 5y - 12y - 21y$$
$$= (5 - 12 - 21)y$$
$$= -28y$$

53a.

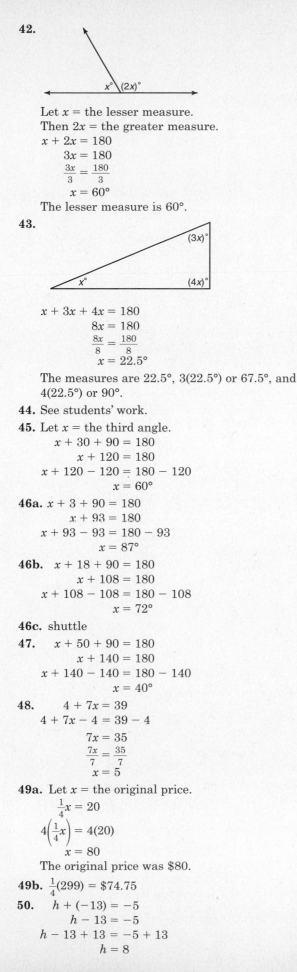

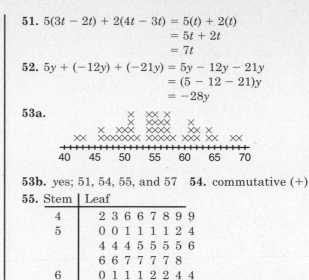

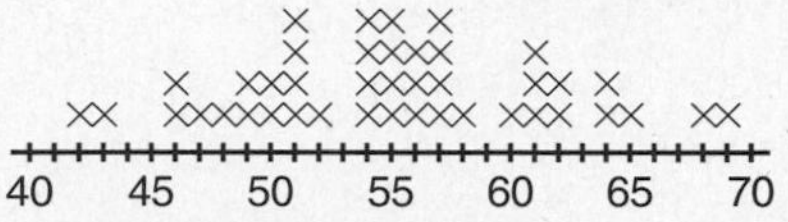

53b. yes; 51, 54, 55, and 57 **54.** commutative (+)

55.

Stem	Leaf
4	2 3 6 6 7 8 9 9
5	0 0 1 1 1 1 2 4
	4 4 4 5 5 5 5 6
	6 6 7 7 7 7 8
6	0 1 1 1 2 2 4 4
	5 8 9

5|2 = 52

3-5 Solving Equations with the Variable on Both Sides

Page 170 Check for Understanding

1a. Sample answer: women are training harder, working out more, and so on.

1b. Sample answer:

Year	Men	Women
1928	111.8	136.8
1948	109.3	130.2
1968	106.7	123.5
1988	104.2	116.9
2008	101.6	110.2
2028	99.1	103.6
2048	96.6	97.0
2068	94.0	90.3

1c. Answers may vary.

2. An identity is true for *all* values of the variable. An equation with no solution is true for *no* values of the variable.

3. Carmen; you begin with the numerals in the innermost grouping symbols – in this case, $(x - 1)$.

4. See students' work.

5. Add $4x$ to each side, subtract 10 from each side, then divide each side by 14.

$$3 - 4x = 10x + 10$$
$$3 - 4x + 4x = 10x + 10 + 4x$$
$$3 = 14x + 10$$
$$3 - 10 = 14x + 10 - 10$$
$$-7 = 14x$$
$$\frac{-7}{14} = \frac{14x}{14}$$
$$-\frac{1}{2} = x$$

6. Add $3y$ to each side, add 10 to each side, then divide each side by 11.

$$8y - 10 = -3y + 2$$
$$8y - 10 + 3y = -3y + 2 + 3y$$
$$11y - 10 = 2$$
$$11y - 10 + 10 = 2 + 10$$
$$11y = 12$$
$$\frac{11y}{11} = \frac{12}{11}$$
$$y = \frac{12}{11}$$

7. Subtract $\frac{1}{5}x$ from each side, subtract 3 from each side, then multiply by $\frac{5}{2}$.

$$\frac{3}{5}x + 3 = \frac{1}{5}x - 7$$
$$\frac{3}{5}x + 3 - \frac{1}{5}x = \frac{1}{5}x - 7 - \frac{1}{5}x$$
$$\frac{2}{5}x + 3 = -7$$
$$\frac{2}{5}x + 3 - 3 = -7 - 3$$
$$\frac{2}{5}x = -10$$
$$\frac{5}{2}\left(\frac{2}{5}\right)x = \frac{5}{2}(-10)$$
$$x = -\frac{50}{2} \text{ or } -25$$

8. Subtract $5.4y$ from each side, add 2.8 to each side, then divide each side by 4.4.

$$5.4y + 8.2 = 9.8y - 2.8$$
$$5.4y + 8.2 - 5.4y = 9.8y - 2.8 - 5.4y$$
$$8.2 = 4.4y - 2.8$$
$$8.2 + 2.8 = 4.4y - 2.8 + 2.8$$
$$11 = 4.4y - 2.8 + 2.8$$
$$11 = 4.4y$$
$$\frac{11}{4.4} = \frac{4.4y}{4.4}$$
$$2.5 = y$$

9. Distribute the 5 on the right side, combine terms. Since the expressions on each side of the equation are the same, the equation is an identity.

$$5x - 7 = 5(x - 2) + 3$$
$$5x - 7 = 5x - 10 + 3$$
$$5x - 7 = 5x - 7$$

all numbers

10. Multiply 4 by $(2x - 1)$ and -10 by $(x - 5)$. Subtract $8x$ from each side, and subtract 50 from each side. Then divide each side by -18.

$$4(2x - 1) = -10(x-5)$$
$$8x - 4 = -10x + 50$$
$$8x - 4 - 8x = -10x + 50 - 8x$$
$$-4 = -18x + 50$$
$$-4 - 50 = -18x + 50 - 50$$
$$-54 = -18x$$
$$\frac{-54}{-18} = \frac{-18x}{-18}$$
$$3 = x$$

11. Let n = the lesser odd integer.
Then $n + 2$ = the greater odd integer.

$$2(n + 2) = 3n - 13$$
$$2n + 4 = 3n - 13$$
$$2n + 4 - 2n = 3n - 13 - 2n$$
$$4 = n - 13$$
$$4 + 13 = n - 13 + 13$$
$$17 = n$$

$$n + 2 = 17 + 2$$
$$n + 2 = 19$$

The consecutive even integers are 17 and 19.

12. $6x + (x - 3) + (3x + 7) = 180$

$$10x + 4 = 180$$
$$10x + 4 - 4 = 180 - 4$$
$$10x = 176$$
$$x = 17.6°$$

The measures are 6(17.6) or 105.6°, 17.6 − 3 or 14.6°, and 3(17.6) + 7 or 59.8°.

13. Let n = the number.

$$\frac{1}{2}n + 16 = \frac{2}{3}n - 4$$
$$\frac{1}{2}n + 16 - \frac{1}{2}n = \frac{2}{3}n - 4 - \frac{1}{2}n$$
$$16 = \frac{4}{6}n - 4 - \frac{3}{6}n$$
$$16 = \frac{1}{6}n - 4$$
$$16 + 4 = \frac{1}{6}n - 4 + 4$$
$$20 = \frac{1}{6}n$$
$$6(20) = 6\left(\frac{1}{6}n\right)$$
$$120 = n$$

The number is 120.

Pages 171–172 Exercises

14.
$$6x + 7 = 8x - 13$$
$$6x + 7 - 6x = 8x - 13 - 6x$$
$$7 = 2x - 13$$
$$7 + 13 = 2x - 13 + 13$$
$$20 = 2x$$
$$\frac{20}{2} = \frac{2x}{2}$$
$$10 = x$$

15.
$$17 + 2n = 21 + 2n$$
$$17 + 2n - 2n = 21 + 2n - 2n$$
$$17 = 21$$

Since 17 = 21 is a false statement, this equation has no solution.

16.
$$\frac{3n - 2}{5} = \frac{7}{10}$$
$$10\left(\frac{3n - 2}{5}\right) = 10\left(\frac{7}{10}\right)$$
$$2(3n - 2) = 7$$
$$6n - 4 = 7$$
$$6n - 4 + 4 = 7 + 4$$
$$6n = 11$$
$$\frac{6n}{6} = \frac{11}{6}$$
$$n \approx 1.83 \text{ or } 1\frac{5}{6}$$

17.
$$\frac{7 + 3t}{4} = -\frac{t}{8}$$
$$8\left(\frac{7 + 3t}{4}\right) = 8\left(-\frac{t}{8}\right)$$
$$2(7 + 3t) = -t$$
$$14 + 6t = -t$$
$$14 + 6t - 6t = -t - 6t$$
$$14 = -7t$$
$$\frac{14}{-7} = \frac{-7t}{-7}$$
$$-2 = t$$

18.
$$13.7b - 6.5 = -2.3b + 8.3$$
$$13.7b - 6.5 + 2.3b = -2.3b + 8.3 + 2.3b$$
$$16b - 6.5 = 8.3$$
$$16b - 6.5 + 6.5 = 8.3 + 6.5$$
$$16b = 14.8$$
$$\frac{16b}{16} = \frac{14.8}{16}$$
$$b = 0.925$$

19. $18 - 3.8x = 7.36 - 1.9x$
$$18 - 3.8x + 3.8x = 7.36 - 1.9x + 3.8x$$
$$18 = 7.36 + 1.9x$$
$$18 - 7.36 = 7.36 + 1.9x - 7.36$$
$$10.64 = 1.9x$$
$$\frac{10.64}{1.9} = \frac{1.9x}{1.9}$$
$$5.6 = x$$

20. $\frac{3}{2}y - y = 4 + \frac{1}{2}y$
$$\frac{1}{2}y = 4 + \frac{1}{2}y$$
$$\frac{1}{2}y - \frac{1}{2}y = 4 + \frac{1}{2}y - \frac{1}{2}y$$
$$0 = 4$$
Since $0 = 4$ is a false statement, this equation has no solution.

21. $\frac{3}{4}n + 16 = 2 - \frac{1}{8}n$
$$\frac{3}{4}n + 16 + \frac{1}{8}n = 2 - \frac{1}{8}n + \frac{1}{8}n$$
$$\frac{6}{8}n + 16 + \frac{1}{8}n = 2$$
$$\frac{7}{8}n + 16 = 2$$
$$\frac{7}{8}n + 16 - 16 = 2 - 16$$
$$\frac{7}{8}n = -14$$
$$\frac{8}{7}\left(\frac{7}{8}n\right) = \frac{8}{7}(-14)$$
$$n = -16$$

22. $-7(x - 3) = -4$
$$-7x + 21 = -4$$
$$-7x + 21 - 21 = -4 - 21$$
$$-7x = -25$$
$$\frac{-7x}{-7} = \frac{-25}{-7}$$
$$x \approx 3.57 \text{ or } 3\tfrac{4}{7}$$

23. $4(x - 2) = 4x$
$$4x - 8 = 4x$$
$$4x - 8 - 4x = 4x - 4x$$
$$-8 = 0$$
Since $-8 = 0$ is a false statement, this equation has no solution.

24. $28 - 2.2y = 11.6y + 262.6$
$$28 - 2.2y + 2.2y = 11.6y + 262.6 + 2.2y$$
$$28 = 13.8y + 262.6$$
$$28 - 262.6 = 13.8y + 262.6 - 262.6$$
$$-234.6 = 13.8y$$
$$\frac{-234.6}{13.8} = \frac{13.8y}{13.8}$$
$$-17 = y$$

25. $1.03x - 4 = -2.15x + 8.72$
$$1.03x - 4 + 2.15x = -2.15x + 8.72 + 2.15x$$
$$3.18x - 4 = 8.72$$
$$3.18x - 4 + 4 = 8.72 + 4$$
$$3.18x = 12.72$$
$$\frac{3.18x}{3.18} = \frac{12.72}{3.18}$$
$$x = 4$$

26. $7 - 3x = x - 4(2 + x)$
$$7 - 3x = x - 8 - 4x$$
$$7 - 3x = -8 - 3x$$
$$7 - 3x + 3x = -8 - 3x + 3x$$
$$7 = -8$$
Since $7 = -8$ is a false statement, this equation has no solution.

27. $6 = 3 + 5(y - 2)$
$$6 = 3 + 5y - 10$$
$$6 = -7 + 5y$$
$$6 + 7 = -7 + 5y + 7$$
$$13 = 5y$$
$$\frac{13}{5} = \frac{5y}{5}$$
$$y = 2.6 \text{ or } 2\tfrac{3}{5}$$

28. $6(y + 2) - 4 = -10$
$$6y + 12 - 4 = -10$$
$$6y + 8 = -10$$
$$6y + 8 - 8 = -10 - 8$$
$$6y = -18$$
$$\frac{6y}{6} = \frac{-18}{6}$$
$$y = -3$$

29. $5 - \frac{1}{2}(b - 6) = 4$
$$5 - \frac{1}{2}b + 3 = 4$$
$$-\frac{1}{2}b + 8 = 4$$
$$-\frac{1}{2}b + 8 - 8 = 4 - 8$$
$$-\frac{1}{2}b = -4$$
$$-2\left(-\frac{1}{2}b\right) = -2(-4)$$
$$b = 8$$

30. $-8(4 + 9x) = 7(-2 - 11x)$
$$32 - 72x = -14 - 77x$$
$$-32 - 72x - 77x = -14 - 77x + 77x$$
$$5x - 32 = -14$$
$$5x - 32 + 32 = -14 + 32$$
$$5x = 18$$
$$\frac{5x}{5} = \frac{18}{5}$$
$$x = 3.6 \text{ or } 3\tfrac{3}{5}$$

31. $2(x - 3) + 5 = 3(x - 1)$
$$2x - 6 + 5 = 3x - 3$$
$$2x - 1 = 3x - 3$$
$$2x - 1 - 2x = 3x - 3 - 2x$$
$$-1 = x - 3$$
$$-1 + 3 = x - 3 + 3$$
$$2 = x$$

32. $4(2a - 8) = \frac{1}{7}(49a + 70)$
$$8a - 32 = 7a + 10$$
$$8a - 32 - 7a = 7a + 10 - 7a$$
$$a - 32 = 10$$
$$a - 32 + 32 = 10 + 32$$
$$a = 42$$

33. $-3(2n - 5) = \frac{1}{2}(-12n + 30)$
$$-6n + 15 = -6n + 15$$
$$-6n + 15 + 6n = -6n + 15 + 6n$$
$$15 = 15$$
Since $15 = 15$ is a true statement, this equation has all numbers as a solution.

34. Let n = the least even integer.
Then $n + 2$ = the next greater even integer, and $n + 4$ = the greatest of the three even integers.
$$3(n + 4) = 2n + 38$$
$$3n + 12 = 2n + 38$$
$$3n + 12 - 2n = 2n + 38 - 2n$$
$$n + 12 = 38$$
$$n + 12 - 12 = 38 - 12$$
$$n = 26$$
$n + 2 = 26 + 2$ $n + 4 = 26 + 4$
$n + 2 = 28$ $n + 4 = 30$
The consecutive even integers are 26, 28, and 30.

35. Let n = the number.

$\frac{1}{5}n + 5n = 7n - 18$

$5\frac{1}{5}n = 7n - 18$

$5\frac{1}{5}n - 7n = 7n - 18 - 7n$

$-1\frac{4}{5}n = -18$

$-\frac{9}{5}n = -18$

$-\frac{5}{9}\left(-\frac{9}{5}n\right) = -\frac{5}{9}\left(-18\right)$

$n = 10$

The number is 10.

36. Let n = the lesser number.
Then $n + 12$ = the greater number.

$\frac{2}{5}(n + 12) = 6 + \frac{1}{3}n$

$\frac{2}{5}n + \frac{24}{5} = 6 + \frac{1}{3}n$

$\frac{2}{5}n + \frac{24}{5} - \frac{2}{5}n = 6 + \frac{1}{3}n - \frac{2}{5}n$

$\frac{24}{5} = 6 + \frac{5}{15}n - \frac{6}{15}n$

$\frac{24}{5} = 6 - \frac{1}{15}n$

$\frac{24}{5} - 6 = 6 - \frac{1}{15}n - 6$

$\frac{24}{5} - \frac{30}{5} = -\frac{1}{15}n$

$-\frac{6}{5} = -\frac{1}{15}n$

$-15\left(-\frac{6}{5}\right) = -15\left(-\frac{1}{15}n\right)$

$18 = n$

$n + 12 = 18 + 12$

$n = 30$

The numbers are 18 and 30.

37.

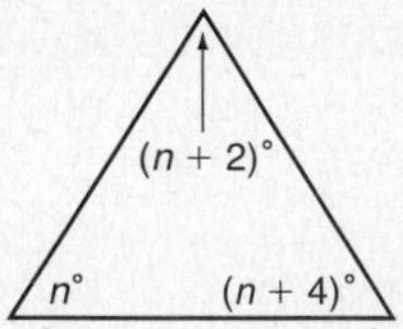

Let n = the least even integer. Then $n + 2$ = the next greater even integer, and $n + 4$ = the greatest of the three even integers.

$n + (n + 2) + (n + 4) = 180$

$3n + 6 = 180$

$3n + 6 - 6 = 180 - 6$

$3n = 174$

$\frac{3n}{3} = \frac{174}{3}$

$n = 58°$

The measures are 58°, 58 + 2 or 60°, and 58 + 4 or 62°.

38.

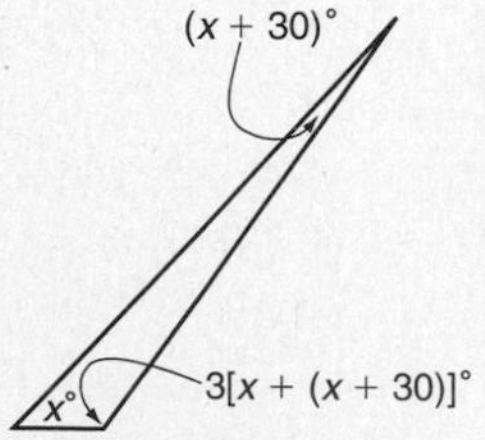

Let x = the measure of the first angle. Then $x + 30$ = the measure of the second angle, and $3[x + (x+30)]$ = the measure of the third angle.

$x + (x + 30) + 3[x + (x + 30)] = 180$

$x + x + 30 + 3[2x + 30] = 180$

$2x + 30 + 6x + 90 = 180$

$8x + 120 = 180$

$8x + 120 - 120 = 180 - 120$

$8x = 60$

$\frac{8x}{8} = \frac{60}{8}$

$x = 7.5°$

The measures are 7.5°, 7.5 + 30 or 37.5°, and 3[7.5 + (7.5 + 30)] or 135°.

39a. $4x + 6 = 4x + 6$
THIS IS AN IDENTY

39b. $5x - 7 = x + 3$; $x = 2.5$

39c. $-3x + 6 = 3x - 6$; $x = 2$

39d. $5.4x + 6.8 = 4.6x + 2.8$; $x = -5$

39e. $2x - 8 = 2x - 6$
NO SOLUTION

40. Let x = the number of years Diophantus lived.
$\frac{1}{6}x + \frac{1}{12}x + \frac{1}{7}x$ is the number of years Diophantus lived before marriage.
$5 + \left(\frac{1}{2}x + 4\right)$ is the number of years Diophantus lived after marriage.

$x = \frac{1}{6}x + \frac{1}{12}x + \frac{1}{7}x + 5 + \frac{1}{2}x + 4$

$x = \frac{14}{84}x + \frac{7}{84}x + \frac{12}{84}x + 5 + \frac{42}{84}x + 4$

$x = \frac{75}{84}x + 9$

$x - \frac{75}{84}x = 9$

$\frac{9}{84}x = 9$

$\frac{84}{9}\left(\frac{9}{84}\right)x = \frac{84}{9}(9)$

$x = 84$

So Diophantus lived 84 years.

41a. Let x = the number of years in which sales of room air conditioners and window fans are equal.

$4.6 - 0.425x = 0.975 + 0.106x$

$4.6 - 0.425x + 0.425x = 0.975 + 0.106x + 0.425x$

$4.6 = 0.975 + 0.531x$

$4.6 - 0.975 = 0.975 + 0.531x - 0.975$

$3.625 = 0.531x$

$\frac{3.625}{0.531} = \frac{0.531x}{0.531}$

$6.827 = x$

6.827 years

41b. Air conditioner sales are decreasing while fan sales are increasing.

42. Let x = the number of years in which the number of households that own dogs and cats is equal.

$34.7 - 0.025x = 27.7 + 0.375x$

$34.7 - 0.025x + 0.025x = 27.7 + 0.375x + 0.025x$

$34.7 = 27.7 + 0.4x$

$34.7 - 27.7 = 27.7 + 0.4x - 27.7$

$7 = 0.4x$

$\frac{7}{0.4} = \frac{0.4x}{0.4}$

$17.5 = x$

17.5 years

43. $180° - 32° = 148°$

44. Let n = the number.

$\frac{6(n - 35) + 87}{3} = 67$

$3\left[\frac{6(n - 35) + 87}{3}\right] = 3(67)$

$6(n - 35) + 87 = 201$

$6n - 210 + 87 = 201$

$6n - 123 = 201$

$6n - 123 + 123 = 201 + 123$

$6n = 324$

$\frac{6n}{6} = \frac{324}{6}$

$n = 54$

The number is 54.

45. $x + 4.2 = 1.5$
$x + 4.2 - 4.2 = 1.5 - 4.2$
$x = -2.7$

46. Let x = the number of years in which Karen is 0.9 times as old as Kristy.
$10 + x = 0.9(15 + x)$
$10 + x = 13.5 + 0.9x$
$10 + x - 0.9x = 13.5 + 0.9x - 0.9x$
$10 + 0.1x = 13.5$
$10 + 0.1x - 10 = 13.5 - 10$
$0.1x = 3.5$
$\frac{0.1x}{0.1} = \frac{3.5}{0.1}$
$x = 35$
35 years

47. $\frac{11}{9} \underline{?} \frac{12}{10}$
$11(10) \underline{?} 9(12)$
$110 > 108$
$\frac{11}{9} > \frac{12}{10}$

48. As students spend more time watching TV, their test scores go down.

49. $14.8 - 3.75 = t$
$11.05 = t$

3-6 Solving Equations and Formulas

Page 175 Check for Understanding

1. $3y + z = am - 4y$
$3y + 4y + z = am - 4y + 4y$
$3y + 4y + z = am$
$(3 + 4)y + z = am$
$7y + z = am$
$\frac{7y + z}{a} = \frac{am}{a}$
$\frac{7y + z}{a} = m$

2. The larger heel absorbs a greater amount of pressure.

3. See students' work.

4. $3x - 4y = 7$
$3x - 4y + 4y = 7 + 4y$
$3x = 7 + 4y$
$\frac{3x}{3} = \frac{7 + 4y}{3}$
$x = \frac{7 + 4y}{3}$

5. $3x - 4y = 7$
$3x - 4y - 3x = 7 - 3x$
$\frac{-4y}{-4} = \frac{7 - 3x}{-4}$
$y = \frac{3x - 7}{4}$

6. $a(y + 1) = b$
$ay + a = b$
$ay + a - a = b - a$
$ay = b - a$
$\frac{ay}{a} = \frac{b - a}{a}$
$y = \frac{b - a}{a}$ or $\frac{b}{a} - 1$

7. $4x + b = 2x + c$
$4x + b - b = 2x + c - b$
$4x = 2x + c - b$
$4x - 2x = 2x + c - b - 2x$
$4x - 2x = c - b$
$(4 - 2)x = c - b$
$2x = c - b$
$\frac{2x}{2} = \frac{c - b}{2}$
$x = \frac{c - b}{2}$

8. $F = G\left(\frac{Mm}{d^2}\right)$
$F(d^2) = G\left(\frac{Mm}{d^2}\right)(d^2)$
$Fd^2 = GMm$
$\frac{Fd^2}{Gm} = \frac{GMm}{Gm}$
$\frac{Fd^2}{Gm} = M$

9. $S = \frac{n}{2}(A + t)$
$2S = 2 \cdot \frac{n}{2}(A + t)$
$2S = n(A + t)$
$2S = nA + nt$
$2S - nt = nA + nt - nt$
$2S - nt = nA$
$\frac{2S - nt}{n} = A$

10. $2x + 12 = 3y - 31$
$2x + 12 + 31 = 3y - 31 + 31$
$2x + 43 = 3y$
$\frac{2x + 43}{3} = \frac{3y}{3}$
$\frac{2x + 43}{3} = y$

Pages 175–177 Exercises

11. $-3x + b = 6x$
$-3x + 3x + b = 6x + 3x$
$b = 9x$
$\frac{b}{9} = \frac{9x}{9}$
$\frac{b}{9} = x$

12. $ex - 2y = 3z$
$ex - 2y + 2y = 3z + 2y$
$ex = 3z + 2y$
$\frac{ex}{e} = \frac{3z + 2y}{e}$
$x = \frac{3z + 2y}{e}$

13. $\frac{y + a}{3} = c$
$3\left(\frac{y + a}{3}\right) = 3(c)$
$y + a = 3c$
$y + a - a = 3c - a$
$y = 3c - a$

14. $\frac{3}{5}y + a = b$
$\frac{3}{5}y + a - a = b - a$
$\frac{3}{5}y = b - a$
$\frac{5}{3}\left(\frac{3}{5}\right)y = \frac{5}{3}(b - a)$
$y = \frac{5(b - a)}{3}$

15. $v = r + at$
$v - r = r + at - r$
$v - r = at$
$\frac{v - r}{t} = \frac{at}{t}$
$\frac{v - r}{t} = a$

16. $y = mx + b$
$y - b = mx + b - b$
$y - b = mx$
$\frac{y - b}{x} = \frac{mx}{x}$
$\frac{y - b}{x} = m$

17. $I = prt$
$\frac{I}{pt} = \frac{prt}{pt}$
$\frac{I}{pt} = r$

18. $\frac{by + 2}{3} = c$
$3\left(\frac{by + 2}{3}\right) = 3 \cdot c$
$by + 2 = 3c$
$by + 2 - 2 = 3c - 2$
$\frac{by}{b} = \frac{3c - 2}{b}$
$y = \frac{3c - 2}{b}$

19. $H = (0.24)\, I^2Rt$

$\frac{H}{0.24I^2t} = \frac{0.24I^2Rt}{0.24I^2t}$

$\frac{H}{0.24I^2t} = R$

20. $P = \frac{E^2}{R}$

$R(P) = \left(\frac{E^2}{R}\right)(R)$

$RP = E^2$

$\frac{RP}{P} = \frac{E^2}{P}$

$R = \frac{E^2}{P}$

21. $4b - 5 = -t$

$4b - 5 + 5 = -t + 5$

$4b = -t + 5$

$\frac{4b}{4} = \frac{-t + 5}{4}$

$b = \frac{-t + 5}{4}$

22. $km + 5x = 6y$

$km + 5x - 5x = 6y - 5x$

$km = 6y - 5x$

$\frac{km}{k} = \frac{6y - 5x}{k}$

$m = \frac{6y - 5x}{k}$

23. $c = \frac{3}{4}y + b$

$c - b = \frac{3}{4}y + b - b$

$c - b = \frac{3}{4}y$

$\frac{4}{3}(c - b) = \frac{4}{3} \cdot \frac{3}{4}y$

$\frac{4}{3}(c - b) = y$

24. $p(t + 1) = -2$

$pt + p = -2$

$pt + p - p = -2 - p$

$pt = -2 - p$

$\frac{pt}{p} = \frac{-2 - p}{p}$

$t = \frac{-2 - p}{p}$ or $-\frac{2}{p} - 1$

25. $\frac{5x + y}{a} = 2$

$\left(\frac{5x + y}{a}\right)a = 2a$

$5x + y = 2a$

$\frac{5x + y}{2} = \frac{2a}{2}$

$\frac{5x + y}{2} = a$

26. $\frac{3ax - n}{5} = -4$

$5\left(\frac{3ax - n}{5}\right) = 5(-4)$

$3ax - n = -20$

$3ax - n + n = -20 + n$

$3ax = -20 + n$

$\frac{3ax}{3a} = \frac{-20 + n}{3a}$

$x = \frac{-20 + n}{3a}$

27. $2x + 12 = 3y - 31$

$2x + 12 - 12 = 3y - 31 - 12$

$2x = 3y - 43$

$\frac{2x}{2} = \frac{3y - 43}{2}$

$x = \frac{3y - 43}{2}$

28. $\frac{5}{8}x = \frac{1}{2}y + 3$

$\frac{5}{8}x - 3 = \frac{1}{2}y + 3 - 3$

$\frac{5}{8}x - 3 = \frac{1}{2}y$

$2\left(\frac{5}{8}x - 3\right) = 2\left(\frac{1}{2}y\right)$

$\frac{5}{4}x - 6 = y$

29. $\frac{2}{3}x + 5 = \frac{1}{2}y - 3$

$\frac{2}{3}x + 5 - 5 = \frac{1}{2}y - 3 - 5$

$\frac{2}{3}x = \frac{1}{2}y - 8$

$\frac{3}{2}\left(\frac{2}{3}\right)x = \frac{3}{2}\left(\frac{1}{2}y - 8\right)$

$x = \frac{3}{4}y - 12$

30. Mercuria's formula = Mrs. Weatherby's approximation.

$\frac{9}{5}C + 32 = 2C + 30$

$\frac{9}{5}C + 32 - \frac{9}{5}C = 2C + 30 - \frac{9}{5}C$

$32 = \frac{10}{5}C - \frac{9}{5}C + 30$

$32 = \frac{1}{5}C + 30$

$32 - 30 = \frac{1}{5}C + 30 - 30$

$2 = \frac{1}{5}C$

$(5)2 = \left(\frac{1}{5}C\right)(5)$

$10° = C$

$F = \frac{9}{5}C + 32$

$F = \frac{9}{5}(10) + 32$

$F = 18 + 32$

$F = 50°$

10°C or 50°F

31. $I = prt$

$= 5000(0.06)(3)$

$= \$900$

32. $d = vt + \frac{1}{2}at^2$

$= 4.5(12) + \frac{1}{2}(0.4)(12)^2$

$= 4.5(12) + \frac{1}{2}(0.4)(144)$

$= 54 + 28.8$

$= 82.8$ meters

33a. $s = \frac{w - 10e}{m}$
$= \frac{420 - 10(6)}{10}$
$= \frac{420 - 60}{10}$
$= \frac{360}{10}$
= 36 words per minute

33b. Clarence, with 74 words per minute

34.
$$\begin{aligned} 2(x-2) &= 3x - (4x-5) \\ 2x - 4 &= 3x - 4x + 5 \\ 2x - 4 &= -x + 5 \\ 2x - 4 + x &= -x + 5 + x \\ 3x - 4 &= 5 \\ 3x - 4 + 4 &= 5 + 4 \\ 3x &= 9 \\ x &= 3 \end{aligned}$$

35. $90° - 85° = 5°$

36. 30 + 50 + 10 + 10 + 15 + 60 = 175 min = 2 h 55 min
9:30 A.M. − (2 h 55 min) = 6:35 A.M.

37. $x \neq 2$

38.

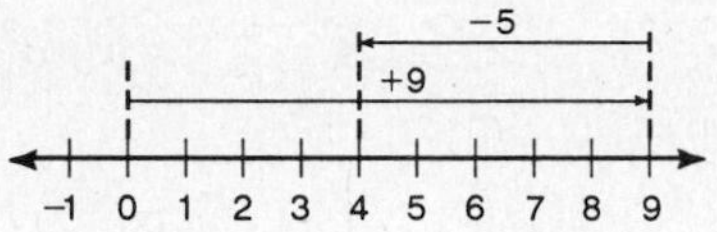

$9 + (-5) = 4$

39.

Replace x with:	$x - 3 > \frac{x+1}{2}$	True or False?
4	$4 - 3 \overset{?}{>} \frac{4+1}{2} \rightarrow 1 \not> \frac{5}{2}$	false
5	$5 + 3 \overset{?}{>} \frac{5+1}{2} \rightarrow 2 \not> 3$	false
6	$6 - 3 \overset{?}{>} \frac{6+1}{2} \rightarrow 3 \not> \frac{7}{2}$	false
7	$7 - 3 \overset{?}{>} \frac{7+1}{2} \rightarrow 4 \not> 4$	false
8	$8 - 3 \overset{?}{>} \frac{8+1}{2} \rightarrow 5 > \frac{9}{2}$	true

Therefore, the solution set for $x - 3 > \frac{x+1}{2}$ is {8}.

40. See students' work.

3-7 Integration: Statistics Measures of Central Tendency

Page 181 Check for Understanding

1. The mean is affected by extreme values, where median is not. Mode is affected by the amount of repetition of values.
2. The mean, since it finds the average amount of the contributions. The mean is affected by extreme values.
3. Count the total number of x's. To find the mean, multiply the number by the number of x's in that column. Then divide by the total number of x's (4.8). To find the median, divide the total number of x's by 2 ($13 \div 2$ or ≈ 7) and count from left to right. The seventh x represents the median (4). The mode is the number with the greatest number of x's in its column (2).
4. Mode; since the data are nonnumeric, the mean and median would have no meaning in this context.
5. See students' work.
6. middle **7.** median **8.** mean **9.** mode

10. mean: $\frac{4 + 6 + 12 + 5 + 8}{5} = \frac{35}{5} = 7$
median: 4, 5, (6), 8, 12 => 6 since it is the middle value
mode: There is no mode since each of the data occur once.

11. mean: $\frac{8 + 8 + 8 + 8 + 9}{5} = \frac{41}{5} = 8.2$
median: 8, 8, (8), 8, 9, => 8 since it is the middle value
mode: 8 since it occurs most often

12. mean:
$\frac{73 + 75 + 82 + 82 + 84 + 90 + 94 + 97 + 99 + 105 + 108 + 114 + 116}{13}$
$= \frac{1219}{13} \approx 93.77$
median: 73, 75, 82, 82, 84, 90, (94), 97, 99, 105, 108, 114, 116 => 94 since it is the middle value
mode: 82 since it occurs most often

13. sample answer: 20, 20, 30, 50, 90, 90

14. sample answer: 65, 65, 70, 70, 73, 77

15a. mean: $\frac{6 + 5 + 4 + 3 + 3 + 3 + 3}{7} = \frac{27}{7} \approx 3.857$
median: 3, 3, 3, (3), 4, 5, 6 => 3 since it is the middle value
mode: 3 since it occurs most often

15b. mean; The mean is affected by extreme values.

Pages 182–183 Exercises

16. mean: $\frac{2 + 4 + 7 + 9 + 12 + 15}{6} = \frac{49}{6} = 8\frac{1}{6}$
median: 2, 4, (7, 9), 12, 15 => $\frac{7+9}{2} = 8$ since it is the average of the two middle values
mode: There is no mode since each of the data occur once.

17. mean: $\frac{300 + 34 + 40 + 50 + 60}{5} = \frac{484}{5} = 96.8$
median: 34, 40, (50), 60, 300 => 50 since it is the middle value
mode: There is no mode since each of the data occur once.

18. mean: $\frac{23 + 23 + 23 + 12 + 12 + 12}{6} = \frac{105}{6} = 17.5$
median: 12, 12, (12, 23), 23, 23 => $\frac{12 + 23}{2} = 17.5$ since it is the average of the two middle values
mode: 12 and 23 since they each occur three times

19. mean: $\dfrac{10+3+17+1+8+6+12+15}{8} = \dfrac{72}{8} = 9$

median: 1, 3, 6, (8, 10,) 12, 15, 17 => $\dfrac{8+10}{2} = 9$ since it is the average of the two middle values

mode: There is no mode since each of the data occur once.

20. mean: $\dfrac{7+19+9+4+7+2}{6} = \dfrac{48}{6} = 8$

median: 2, 4, (7, 7,) 9, 19 => 7 since the two middle values are the same

mode: 7 since it occurs most often

21. mean: $\dfrac{2.1+7.4+13.9+1.6+5.21+3.901}{6} = \dfrac{34.11}{6}$

≈ 5.69

median: 1.6, 2.1, (3.901, 5.21,) 7.4, 13.9 => $\dfrac{3.901+5.21}{2} = 4.56$ since it is the average of the two middle values

mode: There is no mode since each of the data occur once.

22. mean: $\dfrac{\text{sum of 16 values}}{16} = \dfrac{1205}{16} \approx 75.3$

median: 53, 56, 58, 65, 68, 70, 73, (77, 77,) 79, 81, 84, 88, 88, 89, 99 => 77 since the two middle values are the same

mode: 77 and 88 since they both occur twice and all other data occur only once

23. mean: $\dfrac{\text{sum of 18 values}}{18} = \dfrac{3833}{18} \approx 212.94$

median: 218 since the two middle values are the same

mode: 219 since it occurs three times and all other data occur less than three times

24a. Sample answer: 6, 6, 6, 6, 6, 6, 6, 6, 6, 0

24b. Sample answer: 5, 5, 5, 5, 5, 5, 5, 5, 5, 25

24c. not possible

24d. No, because it is always in the middle of the set of data.

25. Let y = largest number.
Let x = average of other numbers.

$\dfrac{9x}{9} = 4$

$x = 4$

$\dfrac{9x+y}{10} = 5$

$10\left(\dfrac{9x+y}{10}\right) = 10(5)$

$9x + y = 50$

$9(4) + y = 50$

$36 + y = 50$

$36 + y - 36 = 50 - 36$

$y = 14$

The number 14 was eliminated.

26a. $\dfrac{(2n+1)+(2n+3)+(2n+5)}{3} = \dfrac{6n+9}{3}$ or $2n+3$

26b. $2n+1$, ($2n+3$,) $2n+5$ => $2n+3$ since it is the middle value

27a. mean

27b. Yes, because the article indicates that the median value is in the middle of the data set.

27c. No, he should have used the term *mean* since the mean can be affected by extremely high values, causing the majority to be below the mean value.

28a. mean: $\dfrac{32+7+150+13+33+10+5+22+3+19}{10} =$

$\dfrac{294}{10} = 29.4$

median: 3, 5, 7, 10, (13, 19,) 22, 32, 33, 150 => $\dfrac{13+19}{2} = \dfrac{32}{2} = 16$ since it is the average of the two middle values

mode: There is no mode since each of the data occur once.

28b. The mean is most representative.

29. mean: $\dfrac{\text{sum of 10 values}}{10} = \dfrac{16{,}606}{10}$ or $1660\frac{3}{5}$

median: 139, 154, 177, 670, (1068, 1085,) 1135, 1234, 3166, 7778 => $\dfrac{1068+1085}{2} = 1076.5$ since it is the average of the two middle values

mode: There is no mode since each of the data occur only once.

30. mean: $\dfrac{\text{sum of heights of 10 buildings}}{10} \approx \dfrac{7980}{10} = 798$

median: $\approx \dfrac{600+650}{2} = 625$ since it is the average of the two middle values

31.

$d = rt$	$d = rt$	$d = rt$
$10 = 30t$	$10 = 50t$	$\dfrac{d}{t} = \dfrac{rt}{t}$
$\dfrac{10}{30} = \dfrac{30t}{30}$	$\dfrac{10}{50} = \dfrac{50t}{50}$	$\dfrac{d}{t} = r$
$\dfrac{1}{3} = t$	$\dfrac{1}{5} = t$	

$r = \dfrac{10+10}{\frac{1}{3}+\frac{1}{5}} = \dfrac{20}{\frac{5}{15}+\frac{3}{15}} = \dfrac{20}{\frac{8}{15}} = 20\left(\dfrac{15}{8}\right) = 37.5$ mph

32. $\dfrac{a+5}{3} = 7x$

$\dfrac{1}{7}\left(\dfrac{a+5}{3}\right) = \dfrac{1}{7}(7x)$

$\dfrac{a+5}{21} = x$

33. $\dfrac{3}{4}n - 3 = 9$

$\dfrac{3}{4}n - 3 + 3 = 9 + 3$

$\dfrac{3}{4}n = 12$

$\dfrac{4}{3}\left(\dfrac{3}{4}\right)n = \dfrac{4}{3}(12)$

$n = 16$

34. $|k| + |m| = |3| + |-6|$
$= 3 + 6$
$= 9$

35.

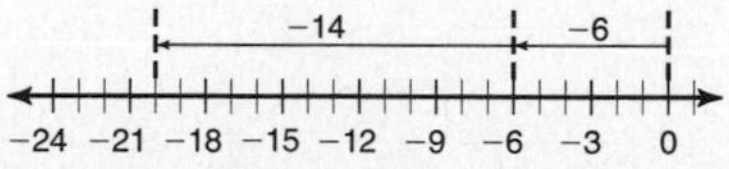

$-6 + (-14) = -20$

36. $(13 + \frac{2}{5} \cdot 5)(3^2 - 2^3)$

$= (13 + 2)(9 - 8)$	substitution (=)
$= (15)(1)$	substitution (=)
$= 15$	identity (×)

37. $5 + 7(ac + 2b) + 2ac = 5 + 7ac + 14b + 2ac$
$= 5 + 7ac + 2ac + 14b$
$= 5 + 9ac + 14b$

Page 183 Mathematics and Society

1. See students' work. **2.** See students' work.

3. See students' work.

Chapter 3 Highlights

Page 185 Understanding and Using the Vocabulary

1. b addition property of equality
2. l subtraction property of equatlity
3. i multiplication property of equality
4. c division property of equality
5. d equilateral triangle **6.** e isosceles triangle
7. k right triangle **8.** j obtuse triangle
9. a acute triangle **10.** f mean
11. g median **12.** h mode

Chapter 3 Study Guide and Assessment

Pages 186–188 Skills and Concepts

13. $r - 21 = -37$
$r - 21 + 21 = -37 + 21$
$r = -16$

14. $14 + c = -5$
$14 + c - 14 = -5 - 14$
$c = -19$

15. $-27 = -6 - p$
$-27 + 6 = -6 - p + 6$
$-21 = -p$
$21 = p$

16. $b + (-14) = 6$
$b - 14 = 6$
$b - 14 + 14 = 6 + 14$
$b = 20$

17. $r + (-11) = -21$
$r - 11 = -21$
$r - 11 + 11 = -21 + 11$
$r = -10$

18. $d - (-1.2) = -7.3$
$d + 1.2 = -7.3$
$d + 1.2 - 1.2 = 7.3 - 1.2$
$d = -8.5$

19. Let n = the number.
$n - 14 = -46$
$n - 14 + 14 = -46 + 14$
$n = -32$
The number is -32.

20. Let n = the other number.
$9 + n = -23$
$9 + n - 9 = -23 - 9$
$n = -32$
The other number is -32.

21. Let n = the number.
$82 + n = -34$
$82 + n - 82 = -34 - 82$
$n = -116$
The number is -116.

22. $6x = -42$
$\frac{6x}{6} = \frac{-42}{6}$
$x = -7$

23. $-7w = -49$
$\frac{-7w}{-7} = \frac{-49}{-7}$
$w = 7$

24. $\frac{3}{4}n = 30$
$\frac{4}{3}\left(\frac{3}{4}n\right) = \frac{4}{3}(30)$
$n = \frac{120}{3}$ or 40

25. $-\frac{3}{5}y = -50$
$-\frac{5}{3}\left(-\frac{3}{5}y\right) = -\frac{5}{3}(50)$
$y = \frac{250}{3}$ or $83\frac{1}{3}$

26. $\frac{5}{2}x = -25$
$\frac{2}{5}\left(\frac{5}{2}\right)x = \frac{2}{5}(-25)$
$x = -10$

27. $\frac{5}{12} = \frac{r}{24}$
$24\left(\frac{5}{12}\right) = 24\left(\frac{r}{24}\right)$
$10 = r$

28. Let n = the number.
$-7n = -56$
$\frac{-7n}{-7} = \frac{-56}{-7}$
$n = 8$
The number is 8.

29. Let n = the number.
$\frac{3}{4}n = -12$
$\frac{4}{3}\left(\frac{3}{4}n\right) = \frac{4}{3}(-12)$
$n = -16$
The number is -16.

30. Let n = the number.
$1\frac{2}{3}n = 1\frac{1}{2}$
$\frac{5}{3}n = \frac{3}{2}$
$\frac{3}{5}\left(\frac{5}{3}n\right) = \frac{3}{5}\left(\frac{3}{2}\right)$
$n = \frac{9}{10}$
The number is $\frac{9}{10}$

31. $4t - 7 = 5$
$4t - 7 + 7 = 5 + 7$
$4t = 12$
$\frac{4t}{4} = \frac{12}{4}$
$t = 3$

32. $6 = 4n + 2$
$6 - 2 = 4n + 2 - 2$
$4 = 4n$
$\frac{4}{4} = \frac{4n}{4}$
$1 = n$

33. $\frac{y}{3} + 6 = -45$
$\frac{y}{3} + 6 - 6 = -45 - 6$
$\frac{y}{3} = -51$
$3\left(\frac{y}{3}\right) = 3(-51)$
$y = -153$

34. $\frac{c}{-4} - 8 = -42$
$\frac{c}{-4} - 8 + 8 = -42 + 8$
$\frac{c}{-4} = -34$
$-4\left(\frac{c}{-4}\right) = -4(-34)$
$c = 136$

35. $\frac{4d + 5}{7} = 7$
$7\left(\frac{4d + 5}{7}\right) = 7(7)$
$4d + 5 = 49$
$4d + 5 - 5 = 49 - 5$
$4d = 44$
$\frac{4d}{4} = \frac{44}{4}$
$d = 11$

36. $\frac{7n + (-1)}{8} = 8$
$8\left(\frac{7n + (-1)}{8}\right) = 8(8)$
$7n + (-1) = 64$
$7n - 1 = 64$
$7n - 1 + 1 = 64 + 1$
$7n = 65$
$\frac{7n}{7} = \frac{65}{7}$
$n = 9\frac{2}{7}$

37. Let n = the number.
$4n - 2n = 100$
$2n = 100$
$\frac{2n}{2} = \frac{100}{2}$
$n = 50$
The number is 50.

38. Let n = the least integer.
Then $n + 1$ = the next greater integer,
and $n + 2$ = the next greater integer,
and $n + 3$ = the greatest of the four integers.

$$\begin{aligned} n + (n + 1) + (n + 2) + (n + 3) &= 130 \\ 4n + 6 &= 130 \\ 4n + 6 - 6 &= 130 - 6 \\ 4n &= 124 \\ \frac{4n}{4} &= \frac{124}{4} \\ n &= 31 \end{aligned}$$

$n + 1 = 31 + 1$ $n + 2 = 31 + 2$ $n + 3 = 31 + 3$
$n + 1 = 32$ $n + 2 = 33$ $n + 3 = 34$

The integers are 31, 32, 33, and 34.

39. Let n = the lesser integer.
Then $n + 1$ = the greater integer.

$$\begin{aligned} 2n + (n + 1) &= 49 \\ 3n + 1 &= 49 \\ 3n + 1 - 1 &= 49 - 1 \\ 3n &= 48 \\ \frac{3n}{3} &= \frac{48}{3} \\ n &= 16 \end{aligned}$$

$$\begin{aligned} n + 1 &= 16 + 1 \\ n + 1 &= 17 \end{aligned}$$

The integers are 16 and 17.

40. $90° - 28° = 62°$
$180° - 28° = 152°$

41. $90° - 69° = 21°$
$180° - 69° = 111°$

42. $(90 - 5x)°$
$(180 - 5x)°$

43. $90° - (y + 20)° = 90° - y - 20° = (70 - y)°$
$180° - (y + 20)° = 180° - y - 20° = (160 - y)°$

44. Let n = the lesser angle.
Then $n + 10$ = the greater angle.

$$\begin{aligned} n + (n + 10) &= 180 \\ 2n + 10 &= 180 \\ 2n + 10 - 10 &= 180 - 10 \\ 2n &= 170 \\ \frac{2n}{2} &= \frac{170}{2} \\ n &= 85° \end{aligned}$$

The angle measures 85 + 10 or 95°.

45. Let n = the greater angle.
Then $\frac{1}{2}n$ = the lesser angle.

$$\begin{aligned} n + \frac{1}{2}n &= 90 \\ 1\frac{1}{2}n &= 90 \\ \frac{3}{2}n &= 90 \\ \frac{2}{3}\left(\frac{3}{2}n\right) &= \frac{2}{3}(90) \\ n &= 60 \end{aligned}$$

The angle measures $\frac{1}{2}(60)$ or 30°.

46.
$$\begin{aligned} x + 16 + 47 &= 180 \\ x + 63 &= 180 \\ x + 63 - 63 &= 180 - 63 \\ x &= 117° \end{aligned}$$

47.
$$\begin{aligned} x + 45 + 120 &= 180 \\ x + 165 &= 180 \\ x + 165 - 165 &= 180 - 165 \\ x &= 15° \end{aligned}$$

48. Let z = the third angle.

$$\begin{aligned} x + y + z &= 180 \\ x + y + z - x - y &= 180 - x - y \\ z &= 180° - x° - y° \text{ or } 180° - (x + y)° \end{aligned}$$

49. Let y = the third angle.

$$\begin{aligned} y + z + (z - 30) &= 180 \\ y &= 180 - (z + z - 30°) \text{ or } (210 - 2z)° \end{aligned}$$

50.
$$\begin{aligned} 4(3 + 5w) &= -11 \\ 12 + 20w &= -11 \\ 12 + 20w - 12 &= -11 - 12 \\ 20w &= -23 \\ \frac{20w}{20} &= \frac{-23}{20} \\ 2 &= -1\frac{3}{20} \end{aligned}$$

51.
$$\begin{aligned} \frac{2}{3}n + 8 &= \frac{1}{3}n - 2 \\ \frac{2}{3}n + 8 - \frac{1}{3}n &= \frac{1}{3}n - 2 - \frac{1}{3}n \\ \frac{1}{3}n + 8 &= -2 \\ \frac{1}{3}n + 8 - 8 &= -2 - 8 \\ \frac{1}{3}n &= -10 \\ 3\left(\frac{1}{3}n\right) &= 3(-10) \\ n &= -30 \end{aligned}$$

52.
$$\begin{aligned} 3x - 2(x + 3) &= x \\ 3x - 2x - 6 &= x \\ x - 6 &= x \\ x - 6 - x &= x - x \\ -6 &= 0 \end{aligned}$$

Since $-6 = 0$ is a false statement, this equation has no solution.

53.
$$\begin{aligned} \frac{4 - x}{5} &= \frac{1}{5}x \\ 5\left(\frac{4 - x}{5}\right) &= 5\left(\frac{1}{5}x\right) \\ 4 - x &= x \\ 4 - x + x &= x + x \\ 4 &= 2x \\ \frac{4}{2} &= \frac{2x}{2} \\ 2 &= x \end{aligned}$$

54. Let n = one number.
Then $25 - n$ = the other number.

$$\begin{aligned} 4n - 12 &= 16 + 2(25 - n) \\ 4n - 12 &= 16 + 50 - 2n \\ 4n - 12 &= 66 - 2n \\ 4n - 12 + 2n &= 66 - 2n + 2n \\ 6n - 12 &= 66 \\ 6n - 12 + 12 &= 66 + 12 \\ 6n &= 78 \\ \frac{6n}{6} &= \frac{78}{6} \\ n &= 13 \end{aligned}$$

The two numbers are 25 − 13 or 12 and 13.

55.
$$\begin{aligned} 5x &= y \\ \frac{5x}{5} &= \frac{y}{5} \\ x &= \frac{y}{5} \end{aligned}$$

56.
$$\begin{aligned} ay - b &= c \\ ay - b + b &= c + b \\ ay &= c + b \\ \frac{ay}{a} &= \frac{c + b}{a} \\ y &= \frac{c + b}{a} \end{aligned}$$

57.
$$\begin{aligned} yx - a &= cx \\ yx - a + a &= cx + a \\ yx &= cx + a \\ yx - cx &= cx + a - cx \\ yx - cx &= a \\ x(y - c) &= a \\ \frac{x(y - c)}{(y - c)} &= \frac{a}{(y - c)} \\ x &= \frac{a}{y - c} \end{aligned}$$

58. $\frac{2y - a}{3} = \frac{a + 3b}{4}$

$12\left(\frac{2y - a}{3}\right) = 12\left(\frac{a + 3b}{4}\right)$

$4(2y - a) = 3(a + 3b)$

$8y - 4a = 3a + 9b$

$8y - 4a + 4a = 3a + 9b + 4a$

$8y = 7a + 9b$

$\frac{8y}{8} = \frac{7a + 9b}{8}$

$y = \frac{7a + 9b}{8}$

59. mean: $\frac{20 + 21 + 18 + 21 + 22 + 22 + 24 + 21 + 20 + 19 + 23}{10}$

$= \frac{210}{10} = 21$

median: 18, 19, 20, 20, 21, 21, 21, 22, 22, 24 => 21 since the two middle values are the same

mode: 21 since it occurs three times and all other data occur less than three times

60. mean: $\frac{16(4.75) + 4(5.50) + 3(6.85) + 6(4.85) + 13(5.25)}{42}$

$= \frac{215.9}{42} \approx \$5.14$

median: The middle value occurs as the average of the 21st and 22nd values when all 42 wages are listed from smallest to largest. There are sixteen workers who earn \$4.75 and six workers who earn \$4.85 for a total of twenty-two workers. Therefore, the median is \$4.85 since it occurs in the middle.

mode: \$4.75 since most workers make that much money per hour

Page 188 Applications and Problem Solving

61a. Let x = the number of years in which people eat the same number of meals in restaurants they order to go.

$71 - 0.7x = 20 + 1.3x$

$71 - 0.7x + 0.7x = 20 + 1.3x + 0.7x$

$71 = 20 + 2x$

$71 - 20 = 20 + 2x - 20$

$51 = 2x$

$\frac{51}{2} = \frac{2x}{2}$

$25.5 = x$

25.5 years

61b. Answers will vary. **62a.** See students' work.

62b. $w = 100 + 6(h - 60)$

$w = 100 + 6h - 360$

$w = 6h - 260$

$w + 260 = 6h - 260 + 260$

$w + 260 = 6h$

$\frac{w + 260}{6} = \frac{6h}{h}$

$\frac{w + 260}{6} = h$

$w = 100 + 5(h - 60)$

$w = 100 + 5h - 300$

$w = 5h - 200$

$w + 200 = 5h - 200 + 200$

$w + 200 = 5h$

$\frac{w + 200}{5} = \frac{5h}{5}$

$\frac{w}{5} + 40 = h$

62c. $h = \frac{w + 260}{6}$

$h = \frac{170 + 260}{6}$

$h = \frac{430}{6}$

$h = 71\frac{2}{3}$ in.

63. Let x = the number of years the average refrigerator lasts.

$x = 2(8) - 2\frac{1}{4}$

$x = 16 - 2\frac{1}{4}$

$x = 13\frac{3}{4}$ years

64a. mean: $\frac{12.5 + 32 + 32 + 32.2 + 43.7 + 56.8 + 73.6}{7}$

$= \frac{282.8}{7} = 40.4$

median: 12.5, 32, 32, 32.2, 43.7, 56.8, 73.6 => 32.2¢ since it is the middle value

mode: 32¢ since it occurs most often

64b. mean: $\frac{13 + 32 + 32 + 32 + 44 + 57 + 74}{7} = \frac{284}{7} = 40.6$¢

median: 13, 32, 32, 32, 44, 57, 74 => 32¢ since it is the middle value

mode: 32¢ since it occurs most often

Page 189 Alternative Assessment: Thinking Critically

- Sample answer: $3x + 2 = 6(x - 4) - 3x$ has no solution since there is no value of the variable that will result in a true equation; when solving the equation, the statement $2 = -4$ results, which is false.
- Sample answer: $7 + 5(x - 1) = 5x + 2$ has an infinite number of solutions since it is true for all values of x; when solving the equation, the expressions on each side are the same: $5x + 2 = 5x + 2$.

Chapter 4 Using Proportional Reasoning

4-1A Modeling Mathematics: Ratios

Page 194

1. See students' work.
2. See students' work.

4-1 Ratios and Proportions

Page 198 Check for Understanding

1. If the cross products of two ratios in a proportion are equal, then the two ratios are equivalent.
2. Sample answer: In the proportion $\frac{x}{2.5} = \frac{3}{4}$, multiply 2.5 and 3, then divide by 4.
3. See students' work.
4. See students' work.
5. $3 \cdot 14 \stackrel{?}{=} 2 \cdot 21$
   $42 = 42$
   So, $\frac{3}{2} = \frac{21}{14}$.
   This is a proportion.
6. $2.3 \cdot 3.6 \stackrel{?}{=} 3.4 \cdot 0.3$
   $8.28 \neq 1.02$
   Since $8.28 \neq 1.02$, $\frac{2.3}{3.4} \neq \frac{2.3}{3.6}$.
   This is not a proportion.
7. $\frac{2}{3} = \frac{8}{x}$
   $2x = 3(8)$
   $2x = 24$
   $x = 12$
8. $\frac{4}{w} = \frac{2}{10}$
   $4(10) = 2w$
   $40 = 2w$
   $20 = w$
9. $\frac{3}{15} = \frac{1}{y}$
   $3y = 15(1)$
   $3y = 15$
   $y = 5$
10. $\frac{5.22}{13.92} = \frac{b}{48}$
   $5.22(48) = 13.92b$
   $250.56 = 13.92b$
   $18 = b$
11. $\frac{1.1}{0.6} = \frac{8.47}{n}$
   $1.1n = 0.6(8.47)$
   $1.1n = 5.082$
   $n = 4.62$
12. $\frac{x}{1.5} = \frac{2.4}{1.6}$
   $1.6x = 1.5(2.4)$
   $1.6x = 3.6$
   $x = 2.25$
13. $\frac{96 \text{ miles}}{6 \text{ gallons}} = \frac{152 \text{ miles}}{x \text{ gallons}}$
   $96x = 912$
   $x = 9.5$
   A 152-mile trip could require 9.5 gallons of gasoline.

Pages 199–200 Exercises

14. $6 \cdot 28 \stackrel{?}{=} 8 \cdot 22$
   $168 \neq 176$
   Since $168 \neq 176$, $\frac{6}{8} \neq \frac{22}{28}$.
   This is not a proportion.
15. $4 \cdot 20 \stackrel{?}{=} 5 \cdot 6$
   $80 = 80$
   So, $\frac{4}{5} = \frac{16}{20}$.
   This is a proportion.
16. $4 \cdot 33 \stackrel{?}{=} 11 \cdot 12$
   $132 = 132$
   So, $\frac{4}{11} = \frac{12}{33}$.
   This is a proportion.
17. $8 \cdot 17 \stackrel{?}{=} 9 \cdot 16$
   $136 \neq 144$
   Since $136 \neq 144$, $\frac{8}{9} \neq \frac{16}{17}$.
   This is not a proportion.
18. $2.1 \cdot 7 \stackrel{?}{=} 3.6 \cdot 5$
   $14.7 \neq 18$
   Since $14.7 \neq 18$, $\frac{2.1}{3.6} \neq \frac{5}{7}$.
   This is not a proportion.
19. $0.4 \cdot 1.4 \stackrel{?}{=} 0.8 \cdot 0.7$
   $0.56 = 0.56$
   So, $\frac{0.4}{0.8} = \frac{0.7}{1.4}$.
   This is a proportion.
20. $\frac{3}{4} = \frac{x}{8}$
   $3 \cdot 8 = 4x$
   $24 = 4x$
   $6 = x$
21. $\frac{a}{45} = \frac{3}{15}$
   $15a = 45 \cdot 3$
   $15a = 135$
   $a = 9$
22. $\frac{x}{9} = \frac{-7}{16}$
   $16y = 9(-7)$
   $16y = -63$
   $y = -\frac{63}{16}$ or -3.938
23. $\frac{3}{5} = \frac{x+2}{6}$
   $3 \cdot 6 = 5(x + 2)$
   $18 = 5x + 10$
   $8 = 5x$
   $x = \frac{8}{5}$ or 1.6
24. $\frac{w+2}{5} = \frac{7}{5}$
   $5(w + 2) = 5 \cdot 7$
   $5w + 10 = 35$
   $5w = 25$
   $w = 5$
25. $\frac{x}{8} = \frac{0.21}{2}$
   $2x = 8 \cdot 0.21$
   $2x = 1.68$
   $x = 0.84$
26. $\frac{5+y}{y-3} = \frac{14}{10}$
   $10(5 + y) = 14(y - 3)$
   $50 + 10y = 14y - 42$
   $50 = 4y - 42$
   $92 = 4y$
   $23 = y$
27. $\frac{m+9}{5} = \frac{m-10}{11}$
   $11(m + 9) = 5(m - 10)$
   $11m + 99 = 5m - 50$
   $6m + 99 = -50$
   $6m = -149$
   $m = -\frac{149}{6}$ or -24.8
28. $\frac{r+7}{-4} = \frac{r-12}{6}$
   $6(r + 7) = -4(r - 12)$
   $6r + 42 = -4r + 48$
   $10r + 42 = 48$
   $10r = 6$
   $r = \frac{6}{10} = \frac{3}{5}$ or 0.6

29. $\frac{85.8}{t} = \frac{70.2}{9}$

$9(85.8) = 70.2t$

$772.2 = 70.2t$

$11 = t$

30. $\frac{z}{33} = \frac{11.75}{35.25}$

$35.25z = 33(11.75)$

$35.25z = 387.75$

$z = 11$

31. $\frac{0.19}{2} = \frac{0.5x}{12}$

$0.19(12) = 2(0.5x)$

$2.28 = x$

32. $\frac{2.405}{3.67} = \frac{g}{1.88}$

$2.405(1.88) = 3.67g$

$4.5214 = 3.67g$

$1.232 = g$

33. $\frac{x}{4.085} = \frac{5}{16.33}$

$16.33x = 5(4.085)$

$16.33x = 20.425$

$x = 1.251$

34. $\frac{3t}{9.65} = \frac{21}{1.066}$

$3t(1.066) = 21(9.65)$

$3.198t = 202.65$

$t = 63.368$

35a.

Louis' age	1	2	3	6	10	20	30
Mariah's age	9	10	11	14	18	28	38

35b. $\frac{9}{1} = 9$, $\frac{10}{2} = 5$, $\frac{11}{3} = 3.\overline{6}$, $\frac{14}{6} = 2.\overline{3}$, $\frac{18}{10} = 1.8$, $\frac{28}{20} = 1.4$, $\frac{38}{30} = 1.2\overline{6}$

35c. $r = \frac{y+8}{y}$

35d. The ratio gets smaller.

35e. No; if the ratio equaled 1, Mariah and Louis would be the same age.

36. $\frac{9 \text{ leaps}}{1 \text{ miles}} = \frac{x \text{ leaps}}{693 \text{ miles}}$

$9(693) = x$

$6237 = x$

It would take 6237 leaps.

37. $\frac{4 \text{ thumbs}}{68 \text{ movies}} = \frac{5 \text{ thumbs}}{x \text{ movies}}$

$4x = 68(5)$

$4x = 340$

$x = 85$

Mr. Ebert rated 85 movies favorably.

38. $\frac{1 \text{ pound denim}}{5 \text{ pairs of jeans}} = \frac{x \text{ pounds denim}}{250 \text{ pairs of jeans}}$

$250 = 5x$

$50 = x$

50 pounds of denim would be left.

39. mean: $\frac{19 + 21 + 18 + 22 + 46 + 18 + 17}{7} = \frac{161}{7} = 23$

median: 17, 18, 18, (19), 21, 22, 46 => 19 since it is the middle value

mode: 18 since it occurs most often

40. $a = \frac{v}{t}$

$t(a) = t\left(\frac{v}{t}\right)$

$at = v$

$\frac{at}{a} = \frac{v}{a}$

$t = \frac{v}{a}$

41. Let x = the number.

$4x - 2x = 100$

$2x = 100$

$\frac{2x}{2} = \frac{100}{2}$

$x = 50$

The number is 50.

42. $-15 + d = 13$

$-15 + d + 15 = 13 + 15$

$d = 28$

43a. 93 **43b.** $9695

43c. more than 40 **43d.** $93 - p$ **43e.** yes

44. $-3 + 2 - 4 - 1 = -6$ or 6 under par

45. $|m - 4| = |-6 - 4|$

$= |-10|$

$= 10$

46. $x^2 + \frac{7}{8}x - \frac{x}{8} = x^2 + \left(\frac{7}{8} - \frac{1}{8}\right)x$

$= x^2 + \frac{6}{8}x$

$= x^2 + \frac{3}{4}x$

4-2 Integration: Geometry Similar Triangles

Page 203 Check for Understanding

1. $\angle R$ and $\angle U$, $\angle S$ and $\angle T$, $\angle Q$ and $\angle V$
2. Sample answer: The measures of their corresponding sides are proportional, and the measures of their corresponding angles are equal.
3. $\angle R$ and $\angle S$, $\angle E$ and $\angle O$, $\angle D$ and $\angle X$

   $\frac{RE}{SO} = \frac{ED}{OX}$, $\frac{RE}{SO} = \frac{RD}{SX}$, $\frac{ED}{OX} = \frac{RD}{SX}$
4. See students' work. **5.** ΔDEF
6. No, the measures of their corresponding angles are not equal.
7. Yes, the measures of their corresponding angles are equal.

8. $\frac{k}{n} = \frac{\ell}{o}$

$\frac{24}{16} = \frac{30}{o}$

$24o = 16(30)$

$24o = 480$

$o = 20$

$\frac{k}{n} = \frac{m}{p}$

$\frac{24}{16} = \frac{15}{p}$

$24p = 16(15)$

$24p = 240$

$p = 10$

9. $\frac{k}{n} = \frac{\ell}{o}$

$\frac{9}{6} = \frac{\ell}{8}$

$9(8) = 6\ell$

$72 = 6\ell$

$12 = \ell$

$\frac{k}{n} = \frac{m}{p}$

$\frac{9}{6} = \frac{m}{4}$

$9(4) = 6m$

$36 = 6m$

$6 = m$

10. $\frac{m}{p} = \frac{k}{n}$

$\frac{1.25}{2.5} = \frac{k}{6}$

$6(1.25) = 2.5k$

$7.5 = 2.5k$

$3 = k$

$\frac{m}{p} = \frac{\ell}{o}$

$\frac{1.25}{2.5} = \frac{4}{o}$

$1.25o = 4(2.5)$

$1.25o = 10$

$o = 8$

11. $\frac{6 \text{ ft tree}}{4 \text{ ft shadow}} = \frac{x \text{ ft flagpole}}{18 \text{ ft shadow}}$

$6(18) = 4x$

$108 = 4x$

$27 = x$

The flagpole is 27 feet high.

Pages 204–205 Exercises

12. ΔPNY **13.** ΔDFE **14.** ΔRQY

15. No, the measures of the corresponding angles are not equal.
16. Yes, the measures of the corresponding angles are equal.
17. Yes, the measures of the corresponding angles are equal.
18. No, the measures of the corresponding angles are not equal.

19. No, the measures of the corresponding angles are not equal.

20. No, the measures of the corresponding angles are not equal.

21.
$\frac{c}{f} = \frac{b}{e}$
$\frac{11}{6} = \frac{b}{4}$
$6b = 4(11)$
$6b = 44$
$b = \frac{44}{6} = \frac{22}{3}$

$\frac{c}{f} = \frac{a}{d}$
$\frac{11}{6} = \frac{a}{5}$
$6a = 5(11)$
$6a = 55$
$a = \frac{55}{6}$

22.
$\frac{a}{d} = \frac{c}{f}$
$\frac{5}{7} = \frac{c}{6}$
$5(6) = 7c$
$30 = 7c$
$\frac{30}{7} = c$

$\frac{a}{d} = \frac{b}{e}$
$\frac{5}{7} = \frac{b}{5}$
$5(5) = 7b$
$25 = 7b$
$\frac{25}{7} = b$

23.
$\frac{c}{f} = \frac{b}{e}$
$\frac{10}{6} = \frac{15}{e}$
$10e = 6(15)$
$10e = 90$
$e = 9$

$\frac{c}{f} = \frac{a}{d}$
$\frac{10}{6} = \frac{17}{d}$
$10d = 102$
$d = \frac{102}{10} = \frac{51}{5}$

24.
$\frac{b}{e} = \frac{c}{f}$
$\frac{13}{7} = \frac{12}{f}$
$13f = 7(12)$
$13f = 84$
$f = \frac{84}{13}$

$\frac{b}{e} = \frac{a}{d}$
$\frac{13}{7} = \frac{16}{d}$
$13d = 7(16)$
$13d = 112$
$d = \frac{112}{13}$

25.
$\frac{b}{e} = \frac{a}{d}$
$\frac{4.5}{3.4} = \frac{a}{2.1}$
$4.5(2.1) = 3.4a$
$9.45 = 3.4a$
$2.78 = a$

$\frac{b}{e} = \frac{c}{f}$
$\frac{4.5}{3.4} = \frac{c}{3.2}$
$4.5(3.2) = 3.4c$
$14.4 = 3.4c$
$4.24 = c$

26.
$\frac{c}{f} = \frac{a}{d}$
$\frac{18}{12} = \frac{a}{18}$
$18(18) = 12a$
$324 = 12a$
$27 = a$

$\frac{c}{f} = \frac{b}{e}$
$\frac{18}{12} = \frac{b}{16}$
$18(16) = 12b$
$288 = 12b$
$24 = b$

27.
$\frac{c}{f} = \frac{a}{d}$
$\frac{5}{2.5} = \frac{12.6}{d}$
$5d = 2.5(12.6)$
$5d = 31.5$
$d = 6.3$

$\frac{c}{f} = \frac{b}{e}$
$\frac{5}{2.5} = \frac{b}{8.1}$
$5(8.1) = 2.5b$
$40.5 = 2.5b$
$16.2 = b$

28.
$\frac{c}{f} = \frac{a}{d}$
$\frac{7.5}{5} = \frac{10.5}{d}$
$7.5d = 5(10.5)$
$7.5d = 52.5$
$d = 7$

$\frac{c}{f} = \frac{b}{e}$
$\frac{7.5}{5} = \frac{15}{e}$
$7.5e = 5(15)$
$7.5e = 75$
$e = 10$

29.
$\frac{b}{e} = \frac{c}{f}$
$\frac{5\frac{1}{2}}{2\frac{3}{4}} = \frac{c}{1\frac{3}{4}}$
$\left(5\frac{1}{2}\right)\left(1\frac{3}{4}\right) = 2\frac{3}{4}c$
$\left(\frac{11}{2}\right)\left(\frac{7}{4}\right) = \frac{11}{4}c$
$\frac{77}{8} = \frac{11}{4}c$
$\frac{7}{2} = c$

$\frac{b}{e} = \frac{a}{d}$
$\frac{5\frac{1}{2}}{2\frac{3}{4}} = \frac{4\frac{1}{4}}{d}$
$5\frac{1}{2}d = \left(2\frac{3}{4}\right)\left(4\frac{1}{4}\right)$
$\frac{11}{2}d = \left(\frac{11}{4}\right)\left(\frac{17}{4}\right)$
$\frac{11}{2}d = \frac{187}{16}$
$d = \frac{17}{8}$

30. $A = \frac{1}{2}bh$

$$\frac{A_{\Delta ABC}}{A_{\Delta DEF}} = \frac{\frac{1}{2}(2b)(2h)}{\frac{1}{2}(3b)(3h)} = \frac{4}{9} \text{ or } 4{:}9$$

31. Sample answer:

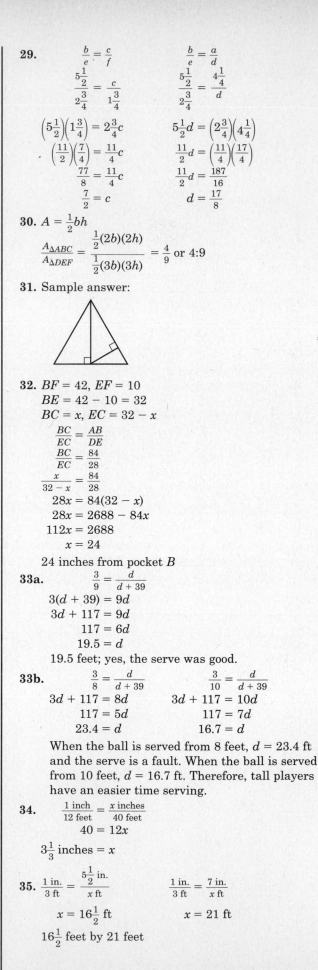

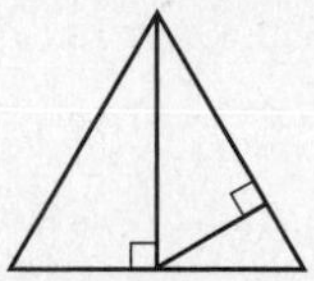

32. $BF = 42$, $EF = 10$
$BE = 42 - 10 = 32$
$BC = x$, $EC = 32 - x$
$\frac{BC}{EC} = \frac{AB}{DE}$
$\frac{BC}{EC} = \frac{84}{28}$
$\frac{x}{32 - x} = \frac{84}{28}$
$28x = 84(32 - x)$
$28x = 2688 - 84x$
$112x = 2688$
$x = 24$

24 inches from pocket B

33a.
$\frac{3}{9} = \frac{d}{d + 39}$
$3(d + 39) = 9d$
$3d + 117 = 9d$
$117 = 6d$
$19.5 = d$

19.5 feet; yes, the serve was good.

33b.
$\frac{3}{8} = \frac{d}{d + 39}$
$3d + 117 = 8d$
$117 = 5d$
$23.4 = d$

$\frac{3}{10} = \frac{d}{d + 39}$
$3d + 117 = 10d$
$117 = 7d$
$16.7 = d$

When the ball is served from 8 feet, $d = 23.4$ ft and the serve is a fault. When the ball is served from 10 feet, $d = 16.7$ ft. Therefore, tall players have an easier time serving.

34.
$\frac{1 \text{ inch}}{12 \text{ feet}} = \frac{x \text{ inches}}{40 \text{ feet}}$
$40 = 12x$
$3\frac{1}{3}$ inches $= x$

35.
$\frac{1 \text{ in.}}{3 \text{ ft}} = \frac{5\frac{1}{2} \text{ in.}}{x \text{ ft}}$
$x = 16\frac{1}{2}$ ft

$\frac{1 \text{ in.}}{3 \text{ ft}} = \frac{7 \text{ in.}}{x \text{ ft}}$
$x = 21$ ft

$16\frac{1}{2}$ feet by 21 feet

36. $7 = 3 - \frac{n}{3}$

$7 - 3 = 3 - \frac{n}{3} - 3$

$4 = -\frac{n}{3}$

$(-3)4 = \left(-\frac{n}{3}\right)(-3)$

$-12 = n$

37. Let x = the number of Ping Pong™ balls.

$\frac{1}{10}x = 16$

$10\left(\frac{1}{10}x\right) = 16(10)$

$x = 160$

160 Ping Pong balls weigh 1 pound.

38. $x + (-8) = -31$

$x - 8 + 8 = -31 + 8$

$x = -23$

39. $\frac{2.5 \text{ million}}{1 \text{ hr}} \cdot \frac{24 \text{ hr}}{1 \text{ day}} = 60\frac{\text{million}}{\text{day}}$ or 60 million per day

$\frac{2.5 \text{ million}}{1 \text{ hr}} \cdot \frac{24 \text{ hr}}{1 \text{ day}} \cdot \frac{7 \text{ days}}{1 \text{ week}} = 420\frac{\text{million}}{\text{week}}$ or 420 million per week

40. $\frac{8}{15} \ \underline{?}\ \frac{9}{16}$

$8(16) \ \underline{?}\ 9(15)$

$128 < 135$

$\frac{8}{15} < \frac{9}{16}$

41. $(9 - 12) \div 7 \cdot 23 = 7 \div 7 \cdot 23$ substitution (=)

$= 1 \cdot 23$ substitution (=)

$= 23$ mult. identity

4-3 Integration: Trigonometry Trigonometric Ratios

Pages 210–211 Check for Understanding

1a. 4 1b. 9

2. sine = $\frac{\text{opposite leg}}{\text{hypotenuse}}$, cosine = $\frac{\text{adjacent leg}}{\text{hypotenuse}}$

3. Use the sine when the opposite side and hypotenuse are known, use the cosine when the adjacent side and hypotenuse are known, and use the tangent when the opposite side and adjacent side are known.

4. angle of elevation: $\angle QRP$; angle of depression: $\angle SPR$

5a. cosine 5b. tangent 5c. sine

6. See students' work.

7. $\sin Y = \frac{6}{10} = 0.600$

$\cos Y = \frac{8}{10} = 0.800$

$\tan Y = \frac{6}{8} = 0.750$

8. $\sin Y = \frac{35}{37} \approx 0.946$

$\cos Y = \frac{12}{37} \approx 0.324$

$\tan Y = \frac{35}{12} \approx 2.917$

9. 0.8192 10. 0.8910 11. 0.1228 12. 16°

13. 46° 14. 68°

15. $\cos x = \frac{17}{21} \approx 0.8095$

$x \approx 36°$

16. $\tan x = \frac{2}{11} \approx 0.1818$

$x \approx 10°$

17. $\angle B = 90° - 40° = 50°$

$\cos 40° = \frac{AC}{16}$ $\quad$ $\sin 40° = \frac{BC}{16}$

$0.7660 \approx \frac{AC}{16}$ $\quad$ $0.6428 \approx \frac{BC}{16}$

$12.3 \text{ m} \approx AC$ $\quad$ $10.3 \text{ m} \approx BC$

18. $\angle B = 90° - 70° = 20°$

$\sin 70° = \frac{9}{AB}$ $\quad$ $\tan 70° = \frac{9}{AC}$

$0.9397 \approx \frac{9}{AB}$ $\quad$ $2.7474 \approx \frac{9}{AC}$

$0.9397AB \approx 9$ $\quad$ $2.7474AC \approx 9$

$AB \approx 9.6 \text{ cm}$ $\quad$ $AC \approx 3.3 \text{ cm}$

19. $\angle A = 90° - 60° = 30°$

$\sin 60° = \frac{AC}{16}$ $\quad$ $\cos 60° = \frac{BC}{16}$

$0.8660 \approx \frac{AC}{16}$ $\quad$ $0.5 = \frac{BC}{16}$

$13.9 \text{ m} \approx AC$ $\quad$ $8 \text{ m} = BC$

20.

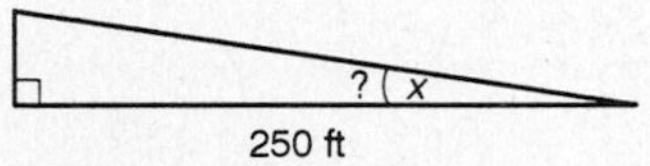

$\tan x = \frac{15}{250}$

$\tan x = 0.06$

$x \approx 3.4°$

Pages 211–214 Exercises

21. $\sin G = \frac{27}{45} = 0.600$

$\cos G = \frac{36}{45} = 0.800$

$\tan G = \frac{27}{36} = 0.750$

22. $\sin G = \frac{16}{65} \approx 0.246$

$\cos G = \frac{63}{65} \approx 0.969$

$\tan G = \frac{16}{63} \approx 0.254$

23. $\sin G = \frac{16}{34} \approx 0.471$

$\cos G = \frac{30}{34} \approx 0.882$

$\tan G = \frac{116}{30} \approx 0.533$

24. $\sin G = \frac{12}{13} \approx 0.923$

$\cos G = \frac{5}{13} \approx 0.385$

$\tan G = \frac{12}{5} = 2.400$

25. $\sin G = \frac{24}{26} \approx 0.923$

$\cos G = \frac{10}{26} \approx 0.385$

$\tan G = \frac{24}{10} = 2.400$

26. $\sin G = \frac{21}{29} \approx 0.724$

$\cos G = \frac{20}{29} \approx 0.690$

$\tan G = \frac{21}{20} \approx 1.050$

27. 0.3584 28. 0.9659 29. 0.9703 30. 1.4826

31. 0.3746 32. 0.5774 33. 33° 34. 40°

35. 22° 36. 73° 37. 62° 38. 84°

39. $\tan x = \frac{9}{2} = 4.5$

$x \approx 77°$

40. $\sin x = \frac{7}{13} \approx 0.5385$

$x \approx 33°$

41. $\tan x = \frac{16}{10} = 1.6$

$x \approx 58°$

42. $\cos x = \frac{9.3}{9.7} \approx 0.9588$

$x \approx 17°$

43.

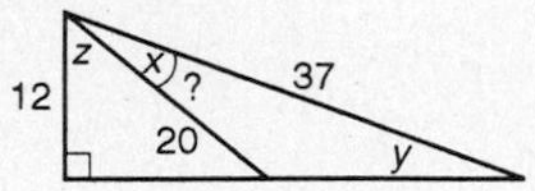

$\sin y = \frac{12}{37}$ $\quad$ $\cos z = \frac{12}{20}$

$\sin y \approx 0.3243$ $\quad$ $\cos z = 0.600$

$y \approx 19°$ $\quad$ $z \approx 53°$

$x = 90° - 53° - 19° = 18°$

44. $\sin x = \frac{12}{18} = 0.6667$

$x = 42°$

45. $\angle B = 90° - 30° = 60°$

$\cos 30° = \frac{BC}{14}$ $\qquad$ $\sin 30° = \frac{BC}{14}$

$0.8660 \approx \frac{BC}{14}$ $\qquad$ $0.5 = \frac{BC}{14}$

$12.1 \text{ m} \approx AC$ $\qquad$ $7 \text{ m} = BC$

46. $\angle A = 90° - 30° = 60°$

$\sin 30° = \frac{AC}{42}$ $\qquad$ $\cos 30° = \frac{BC}{42}$

$0.5 = \frac{AC}{42}$ $\qquad$ $0.8660 \approx \frac{BC}{42}$

$21 \text{ in.} = AC$ $\qquad$ $36.4 \text{ in.} \approx BC$

47. $\angle A = 90° - 45° = 45°$

$\tan 45° = \frac{AC}{6}$ $\qquad$ $\cos 45° = \frac{6}{AB}$

$1 = \frac{AC}{6}$ $\qquad$ $0.7071 \approx \frac{6}{AB}$

$6 \text{ ft} = AC$ $\qquad$ $0.7071AB \approx 6$

$AB \approx 8.5 \text{ ft}$

48. $\angle B = 90° - 29° = 61°$

$\cos 29° = \frac{18}{AB}$ $\qquad$ $\tan 29° = \frac{BC}{18}$

$0.8746 \approx \frac{18}{AB}$ $\qquad$ $0.5543 \approx \frac{BC}{18}$

$0.8746AB \approx 18$ $\qquad$ $10 \text{ m} \approx BC$

$AB \approx 20.6 \text{ m}$

49. $\angle A = 90° - 27° = 63°$

$\sin 27° = \frac{AC}{20}$ $\qquad$ $\cos 27° = \frac{BC}{20}$

$0.4540 \approx \frac{AC}{20}$ $\qquad$ $0.8910 \approx \frac{BC}{20}$

$9.1 \text{ in.} \approx AC$ $\qquad$ $17.8 \text{ in.} \approx BC$

50. $\angle B = 90° - 21° = 69°$

$\cos 21° \approx \frac{13}{AB}$ $\qquad$ $\tan 21° = \frac{BC}{13}$

$0.9336 \approx \frac{13}{AB}$ $\qquad$ $0.3838 \approx \frac{BC}{13}$

$0.9336AB \approx 13$ $\qquad$ $5.0 \text{ in.} \approx BC$

$AB \approx 13.9 \text{ in.}$

51. $\tan A = \frac{5}{12}$ $\qquad$ $\angle B \approx 90° - 23° \approx 67°$

$\tan A \approx 0.4167$

$\angle A \approx 23°$

$\sin 23° = \frac{5}{AB}$

$0.3907 \approx \frac{5}{AB}$

$0.3907AB \approx 5$

$AB \approx 12.8 \text{ ft}$

52. $\tan A = \frac{8}{6}$ $\qquad$ $\angle B \approx 90° - 53° \approx 37°$

$\tan A \approx 1.333$

$\angle A \approx 53°$

$\sin 53° = \frac{8}{AB}$

$0.7986 \approx \frac{8}{AB}$

$0.7986AB \approx 8$

$AB \approx 10 \text{ ft}$

53. $\cos B = \frac{3}{6}$ $\qquad$ $\angle A = 90° - 60° = 30°$

$\cos B = 0.5$

$\angle B = 60°$

$\cos 30° = \frac{AC}{6}$

$0.8660 \approx \frac{AC}{6}$

$5.2 \text{ cm} \approx AC$

54a. SIDE $C = 5$
ANGLE $A = 36.9°$
ANGLE $B = 53.1°$
$\sin A = 0.600$
$\sin B = 0.800$
$\cos A = 0.800$
$\cos B = 0.600$
$\tan A = 0.750$
$\tan B = 1.333$

54b. SIDE $C = 13$
ANGLE $A = 22.6°$
ANGLE $B = 67.4°$
$\sin A = 0.385$
$\sin B = 0.923$
$\cos A = 0.923$
$\cos B = 0.385$
$\tan A = 0.417$
$\tan B = 2.400$

54c. SIDE $C = 44.7$
ANGLE $A = 26.6°$
ANGLE $B = 63.4°$
$\sin A = 0.447$
$\sin B = 0.894$
$\cos A = 0.894$
$\cos B = 0.447$
$\tan A = 0.500$
$\tan B = 2.000$

54d. SIDE $C = 160.1$
ANGLE $A = 51.3°$
ANGLE $B = 38.7°$
$\sin A = 0.781$
$\sin B = 0.625$
$\cos A = 0.625$
$\cos B = 0.781$
$\tan A = 1.250$
$\tan B = 0.800$

55a. $\sin C = \frac{c}{a}$, $\cos B = \frac{c}{a}$ true

55b. $\cos B = \frac{c}{a}$, $\frac{1}{\sin B} = \frac{a}{b}$ false

55c. $\tan C = \frac{c}{b}$, $\frac{\cos C}{\sin C} = \frac{b}{a} \div \frac{c}{a} = \frac{b}{c}$ false

55d. $\tan C = \frac{c}{b}$, $\frac{\sin C}{\cos C} = \frac{c}{a} \div \frac{b}{a} = \frac{c}{b}$ true

55e. $\sin B = \frac{b}{a}$, $(\tan B)(\cos B) = \frac{b}{c} \cdot \frac{c}{a} = \frac{b}{a}$ true

56.

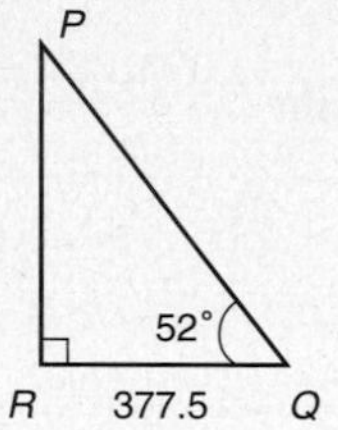

$755 \div 2 = 377.5$

$\tan 52° = \frac{PR}{377.5}$

$1.280 \approx \frac{PR}{377.5}$

$483 \text{ ft} = PR$

57.

$\tan 85° = \frac{x}{65}$

$11.4300 \approx \frac{x}{65}$

$743 \text{ yds} \approx x$

$743(3) = 2229 \text{ ft}$

58. $\frac{100 \text{ m}}{55 \text{ m}} = \frac{(120 + 100) \text{ m}}{DE}$

$100DE = 55(220)$

$100DE = 12{,}100$

$DE = 121 \text{ m}$

The distance across Spring Lake is 121 m.

59. $\frac{x}{5} = \frac{x + 3}{10}$

$10x = 5(x + 3)$

$10x = 5x + 15$

$5x = 15$

$x = 3$

60. 0.183, 0.222, 0.234, 0.240, 0.253, 0.275, 0.286, 0.297, 0.312, 0.333 =>

median $= \frac{0.253 + 0.275}{2} = 0.264$ since it is the average of the two middle values

61. $\frac{2}{5}y + \frac{y}{2} = 9$
$\frac{4}{10}y + \frac{5}{10}y = 9$
$\frac{9}{10}y = 9$
$\left(\frac{10}{9}\right)\left(\frac{9}{10}\right)y = 9\left(\frac{10}{9}\right)$
$y = 10$

62. Let x = the cost per ticket.
$5x = 47.50$
$\frac{5x}{5} = \frac{47.50}{5}$
$x = \$9.50$

63. N, W, Z, Q

64. $\frac{3a+9}{3} = \frac{3a}{3} + \frac{9}{3}$
$= a + 3$

65. $\left(-\frac{2}{3}\right)\left(-\frac{1}{5}\right) = \frac{2}{15}$

66. -21

67. $8x + 2y + x = 8x + x + 2y$
$= (8 + 1)x + 2y$
$= 9x + 2y$

68. $(9 - 2 \cdot 3)^3 - 27 + 9 \cdot 2 = (9 - 6)^3 - 27 + 9 \cdot 2$
$= 3^3 - 27 + 9 \cdot 2$
$= 27 - 27 + 9 \cdot 2$
$= 27 - 27 + 18$
$= 18$

69. $5^3 = 5 \cdot 5 \cdot 5 \cdot = 125$

Page 214 Mathematics and Society

1. Answers will vary. Sample answers: curiosity, determination, a systematic approach, willingness to try new methods, looking for patterns, learning from mistakes, and keeping good records.
2. See students' work.
3. See students' work.

4-4 Percents

Page 218 Check for Understanding

1. They are the same.
2. Enter: 57 [2nd] [%] [X] 42 [=] 23.94
3. The investment of the higher rate may be too risky.
4. The sum of the percents is greater than 100.
5. See students' work.

6. $\frac{3}{4} = \frac{n}{100}$
$300 = 4n$
$75 = n$
75%, 0.75

7. 43%, 0.43

8. $\frac{2}{25} = \frac{n}{100}$
$200 = 25n$
$8 = n$
8%, 0.08

9. $\frac{11}{20} = \frac{r}{100}$
$1100 = 20r$
$55 = r$
11 is 55% of 20.

10. $\frac{45}{80} = \frac{r}{100}$
$4500 = 80r$
$56\frac{1}{4} = r$
$56\frac{1}{4}$% or 56.25% of 80 is 45.

11. $x = \frac{30}{100} \cdot 50$
$x = \frac{1500}{100}$
$x = 15$
15 is 30% of 50.

12. $\frac{x}{100} \cdot 75 = 16$
$\frac{3}{4}x = 16$
$\frac{4}{3}\left(\frac{3}{4}x\right) = \frac{4}{3}(16)$
$x = 21\frac{1}{3}$
$21\frac{1}{3}$% or $21.\overline{3}$% of 75 is 16.

13. $I = prt$
$I = 1500(0.07)\left(\frac{6}{12}\right)$
$I = \$52.50$

14. $I = prt$
$196 = p(0.10)(7)$
$196 = 0.70p$
$\$280 = p$

15. Let n = the amount of money invested at 10%. Then $7200 - n$ = the amount of money invested at 14%.
$0.10n + 0.14(7200 - n) = 960$
$0.10n + 1008 - 0.14n = 960$
$1008 - 0.04n = 960$
$-0.04n = -48$
$n = 1200$
\$1200 at 10%, 7200 − 1200 = \$6000 at 14%

Pages 218–221 Exercises

16. 67%, 0.67

17. $\frac{6}{20} = \frac{x}{100}$
$600 = 20x$
$30 = x$
30%, 0.30

18. $\frac{5}{8} = \frac{x}{100}$
$500 = 8x$
$62.5 = x$
$62\frac{1}{2}$%, 0.625

19. $\frac{7}{10} = \frac{x}{100}$
$700 = 10x$
$70 = x$
70%, 0.70

20. $\frac{5}{6} = \frac{x}{100}$
$500 = 6x$
$0.8\overline{3} = x$
$83\frac{1}{3}$%, $0.8\overline{3}$

21. $\frac{9}{5} = \frac{x}{100}$
$900 = 5x$
$180 = x$
180%, 1.80

22. $\frac{2}{3} = \frac{x}{100}$
$200 = 3x$
$66.\overline{6} = x$
$66\frac{2}{3}$%, $0.\overline{6}$

23. $\frac{25}{40} = \frac{x}{100}$
$2500 = 40x$
$62.5 = x$
$62\frac{1}{2}$%, 0.625

24. $\frac{20}{8} = \frac{x}{100}$
$2000 = 8x$
$250 = x$
250%, 2.5

25. $\frac{35}{70} = \frac{r}{100}$
$3500 = 70r$
$50 = r$
35 is 50% of 70.

26. $\frac{18}{60} = \frac{r}{100}$
$1800 = 60r$
$30 = r$
18 is 30% of 60.

27. $\frac{8}{64} = \frac{r}{100}$
$800 = 64r$
$12.5 = r$
8 is $12\frac{1}{2}$% of 64.

28. $\frac{6}{15} = \frac{r}{100}$
$600 = 15r$
$40 = r$
6 is 40% of 15.

29. $\frac{8}{2} = \frac{r}{100}$
$800 = 2r$
$400 = r$
400% of 2 is 8.

30. $\frac{4.34}{14} = \frac{r}{100}$
$434 = 14r$
$31 = r$
4.34 is 31% of 14.

31. $\frac{x}{100} \cdot 160 = 4$
$\frac{160x}{100} = 4$
$\frac{8}{5}x = 4$
$x = \frac{5}{2}$ or 2.5
4 is 2.5% of 160.

32. $x = \frac{25}{100} \cdot 56$
$x = 14$
25% of 56 is 14.

33. $12 = \frac{16.6}{100} \cdot x$

$72.3 \approx x$

12 is 16.6% of 72.3.

34. $32 = \frac{x}{100} \cdot 80$

$32 = \frac{80x}{100}$

$40 = x$

32 is 40% of 80.

35. $17.56 = \frac{2.5}{100} \cdot x$

$702.4 = x$

17.56 is 2.5% of 702.4.

36. $\frac{x}{100} \cdot 75 = 30$

$\frac{75x}{100} = 30$

$x = 40$

40% of 75 is 30.

37. $64.93 = \frac{x}{100} \cdot 231.90$

$28 = x$

\$64.93 is 28% of \$231.90.

38. $\frac{112}{100} \cdot 500 = x$

$560 = x$

112% of \$500 is \$560.

39. $\frac{81}{100} \cdot 32 = x$

$25.92 = x$

81% of 32 is 25.92.

40. $I = prt$

$5920 = 4000(r)(3)$

$5920 = 12{,}000r$

$0.493 = r$

The rate is 49.3%.

41. $I = prt$

$780 = 6500(r)(1)$

$780 = 6500r$

$0.12 = r$

The rate is 12%.

42. $I = prt$

$I = (3200)(0.09)\left(\frac{18}{12}\right)$

$I = \$432$

43. $I = prt$

$I = 5000(0.125)(5)$

$I = \$3125$

44. $I = prt$

$2160 = (6000)(0.08)t$

$2160 = 480t$

$4.5 = t$

4.5 years

45. $I = prt$

$756 = p(0.09)(3.5)$

$756 = 0.315p$

$\$2400 = p$

46. $x = 2.25y$

$\frac{x}{2.25} = \frac{2.25y}{2.25}$

$0.\overline{4}x = y$

y is $44.\overline{4}\%$ of x.

47. under 18: $\frac{1.6}{4.1} \approx 0.390 \approx 39\%$

18–44: $\frac{1.4}{4.1} \approx 0.341 \approx 34\%$

45–64: $\frac{600{,}000}{4{,}100{,}000} \approx 0.146 \approx 15\%$

65 and older: $\frac{500{,}000}{4{,}100{,}000} \approx 0.122 \approx 12\%$

48. Let n = the amount of money invested at 9%. Then $5000 - n$ = the amount of money invested at 12%.

$0.09n = 0.12(5000 - n) + 198$

$0.09n = 600 - 0.12n + 198$

$0.21n = 798$

$n = 3800$

Melanie invested \$3800 at 9%.

49. Let r = the rate of interest.

$2500 + 0.10(2500) + 6000 + r(6000) = 9440$

$2500 + 250 + 6000 + 6000r = 9440$

$8750 + 6000r = 9440$

$6000r = 690$

$r = 0.115$

They should invest the \$6000 at 11.5%.

50. **Desserts Eaten in the Home**

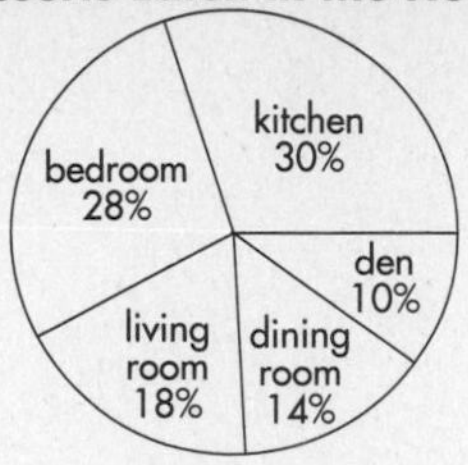

51. $I = prt$

$I = 330(0.198)\left(\frac{1}{12}\right)$

$I = 5.45$

Luke's father will be charged \$5.45.

52.

Topping	Percentage of Calories from Fat
Extra Cheese	$\frac{8(9)}{168} \approx 0.43 \approx 43\%$
Sausage	$\frac{8(9)}{97} \approx 0.74 \approx 74\%$
Pepperoni	$\frac{7(9)}{80} \approx 0.79 \approx 79\%$
Black Olives	$\frac{5(9)}{56} \approx 0.80 \approx 80\%$
Ham	$\frac{2(9)}{41} \approx 0.44 = 44\%$
Onion	$\frac{0.5(9)}{11} \approx 0.41 \approx 41\%$
Green Pepper	$\frac{0(9)}{5} = 0\%$
Mushrooms	$\frac{0(9)}{5} = 0\%$

Black Olives gets the highest percentage of its calories from fat.

53a. chicken marsala: $\frac{21}{100} \cdot 258$ = about 54 people

pizza: $\frac{9}{100} \cdot 258$ = about 23 people

53b. Respondents could choose more than one entree.

54. **U.S. Coins Minted in 1994**

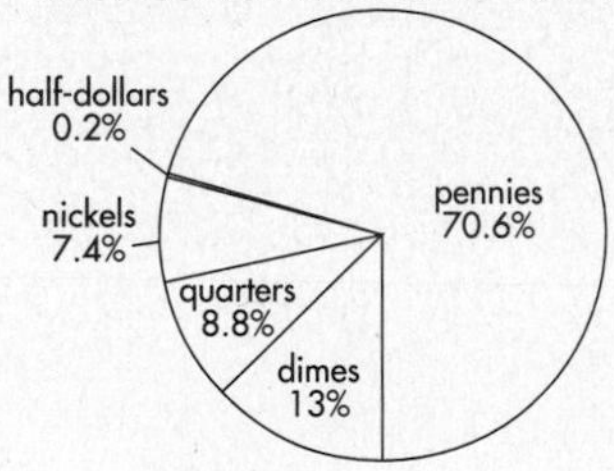

55.

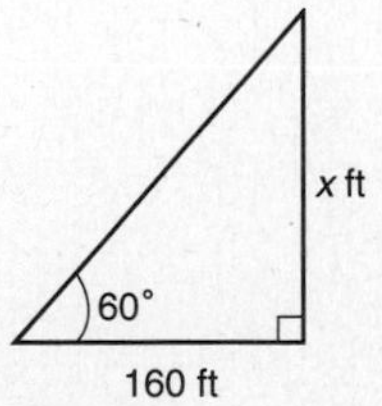

$\tan 60° = \frac{x}{160}$

$1.732 \approx \frac{x}{160}$

$277 \approx x$

The tree is about 277 feet tall.

56. $\frac{a}{r} = \frac{b}{q}$

$\frac{10}{5} = \frac{b}{3}$

$30 = 5b$

$6 = b$

$\frac{a}{r} = \frac{c}{p}$

$\frac{10}{5} = \frac{c}{4}$

$40 = 5c$

$8 = c$

57. $\frac{9}{x - 8} = \frac{4}{5}$

$45 = 4(x - 8)$

$45 = 4x - 32$

$77 = 4x$

$x = \frac{77}{4}$ or 19.25

58. mean: $\frac{\text{sum of 10 values}}{10} = \frac{83}{10} = 8.3$

median: 3, 4, 4, 5, (6, 7) 8, 11, 12, 23 =>
$\frac{6+7}{2} = 6.5$ since it is the average of the middle two values

mode: 4 since it occurs most often

59. $y + (-7.5) = -12.2$
$y - 7.5 + 7.5 = -12.2 + 7.5$
$y = -4.7$

60. total score $= (9 + 8 + 8.5)(3.4)$
$= (25.5)(3.4)$
$= 86.7$

61. $5y + (-12y) + (-21y) = (5 - 12 - 21)y$
$= -28y$

62.

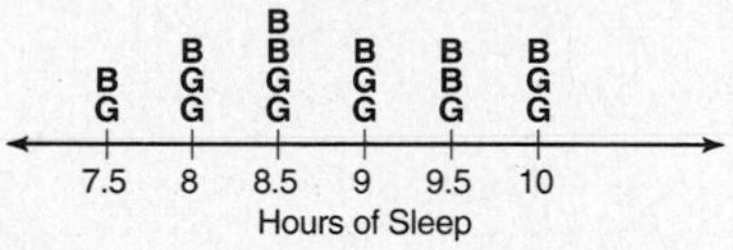

63. $\frac{21-3}{12-3} = x$
$\frac{18}{9} = x$
$2 = x$

64. $19.5 + 5.5 = 25$, $25 + 5.5 = 30.5$, $30.5 + 5.5 = 36$

Page 221 Self Test

1. $\frac{2}{10} = \frac{1}{a}$
$2a = 10$
$a = 5$

2. $\frac{3}{5} = \frac{24}{x}$
$3x = 5(24)$
$3x = 120$
$x = 40$

3. $\frac{y}{4} = \frac{y+5}{8}$
$8y = 4(y + 5)$
$8y = 4y + 20$
$4y = 20$
$y = 5$

4. $\frac{10}{y} = \frac{14}{35}$
$10(35) = 14y$
$350 = 14y$
$25 = y$

$\frac{6}{x} = \frac{14}{35}$
$6(35) = 14x$
$15 = x$

5. $\tan 56° = \frac{17}{b}$
$1.4826 \approx \frac{17}{b}$
$1.4826b \approx 17$
$b \approx 11.5$

$\sin 56° = \frac{17}{c}$
$0.8290 \approx \frac{17}{c}$
$0.8290c \approx 17$
$c \approx 20.5$

$m\angle B = 90° - 56° = 34°$

6. $\tan B = \frac{16}{12}$
$\tan B \approx 1.3333$
$m\angle B \approx 53°$
$m\angle A \approx 90° - 53° \approx 37°$

$\sin B = \frac{16}{c}$
$\sin 53° = \frac{16}{c}$
$0.8 \approx \frac{16}{c}$
$0.8c \approx 16$
$c \approx 20$ mm

7. No, the measures of their corresponding angles are not equal.

8. $36 = \frac{45}{100} \cdot x$
$36 = \frac{45x}{100}$
$80 = x$
36 is 45% of 80.

9. $55 = \frac{x}{100} \cdot 88$
$55 = \frac{88x}{100}$
$62.5 = x$
55 is $62\frac{1}{2}$% or 62.5% of 88.

10. $\frac{6}{100} \cdot 8000 = x$
$480 = x$
$8000 - 480 = 7520$
7520 people had an opinion.

4-5 Percent of Change

Pages 224–225 Check for Understanding

1. Subtract old from new. Divide the result by old. Move decimal point 2 places to the right.

2. Multiply tax rate by original price.

3. $\frac{19{,}705 - 17{,}972}{17{,}972} = \frac{r}{100}$ or $\frac{1733}{17{,}972} = \frac{r}{100}$

4. See students' work.

5. increase
$\frac{70-50}{50} = \frac{r}{100}$
$\frac{20}{50} = \frac{r}{100}$
$20(100) = 50r$
$40 = r$
The percent of increase is 40%.

6. decrease
$\frac{200-172}{200} = \frac{r}{100}$
$\frac{28}{200} = \frac{r}{100}$
$28(100) = 200r$
$14 = r$
The percent of decrease is 14%.

7. decrease
$\frac{72-36}{72} = \frac{r}{100}$
$\frac{36}{72} = \frac{r}{100}$
$36(100) = 72r$
$50 = r$
The percent of decrease is 50%.

8. 15% of \$149 = 0.15(149)
= \$22.35
\$149 − \$22.35 = \$126.65
The discounted price is \$126.65.

9. 10% of \$89.99 = 0.10(89.99)
≈ \$9.00
\$89.99 − \$9.00 = \$80.99
6% of \$80.99 = 0.06(80.99)
≈ \$4.86
\$80.99 + \$4.86 = \$85.85
The total price is \$85.85.

10. 6.5% of \$45 = 0.065(45)
≈ \$2.93
\$45 + \$2.93 = \$47.93
The total price is \$47.93.

11. Let x = the cost of the pictures before taxes.
$x + 0.05x = 205.80$
$1.05x = 205.80$
$x = 196$
The cost of the pictures before taxes was \$196.

Pages 225–227 Exercises

12. decrease

$$\frac{100-59}{100}=\frac{r}{100}$$
$$\frac{41}{100}=\frac{r}{100}$$
$$4100=100r$$
$$41=r$$

The percent of decrease is 41%.

13. increase

$$\frac{549-324}{324}=\frac{r}{100}$$
$$\frac{225}{324}=\frac{r}{100}$$
$$22{,}500=324r$$
$$69\approx r$$

The percent of increase is 69%.

14. increase

$$\frac{152-58}{58}=\frac{r}{100}$$
$$\frac{94}{58}=\frac{r}{100}$$
$$9400=58r$$
$$162\approx r$$

The percent of increase is 162%.

15. decrease

$$\frac{66-30}{66}=\frac{r}{100}$$
$$\frac{36}{66}=\frac{r}{100}$$
$$3600=66r$$
$$55\approx r$$

The percent of decrease is 55%.

16. increase

$$\frac{75-53}{53}=\frac{r}{100}$$
$$\frac{22}{53}=\frac{r}{100}$$
$$2200=53r$$
$$42\approx r$$

The percent of increase is 42%.

17. decrease

$$\frac{15.6-11.4}{15.6}=\frac{r}{100}$$
$$\frac{4.2}{15.6}=\frac{r}{100}$$
$$420=15.6r$$
$$27\approx r$$

The percent of decrease is 27%.

18. decrease

$$\frac{3.78-2.50}{3.78}=\frac{r}{100}$$
$$\frac{1.28}{3.78}=\frac{r}{100}$$
$$128=3.78r$$
$$34\approx r$$

The percent of decrease is 34%.

19. increase

$$\frac{236.4-231.2}{231.2}=\frac{r}{100}$$
$$\frac{5.2}{231.2}=\frac{r}{100}$$
$$520=231.2r$$
$$2\approx r$$

The percent of increase is 2%.

20. increase

$$\frac{137-124}{124}=\frac{r}{100}$$
$$\frac{13}{124}=\frac{r}{100}$$
$$1300=124r$$
$$10\approx r$$

The percent of increase is 10%.

21. 6.5% of \$219 = 0.065(219)
≈ 14.24
\$219 + \$14.24 = \$233.24
The total price is \$233.24.

22. 15% of \$39.99 = 0.15(39.99)
= \$6.00
\$39.99 − \$6.00 = \$33.99
4% of \$33.99 = 0.04(33.99)
≈ \$1.36
\$33.99 + \$1.36 = \$35.35
The total price is \$35.35.

23. 5% of \$19.95 = 0.05(19.95)
≈ \$1.00
\$19.95 − \$1.00 = 18.95
5% of \$18.95 = 0.05(18.95)
≈ 0.95
\$18.95 + \$0.95 = \$19.90
The total price is \$19.90.

24. 7% of \$52.50 = 0.07(52.50)
≈ \$3.68
\$52.50 + \$3.68 = \$56.18
The total price is \$56.18.

25. 20% of \$99.99 = 0.20(99.99)
≈ 20.00
\$99.99 − \$20.00 = \$79.99
6.75% of \$79.99 = 0.0675(79.99)
≈ \$5.40
\$79.99 + \$5.40 = \$85.39
The total price is \$85.39.

26. 10% of \$59 = 0.10(59)
= \$5.90
\$59 − \$5.90 = \$53.10
5.5% of \$53.10 = 0.055(53.10)
≈ \$2.92
\$53.10 + \$2.92 = \$56.02
The total price is \$56.02.

27. 4.5% of \$15.88 = 0.045(15.88)
≈ \$0.71
\$15.88 + \$0.71 = \$16.59
The total price is \$16.59.

28. 6% of \$37.50 = 0.06(37.50)
= \$2.25
\$37.50 + \$2.25 = \$39.75
The total price is \$39.75.

29. 6% of \$29.99 = 0.06(29.99)
≈ \$1.80
\$29.99 − \$1.80 = \$28.19
6.75% of \$28.19 = 0.0675(28.19)
≈ \$1.90
\$28.19 + \$1.90 = \$30.09
The total price is \$30.09.

30a. SUCCESSIVE DISCOUNT, \$60.08
COMBINED DISCOUNT, \$57.85

30b. SUCCESSIVE DISCOUNT, \$152.02
COMBINED DISCOUNT, \$140.97

31. No; see students' work.

32. \$150 − \$125 = \$25 difference
110% of \$25 = 1.10(25) = \$27.50
pay the customer \$27.50

33.

$$\frac{1400-600}{600}=\frac{r}{100}$$
$$\frac{800}{600}=\frac{r}{100}$$
$$80{,}000=600r$$
$$133\approx r$$

The percent increase is 133%.

34. 150% of 3,000,000 = 1.5(3,000,000)
= 4,500,000
There will be 4,500,000 + 3,000,000 or 7,500,000 users in the year 2000.

35. 2:45 = 2 hrs 45 min or 165 min
2:32 = 2 hrs 32 min or 152 min

$$\frac{165-152}{152}=\frac{r}{100}$$
$$\frac{13}{152}=\frac{r}{100}$$
$$1300=152r$$
$$8.6\approx r$$

The percent of increase was 8.6%.

36. 10% of \$360 = 0.10(360)
= \$36
\$360 − \$36 = \$324
5% of \$324 = 0.05(324)
= \$16.20
\$324 − \$16.20 = \$307.80
He would pay \$307.80.

37. Let x = the normal resting length of muscles. Then $x - 0.10x$ or $0.90x$ = the length of muscles in the morning, and $x + 0.10x$ or $1.10x$ = the length of muscles after exercise.
The amount of change in muscle length between morning and after exercise is $1.10x - 0.90x$ or $0.20x$.
$$\frac{\text{amount of increase}}{\text{original length}} = \frac{0.20x}{0.90x} = 0.2\overline{2}$$
There is an increase in muscle length of more than 22%.

38a. no difference; 75% of \$75 = 0.75(75)
= \$56.25
106% of \$56.25 = 1.06 (56.25) = \$59.63
or 106% of \$75 = 1.06 (75) = \$79.50
75% of \$79.50 = 0.75 (79.50) = \$59.63

38b. See students' work.

39. $\frac{9559 - 8500}{9559} = \frac{r}{100}$
$\frac{1059}{9559} = \frac{r}{100}$
$105{,}900 = 9559r$
$11 \approx r$
The percent of decrease is 11%.

40. 75% of 720 = 0.75(720)
= 540
540 seats were filled.

41.
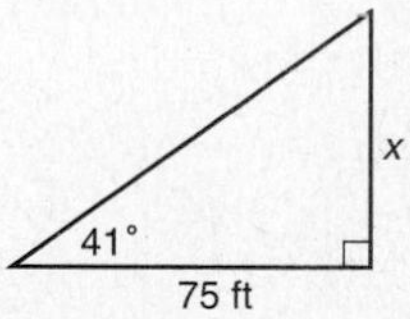

$\tan 41° = \frac{x}{75}$
$0.8693 \approx \frac{x}{75}$
$65 \approx x$
The chimney is about 65 feet tall.

42.
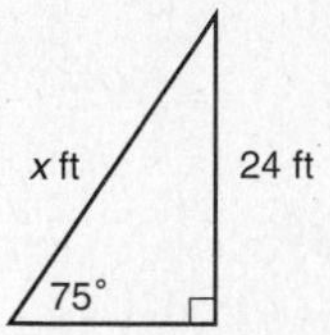

$\sin 75° = \frac{24}{x}$
$0.9659 \approx \frac{24}{x}$
$0.9659x \approx 24$
$x \approx 25$
The ladder must be at least 25 feet long.

43. $0.2x + 1.7 = 3.9$
$0.2x + 1.7 - 1.7 = 3.9 - 1.7$
$0.2x = 2.2$
$\frac{0.2x}{0.2x} = \frac{2.2}{0.2}$
$x = 11$

44. Let x = the measure of the third angle.
$x + 38 + 41 = 180$
$x + 79 = 180$
$x = 101°$
The third angle measures 101°.

45. heavy feeding = $\frac{2}{7} \cdot 2000 \approx 571$ Calories
light feeding = $\frac{1}{7} \cdot 2000 \approx 286$ Calories

46. from 4 to 10, intervals of 0.2
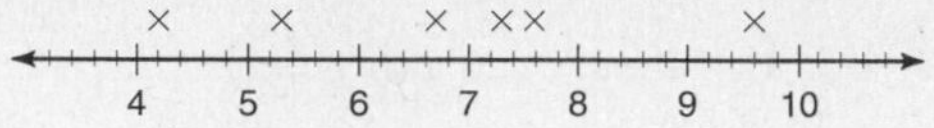

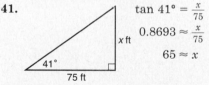

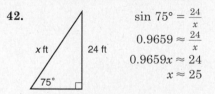

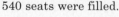

4-6 Integration: Probability Probability and Odds

Page 230 Check for Understanding

1. There is 1 Z tile. It has been chosen, so 0 remain. There are 100 − 25 or 75 tiles from which to select;
$P(\text{selecting a Z}) = \frac{0}{75}$ or 0
2. 7; a natural number less than 7
3. 5:3
4. See students' work.
5. See students' work.
6. 1
7. $\frac{1}{2}$
8. $\frac{1}{6}$
9. $\frac{4}{6} = \frac{2}{3}$
10. 4:2 = 2:1
11. 5:1
12. The number of successes is 3, total number of outcomes is 7. This means the number of failures is 7 − 3 or 4; odds the event will not occur = 4:3.

Pages 231–232 Exercises

13. $\frac{1}{2}$
14. 1
15. $\frac{1}{2}$
16. 0
17. P(roll a multiple of 2 on a die)
$= \frac{\text{roll 2, 4, 6}}{\text{roll 1, 2, 3, 4, 5, 6}} = \frac{3}{6} = \frac{1}{2}$
18. P(birthday in June) = $\frac{1}{12}$
19. There are 11 letters, 2 are the letter b.
P(letter b) = $\frac{2}{11}$
20. There are 11 letters, 9 are not i.
P(not i) = $\frac{9}{11}$
21. There are 11 letters, 0 are the letter e.
P(letter e) = $\frac{0}{11} = 0$
22. There are 11 letters, 4 are vowels.
P(vowel) = $\frac{4}{11}$
23. There are 11 letters, 8 are not b or y.
P(not b or y) = $\frac{8}{11}$
24. There are 11 letters, 2 are a or t.
P(letters a or t) = $\frac{2}{11}$
25. There are 50 quarters, 250 other coins; odds of selecting a quarter = 50:250 or 1:5.
26. There are 100 nickels, 200 other coins; odds of selecting a nickel = 100:200 or 1:2.
27. There are 80 pennies, 220 other coins; odds of selecting a penny = 80:220 or 4:11.
28. There are 200 coins that are not nickels, 100 nickels; odds of not selecting a nickel = 200:100 or 2:1.
29. There are 230 coins that are not dimes, 70 dimes; odds of not selecting a dime = 230:70 or 23:7.
30. There are 150 pennies and dimes, 150 other coins; odds of selecting a penny or dime = 150:150 or 1:1.

31. There are 26 red cards; $P(\text{red card}) = \frac{26}{52} = \frac{1}{2}$.

32. There are 4 queens; $P(\text{queen}) = \frac{4}{52} = \frac{1}{13}$.

33. There are 13 hearts, 39 other cards; odds of selecting a heart = 13:39 or 1:3.

34. There are 50 cards that are not a black 6, 2 black 6's; odds of not selecting a black 6 = 50:2 or 25:1.

35. There are 8 successes and $8 + 5 = 13$ outcomes; $P(\text{event}) = \frac{8}{13}$.

36. There are 2 successes and $3 - 2 = 1$ failure; odds of the event = 2:1.

37. This figure has 15 equal triangles of which 2 are shaded; $P(\text{shaded region}) = \frac{2}{14}$ or $\frac{1}{7}$.

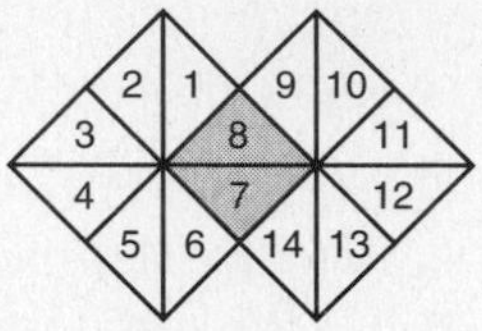

38. This figure has a total area of 19 units of which 6 are not shaded; $P(\text{not in the shaded region}) = \frac{6}{19}$.

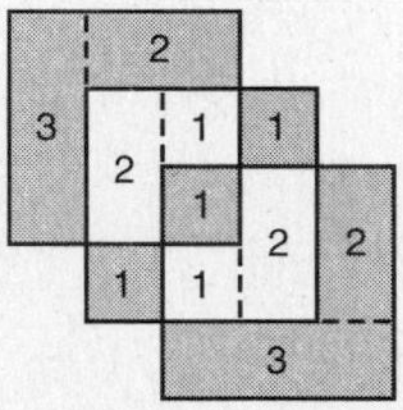

39a. There are 2 Daily Doubles, 28 other squares; odds of choosing a Daily Double square = 2:28 or 1:14.

39b. There are $2 - 1 = 1$ Daily Double squares left and there are $30 - 3 = 27$ squares to choose from on the fourth round; $P(\text{Daily Double or the fourth selection}) = \frac{1}{27}$.

40a. $P(\text{being chosen on the first day}) = \frac{4}{35}$

40b. Four students are chosen per day; by the fourth day $35 - 3(4) = 35 - 12 = 23$ students remain; $P(\text{being chosen on the fourth day}) = \frac{4}{23}$.

41a. Three teams earned 97 points, there are 26 teams total; $P(\text{earning 97 points}) = \frac{3}{26}$.

41b. Eight teams earned less than 80 points, there are 26 teams total; $P(\text{earning less than 80 points}) = \frac{8}{26} = \frac{4}{13}$.

41c. Three teams earned more than 100 points, 23 did not; odds in favor of scoring more than 100 points = 3:23.

42.
$$\frac{300 - 9}{4} = \frac{r}{100}$$
$$\frac{291}{9} = \frac{r}{100}$$
$$29{,}100 = 9r$$
$$3233 \approx r$$
The percent of change is 3233%.

43.

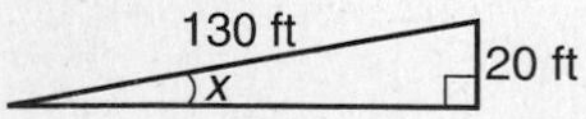

$$\sin x = \frac{20}{130}$$
$$\sin x \approx 0.1538$$
$$x \approx 9°$$

44.
$$\frac{5}{8}x + \frac{3}{5} = x$$
$$\frac{5}{8}x + \frac{3}{5} - \frac{5}{8}x = x - \frac{5}{8}x$$
$$\frac{3}{5} = x - \frac{5}{8}x$$
$$\frac{3}{5} = \frac{8}{8}x - \frac{5}{8}x$$
$$\frac{3}{5} = \frac{3}{8}x$$
$$\frac{8}{3}\left(\frac{3}{5}\right) = \frac{8}{3}\left(\frac{3}{8}\right)x$$
$$\frac{8}{5} = x$$
$\frac{8}{5}$; 1.6

45.

Activity	Amount of Money After Activity	Amount of Money Spent on Activity	Amount of Money Before Activity
Lunch	\$13	\$7	\$20
Haircut	\$20	\$20	\$40
Gasoline	\$40	$40 + \frac{1}{5}x$	x

Solve for x: $40 + \frac{1}{5}x = x$
$$40 = \frac{4}{5}x$$
$$50 = x$$
Kristin originally had \$50.

46. ± 42

47. $\frac{17}{21} + \left(-\frac{13}{21}\right) = \frac{4}{21}$

48a.

Stem	Leaf
1	6 7 7 8 8 8 8 8 9 9 9 9 9 9 9
2	0 0 2 3 4 4 5 5 6 7 7
3	0 2 3 3 5 6
4	5 8
5	5

3|5 = 35

48b. 35 people

48c. $55 - 16 = 39$ years

48d. 19 years

48e. teens

49.
$$8(a - c)^2 + 3 = 8(6 - 3)^2 + 3$$
$$= 8(3)^2 + 3$$
$$= 8(9) + 3$$
$$= 72 + 3$$
$$= 75$$

4-7 Weighted Averages

Page 236 Check for Understanding

1. d = distance, r = rate, t = time
2. to organize information and model the situation
3. See students' work.
4.

	Amount of Solution (mL)	Amount of Copper Sulfate
25% solution	40	0.25(40)
60% solution	x	$0.60x$
30% solution	$40 + x$	$0.30(40 + x)$

$$0.25(40) + 0.60x = 0.30(40 + x)$$
$$10 + 0.60x = 12 + 0.30x$$
$$0.30x = 2$$
$$x \approx 6.7 \text{ mL}$$
Joshua should add about 6.7 mL.

5.

	Number of Dozen	Price Per Dozen	Total Price
peanut butter	$85 + c$	\$6.50	$6.5(85 + c)$
chocolate chip	c	\$9.00	$9c$

$$\begin{aligned} 6.5(85 + c) + 9c &= 4055.50 \\ 552.5 + 6.5c + 9c &= 4055.5 \\ 15.5c &= 3503 \\ c &= 226 \end{aligned}$$

There were 226 dozen chocolate chip cookies sold. There were 85 + 226, or 311 dozen peanut butter cookies sold.

6.

Plane	r	t	d
Eastbound	$\frac{1000}{2} = 500$	2	1000
Southbound	$\frac{1000}{3}$	3	1000

$$M = \frac{500(2) + \frac{1000}{3}(3)}{5} = \frac{2000}{5} \text{ or } 400$$

The average speed of the airplane was 400 miles per hour.

7.

Boat	r	t	d
Yankee Clipper	8	t	$8t$
Riverboat Rover	10	$t - \frac{1}{2}$	$10\left(t - \frac{1}{2}\right)$

$$\begin{aligned} 8t &= 10\left(t - \tfrac{1}{2}\right) \\ 8t &= 10t - 5 \\ 8t + 5 &= 10t \\ 5 &= 2t \\ 2.5 &= t \end{aligned}$$

9:00 A.M. + 2.5 hrs = 11:30 A.M.

At 11:30 A.M. *The Riverboat Rover* will overtake *The Yankee Clipper.*

Pages 237–238 Exercises

8. $$\begin{aligned} 4r + 6(480 - r) &= 2340 \\ 4r + 2880 - 6r &= 2340 \\ 2880 - 2r &= 2340 \\ -2r &= -540 \\ r &= 270 \end{aligned}$$

They sold 270 rolls of solid gift wrap and 480 − 270 or 210 rolls of print gift wrap.

9.

	Number of Coins	Value	Total Value
dimes	$8 + q$	\$0.10	$0.10(8 + q)$
quarters	q	\$0.25	$0.25q$

$$\begin{aligned} 0.10(8 + q) + 0.25q &= 2.55 \\ 0.80 + 0.10q + 0.25q &= 2.55 \\ 0.80 + 0.35q &= 2.55 \\ 0.35q &= 1.75 \\ q &= 5 \end{aligned}$$

Rochelle has 5 quarters.

10.

	Number of Pounds	Price Per Pound	Total Price
walnuts	10	\$4.00	10(4)
cashews	c	\$7.00	7c
mixture	$c + 10$	\$ 5.50	$5.5(c + 10)$

$$\begin{aligned} 10(4) + 7c &= 5.5(c + 10) \\ 40 + 7c &= 5.5c + 55 \\ 1.5c &= 15 \\ c &= 10 \end{aligned}$$

10 pounds of cashews should be mixed with the 10 pounds of walnuts.

11.

	r	t	d
Ryan	57	t	$57t$
Jessica	65	t	$65t$

$$\begin{aligned} 57t + 65t &= 366 \\ 122t &= 366 \\ t &= 3 \end{aligned}$$

In 3 hours they will be 366 miles apart.

12.

	r	t	d
Bart	50	$t - \frac{3}{4}$	$50\left(t - \frac{3}{4}\right)$
Brooke	35	t	$35t$

$$\begin{aligned} 50\left(t - \tfrac{3}{4}\right) &= 35t \\ 50t - 37.5 &= 35t \\ -37.5 &= -15t \\ 2.5 &= t \end{aligned}$$

Bart will catch up with Brooke after 2.5 hours at 9:30 A.M.

13.

	r	t	d
Cyclist 1	20	t	$20t$
Cyclist 2	14	t	$14t$

$$\begin{aligned} 20t - 14t &= 15 \\ 6t &= 15 \\ t &= 2.5 \end{aligned}$$

They will be 15 miles apart after 2.5 hours.

14.

	Number of Tickets	Cost Per Ticket	Total Cost
adults	a	22	$22a$
students	$8 - a$	19	$19(8 - a)$

$$\begin{aligned} 22a + 19(8 - a) &= 167 \\ 22a + 152 - 19a &= 167 \\ 3a + 152 &= 167 \\ 3a &= 15 \\ a &= 5 \end{aligned}$$

The station can buy 5 adult tickets and 8 − 5, or 3 student tickets.

15.

	r	t	d
Pablo	40	5	40(5)
Ricardo	r	5	$5r$

$$\begin{aligned} 40(5) + 30 &= 5r \\ 200 + 30 &= 5r \\ 230 &= 5r \\ 46 &= r \end{aligned}$$

Ricardo must drive 46 miles per hour to catch up to Pablo in 5 hours.

16.

	Amount of Solution (quarts)	Amount of Pure Antifreeze
25% solution	$16 - x$	$0.25(16 - x)$
100% solution	x	$1.0x$
40% solution	16	$0.4(16)$

$$0.25(16 - x) + 1.0x = 0.4(16)$$
$$4 + 0.75x = 6.4$$
$$0.75x = 2.4$$
$$x = 3.2$$

3.2 quarts should be drained off and replaced.

17.

	r	t	d
patrol car	70	$\frac{1}{12}$	$d + \frac{1}{4}$
other car	r	$\frac{1}{12}$	d

$$70\left(\frac{1}{12}\right) = d + \frac{1}{4} \qquad r\left(\frac{1}{12}\right) = d$$
$$\frac{70}{12} = d + \frac{1}{4} \qquad r\left(\frac{1}{12}\right) = \frac{67}{12}$$
$$\frac{67}{12} = d \qquad r = 67$$

The other driver was going 67 miles per hour.

18.

	r	t	d
express	80	t	$80t$
local	48	$t + 2$	$48(t + 2)$

$$80t = 48(t + 2)$$
$$80t = 48t + 96$$
$$32t = 96$$
$$t = 3$$

Ironton and Wildwood are 3(80) or 240 km apart.

19a. $M = \frac{4(4) + 3(2) + 3(1) + 1(4) + 2(3)}{5}$

$= \frac{16 + 6 + 3 + 4 + 6}{5} = \frac{35}{5} = 7$

19b. 4(4) or 16 is the highest rating.

20. $M = \frac{4(2.5) + 3(2)}{4.5} = \frac{10 + 6}{4.5} = \frac{16}{4.5} \approx 3.56$

21. Sample answer: How much pure antifreeze must be mixed with a 20% solution to produce 40 quarts of a 28% solution?

22.

	r	t	d
Monday	40	$t + \frac{1}{60}$	$40\left(t + \frac{1}{60}\right)$
Tuesday	45	$t - \frac{1}{60}$	$45\left(t - \frac{1}{60}\right)$

$$40\left(t + \frac{1}{60}\right) = 45\left(t - \frac{1}{60}\right) \qquad 40\left(\frac{17}{60} + \frac{1}{60}\right) = 40\left(\frac{18}{60}\right)$$
$$40t + \frac{40}{60} = 45t - \frac{45}{60} \qquad = 12$$
$$\frac{85}{60} = 5t$$
$$\frac{17}{60} = t$$

Monica drives 12 miles to work.

23. $P(\text{number less than } 1) = \frac{0}{6} = 0$

24. 60% of 7500 = 0.60(7500)
= 4500

The company sold 7500 + 4500 or 12,000 bats in 1995.

25. Let n = amount invested at 8%.
Then $16{,}000 - n$ = amount invested at 5%.

$$0.08n + 0.05(16{,}000 - n) = 1130$$
$$0.08n + 800 - 0.05n = 1130$$
$$0.03n = 330$$
$$n = 11{,}000$$

Selena should invest \$11,000 at 8%.

26. $\frac{\frac{1}{87}}{1} = \frac{8}{x}$

$\frac{1}{87}x = 8$

$x = 8(87)$ or 696

The real locomotive is $\frac{696}{12}$, or 58 feet long.

27.
$$5.3 - 0.3x = -9.4$$
$$5.3 - 0.3 - 5.3x = -9.4 - 5.3$$
$$-0.3x = -14.7$$
$$x = 49$$

28. $24 = -2a$

$\frac{24}{-2} = \frac{-2a}{-2}$

$-12 = a$

29. associative (+)

4-8 Direct and Inverse Variation

Pages 242–243 Check for Understanding

1. inverse
2. $y = kx$, where $k \neq 0$
3. Divide each side of $y = kx$ by x.
4. No, because growth rates vary widely.
5. inverse, constant of variation = 5
6. direct, constant of variation = -3

7.
$$\frac{y_1}{y_2} = \frac{x_1}{x_2}$$
$$\frac{27}{45} = \frac{6}{x_2}$$
$$27x_2 = 45(6)$$
$$27x_2 = 270$$
$$x_2 = 10$$

Thus, $x = 10$ when $y = 45$.

8.
$$\frac{y_1}{y_2} = \frac{x_1}{x_2}$$
$$\frac{-7}{y_2} = \frac{-14}{20}$$
$$-7(20) = -14y_2$$
$$-140 = -14y_2$$
$$10 = y_2$$

Thus, $y = 10$ when $x = 20$.

9.
$$x_1y_1 = x_2y_2$$
$$11(99) = x_2(11)$$
$$1089 = 11x_2$$
$$99 = x_2$$

Thus, $x = 99$ when $y = 11$.

10.
$$x_1y_1 = x_2y_2$$
$$-2(-6) = 5(y_2)$$
$$12 = 5y_2$$
$$\frac{12}{5} = y_2$$

Thus, $y = \frac{12}{5}$ when $x = 5$.

11.
$$x_1y_1 = x_2y_2$$
$$8x = 10(36 - x)$$
$$8x = 360 - 10x$$
$$18x = 360$$
$$x = 20$$

20 inches from the 8-ounce weight, 36 − 20 or 16 inches from the 10-ounce weight.

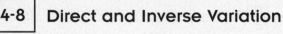

Pages 243–244 Exercises

12. direct, constant of variation = 3.14
13. inverse, constant of variation = 15
14. inverse, constant of variation = 35
15. inverse, constant of variation = 9
16. direct, constant of variation = $\frac{1}{3}$
17. direct, constant of variation = 4

18.
$$\frac{y_1}{y_2} = \frac{x_1}{x_2}$$
$$\frac{-8}{6} = \frac{-3}{x_2}$$
$$-8x_2 = -3(6)$$
$$-8x_2 = -18$$
$$x_2 = 2.25$$
Thus, $x = 2.25$ or $2\frac{1}{4}$ when $y = 6$.

19.
$$\frac{y_1}{y_2} = \frac{x_1}{x_2}$$
$$\frac{12}{21} = \frac{15}{x_2}$$
$$12x_2 = 15(21)$$
$$12x_2 = 315$$
$$x_2 = 26.25$$
Thus, $x = 26.25$ or $26\frac{1}{4}$ when $y = 21$.

20.
$$\frac{y_1}{y_2} = \frac{x_1}{x_2}$$
$$\frac{2.5}{y_2} = \frac{0.5}{20}$$
$$0.5y_2 = 20(2.5)$$
$$0.5y_2 = 50$$
$$y_2 = 100$$
Thus, $y = 100$ when $x = 20$.

21.
$$\frac{y_1}{y_2} = \frac{x_1}{x_2}$$
$$\frac{4}{y_2} = \frac{12}{-24}$$
$$4(-24) = 12y_2$$
$$-96 = 12y_2$$
$$-8 = y_2$$
Thus, $y = -8$ when $x = -24$.

22.
$$\frac{y_1}{y_2} = \frac{x_1}{x_2}$$
$$\frac{-6}{y_2} = \frac{9}{6}$$
$$-6(6) = 9y_2$$
$$-36 = 9y_2$$
$$-4 = y_2$$
Thus, $y = -4$ when $x = 6$.

23.
$$\frac{y_1}{y_2} = \frac{x_1}{x_2}$$
$$\frac{2\frac{2}{3}}{y_2} = \frac{\frac{1}{4}}{1\frac{1}{8}}$$
$$2\frac{2}{3}\left(1\frac{1}{8}\right) = \frac{1}{4}y_2$$
$$\frac{8}{3}\left(\frac{9}{8}\right) = \frac{1}{4}y_2$$
$$3 = \frac{1}{4}y_2$$
$$12 = y_2$$
Thus, $y = 12$ when $x = 1\frac{1}{8}$.

24.
$$x_1y_1 = x_2y_2$$
$$8(9) = 6(y_2)$$
$$72 = 6y_2$$
$$12 = y_2$$
Thus, $y = 12$ when $x = 6$.

25.
$$x_1y_1 = x_2y_2$$
$$2.7(8.1) = 3.6(y_2)$$
$$21.87 = 3.6y_2$$
$$6.075 = y_2$$
Thus, $y = 6.075$ when $x = 3.6$.

26.
$$x_1y_1 = x_2y_2$$
$$-8(24) = 4(y_2)$$
$$-192 = 4y_2$$
$$-48 = y_2$$
Thus, $y = -48$ when $x = 4$.

27.
$$x_1y_1 = x_2y_2$$
$$6.1(4.4) = x_2(3.2)$$
$$26.84 = 3.2x_2$$
$$8.3875 = x_2$$
Thus, $x = 8.3875$ when $y = 3.2$.

28.
$$x_1y_1 = x_2y_2$$
$$\frac{2}{3}(7) = 7(y_2)$$
$$\frac{14}{3} = 7y_2$$
$$\frac{2}{3} = y_2$$
Thus, $y = \frac{2}{3}$ when $x = 7$.

29.
$$x_1y_1 = x_2y_2$$
$$\frac{1}{2}(16) = x_2(32)$$
$$8 = 32x_2$$
$$\frac{1}{4} = x_2$$
Thus, $x = \frac{1}{4}$ when $y = 32$.

30a. It is halved.

30b. It is divided by 3.

31.
$$\frac{y_1}{y_2} = \frac{x_1}{x_2}$$
$$\frac{360}{108} = \frac{60}{x_2}$$
$$360x_2 = 60(108)$$
$$360x_2 = 6480$$
$$x_2 = 18$$
Tara would weigh 18 pounds on the moon.

32.
$$x_1y_1 + x_2y_2 = x_3y_3$$
$$6(115) + 8(120) = 10y_3$$
$$690 + 960 = 10y_3$$
$$1650 = 10y_3$$
$$165 = y_3$$
Kam weighs 165 pounds.

33.
$$x_1y_1 = x_2y_2$$
$$440(2.4) = 660y_2$$
$$1056 = 660y_2$$
$$1.6 = y_2$$
A pitch of 660 vibrations per second has a wavelength of 1.6 feet.

34.

	r	***t***	***d***
Alma	35	t	$35t$
Reiko	42	$t - 1$	$42(t - 1)$

$$35t + 42(t - 1) = 266$$
$$35t + 42t - 42 = 266$$
$$77t - 42 = 266$$
$$77t = 308$$
$$t = 4 \text{ hours}$$
8:00AM + 4 hours = 12:00 noon

They will be 266 miles apart at 12:00 noon.

35. number of successes = 2, number of failures = 3 − 2 = 1; odds that the event will occur = 2:1.

36. Let x = the wholesale price.
$$x + 0.25x = 79$$
$$1.25x = 79$$
$$x = 63.20$$
The wholesale price was $63.20.

37. Let n = the amount invested at 5%. Then 11,700 − n = the amount invested at 7%.
$$0.05n + 0.07(11{,}700 - n) = 733$$
$$0.05n + 819 - 0.07n = 733$$
$$-0.02n + 819 = 733$$
$$-0.02n = -86$$
$$n = 4300$$
Hiroko invested $4300 at 5% and 11,700 − 4300 or $7400 at 7%.

38. $\frac{2x}{5} + \frac{x}{4} = \frac{26}{5}$

$\frac{8x}{20} + \frac{5x}{20} = \frac{26}{5}$

$\frac{13x}{20} = \frac{26}{5}$

$\left(\frac{20}{13}\right)\left(\frac{13x}{20}\right) = \left(\frac{26}{5}\right)\left(\frac{20}{13}\right)$

$x = 8$

39. $\frac{x}{4} + 9 = 6$

$\frac{x}{4} + 9 - 9 = 6 - 9$

$\frac{x}{4} = -3$

$(4)\left(\frac{x}{4}\right) = -3(4)$

$x = -12$

40. $\frac{4a + 32}{4} = \frac{4a}{4} + \frac{32}{4}$

$= a + 8$

Chapter 4 Highlights

Page 245 Understanding and Using the Vocabulary

1. angle of elevation
2. proportion
3. equal, proportional
4. can
5. legs
6. means
7. odds
8. percentage, base
9. inverse variation
10. opposite, adjacent side

Chapter 4 Study Guide and Assessment

Pages 246–248 Skills and Concepts

11. $10 \cdot 45 = 3 \cdot 150$

$450 = 450$

So, $\frac{10}{3} = \frac{150}{45}$.

This is a proportion.

12. $8(1.75) = 7 \cdot 2$

$14 = 14$

So, $\frac{8}{7} = \frac{2}{1.75}$.

This is a proportion.

13. $20 \cdot 4 = 12 \cdot 5$

$80 \neq 60$

Since $80 \neq 60$, $\frac{30}{12} \neq \frac{5}{4}$.

This is not a proportion.

14. $2.7(9.3) = 3.1(8.1)$

$25.11 = 25.11$

So, $\frac{2.7}{3.1} = \frac{8.1}{9.3}$.

This is a proportion.

15. $\frac{6}{15} = \frac{n}{45}$

$6(45) = 15n$

$270 = 15n$

$18 = n$

16. $\frac{x}{11} = \frac{35}{55}$

$55x = 11(35)$

$55x = 385$

$x = 7$

17. $\frac{y + 4}{y - 1} = \frac{4}{3}$

$3(y + 4) = 4(y - 1)$

$3y + 12 = 4y - 4$

$12 = y - 4$

$16 = y$

18. $\frac{z - 7}{6} = \frac{z + 3}{7}$

$7(z - 7) = 6(z + 3)$

$7z - 49 = 6z + 18$

$z - 49 = 18$

$z = 67$

19. $\frac{a}{d} = \frac{c}{f}$

$\frac{10}{d} = \frac{16}{9}$

$10(9) = 16d$

$90 = 16d$

$\frac{45}{8} = d$

$\frac{f}{c} = \frac{e}{b}$

$\frac{9}{16} = \frac{e}{12}$

$9(12) = 16e$

$108 = 16e$

$\frac{27}{4} = e$

20. $\frac{c}{f} = \frac{a}{d}$

$\frac{10}{12} = \frac{8}{d}$

$10d = 12(8)$

$10d = 96$

$d = \frac{48}{5}$

$\frac{c}{f} = \frac{b}{e}$

$\frac{10}{12} = \frac{6}{e}$

$10e = 12(6)$

$10e = 72$

$e = \frac{36}{5}$

21. $\frac{f}{c} = \frac{e}{b}$

$\frac{9}{12} = \frac{11}{b}$

$9b = 12(11)$

$9b = 132$

$b = \frac{44}{3}$

$\frac{c}{f} = \frac{a}{d}$

$\frac{12}{9} = \frac{8}{d}$

$12d = 9(8)$

$12d = 72$

$d = 6$

22. $\frac{f}{c} = \frac{d}{a}$

$\frac{6}{15} = \frac{7}{a}$

$6a = 15(7)$

$6a = 105$

$a = \frac{35}{2}$

$\frac{c}{f} = \frac{b}{e}$

$\frac{15}{6} = \frac{20}{e}$

$15e = 6(20)$

$15e = 120$

$e = 8$

23. $\cos B = \frac{45}{53} \approx 0.528$

24. $\tan A = \frac{28}{45} \approx 0.622$

25. $\sin B = \frac{45}{53} \approx 0.849$

26. $\cos A = \frac{45}{53} \approx 0.849$

27. $\tan B = \frac{45}{28} \approx 1.607$

28. $\sin A = \frac{28}{53} \approx 0.528$

29. 39°
30. 7°
31. 80°
32. 42°

33. $m\angle B = 90° - 45° = 45°$

$\cos 45° = \frac{6}{AB}$

$0.7071 \approx \frac{6}{AB}$

$0.7071AB \approx 6$

$AB \approx 8.5$

$\tan 45° = \frac{BC}{6}$

$1 = \frac{BC}{6}$

$1(6) = BC$

$6 = BC$

34. $m\angle B = 90° - 78° = 12°$

$\cos 78° = \frac{28}{AB}$

$0.2079 \approx \frac{28}{AB}$

$0.2079AB \approx 28$

$AB \approx 134.7$

$\tan 78° = \frac{BC}{28}$

$4.7046 \approx \frac{BC}{28}$

$4.7046(28) \approx BC$

$131.7 \approx BC$

35. $\tan A = \frac{9}{4}$

$\tan A = 2.25$

$m\angle A \approx 66°$

$\tan B = \frac{4}{9}$

$\tan B \approx 0.444$

$m\angle B \approx 24°$

$\sin 66° = \frac{9}{AB}$

$0.9135AB \approx 9$

$AB \approx 9.8$

36. $m\angle B = 90° - 30° = 60°$

$\cos 30° = \frac{AC}{26}$

$0.8660 \approx \frac{AC}{26}$

$0.8660(26) \approx AC$

$22.5 \approx AC$

$\sin 30° = \frac{BC}{26}$

$0.5 = \frac{BC}{26}$

$0.5(26) = BC$

$13 = BC$

37. $\frac{60}{100} = \frac{r}{80}$

$60(80) = 100r$

$4800 = 100r$

$48 = r$

60% of 80 is 48.

38. $\frac{21}{r} = \frac{35}{100}$

$35r = 21(100)$

$35r = 2100$

$r = 60$

21 is 35% of 60.

39. $\frac{84}{96} = \frac{r}{100}$

$84(100) = 96r$

$8400 = 96r$

$87.5 = r$

84 is 87.5% of 96.

40. $\frac{34}{17} = \frac{r}{100}$

$34(100) = 17r$

$3400 = 17r$

$200 = r$

34 is 200% of 17.

41. $\frac{r}{62.7} = \frac{0.3}{100}$

$100r = 62.7(0.3)$

$100r = 18.81$

$r = 0.1881$

0.1881 is 0.3% of 62.7.

42. $\frac{r}{5200} = \frac{0.12}{100}$

$100r = 5200(0.12)$

$100r = 624$

$r = 6.24$

0.12% of $5200 is $6.24.

43. decrease

$\frac{40 - 35}{40} = \frac{r}{100}$

$\frac{5}{40} = \frac{r}{100}$

$500 = 40r$

$12.5 = r$

The percent of decrease is about 13%.

44. increase

$\frac{115 - 97}{97} = \frac{r}{100}$

$\frac{18}{97} = \frac{r}{100}$

$1800 = 97r$

$18.6 \approx r$

The percent of increase is about 19%.

45. increase

$\frac{37.10 - 35}{35} = \frac{r}{100}$

$\frac{2.10}{35} = \frac{r}{100}$

$210 = 35r$

$6 = r$

The percent of increase is 6%.

46. increase

$\frac{88 - 50}{50} = \frac{r}{100}$

$\frac{38}{50} = \frac{r}{100}$

$3800 = 50r$

$76 = r$

The percent of increase is 76%.

47. decrease

$\frac{1500 - 1350}{1500} = \frac{r}{100}$

$\frac{150}{1500} = \frac{r}{100}$

$1500r = 15{,}000$

$r = 10$

The percent of decrease is 10%.

48. decrease

$\frac{12{,}500 - 11{,}800}{12{,}500} = \frac{r}{100}$

$\frac{700}{12{,}500} = \frac{r}{100}$

$12{,}500r = 70{,}000$

$r = 5.6$

The percent of decrease is about 6%.

49. 5.75% of $81 = 0.0575(81)
≈ 4.66

$81 + $4.66 = $85.66

The total price is $85.66.

50. 2% of $21.50 = 0.02(21.50)
= 0.43

$21.50 − $0.43 = $21.07

The total price is $21.07.

51. 6.7% of $8690 = 0.067(8690)
= 582.23

$8690 + $582.23 = $9272.23

The total price is $9272.23.

52. 25% of $89 = 0.25(89)
= 22.25

$89 − $22.25 = $66.75

7% of $66.75 = 0.07(66.75)
≈ 4.67

$66.75 + $4.67 = $71.42

The total price is $71.42.

53. There are 12 letters, 1 is the letter S; $P(\text{letter S}) = \frac{1}{12}$.

54. There are 12 letters, 3 are the letter E; $P(\text{letter E}) = \frac{3}{12}$ or $\frac{1}{4}$.

55. There are 12 letters, 10 are not N; $P(\text{not N}) = \frac{10}{12}$ or $\frac{5}{6}$.

56. There are 12 letters, 3 are the letters R or P; $P(\text{letters R or P}) = \frac{3}{12}$ or $\frac{1}{4}$.

57. There are 50 dimes, 195 other coins; odds of selecting a dime = 50:195 or 10:39.

58. There are 90 pennies, 155 other coins; odds of selecting a penny = 90:155 or 18:31.

59. There are 170 coins that are not nickels, 75 nickels; odds of selecting a nickel = 170:75 or 34:15.

60. There are 125 nickels and dimes, 120 other coins; odds of selecting a nickel or dime = 125:120 or 25:24.

61. $\frac{y_1}{y_2} = \frac{x_1}{x_2}$

$\frac{15}{y_2} = \frac{5}{7}$

$15(7) = 5y_2$

$105 = 5y_2$

$21 = y_2$

Thus, $y = 21$ when $x = 7$.

62. $\frac{y_1}{y_2} = \frac{x_1}{x_2}$

$\frac{35}{y_2} = \frac{175}{75}$

$35(75) = 175y_2$

$2625 = 175y_2$

$15 = y_2$

Thus, $y = 15$ when $x = 75$.

63. $\frac{y_1}{y_2} = \frac{x_1}{x_2}$

$\frac{10}{80} = \frac{0.75}{x_2}$

$10x_2 = 80(0.75)$

$10x_2 = 60$

$x_2 = 6$

Thus, $x = 6$ when $y = 80$.

64. $\frac{y_1}{y_2} = \frac{x_1}{x_2}$

$\frac{3}{y_2} = \frac{99.9}{522.81}$

$3(522.81) = 99.9y_2$

$1568.43 = 99.9y_2$

$15.7 = y_2$

Thus, $y = 15.7$ when $x = 522.81$.

65. $x_1y_1 = x_2y_2$

$28(42) = 56(y_2)$

$1176 = 56y_2$

$21 = y_2$

Thus, $y = 21$ when $x = 56$.

66. $x_1y_1 = x_2y_2$

$5(15) = 3(y_2)$

$75 = 3y_2$

$25 = y_2$

Thus, $y = 25$ when $x = 3$.

67. $x_1y_1 = x_2y_2$

$8(18) = x_2(3)$

$144 = 3x_2$

$48 = x_2$

Thus, $x = 48$ when $y = 3$.

68. $x_1y_1 = x_2y_2$

$175(35) = 75(y_2)$

$6125 = 75y_2$

$81.\overline{6} = y_2$

Thus, $y = 81.\overline{6}$ when $x = 75$.

Page 248 Applications and Problem Solving

69.

	r	*t*	*d*
plane 1	r	3	$3r$
plane 2	$r + 80$	3	$3(r + 80)$

$3r + 3(r + 80) = 2940$

$3r + 3r + 240 = 2940$

$6r + 240 = 2940$

$6r = 2700$

$r = 450$

$r + 80 = 450 + 80$
$= 530$

The rates of the airplanes are 450 mph and 530 mph.

70.

	Number of Pounds	Price Per Pound	Total Price
coffee 1	9	\$8.40	9(8.4)
coffee 2	x	\$7.28	$7.28x$
mixture	$x + 9$	\$7.95	$7.95(x + 9)$

$$9(8.4) + 7.28x = 7.95(x + 9)$$
$$75.6 + 7.28x = 7.95x + 71.55$$
$$75.6 = 0.67x + 71.55$$
$$4.05 = 0.67x$$
$$6.04 \approx x$$

She should mix 6 pounds of the \$7.28 coffee with 9 pounds of the \$8.40 coffee.

Page 249 Alternative Assessment: Thinking Critically

- Sample answer: When rolling a die, the odds of rolling a 6 are 1:5, since there is one chance of success (6) and five chances of failure (1, 2, 3, 4, or 5); the probability of rolling a 6 is $\frac{1}{6}$, since there is one chance of success (6) and six possible outcomes (1, 2, 3, 4, 5, or 6). Both odds and probability measure the chance of an event occurring.
- Sample answer: In a right triangle with acute angles A and B, the opposite side of A is the adjacent side of B.
  $$\sin A = \frac{\text{opposite side of } A}{\text{hypotenuse}} = \frac{\text{adjacent side of } B}{\text{hypotenuse}} = \cos B$$
  Likewise, the adjacent side of A is the opposite side of B.
  $$\cos A = \frac{\text{adjacent side of } A}{\text{hypotenuse}} = \frac{\text{opposite side of } B}{\text{hypotenuse}} = \sin B$$

Cumulative Review, Chapters 1–4

Pages 250–251

1.
$$7(3b + x) = 5a$$
$$21b + 7x = 5a$$
$$21b + 7x - 21b = 5a - 21b$$
$$7x = 5a - 21b$$
$$\frac{7x}{7} = \frac{5a - 21b}{7}$$
$$x = \frac{5a - 21b}{7} \quad \text{D}$$

2.
$$\frac{40 - 35}{40} = \frac{r}{100}$$
$$\frac{5}{40} = \frac{r}{100}$$
$$5(100) = 40r$$
$$500 = 40r$$
$$12.5\% = r \quad \text{B}$$

3.
$$2 - \left(1\tfrac{1}{4} - \tfrac{3}{8} + \tfrac{5}{6}\right) = 2 - \left(\tfrac{30}{24} - \tfrac{9}{24} + \tfrac{20}{24}\right)$$
$$= 2 - \left(\tfrac{41}{24}\right)$$
$$= \tfrac{48}{24} - \tfrac{41}{24}$$
$$= \tfrac{7}{24} \text{ feet} \quad \text{A}$$

4.
$$\frac{ED}{AB} = \frac{DC}{BC}$$
$$\frac{70}{AB} = \frac{80}{120} \quad \text{C}$$

5.
$$\frac{36 \text{ pages}}{2 \text{ hours}} = \frac{135 \text{ pages}}{x \text{ hours}}$$
$$36x = 2(135)$$
$$36x = 270$$
$$x = 7\tfrac{1}{2} \text{ hours} \quad \text{B}$$

6.
$$h = gb^2 - t$$
$$h + t = gb^2 - t + t$$
$$h + t = gb^2 \quad \text{D}$$

7. Let x = the number of prizes.
$$\frac{1}{6} = \frac{x}{180}$$
$$180 = 6x$$
$$30 = x$$
30 prizes are needed. C

8. $\frac{75}{100} = \frac{26.25}{x}$ A

9. Let x = her score for the last game.
$$\frac{(b+2) + (b+3) + (b-2) + (b-1) + x}{5} = b + 2$$
$$\frac{4b + 2 + x}{5} = b + 2$$
$$4b + 2 + x = 5(b + 2)$$
$$4b + 2 + x = 5b + 10$$
$$x = b + 8 \quad \text{D}$$

10. See students' work.

11. Let ℓ = the length of the rectangle.
Then $w = \ell - 5$.
$$P = 2\ell + 2w$$
$$70 = 2\ell + 2(\ell - 5)$$
$$70 = 2\ell + 2\ell - 10$$
$$70 = 4\ell - 10$$
$$80 = 4\ell$$
$$20 = \ell$$
The length is 20 in. and the width is 20 − 5 in.

12. \$428.79 − \$1097.31 + 2(\$691.53) − \$100
= 428.79 − 1097.31 + 1383.06 − 100
= \$614.54
The new balance in Marisa's account was \$614.54.

13. Let n = the amount invested at 12%.
Then $8000 - n$ = the amount invested at 8%.
$$0.12n + 0.08(8000 - n) = 760$$
$$0.12n + 640 - 0.08n = 760$$
$$0.04n + 640 = 760$$
$$0.04n = 120$$
$$n = 3000$$
Maria should invest \$3000 at 12% and \$8000 − \$3000 or \$5000 at 8%.

14. $t = \sqrt{\frac{d^3}{216}} = \sqrt{\frac{12^3}{216}} = \sqrt{\frac{1728}{216}} = \sqrt{8} \approx 2.8$ hrs
4:00 P.M. + 2.8 hrs = 4:00 + 2:48 = 6:48
No, since the rain will end about 6:50 P.M.

15. mean: $\frac{\text{sum of 24 values}}{24} = \frac{1139}{24} = 47.5$
median: 46 since both middle values are the same
mode: 35 and 63 since these values occur four times

16. See students' work.

17. Four years is the term for the President.
150% of 4 = 1.5(4)
= 6 years
The term of office for a United States Senator is 6 years.

18. $x_1y_1 = x_2y_2$
$126x = 154(16 - x)$
$126x = 2464 - 154x$
$280x = 2464$
$x = 8.8$
Shannon is 8.8 ft from the fulcrum.

19. Let x = one angle of a triangle.
Then $x + 15$ = another angle, and
$3[x + (x + 15)]$ = the third angle.
$x + x + 15 + 3[x + (x + 15)] = 180$
$x + x + 15 + 3(2x + 15) = 180$
$x + x + 15 + 6x + 45 = 180$
$8x + 60 = 180$
$8x = 120$
$x = 15$
The three angles measure 15°, 15° + 15° or 30°, and 3(45°) or 135°.

20. An adult blue whale weighs 37(12,000) or 444,000 pounds. A newborn blue whale weighs $\frac{1}{3}$(12,000) or 4000 pounds.
$4000 + 200x = 444,000$
$200x = 440,000$
$x = 2200$
It will take the newborn 2200 days to reach adult weight.

Chapter 5 Graphing Relations and Functions

5-1 The Coordinate Plane

Page 257 Check for Understanding

1. See coordinate plane on page 254.
2. (+, +), I; (−, +), II; (−, −), III; (+, −), IV
3. See students' work.
4. (5, 2); I
5. (−3, −1); III
6. (−2, 3); II
7. (0, −2); none

8–11.

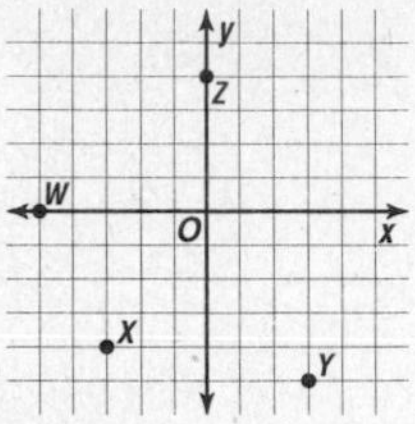

12. (−13, 15)

Pages 257–259 Exercises

13. (−1, −3); III
14. (−2, 0); none
15. (0, 3); none
16. (−4, 5); II
17. (0, 0); none
18. (5, −5); IV
19. (3, −2); IV
20. (2, 5); I
21. (2, 2); I
22. (4, 4); I
23. (−5, 4); II
24. (−2, −5); III

25-36.

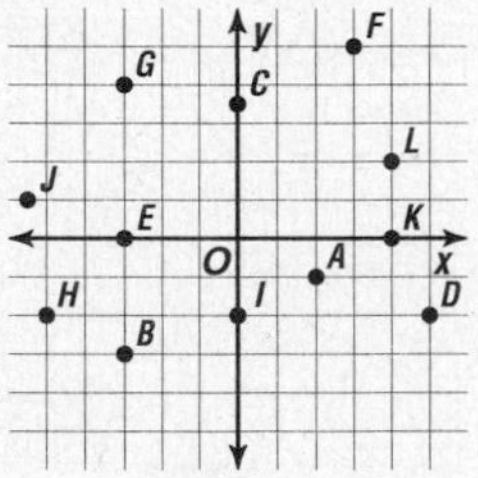

37.

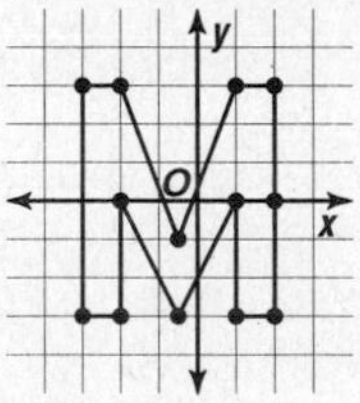

38.

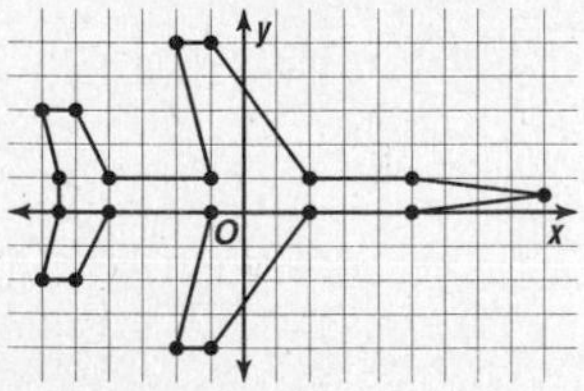

39. See students' work.

40a. If $xy > 0$, then x and y are both positive: Quadrant I, or x and y are both negative: Quadrant III.

40b. If $xy < 0$, then x is negative and y is positive: Quadrant II or x is positive and y is negative: Quadrant IV.

40c. If $xy = 0$, then $x = 0$: y-axis, or $y = 0$: x-axis.

41a. New Orleans 41b. Oregon

41c. Answers may vary. Sample answer: (75°, 40°)

41d. Honolulu, Hawaii 41e. See students' work.

41f. Sample answer: The longitude lines are not the same distance apart; they meet at the poles.

42a. John Kennedy 42b. (1, O) 42c. I-95

42d. (1, P), (1, O), (1, N), (1, M), (1, L), (2, L), (3, L)

43a. See students' work. 43b. See students' work.

44.
$$\frac{y1}{y_2} = \frac{x_1}{x_2}$$
$$\frac{3}{y_2} = \frac{15}{-25}$$
$$3(-25) = 15y_2$$
$$-75 = 15y_2$$
$$-5 = y_2$$

45.

Train	r	t	d
Northbound	40	t	$40t$
Southbound	30	t	$30t$

$$30t + 40t = 245$$
$$70t = 245$$
$$t = 3\tfrac{1}{2}$$

In $3\frac{1}{2}$ hours, the trains will be 245 miles apart.

46. 16°

47. mean: $\frac{5+9+1+2+3}{5} = 4$
median: 1 2 ③ 5 9 => 3 since it is the middle value
mode: none

48. $\frac{4}{5}$

49. $\frac{7a+35}{-7} = \frac{7a}{-7} + \frac{35}{-7}$
$= -a - 5$

50a. 65° 50b. 51° to 72°

51. $7(5a + 3b) - 4a = 7(5a) + 7(3b) - 4a$
$= 35a + 21b - 4a$
$= 35a - 4a + 21b$
$= 31a + 21b$

5-2A Graphing Technology Relations

Page 261 Exercises

1-6.

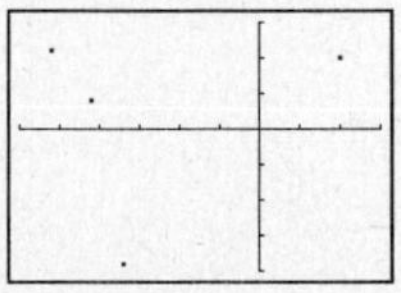

7. They are points on the axes.

8a.

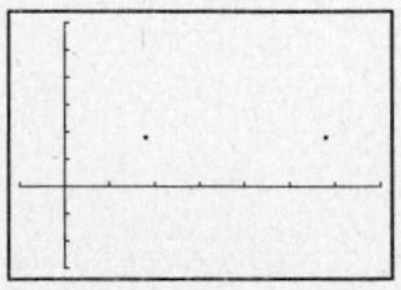

8b. $E(9, -11)$, $F(29, -11)$; $E(9, 29)$, $F(29, 29)$

8c.

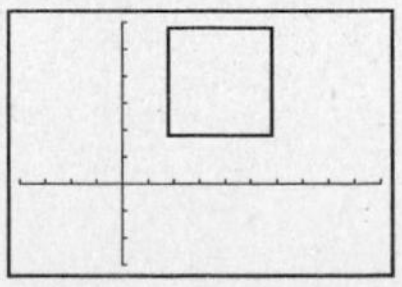

5-2 Relations

Page 266 Check for Understanding

1. The domain values are the *x* values and the range values are the *y* values. If you do not know which is which, your plots will be incorrect.
2. After a high in 1990, the number of deaths seems to be decreasing.
3. The domain of the relation becomes the range of the inverse. The range becomes the domain of the inverse.
4. 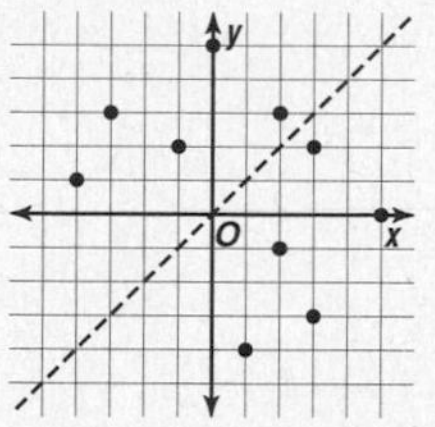

5. D = {0, 1, 2}; R = {2, −2, 4}
6. D = {−4, −2, 0, 2}; R = {2, 0, 4}
7. {(1, 3), (2, 4), (3, 5), (5, 7)}; D = {1, 2, 3, 5}; R = {3, 4, 5, 7}; Inv = {(3, 1), (4, 2), (5, 3), (7, 5)}
8. {(1, 4), (3, −2), (4, 4), (6, −2)}; D = {1, 3, 4, 6}; R = {−2, 4}; Inv = {(4, 1), (−2, 3), (4, 4), (−2, 6)}
9. {(1, 3), (2, 2), (4, 9), (6, 5)}; D − {1, 2, 4, 6}; R = {2, 3, 5, 9}; Inv = {(3, 1), (2, 2), (9, 4), (5, 6)}
10. {(−3, −2), (−2, −1), (0, 0), (1, 1)}; D = (−3, −2, 0, 1}; R = {−2, −1, 0, 1}; Inv = {(−2, −3), (−1, −2), (0, 0), (1, 1)}
11. {(−2, 2), (−1, 1), (0, 1), (1, 1), (1, −1), (2, −1), (3, 1)}; D = {−2, −1, 0, 1, 2, 3}; R = {−1, 1, 2}; Inv = {(2, −2), (1, −1), (1, 0), (1, 1), (−1, 1), (−1, 2), (1, 3)}
12. 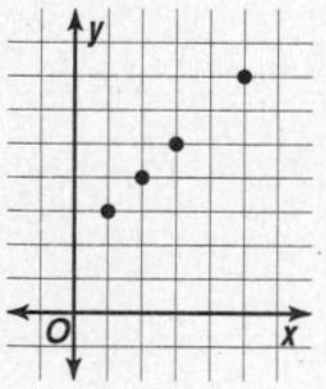

13. 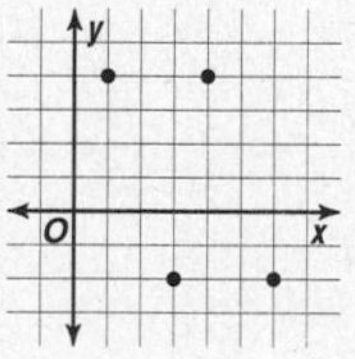

14. 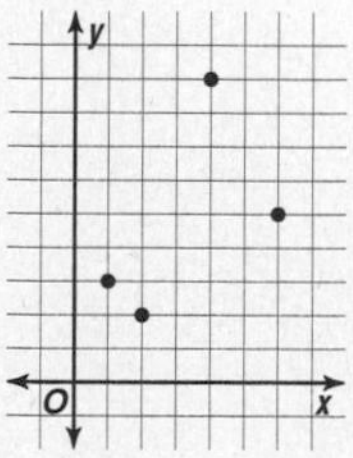

15a. See students' work.

15b. 5.6%

15c. Except for the first 6 months of 1992, the unemployment rate seems to be decreasing.

Pages 267–269 Exercises

16. D = {1, 2, 3}; R = {−7, 3, 5, 9}
17. D = {−5, −2, 1, 3}; R = {7}
18. D = {−9, −4.7, 2.4, 3.1}; R = {−3.6, −1, 2, 3.9}
19. $D = \left\{-5\frac{1}{4}, -3, \frac{1}{2}, 1\frac{1}{2}\right\}$; $R = \left\{-6\frac{2}{7}, -\frac{2}{3}, \frac{1}{4}, \frac{2}{5}\right\}$
20. {(0, 4), (1, 5), (2, 6), (3, 6)}; D = {0, 1, 2, 3}; R = {4, 5, 6}; Inv = {(4, 0), (5, 1), (6, 2), (6, 3)}
21. {(6, 4), (4, −2), (3, 4), (1, −2)}; D = {1, 3, 4, 6}; R = {−2, 4}; Inv = {(4, 6), (−2, 4), (4, 3), (−2, 1)}
22. {(−4, 2), (−2, 0), (0, 2), (2, 4)}; D = {−4, −2, 0, 2}; R = {0, 2, 4}; Inv = {(2, −4), (0, −2), (2, 0), (4, 2)}
23. {(6, 0), (−3, 5), (2,−2), (−3, 3)}; D = {−3, 2, 6}; R = {−2, 0, 3, 5}; Inv = {(0, 6), (5, −3), (−2, 2), (3, −3)}
24. {(5, 2), (−3, 1), (2, 2), (1, 7)}; D = {−3, 1, 2, 5}; R = {1, 2, 7}; Inv = {(2, 5), (1, −3), (2, 2), (7, 1)}
25. {(3, 4), (3, 2), (2, 9), (5, 4), (5, 8), (−7, 2)}; D = {−7, 2, 3, 5}; R = {2, 4, 8, 9}; Inv = {(4, 3), (2, 3), (9, 2), (4, 5), (8, 5), (2, −7)}
26. {(0, 100), (5, 90), (10, 81), (15, 73), (20, 66), (25, 60), (30, 55)}; D = {0, 5, 10, 15, 20, 25, 30}; R= {55, 60, 66, 73, 81, 90, 100}; Inv = {(100, 0), (90, 5), (81, 10), (73, 15), (66, 20), (60, 25) (55, 30)}
27. {(0, 25), (1, 50), (2, 75), (3, 100)}; D = {0, 1, 2, 3}; R = {25, 50, 75, 100}; Inv = {(25, 0), (50, 1), (75, 2), (100, 3)}
28. {(1.25, 68.75), (3.75, 206.25), (4.5, 247.5), (5.5, 302.5), (6, 330)}; D = {1.25, 3.75, 4.5, 5.5, 6}; R = {68.75, 206.25, 247.5, 302.5, 330}; Inv = {(68.75, 1.25), (206.25, 3.75), (247.5, 4.5), (302.5, 5.5), (330, 6)}
29. {(−3, 4), (−2, 2), (−1, −2), (2, 2)}; D = {−3, −2, −1, 2}; R = {−2, 2, 4}; Inv = {(4, −3), (2, −2), (−2, −1), (2, 2)}
30. {(−3, 3), (2, 4), (3, 1), (3, −3), (1, −3), (−2, −3)}; D = {−3, −2, 1, 2, 3}; R = {−3, 1, 3, 4}; Inv = {(3, −3), (4, 2), (1, 3), (−3, 3), (−3, 1), (−3, −2)}
31. {(−3, 3), (−3, −3), (3, 3), (3, −3), (0, 0)}; D = {−3, 0, 3}; R = {−3, 0, 3}; Inv = {(3, −3), (−3, −3), (3, 3), (−3, 3), (0, 0)}
32. {(−3, −2), (−2, −1), (−1, 0), (1, 2), (2, 3), (3, 4)}; D = {−3, −2, −1, 1, 2, 3}; R = {−2, −1, 0, 2, 3, 4}; Inv = {(−2, −3), (−1, −2), (0, −1), (2, 1), (3, 2), (4, 3)}
33. {(−3, 1), (−1, 1), (2, 1), (3, 1), (4, 1)}; D = {−3, −1, 2, 3, 4}; R = {1}; Inv = {(1, −3), (1, −1), (1, 2), (1, 3), (1, 4)}
34. {(−2, 4), (−2, 2), (−2, 0), (2, 0), (2, −2), (2, −4)}; D = {−2, 2}; R = {−4, −2, 0, 2, 4}; Inv = {(4, −2), (2, −2), (0, −2), (0, 2), (−2, 2), (−4, 2)}
35. 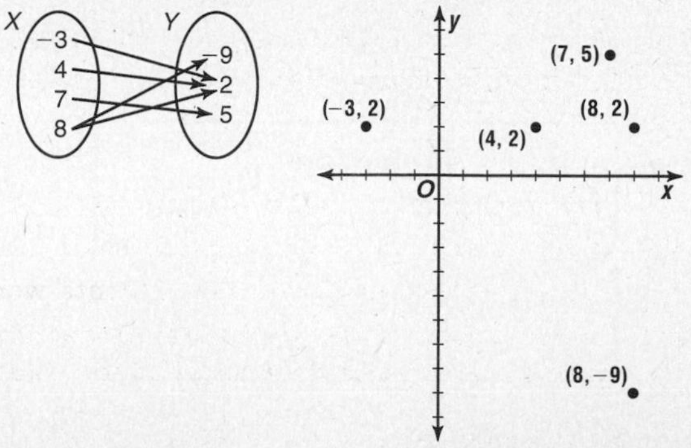

36.
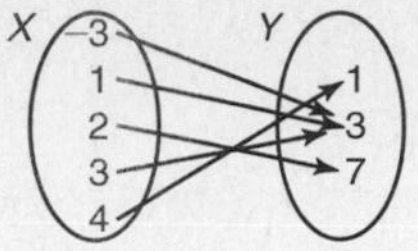

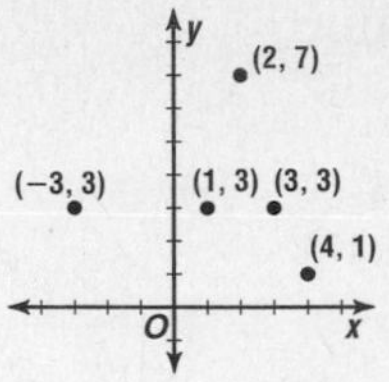

37.
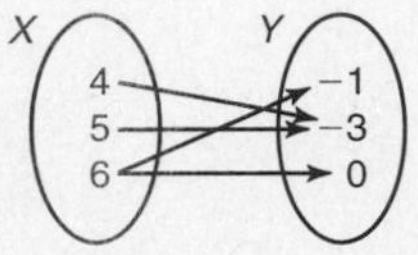

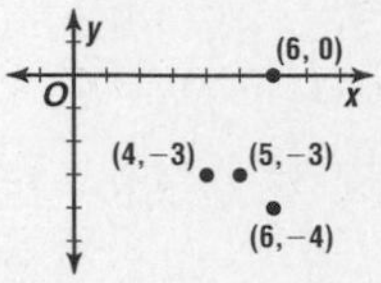

38-40. Windows and graphs may vary. Sample answers are given.

38a. [1991, 1996] by [0, 900]

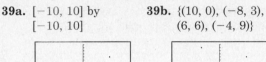

38b. {(77, 1992), (200, 1993), (550, 1994), (880, 1995)}

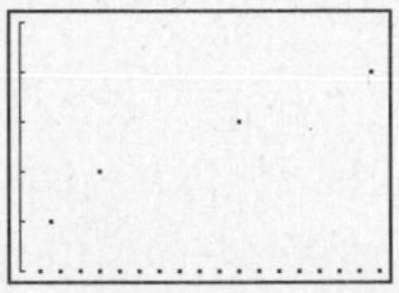

38c. All points lie in Quadrant I.

39a. [−10, 10] by [−10, 10]

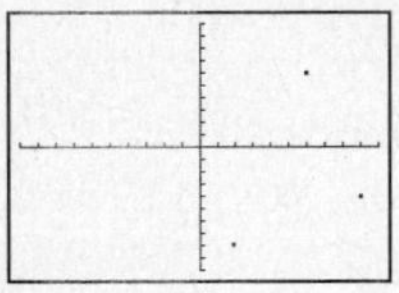

39b. {(10, 0), (−8, 3), (6, 6), (−4, 9)}

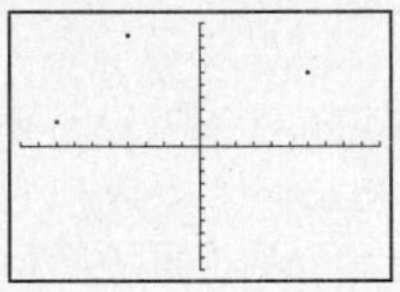

39c.

(x, y)	Quadrant	Inverse's Quadrant
(0, 10)	I	I
(3, −8)	IV	II
(6, 6)	I	I
(9, −4)	IV	II

40a. [−8, 4] by [−4, 36]

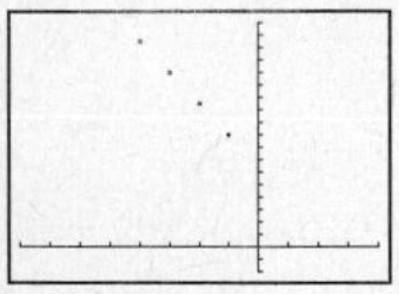

40b. {(18, −1), (23, −2), (28, −3), (33, −4)}

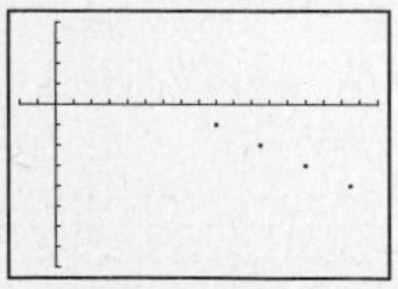

40c.

(x, y)	Quadrant	Inverse's Quadrant
(−1, 18)	II	IV
(−2, 23)	II	IV
(−3, 28)	II	IV
(−4, 33)	II	IV

41. If a point lies in Quadrants I or III, its inverse will lie in the same quadrant as the point. If a point lies in Quadrant II, its inverse lies in Quadrant IV, and vice versa. If a point lies on the x-axis, its inverse lies on the y-axis and vice versa.

42. Relations will vary. Sample answer: {(5, 3), (3, 5), (2, 2), (−4, −2), (−2, −4)}; the graphs are the same.

43a. Sample answer: 157 billion, 191 billion

43b. Sample answer: Retail sales have increased from 1992 to 1994.

43c. Sample answer: As unemployment decreases, retail sales increase because people have more money to spend.

44a.

Number of Weeks	Amount in Account
0	$500
1	$545
2	$590
3	$635
4	$680
5	$725
6	$770
7	$815
8	$860
9	$905
10	$950
11	$995
12	$1040
13	$1085
14	$1130
15	$1175
16	$1220

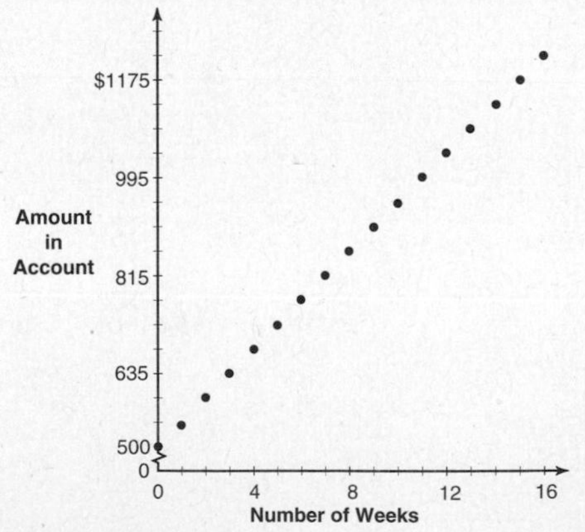

44b. after 16 weeks

45a.

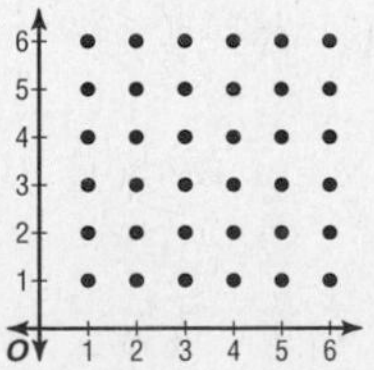

D = {1, 2, 3, 4, 5, 6}; R = {1, 2, 3, 4, 5, 6}

45b. D = R = {1, 2, 3, 4, 5, 6}; relation = inverse

45c. 11 possible sums

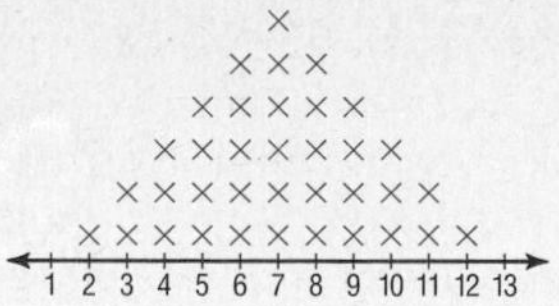

45d.

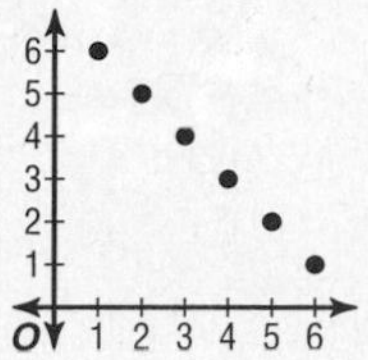

45e. $\frac{6}{36}$ or $\frac{1}{6}$; There are 6 out of 36 ways to roll a sum of 7.

46.

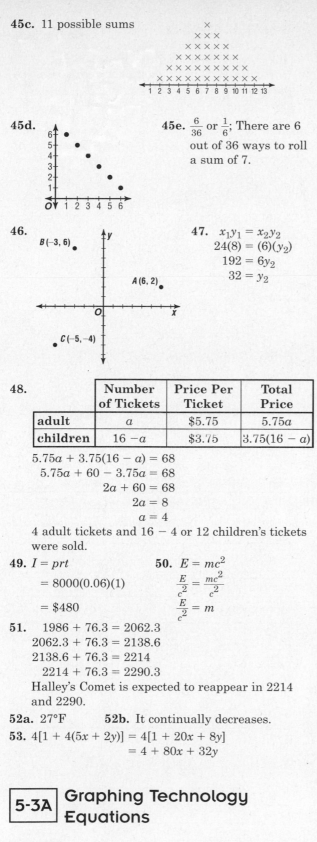

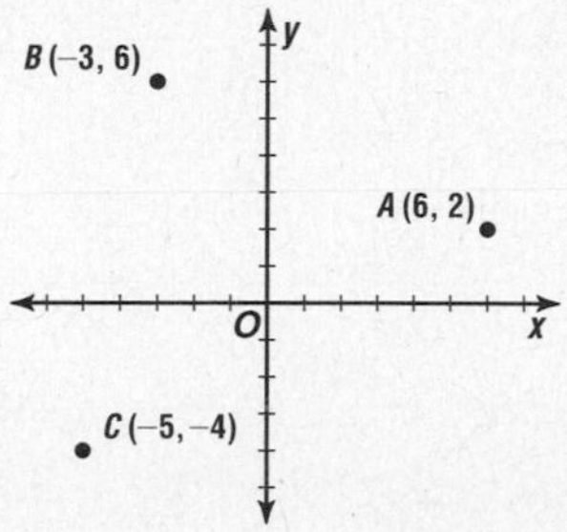

47.

$$x_1y_1 = x_2y_2$$
$$24(8) = (6)(y_2)$$
$$192 = 6y_2$$
$$32 = y_2$$

48.

	Number of Tickets	Price Per Ticket	Total Price
adult	a	\$5.75	$5.75a$
children	$16 - a$	\$3.75	$3.75(16 - a)$

$$5.75a + 3.75(16 - a) = 68$$
$$5.75a + 60 - 3.75a = 68$$
$$2a + 60 = 68$$
$$2a = 8$$
$$a = 4$$

4 adult tickets and 16 − 4 or 12 children's tickets were sold.

49. $I = prt$
$= 8000(0.06)(1)$
$= \$480$

50. $E = mc^2$
$\frac{E}{c^2} = \frac{mc^2}{c^2}$
$\frac{E}{c^2} = m$

51.
$1986 + 76.3 = 2062.3$
$2062.3 + 76.3 = 2138.6$
$2138.6 + 76.3 = 2214$
$2214 + 76.3 = 2290.3$

Halley's Comet is expected to reappear in 2214 and 2290.

52a. 27°F **52b.** It continually decreases.

53. $4[1 + 4(5x + 2y)] = 4[1 + 20x + 8y]$
$= 4 + 80x + 32y$

5-3A Graphing Technology Equations

Page 270

1. Enter: [Y=] 4 [X,T,θ] [−] 7 [2nd] [TblSet] [(−)] 3 [ENTER] 1 [2nd] [TABLE]

{(−3, −19), (−2, −15), (−1, −11), (0, −7), (1, −3), (2, −1), (3, 5)}

2. Enter: [Y=] [X,T,θ] [^] 2 [+] 11 [2nd] [TblSet] [(−)] 3 [ENTER] 1 [2nd] [TABLE]

{−3, 20), (−2, 15), (−1, 12), (0, 11), (1, 12), (2, 15), (3, 20)}

3. Solve for y: $1.2x - y = 6.8$
$-y = -1.2x + 6.8$
$y = 1.2x - 6.8$

Enter: [Y=] 1.2 [X,T,θ] [−] 6.8 [2nd] [TblSet] [(−)] 3 [ENTER] 1 [2nd] [TABLE]

{(−3, −10.4), (−2, −9.2), (−1, −8), (0, −6.8), (1, −5.6), (2, −4.4), (3, −3.2)}

4. Solve for y : $6x + 2y = 12$
$2y = -6x + 12$
$y = -3x + 6$

Enter: [Y=] [(−)] 3 [X,T,θ] [+] 6 [2nd] [TblSet] [(−)] 3 [ENTER] 1 [2nd] [TABLE]

{(−3, 15), (−2, 12), (−1, 9), (0, 6), (1, 3), (2, 0), (3, −3)}

5-3 Equations as Relations

Pages 274–275 Check for Understanding

1a. air, gasoline; air, aluminum, gasoline, lead, silver, steel, water

1b. D = {10, 50, 100, 150}; R = {193, 965, 1930, 2895}

2. not; $1 + 2(-1) \neq 3$

3. $A(-2, -3)$
$-3 = 2(-2) + 1$
$-3 = -3$

$C(-1, -1)$
$-1 = 2(-1) + 1$
$-1 = -1$

$F(1, 3)$
$3 = 2(1) + 1$
$3 = 3$

$G(2, 5)$
$5 = 2(2) + 1$
$5 = 5$

A, C, F, G

4. Length of a side cannot be zero or a negative number.

5. It makes calculating the y value easier.

6. The independent variable's values are chosen or assigned. The dependent variable's value varies with the value of the independent variable. The independent variable is graphed along the horizontal axis, and the dependent variable along the vertical axis.

7.

x	$2x + 3$	y	(x, y)
−2	2(−2) + 3	−1	(−2, −1)
−1	2(−1) + 3	1	(−1, 1)
0	2(0) + 3	3	(0, 3)
1	2(1) + 3	5	(1, 5)
2	2(2) + 3	7	(2, 7)
3	2(3) + 3	9	(3, 9)

8.

b	$\frac{3b-5}{2}$	a	(b, a)
-5	$\frac{3(-5)-5}{2}$	-10	$(-5, -10)$
-2	$\frac{3(-2)-5}{2}$	$-\frac{11}{2}$	$\left(-2, -\frac{11}{2}\right)$
0	$\frac{3(0)-5}{2}$	$-\frac{5}{2}$	$\left(0, -\frac{5}{2}\right)$
2	$\frac{3(2)-5}{2}$	$\frac{1}{2}$	$\left(2, \frac{1}{2}\right)$
5	$\frac{3(5)-5}{2}$	5	$(5, 5)$

9. a, d $\quad 1 + 5y = 2x$
- **a.** $(-7, -3)$ $\quad 1 + 5(-3) \stackrel{?}{=} 2(-7) \Rightarrow -14 = -14$ yes
- **b.** $(7, 3)$ $\quad 1 + 5(3) \stackrel{?}{=} 2(7) \Rightarrow 16 \neq 14$ no
- **c.** $(2,1)$ $\quad 1 + 5(1) \stackrel{?}{=} 2(2) \Rightarrow 6 \neq 4$ no
- **d.** $(-2, -1)$ $\quad 1 + 5(-1) \stackrel{?}{=} 2(-2) \Rightarrow -4 = -4$ yes

10. b, c $\quad 11 - 2y = 3x$
- **a.** $(1, 3)$ $\quad 11 - 2(3) \stackrel{?}{=} 3(1) \Rightarrow 5 \neq 3$ no
- **b.** $(3, 1)$ $\quad 11 - 2(1) \stackrel{?}{=} 3(3) \Rightarrow 9 = 9$ yes
- **c.** $(5, -2)$ $\quad 11 - 2(-2) \stackrel{?}{=} 3(5) \Rightarrow 15 = 15$ yes
- **d.** $(-1, 4)$ $\quad 11 - 2(4) \stackrel{?}{=} 3(-1) \Rightarrow 3 \neq -3$ no

11. Solve for y. $\quad x + 2y = 14$

$$2y = -x + 14$$
$$y = \frac{-x + 14}{2}$$

x	$\frac{-x+14}{2}$	y	(x, y)
-2	$\frac{-(-2)+14}{2}$	8	$(-2, 8)$
-1	$\frac{-(-1)+14}{2}$	7.5	$(-1, 7.5)$
0	$\frac{-(0)+14}{2}$	7	$(0, 7)$
1	$\frac{-(1)+14}{2}$	6.5	$(1, 6.5)$
2	$\frac{-(2)+14}{2}$	6	$(2, 6)$

The solution set is $\{(-2, 8), (-1, 7.5), (0, 7), (1, 6.5), (2, 6)\}$

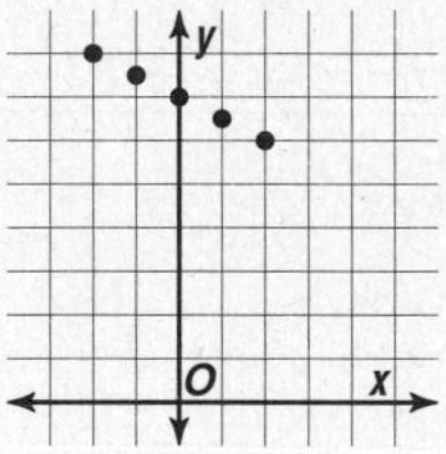

12a. $A = \ell w$

$$36 = \ell w$$
$$\frac{36}{w} = \frac{\ell w}{w}$$
$$\frac{36}{w} = \ell$$

12b. Sample answer:

w	$\frac{36}{w}$	ℓ	(w, ℓ)
1	$\frac{36}{1}$	36	(1, 36)
2	$\frac{36}{2}$	18	(2, 18)
3	$\frac{36}{3}$	12	(3, 12)
4	$\frac{36}{4}$	9	(4, 9)
6	$\frac{36}{6}$	6	(6, 6)

Pages 275–277 Exercises

13. a, c $\quad 3a + b = 8$
- **a.** $(4, -4)$ $\quad 3(4) + (-4) \stackrel{?}{=} 8 \Rightarrow 8 = 8$ yes
- **b.** $(8, 0)$ $\quad 3(8) + (0) \stackrel{?}{=} 8 \Rightarrow 24 \neq 8$ no
- **c.** $(2, 2)$ $\quad 3(2) + (2) \stackrel{?}{=} 8 \Rightarrow 8 = 8$ yes
- **d.** $(3, 1)$ $\quad 3(3) + (1) \stackrel{?}{=} 8 \Rightarrow 10 \neq 8$ no

14. b, c $\quad y = 3x$
- **a.** $(6, 2)$ $\quad 2 \stackrel{?}{=} 3(6) \Rightarrow 2 \neq 18$ no
- **b.** $(-2, -6)$ $\quad -6 \stackrel{?}{=} 3(-2) \Rightarrow -6 = -6$ yes
- **c.** $(0. 0)$ $\quad 0 \stackrel{?}{=} 3(0) \Rightarrow 0 = 0$ yes
- **d.** $(-15, -5)$ $\quad -5 \stackrel{?}{=} 3(-15) \Rightarrow -5 \neq -45$ no

15. a, b $\quad 3a - 8b = -4$
- **a.** $(0, 0.5)$ $\quad 3(0) - 8(0.5) \stackrel{?}{=} -4 \Rightarrow -4 = -4$ yes
- **b.** $(4, 2)$ $\quad 3(4) - 8(2) \stackrel{?}{=} -4 \Rightarrow -4 = -4$ yes
- **c.** $(2, 0.75)$ $\quad 3(2) - 8(0.75) \stackrel{?}{=} -4 \Rightarrow 0 \neq -4$ no
- **d.** $(2, 4)$ $\quad 3(2) - 8(4) \stackrel{?}{=} -4 \Rightarrow -26 \neq -4$ no

16. c, d $\quad x = 3y - 7$
- **a.** $(2, -1)$ $\quad 2 \stackrel{?}{=} 3(-1) - 7 \Rightarrow 2 \neq -10$ no
- **b.** $(2, 4)$ $\quad 2 \stackrel{?}{=} 3(4) - 7 \Rightarrow 2 \neq 5$ no
- **c.** $(-1, 2)$ $\quad -1 \stackrel{?}{=} 3(2) - 7 \Rightarrow -1 = -1$ yes
- **d.** $(2, 3)$ $\quad 2 \stackrel{?}{=} 3(3) - 7 \Rightarrow 2 = 2$ yes

17. c $\quad 2y + 4x = 8$
- **a.** $(10, 2)$ $\quad 2(2) + 4\,(0) \stackrel{?}{=} 8 \Rightarrow 4 \neq 8$ no
- **b.** $(-3, 0.5)$ $\quad 2(0.5) + 4(-3) \stackrel{?}{=} 8 \Rightarrow -11 \neq 8$ no
- **c.** $(2, 0)$ $\quad 2(0) + 4(2) \stackrel{?}{=} 8 \Rightarrow 8 = 8$ yes
- **d.** $(-2, 1)$ $\quad 2(1) + 4(-2) \stackrel{?}{=} 8 \Rightarrow -6 \neq 8$ no

18. a, b, c, d $\quad 3x + 3y = 0$
- **a.** $(1, -1)$ $\quad 3(1) + 3(-1) \stackrel{?}{=} 0 \Rightarrow 0 = 0$ yes
- **b.** $(2, -2)$ $\quad 3(2) + 3(-2) \stackrel{?}{=} 0 \Rightarrow 0 = 0$ yes
- **c.** $(-1, 1)$ $\quad 3(-1) + 3(1) \stackrel{?}{=} 0 \Rightarrow 0 = 0$ yes
- **d.** $(-2, 2)$ $\quad 3(-2) + 3(2) \stackrel{?}{=} 0 \Rightarrow 0 = 0$ yes

19.

x	$4x$	y	(x, y)
-3	$4(-3)$	-12	$(-3, -12)$
-2	$4(-2)$	-8	$(-2, -8)$
0	$4(0)$	0	$(0, 0)$
3	$4(3)$	12	$(3, 12)$
6	$4(6)$	24	$(6, 24)$

$\{(-3, -12), (-2, -8), (0, 0), (3, 12), (6, 24)\}$

20.

x	$3x - 1$	y	(x, y)
-3	$3(-3) - 1$	-10	$(-3, 10)$
-2	$3(-2) - 1$	-7	$(-2, -7)$
0	$3(0) - 1$	-1	$(0, -1)$
3	$3(3) - 1$	8	$(3, 8)$
6	$3(6) - 1$	17	$(6, 17)$

$\{(-3, -10), (-2, -7), (0, -1), (3, 8), (6, 17)\}$

21. Solve for y: $\quad 2x + 2y = 14$

$$2y = -2x + 14$$
$$y = -x + 7$$

x	$-x + 7$	y	(x, y)
-3	$-(-3) + 7$	10	$(-3, 10)$
-2	$-(-2) + 7$	9	$(-2, 9)$
0	$-(0) + 7$	7	$(0, 7)$
3	$-(3) + 7$	4	$(3, 4)$
6	$-(6) + 7$	1	$(6, 1)$

$\{(-3, 10), (-2, 9), (0, 7), (3, 4), (6, 1)\}$

22. Solve for y: $x = 4 + y$

$x - 4 = y$

x	$x - 4$	y	(x, y)
−3	−3 − 4	−7	(−3, −7)
−2	−2 − 4	−6	(−2, −6)
0	0 − 4	−4	(0, −4)
3	3 − 4	−1	(3, −1)
6	6 − 4	2	(6, 2)

{(−3, −7), (−2, −6), (0, −4), (3, −1), (6, 2)}

23. Solve for y: $3x = 13 - 2y$

$3x - 13 = -2y$

$\frac{3x - 13}{-2} = y$

x	$\frac{3x - 13}{-2}$	y	(x, y)
−3	$\frac{3(-3) - 13}{-2}$	11	(−3, 11)
−2	$\frac{3(-2) - 13}{-2}$	9.5	(−2, 9.5)
0	$\frac{3(0) - 13}{-2}$	6.5	(0, 6.5)
3	$\frac{3(3) - 13}{-2}$	2	(3, 2)
6	$\frac{3(6) - 13}{-2}$	−2.5	(6, −2.5)

{(−3, 11), (−2, 9.5), (0, 6.5), (3, 2), (6, −2.5)}

24.

x	$4 - 5x$	y	(x, y)
−3	4 − 5(−3)	19	(−3, 19)
−2	4 − 5(−2)	14	(−2, 14)
0	4 − 5(0)	4	(0, 4)
3	4 − 5(3)	−11	(3, −11)
6	4 − 5(6)	−26	(6, −26)

{(−3, 19), (−2, 14), (0, 4), (3, −11), (6, −26)}

25.

x	$5x + 3$	y	(x, y)
−3	5(−3) + 3	−12	(−3, −12)
−2	5(−2) + 3	−7	(−2, −7)
0	5(0) + 3	3	(0, 3)
3	5(3) + 3	18	(3, 18)
6	5(6) + 3	33	(6, 33)

{(−3, −12), (−2, −7), (0, 3), (3, 18), (6, 33)}

26. Solve for y: $5x - 10y = 40$

$-10y = -5x + 40$

$y = \frac{-5x + 40}{-10}$

x	$\frac{-5x + 40}{-10}$	y	(x, y)
−3	$\frac{-5(-3) + 40}{-10}$	−5.5	(−3, −5.5)
−2	$\frac{-5(-2) + 40}{-10}$	−5	(−2, −5)
0	$\frac{-5(0) + 40}{-10}$	−4	(0, −4)
3	$\frac{-5(3) + 40}{-10}$	−2.5	(3, −2.5)
6	$\frac{-5(6) + 40}{-10}$	−1	(6, −1)

{(−3, −5.5), (−2, −5), (0, −4), (3, −2.5), (6, −1)}

27. Solve for y: $2x + 5y = 3$

$5y = 3 - 2x$

$y = \frac{3 - 2x}{5}$

x	$\frac{3 - 2x}{5}$	y	(x, y)
−3	$\frac{3 - 2(-3)}{5}$	1.8	(−3, 1.8)
−2	$\frac{3 - 2(-2)}{5}$	1.4	(−2, 1.4)
0	$\frac{3 - 2(0)}{5}$	0.6	(0, 0.6)
3	$\frac{3 - 2(3)}{5}$	−0.6	(3, −0.6)
6	$\frac{3 - 2(6)}{5}$	−1.8	(6, −1.8)

{(−3, 1.8), (−2, 1.4), (0, 0.6), (3, −0.6), (6, −1.8)}

28.

x	$3x$	y	(x, y)
−3	3(−3)	−9	(−3, −9)
−2	3(−2)	−6	(−2, −6)
−1	3(−1)	−3	(−1, −3)
0	3(0)	0	(0, 0)
1	3(1)	3	(1, 3)
2	3(2)	6	(2, 6)
3	3(3)	9	(3, 9)

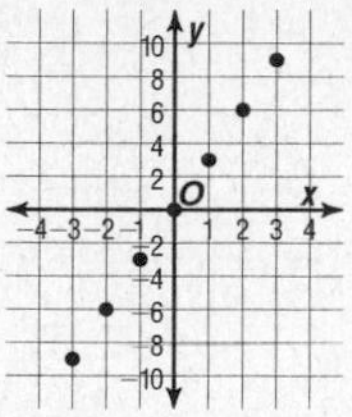

29.

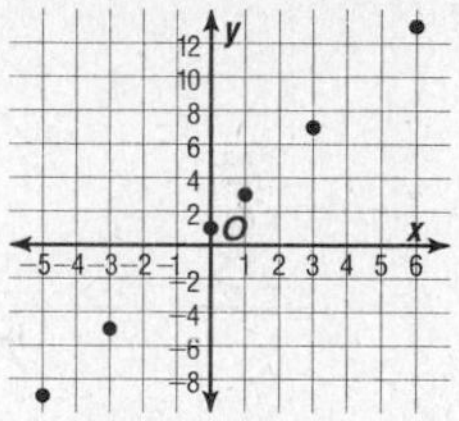

x	$2x + 1$	y	(x, y)
−5	2(−5) + 1	−9	(−5, −9)
−3	2(−3) + 1	−5	(−3, −5)
0	2(0) + 1	1	(0, 1)
1	2(1) + 1	3	(1, 3)
3	2(3) + 1	7	(3, 7)
6	2(6) + 1	13	(6, 13)

30. Solve for y: $3x - 2y = 5$

$-2y = 5 - 3x$

$y = \frac{5 - 3x}{-2}$

x	$\frac{5 - 3x}{-2}$	y	(x, y)
−3	$\frac{5 - 3(-3)}{-2}$	−7	(−3, −7)
−1	$\frac{5 - 3(-1)}{-2}$	−4	(−1, −4)
2	$\frac{5 - 3(2)}{-2}$	0.5	(2, 0.5)
4	$\frac{5 - 3(4)}{-2}$	3.5	(4, 3.5)
7	$\frac{5 - 3(7)}{-2}$	8	(7, 8)

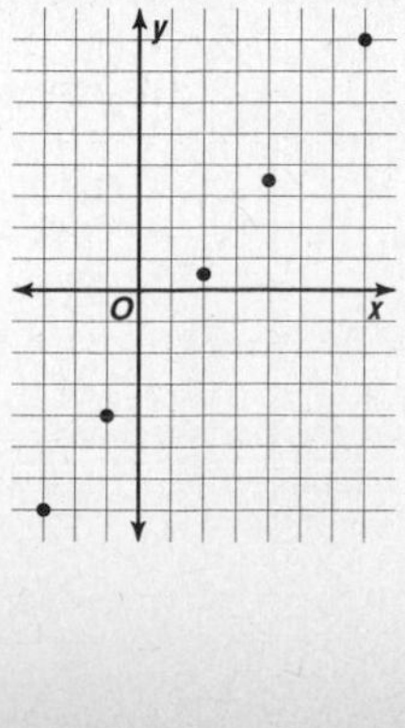

31. Solve for y: $5x = 8 - 4y$

$5x - 8 = -4y$

$\frac{5x - 8}{-4} = y$

x	$\frac{5x-8}{-4}$	y	(x, y)
−2	$\frac{5(-2)-8}{-4}$	4.5	(−2, 4.5)
−1	$\frac{5(-1)-8}{-4}$	3.25	(−1, 3.25)
0	$\frac{5(0)-8}{-4}$	2	(0, 2)
1	$\frac{5(1)-8}{-4}$	0.75	(1, 0.75)
3	$\frac{5(3)-8}{-4}$	−1.75	(3, −1.75)
4	$\frac{5(4)-8}{-4}$	−3	(4, −3)
5	$\frac{5(5)-8}{-4}$	−4.25	(5, −4.25)

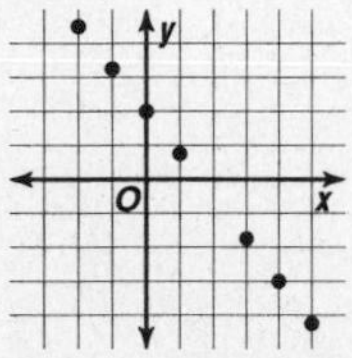

32a. $5(a + b) = 540$

$5a + 5b = 540$

32b. $5a + 5b = 540$

$5a = 540 - 5b$

$a = 108 - b$

32c. Sample answer:

a	$108 - b$	b	(a, b)
1	108 − 1	107	(1,107)
2	108 − 2	106	(2,106)
3	108 − 3	105	(3,105)
4	108 − 4	104	(4,104)
5	108 − 5	103	(5,103)

(1, 107), (2, 106), (3, 105), (4, 104), (5, 103)

33a. $(x + y) + (2x + 3y) = 180$

$3x + 4y = 180$

33b. $3x + 4y = 180$

$4y = 180 - 3x$

$y = 45 - \frac{3}{4}x$

33c. Sample answer:

x	$45 - \frac{3}{4}x$	y	(x, y)
1	$45 - \frac{3}{4}(1)$	44.25	(1, 44.25)
2	$45 - \frac{3}{4}(2)$	43.5	(2, 43.5)
3	$45 - \frac{3}{4}(3)$	42.75	(3, 42.75)
4	$45 - \frac{3}{4}(4)$	42	(4, 42)
5	$45 - \frac{3}{4}(5)$	41.25	(5, 41.25)

(1, 44.25), (2, 43.5), (3, 42.75), (4, 42), (5, 41.25)

34. Solve for x: $y = x + 7$

$y - 7 = x$

y	$y - 7$	x
−2	−2 − 7	−9
−1	−1 − 7	−8
0	0 − 7	−7
2	2 − 7	−5
3	3 − 7	−4

{−9, −8, −7, −5, −4)}

35. Solve for x: $y = 3x$

$\frac{y}{3} = x$

y	$\frac{y}{3}$	x
−2	$-\frac{2}{3}$	$-\frac{2}{3}$
−1	$\frac{1}{3}$	$-\frac{1}{3}$
0	$\frac{0}{3}$	0
2	$\frac{2}{3}$	$\frac{2}{3}$
3	$\frac{3}{3}$	1

$\left\{-\frac{2}{3}, -\frac{1}{3}, 0, \frac{2}{3}, 1\right\}$

36. Solve for x: $6x - y = -3$

$6x = y - 3$

$x = \frac{y - 3}{6}$

y	$\frac{y-3}{6}$	x
−2	$\frac{-2-3}{6}$	$\frac{-5}{6}$
−1	$\frac{-1-3}{6}$	$\frac{-2}{3}$
0	$\frac{0-3}{6}$	$\frac{-1}{2}$
2	$\frac{2-3}{6}$	$\frac{-1}{6}$
3	$\frac{3-3}{6}$	0

$\left\{-\frac{5}{6}, -\frac{2}{3}, -\frac{1}{2}, -\frac{1}{6}, 0\right\}$

37. Solve for x: $5y = 8 - 4x$

$5y - 8 = -4x$

$\frac{5y - 8}{-4} = x$

y	$\frac{5y-8}{-4}$	x
−2	$\frac{5(-2)-8}{-4}$	$\frac{9}{2}$
−1	$\frac{5(-1)-8}{-4}$	$\frac{13}{4}$
0	$\frac{5(0)-8}{-4}$	2
2	$\frac{5(2)-8}{-4}$	$-\frac{1}{2}$
3	$\frac{5(3)-8}{-4}$	$-\frac{7}{4}$

$\left\{-\frac{7}{4}, -\frac{1}{2}, 2, \frac{13}{4}, \frac{9}{2}\right\}$

38.

x	$x^2 - 3x - 10$	y	(x, y)
−3	$(-3)^2 - 3(-3) - 10$	8	(−3, 8)
−1	$(-1)^2 - 3(-1) - 10$	−6	(−1, −6)
0	$(0)^2 - 3(0) - 10$	−10	(0, −10)
1	$(1)^2 - 3(1) - 10$	−12	(1, −12)
3	$(3)^2 - 3(3) - 10$	−10	(3, −10)
5	$(5)^2 - 3(5) - 10$	0	(5, 0)

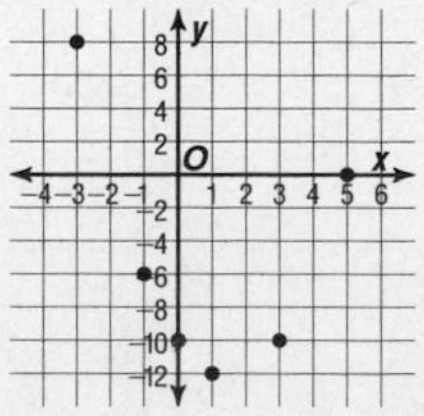

39.

x	x^3	y	(x, y)
-2	$(-2)^3$	-8	$(-2, -8)$
-1	$(-1)^3$	-1	$(-1, -1)$
0	$(0)^3$	0	$(0, 0)$
1	$(1)^3$	1	$(1, 1)$
2	$(2)^3$	8	$(2, 8)$

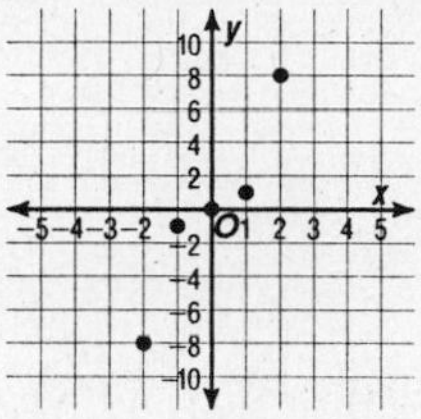

40.

x	3^x	y	(x, y)
1	3^1	3	$(1, 3)$
2	3^2	9	$(2, 9)$
3	3^3	27	$(3, 27)$
4	3^4	81	$(4, 81)$

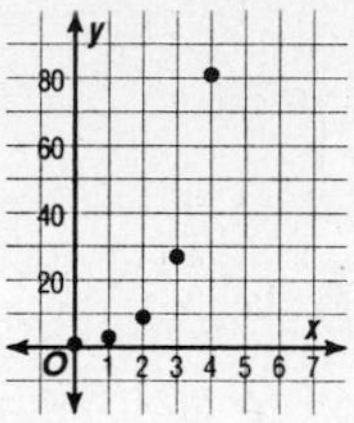

For Exercises 41–44, press [2nd] [TABLE] and use the arrow keys to go to Indpnt:. Highlight Ask.

41. Enter: [Y=] 1.4 [X,T,θ] [−] .76 [2nd] [TABLE] [(−)] 2.5 [ENTER] [(−)] 1.75 [ENTER] 0 [ENTER] 1.25 [ENTER] 3.33 [ENTER]

{(−2.5, −4.26), (−1.75, −3.21), (0, −0.76), (1.25, 0.99), (3.33, 3.902)}

42. Enter: [Y=] 3.5 [X,T,θ] [+] 12 [2nd] [TABLE] [(−)] 125 [ENTER] [(−)] 37 [ENTER] [(−)] 6 [ENTER] 12 [ENTER] 57 [ENTER] 150 [ENTER]

{(−125, −425.5), (−37, −117.5), (−6, −9), (12, 54), (57, 211.5), (150, 537)}

43. Solve for y: $3.6y + 12x = 60$

$$3.6y = 60 - 12x$$
$$y = \frac{60 - 12x}{3.6}$$

Enter: [Y=] [(] 60 [−] 12 [X,T,θ] [)] [÷] 3.6 [2nd] [TABLE] [(−)] 100 [ENTER] [(−)] 30 [ENTER] 0 [ENTER] 120 [ENTER] 360 [ENTER] 720 [ENTER]

{(−100, 350), (−30, 116.67), (0, 16.667), (120, −383.3), (360, −1183), (720, −2383)}
answers to nearest tenth: {(−100, 350), (−30, $116.\overline{6}$), (0, $16.\overline{6}$), (120, $-383.\overline{3}$), (360, $-1183.\overline{3}$), (720, $-2383.\overline{3}$)}

44. Solve for y: $75y + 25x = 100$

$$75y = 100 - 25x$$
$$y = \frac{100 - 25x}{75}$$

Enter: [Y=] [(] 100 [−] 25 [X,T,θ] [)] [÷] 75 [2nd] [TABLE] [(−)] 10 [ENTER] [(−)] 5 [ENTER] 0 [ENTER] 5 [ENTER] 10 [ENTER] 15 [ENTER]

{(−10, 4.6667), (−5, 3), (0, 1.3333), (5, −.3333), (10, −2), (15, −3.667)}
answers to nearest tenth: {(−10, $4.\overline{6}$), (−5, 3), (0, $1.\overline{3}$), (5, $-0.\overline{3}$), (10, −2), (15, $-3.\overline{6}$)}

45a. Solve for x: $y = x^2$

$$\pm\sqrt{y} = x$$

y	$\pm\sqrt{y}$	x
0	0	0
16	$\pm\sqrt{16}$	± 4
36	$\pm\sqrt{36}$	± 6

{−6, −4, 0, 4, 6}

45b. Solve for x: $y = |4x| - 16$

$$y + 16 = |4x|$$
$$\pm\left(\frac{y + 16}{4}\right) = x$$

y	$\pm\left(\frac{y+16}{4}\right)$	x
0	$\pm\left(\frac{0+16}{4}\right)$	± 4
16	$\pm\left(\frac{16+16}{4}\right)$	± 8
36	$\pm\left(\frac{36+16}{4}\right)$	± 13

{−13, −8, −4, 4, 8, 13}

45c. Solve for x: $y = |4x - 16|$

$$\pm y = 4x - 16$$
$$\frac{\pm y + 16}{4} = x$$

y	$\frac{\pm y + 16}{4}$	x
0	$\frac{0 + 16}{4}$	4
16	$\frac{16 + 16}{4}, \frac{-16 + 16}{4}$	8, 0
36	$\frac{36 + 16}{4}, \frac{-36 + 16}{4}$	13, −5

{−5, 0, 4, 8, 13}

46a. The other graphs have points that seem to lie in a straight line. These points do not.

46b. $y = x^2 - 3x - 10$ is U-shaped; $y = x^3$ is both an upward and downward curve; $y = 3^x$ is J-shaped.

47a. $m = DV$

$\frac{m}{V} = \frac{DV}{V}$

$\frac{m}{V} = D$

47b. $D = \frac{m}{V} = \frac{378}{36} = 10.5$ $\qquad D = \frac{m}{V} = \frac{87.5}{125} = 0.7$

silver and gasoline

48a. D: $R > 0$; R: $T > 0$

48b. North America: $T = \frac{70}{3.6} \approx 19$

South America: $T = \frac{70}{2.1} \approx 33$

Europe: $T = \frac{70}{1.3} \approx 54$

Asia: $T = \frac{70}{9.7} \approx 7$ $\qquad$ Africa: $T = \frac{70}{15.1} \approx 5$

48c. in 2000: $248{,}709{,}873(1.036)^{10} = 354{,}234{,}275$;
in 2010: $248{,}709{,}873(1.036)^{20} = 504{,}531{,}323$;
in 2020: $248{,}709{,}873(1.036)^{30} = 718{,}597{,}477$

49.

Women			
L	**3L − 22**	**S**	**(L, S)**
$9\frac{1}{3}$	$3\left(9\frac{1}{3}\right) - 22$	6	$\left(9\frac{1}{3}, 6\right)$
$9\frac{5}{6}$	$3\left(9\frac{5}{6}\right) - 22$	$7\frac{1}{2}$	$\left(9\frac{5}{6}, 7\frac{1}{2}\right)$
$10\frac{1}{6}$	$3\left(10\frac{1}{6}\right) - 22$	$8\frac{1}{2}$	$\left(9\frac{1}{6}, 8\frac{1}{2}\right)$
$10\frac{2}{3}$	$3\left(10\frac{2}{3}\right) - 22$	10	$\left(10\frac{2}{3}, 10\right)$

Men			
L	**3L − 26**	**S**	**(L, S)**
$11\frac{1}{3}$	$3\left(11\frac{1}{3}\right) - 26$	8	$\left(11\frac{1}{3}, 8\right)$
$11\frac{5}{6}$	$3\left(11\frac{5}{6}\right) - 26$	$9\frac{1}{2}$	$\left(11\frac{5}{6}, 9\frac{1}{2}\right)$
$12\frac{1}{3}$	$3\left(12\frac{1}{3}\right) - 26$	11	$\left(12\frac{1}{3}, 11\right)$
$12\frac{5}{6}$	$3\left(12\frac{5}{6}\right) - 26$	$12\frac{1}{2}$	$\left(12\frac{5}{6}, 12\frac{1}{2}\right)$

50a.

Day	Plan A	Plan B
1	\$1	\$0.01
2	\$2	\$0.02
3	\$3	\$0.04
4	\$4	\$0.08
5	\$5	\$0.16
6	\$6	\$0.32
7	\$7	\$0.64
8	\$8	\$1.28
9	\$9	\$2.56
10	\$10	\$5.12
11	\$11	\$10.24
12	\$12	\$20.48
13	\$13	\$40.96
14	\$14	\$81.92
15	\$15	\$163.84
16	\$16	\$327.68
17	\$17	\$655.36
18	\$18	\$1310.72
19	\$19	\$2621.44
20	\$20	\$5242.88
21	\$21	\$10,485.76
22	\$22	\$20,971.52
23	\$23	\$41,943.04
24	\$24	\$83,886.08
25	\$25	\$167,772.16
26	\$26	\$335,544.32
27	\$27	\$671,088.64
28	\$28	\$1,342,177.28
29	\$29	\$2,684,354.56
30	\$30	\$5,368.709.12

50b. On day 12, Plan B exceeds Plan A.

51a.

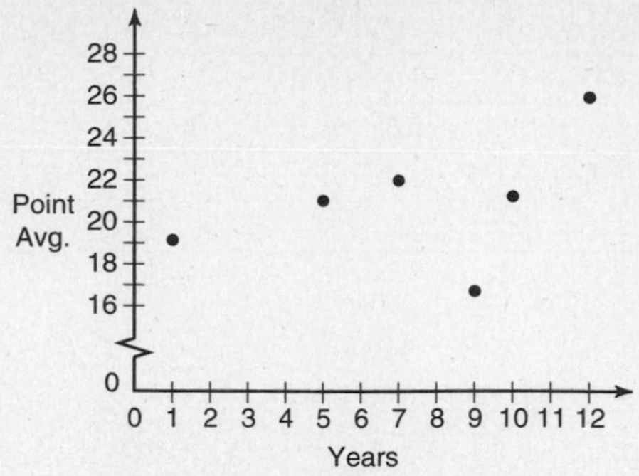

51b. The more years played, the higher the point-per-game average of the player.

52. star

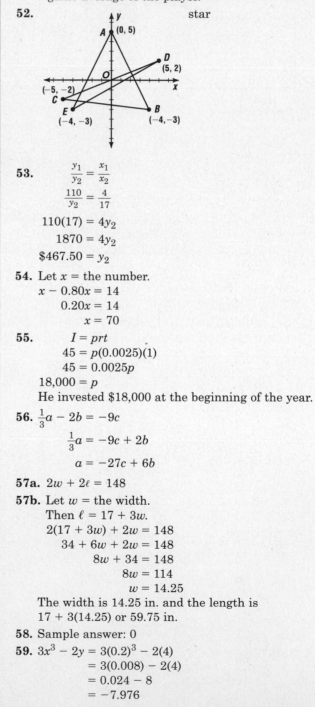

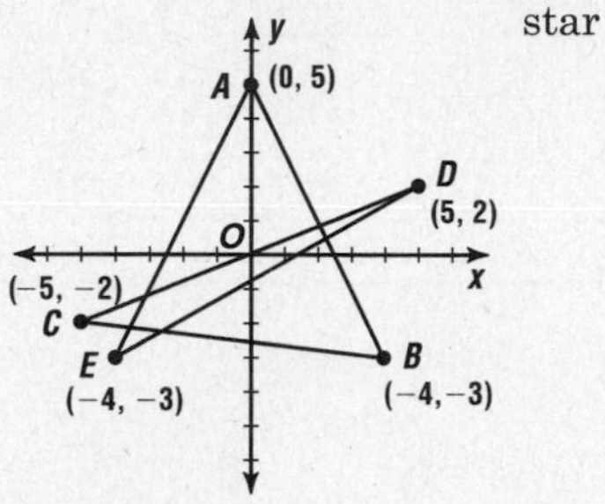

53.

$\frac{y_1}{y_2} = \frac{x_1}{x_2}$

$\frac{110}{y_2} = \frac{4}{17}$

$110(17) = 4y_2$

$1870 = 4y_2$

$\$467.50 = y_2$

54. Let x = the number.

$x - 0.80x = 14$

$0.20x = 14$

$x = 70$

55.

$I = prt$

$45 = p(0.0025)(1)$

$45 = 0.0025p$

$18{,}000 = p$

He invested \$18,000 at the beginning of the year.

56. $\frac{1}{3}a - 2b = -9c$

$\frac{1}{3}a = -9c + 2b$

$a = -27c + 6b$

57a. $2w + 2\ell = 148$

57b. Let w = the width.

Then $\ell = 17 + 3w$.

$2(17 + 3w) + 2w = 148$

$34 + 6w + 2w = 148$

$8w + 34 = 148$

$8w = 114$

$w = 14.25$

The width is 14.25 in. and the length is $17 + 3(14.25)$ or 59.75 in.

58. Sample answer: 0

59. $3x^3 - 2y = 3(0.2)^3 - 2(4)$

$= 3(0.008) - 2(4)$

$= 0.024 - 8$

$= -7.976$

5-4A Graphing Technology Linear Relations and Functions

Page 279 Exercises

1. Enter: [Y=] 3 [X,T,θ] [−] 6 [ZOOM] 6

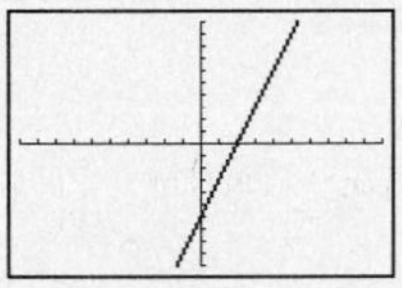

2. Enter: [Y=] .5 [X,T,θ] [−] 4 [ZOOM] 6

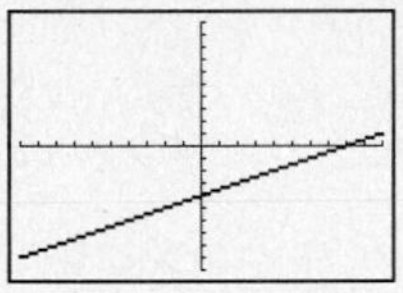

3. Solve for y: $2x - 3y = 5$

$$-3y = -2x + 5$$
$$y = \frac{2x - 5}{3}$$

Enter: [Y=] [(] 2 [X,T,θ] [−] 5 [)] [÷] 3 [ZOOM] 6

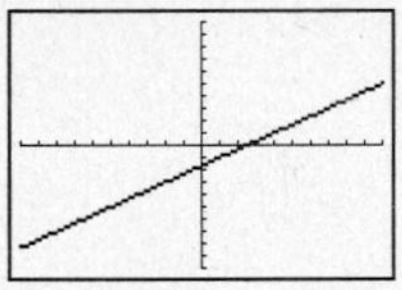

4. Solve for y: $5x + y = 8$

$$y = -5x + 8$$

Enter: [Y=] [(−)] 5 [X,T,θ] [+] 8 [ZOOM] 6

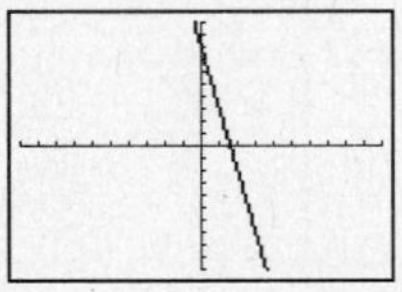

5. Solve for y: $2y - 2x = 3$

$$2y = 2x + 3$$
$$y = x + 1.5$$

Enter: [Y=] [X,T,θ] [+] 1.5 [ZOOM] 6

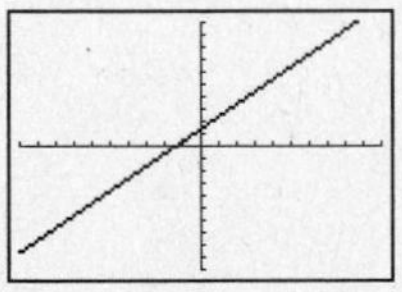

6. Solve for y: $-10x - 2y = -14$

$$-2y = 10x - 14$$
$$y = -5x + 7$$

Enter: [Y=] [(−)] 5 [X,T,θ] [+] 7 [ZOOM] 6

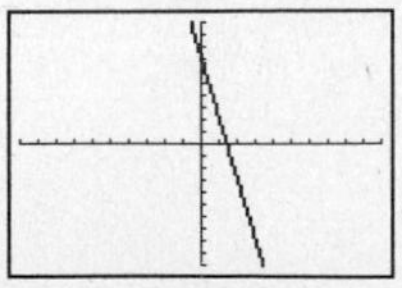

7-10. Answers will vary; sample answers are given.

7a. [−10, 110] by [−5, 15]

7b. Xscl: 10, Yscl: 1

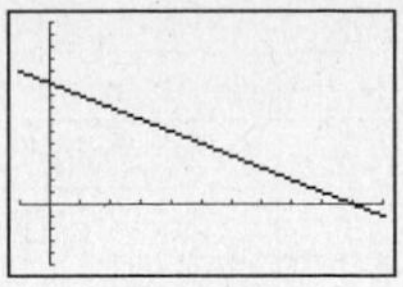

7c. (0, 10), (100, 0), (10, 9)

8a. [−10, 10] by [−5, 20]

8b. Xscl: 1, Yscl: 1

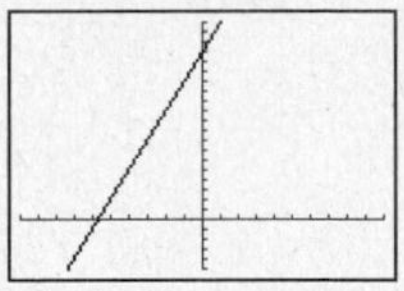

8c. (0, 17), (1, 20), (2, 23)

9a. [−2.5, 0.5] by [−0.05, 0.05]

9b. Xscl: 0.5, Yscl: 0.01

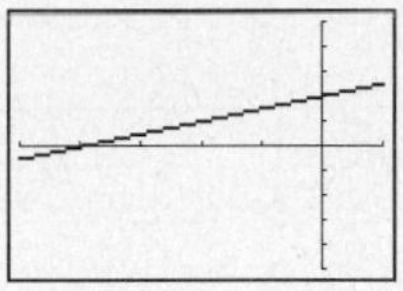

9c. (−2, 0), (0, 0.02), (1, 0.03)

10a. [−1, 1] by [−10, 160]

10b. Xscl: 0.1, Yscl: 10

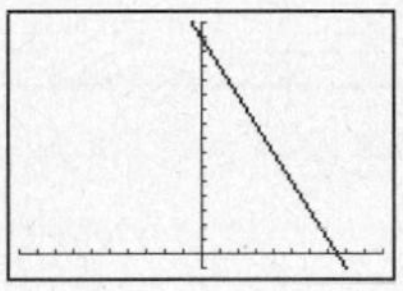

10c. (0, 150), (1, −50), (2, −250)

5-4 Graphing Linear Equations

Page 283 Check for Understanding

1. Because $3 = -2(-1) + 1$ is a true sentence.

2a. horizontal line **2b.** vertical line

2c. slanted line

3. The first graph is a set of points; the second is a line.

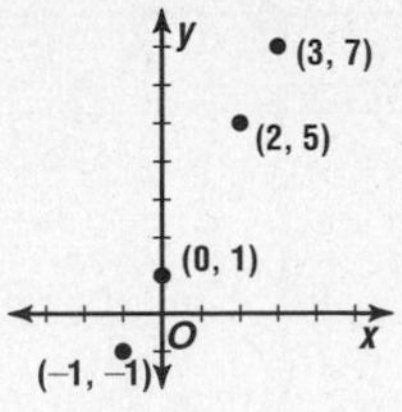

$y = 2x + 1$ for $x = \{-1, 0, 2, 3\}$

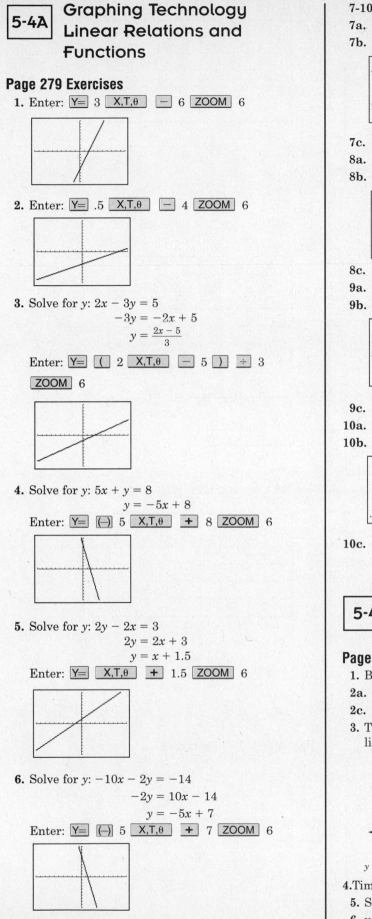

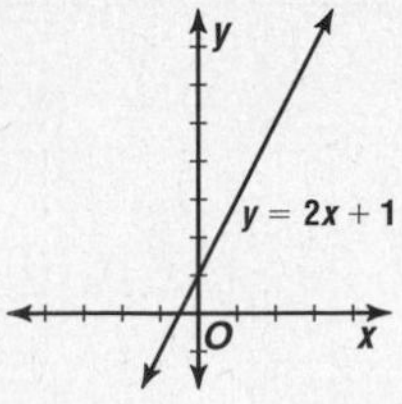

$y = 2x + 1$ for $x \in$ {real numbers}

4. Time and Calories are nonnegative quantities.

5. See students' work.

6. yes; $3x - 5y = 0$

7. yes; $2x + y = 6$

8. no

9. yes; $3x + 2y = 7$

10. Solve for y: $3x + y = 4$

$y = -3x + 4$

x	$-3x + 4$	y	(x, y)
-2	$-3(-2) + 4$	10	$(-2, 10)$
-1	$-3(-1) + 4$	7	$(-1, 7)$
0	$-3(0) + 4$	4	$(0, 4)$
1	$-3(1) + 4$	1	$(1, 1)$
2	$-3(2) + 4$	-2	$(2, -2)$

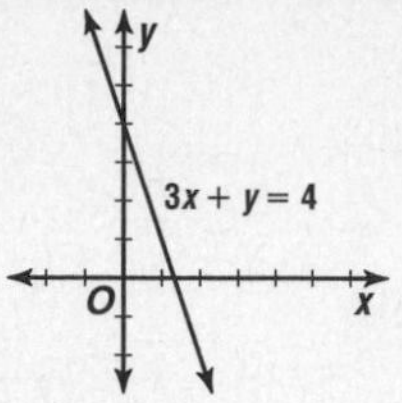

11. Solve for y: $4x + 3y = 12$

$3y = 12 - 4x$

$y = \frac{12 - 4x}{3}$

x	$\frac{12 - 4x}{3}$	y	(x, y)
-3	$\frac{12 - 4(-3)}{3}$	8	$(-3, 8)$
0	$\frac{12 - 4(0)}{3}$	4	$(0, 4)$
3	$\frac{12 - 4(3)}{3}$	0	$(3, 0)$
6	$\frac{12 - 4(6)}{3}$	-4	$(6, -4)$

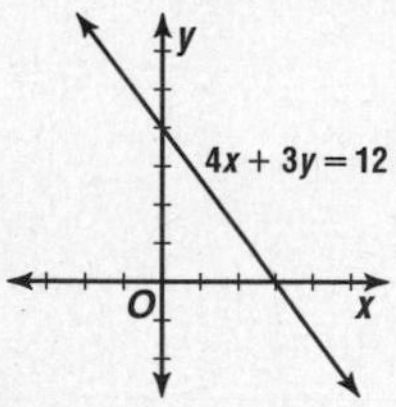

12. Solve for y:

$\frac{1}{2}x = 8 - y$

$\frac{1}{2}x - 8 = -y$

$8 - \frac{1}{2}x = y$

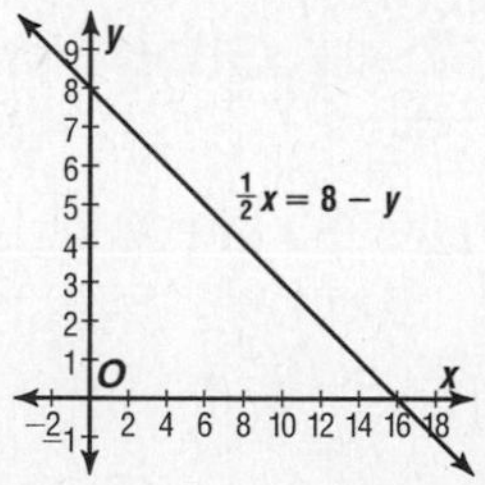

x	$8 - \frac{1}{2}x$	y	(x, y)
-2	$8 - \frac{1}{2}(-2)$	9	$(-2, 9)$
0	$8 - \frac{1}{2}(0)$	8	$(0, 8)$
2	$8 - \frac{1}{2}(2)$	7	$(2, 7)$
4	$8 - \frac{1}{2}(4)$	6	$(4, 6)$
6	$8 - \frac{1}{2}(6)$	5	$(6, 5)$

13. $x = 6$

x	y	(x, y)
6	-1	$(6, -1)$
6	0	$(6, 0)$
6	1	$(6, 1)$
6	2	$(6, 2)$
6	3	$(6, 3)$

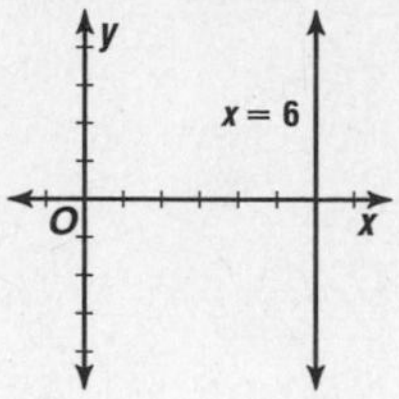

14. $y = -5$

x	y	(x, y)
-2	-5	$(-2, -5)$
-1	-5	$(-1, -5)$
0	-5	$(0, -5)$
1	-5	$(1, -5)$
2	-5	$(2, -5)$

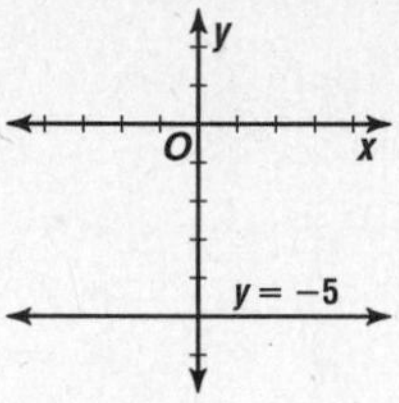

15. Solve for y: $x - y = 0$

$x = y$

x	y	(x, y)
-1	-1	$(-1, -1)$
0	0	$(0, 0)$
1	1	$(1, 1)$
2	2	$(2, 2)$
3	3	$(3, 3)$

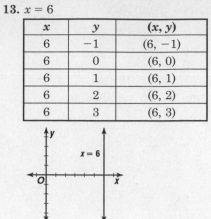

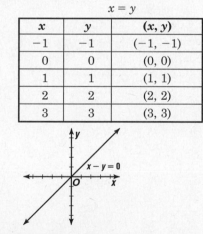

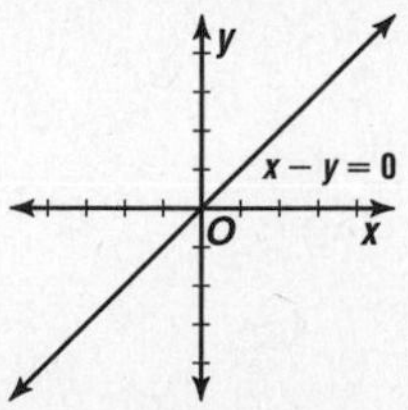

Pages 283–286 Exercises

16. no

17. yes; $\frac{3}{2}x - \frac{2}{3}y = 5$

18. no

19. no

20. yes; $3y = -2$

21. yes; $3x - 2y = 8$

22. yes; $5x = 7$

23. yes; $7x - 7y = 0$

24. no

25. yes; $3m - 2n = 0$

26. yes; $\frac{1}{2}x - \frac{2}{3}y = 10$

27. yes; $6a - 7b = -5$

28. $x + 6 = -5$

$x = -11$

x	y	(x, y)
-11	-1	$(-11, -1)$
-11	0	$(-11, 0)$
-11	1	$(-11, 1)$
-11	2	$(-11, 2)$
-11	3	$(-11, 3)$

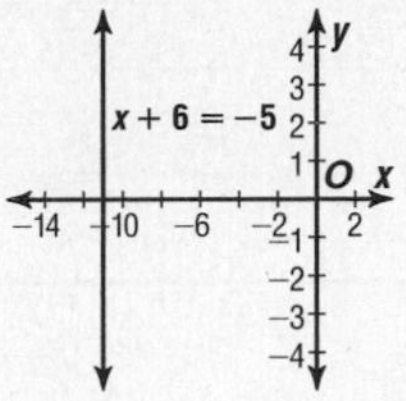

29. $y = 3x + 1$

x	$3x + 1$	y	(x, y)
-2	$3(-2) + 1$	-5	$(-2, -5)$
-1	$3(-1) + 1$	-2	$(-1, -2)$
0	$3(0) + 1$	1	$(0, 1)$
1	$3(1) + 1$	4	$(1, 4)$
2	$3(2) + 1$	7	$(2, 7)$

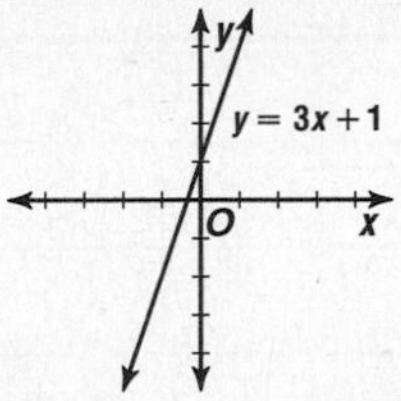

30. Solve for y: $6x + 7 = -14y$

$\frac{6x + 7}{-14} = y$

x	$\frac{6x + 7}{-14}$	y	(x, y)
-1	$\frac{6(-1) + 7}{-14}$	$-\frac{1}{14}$	$\left(-1, -\frac{1}{14}\right)$
0	$\frac{6(0) + 7}{-14}$	$-\frac{1}{2}$	$\left(0, -\frac{1}{2}\right)$
1	$\frac{6(1) + 7}{-14}$	$-\frac{13}{14}$	$\left(1, -\frac{13}{14}\right)$
2	$\frac{6(2) + 7}{-14}$	$-\frac{19}{14}$	$\left(2, -\frac{19}{14}\right)$
3	$\frac{6(3) + 7}{-14}$	$-\frac{25}{14}$	$\left(3, -\frac{25}{14}\right)$

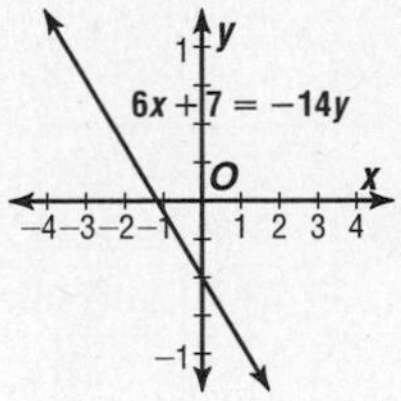

31. Solve for y: $2x + 7y = 9$

$7y = 9 - 2x$

$y = \frac{9 - 2x}{7}$

x	$\frac{9 - 2x}{7}$	y	(x, y)
-2	$\frac{9 - 2(-2)}{7}$	$\frac{13}{7}$	$\left(-2, \frac{13}{7}\right)$
-1	$\frac{9 - 2(-1)}{7}$	$\frac{11}{7}$	$\left(-1, \frac{11}{7}\right)$
0	$\frac{9 - 2(0)}{7}$	$\frac{9}{7}$	$\left(0, \frac{9}{7}\right)$
1	$\frac{9 - 2(1)}{7}$	1	$(1, 1)$
2	$\frac{9 - 2(2)}{7}$	$\frac{5}{7}$	$\left(2, \frac{5}{7}\right)$

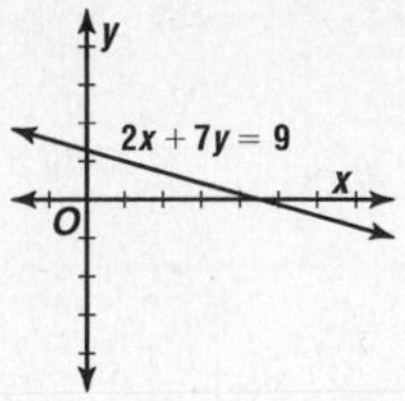

32. Solve for y: $y + 3 = 4$

$y = 1$

x	y	(x, y)
-2	1	$(-2, 1)$
-1	1	$(-1, 1)$
0	1	$(0, 1)$
1	1	$(1, 1)$
2	1	$(2, 1)$

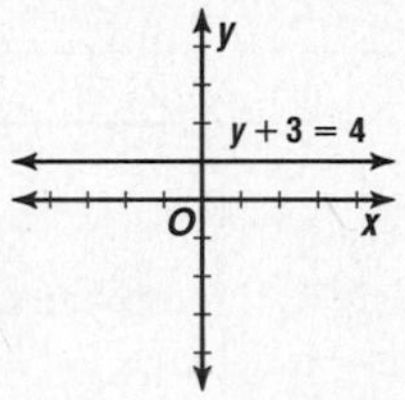

33. Solve for y: $x - 6 = \frac{-1}{3}y$

$-3x + 18 = y$

x	$-3x + 18$	y	(x, y)
-2	$-3(-2) + 18$	24	$(-2, 24)$
-1	$-3(-1) + 18$	21	$(-1, 21)$
0	$-3(0) + 18$	18	$(0, 18)$
1	$-3(1) + 18$	15	$(1, 15)$
2	$-3(2) + 18$	12	$(2, 12)$

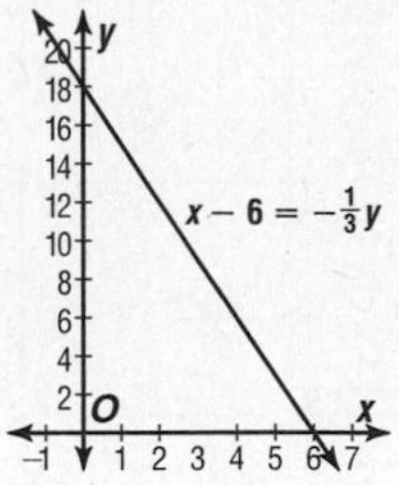

34. Solve for y: $8x - y = 16$

$$-y = 16 - 8x$$
$$y = 8x - 16$$

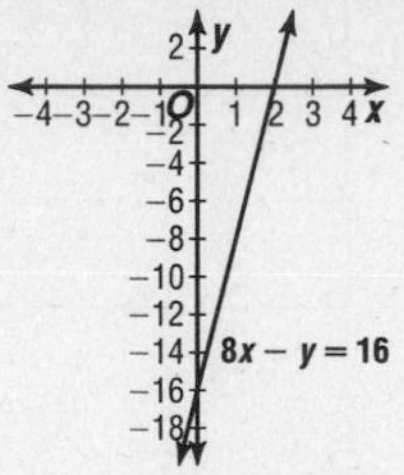

x	$8x - 16$	y	(x, y)
-2	$8(-2) - 16$	-32	$(-2, -32)$
-1	$8(-1) - 16$	-24	$(-1, -24)$
0	$8(0) - 16$	-16	$(0, -16)$
1	$8(1) - 16$	-8	$(1, -8)$
2	$8(2) - 16$	0	$(2, 0)$

35. Solve for y: $3x + 3y = 12$

$$3y = 12 - 3x$$
$$y = 4 - x$$

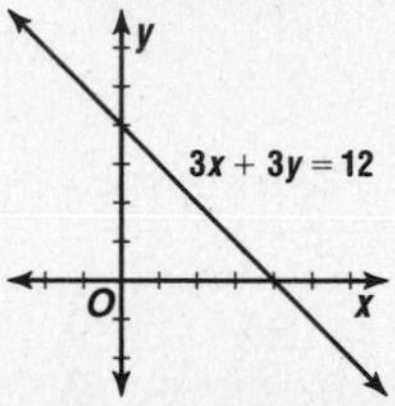

x	$4 - x$	y	(x, y)
-2	$4 - (-2)$	6	$(-2, 6)$
-1	$4 - (-1)$	5	$(-1, 5)$
0	$4 - (0)$	4	$(0, 4)$
1	$4 - (1)$	3	$(1, 3)$
2	$4 - (2)$	2	$(2, 2)$

36. Solve for y: $6x = 24 - 6y$

$$6x - 24 = -6y$$
$$-x + 4 = y$$

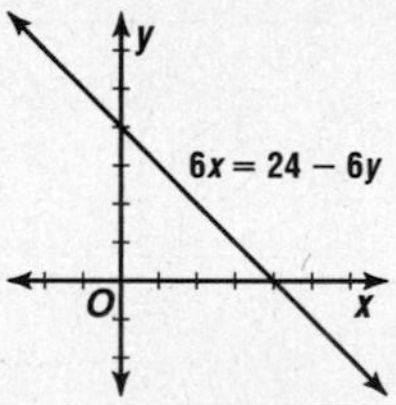

x	$-x + 4$	y	(x, y)
-2	$-(-2) + 4$	6	$(-2, 6)$
-1	$-(-1) + 4$	5	$(-1, 5)$
0	$-(0) + 4$	4	$(0, 4)$
1	$-(1) + 4$	3	$(1, 3)$
2	$-(2) + 4$	2	$(2, 2)$

37. Solve for x: $x - \frac{7}{2} = 0$

$$x = \frac{7}{2}$$

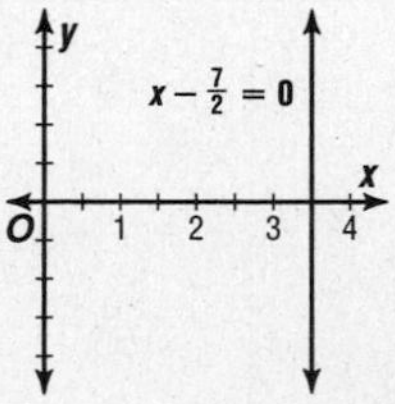

x	y	(x, y)
$\frac{7}{2}$	-2	$\left(\frac{7}{2}, -2\right)$
$\frac{7}{2}$	-1	$\left(\frac{7}{2}, -1\right)$
$\frac{7}{2}$	0	$\left(\frac{7}{2}, 0\right)$
$\frac{7}{2}$	1	$\left(\frac{7}{2}, 1\right)$
$\frac{7}{2}$	2	$\left(\frac{7}{2}, 2\right)$

38. Solve for y: $3x - 4y = 60$

$$-4y = 60 - 3x$$
$$y = -15 + \frac{3}{4}x$$

x	$-15 + \frac{3}{4}x$	y	(x, y)
-4	$-15 + \frac{3}{4}(-4)$	-18	$(-4, -18)$
0	$-15 + \frac{3}{4}(0)$	-15	$(0, -15)$
4	$-15 + \frac{3}{4}(4)$	-12	$(4, -12)$
8	$-15 + \frac{3}{4}(8)$	-9	$(8, -9)$
12	$-15 + \frac{3}{4}(12)$	-6	$(12, -6)$

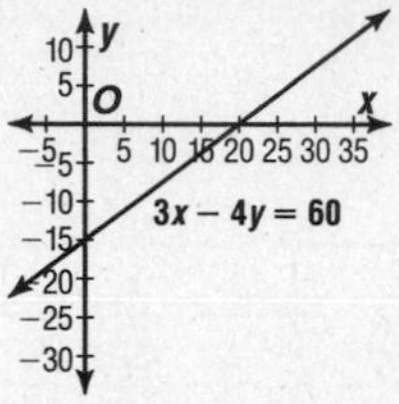

39. Solve for y: $4x - \frac{3}{8}y = 1$

$$-\frac{3}{8}y = 1 - 4x$$
$$y = -\frac{8}{3} + \frac{32}{3}x$$

x	$-\frac{8}{3} + \frac{32}{3}x$	y	(x, y)
-1	$-\frac{8}{3} + \frac{32}{3}(-1)$	$-\frac{40}{3}$	$\left(-1, -\frac{40}{3}\right)$
0	$-\frac{8}{3} + \frac{32}{3}(0)$	$-\frac{8}{3}$	$\left(0, -\frac{8}{3}\right)$
1	$-\frac{8}{3} + \frac{32}{3}(1)$	8	$(1, 8)$
2	$-\frac{8}{3} + \frac{32}{3}(2)$	$\frac{56}{3}$	$\left(2, \frac{56}{3}\right)$
3	$-\frac{8}{3} + \frac{32}{3}(3)$	24	$(3, 24)$

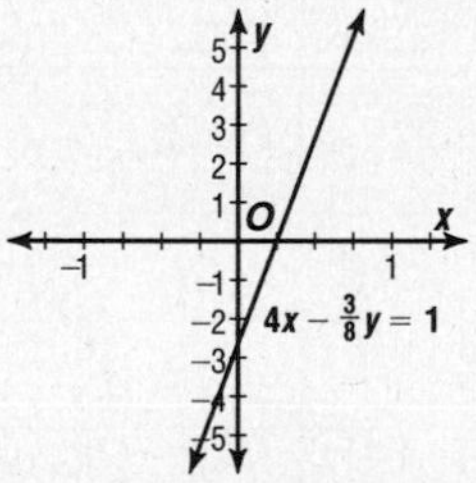

40. Solve for y: $2.5x + 5y = 7.5$

$$5y = 7.5 - 2.5x$$
$$y = 1.5 - 0.5x$$

x	$1.5 - 0.5x$	y	(x, y)
-2	$1.5 - 0.5(-2)$	2.5	$(-2, 2.5)$
-1	$1.5 - 0.5(-1)$	2.0	$(-1, 2.0)$
0	$1.5 - 0.5(0)$	1.5	$(0, 1.5)$
1	$1.5 - 0.5(1)$	1.0	$(1, 1.0)$
2	$1.5 - 0.5(2)$	0.5	$(2, 0.5)$

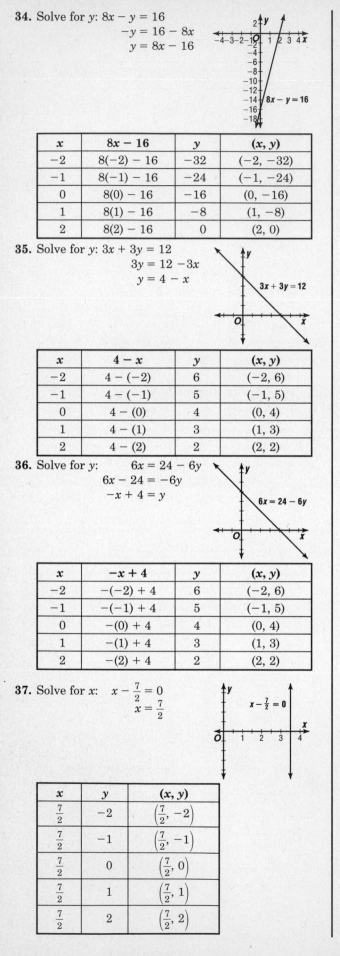

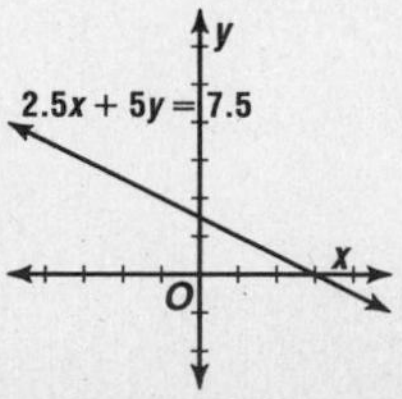

41. Solve for y: $x + 5y = 16$

$$5y = 16 - x$$
$$y = \frac{16 - x}{5}$$

x	$\frac{16 - x}{5}$	y	(x, y)
-1	$\frac{16 - (-1)}{5}$	3.4	$(-1, 3.4)$
0	$\frac{16 - (0)}{5}$	3.2	(0, 3.2)
1	$\frac{16 - 1}{5}$	3	(1, 3)
2	$\frac{16 - 2}{5}$	2.8	(2, 2.8)
3	$\frac{16 - 3}{5}$	2.4	(3, 2.4)

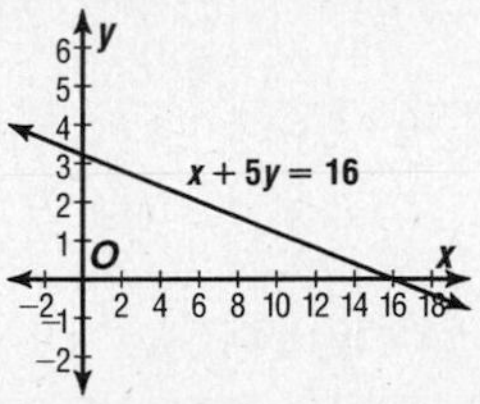

42. Solve for y: $y + 0.25 = 2$

$$y = 1.75$$

x	y	(x, y)
-2	1.75	$(-2, 1.75)$
-1	1.75	$(-1, 1.75)$
0	1.75	(0, 1.75)
1	1.75	(1, 1.75)
2	1.75	(2, 1.75)

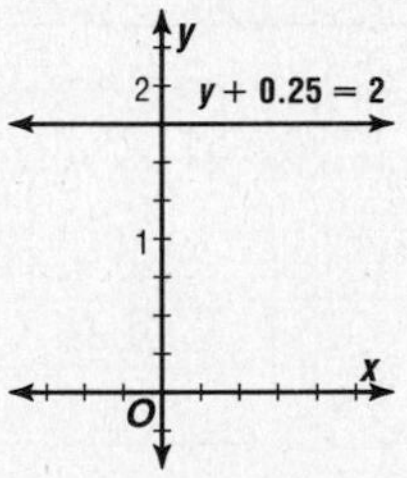

43. Solve for y: $\frac{4x}{3} = \frac{3y}{4} + 1$

$$\frac{4x}{3} - 1 = \frac{3}{4}y$$
$$x - \frac{4}{3} = y$$

x	$x - \frac{4}{3}$	y	(x, y)
-2	$(-2) - \frac{4}{3}$	$-\frac{10}{3}$	$\left(-2, \frac{10}{3}\right)$
-1	$(-1) - \frac{4}{3}$	$-\frac{7}{3}$	$\left(-1, \frac{7}{3}\right)$
0	$(0) - \frac{4}{3}$	$-\frac{4}{3}$	$\left(0, -\frac{4}{3}\right)$
1	$(1) - \frac{4}{3}$	$-\frac{1}{3}$	$\left(1, -\frac{1}{3}\right)$
2	$(2) - \frac{4}{3}$	$\frac{2}{3}$	$\left(2, \frac{2}{3}\right)$

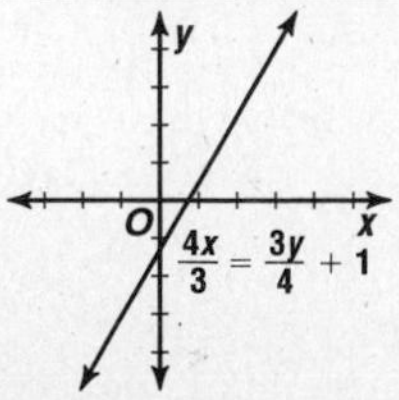

44. Solve for y: $y + \frac{1}{3} = \frac{1}{4}x - 3$

$$y = \frac{1}{4}x - \frac{10}{3}$$

x	$\frac{1}{4}x - \frac{10}{3}$	y	(x, y)
-4	$\frac{1}{4}(-4) - \frac{10}{3}$	$-\frac{13}{3}$	$\left(-4, -\frac{13}{3}\right)$
-2	$\frac{1}{4}(-2) - \frac{10}{3}$	$-\frac{23}{6}$	$\left(-2, -\frac{23}{6}\right)$
0	$\frac{1}{4}(0) - \frac{10}{3}$	$-\frac{10}{3}$	$\left(0, -\frac{10}{3}\right)$
2	$\frac{1}{4}(2) - \frac{10}{3}$	$-\frac{17}{6}$	$\left(2, -\frac{17}{6}\right)$
4	$\frac{1}{4}(4) - \frac{10}{3}$	$-\frac{7}{3}$	$\left(4, -\frac{7}{3}\right)$

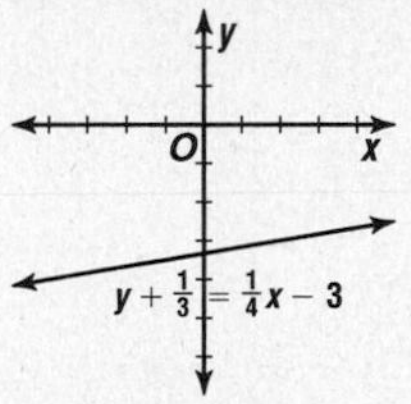

45. Solve for y:

$$\frac{3x}{4} + \frac{y}{2} = 6$$
$$\frac{y}{2} = 6 - \frac{3x}{4}$$
$$y = 12 - \frac{3x}{2}$$

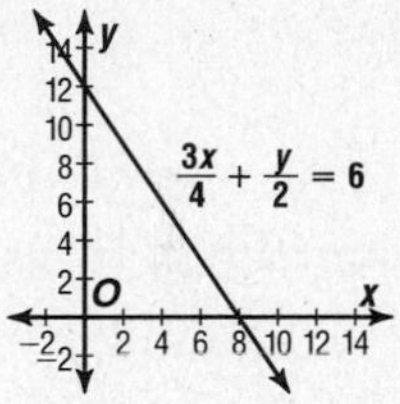

x	$12 - \frac{3x}{2}$	y	(x, y)
-2	$12 - \frac{3(-2)}{2}$	15	$(-2, 15)$
0	$12 - \frac{3(0)}{2}$	12	(0, 12)
2	$12 - \frac{3(2)}{2}$	9	(2, 9)
4	$12 - \frac{3(4)}{2}$	6	(4, 6)
6	$12 - \frac{3(6)}{2}$	3	(6, 3)

46.

x	y
0	4
1	5
2	6
3	7
4	8
5	9

$y = x + 4$

47.

x	y
10	-5
5	-2.5
0	0
-5	2.5
-10	5
-15	7.5

$y = -\frac{1}{2}x$

48.

x	y
0	0
3	6
6	12
9	18
12	24
15	30

$y = 2x$

49.

x	y
-6	5
-4	6
-2	7
0	8
2	9
4	10

$y = \frac{1}{2}x + 8$

50. [−10, 10] by [−10, 10], Xscl: 1, Yscl: 1

Enter: [Y=] 2 [X,T,θ] [+] 4 [ZOOM] 6

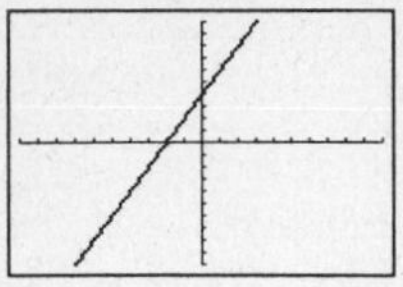

51. Solve for y: $4x - 9y = 45$

$$-9y = 45 - 4x$$
$$y = \frac{-45 + 4x}{9}$$

[−5, 15] by [−10, 10], Xscl: 1, Yscl: 1

Enter: [Y=] [(] [(−)] 45 [+] [X,T,θ] [)] [÷] 9

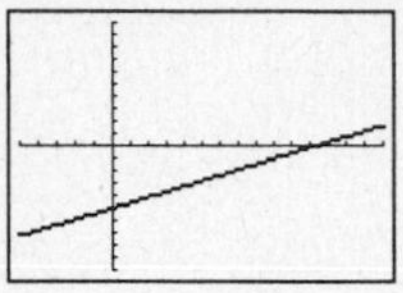

52. Solve for y: $27x + 75y = 100$

$$75y = 100 - 27x$$
$$y = \frac{100 - 27x}{75}$$

[−10, 10] by [−10, 10], Xscl: 1, Yscl: 1

Enter: [Y=] [(] 100 [−] 27 [X,T,θ] [)] [÷] 75 [ZOOM] 6

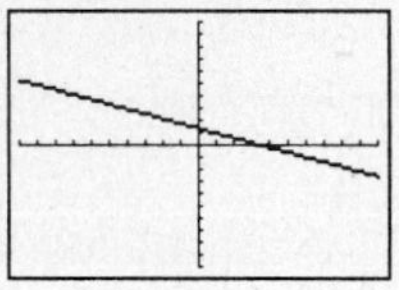

53. Solve for y: $17y = 22$

$$y = \frac{22}{17}$$

[−10, 10] by [−2, 2], Xscl: 1, Yscl: 0.25

Enter: [Y=] 22 [÷] 17 [GRAPH]

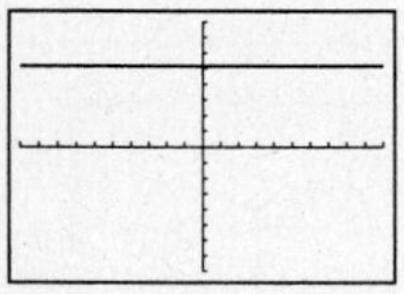

54. Solve for y: $0.2x - 9.7y = 8.9$

$$-9.7y = 8.9 - 0.2x$$
$$y = \frac{-89 + 2x}{97}$$

[−5, 50] by [−1.5, 0.5], Xscl: 5, Yscl: 0.25

Enter: [Y=] [(] [(−)] 89 [+] 2 [X,T,θ] [)] [÷] 97 [GRAPH]

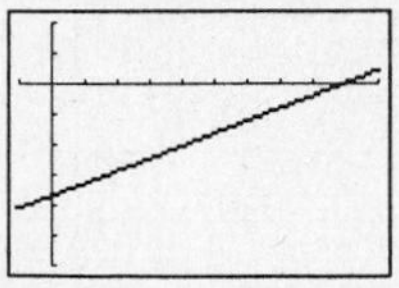

55. Solve for y: $\frac{1}{2}x - \frac{2}{3}y = 10$

$$-\frac{2}{3}y = 10 - \frac{1}{2}x$$
$$y = -15 + \frac{3}{4}x$$

[−5, 25] by [−20, 5], Xscl: 5, Yscl: 5

Enter: [Y=] 0.75 [X,T,θ] [−] 15 [GRAPH]

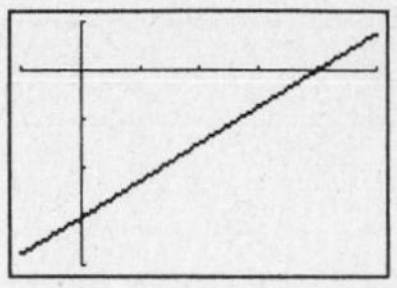

56. Graph of $x = 3$; use the same procedure but change 3 to −25.

57a. Sample answer: Parallel lines that slant upward and intersect the x-axis at −7, −2.5, 0, and 4.5.

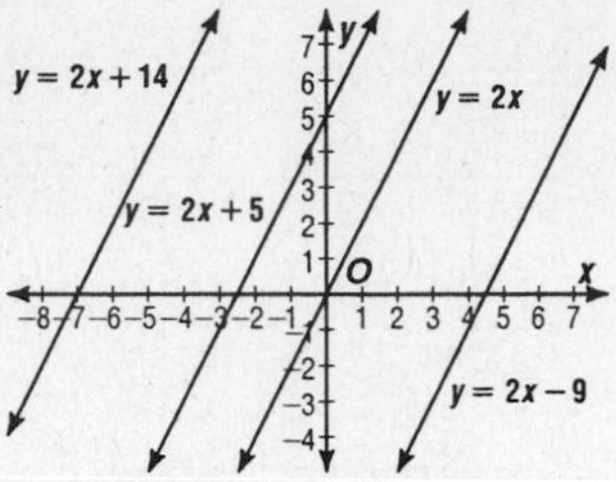

57b. Sample answer: Parallel lines that slant downward and intersect the x-axis at 0, $1\frac{1}{3}$, $2\frac{1}{3}$, and $-3\frac{1}{3}$.

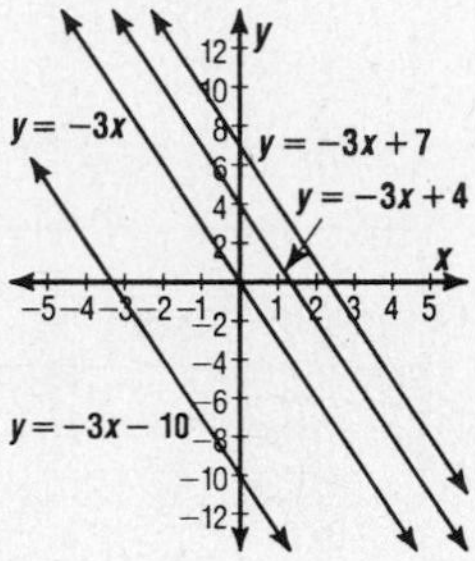

58a. D: $t \geq 0$; R: $y \geq 0$

58b.

t	$0.21t$	y	(t, y)
0	0.21(0)	0	(0, 0)
10	0.21(10)	2.1	(10, 2.1)
20	0.21(20)	4.2	(20, 4.2)
30	0.21(30)	6.3	(30, 6.3)
40	0.21(40)	8.4	(40, 8.4)

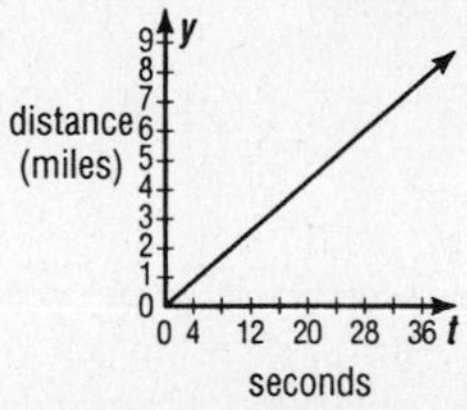

58c. about 14 seconds

59a.

x	$1800 + 0.06x$	y	(x, y)
0	1800 + 0.06(0)	1800	(0, 1800)
800	1800 + 0.06(800)	1848	(800, 1848)
1300	1800 + 0.06(1300)	1878	(1300, 1878)
2000	1800 + 0.06(2000)	1920	(2000, 1920)

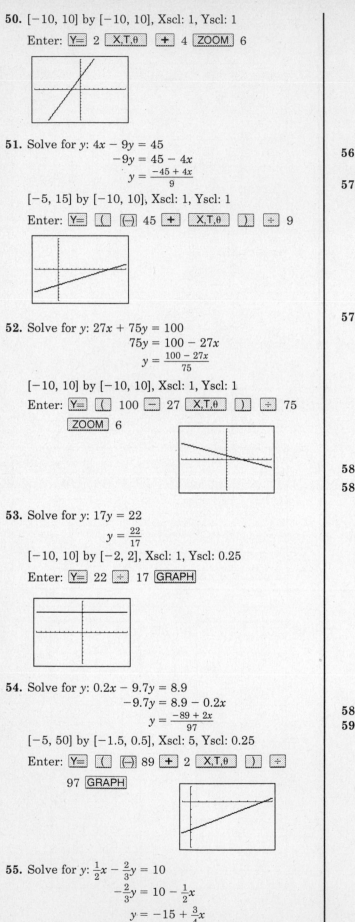

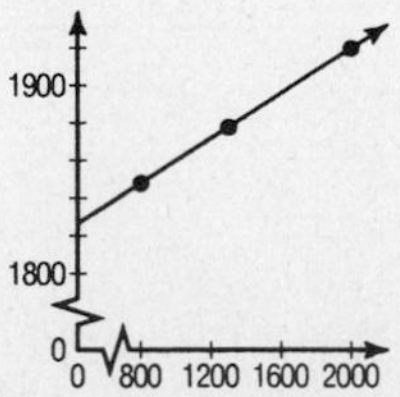

59b. yes, but only if her sales are \$1300 or \$2000 over target

60a. $C = 0.092(68.2)t$

$C = 6.2744t$

t	$6.2744t$	C	(t, C)
0	6.2744(0)	0	(0, 0)
5	6.2744(5)	31	(5, 31)
10	6.2744(10)	63	(10, 63)
15	6.2744(15)	94	(15, 94)
20	6.2744(20)	125	(20, 125)
25	6.2744(25)	157	(25, 157)
30	6.2744(30)	188	(30, 188)
35	6.2744(35)	220	(35, 220)
40	6.2744(40)	251	(40, 251)
45	6.2744(45)	282	(45, 282)
50	6.2744(50)	314	(50, 314)
55	6.2744(55)	345	(55, 345)
60	6.2744(60)	376	(60, 376)

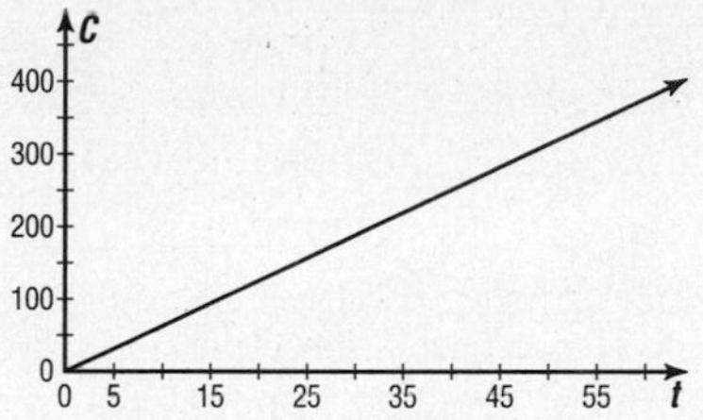

60b. He will burn more Calories in the new routine because $0.092(30)(72.3) + 0.132(30)(72.3) > 0.092(60)(72.3)$.

61. $8x + 2y = 6$

$2y = 6 - 8x$

$y = 3 - 4x$

62.

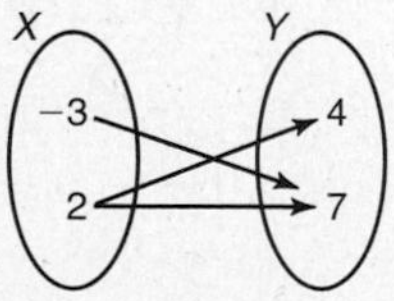

63a.

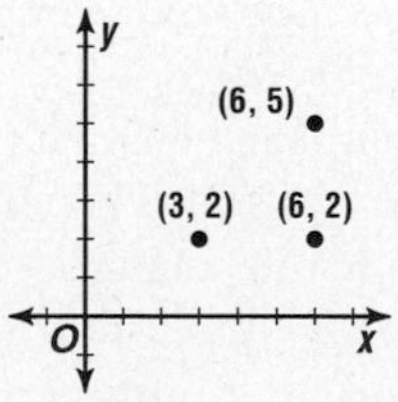

63b. (3, 5)

63c. $|5 - 2| = |3| = 3$

Each side is 3 inches.

$P = 4s$

$= 4(3)$

$= 12$ inches

64. $P(\text{orange}) = \dfrac{14}{24 + 5 + 18 + 14 + 9} = \dfrac{14}{70} = \dfrac{1}{5}$

65. $\dfrac{4.50}{(24.65 + 4.50)} = \dfrac{4.50}{29.15} \approx 0.15$

The percent of discount was about 15%.

66. Let x = the first of the next four finishers, then $x + 1$ = the second of the next four finishers, then $x + 2$ = the third of the next four finishers, and $x + 3$ = the fourth of the next four finishers.

$4 + x + (x + 1) + (x + 2) + (x + 3) = 70$

$4x + 10 = 70$

$4x = 60$

$x = 15$

15th, 15 + 1 = 16th, 15 + 2 = 17th, 15 + 3 = 18th

67. $x + 30 + 30 = 180$

$x + 60 = 180$

$x = 120°$

The angle is 120°.

68. $\dfrac{2 \text{ m}}{0.25 \text{ kg}} = \dfrac{50 \text{ m}}{x \text{ kg}}$

$2x = 50(0.25)$

$2x = 12.5$

$x = 6.25$

50 meters of tubing weigh 6.25 kg.

69. $\dfrac{\frac{-3}{-4}}{-36} = \dfrac{-3}{4} \div -36$

$= \dfrac{-3}{4} \cdot -\dfrac{1}{36}$

$= \dfrac{3}{144}$

$= \dfrac{1}{48}$

70. $-21 + 25 = 31$

Page 286 Self Test

1.

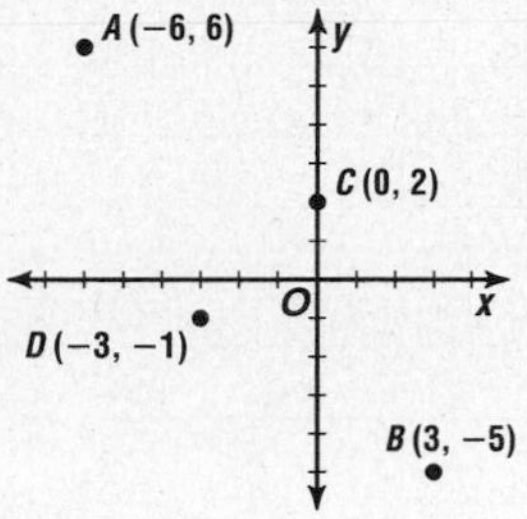

2. {(1, 3), (2, 7), (4, 1), (−3, 3), (−3, −3)}; D = {−3, 1, 2, 4}; R = {−3, 1, 3, 7}; Inv = {(3, 1), (7, 2), (1, 4), (3, −3), (−3, −3)}

3. {(−5, −3), (−1, 4), (4, 4), (4, −3)}; D = {−5, −1, 4}; R = {−3, 4}; Inv = {(−3, −5), (4, −1), (4, 4), (−3, 4)}

4. Solve for y: $3y + 6x = 12$

$3y = 12 - 6x$

$y = 4 - 2x$

x	$4 - 2x$	y
−2	4 − 2(−2)	8
−1	4 − 2(−1)	6
0	4 − 2(0)	4
1	4 − 2(1)	2
3	4 − 2(3)	−2

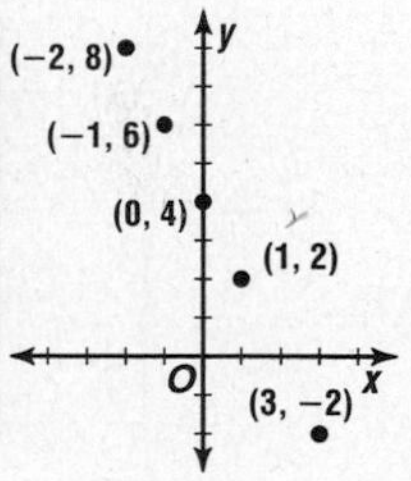

{(−2, 8), (−1, 6), (0, 4), (1, 2), (3, −2)}

5. Solve for b: $2a + 3b = 9$

$3b = 9 - 2a$

$b = \dfrac{4 - 2a}{3}$

$b = 3 - \dfrac{2}{3}a$

a	$3 - \frac{2}{3}a$	b
−2	$3 - \frac{2}{3}(-2)$	$4\frac{1}{3}$
−1	$3 - \frac{2}{3}(-1)$	$3\frac{2}{3}$
0	$3 - \frac{2}{3}(0)$	3
1	$3 - \frac{2}{3}(1)$	$2\frac{1}{3}$
3	$3 - \frac{2}{3}(3)$	1

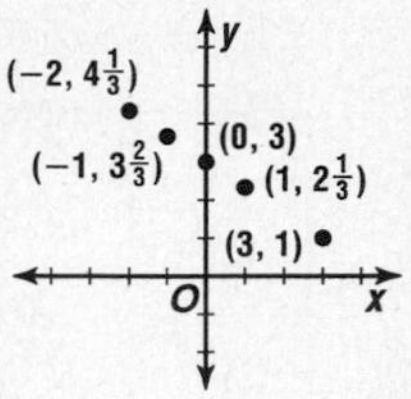

$\left\{\left(-2, 4\frac{1}{3}\right), \left(-1, 3\frac{2}{3}\right), (0, 3), \left(1, 2\frac{1}{3}\right), (3, 1)\right\}$

6. Solve for s: $5r = 8 - 4s$

$$5r - 8 = -4s$$
$$\frac{8 - 5r}{4} = s$$

r	$\frac{8-5r}{4}$	s
-2	$\frac{8-5(-2)}{4}$	$4\frac{1}{2}$
-1	$\frac{8-5(-1)}{4}$	$3\frac{1}{4}$
0	$\frac{8-5(0)}{4}$	2
1	$\frac{8-5(1)}{4}$	$\frac{3}{4}$
3	$\frac{8-5(3)}{4}$	$-1\frac{3}{4}$

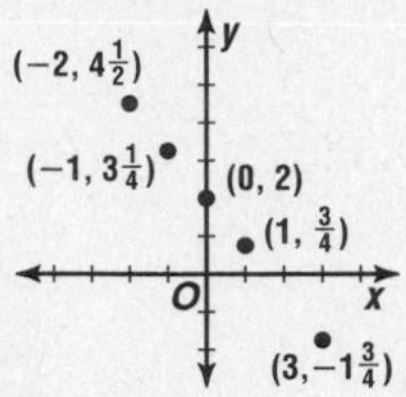

$\left\{\left(-2, 4\frac{1}{2}\right), \left(-1, 3\frac{1}{4}\right), (0, 2), \left(1, \frac{3}{4}\right), \left(3, -1\frac{3}{4}\right)\right\}$

7.

x	$x - 1$	y	(x, y)
-2	$-2 - 1$	-3	$(-2, -3)$
-1	$-1 - 1$	-2	$(-1, -2)$
0	$0 - 1$	-1	$(0, -1)$
1	$1 - 1$	0	$(1, 0)$
2	$2 - 1$	1	$(2, 1)$

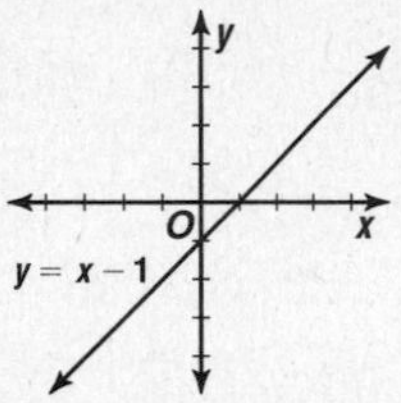

8.

x	$2x - 1$	y	(x, y)
-2	$2(-2) - 1$	-5	$(-2, -5)$
-1	$2(-1) - 1$	-3	$(-1, -3)$
0	$2(0) - 1$	-1	$(0, -1)$
1	$2(1) - 1$	1	$(1, 1)$
2	$2(2) - 1$	3	$(2, 3)$

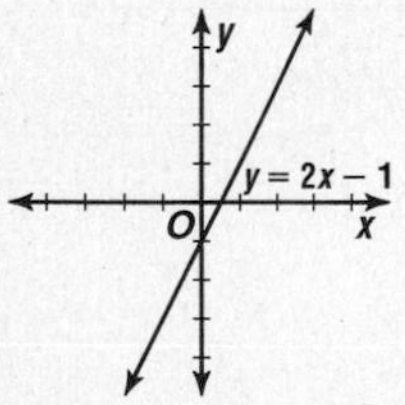

9. Solve for y: $3x + 2y = 4$

$$2y = 4 - 3x$$
$$y = 2 - \frac{3}{2}x$$

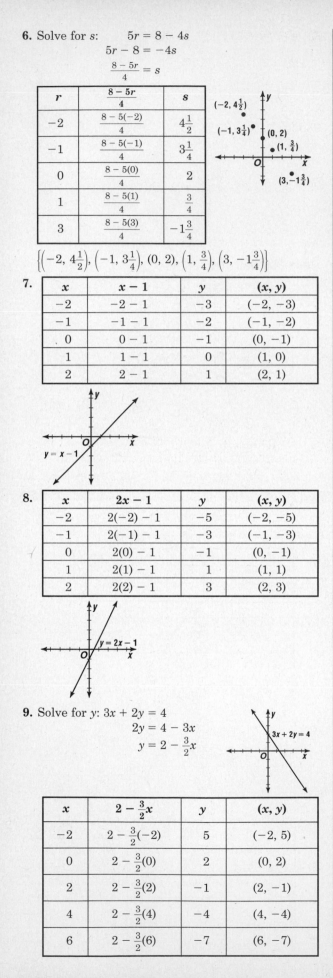

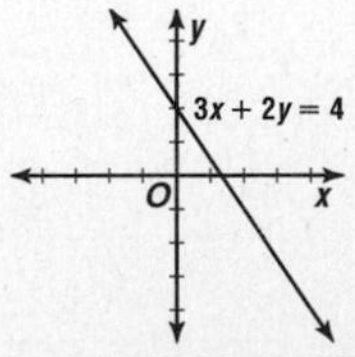

x	$2 - \frac{3}{2}x$	y	(x, y)
-2	$2 - \frac{3}{2}(-2)$	5	$(-2, 5)$
0	$2 - \frac{3}{2}(0)$	2	$(0, 2)$
2	$2 - \frac{3}{2}(2)$	-1	$(2, -1)$
4	$2 - \frac{3}{2}(4)$	-4	$(4, -4)$
6	$2 - \frac{3}{2}(6)$	-7	$(6, -7)$

10. $A = \frac{1}{2}h(b_1 + b_2)$

$$40 = \frac{1}{2}h(5 + 10)$$
$$40 = \frac{1}{2}h(15)$$
$$40 = \frac{15}{2}h$$
$$5.3\overline{3} = h$$

The height is about 5.33 m.

5-5 Functions

Page 291 Check for Understanding

1. A relation is a set of ordered pairs. A function is a relation in which each member of the domain is paired with only one member of the range.
2. The value of one variable is dependent upon the value of the other variable. That is, if w is a function of f, the value of w is dependent upon the value of f in the expression defining w.
3. Substitute 1 for x in the equation and evaluate; $g(1) = 15$.
4. False; $x = 4$ is not a function.
5. Sample answer: If you can draw a vertical line through the graph at any point and it intersects the graph more than once, the graph is not the graph of a function.
6. Yes; for each element of the domain, there is only one corresponding element of the range.
7. No; the element 5 in the domain is paired with both 3 and 4 in the range.
8. Yes; for any given value of x, there is only one value for y.
9. Yes; each element of the domain is paired with exactly one element of the range.
10. No; the element -2 in the domain is paired with both 2 and -5 in the range.
11. Yes; in a table of values, for any given x, there is only one y value that will satisfy the equation.
12. No; in a table of values, for any given x, there are two y values that satisfy the equation.
13. No; the vertical line test fails.
14. a, c

15. $h(-4) = 3(-4) + 2$
$= -12 + 2$
$= -10$

16. $h(2) = 3(2) + 2$
$= 6 + 2$
$= 8$

17. $h(w) = 3(w) + 2$
$= 3w + 2$

18. $h(r - 6) = 3(r - 6) + 2$
$= 3r - 18 + 2$
$= 3r - 16$

Pages 292–294

19. Yes; for any given value of a, there is only one value for b.
20. No; the element -4 in the domain is paired with 3, 2 and 1 in the range.

21. No; for the element 3 in the domain, there are three corresponding elements in the range.

22. Yes; for each element of the domain, there is only one corresponding element in the range.

23. Yes; for any given value of x, there is only one value for y.

24. No; the x value of 1 is paired with a y value of 1 and -2 and the x value of 3 is paired with a y value of 3 and -2.

25. Yes; each element of the domain is paired with exactly one element of the range.

26. No; the element 4 in the domain is paired with 5 and 7 in the range.

27. Yes; each element of the domain is paired with exactly one element of the range.

28. Yes; each element of the domain is paired with exactly one element of the range.

29. Yes; for any given value of x, there is only one value for y that will satisfy the equation.

30. No; a graph of the equation fails the vertical line test.

31. Yes; for any given value of x, there is only one value for y that will satisfy the equation.

32. Yes; for any given value of x, there is only one value for y that will satisfy the equation.

33. No; a graph of the equation fails the vertical line test.

34. Yes; for any given value of x, there is only one value for y that will satisfy the equation.

35. $f(-4) = 4(-4) + 2$
$= -16 + 2$
$= -14$

36. $g(4) = (4)^2 - 2(4)$
$= 16 - 8$
$= 8$

37. $g\left(\frac{1}{5}\right) = \left(\frac{1}{5}\right)^2 - 2\left(\frac{1}{5}\right)$
$= \frac{1}{25} - \frac{2}{5}$
$= \frac{1}{25} - \frac{10}{25}$
$= -\frac{9}{25}$

38. $f\left(\frac{3}{4}\right) = 4\left(\frac{3}{4}\right) + 2$
$= 3 + 2$
$= 5$

39. $g(3.5) = (3.5)^2 - 2(3.5)$
$= 12.25 - 7$
$= 5.25$

40. $f(6.2) = 4(6.2) + 2$
$= 24.8 + 2$
$= 26.8$

41. $3[f(-2)] = 3[4(-2) + 2]$
$= 3(-8 + 2)$
$= 3(-6)$
$= -18$

42. $-6[g(0.4)] = -6[(0.4)^2 - 2(0.4)]$
$= -6(0.16 - 0.8)$
$= -6(-0.64)$
$= 3.84$

43. $g(3b) = (3b)^2 - 2(3b)$
$= 9b^2 - 6b$

44. $f(2y) = 4(2y) + 2$
$= 8y + 2$

45. $-3[g(1)] = -3[(1)^2 - 2(1)]$
$= -3(1 - 2)$
$= -3(-1)$
$= 3$

46. $3[g(2w)] = 3[(2w)^2 - 2(2w)]$
$= 3(4w^2 - 4w)$
$= 12w^2 - 12w$

47. $5[g(a^2)] = 5[(a^2)^2 - 2(a^2)]$
$= 5(a^4 - 2a^2)$
$= 5a^4 - 10a^2$

48. $f(c + 3) = 4(c + 3) + 2$
$= 4c + 12 + 2$
$= 4c + 14$

49. $6[f(p - 2)] = 6[4(p - 2) + 2]$
$= 6(4p - 8 + 2)$
$= 6(4p - 6)$
$= 24p - 36$

50. $-3[f(5w + 2)] = 3[4(5w + 2) + 2]$
$= -3(20w + 8 + 2)$
$= -3(20w + 10)$
$= -60w - 30$

51a. Answers will vary; a sample answer is $f(x) = x$. The function and its inverse have the same graph.

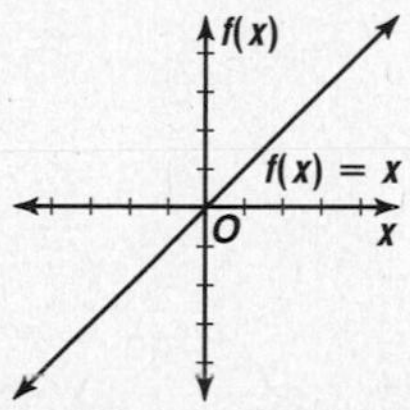

x	$f(x)$	$(x, f(x))$
0	0	(0, 0)
1	1	(1, 1)
2	2	(2, 2)
3	3	(3, 3)

51b. Answers will vary; a sample answer is $f(x) = x^2$.

x	x^2	$f(x)$	$(x, f(x))$
-2	$(-2)^2$	4	$(-2, 4)$
-1	$(-1)^2$	1	$(-1, 1)$
0	$(0)^2$	0	(0, 0)
1	$(1)^2$	1	(1, 1)
2	$(2)^2$	4	(2, 4)

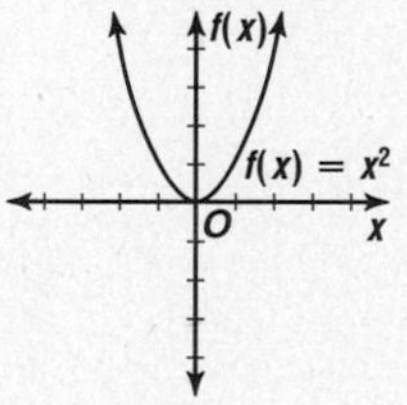

Inv = {(4, −2), (1, −1),(0, 0), (1, 1), (4, 2)}

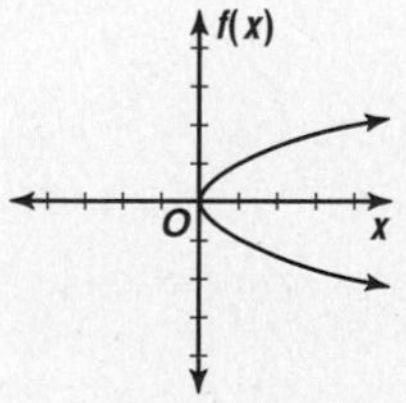

52. b; Each step represents a minute or any part thereof; this graph represents a function since for any given time, there is only one value for cost.

53. a; It is a step function using individual points, since you cannot have a fraction of a T-shirt.

54a.

x	$f(x) = x^2 + 3x + 2$	$f(x)$	$(x, f(x))$
−5	$(-5)^2 + 3(-5) + 2$	12	(−5, 12)
−4	$(-4)^2 + 3(-4) + 2$	6	(−4, 6)
−3	$(-3)^2 + 3(-3) + 2$	2	(−3, 2)
−2	$(-2)^2 + 3(-2) + 2$	0	(−2, 0)
−1	$(-1)^2 + 3(-1) + 2$	0	(−1, 0)
0	$(0)^2 + 3(0) + 2$	2	(0, 2)
1	$(1)^2 + 3(1) + 2$	6	(1, 6)
2	$(2)^2 + 3(2) + 2$	12	(2, 12)

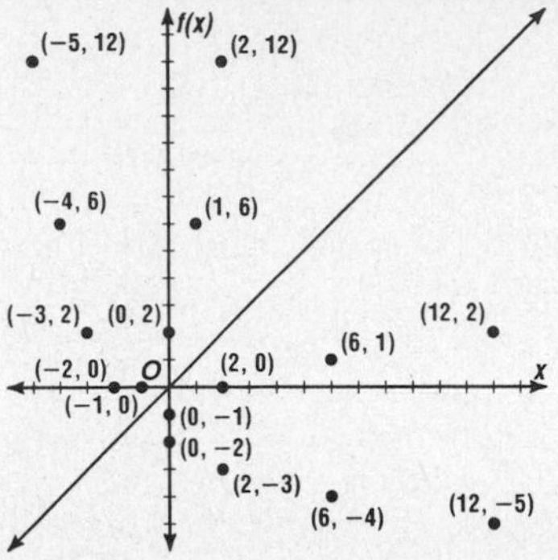

Inv = {(12, −5), (6, −4), (2, −3), (0, −2), (0, −1), (2, 0), (6, 1), (12, 2)}

54b. No; the elements 12, 6, 2, and 0 in the domain are each paired with two values in the range.

54c. The inverse is a reflection of the function with $y = x$ acting as the mirror.

55a. D: $0 \le k \le 24$; R: $0 \le y \le 100$

55b. It is a line.

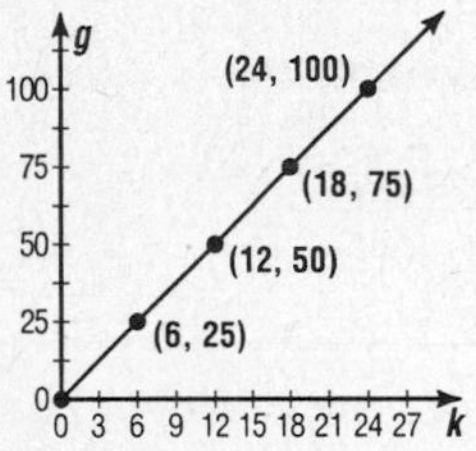

55c. 24 karats

56a. $T = 35d + S$
$= 35(30) + 75$
$= 1050 + 75$
$= 1125$°F

56b. $T = 35d + S$
$= 35(7) + 0$
$= 245$°F

56c. Because the crust is thinnest when measured from the bottom of the ocean and thicker from the tops of mountains.

57a. $B = 0.15(2000 - B)$
$B = 300 - 0.15B$
$1.15B = 300$
$B = \$260.87$

57b. Equations may vary; Sample equation:
$B = 0.15(P - B)$
$B = 0.15P - 0.15B$
$1.15B = 0.15\ P$
$B = \frac{3}{23}P$

P	$\frac{3}{23}P$	B	(P, B)
0	$\frac{3}{23}(0)$	0	(0, 0)
2300	$\frac{3}{23}(2300)$	300	(2300, 300)
4600	$\frac{3}{23}(4600)$	600	(4600, 600)
6900	$\frac{3}{23}(6900)$	900	(6900, 900)
9200	$\frac{3}{23}(9200)$	1200	(9200, 1200)

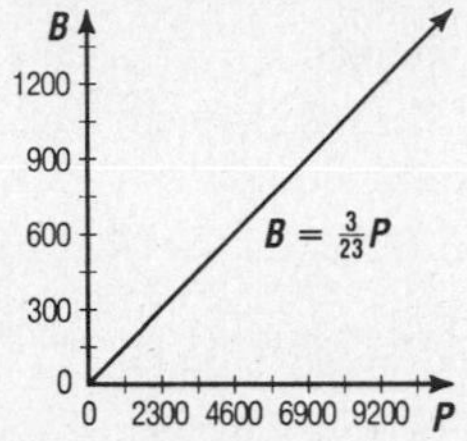

58. Solve for y: $y - x = -5$
$y = x - 5$

x	$x - 5$	y	(x, y)
−2	−2 − 5	−7	(−2, −7)
−1	−1 − 5	−6	(−1, −6)
0	0 − 5	−5	(0, −5)
1	1 − 5	−4	(1, −4)
2	2 − 5	−3	(2, −3)

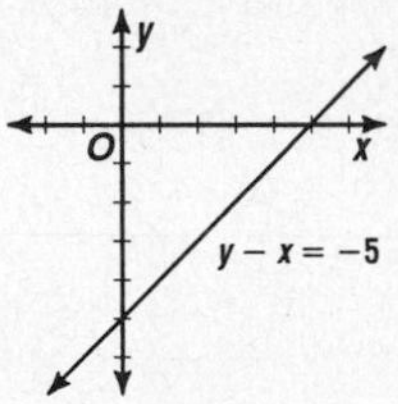

59. Solve for b: $3a - b = 7$
$-b = -3a + 7$
$b = 3a - 7$

a	$3a - 7$	b
−3	3(−3) − 7	−16
−2	3(−2) − 7	−13
4	3(4) − 7	5
6	3(6) − 7	11

{−16, −13, 5, 11}

60. {(1, −1), (9, −5), (6, 4)}

61. P(jack, queen, or king) $= \frac{12}{52} = \frac{3}{13}$

62. $\frac{x}{100} = \frac{44}{89}$

$89x = 4400$

$x \approx 49.4\%$

63. $\sin x = \cos x$

$\frac{\sin x}{\cos x} = \frac{\cos x}{\cos x}$

$\tan x = 1$

$x = 45°$

64. $x + 167 + 4 = 180$

$x + 171 = 180$

$x = 9°$

The third angle measures 9°.

65. $\frac{z}{-4} - 9 = 3$

$\frac{z}{-4} = 12$

$z = -48$

66. $210.87 - 95.25 = \$115.62$

67a.

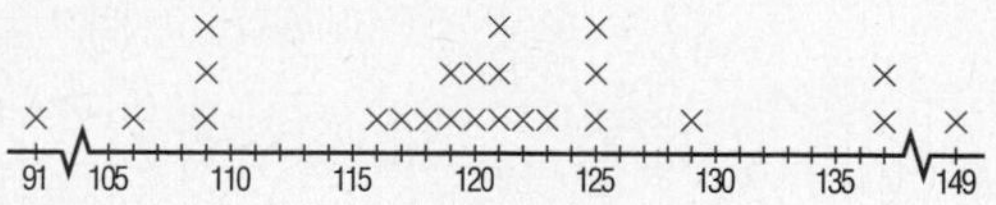

67b. 149

67c. 91

67d. 121 and 125

67e. 13 players

5-6 Writing Equations from Patterns

Pages 298–299 Check for Understanding

1a. upward

1b. downward

2. Test the values of the domain in the equation. If the resulting values match the range, the equation is correct.

3. Yes; she can use points on the line since the line represents all solutions to the equation.

4. Sample answer: $2x + y = 3$; No, $4x + 2y = 6$ and other equivalent equations also have these solutions.

5. $\frac{\text{range differences}}{\text{domain differences}}$ $\quad \frac{14-12}{4-3} = 2 \quad \frac{16-14}{5-4} = 2$

$f(x) = 2x + 6$

6. $\frac{\text{range differences}}{\text{domain differences}}$ $\quad \frac{-3-(-4)}{4-2} = \frac{1}{2} \quad \frac{-2-(-3)}{6-4} = \frac{1}{2}$

$f(x) = \frac{1}{2}x - 5$

7.

x	−5	−3	−1	1	3	5
y	−4	−3	−2	−1	0	1

$\frac{\text{range differences}}{\text{domain differences}}$ $\quad \frac{-3-(-4)}{-3-(-5)} = \frac{1}{2} \quad \frac{-1-(-2)}{1-(-1)} = \frac{1}{2}$

$y = \frac{1}{2}x - \frac{3}{2}$

8.

x	−3	1	3	4
y	−3	1	3	4

$\frac{\text{range differences}}{\text{domain differences}}$ $\quad \frac{4-3}{4-3} = 1 \quad \frac{3-1}{3-1} = \frac{2}{2}$ or 1

$y = x$

9. $\frac{\text{range differences}}{\text{domain differences}}$ $\quad \frac{-8-(-10)}{4-8} = \frac{2}{-4}$ or $-\frac{1}{2}$

$\frac{-7-(-8)}{2-4} = -\frac{1}{2}$

$N(m) = -\frac{1}{2}m - 6$

$N(0) = -\frac{1}{2}(0) - 6$

$= -6$

See students' work.

10a.

water	11	33	66
ice	12	36	72

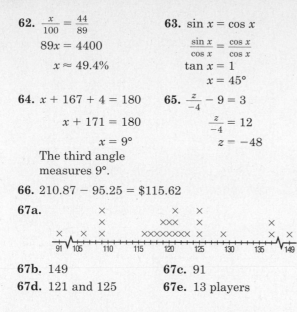

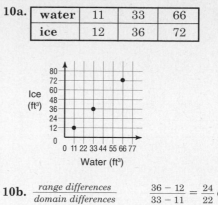

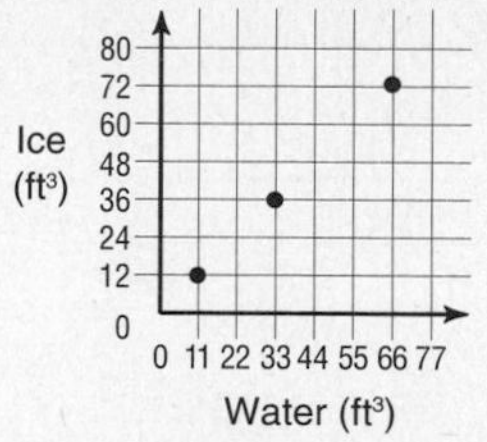

10b. $\frac{\text{range differences}}{\text{domain differences}}$ $\quad \frac{36-12}{33-11} = \frac{24}{22}$ or $\frac{12}{11}$

$\frac{72-36}{66-33} = \frac{36}{33}$ or $\frac{12}{11}$

$f(w) = \frac{12}{11}w$

Pages 299–302 Exercises

11.

x	1	2	3	4	5
$f(x)$	12	24	36	48	60

$f(x) = 12x$

$f(4) = 12(4) = 48$

$f(5) = 12(5) = 60$

12.

x	−4	−2	0	2	4
$g(x)$	−2	−1	0	1	2

$g(x) = \frac{1}{2}x$

$g(0) = \frac{1}{2}(0) = 0$

$g(2) = \frac{1}{2}(2) = 1$

13.

x	−3	−1	1	2	4
$h(x)$	18	8	−2	−7	−17

$h(x) = -5x + 3$

$h(-1) = -5(-1) + 3$ or 8

$h(1) = -5(1) + 3$ or −2

14.

x	−2	0	2	4	6
$p(x)$	0	1	2	3	4

$p(x) = \frac{1}{2}x + 1$

$p(-2) = \frac{1}{2}(-2) + 1$ or 0

$p(0) = \frac{1}{2}(0) + 1$ or 1

15. $\frac{\text{range differences}}{\text{domain differences}} = \frac{10-5}{2-1} = 5$

$f(x) = 5x$

16. $\frac{\text{range differences}}{\text{domain differences}} = \frac{4-1}{2-1} = 3$

$f(n) = 3n - 2$

17. $\frac{\text{range differences}}{\text{domain differences}} = \frac{12-13}{-1-(-2)} = -1$

$g(x) = -x + 11$ or $g(x) = 11 - x$

18. $\frac{\text{range differences}}{\text{domain differences}} = \frac{-3-(-11)}{-2-(-4)} = \frac{8}{2}$ or 4

$m(n) = 4n + 5$

19. $\frac{\text{range differences}}{\text{domain differences}} = \frac{0-(-2)}{6-0} = \frac{2}{6}$ or $\frac{1}{3}$

$h(x) = \frac{1}{3}x - 2$

20. $\frac{\text{range differences}}{\text{domain differences}} = \frac{18-26}{0-(-4)} = \frac{-8}{4}$ or −2

$m(n) = -2n + 18$ or $m(n) = 18 - 2n$

21.

x	−1	0	1
y	3	0	−3

$\frac{\text{range differences}}{\text{domain differences}} \quad \frac{0-3}{0-(-1)} = -3$

$y = -3x$

22.

x	−3	−1	0	1	2
y	−1	1	2	3	4

$\frac{\text{range differences}}{\text{domain differences}} = \frac{2-1}{0-(-1)} = 1$

$y = x + 2$

23.

x	−4	−2	0	2	4
y	−2	−1	0	1	2

$\frac{\text{range differences}}{\text{domain differences}} = \frac{1-0}{2-0} = \frac{1}{2}$

$y = \frac{1}{2}x$

24.

x	0	2	4	6
y	6	4	2	0

$\frac{\text{range differences}}{\text{domain differences}} = \frac{2-4}{4-2} = \frac{-2}{2}$ or -1

$y = -x + 6$

25.

x	2	3	4	5
y	−6	−4	−2	0

$\frac{\text{range differences}}{\text{domain differences}} = \frac{-2-(-4)}{4-3} = 2$

$y = 2x - 10$

26.

x	0	2	4
y	12	6	0

$\frac{\text{range differences}}{\text{domain differences}} = \frac{0-6}{4-2} = \frac{-6}{2}$ or -3

$y = -3x + 12$

27. $xy = -24$

28. $y = x^2 + 1$

29. $y = x^3$

30. $y = \frac{48}{x^2}$

31. y-intercept: $f(0)$, x-intercept: $f(x) = 0$

32. $\frac{\text{range differences}}{\text{domain differences}} = \frac{2}{3}$

x	−3	0	3	6
y	2	4	6	8

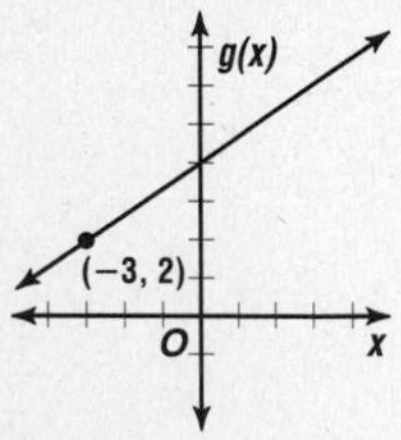

33a. $\frac{\text{range differences}}{\text{domain differences}} \quad \frac{34-0}{2-1} = 34 \quad \frac{68-34}{3-2} = 34$

$f(x) = 34x - 34$

33b. You must go deeper in fresh water to get the same pressure as in ocean water.

34a. Sample answer:

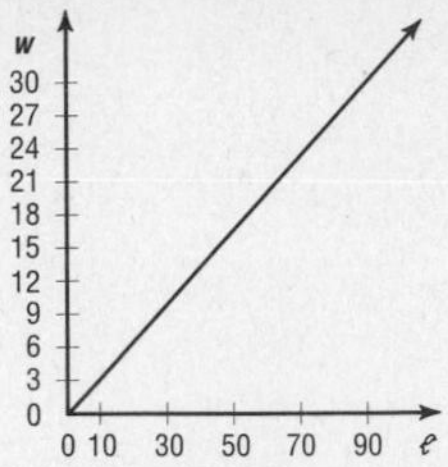

34b. about 16 lb

34c. $W(\ell) = \frac{23}{70}\ell$

34d. $w(50) = \frac{23}{70}(50)$

$= 16.4$ lb, slightly more than estimate

35a. $797 + 327 + 390 = 1514$ C

35b. $(0.138)(80) = 11.04$ C/min

35c.

Minutes	Calories
1	11.04
2	22.08
3	33.12
4	44.16
5	55.2
6	66.24
7	77.28
8	88.32
9	99.36
10	110.4

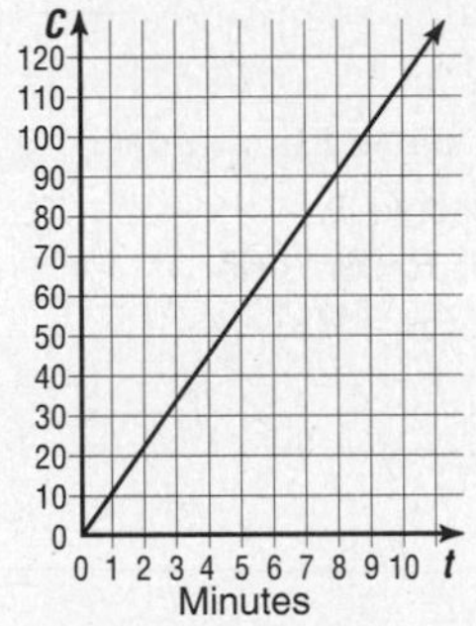

35d. $C(t) = 11.04t$; yes

35e. $C(120) = 11.04(120)$

$= 1324.8$ C burned;

yes, $1514 - 1324.8 = 189.2$ C remaining

36a. $f(12) - \frac{12}{0.2} - 32 = 60 - 32 = 28$ times

36b. $\frac{54 \text{ times}}{3 \text{ hours}} = \frac{x \text{ times}}{1 \text{ hour}}$

$3x = 54$

$x = 18$ times

$18 = \frac{t}{0.2} - 32$

$50 = \frac{t}{0.2}$

$10°\text{C} = t$

37. D = {1, 3, 5};

R = {2, 4, 6}

38. $\frac{16}{100} = \frac{x}{50}$

$16(50) = 100x$

$800 = 100x$

$8 = x$

8 is 16% of 50.

39. $\frac{s}{4} = \frac{s+10}{12}$

$12s = 4(s + 10)$

$12s = 4s + 40$

$8s = 40$

$s = 5$

40. $x + (-7) = 36$

$x + (-7) + 7 = 36 + 7$

$x = 43$

41. 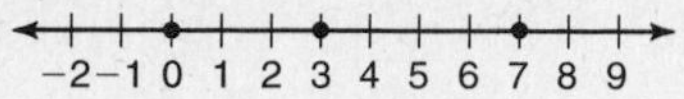

42.

Stem	Leaf
2	3
3	2
4	3 5 7
5	3 7 8 9 9 9
6	0 0 2 2 4 4 5
•	5 6 6 6 6 6 6
•	6 7 8 8 8 8 9
7	0 2 3 4 4 4 4
•	4 4 4 4 5 5 5
•	5 5 5 5 5 5 5

2|3 = 23¢

5-7A Graphing Technology Measures of Variation

Page 304 Exercises

1. Enter: STAT 4 2nd L1 ENTER

Enter: STAT 1

Enter the values into L1, pressing ENTER after each entry.

Enter: STAT ▶ 1 ENTER

Q_1, 14; Med, 17; Q_3, 20.5; R, 23 − 12 = 11;
IQR = $Q_3 - Q_1$ = 20.5 − 14 = 6.5

2. Repeat steps from Exercise 1.
Q_1, 34; Med, 40; Q_3, 45; R, 56 − 10 = 46;
IQR = $Q_3 - Q_1$ = 45 − 34 = 11

3. Repeat steps from Exercise 1.
Q_1, 68; Med, 78; Q_3, 96; R, 99 − 65 = 34;
IQR = $Q_3 - Q_1$ = 96 − 68 = 28

4. Repeat steps from Exercise 1.
Q_1, 45; Med, 65; Q_3, 85; R, 100 − 30 = 70;
IQR = $Q_3 - Q_1$ = 85 − 45 = 40

5. Repeat steps from Exercise 1.
Q_1, 3.4; Med, 5.3; Q_3, 21; R, 78 − 1 = 77;
IQR = $Q_3 - Q_1$ = 21 − 3.4 = 17.6

6. Repeat steps from Exercise 1.
Q_1, 62; Med, 73; Q_3, 77; R, 92 − 55 = 37;
IQR = $Q_3 - Q_1$ = 77 − 62 = 15

7. At least 50% of the data is clustered around the median.

8. Each item of data from Q_1 to Q_3 is the same number.

5-7 Integration: Statistics Measures of Variation

Page 309 Check for Understanding

1. Columbus:

35 38 39 ↑ 49 51 62 ↑ 65 73 77 ↑ 81 83 84

Q_1 = 44 Median = 63.5 Q_3 = 79

IQR = $Q_3 - Q_1$ = 79 − 44 = 35

San Francisco:

56 57 59 ↑ 60 61 63 ↑ 63 64 64 ↑ 65 68 69

Q_1 = 59.5 Median = 63 Q_3 = 64.5

IQR = $Q_3 - Q_1$ = 64.5 − 59.5 = 5

San Francisco, 5; Columbus, 35

2. Outliers may make the mean much higher or lower than the mean of the data excluding the outliers.

3a. Sample answer: the basketball teams

3b. Sample answer: the football team

4. The range in Lesson 5-2 is a set of values that correspond to a set of domain values. Range in this lesson describes the spread of data.

5a. See students' work.

5b. See students' work.

6. 11, 16, 17, 19, 24
range = 24 − 11 − 13 median = 17
$Q_3 = \frac{19 + 24}{2} = 21.5$ $Q_1 = \frac{11 + 16}{2} = 13.5$
IQR = 21.5 − 13.5 = 8

7. 11, 34, 37, 43, 45, 56
range = 56 − 11 = 45 median = $\frac{37 + 43}{2} = 40$
Q_3 = 45 Q_1 = 34
IQR = 45 − 34 = 11
outlier: 1.5(11) = 16.5
34 − 16.5 = 17.5; 11 is an outlier since it is less than 17.5

8. range = 148,000 − 32,500 = $115,500
median = $\frac{50{,}800 + 53{,}000}{2}$ = 51,900
Q_3 = 57,300 Q_1 = 42,700
IQR = 57,300 − 42,700 = 14,600
outlier: 1.5(14,600) = 21,900
57,300 + 21,900 = 79,200; $148,000 is an outlier since it is greater than 79,200

9. range = 48 − 0 = 48 median = 26
Q_3 = 39 Q_1 = 17
IQR = 39 − 17 = 22

10. median = 6′2″ Q_3 = $\frac{6'3'' + 6'4''}{2}$ = 6′3.5″
Q_1 = 5′11″
IQR = 6′3.5″ − 5′11″ = 4.5″

Pages 310–313 Exercises

11. 65, 68, 77, 78, 84, 96, 99
range = 99 − 65 = 34 median = 78
Q_3 = 96 Q_1 = 68
IQR = 96 − 68 = 28

12. 17°, 18°, 19°, 21°, 22°, 46°
range = 46 − 17 = 29 median = 19
Q_3 = 22 Q_1 = 18
IQR = 22 − 18 = 4

13. 0, 2, 2, 4, 4, 6, 6, 8, 8, 10
range = 10 − 0 = 10 median = $\frac{4 + 6}{2}$ = 5
Q_3 = 8 Q_1 = 2
IQR = 8 − 2 = 6

14. 56, 64, 73, 75, 82, 87, 89, 92
range = 92 − 56 = 36 median = $\frac{75 + 82}{2}$ = 78.5
$Q_3 = \frac{87 + 89}{2} = 88$ $Q_1 = \frac{64 + 73}{2} = 68.5$
IQR = 88 − 68.5 = 19.5

15. 29.9, 30.0, 30.1, 30.5, 30.7, 30.8, 31.0, 31.0
range = 31.0 − 29.9 = 1.1
median = $\frac{30.5 + 30.7}{2}$ = 30.6
$Q_3 = \frac{30.8 + 31.0}{2} = 30.9$ $Q_1 = \frac{30.0 + 30.1}{2} = 30.05$
IQR = 30.9 − 30.05 = 0.85

16. 1, 2, 3, 3.2, 3.4, 4, 5, 5, 6, 7, 8, 45, 78
range = 78 − 1 = 77 median = 5
$Q_3 = 8$ $Q_1 = 3.2$
IQR = 8 − 3.2 = 4.8

17. 835, 975, 1005, 1025, 1050, 1055, 1075, 1075, 1095, 1100, 1125, 1125, 1145, 1175
range = 1175 − 835 = 340 median = 1075
$Q_3 = 1125$ $Q_1 = 1025$
IQR = 1125 − 1025 = 100

18. range = 9900 − 5300 = 4600
median = 7700
$Q_3 = \frac{8400 + 8800}{2} = 8600$
$Q_1 = \frac{6500 + 6800}{2} = 6650$
IQR = 8600 − 6650 = 1950

19. range = 232 − 193 = 39 median = 218
$Q_3 = 221$ $Q_1 = 202$
IQR = 221 − 202 = 19

20. range = 9.9 − 5.0 = 4.9
median = $\frac{7.50 + 7.60}{2}$ = 7.55
$Q_3 = \frac{8.3 + 8.5}{2} = 8.4$ $Q_1 = \frac{6.3 + 6.4}{2} = 6.35$
IQR = 8.4 − 6.35 = 2.05

21a. Enter: [STAT] 4 [2nd] [L1] [ENTER]
Enter each number of books in L_1.
Enter: [STAT] 1
Enter: [STAT] [▶] 3 Highlight L_1.
Enter: [STAT] [▶] 1 [ENTER]
Med = 9,198,630
Q_3 = 11,750,000
Q_1 = 5,700,000
Range = 28,000,000 − 4,000,000 = 24,000,000
IQR = $Q_3 - Q_1$ = 11,750,000 − 5,700,000
= 6,050,000

21b. No; the libraries would have accumulated books throughout the years.

22a. Sample answer: {26, 27, 28, 29, 30, 36, 37, 38, 39, 40, 41, 42, 43, 45, 46, 50, 55, 58, 86}

22b. Sample answer: {29, 31, 32, 33, 34, 36, 37, 38, 39, 40, 41, 42, 43, 44, 45, 46, 47, 48, 49}

23. range = 6137 − 2377 = 3760
median = 3224
$Q_3 = \frac{3486 + 4917}{2} = 4201.5$
$Q_1 = \frac{2717 + 2844}{2} = 2780.5$
IQR = 4201.5 − 2780.5 = 1421

24. range = 360,448 − 214,761 = 145,687
median = $\frac{255{,}579 + 269{,}034}{2}$ = 262,306.5
Q_3 = 299,737 Q_1 = 219,683
IQR = 299,737 − 219,683 = 80,054

25. range = 23,651 − 1977 = 21,674
median = 9790
Q_3 = 12,194 Q_1 = 5475
IQR = 12,194 − 5475 = 6719

26. range = 225 − 50 = 175
median = $\frac{120 + 130}{2}$ = 125
$Q_3 = \frac{185 + 190}{2} = 187.5$ $Q_1 = \frac{85 + 100}{2} = 92.5$
IQR = 187.5 − 92.5 = 95

27a.

Males	**Females**
range = 54 − 18 = 36	range = 46 − 23 = 23
$Q_1 = 29$	$Q_1 = 29$
median = $\frac{37 + 38}{2}$ = 37.5	median = $\frac{32 + 34}{2}$ = 33
$Q_3 = \frac{42 + 46}{2} = 44$	$Q_3 = 39$
IQR = 44 − 29 = 15	IQR = 39 − 29 = 10

27b. There are no outliers.

27c. The ages of the top female golfers are less varied than those of the top male golfers.

28a. range = 86.8 − 19.0 = $67.8 million
median = $50.5 million
$Q_3 = \frac{70.0 + 78.2}{2}$ = \$74.1 million
$Q_1 = \frac{27.5 + 30.6}{2}$ = \$29.05 million
IQR = 74.1 − 29.05 = $45.05 million

28b. There are none.

28c. None of these are on the top 20 list.

29a. See students' work. **29b.** See students' work.

29c. See students' work.

30a.

x	0	2	10
y	20	90	370

$\frac{\textit{range differences}}{\textit{domain differences}} = \frac{90 - 20}{2 - 0} = 35$; $y = 35x + 20$

30b. $y = 35(13) + 20$
$y = 455 + 20$
$y = 475°C$

31. c, d $5 - 1.5x = 2y$

31a. (0.1) $5 - 1.5(0) \stackrel{?}{=} 2(1)$ => $5 \neq 2$ no
31b. (8, 2) $5 - 1.5(8) \stackrel{?}{=} 2(2)$ => $-7 \neq 4$ no
31c. $\left(4, -\frac{1}{2}\right)$ $5 - 1.5(4) \stackrel{?}{=} 2\left(-\frac{1}{2}\right)$ => $-1 = -1$ yes
31d. (2, 1) $5 - 1.5(2) \stackrel{?}{=} 2(1)$ => $2 = 2$ yes

32. $\frac{20 \text{ grams}}{1.5 \text{ hours}} = \frac{50 \text{ grams}}{x \text{ hours}}$
$20x = 50(1.5)$
$20x = 75$
$x = 3.75$
Jodi would be able to drive her car 3.75 hours.

33a. $6.2 + p = 9.4$
$p = 3.2$
about 3.2 million people

33b. $6.0 + p = 6.9$
$p = 0.9$
about 0.9 million people

34. $3(-4) + 2(-7) = -12 + (-14)$
$= -26$

Page 313 Mathematics and Society

1. $80 - (-128) = 208°F$
2. No; the wind-chill factor applies to people and animals, but not to inanimate objects.
3. $136 - (-128) = 264°F$
4. The temperature stays the same about half of the time.

Chapter 5 Highlights

Page 315 Understanding and Using the Vocabulary

1. e origin
2. g relation
3. d ordered pairs
4. h *x*-axis
5. j *y*-coordinate
6. f quadrants
7. c linear function
8. a domain
9. b independent variable

Chapter 5 Study Guide and Assessment

Pages 316–318 Skills and Concepts

10–13.

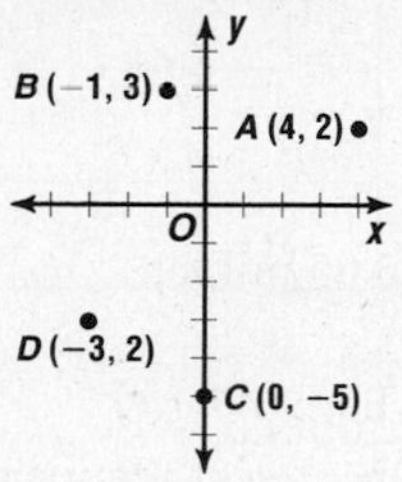

14. (−4, 0); none
15. (2, −1); IV
16. (−1, −4); III
17. (1, 1); I
18. D = {4}, R = {−1, 1, 6}
19. D = {−3, 4}, R = {5, 6}
20. D = {−7, −5, −2}, R = {1}
21. D = {−3, −2, −1, 0}, R = {0, 1, 2}

22.

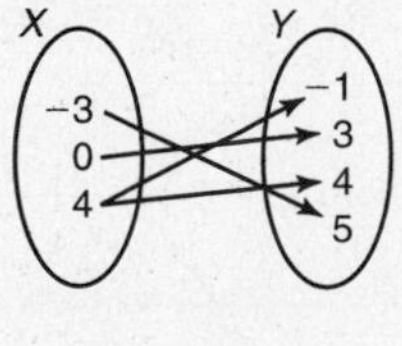

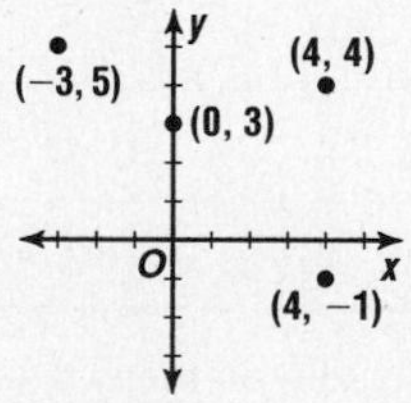

Inv = {(4, 4), (5, −3), (−1, 4), (3, 0)}

23.

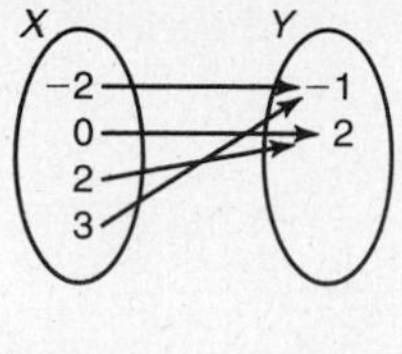

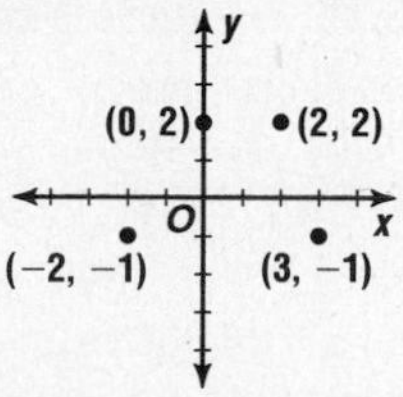

Inv = {(2, 0), (−1, 3), (2, 2), (−1, −2)}

24.

x	$4x + 5$	y	(x, y)
−4	4(−4) + 5	−11	(−4, −11)
−2	4(−2) + 5	−3	(−2, −3)
0	4(0) + 5	5	(0, 5)
2	4(2) + 5	13	(2, 13)
4	4(4) + 5	21	(4, 21)

25. Solve for y: $x - y = 9$

$$-y = 9 - x$$
$$y = x - 9$$

x	$x - 9$	y	(x, y)
−4	−4 − 9	−13	(−4, −13)
−2	−2 − 9	−11	(−2, −11)
0	0 − 9	−9	(0, −9)
2	2 − 9	−7	(2, −7)
4	4 − 9	−5	(4, −5)

26. Solve for y: $3x + 2y = 9$

$$2y = 9 - 3x$$
$$y = \frac{9 - 3x}{2}$$

x	$\frac{9 - 3x}{2}$	y	(x, y)
−4	$\frac{9 - 3(-11)}{2}$	$10\frac{1}{2}$	$\left(-4, 10\frac{1}{2}\right)$
−2	$\frac{9 - 3(-2)}{2}$	$7\frac{1}{2}$	$\left(-2, 7\frac{1}{2}\right)$
0	$\frac{9 - 3(0)}{2}$	$4\frac{1}{2}$	$\left(0, 4\frac{1}{2}\right)$
2	$\frac{9 - 3(2)}{2}$	$1\frac{1}{2}$	$\left(2, 1\frac{1}{2}\right)$
4	$\frac{9 - 3(4)}{2}$	$-1\frac{1}{2}$	$\left(4, -1\frac{1}{2}\right)$

27. Solve for y: $4x - 3y = 0$

$$4x = 3y$$
$$\frac{4}{3}x = y$$

x	$\frac{4}{3}x$	y	(x, y)
−4	$\frac{4}{3}(-4)$	$-5\frac{1}{3}$	$\left(-4, -5\frac{1}{3}\right)$
−2	$\frac{4}{3}(-2)$	$-2\frac{2}{3}$	$\left(-2, -2\frac{2}{3}\right)$
0	$\frac{4}{3}(0)$	0	(0, 0)
2	$\frac{4}{3}(2)$	$2\frac{2}{3}$	$\left(2, 2\frac{2}{3}\right)$
4	$\frac{4}{3}(4)$	$5\frac{1}{3}$	$\left(4, 5\frac{1}{3}\right)$

28.

x	$7 - 3x$	y	(x, y)
−3	7 − 3(−3)	16	(−3, 16)
−2	7 − 3(−2)	13	(−2, 13)
−1	7 − 3(−1)	10	(−1, 10)
0	7 − 3(0)	7	(0, 7)
1	7 − 3(1)	4	(1, 4)
2	7 − 3(2)	1	(2, 1)
3	7 − 3(3)	−2	(3, −2)

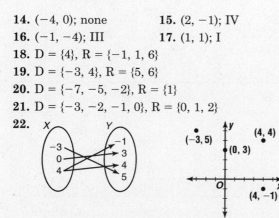

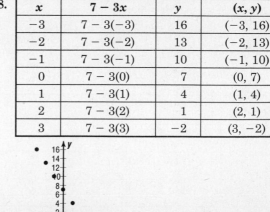

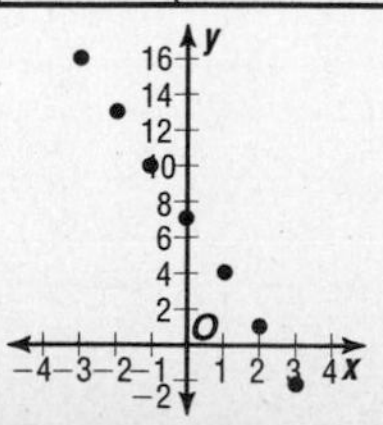

29. Solve for y:

$5x - y = -3$

$-y = -3 - 5x$

$y = 3 + 5x$

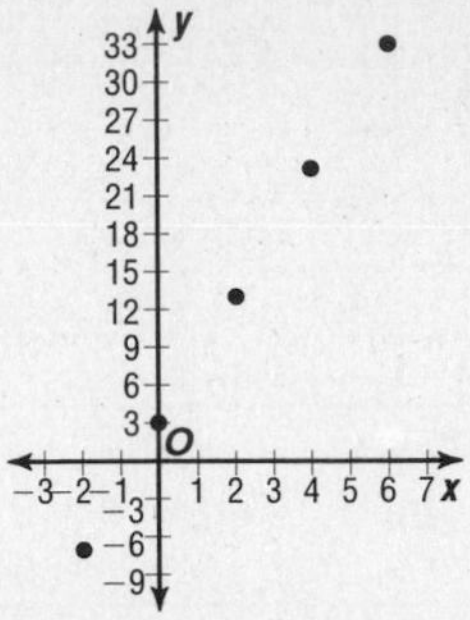

x	$4 + 5x$	y	(x, y)
-2	$3 + 5(-2)$	-7	$(-2, -7)$
0	$3 + 5(0)$	3	$(0, 3)$
2	$3 + 5(2)$	13	$(2, 13)$
4	$3 + 5(4)$	23	$(4, 23)$
6	$3 + 5(6)$	33	$(6, 33)$

30.

x	$-x + 2$	y	(x, y)
0	$-(0) + 2$	2	$(0, 2)$
1	$-(1) + 2$	1	$(1, 1)$
2	$-(2) + 2$	0	$(2, 0)$

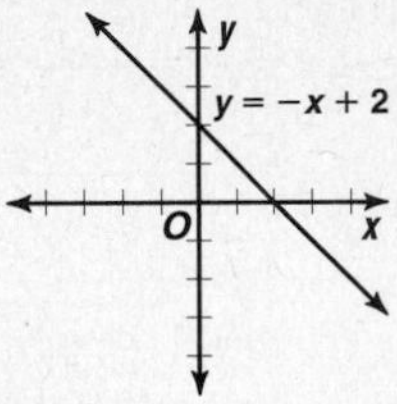

31. Solve for y: $x + 5y = 4$

$5y = 4 - x$

$y = \frac{4 - x}{5}$

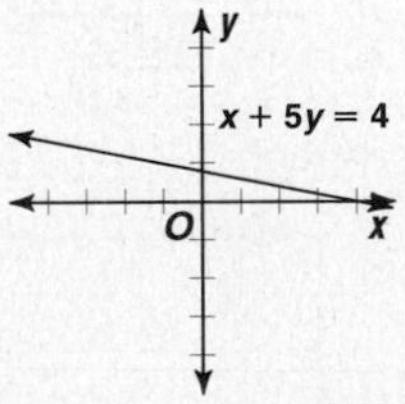

x	$\frac{4 - x}{5}$	y	(x, y)
-1	$\frac{4 - (-1)}{5}$	1	$(-1, 1)$
0	$\frac{4 - 0}{5}$	$\frac{4}{5}$	$\left(0, \frac{4}{5}\right)$
9	$\frac{4 - 9}{5}$	-1	$(9, -1)$

32. Solve for y: $2x - 3y = 6$

$-3y = 6 - 2x$

$y = \frac{2x - 6}{3}$

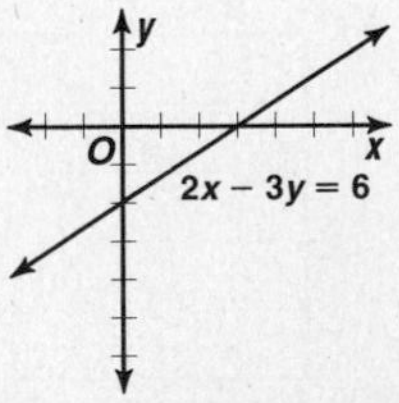

x	$\frac{2x - 6}{3}$	y	(x, y)
0	$\frac{2(0) - 6}{3}$	-2	$(0, -2)$
1	$\frac{2(1) - 6}{3}$	$-\frac{4}{3}$	$\left(1, -\frac{4}{3}\right)$
3	$\frac{2(3) - 6}{3}$	0	$(3, 0)$

33. Solve for y: $5x + 2y = 10$

$2y = 10 - 5x$

$y = \frac{10 - 5x}{2}$

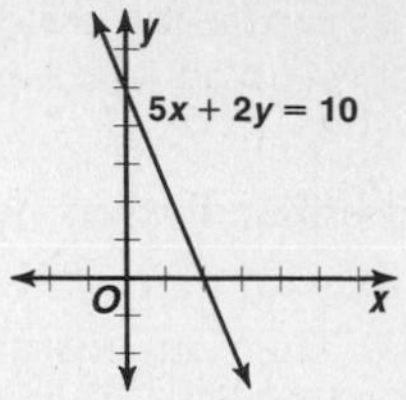

x	$\frac{10 - 5x}{2}$	y	(x, y)
0	$\frac{10 - 5(0)}{2}$	5	$(0, 5)$
1	$\frac{10 - 5(1)}{2}$	$\frac{5}{2}$	$\left(1, \frac{5}{2}\right)$
2	$\frac{10 - 5(2)}{2}$	0	$(2, 0)$

34. Solve for y: $\frac{1}{2}x + \frac{1}{3}y = 3$

$\frac{1}{3}y = 3 - \frac{1}{2}x$

$y = 9 - \frac{3}{2}x$

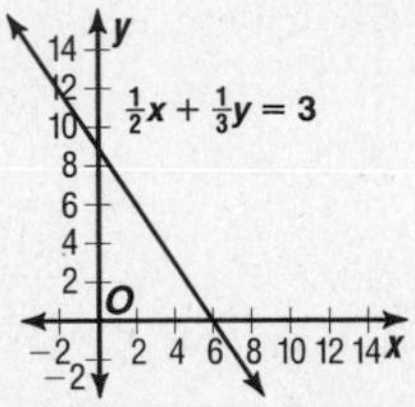

x	$9 - \frac{3}{2}x$	y	(x, y)
-2	$9 - \frac{3}{2}(-2)$	12	$(-2, 12)$
0	$9 - \frac{3}{2}(0)$	9	$(0, 9)$
2	$9 - \frac{3}{2}(2)$	6	$(-2, 6)$

35. Solve for y: $y - \frac{1}{3} = \frac{1}{3}x + \frac{2}{3}$

$y = \frac{1}{3}x + 1$

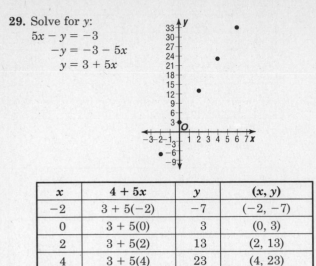

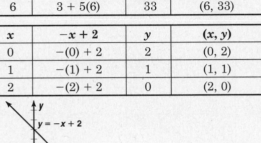

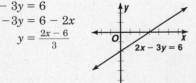

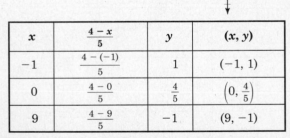

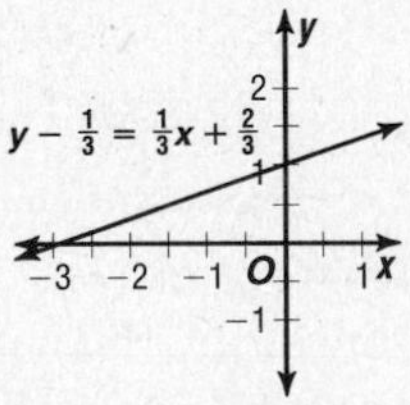

x	$\frac{1}{3}x + 1$	y	(x, y)
-3	$\frac{1}{3}(-3) + 1$	0	$(-3, 0)$
-1	$\frac{1}{3}(-1) + 1$	$\frac{2}{3}$	$\left(-1, \frac{2}{3}\right)$
0	$\frac{1}{3}(0) + 1$	1	$(0, 1)$

36. No; the element 3 in the domain is paired with both -2 and 0 in the range.

37. Yes; for each element in the domain, there is only one corresponding element in the range.

38. Yes; each element of the domain is paired with exactly one element in the range.

39. No; from a table of values, the x value of 5 is paired with the y values of 1 and -1.

40. Yes; a table of values shows that any value of x is paired with one value of y that will satisfy the equation.

41. Yes; a table of values shows that any value of x is paired with one value of y that will satisfy the equation.

42. $g(2) = (2)^2 - (2) + 1$
$= 4 - 2 + 1$
$= 3$

43. $g(-1) = (-1)^2 - (-1) + 1$
$= 1 + 1 + 1$
$= 3$

44. $g\left(\frac{1}{2}\right) = \left(\frac{1}{2}\right)^2 - \frac{1}{2} + 1$
$= \frac{1}{4} - \frac{1}{2} + 1$
$= \frac{3}{4}$

45. $g(a + 1) = (a + 1)^2 - (a + 1) + 1$
$= a^2 + 2a + 1 - a - 1 + 1$
$= a^2 + a + 1$

46. $g(-2a) = (-2a)^2 - (-2a) + 1$
$= 4a^2 + 2a + 1$

47. $2g(a - 3) = 2[(a - 3)^2 - (a - 3) + 1]$
$= 2(a^2 - 6a + 9 - a + 3 + 1)$
$= 2(a^2 - 7a + 13)$
$= 2a^2 - 14a + 26$

48. $\frac{\textit{range differences}}{\textit{domain differences}}$ $\frac{8-5}{1-0} - 3$ $\frac{11-8}{2-1} = 3$
$y = 3x + 5$

49. $\frac{\textit{range differences}}{\textit{domain differences}}$ $\frac{0-(-2)}{4-2} = \frac{2}{2}$ or 1 $\frac{3-1}{7-5} = 1$
$y = x - 4$

50. $\frac{\textit{range differences}}{\textit{domain differences}}$ $\frac{-3-(-1)}{6-3} = -\frac{2}{3}$
$\frac{-7-(-5)}{12-9} = -\frac{2}{3}$
$y = -\frac{2}{3}x + 1$

51. 30, 40, 50, 60, 70, 80, 90, 100
range = 100 − 30 = 70 median = $\frac{60+70}{2} = 65$
$Q_3 = \frac{80+90}{2} = 85$ $Q_1 = \frac{40+50}{2} = 45$
IQR = 85 − 45 = 40

52. 1, 2, 3, 3.2, 3.4, 4, 5, 5, 5.3, 7, 8, 21, 45, 78
range = 78 − 1 = 77 median = 5
$Q_3 = 8$ $Q_1 = 3.2$
IQR = 8 − 3.2 = 4.8

53. 55, 58, 59, 62, 67, 69, 69, 73, 75, 76, 77, 77, 82, 85, 92 range = 92 − 55 = 37 median = 73
$Q_3 = 77$ $Q_1 = 62$
IQR = 77 − 62 = 15

54. 59.8, 63.8, 64.3, 68.6, 70.7, 77.1, 82.3, 88.9, 91.7, 110.5, 111.5, 254.8
range = 254.8 − 59.8 = 195
median = $\frac{77.1+82.3}{2} = 79.7$
$Q_3 = \frac{91.7+110.5}{2} = 101.1$ $Q_1 = \frac{64.3+68.6}{2} = 66.45$
IQR = 101.1 − 66.45 = 34.65

55a.

w	$5w + 56$	s	$(s, 5)$
0	5(0) + 56	56	(0, 56)
1	5(1) + 56	61	(1, 61)
2	5(2) + 56	66	(2, 66)
3	5(3) + 56	71	(3, 71)

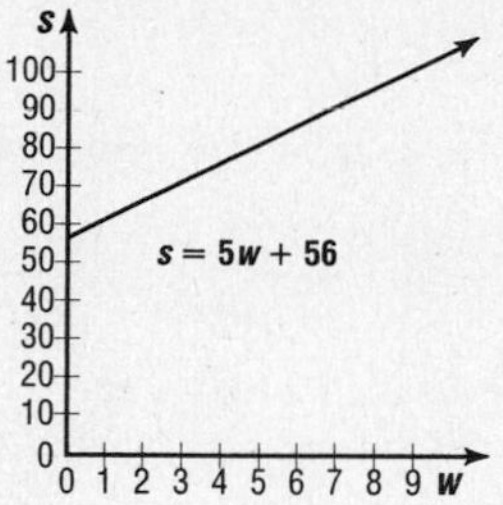

55b. $56

56a.

x	100	160	225
y	41	51.80	63.50

$\frac{\textit{range differences}}{\textit{domain differences}} = \frac{51.80 - 41}{160 - 100} = \frac{10.80}{60} = 0.18$
$y = 0.18x + 23$

56b. $0.18 per mile

57a. range = 14.7 − 5.1 = 9.6 $Q_1 = \frac{5.9+6.1}{2} = 6$
median = $\frac{6.9+7.2}{2} = 7.05$ $Q_3 = \frac{8.2+8.4}{2} = 8.3$
IQR = 8.3 − 6 = 2.3

57b. 1.5 (IQR) = 1.5(2.3)
= 3.45
8.3 + 3.45 = 11.75
6 − 3.45 = 2.55
There are no ratings below 2.55, but there are two ratings above 11.75, 12.6 and 14.7.

Page 319 Alternative Assessment: Thinking Critically

- See students' work.
- Sample answer: {(0, −1), (1, 3), (2, 7), (3, 11)} is a function since each element of the domain is paired with exactly one element of the range; {(6, 7), (0, 9), (8, 1), (6, −2)} is not a function since the element 6 in the domain is paired with both 7 and −2 in the range.

Chapter 6 Analyzing Linear Equations

6-1A Modeling Mathematics: Slope

Page 324

1. $-\frac{1}{2}$
2. $\frac{2-5}{1-3} = \frac{3}{2}$; $\frac{4-2}{1-5} = \frac{2}{-4}$ or $-\frac{1}{2}$; It is the same ratio as the slope of the segments.
3. Sample answer: (3, 3)
4. Sample answer: If $A(a, b)$ and $B(c, d)$ are endpoints of segment AB, then the slope of AB is $\frac{d-b}{c-a}$.
5. Yes; sample answer: suppose the endpoints are $C(-4, -1)$ and $D(-2, -2)$. Let the upper right peg represent (0, 0). To go from C to D, the y value decreases by 1 and the x value increases by 2. The ratio is $-\frac{1}{2}$. If you use the rule from Exercise 3, $\frac{-2-(-1)}{-2-(-4)} = -\frac{1}{2}$. The results are the same.

6-1 Slope

Pages 328–329 Check for Understanding

1. From one point to another, go down 3 units and right 5 units. The slope is $-\frac{3}{5}$.
2. It means that as you travel 100 ft horizontally, your altitude increases 8 ft.
3. Yes, it would affect the sign of the slope.

4a.

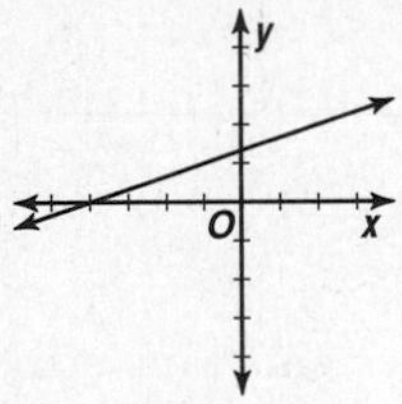

4b.

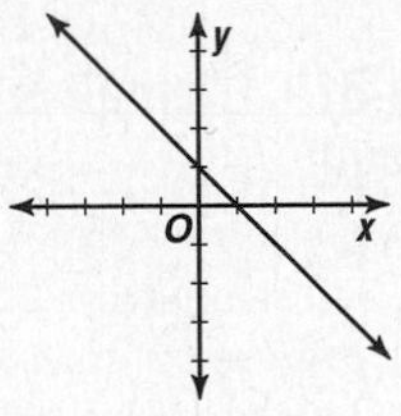

4c.

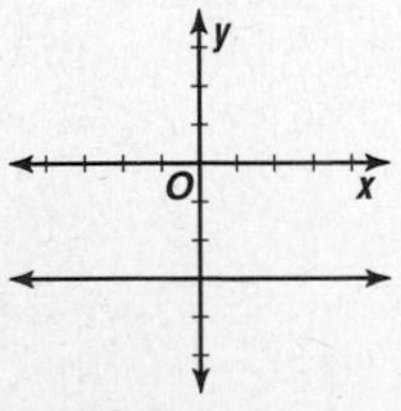

4d.

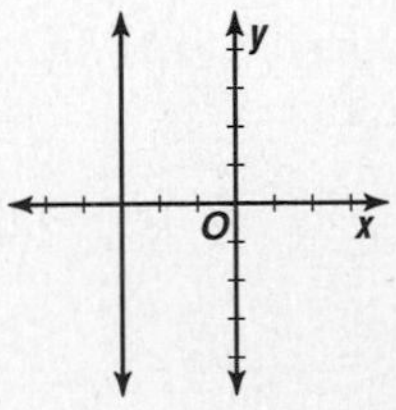

5. The difference in the x values is always 0, and division by 0 is undefined.

6a.

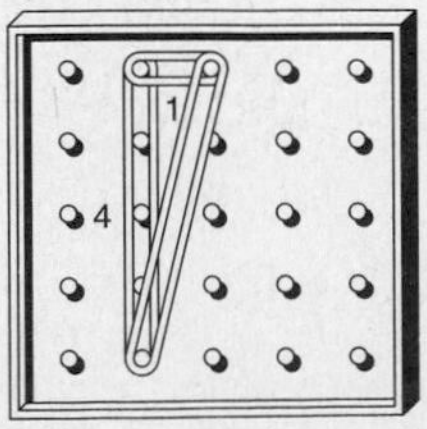

6b.

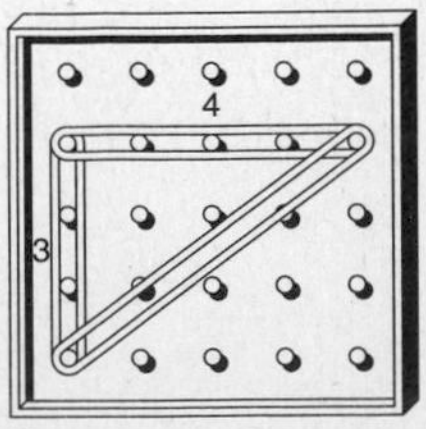

6c.

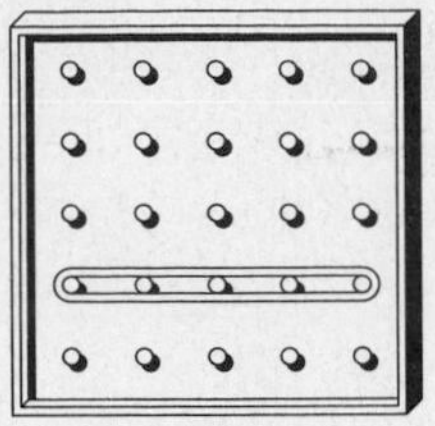

6d.

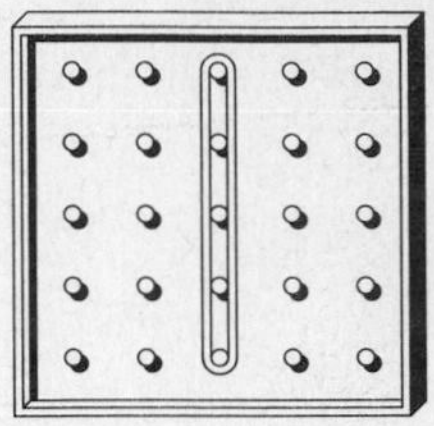

6e.

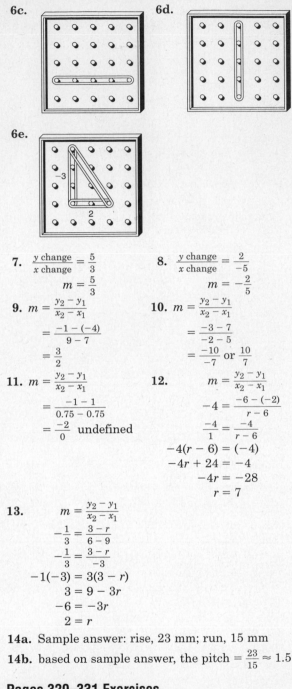

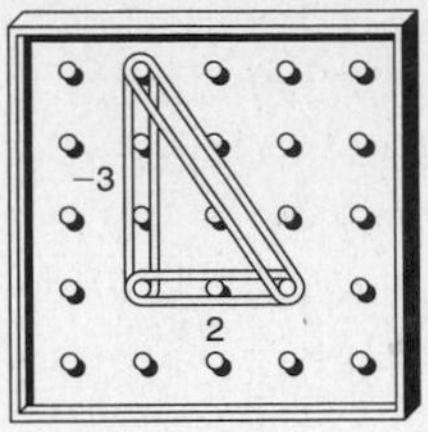

7. $\frac{y \text{ change}}{x \text{ change}} = \frac{5}{3}$
   $m = \frac{5}{3}$

8. $\frac{y \text{ change}}{x \text{ change}} = \frac{2}{-5}$
   $m = -\frac{2}{5}$

9. $m = \frac{y_2 - y_1}{x_2 - x_1}$
   $= \frac{-1-(-4)}{9-7}$
   $= \frac{3}{2}$

10. $m = \frac{y_2 - y_1}{x_2 - x_1}$
   $= \frac{-3-7}{-2-5}$
   $= \frac{-10}{-7}$ or $\frac{10}{7}$

11. $m = \frac{y_2 - y_1}{x_2 - x_1}$
   $= \frac{-1-1}{0.75-0.75}$
   $= \frac{-2}{0}$ undefined

12. $m = \frac{y_2 - y_1}{x_2 - x_1}$
   $-4 = \frac{-6-(-2)}{r-6}$
   $\frac{-4}{1} = \frac{-4}{r-6}$
   $-4(r-6) = (-4)$
   $-4r + 24 = -4$
   $-4r = -28$
   $r = 7$

13. $m = \frac{y_2 - y_1}{x_2 - x_1}$
   $-\frac{1}{3} = \frac{3-r}{6-9}$
   $-\frac{1}{3} = \frac{3-r}{-3}$
   $-1(-3) = 3(3-r)$
   $3 = 9 - 3r$
   $-6 = -3r$
   $2 = r$

14a. Sample answer: rise, 23 mm; run, 15 mm

14b. based on sample answer, the pitch $= \frac{23}{15} \approx 1.5$

Pages 329–331 Exercises

15. $\frac{y \text{ change}}{x \text{ change}} = \frac{1}{-5}$
   $m = -\frac{1}{5}$

16. $\frac{y \text{ change}}{x \text{ change}} = \frac{1}{4}$
   $m = \frac{1}{4}$

17. $\frac{y \text{ change}}{x \text{ change}} = \frac{0}{7}$
   $m = 0$

18. $\frac{y \text{ change}}{x \text{ change}} = \frac{6}{0}$
   undefined

19. $\frac{y \text{ change}}{x \text{ change}} = \frac{1}{1}$
   $m = 1$

20. $\frac{y \text{ change}}{x \text{ change}} = \frac{-6}{1}$
   $m = -6$

21. $m = \frac{y_2 - y_1}{x_2 - x_1}$
   $= \frac{7-3}{9-2}$
   $= \frac{4}{7}$

22. $m = \frac{y_2 - y_1}{x_2 - x_1}$
   $= \frac{-1-(-4)}{5-(-3)}$
   $= \frac{3}{8}$

23. $m = \frac{y_2 - y_1}{x_2 - x_1}$
$= \frac{-3-(-1)}{5-2}$
$= -\frac{2}{3}$

24. $m = \frac{y_2 - y_1}{x_2 - x_1}$
$= \frac{3-6}{-1-2}$
$= \frac{-3}{-3}$ or 1

25. $m = \frac{y_2 - y_1}{x_2 - x_1}$
$= \frac{-1-4}{-5-(-5)}$
$= \frac{-5}{0}$ undefined

26. $m = \frac{y_2 - y_1}{x_2 - x_1}$
$= \frac{3-3}{8-(-2)}$
$= \frac{0}{10}$ or 0

27. $m = \frac{y_2 - y_1}{x_2 - x_1}$
$= \frac{2-(-5)}{4-4}$
$= \frac{7}{0}$ undefined

28. $m = \frac{y_2 - y_1}{x_2 - x_1}$
$= \frac{\frac{1}{2} - \left(-1\frac{1}{2}\right)}{-\frac{1}{2} - 2\frac{1}{2}}$
$= -\frac{2}{3}$

29. $m = \frac{y_2 - y_1}{x_2 - x_1}$
$= \frac{-1 - 1\frac{1}{4}}{-\frac{1}{2} - \frac{3}{4}}$
$= \frac{-2\frac{1}{4}}{-1\frac{1}{4}}$
$= \frac{-\frac{9}{4}}{-\frac{5}{4}}$
$= \frac{9}{5}$

30. $m = \frac{y_2 - y_1}{x_2 - x_1}$
$\frac{4}{3} = \frac{-3-r}{2-5}$
$\frac{4}{3} = \frac{-3-r}{-3}$
$4(-3) = 3(-3-r)$
$-12 = -9 - 3r$
$-3 = -3r$
$1 = r$

31. $m = \frac{y_2 - y_1}{x_2 - x_1}$
$\frac{4}{3} = \frac{3-7}{r-(-2)}$
$\frac{4}{3} = \frac{-4}{r+2}$
$4(r+2) = 3(-4)$
$4r + 8 = -12$
$4r = -20$
$r = -5$

32. $m = \frac{y_2 - y_1}{x_2 - x_1}$
$8 = \frac{r-(-5)}{3-4}$
$\frac{8}{1} = \frac{r+5}{-1}$
$(-1)(8) = r + 5$
$-8 = r + 5$
$-13 = r$

33. $m = \frac{y_2 - y_1}{x_2 - x_1}$
$\frac{-1}{1} = \frac{r-2}{9-6}$
$\frac{-1}{1} = \frac{r-2}{3}$
$-1(3) = r - 2$
$-3 = r - 2$
$-1 = r$

34. $m = \frac{y_2 - y_1}{x_2 - x_1}$
$-\frac{5}{3} = \frac{2-r}{r-4}$
$-5(r-4) = 3(2-r)$
$-5r + 20 = 6 - 3r$
$-2r + 20 = 6$
$-2r = -14$
$r = 7$

35. $m = \frac{y_2 - y_1}{x_2 - x_1}$
$-\frac{2}{9} = \frac{r-5}{-2-r}$
$-2(-2-r) = 9(r-5)$
$4 + 2r = 9r - 45$
$4 = 7r - 45$
$49 = 7r$
$7 = r$

36.

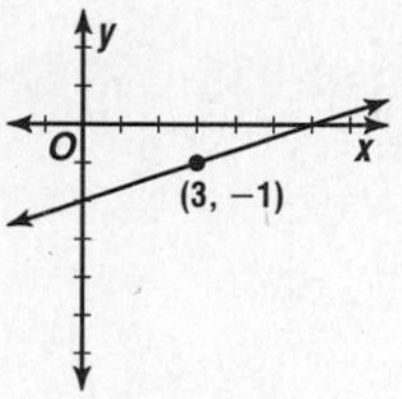

37.

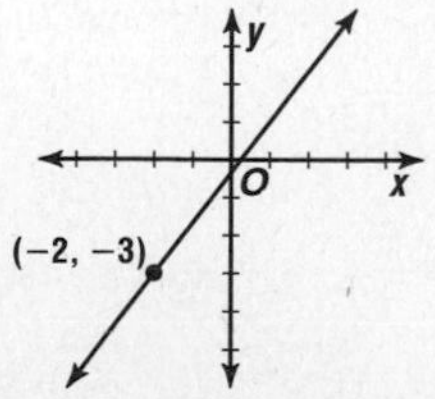

38.

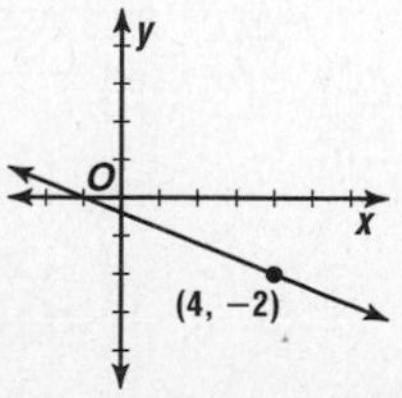

39. Sample answer: (7, 6). The slope of the line containing A and B is -2. Use the slope to go 2 units down and 1 unit to the right of either point.

40. The slope is $\frac{120 \text{ in.}}{30 \text{ ft}} = \frac{10 \text{ ft}}{30 \text{ ft}}$ or $\frac{1}{3}$. Use the slope to figure the length of the support.

distance (in.)	16	32	64	96
length (in.)	$\frac{16}{3}$	$\frac{32}{3}$	$\frac{64}{3}$	$\frac{96}{3}$

41. $\tan A = \frac{5}{100}$
$A \approx 2.8624°$

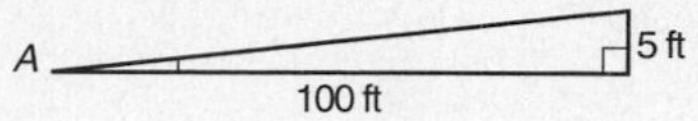

$5.6 \text{ mi} \cdot \frac{5280 \text{ ft}}{1 \text{ mi}} = 29{,}568 \text{ ft}$

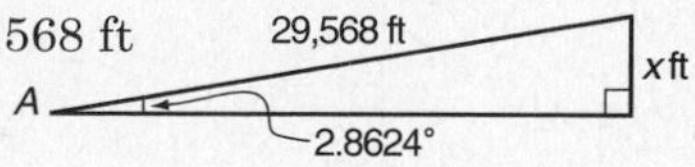

$\sin A = \frac{x}{29{,}568}$
$\sin 2.8624 = \frac{x}{29{,}568}$
$1476.55 \approx x$
The change in elevation is about 1477 feet.

42a. Let s = the number of steps.
$\frac{y \text{ change}}{x \text{ change}} \le \frac{3}{4}$
$\frac{\frac{9(12)}{s}}{10} \le \frac{3}{4}$
$4\left(\frac{108}{s}\right) \le 30$
$\frac{432}{s} \le 30$
$14.4 \le s$
Julio should plan 15 steps.

42b. $\frac{9(12)}{15} = \frac{108}{15} = 7.2$ in.

43. $\frac{y \text{ change}}{x \text{ change}} = \text{upgrade}$
$\frac{y - 11{,}080}{8941} = 0.00895$
$y - 11080 = 8941(0.00895)$
$y - 11{,}080 \approx 80$
$y \approx 11{,}160$ feet

44a. 1 44b. $\frac{3}{2}$ 44c. 1

45. 1, 2, 3, 3.2, 3.4, 4, 5, 5, 5.3, 6, 7, 8, 26, 45, 78
range = 78 − 1 = 77 median = 5
$Q_3 = 8$ $Q_1 = 3.2$
$IQR = Q_3 - Q_1 = 8 - 3.2 = 4.8$

46. $\frac{\textit{range differences}}{\textit{domain differences}} = \frac{11-12}{4-3} = \frac{-1}{1}$ or -1
$f(n) = -n + 15$
$f(1) = -(1) + 15 = 14$
$f(2) = -(2) + 15 = 13$

n	1	2	3	4	5
$f(n)$	14	13	12	11	10

47. $I = prt$

$2430 = 9000(r)(2\frac{1}{4})$

$2430 = 20{,}250r$

$0.12 = r$

$r = 12\%$

48. $\frac{6}{14} = \frac{7}{x-3}$

$6(x-3) = 7(14)$

$6x - 18 = 98$

$6x = 116$

$x = \frac{116}{6} = \frac{58}{3}$

49. $\frac{2}{3}x + 5 = \frac{1}{2}x + 4$

$\frac{1}{6}x + 5 = 4$

$\frac{1}{6}x = -1$

$x = -6$

50. $3x - 8 = 22$

$3x = 30$

$x = 10$

51a. 12 animals

51b.

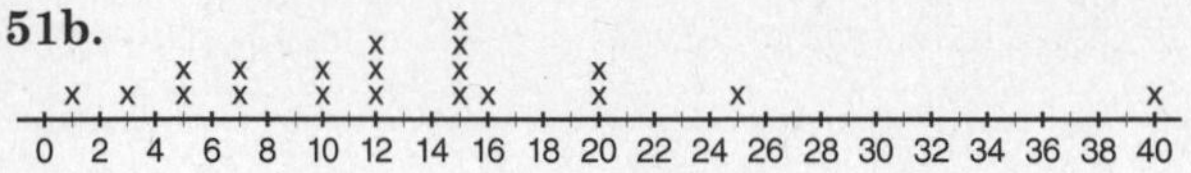

51c. 15 years

51d. 4 animals

52. $29 - 3(9-4) = 29 - 3(5)$

$= 29 - 15$

$= 14$

6-2 Writing Linear Equations in Point-Slope and Standard Forms

Pages 335–336 Check for Understanding

1. x_1 and y_1 are the coordinates of a point through which the line passes.
2. $x = 6$ is a vertical line and $y = 6$ is a horizontal line.
3. There would be no variable in the equation.
4. slope of $\overleftrightarrow{PQ} = \frac{5-2}{2-(-3)} = \frac{3}{5}$.

An equation of the line is $y - 5 = \frac{3}{5}(x-2)$. Try point R in this equation.

$y - 5 = \frac{3}{5}(x-2)$

$12 - 5 = \frac{3}{5}(12-2)$

$7 = \frac{3}{5}(10)$

$7 \neq 6$ Point R does not lie on $\overleftrightarrow{PQ}$.

5. 4; (2, −3)   6. $-\frac{2}{3}$; (−5, −6)   7. 3; (−7, 1)

8. $y - y_1 = m(x - x_1)$

$y - 1 = \frac{2}{3}(x-9)$

9. $y - y_1 = m(x - x_1)$

$y - 4 = -3[x - (-2)]$

$y - 4 = -3(x+2)$

10. $y - y_1 = m(x - x_1)$

$y - 6 = 0[x - (-3)]$

$y - 6 = 0$

$y = 6$

11. $y + 3 = -\frac{3}{4}(x-1)$

$4(y+3) = 4\left(-\frac{3}{4}\right)(x-1)$

$4y + 12 = -3(x-1)$

$4y + 12 = -3x + 3$

$4y = -3x - 9$

$3x + 4y = -9$

12. $y - \frac{1}{2} = \frac{5}{6}(x+2)$

$6\left(y - \frac{1}{2}\right) = 6\left(\frac{5}{6}\right)(x+2)$

$6y - 3 = 5(x+2)$

$6y = 5x + 13$

$-5x + 6y = 13$

$5x - 6y = -13$

13. $y - 3 = 2(x + 1.5)$

$y - 3 = 2x + 3$

$y = 2x + 6$

$-2x + y = 6$

$2x - y = -6$

14. $m = \frac{2-1}{-8-(-6)} = -\frac{1}{2}$

Use (−6, 1).

$y - y_1 = m(x - x_1)$

$y - 1 = -\frac{1}{2}[x - (-6)]$

$y - 1 = -\frac{1}{2}(x+6)$

Use (−8, 2).

$y - y_1 = m(x - x_1)$

$y - 2 = -\frac{1}{2}[x - (-8)]$

$y - 2 = -\frac{1}{2}(x+8)$

standard form: $y - 1 = -\frac{1}{2}(x+6)$

$2(y-1) = 2\left(-\frac{1}{2}\right)(x+6)$

$2y - 2 = -(x+6)$

$2y - 2 = -x - 6$

$2y = -x - 4$

$x + 2y = -4$

15. $m = \frac{2-(-2)}{-8-(-1)} = -\frac{4}{7}$

Use (−1, −2).

$y - y_1 = m(x - x_1)$

$y - (-2) = -\frac{4}{7}[x - (-1)]$

$y + 2 = -\frac{4}{7}(x+1)$

Use (−8, 2).

$y - y_1 = m(x - x_1)$

$y - 2 = -\frac{4}{7}[x - (-8)]$

$y - 2 = -\frac{4}{7}(x+8)$

standard form: $y + 2 = -\frac{4}{7}(x+1)$

$7(y+2) = 7\left(-\frac{4}{7}\right)(x+1)$

$7y + 14 = -4(x+1)$

$7y + 14 = -4x - 4$

$7y = -4x - 18$

$4x + 7y = -18$

16. $m = \frac{8-8}{-2.5-4} = \frac{0}{-6.5} = 0$

Use (4, 8).

$y - y_1 = m(x - x_1)$

$y - 8 = 0(x-4)$

$y - 8 = 0$

Use (−2.5, 8).

$y - y_1 = m(x - x_1)$

$y - 8 = 0[x - (-2.5)]$

$y - 8 = 0$

standard form: $y - 8 = 0$

$y = 8$

17. (1, 1), (6, 4)

$m = \frac{4-1}{6-1} = \frac{3}{5}$

$y - y_1 = m(x - x_1)$

$y - 1 = \frac{3}{5}(x-1)$

$5(y-1) = 5\left(\frac{3}{5}\right)(x-1)$

$5(y-1) = 3(x-1)$

$5y - 5 = 3x - 3$

$5y = 3x + 2$

$-3x + 5y = 2$

$3x - 5y = -2$

Pages 336–338 Exercises

18. $y - y_1 = m(x - x_1)$

$y - 8 = 2(x-3)$

19. $y - y_1 = m(x - x_1)$

$y - 5 = 3(x-4)$

20. $y - y_1 = m(x - x_1)$

$y - (-3) = 1[x - (-4)]$

$y + 3 = x + 4$

21. $y - y_1 = m(x - x_1)$

$y - 1 = -4[x - (-6)]$

$y - 1 = -4(x+6)$

22. $y - y_1 = m(x - x_1)$

$y - 5 = 0(x-0)$

$y - 5 = 0$

23. $y - y_1 = m(x - x_1)$

$y - 3 = -2(x-1)$

24. $y - y_1 = m(x - x_1)$

$y - 5 = \frac{2}{3}(x-3)$

25. $y - y_1 = m(x - x_1)$

$y - (-3) = \frac{3}{4}(x-8)$

$y + 3 = \frac{3}{4}(x-8)$

26. $y - y_1 = m(x - x_1)$

$y - 3 = -\frac{2}{3}[x - (-6)]$

$y - 3 = -\frac{2}{3}(x + 6)$

27. $y - y_1 = m(x - x_1)$

$y - 13 = 4(x - 2)$

$y - 13 = 4x - 8$

$y = 4x + 5$

$-4x + y = 5$

$4x - y = -5$

28. $y - y_1 = m(x - x_1)$

$y - (-3) = 4[x - (-5)]$

$y + 3 = 4(x + 5)$

$y + 3 = 4x + 20$

$y = 4x + 17$

$-4x + y = 17$

$4x - y = -17$

29. $y - y_1 = m(x - x_1)$

$y - 6 = \frac{3}{2}[x - (-4)]$

$y - 6 = \frac{3}{2}(x + 4)$

$2(y - 6) = 2\left(\frac{3}{2}\right)(x + 4)$

$2y - 12 = 3(x + 4)$

$2y - 12 = 3x + 12$

$2y = 3x + 24$

$-3x + 2y = 24$

$3x - 2y = -24$

30. $y - y_1 = m(x - x_1)$

$y - (-7) = 0[x - (-2)]$

$y + 7 = 0$

$y = -7$

31. $y - y_1 = m(x - x_1)$

$y - 2 = -\frac{2}{5}(x - 8)$

$5(y - 2) = 5\left(-\frac{2}{5}\right)(x - 8)$

$5y - 10 = -2(x - 8)$

$5y - 10 = -2x + 16$

$5y = -2x + 26$

$2x + 5y = 26$

32. $x = -5$

33. $m = \frac{-1 - 2}{4 - (-5)} = \frac{-3}{9} = -\frac{1}{3}$

Use $(-5, 2)$.

$y - y_1 = m(x - x_1)$

$y - 2 = -\frac{1}{3}[x - (-5)]$

$y - 2 = -\frac{1}{3}(x + 5)$

Use $(4, -1)$.

$y - y_1 = m(x - x_1)$

$y - (-1) = -\frac{1}{3}(x - 4)$

$y + 1 = -\frac{1}{3}(x - 4)$

34. $m = \frac{4 \quad 1}{7 - 6} = \frac{5}{1} = -5$

Use $(6, 1)$.

$y - y_1 = m(x - x_1)$

$y - 1 = -5(x - 6)$

Use $(7, -4)$.

$y - y_1 = m(x - x_1)$

$y - (-4) = -5(x - 7)$

$y + 4 = -5(x - 7)$

35. $m = \frac{5 - (-1)}{6 - (-8)} = \frac{6}{14} = \frac{3}{7}$

Use $(-8, -1)$.

$y - y_1 = m(x - x_1)$

$y - (-1) = \frac{3}{7}[x - (-8)]$

$y + 1 = \frac{3}{7}(x + 8)$

Use $(6, 5)$.

$y - y_1 = m(x - x_1)$

$y - 5 = \frac{3}{7}(x - 6)$

36. $m = \frac{1 - 3}{5 - 2} = -\frac{2}{3}$

Use $(2, 3)$.

$y - y_1 = m(x - x_1)$

$y - 3 = -\frac{2}{3}(x - 2)$

Use $(5, 1)$.

$y - y_1 = m(x - x_1)$

$y - 1 = -\frac{2}{3}(x - 5)$

37. $m = \frac{-2 - (-2)}{8 - 4} = \frac{0}{4} = 0$

Use $(4, -2)$.

$y - y_1 = m(x - x_1)$

$y - (-2) = 0(x - 4)$

$y + 2 = 0(x - 4)$

Use $(8, -2)$.

$y - y_1 = m(x - x_1)$

$y - (-2) = 0(x - 8)$

$y + 2 = 0(x - 8)$

38. $m = \frac{-4.5 - 3}{-0.5 - 2.5} = \frac{-7.5}{-3} = 2.5$

Use $(2.5, 3)$.

$y - y_1 = m(x - x_1)$

$y - 3 = 2.5(x - 2.5)$

Use $(-0.5, -4.5)$.

$y - y_1 = m(x - x_1)$

$y - (-4.5) = 2.5[x - (-0.5)]$

$y + 4.5 = 2.5(x + 0.5)$

39. $m = \frac{-3 - 5}{12 - 6} = \frac{-8}{6} = -\frac{4}{3}$

$y - y_1 = m(x - x_1)$, using $(6, 5)$

$y - 5 = -\frac{4}{3}(x - 6)$

$3(y - 5) = 3\left(-\frac{4}{3}\right)(x - 6)$

$3y - 15 = -4(x - 6)$

$3y - 15 = -4x + 24$

$3y = -4x + 39$

$4x + 3y = 39$

40. $m = \frac{2 - (-7)}{1 - (-2)} = \frac{9}{3} = 3$

$y - y_1 = m(x - x_1)$, using $(1, 2)$

$y - 2 = 3(x - 1)$

$y - 2 = 3x - 3$

$y = 3x - 1$

$-3x + y = -1$

$3x - y = 1$

41. $m = \frac{-2 - 9}{3 - (-5)} = \frac{-11}{-8} = \frac{11}{8}$

$y - y_1 = m(x - x_1)$, using $(-5, 9)$

$y - 9 = -\frac{11}{8}[x - (-5)]$

$8(y - 9) = 8\left(-\frac{11}{8}\right)(x + 5)$

$8y - 72 = -11(x + 5)$

$8y - 72 = -11x - 55$

$8y = -11x + 17$

$11x + 8y = 17$

42. $m = \frac{3.1 - (-1.3)}{-0.4 - (-0.7)} = \frac{4.4}{-1.1} = -4$

$y - y_1 = m(x - x_1)$, using $(0.7, -1.3)$

$y - (-1.3) = -4(x - 0.7)$

$y + 1.3 = -4x + 2.8$

$y = -4x + 1.5$

$4x + y = 1.5$

43. $m = \dfrac{-\frac{1}{3} - \left(-\frac{5}{6}\right)}{\frac{3}{4} - \left(-\frac{2}{3}\right)} = \dfrac{\frac{3}{6}}{\frac{17}{12}} = \frac{6}{17}$

$y - y_1 = m(x - x_1)$, using $\left(\frac{3}{4}, -\frac{1}{3}\right)$

$y - \left(-\frac{1}{3}\right) = \frac{6}{17}\left(x - \frac{3}{4}\right)$

$17\left(y + \frac{1}{3}\right) = 17\left(\frac{6}{17}\right)\left(x - \frac{3}{4}\right)$

$17y + \frac{17}{3} = 6\left(x - \frac{3}{4}\right)$

$12\left(17y + \frac{17}{3}\right) = (12)(6)\left(x - \frac{3}{4}\right)$

$204y + 68 = 72x - 54$

$204y = 72x + 14$

$-72x + 204y = -122$

$36x - 102y = 61$

44. $m = \dfrac{\frac{16}{5} - 7\frac{2}{3}}{-2 - (-2)} = \dfrac{\frac{67}{15}}{0}$ undefined

$x = -2$

45. $\frac{5-1}{5-9} = \frac{4}{-4}$ or -1

An equation of the line is $(y - 1) = -1(x - 9)$. Let $y = 0$ in the equation and see if $x = 10$.

$0 - 1 = -x + 9$

$-10 = -x$

$10 = x$

(10, 0) lies on the line. Since (10, 0) is a point on the x-axis, the line intersects the x-axis at (10, 0).

46a. *AC*:

$A(-2, 4)$, $C(-4, -3)$

$m = \frac{-3-4}{-4-(-2)} = \frac{-7}{-2} = \frac{7}{2}$

Use (−2, 4).

$y - y_1 = m(x - x_1)$

$y - 4 = \frac{7}{2}[x - (-2)]$

$y - 4 = \frac{7}{2}(x + 2)$ or

Use (−4, −3).

$y - y_1 = m(x - x_1)$

$y - (-3) = \frac{7}{2}[x - (-4)]$

$y + 3 = \frac{7}{2}(x + 4)$

AB:

$A(-2, 4)$, $B(2, -3)$

$m = \frac{-3-4}{-2-(-2)} = -\frac{7}{4}$

Use (−2, 4).

$y - y_1 = m(x - x_1)$

$y - 4 = -\frac{7}{4}[x - (-2)]$

$y - 4 = -\frac{7}{4}(x + 2)$ or

Use (2, −3).

$y - y_1 = m(x - x_1)$

$y - (-3) = 0(x - 2)$

$y + 3 = -\frac{7}{4}(x - 2)$

BC:

$B(2, -3)$, $C(-4, -3)$

$m = \frac{-3-(-3)}{-4-2} = \frac{0}{-6} = 0$

$y - y_1 = m\ (x - x_1)$

$y - (-3) = -\frac{7}{4}(x - 2)$

$y + 3 = 0$

46b. *AC*: $y - 4 = \frac{7}{2}(x + 2)$

$2(y - 4) = 2\left(\frac{7}{2}\right)(x + 2)$

$2y - 8 = 7(x + 2)$

$2y - 8 = 7x + 14$

$2y = 7x + 22$

$-7x + 2y = 22$

$7x - 2y = -22$

AB: $y - 4 = -\frac{7}{4}(x + 2)$

$4(y - 4) = 4\left(-\frac{7}{4}\right)(x + 2)$

$4y - 16 = -7(x + 2)$

$4y - 16 = -7x - 14$

$4y = -7x + 2$

$7x + 4y = 2$

BC: $y + 3 = 0$

$y = -3$

47a. No, for a rise of 30 inches the ramp must be 30 feet long, but there is only 18 feet available.

47b.

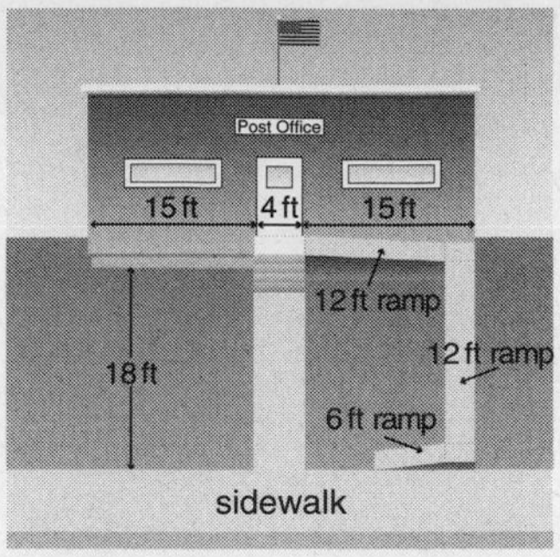

48. $\dfrac{\text{vertical change}}{\text{horizontal change}} = \dfrac{33{,}000 - 7000}{50(5280)} = \dfrac{26{,}000}{264{,}000} \approx 0.0985$

The approximate slope of descent is 9.85%.

49a. range = 32 − 6 = \$0.26

$IQR = Q_3 - Q_1$ = \$0.18 − \$0.09 = \$0.09

49b. 1.5(0.09) = 0.135

0.135 + 0.18 = 0.315

So, \$0.32 is an outlier.

50.

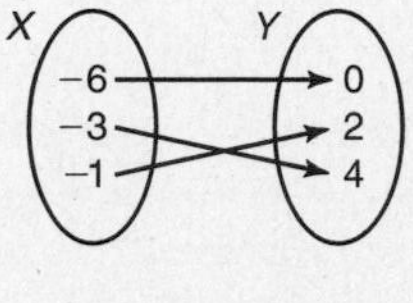

51. $\frac{y_1}{x_1} = \frac{y_2}{x_2}$

$\frac{12}{3} = \frac{y}{7}$

$12(7) = 3y$

$84 = 3y$

$28 = y$

52.

	r	*t*	*d*
plane 1	280	$\frac{2240}{280} = 8$	2240
plane 2	*r*	7	2240

$7r = 2240$

$r = 320$ mph

53. No; because there could be 2 pink and 1 white or 1 pink and 2 white.

54. full: $3000 \cdot \frac{\$27.50}{1000} = \$82.50$

broken: $2500 \cdot \frac{\$38.40}{1000} = \$96$

The full carton is least expensive.

55. associative (+)

6-3 Integration: Statistics Scatter Plots and Best-Fit Lines

Page 343 Check for Understanding

1. If the slope is positive (or negative), the correlation is positive (or negative).

2a–c. Sample answers are given.

2a.

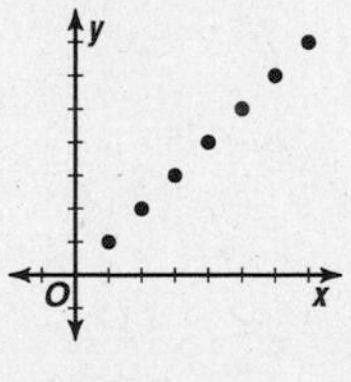

2b.

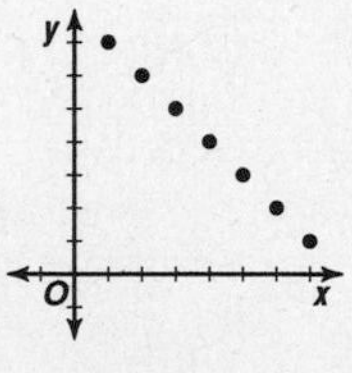

2c.

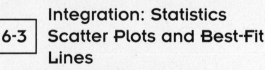

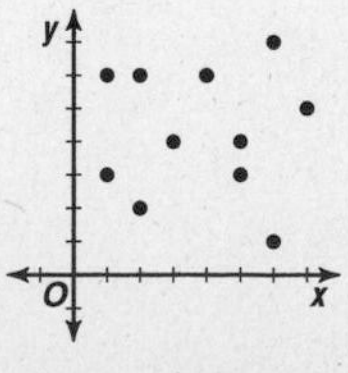

3a–c. Sample answers are given.

3a. height as you age from 0–12 years

3b. the longer you let water boil to volume of water in the pan

3c. the height of an adult to their age

4. how strongly the data are correlated; -1 is very negative; 1 is very positive

5. Sample answer: distance driven vs. gallons of gasoline in tank

6. positive **7.** positive **8.** negative

9a. It gets better. **9b.** yes; negative

9c. (7, 18) and (8, 16)

10a.

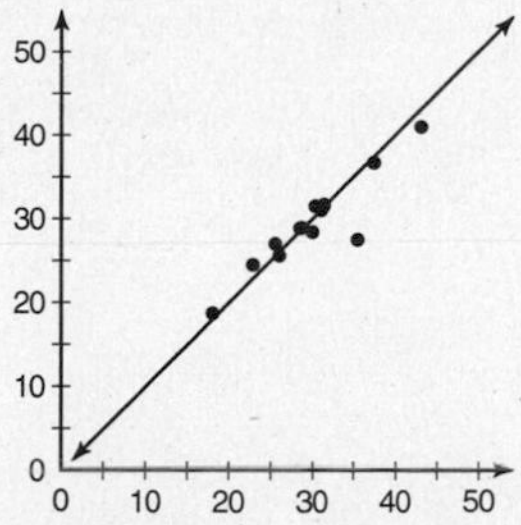

10b. Sample answer: $y = x$

10c. An insect's body temperature closely approximates that of the air around it, and thus, is cold-blooded.

Pages 343–345 Exercises

11. positive	**12.** negative	**13.** no
14. positive	**15.** no	**16.** negative
17. positive	**18.** positive	**19.** negative

20. yes; Sample reason: Dots lie in a horizontal pattern.

21. yes; Sample reason: Dots are grouped in an upward diagonal pattern.

22. no; Sample reason: Dots are everywhere, no linear pattern exists.

23. c; if 1 is correct then 19 are wrong, if 2 are correct, then 18 are wrong and so on. Graph c shows these pairs of numbers.

24a.

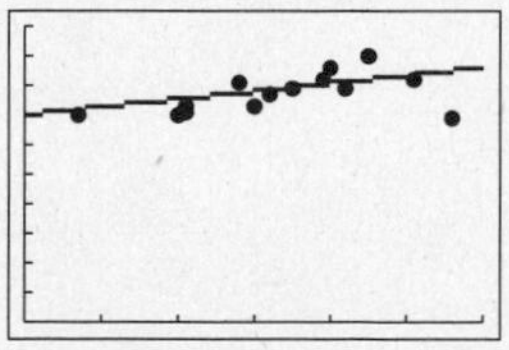

24b. The points seem to be positively correlated.

24c. $y = 2.48x + 68.94$, $r = 0.501$

24d. Sample answer: As the January temperature increases, so does the July temperature.

25a–d. Sample answers are given.

25a. The more taxation increases, the more in debt the government becomes.

25b. You work harder, and your grades go up.

25c. As more money is spent on research, fewer people die of cancer.

25d. comparing the number of professional golfers with the number of holes-in-one

26. See students' work.

27a. The correlation shown by the graph shows a slightly positive correlation between SAT scores and graduation rate.

27b. See students' graphs. Sample equation: $y = 0.89x + 1142.17$

28a.

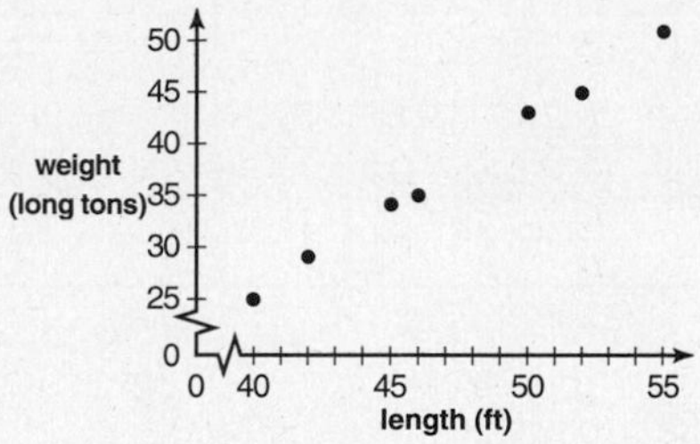

There seems to be a positive correlation between the length and weight of humpback whales.

28b. about 43–45 long tons

28c. 43–46 feet

28d. Yes; sample answer: the point (46, 36) falls in the same general area as the other data.

29a. and 29c.

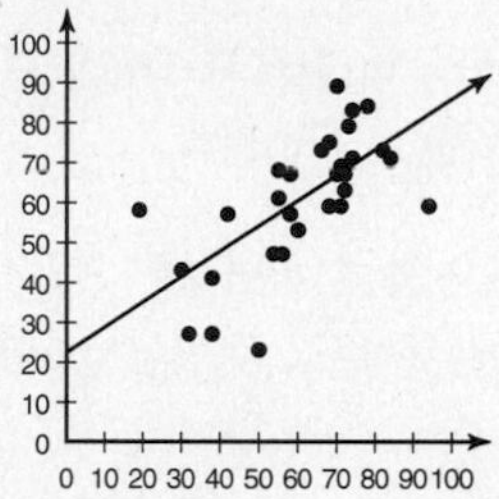

29b. positive

29c. Sample answer: $y = \frac{2}{3}x + 22$

30a–c. See students' work.

31a.

x	209	22
y	30,000	45,000

$$m = \frac{45{,}000 - 30{,}000}{22 - 20} = \frac{15{,}000}{2} = 7500$$

$$y - y_1 = m(x - x_1)$$
$$y - 30{,}000 = 7500(x - 20)$$
$$y - 30{,}000 = 7500x - 150{,}000$$
$$y = 7500x - 120{,}000$$
$$-7500x + y = -120{,}000$$
$$7500x - y = 120{,}000$$

31b.
$$7500x - y = 120{,}000$$
$$7500(18) - y = 120{,}000$$
$$135{,}000 - y = 120{,}000$$
$$-y = -15{,}000$$
$$y = 15{,}000$$

The plane's altitude would be 15,000 feet.

31c. No, it only describes the plane's path in that part of the flight.

32. solve for b: $6b - a = 32$

$$6b = a + 32$$
$$b = \frac{a + 32}{6}$$

a	$\frac{a+32}{6}$	b	(a,b)
-2	$\frac{-2+32}{6}$	5	$(-2, 5)$
-1	$\frac{-1+32}{6}$	$5\frac{1}{6}$	$\left(-1, 5\frac{1}{6}\right)$
0	$\frac{0+32}{6}$	$5\frac{1}{3}$	$\left(0, 5\frac{1}{3}\right)$
2	$\frac{2+32}{6}$	$5\frac{2}{3}$	$\left(2, 5\frac{2}{3}\right)$
5	$\frac{5+32}{6}$	$6\frac{1}{6}$	$\left(5, 6\frac{1}{6}\right)$

33. 75°

34. $1.2(4x - 5y) - 0.2(-1.5x + 8y)$
$= 4.8x - 6.0y + 0.3x - 1.6y$
$= 4.8x + 0.3x - 6.0y - 1.6y$
$= 5.1x - 7.6y$

35. $8.2 - 6.75 = m$
$1.45 = m$

6-4 Writing Linear Equations in Slope-Intercept Form

Pages 349–350 Check for Understanding

1. Let $x = 0$ to find the y-intercept; let $y = 0$ to find the x-intercept; x: $\frac{C}{A}$, y: $\frac{C}{B}$.

2. Sample answer: Direct variation is the slope-intercept form when $b = 0$.

3. Direct variation may be solved by using the formulas $y = kx$ or $\frac{y}{x} = k$, where $k = m$, which represents the slope.

4. Because its slope is undefined.

5. Both; Chuma's equation is the standard form of Taka's slope-intercept form.

6. Sample answer:

(1) Use the y-intercept (3) and slope, $-\frac{2}{5}$.
$y = mx + b$
$y = -\frac{2}{5}x + 3$

(2) Use a point (5, 2) and the slope, $-\frac{2}{5}$.
$y - y_1 = m(x - x_1)$
$y - 2 = -\frac{2}{5}(x - 5)$

(3) Use two points, $(1, -3)$ and $(4, 6)$.
$m = \frac{6-(-3)}{4-1}$ or 3
$y - (-3) = 3(x - 1)$
$y + 3 = 3x - 3$
$y = 3x - 6$

7a. $(x_1, y_1) = (2, 0)$, $(x_2, y_2) = (0, -4)$
$m = \frac{-4-0}{0-2} = 2$

7b. x-intercept: 2, y-intercept: -4

7c. $y = mx + b$
$y = 2x - 4$

8. $3x + 4y = 24$

Let $y = 0$.
$3x + 4(0) = 24$
$3x = 24$
$x = 8$
x-intercept: 8

Let $x = 0$.
$3(0) + 4y = 24$
$4y = 24$
$y = 6$
y-intercept: 6

9. $\frac{3}{4}x - 2y + 7 = 0$

Let $y = 0$.
$\frac{3}{4}x - 2(0) + 7 = 0$
$\frac{3}{4}x + 7 = 0$
$\frac{3}{4}x = -7$
$x = -\frac{28}{3}$
x-intercept: $-\frac{28}{3}$

Let $x = 0$.
$\frac{3}{4}(0) - 2y + 7 = 0$
$-2y + 7 = 0$
$-2y = -7$
$y = \frac{7}{2}$
y-intercept: $\frac{7}{2}$

10. $y = mx + b$
$y = -4x + 5$ slope-intercept
$4x + y = 5$ standard

11. $y = mx + b$
$y = \frac{2}{3}x - 10$ slope-intercept
$3y = 2x - 30$
$-2x + 3y = -30$
$2x - 3y = 30$ standard

12. $m = -3$, $b = 7$

13. $2x + y = -4$
$y = -2x - 4$
$m = -2$, $b = -4$

14. $x = 3y - 2$
$-3y + x = -2$
$-3y = -x - 2$
$y = \frac{1}{3}x + \frac{2}{3}$
$m = \frac{1}{3}$, $b = \frac{2}{3}$

15. $m = \frac{3-1}{-2-8} = \frac{2}{-10} = -\frac{1}{5}$
$y - y_1 = m(x - x_1)$, using (8, 1)
$y - 1 = -\frac{1}{5}(x - 8)$
$5(y - 1) = 5\left(-\frac{1}{5}\right)(x - 8)$
$5y - 5 = -(x - 8)$
$5y - 5 = -x + 8$
$5y = -x + 13$
$x + 5y = 13$

16. $m = \frac{9-7}{1-5} = \frac{2}{-4} = -\frac{1}{2}$
$y - y_1 = m(x - x_1)$, using (5, 7)
$y - 7 = -\frac{1}{2}(x - 5)$
$2(y - 7) = 2\left(-\frac{1}{2}\right)(x - 5)$
$2y - 14 = -(x - 5)$
$2y - 14 = -x + 5$
$2y = -x + 19$
$x + 2y = 19$

17. $y = \frac{11}{3}x$
$y = \frac{11}{3}(12)$
$y = 44$

18a. $y = \frac{1}{4}x + 12$

18b. $y = \frac{1}{4}(6) + 12$
$= 13.5$

The roof is 13.5 feet high at that point.

Pages 350–353 Exercises

19a. $(x_1, y_1) = (-2, 3), (x_2, y_2) = (0, 0)$

$m = \frac{0-3}{0-(-2)} = -\frac{3}{2}$

19b. x-intercept: 0, y-intercept: 0

19c. $y = mx + b$

$y = -\frac{3}{2}x$

20a. $(x_1, y_1) = (3, 0), (x_2, y_2) = (0, 9)$

$m = \frac{9-0}{0-3} = -3$

20b. x-intercept: 3, y-intercept: 9

20c. $y = mx + b$

$y = -3x + 9$

21a. $(x_1, y_1) = (0, -2), (x_2, y_2) = (5, 0)$

$m = \frac{0-(-2)}{5-0} = \frac{2}{5}$

21b. x-intercept: 5, y-intercept: -2

21c. $y = mx + b$

$y = \frac{2}{5}x - 2$

22. $5x - 3y = -12$

Let $y = 0$.	Let $x = 0$.
$5x - 3(0) = -12$	$5(0) - 3y = -12$
$5x = -12$	$-3y = -12$
$x = \frac{-12}{5}$	$y = 4$
x-intercept: $-\frac{12}{5}$	y-intercept: 4

23. $4x + 7y = 8$

Let $y = 0$.	Let $x = 0$.
$4x + 7(0) = 8$	$4(0) + 7y = 8$
$4x = 8$	$7y = 8$
$x = 2$	$y = \frac{8}{7}$
x-intercept: 2	y-intercept: $\frac{8}{7}$

24. $5y - 2 = 2x$

Let $y = 0$.	Let $x = 0$.
$5(0) - 2 = 2x$	$5y - 2 = 2(0)$
$-2 = 2x$	$5y - 2 = 0$
$-1 = x$	$5y = 2$
	$y = \frac{2}{5}$
x-intercept: -1	y-intercept: $\frac{2}{5}$

25. $y - 6x = 5$

Let $y = 0$.	Let $x = 0$.
$0 - 6x = 5$	$y - 6(0) = 5$
$x = -\frac{5}{6}$	$y = 5$
x-intercept: $-\frac{5}{6}$	y-intercept: 5

26. $4y - x = 3$

Let $y = 0$.	Let $x = 0$.
$4(0) - x = 3$	$4y - 0 = 3$
$-x = 3$	$y = \frac{3}{4}$
$x = -3$	
x-intercept: -3	y-intercept: $\frac{3}{4}$

27. $3y = 18$

Let $y = 0$.	Let $x = 0$.
$3(0) = 18$	$3y = 18$
$0 \neq 18$	$y = 6$
x-intercept: none	y-intercept: 6

28.

$y = mx + b$	
$y = 3x + 5$	slope-intercept
$-3x + y = 5$	
$3x - y = -5$	standard

29.

$y = mx + b$	
$y = 7x - 2$	slope-intercept
$-7x + y = -2$	
$7x - y = 2$	standard

30.

$y = mx + b$	
$y = -6x$	slope-intercept
$6x + y = 0$	standard

31.

$y = mx + b$	
$y = -1.5x + 3.75$	slope-intercept
$1.5x + y = 3.75$	
$4(1.5x + y) = 4(3.75)$	
$6x + 4y = 15$	standard

32.

$y = mx + b$	
$y = \frac{1}{4}x - 10$	slope-intercept
$4y = x - 40$	
$-x + 4y = -40$	
$x - 4y = 40$	standard

33.

$y = mx + b$	
$y = -7$	slope-intercept
$y = -7$	standard

34. $3y = 2x - 9$

$y = \frac{2}{3}x - 3$

$m = \frac{2}{3}, b = -3$

35. $5x + 4y = 10$

$4y = -5x + 10$

$y = -\frac{5}{4}x + \frac{5}{2}$

$m = -\frac{5}{4}, b = \frac{5}{2}$

36. $4x - \frac{1}{3}y = -2$

$-\frac{1}{3}y = -4x - 2$

$y = 12x + 6$

$m = 12, b = 6$

37. $\frac{2}{3}x + \frac{1}{6}y = 2$

$\frac{1}{6}y = -\frac{2}{3}x + 2$

$y = -4x + 12$

$m = -4, b = 12$

38. $5(x - 3y) = 2(x + 3)$

$5x - 15y = 2x + 6$

$-15y = -3x + 6$

$y = \frac{1}{5}x - \frac{2}{5}$

$m = \frac{1}{5}, b = -\frac{2}{5}$

39. $4(3x + 9) - 3(5y + 7) = 11$

$12x + 36 - 15y - 21 = 11$

$12x - 15y + 15 = 11$

$-15y = -12x - 4$

$y = \frac{4}{5}x + \frac{4}{15}$

$m = \frac{4}{5}, b = \frac{4}{15}$

40. $m = \frac{5-(-5)}{4-(-3)} = \frac{10}{7}$

$y - y_1 = m(x - x_1)$, using (4, 5)

$y - 5 = \frac{10}{7}(x - 4)$

$7(y - 5) = 7\left(\frac{10}{7}\right)(x - 4)$

$7y - 35 = 10(x - 4)$

$7y - 35 = 10x - 40$

$7y = 10x - 5$

$-10x + 7y = -5$

$10x - 7y = 5$

41. $m = \frac{-2-(-2)}{-4-7} = \frac{0}{-11} = 0$

$y - y_1 = m(x - x_1)$, using (7, −2)

$y - (-2) = 0(x - 7)$

$y + 2 = 0$

$y = -2$

42. $m = \frac{-2-1}{4-(-6)} = -\frac{3}{10}$

$y - y_1 = m(x - x_1)$, using $(-6, 1)$

$y - 1 = -\frac{3}{10}[x - (-6)]$

$10(y - 1) = 10\left(-\frac{3}{10}\right)(x + 6)$

$10y - 10 = -3(x + 6)$

$10y - 10 = -3x - 18$

$10y = -3x - 8$

$3x + 10y = -8$

43. $m = \frac{-6-5}{3-3} = \frac{-11}{0}$ undefined

$x = 3$

44. $m = \frac{9-4}{-5-7} = -\frac{5}{12}$

$y - y_1 = m(x - x_1)$, using $(7, 4)$

$y - 4 = -\frac{5}{12}(x - 7)$

$12(y - 4) = 12\left(-\frac{5}{12}\right)(x - 7)$

$12y - 48 = -5(x - 7)$

$12y - 48 = -5x + 35$

$12y = -5x + 83$

$5x + 12y = 83$

45. $m = \frac{9-9}{-5-2} = 0$

$y - y_1 = m(x - x_1)$, using $(2, 9)$

$y - 9 = 0(x - 2)$

$y - 9 = 0$

$y = 9$

46. $y = -\frac{8}{5}x$

$11 = -\frac{8}{5}x$

$-\frac{55}{8} = x$

47. $y = \frac{11}{24}x$

$y = \frac{11}{24}(36)$

$y = \frac{33}{2}$

48. $y = -\frac{3}{17}x$

$15 = -\frac{3}{17}x$

$-85 = x$

49. $m = \frac{2}{3}$, $(4, 0)$

$y - y_1 = m(x - x_1)$

$y - 0 = \frac{2}{3}(x - 4)$

$y = \frac{2}{3}x - \frac{8}{3}$

50. $(x + 5, x)$

$5x + 3y = 10$

$5(x + 5) - 3(x) = 10$

$5x + 25 - 3x = 10$

$2x + 25 = 10$

$2x = -15$

$x = -\frac{15}{2}$

$x + 5 = -\frac{15}{2} + 5$

$= -\frac{5}{2}$

$\left(-\frac{5}{2}, -\frac{15}{2}\right)$

51. $(3x, x)$

$3x + 7y = -16$

$3(3x) + 7(x) = -16$

$9x + 7x = -16$

$16x = -16$

$x = -1$

$3x = -3$

$(-3, -1)$

52. $(7, 0), (0, -2)$

$m = \frac{-2-0}{0-7} = \frac{2}{7}$

$y = mx + b$

$y = \frac{2}{7}x - 2$

$7y = 2x - 14$

$-2x + 7y = -14$

$2x - 7y = 14$

53a. $y = 2.04x - 21.32$

54. $(p, 0), (0, q)$; $m = \frac{q-0}{0-p} = -\frac{q}{p}$

$y = mx + b$

$y \approx -\frac{qx}{p} + q$

55a. $y = \frac{35}{290}x$

$y = \frac{35}{290}(350)$

$y \approx 42.24$

The volume at 350 K is about 42.24 ft^3.

55b. $y = \frac{200}{300}x$

$180 = \frac{2}{3}x$

$270 = x$

The temperature is 270 K at 180 ft^3.

56a. Sample answer: $m = \frac{73.2 - 67.1}{2000 - 1970} = \frac{6.1}{30} \approx 0.20$

$y - y_1 = m(x - x_1)$, using $(2000, 73.2)$

$y - 73.2 = 0.20(x - 2000)$

$y - 73.2 = 0.20x - 400$

$y = 0.20x - 326.8$

56b. Sample answer:

$m = \frac{80.2 - 74.7}{2000 - 1970} \approx 0.18$

$y - y_1 = m(x - x_1)$, using $(2000, 80.2)$

$y - 80.2 = 0.18(x - 2000)$

$y - 80.2 = 0.18x - 360$

$y = 0.18x - 279.8$

56c–d.

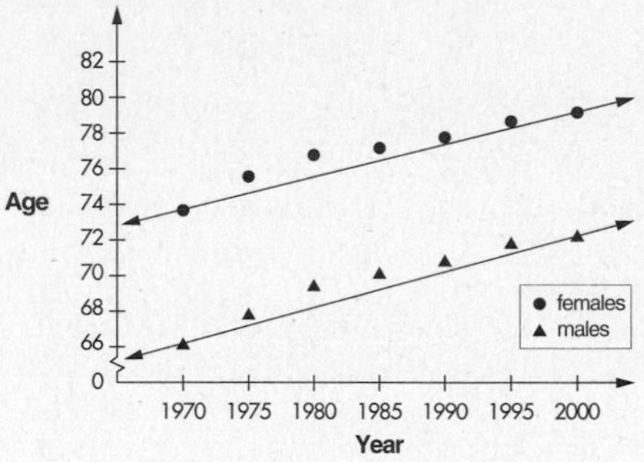

56e. The life expectancy of females is higher than the life expectancy of males and, as time passes, the life expectancy of both increases. According to the graph, at approximately the year 2350, men and women both will have a life expectancy of about 136 years.

56f.

males	females
$y = 0.20x - 326.8$	$y = 0.18x - 279.8$
$y = 0.20(2100) - 326.8$	$y = 0.18(2100) - 279.8$
$y = 93.2$	$y = 98.2$

based on sample equations: males, 93.2; females, 98.2

57a. $(0, 3), (2, 3.20)$

$m = \frac{3.20 - 3}{2 - 0} = \frac{0.2}{2} = 0.1$

$y = mx + b$

$y = 0.1x + 3$

57b. $y = 0.1(25) + 3$

$y = \$5.50$

Go to the other bank, since this one would charge you \$5.50.

58a. and 58b.

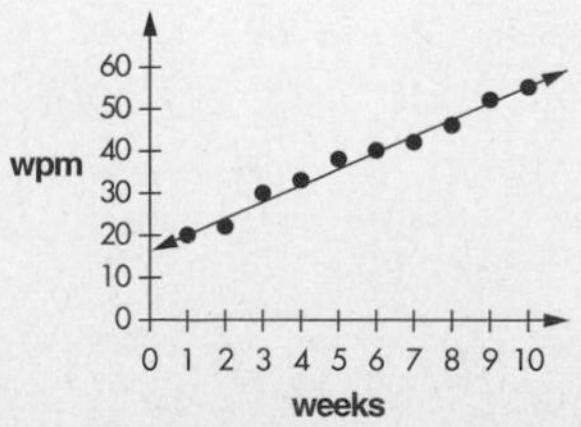

58b. Sample answer:
(4, 33), (7, 45)

$m = \frac{45 - 33}{7 - 4} = \frac{12}{3} = 4$

$y - y_1 = m(x - x_1)$

$y - 33 = 4(x - 4)$

$y - 33 = 4x - 16$

$y = 4x + 17$

58c. $y = 4(12) + 17$

$y = 48 + 17$

$y = 65$

about 65 wpm

58d. There's a limit as to how fast one can type.

59. $m = \frac{3 - 3}{-11 - 14} = \frac{0}{-25}$ or 0

60. $\frac{\text{difference in } n}{\text{difference in } m} = \frac{6 - 9}{2 - 1} = -3$

$n = -3m + 12$ or $n = 12 - 3m$

61.

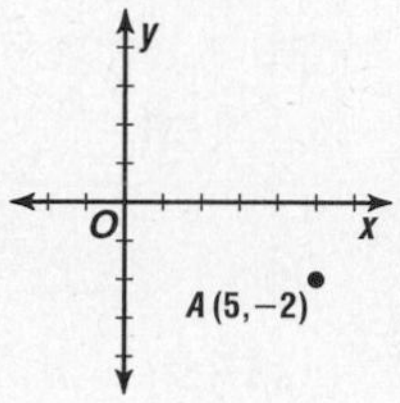

62. $P(\text{black card}) = \frac{26}{52} = \frac{1}{2}$

63. $\frac{9}{25} = \frac{5}{x}$

$9x = 5(25)$

$9x = 125$

$x = \frac{125}{9}$ or 13 ft 11 in.

64. $8x + 2y = 6$

$2y = 6 - 8x$

$\frac{2y}{2} = \frac{6}{2} - \frac{8x}{2}$

$y = 3 - 4x$

65. $-36 = 4z$

$-9 = z$

66. $|a + k| = |-5 + 3|$

$= |-2|$

$= 2$

67. $4(3x + 2) + 2(x + 3) = 12x + 8 + 2x + 6$

$= 14x + 14$

Page 353 Self Test

1. $m = \frac{5 - 10}{-2 - (-7)} = \frac{-5}{5}$ or -1

2. $m = \frac{3 - 3}{-12 - (-6)} = \frac{0}{-6}$ or 0

3. $m = \frac{-15 - 7}{-5 - (-5)} = \frac{-22}{0}$

The slope is undefined.

4. $\frac{-2 - 3}{6 - r} = -\frac{5}{2}$

$\frac{-5}{6 - r} = -\frac{5}{2}$

$-5(2) = -5(6 - r)$

$-10 = -30 + 5r$

$20 = 5r$

$4 = r$

5. $y - y_1 = m(x - x_1)$

$y - 4 = \frac{1}{2}[x - (-6)]$

$y - 4 = \frac{1}{2}(x + 6)$

6. $y - y_1 = m(x - x_1)$

$y - 12 = 0[x - (-12)]$

$y - 12 = 0$

7. $m = \frac{3 - 4}{2 - (-3)} = -\frac{1}{5}$

$y - y_1 = m(x - x_1)$, using (2, 3)

$y - 3 = -\frac{1}{5}(x - 2)$

$5(y - 3) = 5\left(-\frac{1}{5}\right)(x - 2)$

$5y - 15 = -(x - 2)$

$5y - 15 = -x + 2$

$5y = -x + 17$

$x + 5y = 17$

8a. and 8b.

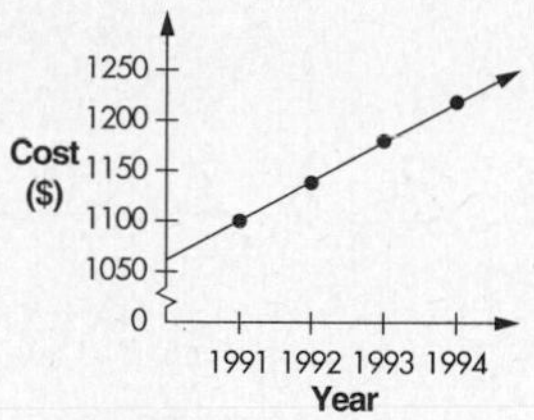

8b. Sample equation: $m = \frac{1183 - 1143}{1993 - 1992} = 40$

$y = mx + b$

$1183 = 40(1993) + b$

$-78{,}537 = b$

$y = 40x - 78{,}537$

8c. positive

8d. Each year the cost of a computer increases.

8e. The number of features on a computer increases more quickly than the cost. Thus, it costs less to buy specific features on a computer now than it did a year ago.

9. $7x + 3y = -42$

Let $y = 0$.

$7x + 3(0) = -42$

$7x = -42$

$x = -6$

x-intercept: -6

Let $x = 0$.

$7(0) + 3y = -42$

$3y = -42$

$y = -14$

y-intercept: -14

10. $m = \frac{0 - (-3)}{6 - 0} = \frac{3}{6} = \frac{1}{2}$

$y = mx + b$

$y = \frac{1}{2}x + (-3)$

$y = \frac{1}{2}x - 3$

6-5A Graphing Technology Families of Linear Graphs

Page 355

1. All graphs are of the family $y = -ax + 0$, where $-a$ represents different negative slopes.

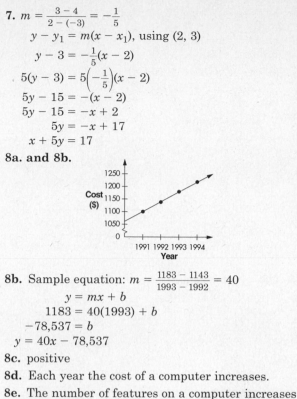

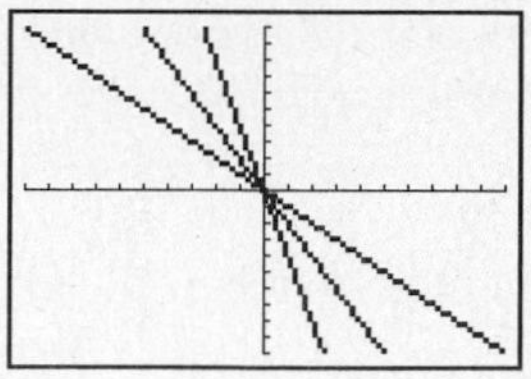

2. All graphs are of the family $y = ax + 0$, where a represents different positive slopes.

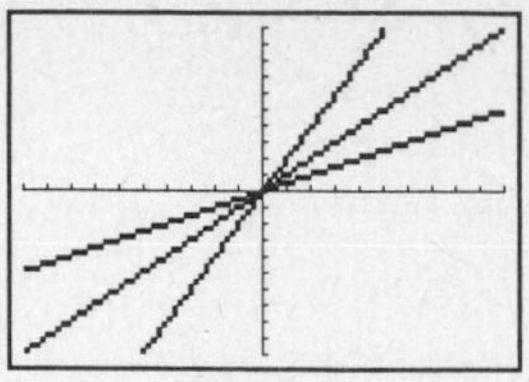

3. All graphs have the same slope, -1, but have different y-intercepts.

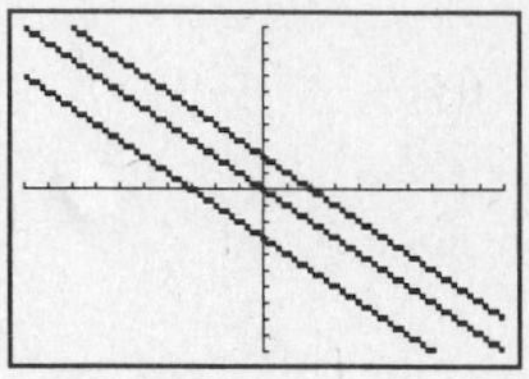

4. Graphs with positive x-coefficients slant upward from left to right. Graphs with negative x-coefficients slant downward from left to right.
5. This graph belongs to the family of graphs in Example 2 since it has a slope of 1.

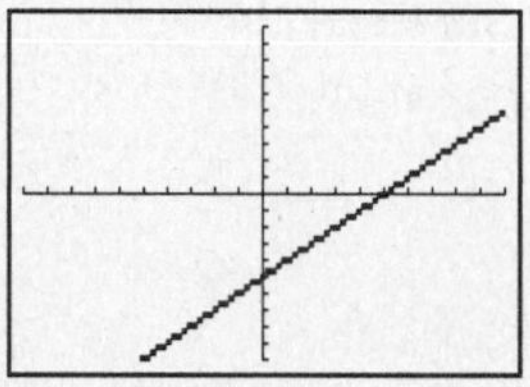

6. This graph belongs to the family of graphs in Exercise 3 since it has a slope of -1.

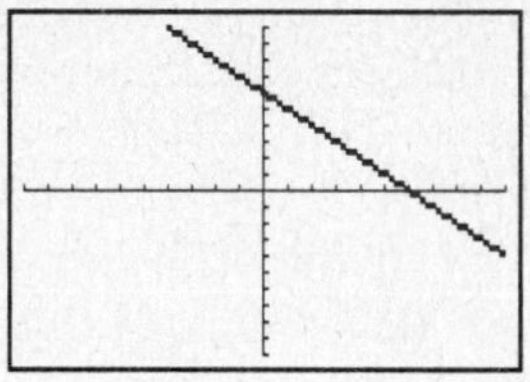

7. This graph belongs to the family of graphs in Exercise 2 since it passes through the origin and has a positive slope.

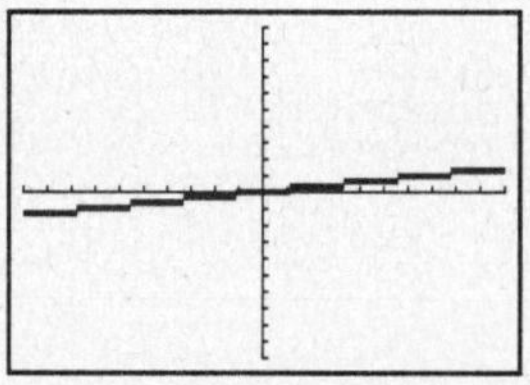

8. This graph has a slope of $\frac{1}{3}$ and a y-intercept of 4. It does not belong to any of the families of graphs.

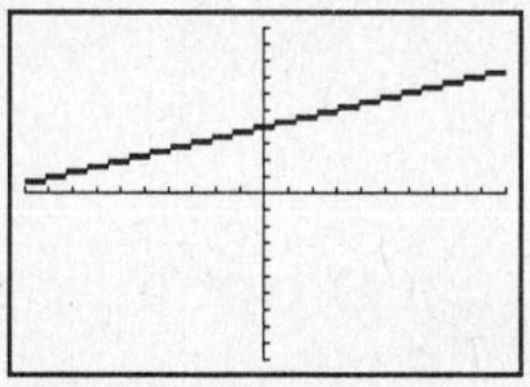

9. Sample answer: $y = -x + 2.5$
10. Sample answer: The value of m tells how the line will slant—upward or downward—and how steep it will be. The value of b tells where the line will intersect the y-axis. See students' work for graphs.

6-5 Graphing Linear Equations

Page 359 Check for Understanding

1. You can graph a line if you know the slope and a point on the line.
2. A twig cannot have a diameter of 0 and have any length at all.
3. Sample answer: For (2, 3) and $m = \frac{2}{3}$, you graph (2, 3) and move 2 units up and 3 units right to plot the second point. You can repeat the movements to find additional points.
4. down 3, right 4; up 3, left 4
5. See students' work.
6. If $x = 0$, $3(0) - 8y = 12$

$$-8y = 12$$
$$y = -\frac{3}{2}$$

If $y = 0$, $3x - 8(0) = 12$

$$3x = 12$$
$$x = 4$$

$\left(0, -\frac{3}{2}\right)$, (4, 0)

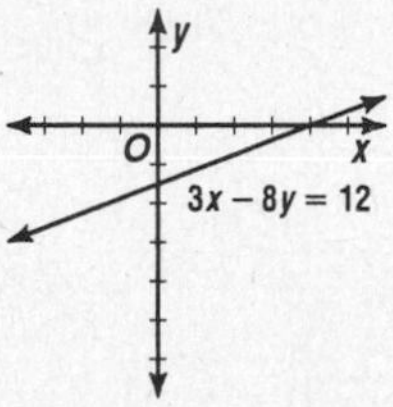

7. $y + 5 = -2(x + 1)$
$y - y_1 = m(x - x_1)$
The slope is -2.
The point is $(-1, -5)$.

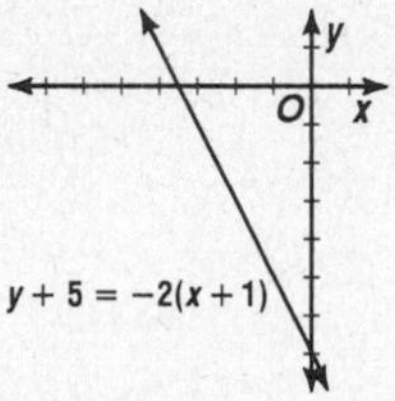

8. $\frac{2}{3}x + \frac{1}{2}y = 3$

$$\frac{1}{2}y = -\frac{2}{3}x + 3$$
$$y = -\frac{4}{3}x + 6$$

The slope is $-\frac{4}{3}$.
The y-intercept is 6.

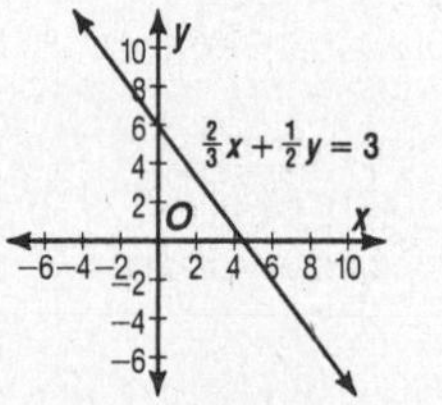

9. $y = 2x - 3$
The y-intercept is -3 and the slope is 2.

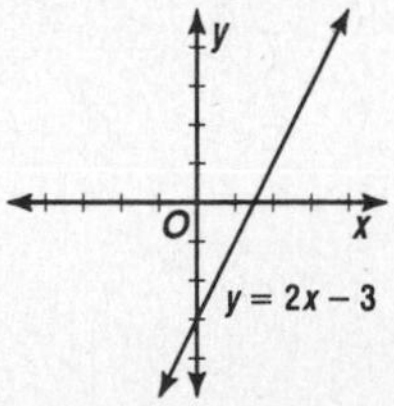

10. $y = \frac{2}{5}x - 4$
The y-intercept is -4 and the slope is $\frac{2}{5}$.

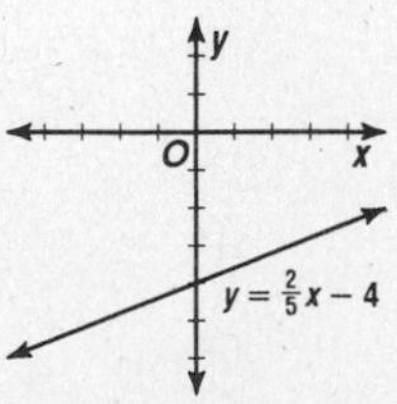

11. $6y + 12 = 18$
$6y = 6$
$y = 1$
The y-intercept is 1, the slope is 0.

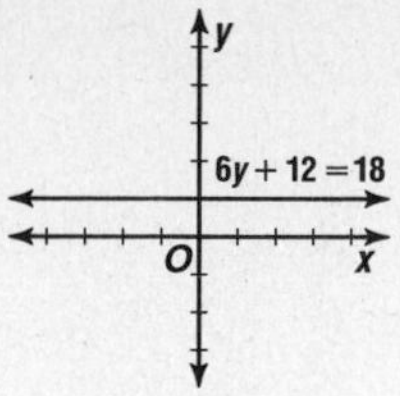

12. $5x = 9$
$x = \frac{9}{5}$
The x-intercept is $\frac{9}{5}$ and the slope is undefined.

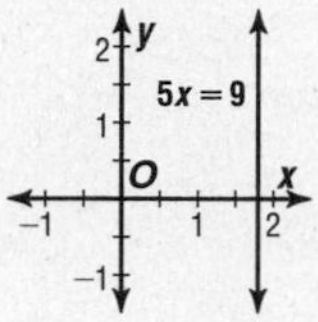

13a, d.

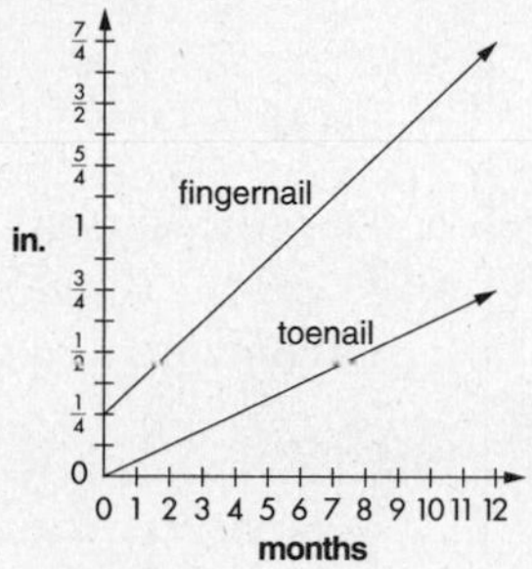

13b. $12\left(\frac{1}{8}\right) + \frac{1}{4} = \frac{7}{4}$ or $1\frac{3}{4}$ inches

13c. $\frac{1}{2}\left(\frac{1}{8}\right) = \frac{1}{16}$ inch

13e. the rate of growth per month

Pages 359–361 Exercises

14. If $x = 0$, $y = -10$.
If $y = 0$,
$0 = 5x - 10$
$10 = 5x$
$2 = x$
$(0, -10)$, $(2, 0)$

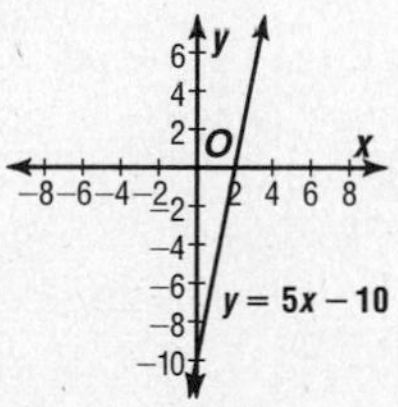

15. If $x = 0$, $y = -9$.
If $y = 0$,
$6x - 0 = 9$
$6x = 9$
$x = \frac{3}{2}$
$(0, -9)$, $\left(\frac{3}{2}, 0\right)$

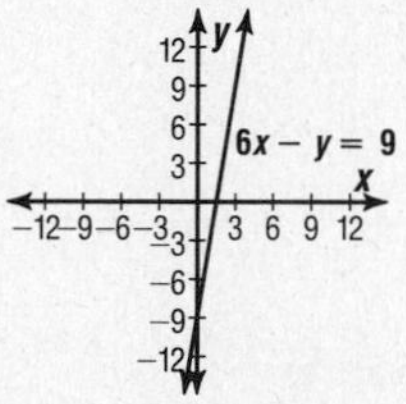

16. If $x = 0$, $\frac{1}{2}(0) - \frac{2}{3}y = -6$
$-\frac{2}{3}y = -6$
$y = 9$
If $y = 0$, $\frac{1}{2}x - \frac{2}{3}(0) = -6$
$\frac{1}{2}x = -6$
$x = -12$
$(0, 9)$, $(-12, 0)$

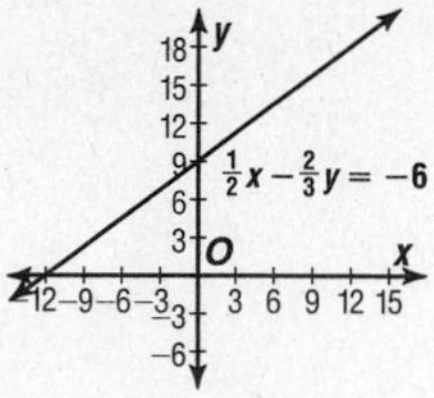

17. $y - y_1 = m(x - x_1)$
$y - 2 = 3(x - 5)$
The slope is 3.
The point is $(5, 2)$.

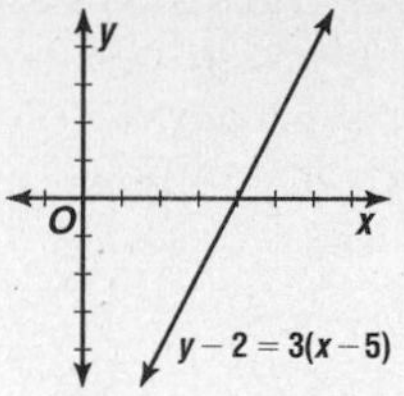

18. $y - y_1 = m(x - x_1)$
$y + 6 = -\frac{3}{2}(x + 5)$
The slope is $-\frac{3}{2}$.
The point is $(-5, -6)$.

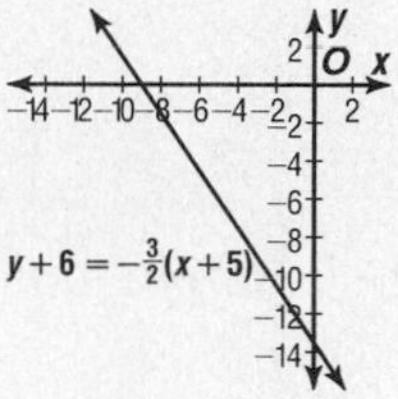

19. $y - y_1 = m(x - x_1)$
$y + \frac{3}{2} = 2(x - 3)$
The slope is 2.
The point is $(3, -\frac{3}{2})$.

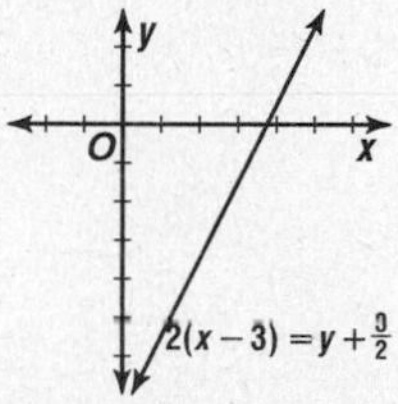

20. $y = -\frac{3}{4}x + 4$

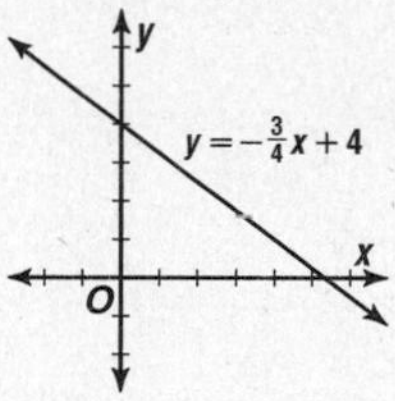

The slope is $-\frac{3}{4}$.
The y-intercept is 4.

21. $2x - 3y = -7$
$-3y = -2x - 7$
$y = \frac{2}{3}x + \frac{7}{3}$
The slope is $\frac{2}{3}$.
The y-intercept is $\frac{7}{3}$.

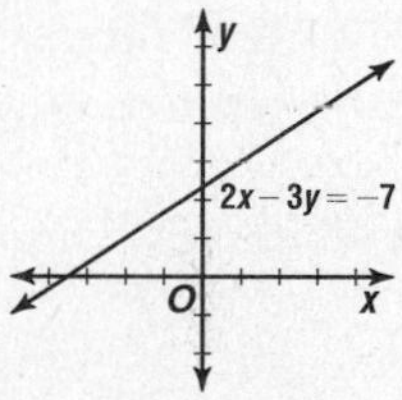

22. $5y + 3 = -5$
$5y = -8$
$y = -\frac{8}{5}$
The slope is 0.
The y-intercept is $-\frac{8}{5}$.

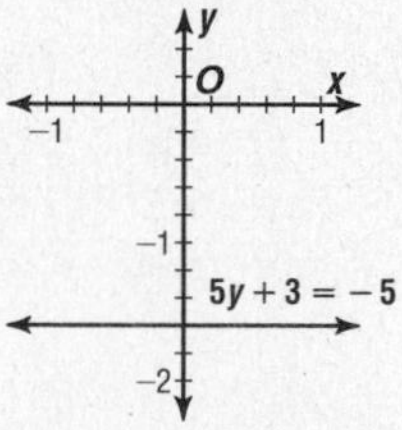

23. $y = 3x - 5$
The slope is 3.
The y-intercept is -5.

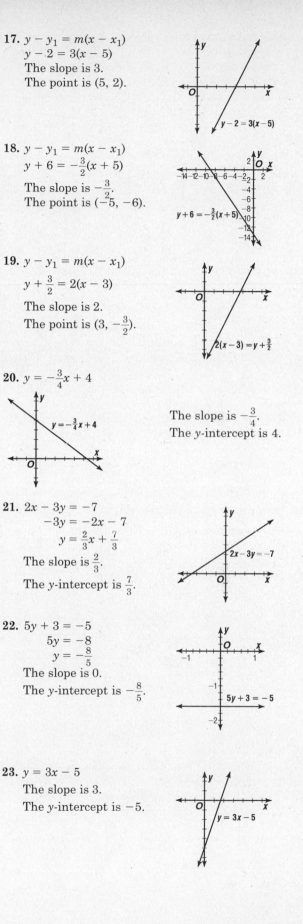

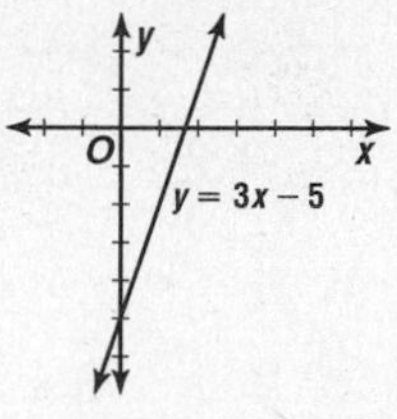

24. $6y + 5 = 5y + 3$
$y + 5 = 3$
$y = -2$
$m = 0$, y-intercept: -2

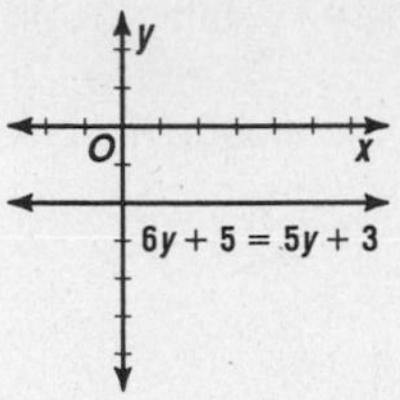

25. $3(y + 4) = -2x$
$3y + 12 = -2x$
$3y = -2x - 12$
$y = -\frac{2}{3}x - 4$
$m = -\frac{2}{3}$, y-intercept: -4

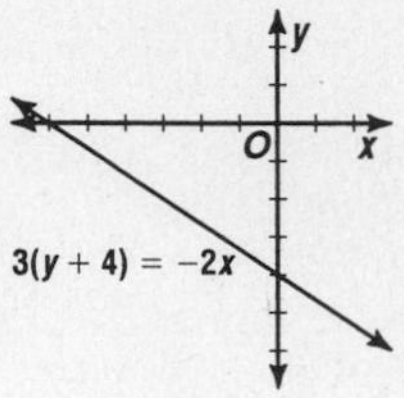

26. $y = \frac{2}{3}x + 1$
$m = \frac{2}{3}$, y-intercept: 1

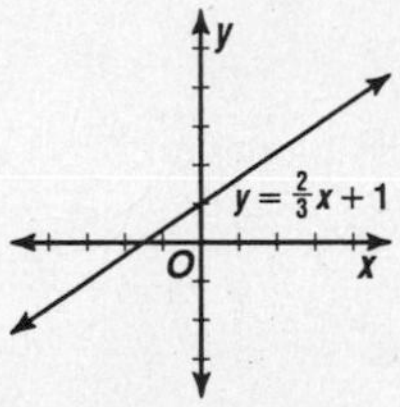

27. $5x + 2y = 20$
If $x = 0$, $5(0) + 2y = 20$
$y = 10$
If $y = 0$, $5x + 2(0) = 20$
$x = 4$
(0, 10), (4, 0)

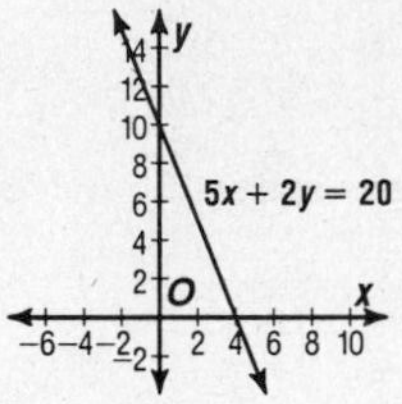

28. $\frac{2}{3}x - y = 4$
$-y = -\frac{2}{3}x + 4$
$y = \frac{2}{3}x - 4$
$m = \frac{2}{3}$, y-intercept: -4

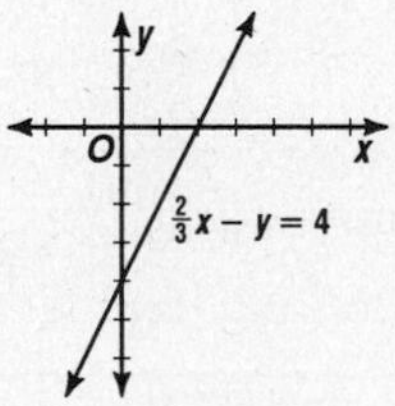

29. Solve for y:
$6x - y = 8$
$-y = -6x + 8$
$y = 6x - 8$
$m = 6$, y-intercept: -8

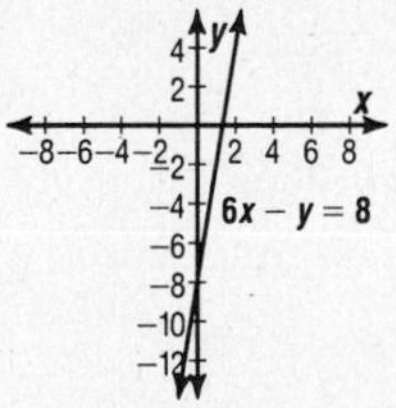

30. $15x - 29y = 429$
$-29y = -15x + 429$
$y = \frac{15}{29}x - \frac{429}{29}$
$m = \frac{15}{29}$, y-intercept: $-\frac{429}{29}$

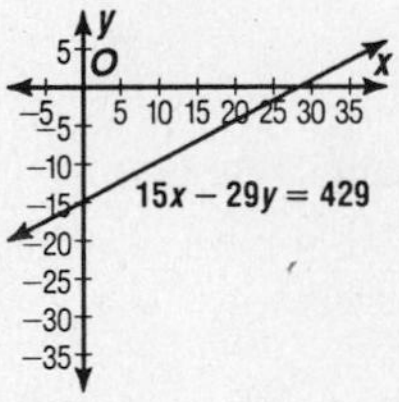

31. $y = 0.17x + 1.75$
$m = 0.17$,
y-intercept: 1.75

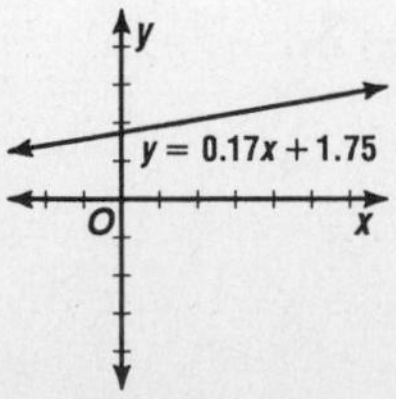

32. $y - y_1 = m(x - x_1)$
$y - 3 = \frac{2}{3}(x - 6)$
$m = \frac{2}{3}$, (6, 3)

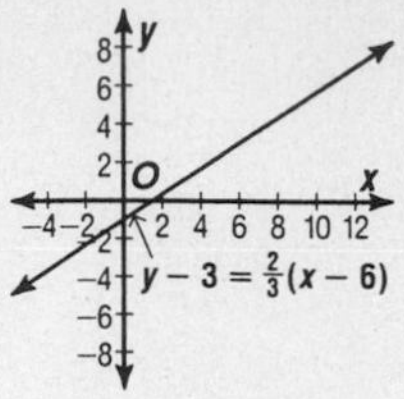

33. $y - y_1 = m(x - x_1)$
$y + 1 = -2(x + 3)$
$m = -2$, $(-3, -1)$

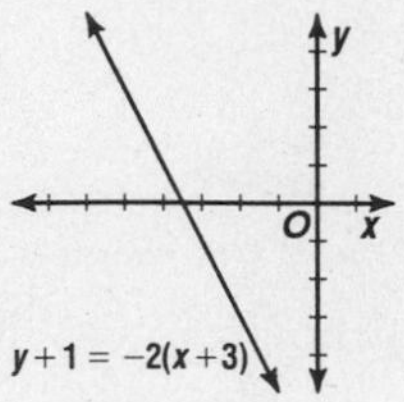

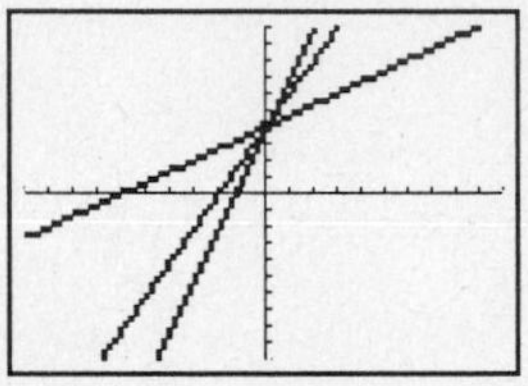

34. This is a family of graphs in which the slope of each graph is positive and the graphs have the same Y-intercept.

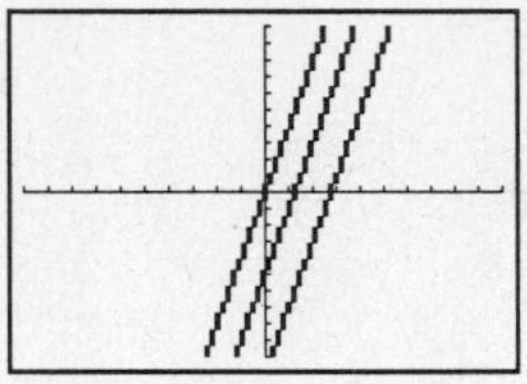

35. This is a family of graphs in which the slope of the graphs is the same and the graphs are parallel.

36. It has the same slope as $y = 3x$. Graph the intercept and use the slope, 3.

37a.

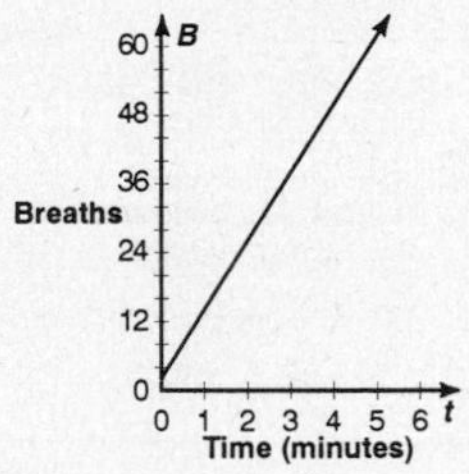

37b. $B = 2 + 12t$
$B = 2 + 12(10)$
$= 2 + 120$
$= 122$ breaths

38a.

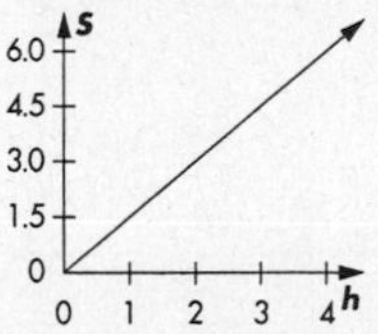

38b. $S = 1.5h$
$30 = 1.5h$
$20 = h$
The height of the tree is 20 feet.

39. $2x - 5y - 10 = 0$
$-5y = -2x + 10$
$y = \frac{2}{5}x - 2$
$m = \frac{2}{5}$, y-intercept: 12
$y = mx + b$
$y = \frac{2}{5}x + 12$

40.

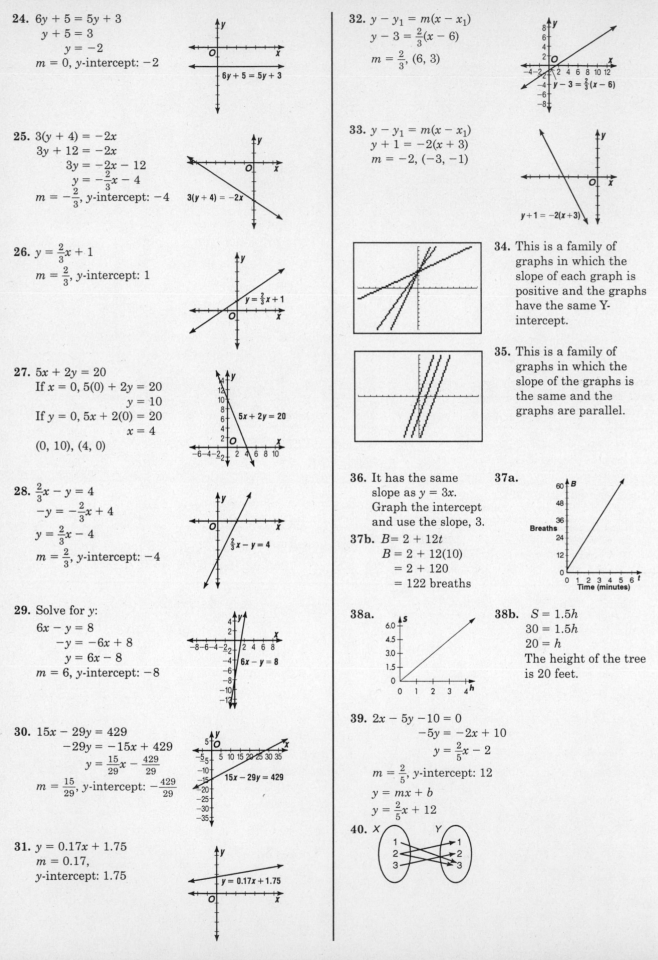

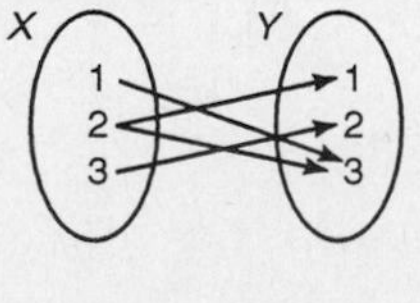

41.

	r	t	d
Art	50	t	$50t$
Jennifer	45	$t - \frac{3}{2}$	$45\left(t - \frac{3}{2}\right)$

$$50t - 45\left(t - \frac{3}{2}\right) = 100$$
$$50t - 45t + \frac{135}{2} = 100$$
$$5t + \frac{135}{2} = 100$$
$$5t = \frac{65}{2}$$
$$t = \frac{13}{2} \text{ or } 6\frac{1}{2} \text{ hours}$$

They will be 100 miles apart at 4:30 P.M.

42. $180° - 87° = 93°$ **43.** $\sqrt{3.24} = 1.8$

44. $-13 + (-9) = -22$ **45.** a number m minus 1

6-6 Integration: Geometry Parallel and Perpendicular Lines

Page 366 Check for Understanding

1a. The slopes are equal.

1b. The slopes are negative reciprocals.

2. Negative reciprocals are two numbers whose product is -1; -2 and $\frac{1}{2}$.

3. The lines from Example 2 have the same slope, and the graph shows that the lines are parallel. The lines from Example 5 have slopes that are negative reciprocals, and the graph shows that the lines are perpendicular.

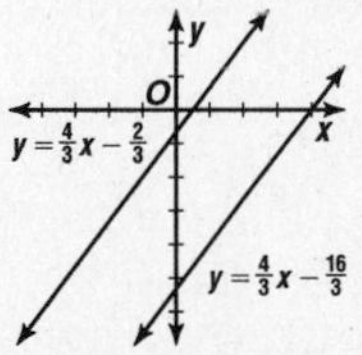

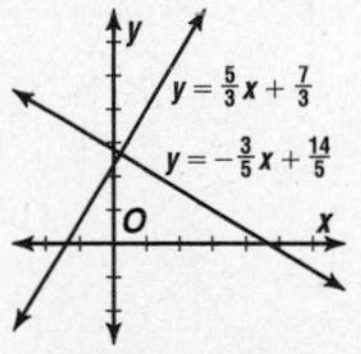

4. If it were not, a and b would be equal.

5a. Slopes are different; relationship is not.

5b. Sample answer: The relationship would not work because there would be no perpendicular lines.

6. $6x - 5y = 11$
$$-5y = -6x + 11$$
$$y = \frac{6}{5}x - \frac{11}{5}$$
$\frac{6}{5}, -\frac{5}{6}$

7. $y = \frac{2}{3}x - \frac{4}{5}$
$\frac{2}{3}, -\frac{3}{2}$

8. $3x = 10y - 3$
$$3x - 10y = -3$$
$$-10y = -3 - 3x$$
$$y = \frac{3}{10} + \frac{3}{10}x$$
$\frac{3}{10}, -\frac{10}{3}$

9. $3x - 7y = 1$
$$-7y = 1 - 3x$$
$$y = \frac{3}{7}x - \frac{1}{7}$$
$m = \frac{3}{5}$

$7x + 3y = 4$
$$3y = -7x + 4$$
$$y = -\frac{7}{3}x + \frac{4}{3}$$
$m = -\frac{7}{3}$

The slopes are negative reciprocals, therefore the lines are perpendicular.

10. $5x - 2y = 6$
$$-2y = -5x + 6$$
$$y = \frac{5}{2}x - 3$$
$m = \frac{5}{2}$

$4y - 10x = -48$
$$4y = 10x - 48$$
$$y = \frac{10}{4}x - 12$$
$$y = \frac{5}{2}x - 12$$
$m = \frac{5}{2}$

The slopes are the same, therefore the lines are parallel.

11. $5x - 6y = 2$
$$-6y = -5x + 2$$
$$y = \frac{5}{6}x - \frac{1}{3}$$
$m = \frac{5}{6}$, $(9, -3)$
$$y - y_1 = m(x - x_1)$$
$$y - (-3) = \frac{5}{6}(x - 9)$$
$$y + 3 = \frac{5}{6}x - \frac{15}{2}$$
$$y = \frac{5}{6}x - \frac{21}{2}$$

12. $2y = 5x - 7$
$$y = \frac{5}{2}x - \frac{7}{2}$$
$m = \frac{5}{2}$, $(0, 4)$
$$y = mx + b$$
$$y = \frac{5}{2}x + 4$$

13. $x - y = 0$
$$x = y$$
$m = 1$, $(7, 2)$
$$y - y_1 = m(x - x_1)$$
$$y - (-2) = 1(x - 7)$$
$$y + 2 = x - 7$$
$$y = x - 9$$

14. $7x + 4y = 23$
$$4y = -7x + 23$$
$$y = -\frac{7}{4}x + \frac{23}{4}$$
$m = \frac{4}{7}$, $(8, 5)$
$$y - y_1 = m(x - x_1)$$
$$y - 5 = \frac{4}{7}(x - 8)$$
$$y - 5 = \frac{4}{7}x - \frac{32}{7}$$
$$y = \frac{4}{7}x + \frac{3}{7}$$

15. $9y = 3 - 5x$
$$y = \frac{1}{3} - \frac{5}{9}x$$
$m = \frac{9}{5}$, $(0, 0)$
$$y = mx + b$$
$$y = \frac{9}{5}x$$

16. $2x - 5y = 3$
$$-5y = -2x + 3$$
$$y = \frac{2}{5}x - \frac{3}{5}$$
$m = -\frac{5}{2}$, $(2, 7)$
$$y - y_1 = m(x - x_1)$$
$$y - 7 = -\frac{5}{2}[x - (-2)]$$
$$y - 7 = -\frac{5}{2}x - 5$$
$$y = -\frac{5}{2}x + 2$$

17. $A(1, 3)$, $C(-1, -3)$ $B(3, -1)$, $D(-3, 1)$
$AC = \frac{-3 - 3}{-1 - 1} = 3$ $BD = \frac{1 - (-1)}{-3 - 3} = -\frac{1}{3}$

The diagonals are perpendicular.

Pages 367–368 Exercises

18. $y = -22x + 11$
$m = -2$

$y + 2x = 23$
$$y = -2x + 23$$
$m = -2$

The slopes are the same, therefore the lines are parallel.

19. $3y = 2x + 14$
$y = \frac{2}{3}x + \frac{14}{3}$
$m = \frac{2}{3}$

$2x - 3y = 2$
$-3y = -2x + 2$
$y = \frac{2}{3}x - \frac{2}{3}$
$m = \frac{2}{3}$

The slopes are the same, therefore the lines are parallel.

20. $y = -5x$
$m = -5$

$y = 5x - 18$
$m = 5$

neither

21. $y = 0.6x + 7$
$m = 0.6$ or $\frac{3}{5}$

$3y = -5x + 30$
$y = \frac{-5}{3}x + 10$
$m = -\frac{5}{3}$

The slopes are negative reciprocals, therefore the lines are perpendicular.

22. $y = 3x + 5$
$m = 3$

$y = 5x + 3$
$m = 5$

neither

23. $y + 6 = -5$
$y = -11$
$m = 0$

$y + x = y + 7$
$x = 7$
slope is undefined

The graph of $y = -11$ is a horizontal line and the graph of $x = 7$ is a vertical line, therefore the lines are perpendicular.

24. $y = x - 2$
$m = 1, (2, -7)$
$y - y_1 = m(x - x_1)$
$y - (-7) = 1(x - 2)$
$y + 7 = x - 2$
$y = x - 9$

25. $y = x + 5$
$m = 1, (2, 3)$
$y - y_1 = m(x - x_1)$
$y - 3 = 1(x - 2)$
$y - 3 = x - 2$
$y = x + 1$

26. $2x + 3y = -1$
$3y = -2x - 1$
$y = -\frac{2}{3}x - \frac{1}{3}$
$m = -\frac{2}{3}, (-5, -4)$
$y - y_1 = m(x - x_1)$
$y - (-4) = -\frac{2}{3}[x - (-5)]$
$y + 4 = -\frac{2}{3}(x + 5)$
$y + 4 = -\frac{2}{3}x - \frac{10}{3}$
$y = -\frac{2}{3}x - \frac{22}{3}$

27. $8x - 7y = 23$
$-7y = -8x + 23$
$y = \frac{8}{7}x - \frac{23}{7}$
$m = \frac{8}{7}, (5, 6)$
$y - y_1 = m(x - x_1)$
$y - 6 = \frac{8}{7}(x - 5)$
$y - 6 = \frac{8}{7}x - \frac{40}{7}$
$y = \frac{8}{7}x + \frac{2}{7}$

28. $y = -2x + 7$
$m = -2, (1, -2)$
$y - y_1 = m(x - x_1)$
$y - (-2) = -2(x - 1)$
$y + 2 = -2x + 2$
$y = -2x$

29. $5x - 2y = -7$
$-2y = -5x - 7$
$y = \frac{5}{2}x + \frac{7}{2}$
$m = \frac{5}{2}, (0, -5)$
$y = mx + b$
$y = \frac{5}{2}x - 5$

30. $x - 3y = 8$
$-3y = -x + 8$
$y = \frac{1}{3}x - \frac{8}{3}$
$m = \frac{1}{3}, (5, -4)$
$y - y_1 = m(x - x_1)$
$y - (-4) = \frac{1}{3}(x - 5)$
$y + 4 = \frac{1}{3}x - \frac{5}{3}$
$y = \frac{1}{3}x - \frac{17}{3}$

31. $2x - 3y = 6$
$-3y = -2x + 6$
$y = \frac{2}{3}x - 2$
$m = \frac{2}{3}, (-3, 2)$
$y - y_1 = m(x - x_1)$
$y - 2 = \frac{2}{3}[x - (-3)]$
$y - 2 = \frac{2}{3}x + 2$
$y = \frac{2}{3}x + 4$

32. $y = -0.5x + 2$
$m = -0.5, (2, -1)$
$y - y_1 = m(x - x_1)$
$y + 1 = -0.5(x - 2)$
$y + 1 = -0.5x + 1$
$y = -0.5x$

33. $2x - 9y = 5$
$-9y = -2x + 5$
$y = \frac{2}{9}x - \frac{5}{9}$
$m = -\frac{9}{2}, (6, -13)$
$y - y_1 = m(x - x_1)$
$y - (-13) = -\frac{9}{2}(x - 6)$
$y + 13 = -\frac{9}{2}x + 27$
$y = -\frac{9}{2}x + 14$

34. $y = \frac{1}{3}x + 2$
$m = -3, (-3, 1)$
$y - y_1 = m(x - x_1)$
$y - 1 = -3[x - (-3)]$
$y - 1 = -3x - 9$
$y = -3x - 8$

35. $3y + x = 3$
$3y = -x + 3$
$y = -\frac{1}{3}x + 1$
$m = 3, (6, -1)$
$y - (-1) = 3(x - 6)$
$y + 1 = 3x - 18$
$y = 3x - 19$

36. $y = \frac{3}{5}x - 4$
$m = -\frac{5}{3}, (6, -2)$
$y - (-2) = -\frac{5}{3}(x - 6)$
$y + 2 = -\frac{5}{3}x + 10$
$y = -\frac{5}{3}x + 8$

37. $5x - y = 3$
$-y = -5x + 3$
$y = 5x - 3$
$m = -\frac{1}{5}, (0, -1)$
$y = mx + b$
$y = -\frac{1}{5}x - 1$

38. $5x - 7 = 3y$
$\frac{5}{3}x - \frac{7}{3} = y$
$m = -\frac{3}{5}, (8, -2)$
$y - y_1 = m(x - x_1)$
$y - (-2) = -\frac{3}{5}(x - 8)$
$y + 2 = -\frac{3}{5}x + \frac{24}{5}$
$y = -\frac{3}{5}x + \frac{14}{5}$

39. $2x - 7y = 12$
$-7y = -2x + 12$
$y = \frac{2}{7}x - \frac{12}{7}$
$m = -\frac{7}{2}, (4, -3)$
$y - y_1 = m(x - x_1)$
$y - (-3) = -\frac{7}{2}(x - 4)$
$y + 3 = -\frac{7}{2}x + 14$
$y = -\frac{7}{2}x + 11$

40. $y = \frac{3}{4}x - 1$
$m = -\frac{4}{3}, (3, 7)$
$y - y_1 = m(x - x_1)$
$y - 7 = -\frac{4}{3}(x - 3)$
$y - 7 = -\frac{4}{3}x + 4$
$y = -\frac{4}{3}x + 11$

41. $3x + 7 = 2x$
$x + 7 = 0$
$x = -7$
$m = 0, (3, -3)$
$y = -3$

42. $x = -5$

43. $m = \frac{5}{4}, (0, 0)$
$y = mx + b$
$y = \frac{5}{4}x$

44. $5x - 3y = 2$
$-3y = -5x + 2$
$y = \frac{5}{3}x - \frac{2}{3}$
$m = -\frac{3}{5}, (3, 0)$
$y - y_1 = m(x - x_1)$
$y - 0 = -\frac{3}{5}(x - 3)$
$y = -\frac{3}{5}x + \frac{9}{5}$

45. $x - 3y = 8$
$-3y = -x + 8$
$y = \frac{1}{3}x - \frac{8}{3}$
$m = \frac{1}{3}, (0, -6)$
$y = mx + b$
$y = \frac{1}{3}x - 6$

46a. line a:

$m = 2, (3, 6)$

$y - y_1 = m(x - x_1)$

$y - 6 = 2(x - 3)$

$y - 6 = 2x - 6$

$y = 2x$

line b:

$m = -\frac{1}{2}, (3, 6)$

$y - y_1 = m(x - x_1)$

$y - 6 = -\frac{1}{2}(x - 3)$

$y - 6 = -\frac{1}{2}x + \frac{3}{2}$

$y = -\frac{1}{2}x + \frac{15}{2}$

46b.

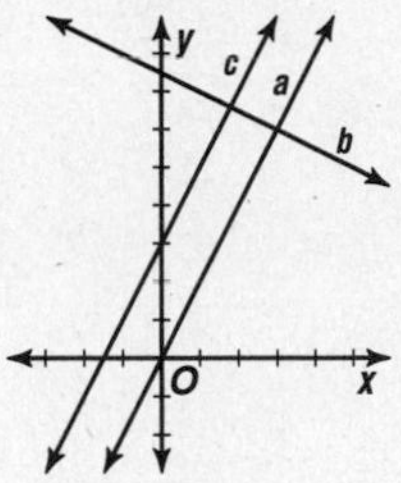

46c. parallel

47. No, because the slope of $\overline{AC}$ is $\frac{6}{7}$ and the slope of $\overline{BD}$ is $-\frac{2}{3}$. These are not negative reciprocals, so the diagonals are not perpendicular.

48a. 10

48b. $m = -\frac{1}{10}, (9, 3)$

$y - y_1 = m(x - x_1)$

$y - 3 = -\frac{1}{10}(x - 9)$

$y - 3 = -\frac{1}{10}x + \frac{9}{10}$

$y = -\frac{1}{10}x + \frac{39}{10}$

$m = 10, (-1, 4)$

$y - y_1 = m(x - x_1)$

$y - 4 = 10[x - (-1)]$

$y - 4 = 10x + 10$

$y = 10x + 14$

49a. $m = \frac{5 - 2}{3 - (-3)} = \frac{1}{2}, (3, 5)$

$y - y_1 = m(x - x_1)$

$y - 5 = \frac{1}{2}(x - 3)$

$y - 5 = \frac{1}{2}x - \frac{3}{2}$

$y = \frac{1}{2}x + \frac{7}{2}$

$m = \frac{5 - 3}{3 - 4} = -2, (3, 5)$

$y - y_1 = m(x - x_1)$

$y - 5 = -2(x - 3)$

$y - 5 = -2x + 6$

$y = -2x + 11$

49b. right or 90° angle

50. If $x = 0$,

$7(0) - 2y = -7$

$y = \frac{7}{2}$ or 3.5

If $y = 0$,

$7x - 2(0) = -7$

$x = -1$

(0, 3.5), (−1, 0)

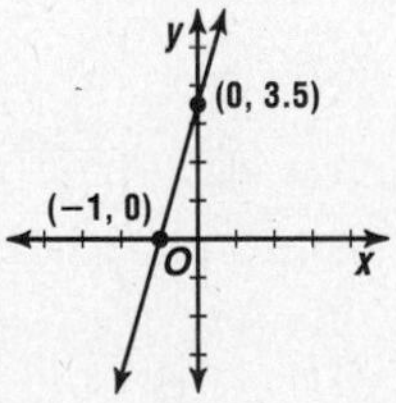

51.

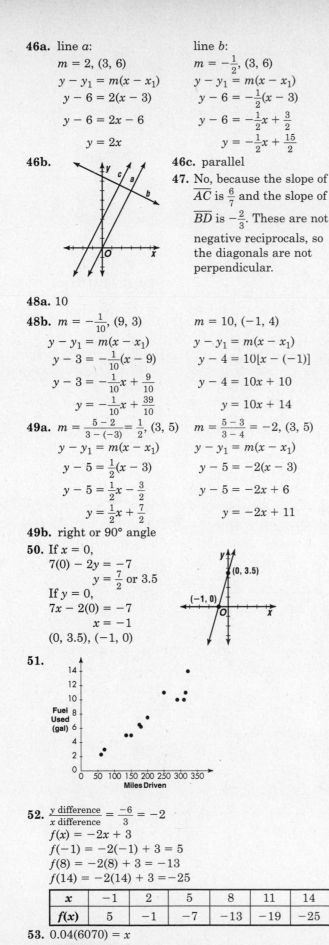

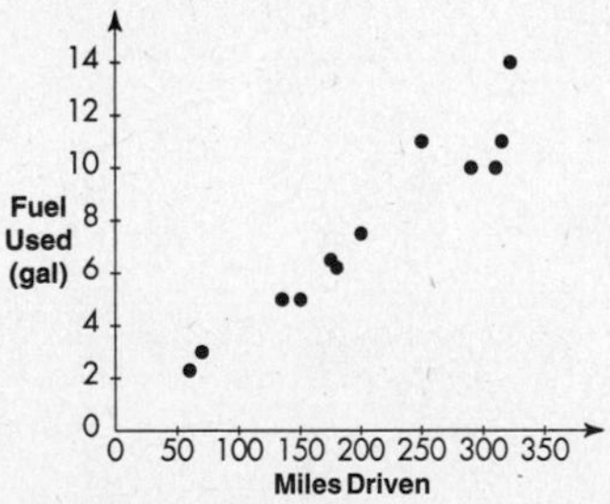

52. $\frac{y \text{ difference}}{x \text{ difference}} = \frac{-6}{3} = -2$

$f(x) = -2x + 3$

$f(-1) = -2(-1) + 3 = 5$

$f(8) = -2(8) + 3 = -13$

$f(14) = -2(14) + 3 = -25$

x	−1	2	5	8	11	14
$f(x)$	5	−1	−7	−13	−19	−25

53. $0.04(6070) = x$

$\$242.80 = x$

54. $16 = \frac{s - 8}{-7}$

$-7(16) = s - 8$

$-112 = s - 8$

$-104 = s$

55a. $\frac{10}{24} = \frac{5}{12}$ pure gold

$1 - \frac{5}{12} = \frac{7}{12}$ not gold

55b. $\frac{2}{3} = \frac{x}{24}$

$2(24) = 3x$

$48 = 3x$

$16 = x$

16-karat gold

56. −0.3005

57. identity (×)

58. $x = 6 + 0.28$

$= 6.28$

6-7 Integration: Geometry Midpoint of a Line Segment

Pages 371–372 Check for Understanding

1a. The x-coordinates will be the same, so calculate the average of the y-coordinates.

1b. The y-coordinates will be the same, so calculate the average of the x-coordinates.

2. $-3 = \frac{0 + x_2}{2}$

$-6 = x_2$

$4 = \frac{-1 + y_2}{2}$

$8 = -1 + y_2$

$9 = y_2$

$C(-6, 9)$

3a-c. See students' work.

4. $\left(\frac{5 + 5}{2}, \frac{-2 + 8}{2}\right) = \left(\frac{10}{2}, \frac{6}{2}\right)$

$= (5, 3)$

5. $\left(\frac{-5 + 8}{2}, \frac{6 + 6}{2}\right) = \left(\frac{3}{2}, \frac{12}{2}\right)$

$= (1.5, 6)$

6. $\left(\frac{6 + 14}{2}, \frac{5 + 7}{2}\right) = \left(\frac{20}{2}, \frac{12}{2}\right)$

$= (10, 6)$

7. $\left(\frac{-9 - (-3)}{2}, \frac{-6 + 8}{2}\right) = \left(-\frac{12}{2}, \frac{2}{2}\right)$

$= (-6, 1)$

8. $-1.5 = \frac{3 + x_2}{2}$

$-3 = 3 + x_2$

$-6 = x_2$

$(-6, 4)$

$5 = \frac{6 + y_2}{2}$

$10 = 6 + y_2$

$4 = y_2$

9. $-7 = \frac{-3 + x_2}{2}$

$-14 = -3 + x_2$

$-11 = x_2$

$(-11, 7)$

$7 = \frac{7 + y_2}{2}$

$14 = 7 + y_2$

$7 = y_2$

10. $5 = \frac{8 + x_2}{2}$

$10 = 8 + x_2$

$2 = x^2$

$(2, 6)$

$\frac{17}{2} = \frac{11 + y_2}{2}$

$34 = 2(11 + y_2)$

$34 = 22 + 2y_2$

$12 = 2y_2$

$6 = y_2$

11. $8 = \frac{8 + x_2}{2}$

$16 = 8 + x_2$

$8 = x_2$

$(8, 9.8)$

$7.15 = \frac{4.5 + y_2}{2}$

$14.30 = 4.5 + y_2$

$9.8 = y_2$

12. $\left(\frac{-10 + 4}{2}, \frac{13 + (-3)}{2}\right)$

$= \left(\frac{-6}{2}, \frac{10}{2}\right)$

$= (-3, 5)$

Pages 372–374 Exercises

13. $\left(\frac{6+19}{2}, \frac{6+6}{2}\right) = \left(\frac{25}{2}, \frac{12}{2}\right)$
$= (12.5, 6)$

14. $\left(\frac{-7+5}{2}, \frac{3+9}{2}\right) = \left(\frac{-2}{2}, \frac{12}{2}\right)$
$= (-1, 6)$

15. $\left(\frac{-5+7}{2}, \frac{9+1}{2}\right) = \left(\frac{2}{2}, \frac{10}{2}\right)$
$= (1, 5)$

16. $\left(\frac{7+11}{2}, \frac{4+(-10)}{2}\right) = \left(\frac{18}{2}, \frac{-6}{2}\right)$
$= (9, -3)$

17. $\left(\frac{8+(-2)}{2}, \frac{-7+11}{2}\right) = \left(\frac{6}{2}, \frac{4}{2}\right)$
$= (3, 2)$

18. $\left(\frac{-8+(-8)}{2}, \frac{1.2+7.4}{2}\right) = \left(\frac{-16}{2}, \frac{8.6}{2}\right)$
$= (-8, 4.3)$

19. $\left(\frac{-3+4}{2}, \frac{9+(-7)}{2}\right) = \left(\frac{1}{2}, \frac{2}{2}\right)$
$= \left(\frac{1}{2}, 1\right)$

20. $\left(\frac{9+2}{2}, \frac{-4+7}{2}\right) = \left(\frac{11}{2}, \frac{3}{2}\right)$

21. $\left(\frac{4.7+(-3.1)}{2}, \frac{-2.9+8.3}{2}\right) = \left(\frac{1.6}{2}, \frac{5.4}{2}\right)$
$= (0.8, 2.7)$

22. $\left(\frac{a+c}{2}, \frac{b+d}{2}\right)$

23. $\left(\frac{6x+2x}{2}, \frac{14y+4y}{2}\right) = \left(\frac{8x}{2}, \frac{18y}{2}\right)$
$= (4x, 9y)$

24. $\left(\frac{-2w+6w}{2}, \frac{-7v+2v}{2}\right) = \left(\frac{4w}{2}, \frac{-5v}{2}\right)$
$= \left(2w, -\frac{5}{2}v\right)$

25. $-7 = \frac{-7+x_2}{2}$ $4 = \frac{8+y_2}{2}$
$-14 = -7 + x_2$ $8 = 8 + y_2$
$-7 = x_2$ $0 = y_2$
$(-7, 0)$

26. $2 = \frac{4+x_2}{2}$ $1 = \frac{2+y_2}{2}$
$4 = 4 + x_2$ $2 = 2 + y_2$
$0 = x_2$ $0 = y_2$
$(0, 0)$

27. $12 = \frac{3+x_2}{2}$ $-6 = \frac{-6+y_2}{2}$
$24 = 3 + x_2$ $-12 = -6 + y_2$
$21 = x_2$ $-6 = y_2$
$(21, -6)$

28. $6 = \frac{5+y_2}{2}$ $4 = \frac{3+y_2}{2}$
$12 = 5 + x_2$ $8 = 3 + y_2$
$7 = x_2$ $5 = y_2$
$(7, 5)$

29. $\frac{1}{2} = \frac{-8+x_2}{2}$ $7 = \frac{4+y_2}{2}$
$1 = -8 + x_2$ $14 = 4 + y_2$
$9 = x_2$ $10 = y_2$
$(9, 10)$

30. $8 = \frac{5+x_2}{2}$ $-7.5 = \frac{-9+y_2}{2}$
$16 = 5 + x_2$ $-15 = -9 + y_2$
$11 = x_2$ $-6 = y_2$
$(11, -6)$

31. $\frac{1}{2} = \frac{\frac{1}{6}+x_2}{2}$ $\frac{1}{3} = \frac{\frac{1}{3}+y_2}{2}$
$1 = \frac{1}{6} + x_2$ $\frac{2}{3} = \frac{1}{3} + y_2$
$\frac{5}{6} = x_2$ $\frac{1}{3} = y_2$
$\left(\frac{5}{6}, \frac{1}{3}\right)$

32. $\frac{x+a}{2} = \frac{a+x_2}{2}$ $\frac{y+b}{2} = \frac{b+y_2}{2}$
$x = x_2$ $y = y_2$
(x, y)

33. $4.4 = \frac{x_2+6.5}{2}$ $-0.7 = \frac{-8.2+y_2}{2}$
$8.8 = x_2 + 6.5$ $-1.4 = -8.2 + y_2$
$2.3 = x_2$ $6.8 = y_2$
$B(2.3, 6.8)$

34. $1.2 = \frac{x_2+5.3}{2}$ $4.5 = \frac{y_2+1.9}{2}$
$2.4 = x_2 + 5.3$ $9 = y_2 + 1.9$
$-2.9 = x_2$ $7.1 = y_2$
$A(-2.9, 7.1)$

35. $\left(\frac{9.7+3.6}{2}, \frac{-5.4+1.7}{2}\right) = \left(\frac{13.3}{2}, \frac{-3.7}{2}\right)$
$P(6.65, -1.85)$

36. $-1.05 = \frac{x_2+(-5.9)}{2}$ $5.85 = \frac{y_2+7.2}{2}$
$-2.1 = x_2 + (-5.9)$ $11.7 = y_2 + 7.2$
$3.8 = x_2$ $4.5 = y_2$
$B(3.8, 4.5)$

37. $\left(\frac{5+(-7)}{2}, \frac{8+2}{2}\right) = \left(-\frac{2}{2}, \frac{10}{2}\right)$
$= (-1, 5)$

38. midpoint of $\overline{AB} = \left(\frac{8+10}{2}, \frac{3+(-5)}{2}\right)$
$= \left(\frac{18}{2}, \frac{-2}{2}\right)$
$= (9, -1)$
midpoint of $\overline{AP} = \left(\frac{8+9}{2}, \frac{3+(-1)}{2}\right)$
$= \left(\frac{17}{2}, \frac{2}{2}\right)$
$= (8.5, 1)$
The coordinates of the point are (8.5, 1).

39. midpoint of $\overline{AB} = \left(\frac{-2+6}{2}, \frac{7+(-5)}{2}\right)$
$= \left(\frac{4}{2}, \frac{2}{2}\right)$
$M(2, 1)$
midpoint of $\overline{AM} = \left(\frac{-2+2}{2}, \frac{7+1}{2}\right)$
$= \left(\frac{0}{2}, \frac{8}{2}\right)$
$P(0, 4)$
midpoint of $\overline{PM} = \left(\frac{2+0}{2}, \frac{1+4}{2}\right)$
$= \left(\frac{2}{2}, \frac{5}{2}\right)$
$= \left(1, \frac{5}{2}\right)$
The coordinates of P are $\left(1, \frac{5}{2}\right)$.

40. The vertices are $W(2, -3)$, $X(6, 2)$, $Y(2, 4)$, and $Z(-2, -1)$. The slope of $\overline{XW}$ = slope of $\overline{YZ} = \frac{5}{4}$. The slope of $\overline{WZ}$ = slope of $\overline{XY} = -\frac{1}{2}$. The opposite sides are parallel, so $WXYZ$ is a parallelogram.

41a. $A(5, 0), C(7, 6)$

midpoint of $\overline{AC} = \left(\frac{7+5}{2}, \frac{0+6}{2}\right)$
$= \left(\frac{12}{2}, \frac{6}{2}\right)$
$= (6, 3)$

$B(13, 0), C(7, 6)$

midpoint of $\overline{BC} = \left(\frac{13+7}{2}, \frac{0+6}{2}\right)$
$= \left(\frac{20}{2}, \frac{6}{2}\right)$
$= (10, 3)$

$N(6, 3), M(10, 3)$

41b. $MN = \frac{3-3}{10-6}$ $= 0$ $\qquad AB = \frac{0-0}{13-5}$ $= 0$

They are parallel, $MN = \frac{1}{2}AB$

42a. $30 = \frac{x_2 + 20}{2}$ $\qquad 60 = \frac{43 + y_2}{2}$

$60 = x_2 + 20$ $\qquad 120 = 43 + y_2$

$40 = x_2$ $\qquad 77 = y_2$

$(40, 77)$

42b. origin $= \left(\frac{0+62}{2}, \frac{0+94}{2}\right)$
$= \left(\frac{62}{2}, \frac{94}{2}\right)$
$= (31, 47)$

42c. Ordered pairs are (y, x) and the origin is in a different place.

43a. $-1 = \frac{2 + y_2}{2}$ $\qquad 5 = \frac{9 + y_2}{2}$

$-2 = 2 + x_2$ $\qquad 10 = 9 + y_2$

$-4 = x_2$ $\qquad 1 = y^2$

$P(-4, 1)$

$6 = \frac{2 + x_2}{2}$ $\qquad 4 = \frac{9 + y_2}{2}$

$12 = 2 + x_2$ $\qquad 8 - 9 + y_2$

$10 = x_2$ $\qquad -1 = y_2$

$Q(10, -1)$

43b. Sample answer: The area of the smaller triangle is $\frac{1}{2}bh$. Since the base of the larger triangle is twice that of the smaller one and the height is also twice the length of the smaller one, the area of the larger is $\frac{1}{2}(2b)(2h)$, or $2bh$. This is 4 times the area of the smaller one.
area $\Delta RPQ = 4(15.5) = 62$ square units

44. $5x - 3y = 7$
$-3y = -5x + 7$
$y = \frac{5}{3}x - \frac{7}{3}$
$m = -\frac{3}{5}, (8, -2)$

$y - y_1 = m(x - x_1)$
$y - (-2) = -\frac{3}{5}(x - 8)$
$y + 2 = -\frac{3}{5}x + \frac{24}{5}$
$y = -\frac{3}{5}x + \frac{14}{5}$

45. $m = \frac{-5-2}{3-(-6)} = -\frac{7}{9}$

$y - y_1 = m(x - x_1)$, using $(3, -5)$
$y - (-5) = -\frac{7}{9}(x - 3)$
$y + 5 = -\frac{7}{9}x + \frac{21}{9}$
$y = -\frac{7}{9}x - \frac{8}{3}$

46. $g(4b) = (4b)^2 - 4b$
$= 16b^2 - 4b$

47. yes; $9x - 6y = 7$ $\qquad$ **48.** 38°

49. $-27 - b = -7$
$-b = 20$
$b = -20$

50a. 10 years old

50b. $a + 10$

50c. no; $4 + 10 \neq 12$

51. $0.2(3x + 0.2) + 0.5(5x + 3)$
$= 0.6x + 0.04 + 2.5x + 1.5$
$= 0.6x + 2.5x + 0.04 + 1.5$
$= 3.1x + 1.54$

Page 374 Mathematics and Society

1. Sample answer: The more people there are on Earth, the more need for the natural resources and the less resources to share. Without conservation of resources, there will not be enough to go around.
2. Sample answers: Less space; less water, power, gas, and other natural resources; smaller yards due to more homes being built; and so on.

3a. $\frac{1000 \text{ refugees}}{1 \text{ day}} \cdot \frac{365 \text{ days}}{1 \text{ year}} = 365{,}000\frac{\text{refugees}}{\text{year}}$

$\frac{2{,}500{,}000}{365{,}000} \approx 6.85$ It would take about 6.85 years.

3b. Sample answer: No, this does not take into account deaths and births that may occur during the immigration.

Chapter 6 Highlights

Page 375 Understanding and Using the Vocabulary

1. parallel
2. point-slope
3. midpoint
4. x-intercept
5. perpendicular
6. rise; run
7. slope-intercept
8. y-intercept
9. slope
10. standard

Chapter 6 Study Guide and Assessment

Pages 376–378 Skills and Concepts

11. $m = \frac{5-3}{2-8}$
$= \frac{2}{-6}$ or $-\frac{1}{3}$

12. $m = \frac{9-5}{-2-(-2)}$
$= \frac{4}{0}$ undefined

13. $m = \frac{4-6}{-8-(-3)}$
$= \frac{-2}{-5}$ or $\frac{2}{5}$

14. $m = \frac{3-3}{-5-4}$
$= \frac{0}{-9}$ or 0

15. $\frac{3}{4} = \frac{3-4}{7-r}$
$\frac{3}{4} = \frac{-1}{7-r}$
$3(7 - r) = 4(-1)$
$21 - 3r = -4$
$-3r = -25$
$r = \frac{25}{3}$

16. $\frac{8}{3} = \frac{r-(-7)}{-2-4}$
$\frac{8}{3} = \frac{r+7}{-6}$
$-48 = 3(r + 7)$
$-48 = 3r + 21$
$-69 = 3r$
$-23 = r$

17. $y - y_1 = m(x - x_1)$
$y - (-3) = -2(x - 4)$
$y + 3 = -2(x - 4)$

18. $y - y_1 = m(x - x_1)$
$y - 5 = 5(x - 8)$

19. $y - y_1 = m(x - x_1)$
$y - 7 = 0[x - (-5)]$
$y - 7 = 0$

20. $y - y_1 = m(x - x_1)$
$y - 2 = \frac{1}{2}(x - 6)$

21. $m = \frac{3-0}{0-(-5)} = \frac{3}{5}$

$y - y_1 = m(x - x_1)$, using (0, 3)

$y - 3 = \frac{3}{5}(x - 0)$

$y - 3 = \frac{3}{5}x$

22. $m = \frac{4-3}{5-6} = -1$

$y - y_1 = m(x - x_1)$, using (6, 3)

$y - 3 = -(x - 6)$

23. $m = \frac{7-1}{-3-4} = -\frac{6}{7}$

$y - y_1 = m(x - x_1)$, using (4, 1)

$y - 1 = -\frac{6}{7}(x - 4)$

24. $m = \frac{-5-4}{2-0} = -\frac{9}{2}$

$y - y_1 = m(x - x_1)$, using (2, −5)

$y - (-5) = -\frac{9}{2}(x - 2)$

$y + 5 = -\frac{9}{2}(x - 2)$

25. $y - y_1 = m(x - x_1)$

$y - (-6) = 3(x - 4)$

$y + 6 = 3x - 12$

$y = 3x - 18$

$-3x + y = -18$

$3x - y = 18$

26. $y - y_1 = m(x - x_1)$

$y - 5 = 0(x - 1)$

$y - 5 = 0$

$y = 5$

27. $y - y_1 = m(x - x_1)$

$y - (-1) = \frac{3}{4}(x - 6)$

$y + 1 = \frac{3}{4}(x - 6)$

$4(y + 1) = 4\left(\frac{3}{4}\right)(x - 6)$

$4y + 4 = 3(x - 6)$

$4y + 4 = 3x - 18$

$4y = 3x - 22$

$-3x + 4y = -22$

$3x - 4y = 22$

28. $x = 8$

29. $m = \frac{5-5}{-2-9} = 0$

$y - y_1 = m(x - x_1)$, using (9, 5)

$y - 5 = 0(x - 9)$

$y - 5 = 0$

$y = 5$

30. $m = \frac{5-0}{0-(-2)} = \frac{5}{2}$

$m = \frac{5}{2}$, (0, 5)

$y = mx + b$

$y = \frac{5}{2}x + 5$

$2y = 5x + 10$

$-5x + 2y = 10$

$5x - 2y = -10$

31. $m = \frac{\frac{2}{3} - \frac{2}{7}}{-2-(-2)} = \frac{\frac{8}{21}}{0}$

The slope is undefined.

$x = -2$

32. $m = \frac{7 - \frac{1}{2}}{-5-0} = \frac{\frac{13}{2}}{-5} = -\frac{13}{10}$

$m = -\frac{13}{10}, \left(0, \frac{1}{2}\right)$

$y = mx + b$

$y = -\frac{13}{10}x + \frac{1}{2}$

$10y = -13x + 5$

$13x + 10y = 5$

33a, 33c.

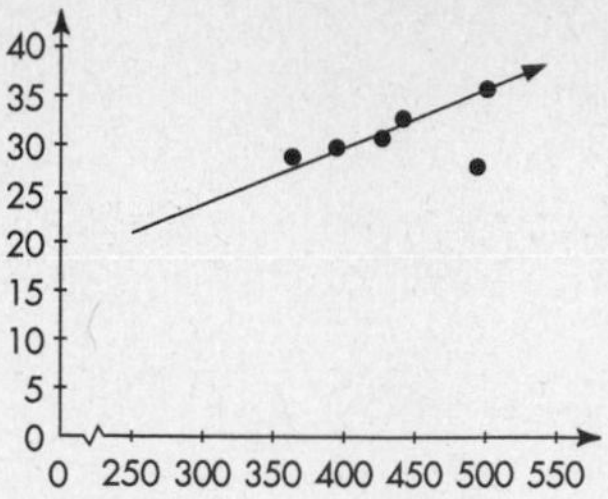

Yes; it is positive.

33b. Sample answer: 35 stories

33c. $y = 0.03x + 21$

34. $y = mx + b$

$y = 2x + 4$

35. $y = mx + b$

$y = -3x + 0$

$y = -3x$

36. $y = mx + b$

$y = -\frac{1}{2}x - 9$

37. $y = mx + b$

$y = 0x + 5.5$

$y = 5.5$

38. $x = 2y - 7$

$x + 7 = 2y$

$\frac{1}{2}x + \frac{7}{2} = y$

$y = \frac{1}{2}x + \frac{7}{2}$

$m = \frac{1}{2}$, y-intercept: $\frac{7}{2}$

39. $8x + y = 4$

$y = -8x + 4$

$m = -8$, y-intercept: 4

40. $y = \frac{1}{4}x + 3$

$m = \frac{1}{4}$, y-intercept: 3

41. $\frac{1}{2}x + \frac{1}{4}y = 3$

$2x + y = 12$

$y = -2x + 12$

$m = -2$, y-intercept: 12

42. $3x - y = 9$

$-y = -3x + 9$

$y = 3x + 9$

$m = 3$, y-intercept: 9

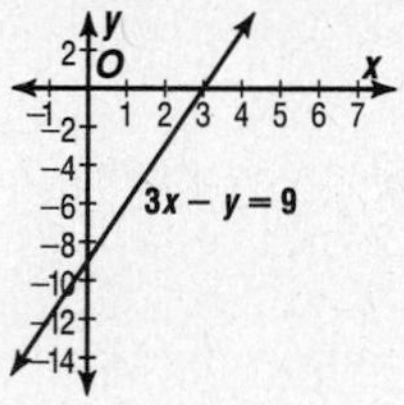

43. $5x + 2y = 12$

$2y = -5x + 12$

$y = -\frac{5}{2}x + 6$

$m = -\frac{5}{2}$, y-intercept: 6

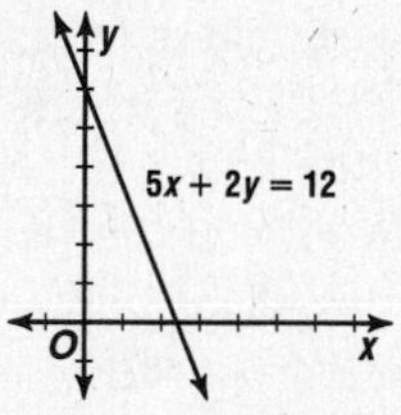

44. $y = \frac{2}{3}x + 4$

$m = \frac{2}{3}$, y-intercept: 4

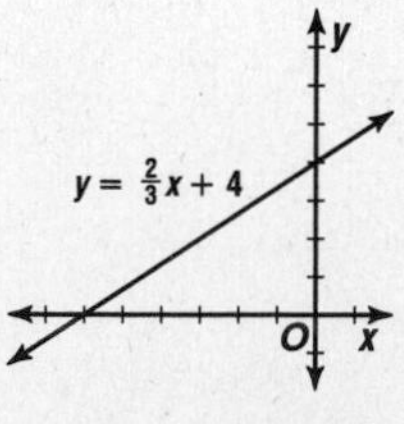

45. $y = -\frac{3}{2}x - 6$

$m = -\frac{3}{2}$, y-intercept: −6

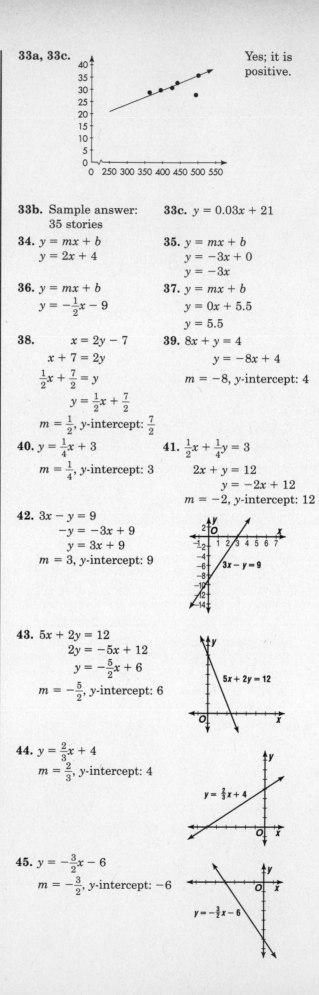

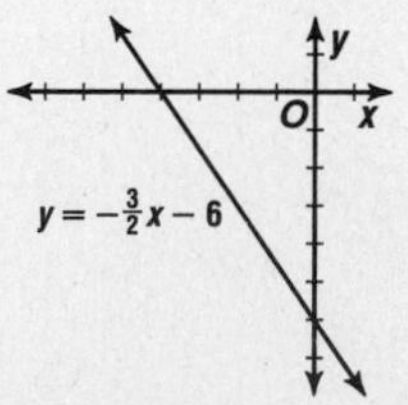

46. $3x + 4y = 6$
$4y = -3x + 6$
$y = -\frac{3}{4}x + \frac{3}{2}$
$m = -\frac{3}{4}$, y-intercept: $\frac{3}{2}$

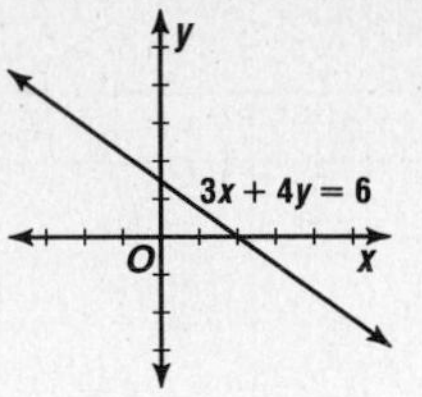

47. $5x - \frac{1}{2}y = 2$
$-\frac{1}{2}y = -5x + 2$
$y = 10x - 4$
$m = 10$, y-intercept: -4

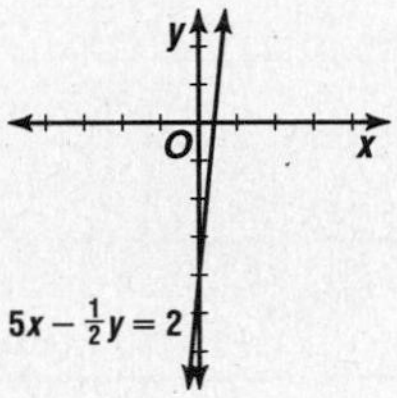

48. $y - y_1 = m(x - x_1)$
$y - 4 = -2(x + 1)$
$m = -2$, $(-1, 4)$

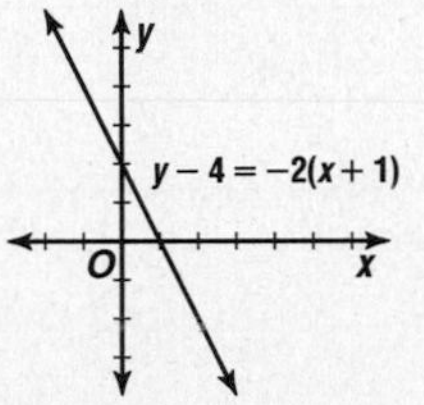

49. $y - y_1 = m(x - x_1)$
$y + 5 = -\frac{3}{4}(x - 6)$
$m = -\frac{3}{4}$, $(6, -5)$

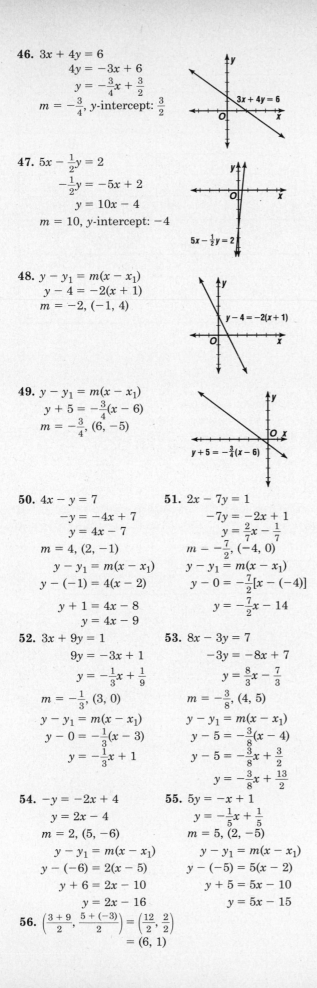

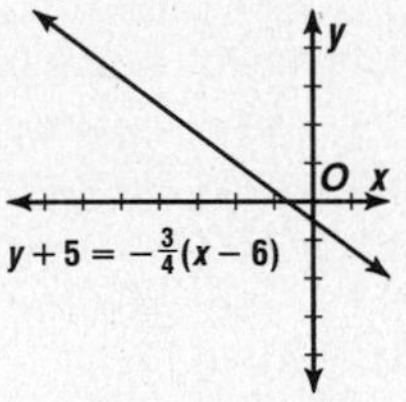

50. $4x - y = 7$
$-y = -4x + 7$
$y = 4x - 7$
$m = 4$, $(2, -1)$
$y - y_1 = m(x - x_1)$
$y - (-1) = 4(x - 2)$
$y + 1 = 4x - 8$
$y = 4x - 9$

51. $2x - 7y = 1$
$-7y = -2x + 1$
$y = \frac{2}{7}x - \frac{1}{7}$
$m - -\frac{7}{2}$, $(-4, 0)$
$y - y_1 = m(x - x_1)$
$y - 0 = -\frac{7}{2}[x - (-4)]$
$y = -\frac{7}{2}x - 14$

52. $3x + 9y = 1$
$9y = -3x + 1$
$y = -\frac{1}{3}x + \frac{1}{9}$
$m = -\frac{1}{3}$, $(3, 0)$
$y - y_1 = m(x - x_1)$
$y - 0 = -\frac{1}{3}(x - 3)$
$y = -\frac{1}{3}x + 1$

53. $8x - 3y = 7$
$-3y = -8x + 7$
$y = \frac{8}{3}x - \frac{7}{3}$
$m = -\frac{3}{8}$, $(4, 5)$
$y - y_1 = m(x - x_1)$
$y - 5 = -\frac{3}{8}(x - 4)$
$y - 5 = -\frac{3}{8}x + \frac{3}{2}$
$y = -\frac{3}{8}x + \frac{13}{2}$

54. $-y = -2x + 4$
$y = 2x - 4$
$m = 2$, $(5, -6)$
$y - y_1 = m(x - x_1)$
$y - (-6) = 2(x - 5)$
$y + 6 = 2x - 10$
$y = 2x - 16$

55. $5y = -x + 1$
$y = -\frac{1}{5}x + \frac{1}{5}$
$m = 5$, $(2, -5)$
$y - y_1 = m(x - x_1)$
$y - (-5) = 5(x - 2)$
$y + 5 = 5x - 10$
$y = 5x - 15$

56. $\left(\frac{3+9}{2}, \frac{5+(-3)}{2}\right) = \left(\frac{12}{2}, \frac{2}{2}\right)$
$= (6, 1)$

57. $\left(\frac{-6+8}{2}, \frac{6+(-11)}{2}\right) = \left(\frac{2}{2}, -\frac{5}{2}\right)$
$= \left(1, -\frac{5}{2}\right)$

58. $\left(\frac{14+2}{2}, \frac{4+0}{2}\right) = \left(\frac{16}{2}, \frac{4}{2}\right)$
$= (8, 2)$

59. $\left(\frac{2+8}{2}, \frac{7+4}{2}\right) = \left(\frac{10}{2}, \frac{11}{2}\right)$
$= \left(5, \frac{11}{2}\right)$

60. $\left(\frac{2+4}{2}, \frac{5+(-1)}{2}\right) = \left(\frac{6}{2}, \frac{4}{2}\right)$
$= (3, 2)$

61. $\left(\frac{10+(-3)}{2}, \frac{4+(-7)}{2}\right) = \left(\frac{7}{2}, -\frac{3}{2}\right)$

62. $11 = \frac{3 + x_2}{2}$
$22 = 3 + x_2$
$19 = x_2$
$(19, 9)$

$7 = \frac{5 + y_2}{2}$
$14 = 5 + y_2$
$9 = y_2$

63. $9 = \frac{x_2 + 5}{2}$
$18 = x_2 + 5$
$13 = x_2$
$(13, 11)$

$7 = \frac{3 + y_2}{2}$
$14 = 3 + y_2$
$11 = y_2$

64. $5 = \frac{x_2 + 4}{2}$
$10 = x_2 + 4$
$6 = x_2$
$(6, -7)$

$-9 = \frac{-11 + y_2}{2}$
$-18 = -11 + y_2$
$-7 = y_2$

65. $3 = \frac{11 - x_2}{2}$
$6 = 11 + x_2$
$-5 = x_2$
$(-5, 20)$

$8 = \frac{-4 + y_2}{2}$
$16 = -4 + y_2$
$20 = y_2$

Page 378 Applications and Problem Solving

66a. $m = \frac{60}{250}$ or $\frac{6}{25}$ **66b.** yes, $\frac{6}{25} < \frac{1}{3}$

67. $d = rt + 80$
$d = 45(t - 2) + 80,\ t > 2$
$d = 45t - 90 + 80$
$d = 45t - 10$

68. lowest (8, 4), highest (6, 7)
midpoint $= \left(\frac{8+6}{2}, \frac{4+7}{2}\right)$
$= \left(\frac{14}{2}, \frac{11}{2}\right)$
$= (7, \$5.50)$

Page 379 Alternative Assessment: Thinking Critically

- Sample answer: $y = -x + 2$; the x-intercept is 2 and the y-intercept is 2. The slope of the line is -1.
- Sample answer: $y = x - 2$; the x-intercept is 2 and the y-intercept is -2. The slope of the line is 1.
- The slopes of lines whose x- and y-intercepts are equal is -1. The slopes of lines whose x- and y-intercepts are opposites is 1.

- x-intercept is s: $(s, 0)$, y-intercept is t: $(0, t)$

$m = \frac{t-0}{0-s}$

$= -\frac{t}{s}$

$y = mx + b$

$y = -\frac{t}{s}x + t$ slope-intercept form

$sy = -tx + st$

$tx + sy = st$ standard form

Cumulative Review, Chapters 1–6

Pages 380–381

1. x is negative and y is negative in Quadrant III. C

2. school (3, 8), friend's house (7, 6)

midpoint $= \left(\frac{3+7}{2}, \frac{8+6}{2}\right)$

$= \left(\frac{10}{2}, \frac{14}{2}\right)$

$= (5, 7)$ A

3. $m = \frac{9-6}{-5-(-3)}$

$= -\frac{3}{2}$ C

4. number damaged = 0.04(100) = 4
number undamaged = 100 − 4 = 96
odds (damaged CD) = number damaged:number undamaged = 4:96 or 1:24 D

5. A vertical line can not intersect the graph in more than one point to be a function. B

6. $(g + h)b = g(b) + h(b)$ A distribution property

7. $y = -\frac{2}{3}x + 2$

$m = -\frac{2}{3}$, y-intercept: 2 D

8. Area $= \frac{1}{2}bc \sin A$

$= \frac{1}{2}(16)(9) \sin 36°$

$\approx 72(0.5878)$

$\approx 42.3 \text{ cm}^2$ B

9. {(−3, −1), (−2, 0), (−1, 3), (0, −1), (1, 0), (1, 1), (2, 2), (3, 1), (3, 2)}

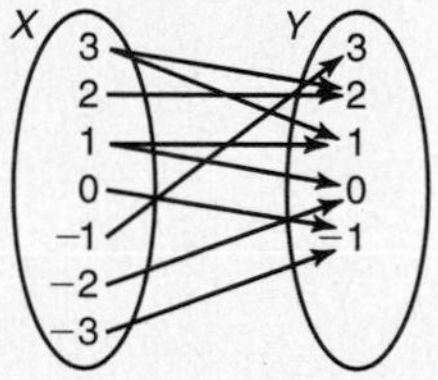

10. $4x - y = 7$

$-y = -4x + 7$

$y = 4x - 7$

$m = -\frac{1}{4}$, $(2, -1)$

$y - y_1 = m(x - x_1)$

$y - (-1) = -\frac{1}{4}(x - 2)$

$y + 1 = -\frac{1}{4}x + \frac{1}{2}$

$y = -\frac{1}{4}x - \frac{1}{2}$

11. mean

$= \frac{59 + 70 + 49 + 62 + 46 + 63 + 71 + 64 + 55 + 68 + 54}{11}$

$= \frac{661}{11}$

$= 60$

The mean temperature is 60°F. Yes, survival is possible.

12. solve for y: $5x + y = 4$

$y = -5x + 4$

x	$-5x + 4$	y	(x, y)
−2	−5(−2) + 4	4	(−2, 14)
−1	−5(−1) + 4	9	(−1, 9)
0	−5(0) + 4	4	(0, 4)
2	−5(2) + 4	−6	(2, −6)
5	−5(5) + 4	−21	(5, 21)

{(−2, 14), (−1, 9), (0, 4), (2, −6), (5, −21)}

13.

Nuts	Number of Pounds	Cost Per Pound	Total Cost
peanuts	12	3	36
cashews	c	6	$6c$
mix	$12 + c$	4.20	$4.2(12 + c)$

$36 + 6c = 4.2(12 + c)$

$36 + 6c = 50.4 + 4.2c$

$1.8c = 14.4$

$c = 8$

8 pounds of cashews

14. $C(v) = 150 + 0.30(v - 100)$

$225 = 150 + 0.30(v - 100)$

$225 = 150 + 0.30v - 30$

$225 = 120 + 0.30v$

$105 = 0.30v$

$350 = v$

She must sell 350 videos each week.

15.

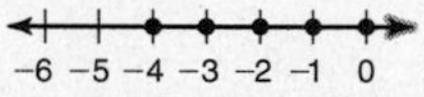

16.

number of minutes	4	6	15
charge	1.72	2.40	5.46

$\frac{\textit{range differences}}{\textit{domain differences}} = \frac{2.40 - 1.72}{6 - 4} = 0.34$

$f(x) = 0.34x + 0.36$

$f(1) = 0.34(1) + 0.36$

$= 0.34 + 0.36$

$= 0.70$

A 1-minute call would cost \$0.70.

17a.

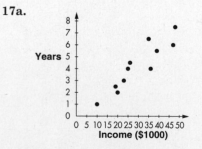

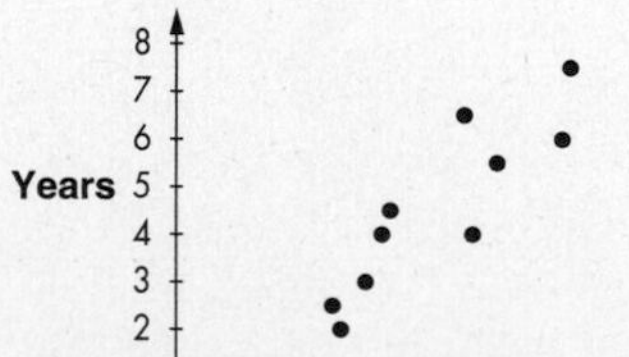

17b. The more years of education you have, the higher your income.

Chapter 7 Solving Linear Inequalities

7-1 Solving Inequalities by Using Addition and Subtraction

Pages 387–388 Check for Understanding

1. Sample answer: $x + 5 < -5$, $x - 5 < -15$, $2x < x - 10$
2. The set of all numbers w such that w is greater than -3.
3. One ($\leq$) includes -7; the other does not.
4. Answers and graphs will vary. Sample answer: The circle on the graph will be filled if the inequality involves $\leq$ or $\geq$. The circle will be open if it involves $>$ or $<$. The arrow goes to the left if it involves $<$ or $\leq$. It goes to the right for $>$ or $\geq$.
5. Yes, sample answer: $x + 6 > x + 8$.
6. See students' work.

7.
$$b - 18 > -3$$
$$b - 18 + 18 > -3 + 18$$
$$b > 15$$
c

8.
$$10 \geq -3 + x$$
$$10 + 3 \geq -3 + 3 + x$$
$$13 \geq x$$
a

9.
$$x + 11 < 6$$
$$x + 11 - 11 < 6 - 11$$
$$x < -5$$
d

10.
$$4c - 3 \leq 5c$$
$$4c - 4c - 3 \leq 5c - 4c$$
$$-3 \leq c$$
b

11.
$$x + 7 > 2$$
$$x + 7 - 7 > 2 - 7$$
$$x > -5$$
$$\{x \mid x > -5\}$$

12.
$$10 \geq x + 8$$
$$10 - 8 \geq x + 8 - 8$$
$$2 \geq x$$
$$\{x \mid x \leq 2\}$$

13.
$$y - 7 < -12$$
$$y - 7 + 7 < -12 + 7$$
$$y < -5$$
$$\{y \mid y < -5\}$$

14.
$$-81 + q > 16 + 2q$$
$$-81 - 16 + q > 16 - 16 + 2q$$
$$-97 + q > 2q$$
$$-97 + q - q > 2q - q$$
$$-97 > q$$
$$\{q \mid q < -97\}$$

15.
$$x - 17 < -13$$
$$x - 17 + 17 < -13 + 17$$
$$x < 4$$
$$\{x \mid x < 4\}$$

16.
$$x + 4 \geq 3$$
$$x + 4 - 4 \geq 3 - 4$$
$$x \geq -1$$
$$\{x \mid x \geq -1\}$$

Pages 388–390 Exercises

17.
$$a - 12 < 6$$
$$a - 12 + 12 < 6 + 12$$
$$a < 18$$
$$\{a \mid a < 18\}$$

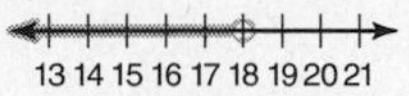

18.
$$m - 3 < -17$$
$$m - 3 + 3 < -17 + 3$$
$$m < -14$$
$$\{m \mid m < -14\}$$

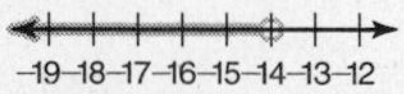

19.
$$2x \leq x + 1$$
$$2x - x \leq x - x + 1$$
$$x \leq 1$$
$$\{x \mid x \leq 1\}$$

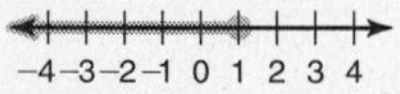

20.
$$-9 + d > 9$$
$$-9 + 9 + d > 9 + 9$$
$$d > 18$$
$$\{d \mid d > 18\}$$

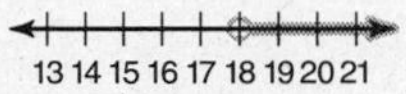

21.
$$x + \frac{1}{3} > 4$$
$$x + \frac{1}{3} - \frac{1}{3} > 4 - \frac{1}{3}$$
$$x > \frac{11}{3}$$
$$\left\{x \mid x > \frac{11}{3}\right\}$$

22.
$$-0.11 \leq n - (-0.04)$$
$$-0.11 \leq n + 0.04$$
$$-0.11 - 0.04 \leq n + 0.04 - 0.04$$
$$-0.15 \leq n$$
$$\{n \mid n \geq -0.15\}$$

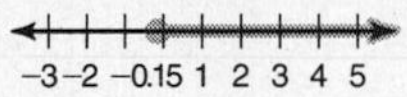

23.
$$2x + 3 > x + 5$$
$$2x + 3 - 3 > x + 5 - 3$$
$$2x > x + 2$$
$$2x - x > x - x + 2$$
$$x > 2$$
$$\{x \mid x > 2\}$$

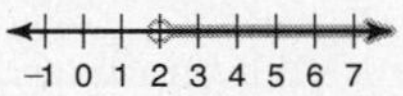

24.
$$7h - 1 \leq 6h$$
$$7h - 1 + 1 \leq 6h + 1$$
$$7h \leq 6h + 1$$
$$7h - 6h \leq 6h - 6h + 1$$
$$h \leq 1$$
$$\{h \mid h \leq 1\}$$

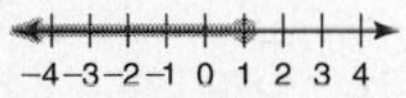

25.
$$x + \frac{1}{8} < \frac{1}{2}$$
$$x + \frac{1}{8} - \frac{1}{8} < \frac{1}{2} - \frac{1}{8}$$
$$x < \frac{3}{8}$$
$$\left\{x \mid x < \frac{3}{8}\right\}$$

26.
$$3x + \frac{4}{5} \leq 4x + \frac{3}{5}$$
$$3x + \frac{4}{5} - \frac{3}{5} \leq 4x + \frac{3}{5} - \frac{3}{5}$$
$$3x + \frac{1}{5} \leq 4x$$
$$3x - 3x + \frac{1}{5} \leq 4x - 3x$$
$$\frac{1}{5} \leq x$$
$$\left\{x \mid x \geq \frac{1}{5}\right\}$$

27.
$$3x - 9 \leq 2x + 6$$
$$3x - 9 + 9 \leq 2x + 6 + 9$$
$$3x \leq 2x + 15$$
$$3x - 2x \leq 2x - 2x + 15$$
$$x \leq 15$$
$$\{x \mid x \leq 15\}$$

28.
$$6w + 4 \geq 5w + 4$$
$$6w + 4 - 4 \geq 5w + 4 - 4$$
$$6w \geq 5w$$
$$6w - 5w \geq 5w - 5w$$
$$w \geq 0$$
$$\{w \mid w \geq 0\}$$

29. $-0.17x - 0.23 < 0.75 - 1.17x$
$-0.17x - 0.23 + 0.23 < 0.75 + 0.23 - 1.17x$
$-0.17x < 0.98 - 1.17x$
$-0.17x + 1.17x < 0.98 - 1.17x + 1.17x$
$x < 0.98$
$\{x \mid x < 0.98\}$

30. $0.8x + 5 \geq 6 - 0.2x$
$0.8x + 5 - 5 \geq 6 - 5 - 0.2x$
$0.8x \geq 1 - 0.2x$
$0.8x + 0.2x \geq 1 - 0.2x + 0.2x$
$x \geq 1$
$\{x \mid x \geq 1\}$

31. $3(r - 2) < 2r + 4$
$3r - 6 < 2r + 4$
$3r - 6 + 6 < 2r + 4 + 6$
$3r < 2r + 10$
$3r - 2r < 2r - 2r + 10$
$r < 10$
$\{r \mid r < 10\}$

32. $-x - 11 \geq 23$
$-x + x - 11 \geq 23 + x$
$-11 \geq 23 + x$
$-11 - 23 \geq 23 - 23 + x$
$-34 \geq x$
$\{x \mid x \leq -34\}$

33. Let x = the number.
$x - (-4) \geq 9$
$x + 4 \geq 9$
$x + 4 - 4 \geq 9 - 4$
$x \geq 5$
$\{x \mid x \geq 5\}$

34. Let x = the number.
$x + 5 \geq 17$
$x + 5 - 5 \geq 17 - 5$
$x \geq 12$
$\{x \mid x \geq 12\}$

35. Let x = the number.
$3x < 2x + 8$
$3x - 2x < 2x - 2x + 8$
$x < 8$
$\{x \mid x < 8\}$

36. Let x = the number.
$21 \geq x + (-2)$
$21 \geq x - 2$
$21 + 2 \geq x - 2 + 2$
$23 \geq x$
$\{x \mid x \leq 23\}$

37. Let x = the other number.
$20 + x < 53$
$20 - 20 + x < 53 - 20$
$x < 33$
$\{x \mid x < 33\}$

38. Let x = the number.
$4x + 7 < 3x$
$4x + 7 - 7 < 3x - 7$
$4x < 3x - 7$
$4x - 3x < 3x - 3x - 7$
$x < -7$
$\{x \mid x < -7\}$

39. Let x = the number.
$2x > x - 6$
$2x - x > x - x - 6$
$x > -6$
$\{x \mid x > -6\}$

40. Let x = one number.
Then $100 - x$ = the other number.
$100 - x \geq x + 16$
$100 - 16 - x \geq x + 16 - 16$
$84 - x \geq x$
$84 - x + x \geq x + x$
$84 \geq 2x$
$42 \geq x$
$\{x \mid x \leq 42\}$

41. $3x \geq 2x + 5$
$3x + 7 \geq 2x + 5 + 7$
$3x + 7 \geq 2x + 12$

42. $3x \geq 2x + 5$
$3x - 10 \geq 2x + 5 - 10$
$3x - 10 \geq 2x - 5$

43. $3x \geq 2x + 5$
$3x - 2 \geq 2x + 5 - 2$
$3x + (-2) \geq 2x + 3$

44. $3x \geq 2x + 5$
$3x - 2x \geq 2x - 2x + 5$
$x \geq 5$
$5 \leq x$

45a. NOT A TRIANGLE, no
45b. THIS IS A TRIANGLE, yes
45c. THIS IS A TRIANGLE, yes
45d. THIS IS A TRIANGLE, yes

46. Answers will vary. Sample answer: $x = 4$, $y = 2$, $t = 3$, $w = 0$
$4 > 2$ and $3 > 0$
$4 - 3 \overset{?}{>} 2 - 0$
$1 > 2$ false

47. The value of x falls between -2.4 and 3.6.

48a. $168 + 46 + 33 + x \geq 320$
$247 + x \geq 320$

48b. $247 + x \geq 320$
$247 - 247 + x \geq 320 - 247$
$x \geq 73$
$\{x \mid x \geq 73\}$

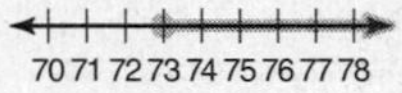

49a. $x + 21.95 + 23.42 + 16.75 \leq 75$
$x + 62.12 \leq 75$
$x + 62.12 - 62.12 \leq 75 - 62.12$
$x \leq \$12.88$
Tanaka can spend \$12.88 or less for his brother's present.

49b. Sample answer: There may be sales tax on his purchases.

50. midpoint: $\left(\frac{-1 + (-5)}{2}, \frac{9 + 5}{2}\right) = \left(\frac{-6}{2}, \frac{14}{2}\right)$
$= (-3, 7)$

51. Solve for y: $x + 7 = 3y$
$\frac{1}{3}x + \frac{7}{3} = y$
$y = \frac{1}{3}x + \frac{7}{3}$
$m = -3$; $(1, 0)$
$y - y_1 = m(x - x_1)$
$y - 0 = -3(x - 1)$
$y = -3x + 3$

52. Solve for y: $\frac{1}{5}y - 3x = 2$
$\frac{1}{5}y = 3x + 2$
$y = 15x + 10$
$m = 15$; $(0, -3)$
$y = mx + b$
$y = 15x - 3$

53. range: $166 - 124 = 42$
Q_1: 131 median: 145
Q_3: 159 IQR: $Q_3 - Q_1 = 159 - 131$
$= 28$

54. solve for y: $4x + 3y = 16$

$$3y = 16 - 4x$$
$$y = \frac{16 - 4x}{3}$$

x	$y = \frac{16 - 4x}{3}$	y	(x, y)
-2	$\frac{16 - 4(-2)}{3}$	8	$(-2, 8)$
-1	$\frac{16 - 4(-1)}{3}$	$\frac{20}{3}$	$\left(-1, \frac{20}{3}\right)$
0	$\frac{16 - 4(0)}{3}$	$\frac{16}{3}$	$\left(0, \frac{16}{3}\right)$
2	$\frac{16 - 4(2)}{3}$	$\frac{8}{3}$	$\left(2, \frac{8}{3}\right)$
5	$\frac{16 - 4(5)}{3}$	$-\frac{4}{3}$	$\left(5, -\frac{4}{3}\right)$

$$\left\{(-2, 8), \left(-1, \frac{20}{3}\right), \left(0, \frac{16}{3}\right), \left(2, \frac{8}{3}\right), \left(5, -\frac{4}{3}\right)\right\}$$

55.
$$\frac{x_1}{x_2} = \frac{y_2}{y_1}$$
$$\frac{3}{8} = \frac{y_2}{32}$$
$$96 = 8y_2$$
$$12 = y_2$$

56.
$$y - \frac{7}{16} = -\frac{5}{8}$$
$$y - \frac{7}{16} + \frac{7}{16} = -\frac{5}{8} + \frac{7}{16}$$
$$y = -\frac{10}{16} + \frac{7}{16}$$
$$y = -\frac{3}{16}$$

57.
$$\frac{6}{13} \ \underline{?}\ \frac{1}{2}$$
$$6(2) \ \underline{?}\ 13(1)$$
$$12 < 13$$
$$\frac{6}{13} < \frac{1}{2}$$

58.

length of side of triangle (units)	number of triangles
8	1
7	3
6	6
5	10
4	15
3	21
2	28
1	36

$1 + 3 + 6 + 10 + 15 + 21 + 28 + 36 = 120$

120 triangles

7-2A Modeling Mathematics: Solving Inequalities

Page 391

1. The symbol in the original problem was $<$ and in the solution was $>$. The variable in the original problem was on the left and in the solution it was on the right side.
2. 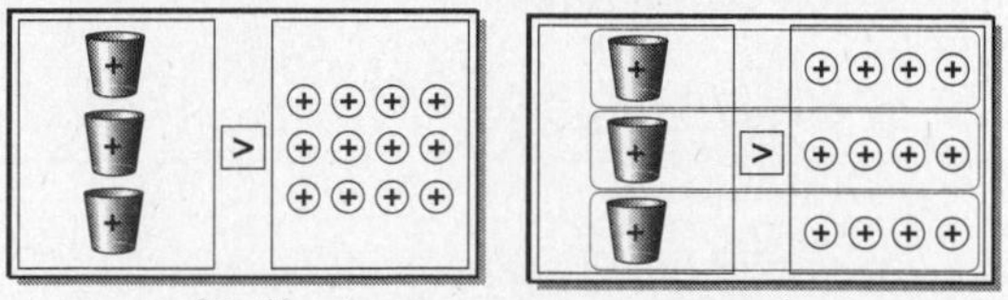

$3x > 12$ $\qquad$ $x > 4$

We do not have any negative cups so the variable remains on the left and the symbol remains $>$.

3. If each side of a true inequality is multiplied by the same positive number, the resulting inequality is also true. If each side of a true inequality is multiplied by the same negative number, the direction of the inequality symbol must be reversed so that the resulting inequality is also true.
4. Yes, dividing by a number is the same as multiplying by its reciprocal.

7-2 Solving Inequalities by Using Multiplication and Division

Pages 395–396 Check for Understanding

1a. False; change $>$ to $<$ in the second inequality.

1b. true

2a. negative **2b.** $-\frac{1}{6}$ **2c.** 90°

3. Utina is correct because the only time the inequality symbol changes in solving an inequality is when you must multiply or divide by a negative to solve for the variable. For example, in $-3x > 12$, the inequality symbol changes. However, in $3x > -12$, the inequality symbol does not.

4-7. Students should use cup and counters to model each step in the solutions.

4.
$$3x < 15$$
$$x < 5$$
$$\{x \mid x < 5\}$$

5.
$$-6x < 18$$
$$-6x + 6x < 18 + 6x$$
$$-18 < 6x$$
$$-3 < x$$
$$\{x \mid x > -3\}$$

6.
$$2x + 6 > x - 7$$
$$2x - x + 6 > x - x - 7$$
$$x + 6 - 6 > -7 - 6$$
$$x > -13$$
$$\{x \mid x > -13\}$$

7.
$$-4x + 8 \geq 14$$
$$-4x + 4x + 8 \geq 14 + 4x$$
$$8 - 14 \geq 14 + 4x - 14$$
$$-3 \geq 2x$$
$$\{x \mid x \leq -1.5\}$$

8a. 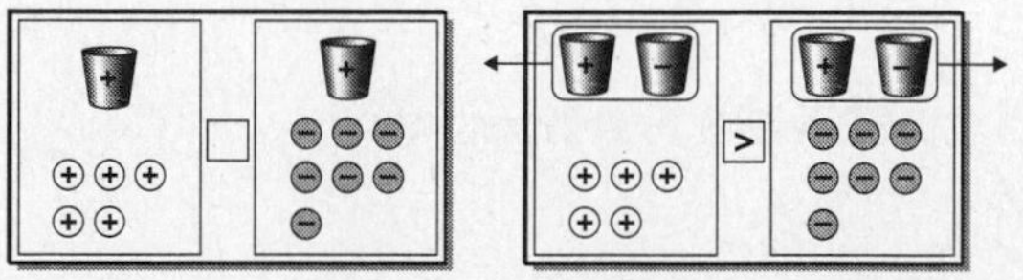

$x + 5$ $\qquad$ $x - 7$ $\qquad$ $x + 5 - x$ $\qquad$ $x - 7 - x$

$5 > -7$

8b. 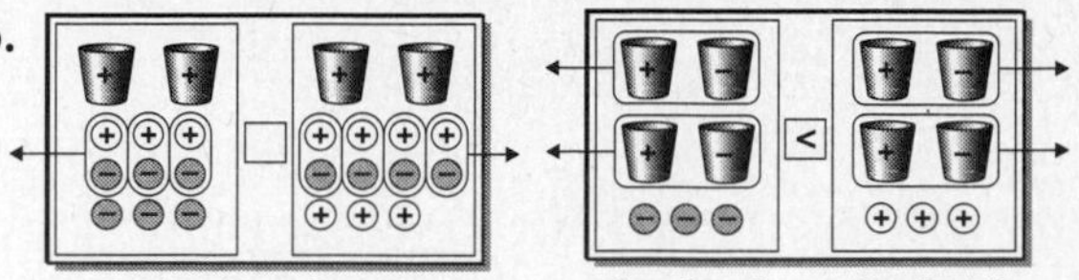

$x + 3 + (x - 6)$ $\qquad$ $(2x + 7) - 4$ $\qquad$ $2x - 2x - 3$ $\qquad$ $2x - 2x + 3$

$-3 < 3$

8c.

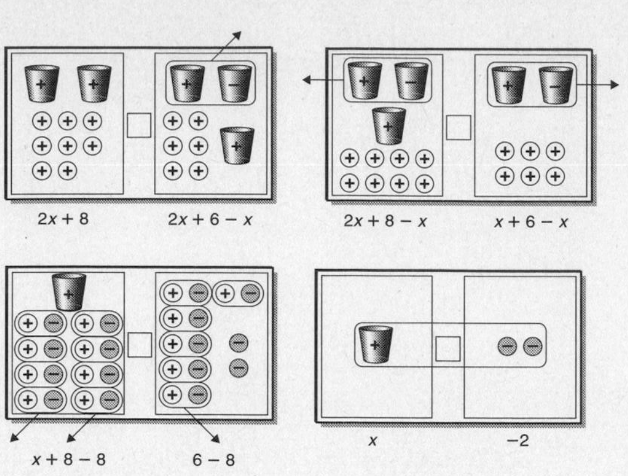

cannot be determined

9. $\times -\frac{1}{6}$, $\div -6$; yes

$-6y \geq -24$

$\frac{-6y}{-6} \leq \frac{-24}{-6}$

$y \leq 4$

$\{y \mid y \leq 4\}$

10. $\times \frac{1}{10}$, $\div 10$; no

$10x > 20$

$\frac{10x}{10} > \frac{20}{10}$

$x > 2$

$\{x \mid x > 2\}$

11. $\times 4$; no

$\frac{x}{4} < -5$

$4\left(\frac{x}{4}\right) < 4(-5)$

$x < -20$

$\{x \mid x < -20\}$

12. $\times -\frac{7}{2}$; yes

$-\frac{2}{7}z \geq -12$

$-\frac{7}{2}\left(-\frac{2}{7}z\right) \leq -\frac{7}{2}(-12)$

$z \leq 42$

$\{z \mid z \leq 42\}$

13. $\frac{4}{5}x < 24$

$\frac{5}{4}\left(\frac{4}{5}x\right) < \frac{5}{4}(24)$

$x < 30$

$\{x \mid x < 30\}$

14. $-\frac{v}{3} \geq 4$

$-3\left(-\frac{v}{3}\right) \leq -3(4)$

$v \leq -12$

$\{v \mid v \leq -12\}$

15. $-0.1t \geq 3$

$\frac{-0.1t}{-0.1} \leq \frac{3}{-0.1}$

$t \leq -30$

$\{t \mid t \leq -30\}$

16. $5y > -25$

$\frac{5y}{5} > -\frac{25}{5}$

$y > -5$

$\{y \mid y > -5\}$

17. Let x = the number.

$\frac{1}{5}x \leq 4.025$

$5\left(\frac{1}{5}x\right) \leq 5(4.025)$

$x \leq 20.125$

$\{x \mid x \leq 20.125\}$

18. Let x = the number.

$-6x < 216$

$\frac{-6x}{-6} > \frac{216}{-6}$

$x > -36$

$\{x \mid x > -36\}$

19. $s \geq 144$

$s \geq 12$

Pages 396–398 Exercises

20. $7a \leq 49$

$\frac{7a}{7} \leq \frac{49}{7}$

$a \leq 7$

$\{a \mid a \leq 7\}$

21. $12b > -144$

$\frac{12b}{12} > -\frac{144}{12}$

$b > -12$

$\{b \mid b > -12\}$

22. $-5w > -125$

$\frac{-5w}{-5} < \frac{-125}{-5}$

$w < 25$

$\{w \mid w < 25\}$

23. $-x \leq 44$

$\frac{-x}{-1} \geq \frac{44}{-1}$

$x \geq -44$

$\{x \mid x \geq -44\}$

24. $4 < -x$

$\frac{4}{-1} > \frac{-x}{-1}$

$-4 > x$

$\{x \mid x < -4\}$

25. $-102 > 17r$

$\frac{-102}{17} > \frac{17r}{17}$

$-6 > r$

$\{r \mid r < -6\}$

26. $\frac{b}{-12} \leq 3$

$-12\left(\frac{b}{-12}\right) \geq -12(3)$

$b \geq -36$

$\{b \mid b \geq -36\}$

27. $\frac{t}{13} < 13$

$13\left(\frac{t}{13}\right) < 13(13)$

$t < 169$

$\{t \mid t < 169\}$

28. $\frac{2}{3}w > -22$

$\frac{3}{2}\left(\frac{2}{3}w\right) > \frac{3}{2}(-22)$

$w > -33$

$\{w \mid w > -33\}$

29. $6 \leq 0.8g$

$\frac{6}{0.8} \leq \frac{0.8g}{0.8}$

$7.5 \leq g$

$\{g \mid g \geq 7.5\}$

30. $-15b < -28$

$\frac{-15b}{-15} > \frac{-28}{-15}$

$b > \frac{28}{15}$

$\left\{b \mid b > \frac{28}{15}\right\}$

31. $-0.049 \leq 0.07x$

$\frac{-0.049}{0.07} \leq \frac{0.07x}{0.07}$

$-0.7 \leq x$

$\{x \mid x \geq -0.7\}$

32. $\frac{3}{7}h < \frac{3}{49}$

$\frac{7}{3}\left(\frac{3}{7}h\right) < \frac{7}{3}\left(\frac{3}{49}\right)$

$h < \frac{1}{7}$

$\left\{h \mid h < \frac{1}{7}\right\}$

33. $\frac{12r}{-4} > \frac{3}{20}$

$-3r > \frac{3}{20}$

$-\frac{1}{3}(-3r) < -\frac{1}{3}\left(\frac{3}{20}\right)$

$r < -\frac{1}{20}$

$\left\{r \mid r < -\frac{1}{20}\right\}$

34. $\frac{3b}{4} \leq \frac{2}{3}$

$\frac{4}{3}\left(\frac{3b}{4}\right) \leq \frac{4}{3}\left(\frac{2}{3}\right)$

$b \leq \frac{8}{9}$

$\left\{b \mid b \leq \frac{8}{9}\right\}$

35. $-\frac{1}{3}x > 9$

$-3\left(-\frac{1}{3}x\right) < -3(9)$

$x < -27$

$\{x \mid x < -27\}$

36. $\frac{y}{6} \geq \frac{1}{2}$

$6\left(\frac{y}{6}\right) \geq 6\left(\frac{1}{2}\right)$

$y \geq 3$

$\{y \mid y \geq 3\}$

37. $\frac{-3m}{4} \leq 18$

$-\frac{4}{3}\left(\frac{-3m}{4}\right) \geq -\frac{4}{3}(18)$

$m \geq -24$

$\{m \mid m \geq -24\}$

38. Let x = the number.

$4x \leq 36$

$\frac{4x}{4} \leq \frac{36}{4}$

$x \leq 9$

$\{x \mid x \leq 9\}$

39. Let x = the number.

$36 \geq \frac{1}{2}x$

$2(36) \geq 2\left(\frac{1}{2}x\right)$

$72 \geq x$

$\{x \mid x \leq 72\}$

40. Let x = the number.

$-3x > 48$

$\frac{-3x}{-3} < \frac{48}{-3}$

$x < -16$

$\{x \mid x < -16\}$

41. Let x = the number.

$\frac{3}{4}x \leq -24$

$\frac{4}{3}\left(\frac{3}{4}x\right) \leq \frac{4}{3}(-24)$

$x \leq -32$

$\{x \mid x \leq -32\}$

42. Let x = the number.

$0.80x < 24$

$\frac{0.80x}{0.80} < \frac{24}{0.80}$

$x < 30$

$\{x \mid x < 30\}$

43. Let x = the other number.

$-8x \leq 144$

$\frac{-8x}{-8} \geq \frac{144}{-8}$

$x \geq -18$

-18 or greater

44. $3x(36) \geq 918$
$108x \geq 918$
$\frac{108x}{108} \geq \frac{918}{108}$
$x \geq 8.5$ feet

45. $3y + 5y + 6y < 100$
$14y < 100$
$\frac{14y}{14} < \frac{100}{14}$
$y < 7.14$ m

46. $24m \geq 16$
$\frac{3}{4}(24m) \geq \frac{3}{4}(16)$
$18m \geq 12$

47. $-9 \leq 15b$
$\frac{5}{3}(-9) \leq \frac{5}{3}(15b)$
$-15 \leq 25b$
$25b \geq -15$

48. $5y < -12$
$4(5y) < 4(-12)$
$20y < -48$

49. $-10a > 21$
$-3(-10a) < -3(21)$
$30a < -63$

50. Answers will vary.
Sample answer: $x = -1$, $y = -2$
$-1 > -2$
$(-1)^2 > (-2)^2$
$1 > 4$ false

51. Let m = the number of miles.
$0.12m \leq 50$
$\frac{0.12m}{0.12} \leq \frac{50}{0.12}$
$m \leq 416\frac{2}{3}$
Mrs. Rodriguez can travel up to 416 miles.

52. $F_e \cdot MA \geq F_r$
$120MA \geq 360$
$\frac{120MA}{120} \geq \frac{360}{120}$
$MA \geq 3$
She needs a mechanical advantage of at least 3.

53. Let x = the number of signatures.
$0.85x \geq 5000$
$\frac{0.85x}{0.85} \geq \frac{5000}{0.85}$
$x \geq 5882.35$
The candidate should get at least 5883 signatures.

54. Let a = the number.
$5a - 4a + 7 \leq 34$
$a + 7 \leq 34$
$a + 7 - 7 \leq 34 - 7$
$a \leq 27$

55. midpoint of $(-5, 5)$ and $(3, -3)$
$= \left(\frac{-5+3}{2}, \frac{5+(-3)}{2}\right)$
$= \left(\frac{-2}{2}, \frac{2}{2}\right)$
$= (-1, 1)$

56. Solve for y: $3x - 6 = -y$
$-3x + 6 = y$
$y = -3x + 6$
parallel: -3; perpendicular: $\frac{1}{3}$

57. $m = \frac{y_2 - y_1}{x_2 - x_1}$
$= \frac{-9 - 3}{4 - (-2)}$
$= \frac{-12}{6} = -2$

58. $\frac{\text{difference in } b}{\text{difference in } a} = \frac{-3 - (-5)}{0 - (-2)} = \frac{2}{2} = 1$
$b = a - 3$

59. Let x = amount she can spend on entertainment.
$x = 0.12(1782 - 325 - 120 - 40)$
$x = 0.12(1297)$
$x = \$155.64$

60. $x = \frac{47}{100}(27)$
$x = 12.69$

61. Let $\ell = 3w - 75$
$P = 2\ell + 2w$
$370 = 2(3w - 75) + 2w$
$370 = 6w - 150 + 2w$
$370 = 8w - 150$
$520 = 8w$
$65 = w$

$\ell = 3w - 75$
$\ell = 3(65) - 75$
$\ell = 195 - 75$
$\ell = 120$

The dimensions are 65 yd by 120 yd.

62. $5y + 3 = 5(1.3) + 3$
$= 6.5 + 3$
$= 9.5$

7-3 Solving Multi-Step Inequalities

Page 402 Check for Understanding

1. Sample answer:
$-3x + 7 < 4x - 5$
$3x - 3x + 7 < 4x - 5 + 3x$
$7 < 7x - 5$
$7 + 5 < 7x - 5 + 5$
$12 < 7x$
$\frac{12}{7} < \frac{7x}{7}$
$\frac{12}{7} < x$ or $x > \frac{12}{7}$

2. $P = 4s$
$4s + 3 \leq 50$

3. Answers will vary. Sample answer: $x + 1 < x - 1$.

4. Add $5w$ to each side. Subtract 29 from each side. Divide each side by 5. The solution is $\left\{w \mid w < -\frac{13}{5}\right\}$.

5. Sample answer: Method 2, because it is shorter.

6a. Students should use cups and counters to model each step in the solutions.
$3 - 4x \geq 15$
$3 - 4x + 4x \geq 15 + 4x$
$3 - 15 \geq 15 + 4x - 15$
$-3 \geq x$

6b. $6x - 1 < 5 + 3x$
$6x - 3x - 1 < 5 + 3x - 3x$
$3x - 1 + 1 < 5 + 1$
$x < 2$

7. $2m + 5 \leq 4m - 1$
$2m + 5 - 2m \leq 4m - 1 - 2m$
$5 \leq 2m - 1$
$5 + 1 \leq 2m - 1 + 1$
$6 \leq 2m$
$\frac{6}{2} \leq \frac{2m}{2}$
$3 \leq m$
$m \geq 3$ c

8. $13r - 11 \geq 7r + 37$
$13r - 11 - 7r \geq 7r + 37 - 7r$
$6r - 11 \geq 37$
$6r - 11 + 11 \geq 37 + 11$
$6r \geq 48$
$\frac{6r}{6} \geq \frac{48}{6}$
$r \geq 8$ b

9.
$$9x + 2 > 20$$
$$9x + 2 - 2 > 20 - 2$$
$$9x > 18$$
$$\frac{9x}{9} > \frac{18}{9}$$
$$x > 2$$
$\{x \mid x > 2\}$

10.
$$-4h + 7 > 15$$
$$-4h + 7 - 7 > 15 - 7$$
$$-4h > 8$$
$$\frac{-4h}{-4} < \frac{8}{-4}$$
$$h < -2$$
$\{h \mid h < -2\}$

11.
$$-2 - \frac{d}{5} < 23$$
$$-2 - \frac{d}{5} + 2 < 23 + 2$$
$$-\frac{d}{5} < 25$$
$$-5\left(-\frac{d}{5}\right) > -5(25)$$
$$d > -125$$
$\{d \mid d > -125\}$

12.
$$6a + 9 < -4a + 29$$
$$6a + 9 + 4a < -4a + 29 + 4a$$
$$10a + 9 < 29$$
$$10a + 9 - 9 < 29 - 9$$
$$10a < 20$$
$$\frac{10a}{10} < \frac{20}{10}$$
$$a < 2$$
$\{a \mid a < 2\}$

13.
$$3x - 1 > 4$$
$$3x - 1 + 1 > 4 + 1$$
$$3x > 5$$
$$\frac{3x}{3} > \frac{5}{3}$$
$$x > \frac{5}{3}$$
$\{2, 3\}$

14.
$$-7a + 6 \leq 48$$
$$-7a + 6 - 6 \leq 48 - 6$$
$$-7a \leq 42$$
$$\frac{-7a}{-7} \geq \frac{42}{-7}$$
$$a \geq -6$$
$\{-6, -5, -4, -3\}$

15a. Let x = one of the integers. Then $x + 2$ = the greater of the two consecutive even integers.
$x + (x + 2) > 75$

15b.
$$2x + 2 > 75$$
$$2x + 2 - 2 > 75 - 2$$
$$2x > 73$$
$$\frac{2x}{2} > \frac{73}{2}$$
$$x > 36.5$$

15c. Answers will vary; sample answer: 38 and 40.

Pages 402–404 Exercises

16.
$$n - 3 \geq \frac{n+1}{2}$$
$$2(n - 3) \geq 2\left(\frac{n+1}{2}\right)$$
$$2n - 6 \geq n + 1$$
$$2n - 6 - n \geq n + 1 - n$$
$$n - 6 \geq 1$$
$$n - 6 + 6 \geq 1 + 6$$
$$n \geq 7$$
$\{7, 8, 9, 10\}$

17.
$$\frac{2(x + 2)}{3} < 4$$
$$3\left[\frac{2(x + 2)}{3}\right] < 3(4)$$
$$2(x + 2) < 12$$
$$2x + 4 < 12$$
$$2x + 4 - 4 < 12 - 4$$
$$2x < 8$$
$$\frac{2x}{2} < \frac{8}{2}$$
$$x < 4$$
$\{-10, -9, \ldots, 2, 3\}$

18.
$$1.3y - 12 < 0.9y + 4$$
$$1.3y - 12 + 12 < 0.9y + 4 + 12$$
$$1.3y < 0.9y + 16$$
$$1.3y - 0.9y < -0.9y + 16 - 0.9y$$
$$0.4y < 16$$
$$\frac{0.4y}{0.4} < \frac{16}{0.4}$$
$$y < 40$$
$\{-10, -9, -8, \ldots, 8, 9, 10\}$

19.
$$-20 \geq 8 + 7k$$
$$-20 - 8 \geq 8 + 7k - 8$$
$$-28 \geq 7k$$
$$\frac{-28}{7} \geq \frac{7k}{7}$$
$$-4 \geq k$$
$\{-10, -9, \ldots, -5, -4\}$

20.
$$2m + 7 > 17$$
$$2m + 7 - 7 > 17 - 7$$
$$2m > 10$$
$$\frac{2m}{2} > \frac{10}{2}$$
$$m > 5$$
$\{m \mid m > 5\}$

21.
$$-3 > -3t + 6$$
$$-3 - 6 > -3t + 6 - 6$$
$$-9 > -3t$$
$$\frac{-9}{-3} < \frac{-3t}{-3}$$
$$3 < t$$
$\{t \mid t > 3\}$

22.
$$-2 - 3x \geq 2$$
$$-2 - 3x + 2 \geq 2 + 2$$
$$-3x \geq 4$$
$$\frac{-3x}{-3} \leq -\frac{4}{3}$$
$$x \leq -\frac{4}{3}$$
$\left\{x \mid x \leq -\frac{4}{3}\right\}$

23.
$$\frac{2}{3}w - 3 \leq 7$$
$$\frac{2}{3}w - 3 + 3 \leq 7 + 3$$
$$\frac{2}{3}w \leq 10$$
$$\frac{3}{2}\left(\frac{2}{3}w\right) \leq \frac{3}{2}(10)$$
$$w \leq 15$$
$\{w \mid w \leq 15\}$

24.
$$7x - 1 < 29 - 2x$$
$$7x - 1 + 2x < 29 - 2x + 2x$$
$$9x - 1 < 29$$
$$9x - 1 + 1 < 29 + 1$$
$$9x < 30$$
$$\frac{9x}{9} < \frac{30}{9}$$
$$x < \frac{10}{3}$$
$\left\{x \mid x < \frac{10}{3}\right\}$

25.
$$8n + 2 - 10n < 20$$
$$2 - 2n < 20$$
$$2 - 2n - 2 < 20 - 2$$
$$-2n < 18$$
$$\frac{-2n}{-2} > \frac{18}{-2}$$
$$n > -9$$
$\{n \mid n > -9\}$

26.
$$2x + 5 < 3x - 7$$
$$2x + 5 - 2x < 3x - 7 - 2x$$
$$5 < x - 7$$
$$5 + 7 < x - 7 + 7$$
$$12 < x$$
$\{x \mid x > 12\}$

27.
$$5 - 4m + 8 + 2m > -17$$
$$13 - 2m > -17$$
$$13 - 2m - 13 > -17 - 13$$
$$-2m > -30$$
$$\frac{-2m}{-2} < \frac{-30}{-2}$$
$$m < 15$$
$\{m \mid m < 15\}$

28. $\frac{2x-3}{5} < 7$

$5\left(\frac{2x-3}{5}\right) < 5(7)$

$2x - 3 < 35$

$2x - 3 + 3 < 35 + 3$

$2x < 38$

$\frac{2x}{2} < \frac{38}{2}$

$x < 19$

$\{x \mid x < 19\}$

29. $x < \frac{2x-15}{3}$

$3(x) < 3\left(\frac{2x-15}{3}\right)$

$3x < 2x - 15$

$3x - 2x < 2x - 15 - 2x$

$x < -15$

$\{x \mid x < -15\}$

30. $9r + 15 \geq 24 + 10r$

$9r + 15 - 9r \geq 24 + 10r - 9r$

$15 \geq 24 + r$

$15 - 24 \geq 24 - 24 + r$

$-9 \geq r$

$\{r \mid r \leq -9\}$

31. $6p - 2 \leq 3p + 12$

$6p - 3p - 2 \leq 3p - 3p + 12$

$3p - 2 \leq 12$

$3p - 2 + 2 \leq 12 + 2$

$3p \leq 14$

$\frac{3p}{3} \leq \frac{14}{3}$

$p \leq \frac{14}{3}$

$\left\{p \mid p \leq \frac{14}{3}\right\}$

32. $4y + 2 < 8y - (6y - 10)$

$4y + 2 < 8y - 6y + 10$

$4y + 2 < 2y + 10$

$4y - 2y + 2 < 2y - 2y + 10$

$2y + 2 < 10$

$2y + 2 - 2 < 10 - 2$

$2y < 8$

$\frac{2y}{2} < \frac{8}{2}$

$y < 4$

$\{y \mid y < 4\}$

33. $3(x - 2) - 8x < 44$

$3x - 6 - 8x < 44$

$-5x - 6 < 44$

$-5x - 6 + 6 < 44 + 6$

$-5x < 50$

$\frac{-5x}{-5} > \frac{50}{-5}$

$x > -10$

$\{x \mid x > -10\}$

34. $3.1q - 1.4 > 1.3q + 6.7$

$3.1q - 1.3q - 1.4 > 1.3q - 1.3q + 6.7$

$1.8q - 1.4 > 6.7$

$1.8q - 1.4 + 1.4 > 6.7 + 1.4$

$1.8q > 8.1$

$\frac{1.8q}{1.8} > \frac{8.1}{1.8}$

$q > 4.5$

$\{q \mid q > 4.5\}$

35. $-5(k + 4) \geq 3(k - 4)$

$-5k - 20 \geq 3k - 12$

$-5k + 5k - 20 \geq 3k + 5k - 12$

$-20 \geq 8k - 12$

$-20 + 12 \geq 8k - 12 + 12$

$-8 \geq 8k$

$\frac{-8}{8} \geq \frac{8k}{8}$

$-1 \geq k$

$\{k \mid k \leq -1\}$

36. $5(2h - 6) - 7(h + 7) > 4h$

$10h - 30 - 7h - 49 > 4h$

$3h - 79 > 4h$

$3h - 3h - 79 > 4h - 3h$

$-79 > h$

$\{h \mid h < -79\}$

37. $7 + 3y > 2(y + 3) - 2(-1 - y)$

$7 + 3y > 2y + 6 + 2 + 2y$

$7 + 3y > 4y + 8$

$7 + 3y - 3y > 4y + 8 - 3y$

$7 > y + 8$

$7 - 8 > y + 8 - 8$

$-1 > y$

$\{y \mid y < -1\}$

38. Let x = the number.

$\frac{2}{3}x - 27 \geq 9$

$\frac{2}{3}x - 27 + 27 \geq 9 + 27$

$\frac{2}{3}x \geq 36$

$\frac{3}{2}\left(\frac{2}{3}x\right) \geq \frac{3}{2}(36)$

$x \geq 54$

$\{x \mid x \geq 54\}$

39. Let x = the number.

$3(x + 7) > 5x - 13$

$3x + 21 > 5x - 13$

$3x - 3x + 21 > 5x - 3x - 13$

$21 > 2x - 13$

$21 + 13 > 2x - 13 + 13$

$34 > 2x$

$\frac{34}{2} > \frac{2x}{2}$

$17 > x$

$\{x \mid x < 17\}$

40. Let x = the first consecutive odd integer. Then $x + 2$ = the greater of the two consecutive odd integers.

$x + (x + 2) \leq 123$

$2x + 2 \leq 123$

$2x + 2 - 2 \leq 123 - 2$

$2x \leq 121$

$x \leq 60.5$

The pair with the greatest sum is 59 and 59 + 2 or 61.

41. Let x = one of the consecutive odd integers. Then $x + 2$ = the greater of the two consecutive odd integers.

$x + (x + 2) \le 18$
$2x + 2 \le 18$
$2x + 2 - 2 \le 18 - 2$
$2x \le 16$
$\frac{2x}{2} \le \frac{16}{2}$
$x \le 8$

The sets of consecutive odd integers are 7 and 7 + 2 or 9; 5 and 5 + 2 or 7; 3 and 3 + 2 or 5; 1 and 1 + 2 or 3.

42. Let x = the first integer. Then $x + 2$ = the next integer, and $x + 4$ = the greatest of the three consecutive even integers.

$x + (x + 2) + (x + 4) < 40$
$3x + 6 < 40$
$3x + 6 - 6 < 40 - 6$
$3x < 34$
$\frac{3x}{3} < \frac{34}{3}$
$x < 11\frac{1}{3}$

The sets of three consecutive positive even integers are 10, 12, 14; 8, 10, 12; 6, 8, 10; 4, 6, 8; 2, 4, 6.

43. $3x + 4 > 2(x + 3) + x$
$3x + 4 > 2x + 6 + x$
$3x + 4 > 3x + 6$
$3x - 3x + 4 > 3x - 3x + 6$
$4 > 6$ false

no solution ($\varnothing$)

44. $3 - 3(y - 2) < 13 - 3(y - 6)$
$3 - 3y + 6 < 13 - 3y + 18$
$-3y + 9 < -3y + 31$
$-3y + 3y + 9 < -3y + 3y + 31$
$9 < 31$ true

$\{y \mid y \text{ is a real number.}\}$

45a–d. Clear the Y= list before each exercise.

45a. Enter: (–) 5 – 8 X,T,θ 2nd TEST 4 59 GRAPH. Using the TRACE function, $y = 1$ up to and including $x = -8$; then $y = 0$. Therefore, $x \le -8$.

45b. Enter: 13 X,T,θ – 11 2nd TEST 3 7 X,T,θ + 37 GRAPH. Using the TRACE function, $y = 0$ up to and including $x = 8$; then $y = 1$. Therefore, $x > 8$.

45c. Enter: 8 X,T,θ – (X,T,θ – 5) 2nd TEST 3 X,T,θ + 17 GRAPH. Using the TRACE function, $y = 0$ up to and including $x = 2$; then $y = 1$. Therefore, $x > 2$.

45d. Enter: (–) 5 (X,T,θ + 4) 2nd TEST 4 3 (X,T,θ – 4) GRAPH. Using the TRACE function, $y = 1$ up to and including $x = -1$; then $y = 0$. Therefore, $x \le -1$.

46. $-3 < x + 2 < 4$
$-3 - 2 < x + 2 - 2 < 4 - 2$
$-5 < x < 2$

the numbers between -5 and 2 or $\{x \mid -5 < x < 2\}$

47. Let x = cost of the meal.

$x + 0.04x + 0.15(x + 0.04x) \le 50$
$x + 0.04x + 0.15x + 0.006x \le 50$
$1.196x \le 50$
$\frac{1.196x}{1.196} \le \frac{50}{1.196}$
$x \le \$41.80$

The couple can spend up to \$41.80.

48. Let x = the number of games.

$1.25(2) + 0.50x \le 10$
$2.50 + 0.50x \le 10$
$2.50 - 2.50 + 0.50x \le 10 - 2.50$
$0.50x \le 7.50$
$\frac{0.50x}{0.50} \le \frac{7.50}{0.50}$
$x \le 15$

They can play up to 15 games.

49. Let x = the amount the school must raise.

$x + 0.40x \ge 800{,}000$
$1.40x \ge 800{,}000$
$\frac{1.40x}{1.40} \ge \frac{800{,}000}{1.40}$
$x \ge 571{,}428.57$

The school must raise at least \$571,428.57.

50. Let x = the selling price of her house.

$x - 0.07x \ge 90{,}000$
$0.93x \ge 90{,}000$
$\frac{0.93x}{0.93} \ge \frac{90{,}000}{0.93}$
$x \ge 96{,}774.19$

The selling price of her house must be at least \$96,774.

51a. Let x = the number of weeks.

$52(400) \le 1.06(400)(52 - x)$
$20{,}800 \le 22{,}048 - 424x$
$-1248 \le -424x$
$\frac{-1248}{-424} \ge \frac{-424x}{-424}$
$2.9 \ge x$

at most 2.9 weeks

51b. $52(575) \le 1.06(575)(52 - x)$
$29{,}900 \le 31{,}694 - 609.5x$
$-1794 \le -609.5x$
$\frac{-1794}{-609.5} \ge \frac{-609.5x}{-609.5}$
$2.9 \ge x$

no change

51c. $52(400) - 120x \le 1.06(400)(52 - x)$
$20{,}800 - 120x \le 22{,}048 - 424x$
$20{,}800 - 20{,}800 - 120x \le 22{,}048 - 20{,}800 - 424x$
$-120x \le 1248 - 424x$
$-120x + 424x \le 1248 - 424x + 424x$
$304x \le 1248$
$\frac{304x}{304} \le \frac{1248}{304}$
$x \le 4.1$

at most 4.1 weeks

52. $2r - 2.1 < -8.7 + r$
$2r - r - 2.1 < -8.7 + r - r$
$r - 2.1 < -8.7$
$r - 2.1 + 2.1 < -8.7 + 2.1$
$r < -6.6$

$\{r \mid r < -6.6\}$

53. $7 - 2y < -y - 3$
$7 - 2y + 2y < -y + 2y - 3$
$7 < y - 3$
$7 + 3 < y - 3 + 3$
$10 < y$
$\{y \mid y > 10\}$

54. $m = \frac{y_2 - y_1}{x_2 - x_1}$
$= \frac{7 - 12}{-2 - (-12)}$
$= \frac{-5}{10}$
$= -\frac{1}{2}$
$m = -\frac{1}{2}; (-12, 12)$

$y - y_1 = m(x - x_1)$
$y - 12 = -\frac{1}{2}[x - (-12)]$
$y - 12 = -\frac{1}{2}x - 6$
$y = -\frac{1}{2}x + 6$

55. $m = -\frac{3}{2}; (2, 4)$
$y - y_1 = m(x - x_1)$
$y - 4 = -\frac{3}{2}(x - 2)$
$2(y - 4) = 2\left[-\frac{3}{2}(x - 2)\right]$
$2y - 8 = -3(x - 2)$
$2y - 8 = -3x + 6$
$2y = -3x + 14$
$3x + 2y = 14$

56. $P(40) = -0.027(40)^2 + 8(40) - 280$
$= -43.2 + 320 - 280$
$= -3.2$
$P(41) = -0.027(41)^2 + 8(41) - 280$
$= -45.387 + 328 - 280$
$= 2.613$
41 cars

57.

y	$3y - 2 = x$	x
-1	$3(-1) - 2$	-5
6	$3(6) - 2$	16
0	$3(0) - 2$	-2
$-\frac{1}{3}$	$3\left(-\frac{1}{3}\right) - 2$	-3
2	$3(2) - 2$	4

$\{-5, -3, -2, 4, 16\}$

58. odds against: odds in favor = 1:4

59. mean: $\frac{\text{sum of 10 games}}{10} = \frac{251}{10} = 25.1$
median: $\frac{22 + 25}{2} = \frac{47}{2} = 23.5$
mode: none

60. $18 - (-34) = 18 + 34$
$= 52$

7-4 Solving Compound Inequalities

Pages 409–410 Check for Understanding

1. Answers will vary. Sample answer: The price of an item is at most \$18.50 but more than \$7.50.
2. $x < -4$ or $x \geq 1$
3. Sample answers: Draw a diagram (helps you to see the solution), make a table (helps you to see a pattern), look for a pattern (determines how the tables relate to the number of people seated).
4. The one containing *and* is true when both inequalities are true; the one containing *or* is true if either inequality is true.
5. Helps you plan the solution; provides the solution.

6.

7. $0 \leq x < 9$
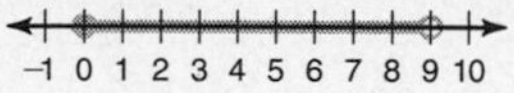

8. $-2 < x < 3$

9. $-3 < x \leq 1$

10. $x < -2$ or $x > 0$

11. The solution is the empty set. There are no numbers greater than 5 but less than -3.

12. $2 \leq y + 6$ and $y + 6 < 8$
$2 - 6 \leq y + 6 - 6$ $\quad$ $y + 6 - 6 < 8 - 6$
$-4 \leq y$ $\quad$ $y < 2$
$\{y \mid -4 \leq y < 2\}$
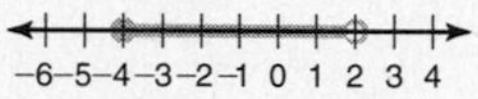

13. $4 + h \leq -3$ or $4 + h \geq 5$
$4 - 4 + h \leq -3 - 4$ $\quad$ $4 - 4 + h \geq 5 - 4$
$h \leq -7$ $\quad$ $h \geq 1$
$\{h \mid h \leq -7 \text{ or } h \geq 1\}$
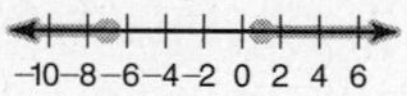

14. $b + 5 > 10$ or $b \geq 0$
$b + 5 - 5 > 10 - 5$
$b > 5$
$\{b \mid b \geq 0\}$

15. $2 + w > 2w + 1 \geq -4 + w$
$2 + w > 2w + 1$
$2 + w - w > 2w - w + 1$
$2 > w + 1$
$2 - 1 > w + 1 - 1$
$1 > w$
and
$2w + 1 \geq -4 + w$
$2w - w + 1 \geq -4 + w - w$
$w + 1 \geq -4$
$w + 1 - 1 \geq -4 - 1$
$w \geq -5$
$\{w \mid 1 > w \geq -5\}$
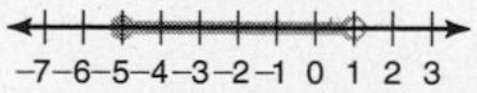

16. $\$0 \leq c \leq \$100$

17. Drawings will vary; 16 pieces.

Pages 410–412 Exercises

18.
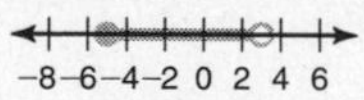

19. $\varnothing$

20.
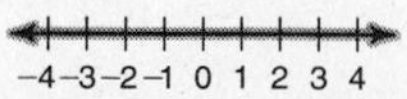

21.
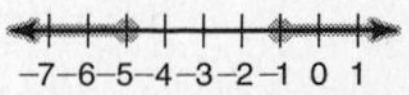

22. 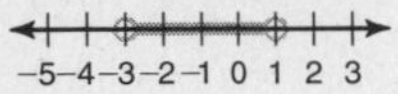

23. 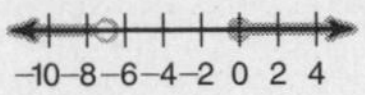

24. $-3 < x < 1$

25. $-4 \le x \le 5$

26. $x < 0$ or $x > 2$

27. $x \le -2$ or $x > 1$

28.
$4m - 5 > 7$ or $4m - 5 < -9$
$4m - 5 + 5 > 7 + 5$ $\quad$ $4m - 5 + 5 < -9 + 5$
$4m > 12$ $\quad$ $4m < -4$
$\frac{4m}{4} > \frac{12}{4}$ $\quad$ $\frac{4m}{4} < \frac{-4}{4}$
$m > 3$ $\quad$ $m < -1$
$\{m \mid m > 3 \text{ or } m < -1\}$

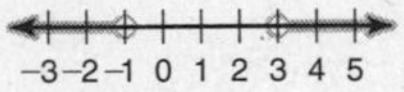

29.
$x - 4 < 1$ and $x + 2 > 1$
$x - 4 + 4 < 1 + 4$ $\quad$ $x + 2 - 2 > 1 - 2$
$x < 5$ $\quad$ $x > -1$
$\{x \mid -1 < x < 5\}$

30.
$y + 6 > -1$ and $y - 2 < 4$
$y + 6 - 6 > -1 - 6$ $\quad$ $y - 2 + 2 < 4 + 2$
$y > -7$ $\quad$ $y < 6$
$\{y \mid -7 < y < 6\}$

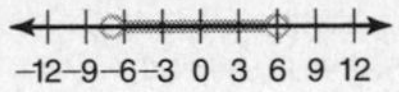

31.
$x + 4 < 2$ or $x - 2 > 1$
$x + 4 - 4 < 2 - 4$ $\quad$ $x - 2 + 2 > 1 + 2$
$x < -2$ $\quad$ $x > 3$
$\{x \mid x < -2 \text{ or } x > 3\}$

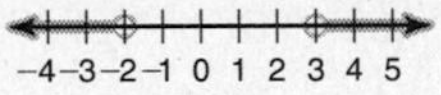

32.
$10 - 2p > 12$ and $7p < 4p + 9$
$10 - 10 - 2p > 12 - 10$ $\quad$ $7p - 4p < 4p + 9 - 4p$
$-2p > 2$ $\quad$ $3p < 9$
$\frac{-2p}{-2} < \frac{2}{-2}$ $\quad$ $\frac{3p}{3} < \frac{9}{3}$
$p < -1$ $\quad$ $p < 3$
$\{p \mid p < -1\}$

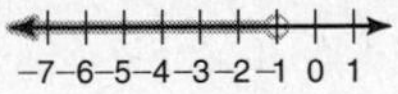

33.
$6 - c > c$ or $3c - 1 < c + 13$
$6 - c + c > c + c$ $\quad$ $3c - c - 1 < c - c + 13$
$6 > 2c$ $\quad$ $2c - 1 < 13$
$\frac{6}{2} > \frac{2c}{2}$ $\quad$ $2c - 1 + 1 < 13 + 1$
$3 > c$ $\quad$ $2c < 14$
$\frac{2c}{2} < \frac{14}{2}$
$c < 7$
$\{c \mid c < 7\}$ 

34. $4 < 2x - 2 < 10$
$4 < 2x - 2$ and $2x - 2 < 10$
$4 + 2 < 2x - 2 + 2$ $\quad$ $2x - 2 + 2 < 10 + 2$
$6 < 2x$ $\quad$ $2x < 12$
$\frac{6}{2} < \frac{2x}{2}$ $\quad$ $\frac{2x}{2} < \frac{12}{2}$
$3 < x$ $\quad$ $x < 6$
$\{x \mid 3 < x < 6\}$

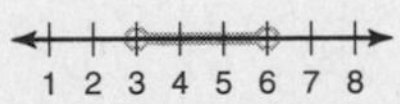

35. $14 < 3h + 2 < 2$
$14 < 3h + 2$ and $3h + 2 < 2$
$14 - 2 < 3h + 2 - 2$ $\quad$ $3h + 2 - 2 < 2 - 2$
$12 < 3h$ $\quad$ $3h < 0$
$\frac{12}{3} < \frac{3h}{3}$ $\quad$ $\frac{3h}{3} < \frac{0}{3}$
$4 < h$ $\quad$ $h < 0$
$\varnothing$

36.
$8 > 5 - 3q$ and $5 - 3q > -13$
$8 - 5 > 5 - 5 - 3q$ $\quad$ $5 - 5 - 3q > -13 - 5$
$3 > -3q$ $\quad$ $-3q > -18$
$\frac{3}{-3} < \frac{-3q}{-3}$ $\quad$ $\frac{-3q}{-3} < \frac{-18}{-3}$
$-1 < q$ $\quad$ $q < 6$
$\{q \mid -1 < q < 6\}$

37.
$-1 + x \le 3$ or $-x \le -4$
$-1 + 1 + x \le 3 + 1$ $\quad$ $\frac{-x}{-1} \ge \frac{-4}{-1}$
$x \le 4$ $\quad$ $x \ge 4$
$\{x \mid x \text{ is a real number}\}$

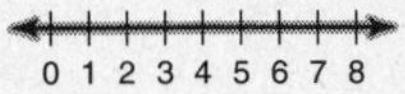

38.
$3n + 11 \le 13$ or $2n \ge 5n - 12$
$3n + 11 - 11 \le 13 - 11$ $\quad$ $2n - 5n \ge 5n - 5n - 12$
$3n \le 2$ $\quad$ $-3n \ge -12$
$\frac{3n}{3} \le \frac{2}{3}$ $\quad$ $\frac{-3n}{-3} \le \frac{-12}{-3}$
$n \le \frac{2}{3}$ $\quad$ $n \le 4$
$\{n \mid n \le 4\}$

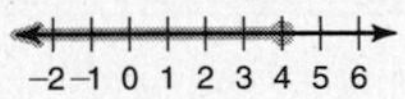

39.
$3y + 1 > 10$ and $y \ne 6$
$3y + 1 - 1 > 10 - 1$
$3y > 9$
$\frac{3y}{3} > \frac{9}{3}$
$y > 3$
$\{y \mid y > 3 \text{ and } y \ne 6\}$

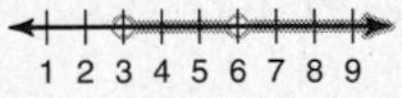

40.
$4z + 8 \ge z + 6$ or $7z - 14 \ge 2z - 4$
$4z - z + 8 \ge z - z + 6$ $\quad$ $7z - 2z - 14 \ge 2z - 2z - 4$
$3z + 8 \ge 6$ $\quad$ $5z - 14 \ge -4$
$3z + 8 - 8 \ge 6 - 8$ $\quad$ $5z - 14 + 14 \ge -4 + 14$
$3z \ge -2$ $\quad$ $5z \ge 10$
$\frac{3z}{3} \ge \frac{-2}{3}$ $\quad$ $\frac{5z}{5} \ge \frac{10}{5}$
$z \ge -\frac{2}{3}$ $\quad$ $z \ge 2$
$\left\{z \,\middle|\, z \ge -\frac{2}{3}\right\}$

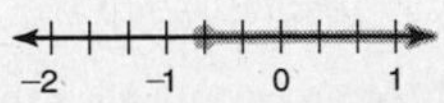

41. $5x + 7 > 2x + 4$

$5x - 2x + 7 > 2x - 2x + 4$

$3x + 7 > 4$

$3x + 7 - 7 > 4 - 7$

$3x > -3$

$\frac{3x}{3} > \frac{-3}{3}$

$x > -1$

or

$3x + 3 < 24 - 4x$

$3x + 4x + 3 < 24 - 4x + 4x$

$7x + 3 < 24$

$7x + 3 - 3 < 24 - 3$

$7x < 21$

$\frac{7x}{7} < \frac{21}{7}$

$x < 3$

$\{x \mid x \text{ is a real number}\}$

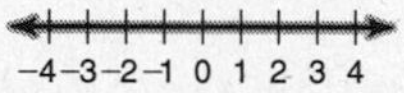

42. $2 - 5(2y - 3) > 2$ or $3y < 2(y - 8)$

$2 - 10y + 15 > 2$ | $3y < 2y - 16$

$-10y + 17 > 2$ | $3y - 2y < 2y - 2y - 16$

$-10y + 17 - 17 > 2 - 17$ | $y < -16$

$-10y > -15$

$\frac{-10y}{-10} < \frac{-15}{-10}$

$y < \frac{3}{2}$

$\left\{y \mid y < \frac{3}{2}\right\}$

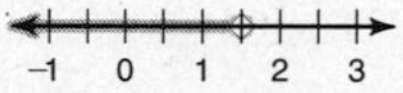

43. $5w > 4(2w - 3)$ and $5(w - 3) + 2 < 7$

$5w > 8w - 12$ | $5w - 15 + 2 < 7$

$5w - 8w > 8w - 8w - 12$ | $5w - 13 < 7$

$-3w > -12$ | $5w - 13 + 13 < 7 + 13$

$\frac{-3w}{-3} < \frac{-12}{-3}$ | $5w < 20$

$w < 4$ | $\frac{5w}{5} < \frac{20}{5}$

$w < 4$

$\{w \mid w < 4\}$

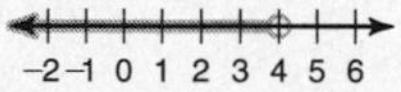

44. Sample answer: $x > -2$ or $x < 4$

45. Sample answer: $x > 5$ and $x < -4$

46. Let d = the distance to the finish line.

$50 < 3d + 5 < 89$

$50 < 3d + 5$ and $3d + 5 < 89$

$50 - 5 < 3d + 5 - 5$ | $3d + 5 - 5 < 89 - 5$

$45 < 3d$ | $3d < 84$

$\frac{45}{3} < \frac{3d}{3}$ | $\frac{3d}{3} < \frac{84}{3}$

$15 < d$ | $d < 28$

$\{d \mid 15 < d < 28\}$

47. Let n = the number.

$n + 2 \le 6$ or $n + 2 \ge 10$

$n + 2 - 2 \le 6 - 2$ | $n + 2 - 2 \ge 10 - 2$

$n \le 4$ | $n \ge 8$

$\{n \mid n \le 4 \text{ or } n \ge 8\}$

48. Let n = the number.

$7 < 2n + 5 < 11$

$7 < 2n + 5$ and $2n + 5 < 11$

$7 - 5 < 2n + 5 - 5$ | $2n + 5 - 5 < 11 - 5$

$2 < 2n$ | $2n < 6$

$\frac{2}{2} < \frac{2n}{2}$ | $\frac{2n}{2} < \frac{6}{2}$

$1 < n$ | $n < 3$

$\{n \mid 1 < n < 3\}$

49. Let n = the number.

$31 \le 6n - 5 \le 37$

$31 \le 6n - 5$ and $6n - 5 \le 37$

$31 + 5 \le 6n - 5 + 5$ | $6n - 5 + 5 \le 37 + 5$

$36 \le 6n$ | $6n \le 42$

$\frac{36}{6} \le \frac{6n}{6}$ | $\frac{6n}{6} \le \frac{42}{6}$

$6 \le n$ | $n \le 7$

$\{n \mid 6 \le n \le 7\}$

50. $3 + y > 2y > -3 - y$

$3 + y > 2y$ and $2y > -3 - y$

$3 + y - y > 2y - y$ | $2y + y > -3 - y + y$

$3 > y$ | $3y > -3$

$\frac{3y}{3} > \frac{-3}{3}$

$y > -1$

$\{y \mid -1 < y < 3\}$

51. $m > 2m - 1 > m - 5$

$m > 2m - 1$

$m - 2m > 2m - 2m - 1$

$-m > -1$

$\frac{-m}{-1} < \frac{-1}{-1}$

$m < 1$

and

$2m - 1 > m - 5$

$2m - 1 - m > m - 5 - m$

$m - 1 > -5$

$m - 1 + 1 > -5 + 1$

$m > -4$

$\{m \mid -4 < m < 1\}$

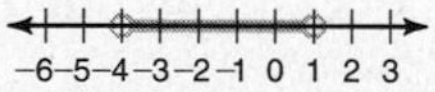

52. Since $x \ne 0$, the following statement must be true for $\frac{5}{x} + 3 > 0$.

$\frac{5}{x} + 3 > 0$ and $x > 0$ or $\frac{5}{x} + 3 > 0$ and $x < 0$

$\frac{5}{x} > -3$ | $\frac{5}{x} > -3$

$5 > -3x$ | $5 < -3x$

$-\frac{5}{3} < x$ and $x > 0$ | $-\frac{5}{3} > x$ and $x < 0$

$x > 0$ or $x < -\frac{5}{3}$

$\{x \mid x < -\frac{5}{3} \text{ or } x > 0\}$

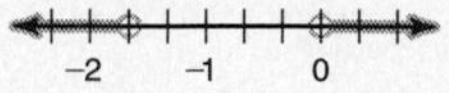

53a. Enter: 3 [+] [X,T,θ] [2nd] [TEST] 5 [(–)] 4 [2nd] [TEST] [▶] 2 3 [+] [X,T,θ] [2nd] [TEST] 3 4 [GRAPH]. Using the TRACE function, $y = 0$ for $-7 \le x \le 1$; $y = 1$ for $x < -7$ and $x > 1$. Therefore, $\{x \mid x < -7 \text{ or } x > 1\}$.

53b. Enter: [(-)] 2 [2nd] [TEST] 6 [X,T,θ] [+] 3 [2nd] [TEST] [▶] 1 [X,T,θ] [+] 3 [2nd] [TEST] 5 4 [GRAPH]. Using the TRACE function, $y = 0$ for $x < 5$ and $x \geq 1$; $y = 1$ for $-5 \leq x < 1$. Therefore, $\{x \mid -5 \leq x < 1\}$.

54. $a \leq 0$

55. $-4 \leq x \leq -1.5$ or $x \geq 2$

56.

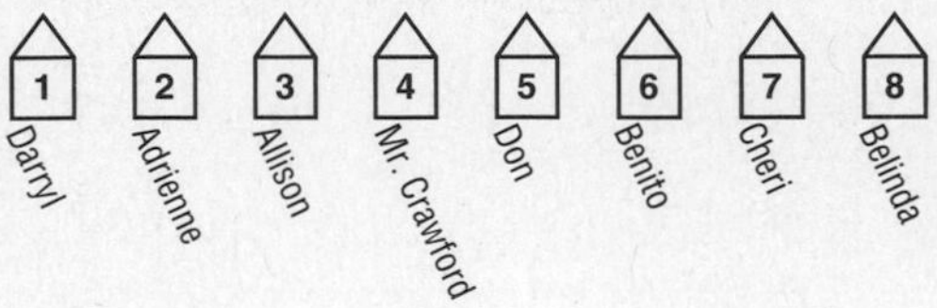

57. $20 < 4.5x < 30$

$20 < 4.5x$ and $4.5x < 30$

$\frac{20}{4.5} < \frac{4.5x}{4.5}$ $\qquad$ $\frac{4.5x}{4.5} < \frac{30}{4.5}$

$4.4 < x$ $\qquad$ $x < 6.7$

$4.4 < x < 6.7$

58. $92 \leq \frac{92 + 96 + 88 + s}{4} \leq 94$

$$92 \leq \frac{92 + 96 + 88 + s}{4}$$
$$4(92) \leq 4\left(\frac{276 + s}{4}\right)$$
$$368 \leq 276 + s$$
$$368 - 276 \leq 276 + s - 276$$
$$92 \leq s$$

and

$$\frac{92 + 96 + 88 + s}{4} = 94$$
$$4\left(\frac{92 + 96 + 88 + s}{4}\right) \leq 4(94)$$
$$276 + s \leq 376$$
$$276 + s - 276 \leq 376 - 276$$
$$s \leq 100$$

$92 \leq s \leq 100$

59. Let m = the number.

$$\frac{3}{4}m - 8 \geq 3$$
$$\frac{3}{4}m - 8 + 8 \geq 3 + 8$$
$$\frac{3}{4}m \geq 11$$
$$\frac{4}{3}\left(\frac{3}{4}m\right) \geq \frac{4}{3}(11)$$
$$m \geq \frac{44}{3}$$

$\{m \mid m \geq \frac{44}{3}\}$

60. Let x = the number.

$$x + 23 \leq 5$$
$$x + 23 - 23 \leq 5 - 23$$
$$x \leq -18$$

$\{x \mid x \leq -18\}$

61.
$$7x - 2 \leq 9x + 3$$
$$7x - 7x - 2 \leq 9x - 7x + 3$$
$$-2 \leq 2x + 3$$
$$-2 - 3 \leq 2x + 3 - 3$$
$$-5 \leq 2x$$
$$2x \geq -5$$

62. Solve for y: $3x - 7y = -3$

$$-7y = -3x - 3$$
$$y = \frac{3}{7}x + \frac{3}{7}$$

$m = \frac{3}{7}$

63. $x = 2y - 4$

Let $x = 0$.
$0 = 2y - 4$
$4 = 2y$
$2 = y$
$(0, 2)$

Let $y = 0$.
$x = 2(0) - 4$
$x = -4$
$(-4, 0)$

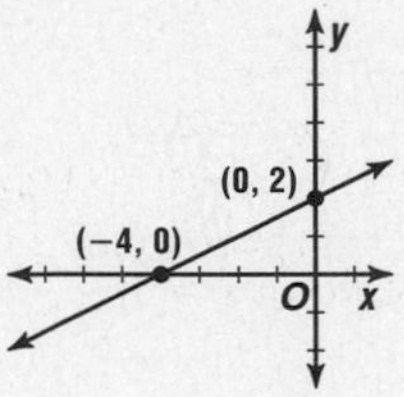

64. $m = \frac{5 - 1}{0 - 2} = \frac{4}{-2} = -2$

$$y - y_1 = m(x - x_1)$$
$$y - 5 = -2(x - 0)$$
$$y - 5 = -2x$$
$$y = -2x + 5$$
$$f(x) = -2x + 5$$

65.

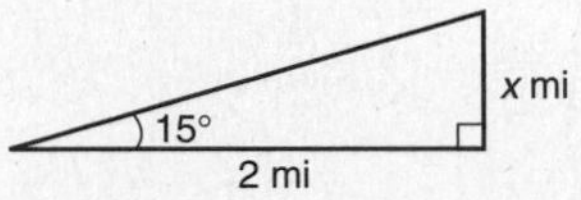

$\tan 15° = \frac{x}{2}$

$0.2679 \approx \frac{x}{2}$

$0.54 \approx x$

The hot-air balloon is a little more than half a mile away.

66.
$$\frac{4m - 3}{-2} = 12$$
$$-2\left(\frac{4m - 3}{-2}\right) = -2(12)$$
$$4m - 3 = -24$$
$$4m - 3 + 3 = -24 + 3$$
$$4m = -21$$
$$m = -\frac{21}{4}$$

67. $-17px + 22bg + 35px + (-37bg)$
$= -17px + 35px + 22bg + (-37bg)$
$= 18px - 15bg$

68. $3ab - c^2 = 3(6)(4) - (3)^2$
$= 72 - 9$
$= 63$

Page 412 Self Test

1.
$$y + 15 \geq -2$$
$$y + 15 - 15 \geq -2 - 15$$
$$y \geq -17$$

$\{y \mid y \geq -17\}$

2. $-102 > 17r$

$$\frac{-102}{17} > \frac{17r}{17}$$
$$-6 > r$$

$\{r \mid r < -6\}$

3.
$$5 - 6n > -19$$
$$5 - 5 - 6n > -19 - 5$$
$$-6n > -24$$
$$\frac{-6n}{-6} < \frac{-24}{-6}$$
$$n < 4$$

$\{n \mid n < 4\}$

4.
$$\frac{11 - 6w}{5} > 10$$
$$5\left(\frac{11 - 6w}{5}\right) > 5(10)$$
$$11 - 6w > 50$$
$$11 - 11 - 6w > 50 - 11$$
$$-6w > 39$$
$$\frac{-6w}{-6} < \frac{39}{-6}$$
$$w < -6.5$$

$\{w \mid w < -6.5\}$

5. $7(g + 8) < 3(g + 12)$
$$7g + 56 < 3g + 36$$
$$7g - 3g + 56 < 3g - 3g + 36$$
$$4g + 56 < 36$$
$$4g + 56 - 56 < 36 - 56$$
$$4g < -20$$
$$\frac{4g}{4} < \frac{-20}{4}$$
$$g < -5$$
$\{g \mid g < -5\}$

6. $0.1y - 2 \le 0.3y - 5$
$$0.1y - 0.1y - 2 \le 0.3y - 0.1y - 5$$
$$-2 \le 0.2y - 5$$
$$-2 + 5 \le 0.2y - 5 + 5$$
$$3 \le 0.2y$$
$$\frac{3}{0.2} \le \frac{0.2y}{0.2}$$
$$15 \le y$$
$\{y \mid y \ge 15\}$

7. $4 \ge x - 1 \ge -3$

$4 \ge x - 1$	and	$x - 1 \ge -3$
$4 + 1 \ge x - 1 + 1$		$x - 1 + 1 \ge -3 + 1$
$5 \ge x$		$x \ge -2$

$\{x \mid 5 \ge x \ge -2\}$ c

8.

$8 + 3t < 2$	or	$-12 < 11t - 1$
$8 - 8 + 3t < 2 - 8$		$-12 + 1 < 11t - 1 + 1$
$3t < -6$		$-11 < 11t$
$\frac{3t}{3} < \frac{-6}{3}$		$\frac{-11}{11} < \frac{11t}{11}$
$t < -2$		$-1 < t$

$\{t \mid t < -2 \text{ or } t > -1\}$

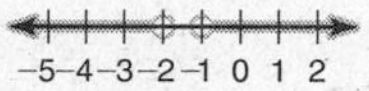

9. $\frac{18 + 15 + 30 + x}{4} \ge 20$
$$4\left(\frac{18 + 15 + 30 + x}{4}\right) \ge 4(20)$$
$$63 + x \ge 80$$
$$63 + x - 63 \ge 80 - 63$$
$$x \ge 17$$
She must score more than 17 points.

10a. (2, 1), (2, 3), (2, 5), (4, 1), (4, 3), (4, 5), (6, 1), (6, 3), (6, 5)

10b. (2, 5), (4, 3), (6, 1); 3 possibilities have a sum of 7

7-5 Integration: Probability Compound Events

Pages 415–416 Check for Understanding

1.

H	H	HH
	T	HT
T	H	TH
	T	TT

2. See students' work.

3. A compound event consists of two or more simple events. Tossing a coin is a simple event while tossing two coins is a compound event.

4. Answers may vary. Sample answer: The one in Example 2 involves two events while the one in Example 3 involves as many as three events.

5. See students' work.

6. $\frac{1}{6} \cdot \frac{1}{6} \cdot \frac{1}{6} \cdot \frac{1}{6} \cdot \frac{1}{6} = \frac{1}{7776}$ or 0.0001286

7a.

burger	soup	lemonade	burger, soup, lemonade
		soft drink	burger, soup, soft drink
	salad	lemonade	burger, salad, lemonade
		soft drink	burger, salad, soft drink
	French fries	lemonade	burger, French fries, lemonade
		soft drink	burger, French fries, soft drink
sandwich	soup	lemonade	sandwich, soup, lemonade
		soft drink	sandwich, soup, soft drink
	salad	lemonade	sandwich, salad, lemonade
		soft drink	sandwich, salad, soft drink
	French fries	lemonade	sandwich, French fries, lemonade
		soft drink	sandwich, French fries, soft drink
taco	soup	lemonade	taco, soup, lemonade
		soft drink	taco, soup, soft drink
	salad	lemonade	taco, salad, lemonade
		soft drink	taco, salad, soft drink
	French fries	lemonade	taco, French fries, lemonade
		soft drink	taco, French fries, soft drink
pizza	soup	lemonade	pizza, soup, lemonade
		soft drink	pizza, soup, soft drink
	salad	lemonade	pizza, salad, lemonade
		soft drink	pizza, salad, soft drink
	French fries	lemonade	pizza, French fries, lemonade
		soft drink	pizza, French fries, soft drink

7b. $\frac{8}{24} = \frac{1}{3}$ or $0.\overline{3}$

7c. $\frac{2}{24} = \frac{1}{12}$ or $0.08\overline{3}$

7d. $\frac{1}{24}$ or $0.041\overline{6}$

Pages 416–419 Exercises

8a. Let 1–5 represent the roads, and let A and B represent the doors.

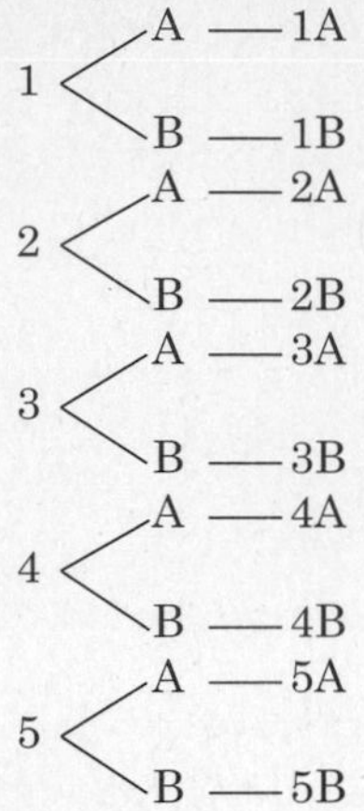

8b. $\frac{1}{10}$ or 0.1 **9a.** 3(5) = 15 **9b.** $\frac{3}{15} = \frac{1}{5}$ or 0.2

10. 3(2) = 6 possible combinations; $\frac{1}{6}$ or $0.1\overline{6}$

11. $\frac{1}{3}$ or $0.\overline{3}$

12a. Diagrams may vary. Sample answer:

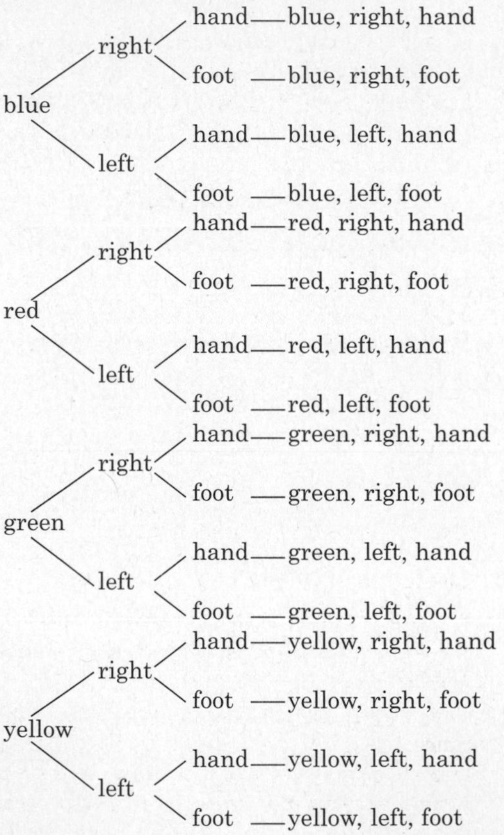

12b. $\frac{1}{16}$ or 0.0625

13a. R3-G5, R3-R10, R3-B10, R3-G1, R3-Y14, B3-G5, B3-R10, B3-B10, B3-G1, B3-Y14, R5-G5, R5-R10, R5-B10, R5-G1, R5-Y14, R14-G5, R14-R10, R14-B10, R14-G1, R14-Y14, Y10-G5, Y10-R10, Y10-B10, Y10-G1, Y10-Y14

13b. R5-R10, R14-R10, R3-R10: $\frac{3}{25}$ or 0.12

13c. Y10-R10, Y10-B10: $\frac{2}{25}$ or 0.08

13d. 0

13e. $\frac{14}{25}$ or 0.56

14a.

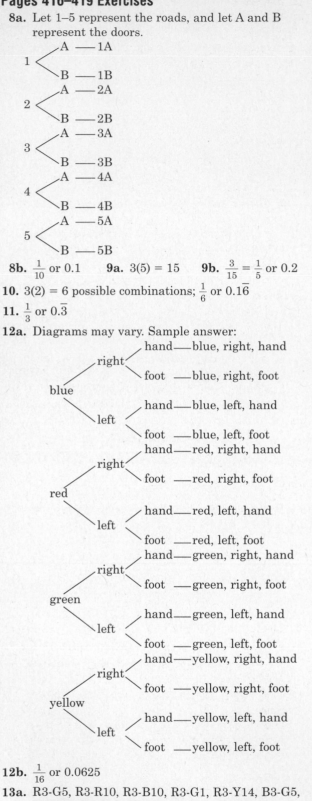

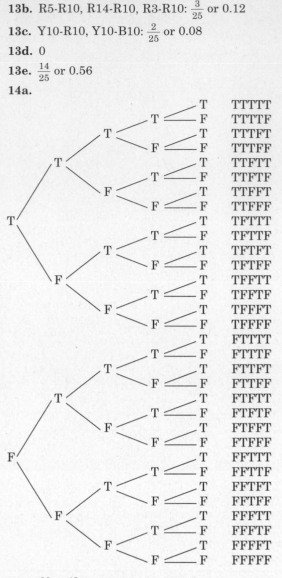

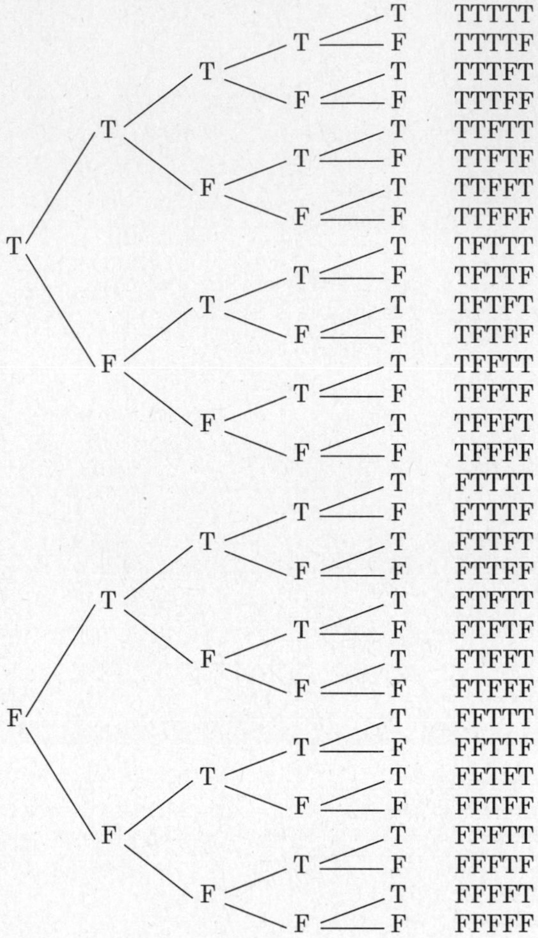

14b. $\frac{26}{32} = \frac{13}{16}$ or 0.8125

14c. Answers will vary. See students' work.

15a. (0.487)(0.487)(0.487)(0.487) ≈ 0.056 or about 5.6%

15b. 4(0.487)(0.513)(0.513)(0.513) ≈ 0.263 or about 26.3%

15c. See students' work.

16. 0.45(0.31) = 0.1395 or about 14%

17. *P*(drives when oversleeps) + *P*(drives when does not oversleep) = (0.2)(0.8) + (0.8)(0.2) = 0.32 or 32%

18a. See students' work; 30 outcomes

18b. $\frac{6}{30} = \frac{1}{5}$

19. $88 \le \frac{88 + 90 + 91 + x}{4} \le 92$

$$88 \le \frac{269 + x}{4}$$
$$4(88) \le 4\left(\frac{269 + x}{4}\right)$$
$$352 \le 269 + x$$
$$352 - 269 \le 269 + x - 269$$
$$83 \le x$$

and

$$\frac{269 + x}{4} \le 92$$
$$4\left(\frac{269 + x}{4}\right) \le 4(92)$$
$$269 + x \le 368$$
$$269 + x - 269 \le 368 - 269$$
$$x \le 99$$

$\{x \mid 83 \le x \le 99\}$; She must receive between 83 and 99, inclusive, on the fourth test.

20. Let n = the number.

$$\frac{2}{3}n > 99$$
$$\frac{3}{2}\left(\frac{2}{3}n\right) > \frac{3}{2}(99)$$
$$n > 148.5$$

$\{n \mid n > 148.5\}$

21. Solve for y:

$$3x - y = 9$$
$$-y = -3x + 9$$
$$y = 3x - 9$$

$m = 3$; y-intercept: -9

22. $8r - 7t + 2 = 5(r + 2t) - 9$

$$8r - 7t + 2 = 5r + 10t - 9$$
$$3r - 7t + 2 = 10t - 9$$
$$3r + 2 = 17t - 9$$
$$3r = 17t - 11$$
$$r = \frac{17t - 11}{3}$$

23a. 50° **23b.** 180° − 50° = 130° **23c.** yes

Page 419 Mathematics and Society

1. The computer's speed can evaluate several options for this and future moves better than the best of players.
2. First choose a level a little above your level to stimulate your playing skills. Next choice would be at your level to improve your technique and speed. Playing at a level far above your level might be too frustrating.
3. See students' work.
4. The computer tests all combinations of possible moves now and in the future. It is programmed to take into consideration the likelihood of certain combinations of moves. Those combinations that are least likely can probably be ignored as possibilities for your opponent's next move.

7-6 Solving Open Sentences Involving Absolute Value

Page 423 Check for Understanding

1. You can graph the meaning of the absolute value inequality on a number line, or you can solve the compound inequality it represents algebraically.
2. $|x + 7| > 4$ is solved as $x + 7 > 4$ or $x + 7 < -4$; $|x + 7| < 4$ is solved as $x + 7 < 4$ and $x + 7 > -4$.
3. $n = -x$
4. Yes, it will always be $\varnothing$.
5. $|x - 7| = 2$

$x - 7 = 2$ or $x - 7 = -2$

$x - 7 + 7 = 2 + 7$ $\quad$ $x - 7 + 7 = -2 + 7$

$x = 9$ $\quad$ $x = 5$

$\{5, 9\}$ c

6. $|x - 2| > 4$

$x - 2 < -4$ or $x - 2 > 4$

$x - 2 + 2 < -4 + 2$ $\quad$ $x - 2 + 2 > 4 + 2$

$x < -2$ $\quad$ $x > 6$

$\{x \mid x < -2 \text{ or } x > 6\}$ d

7. $|y| = 3$

$y = 3$ or $y = -3$ c

8. $|y| > 3$

$y < -3$ or $y > 3$ a

9. $|y| < 3$

$y > -3$ and $y < 3$

$\{y \mid -3 < y < 3\}$ d

10. $|y| \le 3$

$y \ge -3$ and $y \le 3$

$\{y \mid -3 \le y \le 3\}$ b

11. $|m| \ge 5$

$m \le -5$ or $m \ge 5$

$\{m \mid m \le -5 \text{ or } m \ge 5\}$

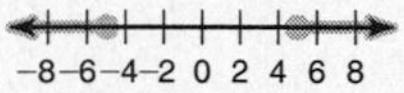

12. $|n| < 6$

$n > -6$ and $n < 6$

$\{n \mid -6 < n < 6\}$

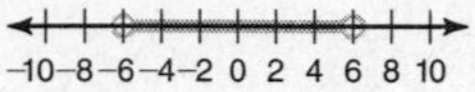

13. $|r + 3| < 6$

$r + 3 > -6$ and $r + 3 < 6$

$r + 3 - 3 > -6 - 3$ $\quad$ $r + 3 - 3 < 6 - 3$

$r > -9$ $\quad$ $r < 3$

$\{r \mid -9 < r < 3\}$

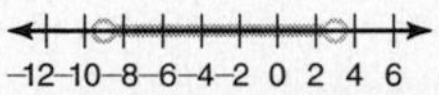

14. $|8 - t| \ge 3$

$8 - t \le -3$ or $8 - t \ge 3$

$8 - 8 - t \le -3 - 8$ $\quad$ $8 - 8 - t \ge 3 - 8$

$-t \le -11$ $\quad$ $-t \ge -5$

$\frac{-t}{-1} \ge \frac{-11}{-1}$ $\quad$ $\frac{-t}{-1} \le \frac{-5}{-1}$

$t \ge 11$ $\quad$ $t \le 5$

$\{t \mid t \le 5 \text{ or } t \ge 11\}$

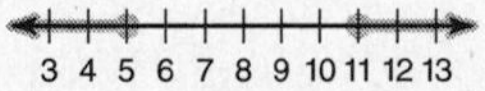

15. The center point between the points $x = -2$ and $x = 2$ is $\frac{-2 + 2}{2}$ or 0. Since 0 is 2 units from -2 and 2 units from 2, the distance between x and 0 is 2. Therefore, $|x - 0| = 2$ or $|x| = 2$.
16. The center point of the graph is $\frac{4 + (-2)}{2}$ or 1. Since 1 is 3 units from -2 and 3 units from 4, and x represents a number between -2 and 4 inclusive, the distance between x and 1 must be less than or equal to 3. Therefore, $|x - 1| \le 3$.

Pages 424–426 Exercises

17. $|y - 2| = 4$

$y - 2 = 4$ or $y - 2 = -4$

$y - 2 + 2 = 4 + 2$ $\quad$ $y - 2 + 2 = -4 + 2$

$y = 6$ $\quad$ $y = -2$

$\{-2, 6\}$

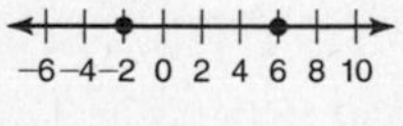

18. $|3 - 3x| = 0$

$3 - 3x = 0$

$3 - 3 - 3x = 0 - 3$

$-3x = -3$

$\frac{-3x}{-3} = \frac{-3}{-3}$

$x = 1$

$\{1\}$

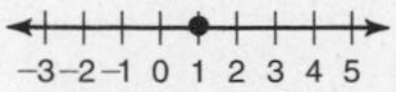

19. $|7x = 2| = -2$

There can be no expression whose absolute set is equal to a negative value. The solution is $\varnothing$.

20. $|w + 8| \geq 1$

$w + 8 \leq -1$ or $w + 8 \geq 1$

$w + 8 - 8 \leq -1 - 8$ $\quad$ $w + 8 - 8 \geq 1 - 8$

$w \leq -9$ $\quad$ $w \geq -7$

$\{w \mid w \leq -9 \text{ or } w \geq -7\}$

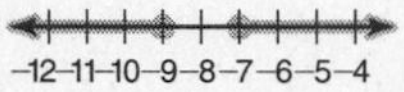

21. $|2 - y| \leq 1$

$2 - y \geq -1$ and $2 - y \leq 1$

$2 - 2 - y \geq -1 - 2$ $\quad$ $2 - 2 - y \leq 1 - 2$

$-y \geq -3$ $\quad$ $-y \leq -1$

$\frac{-y}{-1} \leq \frac{-3}{-1}$ $\quad$ $\frac{-y}{-1} \geq \frac{-1}{-1}$

$y \leq 3$ $\quad$ $y \geq 1$

$\{y \mid 1 \leq y \leq 3\}$

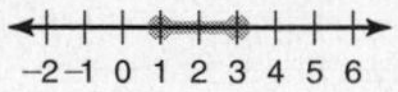

22. $|t + 4| \geq 3$

$t + 4 \leq -3$ or $t + 4 \geq 3$

$t + 4 - 4 \leq -3 - 4$ $\quad$ $t + 4 - 4 \geq 3 - 4$

$t \leq -7$ $\quad$ $t \geq -1$

$\{t \mid t \leq -7 \text{ or } t \geq -1\}$

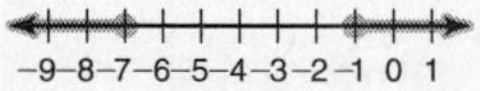

23. $|4y - 8| > 0$

There can be no expression whose absolute value is less than zero. The solution is $\varnothing$.

24. $|2x + 5| < 4$

$2x + 5 > -4$ and $2x + 5 < 4$

$2x + 5 - 5 > -4 - 5$ $\quad$ $2x + 5 - 5 < 4 - 5$

$2x > -9$ $\quad$ $2x < -1$

$\frac{2x}{2} > \frac{-9}{2}$ $\quad$ $\frac{2x}{2} < \frac{-1}{2}$

$x > -\frac{9}{2}$ $\quad$ $x < -\frac{1}{2}$

$\left\{x \mid -\frac{9}{2} < x < -\frac{1}{2}\right\}$

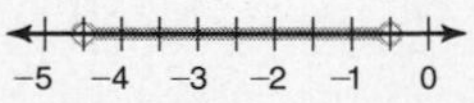

25. $|3e - 7| < 2$

$3e - 7 > -2$ and $3e - 7 < 2$

$3e - 7 + 7 > -2 + 7$ $\quad$ $3e - 7 + 7 < 2 + 7$

$3e > 5$ $\quad$ $3e < 9$

$\frac{3e}{3} > \frac{5}{3}$ $\quad$ $\frac{3e}{3} < \frac{9}{3}$

$e > \frac{5}{3}$ $\quad$ $e < 3$

$\left\{e \mid \frac{5}{3} < e < 3\right\}$

26. $|3x + 4| < 8$

$3x + 4 > -8$ and $3x + 4 < 8$

$3x + 4 - 4 > -8 - 4$ $\quad$ $3x + 4 - 4 < 8 - 4$

$3x > -12$ $\quad$ $3x < 4$

$\frac{3x}{3} > \frac{-12}{3}$ $\quad$ $\frac{3x}{3} < \frac{4}{3}$

$x > -4$ $\quad$ $x < \frac{4}{3}$

$\left\{x \mid -4 < x < \frac{4}{3}\right\}$

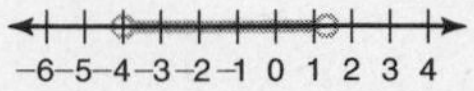

27. $|1 - 3y| > -2$

$1 - 3y > -2$ or $1 - 3y < 2$

$1 - 3y - 1 > -2 - 1$ $\quad$ $1 - 3y - 1 < 2 - 1$

$-3y > -3$ $\quad$ $-3y < 1$

$\frac{-3y}{-3} < \frac{-3}{-3}$ $\quad$ $\frac{-3y}{-3} > \frac{1}{-3}$

$y < 1$ $\quad$ $y > -\frac{1}{3}$

{all numbers}

28. $3 + |x| > 3$

$3 - 3 + |x| > 3 - 3$

$|x| > 0$

$x < 0$ or $x > 0$

$\{x \mid x \neq 0\}$

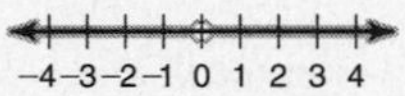

29. $|8 - (w - 1)| \leq 9$

$|8 - w + 1| \leq 9$

$|9 - w| \leq 9$

$9 - w \geq -9$ and $9 - w \leq 9$

$9 - 9 - w \geq -9 - 9$ $\quad$ $9 - 9 - w \leq 9 - 9$

$-w \geq -18$ $\quad$ $-w \leq 0$

$\frac{-w}{-1} \leq \frac{-18}{-1}$ $\quad$ $\frac{-w}{-1} \geq \frac{0}{-1}$

$w \leq 18$ $\quad$ $w \geq 0$

$\{w \mid 0 \leq w \leq 18\}$

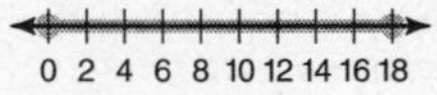

30. $|6 - (11 - b)| = -3$

There can be no expression whose absolute value is equal to a negative value. The solution is $\varnothing$.

31. $|2.2y - 1.1| = 5.5$

$2.2y - 1.1 = 5.5$

$2.2y - 1.1 + 1.1 = -5.5 + 1.1$

$2.2y = 6.6$

$\frac{2.2y}{2.2} = \frac{6.6}{2.2}$

$y = 3$

or

$2.2y - 1.1 = -5.5$

$2.2y - 1.1 + 1.1 = 5.5 + 1.1$

$2.2y = -4.4$

$\frac{2.2y}{2.2} = \frac{-4.4}{2.2}$

$y = -2$

$\{-2, 3\}$

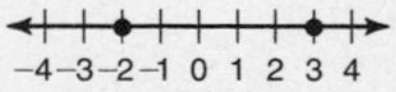

32. $|3r - 0.5| \geq 5.5$

$$3r - 0.5 \leq -5.5$$
$$3r - 0.5 + 0.5 \leq -5.5 + 0.5$$
$$3r \leq -5$$
$$\frac{3r}{3} \leq \frac{-5}{3}$$
$$r \leq -\frac{5}{3} \text{ or } -1.\overline{6}$$

or

$$3r - 0.5 \geq 5.5$$
$$3r - 0.5 + 0.5 \geq 5.5 + 0.5$$
$$3r \geq 6$$
$$\frac{3r}{3} \geq \frac{6}{3}$$
$$r \geq 2$$

$\{r \mid r \leq 1.\overline{6} \text{ or r} \geq 2\}$

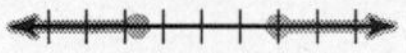

33. $\left|\frac{2-3x}{5}\right| \geq 2$

$$\frac{2-3x}{5} \leq -2 \quad \text{or} \quad \frac{2-3x}{5} \geq 2$$
$$5\left(\frac{2-3x}{5}\right) \leq 5(-2) \qquad 5\left(\frac{2-3x}{5}\right) \geq 2(5)$$
$$2 - 3x \leq -10 \qquad 2 - 3x \geq 10$$
$$2 - 2 - 3x \leq -10 - 2 \qquad 2 - 2 - 3x \geq 10 - 2$$
$$-3x \leq -12 \qquad -3x \geq 8$$
$$\frac{-3x}{-3} \geq \frac{-12}{-3} \qquad \frac{-3x}{-3} \leq \frac{8}{-3}$$
$$x \geq 4 \qquad x \leq -\frac{8}{3}$$

$\{x \mid x \leq -\frac{8}{3} \text{ or } x \geq 4\}$

34. $\left|\frac{1}{2} - 3p\right| < \frac{7}{2}$

$$\frac{1}{2} - 3p > -\frac{7}{2} \quad \text{and} \quad \frac{1}{2} - 3p < \frac{7}{2}$$
$$\frac{1}{2} - 3p - \frac{1}{2} > -\frac{7}{2} - \frac{1}{2} \qquad \frac{1}{2} - 3p - \frac{1}{2} < \frac{7}{2} - \frac{1}{2}$$
$$-3p > -4 \qquad -3p < 3$$
$$\frac{-3p}{-3} < \frac{-4}{-3} \qquad \frac{-3p}{-3} > \frac{3}{-3}$$
$$p < \frac{4}{3} \qquad p > -1$$

$\left\{p \mid -1 < p < \frac{4}{3}\right\}$

35. $|p - 1| \leq 0.01$ **36.** $|s - 55| \leq 3$

37. $|t - 50| > 50$

38. The center point between the points $x = -2$ and $x = 6$ is $\frac{-2+6}{2}$ or 2. Since 2 is 4 units from -2 and 4 units from 6, the distance between x and 2 is 4. Therefore, $|x - 2| = 4$.

39. The center point between the points $x = -4$ and $x = 2$ is $\frac{-4+2}{2}$ or -1. Since -1 is 3 units from -4 and 3 units from 2, the distance between x and -1 is 3. Therefore, $|x - (-1)| = 3$ or $|x + 1| = 3$.

40. The center point between $x \leq -2$ and $x \geq 2$ is $\frac{-2+2}{2}$ or 0. Since 0 is 2 units from -2 and 2 units from 2, and x represents a number less than or equal to -2 or greater than or equal to 2, the distance between x and 0 must be greater than or equal to 2. Therefore, $|x - 0| \geq 2$ or $|x| \geq 2$.

41. The center point of the graph is $\frac{2+0}{2}$ or 1. Since 1 is 1 unit from 0 and 1 unit from 2, and x represents a number between 0 and 2 inclusive, the distance between x and 1 must be less than or equal to 1. Therefore, $|x - 1| \leq 1$.

42. The center point of the graph is $\frac{-4+2}{2}$ or -1. Since -1 is 3 units from -4 and 3 units from 2, and x represents a number between -4 and 2, the distance between x and -1 must be less than 3. Therefore, $|x - (-1)| < 3$ or $|x + 1| < 3$.

43. The center point between $x \leq 5$ and $x \geq 11$ is $\frac{11+5}{2}$ or 8. Since 8 is 3 units from 5 and 3 units from 11, and x represents a number less than or equal to 5 or greater than or equal to 11, the distance between x and 8 must be greater than or equal to 3. Therefore, $|x - 8| \geq 3$.

44. $|x| < 4$
$x > -4$ and $x < 4$
$\{x \mid -4 < x < 4\}$
$\{-3, -2, -1, 0, 1, 2, 3\}$

45. $|x| \leq 2$
$x \geq -2$ and $x \leq 2$
$\{x \mid -2 \leq x \leq 2\}$
$\{-2, -1, 0, 1, 2\}$

46. Using the answer to 44 as an example, we see that there are 7 or $2(4) - 1$ solutions to 44. Thus, if $|x| < a$, there are $2a - 1$ integer solutions.

47. Using the answer to 45 as an example, we see that there are 5 or $2(2) + 1$ solutions to 45. Thus, if $|x| \leq a$, there are $2a + 1$ integer solutions.

48. $|y - 3| = |2 + y|$

$$y - 3 = 2 + y \quad \text{or} \quad y - 3 = -(2 + y)$$
$$y - y - 3 = 2 + y - y \qquad y - 3 = -2 - y$$
$$-3 \neq 2 \qquad y + y - 3 = -2 - y + y$$
$$2y - 3 = -2$$
$$2y - 3 + 3 = -2 + 3$$
$$2y = 1$$
$$\frac{2y}{2} = \frac{1}{2}$$
$$y = \frac{1}{2}$$

or

$$-(y - 3) = 2 + y$$
$$-y + 3 = 2 + y$$
$$-y + y + 3 = 2 + y + y$$
$$3 = 2 + 2y$$
$$3 - 2 = 2 + 2y - 2$$
$$1 = 2y$$
$$\frac{1}{2} = \frac{2y}{2}$$
$$\frac{1}{2} = y$$

or

$$-(y - 3) = -(2 + y)$$
$$-y + 3 = -2 - y$$
$$-y + y + 3 = -2 - y + y$$
$$3 \neq -2$$

The solution is $\left\{\frac{1}{2}\right\}$.

49. $a \neq 0$; never

50. The center point of the graph of this inequality is $\frac{8+12}{2}$ or 10. Since 10 is 2 units from 8 and 2 units from 12, and x represents a number between 8 and 12 inclusive, the distance between x and 10 must be less than or equal to 2. Therefore, $|x - 10| \leq 2$.

51. $|x| \le 6$

$x \le -6$ and $x \ge 6$

$\{-6, -5, -4, -3, -2, -1, 0, 1, 2, 3, 4, 5, 6\}$

$P(|x| \text{ being a factor of } 18) = \frac{8}{13}$ or 0.61

52. $-257 - 2 < t < 257 - 2$

$-259°C < t < 255°C$

53. $59 - 7 \le s \le 59 + 7$

no; $52 \le s \le 66$

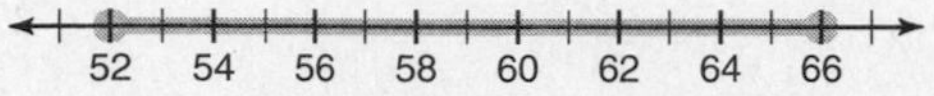

54. $|300 - t| \le 2.5$

$300 - t \le 2.5$

$300 - t - 300 \le 2.5 - 300$

$-t \le -297.5$

$\frac{-t}{-1} \ge \frac{-297.5}{-1}$

$t \ge 297.5$

and

$300 - t \ge -2.5$

$300 - t - 300 \ge -2.5 - 300$

$-t \ge -302.5$

$\frac{-t}{-1} \ge \frac{-302.5}{-1}$

$t \le 302.5$

$297.5 \le t \le 302.5$ minutes

55. $18{,}000 - 1500 \le p \le 18{,}000$

$\$16{,}500 \le p \le \$18{,}000$

56a. $2.40 \le s \le 43.00$; The center point of the graph of this inequality is $\frac{2.40 + 43.00}{2}$ or 22.70. Since 22.70 is 22.70 − 2.40 or 20.30 units from 2.40 and 43.00 − 22.70 or 20.30 units from 43.00 inclusive, the distance between s and 22.70 must be less than or equal to 20.30. Therefore, $|s - 22.70| \le 20.30$.

56b. $22 \le s \le 43$; The center point of the graph of this inequality is $\frac{22 + 43}{2}$ or 32.50. Since 32.50 is 32.50 − 22 or 10.50 units from 22 and 43 − 32.50 or 10.50 units from 43 and since s represents a number between 22 and 43 inclusive, the distance between s and 32.50 must be less than or equal to 10.50. Therefore, $|s - 32.50| \le 10.50$.

56c. See students' work.

57a. See students' work for diagram. List of outcomes: BBBB, BBBG, BBGB, BBGG, BGBB, BGBG, BGGB, BGGG, GBBB, GBBG, GBGB, GBGG, GGBB, GGBG, GGGB, and GGGG.

57b. $\frac{1}{16}$ or 0.0625, $\frac{1}{16}$ or 0.0625

57c. $\frac{6}{16} = \frac{3}{8}$ or 0.375

58. $1700 < p - 0.12p < 2200$

$1700 < 0.88p$ and $0.88p < 2200$

$\frac{1700}{0.88} < \frac{0.88p}{0.88}$ $\quad$ $\frac{0.88p}{0.88} < \frac{2200}{0.88}$

$1932 < p$ $\quad$ $p < 2500$

$\$1932 < p < \$2500$

59. $10x - 2 \ge 4(x - 2)$

$10x - 2 \ge 4x - 8$

$10x - 4x - 2 \ge 4x - 4x - 8$

$6x - 2 \ge -8$

$6x - 2 + 2 \ge -8 + 2$

$6x \ge -6$

$\frac{6x}{6} \ge \frac{-6}{6}$

$x \ge -1$

$\{x \mid x \ge -1\}$

60. $396 > -11t$

$\frac{396}{-11} < \frac{-11t}{-11}$

$-36 < t$

$\{t \mid t > -36\}$

61. $-11 \le k - (-4)$

$-11 \le k + 4$

$-11 - 4 \le k + 4 - 4$

$-15 \le k$

$\{k \mid k \ge -15\}$

62. midpoint $= \left(\frac{-4 + 10}{2}, \frac{1 + 3}{2}\right)$

$= \left(\frac{6}{2}, \frac{4}{2}\right)$

$= (3, 2)$

63. Let $x = 0$.

$2x - 9 = 2y$

$2(0) - 9 = 2y$

$-9 = 2y$

$\frac{-9}{2} = y$

$\left(0, -\frac{9}{2}\right)$

Let $y = 0$.

$2x - 9 = 2y$

$2x - 9 = 2(0)$

$2x - 9 = 0$

$2x = 9$

$x = \frac{9}{2}$

$\left(\frac{9}{2}, 0\right)$

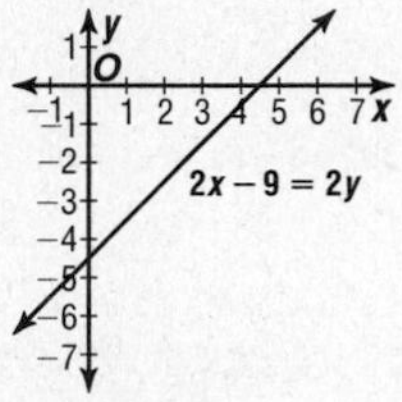

64. $\frac{5 \text{ ft}}{2 \text{ in.}} = \frac{4 \text{ ft}}{x \text{ in.}}$

$5x = 4(2)$

$5x = 8$

$x = \frac{8}{5}$ or 1.6

$\frac{5 \text{ ft}}{2 \text{ in.}} = \frac{3 \text{ ft}}{x \text{ in.}}$

$5x = 3(2)$

$5x = 6$

$x = \frac{6}{5}$ or 1.2

1.2 in.; 1.6 in.

65. $2m + \frac{3}{4}n = \frac{1}{2}m - 9$

$2m - \frac{1}{2}m + \frac{3}{4}n = \frac{1}{2}m - \frac{1}{2}m - 9$

$\frac{3}{2}m + \frac{3}{4}n = -9$

$\frac{3}{2}m + \frac{3}{4}n - \frac{3}{4}n = -9 - \frac{3}{4}n$

$\frac{3}{2}m = -9 - \frac{3}{4}n$

$\frac{2}{3}\left(\frac{3}{2}m\right) = \frac{2}{3}\left(-9 - \frac{3}{4}n\right)$

$m = -6 - \frac{n}{2}$

66. $\frac{-42r + 18}{3} = \frac{-42r}{3} + \frac{18}{3}$

$= -14r + 6$

7-7 Integration: Statistics Box-and-Whisker Plots

Pages 429–430 Check for Understanding

1. Scale must be large enough to include the least and greatest values.

2. LV and Q_1; Q_3 and GV **3.** the median

4a. 25% **4b.** 90 − 120 **4c.** none

5. Sample answer: quartiles, interquartile range, outliers, whether the data are clustered or diverse; individual point of data, number of data

6a.

	1985	1992
median:	14.0	13.1
Q_3:	18.0	15.7
Q_1:	11.9	11.9
IQR:	18.0 − 11.9 = 6.1	15.7 − 11.9 = 3.8

6b. For 1985:

$x \geq Q_3 + 1.5(IQR)$ or $x \leq Q_1 - 1.5(IQR)$
$x \geq 18 + 1.5(6.1)$ $\quad x \leq 11.9 - 1.5(6.1)$
$x \geq 27.5$ $\quad x \leq 2.75$
There are no outliers.

For 1992:

$x \geq Q_3 + 1.5(IQR)$ or $x \leq Q_1 - 1.5(IQR)$
$x \geq 15.7 + 1.5(3.8)$ $\quad x \leq 11.9 - 1.5(38)$
$x \geq 21.4$ $\quad x \leq 6.2$
The outliers are 21.5 and 23.3.

6c.

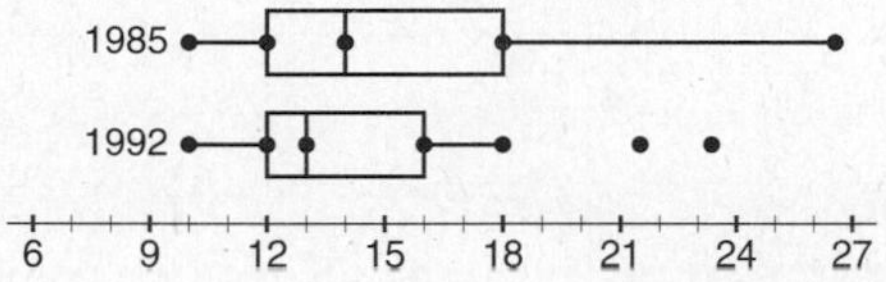

6d. 1992; because the plot is not as wide.

7a.

	A	B
LV:	25	20
GV:	65	70
Q_1:	30	40
Q_3:	60	60
median:	40	45

7b. B

7c. IQR of A: 60 − 30 = 30
IQR of B: 60 − 40 = 20
A has the greatest interquartile range.

7d. range of A: 65 − 25 = 40
range of B: 70 − 20 = 50
B has the greatest range.

Pages 430–432 Exercises

8a. range of A: 750 − 300 = 450
range of B: 525 − 350 = 175
A had the most varied results.

8b. yes; A; the outlier was 750.

8c. about the same, 425

8d. B; The lives of the bulbs were more consistent.

9a. $Q_2 = \frac{6+7}{2} = 6.5$
$Q_3 = 16$
$Q_1 = 5$
$IQR = 16 - 5 = 11$

9b. $x \geq Q_3 + 1.5(IQR)$ $\quad x \leq Q_1 - 1.5(IQR)$
$x \geq 16 + 1.5(11)$ $\quad x \leq 5 - 1.5(11)$
$x \geq 32.5$ $\quad x \leq -11.5$
There are no outliers.

9c.

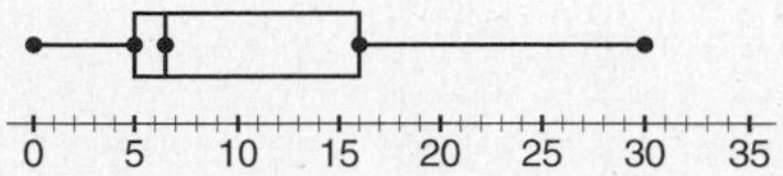

10. LV: 6
Q_1: $\frac{8+12}{2} = 10$
Q_2: 14
Q_3: $\frac{16+18}{2} = 17$
GV: 25
IQR: 17 − 10 = 7
Outliers: $x \geq 17 + 1.5(7)$ $\quad x \leq 10 - 1.5(7)$
$x \geq 27.5$ $\quad x \leq -0.5$
There are no outliers.

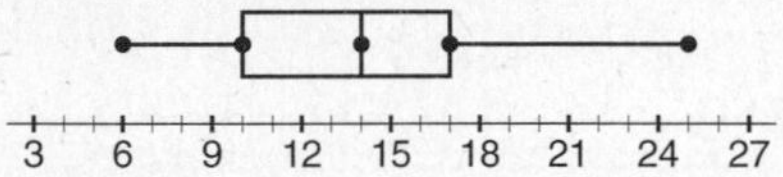

11a. LV:1
Q_1: 1
Q_2: 3
Q_3: 8
GV: 96
IQR: 8 − 1 = 7
Outliers: $x \geq 8 + 1.5(7)$ $\quad x \leq 1 - 1.5(7)$
$x \geq 18.5$ $\quad x \leq -9.5$
The outliers are 19, 23, 25, 27, and 96.

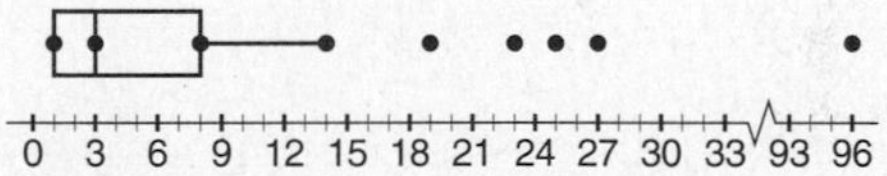

11b. clustered with lots of outliers

11c. There are four western states that have more American Indian people than other states.

11d. The median is 3. The mean of 8.8 is greater than the median.

12a. LV: 6
Q_1: 13
Q_2: 22
Q_3: $\frac{38+57}{2} = 47.5$
GV: 101
IQR: 47.5 − 13 = 34.5
Outliers: $x \geq 47.5 + 1.5(34.5)$
$x \geq 99.25$
$x \leq 13 - 1.5(34.5)$
$x \leq -38.75$
The only outlier is 101.

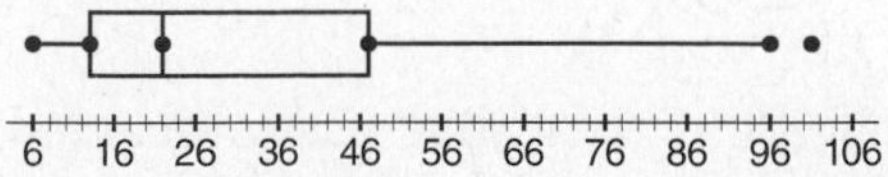

12b. median: 22 **12c.** PA **12d.** the upper half

13a.

Male	**Female**
LV: 18.3	LV: 16
Q1: 18.35	Q1: 16.1
Q2: 18.5	Q2: 16.1
Q3: 20.45	Q3: 19.3
GV: 20.6	GV: 19.6

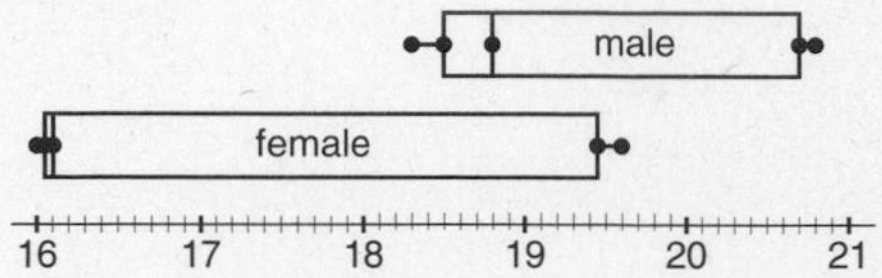

Male data are more condensed and generally higher than female data.

13b. 1990; See students' work.

14a–b.

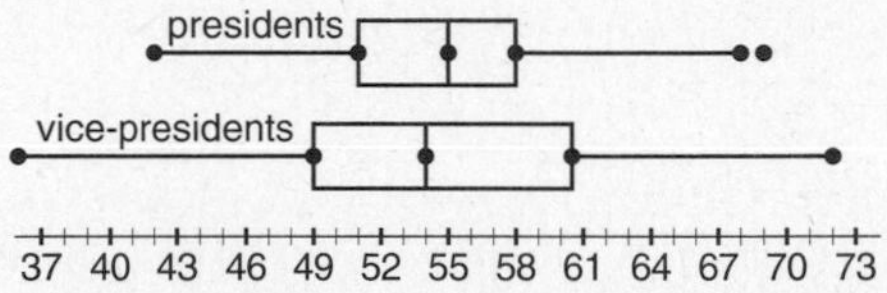

14c. The presidents seem more clustered because the box portion, representing 50% of the data, is narrower.

14d. ages 66–72, assuming no vice-president age 66 or 67 succeeded a president during the president's term

15. Sample answer: Class A appears to be a more difficult class than Class B because the students don't do as well.

16. $18(15) \le d \le 21(15)$

$270 \le d \le 315$

270 to 315 miles

17.

$2m - 3 > 7$	or	$2m + 7 > 9$
$2m - 3 + 3 > 7 + 3$		$2m + 7 - 7 > 9 - 7$
$2m > 10$		$2m > 2$
$\frac{2m}{2} > \frac{10}{2}$		$\frac{2m}{2} > \frac{2}{2}$
$m > 5$		$m > 1$

$\{m \mid m > 1\}$

18. $m = \frac{-2 - 7}{1 - 4} = \frac{-9}{-3}$ or 3

$m = 3$; (4, 7)

$y - y_1 = m(x - x_1)$

$y - 7 = 3(x - 4)$

$y - 7 = 3x - 12$

$y - 7 + 12 = 3x - 12 + 12$

$y + 5 = 3x$

$5 = 3x - y$

$3x - y = 5$

19.

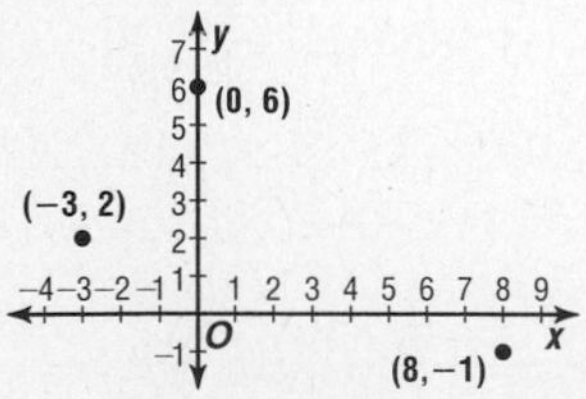

20. $\frac{6}{x - 3} = \frac{3}{4}$

$6(4) = 3(x - 3)$

$24 = 3x - 9$

$24 + 9 = 3x - 9 + 9$

$33 = 3x$

$11 = x$

7-7B Graphing Technology Box-and-Whisker Plots

Page 434 Exercises

1. women identifying objects with left hand
2. With the left hand; the data are clustered.
3. The left hand data are more clustered.
4. females
5. males
6. It does not agree. Sample reason: Adults may have better recognition skills or there may have been a large number of left-handed people in the sample.

7-8A Graphing Technology Graphing Inequalities

Page 435 Exercises

1. Enter: [2nd] [DRAW] 7 [X,T,θ] , [+] 2 [,] 10 [)] [ENTER]

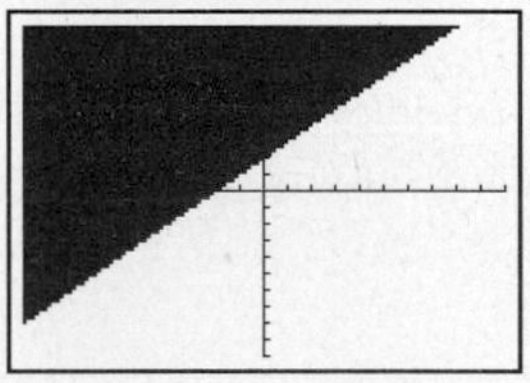

2. Enter: [2nd] [DRAW] 7 [(−)] 10 [,] [(−)] 2 [X,T,θ] [−] 4 [)] [ENTER]

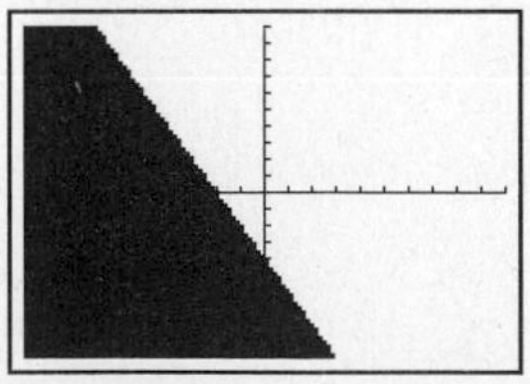

3. Solve for y: $y + 1 \le 0.5x$

$y \le 0.5x - 1$

Enter: [2nd] [DRAW] 7 [(−)] 10 [,] .5 [X,T,θ] [−] 1 [)] [ENTER]

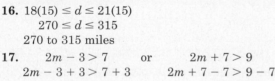

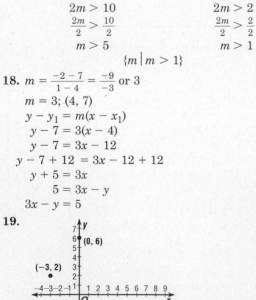

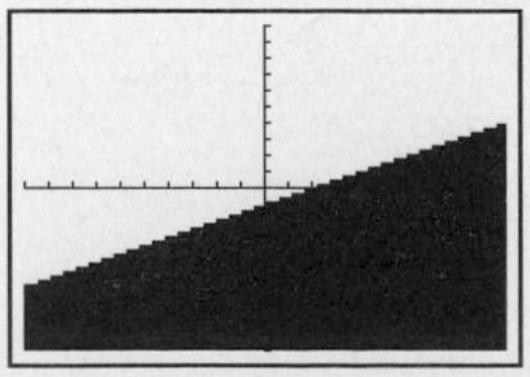

4. Enter: 2nd DRAW 7 4 X,T,θ , 10) ENTER

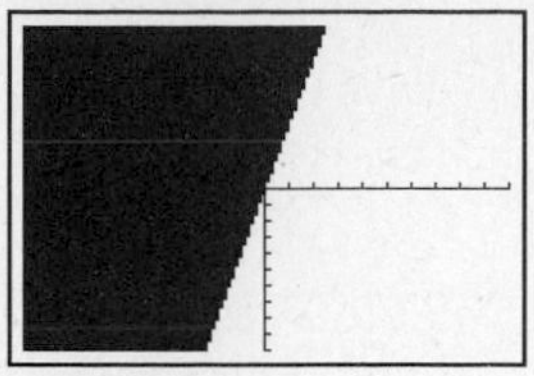

5. Solve for y: $x + y \leq 0$

$y \leq -x$

Enter: 2nd DRAW 7 (−) 10 , (−) X,T,θ) ENTER

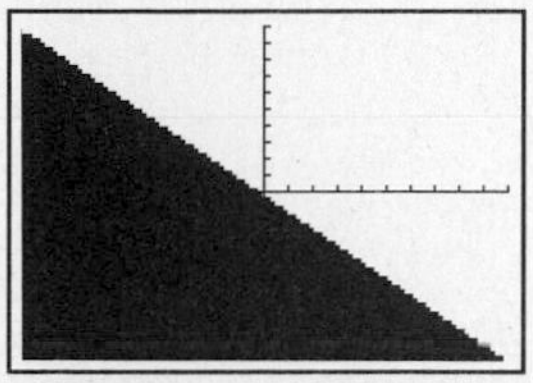

6. Solve for y: $2y + x \geq 4$

$2y \geq -x + 4$

$y \geq -0.5x + 2$

Enter: 2nd DRAW 7 (−) .5 X,T,θ + 2 , 10) ENTER

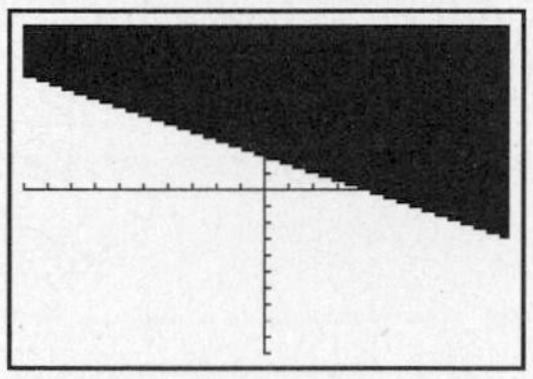

7. Solve for y: $3x + y \leq 18$

$y = -3x + 18$

Enter: 2nd DRAW 7 (−) 10 , (−) 3 X,T,θ + 18) ENTER

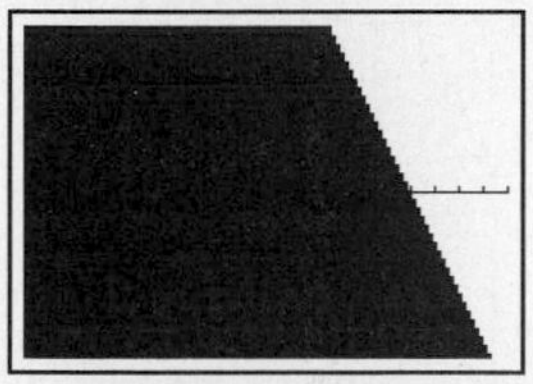

8. Enter: 2nd DRAW 7 3 , 10) ENTER

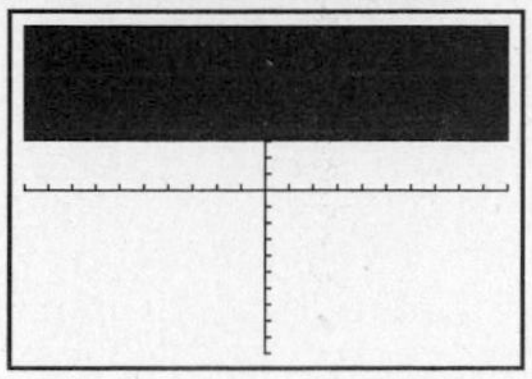

9. Solve for y: $0.2x + 0.1y \leq 1$

$0.1y \leq -0.2x + 1$

$y \leq -2x + 10$

Enter: 2nd DRAW 7 (−) 10 , (−) 2 X,T,θ + 10) ENTER

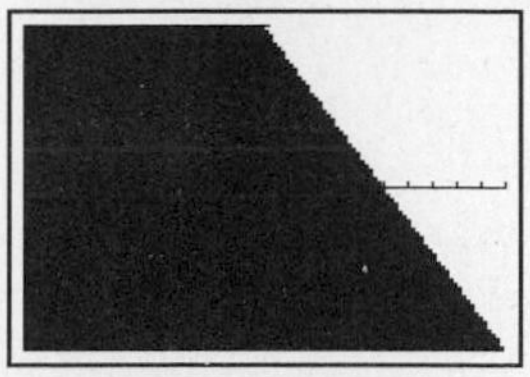

7-8 Graphing Inequalities in Two Variables

Page 439 Check for Understanding

1a.

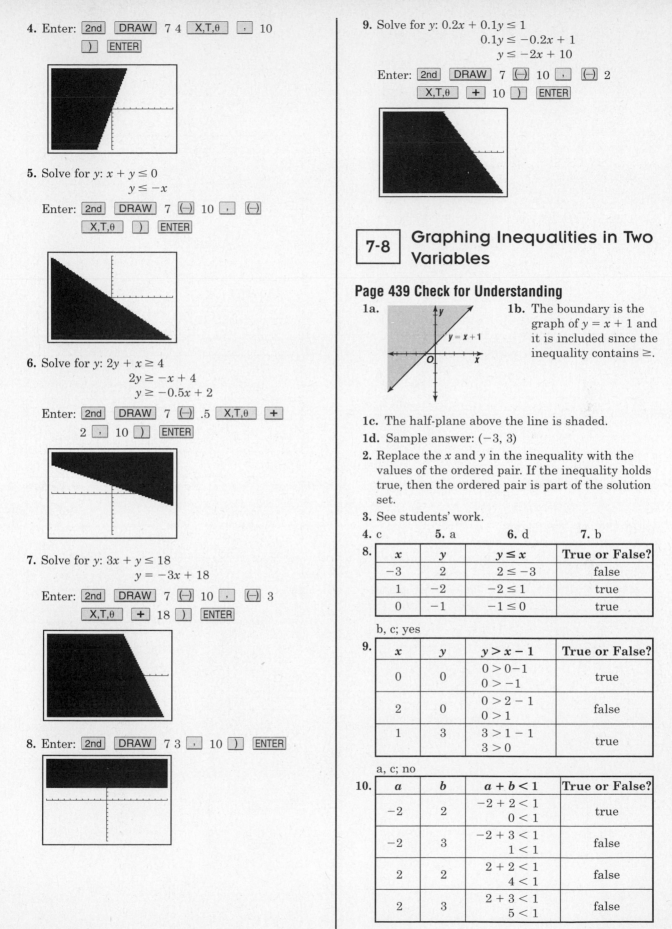

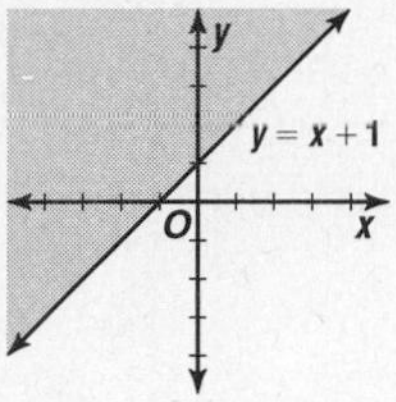

1b. The boundary is the graph of $y = x + 1$ and it is included since the inequality contains $\geq$.

1c. The half-plane above the line is shaded.

1d. Sample answer: $(-3, 3)$

2. Replace the x and y in the inequality with the values of the ordered pair. If the inequality holds true, then the ordered pair is part of the solution set.

3. See students' work.

4. c   5. a   6. d   7. b

8.

x	y	$y \leq x$	True or False?
-3	2	$2 \leq -3$	false
1	-2	$-2 \leq 1$	true
0	-1	$-1 \leq 0$	true

b, c; yes

9.

x	y	$y > x - 1$	True or False?
0	0	$0 > 0-1$ $0 > -1$	true
2	0	$0 > 2 - 1$ $0 > 1$	false
1	3	$3 > 1 - 1$ $3 > 0$	true

a, c; no

10.

a	b	$a + b < 1$	True or False?
-2	2	$-2 + 2 < 1$ $0 < 1$	true
-2	3	$-2 + 3 < 1$ $1 < 1$	false
2	2	$2 + 2 < 1$ $4 < 1$	false
2	3	$2 + 3 < 1$ $5 < 1$	false

$\{-2, 2\}$

11. Test (0, 0): $y > 3$
$0 > 3$ false
Test (0, 4): $4 > 3$ true
Shade the half-plane containing (0, 4).

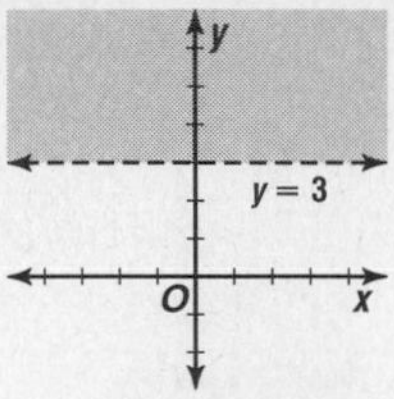

12. Solve for y:
$x + y > 1$
$y > -x + 1$
Test (0, 0): $0 > -0 + 1$ false
Test (0, 2): $2 > -0 + 1$ true
Shade the half-plane containing (0, 2).

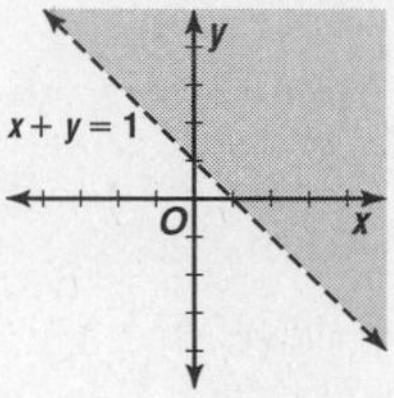

13. Solve for y:
$2x + 3y \geq -2$
$3y \geq -2x - 2$
$y \geq -\frac{2}{3}x - \frac{2}{3}$
Test (0, 0):
$0 \geq -\frac{2}{3}(0) - \frac{2}{3}$ true
Shade the half-plane containing (0, 0).

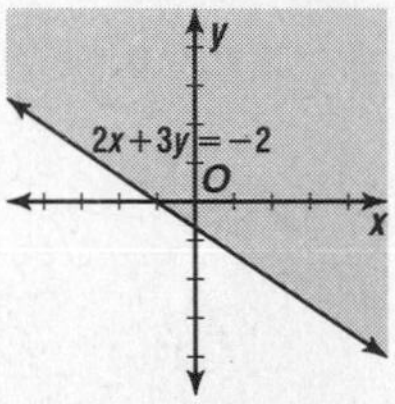

14. Solve for y:
$-x < -y$
$\frac{-x}{-1} > \frac{-y}{-1}$
$x > y$
$y < x$
Test (0, −1):
$-1 < 0$ true
Shade the half-plane containing (0, −1).

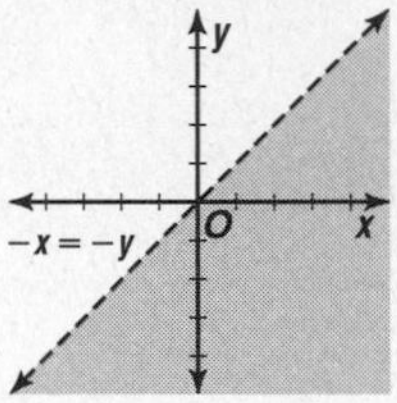

Pages 439–441 Exercises

15.

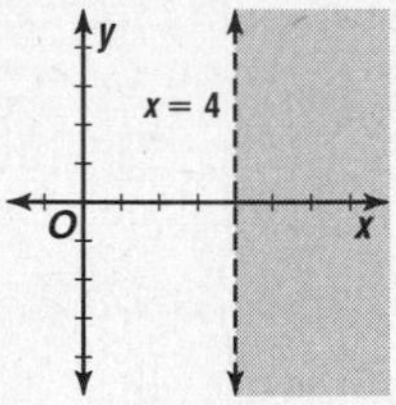

Test (5, 0):
$x > 4$
$5 > 4$ true
Shade the half-plane containing (5, 0).

16.

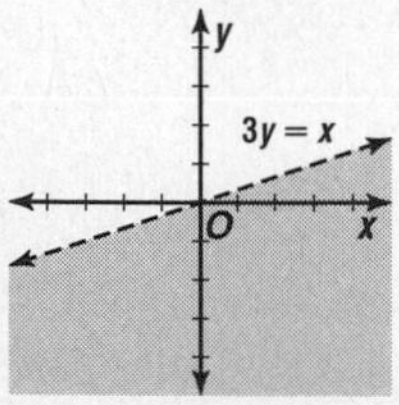

Test (0, −1):
$3y < x$
$3(-1) < 0$
$-3 < 0$ true
Shade the half-plane containing (0, −1).

17.

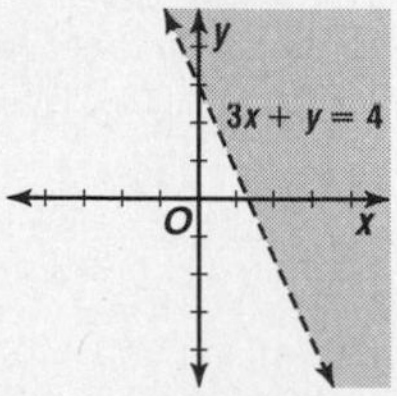

Test (2, 2):
$3x + y > 4$
$3(2) + 2 > 4$
$6 + 2 > 4$
$8 > 4$ true
Shade the half-plane containing (2, 2).

18.

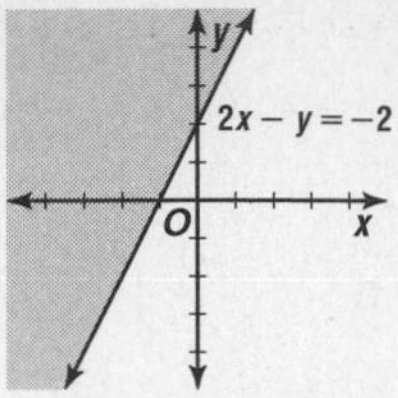

Test (0, 3):
$2x - y \leq -2$
$2(0) - 3 \leq -2$
$-3 \leq -2$ true
Shade the half-plane containing (0, 3).

19.

x	y	$y < 3x$	True or False?
−3	1	$1 < -3(3)$ $1 < -9$	false
−3	2	$2 < -3(3)$ $2 < -9$	false
1	1	$1 < 3(1)$ $1 < 3$	true
1	2	$2 < 3(1)$ $2 < 3$	true

{(1, 1), (1, 2)}

20.

x	y	$y - x > 0$	True or False?
1	1	$1 - 1 > 0$ $0 > 0$	false
1	2	$2 - 1 > 0$ $1 > 0$	true
4	1	$1 - 4 > 0$ $-3 > 0$	false
4	2	$2 - 4 > 0$ $-2 > 0$	false

{(1, 2)}

21.

x	y	$2y + x \geq 4$	True or False?
−1	−3	$2(-3) - 1 \geq 4$ $-7 \geq 4$	false
−1	0	$2(0) - 1 \geq 4$ $-1 \geq 4$	false
−2	−3	$2(-3) - 2 \geq 4$ $-8 \geq 4$	false
−2	0	$2(0) - 2 \geq 4$ $-2 \geq 4$	false

$\varnothing$

22.

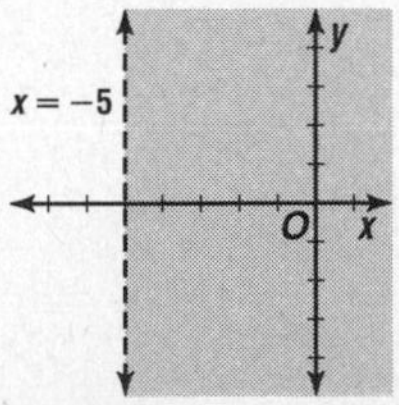

Test (0, 0):
$x > -5$
$0 > -5$ true
Shade the half-plane containing (0, 0).

23.

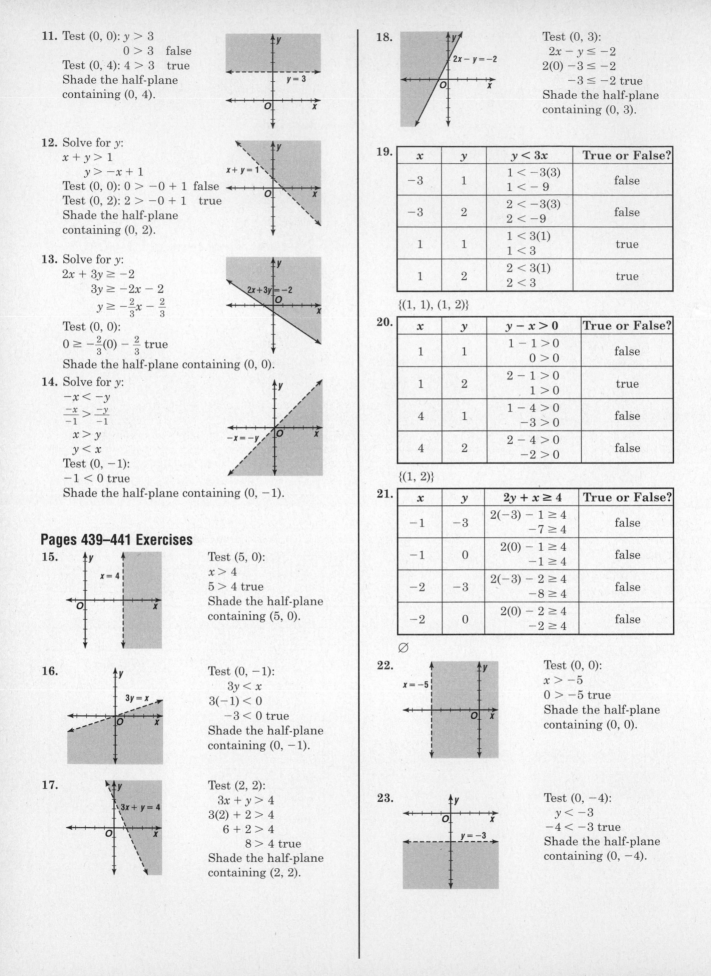

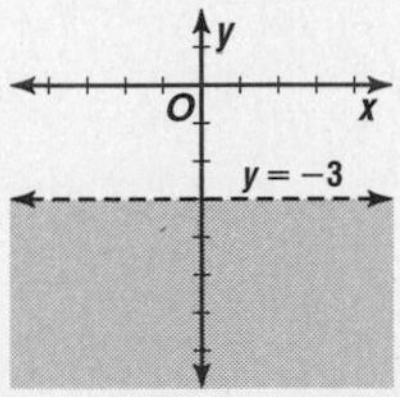

Test (0, −4):
$y < -3$
$-4 < -3$ true
Shade the half-plane containing (0, −4).

24.

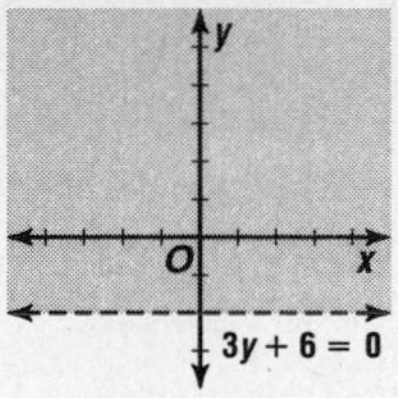

Solve for y: $3y + 6 > 0$

$3y > -6$

$y > -2$

Test (0, 0):

$y > -2$

$0 > -2$ true

Shade the half-plane containing (0, 0).

25.

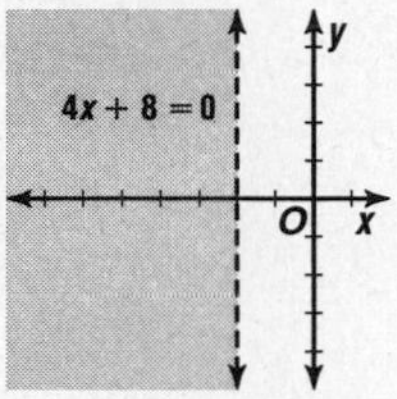

Solve for x: $4x + 8 < 0$

$4x < -8$

$x < -2$

Test (−3, 0):

$-3 < -2$ true

Shade the half-plane containing (−3, 0).

26.

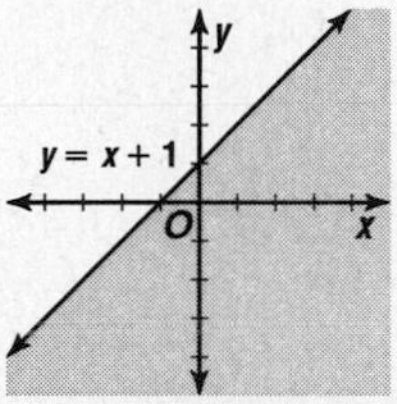

Test (0, 0):

$y \le x + 1$

$0 \le 0 + 1$

$0 \le 1$ true

Shade the half-plane containing (0, 0).

27.

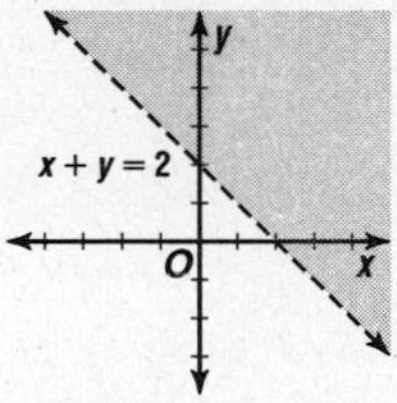

Solve for y:

$x + y > 2$

$y > -x + 2$

Test (0, 3):

$3 > 0 + 2$

$3 > 2$ true

Shade the half-plane containing (0, 3).

28.

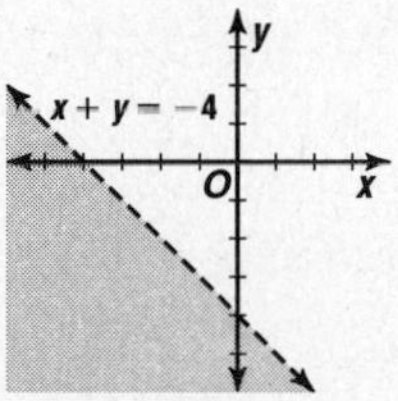

Solve for y:

$x + y < -4$

$y < -x - 4$

Test (−5, 0):

$0 < -(-5) - 4$

$0 < 1$ true

Shade the half-plane containing (−5, 0).

29.

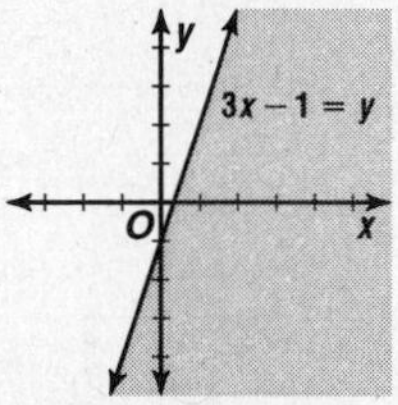

Test (1, 0):

$3x - 1 \ge y$

$3(1) - 1 \ge 0$

$2 \ge 0$ true

Shade the half-plane containing (1, 0).

30.

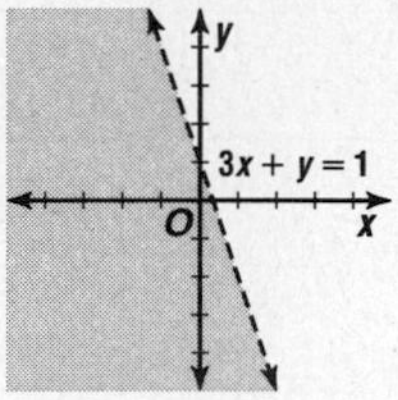

Solve for y:

$3x + y < 1$

$y < -3x + 1$

Test (0, 0):

$0 < -3\,(0) + 1$

$0 < 1$ true

Shade the half-plane containing (0, 0).

31.

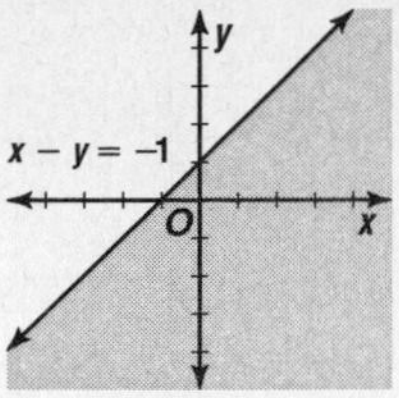

Solve for y:

$x - y \ge -1$

$-y \ge -x - 1$

$\frac{-y}{-1} \le \frac{-x}{-1} - \frac{1}{-1}$

Test (0, 0):

$y \le x + 1$

$0 \le 0 + 1$

$0 \le 1$ true

Shade the half-plane containing (0, 0).

32.

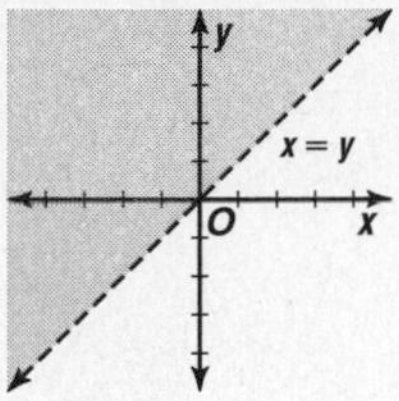

Test (0, 1):

$x < 1$

$0 < 1$ true

Shade the half-plane containing (0, 1).

33.

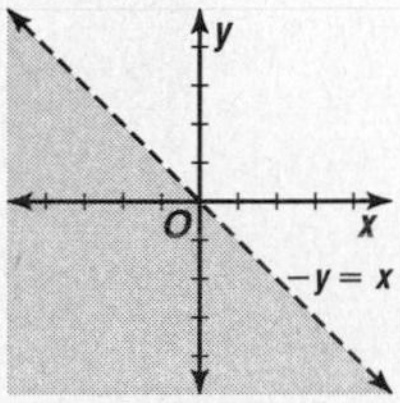

Solve for y:

$-y > x$

$\frac{-y}{-1} < \frac{x}{-1}$

$y < -x$

Test (−1, 0):

$0 < -(-1)$

$0 < 1$ true

Shade the half-plane containing (−1, 0).

34.

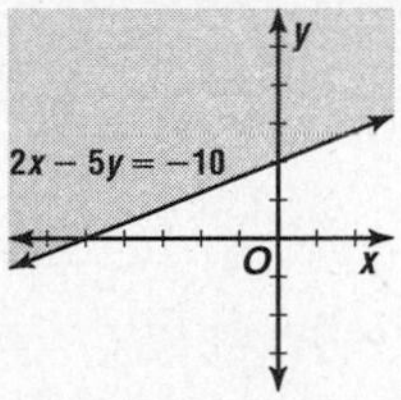

Solve for y:

$2x - 5y \le -10$

$-5y \le -2x - 10$

$\frac{-5y}{-5} \ge \frac{-2x}{-5} \frac{-10}{-5}$

$y \ge \frac{2x}{5} + 2$

Test (0, 3):

$3 \ge \frac{2(0)}{5} + 2$

$3 \ge 2$ true

Shade the half-plane containing (0, 3).

35.

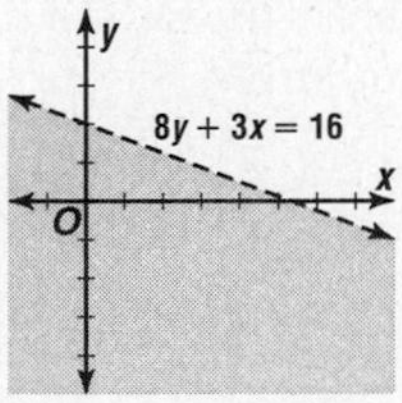

Solve for y:

$8y + 3x < 16$

$8y < -3x + 16$

$\frac{8y}{8} < \frac{-3x}{8} + \frac{16}{8}$

$y < \frac{-3x}{8} + 2$

Test (0, 0):

$0 < \frac{-3(0)}{8} + 2$

$0 < 2$ true

Shade the half-plane containing (0, 0).

36. $|y| \ge 2$

$y \le -2$ or $y \ge 2$

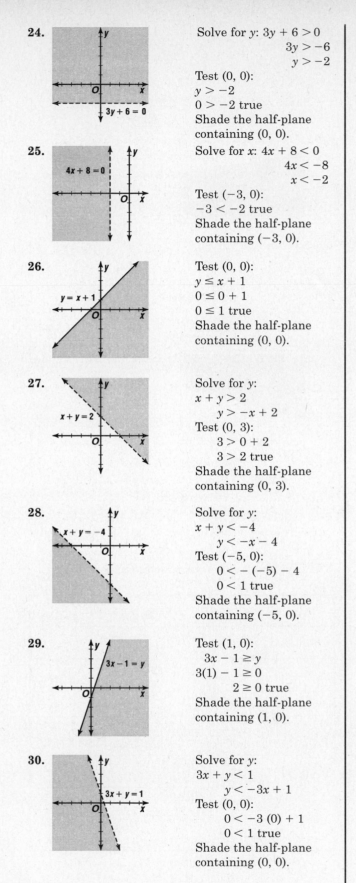

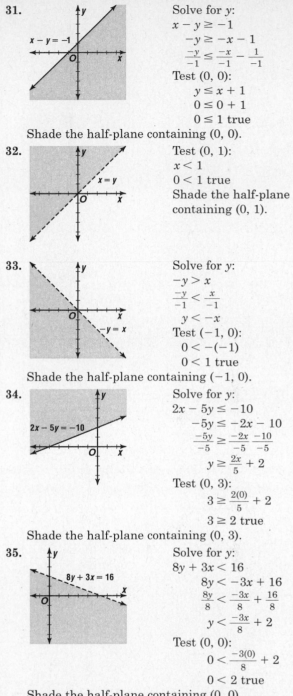

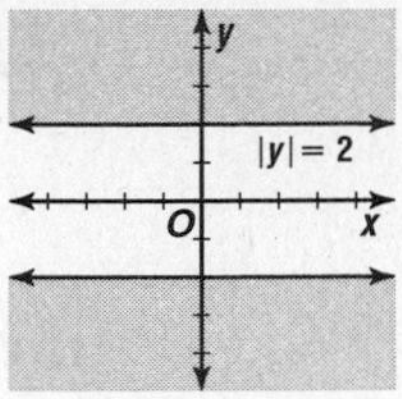

Only one of the two shaded areas will be a solution at any one time.

37. $y > |x + 2|$

$y > x + 2$ or $-y < x + 2$

$y > -x - 2$

Test (0, 3):

$y > x + 2$	$y > -x - 2$
$3 > 0 + 2$	$3 > -0 - 2$
$3 > 2$ true	$3 > -2$ true
Shade the half-plane containing (0, 3).	Shade the half-plane containing (0, 3).

The solution is the intersection of these two shaded areas.

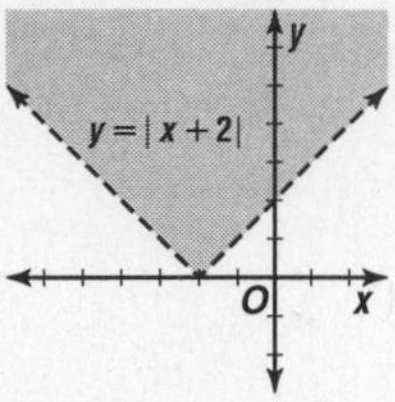

38. $y > 2$ and $x < 3$

Test (0, 4):	Test (0, 0):
$4 > 2$ true	$0 < 3$ true
Shade the half-plane containing (0,4).	Shade the half-plane containing (0, 0).

The solution is the intersection of these two shaded areas.

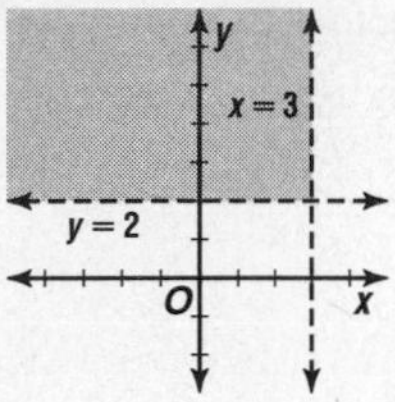

39. $y \leq -x$ and $x \geq -3$

Test (0, −1): $0 \leq -(-1)$	Test (0, 0): $0 \geq -3$
$0 < 1$ true	true
Shade the half-plane containing (0, −1).	Shade the half-plane containing (0, 0).

The solution is the intersection of these two shaded areas.

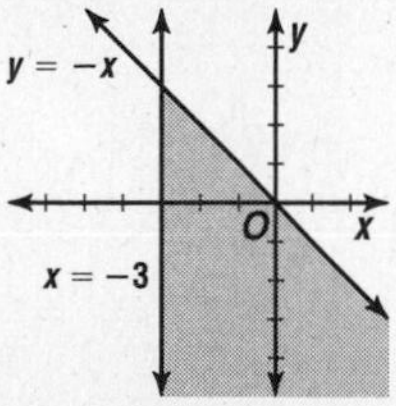

40. Enter: [2nd] [DRAW] 7 [X,T,θ] [−] 1 [,] 10 [)] [ENTER]

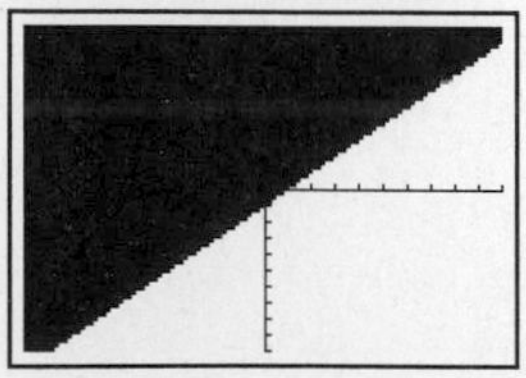

41. Solve for y: $4y + x < 16$

$$4y < -x + 16$$
$$\frac{4y}{4} < \frac{-x}{4} + \frac{16}{4}$$
$$y < -0.25x + 4$$

Enter: [2nd] [DRAW] 7 [(−)] 10 [,] [(−)] .25 [X,T,θ] [+] 4 [)] [ENTER]

42. Solve for y: $x - 2y < 4$

$$-2y < -x + 4$$
$$\frac{-2y}{-2} > \frac{-x}{-2} + \frac{4}{-2}$$
$$y > 0.5x - 2$$

Enter: [2nd] [DRAW] 7 .5 [X,T,θ] [−] 2 [,] 10 [)] [ENTER]

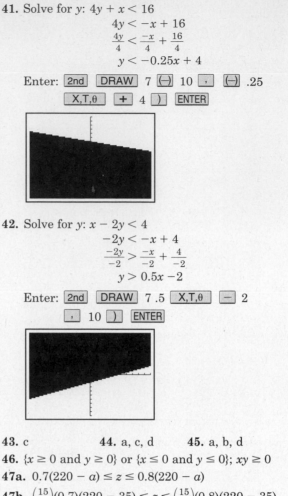

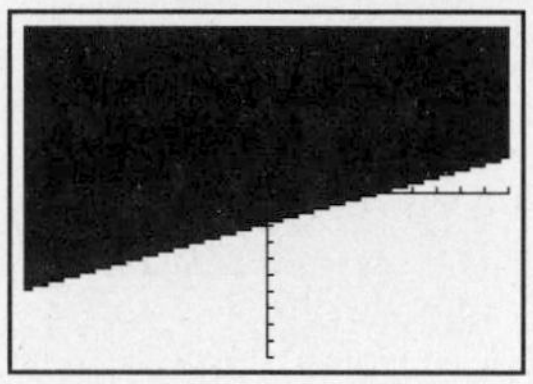

43. c **44.** a, c, d **45.** a, b, d

46. $\{x \geq 0$ and $y \geq 0\}$ or $\{x \leq 0$ and $y \leq 0\}$; $xy \geq 0$

47a. $0.7(220 - a) \leq z \leq 0.8(220 - a)$

47b. $\left(\frac{15}{60}\right)(0.7)(220 - 35) \leq z \leq \left(\frac{15}{60}\right)(0.8)(220 - 35)$

$$(0.25)(0.7)(185) \leq z \leq (0.25)(0.8)(185)$$
$$32 \leq z \leq 37$$

47c. improve cardiovascular conditioning

48a.

Year	x	y	$x + 350 > y$	True or False?
1987–88	14	278	$14 + 350 > 278$ $364 > 278$	true
1988–89	8	322	$8 + 350 > 322$ $358 > 322$	true
1989–90	10	260	$10 + 350 > 260$ $360 > 260$	true
1990–91	11	366	$11 + 350 > 366$ $361 > 366$	false
1991–92	15	401	$15 + 350 > 401$ $365 > 401$	false
1992–93	19	569	$19 + 350 > 569$ $369 > 569$	false
1993–94	21	553	$21 + 350 > 553$ $371 > 553$	false

1987–88, 1988–89, 1989–90

48b.

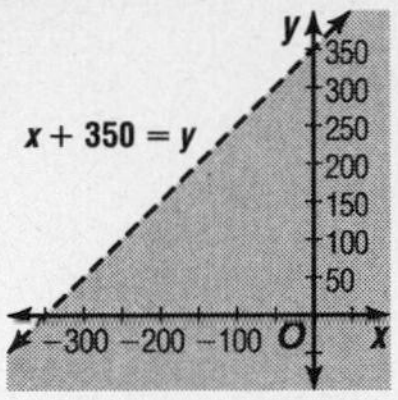

48c. See students' work.

49. LV: 260   Outliers:

Q1: 278 $x \geq 553 + 1.5(275)$

Q2: 366 $x \geq 965.5$

$x \leq 278 - 1.5(275)$

Q3: 553 $x \leq -134.5$

GV: 569   There are no outliers.

IQR = 553 − 278 = 275

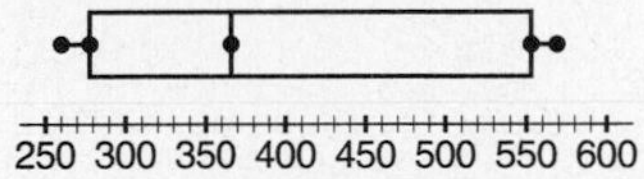

50.

$$5 - |2x - 7| > 2$$
$$5 - 5 - |2x - 7| > 2 - 5$$
$$-|2x - 7| > -3$$
$$|2x - 7| < 3$$

$2x - 7 > -3$ and $2x - 7 < 3$

$2x - 7 + 7 > -3 + 7$ $2x - 7 + 7 < 3 + 7$

$2x > 4$ $2x < 10$

$\frac{2x}{2} > \frac{4}{2}$ $\frac{2x}{2} < \frac{10}{2}$

$x > 2$ $x < 5$

$\{x \mid 2 < x < 5\}$

51. solve for y:

$8x - 2y = 7$

$-2y = -8x + 7$

$\frac{-2y}{-2} = \frac{-8x}{-2} + \frac{7}{-2}$

$y = 4x - \frac{7}{2}$

$m = 4$

$y = mx + b$

$y = 4x - 2$

solve for y:

$2x - 9y = 18$

$-9y = -2x + 18$

$\frac{-9y}{-9} = \frac{-2x}{-9} + \frac{18}{-9}$

$y = \frac{2x}{9} - 2$

y-intercept: −2

52.

$$m = \frac{y_2 - y_1}{x_2 - x_1}$$
$$4 = \frac{4 - r}{r - (-4)}$$
$$\frac{4}{1} = \frac{4 - r}{r + 4}$$
$$4(r + 4) = 4 - r$$
$$4r + 16 = 4 - r$$
$$4r + r + 16 = 4 - r + r$$
$$5r + 16 = 4$$
$$5r + 16 - 16 = 4 - 16$$
$$5r = -12$$
$$r = -\frac{12}{5}$$

53. solve for y:

$-y + \frac{2}{7}x = 1$

$-y = -\frac{2}{7}x + 1$

$y = \frac{2}{7}x - 1$

$m = \frac{2}{7}$, y-intercept: −1

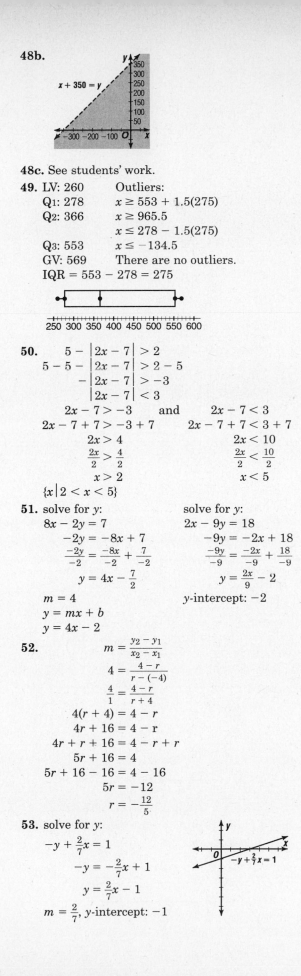

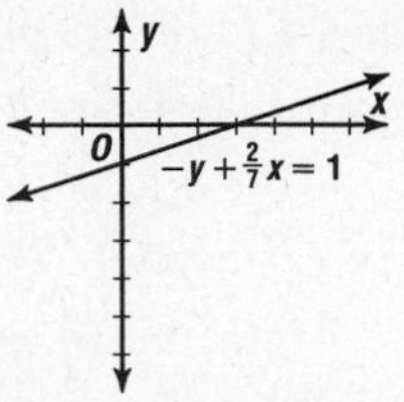

54. $\{(-1, 4), (2, 3), (0, -4), (9, 17)\}$

55. $x = 0.985(140.32)$

$x = \$138.22$

56. Let x = the first consecutive integer.
Then $x + 1$ = the next integer
and $x + 2$ = the greatest of the integers.

$$x + (x + 1) + (x + 2) = 87$$
$$3x + 3 = 87$$
$$3x = 84$$
$$x = 28$$

$x + 1 = 28 + 1 = 29$ $x + 2 = 28 + 2 = 30$

The three consecutive integers are 28, 29, and 30.

Chapter 7 Study Guide and Assessment

Page 443 Understanding and Using the Vocabulary

1. h multiplication property for inequality
2. b addition property for inequality
3. i set builder rotation
4. c compound inequality, k union
5. c compound inequality, f intersection
6. j subtraction property for inequality
7. d division property for inequality
8. e greater than   **9.** g less than
10. c compound inequality, f intersection
11. a absolute value inequality

Pages 444–446 Skills and Concepts

12.

$$r + 7 > -5$$
$$r + 7 - 7 > -5 - 7$$
$$r > -12$$

$\{r \mid r > -12\}$

13.

$$-35 + 6n < 7n$$
$$-35 + 6n - 6n < 7n - 6n$$
$$-35 < n$$

$\{n \mid n > -35\}$

14.

$$2t - 0.3 \leq 5.7 + t$$
$$2t - t - 0.3 \leq 5.7 + t - t$$
$$t - 0.3 \leq 5.7$$
$$t + 0.3 - 0.3 \leq 5.7 + 0.3$$
$$t \leq 6$$

$\{t \mid t \leq 6\}$

15.

$$-14 + p \geq 4 - (-2p)$$
$$-14 + p \geq 4 + 2p$$
$$-14 + p - p \geq 4 + 2p - p$$
$$-14 \geq 4 + p$$
$$-14 - 4 \geq 4 - 4 + p$$
$$-18 \geq p$$

$\{p \mid p \leq -18\}$

16. Let n = the number.

$$n - 3 \geq 2$$
$$n - 3 + 3 \geq 2 + 3$$
$$n \geq 5$$

$\{n \mid n \geq 5\}$

17. let n = the number.

$$3n > 4n - 8$$
$$3n - 4n > 4n - 4n - 8$$
$$-n > -8$$
$$\frac{-n}{-1} < \frac{-8}{-1}$$
$$n < 8$$

$\{n \mid n < 8\}$

18. $7x \ge -56$

$\frac{7x}{7} \ge \frac{-56}{7}$

$x \ge -8$

$\{x \mid x \ge -8\}$

19. $90 \le -6w$

$\frac{90}{-6} \ge \frac{-6w}{-6}$

$-15 \ge w$

$\{w \mid w \le -15\}$

20. $\frac{2}{3}k \ge \frac{2}{15}$

$\frac{3}{2}\left(\frac{2}{3}k\right) \ge \frac{3}{2}\left(\frac{2}{15}\right)$

$k \ge \frac{1}{5}$

$\left\{k \mid k \ge \frac{1}{5}\right\}$

21. $9.6 < 0.3x$

$\frac{9.6}{0.3} < \frac{0.3x}{0.3}$

$32 < x$

$\{x \mid x > 32\}$

22. Let n = the number.

$6n \le 32.4$

$\frac{6n}{6} \le \frac{32.4}{6}$

$n \le 5.4$

$\{n \mid n \le 5.4\}$

23. Let n = the number.

$-\frac{3}{4}n \le 30$

$-\frac{4}{3}\left(\frac{-3}{4}n\right) \ge -\frac{4}{3}(30)$

$n \ge -40$

$\{n \mid n \ge -40\}$

24. $\frac{x-5}{3} > -3$

$3\left(\frac{x-5}{3}\right) > 3(-3)$

$x - 5 > -9$

$x - 5 + 5 > -9 + 5$

$x > -4$

$\{-3, -2, -1, \ldots 4, 5\}$

25. $3x \le -4x + 7$

$3x + 4x \le -4x + 4x + 7$

$7x \le 7$

$\frac{7x}{7} \le \frac{7}{7}$

$x \le 1$

$\{-5, -4, \ldots 0, 1\}$

26. $2r - 3.1 > 0.5$

$2r - 3.1 + 3.1 > 0.5 + 3.1$

$2r > 3.6$

$\frac{2r}{2} > \frac{3.6}{2}$

$r > 1.8$

$\{r \mid r > 1.8\}$

27. $4y - 11 \ge 8y + 7$

$4y - 4y - 11 \ge 8y - 4y + 7$

$-11 \ge 4y + 7$

$-11 - 7 \ge 4y + 7 - 7$

$-18 \ge 4y$

$-\frac{18}{4} \ge \frac{4y}{4}$

$-\frac{9}{2} \ge y$

$\left\{y \mid y \le -\frac{9}{2}\right\}$

28. $-3(m - 2) > 12$

$-3m + 6 > 12$

$-3m + 6 - 6 > 12 - 6$

$-3m > 6$

$\frac{-3m}{3} < \frac{6}{-3}$

$m < -2$

$\{m \mid m < -2\}$

29. $-5x + 3 < 3x + 23$

$-5x + 5x + 3 < 3x + 5x + 23$

$3 < 8x + 23$

$3 - 23 < 8x + 23 - 23$

$-20 < 8x$

$\frac{-20}{8} < \frac{8x}{8}$

$-\frac{5}{2} < x$

$\left\{x \mid x > -\frac{5}{2}\right\}$

30. $4(n - 1) < 7n + 8$

$4n - 4 < 7n + 8$

$4n - 4n - 4 < 7n - 4n + 8$

$-4 < 3n + 8$

$-4 - 8 < 3n + 8 - 8$

$-12 < 3n$

$\frac{-12}{3} < \frac{3n}{3}$

$-4 < n$

$\{n \mid n > -4\}$

31. $0.3(z - 4) \le 0.8(0.2z + 2)$

$0.3z - 1.2 \le 0.16z + 1.6$

$0.3z - 0.16z - 1.2 \le 0.16z - 0.16z + 1.6$

$0.14z - 1.2 \le 1.6$

$0.14z - 1.2 + 1.2 \le 1.6 + 1.2$

$0.14z \le 2.8$

$\frac{0.14z}{0.14} \le \frac{2.8}{0.14}$

$z \le 20$

$\{z \mid z \le 20\}$

32. $x - 5 < -2$ and $x - 5 > 2$

$x - 5 + 5 < -2 + 5$ | $x - 5 + 5 > 2 + 5$

$x < 3$ | $x > 7$

$\varnothing$

33. $2a + 5 \le 7$ or $2a \ge a - 3$

$2a + 5 \le 7 - 5$ | $2a - a \ge a - a - 3$

$2a \le 2$ | $a \ge -3$

$\frac{2a}{2} \le \frac{2}{2}$

$a \le 1$

$\{a \mid a$ is a real number$\}$

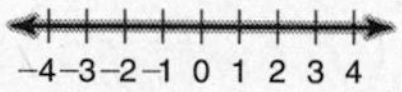

34. $4r \ge 3r + 7$ and $3r + 7 < r + 29$

$4r - 3r \ge 3r - 3r + 7$ | $3r - r + 7 < r - r + 29$

$r \ge 7$ | $2r + 7 < 29$

$2r + 7 - 7 < 29 - 7$

$2r < 22$

$\frac{2r}{2} < \frac{22}{2}$

$r < 11$

$\{r \mid 7 \le r < 11\}$

35. $-2b - 4 \ge 7$ or $-5 + 3b \le 10$

$-2b + 4 - 4 \ge 7 + 4$ | $-5 + 5 + 3b \le 10 + 5$

$-2b \ge 11$ | $3b \le 15$

$\frac{-2b}{-2} \le \frac{11}{-2}$ | $\frac{3b}{3} \le \frac{15}{3}$

$b \le -\frac{11}{2}$ | $b \le 5$

$\{b \mid b \le 5\}$

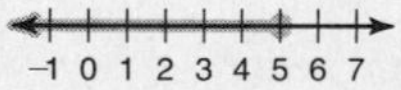

36. $a \neq 6$ and $3a + 1 > 10$

$3a + 1 - 1 > 10 - 1$

$3a > 9$

$\frac{3a}{3} > \frac{9}{3}$

$a > 3$

$\{a \mid a > 3 \text{ and } a \neq 6\}$

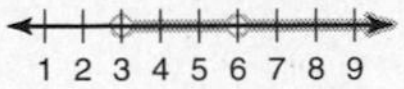

37a–f.

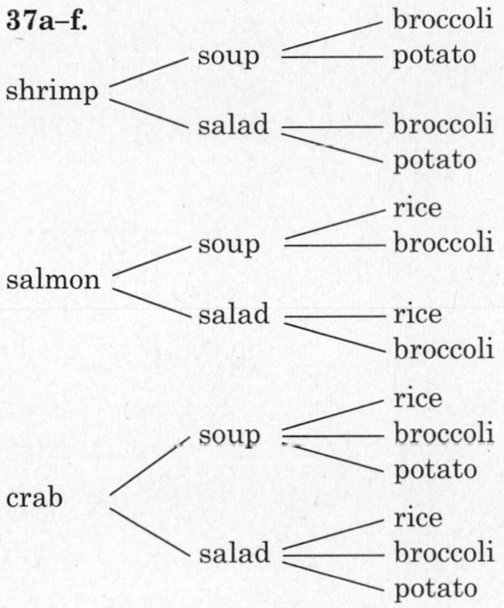

37a. $\frac{4}{14} = \frac{2}{7}$ **37b.** $\frac{7}{14} = \frac{1}{2}$ **37c.** $\frac{4}{14} = \frac{2}{7}$

37d. 0 **37e.** $\frac{3}{14}$ **37f.** $\frac{1}{14}$

38. **First Choice** **Second Choice** **Number of Matching Pairs**

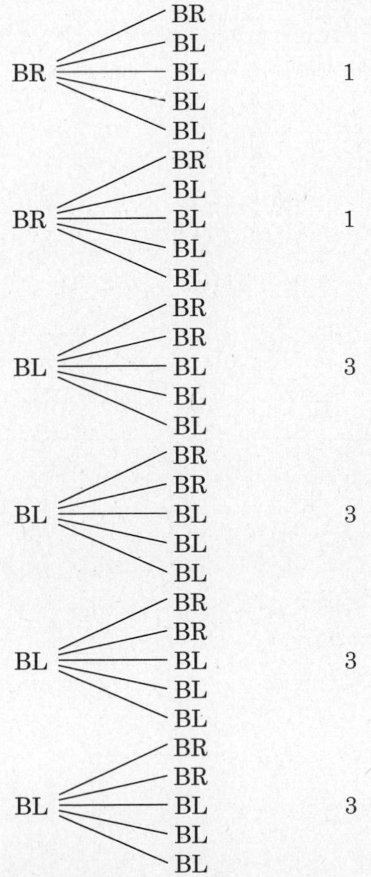

$\frac{14}{30} = \frac{7}{15} \approx 0.4\overline{6}$

39. $|y + 5| > 0$

$y + 5 > 0$ or $y + 5 < 0$

$y + 5 - 5 > 0$ $y + 5 - 5$

$< 0 - 5$

$y > -5$ $y < -5$

$\{y \mid y > -5 \text{ or } y < -5\}$

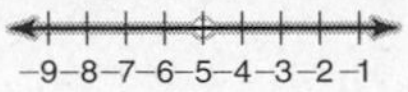

40. $|1 - n| \leq 5$

$1 - n \geq -5$ and $1 - n \leq 5$

$-1 + 1 - n \geq -5 - 1$ $1 - 1 - n \leq 5 - 1$

$-n \geq -6$ $-n \leq 4$

$\frac{-n}{-1} \leq \frac{-6}{-1}$ $\frac{-n}{-1} \geq \frac{4}{-1}$

$n \leq 6$ $n \geq -4$

$\{n \mid 6 \geq n \geq -4\}$

41. $|4k + 2| \leq 14$

$4k + 2 \geq -14$ and $4k + 2 \leq 14$

$4k + 2 - 2 \geq -14 - 2$ $4k + 2 - 2 \leq 14 - 2$

$4k \geq -16$ $4k \leq 12$

$\frac{4k}{4} \geq \frac{-16}{4}$ $\frac{4k}{4} \leq \frac{12}{4}$

$k \geq -4$ $k \leq 3$

$\{k \mid 3 \geq k \geq -4\}$

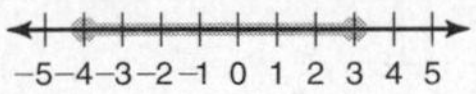

42. $|3x - 12| < 12$

$3x - 12 > -12$ and $3x - 12 < 12 + 12$

$3x - 12 + 12 > -12 + 12$ $3x - 12 + 12 < 12 + 12$

$3x > 0$ $3x < 24$

$\frac{3x}{3} > \frac{0}{3}$ $\frac{3x}{3} < \frac{24}{3}$

$x > 0$ $x < 8$

$\{x \mid 0 < x < 8\}$

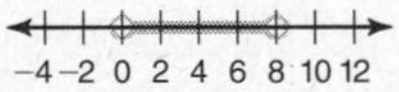

43. $|13 - 5y| \geq 8$

$13 - 5y \leq -8$ or $13 - 5y \geq 8$

$13 - 13 - 5y \leq -8 - 13$ $13 - 13 - 5y \geq 8 - 13$

$-5y \leq -21$ $-5y \geq -5$

$\frac{-5y}{-5} \geq \frac{-21}{-5}$ $\frac{-5y}{-5} \leq \frac{-5}{-5}$

$y \geq \frac{21}{5}$ $y \leq 1$

$\{y \mid y \geq \frac{21}{5} \text{ or } y \leq 1\}$

44. $\left|2p - \frac{1}{2}\right| > \frac{9}{2}$

$2p - \frac{1}{2} < -\frac{9}{2}$ or $2p - \frac{1}{2} > \frac{9}{2}$

$2p - \frac{1}{2} + \frac{1}{2} < \frac{9}{2} + \frac{1}{2}$ $2p - \frac{1}{2} + \frac{1}{2} > \frac{9}{2} + \frac{1}{2}$

$2p < -4$ $2p > 5$

$\frac{2p}{2} < \frac{-4}{2}$ $\frac{2p}{2} > \frac{5}{2}$

$p < -2$ $p > \frac{5}{2}$

$\left\{p \mid p < -2 \text{ or } p > \frac{5}{2}\right\}$

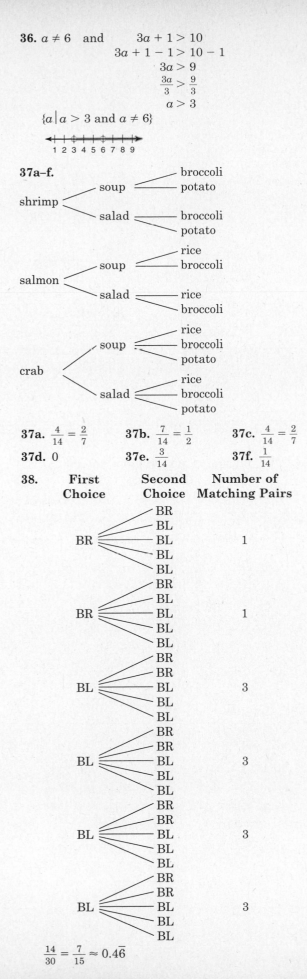

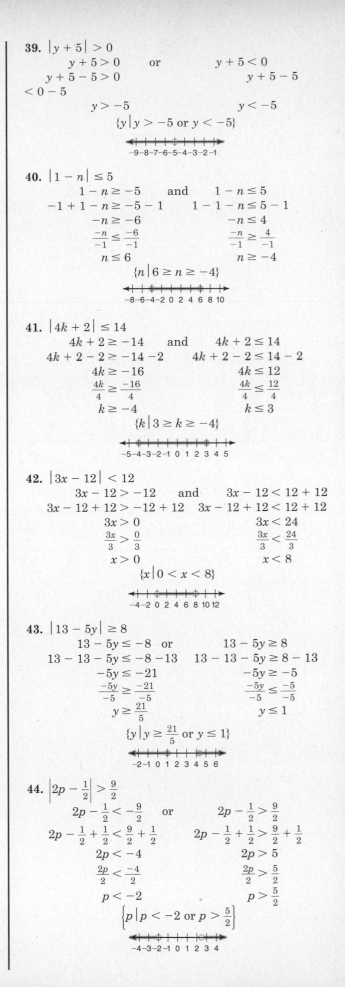

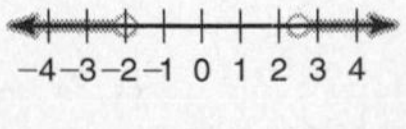

45. LV: 125

Q1: $\frac{200 + 212}{2} = 206$

Q2: 239

Q3: $\frac{250 + 274}{2} = 262$

GV: 348

IQR: 56

Outliers:

$x \geq 262 + 1.5(56)$

$x \geq 346$

$x \leq 206 - 1.5(56)$

$x \leq 122$

350 is an outlier.

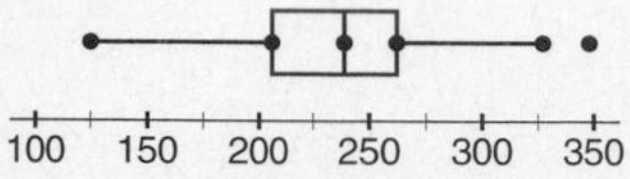

46. yes, 348

47.

x	y	$3x + 4y < 7$	True or False?
1	1	$3(1) + 4(1) < 7$ $7 < 7$	false
2	−1	$3(2) + 4(-1) < 7$ $2 < 7$	true
−1	1	$3(-1) + 4(1) < 7$ $1 < 7$	true
−2	4	$3(-2) + 4(4) < 7$ $10 < 7$	false

{(2, −1), (−1, 1)}

48.

x	y	$4y - 8 \geq 0$	True or False?
5	−1	$4(-1) - 8 \geq 0$ $-12 \geq 0$	false
0	2	$4(2) - 8 \geq 0$ $0 \geq 0$	true
2	5	$4(5) - 8 \geq 0$ $12 \geq 0$	true
−2	0	$4(0) - 8 \geq 0$ $-8 \geq 0$	false

{(0, 2), (2, 5)}

49.

x	y	$-2x < 8 - y$	True or False?
5	10	$-2(5) < 8 - 10$ $-10 < -2$	true
3	6	$-2(3) < 8 - 6$ $-6 < 2$	true
−4	0	$-2(-4) < 8 - 0$ $8 < 8$	false
−3	6	$-2(-3) < 8 - 6$ $6 < 2$	false

{(5, 10), (3, 6)}

50. Solve for y: $x + 2y > 5$

$2y > -x + 5$

$\frac{2y}{2} > -\frac{x}{2} + \frac{5}{2}$

$y > -\frac{x}{2} + \frac{5}{2}$

Test (0, 4): $4 > \frac{0}{2} + \frac{5}{2}$

$4 > \frac{5}{2}$ true

Shade the half-plane containing (0, 4).

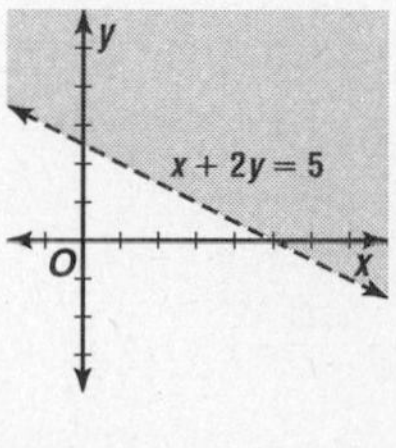

51. Solve for y: $4x - y \leq 8$

$-y \leq -4x + 8$

$\frac{-y}{-1} \geq \frac{-4x}{-1} + \frac{8}{-1}$

$y \geq 4x - 8$

Test (0, 0): $0 \geq 4(0) - 8$

$0 \geq -8$ true

Shade the half-plane containing (0, 0).

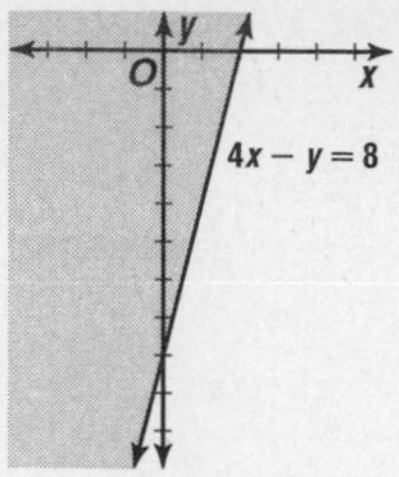

52. Solve for y: $\frac{1}{2}y \geq x + 4$

$2\left(\frac{1}{2}y\right) \geq 2(x + 4)$

$y \geq 2x + 8$

Test (0, 9): $9 \geq 2(0) + 8$

$9 \geq 8$ true

Shade the half-plane containing (0, 9).

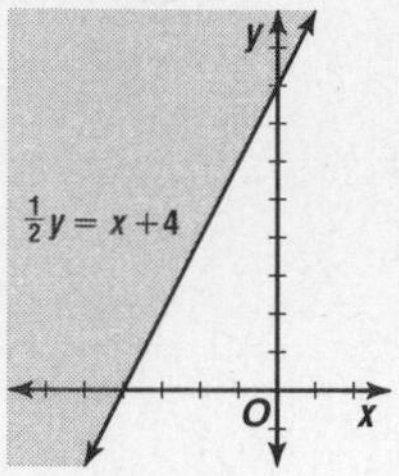

53. Solve for y: $3x - 2y < 6$

$-2y < -3x + 6$

$\frac{-2y}{-2} > \frac{-3x}{-2} + \frac{6}{-2}$

$y > \frac{3x}{2} - 3$

Test (0, 0): $0 > \frac{3}{2}(0) - 3$

$0 > -3$ true

Shade the half-plane containing (0, 0).

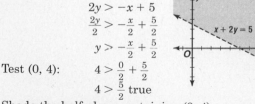

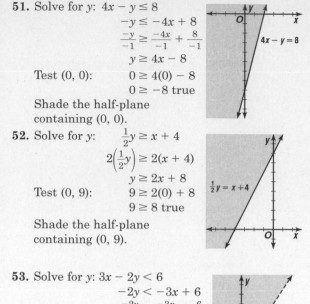

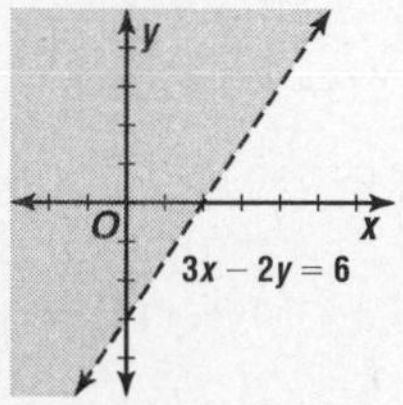

Page 446 Applications and Problem Solving

54. Let x = the first integer.

Then $x + 1$ = the next integer

and $x + 2$ = the greatest of the three integers.

$x + (x + 1) + (x + 2) < 100$

$3x + 3 < 100$

$3x + 3 - 3 < 100 - 3$

$3x < 97$

$\frac{3x}{3} < \frac{97}{3}$

$x < 32\frac{1}{3}$

$x = 32$ $\quad x + 1 = 32 + 1 = 33$ $\quad x + 2 = 32 + 2 = 34$

The three integers are 32, 33, and 34.

55. $55 \leq 1.5x + 30 \leq 60$

$55 \leq 1.5x + 30$

$55 - 30 \leq 1.5x + 30 - 30$

$25 \leq 1.5x$

$\frac{25}{1.5} \leq \frac{1.5x}{1.5}$

$16\frac{2}{3} \leq x$

and

$1.5x + 30 \leq 60$

$1.5x + 30 - 30 \leq 60 - 30$

$1.5x \leq 30$

$\frac{1.5x}{1.5} \leq \frac{30}{1.5}$

$x \leq 20$

17 to 20 books

56a–c.

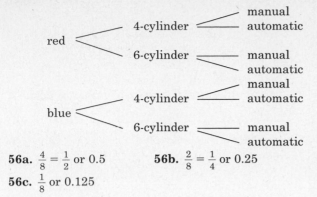

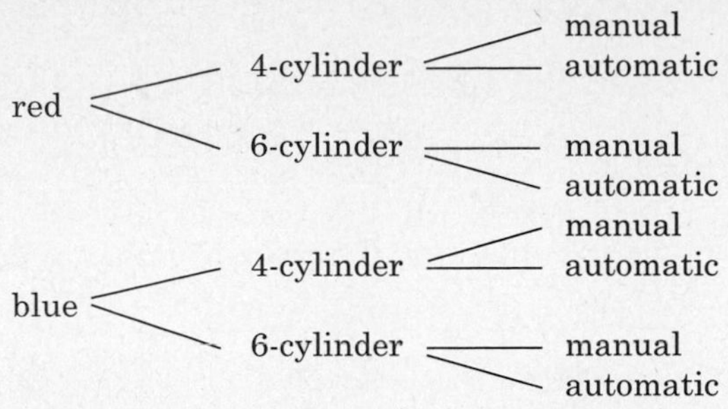

56a. $\frac{4}{8} = \frac{1}{2}$ or 0.5

56b. $\frac{2}{8} = \frac{1}{4}$ or 0.25

56c. $\frac{1}{8}$ or 0.125

Page 447 Alternative Assessment: Thinking Critically

- If each side of a true inequality is multiplied or divided by the same positive number, the resulting inequality is also true. If each side of the inequality is multiplied or divided by the same negative number, the direction of the inequality must be reversed so that the resulting inequality is also true.

  If you add a positive or negative number to each side of a true inequality or subtract a positive or negative number from each side of a true inequality, the resulting equation is also true.
- There is no solution if $a \leq 0$.

Chapter 8 Solving Systems of Linear Equations and Inequalities

8-1A Graphing Technology Systems of Equations

Page 453 Exercises

1. Enter: [Y=] [X,T,θ] [+] 7 [ENTER] [(-)] [X,T,θ] [+] 9 [ZOOM] 8
   Using the TRACE function, the solution is (1, 8).
2. Solve for y:
   $x + y = 27$ $\quad$ $3x - y = 41$
   $y = -x + 27$ $\quad$ $-y = -3x + 41$
   $y = 3x - 41$
   Enter: [Y=] [(-)] [X,T,θ] [+] 27 [ENTER] 3 [X,T,θ] [−] 41 [ZOOM] 8
   Using the TRACE function, the solution is (17, 10).
3. Enter: [Y=] 3 [X,T,θ] [−] 4 [ENTER] [(-)] .5 [X,T,θ] [+] 6 [ZOOM] 6
   Use the INTERSECT feature by pressing: [2nd] [CALC] 5 [ENTER] [ENTER] [ENTER].
   The solution is (2.86, 4.57).
4. Solve for y: $x - y = 6$
   $-y = -x + 6$
   $y = x - 6$
   Enter: [Y=] [X,T,θ] [−] 6 [ENTER] 9 [ZOOM] 8
   Using the TRACE function, the solution is (15, 9).
5. Solve for y: $x + y = 5.35$ $\quad$ $3x - y = 3.75$
   $y = -x + 5.35$ $\quad$ $-y = -3x + 3.75$
   $y = 3x - 3.75$
   Enter: [Y=] [(-)] [X,T,θ] [+] 5.35 [ENTER] 3 [X,T,θ] [−] 3.75 [ZOOM] 6
   Use the INTERSECT feature by pressing [2nd] [CALC] 5 [ENTER] [ENTER] [ENTER].
   The solution is (2.28, 3.08).
6. Solve for y:
   $5x - 4y = 26$ $\quad$ $4x + 2y = 53.3$
   $-4y = -5x + 26$ $\quad$ $2y = -4x + 53.3$
   $y = 1.25x - 6.5$ $\quad$ $y = -2x + 26.65$
   Enter: [Y=] 1.25 [X,T,θ] [−] 6.5 [ENTER] [(-)] 2 [X,T,θ] [+] 26.65 [ZOOM] 6
   Use the INTERSECT feature by pressing [2nd] [CALC] 5 [ENTER] [ENTER] [ENTER].
   The solution is (10.2, 6.25).
7. Solve for y:
   $2x + 3y = 11$ $\quad$ $4x + y = -6$
   $3y = -2x + 11$ $\quad$ $y = -4x - 6$
   $y = -\frac{2}{3}x + \frac{11}{3}$
   Enter: [Y=] [(-)] [(] 2 [÷] 3 [)] [X,T,θ] [+] 11 [÷] 3 [ENTER] [(-)] 4 [X,T,θ] [−] 6 [ZOOM] 6
   Use the INTERSECT feature by pressing [2nd] [CALC] 5 [ENTER] [ENTER] [ENTER].
   The solution is (−2.9, 5.6).
8. Solve for y: $2.93x + y = 6.08$
   $y = -2.93x + 6.08$
   $8.32x - y = 4.11$
   $-y = -8.32x + 4.11$
   $y = 8.32x - 4.11$
   Enter: [Y=] [(-)] 2.93 [X,T,θ] [+] 6.08 [ENTER] 8.32 [X,T,θ] [−] 4.11 [ZOOM] 6
   Use the INTERSECT feature by pressing [2nd] [CALC] 5 [ENTER] [ENTER] [ENTER].
   The solution is (0.91, 3.43).
9. Solve for y: $125x - 200y = 800$
   $-200y = -125x + 800$
   $y = 0.625x - 4$
   $65x - 20y = 140$
   $-20y = -65x + 140$
   $y = 3.25x - 7$
   Enter: [Y=] .625 [X,T,θ] [−] 4 [ENTER] 3.25 [X,T,θ] [−] 7 [ZOOM] 6
   Use the INTERSECT feature by pressing [2nd] [CALC] 5 [ENTER] [ENTER] [ENTER].
   The solution is (1.14, −3.29).
10. Solve for y: $0.22x + 0.15y = 0.30$
    $0.15y = -0.22x + 0.30$
    $y = -\frac{22}{15}x + 2$
    $-0.33x + y = 6.22$
    $y = 0.33x + 6.22$
    Enter: [Y=] [(-)] [(] 22 [÷] 15 [)] [X,T,θ] [+] 2 [ENTER] .33 [X,T,θ] [+] 6.22 [ZOOM] 6
    Use the INTERSECT feature by pressing [2nd] [CALC] 5 [ENTER] [ENTER] [ENTER].
    The solution is (−2.35, 5.44).

8-1 Graphing Systems of Equations

Page 458 Check for Understanding

1. (2, 4); The graphs intersect at the point (2, 4) and (2, 4) is a solution of both equations.
2. Find an ordered pair that satisfies both equations.
3. The graphs are the same line.

4. Sample answer: (3, 0), (4, 1)

check: $x - y = 3$ $2x - 2y = 6$
$4 - 1 \stackrel{?}{=} 3$ $2(4) - 2(1) \stackrel{?}{=} 6$
$3 = 3$ ✔ $8 - 2 \stackrel{?}{=} 6$
$6 = 6$ ✔

check: $x - y = 3$ $2x - 2y = 6$
$3 - 0 \stackrel{?}{=} 3$ $2(3) - 2(0) \stackrel{?}{=} 6$
$3 = 3$ ✔ $6 - 0 \stackrel{?}{=} 6$
$6 = 6$ ✔

5. Sample answer: $x + y = 2$
$x - y = -8$

6. Graphs will vary, but lines must be parallel. Sample graph:

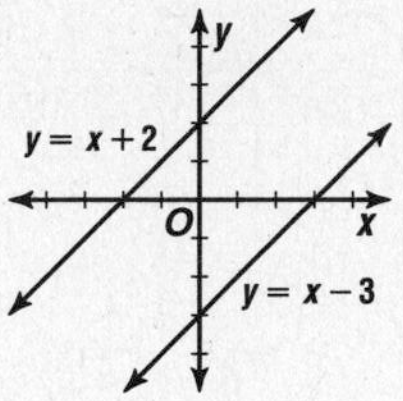

7. See students' work.

8. one solution; (4, 1)

9. no solution

10. one solution; (−3, 8)

11. one solution; (−6, 2)

12. $x - y = 6$ $2x + y = 0$
$-2 - (-4) \stackrel{?}{=} 6$ $2(-4) - 4 \stackrel{?}{=} 0$
$-2 + 4 \neq 6$ $-8 - 4 \neq 0$
no

13. $2x - y = 4$ $3x + y = 1$
$2(1) - (-2) \stackrel{?}{=} 4$ $3(1) + (-2) \stackrel{?}{=} 1$
$2 + 2 \stackrel{?}{=} 4$ $3 + (-2) \stackrel{?}{=} 1$
$4 = 4$ ✔ $1 = 1$ ✔
yes

14.

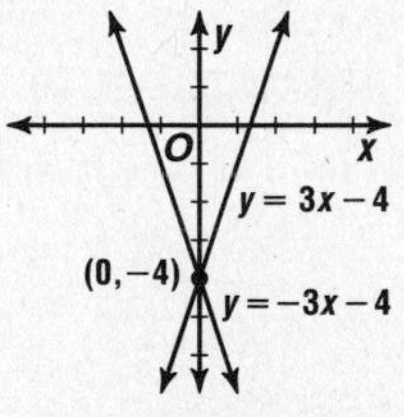

one solution; (0, −4)

15.

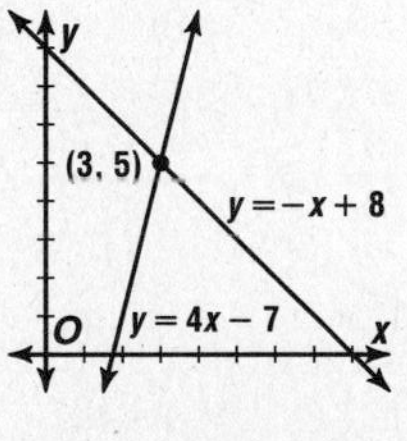

one solution; (3, 5)

16. $x + 2y = 5$
$x - x + 2y = 5 - x$
$2y = -x + 5$
$\frac{2y}{2} = -\frac{x}{2} + \frac{5}{2}$
$y = -\frac{1}{2}x + \frac{5}{2}$

$2x + 4y = 2$
$2x - 2x + 4y = 2 - 2x$
$4y = -2x + 2$
$\frac{4y}{4} = -\frac{2x}{4} + \frac{2}{4}$
$y = -\frac{1}{2}x + \frac{1}{2}$

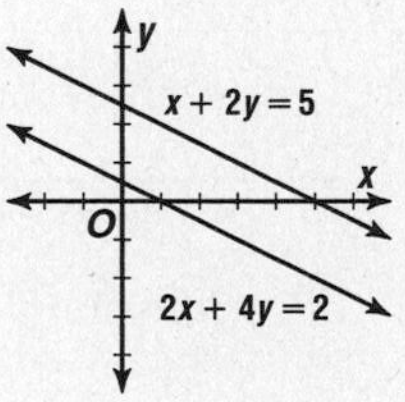

no solution

17. $y = -6$

$4x + y = 2$
$4x - 4x + y = 2 - 4x$
$y = -4x + 2$

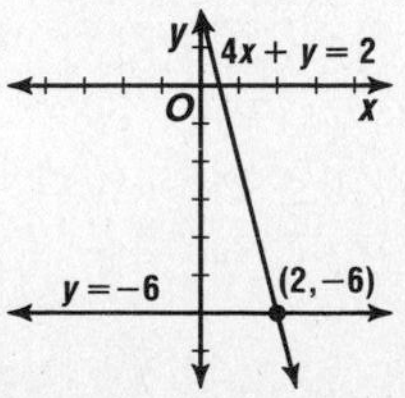

one solution; (2, −6)

18. $-4x - 6y = -8$
$-4x + 4x - 6y = -8 + 4x$
$-6y = 4x - 8$
$\frac{-6y}{-6} = \frac{4x}{-6} - \frac{8}{-6}$
$y = -\frac{2}{3}x + \frac{4}{3}$

$2x + 3y = 4$
$2x - 2x + 3y = 4 - 2x$
$3y = -2x + 4$
$\frac{3y}{3} = -\frac{2x}{3} + \frac{4}{3}$
$y = -\frac{2}{3}x + \frac{4}{3}$

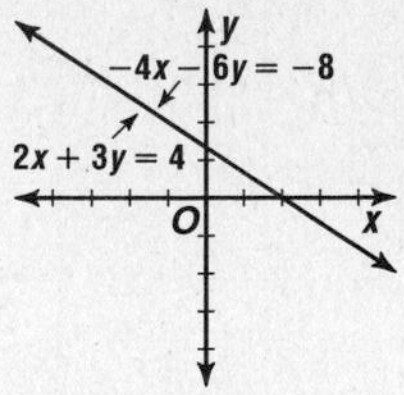

infinitely many solutions

19. $2x + y = -4$
$2x - 2x + y = -4 - 2x$
$y = -2x - 4$
$5x + 3y = -6$
$5x - 5x + 3y = -6 - 5x$
$3y = -5x - 6$
$\frac{3y}{3} = -\frac{5}{3}x - \frac{6}{3}$
$y = -\frac{5}{3}x - 2$

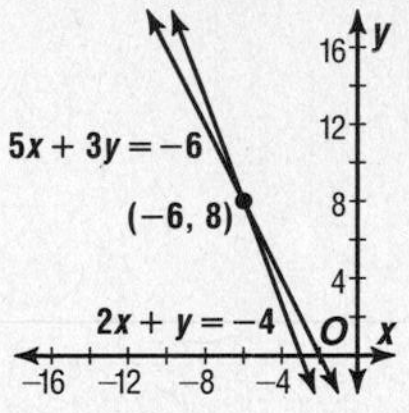

one solution; (−6, 8)

20a–b.

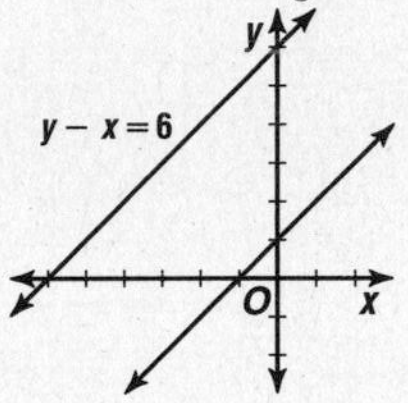

20c. The graphs of the system are parallel lines. The system has no solution and is inconsistent.

Pages 459–461 Exercises

21. one solution; (3, −1)

22. one solution; (6, 2)

23. no solution

24. one solution; (9, 5)

25. one solution; (3, 3)

26. one solution; (9, 1)

27.

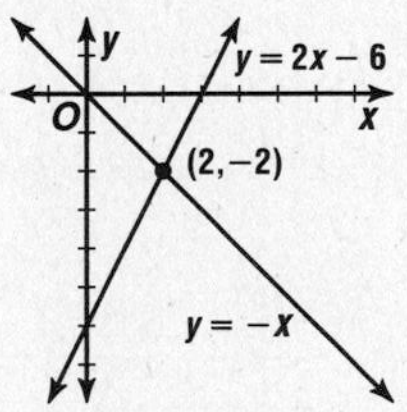

one solution; (2, −2)

28.

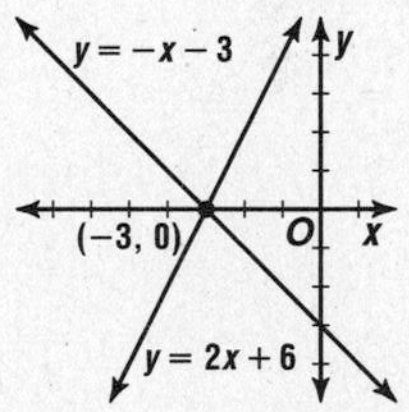

one solution; (−3, 0)

29. $y = 4x + 7$

$x + y = 2$
$x - x + y = 2 - x$
$y = -x + 2$

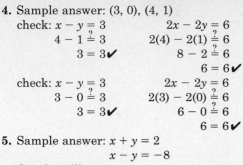

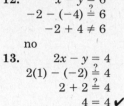

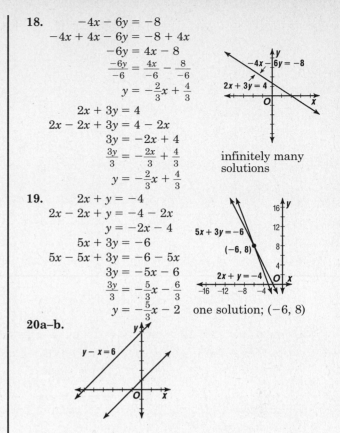

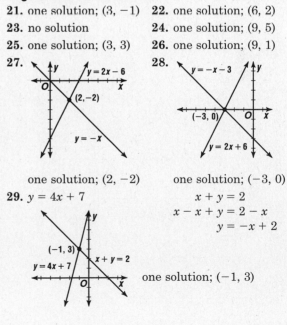

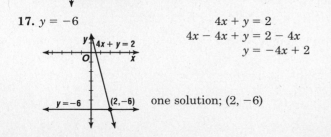

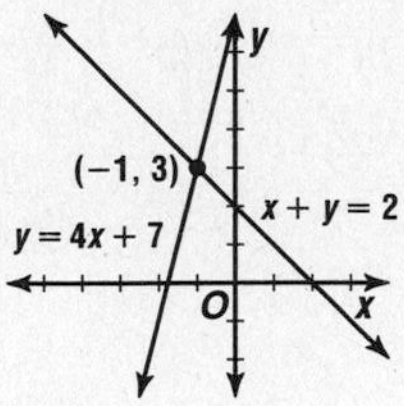

one solution; (−1, 3)

30. $y = \frac{1}{2}x$

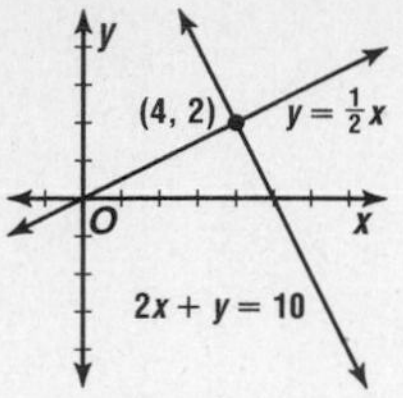

$$2x + y = 10$$
$$2x - 2x + y = 10 - 2x$$
$$y = -2x + 10$$

one solution; (4, 2)

31.
$$x + y = 2$$
$$x - x + y = 2 - x$$
$$y = -x + 2$$

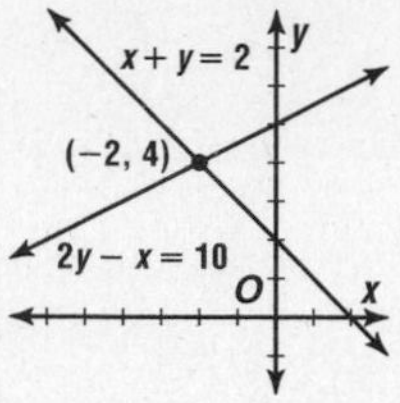

$$2y - x = 10$$
$$2y - x + x = 10 + x$$
$$2y = x + 10$$
$$\frac{2y}{2} = \frac{x}{2} + \frac{10}{2}$$
$$y = \frac{1}{2}x + 5$$

one solution; (−2, 4)

32.
$$3x + 2y = 12$$
$$3x - 3x + 2y = 12 - 3x$$
$$2y = -3x + 12$$
$$\frac{2y}{2} = \frac{-3x}{2} + \frac{12}{2}$$
$$y = -\frac{3}{2}x + 6$$
$$3x + 2y = 6$$
$$3x - 3x + 2y = 6 - 3x$$
$$2y = -3x + 6$$
$$\frac{2y}{2} = \frac{-3x}{2} + \frac{6}{2}$$
$$y = -\frac{3}{2}x + 3$$

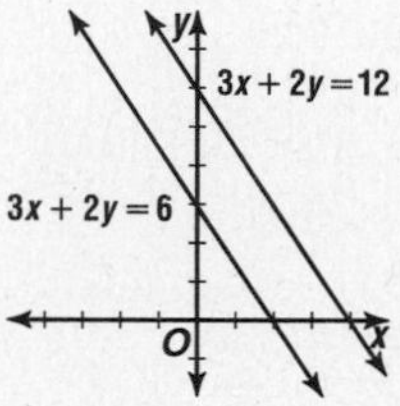

no solution

33.
$$3x + y = 6$$
$$3x - 3x + y = 6 - 3x$$
$$y = -3x + 6$$
$$x - 2y = 2$$
$$x - x - 2y = 2 - x$$
$$-2y = -x + 2$$
$$\frac{-2y}{-2} = \frac{-x}{-2} + \frac{2}{-2}$$
$$y = \frac{1}{2}x - 1$$

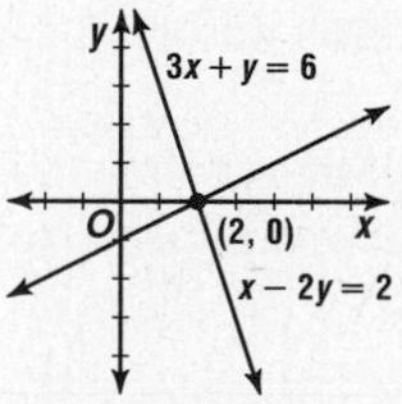

one solution; (2, 0)

34.
$$x - y = 2$$
$$x - x - y = 2 - x$$
$$-y = -x + 2$$
$$y = x - 2$$
$$3y + 2x = 9$$
$$3y + 2x - 2x = 9 - 2x$$
$$3y = -2x + 9$$
$$\frac{3y}{3} = \frac{-2x}{3} + \frac{9}{3}$$
$$y = -\frac{2}{3}x + 3$$

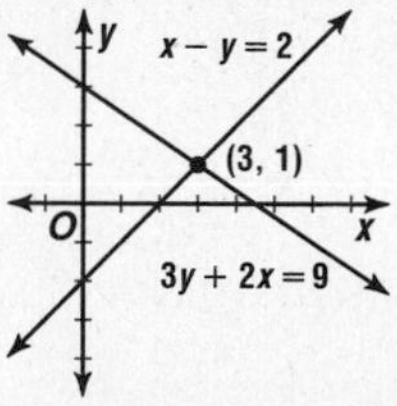

one solution; (3, 1)

35.
$$3x + y = 3$$
$$3x - 3x + y = 3 - 3x$$
$$y = -3x + 3$$
$$2y = -6x + 6$$
$$\frac{2y}{2} = -\frac{6x}{2} + \frac{6}{2}$$
$$y = -3x + 3$$

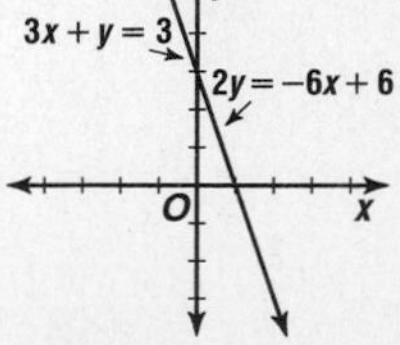

infinitely many solutions

36. $y = x - 4$

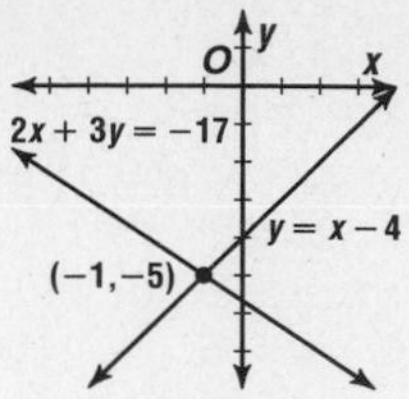

$$2x + 3y = -17$$
$$2x - 2x + 3y = -17 - 2x$$
$$3y = -2x - 17$$
$$\frac{3y}{3} = \frac{-2x}{3} - \frac{17}{3}$$
$$y = -\frac{2}{3}x - \frac{17}{3}$$

one solution; (−1, −5)

37. $y = \frac{2}{3}x - 5$

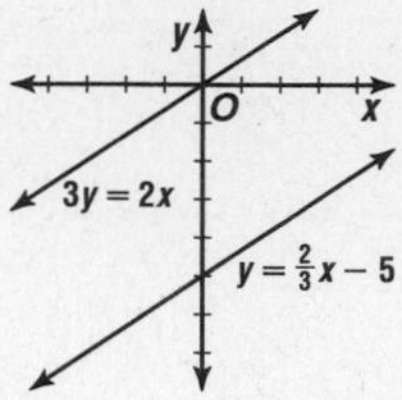

$$3y = 2x$$
$$\frac{3y}{3} = \frac{2x}{3}$$
$$y = \frac{2}{3}x$$

no solution

38.
$$5x - 8y = -17$$
$$5x - 5x - 8y = -17 - 5x$$
$$-8y = -5x - 17$$
$$\frac{-8y}{-8} = \frac{-5x}{-8} - \frac{17}{-8}$$
$$y = \frac{5}{8}x + \frac{17}{8}$$
$$4x + 3y = 24$$
$$4x - 4x + 3y = 24 - 4x$$
$$3y = -4x + 24$$
$$\frac{3y}{3} = -\frac{4x}{3} + \frac{24}{3}$$
$$y = -\frac{4}{3}x + 8$$

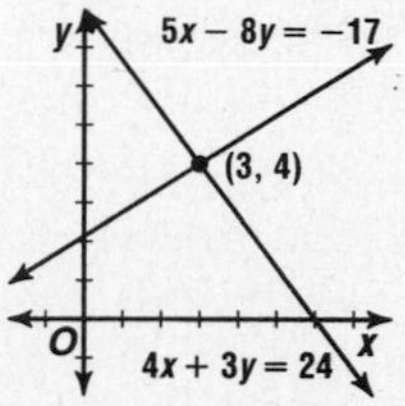

one solution; (3, 4)

39. $y = \frac{1}{2}x + 2$

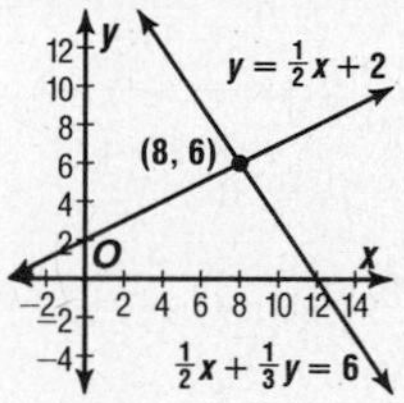

$$\frac{1}{2}x + \frac{1}{3}y = 6$$
$$\frac{1}{2}x - \frac{1}{2}x + \frac{1}{3}y = 6 - \frac{1}{2}x$$
$$\frac{1}{3}y = -\frac{1}{2}x + 6$$
$$3\left(\frac{1}{3}y\right) = 3\left(-\frac{1}{2}x + 6\right)$$
$$y = -\frac{3}{2}x + 18$$

one solution; (8, 6)

40.
$$6 - \frac{3}{8}y = x$$
$$6 - 6 - \frac{3}{8}y = x - 6$$
$$-\frac{3}{8}y = x - 6$$
$$-\frac{8}{3}\left(-\frac{3}{8}y\right) = -\frac{8}{3}(x - 6)$$
$$y = -\frac{8}{3}x + 16$$
$$\frac{2}{3}x + \frac{1}{4}y = 4$$
$$\frac{2}{3}x - \frac{2}{3}x + \frac{1}{4}y = 4 - \frac{2}{3}x$$
$$\frac{1}{4}y = -\frac{2}{3}x + 4$$
$$4\left(\frac{1}{4}y\right) = 4\left(-\frac{2}{3}x + 4\right)$$
$$y = -\frac{8}{3}x + 16$$

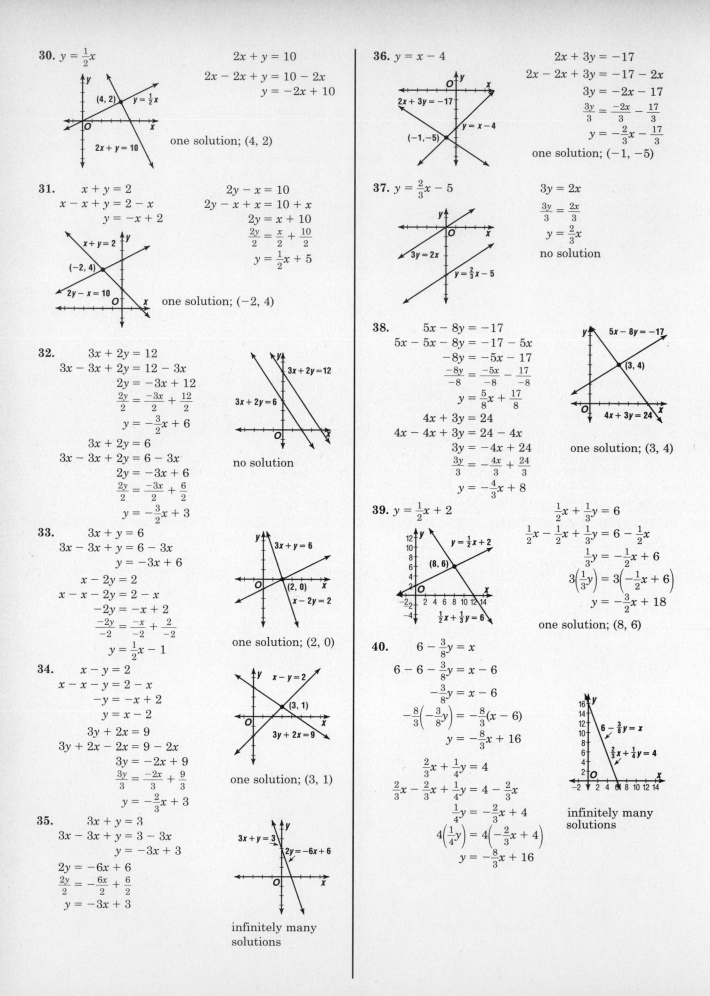

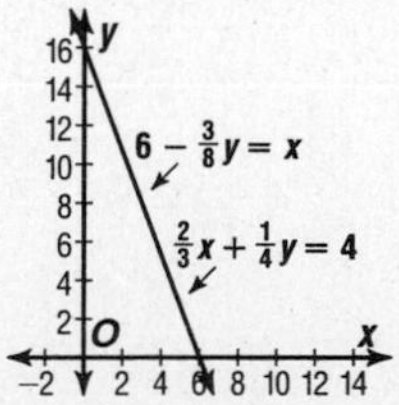

infinitely many solutions

41.
$$2x + 4y = 2$$
$$2x - 2x + 4y = 2 - 2x$$
$$4y = -2x + 2$$
$$\frac{4y}{4} = -\frac{2x}{4} + \frac{2}{4}$$
$$y = -\frac{1}{2}x + \frac{1}{2}$$
$$3x + 6y = 3$$
$$3x - 3x + 6y = 3 - 3x$$
$$6y = -3x + 3$$
$$\frac{6y}{6} = -\frac{3x}{6} + \frac{3}{6}$$
$$y = -\frac{1}{2}x + \frac{1}{2}$$

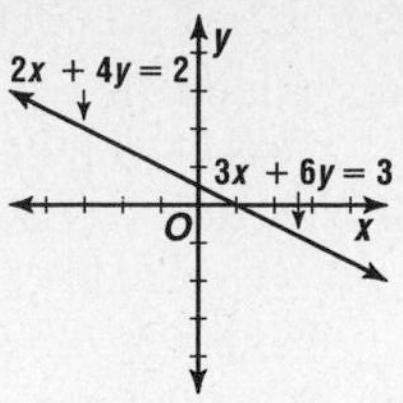

infinitely many solutions

42.

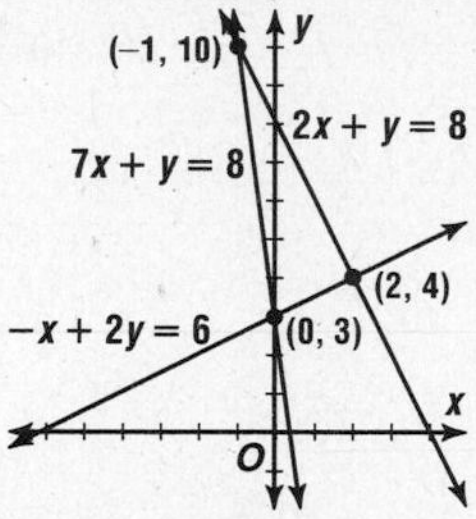

(2, 4), (0, 3), (−1, 10)

43.

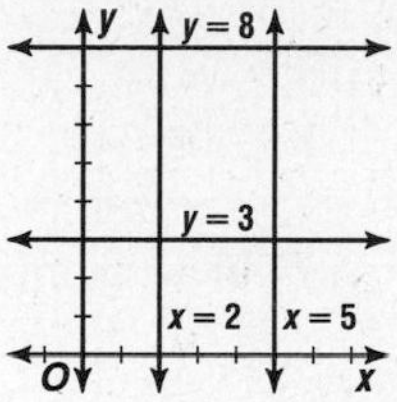

$A = \ell w$
$= 5(3)$
$= 15$ square units

44. Enter: [Y=] [X,T,θ] [+] 2 [ENTER] [(–)] [X,T,θ] [–] 1 [ZOOM] 6

Use the INTERSECT feature by pressing [2nd] [CALC] 5 [ENTER] [ENTER] [ENTER].
The solution is (−1.50, 0.50).

45. Enter: [Y=] [(] 1 [÷] 4 [)] [X,T,θ] [–] 3 [ENTER] [(–)] [(] 1 [÷] 3 [)] [X,T,θ] [–] 2 [ZOOM] 6

Use the INTERSECT feature by pressing [2nd] [CALC] 5 [ENTER] [ENTER] [ENTER].
The solution is (1.71, −2.57).

46. Solve for y: $6x + y = 5$
$y = -6x + 5$

Enter: [Y=] [(–)] 6 [X,T,θ] [+] 5 [ENTER] 9 [+] 3 [X,T,θ] [ZOOM] 6

Use the INTERSECT feature by pressing [2nd] [CALC] 5 [ENTER] [ENTER] [ENTER].
The solution is (−0.44, 7.67).

47. Solve for y: $3 + y = x$ $\quad 2 + y = 5x$
$y = x - 3 \quad y = 5x - 2$

Enter: [Y=] [X,T,θ] [–] 3 [ENTER] 5 [X,T,θ] [–] 2 [ZOOM] 6

Use the INTERSECT feature by pressing [2nd] [CALC] 5 [ENTER] [ENTER] [ENTER].
The solution is (−0.25, −3.25).

48. Yes, the lines are coincident.

49.
$$Ax + y = 5$$
$$A(-1) + (2) = 5$$
$$-A + 2 = 5$$
$$-A = 3$$
$$A = -3$$
$$Ax + By = 7$$
$$A(-1) + B(2) = 7$$
$$-A + 2B = 7$$
$$-(-3) + 2B = 7$$
$$2B = 4$$
$$B = 2$$

50a. The number of toys sold for which expenses equal income.

50b. After selling more than 1000 toys; the line representing income is above the line representing expenses, so income is greater than expenses.

50c. When selling fewer than 1000 toys; the line representing expenses is above the line representing income, so expenses are greater than income.

51.

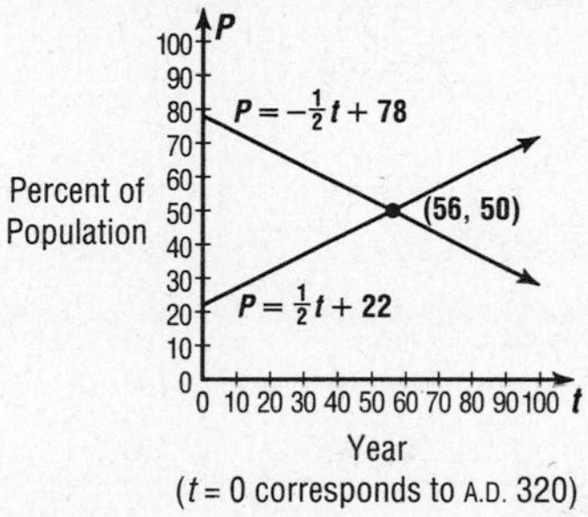

$t = 56$
A.D. 320 + 56 = A.D. 376

52. Solve for y:

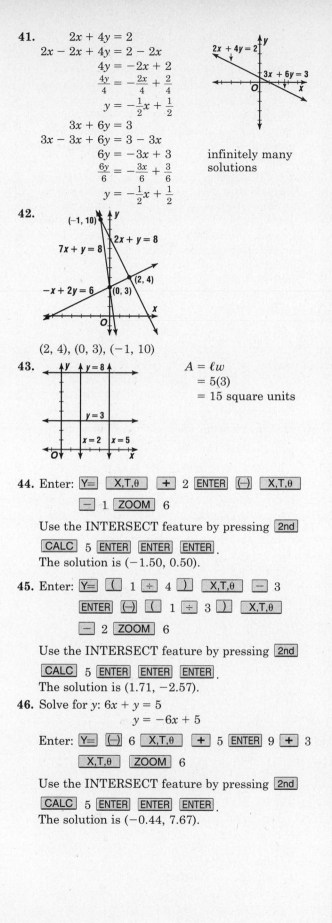

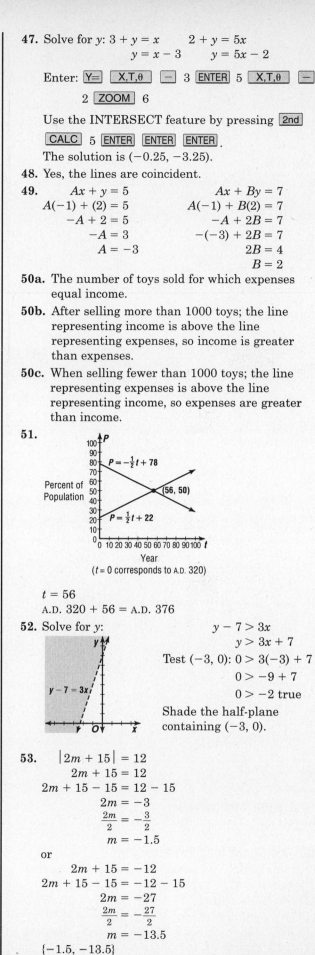

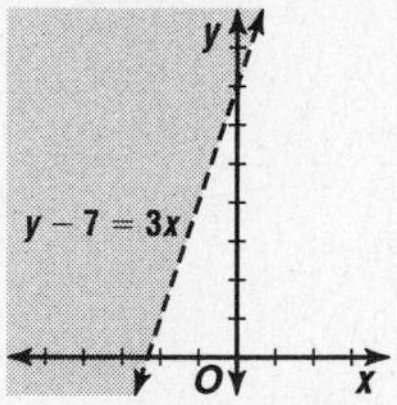

$$y - 7 > 3x$$
$$y > 3x + 7$$
Test (−3, 0): $0 > 3(-3) + 7$
$$0 > -9 + 7$$
$$0 > -2 \text{ true}$$
Shade the half-plane containing (−3, 0).

53.
$$|2m + 15| = 12$$
$$2m + 15 = 12$$
$$2m + 15 - 15 = 12 - 15$$
$$2m = -3$$
$$\frac{2m}{2} = -\frac{3}{2}$$
$$m = -1.5$$
or
$$2m + 15 = -12$$
$$2m + 15 - 15 = -12 - 15$$
$$2m = -27$$
$$\frac{2m}{2} = -\frac{27}{2}$$
$$m = -13.5$$
$\{-1.5, -13.5\}$

54.
$$10p - 14 < 8p - 17$$
$$10p - 8p - 14 < 8p - 8p - 17$$
$$2p - 14 < -17$$
$$2p - 14 + 14 < -17 + 14$$
$$2p < -3$$
$$\frac{2p}{2} < \frac{-3}{2}$$
$$p < -\frac{3}{2}$$
$$\left\{p \mid p < -\frac{3}{2}\right\}$$

55.
$$m = -2; (2, -2)$$
$$y - y_1 = m(x - x_1)$$
$$y - (-2) = -2(x - 2)$$
$$y + 2 = -2x + 4$$
$$y = -2x + 2$$

56. range: $467 - 433 = 34$
median: $\frac{444 + 449}{2} = 446.5$
Q3: 457
Q1: 439
IQR: $Q_3 - Q_1 = 457 - 439 = 18$

57.
$$I = Prt$$
Martin's account: $I = 5000(0.1)(1)$
$$I = \$500$$
Patricia's interest: $\$500 - \$125 = \$375$
$$I = Prt$$
$$375 = 5000(r)(1)$$
$$\frac{375}{5000} = r$$
$$0.075 = r$$
Patricia's annual interest rate was 7.5% or $7\frac{1}{2}$%.

58.
$$\frac{a - x}{-3} = \frac{-2}{b}$$
$$b(a - x) = -3(-2)$$
$$ba - bx = 6$$
$$ba - bx - ba = 6 - ba$$
$$-bx = 6 - ba$$
$$\frac{-bx}{-b} = \frac{6}{-b} - \frac{ba}{-b}$$
$$x = -\frac{6}{b} + a$$

59a. how many three- and four-bedroom homes will be built

59b. $100 - h$ or $4h$

59c. $4(20) = 80$ homes

60.
$$\frac{6ab}{3x + 2y} = \frac{6(6)(4)}{3(0.2) + 2(1.3)}$$
$$= \frac{144}{0.6 + 2.6}$$
$$= \frac{144}{3.2}$$
$$= 45$$

8-2 Substitution

Page 466 Check for Understanding

1. From the first equation, y is equal to $2x - 4$, and y must have the same value in both equations.
2. There is no solution.
3. The graphs of both equations have the same slope, 9, but different y-intercepts, so the lines are parallel and the system has no solution.
4. Answers will vary.

5a. Yolanda is walking faster than Adele and catches up after about 5 seconds; 1 solution.

5b. Yolanda never catches up with Adele because they both are walking at the same rate, and Adele has a 30-ft headstart; no solution.

5c. Yolanda never catches up with Adele because Adele is walking at a faster rate and has a 30-ft headstart.

6. Model the system $3x + 2y = 9$ and $y = 2x - 6$ by placing 3 cups and two sets of 2 cups and 6 negative counters on the left side of the equation mat. Place 9 positive counters on the right side of the mat. Add 12 positive counters to each side and remove the zero pairs. Each remaining cup is paired with 3 positive counters. Therefore, $x = 3$. Substitute 3 for x in the equation $y = 2x - 6$ to solve for y. $y = 2(3) - 6$ or 0. Therefore, $y = 0$. The solution is (3, 0).

7.
$$x + 4y = 8 \qquad x + 4y = 8$$
$$x = 8 - 4y \qquad 4y = 8 - x$$
$$y = 2 - \frac{1}{4}x$$

8.
$$3x - 5y = 12 \qquad 3x - 5y = 12$$
$$3x = 12 + 5y \qquad -5y = 12 - 3x$$
$$x = 4 + \frac{5}{3}y \qquad y = -\frac{12}{5} + \frac{3}{5}x$$

9.
$$0.8x + 6 = -0.75y \qquad 0.8x + 6 = -0.75y$$
$$0.8x = -0.75y - 6 \qquad \frac{0.8x}{-0.75} + \frac{6}{-0.75} = \frac{-0.75y}{-0.75}$$
$$\frac{0.8x}{0.8} = \frac{-0.75y}{0.8} - \frac{6}{0.8} \qquad -\frac{0.8}{0.75}x - 8 = y$$
$$x = \frac{-0.75}{0.8}y - 7.5 \qquad y = -\frac{0.8}{0.75}x - 8$$

10.
$$x + 2y = -21 \qquad y = 3x$$
$$x + 2(3x) = -21 \qquad y = 3(-3)$$
$$x + 6x = -21 \qquad y = -9$$
$$7x = -21$$
$$x = -3$$
$(-3, -9)$

11.
$$4x + 2y = 15 \qquad x = 2y$$
$$4(2y) + 2y = 15 \qquad x = 2\left(\frac{3}{2}\right)$$
$$8y + 2y = 15 \qquad x = 3$$
$$10y = 15$$
$$y = \frac{3}{2}$$
$\left(3, \frac{3}{2}\right)$

12.
$$x + 5y = -3$$
$$x = -3 - 5y$$
$$3x - 2y = 8 \qquad x = -3 - 5y$$
$$3(-3 - 5y) - 2y = 8 \qquad x = -3 - 5(-1)$$
$$-9 - 15y - 2y = 8 \qquad x = -3 + 5$$
$$-9 - 17y = 8 \qquad x = 2$$
$$-17y = 17$$
$$y = -1$$
$(2, -1)$

13.
$$4x + y = 11$$
$$y = -4x + 11$$
$$8x + 2y = 13$$
$$8x + 2(-4x + 11) = 13$$
$$8x - 8x + 22 = 13$$
$$22 = 13$$
no solution

14. $-3x + y = -9$

$y = 3x - 9$

$2x - y = -4$
$2x - (3x - 9) = -4$
$2x - 3x + 9 = -4$
$-x + 9 = -4$
$-x = -13$
$x = 13$

$y = 3x - 9$
$y = 3(13) - 9$
$y = 39 - 9$
$y = 30$

$(13, 30)$

15. $6x - 2y = -4$
$6x - 2(3x + 2) = -4$
$6x - 6x - 4 = -4$
$-4 = -4$

infinitely many

16a. Let x = the number of $12 CDs.
Let y = the number of $10 CDs.
$x + y = 500$
$12x + 10y = 5750$

16b. $x + y = 500$

$y = 500 - x$

$12x + 10y = 5750$
$12x + 10(500 - x) = 5750$
$12x + 5000 - 10x = 5750$
$2x + 5000 = 5750$
$2x = 750$
$x = 375$

$y = 500 - x$
$y = 500 - 375$
$y = 125$

$12: 375; $10: 125

Pages 467–468 Exercises

17. $y = 3x - 8$
$4 - x = 3x - 8$
$4 - x + x = 3x + x - 8$
$4 = 4x - 8$
$4 + 8 = 4x - 8 + 8$
$12 = 4x$
$3 = x$

$y = 4 - x$
$y = 4 - 3$
$y = 1$

$(3, 1)$

18. $2x + 7y = 3$
$2(1 - 4y) + 7y = 3$
$2 - 8y + 7y = 3$
$2 - y = 3$
$-y = 1$
$y = -1$

$x = 1 - 4y$
$x = 1 - 4(-1)$
$x = 1 + 4$
$x = 5$

$(5, -1)$

19. $x + y = 0$

$y = -x$

$3x + y = -8$
$3x + (-x) = -8$
$2x = -8$
$x = -4$

$y = -x$
$y = -(-4)$
$y = 4$

$(-4, 4)$

20. $4c = 3d + 3$
$4(d - 1) = 3d + 3$
$4d - 4 = 3d + 3$
$4d - 3d - 4 = 3d - 3d + 3$
$d - 4 = 3$
$d = 7$

$c = d - 1$
$c = 7 - 1$
$c = 6$

$(6, 7)$

21. $4x + 5y = 11$
$4x + 5(3x - 13) = 11$
$4x + 15x - 65 = 11$
$19x - 65 = 11$
$19x = 76$
$x = 4$

$y = 3x - 13$
$y = 3(4) - 13$
$y = 12 - 13$
$y = -1$

$(4, -1)$

22. $x - 3y = 1$

$x = 1 + 3y$

$3x - 5y = 11$
$3(1 + 3y) - 5y = 11$
$3 + 9y - 5y = 11$
$3 + 4y = 11$
$4y = 8$
$y = 2$

$x = 1 + 3y$
$x = 1 + 3(2)$
$x = 1 + 6$
$x = 7$

$(7, 2)$

23. $c - 5d = 2$

$c = 2 + 5d$

$2(2 + 5d) + d = 4$
$4 + 10d + d = 4$
$4 + 11d = 4$
$11d = 0$
$d = 0$

$c = 2 + 5d$
$c = 2 + 5(0)$
$c = 2 + 0$
$c = 2$

$(2, 0)$

24. $x + 2y = 6$

$x = 6 - 2y$

$3x - 2y = 12$
$3(6 - 2y) - 2y = 12$
$18 - 6y - 2y = 12$
$18 - 8y = 12$
$-8y = -6$
$y = \frac{3}{4}$

$x = 6 - 2y$
$x = 6 - 2\left(\frac{3}{4}\right)$
$x = 6 - \frac{3}{2}$
$x = \frac{12}{2} - \frac{3}{2}$
$x = \frac{9}{2}$

$\left(\frac{9}{2}, \frac{3}{4}\right)$

25. $x + 3y = 12$

$x = 12 - 3y$

$x - y = 8$
$(12 - 3y) - y = 8$
$12 - 4y = 8$
$-4y = -4$
$y = 1$

$x = 12 - 3y$
$x = 12 - 3(1)$
$x = 12 - 3$
$x = 9$

$(9, 1)$

26. $x - 3y = 0$

$x = 3y$

$3x + y = 7$
$3(3y) + y = 7$
$9y + y = 7$
$10y = 7$
$y = \frac{7}{10}$

$x = 3y$
$x = 3\left(\frac{7}{10}\right)$
$x = \frac{21}{10}$

$\left(\frac{21}{10}, \frac{7}{10}\right)$

27. $5r - s = 5$

$-s = 5 - 5r$

$s = -5 + 5r$

$-4r + 5s = 17$
$-4r + 5(-5 + 5r) = 17$
$-4r - 25 + 25r = 17$
$21r - 25 = 17$
$21r = 42$
$r = 2$

$s = -5 + 5r$
$s = -5 + 5(2)$
$s = -5 + 10$
$s = 5$

$(2, 5)$

28. $-3x + y = 15$

$y = 15 + 3x$

$$\begin{aligned} 2x + 3y &= 1 \\ 2x + 3(15 + 3x) &= 1 \\ 2x + 45 + 9x &= 1 \\ 11x + 45 &= 1 \\ 11x &= -44 \\ x &= -4 \end{aligned} \qquad \begin{aligned} y &= 15 + 3x \\ y &= 15 + 3(-4) \\ y &= 15 - 12 \\ y &= 3 \end{aligned}$$

$(-4, 3)$

29. $x - 8y = -12$

$x = -12 + 8y$

$$\begin{aligned} 8x + 6y &= 44 \\ 8(-12 + 8y) + 6y &= 44 \\ -96 + 64y + 6y &= 44 \\ -96 + 70y &= 44 \\ 70y &= 140 \\ y &= 2 \end{aligned} \qquad \begin{aligned} x &= -12 + 8y \\ x &= -12 + 8(2) \\ x &= -12 + 16 \\ x &= 4 \end{aligned}$$

$(4, 2)$

30. $2x + y = 104$

$y = -2x + 104$

$$\begin{aligned} 0.5x - 2y &= 17 \\ 0.5x - 2(-2x + 104) &= 17 \\ 0.5x + 4x - 208 &= 17 \\ 4.5x - 208 &= 17 \\ 4.5x &= 225 \\ x &= 50 \end{aligned} \qquad \begin{aligned} y &= -2x + 104 \\ y &= -2(50) + 104 \\ y &= -100 + 104 \\ y &= 4 \end{aligned}$$

$(50, 4)$

31. $-0.3x + y = 0.5$

$y = 0.5 + 0.3x$

$$\begin{aligned} 0.5x - 0.3y &= 1.9 \\ 0.5x - 0.3(0.5 + 0.3x) &= 1.9 \\ 0.5x - 0.15 - 0.09x &= 1.9 \\ 0.41x - 0.15 &= 1.9 \\ 0.41x &= 2.05 \\ x &= 5 \end{aligned} \qquad \begin{aligned} y &= 0.5 + 0.3x \\ y &= 0.5 + 0.3(5) \\ y &= 0.5 + 1.5 \\ y &= 2 \end{aligned}$$

$(5, 2)$

32.

$$\begin{aligned} 2x - y &= 6 \\ 2\left(\tfrac{1}{2}y + 3\right) - y &= 6 \\ y + 6 - y &= 6 \\ 6 &= 6 \end{aligned}$$

infinitely many

33.

$$\begin{aligned} y &= 2x - 1 \\ \tfrac{1}{2}x + 3 &= 2x - 1 \\ 2\left(\tfrac{1}{2}x + 3\right) &= 2(2x - 1) \\ x + 6 &= 4x - 2 \\ x - x + 6 &= 4x - x - 2 \\ 6 &= 3x - 2 \\ 8 &= 3x \\ \tfrac{8}{3} &= x \end{aligned} \qquad \begin{aligned} y &= 2x - 1 \\ y &= 2\left(\tfrac{8}{3}\right) - 1 \\ y &= \tfrac{16}{3} - \tfrac{3}{3} \\ y &= \tfrac{13}{3} \end{aligned}$$

$\left(\frac{8}{3}, \frac{13}{3}\right)$

34.

$$\begin{aligned} 3x - 5y &= 15 \\ 3x - 5\left(\tfrac{3}{5}x\right) &= 15 \\ 3x - 3x &= 15 \\ 0 &= 15 \end{aligned}$$

no solution

35.

$$\begin{aligned} x + y + z &= -54 \\ (-6y) + y + (14y) &= -54 \\ 9y &= -54 \\ y &= -6 \end{aligned}$$

$$\begin{aligned} x &= -6y \\ x &= -6(-6) \\ x &= 36 \end{aligned} \qquad \begin{aligned} z &= 14y \\ z &= 14(-6) \\ z &= -84 \end{aligned}$$

$(36, -6, -84)$

36.

$$\begin{aligned} 2x + 3y - z &= 17 \\ (z + 2) + 3(-3z - 7) - z &= 17 \\ z + 2 - 9z - 21 - z &= 17 \\ -9z - 19 &= 17 \\ -9z &= 36 \\ z &= -4 \end{aligned}$$

$$\begin{aligned} y &= -3z - 7 \\ y &= -3(-4) - 7 \\ y &= 12 - 7 \\ y &= 5 \end{aligned} \qquad \begin{aligned} 2x &= z + 2 \\ 2x &= -4 + 2 \\ 2x &= -2 \\ x &= -1 \end{aligned}$$

$(-1, 5, -4)$

37. $x + 2z = 2$ $\qquad y + 3z = 9$

$x = 2 - 2z$ $\qquad y = 9 - 3z$

$$\begin{aligned} 12x - y + 7z &= 99 \\ 12(2 - 2z) - (9 - 3z) + 7z &= 99 \\ 24 - 24z - 9 + 3z + 7z &= 99 \\ 15 - 14z &= 99 \\ -14z &= 84 \\ z &= -6 \end{aligned}$$

$$\begin{aligned} x &= 2 - 2z \\ x &= 2 - 2(-6) \\ x &= 2 + 12 \\ x &= 14 \end{aligned} \qquad \begin{aligned} y &= 9 - 3z \\ y &= 9 - 3(-6) \\ y &= 9 + 18 \\ y &= 27 \end{aligned}$$

$(14, 27, -6)$

38. Let t = the tens digit.
Let u = the units digit.
Then $10t + u$ = a two-digit integer.

$$\begin{aligned} 10t + u - 36 &= 10u + t \\ 10t - t + u - 36 &= 10u + t - t \\ 9t + u - u - 36 &= 10u - u \\ 9t - 36 &= 9u \\ \tfrac{9t}{9} - \tfrac{36}{9} &= \tfrac{9u}{9} \\ t - 4 &= u \end{aligned}$$

If $t = 1$, $u = -3$ no	$t = 6$, $u = 2$ yes
$t = 2$, $u = -2$ no	$t = 7$, $u = 3$ yes
$t = 3$, $u = -1$ no	$t = 8$, $u = 4$ yes
$t = 4$, $u = 0$ yes	$t = 9$, $u = 5$ yes
$t = 5$, $u = 1$ yes	

If t = 1, 2, or 3, the number is negative. The integers that make the statement true are 40, 51, 62, 73, 84, and 95.

39a. Let x = the number of tickets.

$y = 1000 + 5x$, $y = 13x$

39b.

$$\begin{aligned} 13x &= 1000 + 5x \\ 13x - 5x &= 1000 + 5x - 5x \\ 8x &= 1000 \\ x &= 125 \end{aligned}$$

They need to sell 125 tickets to break even.

40. Let x = the number of gallons cream containing 25% butterfat.
Let y = the number of gallons of milk containing $3\frac{1}{2}$% butterfat.

	25% Cream	$3\frac{1}{2}$% Butterfat	$12\frac{1}{2}$% Butterfat
Total Gallons	x	y	50
Gallons of Butterfat	$0.25x$	$0.035y$	$0.125(50)$

$x + y = 50$
$x = 50 - y$
$0.25x + 0.035y = 0.125(50)$
$0.25(50 - y) + 0.035y = 0.125(50)$
$12.5 - 0.25y + 0.035y = 6.25$
$12.5 - 0.215y = 6.25$
$-0.215y = -6.25$
$y = 29.07$
$x = 50 - y$
$x = 50 - 29.07$
$x = 20.93$
20.93 gal of cream, 29.07 gal of milk

41a. Let x = the number of years.
$39.1 - 0.20x = 36.45 - 0.10x$
$39.1 - 0.20x + 0.20x = 36.45 - 0.10x + 0.20x$
$39.1 = 36.45 + 0.10x$
$39.1 - 36.45 = 36.45 - 36.45 + 0.10x$
$2.65 = 0.10x$
$26.5 = x$
26.5 years

41b. $39.1 - 0.20x = 39.1 - 0.20(26.5)$
$= 39.1 - 5.3$
$= 33.8$ seconds

41c. See students' work.

42. $3000 = 0.80S$ $\qquad x = 0.20S$
$\frac{3000}{0.80} = \frac{0.80S}{0.80}$ $\qquad x = 0.20(3750)$
$3750 = S$ $\qquad x = 750$
The value of stock issued to Ms. Eppick would be \$750.

43a.

	75% Gold (18-carat)	50% Gold (12-carat)	58% Gold (14-carat)
Total Grams	x	y	300
Grams of pure gold	$0.75x$	$0.50y$	$0.58(300)$

43b. $x + y = 300$
$0.75x + 0.50y = 0.58(300)$

43c. $x + y = 300$
$y = 300 - x$
$0.75x + 0.50(300 - x) = 0.58(300)$ $\qquad y = 300 - x$
$0.75x + 150 - 0.50x = 174$ $\qquad y = 300 - 96$
$0.25x + 125 = 174$ $\qquad y = 204$
$0.25x = 24$
$x = 96$
96 grams of 18-carat gold, 204 grams of 12-carat gold

44. 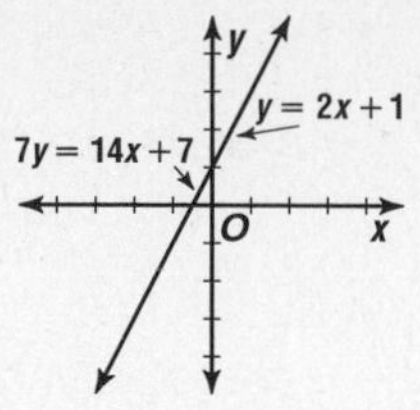

infinitely many solutions

45. Let x = the number of shares.
$14x \leq 0.60(885)$
$14x \leq 531$
$\frac{14x}{14} \leq \frac{531}{14}$
$x \leq 37.9$
37 shares

46. $m = \frac{1}{5}$; y-intercept: -3

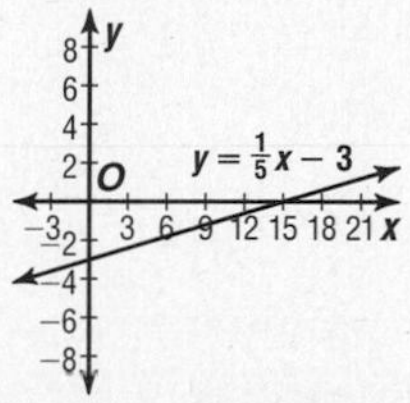

47.

a	$3a - 4$	b	(a, b)
-1	$3(-1) - 4$	-7	$(-1, -7)$
4	$3(4) - 4$	8	$(4, 8)$
7	$3(7) - 4$	17	$(7, 17)$
13	$3(13) - 4$	35	$(13, 35)$

$\{(-1, -7), (4, 8), (7, 17), (13, 35)\}$

48. $94 - 0.25(94) = 94 - 23.5$
$= 70.5$

49. $-8 - 12x = 28$
$-8 + 8 - 12x = 28 + 8$
$-12x = 36$
$\frac{-12x}{-12} = \frac{36}{-12}$
$x = -3$

50. 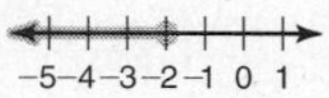

51. $m - 12$

8-3 Elimination Using Addition and Subtraction

Page 472 Check for Understanding

1a. When the coefficients of one of the variable are the same.

1b. When the coefficients of one of the variables are additive inverses of each other.

2. The result is $0 = 45$, which is false. Thus, the system has no solution.

2b. The graph is two parallel lines.

3. Both are correct. If the resulting statement is false, there is no solution. If the resulting statement is true, there is an infinite number of solutions.

4a. Sample answer: $(-3, 4)$

4b.
$$\begin{aligned} 4y + 2x &= 10 \\ (-)\ 4y + 12x &= -24 \\ \hline -10x &= 34 \\ x &= -3.4 \end{aligned} \qquad \begin{aligned} 4y + 2x &= 10 \\ 4y + 2(-3.4) &= 10 \\ 4y - 6.8 &= 10 \\ 4y &= 16.8 \\ y &= 4.2 \end{aligned}$$

$(-3.4, 4.2)$

5. addition
$$\begin{aligned} 3x - 5y &= 3 \\ (+)\ 4x + 5y &= 4 \\ \hline 7x &= 7 \\ x &= 1 \end{aligned} \qquad \begin{aligned} 3x - 5y &= 3 \\ 3(1) - 5y &= 3 \\ 3 - 5y &= 3 \\ -5y &= 0 \\ y &= 0 \end{aligned}$$

The solution is $(1, 0)$.

6. substitution
$$\begin{aligned} 3x + 2y &= 7 \\ 3x + 2(4x - 2) &= 7 \\ 3x + 8x - 4 &= 7 \\ 11x - 4 &= 7 \\ 11x &= 11 \\ x &= 1 \end{aligned} \qquad \begin{aligned} y &= 4x - 2 \\ y &= 4(1) - 2 \\ y &= 4 - 2 \\ y &= 2 \end{aligned}$$

The solution is $(1, 2)$.

7. subtraction
$$\begin{aligned} -4m + 2n &= 6 \\ (-)\ -4m + n &= 8 \\ \hline n &= -2 \end{aligned} \qquad \begin{aligned} -4m + 2n &= 6 \\ -4m + 2(-2) &= 6 \\ -4m - 4 &= 6 \\ -4m &= 10 \\ m &= -\tfrac{5}{2} \end{aligned}$$

The solution is $\left(-\frac{5}{2}, -2\right)$.

8. subtraction
$$\begin{aligned} 8a + b &= 1 \\ (-)\ 8a - 3b &= 3 \\ \hline 4b &= -2 \\ b &= -\tfrac{1}{2} \end{aligned} \qquad \begin{aligned} 8a + b &= 1 \\ 8a + \left(-\tfrac{1}{2}\right) &= 1 \\ 8a &= \tfrac{3}{2} \\ a &= \tfrac{3}{16} \end{aligned}$$

The solution is $\left(\frac{3}{16}, -\frac{1}{2}\right)$.

9. substitution
$$\begin{aligned} 3x + y &= 7 \\ y &= 7 - 3x \\ 2x + 5y &= 22 \\ 2x + 5(7 - 3x) &= 22 \\ 2x + 35 - 15x &= 22 \\ 35 - 13x &= 22 \\ -13x &= -13 \\ x &= 1 \end{aligned} \qquad \begin{aligned} y &= 7 - 3x \\ y &= 7 - 3(1) \\ y &= 7 - 3 \\ y &= 4 \end{aligned}$$

The solution is $(1, 4)$.

10. substitution
$$\begin{aligned} 2b + 4c &= 8 \\ 2(c - 2) + 4c &= 8 \\ 2c - 4 + 4c &= 8 \\ 6c - 4 &= 8 \\ 6c &= 12 \\ c &= 2 \end{aligned} \qquad \begin{aligned} c - 2 &= b \\ 2 - 2 &= b \\ 0 &= b \end{aligned}$$

The solution is $(0, 2)$.

11. Let x = the first number.
Let y = the second number.
$$\frac{x + y}{2} = 28 \rightarrow \tfrac{1}{2}x + \tfrac{1}{2}y = 28$$
$$3x = \tfrac{1}{2}y \rightarrow (+)\ 3x - \tfrac{1}{2}y = 0$$
$$\begin{aligned} \tfrac{7}{2}x &= 28 \\ x &= 8 \end{aligned}$$
$$\begin{aligned} \tfrac{1}{2}x + \tfrac{1}{2}y &= 28 \\ \tfrac{1}{2}(8) + \tfrac{1}{2}y &= 28 \\ 4 + \tfrac{1}{2}y &= 28 \\ \tfrac{1}{2}y &= 24 \\ y &= 48 \end{aligned}$$

The numbers are 8 and 48.

Pages 472–474 Exercises

12a. $(-2, 1)$

12b.
$$\begin{aligned} y + 3x &= -5 \\ (+)\ 2y - 3x &= 9 \\ \hline 3y &= 4 \\ y &= \tfrac{4}{3} \end{aligned} \qquad \begin{aligned} y + 3x &= -5 \\ \tfrac{4}{3} + 3x &= -5 \\ 3x &= -\tfrac{15}{3} - \tfrac{4}{3} \\ 3x &= -\tfrac{19}{3} \\ x &= -\tfrac{19}{9} \end{aligned}$$

The solution is $\left(-\frac{19}{9}, \frac{4}{3}\right)$.

13a. $(1, -4)$

13b.
$$\begin{aligned} 1.6y + 2.7x &= -3 \\ (-)\ 1.6y + 8.9x &= 5 \\ \hline -6.2x &= -8 \\ x &= 1.29 \end{aligned} \qquad \begin{aligned} 1.6y + 2.7x &= -3 \\ 1.6y + 2.7(1.29) &= -3 \\ 1.6y + 3.483 &= -3 \\ 1.6y &= -6.483 \\ y &= -4.05 \end{aligned}$$

The solution is $(1.29, -4.05)$.

14a. $(-2, 3)$

14b.
$$\begin{aligned} 2y - 3x &= 12 \\ (-)\ 2y + 6x &= -5 \\ \hline -9x &= 17 \\ x &= -\tfrac{17}{9} \end{aligned} \qquad \begin{aligned} 2y - 3x &= 12 \\ 2y - 3\left(-\tfrac{17}{9}\right) &= 12 \\ 2y + \tfrac{17}{3} &= 12 \\ 2y &= \tfrac{36}{3} - \tfrac{17}{3} \\ 2y &= \tfrac{19}{3} \\ y &= \tfrac{19}{6} \end{aligned}$$

The solution is $\left(-\frac{17}{9}, \frac{19}{6}\right)$.

15. addition
$$\begin{aligned} x + y &= 8 \\ (+)\ x - y &= 4 \\ \hline 2x &= 12 \\ x &= 6 \end{aligned} \qquad \begin{aligned} x + y &= 8 \\ 6 + y &= 8 \\ y &= 2 \end{aligned}$$

The solution is $(6, 2)$.

16. addition
$$\begin{aligned} 2r + s &= 5 \\ (+)\ r - s &= 1 \\ \hline 3r &= 6 \\ r &= 2 \end{aligned} \qquad \begin{aligned} 2r + s &= 5 \\ 2(2) + s &= 5 \\ 4 + s &= 5 \\ s &= 1 \end{aligned}$$

The solution is $(2, 1)$.

17. subtraction

$$\begin{array}{rrl} & x - 3y = & 7 \\ (-) & x + 2y = & 2 \\ \hline & -5y = & 5 \\ & y = & -1 \end{array} \qquad \begin{aligned} x - 3y &= 7 \\ x - 3(-1) &= 7 \\ x + 3 &= 7 \\ x &= 4 \end{aligned}$$

The solution is $(4, -1)$.

18. subtraction

$$\begin{array}{rrl} & 3x + y = & 5 \\ (-) & 2x + y = & 10 \\ \hline & x \quad = & -5 \end{array} \qquad \begin{aligned} 3x + y &= 5 \\ 3(-5) + y &= 5 \\ -15 + y &= 5 \\ y &= 20 \end{aligned}$$

The solution is $(-5, 20)$.

19. subtraction

$$\begin{array}{rrl} & 5s + 2t = & 6 \\ (-) & 9s + 2t = & 22 \\ \hline & -4s = & -16 \\ & s = & 4 \end{array} \qquad \begin{aligned} 5s + 2t &= 6 \\ 5(4) + 2t &= 6 \\ 20 + 2t &= 6 \\ 2t &= -14 \\ t &= -7 \end{aligned}$$

The solution is $(4, -7)$.

20. addition or subtraction

$$\begin{array}{rrl} & 4x - 3y = & 12 \\ (+) & 4x + 3y = & 24 \\ \hline & 8x \quad = & 36 \\ & x = & \frac{9}{2} \end{array} \qquad \begin{aligned} 4x - 3y &= 12 \\ 4\left(\tfrac{9}{2}\right) - 3y &= 12 \\ 18 - 3y &= 12 \\ -3y &= -6 \\ y &= 2 \end{aligned}$$

The solution is $\left(\frac{9}{2}, 2\right)$.

21. addition

$$\begin{array}{rrl} & 2x + 3y = & 13 \\ (+) & x - 3y = & 2 \\ \hline & 3x \quad = & 15 \\ & x = & 5 \end{array} \qquad \begin{aligned} 2x + 3y &= 13 \\ 2(5) + 3y &= 13 \\ 10 + 3y &= 13 \\ 3y &= 3 \\ y &= 1 \end{aligned}$$

The solution is $(5, 1)$.

22. subtraction

$$\begin{array}{rrl} & 2m - 5n = & -6 \\ (-) & 2m - 7n = & -14 \\ \hline & 2n = & 8 \\ & n = & 4 \end{array} \qquad \begin{aligned} 2m - 5n &= -6 \\ 2m - 5(4) &= -6 \\ 2m - 20 &= -6 \\ 2m &= 14 \\ m &= 7 \end{aligned}$$

The solution is $(7, 4)$.

23. substitution

$$\begin{aligned} x - 2y &= 7 \\ x &= 7 + 2y \\ -3x + 6y &= -21 \\ -3(7 + 2y) + 6y &= -21 \\ -21 - 6y + 6y &= -21 \\ -21 &= -21 \end{aligned}$$

There are infinitely many solutions.

24. subtraction

$$\begin{array}{rrl} & 3r - 5s = & -35 \\ (-) & 2r - 5s = & -30 \\ \hline & r = & -5 \end{array} \qquad \begin{aligned} 3r - 5s &= -35 \\ 3(-5) - 5s &= -35 \\ -15 - 5s &= -35 \\ -5s &= -20 \\ s &= 4 \end{aligned}$$

The solution is $(-5, 4)$.

25. subtraction

$$\begin{array}{rrl} & 13a + 5b = & -11 \\ (-) & 13a + 11b = & 7 \\ \hline & -6b = & -18 \\ & b = & 3 \end{array} \qquad \begin{aligned} 13a + 5b &= -11 \\ 13a + 5(3) &= -11 \\ 13a + 15 &= -11 \\ 13a &= -26 \\ a &= -2 \end{aligned}$$

The solution is $(-2, 3)$.

26. subtraction

$$\begin{aligned} a - 2b - 5 = 0 &\rightarrow \\ 3a - 2b - 9 = 0 &\rightarrow \end{aligned} \qquad \begin{array}{rrl} & a - 2b = & 5 \\ (-) & 3a - 2b = & 9 \\ \hline & -2a \quad = & -4 \\ & a = & 2 \end{array}$$

$$\begin{aligned} a - 2b &= 5 \\ 2 - 2b &= 5 \\ -2b &= 3 \\ b &= -\tfrac{3}{2} \end{aligned}$$

The solution is $\left(2, -\frac{3}{2}\right)$.

27. subtraction

$$\begin{aligned} 4x = 7 - 5y &\rightarrow \\ 8x = 9 - 5y &\rightarrow \end{aligned} \qquad \begin{array}{rrl} & 4x + 5y = & 7 \\ (-) & 8x + 5y = & 9 \\ \hline & -4x = & -2 \\ & x = & \frac{1}{2} \end{array}$$

$$\begin{aligned} 4x + 5y &= 7 \\ 4\left(\tfrac{1}{2}\right) + 5y &= 7 \\ 2 + 5y &= 7 \\ 5y &= 5 \\ y &= 1 \end{aligned}$$

The solution is $\left(\frac{1}{2}, 1\right)$.

28. substitution

$$\begin{aligned} \tfrac{2}{3}x + y &= 7 \\ y &= 7 - \tfrac{2}{3}x \\ \tfrac{10}{3}x + 5y &= 11 \\ \tfrac{10}{3}x + 5\left(7 - \tfrac{2}{3}x\right) &= 11 \\ \tfrac{10}{3}x + 35 - \tfrac{10}{3}x &= 11 \\ 35 &\neq 11 \end{aligned}$$

There is no solution.

29. addition

$$\begin{array}{rrl} & \frac{3}{5}c - \frac{1}{5}d = & 9 \\ (+) & \frac{7}{5}c + \frac{1}{5}d = & 11 \\ \hline & 2c \quad = & 20 \\ & c = & 10 \end{array} \qquad \begin{aligned} \tfrac{3}{5}c - \tfrac{1}{5}d &= 9 \\ \tfrac{3}{5}(10) - \tfrac{1}{5}d &= 9 \\ 6 - \tfrac{1}{5}d &= 9 \\ -\tfrac{1}{5}d &= 3 \\ d &= -15 \end{aligned}$$

The solution is $(10, -15)$.

30. substitution

$$\begin{aligned} 0.3m &= 0.45 - 0.1n \\ m &= 1.5 - \tfrac{0.1}{0.3}n \\ 0.6m - 0.2n &= 0.9 \\ 0.6\left(1.5 - \tfrac{0.1}{0.3}n\right) - 0.2n &= 0.9 \\ 0.9 - 0.2n - 0.2n &= 0.9 \\ 0.9 - 0.4n &= 0.9 \\ -0.4n &= 0 \\ n &= 0 \end{aligned}$$

$$\begin{aligned} m &= 1.5 - \tfrac{0.1}{0.3}n \\ m &= 1.5 - \tfrac{0.1}{0.3}(0) \\ m &= 1.5 - 0 \\ m &= 1.5 \end{aligned}$$

The solution is $(1.5, 0)$.

31. addition

$$\begin{array}{rl} 1.44x - 3.24y &= -5.58 \\ (+)\ 1.08x + 3.24y &= 9.99 \\ \hline 2.52x &= 4.41 \\ x &= 1.75 \end{array}$$

$$\begin{aligned} 1.44x - 3.24y &= -5.58 \\ 1.44(1.75) - 3.24y &= -5.58 \\ 2.52 - 3.24y &= -5.58 \\ -3.24y &= -8.1 \\ y &= 2.5 \end{aligned}$$

The solution is (1.75, 2.5).

32. subtraction

$$\begin{array}{rl} 7.2m + 4.5n &= 129.06 \\ (-)\ 7.2m + 6.7n &= 136.54 \\ \hline -2.2n &= 7.48 \\ n &= 3.4 \end{array}$$

$$\begin{aligned} 7.2m + 4.5n &= 129.06 \\ 7.2m + 4.5(3.4) &= 129.06 \\ 7.2m + 15.3 &= 129.06 \\ 7.2m &= 113.76 \\ m &= 15.8 \end{aligned}$$

The solution is (15.8, 3.4).

33. Let x = the first number.
Let y = the second number.

$x + y = 64 \rightarrow$
$x - y = 42 \rightarrow$

$$\begin{array}{rl} x + y &= 64 \\ (+)\ x - y &= 42 \\ \hline 2x &= 106 \\ x &= 53 \end{array}$$

$$\begin{aligned} x + y &= 64 \\ 53 + y &= 64 \\ y &= 11 \end{aligned}$$

The two numbers are 11 and 53.

34. Let x = the first number.
Let y = the second number.

$x + y = 18 \rightarrow$
$x - y = 22 \rightarrow$

$$\begin{array}{rl} x + y &= 18 \\ (+)\ x - y &= 22 \\ \hline 2x &= 40 \\ x &= 20 \end{array}$$

$$\begin{aligned} x + y &= 18 \\ 20 + y &= 18 \\ y &= -2 \end{aligned}$$

The two numbers are 20 and −2.

35. Let x = the first number.
Let y = the second number.

$2x + y = 18 \rightarrow$
$4x - y = 12 \rightarrow$

$$\begin{array}{rl} 2x + y &= 18 \\ (+)\ 4x - y &= 12 \\ \hline 6x &= 30 \\ x &= 5 \end{array}$$

$$\begin{aligned} 2x + y &= 18 \\ 2(5) + y &= 18 \\ 10 + y &= 18 \\ y &= 8 \end{aligned}$$

The two numbers are 5 and 8.

36.

$$\begin{array}{rl} x + y &= 11 \\ (+)\ x - y &= 5 \\ \hline 2x &= 16 \\ x &= 8 \end{array}$$

$$\begin{aligned} x + y &= 11 \\ 8 + y &= 11 \\ y &= 3 \end{aligned}$$

$$\begin{aligned} xy &= (8)(3) \\ xy &= 24 \end{aligned}$$

37.

$$\begin{array}{rl} x + y &= 5 \\ (-)\ y + z &= 10 \\ \hline x - z &= -5 \\ (+)\ x + z &= 9 \\ \hline 2x &= 4 \\ x &= 2 \end{array}$$

$$\begin{aligned} x + y &= 5 \\ 2 + y &= 5 \\ y &= 3 \end{aligned}$$

$$\begin{aligned} y + z &= 10 \\ 3 + z &= 10 \\ z &= 7 \end{aligned}$$

The solution is (2, 3, 7).

38.

$$\begin{array}{rl} 2x + y + z &= 13 \\ (+)\ x - y + 2z &= 8 \\ \hline 3x + 3z &= 21 \\ (+)\ 4x - 3z &= 7 \\ \hline 7x &= 28 \\ x &= 4 \end{array}$$

$$\begin{aligned} 4x - 3z &= 7 \\ 4(4) - 3z &= 7 \\ 16 - 3z &= 7 \\ -3z &= -9 \\ z &= 3 \end{aligned}$$

$$\begin{aligned} 2x + y + z &= 13 \\ 2(4) + y + 3 &= 13 \\ 8 + y + 3 &= 13 \\ 11 + y &= 13 \\ y &= 2 \end{aligned}$$

The solution is (4, 2, 3).

39.

$$\begin{array}{rl} y + 3z &= 9 \\ (+)\ 12x - y + 7z &= 99 \\ \hline 12x + 10z &= 108 \end{array}$$

$$\begin{aligned} x + 2z &= 2 \\ x &= 2 - 2z \end{aligned}$$

$$\begin{aligned} 12x + 10z &= 108 \\ 12(2 - 2z) + 10z &= 108 \\ 24 - 24z + 10z &= 108 \\ 24 - 14z &= 108 \\ -14z &= 84 \\ z &= -6 \end{aligned}$$

$$\begin{aligned} x + 2z &= 2 \\ x + 2(-6) &= 2 \\ x - 12 &= 2 \\ x &= 14 \end{aligned}$$

$$\begin{aligned} y + 3z &= 9 \\ y + 3(-6) &= 9 \\ y - 18 &= 9 \\ y &= 27 \end{aligned}$$

The solution is (14, 27, −6).

40.

$$\begin{aligned} Ax + By &= 7 \\ A(4) + B(-1) &= 7 \\ 4A - B &= 7 \end{aligned}$$

$$\begin{aligned} Ax - By &= 9 \\ A(4) - B(-1) &= 9 \\ 4A + B &= 9 \end{aligned}$$

$$\begin{array}{rl} 4A - B &= 7 \\ (+)\ 4A + B &= 9 \\ \hline 8A &= 16 \\ A &= 2 \end{array}$$

$$\begin{aligned} 4A - B &= 7 \\ 4(2) - B &= 7 \\ 8 - B &= 7 \\ -B &= -1 \\ B &= 1 \end{aligned}$$

The solution is (2, 1).

41. Let x = the time for José and let y = the time for Ling.

$$\begin{aligned} x + y &= 2.6 \\ y &= x + 0.3 \end{aligned}$$

$$\begin{aligned} x + y &= 2.6 \\ x + (x + 0.3) &= 2.6 \\ 2x + 0.3 &= 2.6 \\ 2x &= 2.3 \\ x &= 1.15 \end{aligned}$$

$$\begin{aligned} y &= x + 0.3 \\ y &= 1.15 + 0.3 \\ y &= 1.45 \end{aligned}$$

José, 1.15 hours or 1 hour, 9 minutes;
Ling, 1.45 hours or 1 hour, 27 minutes.

42a.

$$\begin{array}{rl} 13x + 10y &= 9600 \\ (+)\ 3x - 10y &= 1500 \\ \hline 16x &= 11{,}100 \\ x &= 693.75 \end{array}$$

$$\begin{aligned} 13x + 10y &= 9600 \\ 13(693.75) + 10y &= 9600 \\ 9018.75 + 10y &= 9600 \\ 10y &= 581.25 \\ y &= 58.125 \end{aligned}$$

(693.75, 58.125)

42b.

$$\begin{array}{rl} 13x - 10y &= 0 \\ (+)\ 13x + 10y &= 9600 \\ \hline 26x &= 9600 \\ x &= 369.2 \end{array}$$

$$\begin{aligned} 13x - 10y &= 0 \\ 13(396.2) - 10y &= 0 \\ 4800 - 10y &= 0 \\ -10y &= -4800 \\ y &= 480 \end{aligned}$$

(369.2, 480); The height of the pyramid is 480 ft.

43.

	25% Acid	50% Acid	34% Acid
Total Gallons	x	y	500
Gallons of Acid	$0.25x$	$0.50y$	$0.34(500)$

$x + y = 500$
$x = 500 - y$
$0.25x + 0.50y = 0.34(500)$
$0.25(500 - y) + 0.50y = 170$
$125 - 0.25y + 0.50y = 170$
$125 + 0.25y = 170$
$0.25y = 45$
$y = 180$

$x = 500 - y$
$x = 500 - 180$
$x = 320$

320 gallons of 25% acid solution and 180 gallons of 50% acid solution should be used.

44. $5 - 8h \le 9$
$5 - 5 - 8h \le 9 - 5$
$-8h \le 4$
$\frac{-8h}{-8} \ge \frac{4}{-8}$
$h \ge -\frac{1}{2}$
$\left\{h \mid h \ge -\frac{1}{2}\right\}$

45. $m = \frac{y_2 - y_1}{x_2 - x_1}$
$= \frac{0 - (-9)}{-1 - 2}$
$= \frac{9}{-3}$
$= -3$

46. $6x - \frac{1}{2}y = -10$
$-\frac{1}{2}y = -6x - 10$
$-2\left(-\frac{1}{2}y\right) = -2(-6x - 10)$
$y = 12x + 20$

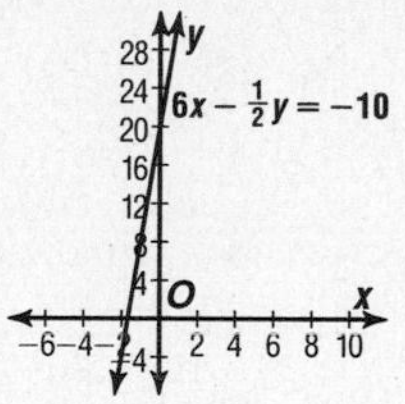

$m = 12$; y-intercept: 20

47. $-2(3t + 1) = 5$
$-6t - 2 = 5$
$-6t = 7$
$t = -\frac{7}{6}$

48. $\sqrt{15} \approx 3.87$

49. substitution (=)

Page 474 Self Test

1. $3x + y = 1$
$3x - 3x + y = 1 - 3x$
$y = -3x + 1$

$x - y = 3$
$x - x - y = 3 - x$
$-y = -x + 3$
$y = x - 3$

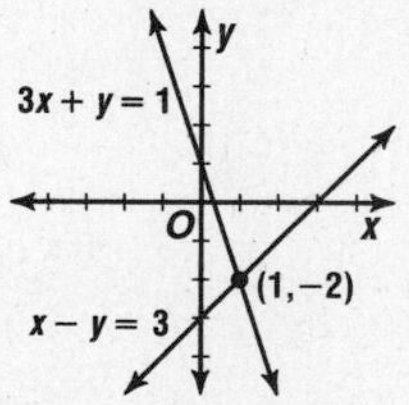

one solution; (1, −2)

2. $3y = 7 + 2x$
$\frac{3y}{3} = \frac{7}{3} + \frac{2x}{3}$
$y = \frac{2}{3}x + \frac{7}{3}$

$2x - 3y = 7$
$2x - 2x - 3y = 7 - 2x$
$-3y = -2x + 7$
$\frac{-3y}{-3} = \frac{-2x}{-3} + \frac{7}{-3}$
$y = \frac{2}{3}x - \frac{7}{3}$

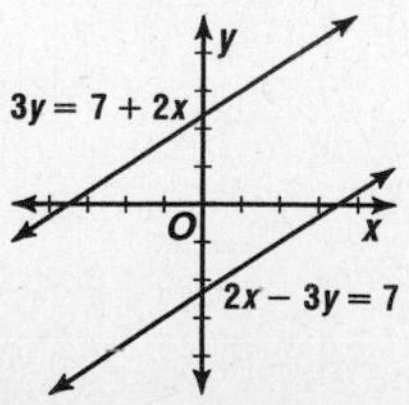

no solution

3. $4x + y = 12$
$4x - 4x + y = 12 - 4x$
$y = -4x + 12$

$x = 3 - \frac{1}{4}y$
$x + \frac{1}{4}y = 3 - \frac{1}{4}y + \frac{1}{4}y$
$x + \frac{1}{4}y = 3$
$x - x + \frac{1}{4}y = 3 - x$
$\frac{1}{4}y = -x + 3$
$4\left(\frac{1}{4}y\right) = 4(-x + 3)$
$y = -4x + 12$

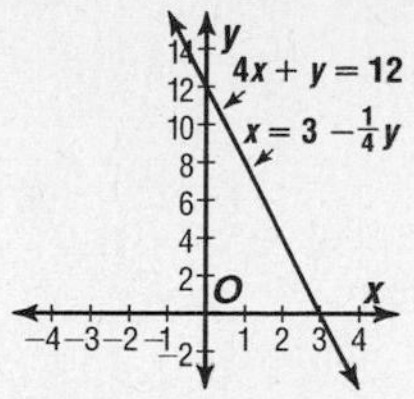

infinitely many solutions

4. $x + 2y = 22$
$x + 2(5x) = 22$
$x + 10x = 22$
$11x = 22$
$x = 2$

$y = 5x$
$y = 5(2)$
$y = 10$

(2, 10)

5. Solve for y: $y - 3x = 20$
$y = 20 + 3x$

$2y - x = -5$
$2(20 + 3x) - x = -5$
$40 + 6x - x = -5$
$40 + 5x = -5$
$5x = -45$
$x = -9$

$y = 20 + 3x$
$y = 20 + 3(-9)$
$y = 20 + (-27)$
$y = -7$

(−9, −7)

6. Solve for x: $x + \frac{8}{3}y = 12$
$x = 12 - \frac{8}{3}y$

$3x + 2y = 18$
$3\left(12 - \frac{8}{3}y\right) + 2y = 18$
$36 - 8y + 2y = 18$
$36 - 6y = 18$
$-6y = -18$
$y = 3$

$x = 12 - \frac{8}{3}y$
$x = 12 - \frac{8}{3}(3)$
$x = 12 - 8$
$x = 4$

(4, 3)

7. $x - y = -5$
$(+)\ x + y = 25$
$2x = 20$
$x = 10$

$x - y = -5$
$10 - y = -5$
$-y = -15$
$y = 15$

(10, 15)

8. $3x + 5y = 14$
$(+)\ 2x - 5y = 1$
$5x = 15$
$x = 3$

$3x + 5y = 14$
$3(3) + 5y = 14$
$9 + 5y = 14$
$5y = 5$
$y = 1$

(3, 1)

9. $5x + 4y = 12$
$(-)\ 3x + 4y = 4$
$2x = 8$
$x = 4$

$5x + 4y = 12$
$5(4) + 4y = 12$
$20 + 4y = 12$
$4y = -8$
$y = -2$

(4, −2)

10. Let x = the cost for members and let y = the cost for nonmembers.

$$\begin{array}{lcr} 3x + 3y = 180 & \rightarrow & 3x + 3y = 180 \\ 5x + 3y = 210 & \rightarrow & \underline{(-)\ 5x + 3y = 210} \\ & & -2x \quad = -30 \\ & & x = \quad 15 \end{array}$$

$$\begin{aligned} 3x + 3y &= 180 \\ 3(15) + 3y &= 180 \\ 45 + 3y &= 180 \\ 3y &= 135 \\ y &= 45 \end{aligned}$$

The cost is \$15 for members and \$45 for nonmembers.

8-4 Elimination Using Multiplication

Pages 478–479 Check for Understanding

1. See students' work.
2. To make either the x-term or y-term coefficients additive inverses.
3. Sample answer: $3x + 5y = 7$, $4x - 10y = 1$
4. See students' work.
5. Multiply the first equation by -3, then add.

$$\begin{array}{lcr} x + 5x = 4 & \rightarrow & -3x - 15y = -12 \\ 3x - 7y = -10 & \rightarrow & \underline{(+)\ 3x - 7y = -10} \\ & & -22y = -22 \\ & & y = \quad 1 \end{array}$$

$$\begin{aligned} x + 5y &= 4 \\ x + 5(1) &= 4 \\ x + 5 &= 4 \\ x &= -1 \end{aligned}$$

The solution is $(-1, 1)$.

6. Multiply the first equation by 3, multiply the second equation by -2, then add.

$$\begin{array}{lcr} 2x - y = 6 & \rightarrow & 6x - 3y = 18 \\ 3x + 4y = -2 & \rightarrow & \underline{(+)\ -6x - 8y = \quad 4} \\ & & -11y = 22 \\ & & y = -2 \end{array}$$

$$\begin{aligned} 2x - y &= 6 \\ 2x - (-2) &= 6 \\ 2x + 2 &= 6 \\ 2x &= 4 \\ x &= 2 \end{aligned}$$

The solution is $(2, -2)$.

7. Multiply the second equation by 5, then add.

$$\begin{array}{lcr} -5x + 3y = 6 & \rightarrow & -5x + 3y = \quad 6 \\ x - y = 4 & \rightarrow & \underline{(+)\ 5x - 5y = 20} \\ & & -2y - 26 \\ & & y = -13 \end{array}$$

$$\begin{aligned} x - y &= 4 \\ x - (-13) &= 4 \\ x + 13 &= 4 \\ x &= -9 \end{aligned}$$

The solution is $(-9, -13)$.

8. Multiply the first equation by 5, multiply the second equation by -7, then add.

$$\begin{array}{lcr} 4x + 7y = 6 & \rightarrow & 20x + 35y = \quad 30 \\ 6x + 5y = 20 & \rightarrow & \underline{(+)\ -42x - 35y = -140} \\ & & -22x \quad = -110 \\ & & x = 5 \end{array}$$

$$\begin{aligned} 4x + 7y &= 6 \\ 4(5) + 7y &= 6 \\ 20 + 7y &= 6 \\ 7y &= -14 \\ y &= -2 \end{aligned}$$

The solution is $(5, -2)$.

9. Multiply the first equation by 5, multiply the second equation by -8, then add.

$$\begin{array}{lcr} 3x - 8y = 13 & \rightarrow & 15x - 40y = \quad 65 \\ 4x - 5y = 6 & \rightarrow & \underline{(+)\ -32x + 40y = -48} \\ & & -17x \quad = \quad 17 \\ & & x = -1 \end{array}$$

$$\begin{aligned} 3x - 8y &= 13 \\ 3(-1) - 8y &= 13 \\ -3 - 8y &= 13 \\ -8y &= 16 \\ y &= -2 \end{aligned}$$

The solution is $(-1, -2)$.

10. Multiply the first equation by 4, multiply the second equation by 3, then add.

$$\begin{array}{lcr} 2x - 3y = 2 & \rightarrow & 8x - 12y = \quad 8 \\ 5x + 4y = 28 & \rightarrow & \underline{(+)\ 15x + 12y = 84} \\ & & 23x \quad = 92 \\ & & x = 4 \end{array}$$

$$\begin{aligned} 2x - 3y &= 2 \\ 2(4) - 3y &= 2 \\ 8 - 3y &= 2 \\ -3y &= -6 \\ y &= 2 \end{aligned}$$

The solution is $(4, 2)$.

11. b elimination using addition or subtraction

$$\begin{array}{rcr} 3x - 7y = \quad 6 & \quad & 3x - 7y = 6 \\ \underline{(+)\ 2x + 7y = \quad 4} & & 3(2) - 7y = 6 \\ 5x \quad = 10 & & 6 - 7y = 6 \\ x = 2 & & -7y = 0 \\ & & y = 0 \end{array}$$

The solution is $(2, 0)$.

12 a substitution

$$\begin{array}{rcl} 3x - 2y = -7 & \quad & y = 4x + 11 \\ 3x - 2(4x + 11) = -7 & & y = 4(-3) + 11 \\ 3x - 8x - 22 = -7 & & y = -12 + 11 \\ -5x - 22 = -7 & & y = -1 \\ -5x = 15 & & \\ x = -3 & & \end{array}$$

The solution is $(-3, -1)$.

13. c elimination using multiplication

$$\begin{array}{lcr} 4x + 3y = 19 & \rightarrow & 16x + 12y = \quad 76 \\ 3x - 4y = 8 & \rightarrow & \underline{(+)\ 9x - 12y = \quad 24} \\ & & 25x \quad = 100 \\ & & x = 4 \end{array}$$

$$\begin{aligned} 4x + 3y &= 19 \\ 4(4) + 3y &= 19 \\ 16 + 3y &= 19 \\ 3y &= 3 \\ y &= 1 \end{aligned}$$

The solution is $(4, 1)$.

14a–b.

	r	t	d	$rt = d$
Downstream	$r + c$	2	36	$2r + 2c = 36$
Upstream	$r - c$	3	36	$3r - 3c = 36$

$$\begin{array}{lrl} 2r + 2c = 36 \text{ (Multiply by 3.)} & & 6r + 6c = 108 \\ 3r - 3c = 36 \text{ (Multiply by 2.)} & (+) & 6r - 6c = 72 \\ \hline & & 12r = 180 \\ & & r = 15 \end{array}$$

14a. The rate of the riverboat in still water is 15 mph.

14b.
$$\begin{aligned} 2r + 2c &= 36 \\ 2(15) + 2c &= 36 \\ 30 + 2c &= 36 \\ 2c &= 6 \\ c &= 3 \end{aligned}$$
The rate of the current is 3 mph.

Pages 479–481 Exercises

15.
$$\begin{array}{lcl} 2x + y = 5 & \rightarrow & 4x + 2y = 10 \\ 3x - 2y = 4 & \rightarrow & (+)\ 3x - 2y = 4 \\ \hline & & 7x = 14 \\ & & x = 2 \end{array}$$
$$\begin{aligned} 2x + y &= 5 \\ 2(2) + y &= 5 \\ 4 + y &= 5 \\ y &= 1 \end{aligned}$$
The solution is (2, 1).

16.
$$\begin{array}{lcl} 4x - 3y = 12 & \rightarrow & 4x - 3y = 12 \\ x + 2y = 14 & \rightarrow & (+)\ -4x - 8y = -56 \\ \hline & & -11y = -44 \\ & & y = 4 \end{array}$$
$$\begin{aligned} x + 2y &= 14 \\ x + 2(4) &= 14 \\ x + 8 &= 14 \\ x &= 6 \end{aligned}$$
The solution is (6, 4).

17.
$$\begin{array}{lcl} 3x - 2y = 19 & \rightarrow & 6x - 4y = 38 \\ 5x + 4y = 17 & \rightarrow & (+)\ 5x + 4y = 17 \\ \hline & & 11x = 55 \\ & & x = 5 \end{array}$$
$$\begin{aligned} 3x - 2y &= 19 \\ 3(5) - 2y &= 19 \\ 15 - 2y &= 19 \\ -2y &= 4 \\ y &= -2 \end{aligned}$$
The solution is (5, −2).

18.
$$\begin{array}{lcl} 9x = 5y - 2 & \rightarrow & 9x - 5y = -2 \\ 3x = 2y - 2 & \rightarrow & (+)\ -9x + 6y = 6 \\ \hline & & y = 4 \end{array}$$
$$\begin{aligned} 9x &= 5y - 2 \\ 9x &= 5(4) - 2 \\ 9x &= 20 - 2 \\ 9x &= 18 \\ x &= 2 \end{aligned}$$
The solution is (2, 4).

19.
$$\begin{array}{lcl} 7x + 3y = -1 & \rightarrow & 7x + 3y = -1 \\ 4x + y = 3 & \rightarrow & (+)\ -12x - 3y = -9 \\ \hline & & -5x = -10 \\ & & x = 2 \end{array}$$
$$\begin{aligned} 7x + 3y &= -1 \\ 7(2) + 3y &= -1 \\ 14 + 3y &= -1 \\ 3y &= -15 \\ y &= -5 \end{aligned}$$
The solution is (2, −5).

20.
$$\begin{array}{lcl} 6x - 5y = 27 & \rightarrow & 12x - 10y = 54 \\ 3x + 10y = -24 & \rightarrow & (+)\ 3x + 10y = -24 \\ \hline & & 15x = 30 \\ & & x = 2 \end{array}$$
$$\begin{aligned} 6x - 5y &= 27 \\ 6(2) - 5y &= 27 \\ 12 - 5y &= 27 \\ -5y &= 15 \\ y &= -3 \end{aligned}$$
The solution is (2, −3).

21.
$$\begin{array}{lcl} 8x - 3y = -11 & \rightarrow & 8x - 3y = -11 \\ 2x - 5y = 27 & \rightarrow & (+)\ -8x + 20y = -108 \\ \hline & & 17y = -119 \\ & & y = -7 \end{array}$$
$$\begin{aligned} 8x - 3y &= -11 \\ 8x - 3(-7) &= -11 \\ 8x + 21 &= -11 \\ 8x &= -32 \\ x &= -4 \end{aligned}$$
The solution is (−4, −7).

22.
$$\begin{array}{lcl} 11x - 5y = 80 & \rightarrow & -33x + 15y = -240 \\ 9x - 15y = 120 & \rightarrow & (+)\ 9x - 15y = 120 \\ \hline & & -24x = -120 \\ & & x = 5 \end{array}$$
$$\begin{aligned} 11x - 5y &= 80 \\ 11(5) - 5y &= 80 \\ 55 - 5y &= 80 \\ -5y &= 25 \\ y &= -5 \end{aligned}$$
The solution is (5, −5).

23.
$$\begin{array}{lcl} 4x - 7y = 10 & \rightarrow & 8x - 14y = 20 \\ 3x + 2y = -7 & \rightarrow & (+)\ 21x + 14y = -49 \\ \hline & & 29x = -29 \\ & & x = -1 \end{array}$$
$$\begin{aligned} 4x - 7y &= 10 \\ 4(-1) - 7y &= 10 \\ -4 - 7y &= 10 \\ -7y &= 14 \\ y &= -2 \end{aligned}$$
The solution is (−1, −2).

24.
$$\begin{array}{lcl} 3x - \frac{1}{2}y = 10 & \rightarrow & 6x - y = 20 \\ 5x + \frac{1}{4}y = 8 & \rightarrow & (+)\ 20x + y = 32 \\ \hline & & 26x = 52 \\ & & x = 2 \end{array}$$
$$\begin{aligned} 3x - \tfrac{1}{2}y &= 10 \\ 3(2) - \tfrac{1}{2}y &= 10 \\ 6 - \tfrac{1}{2}y &= 10 \\ -\tfrac{1}{2}y &= 4 \\ y &= -8 \end{aligned}$$
The solution is (2, −8).

25. $2x + \frac{2}{3}y = 4 \rightarrow 6x + 2y = 12$

$x - \frac{1}{2}y = 7 \rightarrow (+)\ 4x - 2y = 28$

$10x = 40$

$x = 4$

$2x + \frac{2}{3}y = 4$

$2(4) + \frac{2}{3}y = 4$

$8 + \frac{2}{3}y = 4$

$\frac{2}{3}y = -4$

$\frac{3}{2}\left(\frac{2}{3}y\right) = \frac{3}{2}(-4)$

$y = -6$

The solution is (4, −6).

26. $\frac{2x+y}{3} = 15 \rightarrow 2x + y = 45$

$\frac{3x-y}{5} = 1 \rightarrow (+)\ 3x - y = 5$

$5x = 50$

$x = 10$

$2x + y = 45$

$2(10) + y = 45$

$20 + y = 45$

$y = 25$

The solution is (10, 25).

27. $7x + 2y = 3(x + 16)$ $\quad$ $x + 16 = 5y + 3x$

$7x + 2y = 3x + 48$ $\quad$ $-2x + 16 = 5y$

$4x + 2y = 48$ $\quad$ $-2x = 5y - 16$

$-2x - 5y = -16$

$4x + 2y = 48 \rightarrow 4x + 2y = 48$

$-2x - 5y = -16 \rightarrow (+)\ -4x - 10y = -32$

$-8y = 16$

$y = -2$

$4x + 2y = 48$

$4x + 2(-2) = 48$

$4x - 4 = 48$

$4x = 52$

$x = 13$

The solution is (13, −2).

28. $0.4x + 0.5y = 2.5 \rightarrow 2.8x + 3.5y = 17.5$

$1.2x - 3.5y = 2.5 \rightarrow (+)\ 1.2x - 3.5y = 2.5$

$4.0x = 20.0$

$x = 5$

$0.4x + 0.5y = 2.5$

$0.4(5) + 0.5y = 2.5$

$2.0 + 0.5y = 2.5$

$0.5y = 0.5$

$y = 1$

The solution is (5, 1).

29. $1.8x - 0.3y = 14.4 \rightarrow -3.6x + 0.6y = -28.8$

$x - 0.6y = 2.8 \rightarrow (+)x - 0.6y = 2.8$

$-2.6x = -26$

$x = 10$

$x - 0.6y = 2.8$

$10 - 0.6y = 2.8$

$-0.6y = -7.2$

$y = 12$

The solution is (10, 12).

30. Let t = the tens digit.
Let u = the units digit.
Then $10t + u$ = the original number.

$t + u = 14$ $\quad$ $10u + t = 10t + u - 18$

$9u - 9t = -18$

$t + u = 14 \rightarrow 9u + 9t = 126$

$9u - 9t = -18 \rightarrow (+)\ 9u - 9t = -18$

$18u = 108$

$u = 6$

$t + u = 14$

$t + 6 = 14$

$t = 8$

The original number is 10(8) + 6 or 86.

31. Let x = the first number.
Let y = the second number.

$3x = 2y$ $\quad$ $2x = 3 + y$

$3x - 2y = 0$ $\quad$ $2x - y = 3$

$3x - 2y = 0 \rightarrow 3x - 2y = 0$

$2x - y = 3 \rightarrow (+)\ -4x + 2y = -6$

$-x = -6$

$x = 6$

$3x - 2y = 0$

$3(6) - 2y = 0$

$18 - 2y = 0$

$-2y = -18$

$y = 9$

The numbers are 6 and 9.

32. Let t = the tens digit.
Let u = the units digit.
Then $10t + u$ = the original number, and
$10u + t$ = the new number.

$\frac{t}{u} = \frac{1}{4}$ $\quad$ $(10u + t) + (10t + u) = 110$

$4t = u$ $\quad$ $11t + 11u = 110$

$4t - u = 0$

$4t - u = 0 \rightarrow 44t - 11u = 0$

$11t + 11u = 110 \rightarrow (+)\ 11t + 11u = 110$

$55t = 110$

$t = 2$

$4t - u = 0$

$4(2) - u = 0$

$8 - u = 0$

$-u = -8$

$u = 8$

The original number is 10(2) + 8 or 28.

33. elimination using addition

$9x - 8y = 17$ $\quad$ $9x - 8y = 17$

$(+)\ 4x + 8y = 9$ $\quad$ $9(2) - 8y = 17$

$13x = 26$ $\quad$ $18 - 8y = 17$

$x = 2$ $\quad$ $-8y = -1$

$y = \frac{1}{8}$

The solution is $\left(2, \frac{1}{8}\right)$.

34. elimination using multiplication

$$\begin{aligned} 3x - 4y &= -10 &\rightarrow\quad 6x - 8y &= -20 \\ 5x + 8y &= -2 &\rightarrow\quad (+)\ 5x + 8y &= -2 \\ & & 11x \quad &= -22 \\ & & x &= -2 \end{aligned}$$

$$\begin{aligned} 3x - 4y &= -10 \\ 3(-2) - 4y &= -10 \\ -6 - 4y &= -10 \\ -4y &= -4 \\ y &= 1 \end{aligned}$$

The solution is $(-2, 1)$.

35. substitution or elimination using multiplication

$$\begin{aligned} x + 2y &= -1 &\rightarrow\quad -2x - 4y &= 2 \\ 2x + 4y &= -2 &\rightarrow\quad (+)\ 2x + 4y &= -2 \\ & & 0 &= 0 \end{aligned}$$

There are infinitely many solutions.

36. elimination using multiplication

$$\begin{aligned} 5x + 3y &= 12 &\rightarrow\quad 25x + 15y &= 60 \\ 4x - 5y &= 17 &\rightarrow\quad (+)\ 12x - 15y &= 51 \\ & & 37x \quad &= 111 \\ & & x &= 3 \end{aligned}$$

$$\begin{aligned} 5x + 3y &= 12 \\ 5(3) + 3y &= 12 \\ 15 + 3y &= 12 \\ 3y &= -3 \\ y &= -1 \end{aligned}$$

The solution is $(3, -1)$.

37. elimination using subtraction

$$\begin{aligned} \tfrac{2}{3}x - \tfrac{1}{2}y &= 14 \\ (-)\ \tfrac{5}{6}x - \tfrac{1}{2}y &= 18 \\ -\tfrac{1}{6}x \quad &= -4 \\ x &= 24 \end{aligned}$$

$$\begin{aligned} \tfrac{2}{3}x - \tfrac{1}{2}y &= 14 \\ \tfrac{2}{3}(24) - \tfrac{1}{2}y &= 14 \\ 16 - \tfrac{1}{2}y &= 14 \\ -\tfrac{1}{2}y &= -2 \\ y &= 4 \end{aligned}$$

The solution is $(24, 4)$.

38. elimination using multiplication

$$\begin{aligned} \tfrac{1}{2}x - \tfrac{2}{3}y &= \tfrac{7}{3} &\rightarrow\quad -\tfrac{3}{2}x + 2y &= -7 \\ \tfrac{3}{2}x + 2y &= -25 &\rightarrow\quad (+)\ \tfrac{3}{2}x + 2y &= -25 \\ & & 4y &= -32 \\ & & y &= -8 \end{aligned}$$

$$\begin{aligned} \tfrac{1}{2}x - \tfrac{2}{3}y &= \tfrac{7}{3} \\ \tfrac{1}{2}x - \tfrac{2}{3}(-8) &= \tfrac{7}{3} \\ \tfrac{1}{2}x + \tfrac{16}{3} &= \tfrac{7}{3} \\ \tfrac{1}{2}x &= -\tfrac{9}{3} \\ x &= -6 \end{aligned}$$

The solution is $(-6, -8)$.

39.

$$\begin{aligned} \frac{1}{x-5} - \frac{3}{y+6} &= 0 \\ \frac{1}{x-5} &= \frac{3}{y+6} \\ 1(y + 6) &= 3(x - 5) \\ y + 6 &= 3x - 15 \\ -3x + y + 6 &= -15 \\ -3x + y &= -21 \end{aligned}$$

$$\begin{aligned} \frac{2}{x+7} - \frac{1}{y-3} &= 0 \\ \frac{2}{x+7} &= \frac{1}{y-3} \\ 2(y - 3) &= 1(x + 7) \\ 2y - 6 &= x + 7 \\ -x + 2y - 6 &= 7 \\ -x + 2y &= 13 \end{aligned}$$

$$\begin{aligned} -3x + y &= -21 &\rightarrow\quad 6x - 2y &= 42 \\ -x + 2y &= 13 &\rightarrow\quad (+)\ -x + 2y &= 13 \\ & & 5x \quad &= 55 \\ & & x &= 11 \end{aligned}$$

$$\begin{aligned} -3x + y &= -21 \\ -3(11) + y &= -21 \\ -33 + y &= -21 \\ y &= 12 \end{aligned}$$

The solution is $(11, 12)$.

40.

$$\begin{aligned} \frac{2}{x} + \frac{3}{y} &= 16 &\rightarrow\quad \frac{2}{x} + \frac{3}{y} &= 16 \\ \frac{1}{x} + \frac{1}{y} &= 7 &\rightarrow\quad (+)\ -\frac{2}{x} - \frac{2}{y} &= 14 \\ & & \frac{1}{y} &= 2 \\ & & 1 &= 2y \\ & & y &= \frac{1}{2} \end{aligned}$$

$$\begin{aligned} \frac{2}{x} + \frac{3}{y} &= 16 \\ \frac{2}{x} + \frac{3}{\frac{1}{2}} &= 16 \\ \frac{2}{x} + 6 &= 16 \\ \frac{2}{x} &= 10 \\ 10x &= 2 \\ x &= \frac{1}{5} \end{aligned}$$

The solution is $\left(\frac{1}{5}, \frac{1}{2}\right)$.

41.

$$\begin{aligned} \frac{1}{x-y} &= \frac{1}{y} \\ y &= x - y \\ 2y - x &= 0 \end{aligned}$$

$$\begin{aligned} \frac{1}{x-y} &= 2 \\ 2(x + y) &= 1 \\ 2x + 2y &= 1 \end{aligned}$$

$$\begin{aligned} 2x + 2y &= 1 &\rightarrow\quad 2x + 2y &= 1 \\ -x + 2y &= 0 &\rightarrow\quad (+)\ -2x + 4y &= 0 \\ & & 6y &= 1 \\ & & y &= \frac{1}{6} \end{aligned}$$

$$\begin{aligned} 2y - x &= 0 \\ 2\left(\frac{1}{6}\right) - x &= 0 \\ \frac{1}{3} - x &= 0 \\ -x &= -\frac{1}{3} \\ x &= \frac{1}{3} \end{aligned}$$

The solution is $\left(\frac{1}{3}, \frac{1}{6}\right)$.

42a. Enter: 8, 2, 0, 12, 3, 0 INFINITELY MANY

42b. Enter: 1, −2, 5, 3, −5, 8 X = −9, Y = −7

42c. Enter: 5, 5, 16, 2, 2, 5 NO SOLUTION

42d. Enter: 7, −3, 5, 14, −6, 10 INFINITELY MANY

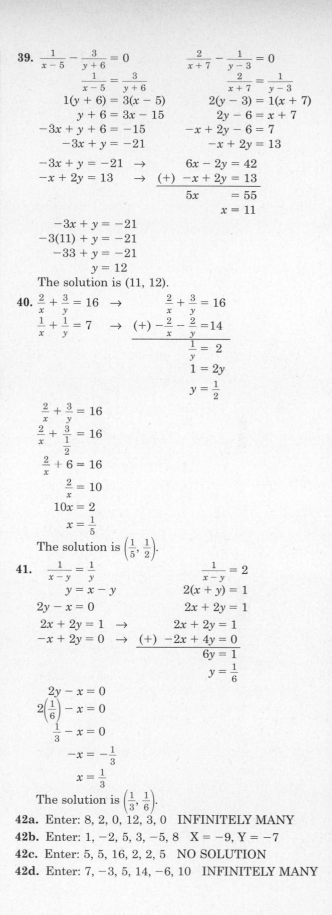

43. $5x + 4y = 18 \rightarrow \quad -10x - 8y = -36$
$2x + 9y = 59 \rightarrow \quad (+)\ 10x + 45y = 295$

$$37y = 259$$
$$y = 7$$

$$\begin{aligned} 5x + 4y &= 18 \\ 5x + 4(7) &= 18 \\ 5x + 28 &= 18 \\ 5x &= -10 \\ x &= -2 \end{aligned}$$

$(-2, 7)$

$3x - 5y = -4 \rightarrow \quad 12x - 20y = -16$
$5x + 4y = 18 \rightarrow \quad (+)\ 25x + 20y = 90$

$$37x = 74$$
$$x = 2$$

$$\begin{aligned} 3x - 5y &= -4 \\ 3(2) - 5y &= -4 \\ 6 - 5y &= -4 \\ -5y &= -10 \\ y &= 2 \end{aligned}$$

$(2, 2)$

$2x + 9y = 59 \rightarrow \quad -6x - 27y = -177$
$3x - 5y = -4 \rightarrow \quad (+)\ 6x - 10y = -8$

$$-37y = -185$$
$$y = 5$$

$$\begin{aligned} 2x + 9y &= 59 \\ 2x + 9(5) &= 59 \\ 2x + 45 &= 59 \\ 2x &= 14 \\ x &= 7 \end{aligned}$$

$(7, 5)$

The vertices are $(-2, 7)$, $(2, 2)$, and $(7, 5)$.

44. $-5x + 7y = 0 \rightarrow \quad -15x + 21y = 0$
$3x + 8y = 305 \rightarrow \quad (+)\ 15x + 40y = 1525$

$$61y = 1525$$
$$y = 25$$

$$\begin{aligned} -5x + 7y &= 0 \\ -5x + 7(25) &= 0 \\ -5x + 175 &= 0 \\ -5x &= -175 \\ x &= 35 \end{aligned}$$

The coordinates are (35, 25).

45. Let x = the number of 2-seat tables and let y = the number of 4-seat tables.

$x + y = 17 \rightarrow \quad -2x - 2y = -34$
$2x + 4y = 56 \rightarrow \quad (+)\ 2x + 4y = 56$

$$2y = 22$$
$$y = 11$$

$$\begin{aligned} x + y &= 17 \\ x + 11 &= 17 \\ x &= 6 \end{aligned}$$

They should buy 6 2-seat tables, and 11 4-seat tables.

46. Let x = the rate per minute for peak and let y = the rate per minute for nonpeak.

$45x + 50y = 27.75 \rightarrow \quad -135x - 150y = -83.25$
$70x + 30y = 36.00 \rightarrow \quad (+)\ 350x + 150y = 180.00$

$$215x = 96.75$$
$$x = 0.45$$

$$\begin{aligned} 70x + 30y &= 36.00 \\ 70(0.45) + 30y &= 36.00 \\ 31.5 + 30y &= 36.00 \\ 30y &= 4.50 \\ y &= 0.15 \end{aligned}$$

The rate per minute is \$0.45 for peak minutes and \$0.15 for nonpeak minutes.

47. $$\begin{aligned} 2x - y &= 10 \\ -y &= -2x + 10 \\ y &= 2x - 10 \end{aligned}$$

$$\begin{aligned} 5x + 3y &= 3 \\ 5x + 3(2x - 10) &= 3 \\ 5x + 6x - 30 &= 3 \\ 11x - 30 &= 3 \\ 11x &= 33 \\ x &= 3 \end{aligned}$$

$$\begin{aligned} y &= 2x - 10 \\ y &= 2(3) - 10 \\ y &= 6 - 10 \\ y &= -4 \end{aligned}$$

$(3, -4)$

48. 35

49. $P(\text{Paul last}) = \frac{1}{3}$

50. $$\begin{aligned} m &= \left(\frac{x_1 + x_2}{2}, \frac{y_1 + y_2}{2}\right) \\ &= \left(\frac{1 + (-3)}{2}, \frac{6 + 4}{2}\right) \\ &= \left(\frac{-2}{2}, \frac{10}{2}\right) \\ &= (-1, 5) \end{aligned}$$

51. Let y = yards headstart for Marcus.

Alfonso's rate $= \frac{440}{55}$ Marcus' rate $= \frac{440}{88}$

$rt = d$ and both must cover 440 yards in 55 seconds.

$$\begin{aligned} \left(\frac{440}{55}\right)55 &= \left(\frac{440}{88}\right)55 + y \\ 440 &= 275 + y \\ 165 &= y \end{aligned}$$

Marcus gets a 165 yard headstart.

52. $$\begin{aligned} 12m &= 4 \\ \frac{12m}{4} &= \frac{4}{4} \\ 3m &= 1 \end{aligned}$$

53. $\frac{4 \text{ sticks}}{1 \text{ pound}} \times \frac{\frac{1}{2} \text{ cup}}{1 \text{ stick}} = \frac{2 \text{ cups}}{1 \text{ pound}}$; 2 cups

54. $$\begin{aligned} 288 \div [3(9 + 3)] &= 288 \div [3(12)] \\ &= 288 \div 36 \\ &= 8 \end{aligned}$$

Page 481 Mathematics and Society

1. The infrared detection system can measure the heights of persons entering and leaving the store, and uses the height measurements to attempt to differentiate between adults and children. The higher the ratio of adults to children, the more checkout clerks would be needed.
2. Sample answer: The age and gender factors may not, by themselves, yield any useful data. Even if there were measurable differences, it may be too complicated and costly to include them in the system. For example, the device can count people in the ShopperTrak system, but it can't detect age or gender.

8-5 Graphing Systems of Inequalities

Pages 484–485 Check for Understanding

1. A boundary line is included in the graph if the inequality is $\le$ or $\ge$ and not included if the inequality is $<$ or $>$.
2. Rolanda is correct; Sample answer: $y < 2x + 4$ and $y > x - 1$; the solution of $y = 2x + 4$ and $y = x - 1$, $(-5, 6)$, is not a solution to the system of inequalities.
3. Sample answer: $y < x + 1$ and $y > x + 3$. There is no intersection.

4a. yes **4b.** yes **4c.** no **4d.** no

5. Answers will vary.

6. 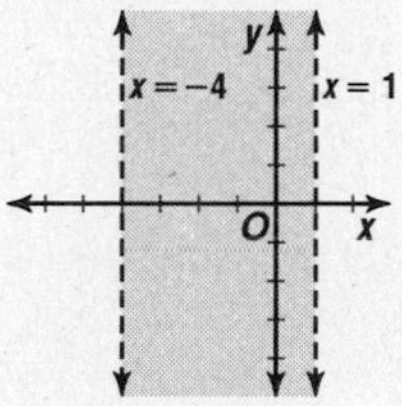

7. 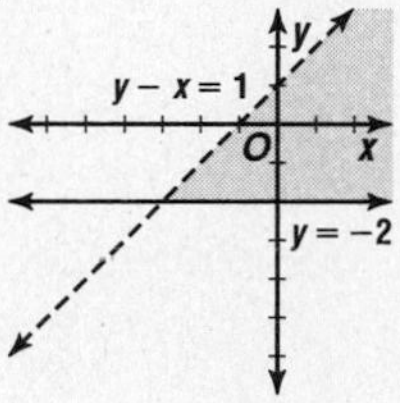

8. 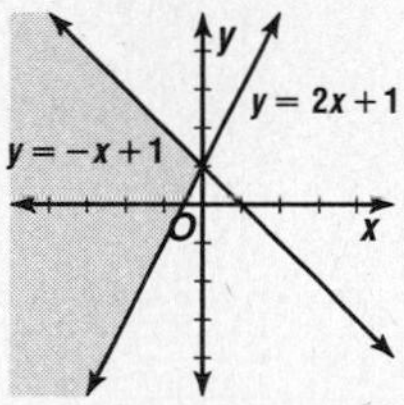

9. 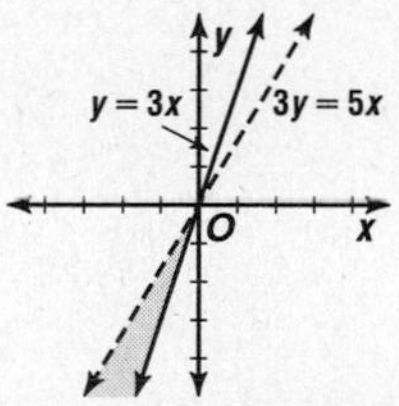

10. $y - x < 1$
$y < x + 1$
$y - x > 3$
$y > x + 3$

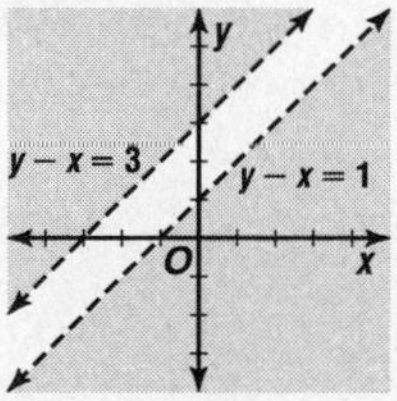

11. $2x + y \le 4$
$y \le -2x + y$
$3x - y \ge 6$
$-y \ge -3x + 6$
$y \le 3x - 6$

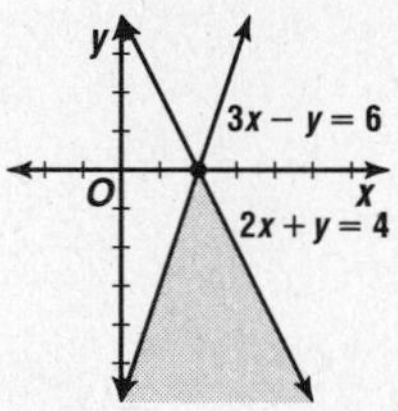

12. $(3, 0), (0, 3)$
$m = \frac{3-0}{0-3} = -1$
$y = mx + b$
$y = -x + 3$
$y \le -x + 3$

$(-3, 0), (0, 3)$
$m = \frac{3-0}{0-(-3)} = 1$
$y = mx + b$
$y = x + 3$
$y \le x + 3$

13. $(0, 0)\ (1, 1)$
$m = \frac{1-0}{1-0} = 1$
$y = mx + b$
$y = x$
$y > x$

$(-4, 0), (0, 4)$
$m = \frac{4-0}{0-(-4)} = 1$
$y = mx + b$
$y = x + 4$
$y \le x + 4$

14. Let x = the number of pepperoni pizzas and let y = the number of supreme pizzas.
$x + y \ge 6$
$9.95x + 12.95y \le 90$
Sample answer:
7 pepperoni, 1 supreme;
5 pepperoni, 3 supreme;
2 pepperoni, 5 supreme

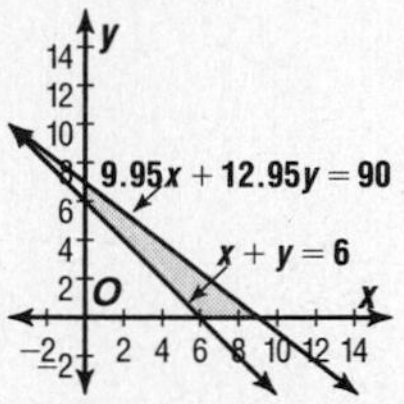

Pages 485–486 Exercises

15. 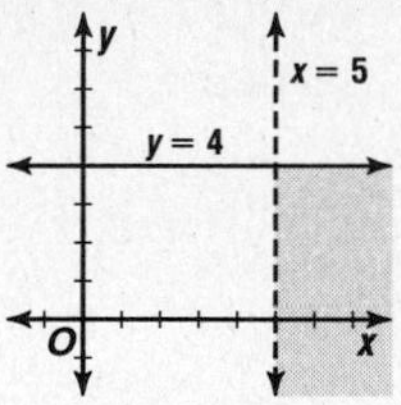

16. 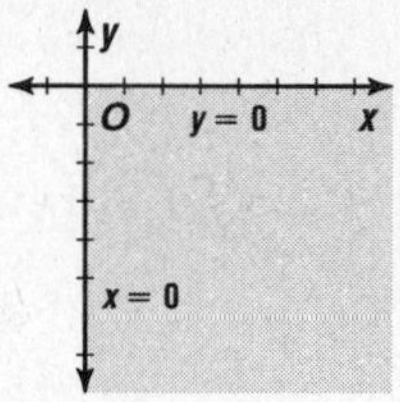

17. 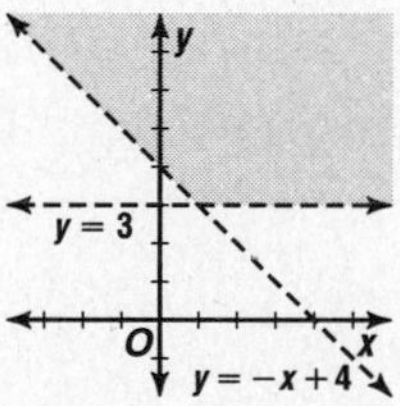

18. $x \le 2$
$y - 4 \ge 5$
$y \ge 9$

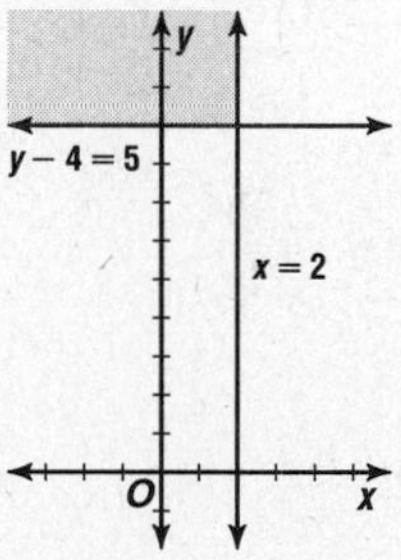

19. $x \ge 2$
$y + x \le 5$
$y \le -x + 5$

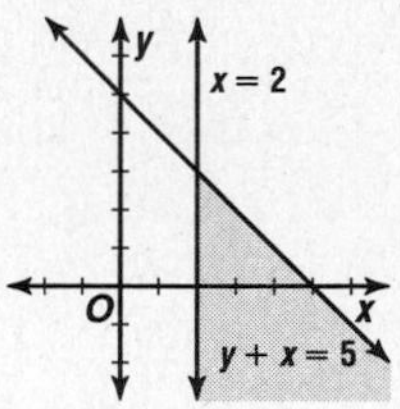

20. $y < -3$
$x - y > 1$
$-y > -x - 1$
$y < x + 1$

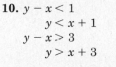

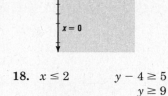

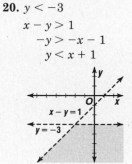

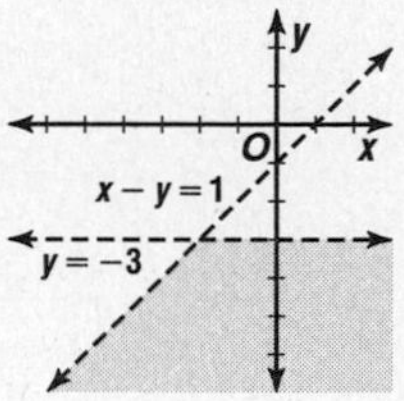

21. 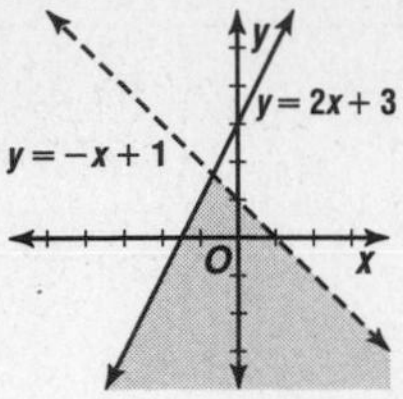

22. $y - x < 3$
$y < x + 3$
$y - x \geq 2$
$y \geq x + 2$

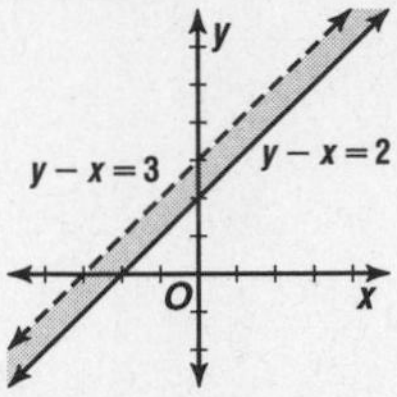

23. $y \geq 3x$
$7y < 2x$
$y < \frac{2}{7}x$

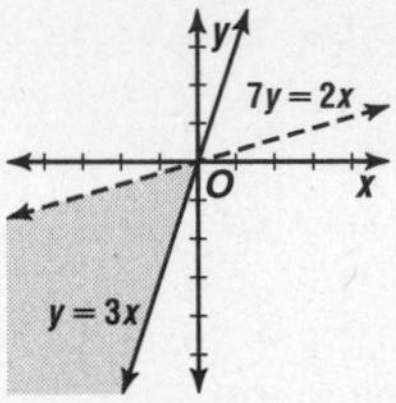

24. $x - y < -1$
$-y < -x - 1$
$y > x + 1$
$x - y > 3$
$-y > -x + 3$
$y < x - 3$

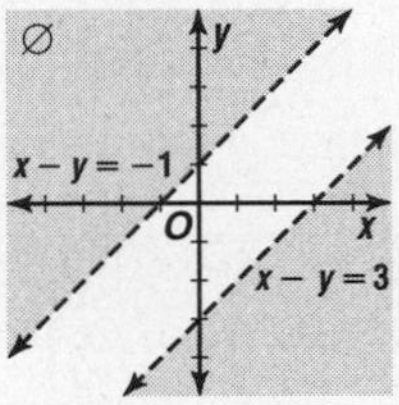

25. $2y + x < 6$
$2y < -x + 6$
$y < -\frac{1}{2}x + 3$
$3x - y > 4$
$-y > -3x + 4$
$y < 3x - 4$

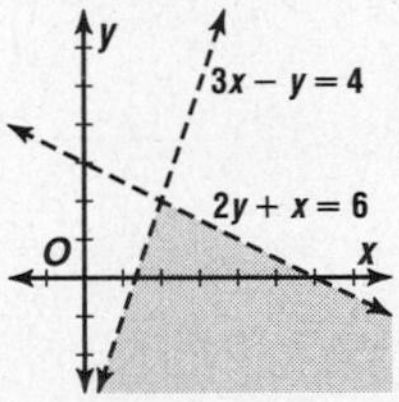

26. $3x - 4y < 1$
$-4y < -3x + 1$
$y > \frac{3}{4}x - \frac{1}{4}$
$x + 2y \leq 7$
$2y \leq -x + 7$
$y \leq -\frac{1}{2}x + \frac{7}{2}$

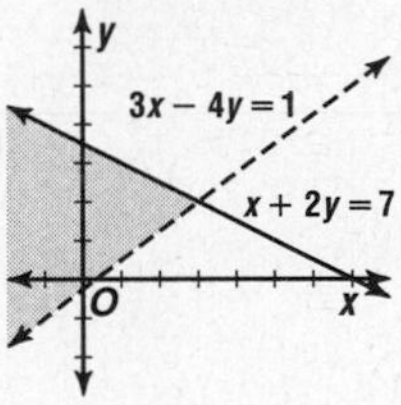

27. $y - 4 > x$
$y > x + 4$
$y + x < 4$
$y < -x + 4$

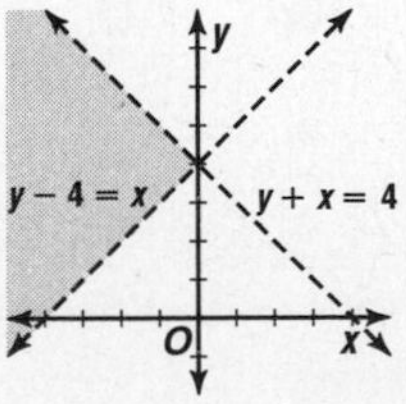

28. $5y \geq 3x + 10$
$y \geq \frac{3}{5}x + 2$
$2y \leq 4x - 10$
$y \leq 2x - 5$

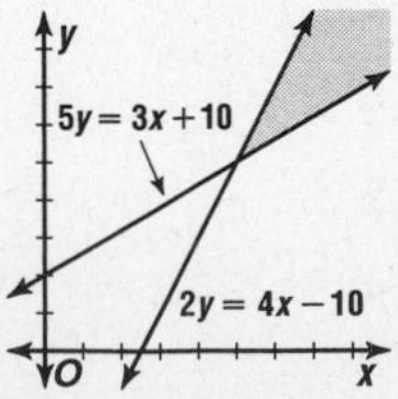

29. $y + 2 \leq x$
$y \leq x - 2$
$2y - 3 > 2x$
$2y > 2x + 3$
$y > x + \frac{3}{2}$

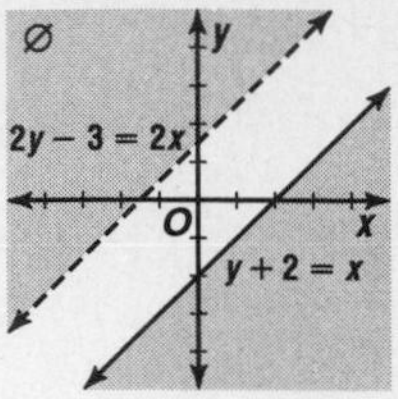

30. $2x + y \geq -4$
$y \geq -2x - 4$
$-5x + 2y < 1$
$2y < 5x + 1$
$y < \frac{5}{2}x + \frac{1}{2}$

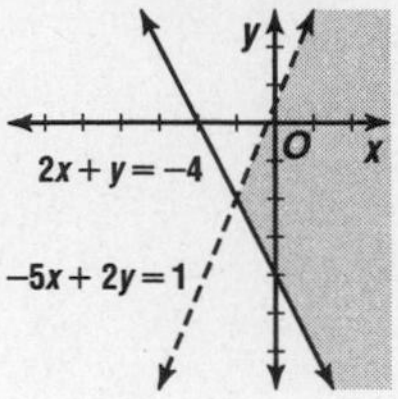

31. $x + y > 4$
$y > -x + 4$
$-2x + 3y < -12$
$3y < 2x - 12$
$y < \frac{2}{3}x - 4$

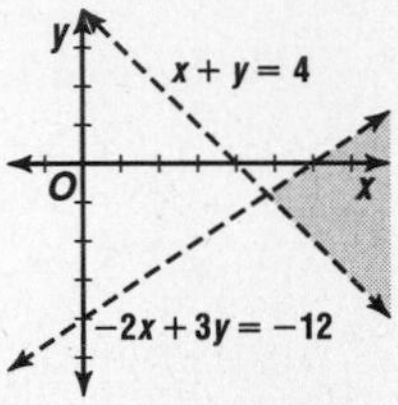

32. $-4x + 5y \leq 41$
$5y \leq 4x + 41$
$y \leq \frac{4}{5}x + \frac{41}{5}$
$x + y > -1$
$y > -x - 1$

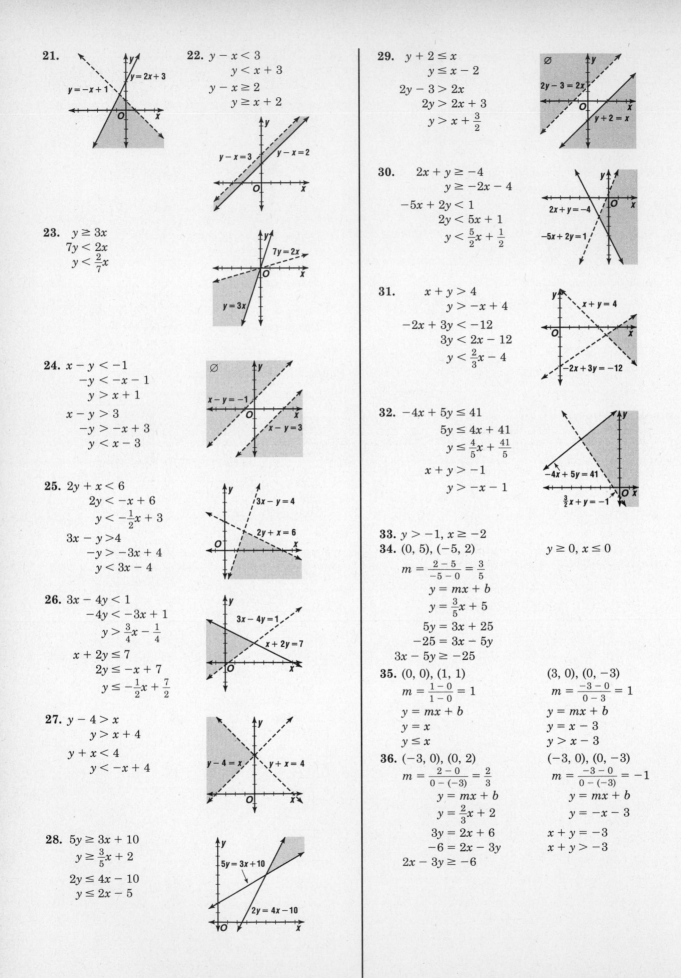

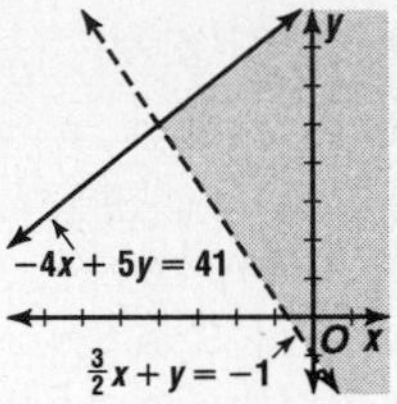

33. $y > -1$, $x \geq -2$ $\quad$ $y \geq 0$, $x \leq 0$

34. (0, 5), (−5, 2)
$m = \frac{2-5}{-5-0} = \frac{3}{5}$
$y = mx + b$
$y = \frac{3}{5}x + 5$
$5y = 3x + 25$
$-25 = 3x - 5y$
$3x - 5y \geq -25$

35. (0, 0), (1, 1)
$m = \frac{1-0}{1-0} = 1$
$y = mx + b$
$y = x$
$y \leq x$

(3, 0), (0, −3)
$m = \frac{-3-0}{0-3} = 1$
$y = mx + b$
$y = x - 3$
$y > x - 3$

36. (−3, 0), (0, 2)
$m = \frac{2-0}{0-(-3)} = \frac{2}{3}$
$y = mx + b$
$y = \frac{2}{3}x + 2$
$3y = 2x + 6$
$-6 = 2x - 3y$
$2x - 3y \geq -6$

(−3, 0), (0, −3)
$m = \frac{-3-0}{0-(-3)} = -1$
$y = mx + b$
$y = -x - 3$
$x + y = -3$
$x + y > -3$

37. (6, 0), (0, 3)

$m = \frac{3-0}{0-6} = -\frac{1}{2}$

$y = mx + b$

$y = -\frac{1}{2}x + 3$

$-2y = x - 6$

$6 = x + 2y$

$x + 2y \le 6$

$x \ge 0, y \ge 0$

38. (−3, 0), (0, 4)

$m = \frac{4-0}{0-(-3)} = \frac{4}{3}$

$y = mx + b$

$y = \frac{4}{3}x + 4$

$3y = 4x + 12$

$-12 = 4x - 3y$

$4x - 3y \ge -12$

(2, 0), (0, 1)

$m = \frac{1-0}{0-2} = -\frac{1}{2}$

$y = mx + b$

$y = -\frac{1}{2}x + 1$

$2y = -x + 2$

$x + 2y = 2$

$x + 2y \ge 2$

(2, 0), (0, 4)

$m = \frac{4-0}{0-2} = -2$

$y = mx + b$

$y = -2x + 4$

$2x + y = 4$

$2x + y \le 4$

39. $x - 2y \le 2$

$-2y \le -x + 2$

$y \ge \frac{1}{2}x - 1$

$3x + 4y \le 12$

$4y \le -3x + 12$

$y \le -\frac{3}{4}x + 12$

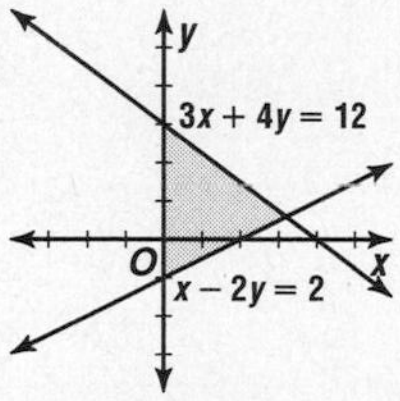

40. $x - y \le 5$

$-y \le -x + 5$

$y \ge x - 5$

$5x + 3y \ge -6$

$3y \ge -5x - 6$

$y \ge -\frac{5}{3}x - 2$

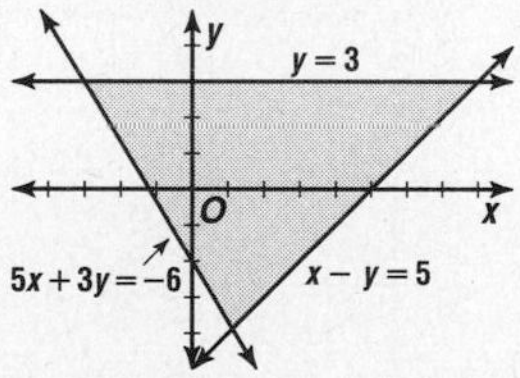

41. $4y > x$

$y > \frac{1}{4}x$

$2x - y < -9$

$-y < -2x - 9$

$y > 2x + 9$

$x + 3y < 9$

$3y < -x + 9$

$y < -\frac{1}{3}x + 3$

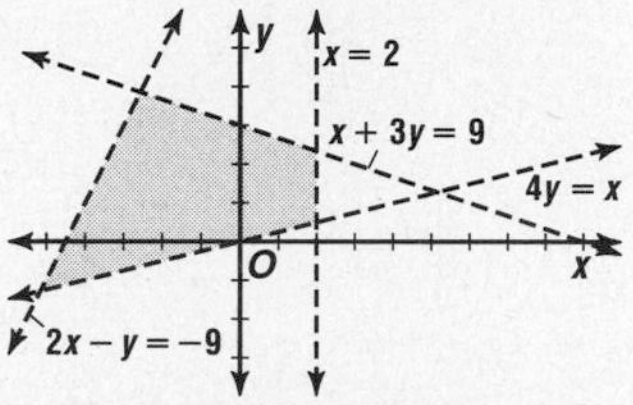

42. Enter: [2nd] [DRAW] 7

3 [X,T,θ] [−] 6 [,]

[X,T,θ] [+] 1 [)]

[ENTER]

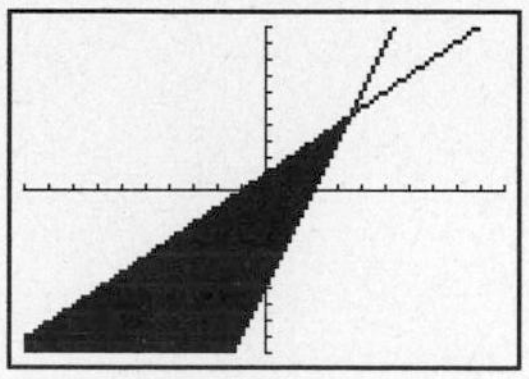

43. Enter: [2nd] [DRAW]

7 [(−)] [X,T,θ] [−] 4 [,]

[X,T,θ] [+] 9 [)]

[ENTER]

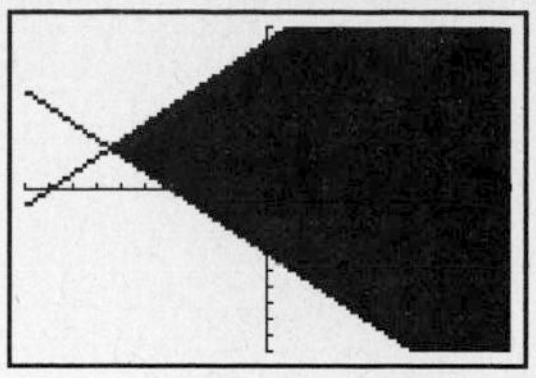

44. Enter: [2nd] [DRAW] 7

7 [X,T,θ] [+] 15 [,] 2

[X,T,θ] [+] 10 [)]

[ENTER]

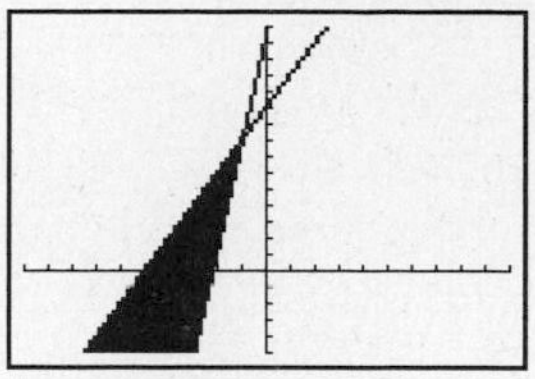

45. $|y| \le 3$

$y \ge -3$ and $y \le 3$

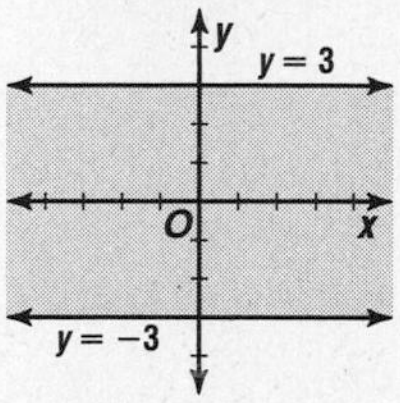

46. Let x = the number of ounces of mozzarella and let y = the number of ounces of Swiss.

$x + y \le 8$

$147x + 219y \ge 1200$

Sample answers:

3 ounces of mozzarella, 4 ounces of Swiss;

4 ounces of mozzarella, 3 ounces of Swiss;

5 ounces of mozzarella, 3 ounces of Swiss

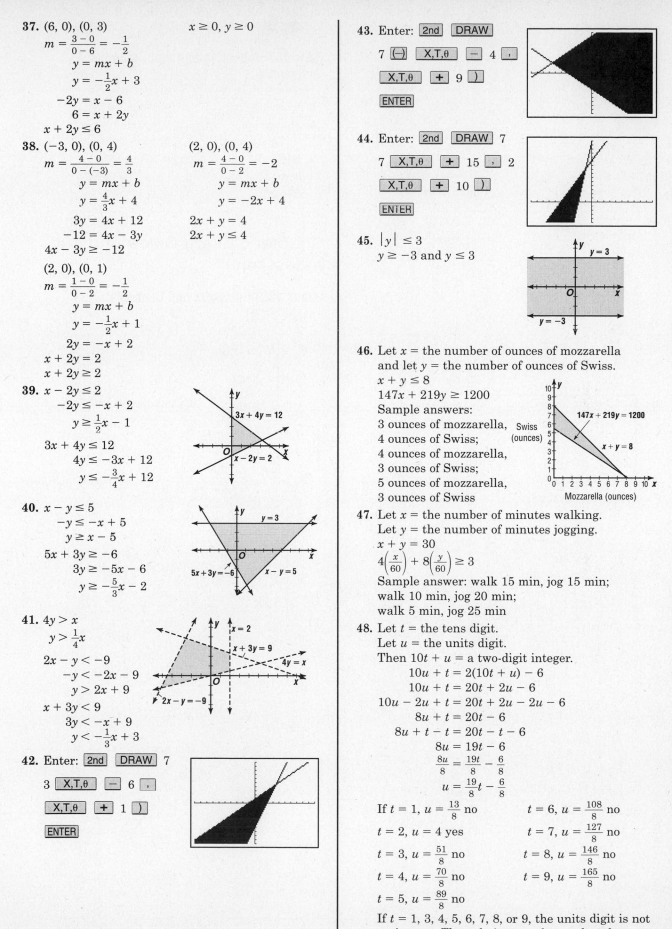

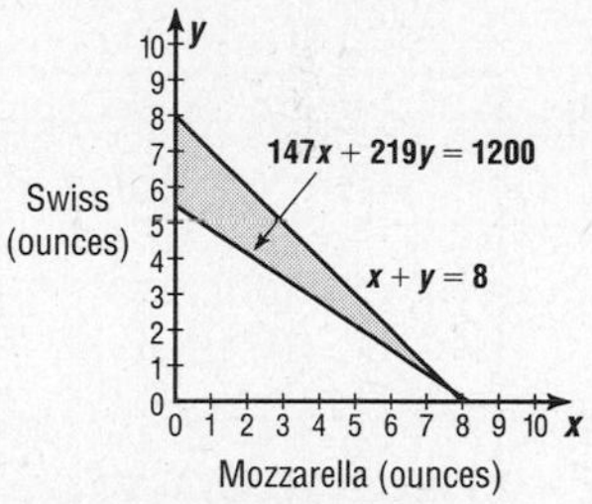

47. Let x = the number of minutes walking.

Let y = the number of minutes jogging.

$x + y = 30$

$4\left(\frac{x}{60}\right) + 8\left(\frac{y}{60}\right) \ge 3$

Sample answer: walk 15 min, jog 15 min;

walk 10 min, jog 20 min;

walk 5 min, jog 25 min

48. Let t = the tens digit.

Let u = the units digit.

Then $10t + u$ = a two-digit integer.

$10u + t = 2(10t + u) - 6$

$10u + t = 20t + 2u - 6$

$10u - 2u + t = 20t + 2u - 2u - 6$

$8u + t = 20t - 6$

$8u + t - t = 20t - t - 6$

$8u = 19t - 6$

$\frac{8u}{8} = \frac{19t}{8} - \frac{6}{8}$

$u = \frac{19}{8}t - \frac{6}{8}$

If $t = 1$, $u = \frac{13}{8}$ no

$t = 2$, $u = 4$ yes

$t = 3$, $u = \frac{51}{8}$ no

$t = 4$, $u = \frac{70}{8}$ no

$t = 5$, $u = \frac{89}{8}$ no

$t = 6$, $u = \frac{108}{8}$ no

$t = 7$, $u = \frac{127}{8}$ no

$t = 8$, $u = \frac{146}{8}$ no

$t = 9$, $u = \frac{165}{8}$ no

If t = 1, 3, 4, 5, 6, 7, 8, or 9, the units digit is not an integer. The only integer that makes the statement true is 10(2) + 4 or 24.

49. Let x = the number of \$5 bills.
Let y = the number of \$20 bills.

$$\begin{aligned} x + y &= 12 &\rightarrow\quad -5x - 5y &= -60 \\ 5x + 20y &= 180 &\rightarrow\quad (+)\ 5x + 20y &= 180 \\ & & \hline 15y &= 120 \\ & & y &= 8 \end{aligned}$$

$$\begin{aligned} x + y &= 12 \\ x + 8 &= 12 \\ x &= 4 \end{aligned}$$

She received 4 \$5 bills and 8 \$20 bills.

50. $4 > 4a + 12 > 24$

$$\begin{aligned} 4 &> 4a + 12 \quad \text{and} \quad & 4a + 12 &> 24 \\ -8 &> 4a & 4a &> 12 \\ -2 &> a & a &> 3 \end{aligned}$$

$\{a \mid -2 > a > 3\}$

51. $m = \frac{5-3}{-1-3} = \frac{2}{-4} = -\frac{1}{2}$

$$\begin{aligned} y - y_1 &= m(x - x_1) \\ y - 3 &= -\tfrac{1}{2}(x - 3) \\ y - 3 &= -\tfrac{1}{2}x + \tfrac{3}{2} \\ y &= -\tfrac{1}{2}x + \tfrac{3}{2} + 3 \\ y &= -\tfrac{1}{2}x + \tfrac{9}{2} \end{aligned}$$

52.

x	$-\frac{1}{2}x + 3$	y
2	$-\frac{1}{2}(2) + 3$	2
4	$-\frac{1}{2}(4) + 3$	1
6	$-\frac{1}{2}(6) + 3$	0

{2, 1, 0}

53.
$$\begin{aligned} x + 0.40x &= 14 \\ 1.40x &= 14 \\ x &= 10 \end{aligned}$$

54. distance = rate · time
Let t = time it takes Paloma to get to work.

$$\begin{aligned} \tfrac{40}{60} \cdot (t + 1) &= \tfrac{45}{60} \cdot (t - 1) \\ \tfrac{40t}{60} + \tfrac{40}{60} &= \tfrac{45t}{60} - \tfrac{45}{60} \\ \tfrac{40t}{60} - \tfrac{40t}{60} + \tfrac{40}{60} &= \tfrac{45t}{60} - \tfrac{40t}{60} - \tfrac{45}{60} \\ \tfrac{40}{60} &= \tfrac{5t}{60} - \tfrac{45}{60} \\ \tfrac{40}{60} + \tfrac{45}{60} &= \tfrac{5t}{60} - \tfrac{45}{60} + \tfrac{45}{60} \\ \tfrac{85}{60} &= \tfrac{5t}{60} \\ \tfrac{60}{5}\left(\tfrac{85}{60}\right) &= \tfrac{60}{5}\left(\tfrac{5t}{60}\right) \\ 17 &= t \end{aligned}$$

It takes Paloma 17 minutes to get to work.

distance $= \frac{40}{60}(17 + 1) = 12$; Paloma drives 12 miles to work.

55. Let y = the number of yards gained in both games; $y = 134 + (134 - 17)$

56. associative (×)

Chapter 8 Highlights

Page 487 Understanding and Using the Vocabulary

1. substitution
2. independent
3. inconsistent
4. dependent
5. elimination
6. parallel lines
7. infinitely many
8. consistent
9. no
10. intersection
11. second

Chapter 8 Study Guide and Assessment

Pages 488–490 Skills and Concepts

12. $y = 2x - 7$ $\quad x + y = 11$
$\qquad\qquad\qquad\quad y = -x + 11$

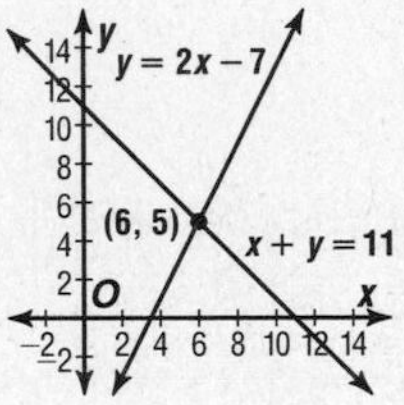

The solution is (6, 5).

13.
$$\begin{aligned} 2y - 8 &= -x & x + 2y &= 6 \\ 2y &= -x + 8 & 2y &= -x + 6 \\ y &= -\tfrac{1}{2}x + 4 & y &= -\tfrac{1}{2}x + 3 \end{aligned}$$

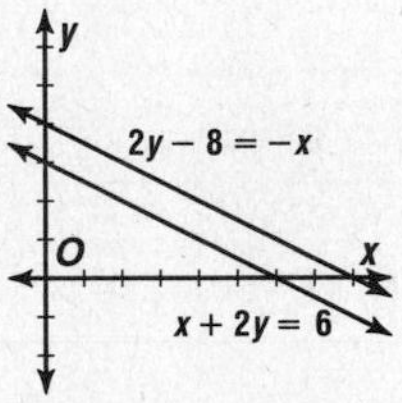

There is no solution.

14.
$$\begin{aligned} 3x + y &= -8 & x + 6y &= 3 \\ y &= -3x - 8 & 6y &= -x + 3 \\ & & y &= -\tfrac{1}{6}x + \tfrac{1}{2} \end{aligned}$$

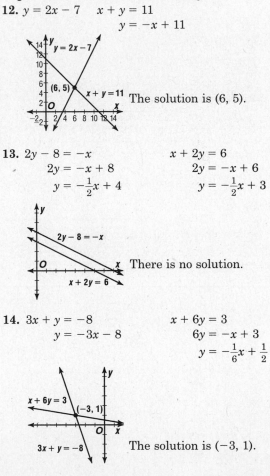

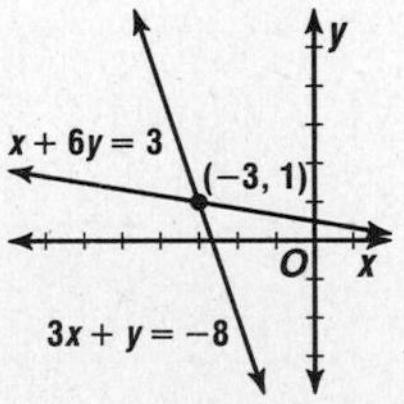

The solution is (–3, 1).

15. $5x - 3y = 11$
$-3y = -5x + 11$
$y = \frac{5}{3}x - \frac{11}{3}$

$2x + 3y = -25$
$3y = -2x - 25$
$y = -\frac{2}{3}x - \frac{25}{3}$

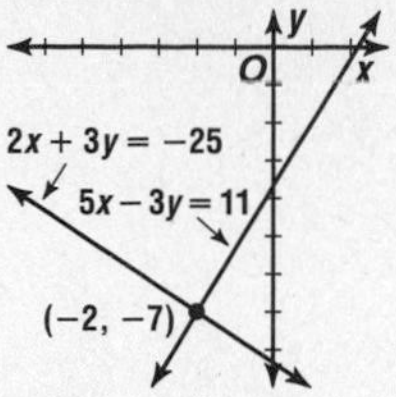

The solution is $(-2, -7)$.

16. $x - y = 9$
$-y = -x + 9$
$y = x - 9$

$x + y = 11$
$y = -x + 11$

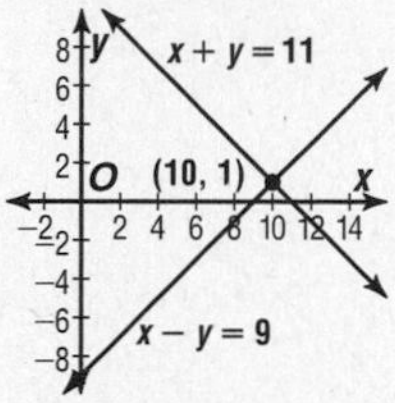

one solution; $(10, 1)$

17. $9x + 2 = 3y$
$3x + \frac{2}{3} = y$

$y - 3x = 8$
$y = 3x + 8$

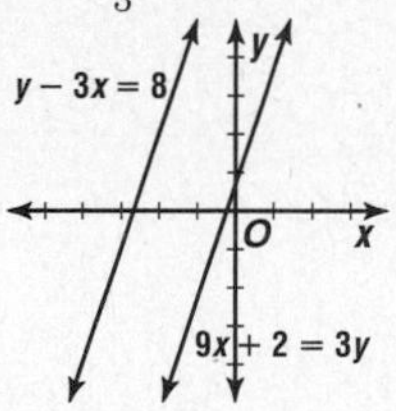

no solution

18. $2x - 3y = 4$
$-3y = -2x + 4$
$y = \frac{2}{3}x - \frac{4}{3}$

$6y = 4x - 8$
$y = \frac{2}{3}x - \frac{4}{3}$

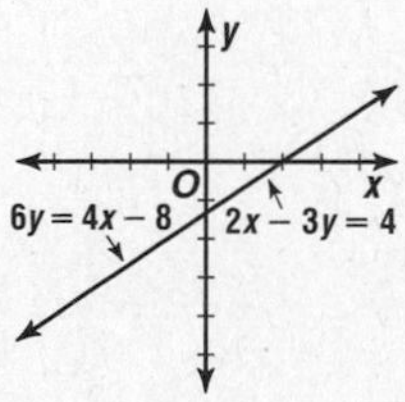

infinitely many solutions

19. $3x - y = 8$
$-y = -3x + 8$
$y = 3x - 8$

$3x = 4 - y$
$3x - 4 = -y$
$-3x + 4 = y$

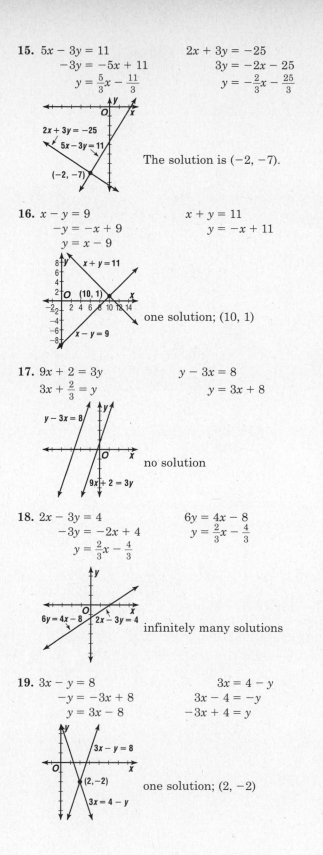

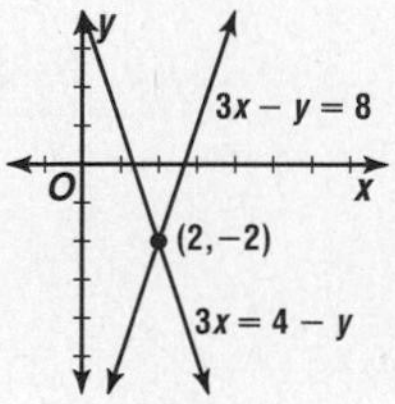

one solution; $(2, -2)$

20. $m - n = 8$
$m = 8 + n$

$2m + n = 1$
$2(8 + n) + n = 1$
$16 + 2n + n = 1$
$16 + 3n = 1$
$3n = -15$
$n = -5$

$m = 8 + n$
$m = 8 + (-5)$
$m = 3$

The solution is $(3, -5)$.

21. $3a + b = 2$
$b = 2 - 3a$

$3a - 2b = -4$
$3a - 2(2 - 3a) = -4$
$3a - 4 + 6a = -4$
$9a - 4 = -4$
$9a = 0$
$a = 0$

$b = 2 - 3a$
$b = 2 - 3(0)$
$b = 2 - 0$
$b = 2$

The solution is $(0, 2)$.

22. $2x + 4y = 6$
$2(3 - 2y) + 4y = 6$
$6 - 4y + 4y - 6$
$6 = 6$

There are infinitely many solutions.

23. $3x - y = 1$
$-y = 1 - 3x$
$y = -1 + 3x$

$2x + 4y = 3$
$2x + 4(-1 + 3x) = 3$
$2x - 4 + 12x = 3$
$14x - 4 = 3$
$14x = 7$
$x = \frac{1}{2}$

$y = -1 + 3x$
$y = -1 + 3\left(\frac{1}{2}\right)$
$y = -1 + \frac{3}{2}$
$y = \frac{1}{2}$

The solution is $\left(\frac{1}{2}, \frac{1}{2}\right)$.

24.
$$\begin{array}{rr} & x + 2y = 6 \\ (-) & x - 3y = -4 \\ \hline & 5y = 10 \\ & y = 2 \end{array}$$

$x + 2y = 6$
$x + 2(2) = 6$
$x + 4 = 6$
$x = 2$

The solution is $(2, 2)$.

25.
$$\begin{array}{rr} & 2m - n = 5 \\ (+) & 2m + n = 3 \\ \hline & 4m = 8 \\ & m = 2 \end{array}$$

$2m - n = 5$
$2(2) - n = 5$
$4 - n = 5$
$-n = 1$
$n = -1$

The solution is $(2, -1)$.

26.
$$\begin{array}{r} 3x - y = 11 \\ (+)\ x + y = 5 \\ \hline 4x = 16 \\ x = 4 \end{array} \qquad \begin{array}{r} 3x - y = 11 \\ 3(4) - y = 11 \\ 12 - y = 11 \\ -y = -1 \\ y = 1 \end{array}$$
The solution is (4, 1).

27.
$$\begin{array}{r} 3s + 6r = 33 \\ (-)\ -9s + 6r = 21 \\ \hline 12s = 12 \\ s = 1 \end{array} \qquad \begin{array}{r} 3s + 6r = 33 \\ 3(1) + 6r = 33 \\ 3 + 6r = 33 \\ 6r = 30 \\ r = 5 \end{array}$$
The solution is (5, 1).

28.
$$\begin{array}{r} 3x + 7y = -1 \\ (-)\ 6x + 7y = 0 \\ \hline -3x = -1 \\ x = \frac{1}{3} \end{array} \qquad \begin{array}{r} 3x + 7y = -1 \\ 3\left(\frac{1}{3}\right) + 7y = -1 \\ 1 + 7y = -1 \\ 7y = -2 \\ y = -\frac{2}{7} \end{array}$$
The solution is $\left(\frac{1}{3}, -\frac{2}{7}\right)$.

29.
$$\begin{array}{r} 12x - 9y = 114 \\ (-)\ 12x + 7y = 82 \\ \hline -16y = 32 \\ y = -2 \end{array} \qquad \begin{array}{r} 12x - 9y = 114 \\ 12x - 9(-2) = 114 \\ 12x + 18 = 114 \\ 12x = 96 \\ x = 8 \end{array}$$
The solution is (8, −2).

30.
$$\begin{array}{rcr} x - 5y = 0 & \rightarrow & -2x + 10y = 0 \\ 2x - 3y = 7 & \rightarrow & (+)\ 2x - 3y = 7 \\ \cline{3-3} & & 7y = 7 \\ & & y = 1 \end{array}$$
$$\begin{array}{r} x - 5y = 0 \\ x - 5(1) = 0 \\ x - 5 = 0 \\ x = 5 \end{array}$$
The solution is (5, 1).

31.
$$\begin{array}{rcr} x - 2y = 5 & \rightarrow & -3x + 6y = -15 \\ 3x - 5y = 8 & \rightarrow & (+)\ 3x - 5y = 8 \\ \cline{3-3} & & y = -7 \end{array}$$
$$\begin{array}{r} x - 2y = 5 \\ x - 2(-7) = 5 \\ x + 14 = 5 \\ x = -9 \end{array}$$
The solution is (−9, −7).

32.
$$\begin{array}{rcr} 2x + 3y = 8 & \rightarrow & 2x + 3y = 8 \\ x - y = 2 & \rightarrow & (+)\ 3x - 3y = 6 \\ \cline{3-3} & & 5x = 14 \\ & & x = \frac{14}{5} \end{array}$$
$$\begin{array}{r} x - y = 2 \\ \frac{14}{5} - y = 2 \\ -y = \frac{10}{5} - \frac{14}{5} \\ -y = -\frac{4}{5} \\ y = \frac{4}{5} \end{array}$$
The solution is $\left(\frac{14}{5}, \frac{4}{5}\right)$.

33.
$$\begin{array}{rcr} -5x + 8y = 21 & \rightarrow & -10x + 16y = 42 \\ 10x + 3y = 15 & \rightarrow & (+)\ 10x + 3y = 15 \\ \cline{3-3} & & 19y = 57 \\ & & y = 3 \end{array}$$
$$\begin{array}{r} -5x + 8y = 21 \\ -5x + 8(3) = 21 \\ -5x + 24 = 21 \\ -5x = -3 \\ x = \frac{3}{5} \end{array}$$
The solution is $\left(\frac{3}{5}, 3\right)$.

34.
$$\begin{array}{rcr} 5m + 2n = -8 & \rightarrow & -15m - 6n = 24 \\ 4m + 3n = 2 & \rightarrow & (+)\ 8m + 6n = 4 \\ \cline{3-3} & & -7m = 28 \\ & & m = -4 \end{array}$$
$$\begin{array}{r} 5m + 2n = -8 \\ 5(-4) + 2n = -8 \\ -20 + 2n = -8 \\ 2n = 12 \\ n = 6 \end{array}$$
The solution is (−4, 6).

35.
$$\begin{array}{rcr} 6x + 7y = 5 & \rightarrow & 6x + 7y = 5 \\ 2x - 3y = 7 & \rightarrow & (+)\ -6x + 9y = -21 \\ \cline{3-3} & & 16y = -16 \\ & & y = -1 \end{array}$$
$$\begin{array}{r} 6x + 7y = 5 \\ 6x + 7(-1) = 5 \\ 6x - 7 = 5 \\ 6x = 12 \\ x = 2 \end{array}$$
The solution is (2, −1).

36.
$$y = 2x \qquad \begin{array}{r} x + 2y = 8 \\ x + 2(2x) = 8 \\ x + 4x = 8 \\ 5x = 8 \\ x = \frac{8}{5} \end{array} \qquad \begin{array}{r} y = 2x \\ y = 2\left(\frac{8}{5}\right) \\ y = \frac{16}{5} \end{array}$$
The solution is $\left(\frac{8}{5}, \frac{16}{5}\right)$.

37.
$$\begin{array}{rcr} 9x + 8y = 7 & \rightarrow & -18x - 16y = -14 \\ 18x - 15y = 14 & \rightarrow & (+)\ 18x - 15y = 14 \\ \cline{3-3} & & -31y = 0 \\ & & y = 0 \end{array}$$
$$\begin{array}{r} 9x + 8y = 7 \\ 9x + 8(0) = 7 \\ 9x + 0 = 7 \\ 9x = 7 \\ x = \frac{7}{9} \end{array}$$
The solution is $\left(\frac{7}{9}, 0\right)$.

38. $2x - y = 36 \rightarrow$ $2x - y = 36$
$3x - 0.5y = 26 \rightarrow$ $(+)\ -6x + y = -52$

$-4x = -16$
$x = 4$

$2x - y = 36$
$2(4) - y = 36$
$8 - y = 36$
$-y = 28$
$y = -28$

The solution is $(4, -28)$.

39. $3x + 5y = 2x$
$3x - 2x + 5y = 2x - 2x$
$x + 5y = 0$

$x + 3y = y$
$x + 3y - y = y - y$
$x + 2y = 0$

$x + 5y = 0$
$(-)\ x + 2y = 0$
$3y = 0$
$y = 0$

$x + 5y = 0$
$x + 5(0) = 0$
$x + 0 = 0$
$x = 0$

The solution is $(0, 0)$.

40. $5x - 2y = 23$
$(+)\ 5x + 2y = 17$
$10x = 40$
$x = 4$

$5x - 2y = 23$
$5(4) - 2y = 23$
$20 - 2y = 23$
$-2y = 3$
$y = -\frac{3}{2}$

The solution is $\left(4, -\frac{3}{2}\right)$.

41. $2x + y = 3x - 15$
$2x - 3x + y = 3x - 3x - 15$
$-x + y = -15$

$x + 5 = 4y + 2x$
$x - 2x + 5 = 4y + 2x - 2x$
$-x + 5 = 4y$
$-x - 4y + 5 = 4y - 4y$
$-x - 4y + 5 - 5 = -5$
$-x - 4y = -5$

$-x + y = -15$
$(-)\ -x - 4y = -5$
$5y = -10$
$y = -2$

$-x + y = -15$
$-x + (-2) = -15$
$-x = -13$
$x = 13$

The solution is $(13, -2)$.

42. $y < 3x$
$x + 2y \geq -21$
$2y \geq -x - 21$
$y \geq -\frac{1}{2}x - \frac{21}{2}$

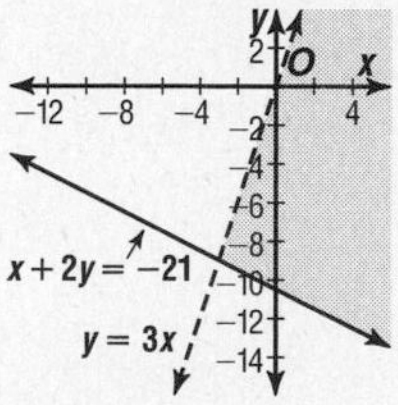

43.

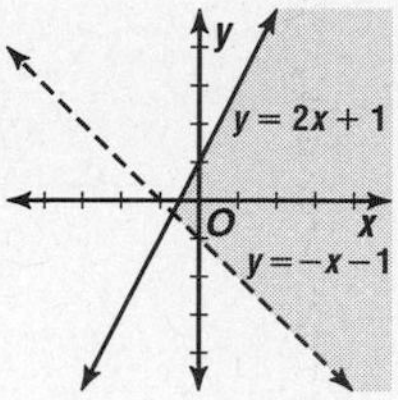

44. $2x + y < 9$
$y < -2x + 9$

$x + 11y < -6$
$11y < -x - 6$
$y < -\frac{1}{11}x - \frac{6}{11}$

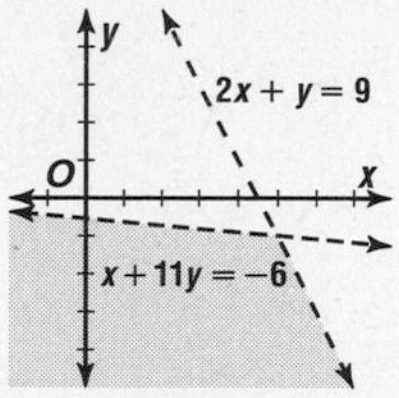

45. $x \geq 1$
$y + x \leq 3$

$y + x \leq 3$
$y \leq -x + 3$

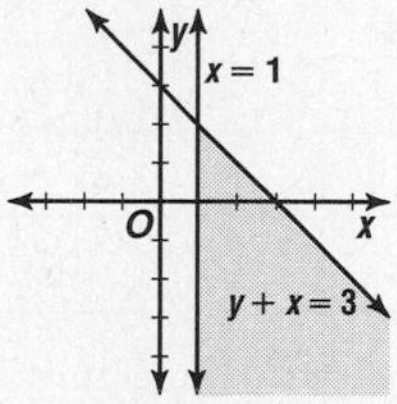

46.

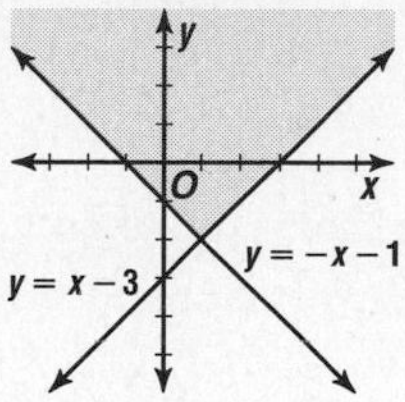

47. $x - 2y \leq -4$
$-2y \leq -x - 4$
$y \geq \frac{1}{2}x + 2$

$4y < 2x - 4$
$y < \frac{1}{2}x - 1$

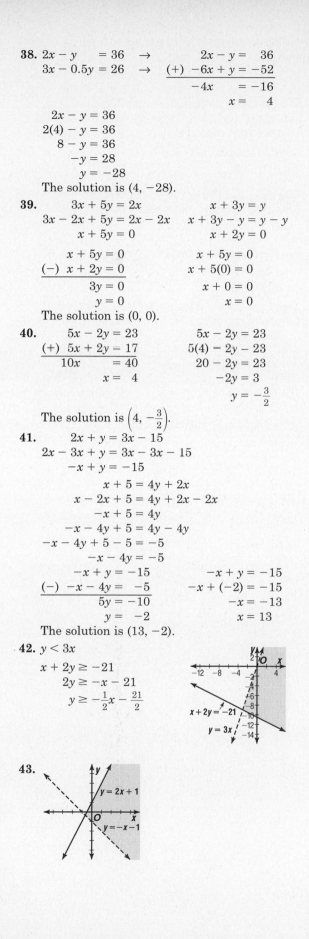

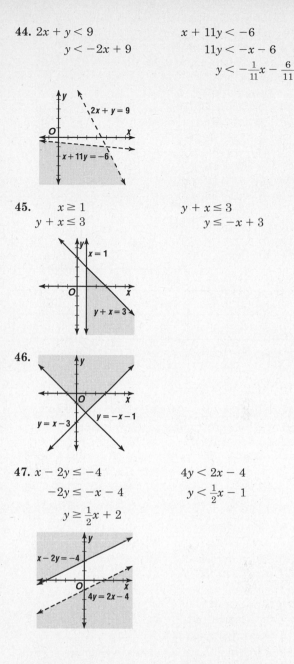

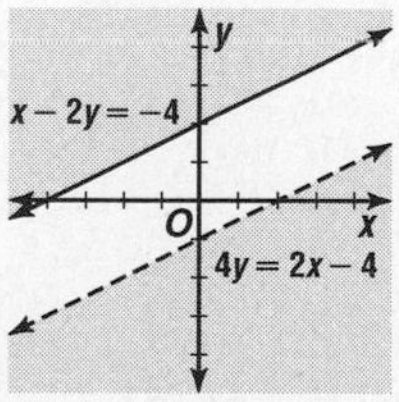

Page 490 Applications and Problem Solving

48a. Let h = the height and let t = the time.

$h = 10 + 15t$
$h = 150 - 20t$

$10 + 15t = 150 - 20t$
$35t = 140$
$t = 4$

4 min

48b. $h = 10 + 15t$
$h = 10 + 15(4)$
$h = 10 + 60$
$h = 70$
70 m

49. Let t = the tens digit.
Let u = the units digit.
Then $10t + u$ = a two-digit number.

$$\begin{aligned} 10t + u &= 7u \\ 10t - 6u &= 0 \\ 10t + u + 18 &= 10u + t \\ 9t - 9u &= -18 \\ 9t &= -18 + 9u \\ t &= -2 + u \end{aligned}$$

$$\begin{aligned} 10t - 6u &= 0 \\ 10(-2 + u) - 6u &= 0 \\ -20 + 10u - 6u &= 0 \\ -20 + 4u &= 0 \\ 4u &= 20 \\ u &= 5 \end{aligned} \qquad \begin{aligned} t &= -2 + u \\ t &= -2 + 5 \\ t &= 3 \end{aligned}$$

The number is $10(3) + 5$ or 35.

50.

	r	t	$rt = d$
Original Trip	40	t	$40t$
Return Trip	56	$t - 2$	$56t - 112$

$$\begin{aligned} 40t &= 56t - 112 \\ -16t &= -112 \\ t &= 7 \end{aligned} \qquad \begin{aligned} d &= rt \\ &= 40t \\ &= 40(7) \\ &= 280 \end{aligned}$$

Mrs. Sumner lives 280 miles from Fullerton.

51a. Let n = the cost of a 1-night stay and let m = the cost per meal.

$$\begin{aligned} 2n + 3m &= 195 &\rightarrow\quad -6n - 9m &= -585 \\ 3n + 5m &= 300 &\rightarrow\quad (+)\ 6n + 10m &= 600 \\ & & m &= 15 \end{aligned}$$

$$\begin{aligned} 2n + 3m &= 195 \\ 2n + 3(15) &= 195 \\ 2n + 45 &= 195 \\ 2n &= 150 \\ n &= 75 \end{aligned}$$

The cost is \$75.

51b.

$$\begin{aligned} 2n + 3m &= 195 \\ 2(75) + 3m &= 195 \\ 150 + 3m &= 195 \end{aligned} \qquad \begin{aligned} 3m &= 45 \\ m &= 15 \end{aligned}$$

The cost per meal is \$15.

52. Let c = the number of pounds of cashews.
Let p = the number of pounds of peanuts.

$5c + 3p \leq 24$
$c + p \geq 5$

Answers will vary. Possible solutions: 1 lb of cashews, 6 lb of peanuts; 3 lb of cashews, 3 lb of peanuts; 4 lb of cashews, 1 lb of peanuts

Page 491 Alternative Assessment: Thinking Critically

- When the elimination or substitution method yields a false equation such as $8 = 0$, the system is inconsistent. When the elimination or substitution method yields a true equation such as $0 = 0$, the system is consistent and dependent.
- Sample answer: $y = \frac{1}{2}x - 2$
  $y = \frac{1}{2}x + 2$
  The lines must be parallel; therefore, the slopes are equal and the y-intercepts are not equal.

Cumulative Review, Chapters 1–8

Pages 492–493

1. There are infinitely many solutions when the graphs of the equations have the same slope and intercepts. D

2.
$$\begin{aligned} \frac{2\text{ cm}}{5\text{ km}} &= \frac{x}{15.75\text{ km}} \\ 2(15.75) &= 5x \\ 31.5 &= 5x \\ x &= 6.3\text{ cm} \end{aligned}$$
C

3.
$$\begin{aligned} 2x - y &< 6 \\ -y &< -2x + 6 \\ y &> 2x - 6 \end{aligned}$$
C

4. Let t = the tens digit.
Let u = the units digit.
Then $10t + u$ = a two-digit number.

$$\begin{aligned} u &= 2t + 1 \\ t + u &= 7 \end{aligned} \qquad \begin{aligned} t + u &= 7 \\ t + (2t + 1) &= 7 \\ 3t + 1 &= 7 \\ 3t &= 6 \\ t &= 2 \end{aligned} \qquad \begin{aligned} u &= 2t + 1 \\ u &= 2(2) + 1 \\ u &= 4 + 1 \\ u &= 5 \end{aligned}$$

The number is $10(2) + 5$ or 25. A

5. B. Region B

6. Let x = the score on the fifth test.

$$\begin{aligned} \frac{85 + 89 + 90 + 81 + x}{5} &\geq 87 \\ 345 + x &\geq 435 \\ x &\geq 90 \end{aligned}$$

at least 90 points B

7.
$$\begin{aligned} x_1y_1 &= x_2y_2 \\ 10(512) &= 8y_2 \\ 5120 &= 8y_2 \\ 640 &= y_2 \end{aligned}$$

640 cycles per second D

8.
$$\begin{aligned} \frac{3\frac{1}{2} + 5 + 4\frac{1}{8} + 7\frac{3}{4} + 4 + 6\frac{5}{8}}{6} &= \frac{29 + \left(\frac{1}{2} + \frac{1}{8} + \frac{3}{4} + \frac{5}{8}\right)}{6} \\ &= \frac{29 + \left(\frac{4}{8} + \frac{1}{8} + \frac{6}{8} + \frac{5}{8}\right)}{6} \\ &= \frac{31}{6} \\ &= 5\frac{1}{6} \end{aligned}$$
A

9. Let x = the number of miles walked.
Let y = the number of miles he ran.

$x + y = 16$ $\qquad$ $x + y = 16$
$y = 2x + 1$ $\qquad$ $x + (2x + 1) = 16$

$$3x + 1 = 16$$
$$3x = 15$$
$$x = 5$$

$y = 2x + 1$
$y = 2(5) + 1$
$y = 10 + 1$
$y = 11$

Eric ran 11 miles and walked 5 miles.

10. 125, 199, 200, 212, 220, 230, (239) 240, 240, 250, 274, 327, 348

LV = 125
GV = 348
median = 239

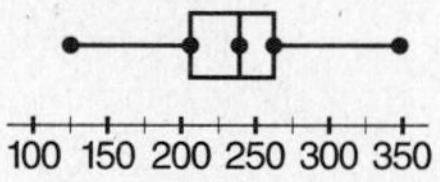

$Q_3 = \frac{250 + 274}{2} = 262$

$Q_1 = \frac{200 + 212}{2} = 206$

outliers: $1.5(56) + 262 = 346$; $348 > 346$, 348 is an outlier

$206 - 1.5(56) = 122$; no outliers below 122

11. Let x = the first consecutive odd integer.
Then $x + 2$ = the second integer,
and $x + 4$ = the third integer.

$$x + (x + 2) + (x + 4) = 81$$
$$3x + 6 = 81$$
$$3x = 75$$
$$x = 25$$

$x + 2 = 25 + 2 = 27$ $\qquad$ $x + 4 = 25 + 4 = 29$

The three consecutive odd integers are 25, 27, and 29.

12. Let h = the cost of a hot dog.
Let s = the cost of a soda.

$6h + 45 = 6.70 \rightarrow -18h - 12s = -20.10$
$4h + 3s = 4.65 \rightarrow (+)\ 16h + 12s = 18.60$

$$-2h = -1.50$$
$$h = 0.75$$

$6h + 4s = 6.70$
$6(0.75) + 4s = 6.70$
$4.5 + 4s = 6.70$
$4s = 2.20$
$s = 0.55$

The hot dogs are \$0.75 and the sodas are \$0.55 each.

13.

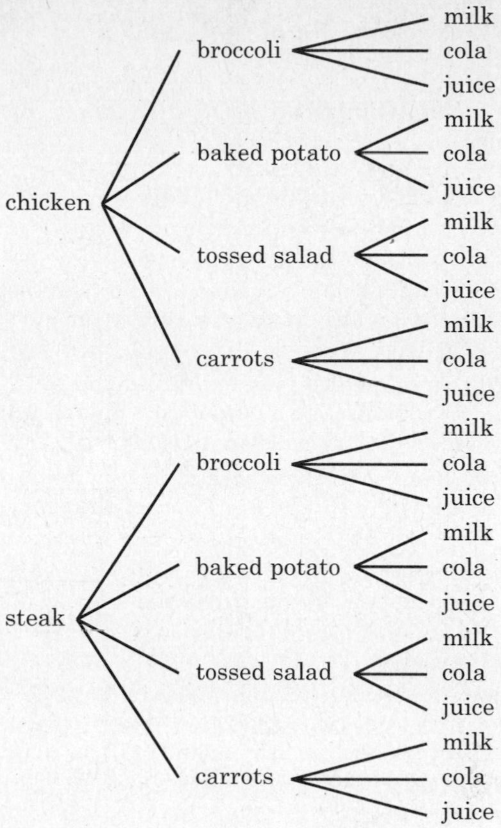

14. Let I = the amount spent on Isabel's gift.
Let S = the amount spent on Sarah's gift.

$I \geq S + 5$
$S + I \leq 56$

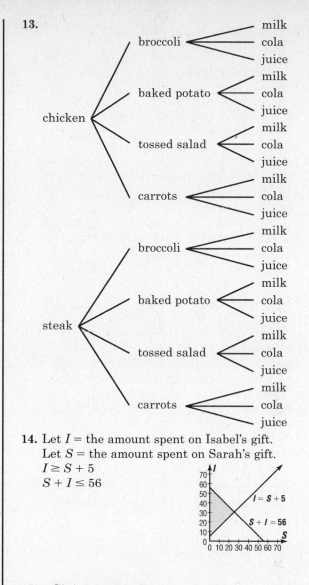

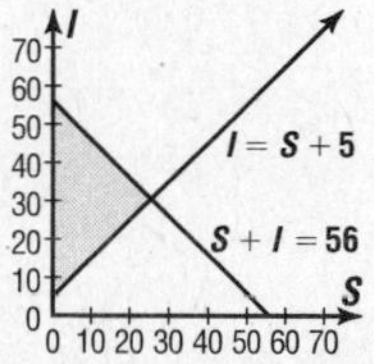

15. $C(m) = 31 + 0.13m$
$C(110) = 31 + 0.13(110)$
$= 31 + 14.30$
$= 45.30$

The cost of the car rental is \$45.30.

16. See students' work. **17.** See students' work.

Chapter 9 Exploring Polynomials

9-1 Multiplying Monomials

Page 499 Check for Understanding

1a. When numbers with the same base are multiplied, the exponents are added.

1b. When a number is raised to a power and then raised to another power, the two exponents are multiplied.

1c. When two numbers are multiplied and the product is raised to a power, each number can be raised to the power before multiplying.

2. If the bases are different you cannot add the exponents. $2^3 \cdot 3^2 = 8 \cdot 9 = 72$ is not the same as $(2 \cdot 3)^{3+2}$ or 6^5.

3. Taryn is correct. When numbers with the same base are multiplied, the exponents are added; $10^4 \times 10^5 = 10^{4+5} = 10^9$, the bases are not multiplied.

4. Answers will vary. Sample answers: 2^6, $(2^3)^2$, $2^2 \times 2^4$, 2×2^5, $2^3 \times 2^3$, $(2^2)^2 \times 2^2$

5. $2d^3 \stackrel{?}{=} (2d)^3$
$2d^3 \stackrel{?}{=} 2^3d^3$
$2d^3 \neq 8d^3$ no

6. $(xy)^2 \stackrel{?}{=} x^2y^2$
$x^2y^2 = x^2y^2$ yes

7. $-x^2 \stackrel{?}{=} (-x)^2$
$-x^2 \stackrel{?}{=} -x \cdot -x$
$-x^2 \neq x^2$ no

8. $5(y^2)^2 \stackrel{?}{=} 25y^4$
$5y^4 \neq 25y^4$ no

9. $a^4(a^7)a = a^{4+7+1}$
$= a^{12}$

10. $(xy^4)(x^2y^3) = x^{1+2}y^{4+3}$
$= x^3y^7$

11. $[(3^2)^4]^2 = [3^8]^2$
$= 3^{16}$ or 43,046,721

12. $(2a^2b)^2 = 2^2(a^2)^2b^2$
$= 4a^4b^2$

13. $(-27ay^3)\left(-\frac{1}{3}ay^3\right) = \left[-27 \cdot \left(-\frac{1}{3}\right)\right](a \cdot a)(y^3 \cdot y^3)$
$= 9a^{1+1}y^{3+3}$
$= 9a^2y^6$

14. $(2x^2)^2\left(\frac{1}{2}y^2\right)^2 = 2^2(x^2)^2\left(\frac{1}{2}\right)^2(y^2)^2$
$= (4x^4)\left(\frac{1}{4}y^4\right)$
$= \left(4 \cdot \frac{1}{4}\right)x^4y^4$
$= x^4y^4$

15. $A = \ell w$
$= 3a^2b(5a^2b^2)$
$= (3 \cdot 5)(a^2 \cdot a^2)(b \cdot b^2)$
$= 15a^{2+2}b^{1+2}$
$= 15a^4b^3$

Pages 499–500 Exercises

16. $b^3(b)(b^5) = b^{3+1+5}$
$= b^9$

17. $(m^3n)(mn^2) = (m^3 \cdot m)(n \cdot n^2)$
$= m^{3+1}n^{1+2}$
$= m^4n^3$

18. $(a^2b)(a^5b^4) = (a^2 \cdot a^5)(b \cdot b^4)$
$= a^{2+5}b^{1+4}$
$= a^7b^5$

19. $[(2^3)^2]^2 = (2^6)^2$
$= 2^{12}$ or 4096

20. $(3x^4y^3)(4x^4y) = (3 \cdot 4)(x^4 \cdot x^4)(y^3 \cdot y)$
$= 12x^{4+4}y^{3+1}$
$= 12x^8y^4$

21. $(a^3x^2)^4 = (a^3)^4(x^2)^4$
$= a^{12}x^8$

22. $m^7(m^3b^2) = (m^7 \cdot m^3)(b^2)$
$= m^{7+3}b^2$
$= m^{10}b^2$

23. $(3x^2y^2z)(2x^2y^2z^3) = (3 \cdot 2)(x^2 \cdot x^2)(y^2 \cdot y^2)(z \cdot z^3)$
$= 6x^{2+2}y^{2+2}z^{1+3}$
$= 6x^4y^4z^4$

24. $(0.6d)^3 = 0.6^3d^3$
$= 0.216d^3$

25. $(ab)(ac)(bc) = (a \cdot a)(b \cdot b)(c \cdot c)$
$= a^{1+1}b^{1+1}c^{1+1}$
$= a^2b^2c^2$

26. $-\frac{5}{6}c(12a^3) = \left(-\frac{5}{6} \cdot 12\right)(a^3 \cdot c)$
$= -10a^3c$

27. $\left(\frac{2}{5}d\right)^2 = \left(\frac{2}{5}\right)^2d^2$
$= \frac{4}{25}d^2$

28. $-3(ax^3y)^2 = -3a^2(x^3)^2y^2$
$= -3a^2x^6y^2$

29. $(0.3x^3y^2)^2 = 0.3^2(x^3)^2(y^2)^2$
$= 0.09x^6y^4$

30. $(-3ab)^3(2b^3) = (-3)^3a^3b^3(2b^3)$
$= -27a^3b^3(2b^3)$
$= (-27 \cdot 2)a^3(b^3 \cdot b^3)$
$= -54a^3b^{3+3}$
$= -54a^3b^6$

31. $\left(\frac{3}{10}y^2\right)^2(10y^2)^3 = \left(\frac{3}{10}\right)^2(y^2)^2 10^3(y^2)^3$
$= \frac{9}{100}(y^4)(1000)(y^6)$
$= \left(\frac{9}{100} \cdot 1000\right)(y^4 \cdot y^6)$
$= 90y^{4+6}$
$= 90y^{10}$

32. $(3x^2)^2\left(\frac{1}{3}y^2\right)^2 = 3^2(x^2)^2\left(\frac{1}{3}\right)^2(y^2)^2$
$= 9x^4\left(\frac{1}{9}\right)y^4$
$= \left(9 \cdot \frac{1}{9}\right)x^4y^4$
$= x^4y^4$

33. $\left(\frac{2}{5}a\right)^2(25a)(13b)\left(\frac{1}{13}b^4\right)$
$= \left(\frac{2}{5}\right)^2a^2(25a)(13b)\left(\frac{1}{13}b^4\right)$
$= \frac{4}{25}a^2(25a)(13b)\left(\frac{1}{13}b^4\right)$
$= \left(\frac{4}{25} \cdot 25 \cdot 13 \cdot \frac{1}{13}\right)(a^2 \cdot a)(b \cdot b^4)$
$= 4a^{2+1}b^{1+4}$
$= 4a^3b^5$

34. $(3a^2)^3 + 2(a^3)^2$
$= 3^3(a^2)^3 + 2a^6$
$= 27a^6 + 2a^6$
$= (27 + 2)a^6$
$= 29a^6$

35. $(-2x^3)^3 - (2x)^9$
$= (-2)^3(x^3)^3 - 2^9x^9$
$= -8x^9 - 512x^9$
$= (-8 - 512)x^9$
$= -520x^9$

36. For example, $(x + y)^2 = (x + y)(x + y)$ and not $x^2 + y^2$.

37. -2^4 equals $-(2)(2)(2)(2)$ or -16 and $(-2)^4$ equals $(-2)(-2)(-2)(-2)$ or 16.

38a. $T = p\left[\frac{(1+r)^t - 1}{r}\right]$

$p = 300,\ r = 0.23,\ t = 12$

$T = 300\left[\frac{(1+0.23)^{12} - 1}{0.23}\right]$

$\approx \$14,336.30$

38b. Total value = amount of money made + value of initial investment
= 14,336.30 + 1474.91
= $15,811.21

39.

Number of Lines	Number of Parts
1	4
2	7
3	10
4	13
.	.
.	.
.	.
n	$3n + 1$
.	.
.	.
.	.
100	301

$3n + 1 = 3(100) + 1$
$= 301$ parts

40. $x \le 2,\ y \ge 2$

41. $x + 2y = 0$

$2y = -x + 0$

$y = -\frac{1}{2}x$

$y + 3 = -x$

$y = -x - 3$

one solution; $(-6, 3)$

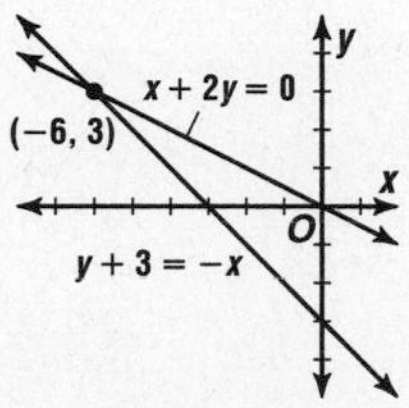

42. Let x = the number of boxes of cards to be printed.

$11 + 6x \le 150$

$11 - 11 + 6x \le 150 - 11$

$6x \le 139$

$x \le 23\frac{1}{6}$

23 boxes (100 cards per box) = 2300
Mr. Martinez can have 2300 cards printed.

43. $\frac{\text{change in } n}{\text{change in } m} = \frac{-3 - (-5)}{-2 - (-3)} = 2$

$n = 2m + 1$

m	-3	-2	-1	0	1
n	-5	-3	-1	1	3

44.

Time of Arrival	r	t	$r \cdot t = d$
11:00	36	t	$36t$
9:00	54	$t - 2$	$54t - 108$
10:00	r	$t - 1$	$r(t - 1)$

$36t = 54t - 108$
$-18t = -108$
$t = 6$ hr
$36t = d$
$36(6) = 216$ mi

$r(t - 1) = d$
$r(6 - 1) = 216$
$r(5) = 216$
$\frac{5r}{5} = \frac{216}{5}$
$r = 43.2$ mph

45. $180° - 44° = 136°$

46. -2

47. $0.3(0.2 + 3y) + 0.21y = 0.3(0.2) + 0.3(3y) + 0.21y$
$= 0.06 + 0.9y + 0.21y$
$= 0.06 + 1.11y$

9-2 Dividing by Monomials

Pages 503–504 Check for Understanding

1. $\frac{0^m}{0^m} \ne 0^{m-m}$, because $0^m = 0$ and division by 0 is not defined.
2. Division by 0 is not defined.
3. Since each number is obtained by dividing the previous number by 3, $3^1 = 3$ and $3^0 = 1$.
4. Divide the previous number by 5.

5^5	5^4	5^3	5^2	5^1	5^0	5^{-1}	5^{-2}	5^{-3}	5^{-4}
3125	625	125	25	5	1	$\frac{1}{5}$	$\frac{1}{25}$	$\frac{1}{125}$	$\frac{1}{625}$

5. See students' work.
6. See students' work.

7. $11^{-2} = \frac{1}{11^2}$
$= \frac{1}{121}$

8. $(6^{-2})^2 = 6^{-4}$
$= \frac{1}{6^4}$
$= \frac{1}{1296}$

9. $\left(\frac{1}{4} \cdot \frac{2}{3}\right)^{-2} = \left(\frac{1}{6}\right)^{-2}$
$= 6^2$
$= 36$

10. $a^4(a^{-7})(a^0) = a^{4-7+0}$
$= a^{-3}$
$= \frac{1}{a^3}$

11. $\frac{6r^3}{r^7} = 6r^{3-7}$
$= 6r^{-4}$
$= \frac{6}{r^4}$

12. $\frac{(a^7b^2)^2}{(a^{-2}b)^{-2}} = \frac{(a^7)^2(b^2)^2}{(a^{-2})^{-2}(b^{-2})}$
$= \frac{a^{14}b^4}{a^4b^{-2}}$
$= \left(\frac{a^{14}}{a^4}\right)\left(\frac{b^4}{b^{-2}}\right)$
$= a^{14-4}b^{4-(-2)}$
$= a^{10}b^6$

13. $\frac{\text{area of circle}}{\text{area of square}} = \frac{\pi r^2}{(2r)^2} = \frac{\pi r^2}{2^2r^2} = \frac{\pi}{4}$

Pages 504–505 Exercises

14. $a^0b^{-2}c^{-1} = (1)\left(\frac{1}{b^2}\right)\left(\frac{1}{c}\right)$
$= \frac{1}{b^2c}$

15. $\frac{a^0}{a^{-2}} = a^{0-(-2)}$
$= a^2$

16. $\frac{5n^5}{n^8} = 5n^{5-8}$
$= 5n^{-3}$
$= \frac{5}{n^3}$

17. $\frac{m^2}{m^{-4}} = m^{2-(-4)}$
$= m^6$

18. $\frac{b^5d^2}{b^3d^8} = \left(\frac{b^5}{b^3}\right)\left(\frac{d^2}{d^8}\right)$
$= b^{5-3}d^{2-8}$
$= b^2d^{-6}$
$= \frac{b^2}{d^6}$

19. $\frac{10m^4}{30m} = \frac{1}{3}\left(\frac{m^4}{m^1}\right)$
$= \frac{1}{3}m^{4-1}$
$= \frac{1}{3}m^3$
$= \frac{m^3}{3}$

20. $\begin{aligned}\frac{(-y)^5m^8}{y^3m^{-7}} &= \frac{-y^5m^8}{y^3m^{-7}}\\ &= \left(\frac{-y^5}{y^3}\right)\left(\frac{m^8}{m^{-7}}\right)\\ &= -y^{5-3}m^{8-(-7)}\\ &= -y^2m^{15}\end{aligned}$

21. $\begin{aligned}\frac{b^6c^5}{b^{14}c^2} &= \left(\frac{b^6}{b^{14}}\right)\left(\frac{c^5}{c^2}\right)\\ &= b^{6-14}c^{5-2}\\ &= b^{-8}c^3\\ &= \frac{c^3}{b^8}\end{aligned}$

22. $\begin{aligned}\frac{22a^2b^5c^7}{-11abc^2} &= \left(\frac{22}{-11}\right)\left(\frac{a^2}{a}\right)\left(\frac{b^5}{b}\right)\left(\frac{c^7}{c^2}\right)\\ &= -2a^{2-1}b^{5-1}c^{7-2}\\ &= -2ab^4c^5\end{aligned}$

23. $\begin{aligned}\frac{(a^{-2}b^3)^2}{(a^2b)^{-2}} &= \frac{(a^{-2})^2(b^3)^2}{(a^2)^{-2}b^{-2}}\\ &= \frac{a^{-4}b^6}{a^{-4}b^{-2}}\\ &= \left(\frac{a^{-4}}{a^{-4}}\right)\left(\frac{b^6}{b^{-2}}\right)\\ &= a^{-4-(-4)}b^{6-(-2)}\\ &= a^0b^8\\ &= b^8\end{aligned}$

24. $\begin{aligned}\frac{7x^3z^5}{4z^{15}} &= \frac{7}{4}x^3\frac{z^5}{z^{15}}\\ &= \frac{7}{4}x^3z^{5-15}\\ &= \frac{7}{4}x^3z^{-10}\\ &= \frac{7x^3}{4z^{10}}\end{aligned}$

25. $\begin{aligned}\frac{(-r)^5s^8}{r^5s^2} &= \frac{-r^5s^8}{r^5s^2}\\ &= \left(\frac{-r^5}{r^5}\right)\left(\frac{s^8}{s^2}\right)\\ &= -r^{5-5}s^{8-2}\\ &= -r^0s^6\\ &= -s^6\end{aligned}$

26. $\begin{aligned}\frac{(r^{-4}k^2)^2}{(5k^2)^2} &= \frac{(r^{-4})^2(k^2)^2}{(5^2)(k^2)^2}\\ &= \frac{r^{-8}k^4}{25k^4}\\ &= \frac{1}{25}\left(\frac{1}{r^8}\right)\left(\frac{k^4}{k^4}\right)\\ &= \frac{1}{25}\left(\frac{1}{r^8}\right)k^{4-4}\\ &= \frac{1}{25r^8}(k^0)\\ &= \frac{1}{25r^8}\end{aligned}$

27. $\begin{aligned}\frac{16b^4}{-4bc^3} &= \left(\frac{16}{-4}\right)\left(\frac{b^4}{b}\right)\left(\frac{1}{c^3}\right)\\ &= \frac{-4b^{4-1}}{c^3}\\ &= -\frac{4b^3}{c^3}\end{aligned}$

28. $\begin{aligned}\frac{27a^4b^6c^9}{15a^3c^{15}} &= \left(\frac{27}{15}\right)\left(\frac{a^4}{a^3}\right)(b^6)\left(\frac{c^9}{c^{15}}\right)\\ &= \frac{9}{5}a^{4-3}b^6c^{9-15}\\ &= \frac{9}{5}ab^6c^{-6}\\ &= \frac{9ab^6}{5c^6}\end{aligned}$

29. $\begin{aligned}\frac{(4a^{-1})^{-2}}{(2a^4)^2} &= \frac{4^{-2}(a^{-1})^{-2}}{2^2(a^4)^2}\\ &= \frac{4^{-2}a^2}{4a^8}\\ &= (4^{-2-1})\ a^{2-8}\\ &= 4^{-3}a^{-6}\\ &= \frac{1}{4^3a^6}\\ &= \frac{1}{64a^6}\end{aligned}$

30. $\left(\frac{3m^2n^2}{6m^{-1}k}\right)^0 = 1$

31. $\begin{aligned}\frac{r^{-5}s^{-2}}{(r^2s^5)^{-1}} &= \frac{r^{-5}s^{-2}}{(r^2)^{-1}(s^5)^{-1}}\\ &= \frac{r^{-5}s^{-2}}{r^{-2}s^{-5}}\\ &= \left(\frac{r^{-5}}{r^{-2}}\right)\left(\frac{s^{-2}}{s^{-5}}\right)\\ &= r^{-5-(-2)}s^{-2-(-5)}\\ &= r^{-3}s^3\\ &= \frac{s^3}{r^3}\end{aligned}$

32. $\begin{aligned}\left(\frac{7m^{-1}n^3}{n^2r^{-1}}\right)^{-1} &= \frac{7^{-1}(m^{-1})^{-1}(n^3)^{-1}}{(n^2)^{-1}(r^{-1})^{-1}}\\ &= \frac{1mn^{-3}}{7n^{-2}r}\\ &= \left(\frac{1}{7}\right)(m)\left(\frac{n^{-3}}{n^{-2}}\right)\left(\frac{1}{r}\right)\\ &= \frac{1}{7}mn^{-3-(-2)}\left(\frac{1}{r}\right)\\ &= \frac{mn^{-1}}{7r}\\ &= \frac{m}{7rn}\end{aligned}$

33. $\begin{aligned}\frac{(-b^{-1}c)^0}{4a^{-1}c^2} &= \frac{1}{4a^{-1}c^2}\\ &= \frac{a}{4c^2}\end{aligned}$

34. $\begin{aligned}\left(\frac{3xy^{-2}z}{4x^{-2}y}\right)^{-2} &= \frac{3^{-2}x^{-2}(y^{-2})^{-2}z^{-2}}{4^{-2}(x^{-2})^{-2}y^{-2}}\\ &= \frac{4^2x^{-2}y^4z^{-2}}{3^2x^4y^{-2}}\\ &= \left(\frac{16}{9}\right)\left(\frac{x^{-2}}{x^4}\right)\left(\frac{y^4}{y^{-2}}\right)(z^{-2})\\ &= \frac{16x^{-2-4}y^{4-(-2)}}{9z^2}\\ &= \frac{16x^{-6}y^6}{9z^2}\\ &= \frac{16y^6}{9x^6z^2}\end{aligned}$

35. $m^3(m^n) = m^{3+n}$

36. $\begin{aligned}y^{2c}(y^{5c}) &= y^{2c+5c}\\ &= y^{7c}\end{aligned}$

37. $\begin{aligned}(3^{2x+1})(3^{2x-7}) &= 3^{2x+1+2x-7}\\ &= 3^{4x-6}\end{aligned}$

38. $\begin{aligned}\frac{r^{y-2}}{r^{y+3}} &= r^{y-2-(y+3)}\\ &= r^{y-2-y-3}\\ &= r^{-5}\\ &= \frac{1}{r^5}\end{aligned}$

39. $\begin{aligned}\frac{(q^{y-7})^2}{(q^{y+2})^2} &= \frac{q^{2y-14}}{q^{2y+4}}\\ &= q^{(2y-14)-(2y+4)}\\ &= q^{2y-14-2y-4}\\ &= q^{-18}\\ &= \frac{1}{q^{18}}\end{aligned}$

40. $\begin{aligned}\frac{y^x}{y^{a-x}} &= y^{x-(a-x)}\\ &= y^{x-a+x}\\ &= y^{2x-a}\end{aligned}$

41. $P = A\left[\frac{i}{1-(1+i)^{-n}}\right]$

down payment $= 0.10(180{,}000) = 18{,}000$

$A = 180{,}000 - 18{,}000 = 162{,}000$

$n = 30(12) = 360$

$i = \frac{8.6\%}{12} = \frac{0.086}{12}$

$P = 162{,}000\left[\frac{\frac{0.086}{12}}{1-\left(\frac{1+0.086}{12}\right)-360}\right]$

$= 162{,}000(0.0077601)$

$\approx \$1257.14$

42. $B = P\left[\frac{1-(1+i)^{k-n}}{i}\right]$

$k = 20,\ n = 48,\ i = \frac{9.6\%}{12} = 0.8\%$ or 0.008

$B = 265.86\left[\frac{1-(1+0.008)^{20-48}}{0.008}\right]$

$B = 265.86\left[\frac{1-1.008^{-28}}{0.008}\right]$

$B \approx 265.86(24.9965)$

$B \approx \$6645.57$

43. $(2a^3)(7ab^2)^2 = (2a^3)(7^2)a^2(b^2)^2$
$= 2a^3(49)a^2b^4$
$= 98a^3a^2b^4$
$= 98a^{3+2}b^4$
$= 98a^5b^4$

44. Let x = rate of plane in still air.
Let y = rate of wind.

	r	t	d	$rt = d$
Downwind	$x + y$	$\frac{40}{60} = \frac{2}{3}$	300	$\frac{2}{3}x + \frac{2}{3}y = 300$
Upwind	$x - y$	$\frac{45}{60} = \frac{3}{4}$	300	$\frac{3}{4}x - \frac{3}{4}y = 300$

$\frac{2}{3}x + \frac{2}{3}y = 300$ (Multiply by 9.) $\quad 6x + 6y = 2700$
$\frac{3}{4}x - \frac{3}{4}y = 300$ (Multiply by 8.) $\quad (+)\ 6x - 6y = 2400$
$12x = 5100$
$x = 425$

The air speed of the plane is 425 mph.

45. The center point of the graph is $\frac{2 + (-4)}{2}$ or -1. Since -1 is 3 units from -4 and 3 units from 2, and x represents a number between -4 and 2, the distance between x and -1 must be less than 3. Therefore, $|x - (-1)| < 3$ or $|x + 1| < 3$.

46. $-\frac{2}{5} > \frac{4z}{7}$
$\frac{7}{4}\left(-\frac{2}{5}\right) > \frac{7}{4}\left(\frac{4z}{7}\right)$
$-\frac{7}{10} > z$

47. midpoint $= \left(\frac{5+1}{2}, \frac{-3+(-7)}{2}\right)$
$= \left(\frac{6}{2}, \frac{-10}{2}\right)$
$= (3, -5)$

48. Let x = the cost of the dress before tax.
$x + 0.06x = 32.86$
$1.06x = 32.86$
$x = 31$
The cost of the dress before tax was $31.00.

49. $\frac{4 - x}{3 + x} = \frac{16}{25}$
$25(4 - x) = 16(3 + x)$
$100 - 25x = 48 + 16x$
$100 = 48 + 41x$
$52 = 41x$
$\frac{52}{41} = x$

50. $4ly - (-41y) = 41y + 41y$
$= 82y$

9-3 Scientific Notation

Page 509 Check for Understanding

1. when the number is greater than or equal to 10
2. when the number is less than 1
3. In your head, first multiply 1.2 and 4 and then multiply 10^5 and 10^8. The answer is 4.8×10^{13}.
4. In your head, first divide 4.4 by 4 and then divide 10^4 by 10^7. The answer is 1.1×10^{-3}.
5. $4.34 \times 10^7 = 4.34 \times 10{,}000{,}000 = 43{,}400{,}000$
$1515 = 1.515 \times 10^3$
6. $9.46 \times 10^7 = 9.46 \times 10{,}000{,}000 = 94{,}600{,}000$
$3963 = 3.963 \times 10^3$
7. $5.07 \times 10^8 = 5.07 \times 100{,}000{,}000 = 507{,}000{,}000$
$44{,}419 = 4.4419 \times 10^4$
8. $1.8597 \times 10^9 = 1.8597 \times 1{,}000{,}000{,}000$
$= 1{,}859{,}700{,}000$
$15{,}881 = 1.5881 \times 10^4$
9. $4.5514 \times 10^9 = 4.5514 \times 1{,}000{,}000{,}000$
$= 4.551{,}400{,}000$
$714 = 7.14 \times 10^2$
10. 5.09×10^{-5} cm
11. 1.672×10^{-21} mg
12. 1.1×10^{-4} mm
13. 4×10^{-6} in.
14. $(3.24 \times 10^3)(6.7 \times 10^4) = (3.24 \times 6.7)(10^3 \times 10^4)$
$= 21{,}708 \times 10^7$
$= 2.1708 \times 10^8$ or $217{,}080{,}000$
15. $(0.2 \times 10^{-3})(31 \times 10^{-4}) = (0.2 \times 31)(10^{-3} \times 10^{-4})$
$= 6.2 \times 10^{-7}$ or 0.00000062
16. $\frac{8.1 \times 10^2}{2.7 \times 10^{-3}} = \left(\frac{8.1}{2.7}\right)\left(\frac{10^2}{10^{-3}}\right)$
$= 3 \times 10^5$ or $300{,}000$
17. $\frac{52{,}440{,}000{,}000}{(2.3 \times 10^6)(38 \times 10^{-5})} = \frac{5.244 \times 10^{10}}{(2.3 \times 38)(10^6 \times 10^{-5})}$
$= \frac{5.244 \times 10^{10}}{87.4 \times 10^1}$
$= \left(\frac{5.244}{87.4}\right)\left(\frac{10^{10}}{10^1}\right)$
$= 0.06 \times 10^9$
$= 6 \times 10^7$ or $60{,}000{,}000$

Pages 509–512 Exercises

18. $9500 = 9.5 \times 1000$
$= 9.5 \times 10^3$
19. $0.0095 = 9.5 \times 0.001$
$= 9.5 \times \frac{1}{1000}$
$= 9.5 \times \frac{1}{10^3}$
$= 9.5 \times 10^{-3}$
20. $56.9 = 5.69 \times 10$
21. $87{,}600{,}000{,}000 = 8.76 \times 10{,}000{,}000{,}000$
$= 8.76 \times 10^{10}$
22. $0.000000000761 = 7.61 \times 0.0000000001$
$= 7.61 \times \frac{1}{10^{10}}$
$= 7.61 \times 10^{-10}$
23. $312{,}720{,}000 = 3.1272 \times 100{,}000{,}000$
$= 3.1272 \times 10^8$
24. 0.00000008
$= 8.0 \times 0.00000001$
$= 8 \times \frac{1}{10^8}$
$= 8 \times 10^{-8}$
25. 0.090909
$= 9.0909 \times 0.01$
$= 9.0909 \times \frac{1}{10^2}$
$= 9.0909 \times 10^{-2}$
26. $355 \times 10^7 = (3.55 \times 10^2) \times 10^7$
$= 3.55 \times 10^{2+7}$
$= 3.55 \times 10^9$
27. $78.6 \times 10^3 = (7.86 \times 10) \times 10^3$
$= 7.86 \times 10^{1+3}$
$= 7.86 \times 10^4$

28. $112 \times 10^{-8} = (1.12 \times 10^2) \times 10^{-8}$
$= 1.12 \times 10^{2+(-8)}$
$= 1.12 \times 10^{-6}$

29. $0.007 \times 10^{-7} = (7 \times 10^{-3}) \times 10^{-7}$
$= 7 \times 10^{-3+(-7)}$
$= 7 \times 10^{-10}$

30. $7830 \times 10^{-2} = (7.830 \times 10^3) \times 10^{-2}$
$= 7.830 \times 10^{3+(-2)}$
$= 7.83 \times 10$

31. $0.99 \times 10^{-5} = (9.9 \times 10^{-1}) \times 10^{-5}$
$= 9.9 \times 10^{-1+(-5)}$
$= 9.9 \times 10^{-6}$

32. $(6.4 \times 10^3)(7 \times 10^2) = (6.4 \times 7)(10^3 \times 10^2)$
$= 44.8 \times 10^5$
$= 4.48 \times 10^6$ or 4,480,000

33. $(4 \times 10^2)(15 \times 10^{-6}) = (4 \times 15)(10^2 \times 10^{-6})$
$= 60 \times 10^{-4}$
$= 6 \times 10^{-3}$ or 0.006

34. $360(5.8 \times 10^7) = (3.6 \times 10^2)(5.8 \times 10^7)$
$= (3.6 \times 5.8)(10^2 \times 10^7)$
$= 20.88 \times 10^9$
$= 2.088 \times 10^{10}$ or 20,880,000,000

35. $(5.62 \times 10^{-3})(16 \times 10^{-5})$
$= (5.62 \times 16)(10^{-3} \times 10^{-5})$
$= 89.92 \times 10^{-8}$
$= 8.992 \times 10^{-7}$ or 0.0000008992

36. $\frac{6.4 \times 10^9}{1.6 \times 10^2} = \left(\frac{6.4}{1.6}\right)\left(\frac{10^9}{10^2}\right)$
$= 4 \times 10^7$ or 40,000,000

37. $\frac{9.2 \times 10^3}{2.3 \times 10^5} = \left(\frac{9.2}{2.3}\right)\left(\frac{10^3}{10^5}\right)$
$= 4 \times 10^{-2}$ or 0.04

38. $\frac{1.035 \times 10^{-3}}{4.5 \times 10^2} = \left(\frac{1.035}{4.5}\right)\left(\frac{10^{-3}}{10^2}\right)$
$= 0.23 \times 10^{-5}$
$= 2.3 \times 10^{-6}$ or 0.0000023

39. $\frac{2.795 \times 10^{-7}}{4.3 \times 10^{-2}} = \left(\frac{2.795}{4.3}\right)\left(\frac{10^{-7}}{10^{-2}}\right)$
$= 0.65 \times 10^{-5}$
$= 6.5 \times 10^{-6}$ or 0.0000065

40. $\frac{3.6 \times 10^2}{1.2 \times 10^7} = \left(\frac{3.6}{1.2}\right)\left(\frac{10^2}{10^7}\right)$
$= 3 \times 10^{-5}$ or 0.00003

41. $\frac{5.412 \times 10^{-2}}{8.2 \times 10^3} = \left(\frac{5.412}{8.2}\right)\left(\frac{10^{-2}}{10^3}\right)$
$= 0.66 \times 10^{-5}$
$= 6.6 \times 10^{-6}$ or 0.0000066

42. $\frac{(35{,}921{,}000)(62 \times 10^3)}{3.1 \times 10^5} = \frac{(3.5921 \times 10^7)(62 \times 10^3)}{3.1 \times 10^5}$
$= \frac{(3.5921 \times 62)(10^7 \times 10^3)}{3.1 \times 10^5}$
$= \frac{222.7102 \times 10^{10}}{3.1 \times 10^5}$
$= \left(\frac{222.7102}{3.1}\right)\left(\frac{10^{10}}{10^5}\right)$
$= 71.842 \times 10^5$
$= 7.1842 \times 10^6$ or 7,184,200

43. $\frac{1.6464 \times 10^5}{(98{,}000)(14 \times 10^3)} = \frac{1.6464 \times 10^5}{(9.8 \times 10^4)(14 \times 10^3)}$
$= \frac{1.6464 \times 10^5}{(9.8 \times 14)(10^4 \times 10^3)}$
$= \frac{1.6464 \times 10^5}{137.2 \times 10^7}$
$= \left(\frac{1.6464}{137.2}\right)\left(\frac{10^5}{10^7}\right)$
$= 0.012 \times 10^{-2}$
$= 1.2 \times 10^{-4}$ or 0.00012

44-47. Put the calculator in scientific mode.

44. Enter: 4.8 [×] 10 [^] 6 [×] 5.73 [×] 10 [^] 2 [ENTER] 2.7504E9 or 2.7504×10^9

45. Enter: 5.07 [×] 10 [^] [(–)] 4 [×] 4.8 [×] 10 [^] 2 [ENTER] 2.4336E–1 or 2.4336×10^{-1}

46. Enter: [(] 9.1 [×] 10 [^] 6 [)] [÷] [(] 2.6 [×] 10 [^] 10 [ENTER] 3.5E–4 or 3.5×10^{-4}

47. Enter: [(] 9.66 [×] 10 [^] 3 [)] [÷] [(] 3.45 [×] 10 [^] [(–)] 2 [)] [ENTER] 2.8E5 or 2.8×10^5

48a. : Prompt A, B, C
: Disp " (A^2B^3C^4) = ", (A^2B^3C^4)
1.416E7

48b. : Prompt A, B
: Disp " (–2A)^2(4B)^3 = ", (–2A)^2(4B)^3
8.84736E5

48c. : Prompt A, B
: Disp " (4A^2B^4)^3 = ", (4A^2B^4)^3
5.706E14

48d. : Disp " (AC)^3 + (3B)^2 = ", (AC)^3 + (3B)^2
3.3092E4

49a. Sample answer: overflow

49b. Multiply 3.7 and 5.6 and multiply 10^{112} and 10^{10}. Then write the product in scientific notation.

49c. $(3.7 \times 10^{112})(5.6 \times 10^{10})$
$= (3.7 \times 5.6)(10^{112} \times 10^{10})$
$= 20.72 \times 10^{122}$
$= 2.072 \times 10^{123}$

50. $\frac{23}{3.5 \times 10^{-6}}$

Enter: 23 [÷] [(] 3.5 [×] 10 [^] [(–)] 6 [)] [ENTER]

6,571,428.571 or about 6.57×10^6 times greater

51. 1,000,000,000,001

52. 1.5309×10^7; 9.227×10^6; 9.022×10^6; 5.460×10^6; 5.153×10^6

53. $(25 \times 10^9)(270 \times 10^6)$

Enter: 25 [×] 10 [^] 9 [×] 270 [×] 10 [^] 6 [ENTER]

6.75×10^{18} molecules

54a. $(3 \times 10^{-4}) \times 1000 = 3 \times 10^{-4} \times 10^3$
$= 3 \times 10^{-1}$
$= 0.3$

$(2 \times 10^{-3}) \times 10^3 = 2 \times 10^0$
$= 2 \times 1$
$= 2$

0.3 mm to 2 mm

54b. The smallest bacteria would probably not be seen with such a microscope.

55a. $\frac{(4.325 \times 10^{11})}{(4.8 \times 10^9)(365)} = \left(\frac{4.325}{4.8 \cdot 365}\right)\left(\frac{10^{11}}{10^9}\right)$
$\approx 0.0025 \times 10^2$ or about 0.25 kg

55b. Answers may vary.

56. $\frac{24x^2y^7z^3}{-6x^2y^3z} = \left(\frac{24}{-6}\right)\left(\frac{x^2}{x^2}\right)\left(\frac{y^7}{y^3}\right)\left(\frac{z^3}{z}\right)$
$= -4y^4z^2$

57.

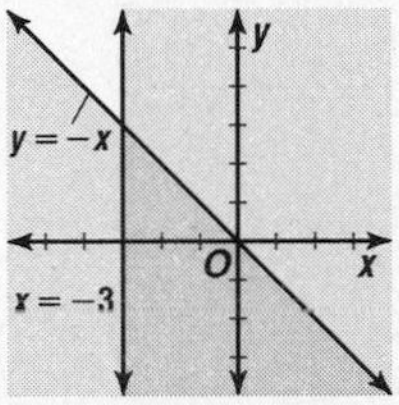

58.
$x - 3y = 8$
$(2y - 12) - 3y = 8$
$-y - 12 = 8$
$-y = 20$
$y = -20$

$x = 2y - 12$
$x = 2(-20) - 12$
$x = -40 - 12$
$x = -52$

$(-52, -20)$

59. 25%

60.

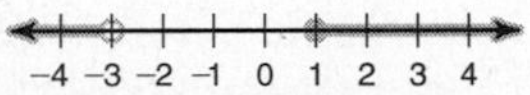

61. $5x + 5y = 35$
$5y = -5x + 35$
$y = -x + 7$

$m = 1; (-3, 2)$
$y - y_1 = m(x - x_1)$
$y - 2 = x - (-3)$
$y - 2 = x + 3$
$y = x + 5$

62. slope $= \frac{\text{vertical change}}{\text{horizontal change}}$
$= \frac{(4500 - 37{,}000)\text{ ft}}{140\text{mi}}$
$\approx -232.14\ \frac{\text{ft}}{\text{mi}}$

$-232.14\ \frac{\text{ft}}{\text{mi}} \times \frac{1\text{ mi}}{5280\text{ ft}} \approx -0.044$

63. Yes, each domain value has a unique range value.

64. $\{4, 0, 21, 13, 3\}$

65. 27°

66. mean $= \frac{26.89 + 26.27 + 25.18 + 25.63 + 27.16 + 27.18}{6}$
$= 26.385$

25.18, 25.63, 26.27, 26.89, 27.16, 27.18

median: $\frac{26.27 + 26.89}{2} = 26.58$

67.
$x - 44 = -207$
$x - 44 + 44 = -207 + 44$
$x = -163$

Page 512 Mathematics and Society

1. $\frac{511{,}366 \times 5280 \times 5280}{1.8 \times 10^9} = 7920$ ft^2 per slice; this is clearly not a reasonable answer. One or more of the figures stated in the article must be incorrect.

2. See students' work; the problem can be made more manageable by using scientific notation to arrive at the solution.

3. See students' work.

9-4A Modeling Mathematics: Polynomials

Page 513

1.

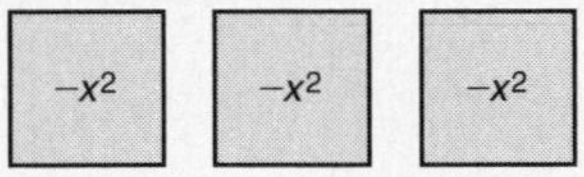

2.

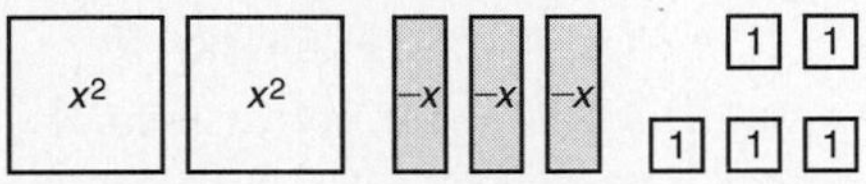

3.

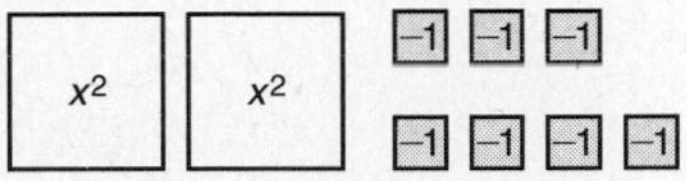

4.

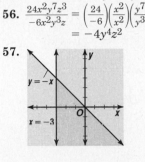

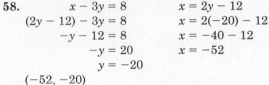

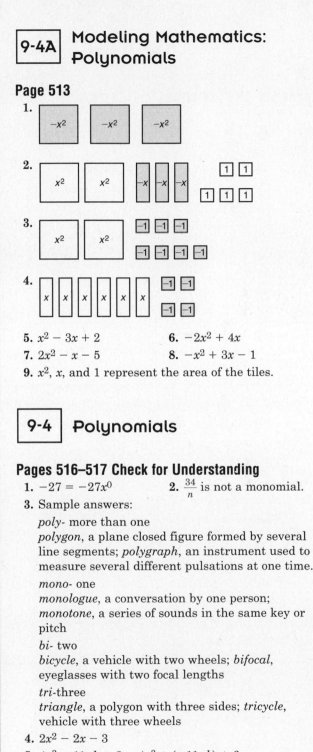

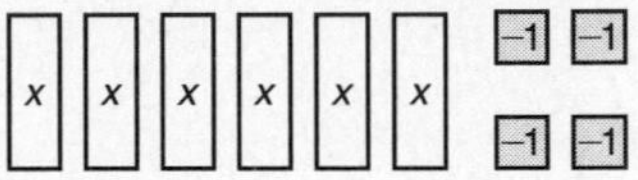

5. $x^2 - 3x + 2$

6. $-2x^2 + 4x$

7. $2x^2 - x - 5$

8. $-x^2 + 3x - 1$

9. x^2, x, and 1 represent the area of the tiles.

9-4 Polynomials

Pages 516–517 Check for Understanding

1. $-27 = -27x^0$

2. $\frac{34}{n}$ is not a monomial.

3. Sample answers:

poly- more than one
polygon, a plane closed figure formed by several line segments; *polygraph*, an instrument used to measure several different pulsations at one time.

mono- one
monologue, a conversation by one person; *monotone*, a series of sounds in the same key or pitch

bi- two
bicycle, a vehicle with two wheels; *bifocal*, eyeglasses with two focal lengths

*tri-*three
triangle, a polygon with three sides; *tricycle*, vehicle with three wheels

4. $2x^2 - 2x - 3$

5. $4x^3 - 11ab + 6 = 4x^3 + (-11ab) + 6$
yes; trinomial

6. no; $\frac{y}{x^2}$ is not a monomial

7. $4c + ab - c = 3c + ab$; yes; binomial

8. 1

9. 0

10. The degree of $42x^{12}y^3$ is 15.
The degree of $-23x^8y^6$ is 14.
Thus, the degree of $42x^{12}y^3 - 23x^8y^6$ is 15.

11. $x^8 - 12x^6 + 5x^3 - 11x$

12. $y^4x - x^2 + y^5x^3 + yx^5$ **13a.** $\ell w - \pi r^2 - s^2$

13b. $\ell w - \pi r^2 - s^2 = 15(8) - \pi(2)^2 - (4)^2$
$= 120 - 4\pi - 16$
$\approx 120 - 12.57 - 16$
≈ 91.43 square units

Pages 517–519 Exercises

14. yes; monomial

15. $x^2 - \frac{1}{3}x + \frac{y}{234} = x^2 + \left(-\frac{1}{3}x\right) + \frac{y}{234}$; yes; trinomial

16. no

17. $5a - 6b - 3a = 2a + (-6b)$; yes; binomial

18. no; $\frac{7}{t}$ is not a monomial **19.** yes; trinomial

20. 2 **21.** 5 **22.** 0

23. The degree of m^2 is 2.
The degree of n^3 is 3.
Thus, the degree of $m^2 + n^3$ is 3.

24. The degree of x^2y^3z is 6.
The degree of $-4x^3z$ is 4.
Thus, the degree of $x^2y^3z - 4x^3z$ is 6.

25. The degree of $3x^2y^3z^4$ is 9.
The degree of $-18a^5f^3$ is 8.
Thus, the degree of $3x^2y^3z^4 - 18a^5f^3$ is 9.

26. The degree of $8r$ is 1.
The degree of $-7y$ is 1.
The degree of $5d$ is 1.
The degree of $-6h$ is 1.
Thus, the degree of $8r - 7y + 5d - 6h$ is 1.

27. The degree of 9 is 0.
The degree of t^2 is 2.
The degree of $-s^2t^2$ is 4.
The degree of rs^2t is 4.
Thus, the degree of $9 + t^2 - s^2t^2 + rs^2t$ is 4.

28. The degree of $-4yzw^4$ is 6.
The degree of $10x^4z^2w$ is 7.
Thus, the degree of $-4yzw^4 + 10x^4z^2w$ is 7.

29. $x^5 + 3x^3 + 5$ **30.** $-2x^5 - 9x^2y + 8x + 5$

31. $-x^7 + abx^2 - bcx + 34$

32. $\frac{12}{19}x^{12} - 14x^7 + 9ax^2 + 7a^3x$

33. $1 + x^2 + x^3 + x^5$ **34.** $y^4 + 3xy^4 - x^2y^3 + 4x^3y$

35. $7a^3x + \frac{2}{3}x^2 - 8a^3x^3 + \frac{1}{5}x^5$

36. $4 + \frac{2}{3}x - x^2 + \frac{3}{4}x^3y$

37. $a(2b) + \frac{1}{2}\pi r^2 + \frac{1}{2}\pi r^2$
$= 2ab + \pi r^2$
$= 2ab + \pi b^2$

$2ab + \pi b^2$
$= 2(20)(6) + \pi(6)^2$
$= 240 + 36\pi$
≈ 353.10 square units

38. $a(2r) - \pi r^2 = 2ar - \pi r^2$
$= 2(20)(5) - \pi(5)^2$
$= 200 - 25\pi$
≈ 121.46 square units

39. $ab - 4x^2 = (20)(6) - 4(1)^2$
$= 120 - 4$
$= 116$ square units

40. $(2c)b - \frac{1}{2}\pi c^2 = 2bc - \frac{1}{2}\pi c^2$
$= 2(6)(2) - \frac{1}{2}\pi(2)^2$
$= 24 - \frac{1}{2}(4)\pi$
$= 24 - 2\pi$
≈ 17.72 square units

41a. See students' work.

41b. $8a^4 + 9a^3 + 4a^2 + 3a^1 + 5a^0$

42. first year:
25,000 + 25,000(0.075) + 2000 = 28,875
second year:
28,875 + 28,875(0.075) + 2000 ≈ 33,040.63
third year:
33,040.63 + 33,040.63(0.075) + 2000 ≈ 37,518.68
fourth year:
37,518.68 + 37,518.68(0.075) +2000 ≈ 42,332.58
fifth year:
42,332.58 + 42,332.58(0.075) + 2000 ≈ 47,507.52
sixth year:
47,507.52 + 47,507.52(0.075) + 2000 ≈ 53,070.58
Yes; after 6 years she has $53,070.58.

43. $14x^3 - 17x^2 - 16x + 34$
$= 14(2.75)^3 - 17(2.75)^2 - 16(2.75) + 34$
≈ 153 eggs

44a. $V = \pi r^2h + \frac{1}{2}\left(\frac{4}{3}\right)\pi r^3$
$= \pi r^2h + \frac{2}{3}\pi r^3$

44b. $V = \pi r^2h + \frac{2}{3}\pi r^3$
$= \pi(8)^2(40) + \frac{2}{3}\pi(8)^3$
$\approx 9114.81 \text{ ft}^3$

45. $42{,}350 = 4.235 \times 10{,}000$
$= 4.235 \times 10^4$

46.
$$\begin{array}{rl} & \frac{3}{2}x + \frac{1}{5}y = 5 \\ (+) & \frac{3}{4}x - \frac{1}{5}y = -5 \\ \hline & \frac{9}{4}x \quad = 0 \\ & x = 0 \end{array}$$

$$\begin{aligned} \frac{3}{2}x + \frac{1}{5}y &= 5 \\ \frac{3}{2}(0) + \frac{1}{5}y &= 5 \\ 0 + \frac{1}{5}y &= 5 \\ y &= 25 \end{aligned}$$

(0, 25)

47. Let x = the integer.
$55 < 6.5x + 11 < 75$
$55 < 6.5x + 11$ and $6.5x + 11 < 75$
$44 < 6.5x$ $\quad 6.5x < 64$
$6.8 < x$ $\quad x < 9.8$
The possible integers are 7, 8, and 9.

48. Let x = the number of months.
$y = 3250x$
$y = 3250(12)$
$y = 39{,}000$
39,000 covers

49. Solve for y: $4x + 3y = 12$

$$3y = 12 - 4x$$

$$y = \frac{12 - 4x}{3}$$

x	$\frac{12 - 4x}{3}$	y	(x, y)
-3	$\frac{12 - 4(-3)}{3}$	8	$(-3, 8)$
1	$\frac{12 - 4(1)}{3}$	$\frac{8}{3}$	$\left(1, \frac{8}{3}\right)$
3	$\frac{12 - 4(3)}{3}$	0	$(3, 0)$
9	$\frac{12 - 4(9)}{3}$	-8	$(9, -8)$

$\{(-3, 8), \left(1, \frac{8}{3}\right), (3, 0), (9, -8)\}$

50. Fridays in March have a 3 in the numeral: 3, 13, 23, 30, 31

P(birthday has a 3 in the numeral)

$= \frac{\text{number of days with a 3 in the numeral}}{\text{total number of days in March}}$

$= \frac{5}{31}$

51. $\frac{5}{36} = \frac{x}{45}$

$5(45) = 36x$

$225 = 36x$

$6.25 = x$

$\$45 - \$6.25 = \$38.75$

52. $ax - by = 2cz$

$-by = 2cz - ax$

$\frac{-by}{-b} = \frac{2cz - ax}{-b}$

$y = \frac{ax - 2cz}{b}$

9-5A Modeling Mathematics: Adding and Subtracting Polynomials

Page 521

1.

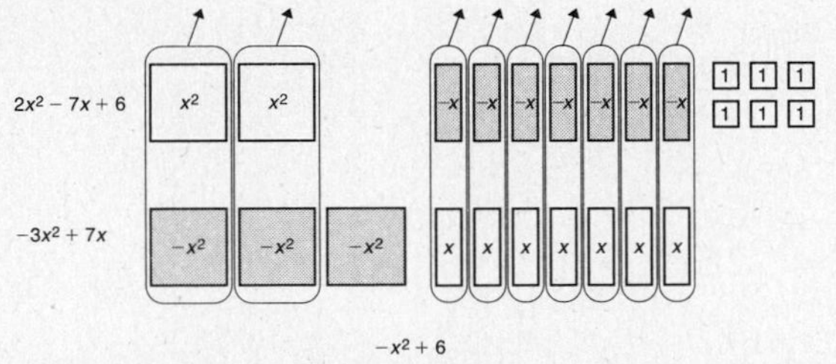

2.

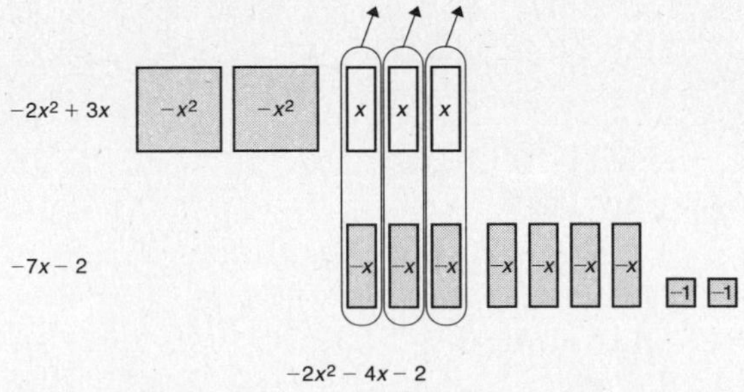

3.

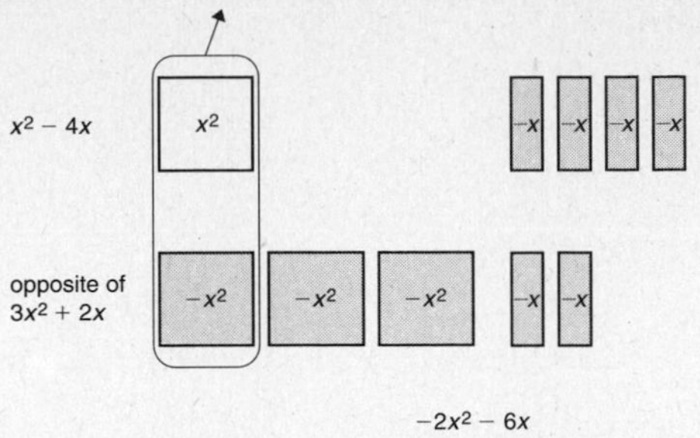

4.

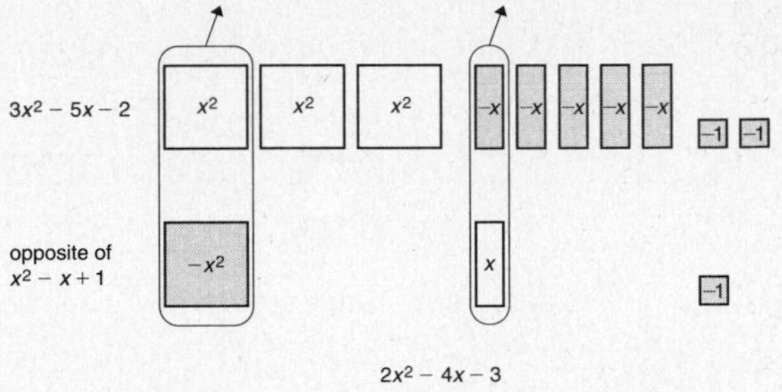

5.

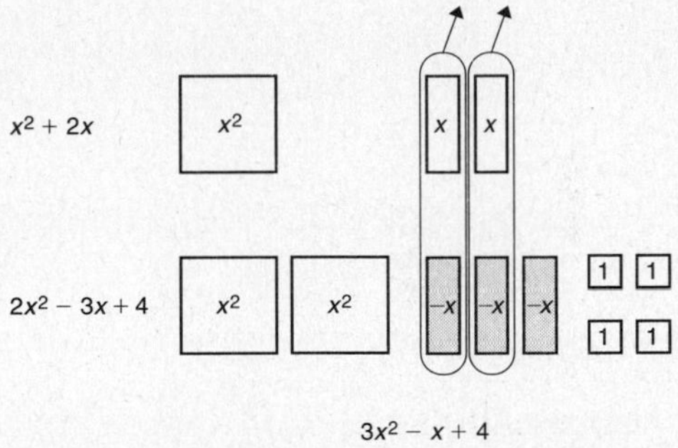

6.

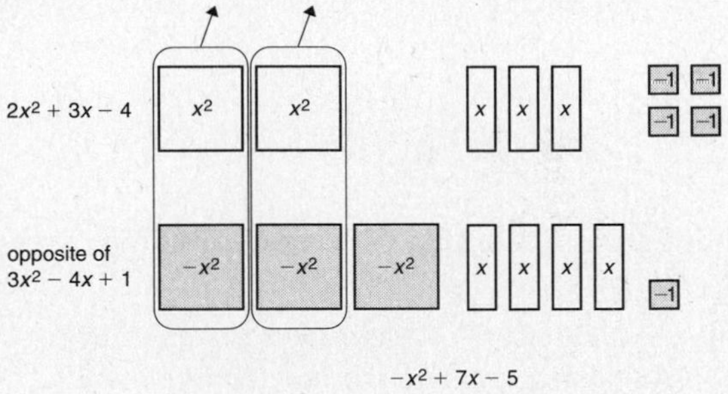

7. true

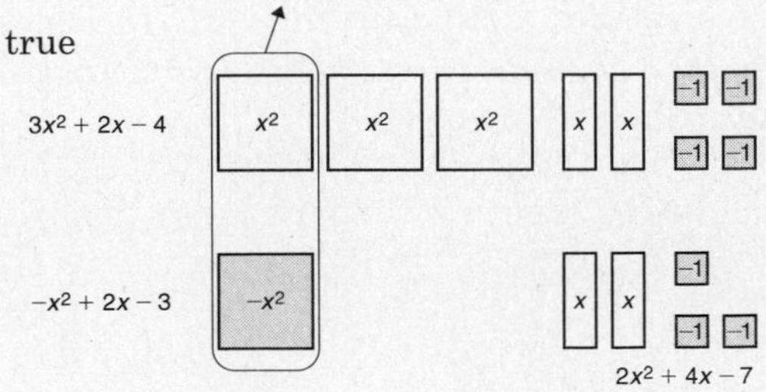

8. false

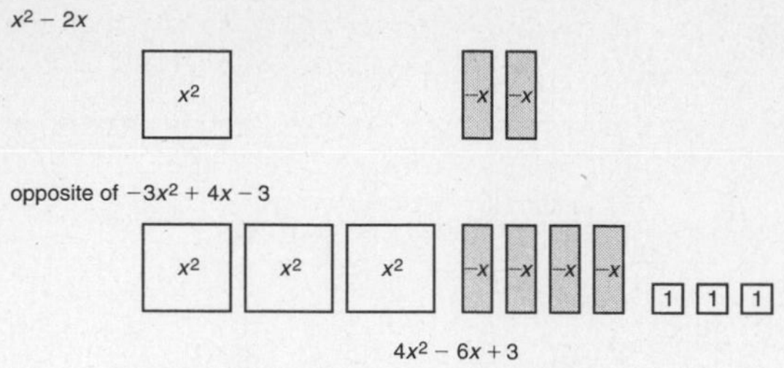

9. Method from Activity 2:

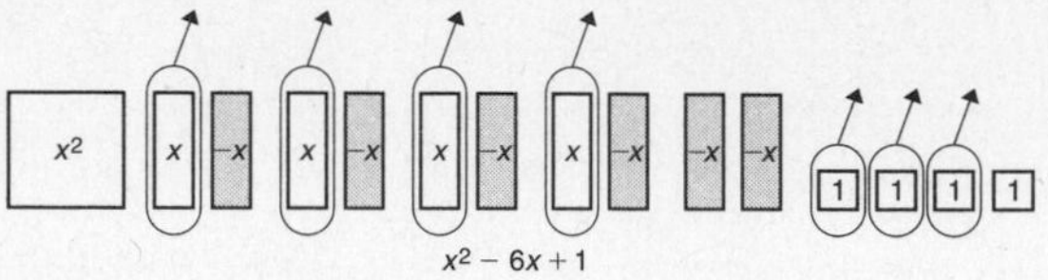

You need to add zero pairs so that you can remove 4 green x-tiles.

Method from Activity 3:

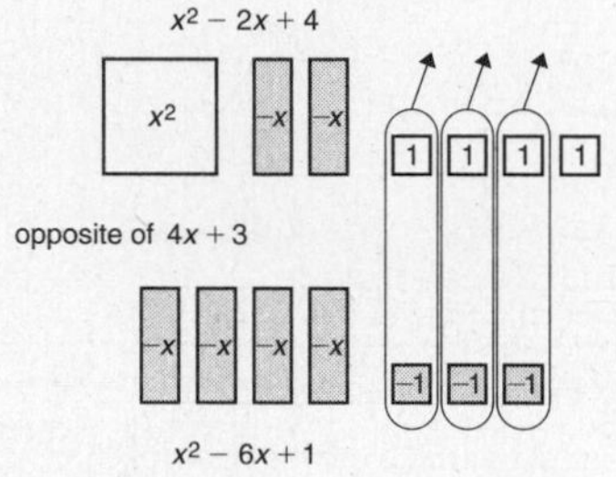

You remove all zero pairs to find the difference in simplest form.

9-5 Adding and Subtracting Polynomials

Pages 524–525 Check for Understanding

1. Align like terms.
2. Sample answer: $2a^2b^3$, $-4a^2b^3$, a^2b^3; $-a^2b^3$
3. Add your answer to the polynomial being subtracted. The sum should equal the first polynomial.
4. Find the additive inverse of the polynomial being subracted and then add.

5a.

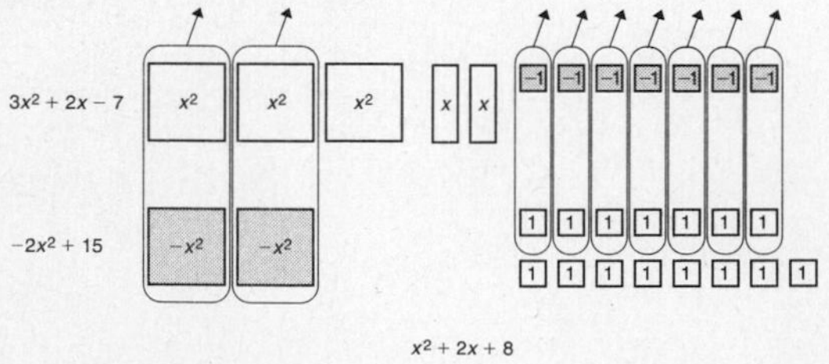

5b.

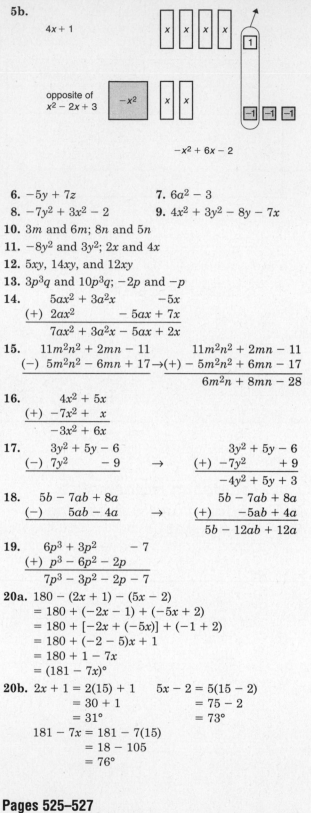

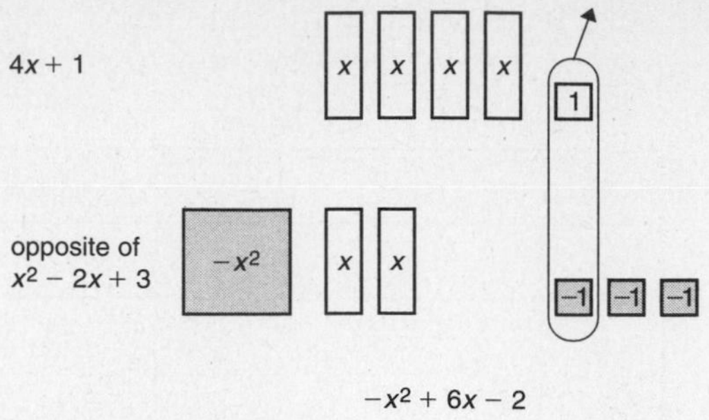

6. $-5y + 7z$
7. $6a^2 - 3$
8. $-7y^2 + 3x^2 - 2$
9. $4x^2 + 3y^2 - 8y - 7x$
10. $3m$ and $6m$; $8n$ and $5n$
11. $-8y^2$ and $3y^2$; $2x$ and $4x$
12. $5xy$, $14xy$, and $12xy$
13. $3p^3q$ and $10p^3q$; $-2p$ and $-p$

14.
$$\begin{array}{rl} & 5ax^2 + 3a^2x \qquad\quad -5x \\ (+) & 2ax^2 \qquad\quad - 5ax + 7x \\ \hline & 7ax^2 + 3a^2x - 5ax + 2x \end{array}$$

15.
$$\begin{array}{rl} & 11m^2n^2 + 2mn - 11 \\ (-) & 5m^2n^2 - 6mn + 17 \end{array} \rightarrow \begin{array}{rl} & 11m^2n^2 + 2mn - 11 \\ (+) & -5m^2n^2 + 6mn - 17 \\ \hline & 6m^2n + 8mn - 28 \end{array}$$

16.
$$\begin{array}{rl} & 4x^2 + 5x \\ (+) & -7x^2 + x \\ \hline & -3x^2 + 6x \end{array}$$

17.
$$\begin{array}{rl} & 3y^2 + 5y - 6 \\ (-) & 7y^2 \qquad - 9 \end{array} \rightarrow \begin{array}{rl} & 3y^2 + 5y - 6 \\ (+) & -7y^2 \qquad + 9 \\ \hline & -4y^2 + 5y + 3 \end{array}$$

18.
$$\begin{array}{rl} & 5b - 7ab + 8a \\ (-) & 5ab - 4a \end{array} \rightarrow \begin{array}{rl} & 5b - 7ab + 8a \\ (+) & -5ab + 4a \\ \hline & 5b - 12ab + 12a \end{array}$$

19.
$$\begin{array}{rl} & 6p^3 + 3p^2 \qquad - 7 \\ (+) & p^3 - 6p^2 - 2p \\ \hline & 7p^3 - 3p^2 - 2p - 7 \end{array}$$

20a.
$$\begin{aligned} & 180 - (2x + 1) - (5x - 2) \\ &= 180 + (-2x - 1) + (-5x + 2) \\ &= 180 + [-2x + (-5x)] + (-1 + 2) \\ &= 180 + (-2 - 5)x + 1 \\ &= 180 + 1 - 7x \\ &= (181 - 7x)^\circ \end{aligned}$$

20b.
$$\begin{aligned} 2x + 1 &= 2(15) + 1 \\ &= 30 + 1 \\ &= 31^\circ \end{aligned} \qquad \begin{aligned} 5x - 2 &= 5(15 - 2) \\ &= 75 - 2 \\ &= 73^\circ \end{aligned}$$
$$\begin{aligned} 181 - 7x &= 181 - 7(15) \\ &= 18 - 105 \\ &= 76^\circ \end{aligned}$$

Pages 525–527

21.
$$\begin{array}{rl} & 4x^2 + 5xy - 3y^2 \\ (+) & 6x^2 + 8xy + 3y^2 \\ \hline & 10x^2 + 13xy \end{array}$$

22.
$$\begin{array}{rl} & 6x^2y^2 - 3xy - 7 \\ (-) & 5x^2y^2 + 2xy + 3 \end{array} \rightarrow \begin{array}{rl} & 6x^2y^2 - 3xy - 7 \\ (+) & -5x^2y^2 - 2xy - 3 \\ \hline & x^2y^2 - 5xy - 10 \end{array}$$

23. $\begin{array}{r} a^3 \qquad\qquad\qquad - b^3 \\ (+)\ 3a^3 + 2a^2b - b^2 + 2b^3 \\ \hline 4a^3 + 2a^2b - b^2 + b^3 \end{array}$

24. $\begin{array}{r} 3a^2 \qquad - 8 \\ (-)\ 5a^2 + 2a + 7 \\ \hline \end{array} \rightarrow \begin{array}{r} 3a^2 \qquad\quad - 8 \\ (+)\ -5a^2 - 2a - 7 \\ \hline -2a^2 - 2a - 15 \end{array}$

25. $\begin{array}{r} 3a + 2b - 7c \\ -4a + 6b + 9c \\ (+)\ -3a - 2b - 7c \\ \hline -4a + 6b - 5c \end{array}$

26. $\begin{array}{r} 2x^2 - 5x + 7 \\ 5x^2 \qquad - 3 \\ (+)\ x^2 - x + 11 \\ \hline 8x^2 - 6x + 15 \end{array}$

27. $\begin{array}{r} 5a - 6m \\ (-)\ 2a + 5m \\ \hline \end{array} \rightarrow \begin{array}{r} 5a - 6m \\ (+)\ -2a - 5m \\ \hline 3a - 11m \end{array}$

28. $\begin{array}{r} 3 + 2a + a^2 \\ (+)\ 5 - 8a + a^2 \\ \hline 8 - 6a + 2a^2 \end{array}$

29. $\begin{array}{r} n^2 + 5n + 13 \\ (+)\ -3n^2 + 2n - 8 \\ \hline -2n^2 + 7n + 5 \end{array}$

30. $\begin{array}{r} 5x^2 \qquad - 4 \\ (-)\ 3x^2 + 8x + 4 \\ \hline \end{array} \rightarrow \begin{array}{r} 5x^2 \qquad - 4 \\ (+)\ -3x^2 - 8x - 4 \\ \hline 2x^2 - 8x - 8 \end{array}$

31. $\begin{array}{r} 13x + 9y \\ (-)\qquad 11y \\ \hline \end{array} \rightarrow \begin{array}{r} 13x + 9y \\ (+)\qquad -11y \\ \hline 13x - 2y \end{array}$

32. $\begin{array}{r} 5ax^2 + 3ax \\ (-)\ 2ax^2 - 8ax + 4 \\ \hline \end{array} \rightarrow \begin{array}{r} 5ax^2 + 3ax \\ (+)\ -2ax^2 + 8ax - 4 \\ \hline 3ax^2 + 11ax - 4 \end{array}$

33. $\begin{array}{r} 3y^3 + 4y - 7 \\ (+)\ -4y^3 - y + 10 \\ \hline -y^3 + 3y + 3 \end{array}$

34. $\begin{array}{r} 7p^2 - p - 7 \\ (-)\ p^2 \qquad + 11 \\ \hline \end{array} \rightarrow \begin{array}{r} 7p^2 - p - 7 \\ (+)\ -p^2 \qquad - 11 \\ \hline 6p^2 - p - 18 \end{array}$

35. $\begin{array}{r} 4z^3 \qquad\quad + 5z \\ (+)\qquad -2z^2 - 4z \\ \hline 4z^3 - 2z^2 + z \end{array}$

36. $\begin{array}{r} x^3 + 4x^2 - 7x - 2 \\ (-)\qquad 2x^2 - 9x + 4 \\ \hline \end{array} \rightarrow \begin{array}{r} x^3 + 4x^2 - 7x - 2 \\ (+)\qquad - 2x^2 + 9x - 4 \\ \hline x^3 + 2x^2 + 2x - 6 \end{array}$

37. $5x + 2y - (x + 2y) - (2x - 3y)$
$= 5x + 2y + (-x - 2y) + (-2x + 3y)$
$= (5x - x - 2x) + (2y - 2y + 3y)$
$= (5 - 1 - 2)x + (2 - 2 + 3)y$
$= 2x + 3y$

38. $13x^2 - 14x + 12 - (17x - 7) - (3x^2 + 5)$
$= 13x^2 - 14x + 12 + (-17x + 7) + (-3x^2 - 5)$
$= (13x^2 - 3x^2) + (-14x - 17x) + (12 + 7 - 5)$
$= (13 - 3)x^2 + (-14 - 17)x + 14$
$= 10x^2 - 31x + 14$

39. $360 - (4x + 12) - (8x - 10) - (6x + 5)$
$= 360 + (-4x - 12) + (-8x + 10) + (-6x - 5)$
$= (360 - 12 + 10 - 5) + (-4x - 8x - 6x)$
$= 353 + (-4 - 8 - 6)x$
$= 353 - 18x$

40. $360 - (x^2 - 2) - (x^2 + 5x - 9) - (-8x - 42)$
$= 360 + (-x^2 + 2) + (-x^2 - 5x + 9) + (8x + 42)$
$= (360 + 2 + 9 + 42) + (-x^2 - x^2) + (-5x + 8x)$
$= 413 + (-1 - 1)x^2 + (-5 + 8)x$
$= 413 - 2x^2 + 3x$

41. $-(2n^2 + n - 4) = -2n^2 - n + 4$

42a. $(60 - 2x) + (40 - 2x) + (40 - 2x) + x + x \leq 108$
$(60 + 40 + 40) + (-2x - 2x - 2x + x + x) \leq 108$
$140 + (-2 - 2 - 2 + 1 + 1)x \leq 108$
$140 - 4x \leq 108$
$-4x \leq -32$
$x \geq 8$

42b. 19 inches

42c. 8488 sq. in.; 836 sq. in.

42d. As height increases, volume decreases.

43. $50x \cdot x + 89x \cdot x + 66x \cdot x + 110x \cdot x + 110x \cdot x + 89x \cdot x + 66x \cdot x + 89x \cdot x + 50x \cdot x$
$= 50x^2 + 89x^2 + 66x^2 + 110x^2 + 110x^2 + 89x^2 + 66x^2 + 89x^2 + 50x^2$
$= 719x^2$ cubic stories

44a. 1, 4, 9, 16, 25

44b. square numbers

44c. 36, 49, 64

44d. square numbers less than or equal to n

45. $-3x - 2x^3 + 4x^5$

46. $P\left[\frac{1 - (1 + r)^{k - n}}{r}\right] = 256\left[\frac{1 - (1 + 0.01)^{20 - 60}}{0.01}\right]$
$= 256(32.8347)$
$= \$8405.68$

47. $5x - 3y = 12$
$-3y = -5x + 12$
$y = \frac{5}{3}x - 4$

$2x - 5y = 1$
$-5y = -2x + 1$
$y = \frac{2}{5}x - \frac{1}{5}$

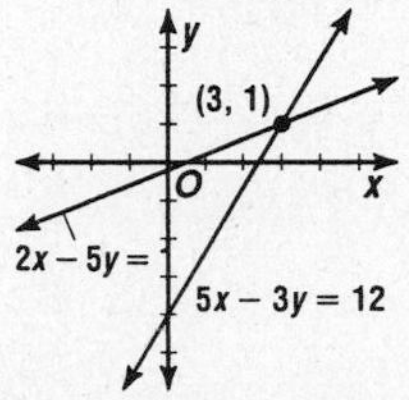

The solution is (3, 1).

48. 135

49. Sample answer: Let h = the number of hours for the repair and let c = the total charge; $c = 34h + 15$.

50. Let x = the money the owners received.
$x + 0.065x = 145{,}000$
$1.065x = 145{,}000$
$x = \$136{,}150$

51. $\frac{-3n - (-4)}{-6} = -9$
$-6\left(\frac{-3n + 4}{-6}\right) = -6(-9)$
$-3n + 4 = 54$
$-3n = 50$
$n = -\frac{50}{3}$

52. $12 \div \left(2\frac{1}{2}\right) = 12 \div \left(\frac{5}{2}\right)$
$= 12 \cdot \frac{2}{5}$
$= \frac{24}{5}$ or $4\frac{4}{5}$

4 tennis balls

Page 527 Self Test

1. $(-2n^4y^3)(3ny^4) = (-2 \cdot 3)(n^4 \cdot n)(y^3y^4)$
$= -6n^{4+1}y^{3+4}$
$= -6n^5y^7$

2. $(-3a^2b^5)^2 = (-3)^2(a^2)^2(b^5)^2$
$= 9a^4b^{10}$

3. $\frac{24a^3b^6}{-2a^2b^2} = \left(\frac{24}{-2}\right)\left(\frac{a^3}{a^2}\right)\left(\frac{b^6}{b^2}\right)$
$= -12a^{3-2}b^{6-2}$
$= -12ab^4$

4. $\frac{(5r^{-1}s)^3}{(s^2)^3} = \frac{5^3r^{-3}s^3}{s^6}$
$= 125r^{-3}\left(\frac{s^3}{s^6}\right)$
$= 125r^{-3}s^{3-6}$
$= 125r^{-3}s^{-3}$
$= \frac{125}{r^3s^3}$

5. $5{,}670{,}000 = 5.67 \times 1{,}000{,}000$
$= 5.67 \times 10^6$

6. $0.86 \times 10^{-4} = 8.6 \times 0.01 \times 10^{-4}$
$= 8.6 \times 10^{-1} \times 10^{-4}$
$= 8.6 \times 10^{-5}$

7. $\frac{2.85 \times 10^9}{186{,}000} = \frac{2.85 \times 10^9}{1.86 \times 10^5}$
$= \left(\frac{2.85}{1.86}\right)\left(\frac{10^9}{10^5}\right)$
$\approx 1.53 \times 10^4$ sec

$1.53 \times 10^4 \text{ sec}\left(\frac{1 \text{ hr}}{3600 \text{ sec}}\right)$
$= \frac{1.53 \times 10^4}{3.6 \times 10^3}$
$= \left(\frac{1.53}{3.6}\right)\left(\frac{10^4}{10^3}\right)$
$= 0.425 \times 10$
$= 4.25$ hours

8. The degree of $11x^2$ is 2.
The degree of $7ax^3$ is 4.
The degree of $-3x$ is 1.
The degree of $2a$ is 1.
Thus, the degree of $11x^2 + 7ax^3 - 3x + 2a$ is 4;
$2a - 3x + 11x^2 + 7ax^3$

9.
$$\begin{array}{r} x^2 + 3x - 5 \\ (+)\ 4x^2 - 7x - 9 \\ \hline 5x^2 - 4x - 14 \end{array}$$

10.
$$\begin{array}{r} 2a - 7 \\ (-)\ 2a^2 + 8a - 11 \\ \hline \end{array} \rightarrow \begin{array}{r} 2a - 7 \\ (+)\ -2a^2 - 8a + 11 \\ \hline -2a^2 - 6a + 4 \end{array}$$

9-6A Modeling Mathematics: Multiplying a Polynomial by a Monomial

Page 528

1.
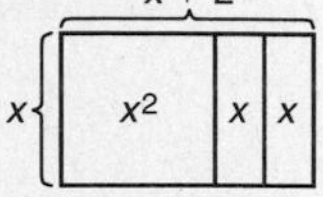

$x^2 + 2x$

2.
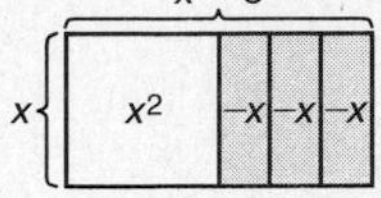

$x^2 - 3x$

3.
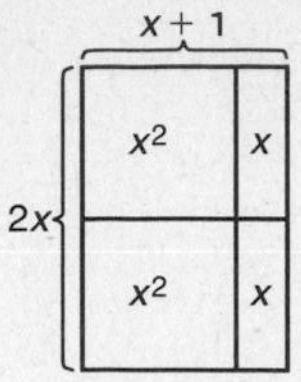

$2x^2 + 2x$

4.
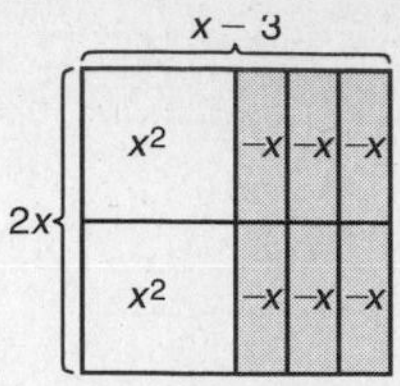

$2x^2 - 6x$

5.
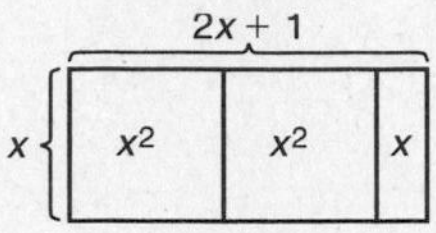

$2x^2 + x$

6.
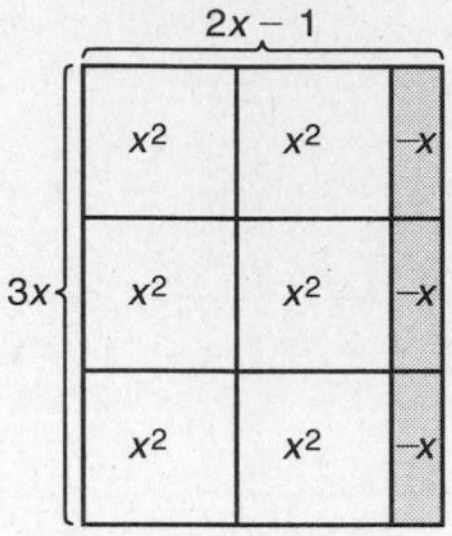

$6x^2 - 3x$

7. true
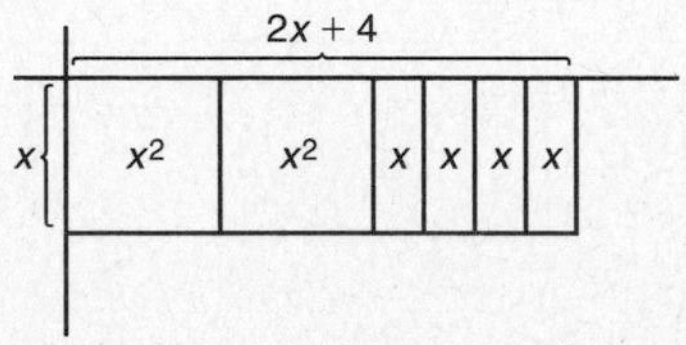

8. false
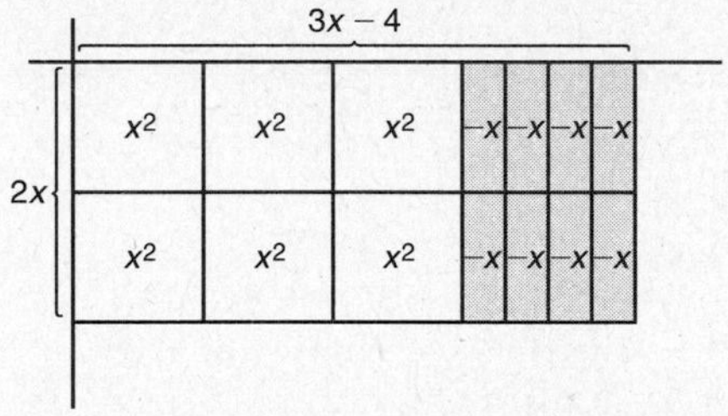

9a. $3x$ and $x + 15$

9b. $3x(x + 15) = (3x^2 + 45x)$ square feet
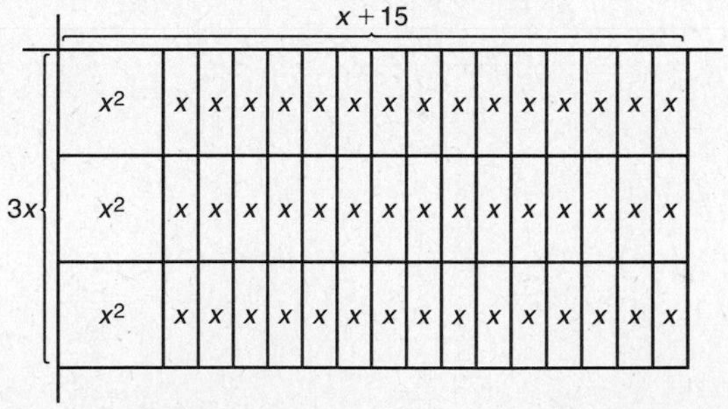

9-6 Multiplying a Polynomial by a Monomial

Pages 531–532 Check for Understanding

1. distributive property

2a. Multiply 7 times $x^2 + 14x$.

2b. $7x^2 + 98x$

2c. $7x^2 + 98x = 7(8)^2 + 98(8)$
$= 7(64) + 98(8)$
$= 448 + 784$
$= 1232 \text{ in}^2$

3a. Replace x with $\frac{19}{11}$ and check to see if both sides of the equation represent the same number.

3b.
$$x(x+3) + 7x - 5 = x(8+x) - 9x + 14$$
$$\frac{19}{11}\left(\frac{19}{11}+3\right) + 7\left(\frac{19}{11}\right) - 5 = \frac{19}{11}\left(8+\frac{19}{11}\right) - 9\left(\frac{19}{11}\right) + 14$$
$$\frac{19}{11}\left(\frac{52}{11}\right) + \frac{133}{11} - \frac{55}{11} = \frac{19}{11}\left(\frac{107}{11}\right) - \frac{171}{11} + \frac{154}{11}$$
$$\frac{988}{121} + \frac{1463}{121} - \frac{605}{121} = \frac{2033}{121} - \frac{1881}{121} + \frac{1694}{121}$$
$$\frac{1846}{121} = \frac{1846}{121}$$

4a.

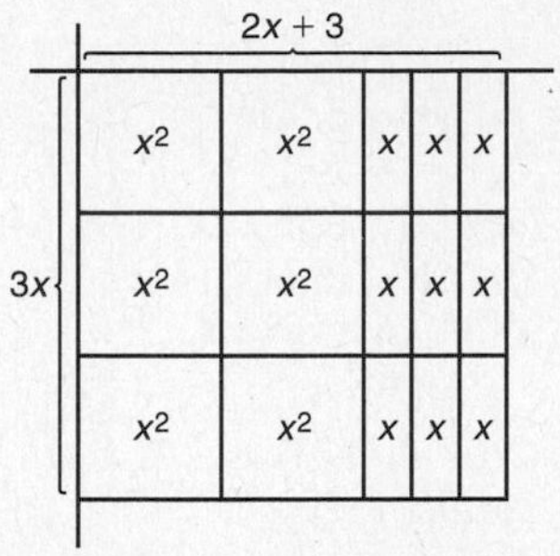

4b. $6x^2 + 9x$

5. $-7b(9b^3c + 1) = -7b(9b^3c) + (-7b)(1)$
$= -63b^4c - 7b$

6. $4a^2(-8a^3c + c - 11)$
$= 4a^2(-8a^3c) + 4a^2(c) + 4a^2(-11)$
$= -32a^5c + 4a^2c - 44a^2$

7.
$$\begin{array}{r} 5y - 13 \\ (\times)\quad 2y \\ \hline 10y^2 - 26y \end{array}$$

8.
$$\begin{array}{r} 2ab - 5a \\ (\times)\quad 11ab \\ \hline 22a^2b^2 - 55a^2b \end{array}$$

9. $w(3w - 5) + 3w = w(3w) - w(5) + 3w$
$= 3w^2 - 5w + 3w$
$= 3w^2 - 2w$

10. $4y(2y^3 - 8y^2 + 2y + 9) - 3(y^2 + 8y)$
$= 4y(2y^3) - 4y(8y^2) + 4y(2y) + 4y(9) - 3y^2 - 3(8y)$
$= 8y^4 - 32y^3 + 8y^2 + 36y - 3y^2 - 24y$
$= 8y^4 - 32y^3 + 5y^2 + 12y$

11.
$12(b + 14) - 20b = 11b + 65$
$12b + 12(14) - 20b = 11b + 65$
$12b + 168 - 20b = 11b + 65$
$168 - 8b = 11b + 65$
$168 = 19b + 65$
$103 = 19b$
$\frac{103}{19} = b$

12.
$x(x - 4) + 2x = x(x + 12) - 7$
$x(x) - x(4) + 2x = x(x) + x(12) - 7$
$x^2 - 4x + 2x = x^2 + 12x - 7$
$x^2 - 2x = x^2 + 12x - 7$
$-14x = -7$
$x = \frac{1}{2}$

13a. $a(a + 1) = a(a) + a(1)$
$= a^2 + a$

13b. $a(a + 2) = a(a) + a(2)$
$= a^2 + 2a$

Pages 532–533 Exercises

14. $-7(2x + 9) = -7(2x) + (-7)(9)$
$= -14x - 63$

15. $\frac{1}{3}x(x - 27) = \frac{1}{3}x(x) - \frac{1}{3}x(27)$
$= \frac{1}{3}x^2 - 9x$

16. $3st(5s^2 + 2st) = 3st(5s^2) + 3st(2st)$
$= 15s^3t + 6s^2t^2$

17. $-4m^3(5m^2 + 2m) = -4m^3(5m^2) + (-4m^3)(2m)$
$= -20m^5 - 8m^4$

18. $3d(4d^2 - 8d - 15) = 3d(4d^2) - 3d(8d) - 3d(15)$
$= 12d^3 - 24d^2 - 45d$

19. $5m^3(6m^2 - 8mn + 12n^3)$
$= 5m^3(6m^2) - 5m^3(8mn) + 5m^3(12n^3)$
$= 30m^5 - 40m^4n + 60m^3n^3$

20. $7x^2y(5x^2 - 3xy + y)$
$= 7x^2y(5x^2) - 7x^2y(3xy) + 7x^2y(y)$
$= 35x^4y - 21x^3y^2 + 7x^2y^2$

21. $-4d(7d^2 - 4d + 3)$
$= -4d(7d^2) - (-4d)(4d) + (-4d)(3)$
$= -28d^3 + 16d^2 - 12d$

22. $2m^2(5m^2 - 7m + 8)$
$= 2m^2(5m^2) - 2m^2(7m) + 2m^2(8)$
$= 10m^4 - 14m^3 + 16m^2$

23. $-8rs(4rs + 7r - 14s^2)$
$= -8rs(4rs) + (-8rs)(7r) - (-8rs)(14s^2)$
$= -32r^2s^2 - 56r^2s + 112rs^3$

24. $-\frac{3}{4}ab^2\left(\frac{1}{3}abc + \frac{4}{9}a - 6\right)$
$= -\frac{3}{4}ab^2\left(\frac{1}{3}abc\right) + \left(-\frac{3}{4}ab^2\right)\left(\frac{4}{9}a\right) - \left(-\frac{3}{4}ab^2\right)(6)$
$= -\frac{1}{4}a^2b^3c - \frac{1}{3}a^2b^2 + \frac{9}{2}ab^2$

25. $\frac{4}{5}x^2\left(9xy + \frac{5}{4}x - 30y\right)$
$= \frac{4}{5}x^2(9xy) + \frac{4}{5}x^2\left(\frac{5}{4}x\right) - \frac{4}{5}x^2(30y)$
$= \frac{36}{5}x^3y + x^3 - 24x^2y$

26. $b(4b - 1) + 10b = b(4b) - b(1) + 10b$
$= 4b^2 - b + 10b$
$= 4b^2 + 9b$

27. $3t(2t - 4) + 6(5t^2 + 2t - 7)$
$= 3t(2t) - 3t(4) + 6(5t^2) + 6(2t) - 6(7)$
$= 6t^2 - 12t + 30t^2 + 12t - 42$
$= 6t^2 + 30t^2 - 12t + 12t - 42$
$= 36t^2 - 42$

28. $8m(-9m^2 + 2m - 6) + 11(2m^3 - 4m + 12)$
$= 8m(-9m^2) + 8m(2m) + 8m(-6) + 11(2m^3) - 11(4m) + 11(12)$
$= -72m^3 + 16m^2 - 48m + 22m^3 - 44m + 132$
$= -72m^3 + 22m^3 + 16m^2 - 48m - 44m + 132$
$= -50m^3 + 16m^2 - 92m + 132$

29. $8y(11y^2 - 2y + 13) - 9(3y^3 - 7y + 2)$
$= 8y(11y^2) - 8y(2y) + 8y(13) - 9(3y^3) - 9(-7y) - 9(2)$
$= 88y^3 - 16y^2 + 104y - 27y^3 + 63y - 18$
$= 88y^3 - 27y^3 - 16y^2 + 104y + 63y - 18$
$= 61y^3 - 16y^2 + 167y - 18$

30. $\frac{3}{4}t(8t^3 + 12t - 4) + \frac{3}{2}(8t^2 - 9t)$
$= \frac{3}{4}t(8t^3) + \frac{3}{4}t(12t) - \frac{3}{4}t(4) + \frac{3}{2}(8t^2) - \frac{3}{2}(9t)$
$= 6t^4 + 9t^2 - 3t + 12t^2 - \frac{27}{2}t$
$= 6t^4 + 9t^2 + 12t^2 - 3t - \frac{27}{2}t$
$= 6t^4 + 21t^2 - \frac{33}{2}t$

31. $6a^2(3a - 4) + 5a(7a^2 - 6a + 5) - 3(a^2 + 6a)$
$= 6a^2(3a) - 6a^2(4) + 5a(7a^2) - 5a(6a) + 5a(5) - 3(a^2) - 3(6a)$
$= 18a^3 - 24a^2 + 35a^3 - 30a^2 + 25a - 3a^2 - 18a$
$= 18a^3 + 35a^3 - 24a^2 - 30a^2 - 3a^2 + 25a - 18a$
$= 53a^3 - 57a^2 + 7a$

32. $2(5w - 12) = 6(-2w + 3) + 2$
$2(5w) - 2(12) = 6(-2w) + 6(3) + 2$
$10w - 24 = -12w + 18 + 2$
$10w - 24 = -12w + 20$
$22w - 24 = 20$
$22w = 44$
$w = 2$

33. $7(x - 12) = 13 + 5(3x - 4)$
$7(x) - 7(12) = 13 + 5(3x) - 5(4)$
$7x - 84 = 13 + 15x - 20$
$7x - 84 = -7 + 15x$
$-77 = 8x$
$-\frac{77}{8} = x$

34. $\frac{1}{2}(2d - 34) = \frac{2}{3}(6d - 27)$
$\frac{1}{2}(2d) - \frac{1}{2}(34) = \frac{2}{3}(6d) - \frac{2}{3}(27)$
$d - 17 = 4d - 18$
$-17 = 3d - 18$
$1 = 3d$
$\frac{1}{3} = d$

35. $p(p + 2) + 3p = p(p - 3)$
$p(p) + p(2) + 3p = p(p) - p(3)$
$p^2 + 2p + 3p = p^2 - 3p$
$p^2 + 5p = p^2 - 3p$
$5p = -3p$
$8p = 0$
$p = 0$

36. $y(y + 12) - 8y = 14 + y(y - 4)$
$y(y) + y(12) - 8y = 14 + y(y) + y(-4)$
$y^2 + 12y - 8y = 14 + y^2 - 4y$
$y^2 + 4y = 14 + y^2 - 4y$
$4y = 14 - 4y$
$8y = 14$
$y = \frac{7}{4}$

37. $x(x - 3) - x(x + 4) = 17x - 23$
$x(x) - x(3) - x(x) - x(4) = 17x - 23$
$x^2 - 3x - x^2 - 4x = 17x - 23$
$-7x = 17x$
$-24x = -23$
$x = \frac{23}{24}$

38. $a(a + 8) - a(a + 3) - 23 = 3a + 11$
$a(a) + a(8) - a(a) - a(3) - 23 = 3a + 11$
$a^2 + 8a - a^2 - 3a - 23 = 3a + 11$
$5a - 23 = 3a + 11$
$2a - 23 = 11$
$2a = 34$
$a = 17$

39. $t(t - 12) + t(t + 2) + 25 = 2t(t + 5) - 15$
$t(t) - t(12) + t(t) + t(2) + 25 = 2t(t) + 2t(5) - 15$
$t^2 - 12t + t^2 + 2t + 25 = 2t^2 + 10t - 15$
$2t^2 - 10t + 25 = 2t^2 + 10t - 15$
$-10t + 25 = 10t - 15$
$25 = 20t - 15$
$40 = 20t$
$2 = t$

40. $3x(x + 2) - 2x(x) = 3x(x) + 3x(2) - 2x^2$
$= 3x^2 + 6x - 2x^2$
$= x^2 + 6x$

41. $4p(4p + 8) - p(p) = 4p(4p) + 4p(8) - p^2$
$= 16p^2 + 32p - p^2$
$= 15p^2 + 32p$

42. $3a^2(4a + b + 5) - 10(2a^2b - b - 1)$
$= 3a^2(4a) + 3a^2(b) + 3a^2(5) - 10(2a^2b) - 10(-b) - 10(-1)$
$= 12a^3 + 3a^2b + 15a^2 - 20a^2b + 10b + 10$
$= 12a^3 - 17a^2b + 15a^2 + 10b + 10$

43. Sample answer: $1(8a^2b + 18ab)$
$a(8ab + 18b)$
$b(8a^2 + 18a)$
$2(4a^2b + 9ab)$
$(2a)(4ab + 9b)$
$(2b)(4a^2 + 9a)$
$(ab)(8a + 18)$
$(2ab)(4a + 9)$

44a. $7y(2y + 1) = 7y(2y) + 7y(1)$
$= 14y^2 + 7y$

44b. $14y^2 + 7y = 14(9)^2 + 7(9)$
$= 14(81) + 63$
$= 1134 + 63$
$= 1197 \text{ in}^2$

45. $t[2.75 + 1.25(m - 1)] = 2.75t + 1.25mt - 1.25t$
$= 1.50t + 1.25mt$

46. If she can spend \$820, and concrete costs \$20 per square yard, then she can buy $\frac{820}{20}$ or 41 square yards of concrete.
Let x = width of walkway in yards;
$\frac{42}{3} + 2x$ or $14 + 2x$ = length of garden and walkway (in yards);
$\frac{24}{3} + \frac{3}{3}$ or 9 = width of garden and walkway (in yards).
$9(14 + 2x) - 8(14) = 41$
$126 + 18x - 112 = 41$
$18x = 27$
$x = 1.5$ yd or 4.5 ft

47a.

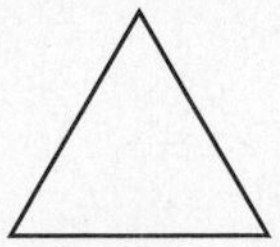

0 diagonals
$\frac{1}{2}(3)(3 - 3) = \frac{1}{2}(3)(0)$
$= 0$

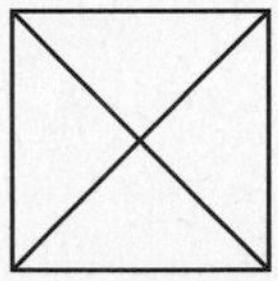

2 diagonals
$\frac{1}{2}(4)(4 - 3) = \frac{1}{2}(4)(1)$
$= 2$

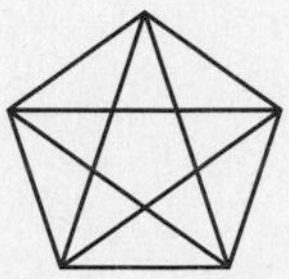

5 diagonals
$\frac{1}{2}(5)(5 - 3) = \frac{1}{2}(5)(2)$
$= 5$

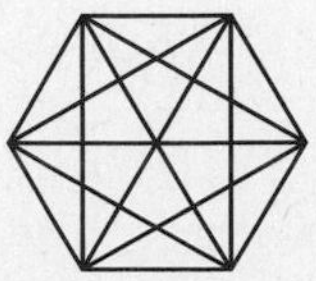

9 diagonals
$\frac{1}{2}(6)(6 - 3) = \frac{1}{2}(6)(3)$
$= 9$

47b. $\frac{1}{2}n(n - 3) = \frac{1}{2}n(n) - \frac{1}{2}n(3)$
$= \frac{1}{2}n^2 - \frac{3}{2}n$

47c. $\frac{1}{2}n^2 - \frac{3}{2}n = \frac{1}{2}(15)^2 - \frac{3}{2}(15)$
$= \frac{1}{2}(225) - \frac{45}{2}$
$= \frac{225 - 45}{2}$
$= \frac{180}{2}$
$= 90$ diagonals

48. $(3a - 4ab + 7b) - (7a - 3b)$
$= 3a - 4ab + 7b - 7a + 3b$
$= 3a - 7a - 4ab + 3b + 7b$
$= (3 - 7)a - 4ab + (3 + 7)b$
$= -4a - 4ab + 10b$

49.

	50% Glycol	30% Glycol	45% Glycol
Total Gallons	x	y	100
Gallons of Glycol	$0.50x$	$0.30y$	$0.45(100)$

$x + y = 100$
$0.50x + 0.30y = 0.45(100)$
$0.50x + 0.30y = 45$
$0.50x + 0.30(100 - x) = 45$
$0.50x + 30 - 0.30x = 45$
$0.20x + 30 = 45$
$0.20x = 15$
$x = 75$ $y = 100 - 75$
$y = 25$

Thus, 75 gallons of 50% glycol and 25 gallons of 30% glycol should be used.

50. $m = \frac{0 - 5}{-3 - 1} = \frac{-5}{-4} = \frac{5}{4}$

51. $g(x) = x^2 + 2x$
$g(a - 1) = (a - 1)^2 + 2(a - 1)$
$= (a - 1)(a - 1) + 2a - 2$
$= a(a - 1) - 1(a - 1) + 2a - 2$
$= a^2 - a - a + 1 + 2a - 2$
$= a^2 - 2a + 2a + 1 - 2$
$= a^2 - 1$

52. $2x - y = 8$
$-y = -2x + 8$
$y = 2x - 8$

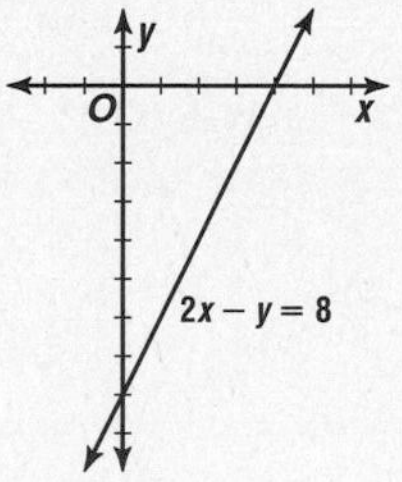

53. $\frac{\$340}{4 \text{ days}} = \frac{\$935}{x \text{ days}}$
$340x = 4(935)$
$340x = 3740$
$x = 11$ days

54. Let x = the angle and let $90 - x$ = the complement.
$x = (90 - x) - 44$
$x = 90 - x - 44$
$x = 46 - x$
$2x = 46$
$x = 23°$

55. $(15x)^3 - y = [15(0.2)]^3 - (1.3)$
$= 3^3 - 1.3$
$= 27 - 1.3$
$= 25.7$

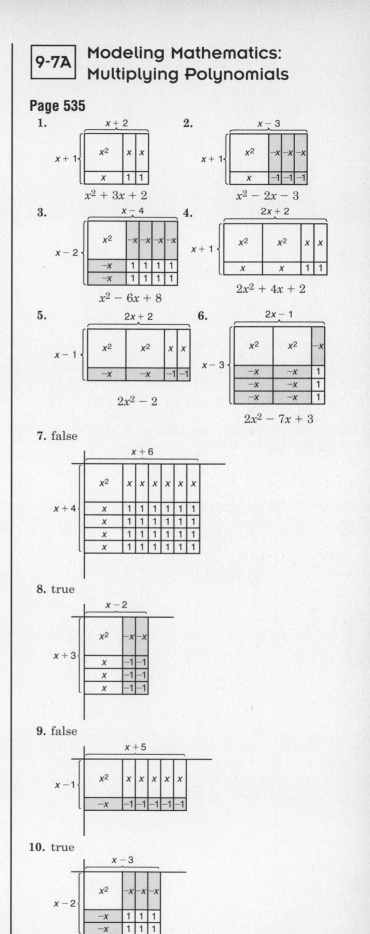

9-7A Modeling Mathematics: Multiplying Polynomials

Page 535

1.

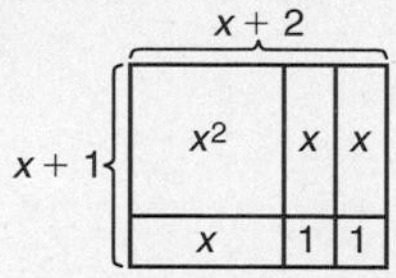

$x^2 + 3x + 2$

2.

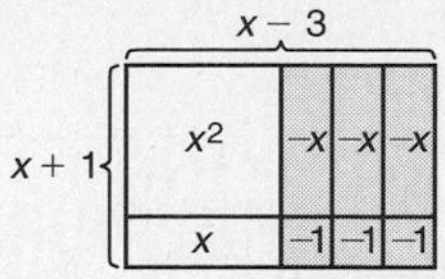

$x^2 - 2x - 3$

3.

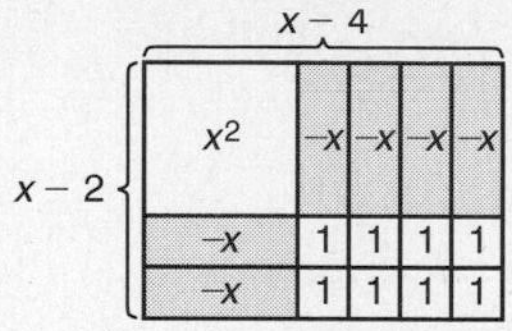

$x^2 - 6x + 8$

4.

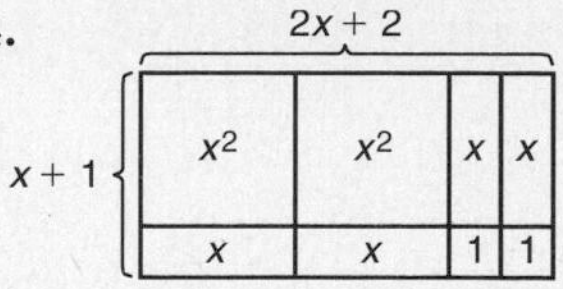

$2x^2 + 4x + 2$

5.

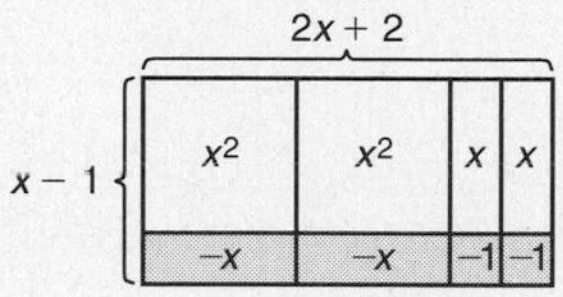

$2x^2 - 2$

6.

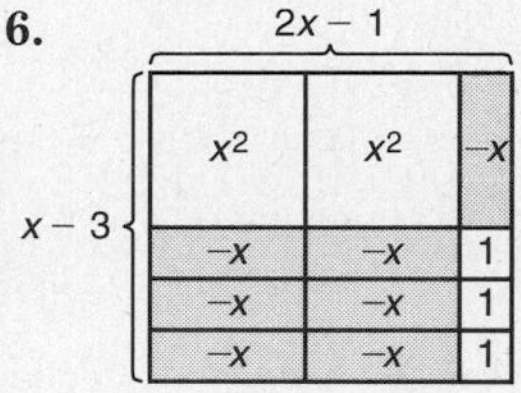

$2x^2 - 7x + 3$

7. false

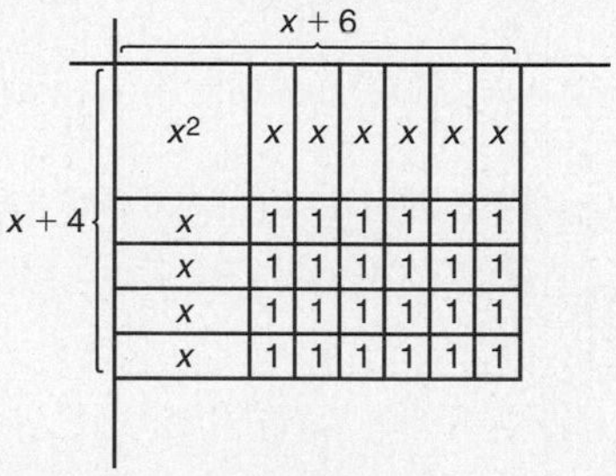

8. true

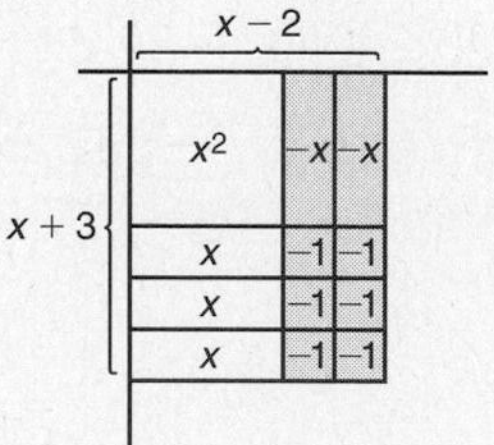

9. false

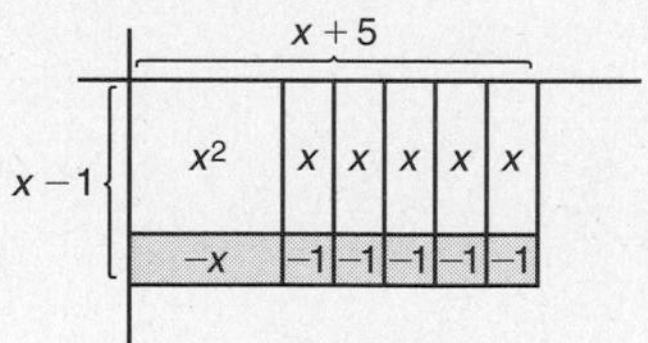

10. true

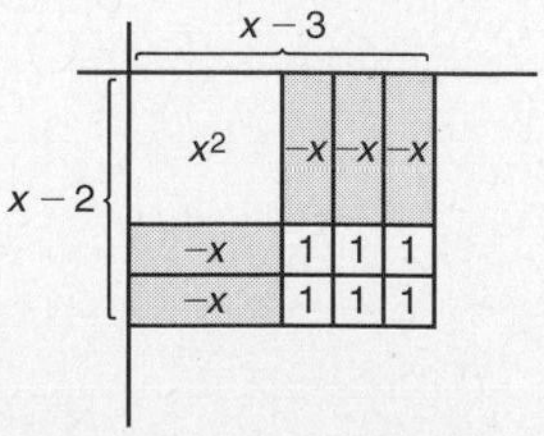

11. By the distributive property, $(x + 3)(x + 2) = x(x + 2) + 3(x + 2)$. The top row represents $x(x + 2)$ or $x^2 + 2x$. The bottom row represents $3(x + 2)$ or $3x + 6$.

9-7 Multiplying Polynomials

Pages 538–539 Check for Understanding

1a. Sample answer:

$(42)(27) = (40 + 2)(20 + 7)$

F O I L

$= 40(20) + 40(7) + 2(20) + 2(7)$
$= 800 + 280 + 40 + 14$
$= 1134$

1b. Sample answer:

$4\frac{1}{2} \cdot 6\frac{3}{4} = \left(4 + \frac{1}{2}\right)\left(6 + \frac{3}{4}\right)$

F O I L

$= 4(6) + 4\left(\frac{3}{4}\right) + \frac{1}{2}(6) + \frac{1}{2}\left(\frac{3}{4}\right)$
$= 24 + 3 + 3 + \frac{3}{8}$
$= 30\frac{3}{8}$

2. See students' work.

3.

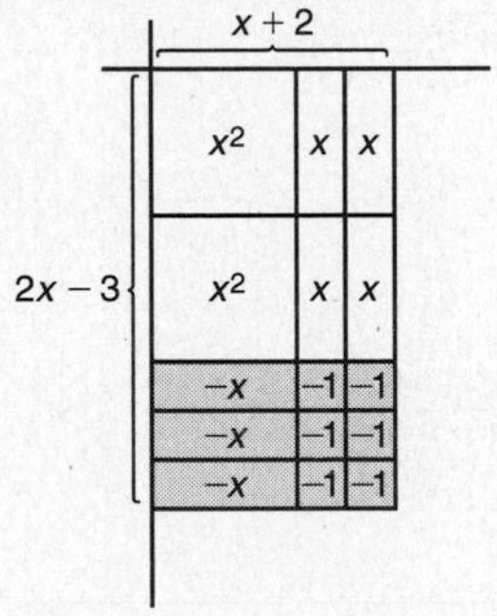

4. Sample answer: $(a + x)(2x + 3)$

5. $(d + 2)(d + 8) = (d)(d) + (d)(8) + (2)(d) + (2)(8)$
$= d^2 + 8d + 2d + 16$
$= d^2 + 10d + 16$

6. $(r - 5)(r - 11)$
$= (r)(r) + (r)(-11) + (-5)(r) + (-5)(-11)$
$= r^2 - 11r - 5r + 55$
$= r^2 - 16r + 55$

7. $(y + 3)(y - 7) = (y)(y) + (y)(-7) + (3)(y) + (3)(-7)$
$= y^2 - 7y + 3y - 21$
$= y^2 - 4y - 21$

8. $(3p - 5)(5p + 2)$
$= (3p)(5p) + (3p)(2) + (-5)(5p) + (-5)(2)$
$= 15p^2 + 6p - 25p - 10$
$= 15p^2 - 19p - 10$

9. $(2x - 1)(x + 5)$
$= (2x)(x) + 2x(5) + (-1)(x) + (-1)(5)$
$= 2x^2 + 10x - x - 5$
$= 2x^2 + 9x - 5$

10. $(2m + 5)(3m - 8)$
$= (2m)(3m) + (2m)(-8) + (5)(3m) + (5)(-8)$
$= 6m^2 - 16m + 15m - 40$
$= 6m^2 - m - 40$

11. $(2a + 3b)(5a - 2b)$
$= (2a)(5a) + (2a)(-2b) + (3b)(5a) + (3b)(-2b)$
$= 10a^2 - 4ab + 15ab - 6b^2$
$= 10a^2 + 11ab - 6b^2$

12. $(2x - 5)(3x^2 - 5x + 4)$
$= 2x(3x^2 - 5x + 4) - 5(3x^2 - 5x + 4)$
$= (6x^3 - 10x^2 + 8x) - (15x^2 - 25x + 20)$
$= 6x^3 - 10x^2 + 8x - 15x^2 + 25x - 20$
$= 6x^3 - 25x^2 + 33x - 20$

13a. $a(a + 1)(a + 2)$
$= a[(a)(a) + (a)(2) + (1)(a) + (1)(2)]$
$= a(a^2 + 2a + a + 2)$
$= a(a^2 + 3a + 2)$
$= a^3 + 3a^2 + 2a$

13b. See students' work.

13c. See students' work. The result is the same as the product in part b.

Pages 539–541 Exercises

14. $(y + 5)(y + 7) = (y)(y) + (y)(7) + (5)(y) + (5)(7)$
$= y^2 + 7y + 5y + 35$
$= y^2 + 12y + 35$

15. $(c - 3)(c - 7)$
$= (c)(c) + (c)(-7) + (-3)(c) + (-3)(-7)$
$= c^2 - 7c - 3c + 21$
$= c^2 - 10c + 21$

16. $(x + 4)(x - 8) = (x)(x) + (x)(-8) + (4)(x) + (4)(-8)$
$= x^2 - 8x + 4x - 32$
$= x^2 - 4x - 32$

17. $(w + 3)(w - 9)$
$= (w)(w) + (w)(-9) + (3)(w) + (3)(-9)$
$= w^2 - 9w + 3w - 27$
$= w^2 - 6w - 27$

18. $(2a - 1)(a + 8)$
$= (2a)(a) + (2a)(8) + (-1)(a) + (-1)(8)$
$= 2a^2 + 16a - a - 8$
$= 2a^2 + 15a - 8$

19. $(5b - 3)(2b + 1)$
$= (5b)(2b) + (5b)(1) + (-3)(2b) + (-3)(1)$
$= 10b^2 + 5b - 6b - 3$
$= 10b^2 - b - 3$

20. $(11y + 9)(12y + 6)$
$= (11y)(12y) + (11y)(6) + (9)(12y) + (9)(6)$
$= 132y^2 + 66y + 108y + 54$
$= 132y^2 + 174y + 54$

21. $(13x - 3)(13x + 3)$
$= (13x)(13x) + (13x)(3) + (-3)(13x) + (-3)(3)$
$= 169x^2 + 39x - 39x - 9$
$= 169x^2 - 9$

22. $(8x + 9y)(3x + 7y)$
$= (8x)(3x) + (8x)(7y) + (9y)(3x) + (9y)(7y)$
$= 24x^2 + 56xy + 27xy + 63y^2$
$= 24x^2 + 83xy + 63y^2$

23. $(0.3v - 7)(0.5v + 2)$
$= (0.3v)(0.5v) + (0.3v)(2) + (-7)(0.5v) + (-7)(2)$
$= 0.15v^2 + 0.6v - 3.5v - 14$
$= 0.15v^2 - 2.9v - 14$

24. $\left(3x + \frac{1}{3}\right)\left(2x - \frac{1}{9}\right)$
$= (3x)(2x) + (3x)\left(-\frac{1}{9}\right) + \left(\frac{1}{3}\right)(2x) + \left(\frac{1}{3}\right)\left(-\frac{1}{9}\right)$
$= 6x^2 - \frac{1}{3}x + \frac{2}{3}x - \frac{1}{27}$
$= 6x^2 + \frac{1}{3}x - \frac{1}{27}$

25. $\left(a - \frac{2}{3}b\right)\left(\frac{2}{3}a + \frac{1}{2}b\right)$
$= (a)\left(\frac{2}{3}a\right) + (a)\left(\frac{1}{2}b\right) + \left(-\frac{2}{3}b\right)\left(\frac{2}{3}a\right) + \left(-\frac{2}{3}b\right)\left(\frac{1}{2}b\right)$
$= \frac{2}{3}a^2 + \frac{1}{2}ab - \frac{4}{9}ab - \frac{1}{3}b^2$
$= \frac{2}{3}a^2 + \frac{1}{18}ab - \frac{1}{3}b^2$

26. $(2r + 0.1)(5r - 0.3)$
$= (2r)(5r) + (2r)(-0.3) + (0.1)(5r) + (0.1)(-0.3)$
$= 10r^2 - 0.6r + 0.5r - 0.03$
$= 10r^2 - 0.1r - 0.03$

27. $(0.7p + 2q)(0.9p + 3q)$
$= (0.7p)(0.9p) + (0.7p)(3q) + (2q)(0.9p) + (2q)(3q)$
$= 0.63p^2 + 2.1pq + 1.8pq + 6q^2$
$= 0.63p^2 + 3.9pq + 6q^2$

28. $(x + 7)(x^2 + 5x - 9)$
$= x(x^2 + 5x - 9) + 7(x^2 + 5x - 9)$
$= (x^3 + 5x^2 - 9x) + (7x^2 + 35x - 63)$
$= x^3 + 5x^2 + 7x^2 - 9x + 35x - 63$
$= x^3 + 12x^2 + 26x - 63$

29. $(3x - 5)(2x^2 + 7x - 11)$
$= 3x(2x^2 + 7x - 11) - 5(2x^2 + 7x - 11)$
$= (6x^3 + 21x^2 - 33x) - (10x^2 + 35x - 55)$
$= 6x^3 + 21x^2 - 33x - 10x^2 - 35x + 55$
$= 6x^3 + 21x^2 - 10x^2 - 33x - 35x + 55$
$= 6x^3 + 11x^2 - 68x + 55$

30.
$$\begin{array}{lr} & a^2 - 3a + 11 \\ (\times) & 5a + 2 \\ \hline & 2a^2 - 6a + 22 \\ & 5a^3 - 15a^2 + 55a \quad \\ \hline & 5a^3 - 13a^2 + 49a + 22 \end{array}$$

31.
$$\begin{array}{lr} & 3x^2 - 7x + 2 \\ (\times) & 3x - 8 \\ \hline & -24x^2 + 56x - 16 \\ & 9x^3 - 21x^2 + 6x \quad \\ \hline & 9x^3 - 45x^2 + 62x - 16 \end{array}$$

32.
$$\begin{array}{lr} & 5x^2 + 8x - 11 \\ (\times) & x^2 - 2x - 1 \\ \hline & -5x^2 - 8x + 11 \\ & -10x^3 - 16x^2 + 22x \quad \\ & 5x^4 + 8x^3 - 11x^2 \quad\quad \\ \hline & 5x^4 - 2x^3 - 32x^2 + 14x + 11 \end{array}$$

33.
$$\begin{array}{lr} & 5d^2 - 6d + 9 \\ (\times) & 4d^2 + 3d + 11 \\ \hline & 55d^2 - 66d + 99 \\ & 15d^3 - 18d^2 + 27d \quad \\ & 20d^4 - 24d^3 + 36d^2 \quad\quad \\ \hline & 20d^4 - 9d^3 + 73d^2 - 39d + 99 \end{array}$$

34.
$$\begin{array}{lr} & x^2 - 8x - 1 \\ (\times) & 2x^2 - 4x + 9 \\ \hline & 9x^2 - 72x - 9 \\ & -4x^3 + 32x^2 + 4x \quad \\ & 2x^4 - 16x^3 - 2x^2 \quad\quad \\ \hline & 2x^4 - 20x^3 + 39x^2 - 68x - 9 \end{array}$$

35.
$$\begin{array}{lr} & 5x^2 - x - 4 \\ (\times) & 2x^2 + x + 12 \\ \hline & 60x^2 - 12x - 48 \\ & 5x^3 - x^2 - 4x \quad \\ & 10x^4 - 2x^3 - 8x^2 \quad\quad \\ \hline & 10x^4 + 3x^3 + 51x^2 - 16x - 48 \end{array}$$

36.
$$\begin{array}{lr} & -7b^3 + 2b - 3 \\ (\times) & 5b^2 - 2b + 4 \\ \hline & -28b^3 + 8b - 12 \\ & 14b^4 - 4b^2 + 6b \quad \\ & -35b^5 + 10b^3 - 15b^2 \quad\quad \\ \hline & -35b^5 + 14b^4 - 18b^3 - 19b^2 + 14b - 12 \end{array}$$

37.
$$\begin{array}{lr} & a^2 + 2a + 5 \\ (\times) & a^2 - 3a - 7 \\ \hline & -7a^2 - 14a - 35 \\ & -3a^3 - 6a^2 - 15a \quad \\ & a^4 + 2a^3 + 5a^2 \quad\quad \\ \hline & a^4 - a^3 - 8a^2 - 29a - 35 \end{array}$$

38. $V = (2a - 2)(a + 1)(a + 5)$
$= (2a - 2)[(a)(a) + (a)(5) + (1)(a) + (1)(5)]$
$= (2a - 2)(a^2 + 5a + a + 5)$
$= (2a - 2)(a^2 + 6a + 5)$
$= 2a(a^2 + 6a + 5) - 2(a^2 + 6a + 5)$
$= (2a^3 + 12a^2 + 10a) - (2a^2 + 12a + 10)$
$= 2a^3 + 12a^2 + 10a - 2a^2 - 12a - 10$
$= 2a^3 + 10a^2 - 2a - 10$

39. $V = (3y)(3y)(7y + 3) - (2y)(6)(7y + 3)$
$= 9y^2(7y + 3) - 12y(7y + 3)$
$= 63y^3 + 27y^2 - 84y^2 - 36y$
$= 63y^3 - 57y^2 - 36y$

40. $V = (4)(x)(3x)(x + 1) + (x)(x)(3x)$
$= 12x^2(x + 1) + 3x^3$
$= 12x^3 + 12x^2 + 3x^3$
$= 15x^3 + 12x^2$

41a.

$\ell = 2a - 2$	$w = a + 5$	$h = a + 1$
$= 2(15) - 2$	$= 15 + 5$	$= 15 + 1$
$= 30 - 2$	$= 20$ cm	$= 16$ cm
$= 28$ cm		

41b. $V = \ell wh$
$= 28(20)(16)$
$= 8960 \text{ cm}^3$

41c. $2a^3 + 10a^2 - 2a - 10$
$= 2(15)^3 + 10(15)^2 - 2(15) - 10$
$= 2(3375) + 10(225) - 30 - 10$
$= 6750 + 2250 - 30 - 10$
$= 8960$

41d. They are the same measure.

42. $AC + B = (3x + 4)(x^2 + 3x - 2) + (x^2 + 2)$
$= 3x(x^2 + 3x - 2) + 4(x^2 + 3x - 2) + (x^2 + 2)$
$= (3x^3 + 9x^2 - 6x) + (4x^2 + 12x - 8) + (x^2 + 2)$
$= 3x^3 + 9x^2 + 4x^2 + x^2 - 6x + 12x - 8 + 2$
$= 3x^3 + 14x^2 + 6x - 6$

43. $2B(3A - 4C)$
$= 2(x^2 + 2)[3(3x + 4) - 4(x^2 + 3x - 2)]$
$= (2x^2 + 4)[(9x + 12) - (4x^2 + 12x - 8)]$
$= (2x^2 + 4)(9x + 12 - 4x^2 - 12x + 8)$
$= (2x^2 + 4)(-4x^2 - 12x + 9x + 12 + 8)$
$= (2x^2 + 4)(-4x^2 - 3x + 20)$
$= 2x^2(-4x^2 - 3x + 20) + 4(-4x^2 - 3x + 20)$
$= (-8x^4 - 6x^3 + 40x^2) + (-16x^2 - 12x + 80)$
$= -8x^4 - 6x^3 + 40x^2 - 16x^2 - 12x + 80$
$= -8x^4 - 6x^3 + 24x^2 - 12x + 80$

44.
$ABC = (3x + 4)(x^2 + 2)(x^2 + 3x - 2)$
$= [(3x)(x^2) + (3x)(2) + (4)(x^2) + (4)(2)](x^2 + 3x - 2)$
$= (3x^3 + 6x + 4x^2 + 8)(x^2 + 3x - 2)$
$= (3x^3 + 4x^2 + 6x + 8)(x^2 + 3x - 2)$
$= 3x^3(x^2 + 3x - 2) + 4x^2(x^2 + 3x - 2) +$
$6x(x^2 + 3x - 2) + 8(x^2 + 3x - 2)$
$= (3x^5 + 9x^4 - 6x^3) + (4x^4 + 12x^3 - 8x^2) +$
$(6x^3 + 18x^2 - 12x) + (8x^2 + 24x - 16)$
$= 3x^5 + 9x^4 + 4x^4 - 6x^3 + 12x^3 + 6x^3 - 8x^2 +$
$18x^2 + 8x^2 - 12x + 24x - 16$
$= 3x^5 + 13x^4 + 12x^3 + 18x^2 + 12x - 16$

45. $(A + B)(B - C)$
$= [(3x + 4) + (x^2 + 2)][(x^2 + 2) - (x^2 + 3x - 2)]$
$= (x^2 + 3x + 6)[x^2 + 2 - x^2 - 3x + 2]$
$= (x^2 + 3x + 6)(-3x + 4)$
$= x^2(-3x + 4) + 3x(-3x + 4) + 6(-3x + 4)$
$= (-3x^3 + 4x^2) + (-9x^2 + 12x) + (-18x + 24)$
$= -3x^3 + 4x^2 - 9x^2 + 12x - 18x + 24$
$= -3x^3 - 5x^2 - 6x + 24$

46. $(w + 5 + 4 + 4)(w + 4 + 4) - w(w + 5) = 424$
$(w + 13)(w + 8) - (w^2 + 5w) = 424$
$[(w)(w) + (w)(8) + (13)(w) + (13)(8)] - w^2 - 5w = 424$
$(w^2 + 8w + 13w + 104) - w^2 - 5w = 424$
$w^2 + 21w + 104 - w^2 - 5w = 424$
$16w + 104 = 424$
$16w = 320$
$w = 20$

$w + 5 = 20 + 5$
$= 25$
20 yd by 25 yd

47a. Sample answer: $x - 2$, $x + 3$

47b. Sample answer:
$(x - 2)(x + 3) = (x)(x) + (x)(3) + (-2)(x) + (-2)(3)$
$= x^2 + 3x - 2x - 6$
$= x^2 + x - 6$

47c. present office: $8 \times 8 = 64$ sq ft
new office: $x^2 + x - 6 = 8^2 + 8 - 6$
$= 66$ sq ft
$66 - 64 = 2$ sq ft
His new office will be larger by 2 sq ft.

48. $\frac{3}{4}a(6a + 12) = \frac{3}{4}a(6a) + \frac{3}{4}a(12)$
$= \frac{9}{2}a^2 + 9a$

49. $6 - 9y < -10y$
$6 < -y$
$-6 > y$
$\{y \mid y < -6\}$

50. $50\% = \frac{50}{100}$ or $\frac{1}{2}$
$\frac{1}{2} = \frac{1015}{x}$
$x = 2(1015)$
$x = 2030$ ft

51. $\frac{\text{change in } y}{\text{change in } x} = \frac{1 - (-1)}{0 - (-1)} = 2$
$y = 2x + 1$

52. $\{8, 4, 6, 5\}$; $\{1, 2, -4, -3, 0\}$;
$\{(1, 8), (2, 4), (-4, 6), (-3, 5), (0, 6)\}$

53. $\frac{2}{6} = \frac{a}{12}$
$2(12) = 6a$
$24 = 6$
$4 = a$

$\frac{2}{6} = \frac{3}{y}$
$2y = 18$
$y = 9$

54. mean: $\frac{299 + 369 + 359 + 228 + 525 + 398}{6} = \frac{2178}{6} = \$363$
228, 299, 359, 369, 398, 525
median: $\frac{359 + 369}{2} = \$364$

55. $C = \frac{5}{9}(F - 32)$
$= \frac{5}{9}(59 - 32)$
$= \frac{5}{9}(27)$
$= 15°C$

56. $\frac{3}{4}s = 6$
$\frac{4}{3}\left(\frac{3}{4}s\right) = \frac{4}{3}(6)$
$s = 8$

9-8 Special Products

Page 546 Check for Understanding

1. The middle terms have different signs.
2. The square of a difference is $(a - b)^2$, which equals $a^2 - 2ab + b^2$. The difference of two squares is the product $(a + b)(a - b)$ or $a^2 - b^2$.
3. $(30 - 1)(30 + 1) = 900 - 1$ or 899

4a.

	x	y
x	x^2	xy
y	xy	y^2

4b.

	x	$-y$
x	x^2	$-xy$
$-y$	$-xy$	y^2

5. $(a - b)^2 = a^2 - 2ab + b^2$
6. $(2x + 3y)^2 = (2x)^2 + 2(2x)(3y) + (3y)^2$
$= 4x^2 + 12xy + 9y^2$
7. $(m - 3n)^2 = (m)^2 - 2(m)(3n) + (3n)^2$
$= m^2 - 6mn + 9n^2$
8. $(2a + 3)(2a - 3) = (2a)^2 - (3)^2$
$= 4a^2 - 9$
9. $(m^2 + 4n)^2 = (m^2)^2 + 2(m^2)(4n) + (4n)^2$
$= m^4 + 8m^2n + 16n^2$
10. $(4y + 2z)(4y - 2z) = (4y)^2 - (2z)^2$
$= 16y^2 - 4z^2$
11. $(5 - x)^2 = (5)^2 - 2(5)(x) + (x)^2$
$= 25 - 10x + x^2$
12. $[(2x + 5) + (2x + 5)]^2$
$= (4x + 10)^2$
$= (4x)^2 + 2(4x)(10) + (10)^2$
$= 16x^2 + 80x + 100$ square units

Pages 546–547 Exercises

13. $(x + 4y)^2 = (x)^2 + 2(x)(4y) + (4y)^2$
$= x^2 + 8xy + 16y^2$

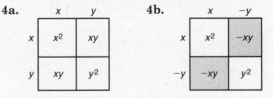

14. $(m - 2n)^2 = (m)^2 - 2(m)(2n) + (2n)^2$
$= m^2 - 4mn + 4n^2$

15. $(3b - a)^2 = (3b)^2 - 2(3b)(a) + (a)^2$
$= 9b^2 - 6ab + a^2$

16. $(3x + 5)(3x - 5) = (3x)^2 - (5)^2$
$= 9x^2 - 25$

17. $(9p - 2q)(9p + 2q) = (9p)^2 - (2q)^2$
$= 81p^2 - 4q^2$

18. $(5s + 6t)^2 = (5s)^2 + 2(5s)(6t) + (6t)^2$
$= 25s^2 + 60st + 36t^2$

19. $(5b - 12a)^2 = (5b)^2 - 2(5b)(12a) + (12a)^2$
$= 25b^2 - 120ab + 144a^2$

20. $(2a + 0.5y)^2 = (2a)^2 + 2(2a)(0.5y) + (0.5y)^2$
$= 4a^2 + 2ay + 0.25y^2$

21. $(x^3 + a^2)^2 = (x^3)^2 + 2(x^3)(a^2) + (a^2)^2$
$= x^6 + 2x^3a^2 + a^4$

22. $\left(\frac{1}{2}b^2 - a^2\right)^2 = \left(\frac{1}{2}b^2\right)^2 - 2\left(\frac{1}{2}b^2\right)(a^2) + (a^2)^2$
$= \frac{1}{4}b^4 - a^2b^2 + a^4$

23. $(8x^2 - 3y)(8x^2 + 3y) = (8x^2)^2 - (3y)^2$
$= 64x^4 - 9y^2$

24. $(7c^2 + d^3)(7c^2 - d^3) = (7c^2)^2 - (d^3)^2$
$= 49c^4 - d^6$

25. $(1.1g + h^5)^2 = (1.1g)^2 + 2(1.1g)(h^5) + (h^5)^2$
$= 1.21g^2 + 2.2gh^5 + h^{10}$

26. $(9 - z^9)(9 + z^9) = (9)^2 - (z^9)^2$
$= 81 - z^{18}$

27. $\left(\frac{4}{3}x^2 - y\right)\left(\frac{4}{3}x^2 + y\right) = \left(\frac{4}{3}x^2\right)^2 - (y)^2$
$= \frac{16}{9}x^4 - y^2$

28. $\left(\frac{1}{3}v^2 - \frac{1}{2}w^3\right)^2 = \left(\frac{1}{3}v^2\right)^2 - 2\left(\frac{1}{3}v^2\right)\left(\frac{1}{2}w^3\right) + \left(\frac{1}{2}w^3\right)^2$
$= \frac{1}{9}v^4 - \frac{1}{3}v^2w^3 + \frac{1}{4}w^6$

29. $(3x + 1)(3x - 1)(x - 5)$
$= [(3x)^2 - (1)^2](x - 5)$
$= (9x^2 - 1)(x - 5)$
$= (9x^2)(x) + (9x^2)(-5) + (-1)(x) + (-1)(-5)$
$= 9x^3 - 45x^2 - x + 5$

30. $(x - 2)(x + 5)(x + 2)(x - 5)$
$= [(x - 2)(x + 2)][(x + 5)(x - 5)]$
$= [(x)^2 - (2)^2][(x)^2 - (5)^2]$
$= (x^2 - 4)(x^2 - 25)$
$= (x^2)(x^2) + (x^2)(-25) + (-4)(x^2) + (-4)(-25)$
$= x^4 - 25x^2 - 4x^2 + 100$
$= x^4 - 29x^2 + 100$

31. $(a + 3b)^3$
$= (a + 3b)(a + 3b)^2$
$= (a + 3b)[(a^2 + 2(a)(3b) + (3b)^2]$
$= (a + 3b)(a^2 + 6ab + 9b^2)$
$= a(a^2 + 6ab + 9b^2) + 3b(a^2 + 6ab + 9b^2)$
$= (a^3 + 6a^2b + 9ab^2) + (3a^2b + 18ab^2 + 27b^3)$
$= a^3 + 6a^2b + 3a^2b + 9ab^2 + 18ab^2 + 27b^3$
$= a^3 + 9a^2b + 27ab^2 + 27b^3$

32. $(2m - n)^4$
$= (2m - n)^2(2m - n)^2$
$= [(2m)^2 - 2(2m)(n) + (n)^2][(2m)^2 - 2(2m)(n) + (n)^2]$
$= (4m^2 - 4mn + n^2)(4m^2 - 4mn + n^2)$
$= 4m^2(4m^2 - 4mn + n^2) - 4mn(4m^2 - 4mn + n^2) + n^2(4m^2 - 4mn + n^2)$
$= (16m^4 - 16m^3n + 4m^2n^2) - (16m^3n - 16m^2n^2 + 4mn^3) + (4m^2n^2 - 4mn^3 + n^4)$
$= 16m^4 - 16m^3n - 16m^3n + 4m^2n^2 + 16m^2n^2 + 4m^2n^2 - 4mn^3 - 4mn^3 + n^4$
$= 16m^4 - 32m^3n + 24m^2n^2 - 8mn^3 + n^4$

33.

	x	y	z
x	x^2	xy	xz
y	xy	y^2	yz
z	xz	yz	z^2

$(x + y + z)^2 = x^2 + y^2 + z^2 + 2xy + 2yz + 2xz$

34a.

	t	t
T	Tt	Tt
t	tt	tt

34b. 50% **34c.** 50% **34d.** 0%

35a. $\pi(s + 4)^2 - \pi(s + 3)^2$
$= \pi(s^2 + 8s + 16) - \pi(s^2 + 6s + 9)$
$= (\pi s^2 + 8\pi s + 16\pi) - (\pi s^2 + 6\pi s + 9\pi)$
$= \pi s^2 + 8\pi s + 16\pi - \pi s^2 - 6\pi s - 9\pi$
$= 2\pi s + 7\pi$ square meters

35b. $A = \pi r^2$
$= \pi(3)^2$
$= 9\pi$
≈ 28.27 square meters

35c. $2\pi s + 7\pi = 2\pi(3) + 7\pi$
$= 6\pi + 7\pi$
$= 13\pi$
≈ 40.84 square meters

36. $(x)(x) - (x - 0.75 - 0.75)(x - 0.75 - 0.75) = 33.75$
$x^2 - (x - 1.5)^2 = 33.75$
$x^2 - [(x)^2 - 2(x)(1.5) + (1.5)^2] = 33.75$
$x^2 - (x^2 - 3x + 2.25) = 33.75$
$x^2 - x^2 + 3x - 2.25 = 33.75$
$3x - 2.25 = 33.75$
$3x = 36$
$x = 12$

The dimensions of the photograph were 12 in. by 12 in.

37. $(3t - 3)(2t + 1)$
$= (3t)(2t) + (3t)(1) + (-3)(2t) + (-3)(1)$
$= 6t^2 + 3t - 6t - 3$
$= 6t^2 - 3t - 3$

38. $-13z > -1.04$
$\frac{-13z}{-13} < \frac{-1.04}{-13}$
$z < 0.08$
$\{z \mid z < 0.08\}$

39a.

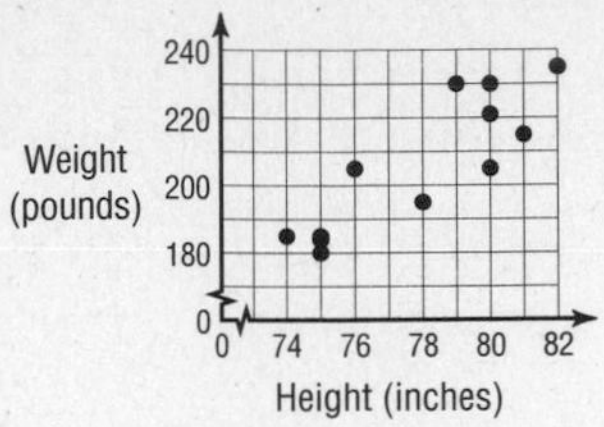

39b. the taller the player, the greater the weight

40.
$$\begin{aligned} y - y_1 &= m(x - x_1) \\ y - 1 &= \tfrac{2}{7}(x - 3) \\ 7(y - 1) &= 7\left(\tfrac{2}{7}\right)(x - 3) \\ 7y - 7 &= 2(x - 3) \\ 7y - 7 &= 2x - 6 \\ -1 &= 2x - 7y \\ 2x - 7y &= -1 \end{aligned}$$

41.

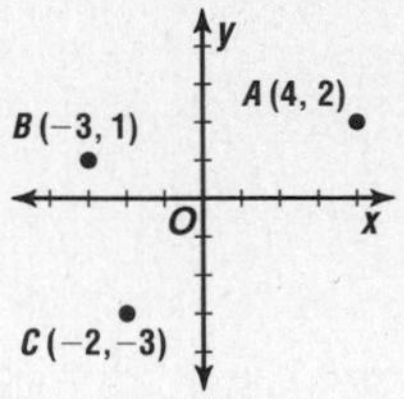

42.
$$\begin{aligned} I^2R &= P \\ I^2(4.5) &= 1500 \\ I^2 &= \tfrac{1500}{4.5} \\ I^2 &\approx 333.33 \\ I &\approx 18.26 \text{ amperes} \end{aligned}$$

43. $5(9 \div 3^2) = 5(9 \div 9)$
$= 5(1)$
$= 5$

Chapter 9 Highlights

Page 549 Understanding and Using the Vocabulary

1. e negative exponent
2. b difference of squares
3. h quotient of powers
4. d monomial
5. i trinomial
6. j zero exponent
7. f polynomial
8. c FOIL method
9. a binomial
10. g product of powers

Chapter 9 Study Guide and Assessment

Pages 550–552 Skills and Concepts

11. $y^3 \cdot y^3 \cdot y = y^{3+3+1}$
$= y^7$

12. $(3ab)(-4a^2b^3) = (3 \cdot -4)(a \cdot a^2)(b \cdot b^3)$
$= -12a^{1+2}b^{1+3}$
$= -12a^3b^4$

13. $(-4a^2x)(-5a^3x^4) = (-4 \cdot -5)(a^2 \cdot a^3)(x \cdot x^4)$
$= 20a^{2+3}x^{1+4}$
$= 20a^5x^5$

14. $(4a^2b)^3 = (4)^3(a^2)^3(b)^3$
$= 64a^6b^3$

15. $(-3xy)^2(4x)^3 = (-3)^2(x)^2(y)^2(4)^3(x)^3$
$= (9)x^2y^2(64)x^3$
$= 576x^{2+3}y^2$
$= 576x^5y^2$

16. $(-2c^2d)^4(-3c^2)^3 = (-2)^4(c^2)^4(d)^4(-3)^3(c^2)^3$
$= 16c^8d^4(-27)c^6$
$= -432c^{8+6}d^4$
$= -432c^{14}d^4$

17. $-\frac{1}{2}(m^2n^4)^2 = -\frac{1}{2}(m^2)^2(n^4)^2$
$= -\frac{1}{2}m^4n^8$

18. $(5a^2)^3 + 7(a^6) = (5)^3(a^2)^3 + 7a^6$
$= 125a^6 + 7a^6$
$= 132a^6$

19. $\frac{y^{10}}{y^6} = y^{10-6}$
$= y^4$

20. $\frac{(3y)^0}{6a} = \frac{1}{6a}$

21. $\frac{42b^7}{14b^4} = 3b^{7-4}$
$= 3b^3$

22. $\frac{27b^{-2}}{14b^{-3}} = \frac{27b^{-2-(-3)}}{14} = \frac{27b}{14}$

23. $\frac{(3a^3bc^2)^2}{18a^2b^3c^4} = \frac{(3)^2(a^3)^2(b)^2(c^2)^2}{18a^2b^3c^4}$
$= \frac{9a^6b^2c^4}{18a^2b^3c^4}$
$= \frac{1a^{6-2}b^{2-3}}{2}$
$= \frac{a^4b^{-1}}{2}$
$= \frac{a^4}{2b}$

24. $\frac{-16a^3b^2x^4y}{-48a^4bxy^3} = \frac{1a^{3-4}b^{2-1}x^{4-1}y^{1-3}}{3}$
$= \frac{a^{-1}bx^3y^{-2}}{3}$
$= \frac{bx^3}{3ay^2}$

25. $240{,}000 = 2.4 \times 100{,}000$
$= 2.4 \times 10^5$

26. $0.000314 = 3.14 \times 0.0001$
$= 3.14 \times 10^{-4}$

27. $4{,}880{,}000{,}000 = 4.88 \times 1{,}000{,}000{,}000$
$= 4.88 \times 10^9$

28. $0.00000187 = 1.87 \times 0.000001$
$= 1.87 \times 10^{-6}$

29. $796 \times 10^3 = (7.96 \times 100) \times 10^3$
$= 7.96 \times 10^2 \times 10^3$
$= 7.96 \times 10^5$

30. $0.03434 \times 10^{-2} = (3.434 \times 0.01) \times 10^{-2}$
$= 3.434 \times 10^{-2} \times 10^{-2}$
$= 3.434 \times 10^{-4}$

31. $(2 \times 10^5)(3 \times 10^6) = (2 \times 3)(10^5 \times 10^6)$
$= 6 \times 10^{11}$

32. $(3 \times 10^3)(1.5 \times 10^6) = (3 \times 1.5)(10^3 \times 10^6)$
$= 4.5 \times 10^9$

33. $\frac{5.4 \times 10^3}{0.9 \times 10^4} = \frac{5.4}{0.9} \times \frac{10^3}{10^4}$
$= 6 \times 10^{-1}$

34. $\frac{8.4 \times 10^{-6}}{1.4 \times 10^{-9}} = \frac{8.4}{1.4} \times \frac{10^{-6}}{10^{-9}}$
$= 6 \times 10^3$

35. $(3 \times 10^2)(5.6 \times 10^{-4}) = (3 \times 5.6)(10^2 \times 10^{-4})$
$= 16.8 \times 10^{-2}$
$= 1.68 \times 10 \times 10^{-2}$
$= 1.68 \times 10^{-1}$

36. $34(4.7 \times 10^5) = (3.4 \times 10)(4.7 \times 10^5)$
$= (3.4 \times 4.7)(10 \times 10^5)$
$= (15.98)(10^6)$
$= 1.598 \times 10 \times 10^6$
$= 1.598 \times 10^7$

37. degree of n: 1
degree of $-2p^2$: 2
degree of $n - 2p^2$: 2

38. degree of $29n^2$: 2
degree of $17n^2t^2$: 2 + 2 or 4
degree of $29n^2 + 17n^2t^2$: 4

39. degree of $4xy$: 1 + 1 or 2
degree of $9x^3z^2$: 3 + 2 or 5
degree of $17rs^3$: 1 + 3 or 4
degree of $4xy + 9x^3z^2 + 17rs^3$: 5

40. degree of $-6x^5y$: 5 + 1 or 6
degree of $-2y^4$: 4
degree of 4: 0
degree of $-8y^2$: 2
degree of $-6x^5y - 2y^4 + 4 - 8y^2$: 6

41. degree of $3ab^3$: 1 + 3 or 4
degree of $-5a^2b^2$: 2 + 2 or 4
degree of $4ab$: 1 + 1 or 2
degree of $3ab^3 - 5a^2b^2 + 4ab$: 4

42. degree of $19m^3n^4$: 3 + 4 or 7
degree of $21m^5n^2$: 5 + 2 or 7
degree of $19m^3n^4 + 21m^5n^2$: 7

43. $3x^4 + x^2 - x - 5$

44. $-4x^4 + 5x^3y^2 - 2x^2y^3 + xy - 27$

45.
$$\begin{array}{r} 2x^2 - 5x + 7 \\ \underline{(-)\ 3x^3 + x^2 \qquad + 2} \end{array} \rightarrow \begin{array}{r} 2x^2 - 5x + 7 \\ \underline{(+)\ -3x^3 - x^2 \qquad - 2} \\ -3x^3 + x^2 - 5x + 5 \end{array}$$

46.
$$\begin{array}{r} x^2 - 6xy + 7y^2 \\ \underline{(+)\ 3x^2 + xy - y^2} \\ 4x^2 - 5xy + 6y^2 \end{array}$$

47.
$$\begin{array}{r} 11m^2n^2 + 4mn - 6 \\ \underline{(+)\ 5m^2n^2 - 6mn + 17} \\ 16m^2n^2 - 2mn + 11 \end{array}$$

48.
$$\begin{array}{r} 7z^2 + \qquad 4 \\ \underline{(-)\ 3z^2 + 2z - 6} \end{array} \rightarrow \begin{array}{r} 7z^2 + \qquad 4 \\ \underline{(+)\ -3z^2 - 2z + 6} \\ 4z^2 - 2z + 10 \end{array}$$

49.
$$\begin{array}{r} 13m^4 - 7m - 10 \\ \underline{(+)\ 8m^4 - 3m + 9} \\ 21m^4 - 10m - 1 \end{array}$$

50.
$$\begin{array}{r} -5p^2 + 3p + 49 \\ \underline{(-)\ 2p^2 + 5p + 24} \end{array} \rightarrow \begin{array}{r} -5p^2 + 3p + 49 \\ \underline{(+)\ -2p^2 - 5p - 24} \\ -7p^2 - 2p + 25 \end{array}$$

51. $4ab(3a^2 - 7b^2) = 4ab(3a^2) - 4ab(7b^2)$
$= 12a^3b - 28ab^3$

52. $7xy(x^2 + 4xy - 8y^2)$
$= 7xy(x^2) + 7xy(4xy) - 7xy(8y^2)$
$= 7x^3y + 28x^2y^2 - 56xy^3$

53. $4x^2y(2x^3 - 3x^2y^2 + y^4)$
$= 4x^2y(2x^3) - 4x^2y(3x^2y^2) + 4x^2y(y^4)$
$= 8x^5y - 12x^4y^3 + 4x^2y^5$

54. $5x^3(x^4 - 8x^2 + 16) = 5x^3(x^4) - 5x^3(8x^2) + 5x^3(16)$
$= 5x^7 - 40x^5 + 80x^3$

55. $2x(x - y^2 + 5) - 5y^2(3x - 2)$
$= 2x(x) - 2x(y^2) + 2x(5) - 5y^2(3x) - 5y^2(-2)$
$= 2x^2 - 2xy^2 + 10x - 15xy^2 + 10y^2$
$= 2x^2 - 17xy^2 + 10x + 10y^2$

56. $x(3x - 5) + 7(x^2 - 2x + 9)$
$= (x)(3x) - (x)(5) + 7(x^2) - 7(2x) + 7(9)$
$= 3x^2 - 5x + 7x^2 - 14x + 63$
$= 10x^2 - 19x + 63$

57. $(r - 3)(r + 7) = (r)(r) + (r)(7) + (-3)(r) + (-3)(7)$
$= r^2 + 7r - 3r - 21$
$= r^2 + 4r - 21$

58. $(x + 5)(3x - 2)$
$= (x)(3x) + (x)(-2) + (5)(3x) + (5)(-2)$
$= 3x^2 - 2x + 15x - 10$
$= 3x^2 + 13x - 10$

59. $(4x - 3)(x + 4)$
$= (4x)(x) + (4x)(4) + (-3)(x) + (-3)(4)$
$= 4x^2 + 16x - 3x - 12$
$= 4x^2 + 13x - 12$

60. $(2x + 5y)(3x - y)$
$= (2x)(3x) + (2x)(-y) + (5y)(3x) + (5y)(-y)$
$= 6x^2 - 2xy + 15xy - 5y^2$
$= 6x^2 + 13xy - 5y^2$

61. $(3x + 0.25)(6x - 0.5)$
$= (3x)(6x) + (3x)(-0.5) + (0.25)(6x) + (0.25)(-0.5)$
$= 18x^2 - 1.5x + 1.5x - 0.125$
$= 18x^2 - 0.125$

62. $(5r - 7s)(4r + 3s)$
$= (5r)(4r) + (5r)(3s) + (-7s)(4r) + (-7s)(3s)$
$= 20r^2 + 15rs - 28rs - 21s^2$
$= 20r^2 - 13rs - 21s^2$

63.
$$\begin{array}{r} x^2 + 7x - 9 \\ \underline{(\times) \qquad\qquad 2x + 1} \\ x^2 + 7x - 9 \\ \underline{2x^3 + 14x^2 - 18x \qquad} \\ 2x^3 + 15x^2 - 11x - 9 \end{array}$$

64.
$$\begin{array}{r} a^2 - 17ab - 3b^2 \\ \underline{(\times) \qquad\qquad 2a + b} \\ a^2b - 17ab^2 - 3b^3 \\ \underline{2a^3 - 34a^2b - 6ab^2 \qquad} \\ 2a^3 - 33a^2b - 23ab^2 - 3b^3 \end{array}$$

65. $(x - 6)(x + 6) = (x)^2 - (6)^2$
$= x^2 - 36$

66. $(7 - 2x)(7 + 2x) = (7)^2 - (2x)^2$
$= 49 - 4x^2$

67. $(4x + 7)^2 = (4x)^2 + 2(4x)(7) + (7)^2$
$= 16x^2 + 56x + 49$

68. $(8x - 5)^2 = (8x)^2 - 2(8x)(5) + (5)^2$
$= 64x^2 - 80x + 25$

69. $(5x - 3y)(5x + 3y) = (5x)^2 - (3y)^2$
$= 25x^2 - 9y^2$

70. $(a^2 + b)^2 = (a^2)^2 + 2(a^2)(b) + (b)^2$
$= a^4 + 2a^2b + b^2$

71. $(6a - 5b)^2 = (6a)^2 - 2(6a)(5b) + (5b)^2$
$= 36a^2 - 60ab + 25b^2$

72. $(3m + 4n)^2 = (3m)^2 + 2(3m)(4n) + (4n)^2$
$= 9m^2 + 24mn + 16n^2$

Page 552 Applications and Problem Solving

73. $B = P\left[\frac{1 - (1 + i)^{k - n}}{i}\right]$

$i = \frac{8.7\%}{12} = \frac{0.087}{12}$ $\quad k = 25$

$n = 36$ $\quad B = 3216.27$

$$3216.27 = P\left[\frac{1 - \left(1 + \frac{0.087}{12}\right)^{25 - 36}}{\frac{0.087}{12}}\right]$$

$3216.27 \approx P(10.54)$

$\$305.26 \approx P$

74. $\frac{19{,}500{,}000}{6500} = \frac{1.95 \times 10{,}000{,}000}{6.5 \times 1000}$

$= \frac{1.95}{6.5} \times \frac{10^7}{10^3}$

$= 0.3 \times 10^4$

$= 0.1 \times 10^4$

$= 3 \times 10^{-1} \times 10^4$

$= 3 \times 10^3$

about 3×10^3 Calories

75. first year:

10,000 + 10,000(0.06) + 1000 = 11,600

second year:

11,600 + 11,600(0.06) + 1000 = 13,296

third year:

13,296 + 13,296(0.06) + 1000 = 15,093.76

fourth year:

15,093.76 + 15,093.76(0.06) + 1000 ≈ 16,999.39

fifth year:

16,999.39 + 16,999.39(0.06) + 1000 ≈ 19,019.35

sixth year:

19,019.35 + 19.019.35(0.06) + 1000 ≈ 21,160.51

No; his money doubles after six years.

Page 553 Alternative Assessment: Thinking Critically

- No; $(-b)^2 = (-b)(-b)$

  $= b^2$

  Sample answer: $b = 3$

  $(-b)^2 = -b^2$

  $(-3)^2 \stackrel{?}{=} -3^2$

  $(-3)(-3) \stackrel{?}{=} -(3^2)$

  $9 \neq -9$

- No, except for $m = 1$: $(a + b)^m = a^m + b^m$

  $(a + b)^1 \stackrel{?}{=} a^1 + b^1$

  $a + b = a + b$

  For $m = 2$: $(a + b)^m = a^m + b^m$

  $(a + b)^2 \stackrel{?}{=} a^2 + b^2$

  $a^2 + 2ab + b^2 \neq a^2 + b^2$

Chapter 10 Using Factoring

10-1 Factors and Greatest Common Factors

Page 561 Check for Understanding

1.

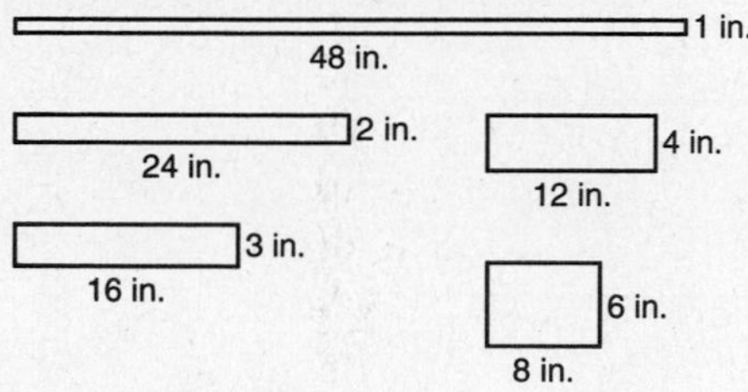

2. No; 4 is not prime.

3. No; the GCF of 4 and 9 is 1, but neither number is prime.

4. See students' work.

5. 4: 1×4, 2×2
factors: 1, 2, 4

6. 56: 1×56, 4×14, 2×28, 7×8
factors: 1, 2, 4, 7, 8, 14, 28, 56

7. prime

8. composite; $39 = 3 \cdot 13$

9. $-30 = -1 \cdot 30$
$= -1 \cdot 2 \cdot 15$
$= -1 \cdot 2 \cdot 3 \cdot 5$

10. $22m^2n = 2 \cdot 11 \cdot m \cdot m \cdot n$

11. $4 = 2 \cdot 2$
$12 = 2 \cdot 2 \cdot 3$
GCF: $2 \cdot 2$ or 4

12. $10 = 2 \cdot 5$
$15 = 3 \cdot 5$
GCF: 5

13. $24d^2 = 2 \cdot 2 \cdot 2 \cdot 3 \cdot d \cdot d$
$30c^2d = 2 \cdot 3 \cdot 5 \cdot c \cdot c \cdot d$
GCF: $2 \cdot 3 \cdot d$ or $6d$

14. $18 = 2 \cdot 3 \cdot 3$
$35 = 5 \cdot 7$
GCF: 1

15. $-20gh = -1 \cdot 2 \cdot 2 \cdot 5 \cdot g \cdot h$
$36g^2h^2 = 2 \cdot 2 \cdot 3 \cdot 3 \cdot g \cdot g \cdot h \cdot h$
GCF: $2 \cdot 2 \cdot g \cdot h$ or $4gh$

16. $30a^2 = 2 \cdot 3 \cdot 5 \cdot a \cdot a$
$42a^3 = 2 \cdot 3 \cdot 7 \cdot a \cdot a \cdot a$
$54a^3b: 2 \cdot 3 \cdot 3 \cdot 3 \cdot a \cdot a \cdot a \cdot b$
GCF: $2 \cdot 3 \cdot a \cdot a$ or $6a^2$

17.

$A = lw$	$2l + 2w = P$
$96 = 96 \cdot 1$	$2(96) + 2(1) = 194$
$96 = 48 \cdot 2$	$2(48) + 2(2) = 100$
$96 = 32 \cdot 3$	$2(32) + 2(3) = 70$
$96 = 24 \cdot 4$	$2(24) + 2(4) = 56$
$96 = 16 \cdot 6$	$2(16) + 2(6) = 44$
$96 = 12 \cdot 8$	$2(12) + 2(8) = 40$

The minimum perimeter is $2(12) + 2(8)$ or 40 in.

Pages 561–563 Exercises

18. 25: 1×25, 5×5
factors: 1, 5, 25

19. 67: 1×67
factors: 1, 67

20. 36: 1×36, 2×18, 3×12, 4×9, 6×6
factors: 1, 2, 3, 4, 6, 9, 12, 18, 36

21. 80: 1×80, 2×40, 4×20, 5×16, 8×10
factors: 1, 2, 4, 5, 8, 10, 16, 20, 40, 80

22. 400: 1×400, 2×200, 4×100, 5×80, 8×50, 10×40, 16×25, 20×20
factors: 1, 2, 4, 5, 8, 10, 16, 20, 25, 40, 50, 80, 100, 200, 400

23. 950: 1×950, 5×190, 10×95, 19×50, 25×38
factors: 1, 5, 10, 19, 25, 38, 50, 95, 190, 950

24. prime

25. composite; $63 = 3 \cdot 21$
$= 3 \cdot 3 \cdot 7$ or $3^2 \cdot 7$

26. composite; $91 = 7 \cdot 13$

27. prime

28. composite; $304 = 2 \cdot 152$
$= 2 \cdot 2 \cdot 76$
$= 2 \cdot 2 \cdot 2 \cdot 38$
$= 2 \cdot 2 \cdot 2 \cdot 2 \cdot 19$ or $2^4 \cdot 19$

29. composite; $1540 = 2 \cdot 770$
$= 2 \cdot 2 \cdot 385$
$= 2 \cdot 2 \cdot 5 \cdot 77$
$= 2 \cdot 2 \cdot 5 \cdot 7 \cdot 11$ or $2^2 \cdot 5 \cdot 7 \cdot 11$

30. $-70 = -1 \cdot 70$
$= -1 \cdot 2 \cdot 35$
$= -1 \cdot 2 \cdot 5 \cdot 7$

31. $-117 = -1 \cdot 117$
$= -1 \cdot 3 \cdot 39$
$= -1 \cdot 3 \cdot 3 \cdot 13$

32. $66z^2 = 2 \cdot 33 \cdot z \cdot z$
$= 2 \cdot 3 \cdot 11 \cdot z \cdot z$

33. $4b^3d^2 = 2 \cdot 2 \cdot b \cdot b \cdot b \cdot d \cdot d$

34. $-102x^3y = -1 \cdot 102 \cdot x \cdot x \cdot x \cdot y$
$= -1 \cdot 2 \cdot 51 \cdot x \cdot x \cdot x \cdot y$
$= -1 \cdot 2 \cdot 3 \cdot 17 \cdot x \cdot x \cdot x \cdot y$

35. $-98a^2b = -1 \cdot 98 \cdot a \cdot a \cdot b$
$= -1 \cdot 2 \cdot 49 \cdot a \cdot a \cdot b$
$= -1 \cdot 2 \cdot 7 \cdot 7 \cdot a \cdot a \cdot b$

36. $18 = 2 \cdot 3 \cdot 3$
$36 = 2 \cdot 2 \cdot 3 \cdot 3$
GCF: $2 \cdot 3 \cdot 3$ or 18

37. $18 = 2 \cdot 3 \cdot 3$
$45 = 3 \cdot 3 \cdot 5$
GCF: $3 \cdot 3$ or 9

38. $84 = 2 \cdot 2 \cdot 3 \cdot 7$
$96 = 2 \cdot 2 \cdot 2 \cdot 2 \cdot 2 \cdot 3$
GCF: $2 \cdot 2 \cdot 3$ or 12

39. $28 = 2 \cdot 2 \cdot 7$
$75 = 3 \cdot 5 \cdot 5$
GCF: 1

40. $-34 = -1 \cdot 2 \cdot 17$
$51 = 3 \cdot 17$
GCF: 17

41. $95 = 5 \cdot 19$
$-304 = -1 \cdot 2 \cdot 2 \cdot 2 \cdot 2 \cdot 19$
GCF: 19

42. $17a = 17 \cdot a$
$34a^2 = 2 \cdot 17 \cdot a \cdot a$
GCF: $17a$

43. $21p^2q = 3 \cdot 7 \cdot p \cdot p \cdot q$
$35pq^2 = 5 \cdot 7 \cdot p \cdot q \cdot q$
GCF: $7pq$

44. $12an^2 = 2 \cdot 2 \cdot 3 \cdot a \cdot n \cdot n$
$40a^4 = 2 \cdot 2 \cdot 2 \cdot 5 \cdot a \cdot a \cdot a \cdot a$
GCF: $2 \cdot 2 \cdot a$ or $4a$

45. $-60r^2s^2t^2 = -1 \cdot 2 \cdot 2 \cdot 3 \cdot 5 \cdot r \cdot r \cdot s \cdot s \cdot t \cdot t$
$45r^3t^3 = 3 \cdot 3 \cdot 5 \cdot r \cdot r \cdot r \cdot t \cdot t \cdot t$
GCF: $3 \cdot 5 \cdot r \cdot r \cdot t \cdot t = 15r^2t^2$

46. $18 = 2 \cdot 3 \cdot 3$
$30 = 2 \cdot 3 \cdot 5$
$54 = 2 \cdot 3 \cdot 3 \cdot 3$
GCF: $2 \cdot 3$ or 6

47. $24 = 2 \cdot 2 \cdot 2 \cdot 3$
$84 = 2 \cdot 2 \cdot 3 \cdot 7$
$168 = 2 \cdot 2 \cdot 2 \cdot 3 \cdot 7$
GCF: $2 \cdot 2 \cdot 3$ or 12

48. $14a^2b^3 = 2 \cdot 7 \cdot a \cdot a \cdot b \cdot b \cdot b$
$20a^3b^2c = 2 \cdot 2 \cdot 5 \cdot a \cdot a \cdot a \cdot b \cdot b \cdot c$
$35ab^3c^2 = 5 \cdot 7 \cdot a \cdot b \cdot b \cdot b \cdot c \cdot c$
GCF: $a \cdot b \cdot b$ or ab^2

49. $18x^2 = 2 \cdot 3 \cdot 3 \cdot x \cdot x$
$30x^3y^2 = 2 \cdot 3 \cdot 5 \cdot x \cdot x \cdot x \cdot y \cdot y$
$54y^3 = 2 \cdot 3 \cdot 3 \cdot 3 \cdot y \cdot y \cdot y$
GCF: $2 \cdot 3$ or 6

50. $14a^2b^2 = 2 \cdot 7 \cdot a \cdot a \cdot b \cdot b$
$18ab = 2 \cdot 3 \cdot 3 \cdot a \cdot b$
$2a^3b^3 = 2 \cdot a \cdot a \cdot a \cdot b \cdot b \cdot b$
GCF: $2ab$

51. $32m^2n^3 = 2 \cdot 2 \cdot 2 \cdot 2 \cdot 2 \cdot m \cdot m \cdot n \cdot n \cdot n$
$8m^2n = 2 \cdot 2 \cdot 2 \cdot m \cdot m \cdot n$
$56m^3n^2 = 2 \cdot 2 \cdot 2 \cdot 7 \cdot m \cdot m \cdot m \cdot n \cdot n$
GCF: $2 \cdot 2 \cdot 2 \cdot m \cdot m \cdot n$ or $8m^2n$

52. $6b^2c$
53. $-12x^3yz^2$
54. $6a^3b^2$
55. $3m^2n$

56. $A = w \cdot \ell$
$116 = 1 \cdot 116$
$116 = 2 \cdot 58$
$116 = 4 \cdot 29$
The possible dimensions are 1 in. by 116 in., 2 in. by 58 in., and 4 in. by 29 in.

57. $A = \ell w$
$1363 = 29 \cdot 47$
The dimensions are 29 cm by 47 cm.

58. See students' work.

59. 3, 5; 5, 7; 11, 13; 17, 19; 29, 31; 41, 43; 59, 61; 71, 73

60a. GCF IS 28
60b. GCF IS 29
60c. GCF IS 1
60d. GCF IS 54
60e. GCF IS 81
60f. GCF IS 85

61a. $2b^3 \times 1 \times 1$
$2b^2 \times b \times 1$
$2b \times b \times b$
$b^3 \times 2 \times 1$
$b^2 \times 2b \times 1$
$b^2 \times 2 \times b$

61b. See students' work.

61c. $4b^3 + 1$ or 865
$2b^3 + 2b^2 + 1$ or 505
$5b^2$ or 180
$3b^3 + 2$ or 650
$2b^3 + b^2 + b$ or 474
$b^3 + 2b^2 + 2b$ or 300

61d. Though the volume remains constant, the surface areas vary greatly.

62. 5 rows of 20 plants, 10 rows of 10 plants, 20 rows of 5 plants

63. Each square of sod is 2×2 yd or 4 yd².
Therefore, $\frac{6000 \text{ yd}^2}{4 \text{ yd}^2} = 1500$ squares of sod

64. $(1.1x + y)^2 = (1.1x)^2 + 2(1.1x)(y) + (y)^2$
$= 1.21x^2 + 2.2xy + y^2$

65. $\frac{12b^5}{4b^4} = 3b^{5-4}$
$= 3b$

66.

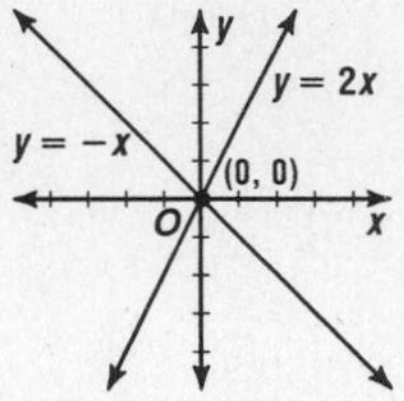

(0, 0)

67.

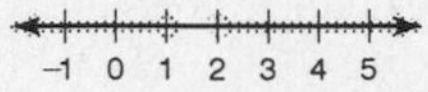

68. $16x < 96$
$\frac{16x}{16} < \frac{96}{16}$
$x < 6$

69. $m = \frac{8 - (-2)}{4 - 4} = \frac{10}{0}$ or undefined
$x = 4$

70. $8x - y = 16$
$-y = -8x + 16$
$y = 8x - 16$

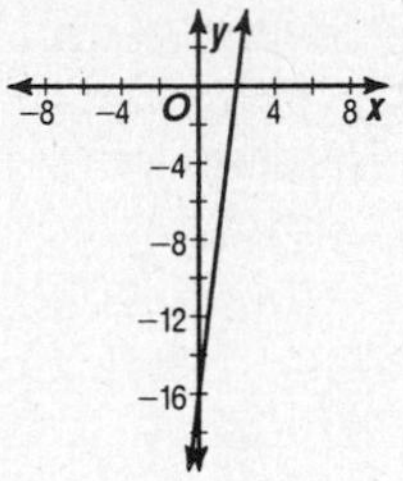

71. $50x = 75(16 - x)$
$50x = 1200 - 75x$
$125x = 1200$
$x = \frac{1200}{125}$ or $9\frac{3}{5}$
The 50-pound weight is $9\frac{3}{5}$ feet from the fulcrum.

72. $\frac{112}{74} = \frac{x}{25}$
$112(25) = 74x$
$2800 = 74x$
$37.8 = x$
A wave brought on by a 25-mph wind could reach 37.8 feet.

73. $9 = x + 13$
$9 - 13 = x + 13 - 13$
$-4 = x$

74. the number z to the seventh power added to 2

Page 563 Mathematics and Society

1. See students' work.
2. See students' work.

10-2A Modeling Mathematics: Factoring Using the Distributive Property

Page 564

1.

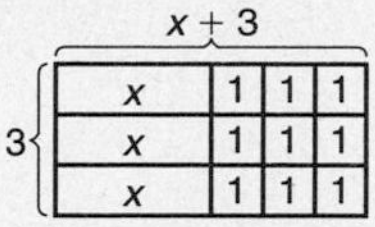

$3x + 9 = 3(x + 3)$

2.

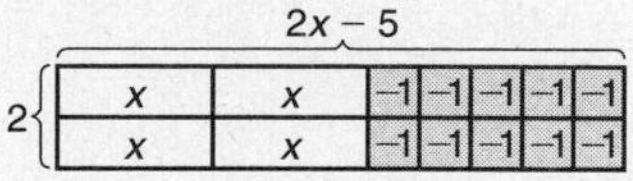

$4x - 10 = 2(2x - 5)$

3.

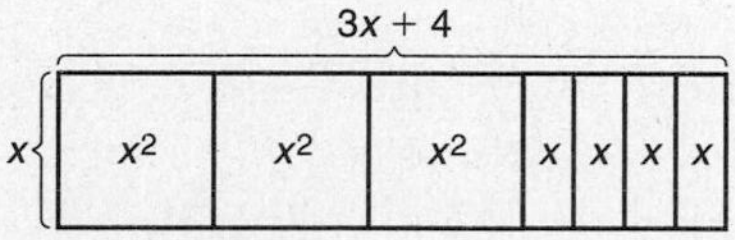

$3x^2 + 4x = x(3x + 4)$

4.

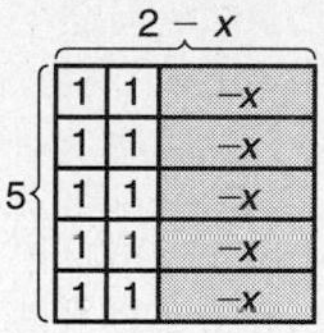

$10 - 5x = 5(2 - x)$

5. no

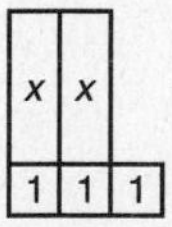

6. yes

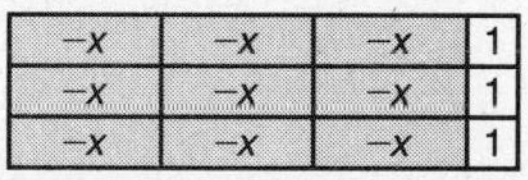

7. yes

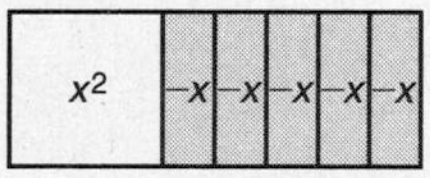

8. no

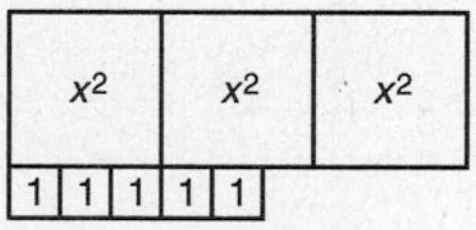

9. Binomials can be factored if they can be represented by a rectangle. Examples: $4x + 4$ can be factored and $4x + 3$ cannot be factored.

10-2 Factoring Using the Distributive Property

Pages 568–569 Check for Understanding

1a. $2(4d^2 - 7d)$, $d(8d - 14)$, $2d(4d - 7)$

1b. $2d(4d - 7)$; $2d$ is the GCF of $8d^2$ and $14d$.

2a. $ac + ad + bc + bd$ 2b. $(a + b)(c + d)$

2c. They are equal.

3. distributive, associative, commutative

4. $(4gh + 8h) + (3g + 6)$, $(4gh + 3g) + (8h + 6)$

5. $-(7p^2 - q) = -7p^2 + q$ or $q - 7p^2$

6.

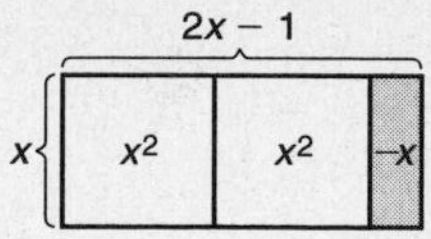

$2x^2 - x = x(2x - 1)$

7. $3y^2 = 3 \cdot y \cdot y$
$12 = 2 \cdot 2 \cdot 3$
GCF: 3

8. $5n = 5 \cdot n$
$-n^2 = -1 \cdot n \cdot n$
GCF: n

9. $5a = 5 \cdot a$
$3b = 3 \cdot b$
GCF: 1

10. $6mn = 2 \cdot 3 \cdot m \cdot n$
$15m^2 = 3 \cdot 5 \cdot m \cdot m$
GCF: $3m$

11. $12x^2y^2 = 2 \cdot 2 \cdot 3 \cdot x \cdot x \cdot y \cdot y$
$-8xy^2 = -1 \cdot 2 \cdot 2 \cdot 2 \cdot x \cdot y \cdot y$
GCF: $2 \cdot 2 \cdot x \cdot y \cdot y$ or $4xy^2$

12. $4x^2y = 2 \cdot 2 \cdot x \cdot x \cdot y$
$-6xy^2 = -1 \cdot 2 \cdot 3 \cdot x \cdot y \cdot y$
GCF: $2 \cdot x \cdot y$ or $2xy$

13. $(a + b)(x + y)$ 14. $(3m + 5n)(a - 2b)$

15. $(x - y)(3a + 4b)$ 16. $(x^2 + 1)(a^2 + b^2)$

17. $3t$ 18. $3x - 5y$

19. $29xy = 29 \cdot x \cdot y$
$-3x = -1 \cdot 3 \cdot x$
GCF: x
$29xy - 3x = x(29y) + x(-3)$
$= x(29y - 3)$

20. $x^5y = x \cdot x \cdot x \cdot x \cdot x \cdot y$
$-x = -1 \cdot x$
GCF: x
$x^5y - x = x(x^4y) + x(-1)$
$= x(x^4y - 1)$

21. $3c^2d = 3 \cdot c \cdot c \cdot d$
$-6c^2d^2 = -1 \cdot 2 \cdot 3 \cdot c \cdot c \cdot d \cdot d$
GCF: $3 \cdot c \cdot c \cdot d$ or $3c^2d$
$3c^2d - 6c^2d^2 = 3c^2d(1) + 3c^2d(-2d)$
$= 3c^2d(1 - 2d)$

22. $ay - ab + cb - cy = (ay - ab) + (cb - cy)$
$= a(y - b) + c(b - y)$
$= a(y - b) + c(-1)(y - b)$
$= a(y - b) - c(y - b)$
$= (a - c)(y - b)$

23. $rx + 2ry + kx + 2ky = (rx + 2ry) + (kx + 2ky)$
$= r(x + 2y) + k(x + 2y)$
$= (r + k)(x + 2y)$

24. $5a - 10a^2 + 2b - 4ab = (5a - 10a^2) + (2b - 4ab)$
$= 5a(1 - 2a) + 2b(1 - 2a)$
$= (5a + 2b)(1 - 2a)$

25a. $g = \frac{1}{2}n^2 - \frac{1}{2}n$
$g = \frac{1}{2}n(n - 1)$

25b. $g = \frac{1}{2}(14)(14 - 1)$
$= \frac{1}{2}(14)(13)$
$= 7(13)$
$= 91$ games

25c. $g = \frac{1}{2}n(n - 1)$
$= \frac{1}{2}(7)(7 - 1)$
$= \frac{1}{2}(7)(6)$
$= \frac{1}{2}(42)$
$= 21$
$21 \cdot 3 = 63$ games

Pages 569–571 Exercises

26. $2g$

27. $8rs$

28. $11p$

29. $2y - 5$

30. $a + 3b$

31. $5k - 7p$

32. $9t^2 = 3 \cdot 3 \cdot t \cdot t$
$36t = 2 \cdot 2 \cdot 3 \cdot 3 \cdot t$
GCF: $3 \cdot 3 \cdot t$ or $9t$
$9t^2 + 36t = 9t(t) + 9t(4)$
$= 9t(t + 4)$

33. $14xz = 2 \cdot 7 \cdot x \cdot z$
$-18xz^2 = -1 \cdot 2 \cdot 3 \cdot 3 \cdot x \cdot z \cdot z$
GCF: $2xz$
$14xz + 18xz^2 = 2xz(7) + 2xz(-9z)$
$= 2xz(7 - 9z)$

34. $15xy^3 = 3 \cdot 5 \cdot x \cdot y \cdot y \cdot y$
$y^4 = y \cdot y \cdot y \cdot y$
GCF: $y \cdot y \cdot y$ or y^3
$15xy^3 + y^4 = y^3(15x) + y^3(y)$
$= y^3(15x + y)$

35. $17a = 17 \cdot a$
$-41a^2b = -1 \cdot 41 \cdot a \cdot a \cdot b$
GCF: a
$17a - 41a^2b = a(17) + a(-41ab)$
$= a(17 - 41ab)$

36. $2ax + 6xc + ba + 3bc = (2ax + 6xc) + (ba + 3bc)$
$= 2x(a + 3c) + b(a + 3c)$
$= (2x + b)(a + 3c)$

37. $2my + 7x + 7m + 2xy = (2my + 2xy) + (7m + 7x)$
$= 2y(m + x) + 7(m + x)$
$= (2y + 7)(m + x)$

38. $3m^2 - 5m^2p + 3p^2 - 5p^3$
$= (3m^2 - 5m^2p) + (3p^2 - 5p^3)$
$= m^2(3 - 5p) + p^2(3 - 5p)$
$= (m^2 + p^2)(3 - 5p)$

39. $3x^3y = 3 \cdot x \cdot x \cdot x \cdot y$
$-9xy^2 = -1 \cdot 3 \cdot 3 \cdot x \cdot y \cdot y$
$36xy = 2 \cdot 2 \cdot 3 \cdot 3 \cdot x \cdot y$
GCF: $3 \cdot x \cdot y$ or $3xy$
$3x^3y - 9xy^2 + 36xy = 3xy(x^2) + 3xy(-3y) + 3xy(12)$
$= 3xy(x^2 - 3y + 12)$

40. $5a^2 - 4ab + 12b^3 - 15ab^2$
$= (5a^2 - 4ab) + (12b^3 - 15ab^2)$
$= a(5a - 4b) + 3b^2(4b - 5a)$
$= a(5a - 4b) + 3b^2(-1)(5a - 4b)$
$= a(5a - 4b) - 3b^2(5a - 4b)$
$= (a - 3b^2)(5a - 4b)$

41. $2x^3 - 5xy^2 - 2x^2y + 5y^3$
$= (2x^3 - 2x^2y) + (-5xy^2 + 5y^3)$
$= 2x^2(x - y) + (-5y^2)(x - y)$
$= 2x^2(x - y) - 5y^2(x - y)$
$= (2x^2 - 5y^2)(x - y)$

42. $12ax = 2 \cdot 2 \cdot 3 \cdot a \cdot x$
$20bx = 2 \cdot 2 \cdot 5 \cdot b \cdot x$
$32cx = 2 \cdot 2 \cdot 2 \cdot 2 \cdot 2 \cdot c \cdot x$
GCF: $2 \cdot 2 \cdot x$ or $4x$
$12ax + 20bx + 32cx = 4x(3a) + 4x(5b) + 4x(8c)$
$= 4x(3a + 5b + 8c)$

43. $4ax - 14bx + 35by - 10ay$
$= (4ax - 14bx) + (35by - 10ay)$
$= 2x(2a - 7b) + 5y(7b - 2a)$
$= 2x(2a - 7b) + 5y(-1)(2a - 7b)$
$= 2x(2a - 7b) - 5y(2a - 7b)$
$= (2x - 5y)(2a - 7b)$

44. $3my - ab + am - 3by$
$= (3my + am) + (-ab - 3by)$
$= m(3y + a) + (-b)(a + 3y)$
$= m(3y + a) - b(3y + a)$
$= (m - b)(3y + a)$

45. $28a^2b^2c^2 = 2 \cdot 2 \cdot 7 \cdot a \cdot a \cdot b \cdot b \cdot c \cdot c$
$21a^2bc^2 = 3 \cdot 7 \cdot a \cdot a \cdot b \cdot c \cdot c$
$-14abc = -1 \cdot 2 \cdot 7 \cdot a \cdot b \cdot c$
GCF: $7abc$
$28a^2b^2c^2 + 21a^2bc^2 - 14abc$
$= 7abc(4abc) + 7abc(3ac) + 7abc(-2)$
$= 7abc(4abc + 3ac - 2)$

46. $6a^2 - 6ab + 3bc - 3ca = (6a^2 - 6ab) + (3bc - 3ca)$
$= 6a(a - b) + 3c(b - a)$
$= 6a(a - b) + 3c(-1)(a - b)$
$= 6a(a - b) - 3c(a - b)$
$= (6a - 3c)(a - b)$
$= 3(2a - c)(a - b)$

47. $12mx - 8m + 6rx - 4r = (12mx - 8m) + (6rx - 4r)$
$= 4m(3x - 2) + 2r(3x - 2)$
$= (4m + 2r)(3x - 2)$
$= 2(2m + r)(3x - 2)$

48. $2ax + bx - 6ay - 3by - bz - 2az$
$= (2ax + bx) + (-6ay - 3by) + (-2az - bz)$
$= x(2a + b) - 3y(2a + b) - z(2a + b)$
$= (x - 3y - z)(2a + b)$

49. $7ax + 7bx + 3at + 3bt - 4a - 4b$
$= (7ax + 7bx) + (3at + 3bt) + (-4a - 4b)$
$= 7x(a + b) + 3t(a + b) - 4(a + b)$
$= (7x + 3t - 4)(a + b)$

50. $(a + 2 + 2)(b + 2 + 2) - ab$
$= (a + 4)(b + 4) - ab$
$= ab + 4a + 4b + 16 - ab$
$= 4a + 4b + 16$
$= 4(a) + 4(b) + 4(4)$
$= 4(a + b + 4)$

51. $A = (a + d + d + 4 + 4)(c + 4 + 4) - a(c - b) - cd - cd - 4b$
$= (a + 2d + 8)(c + 8) - ac + ab - 2cd - 4b$
$= ac + 2cd + 8c + 8a + 16d + 64 - ac + ab - 2cd - 4b$
$= 8a - 4b + 8c + 16d + ab + 64$

52. $4r(2r) - 2\pi r^2 = 8r^2 - 2\pi r^2$
$= 2r^2(4) + 2r^2(-\pi)$
$= 2r^2(4 - \pi)$

53. $4r(4r) - 4\pi r^2 = 16r^2 - 4\pi r^2$
$= 4r^2(4) + 4r^2(-\pi)$
$= 4r^2(4 - \pi)$

54. $5xy + 15x - 6y - 18 = (5xy + 15x) + (-6y - 18)$
$= 5x(y + 3) - 6(y + 3)$
$= (5x - 6)(y + 3)$
$(5x - 6)$ cm by $(y + 3)$ cm

55. $4z^2 - 24z - 18m + 3mz$
$= (4z^2 - 24z) + (-18m + 3mz)$
$= 4z(z - 6) + 3m(-6 + z)$
$= 4z(z - 6) + 3m(z - 6)$
$= (4z + 3m)(z - 6)$
$(4z + 3m)$ cm by $(z - 6)$ cm

56. $s = \frac{12x + 20y}{4}$ $\quad A = s^2$
$= 3x + 5y$ $\quad = (3x + 5y)^2$
$= (3x)^2 + 2(3x)(5y) + (5y)^2$
$= (9x^2 + 30xy + 25y^2)$ in^2

57. Sample answer:
$(3a + 2b)(ab + 6)$, $(3a + ab)(2b + 6)$,
$(2b + ab)(3a + 6)$

58. Let w = original width and let
$2w + 5$ = original length.
original area $= w(2w + 5)$
$= 2w^2 + 5w$
new area $= (2w + 5 + 4)(2w)$
$= (2w + 9)(2w)$
$= 4w^2 + 18w$
new area   original area
$= (4w^2 + 18w) - (2w^2 + 5w)$
$= 4w^2 + 18w - 2w^2 - 5w$
$= 4w^2 - 2w^2 + 18w - 5w$
$= 2w^2 + 13w$
$= w(2w) + w(13)$
$= w(2w + 13)$ ft^2

59.

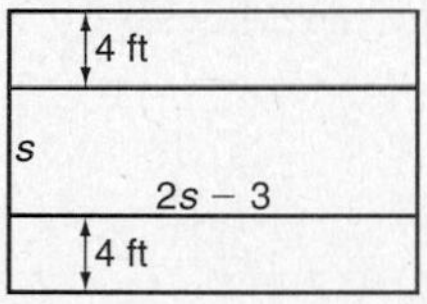

Let s = length of shorter side without path.
Then $s + 4 + 4$ or $s + 8$ = length of shorter side with path, and $2s - 3$ = length of longer side.

$A = \ell w$
$= (2s - 3)(s + 8)$

60a. $x + 75 = 69 + 75$
$= 144$ m

60b. $x(x + 75) = 69(69 + 75)$
$= 69(144)$
$= 9936$ m^2

60c. $[w(w + 52)]$ m^2

60d. $w(w + 52) = 68(68 + 52)$
$= 68(120)$
$= 8160$ m^2

60e. Rugby Union

61. A = 220 = (2) · (2) · 5 · (11)
C = 264 = (2) · (2) · 2 · 3 · (11)
GCF: 2 · 2 · 11 or 44
A = 220 = 2 · 2 · (5) · (11)
C sharp = 275 = 5 · (5) · (11)
GCF: 5 · 11 or 55
C = 264 = 2 · 2 · 2 · 3 · (11)
C sharp = 275 = 5 · 5 · (11)
GCF: 11
closest harmony: A and C sharp

62a. $\frac{248{,}200{,}000}{3{,}540{,}000} = \frac{2.482 \times 100{,}000{,}000}{3.54 \times 1{,}000{,}000}$
$= \frac{2.482 \times 10^8}{3.54 \times 10^6}$
$\approx 0.7 \times 10^{8-6}$
$\approx 7 \times 0.1 \times 10^2$
$\approx 7 \times 10^{-1} \times 10^2$
$\approx 7 \times 10^1$ or about 70 people

62b. $\frac{220{,}000{,}000{,}000}{248{,}200{,}000} = \frac{2.2 \times 100{,}000{,}000{,}000}{2.482 \times 100{,}000{,}000}$
$= \frac{2.2 \times 10^{11}}{2.482 \times 10^8}$
$\approx 0.88638 \times 10^{11-8}$
$\approx 0.88638 \times 10^3$
$\approx \$886.38$

63.

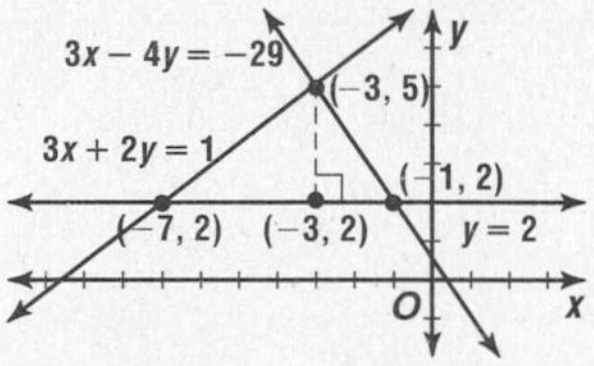

$3x - 4y = -29$
$(-)3x + 2y = 1$
$-6y = -30$
$y = 5$

$3x - 4(5) = -29$
$3x - 20 = -29$
$3x = -9$
$x = -3$

$A = \frac{1}{2}bh$
$= \frac{1}{2}(x_2 - x_1)(y_2 - y_1)$
$= \frac{1}{2}[-1 - (-7)](5 - 2)$
$= \frac{1}{2}(18)$
$= 9$

64a. Q1: 56,700
median: $\frac{59{,}100 + 60{,}500}{2} = 59{,}800$
Q3: 91,300
LV: 55,800
GV: 148,000

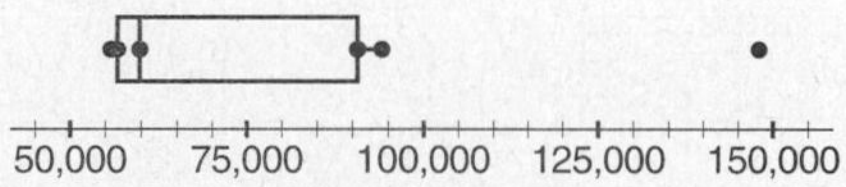

64b. $x \geq$ Q3 + 1.5(IQR)
$x \geq 91{,}300 + 1.5(34{,}600)$
$x \geq 91{,}300 + 51{,}900$
$x \geq 143{,}200$
$x \leq$ Q1 − 1.5(IQR)
$x \leq 56{,}700 = 1.5(34{,}600)$
$x \leq 56{,}700 - 51{,}900$
$x \leq 4800$
outlier: \$148,000

65. $17.42 - 7.029z \geq 15.766 - 8.029z$
$-7.029z \geq -1.654 - 8.029z$
$z \geq -1.654$
$\{z \mid z \geq -1.654\}$

66. midpoint of $\overline{AB} = \left(\frac{5 + 7}{2}, \frac{-2 + 3}{2}\right)$
$= \left(\frac{12}{2}, \frac{1}{2}\right)$
$= \left(6, \frac{1}{2}\right)$

67. Solve for b: $3a + 2b = 11$

$$2b = 11 - 3a$$
$$b = \frac{11 - 3a}{2}$$

a	$\frac{11 - 3a}{2}$	b	(a, b)
-3	$\frac{11 - (3)(-3)}{2}$	10	$(-3, 10)$
0	$\frac{11 - 3(0)}{2}$	$\frac{11}{2}$	$\left(0, \frac{11}{2}\right)$
1	$\frac{11 - 3(1)}{2}$	4	$(1, 4)$
2	$\frac{11 - 3(2)}{2}$	$\frac{5}{2}$	$\left(2, \frac{5}{2}\right)$
5	$\frac{11 - 3(5)}{2}$	-2	$(5, -2)$

$\left\{(-3, 10), \left(0, \frac{11}{2}\right), (1, 4), \left(2, \frac{5}{2}\right), (5, -2)\right\}$

68. Let x = the number.

$$14 = x - 0.50x$$
$$14 = 0.50x$$
$$28 = x$$

The number is 28.

69. $4x + 3y = 7$

$$3y = -4x + 7$$
$$y = -\frac{4}{3}x + \frac{7}{3}$$

70. $\frac{5}{2}x = -25$

$$\frac{2}{5}\left(\frac{5}{2}x\right) = \frac{2}{5}(-25)$$
$$x = -10$$

71. $(2^5 - 5^2) + (4^2 - 2^4) = (32 - 25) + (16 - 16)$
$$= 7 + 0$$
$$= 7$$

10-3A Modeling Mathematics: Factoring Trinomials

Page 573

1.

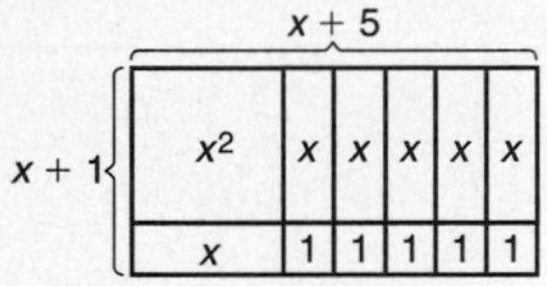

$x^2 + 6x + 5 = (x + 1)(x + 5)$

2.

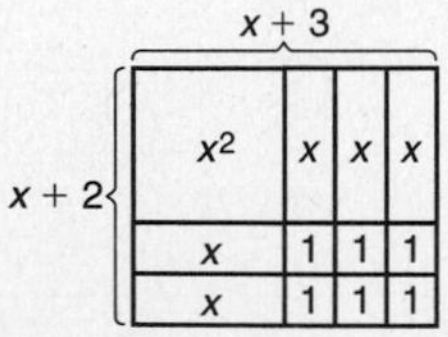

$x^2 + 5x + 6 = (x + 2)(x + 3)$

3.

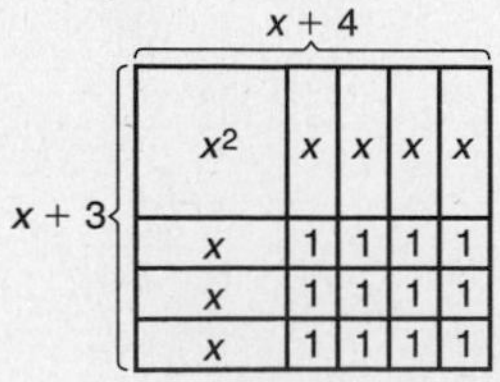

$x^2 + 7x + 12 =$
$(x + 3)(x + 4)$

4.

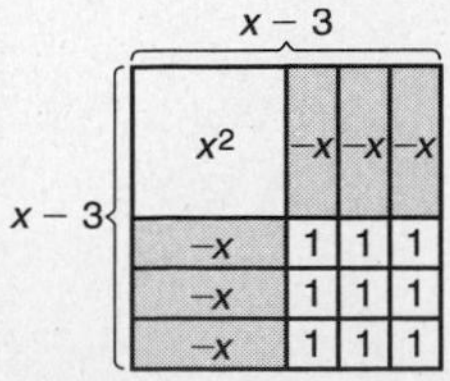

$x^2 - 6x + 9 =$
$(x - 3)(x - 3)$

5.

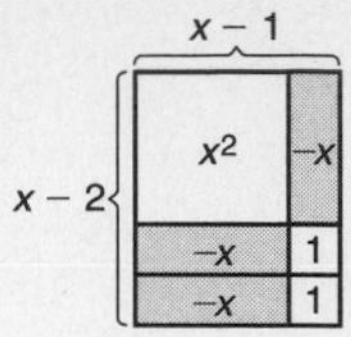

$x^2 - 3x + 2 =$
$(x - 1)(x - 2)$

6.

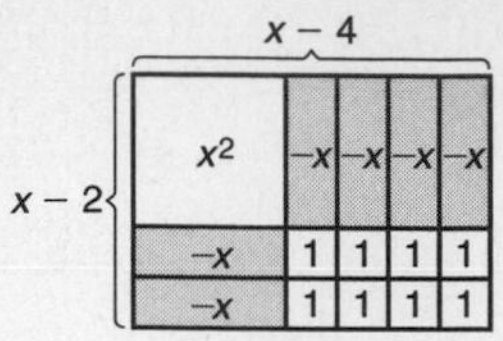

$x^2 - 6x + 8 =$
$(x - 2)(x - 4)$

7.

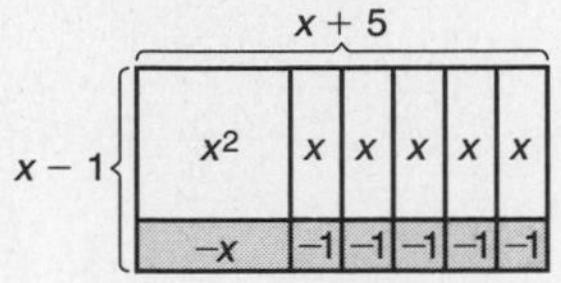

$x^2 + 4x - 5 = (x - 1)(x + 5)$

8.

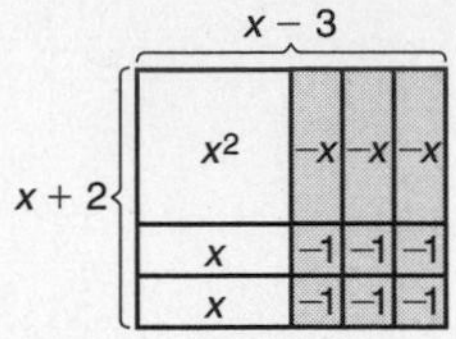

$x^2 - x - 6 = (x + 2)(x - 3)$

9. yes

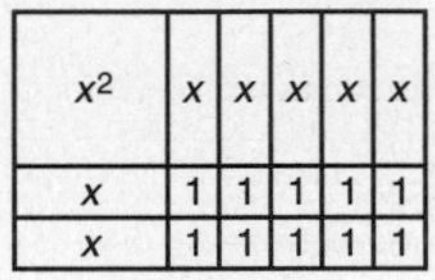

10. no

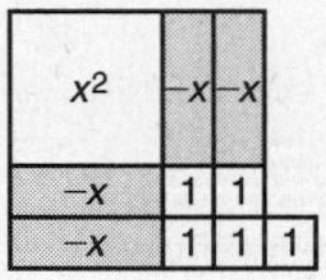

11. no

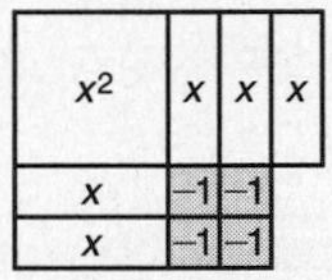

12. no

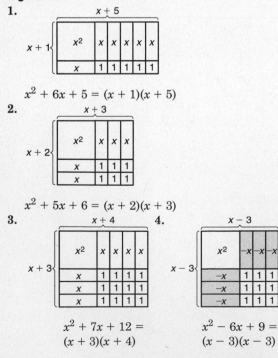

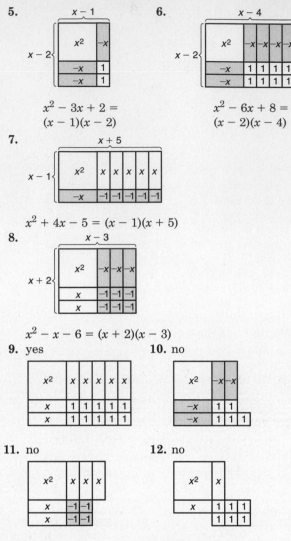

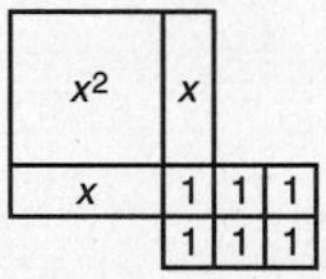

13. Trinomials can be factored if they can be represented by a rectangle. Sample answers: $x^2 + 4x + 4$ can be factored and $x^2 + 6x + 4$ cannot be factored.

10-3 Factoring Trinomials

Pages 578–579 Check for Understanding

1. So you do not waste time trying the same guess twice. It also helps you to make better guesses.

2. See students' work.

3a. It shows that the missing areas must have a sum of $8x$.

3b. $x^2 + 8x + 12 = x^2 + (2 + 6)x + 12$
$$= x^2 + 2x + 6x + 12$$
$$= (x^2 + 2x) + (6x + 12)$$
$$= x(x + 2) + 6(x + 2)$$
$$= (x + 6)(x + 2)$$

4.

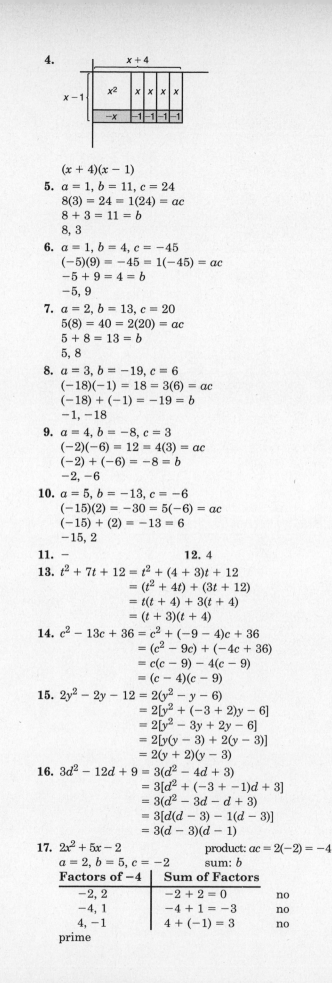

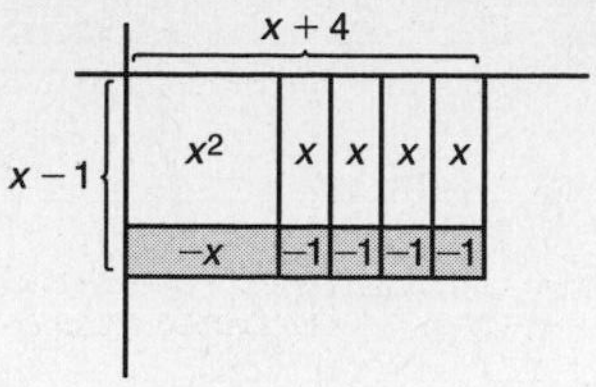

$(x + 4)(x - 1)$

5. $a = 1, b = 11, c = 24$
$8(3) = 24 = 1(24) = ac$
$8 + 3 = 11 = b$
$8, 3$

6. $a = 1, b = 4, c = -45$
$(-5)(9) = -45 = 1(-45) = ac$
$-5 + 9 = 4 = b$
$-5, 9$

7. $a = 2, b = 13, c = 20$
$5(8) = 40 = 2(20) = ac$
$5 + 8 = 13 = b$
$5, 8$

8. $a = 3, b = -19, c = 6$
$(-18)(-1) = 18 = 3(6) = ac$
$(-18) + (-1) = -19 = b$
$-1, -18$

9. $a = 4, b = -8, c = 3$
$(-2)(-6) = 12 = 4(3) = ac$
$(-2) + (-6) = -8 = b$
$-2, -6$

10. $a = 5, b = -13, c = -6$
$(-15)(2) = -30 = 5(-6) = ac$
$(-15) + (2) = -13 = 6$
$-15, 2$

11. $-$

12. 4

13. $t^2 + 7t + 12 = t^2 + (4 + 3)t + 12$
$= (t^2 + 4t) + (3t + 12)$
$= t(t + 4) + 3(t + 4)$
$= (t + 3)(t + 4)$

14. $c^2 - 13c + 36 = c^2 + (-9 - 4)c + 36$
$= (c^2 - 9c) + (-4c + 36)$
$= c(c - 9) - 4(c - 9)$
$= (c - 4)(c - 9)$

15. $2y^2 - 2y - 12 = 2(y^2 - y - 6)$
$= 2[y^2 + (-3 + 2)y - 6]$
$= 2[y^2 - 3y + 2y - 6]$
$= 2[y(y - 3) + 2(y - 3)]$
$= 2(y + 2)(y - 3)$

16. $3d^2 - 12d + 9 = 3(d^2 - 4d + 3)$
$= 3[d^2 + (-3 + -1)d + 3]$
$= 3(d^2 - 3d - d + 3)$
$= 3[d(d - 3) - 1(d - 3)]$
$= 3(d - 3)(d - 1)$

17. $2x^2 + 5x - 2$ product: $ac = 2(-2) = -4$
$a = 2, b = 5, c = -2$ sum: b

Factors of −4	Sum of Factors	
$-2, 2$	$-2 + 2 = 0$	no
$-4, 1$	$-4 + 1 = -3$	no
$4, -1$	$4 + (-1) = 3$	no

prime

18. $6p^2 + 15p - 9 = 3(2p^2 + 5p - 3)$
$= 3[2p^2 + (6 - 1)p - 3]$
$= 3(2p^2 + 6p - p - 3)$
$= 3[2p(p + 3) - 1(p + 3)]$
$= 3(2p - 1)(p + 3)$

19.

Factors of 1(14) or 14	Sum of Factors (k)
$7, 2$	$7 + 2 = 9$
$-7, -2$	$-7 + (-2) = -9$
$14, 1$	$14 + 1 = 15$
$-14, -1$	$-14 + (-1) = -15$

$9, -9, 15, -15$

20.

Factors of 2(−3) or 6	Sum of Factors (k)
$-2, 3$	$-2 + 3 = 1$
$2, -3$	$2 + (-3) = -1$
$-1, 6$	$-1 + 6 = 5$
$1, -6$	$1 + (-6) = -5$

$1, -1, 5, -5$

21. $3x^2 + 14x + 15 = 3x^2 + (9 + 5)x + 15$
$= 3x^2 + 9x + 5x + 15$
$= (3x^2 + 9x) + (5x + 15)$
$= 3x(x + 3) + 5(x + 3)$
$= (3x + 5)(x + 3)$

new width $= (x + 3 - 3) = x$
new length $= (3x + 5 - 3) = 3x + 2$
Area $= x(3x + 2)$
$= (3x^2 + 2x)$ m²

Pages 579–580 Exercises

22. +

23. $-$

24. $4y$

25. 5

26. $2x$

27. 5

28. $b^2 + 7b + 12 = b^2 + (4 + 3)b + 12$
$= b^2 + 4b + 3b + 12$
$= (b^2 + 4b) + (3b + 12)$
$= b(b + 4) + 3(b + 3)$
$= (b + 3)(b + 4)$

29. $m^2 - 14m + 40 = m^2 + (-10 - 4)m + 40$
$= m^2 - 10m - 4m + 40$
$= (m^2 - 10m) + (-4m + 40)$
$= m(m - 10) - 4(m - 10)$
$= (m - 4)(m - 10)$

30. $z^2 - 5z - 24 = z^2 + (3z - 8z) - 24$
$= z^2 + 3z - 8z - 24$
$= (z^2 + 3z) + (-8z - 24)$
$= z(z + 3) - 8(z + 3)$
$= (z - 8)(z + 3)$

31. prime

32. $s^2 + 3s - 180 = s^2 + (-12 + 15)s - 180$
$= s^2 + (-12s) + 15s - 180$
$= (s^2 - 12s) + (15s - 180)$
$= s(s - 12) + 15(s - 12)$
$= (s - 12)(s + 15)$

33. $2x^2 + x - 21 = 2x^2 + (-6 + 7)x - 21$
$= 2x^2 - 6x + 7x - 21$
$= (2x^2 - 6x) + (7x - 21)$
$= 2x(x - 3) + 7(x - 3)$
$= (2x + 7)(x - 3)$

34. $7a^2 + 22a + 3 = 7a^2 + (21 + 1)a + 3$
$= 7a^2 + 21a + a + 3$
$= (7a^2 + 21a) + (a + 3)$
$= 7a(a + 3) + 1(a + 3)$
$= (7a + 1)(a + 3)$

35. $2x^2 - 5x - 12 = 2x^2 + (-8 + 3)x - 12$
$= 2x^2 - 8x + 3x - 12$
$= (2x^2 - 8x) + (3x - 12)$
$= 2x(x - 4) + 3(x - 4)$
$= (2x + 3)(x - 4)$

36. prime

37. $4n^2 - 4n - 35 = 4n^2 + (10 - 14)n - 35$
$= 4n^2 + 10n - 14n - 35$
$= (4n^2 + 10n) + (-14n - 35)$
$= 2n(2n + 5) - 7(2n + 5)$
$= (2n - 7)(2n + 5)$

38. $72 - 26y + 2y^2 = 2(36 - 13y + y^2)$
$= 2[36 + (-9 - 4)y + y^2]$
$= 2(36 - 9y - 4y + y^2)$
$= 2[(36 - 9y) - (4y - y^2)]$
$= 2[9(4 - y) - y(4 - y)]$
$= 2(9 - y)(4 - y)$

39. $10 + 19m + 6m^2 = 10 + (4 + 15)m + 6m^2$
$= 10 + 4m + 15m + 6m^2$
$= (10 + 4m) + (15m + 6m^2)$
$= 2(5 + 2m) + 3m(5 + 2m)$
$= (2 + 3m)(5 + 2m)$

40. $a^2 + 2ab - 3b^2 = a^2 + (-1 + 3)ab - 3b^2$
$= a^2 - ab + 3ab - 3b^2$
$= (a^2 - ab) + (3ab - 3b^2)$
$= a(a - b) + 3b(a - b)$
$= (a + 3b)(a - b)$

41. prime

42. $15x^2 - 13xy + 2y^2 = 15x^2 + (-10 - 3)xy + 2y^2$
$= 15x^2 - 10xy - 3xy + 2y^2$
$= (15x^2 - 10xy) + (-3xy + 2y^2)$
$= 5x(3x - 2y) - y(3x - 2y)$
$= (5x - y)(3x - 2y)$

43. $12x^3 + 2x^2 - 80x = 2x(6x^2 + x - 40)$
$= 2x[6x^2 + (-15 + 16)x - 40]$
$= 2x(6x^2 - 15x + 16x - 40)$
$= 2x[(6x^2 - 15x) + (16x - 40)]$
$= 2x[3x(2x - 5) + 8(2x - 5)]$
$= 2x(3x + 8)(2x - 5)$

44. $5a^3b^2 + 11a^2b^2 - 36ab^2$
$= ab^2(5a^2 + 11a - 36)$
$= ab^2\ [5a^2 + (20 - 9)a - 36]$
$= ab^2\ [5a^2 + 20a - 9a - 36]$
$= ab^2[(5a^2 + 20a) - (9a + 36)]$
$= ab^2[5a(a + 4) - 9(a + 4)]$
$= ab^2(5a - 9)(a + 4)$

45. $20a^4b - 58a^3b^2 + 42a^2b^3$
$= 2a^2b(10a^2 - 29ab + 21b^2)$
$= 2a^2b[10a^2 + (-15 - 14)ab + 21b^2]$
$= 2a^2b[10a^2 - 15ab - 14ab + 21b^2]$
$= 2a^2b[(10a^2 - 15ab) + (-14ab + 21b^2)]$
$= 2a^2b[5a(2a - 3b) - 7b(2a - 3b)]$
$= 2a^2b(5a - 7b)(2a - 3b)$

46.

Factors of 1(−13) or −13	**Sum of Factors (*k*)**
−13, 1	−13 + 1 = −12
13, −1	13 + (−1) = 12

12, −12

47.

Factors of 1(10) or 10	**Sum of Factors (*k*)**
2, 5	2 + 5 = 7
−2, −5	−2 + (−5) = −7
1, 10	1 + 10 = 11
−1, −10	−1 + (−10) = −11

7, −7, 11, −11

48.

Factors of 2(12) or 24	**Sum of Factors (*k*)**
1, 24	1 + 24 = 25
−1, −24	−1 + (−24) = −25
2, 12	2 + 12 = 14
−2, −12	−2 + (−12) = −14
3, 8	3 + 8 = 11
−3, −8	−3 + (−8) = −11
4, 6	4 + 6 = 10
−4, −6	−4 + (−6) = −10

10, −10, 11, −11, 14, −14, 25, −25

49.

Factors of 3(−14) or −42	**Sum of Factors (*k*)**
1, −42	1 + (−42) = −41
−1, 42	(−1) + 42 = 41
2, −21	2 + (−21) = −19
−2, 21	−2 + 21 = 19
3, −14	3 + (−14) = −11
−3, 14	−3 + 14 = 11
6, −7	6 + (−7) = −1
−6, 7	−6 + 7 = 1

1, −1, 11, −11, 19, −19, 41, −41

50.

Sum of Factors (8)	**Product (*k*)**
7 + 1	7(1) = 7
6 + 2	6(2) = 12
3 + 5	3(5) = 15
4 + 4	4(4) = 16

7, 12, 15, 16

51.

Sum of Factors (−5)	**Product (*k*)**
−2 + (−3)	(−2)(−3) = 6
−4 + (−1)	(−4)(−1) = 4

6, 4

52. $6x^2 - 31x + 35 = 6x^2 + (-21 - 10)x + 35$
$= 6x^2 - 21x - 10x + 35$
$= (6x^2 - 21x) + (-10x + 35)$
$= 3x(2x - 7) - 5(2x - 7)$
$= (3x - 5)(2x - 7)$
$= [3(4) - 5][2(4) - 7]$ *Let x = 4.*
$= (12 - 5)(8 - 7)$
$= 7(1)$
$= 7\ \text{in}^2$

53. $15r^3 - 17r^2 - 42r = r(15r^2 - 17r - 42)$
$= r[15r^2 + (-35 + 18)r - 42]$
$= r(15r^2 - 35r + 18r - 42)$
$= r[(15r^2 - 35r) + (18r - 42)]$
$= r[5r(3r - 7) + 6(3r - 7)]$
$= r(5r + 6)(3r - 7)$

r cm, $(5r + 6)$ cm, $(3r - 7)$ cm

54. Press [Y=]. Enter $x^2 - 2x - 15$ for Y1 and $(x - 5)(x + 3)$ for Y2. Press [ZOOM] 6.
yes

55. Press $\boxed{Y=}$. Enter $2x^2 + x - 3$ for Y1 and $(2x - 1)(x + 3)$ for Y2. Press $\boxed{\text{ZOOM}}$ 6.
no; $(2x + 3)(x - 1)$

56. Press $\boxed{Y=}$. Enter $3x^2 - 4x - 4$ for Y1 and $(3x - 2)(x + 2)$ for Y2. Press $\boxed{\text{ZOOM}}$ 6.
no; $(3x + 2)(x - 2)$

57. Press $\boxed{Y=}$. Enter $x^2 - 6x + 9$ for Y1 and $(x + 3)(x - 3)$ for Y2. Press $\boxed{\text{ZOOM}}$ 6.
no; $(x - 3)(x - 3)$

58a. Sample answers:
$16,\ x^2 + 8x + 16 = (x + 4)(x + 4);$
$12,\ x^2 + 8x + 12 = (x + 6)(x + 2);$
$7,\ x^2 + 8x + 7 = (x + 7)(x + 1)$

58b. Sample answers:
$9,\ x^2 + 9x - 10 = (x + 10)(x - 1);$
$3,\ x^2 + 3x - 10 = (x + 5)(x - 2);$
$-3,\ x^2 + (-3)x - 10 = (x - 5)(x + 2)$

59.
$$\begin{aligned} 45x^2 - 174x + 144 &= 3(15x^2 - 58x + 48) \\ &= 3[15x^2 + (-40 - 18)x + 48] \\ &= 3(15x^2 - 40x - 18x + 48) \\ &= 3[5x(3x - 8) - 6(3x - 8)] \\ &= 3(5x - 6)(3x - 8) \end{aligned}$$
Let $x = 3$.
$$\begin{aligned} V &= [3(5 \cdot 3 - 6)(3 \cdot 3 - 8)] \\ V &= [3(15 - 6)(9 - 8)] \\ V &= 3(9)(1) \\ V &= 27 \text{ ft}^3 \end{aligned}$$

60.

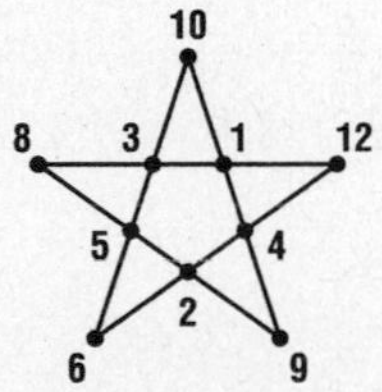

61. sales during 1st hour $= 4x$
sales during 2nd hour $= 8(x - 5)$
$$\begin{aligned} \text{total sales} &= 4x + 8(x - 5) \\ &= 4x + 8x - 40 \\ &= 12x - 40 \end{aligned}$$
$12x - 40 = 4(3x - 10)$
$\frac{12x - 40}{4} = (3x - 10)$
He would have had to sell $(3x - 10)$ shares at \$4 per share.

62. degree of $7x^3$: 3
degree of $4xy$: 1 + 1 or 2
degree of $3xz^3$: 1 + 3 or 4
The degree of $7x^3 + 4xy + 3xz^3$ is 4.

63.
$$\begin{aligned} 2x &= 4 - 3y & &\rightarrow & 3y + 2x &= 4 \\ 3y - x &= -11 & &\rightarrow & (-)\ 3y - x &= -11 \\ & & & & 3x &= 15 \\ & & & & x &= 5 \end{aligned}$$
$$\begin{aligned} 2x &= 4 - 3y \\ 2(5) &= 4 - 3y \\ 10 &= 4 - 3y \\ 6 &= -3y \\ -2 &= y \end{aligned}$$
$(5, -2)$

64. $|2y - 7| \geq -6$
$2y - 7 \geq -6$ or $2y - 7 \leq 6$
$2y \geq 1$ $\qquad 2y \leq 13$
$y \geq \frac{1}{2}$ $\qquad y \leq \frac{13}{2}$
{all numbers}

65.
$$\begin{aligned} 2x + 3y &= 1 \\ 3y &= -2x + 1 \\ y &= -\tfrac{2}{3}x + \tfrac{1}{3} \end{aligned}$$
$m = -\frac{2}{3}$; $(4, 2)$
$$\begin{aligned} y - y_1 &= m(x - x_1) \\ y - 2 &= -\tfrac{2}{3}(x - 4) \\ y - 2 &= -\tfrac{2}{3}x + \tfrac{8}{3} \\ y &= -\tfrac{2}{3}x + \tfrac{14}{3} \end{aligned}$$

66.
$$\begin{aligned} m &= \frac{9 - 6}{-5 - (-3)} \\ &= -\frac{3}{2} \end{aligned}$$

67. D = {0, 1, 2}; R = {2, −2, 4}

68. Let x = amount of surface covered by land.
$$\begin{aligned} x + 3x &= 100\% \\ x + 3x &= 1 \\ 4x &= 1 \\ x &= \tfrac{1}{4} \end{aligned} \qquad \begin{aligned} 3x &= 3\left(\tfrac{1}{4}\right) \\ &= \tfrac{3}{4} \\ &= 75\% \end{aligned}$$

69. $180° - 90° = 90°$

70. 12 noon to 2:00 A.M. = +14 hr
7:30 A.M. + 14 hr = 9:30 P.M.
Oct 26 at 9:30 P.M.

71.
$$\begin{aligned} 3(x + 2y) - 2y &= 3(x) + 3(2y) - 2y \\ &= 3x + 6y - 2y \\ &= 3x + 4y \end{aligned}$$

Page 580 Self Test

1. $50n^4 = 2 \cdot 5 \cdot 5 \cdot n \cdot n \cdot n \cdot n$
$40n^2p^2 = 2 \cdot 2 \cdot 2 \cdot 5 \cdot n \cdot n \cdot p \cdot p$
GCF: $2 \cdot 5 \cdot n \cdot n$ or $10n^2$

2. $15abc = 3 \cdot 5 \cdot a \cdot b \cdot c$
$35a^2c = 5 \cdot 7 \cdot a \cdot a \cdot c$
$105a = 3 \cdot 5 \cdot 7 \cdot a$
GCF: $5a$

3. $18xy^2 = 2 \cdot 3 \cdot 3 \cdot x \cdot y \cdot y$
$-24x^2y = -1 \cdot 2 \cdot 2 \cdot 2 \cdot 3 \cdot x \cdot x \cdot y$
GCF: $2 \cdot 3 \cdot x \cdot y$ or $6xy$
$$\begin{aligned} 18xy^2 - 24x^2y &= 6xy(3y) + 6xy(-4x) \\ &= 6xy(3y - 4x) \end{aligned}$$

4.
$$\begin{aligned} 2ab + 2am - b - m &= (2ab + 2am) + (-b - m) \\ &= 2a(b + m) - 1(b + m) \\ &= (2a - 1)(b + m) \end{aligned}$$

5.
$$\begin{aligned} 2q^2 - 9q - 18 &= 2q^2 + (-12 + 3)q - 18 \\ &= 2q^2 - 12q + 3q - 18 \\ &= 2q(q - 6) + 3(q - 6) \\ &= (2q + 3)(q - 6) \end{aligned}$$

6. prime

7.
$$\begin{aligned} 3y^2 - 8y + 5 &= 3y^2 + (-3 + -5)y + 5 \\ &= 3y^2 - 3y - 5y + 5 \\ &= 3y(y - 1) - 5(y - 1) \\ &= (3y - 5)(y - 1) \end{aligned}$$

8. $27m^2n^2 = 3 \cdot 3 \cdot 3 \cdot m \cdot m \cdot n \cdot n$
$-75mn = -1 \cdot 3 \cdot 5 \cdot 5 \cdot m \cdot n$
GCF: $3mn$
$27m^2n^2 - 75mn = 3mn(9mn) + 3mn(-25)$
$= 3mn(9mn - 25)$

9. 41,312,432 or 23,421,314

10. $x^2 - x - 6 = x^2 + (-3 + 2)x - 6$
$= (x^2 - 3x) + (2x - 6)$
$= x(x - 3) + 2(x - 3)$
$= (x + 2)(x - 3)$
New Area $= (x + 2 + 9)(x - 3 + 9)$
$= (x + 11)(x + 6)$
$= x^2 + 6x + 11x + 66$
$= (x^2 + 17x + 66)$ m^2

10-4 Factoring Differences of Squares

Page 584 Check for Understanding

1. Each term of the binomial is a perfect square, and the binomial can be written as a difference of terms.
2. Sample answer: $a^2 - 25 = (a - 5)(a + 5)$
3. Write the binomial as a trinomial where the coefficient of the middle term is 0, and then factor this trinomial.
4. Patsy; if 7 is factored from each term, the binomial factor is the difference of squares $4f^2 - g^2$.
5. $\frac{15}{16} \cdot \frac{17}{16} = \frac{(16-1)(16+1)}{16^2}$
$= \frac{16^2 - 1^2}{16^2}$
$= \frac{255}{256}$
6. 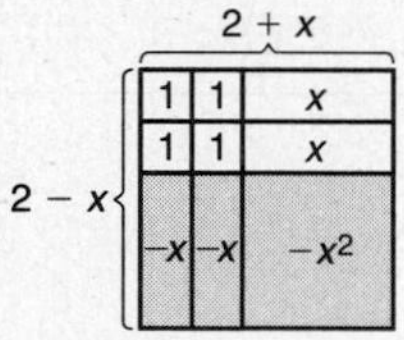

$4 - x^2 = (2 - x)(2 + x)$
7. $p^2 - 49q^2 = (p)^2 - (7q)^2$; yes
8. $25a^2 - 81b^4 = (5a)^2 - (9b^2)^2$; yes
9. no
10. c $(2x - 5)(2x + 5)$
11. d $4(2x - 1)(2x + 1)$
12. b $(5x - 2)(5x + 2)$
13. a $25(x - 1)(x + 1)$
14. $t^2 - 25 = (t)^2 - (5)^2$
$= (t - 5)(t + 5)$
15. $1 - 16g^2 = (1)^2 - (4g)^2$
$= (1 - 4g)(1 + 4g)$
16. prime
17. $20m^2 - 45n^2 = 5(4m^2 - 9n^2)$
$= 5[(2m)^2 - (3n)^2]$
$= 5(2m - 3n)(2m + 3n)$
18. $(a + b)^2 - c^2 = (a + b - c)(a + b + c)$
19. $x^4 - y^4 = (x^2)^2 - (y^2)^2$
$= (x^2 + y^2)(x^2 - y^2)$
$= (x - y)(x + y)(x^2 + y^2)$
20. $(20 - 3)(20 + 3) = 20^2 - 3^2$
$= 400 - 9$
$= 391$
21. $x - y = 3$
$x^2 - y^2 = 15$
$(x - y)(x + y) = 15$
$3(x + y) = 15$
$x + y = 5$
The sum of the numbers is 5.

Pages 584–586 Exercises

22. $w^2 - 81 = (w)^2 - (9)^2$
$= (w - 9)(w + 9)$
23. $4 - v^2 = (2)^2 - (v)^2$
$= (2 - v)(2 + v)$
24. $4q^2 - 9 = (2q)^2 - (3)^2$
$= (2q - 3)(2q + 3)$
25. $100d^2 - 1 = (10d)^2 - (1)^2$
$= (10d - 1)(10d + 1)$
26. $16a^2 - 25b^2 = (4a)^2 - (5b)^2$
$= (4a - 5b)(4a + 5b)$
27. $2z^2 - 98 = 2(z^2 - 49)$
$= 2[(z)^2 - (7)^2]$
$= 2(z - 7)(z + 7)$
28. $9g^2 - 75 = 3(3g^2 - 25)$
29. prime
30. $8x^2 - 18 = 2(4x^2 - 9)$
$= 2[(2x)^2 - (3)^2]$
$= 2(2x - 3)(2x + 3)$
31. $17 - 68k^2 = 17(1 - 4k^2)$
$= 17[(1)^2 - (2k)^2]$
$= 17(1 - 2k)(1 + 2k)$
32. $25y^2 - 49z^4 = (5y)^2 - (7z^2)^2$
$= (5y - 7z^2)(5y + 7z^2)$
33. prime
34. $-16 + 49h^2 = 49h^2 - 16$
$= (7h)^2 - (4)^2$
$= (7h - 4)(7h + 4)$
35. prime
36. $-9r^2 + 81 = 81 - 9r^2$
$= 9(9 - r^2)$
$= 9[(3)^2 - (r)^2]$
$= 9(3 - r)(3 + r)$
37. $a^2x^2 - 0.64y^2 = (ax)^2 - (0.8y)^2$
$= (ax + 0.8y)(ax - 0.8y)$
38. $\frac{1}{16}x^2 - 25z^2 = \left(\frac{1}{4}x\right)^2 - (5z)^2$
$= \left(\frac{1}{4}x + 5z\right)\left(\frac{1}{4}x - 5z\right)$
39. $\frac{9}{2}a^2 - \frac{49}{2}b^2 = \frac{1}{2}(9a^2 - 49b^2)$
$= \frac{1}{2}[(3a)^2 - (7b)^2]$
$= \frac{1}{2}(3a + 7b)(3a - 7b)$
40. $(4p - 9q)^2 - 1 = (4p - 9q + 1)(4p - 9q - 1)$
41. $(a + b)^2 - (c + d)^2 = (a + b + c + d)[a + b - (c + d)]$
$= (a + b + c + d)(a + b - c - d)$
42. $25x^2 - (2y - 7z)^2 = (5x)^2 - (2y - 7z)^2$
$= (5x + 2y - 7z)[5x - (2y - 7z)]$
$= (5x + 2y - 7z)(5x - 2y + 7z)$

43. $x^8 - 16y^4 = (x^4)^2 - (4y^2)^2$
$= (x^4 - 4y^2)(x^4 + 4y^2)$
$= [(x^2)^2 - (2y)^2](x^4 + 4y^2)$
$= (x^2 - 2y)(x^2 + 2y)(x^4 + 4y^2)$

44. $a^6 - a^2b^4 = a^2(a^4 - b^4)$
$= a^2[(a^2)^2 - (b^2)^2]$
$= a^2(a^2 - b^2)(a^2 + b^2)$
$= a^2(a - b)(a + b)(a^2 + b^2)$

45. $a^4 + a^2b^2 - 20b^4 = a^4 + (-4 + 5)a^2b^2 - 20b^4$
$= a^4 - 4a^2b^2 + 5a^2b^2 - 20b^4$
$= (a^4 - 4a^2b^2) + (5a^2b^2 - 20b^4)$
$= a^2(a^2 - 4b^2) + 5b^2(a^2 - 4b^2)$
$= (a^2 + 5b^2)(a^2 - 4b^2)$
$= (a^2 + 5b^2)[(a)^2 - (2b)^2]$
$= (a^2 + 5b^2)(a - 2b)(a + 2b)$

46. $29 \times 31 = (30 - 1)(30 + 1)$
$= 30^2 - 1^2$
$= 900 - 1$
$= 899$

47. $24 \times 26 = (25 - 1)(25 + 1)$
$= 25^2 - 1^2$
$= 625 - 1$
$= 624$

48. $94 \times 106 = (100 - 6)(100 + 6)$
$= 100^2 - 36$
$= 10{,}000 - 36$
$= 9964$

49. $(2a)^2 - (b)^2 = (2a - b)(2a + b)$
$(2a - b)$ in., $(2a + b)$ in.

50. $\pi r^2 - \pi(5)^2 = \pi(r^2 - 5^2)$
$= \pi(r - 5)(r + 5)$
$(\pi r - 5\pi)$ cm, $(r + 5)$ cm or $(r - 5)$ cm, $(\pi r + 5\pi)$ cm

51. $(x + 1)^2 - 3^2 = (x + 1 - 3)(x + 1 + 3)$
$= (x - 2)(x + 4)$
$(x - 2)$ ft, $(x + 4)$ ft

52. $7mp^2 + 2np^2 - 7mr^2 - 2nr^2$
$= (7mp^2 + 2np^2) + (-7mr^2 - 2nr^2)$
$= p^2(7m + 2n) - r^2(7m + 2n)$
$= (p^2 - r^2)(7m + 2n)$
$= (p - r)(p + r)(7m + 2n)$
$(p - r)$ cm, $(p + r)$ cm, $(7m + 2n)$ cm

53. $5a^3 - 125ab^2 - 75b^3 + 3a^2b$
$= (5a^3 - 125ab^2) + (-75b^3 + 3a^2b)$
$= 5a(a^2 - 25b^2) + 3b(a^2 - 25b^2)$
$= (5a + 3b)(a^2 - 25b^2)$
$= (5a + 3b)[(a)^2 - (5b)^2]$
$= (5a + 3b)(a - 5b)(a + 5b)$
$(a - 5b)$ in., $(a + 5b)$ in., $(5a + 3b)$ in.

54.

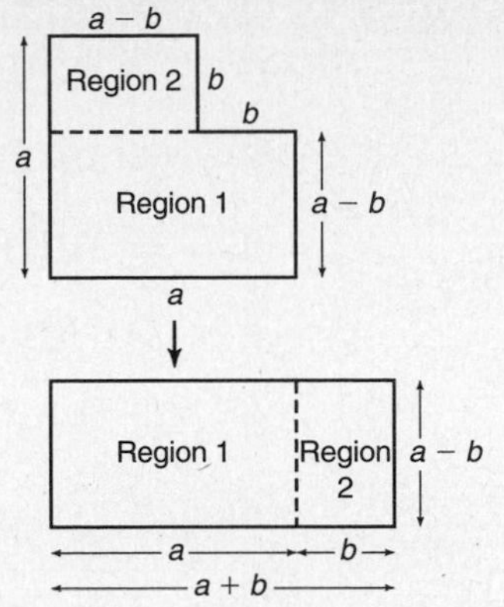

55a. Let x = a side of a square.
Then $x + 5$ = the length and $x - 5$ = the width of the rectangle.
$A_{\text{square}} = x^2$
$A_{\text{rectangle}} = (x + 5)(x - 5)$
$= x^2 - 25$
The square has the greater area.

55b. $x^2 - (x^2 - 25) = x^2 - x^2 + 25 = 25 \text{ cm}^2$

56. $7^2 = 49 = (1)(49)$
$= (25 - 24)(25 + 24)$ $\qquad \frac{1 + 49}{2} = 25$
$= 25^2 - 24^2$
7, 24, 25

57. $9^2 = 81 = (3)(27)$
$= (15 - 12)(15 + 12)$ $\qquad \frac{3 + 27}{2} = 15$
$= 15^2 - 12^2$
9, 12, 15

58. Let x = the length of the missing side.
$(3a + 2)^2 = (a + 1)^2 + x^2$
$(3a)^2 + 2(3a)(2) + (2)^2 = (a)^2 + 2(1)(a) + (1)^2 + x^2$
$9a^2 + 12a + 4 = a^2 + 2a + 1 + x^2$
$8a^2 + 10a + 3 = x^2$
$8a^2 + (6 + 4)a + 3 = x^2$
$8a^2 + 6a + 4a + 3 = x^2$
$(8a^2 + 6a) + (4a + 3) = x^2$
$2a(4a + 3) + 1(4a + 3) = x^2$
$(2a + 1)(4a + 3) = x^2$

59. $3.16 + 1.50 + 1.25 + 1.20 = 7.11$
$3.16 \cdot 1.50 \cdot 1.25 \cdot 1.20 = 7.11$
The items cost \$3.16, \$1.50, \$1.25, and \$1.20.

60. $(n^2 + 5n + 3) + (2n^2 + 8n + 8)$
$= (n^2 + 2n^2) + (5n + 8n) + (3 + 8)$
$= 3n^2 + 13n + 11$

61.
$x + y = 20 \rightarrow \quad -0.4x - 0.4y = -8$
$0.4x + 0.15y = 4 \rightarrow \quad (+)\ 0.4x + 0.15y = 4$
$-0.25y = -4$
$y = 16$

$x + y = 20$
$x + 16 = 20$
$x = 4$
(4, 16)

62. **Coin 1 Coin 2 Coin 3 Coin 4 Outcomes**

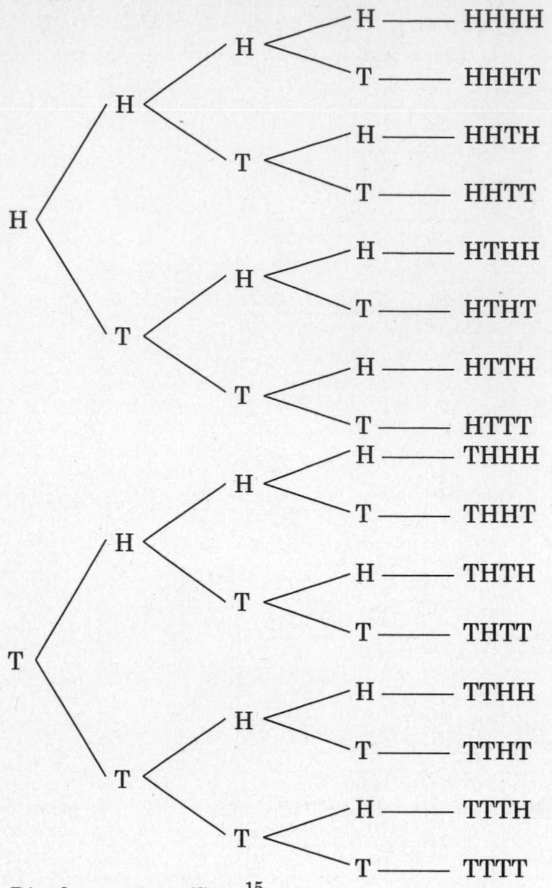

$P(\text{at least one tail}) = \frac{15}{16}$

63. $6x - 3y = 6$
$-3y = -6x + 6$
$y = 2x - 2$

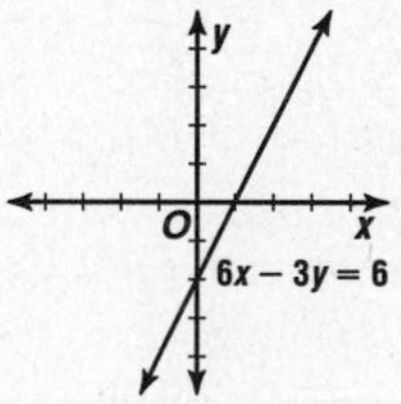

64. $\frac{\text{change in } b}{\text{change in } a} = \frac{4-1}{2-1} = 3$
$b = 3a - 2$

65.

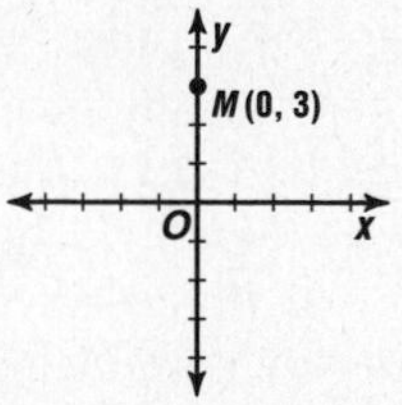

66. $\sin Y = \frac{8}{17} \approx 0.471$
$\cos Y = \frac{15}{17} \approx 0.882$
$\tan Y = \frac{8}{15} \approx 0.533$

67. mean: $\frac{257.6}{50} = 5.14$
median: 3.6
mode: 0.6

68a. $a + 10$

68b. $a + 1$

68c. no; $12 - 4 \neq 10$

10-5 Perfect Squares and Factoring

Page 591 Check for Understanding

1a.

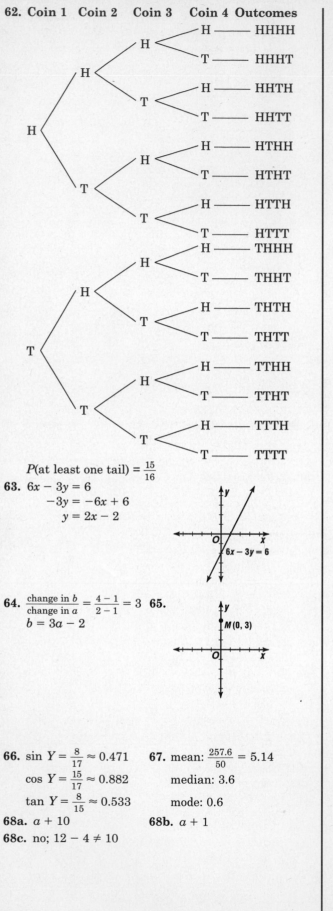

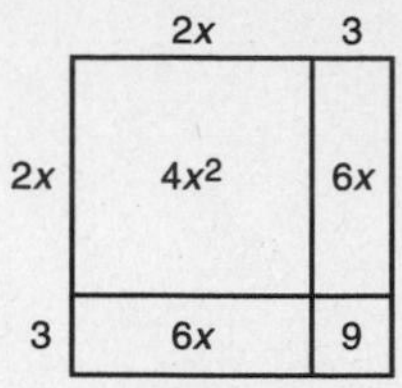

1b. It is a trinomial that can be represented by a square.

2a. See students' work.

2b. Sample answer: $x^2 + 2x + 1 = (x + 1)^2$

3a. Factor out the GCF of the terms.

3b. The other factoring patterns will be more apparent after the GCF has been factored out.

4. Samuel; $(a^2 - 1)$ can be factored as $(a - 1)(a + 1)$.

5. Multiplying and factoring polynomials are inverse operations; see students' work.

6. 5 **7.** $8a$ **8.** $9n$ **9.** $6c$

10. $t^2 + 18t + 81 = (t)^2 + 2(t)(9) + (9)^2$
$= (t + 9)^2$
yes; $(t + 9)^2$

11. $4n^2 - 28n + 49 = (2n)^2 - 2(2n)(7) + (7)^2$
$= (2n - 7)^2$
yes; $(2n - 7)^2$

12. -25 is not a perfect square; no

13. $16b^2 - 56bc + 49c^2 = (4b)^2 - 2(4b)(7c) + (7c)^2$
$= (4b - 7c)^2$
yes; $(4b - 7c)^2$

14. $15g^2 + 25 = 5(3g^2 + 5)$

15. $4a^2 - 36b^2 = 4(a^2 - 9b^2)$
$= 4[(a)^2 - (3b)^2]$
$= 4(a - 3b)(a + 3b)$

16. prime

17. $50g^2 + 40g + 8 = 2(25g^2 + 20g + 4)$
$= 2[(5g)^2 + 2(5g)(2) + (2)^2]$
$= 2(5g + 2)^2$

18. $9t^3 + 66t^2 - 48t = 3t(3t^2 + 22t - 16)$
$= 3t[3t^2 + (24 - 2)t - 16]$
$= 3t(3t^2 + 24t - 2t - 16)$
$= 3t[3t(t + 8) - 2(t + 8)]$
$= 3t(3t - 2)(t + 8)$

19. $20a^2x - 4a^2y - 45xb^2 + 9yb^2$
$= (20a^2x - 4a^2y) + (-45xb^2 + 9yb^2)$
$= 4a^2(5x - y) - 9b^2(5x - y)$
$= (4a^2 - 9b^2)(5x - y)$
$= [(2a)^2 - (3b)^2](5x - y)$
$= (2a - 3b)(2a + 3b)(5x - y)$

20a. Let v^2 = the missing value.
$24x = 2(3x)(v)$
$24x = 6xv$
$\frac{24x}{6x} = v$
$4 = v$
$16 = v^2$
The missing value is 16.

20b.

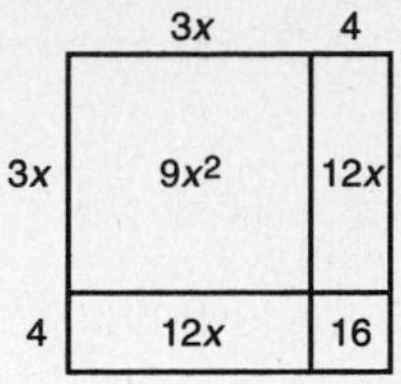

Pages 591–593 Exercises

21. $r^2 - 8r + 16 = (r)^2 - 2(r)(4) + (4)^2$
$= (r - 4)^2$
yes; $(r - 4)^2$

22. $50d \stackrel{?}{=} 2(d)(15)$
$50d \neq 30d$ no

23. $49p^2 - 28p + 4 = (7p)^2 - 2(7p)(2) + (2)^2$
$= (7p - 2)^2$
yes; $(7p - 2)^2$

24. $4y^2 + 12yz + 9z^2 = (2y)^2 + 2(2y)(3z) + (3z)^2$
$= (2y + 3z)^2$
yes; $(2y + 3z)^2$

25. $42st \stackrel{?}{=} 2(7s)(6t)$
$42st \neq 84st$ no

26. $-4z^2$ is not a perfect square; no

27. $4m^2 + 4mn + n^2 = (2m)^2 + 2(2m)(n) + (n)^2$
$= (2m + n)^2$
yes; $(2m + n)^2$

28. $81t^2 - 180t + 100 = (9t)^2 - 2(9t)(10) + (10)^2$
$= (9t - 10)^2$
yes; $(9t - 10)^2$

29. $2g^2$ is not a perfect square; no

30. $1 + 100h^2 + 20h = 100h^2 + 20h + 1$
$= (10h)^2 + 2(10h)(1) + (1)^2$
$= (10h + 1)^2$
yes; $(10h + 1)^2$

31. $72b \stackrel{?}{=} 2(8b)(9)$
$72b \neq 144b$ no

32. $9a^2 - 24a + 16 = (3a)^2 - 2(3a)(4) + (4)^2$
$= (3a - 4)^2$
yes; $(3a - 4)^2$

33. $\frac{1}{4}a^2 + 3a + 9 = \left(\frac{1}{2}a\right)^2 + 2\left(\frac{1}{2}a\right)(3) + (3)^2$
$= \left(\frac{1}{2}a + 3\right)^2$
yes; $\left(\frac{1}{2}a + 3\right)^2$

34. $\frac{4}{9}x^2 - \frac{16}{3}x + 16 = \left(\frac{2}{3}x\right)^2 - 2\left(\frac{2}{3}x\right)(4) + (4)^2$
$= \left(\frac{2}{3}x - 4\right)^2$
yes; $\left(\frac{2}{3}x - 4\right)^2$

35. $45a^2 - 32ab = a(45a - 32b)$

36. $c^2 - 5c + 6 = c^2 + (-2 - 3)c + 6$
$= (c^2 - 2c) + (-3c + 6)$
$= c(c - 2) - 3(c - 2)$
$= (c - 3)(c - 2)$

37. $v^2 - 30v + 225 = (v)^2 - 2(v)(15) + (15)^2$
$= (v - 15)^2$

38. $m^2 - p^4 = (m)^2 - (p^2)^2$
$= (m - p^2)(m + p^2)$

39. prime

40. $3a^2b + 6ab + 9ab^2 = 3ab(a) + 3ab(2) + 3ab(3b)$
$= 3ab(a + 2 + 3b)$

41. $3y^2 - 147 = 3(y^2 - 49)$
$= 3[(y)^2 - (7)^2]$
$= 3(y - 7)(y + 7)$

42. $20n^2 + 34n + 6 = 2(10n^2 + 17n + 3)$
$= 2[10n^2 + (15 + 2)n + 3]$
$= 2[10n^2 + 15n + 2n + 3]$
$= 2[5n(2n + 3) + 1(2n + 3)]$
$= 2(5n + 1)(2n + 3)$

43. $18a^2 - 48a + 32 = 2(9a^2 - 24a + 16)$
$= 2[(3a)^2 - 2(3a)(4) + (4)^2]$
$= 2(3a - 4)^2$

44. $3m^3 + 48m^2n + 192mn^2$
$= 3m(m^2 + 16mn + 64n^2)$
$= 3m[(m)^2 + 2(m)(8n) + (8n)^2]$
$= 3m(m + 8n)^2$

45. $x^2y^2 - y^2 - z^2 + x^2z^2 = (x^2y^2 - y^2) + (-z^2 + x^2z^2)$
$= y^2(x^2 - 1) + z^2(-1 + x^2)$
$= y^2(x^2 - 1) + z^2(x^2 - 1)$
$= (y^2 + z^2)(x^2 - 1)$
$= (y^2 + z^2)(x - 1)(x + 1)$

46. prime

47. $4a^3 + 3a^2b^2 + 8a + 6b^2$
$= (4a^3 + 3a^2b^2) + (8a + 6b^2)$
$= a^2(4a + 3b^2) + 2(4a + 3b^2)$
$= (a^2 + 2)(4a + 3b^2)$

48. $(x + y)^2 - (w - z)^2$
$= [(x + y) - (w - z)][(x + y) + (w - z)]$
$= (x + y - w + z)(x + y + w - z)$

49. $0.7p^2 - 3.5pq + 4.2q^2$
$= 0.7(p^2 - 5pq + 6q^2)$
$= 0.7[p^2 + (-2 - 3)pq + 6q^2]$
$= 0.7(p^2 - 2pq - 3pq + 6q^2)$
$= 0.7[p(p - 2q) - 3q(p - 2q)]$
$= 0.7(p - 3q)(p - 2q)$

50. $(x + 2y)^2 - 3(x + 2y) + 2$
$= [(x + 2y)^2 + (-2 - 1)(x + 2y) + 2]$
$= [(x + 2y)^2 - 2(x + 2y) - 1(x + 2y) + 2]$
$= [(x + 2y)(x + 2y - 2) - 1(x + 2y - 2)]$
$= (x + 2y - 1)(x + 2y - 2)$

51. $g^4 + 6g^3 + 9g^2 - 3g^2h - 18gh - 27h$
$= g^2(g^2 + 6g + 9) - 3h(g^2 + 6g + 9)$
$= (g^2 - 3h)(g^2 + 6g + 9)$
$= (g^2 - 3h)[(g)^2 + 2(g)(3) + (3)^2]$
$= (g^2 - 3h)(g + 3)^2$

52. $12mp^2 - 15np^2 - 16m + 20np - 16mp + 20n$
$= (12mp^2 - 16mp - 16m) + (-15np^2 + 20np + 20n)$
$= 4m(3p^2 - 4p - 4) - 5n(3p^2 - 4p - 4)$
$= (4m - 5n)(3p^2 - 4p - 4)$
$= (4m - 5n)[3p^2 + (-6 + 2)p - 4]$
$= (4m - 5n)(3p^2 - 6p + 2p - 4)$
$= (4m - 5n)[3p(p - 2) + 2(p - 2)]$
$= (4m - 5n)(3p + 2)(p - 2)$

53. $25t^2 - kt + 121 = (5t)^2 + 2(55)(t) + (11)^2$
$-kt = 2(55)t$
$-kt = 110t$
$k = -110$
$25t^2 - kt + 121 = (5t)^2 - 2(55)(t) + (11)^2$
$-kt = -2(55)t$
$-kt = -110t$
$k = 110$
$-110, 110$

54. $64x^2 - 16xy + k = (8x)^2 - 2(8x)(y) + (y)^2$
$k = y^2$

55. $ka^2 - 72ab + 144b^2 = (3a)^2 - 2(12)(3)ab + (12b)^2$
$ka^2 = (3a)^2$
$ka^2 = 9a^2$
$k = 9$

56. $169n^2 + knp + 100p^2$
$= (13n)^2 - 2(13n)(10p) + (10p)^2$
$knp = -2(13n)(10p)$
$knp = -260np$
$k = 260$
$169n^2 + knp + 100p^2$
$= (13n)^2 + 2(13n)(10p) + (10p)^2$
$knp = 2(13n)(10p)$
$knp = 260np$
$k = 260$
$-260, 260$

57. $A = \pi r^2 = (9y^2 + 78y + 169)\pi$
$\pi r^2 = [(3y)^2 + 2(3y)(13) + (13)^2]\pi$
$\pi r^2 = (3y + 13)^2\pi$
$r = 3y + 13$
$d = 2r$
$= 2(3y + 13)$
$= (6y + 26)$ cm

58. $x^3y - 63y^2 + 7x^2 - 9xy^3$
$= (x^3y + 7x^2) + (-9xy^3 - 63y^2)$
$= x^2(xy + 7) - 9y^2(xy + 7)$
$= (x^2 - 9y^2)(xy + 7)$
$= [(x)^2 - (3y)^2](xy + 7)$
$= (x - 3y)(x + 3y)(xy + 7)$
$(x - 3y)$ in., $(x + 3y)$ in., $(xy + 7)$ in.

59. $(16x^2 - 56x + 49) = (4x)^2 - 2(4x)(7) + (7)^2$
$= (4x - 7)^2$
$A = \frac{1}{2}(4x - 7 + 3)(4x - 7)$
$= \frac{1}{2}(4x - 4)(4x - 7)$
$= (2x - 2)(4x - 7)$
$= 8x^2 - 14x - 8x + 14$
$= (8x^2 - 22x + 14)$ cm^2

60. $(81 - 90x + 25x^2) = 25x^2 - 90x + 81$
$= (5x - 9)^2$
Length of side is $5x - 9$.
If $x = 2$, $5x - 9 = 5(2) - 9 = 1$.
Smallest possible perimeter is $4 \cdot 1 = 4$ m.

61a. $\sqrt{a^2 - 2ab + b^2} = \sqrt{(a - b)^2}$
$a - b \geq 0$
$a \geq b$

61b. $\sqrt{(a - b)^2} = -(a - b)$ if $a - b \leq 0$
$a \leq b$

61c. if $a - b = 0$ or $a = b$

62. $(w)^2 + 2(w)(30) + (30)^2 = (w + 30)^2$
$(w + 30)$ yd

63a. $p + 2pr + pr^2$
$= 1000 + 2(1000)(0.08) + (1000)(0.08)^2$
$= 1000 + 160 + 6.4$
$= \$1166.40$

63b. $p + 2pr + pr^2 = p(1 + 2r + r^2)$
$= p[1 + 2(1)(r) + (r)^2]$
$= p(1 + r)^2$

63c. $p(1 + r)^2 = 1000(1 + 0.7)^2$
$= 1000(1.07)^2$
$= \$1144.90$

63d. See students' work.

64. $45x^2 - 20y^2z^2 = 5(9x^2 - 4y^2z^2)$
$= 5[(3x)^2 - (2yz)^2]$
$= 5(3x - 2yz)(3x + 2yz)$

65. $2.5t(8t - 12) + 5.1(6t^2 + 10t - 20)$
$= 20t^2 - 30t + 30.6t^2 + 51t - 102$
$= 50.6t^2 + 21t - 102$

66. $(3a^2)(4a^3) = (3 \cdot 4)(a^2 \cdot a^3)$
$= 12a^{2+3}$
$= 12a^5$

67. Let x = the number of hours he works at the store and let y = the hours he mows the lawn.
$x + y \leq 30$
$5x + 7.5y \geq 175$
$y < 20$
He could work 20 hours.

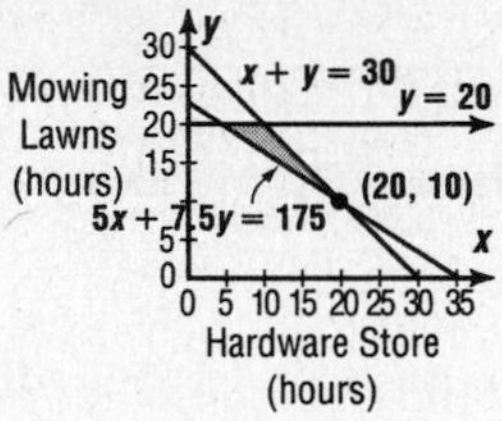

68. $F = \frac{9}{5}C + 32$
$F \geq \frac{9}{5}(35) + 32$ and $F \leq \frac{9}{5}(40) + 32$
$F \geq 9(7) + 32$ $\quad F \leq 9(8) + 32$
$F \geq 63 + 32$ $\quad F \leq 72 + 32$
$F \geq 95°$ $\quad F \leq 104°$
$95° \leq F \leq 104°$

69a.

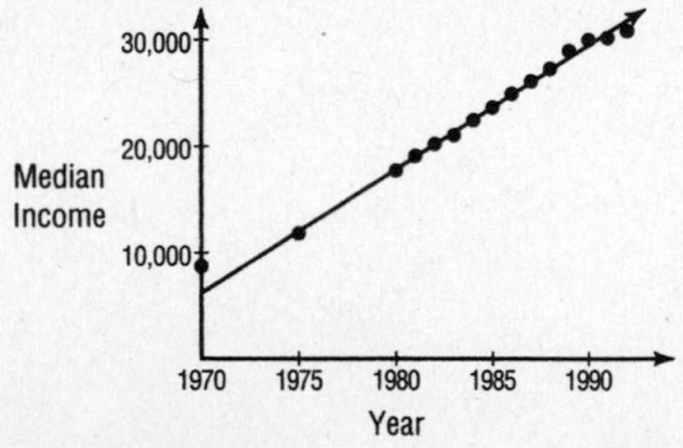

69b. Sample answer: Yes; $I = 1200y + 6000$, where I is the median income and y is the number of years since 1970.

69c. See students' work.

70. range = greatest value − least value
$= 31.2 - 0.5$
$= 30.7$
interquartile range $= Q_3 - Q_1$
$= 6 - 1.4$
$= 4.6$

71. odds of selecting a club
= number of clubs:number of non-clubs
= 13:39
= 1:3

72. $\frac{5}{11} = \frac{b}{14}$ $\qquad$ $\frac{5}{11} = \frac{c}{6}$
$70 = 11b$ $\qquad$ $30 = 11c$
$\frac{70}{11} = b$ $\qquad$ $\frac{30}{11} = c$

73. Let x = the height of the statue.
Then $x - 2$ = the height of the pedestal.
$x + (x - 2) = 302$
$2x - 2 = 302$
$2x = 304$
$x = 152$
The statue is 152 ft tall.

74. $82(50.4) = 4132.8$
4133 points

10-6 Solving Equations by Factoring

Page 598 Check for Understanding

1. At least one of the factors equals 0.
2. equations that can be written as a product of factors that equal 0
3. No; the division would eliminate -3 as a solution.
4. Caitlin; the zero product property only works for 0. If you multiply two numbers and get 8, that does not mean one of the numbers must have been 8.
5. $g(g + 5) = 0$
$g = 0$ or $g + 5 = 0$
$g = -5$
The solution set is $\{0, -5\}$.
6. $(n - 4)(n + 2) = 0$
$n - 4 = 0$ or $n + 2 = 0$
$n = 4$ $\qquad$ $n = -2$
The solution set is $\{4, -2\}$.
7. $5m = 3m^2$
$0 = 3m^2 - 5m$
$0 = m(3m - 5)$
$m = 0$ or $3m - 5 = 0$
$3m = 5$
$m = \frac{5}{3}$
The solution set is $\left\{0, \frac{5}{3}\right\}$.
8. $x^2 = 5x + 14$
$x^2 - 5x - 14 = 0$
$(x + 2)(x - 7) = 0$
$x + 2 = 0$ or $x - 7 = 0$
$x = -2$ $\qquad$ $x = 7$
The solution set is $\{-2, 7\}$.
9. $7r^2 = 70r - 175$
$7r^2 - 70r + 175 = 0$
$7(r^2 - 10r + 25) = 0$
$7(r - 5)(r - 5) = 0$
$r - 5 = 0$
$r = 5$
The solution set is $\{5\}$.
10. $a^3 - 29a^2 = -28a$
$a^3 - 29a^2 + 28a = 0$
$a(a^2 - 29a + 28) = 0$
$a(a - 1)(a - 28) = 0$
$a = 0$ or $a - 1 = 0$ or $a - 28 = 0$
$a = 1$ $\qquad$ $a = 28$
The solution set is $\{0, 1, 28\}$.
11. $(2x - 1)(2x + 9) - x(x) = 195$
$4x^2 + 18x - 2x - 9 - x^2 = 195$
$3x^2 + 16x - 9 = 195$
$3x^2 + 16x - 204 = 0$
$(3x + 34)(x - 6) = 0$
$3x + 34 = 0$ or $x - 6 = 0$
$3x = -34$ $\qquad$ $x = 6$
$x = \frac{-34}{3}$
$x = 6$

12a. $h = vt - 16t^2$
$0 = 151t - 16t^2$
$0 = t(151 - 16t)$
$t = 0$ or $151 - 16t = 0$
$151 - 16l$
$9.4375 = t$
about 9.44 seconds

12b. $t \approx \frac{1}{2}(9.44) = 4.72$ sec
$h = vt - 16t^2$
$h = 151(4.72) - 16(4.72)^2$
$h = 356$ feet

Pages 598–600 Exercises

13. $x(x - 24) = 0$
$x = 0$ or $x - 24 = 0$
$x = 24$
The solution set is $\{0, 24\}$.
14. $(q + 4)(3q - 15) = 0$
$q + 4 = 0$ or $3q - 15 = 0$
$q = -4$ $\qquad$ $3q = 15$
$q = 5$
The solution set is $\{-4, 5\}$.
15. $(2x - 3)(3x - 8) = 0$
$2x - 3 = 0$ or $3x - 8 = 0$
$2x = 3$ $\qquad$ $3x = 8$
$x = \frac{3}{2}$ $\qquad$ $x = \frac{8}{3}$
The solution set is $\left\{\frac{3}{2}, \frac{8}{3}\right\}$.
16. $(4a + 5)(3a - 7) = 0$
$4a + 5 = 0$ or $3a - 7 = 0$
$4a = -5$ $\qquad$ $3a = 7$
$a = -\frac{5}{4}$ $\qquad$ $a = \frac{7}{3}$
The solution set is $\left\{-\frac{5}{4}, \frac{7}{3}\right\}$.
17. $a^2 + 13a + 36 = 0$
$(a + 9)(a + 4) = 0$
$a + 9 = 0$ or $a + 4 = 0$
$a = -9$ $\qquad$ $a = -4$
The solution set is $\{-9, -4\}$.
18. $x^2 - x - 56 = 0$
$(x + 7)(x - 8) = 0$
$x + 7 = 0$ or $x - 8 = 0$
$x = -7$ $\qquad$ $x = 8$
The solution set is $\{-7, 8\}$.

19. $y^2 - 64 = 0$
$(y+8)(y-8) = 0$
$y + 8 = 0$ or $y - 8 = 0$
$y = -8$ $y = 8$
The solution set is $\{-8, 8\}$.

20. $5s - 2s^2 = 0$
$s(5 - 2s) = 0$
$s = 0$ or $5 - 2s = 0$
$5 = 2s$
$\frac{5}{2} = s$
The solution set is $\left\{0, \frac{5}{2}\right\}$.

21. $3z^2 = 12z$
$3z^2 - 12z = 0$
$3z(z - 4) = 0$
$3z = 0$ or $z - 4 = 0$
$z = 0$ $z = 4$
The solution set is $\{0, 4\}$.

22. $m^2 - 24m = -124$
$m^2 - 24m + 124 = 0$
$(m - 12)^2 = 0$
$(m - 12)(m - 12) = 0$
$m - 12 = 0$
$m = 12$
The solution set is $\{12\}$.

23. $6q^2 + 5 = -17q$
$6q^2 + 17q + 5 = 0$
$(3q + 1)(2q + 5) = 0$
$3q + 1 = 0$ or $2q + 5 = 0$
$3q = -1$ $2q = -5$
$q = -\frac{1}{3}$ $q = -\frac{5}{2}$
The solution set is $\left\{-\frac{1}{3}, -\frac{5}{2}\right\}$.

24. $5b^3 + 34b^2 = 7b$
$5b^3 + 34b^2 - 7b = 0$
$b(5b^2 + 34b - 7) = 0$
$b(5b - 1)(b + 7) = 0$
$b = 0$ or $5b - 1 = 0$ or $b + 7 = 0$
$5b = 1$ $b = -7$
$b = \frac{1}{5}$
The solution set is $\left\{-7, 0, \frac{1}{5}\right\}$.

25. $\frac{x^2}{12} - \frac{2x}{3} - 4 = 0$
$x^2 - 8x - 48 = 0$
$(x - 12)(x + 4) = 0$
$x - 12 = 0$ or $x + 4 = 0$
$x = 12$ $x = -4$
The solution set is $\{12, -4\}$.

26. $t^2 - \frac{t}{6} = \frac{35}{6}$
$6t^2 - t = 35$
$6t^2 - t - 35 = 0$
$(3t + 7)(2t - 5) = 0$
$3t + 7 = 0$ or $2t - 5 = 0$
$3t = -7$ $2t = 5$
$t = -\frac{7}{3}$ $t = \frac{5}{2}$
The solution set is $\left\{-\frac{7}{3}, \frac{5}{2}\right\}$.

27. $n^3 - 81n = 0$
$n(n^2 - 81) = 0$
$n(n - 9)(n + 9) = 0$
$n = 0$ or $n - 9 = 0$ or $n + 9 = 0$
$n = 9$ $n = -9$
The solution set is $\{-9, 0, 9\}$.

28. $(x + 8)(x + 1) = -12$
$x^2 + 8x + x + 8 = -12$
$x^2 + 9x + 8 = -12$
$x^2 + 9x + 20 = 0$
$(x + 4)(x + 5) = 0$
$x + 4 = 0$ or $x + 5 = 0$
$x = -4$ $x = -5$
The solution set is $\{-4, -5\}$.

29. $(r - 1)(r - 1) = 36$
$r^2 - r - r + 1 = 36$
$r^2 - 2r + 1 = 36$
$r^2 - 2r - 35 = 0$
$(r + 5)(r - 7) = 0$
$r + 5 = 0$ or $r - 7 = 0$
$r = -5$ $r = 7$
The solution set is $\{-5, 7\}$.

30. $(3y + 2)(y + 3) = y + 14$
$3y^2 + 9y + 2y + 6 = y + 14$
$3y^2 + 11y + 6 = y + 14$
$3y^2 + 10y - 8 = 0$
$(y + 4)(3y - 2) = 0$
$y + 4 = 0$ or $3y - 2 = 0$
$y = -4$ $3y = 2$
$y = \frac{2}{3}$
The solution set is $\left\{-4, \frac{2}{3}\right\}$.

31. Let x = the first of two consecutive even integers.
Then $x + 2$ = the second even integer.
$x(x + 2) = 168$ If $x = -14$,
$x^2 + 2x = 168$ $x + 2 = -14 + 2 = -12$.
$x^2 + 2x - 168 = 0$ If $x = 12$
$(x + 14)(x - 12) = 0$ $x + 2 = 12 + 2 = 14$
$x + 14 = 0$ or $x - 12 = 0$
$x = -14$ $x = 12$
-14 and -12 or 12 and 14

32. Let x = the first of two consecutive odd integers.
Then $x + 2$ = the second odd integer.
$x(x + 2) = 1023$ If $x = -33$,
$x^2 + 2x = 1023$ $x + 2 = -33 + 2 = -31$
$x^2 + 2x - 1023 = 0$ If $x = 31$,
$(x + 33)(x - 31) = 0$ $x + 2 = 31 + 2 = 33$
$x + 33 = 0$ or $x - 31 = 0$
$x = -33$ $x = 31$
-33 and -31 or 31 and 33

33. $A = \frac{1}{2}bh$
$40 = \frac{1}{2}(2h + 6)(h)$
$40 = (h + 3)h$
$40 = h^2 + 3h$
$0 = h^2 + 3h - 40$
$0 = (h + 8)(h - 5)$
$h + 8 = 0$ or $h - 5 = 0$
$h = -8$ $h = 5$
The height is 5 cm.

34. $x = 0, x = -3, \quad x = 7$

$x + 3 = 0 \quad x - 7 = 0$

$x(x + 3)(x - 7) = 0$

$x(x^2 - 7x + 3x - 21) = 0$

$x(x^2 - 4x - 21) = 0$

$x^3 - 4x^2 - 21x = 0$

35a. $a^2 + 5a = 6$

$a^2 + 5a - 6 = 0$

$(a + 6)(a - 1) = 0$

$a + 6 = 0$ or $a - 1 = 0$

$a = -6 \quad a = 1$

$\{-6, 1\}$

$|2x + 5| = 7$

$2x + 5 = 7$ or $2x + 5 = -7$

$2x = 2 \quad 2x = -12$

$x = 1 \quad x = -6$

$\{-6, 1\}$

35b. They are equivalent; they have the same solutions.

36. $P = 2\ell + 2w \quad A = \ell w$

$30 = 2\ell + 2w \quad 54 = \ell(15 - \ell)$

$15 = \ell + w \quad 54 = 15\ell - \ell^2$

$15 - \ell = w \quad \ell^2 - 15\ell + 54 = 0$

$(\ell - 9)(\ell - 6) = 0$

$\ell - 9 = 0$ or $\ell - 6 = 0$

$\ell = 9 \quad \ell = 6$

$15 - \ell = 15 - 9 = 6$

The dimensions should be 9 ft by 6 ft.

37a. $h = 16t^2$

$180 = 16t^2$

$11.25 = t^2$

$3.35 = t$

about 3.35 s

37b. His ideas about falling objects differed from what most people thought to be true. He believed that Earth is a moving planet and that the sun and planets did not revolve around Earth.

38. Sample answer: Agree, since a nozzle speed of 215.16 ft/s should launch an object to a height of about 723 ft in a vacuum. Because of wind resistance, it may only go to 625 feet.

39. $h = vt - 16t^2$

$0 = 2400t - 16t^2$

$0 = 16t(150 - t)$

$16t = 0$ or $150 - t = 0$

$t = 0 \quad 150 = t$

$t = \frac{1}{2}(150) = 75$

$h = vt - 16t^2 + 180$

$h = 2400(75) - 16(75)^2 + 180$

$h = 1{,}800{,}000 - 90{,}000 + 180$

$h \approx 90{,}180$ ft or $\frac{90{,}180}{5280} = 17$ mi

40. $h = 16t^2$

$880 = 16t^2$

$55 = t^2$

$7.4 = t$

Yes, the keys will hit the river within 8 seconds.

41. Let x = the width of the strip.

$(6 - 2x)(5 - 2x) = \frac{2}{3}(30)$

$30 - 12x - 10x + 4x^2 = 10$

$4x^2 - 22x + 30 = 10$

$4x^2 - 22x + 20 = 0$

$2(2x^2 - 11x + 10) = 0$

$2(2x - 1)(x - 5) = 0$

$2x - 1 = 0 \quad x - 5 = 0$

$2x = 1 \quad x = 5$

$x = \frac{1}{2}$ or 0.5

The width of the strip of land is 0.5 km.

42. $100x^2 + 20x + 1 = (10x)^2 + 2(10x)(1) + (1)^2$

$= (10x + 1)^2$

43. $(5q + 2r)(8q - 3r) = 40q^2 - 15qr + 16qr - 6r^2$

$= 40q^2 + qr - 6r^2$

44. $9x + 4 < 7 - 13x$

$22x + 4 < 7$

$22x < 3$

$x < \frac{3}{22}$

$\left\{x \mid x < \frac{3}{22}\right\}$

45. $2x - 7y = 28$

Let $y = 0$. | Let $x = 0$:

$2x - 7(0) = 28 \quad 2(0) - 7y = 28$

$2x = 24 \quad -7y = 28$

$x = 14 \quad y = -4$

x-intercept: 14 | y-intercept: -4

46.

s	4	2	0	−2	−4
$r(s)$	19	11	3	−5	−13

$\frac{\text{change in } r(s)}{\text{change in } s} = \frac{11 - 19}{2 - 4} = \frac{-8}{-2} = 4$

$r(s) = 4s + 3$

$r(-2) = 4(2) + 3 \quad r(-4) = 4(-4) + 3$

$= -8 + 3 \quad = -16 + 3$

$= -5 \quad = -13$

47. $\frac{60 \text{ mi}}{1 \text{ hr}} \cdot \frac{5280 \text{ ft}}{1 \text{ mi}} \cdot \frac{1 \text{ hr}}{60 \text{ min}} = 5280$ ft/sec

$d = rt$

$22{,}996 = 5280t$

$4.355 \approx t$

4.355 minutes or about 4 minutes 21 seconds

48. $400 + 9x = 12(x + 25) \quad 400 + 9\left(\frac{100}{3}\right)$

$400 + 9x = 12x + 300 \quad = 400 + 300$

$100 = 3x \quad = 700$

$\frac{100}{3} = x$

The sofa costs \$700.

Chapter 10 Highlights

Page 601 Understanding and Using the Vocabulary

1. false, composite
2. true
3. false, sample answer: 64
4. true
5. false, $2^4 \cdot 3$

6. false, difference of squares
7. true
8. false, sample answer: $x^2 + 2x + 2$
9. false, zero product property
10. true

Chapter 10 Study Guide and Assessment

Pages 602–604 Skills and Concepts

11. composite
$28 = 2 \cdot 14$
$= 2 \cdot 2 \cdot 7$ or $2^2 \cdot 7$

12. composite
$33 = 3 \cdot 11$

13. composite
$150 = 2 \cdot 75$
$= 2 \cdot 3 \cdot 25$
$= 2 \cdot 3 \cdot 5 \cdot 5$ or $2 \cdot 3 \cdot 5^2$

14. prime

15. prime

16. composite
$378 = 2 \cdot 189$
$= 2 \cdot 3 \cdot 63$
$= 2 \cdot 3 \cdot 3 \cdot 21$
$= 2 \cdot 3 \cdot 3 \cdot 3 \cdot 7$ or $2 \cdot 3^3 \cdot 7$

17. $35 = ⑤ \cdot 7$
$30 = 2 \cdot 3 \cdot ⑤$
GCF: 5

18. $12 = ② \cdot 2 \cdot 3$
$18 = ② \cdot 3 \cdot 3$
$40 = ② \cdot 2 \cdot 2 \cdot 5$
GCF: 2

19. $12ab = ② \cdot ② \cdot 3 \cdot ⓐ \cdot ⓑ$
$-4a^2b^2 = -1 \cdot ② \cdot ② \cdot ⓐ \cdot a \cdot ⓑ \cdot b$
GCF: $2 \cdot 2 \cdot a \cdot b$ or $4ab$

20. $16mrt = ② \cdot 2 \cdot 2 \cdot 2 \cdot ⓜ \cdot ⓡ \cdot t$
$30m^2r = ② \cdot 3 \cdot 5 \cdot m \cdot ⓜ \cdot ⓡ$
GCF: $2mr$

21. $20n^2 = 2 \cdot 2 \cdot ⑤ \cdot ⓝ \cdot n$
$25np^5 = 5 \cdot ⑤ \cdot ⓝ \cdot p \cdot p \cdot p \cdot p \cdot p$
GCF: $5n$

22. $60x^2y^2 = 2 \cdot 2 \cdot 3 \cdot ⑤ \cdot ⓧ \cdot x \cdot y \cdot y$
$35xz^3 = ⑤ \cdot 7 \cdot ⓧ \cdot z \cdot z \cdot z$
GCF: $5x$

23. $56x^3y = 2 \cdot 2 \cdot 2 \cdot ⑦ \cdot ⓧ \cdot ⓧ \cdot x \cdot y$
$49ax^2 = 7 \cdot ⑦ \cdot a \cdot ⓧ \cdot ⓧ$
GCF: $7 \cdot x \cdot x$ or $7x^2$

24. $6a^2 = 2 \cdot ③ \cdot a \cdot a$
$18b^2 = 2 \cdot ③ \cdot 3 \cdot b \cdot b$
$9b^3 = 3 \cdot ③ \cdot b \cdot b \cdot b$
GCF: 3

25. $13x = ⑬ \cdot x$
$26y = 2 \cdot ⑬ \cdot y$
GCF: 13
$13x + 26y = 13(x) + 13(2y)$
$= 13(x + 2y)$

26. $6x^2y = ② \cdot ③ \cdot x \cdot x \cdot y$
$12xy = ② \cdot 2 \cdot ③ \cdot x \cdot y$
$6 = ② \cdot ③$
GCF: $2 \cdot 3$ or 6
$6x^2y + 12xy + 6 = 6(x^2y) + 6(2xy) + 6(1)$
$= 6(x^2y + 2xy + 1)$

27. $24a^2b^2 = 2 \cdot ② \cdot 2 \cdot ③ \cdot ⓐ \cdot a \cdot ⓑ \cdot b$
$-18ab = -1 \cdot ② \cdot ③ \cdot 3 \cdot ⓐ \cdot ⓑ$
GCF: $2 \cdot 3 \cdot a \cdot b = 6ab$
$24a^2b^2 - 18ab = 6ab(4ab) - 6ab(3)$
$= 6ab(4ab - 3)$

28. $26ab = ② \cdot 13 \cdot ⓐ \cdot b$
$18ac = ② \cdot 3 \cdot 3 \cdot ⓐ \cdot c$
$32a^2 = ② \cdot 2 \cdot 2 \cdot 2 \cdot 2 \cdot ⓐ \cdot a$
GCF: $2a$
$26ab + 18ac + 32a^2 = 2a(13b) + 2a(9c) + 2a\,(16a)$
$= 2a(13b + 9c + 16a)$

29. $36p^2q^2 = ② \cdot ② \cdot 3 \cdot ③ \cdot ⓟ \cdot p \cdot ⓠ \cdot q$
$-12pq = -1 \cdot ② \cdot ② \cdot ③ \cdot ⓟ \cdot ⓠ$
GCF: $2 \cdot 2 \cdot 3 \cdot p \cdot q$ or $12pq$
$36p^2q^2 - 12pq = 12pq(3pq) + 12pq(-1)$
$= 12pq(3pq - 1)$

30. $a = ⓐ$
$a^2b = ⓐ \cdot a \cdot b$
$a^3b^3 = ⓐ \cdot a \cdot a \cdot b \cdot b \cdot b$
GCF: a
$a + a^2b + a^3b^3 = a(1) + a(ab) + a(a^2b^3)$
$= a(1 + ab + a^2b^3)$

31. $a^2 - 4ac + ab - 4bc = (a^2 - 4ac) + (ab - 4bc)$
$= a(a - 4c) + b(a - 4c)$
$= (a + b)(a - 4c)$

32. $4rs + 12ps + 2mr + 6mp$
$= (4rs + 12ps) + (2mr + 6mp)$
$= 4s(r + 3p) + 2m(r + 3p)$
$= (4s + 2m)(r + 3p)$
$= 2(2s + m)(r + 3p)$

33. $16k^3 - 4k^2p^2 - 28kp + 7p^3$
$= (16k^3 - 4k^2p^2) + (-28kp + 7p^3)$
$= 4k^2(4k - p^2) + 7p(-4k + p^2)$
$= 4k^2(4k - p^2) + 7p(-1)(4k - p^2)$
$= 4k^2(4k - p^2) - 7p(4k - p^2)$
$= (4k^2 - 7p)(4k - p^2)$

34. $dm + mr + 7r + 7d = (dm + mr) + (7r + 7d)$
$= m(d + r) + 7(r + d)$
$= (m + 7)(d + r)$

35. $24am - 9an + 40bm - 15bn$
$= (24am - 9an) + (40bm - 15bn)$
$= 3a(8m - 3n) + 5b(8m - 3n)$
$= (3a + 5b)(8m - 3n)$

36. $a^3 - a^2b + ab^2 - b^3 = (a^3 - a^2b) + (ab^2 - b^3)$
$= a^2(a - b) + b^2(a - b)$
$= (a^2 + b^2)(a - b)$

37. $y^2 + 7y + 12 = y^2 + (4 + 3)y + 12$
$= y^2 + 4y + 3y + 12$
$= (y^2 + 4y) + (3y + 12)$
$= y(y + 4) + 3(y + 3)$
$= (y + 3)(y + 4)$

38. $x^2 - 9x - 36 = x^2 + [3 + (-12)]x - 36$
$= x^2 + 3x - 12x - 36$
$= (x^2 + 3x) + (-12x - 36)$
$= x(x + 3) - 12(x + 3)$
$= (x - 12)(x + 3)$

39. prime

40. $b^2 + 5b - 6 = b^2 + (-1 + 6)b - 6$
$= b^2 - b + 6b - 6$
$= (b^2 - b) + (6b - 6)$
$= b(b - 1) + 6(b - 1)$
$= (b + 6)(b - 1)$

41. $2r^2 - 3r - 20 = 2r^2 + [5 + (-8)]r - 20$
$= 2r^2 + 5r - 8r - 20$
$= (2r^2 + 5r) + (-8r - 20)$
$= r(2r + 5) - 4(2r + 5)$
$= (r - 4)(2r + 5)$

42. $3a^2 - 13a + 14 = 3a^2 + [-6 + (-7)]a + 14$
$= 3a^2 - 6a - 7a + 14$
$= (3a^2 - 6a) + (-7a + 14)$
$= 3a(a - 2) - 7(a - 2)$
$= (3a - 7)(a - 2)$

43. $b^2 - 16 = (b)^2 - (4)^2$
$= (b - 4)(b + 4)$

44. $25 - 9y^2 = (5)^2 - (3y)^2$
$= (5 - 3y)(5 + 3y)$

45. $16a^2 - 81b^4 = (4a)^2 - (9b^2)^2$
$= (4a - 9b^2)(4a + 9b^2)$

46. $2y^3 - 128y = 2y(y^2 - 64)$
$= 2y[(y)^2 - (8)^2]$
$= 2y(y - 8)(y + 8)$

47. prime

48. $\frac{1}{4}n^2 - \frac{9}{16}r^2 = \left(\frac{1}{2}n\right)^2 - \left(\frac{3}{4}r\right)^2$
$= \left(\frac{1}{2}n - \frac{3}{4}r\right)\left(\frac{1}{2}n + \frac{3}{4}r\right)$

49. $a^2 + 18a + 81 = (a)^2 + 2(a)(9) + (9)^2$
$= (a + 9)^2$

50. $9k^2 - 12k + 4 = (3k)^2 - 2(3k)(2) + (2)^2$
$= (3k - 2)^2$

51. $4 - 28r + 49r^2 = (2)^2 - 2(2)(7r) + (7r)^2$
$= (2 - 7r)^2$

52. $32n^2 - 80n + 50 = 2(16n^2 - 40n + 25)$
$= 2[(4n)^2 - 2(4n)(5) + (5)^2]$
$= 2(4n - 5)^2$

53. $6b^3 - 24b^2g + 24bg^2 = 6b(b^2 - 4bg + 4g^2)$
$= 6b[(b)^2 - 2(b)(2g) + (2g)^2]$
$= 6b(b - 2g)^2$

54. $49m^2 - 126m + 81 = (7m)^2 - 2(7m)(9) + (9)^2$
$= (7m - 9)^2$

55. $25x^2 - 120x + 144 = (5x)^2 - 2(5x)(12) + (12)^2$
$= (5x - 12)^2$

56. $y(y + 11) = 0$
$y = 0$ or $y + 11 = 0$
$y = -11$
The solution set is $\{0, -11\}$.

57. $(3x - 2)(4x + 7) = 0$
$3x - 2 = 0$ or $4x + 7 = 0$
$3x = 2$; $4x = -7$
$x = \frac{2}{3}$; $x = -\frac{7}{4}$
The solution set is $\left\{\frac{2}{3}, -\frac{7}{4}\right\}$.

58. $2a^2 - 9a = 0$
$a(2a - 9) = 0$
$a = 0$ or $2a - 9 = 0$
$2a = 9$
$a = \frac{9}{2}$
The solution set is $\left\{0, \frac{9}{2}\right\}$.

59. $n^2 = -17n$
$n^2 + 17n = 0$
$n(n + 17) = 0$
$n = 0$ or $n + 17 = 0$
$n = -17$
The solution set is $\{0, -17\}$.

60. $\frac{3}{4}y = \frac{1}{2}y^2$
$0 = \frac{1}{2}y^2 - \frac{3}{4}y$
$0 = \frac{1}{2}y(y - \frac{3}{2})$
$\frac{1}{2}y = 0$ or $y - \frac{3}{2} = 0$
$y = 0$; $y = \frac{3}{2}$
The solution set is $\left\{0, \frac{3}{2}\right\}$.

61. $y^2 + 13y + 40 = 0$
$(y + 5)(y + 8) = 0$
$y + 5 = 0$ or $y + 8 = 0$
$y = -5$; $y = -8$
The solution set is $\{-5, -8\}$.

62. $2m^2 + 13m = 24$
$2m^2 + 13m - 24 = 0$
$(m + 8)(2m - 3) = 0$
$m + 8 = 0$ or $2m - 3 = 0$
$m = -8$; $2m = 3$
$m = \frac{3}{2}$
The solution set is $\left\{-8, \frac{3}{2}\right\}$.

63. $25r^2 + 4 = -20r$
$25r^2 + 20r + 4 = 0$
$(5r + 2)^2 = 0$
$5r + 2 = 0$
$5r = -2$
$r = -\frac{2}{5}$
The solution set is $\left\{-\frac{2}{5}\right\}$.

Page 604 Applications and Problem Solving

64. $4m^2 - 3mp + 3p - 4m$
$= (4m^2 - 3mp) + (3p - 4m)$
$= m(4m - 3p) + 1(3p - 4m)$
$= m(4m - 3p) - 1(4m - 3p)$
$= (m - 1)(4m - 3p)$
$(4m - 3p)$ by $(m - 1)$

65. $(3 \cdot 8 \cdot 4)(4) = 96(4)$
$= 384$
The number is 384.

66. Let x = the original length of sides of photograph.

$$x(x) - (x-2)(x-4) = 64$$
$$x^2 - (x^2 - 4x - 2x + 8) = 64$$
$$x^2 - (x^2 - 6x + 8) = 64$$
$$x^2 - x^2 + 6x - 8 = 64$$
$$6x - 8 = 64$$
$$6x = 72$$
$$x = 12$$

The original dimensions were 12 in. by 12 in.

67.

			3
×		5	4
	1	6	2

68. $A = \ell w$

$16x^2 - 9 = (4x)^2 - (3)^2$
$= (4x+3)(4x-3)$

$P = 2\ell + 2w$
$= 2(4x+3) + 2(4x-3)$
$= 8x + 6 + 8x - 6$
$= 16x$

69. Let x = the first consecutive odd integer and let $x + 2$ = the second integer.

$$x(x+2) = 99$$
$$x^2 + 2x = 99$$
$$x^2 + 2x - 99 = 0$$
$$(x-9)(x+11) = 0$$

$x - 9 = 0$ or $x + 11 = 0$
$x = 9$ $\quad$ $x = -11$
$x + 2 = 9 + 2$ $\quad$ $x + 2 = -11 + 2$
$= 11$ $\quad$ $= -9$

9, 11; −11, −9

Page 605 Alternative Assessment: Thinking Critically

- $24 = 2 \cdot 12 = 4 \cdot 6$ $\quad$ $30 = 3 \cdot 10 = 2 \cdot 15$
  $12 - 2 = 4 + 6$ $\quad$ $15 - 2 = 10 + 3$
  $54 = 3 \cdot 18 = 6 \cdot 9$ $\quad$ $60 = 30 \cdot 2 = 5 \cdot 12$
  $18 - 3 = 6 \cdot 9$ $\quad$ $20 - 3 = 5 + 12$
  $96 = 4 \cdot 24 = 8 \cdot 12$
  $24 - 4 = 8 + 12$
- $x = \frac{2}{3}$ $\quad$ $x = -1$
  $3x = 2$ $\quad$ $x + 1 = 0$
  $3x - 2 = 0$
  $(3x-2)(x+1) = 0$
  $3x^2 + 3x - 2x - 2 = 0$
  $3x^2 + x - 2 = 0$

Cumulative Review, Chapters 1–10

Pages 606–607

1. Let x = the number.

$$8x - x^2 = 2x$$
$$0 = x^2 - 6x$$
$$0 = x(x-6)$$

$x = 0$ or $x - 6 = 0$
$x = 6$

A. 0 or 6

2. C. $|d - 2| \le 0.04$

3. D. $4t(t+3) - (t+1)$

4. $A = \frac{1}{2}h(a+b)$

$\frac{2A}{a+b} = h(a+b)$

$\frac{2A}{a+b} = h$

A. $h = \frac{2A}{a+b}$

5.

	r	t	d
going	42	t	$42t$
coming back	56	$7 - t$	$392 - 56t$

$42t = 392 - 56t$ $\quad$ $42t = d$
$98t = 392$ $\quad$ $42(4) = d$
$t = 4$ $\quad$ $168 = d$

B. 168 miles

6. B. An outlier will only affect the mean of a set of data.

7. $y^2 + 12y + 27 = (y+9)(y+3)$
$6x^2 - 11x + 4 = (3x-4)(2x-1)$
$h^2 + 5h - 8$ $\quad$ prime
$9k^2 + 30km + 25m^2 = (3k+5m)^2$
C. $h^2 + 5h - 8$

8. $m = \frac{5-(-4)}{9-(-3)} = \frac{9}{12}$ or $\frac{3}{4}$

$y = \frac{3}{4}x - \frac{7}{4}$ $\quad$ D

9. $\frac{(b+2)+(b+3)+(b-2)+(b-1)+x}{5} = b + 2$

$$4b + 2 + x = 5(b+2)$$
$$4b + 2 + x = 5b + 10$$
$$x = b + 8 \quad \text{A}$$

10. $P = 4s = 20m + 32p$
$4s = 4(5m + 8p)$
$s = 5m + 8p$
$A = s^2$
$= (5m + 8p)^2$
$= (5m)^2 + 2(5m)(8p) + (8p)^2$
$= 25m^2 + 80mp + 64p^2$

11. Let x = the cost of a cookie.
Then $3x + 4$ = the cost of a pie and
$2(3x + 4)$ = the cost of a cake.

$$2(3x+4) + 3(3x+4) + 4x = 24.75$$
$$6x + 8 + 9x + 12 + 4x = 24.75$$
$$19x + 20 = 24.75$$
$$19x = 4.75$$
$$x = 0.25$$

$3x + 4 = 3(0.25) + 4$ $\quad$ $2(3x+4) = 2[3(0.25) + 4]$
$= 0.75 + 4$ $\quad$ $= 2(4.75)$
$= 4.75$ $\quad$ $= 9.50$

cake: \$9.50, pie: \$4.75, cookie: \$0.25

12. $3g^2 - 10gh - 8h^2 = 3g^2 + (-12 + 2)gh - 8h^2$
$= (3g^2 - 12gh) + (2gh - 8h^2)$
$= 3g(g - 4h) + 2h(g - 4h)$
$= (3g + 2h)(g - 4h)$

13. Let x = the number of notebooks sold at 95¢ and let $264 - x$ = the number sold at \$1.25.

$$\begin{aligned} 0.95x + 1.25(264 - x) &= 297 \\ 0.95x + 330 - 1.25x &= 297 \\ 330 - 0.30x &= 297 \\ -0.30x &= -33 \\ x &= 110 \end{aligned}$$

$$\begin{aligned} 264 - x &= 264 - 110 \\ &= 154 \end{aligned}$$

110 at 95¢, 154 at \$1.25

14.
$$\begin{aligned} (8 + x)(12 + x) &= 69 + 8(12) \\ 96 + 8x + 12x + x^2 &= 69 + 96 \\ x^2 + 20x + 96 &= 165 \\ x^2 + 20x - 69 &= 0 \\ (x + 23)(x - 3) &= 0 \end{aligned}$$

$x + 23 = 0$ or $x - 3 = 0$

$x = -23$ $\quad$ $x = 3$

$8 + 3 = 11,\ 12 + 3 = 15$

The dimensions of the new photograph are 11 cm by 15 cm.

15.
$$\begin{aligned} 2(14.20) + x &\leq 50 \\ 28.40 + x &\leq 50 \\ x &\leq 21.60 \end{aligned}$$

\$21.60 or less

16.
$$\begin{aligned} x - y &= 3 \\ x^2 - y^2 &= 15 \\ (x + y)(x - y) &= 15 \\ (x + y)(3) &= 15 \\ x + y &= 5 \end{aligned}$$

The sum of the numbers is 5.

17. Let w = original width.
Then $8w$ = original length.

$$\begin{aligned} 8w(w) - 162 &= (w - 2)(8w - 10) \\ 8w^2 - 162 &= 8w^2 - 10w - 16w + 20 \\ 8w^2 - 162 &= 8w^2 - 26w + 20 \\ -162 &= -26w + 20 \\ -182 &= -26w \\ 7 &= w \end{aligned}$$

$$\begin{aligned} 8w &= 8(7) \\ &= 56 \end{aligned}$$

The original dimensions were 7 m by 56 m.

18. $18(15) = 270$
$21(15) = 315$
270 to 315 miles

19.
$$\begin{aligned} &8x^2 + x + 15 - (2x^2 - 5x + 7) - (x^2 - x + 11) \\ &= 8x^2 + x + 15 - 2x^2 + 5x - 7 - x^2 + x - 11 \\ &= 8x^2 - 2x^2 - x^2 + x + 5x + x + 15 - 7 - 11 \\ &= 5x^2 + 7x - 3 \end{aligned}$$

20.
$$\begin{aligned} V &= \ell wh \\ 1350 &= x(2x)(3) \\ 1350 &= 6x^2 \\ 225 &= x^2 \\ 15 &= x \end{aligned}$$

$$\begin{aligned} 2x &= 2(15) \\ &= 30 \end{aligned}$$

The dimensions should be 3 in. by 30 in. **by 15 in.**

21. Let w = original width.
Then $5w$ = original length.

$$\begin{aligned} 5w(w) - 132 &= (w - 4)(5w + 7) \\ 5w^2 - 132 &= 5w^2 + 7w - 20w - 28 \\ 5w^2 - 132 &= 5w^2 - 13w - 28 \\ -132 &= -13w - 28 \\ -104 &= -13w \\ 8 &= w \end{aligned}$$

$$\begin{aligned} 5w &= 5(8) \\ &= 40 \end{aligned}$$

The original dimensions were 8 m by 40 m.

Chapter 11 Exploring Quadratic and Exponential Functions

11-1A Graphing Technology Quadratic Functions

Page 610

1. Enter: Y= X,T,θ x^2 + 16 X,T,θ + 59 ZOOM 8 ENTER
   The coordinates of the vertex are (−8, −5).

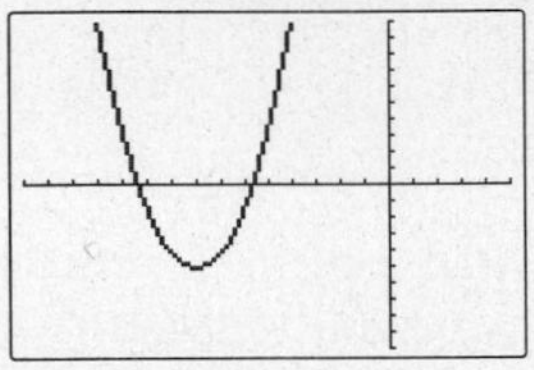

2. Enter: Y= 12 X,T,θ x^2 + 18 X,T,θ + 10 ZOOM 8 ENTER
   The coordinates of the vertex are (−0.75, 3.25).

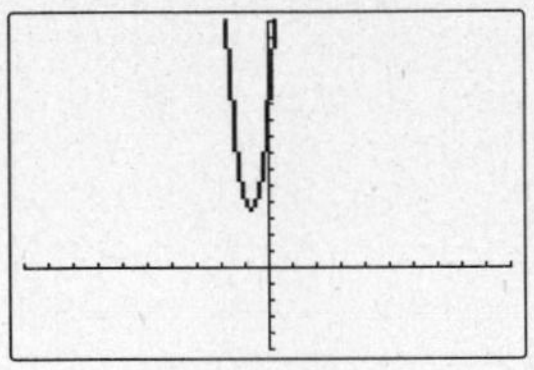

3. Enter: Y= X,T,θ x^2 − 10 X,T,θ + 25 ZOOM 8 ENTER
   The coordinates of the vertex are (5, 0).

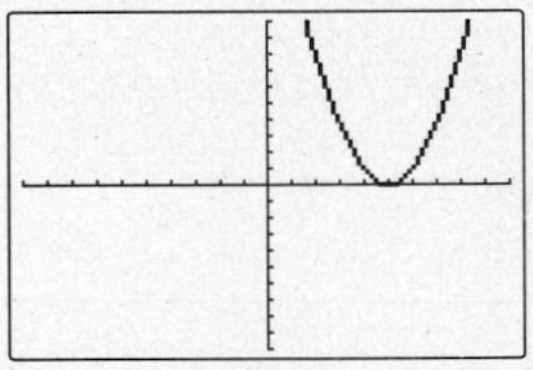

4. Enter: Y= (−) 2 X,T,θ x^2 − 8 X,T,θ − 1 ZOOM 8 ENTER
   The coordinates of the vertex are (−2, 7).

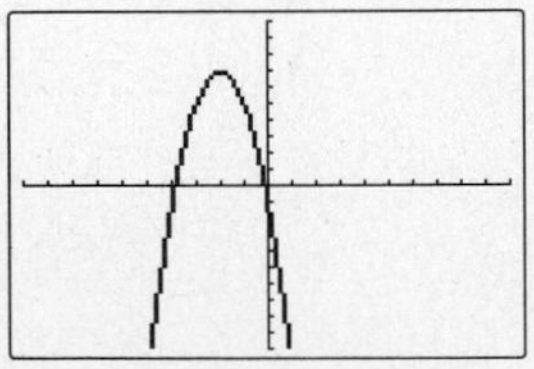

5. Enter: Y= 2 (X,T,θ − 10) ^ 2 + 14 ZOOM 8 ENTER
   The coordinates of the vertex are (10,14).

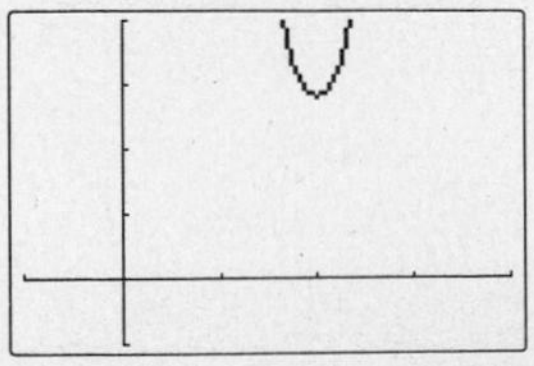

6. Enter: Y= (−) .5 X,T,θ x^2 − 2 X,T,θ + 3 ZOOM 8 ENTER
   The coordinates of the vertex are (−2, 5).

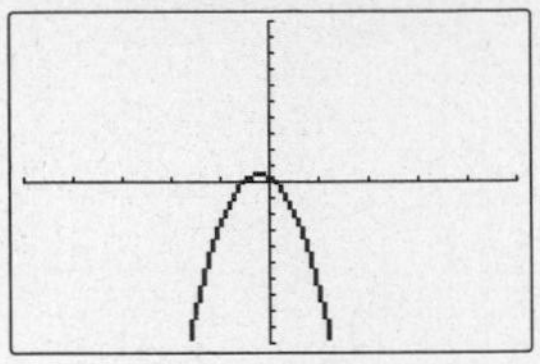

11-1 Graphing Quadratic Functions

Pages 614–615 Check for Understanding

1. 630 ft
2. Sample answer: Once you determine the axis of symmetry, there is a matching point on the other side of the axis for each point you find on one side. Suppose the axis is $x = 4$ and one point is (−2, 3). −2 is 6 units left of the axis; another point is 6 units right of the axis with the same y-coordinate, that is, (10, 3).
3. If (p, q) is the vertex, $x = p$ is the equation of the axis of symmetry.
4. Angie is correct. The graph of $y = (-x)^2$ is the same graph as $y = x^2$, which opens upward from the origin. The graph of $y = -x^2$ opens downward from the origin.

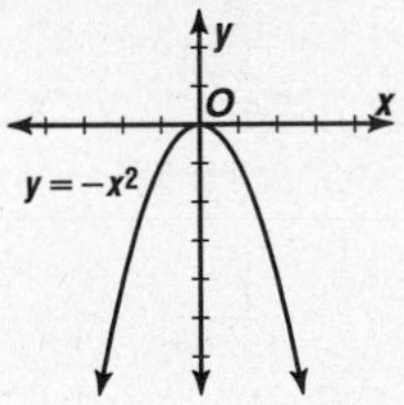

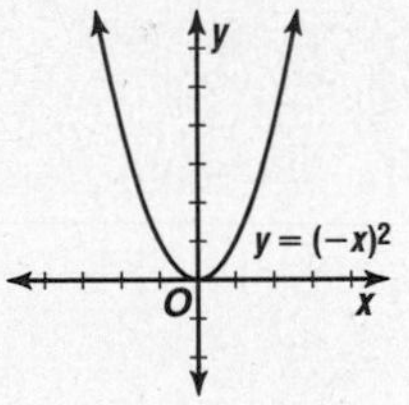

5. If the coefficient of x^2 is positive, it is a minimum. If the coefficient is negative, it is a maximum.
6. It opens downward; $x = 2$.

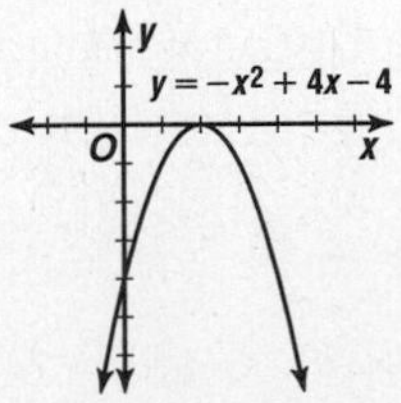

7. $y = x^2 + 2$, $a = 1$, $b = 0$
   axis of symmetry: $x = -\frac{b}{2a} = -\frac{0}{2(1)}$ or $x = 0$
   $y = x^2 + 2$
   $= (0)^2 + 2$
   $= 0 + 2$
   $= 2$
   The coordinates of the vertex are (0, 2), minimum.

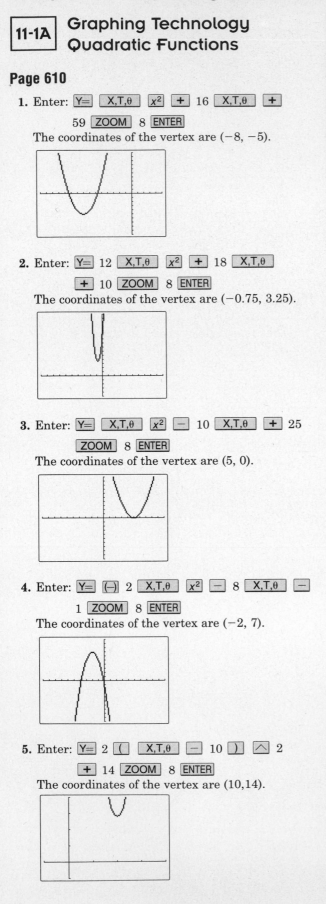

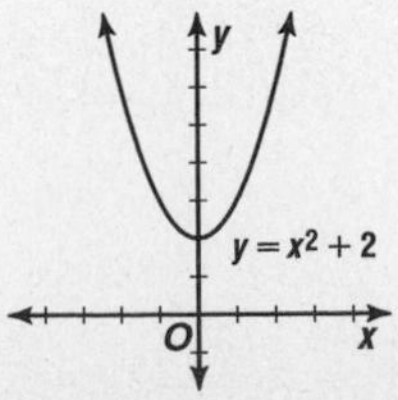

8. $y = -2x^2$, $a = -2$, $b = 0$

axis of symmetry: $x = -\frac{b}{2a} = -\frac{0}{2(-2)}$ or $x = 0$

$y = -2x^2$

$= -2(0)^2$

$= 0$

The coordinates of the vertex are (0, 0), maximum.

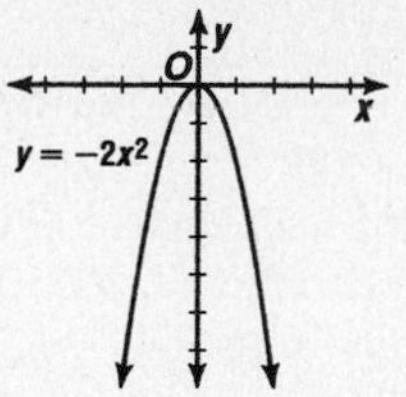

9. $y = x^2 + 4x - 9$, $a = 1$, $b = 4$

axis of symmetry: $x = -\frac{b}{2a} = -\frac{(4)}{2(1)}$ or $x = -2$

$y = x^2 + 4x - 9$

$= (-2)^2 + 4(-2) - 9$

$= 4 - 8 - 9$

$= -13$

The coordinates of the vertex are $(-2, -13)$, minimum.

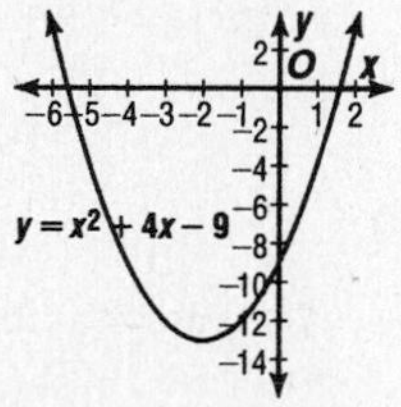

10. $y = x^2 - 14x + 13$, $a = 1$, $b = -14$

axis of symmetry: $x = -\frac{b}{2a} = -\frac{(-14)}{2(1)}$ or $x = 7$

$y = x^2 - 14x + 13$

$= (7)^2 - 14(7) + 13$

$= 49 - 98 + 13$

$= -36$

The coordinates of the vertex are $(7, -36)$, minimum.

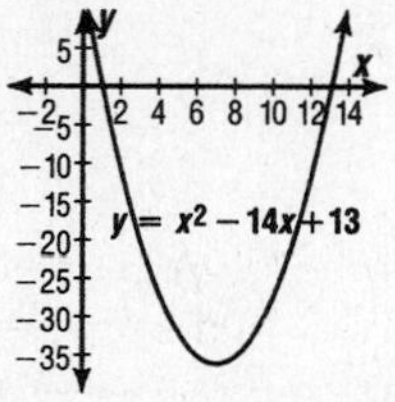

11. $y = -x^2 + 5x + 6$, $a = -1$, $b = 5$

axis of symmetry: $x = -\frac{b}{2a} = -\frac{(5)}{2(-1)}$ or $x = 2.5$

$y = -x^2 + 5x + 6$

$= -(2.5)^2 + 5(2.5) + 6$

$= -6.25 + 12.5 + 6$

$= 12.25$

The coordinates of the vertex are (2.5, 12.25), maximum.

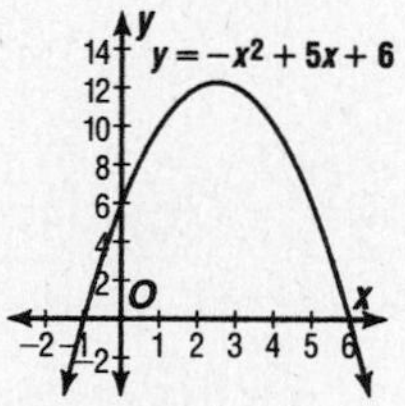

12. $y = -2x^2 + 4x + 6.5$, $a = -2$, $b = 4$

axis of symmetry: $x = -\frac{b}{2a} = -\frac{(4)}{2(-2)}$ or $x = 1$

$y = -2x^2 + 4x + 6.5$

$= -2(1)^2 + 4(1) + 6.5$

$= -2 + 4 + 6.5$

$= 8.5$

The coordinates of the vertex are (1, 8.5), maximum.

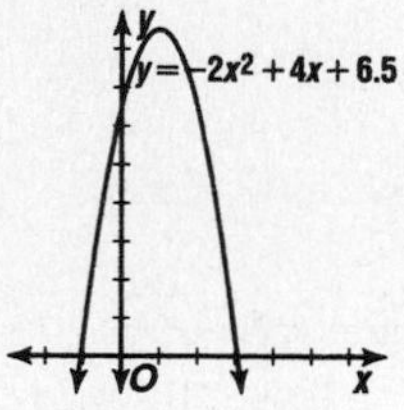

13. $f(x) = x^2 + 6x + 9$, $a = 1$, $b = 6$

axis of symmetry: $x = -\frac{b}{2a} = -\frac{6}{2(1)}$ or -3

$y = x^2 + 6x + 9$

$= (-3)^2 + 6(-3) + 9$

$= 9 - 18 + 9$

$= 0$

The coordinates of the vertex are $(-3, 0)$, minimum.

Thus, $f(x) = x^2 + 6x + 9$ describes the graph; c.

14a. $H(t) = v_0t - \frac{1}{2}gt^2 + h_0$

$= 40t - \frac{1}{2}(32)t^2 + 3$

$= -16t^2 + 40t + 3$, $a = -16$, $b = 40$

axis of symmetry: $x = -\frac{b}{2a} = -\frac{(40)}{2(-16)}$ or 1.25

1.25 s

14b. $H(1.25) = -16(1.25)^2 + 40(1.25) + 3$

$= -25 + 50 + 3$

$= 28$ ft

Pages 615–617 Exercises

15. $y = 4x^2$, $a = 4$, $b = 0$

axis of symmetry: $x = -\frac{b}{2a} = -\frac{(0)}{2(4)}$ or $x = 0$

$y = 4x^2$

$= 4(0)^2$

$= 0$

The coordinates of the vertex are (0, 0), minimum.

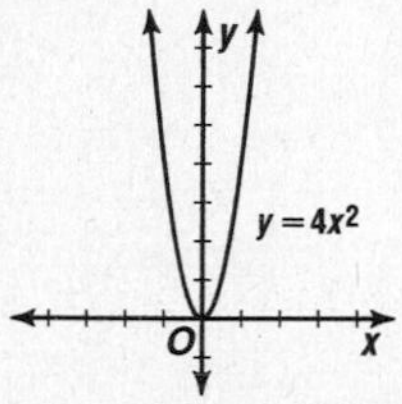

16. $y = -x^2 + 4x - 1$, $a = -1$, $b = 4$

axis of symmetry: $x = -\frac{b}{2a} = -\frac{4}{2(-1)}$ or $x = 2$

$y = x^2 + 4x - 1$

$= (2)^2 + 4(2) - 1$

$= -4 + 8 - 1$

$= 3$

The coordinates of the vertex are (2, 3), maximum.

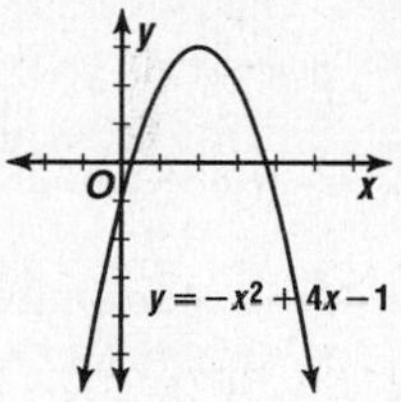

17. $y = x^2 + 2x + 18$, $a = 1$, $b = 2$

axis of symmetry: $x = -\frac{b}{2a} = -\frac{(2)}{2(1)}$ or $x = -1$

$y = x^2 + 2x + 18$

$= (-1)^2 + 2(-1) + 18$

$= 1 - 2 + 18$

$= 17$

The coordinates of the vertex are $(-1, 17)$, minimum.

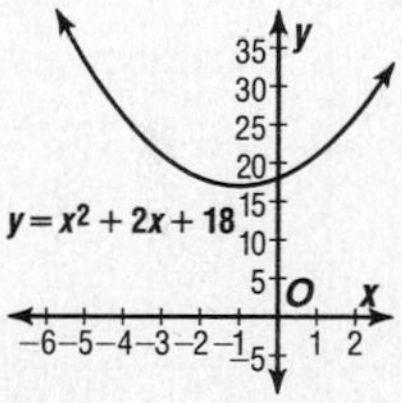

18. $y = x^2 - 3x - 10$, $a = 1$, $b = -3$

axis of symmetry: $x = -\frac{b}{2a} = -\frac{(-3)}{2(1)}$ or $x = \frac{3}{2}$

$y = x^2 - 3x - 10$

$= \left(\frac{3}{2}\right)^2 - 3\left(\frac{3}{2}\right) - 10$

$= \frac{9}{4} - \frac{9}{2} - 10$

$= -\frac{49}{4}$

The coordinates of the vertex are $\left(\frac{3}{2}, -\frac{49}{4}\right)$, minimum.

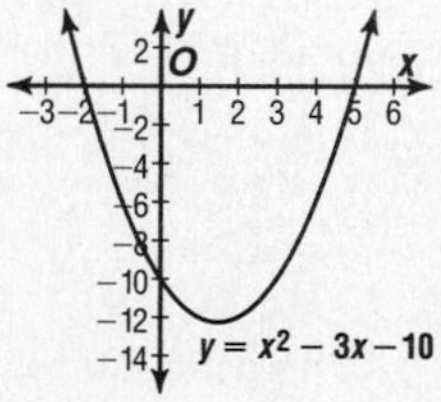

19. $y = x^2 - 5$, $a = 1$, $b = 0$

axis of symmetry: $x = -\frac{b}{2a} = -\frac{(0)}{2(1)}$ or $x = 0$

$y = x^2 - 5$

$= (0)^2 - 5$

$= -5$

The coordinates of the vertex are $(0, -5)$, minimum.

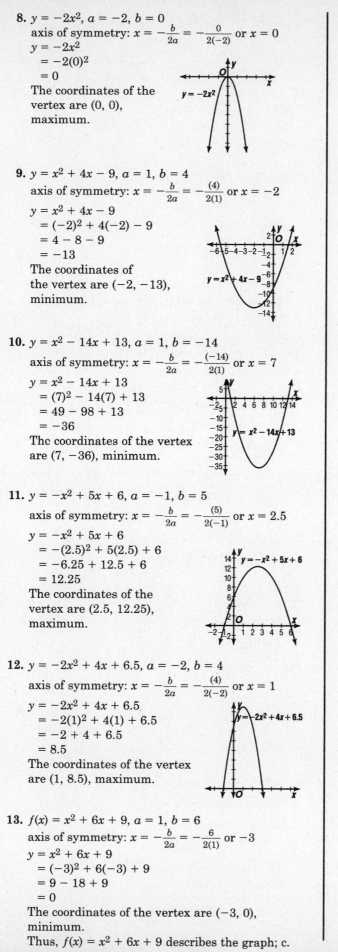

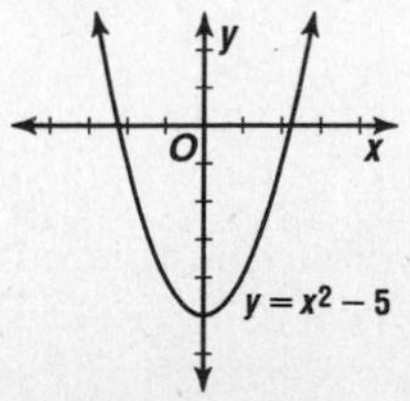

20. $y = 4x^2 + 16$, $a = 4$, $b = 0$

axis of symmetry: $x = -\frac{b}{2a} = -\frac{(0)}{2(4)}$ or $x = 0$

$y = 4x^2 + 16$
$= 4(0)^2 + 16$
$= 0 + 16$
$= 16$

The coordinates of the vertex are (0, 16), minimum.

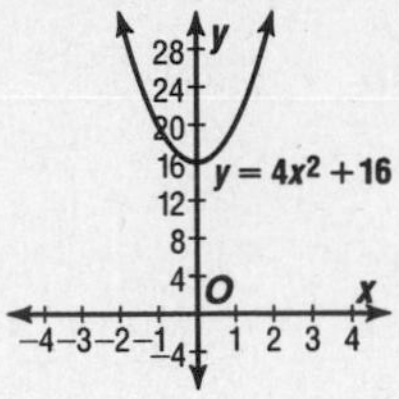

21. $y = 2x^2 + 12x - 11$, $a = 2$, $b = 12$

axis of symmetry: $x = -\frac{b}{2a} = -\frac{(12)}{2(2)}$ or $x = -3$

$y = 2x^2 + 12x - 11$
$= 2(-3)^2 + 12(-3) - 11$
$= 18 - 36 - 11$
$= -29$

The coordinates of the vertex are (−3, −29), minimum.

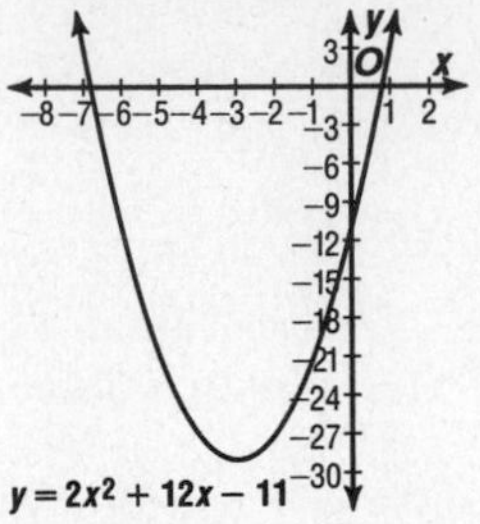

22. $y = 3x^2 + 24x + 80$, $a = 3$, $b = 24$

axis of symmetry: $x = -\frac{b}{2a} = -\frac{(24)}{2(3)}$ or $x = -4$

$y = 3x^2 + 24x + 80$
$= 3(-4)^2 + 24(-4) + 80$
$= 48 - 96 + 80$
$= 32$

The coordinates of the vertex are (−4, 32), minimum.

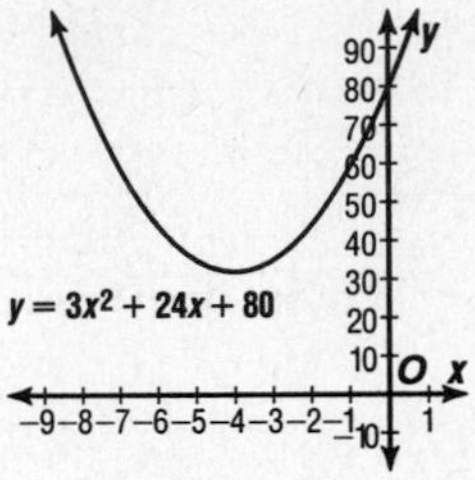

23. $y = x^2 - 25$, $a = 1$, $b = 0$

axis of symmetry: $x = -\frac{b}{2a} = -\frac{(0)}{2(1)}$ or $x = 0$

$y = x^2 - 25$
$= (0)^2 - 25$
$= -25$

The coordinates of the vertex are (0, −25), minimum.

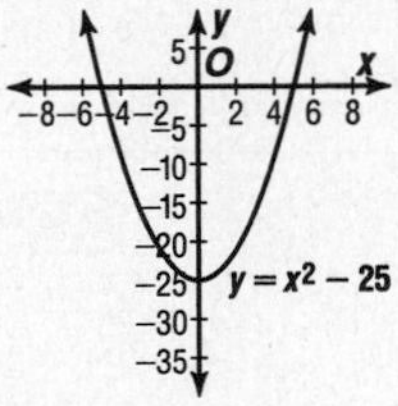

24. $y = 15 - 6x - x^2$, $a = -1$, $b = -6$

axis of symmetry: $x = -\frac{b}{2a} = -\frac{(-6)}{2(-1)}$ or $x = -3$

$y = 15 - 6x - x^2$
$= 15 - 6(-3) - (-3)^2$
$= 15 + 18 - 9$
$= 24$

The coordinates of the vertex are (−3, 24), maximum.

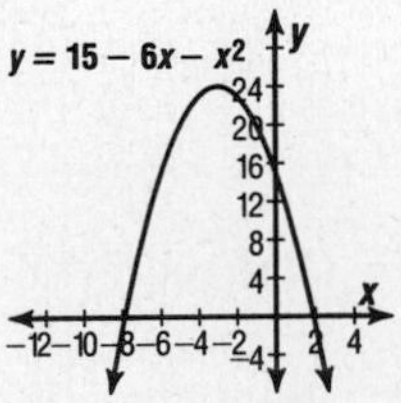

25. $y = -3x^2 - 6x + 4$, $a = -3$, $b = -6$

axis of symmetry: $x = -\frac{b}{2a} = -\frac{(-6)}{2(-3)}$ or $x = -1$

$y = -3x^2 - 6x + 4$
$= -3(-1)^2 - 6(-1) + 4$
$= -3 + 6 + 4$
$= 7$

The coordinates of the vertex are (−1, 7), maximum.

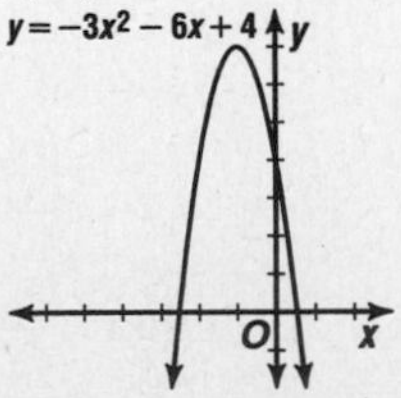

26. $y = 5 + 16x - 2x^2$, $a = -2$, $b = 16$

axis of symmetry: $x = -\frac{b}{2a} = -\frac{(16)}{2(-2)}$ or $x = 4$

$y = 5 + 16x - 2x^2$
$= 5 + 16(4) - 2(4)^2$
$= 5 + 64 - 32$
$= 37$

The coordinates of the vertex are (4, 37), maximum.

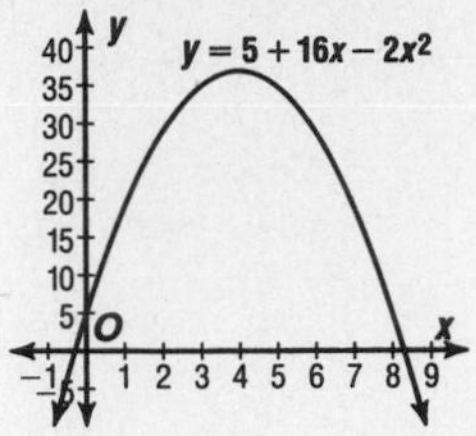

27. $y = 3(x + 1)^2 - 20$
$= 3(x^2 + 2x + 1) - 20$
$= 3x^2 + 6x - 17$, $a = 3$, $b = 6$

axis of symmetry: $x = -\frac{b}{2a} = -\frac{(6)}{2(3)}$ or $x = -1$

$y = 3x^2 + 2x - 1$
$= 3(-1 + 1)^2 - 20$
$= 0 - 20$
$= -20$

The coordinates of the vertex are (−1, −20), minimum.

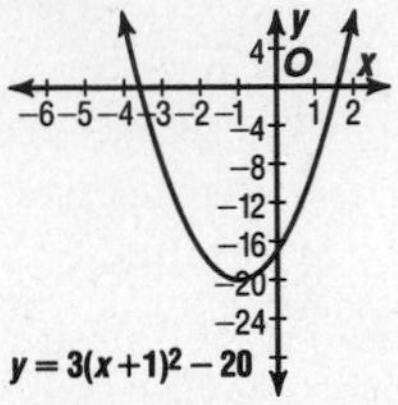

28. $y = -(x - 2)^2 + 1$
$= -(x^2 - 4x + 4) + 1$
$= -x^2 + 4x - 3$, $a = -1$, $b = 4$

axis of symmetry: $x = -\frac{b}{2a} = -\frac{(4)}{2(-1)}$ or $x = 2$

$y = -x^2 + 4x - 3$
$= -(2 - 2)^2 + 1$
$= 0 + 1$
$= 1$

The coordinates of the vertex are (2, 1), maximum.

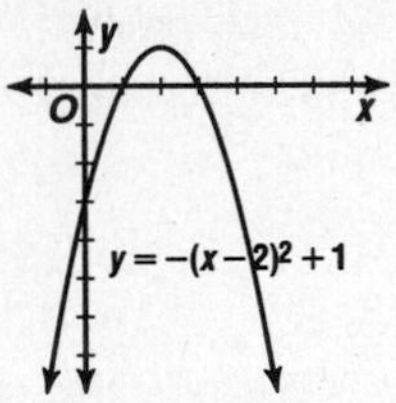

29. $y = \frac{2}{3}(x + 1)^2 - 1$
$= \frac{2}{3}(x^2 + 2x + 1) - 1$
$= \frac{2}{3}x^2 + \frac{4}{3}x - \frac{1}{3}$, $a = \frac{2}{3}$, $b = \frac{4}{3}$

axis of symmetry: $x = -\frac{b}{2a} = -\frac{\frac{4}{3}}{2\left(\frac{2}{3}\right)}$ or $x = -1$

$y = \frac{2}{3}(x + 1)^2 - 1$
$= \frac{2}{3}(-1 + 1)^2 - 1$
$= 0 - 1$
$= -1$

The coordinates of the vertex are (−1, −1), minimum.

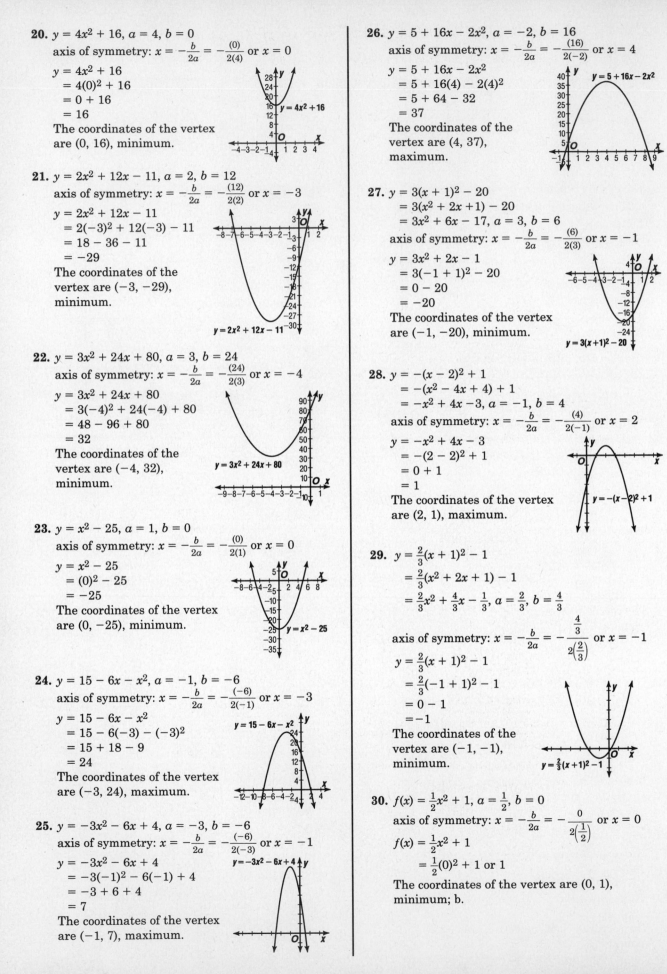

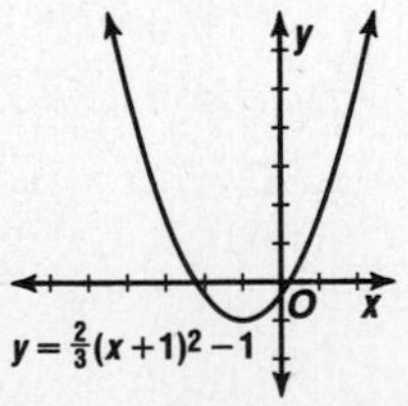

30. $f(x) = \frac{1}{2}x^2 + 1$, $a = \frac{1}{2}$, $b = 0$

axis of symmetry: $x = -\frac{b}{2a} = -\frac{0}{2\left(\frac{1}{2}\right)}$ or $x = 0$

$f(x) = \frac{1}{2}x^2 + 1$
$= \frac{1}{2}(0)^2 + 1$ or 1

The coordinates of the vertex are (0, 1), minimum; b.

31. $f(x) = -\frac{1}{2}x^2 + 1$, $a = -\frac{1}{2}$, $b = 0$

axis of symmetry: $x = -\frac{b}{2a} = -\frac{0}{2\left(\frac{1}{2}\right)}$ or $x = 0$

$f(x) = -\frac{1}{2}x^2 + 1$

$= -\frac{1}{2}(0)^2 + 1$ or 1

The coordinates of the vertex are (0, 1), maximum; c.

32. $f(x) = \frac{1}{2}x^2 - 1$, $a = \frac{1}{2}$, $b = 0$

axis of symmetry: $x = -\frac{b}{2a} = -\frac{0}{2\left(\frac{1}{2}\right)}$ or $x = 0$

$f(x) = \frac{1}{2}x^2 - 1$

$= \frac{1}{2}(0)^2 - 1$ or -1

The coordinates of the vertex are (0, −1), minimum; a.

33. $y + 2 = x^2 - 10x + 25$

$y = x^2 - 10x + 23$, $a = 1$, $b = -10$

axis of symmetry: $x = -\frac{b}{2a} = -\frac{(-10)}{2(1)}$ or 5

$y = x^2 - 10x + 23$

$= (5)^2 - 10(5) + 23$

$= 25 - 50 + 23$ or -2

The coordinates of the vertex are (5, −2), minimum.

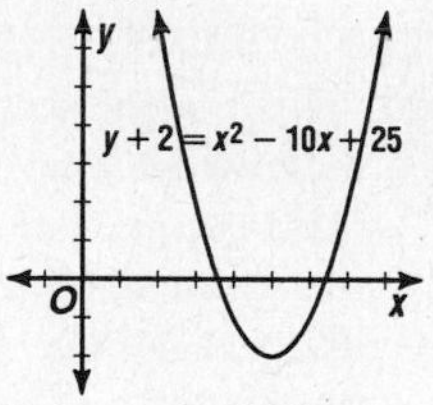

34. $y + 1 = 3x^2 + 12x + 12$

$y = 3x^2 + 12x + 11$, $a = 3$, $b = 12$

axis of symmetry: $x = -\frac{b}{2a} = -\frac{(12)}{2(3)}$ or -2

$y = 3x^2 + 12x + 11$

$= 3(-2)^2 + 12(-2) + 11$

$= 12 - 24 + 11$ or -1

The coordinates of the vertex are (−2, −1), minimum.

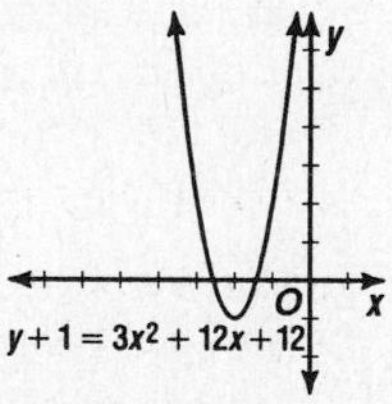

35. $y + 3 = -2(x - 4)^2$

$y + 3 = -2(x^2 - 8x + 16)$

$y + 3 = -2x^2 + 16x - 32$

$y = -2x^2 + 16x - 35$, $a = -2$, $b = 16$

axis of symmetry: $x = -\frac{b}{2a} = -\frac{(16)}{2(-2)}$ or 4

$y = -2x^2 + 16x - 35$

$= -2(4)^2 + 16(4) - 35$

$= -32 + 64 - 35$ or -3

The coordinates of the vertex are (4, −3), maximum.

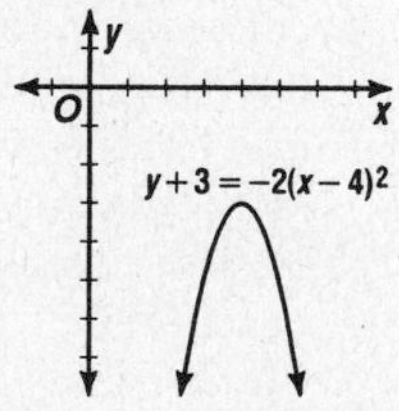

36. $y - 5 = \frac{1}{3}(x + 2)^2$

$y - 5 = \frac{1}{3}(x^2 + 4x + 4)$

$y = \frac{1}{3}x^2 + \frac{4}{3}x + \frac{19}{3}$, $a = \frac{1}{3}$, $b = \frac{4}{3}$

axis of symmetry: $x = -\frac{b}{2a} = -\frac{\left(\frac{4}{3}\right)}{2\left(\frac{1}{3}\right)}$ or -2

$y = \frac{1}{3}x^2 + \frac{4}{3}x + \frac{19}{3}$

$= \frac{1}{3}(-2)^2 + \frac{4}{3}(-2) + \frac{19}{3}$

$= \frac{4}{3} - \frac{8}{3} + \frac{19}{3}$ or 5

The coordinates of the vertex are (−2, 5), minimum.

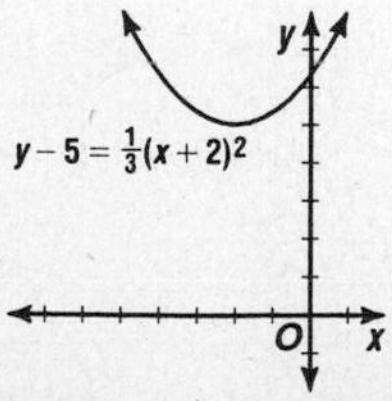

37. Find the line half-way between $x = -6$ and $x = 4$.

$x = \frac{-6 + 4}{2} = \frac{-2}{2}$ or $x = -1$

38. Find the distance between (−4, −3) and $x = -11$. $-4 - (-11) = 7$; The vertex is 7 units from each x-intercept. The other x-intercept is $-4 + 7$ or 3.

39. Find the line half-way between (−8, 7) and (12, 7).

$x = \frac{-8 + 12}{2} = \frac{4}{2}$ or $x = 2$

40. Sample answer:
$x = -2.00$, (−2.00, 12)

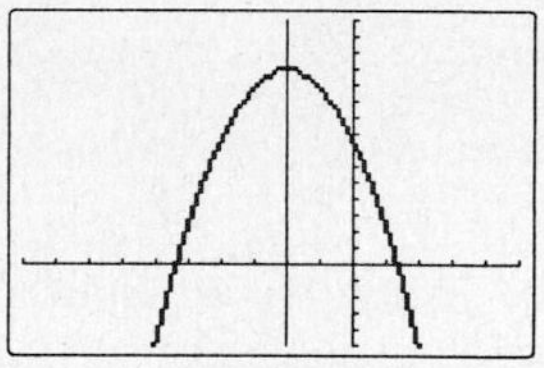

41. Sample answer:
$x = -1.10$,
(−1.10, 125.8)

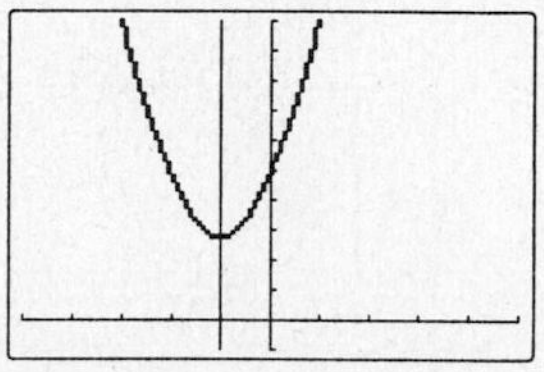

42. Sample answer:
$x = -268.04$,
(−268.04, −1719.47)

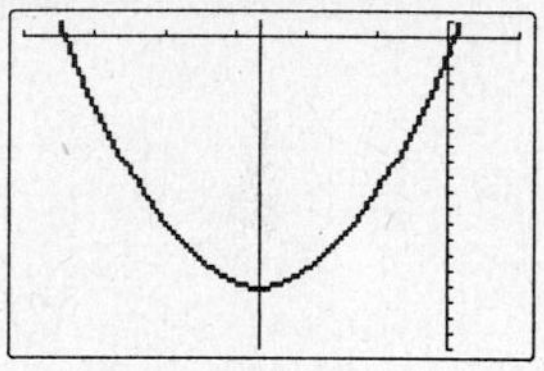

43. Sample answer:
$x = -0.15$,
(−0.15, 90.14)

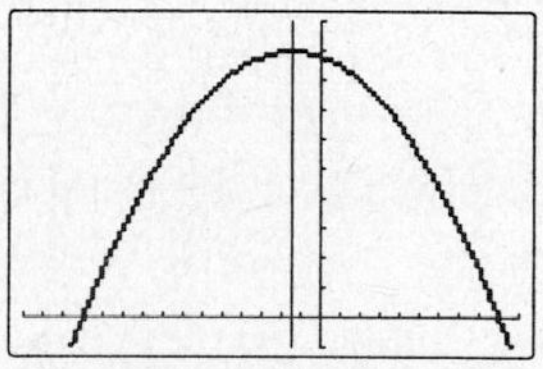

44. (−3, 11), (2, 6);
See students' work.

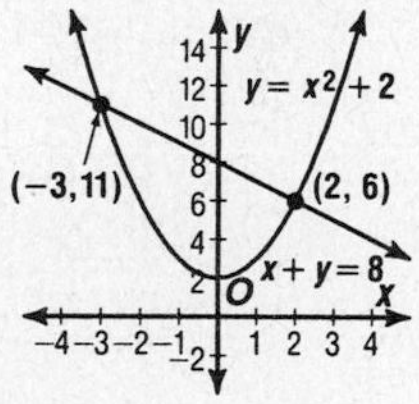

45a.

Year	t	$U(t)$
1970	0	329.96
1975	5	370.31
1980	10	559.16
1985	15	896.51
1990	20	1382.36
1993	23	1745.15

45b. D: $0 \le t \le 23$; R: $326 < U(t) < 1746$

45c.

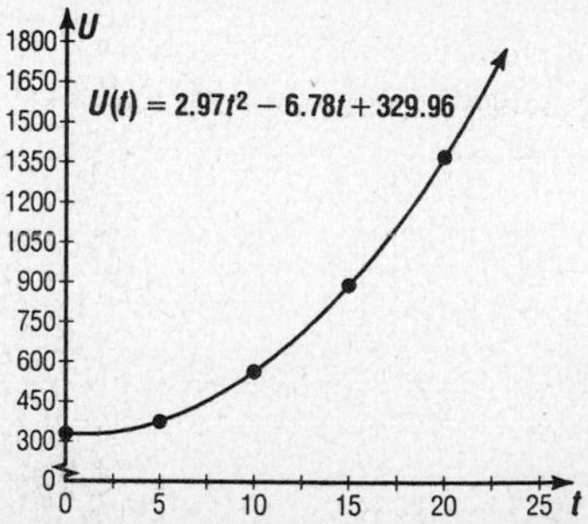

45c. See students' work.

46a. $H(t) = v_0t - \frac{1}{2}gt^2 + h_0$

$H(t) = 80t - \frac{1}{2}(32)t^2 + 2$

$H(t) = 80t - 16t^2 + 2$

46b. $H(1) = 80(1) - 16(1)^2 + 2$
$= 80 - 16 + 2$ or 66 ft

$H(2) = 80(2) - 16(2)^2 + 2$
$= 160 - 64 + 2$ or 98 ft

$H(3) = 80(3) - 16(3)^2 + 2$
$= 240 - 144 + 2$ or 98 ft

46c. $H(t) = 80t - 16t^2 + 2$, $a = -16$, $b = 80$

$x = -\frac{b}{2a} = -\frac{(80)}{2(-16)}$ or 2.5

$2(2.5) = 5$; about 5 seconds

47. Let x = width of the strip.

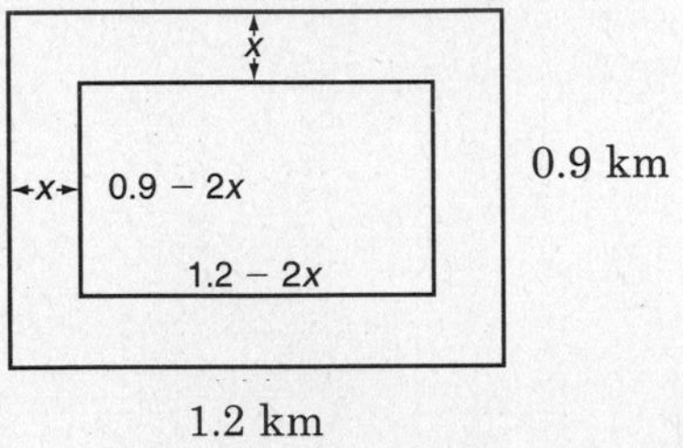

$(0.9 - 2x)(1.2 - 2x) = \frac{1}{2}(1.2)(0.9)$

$1.08 - 1.8x - 2.4x + 4x^2 = 0.54$

$4x^2 - 4.2x + 0.54 = 0$

$x^2 - 1.05x + 0.135 = 0$

$(x - 0.15)(x - 0.9) = 0$

$x - 0.15 = 0$ or $x - 0.9 = 0$

$x = 0.15$ $\quad x = 0.9$

The width of the strip is 0.15 km.

48. $(x - 4)(x - 8) = x^2 - 8x - 4x + 32$
$= x^2 - 12x + 32$

49a. $6.79 \times 10^3 = 6.79 \times 1000$
$= 6790$

49b. $227{,}920{,}000 = 2.2792 \times 100{,}000{,}000$
$= 2.2792 \times 10^8$

50. $3x + 4y = -25 \rightarrow 9x + 12y = -75$

$2x - 3y = 6 \rightarrow (+)\ 8x - 12y = 24$

$17x = -51$

$x = -3$

$3x + 4y = -25$

$3(-3) + 4y = -25$

$-9 + 4y = -25$

$4y = -16$

$y = -4$

The solution is $(-3, -4)$.

51a. LV = 6.00 GV = 43.00

median = 12.13

$Q_1 = 10.40$ $\quad Q_3 = 18.00$

$IQR = Q_3 - Q_1 = 18.00 - 10.40 = 7.60$

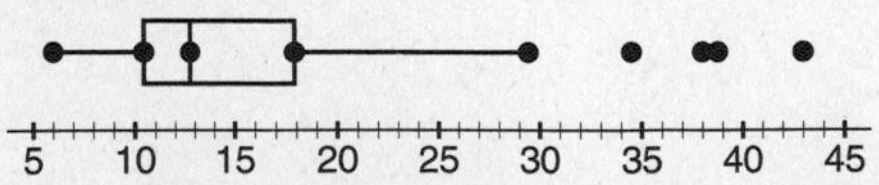

51b. $x \geq Q_3 + 1.5(IQR)$ or $x \leq Q_1 - 1.5(IQR)$

$x \geq 18.00 + 1.5(7.60)$ $\quad x \leq 10.4 - 1.5(7.60)$

$x \geq 18.00 + 11.4$ $\quad x \leq -1.4$

$x \geq 29.4$

34.5, 38, 38.7, 43

52.

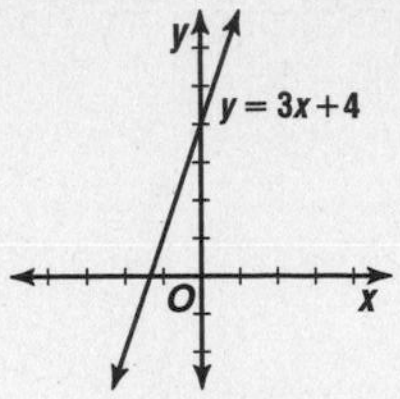

53. $3x = -15$

$\frac{3x}{3} = \frac{-15}{3}$

$x = -5$

54. $3(2) = 6$

$6(2) = 12$

$12(2) = 24$

$24(2) = 48$

$48(2) = 96$

48, 96

11-1B Graphing Technology Families of Parabolas

Page 619 Exercises

1. All the graphs open downward from the origin. $y = -2x^2$ is narrower than $y = -x^2$, and $y = -5x^2$ is the narrowest.

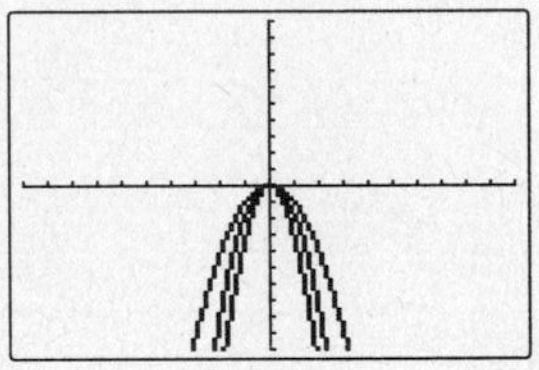

2. All the graphs open downward from the origin. $y = -0.3x^2$ is wider than $y = -x^2$, and $y = -0.7x^2$ is the widest.

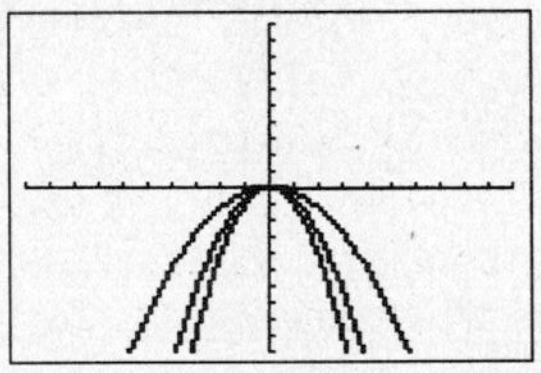

3. All open downward, have the same shape, and have vertices along the x-axis. However, each vertex is different.

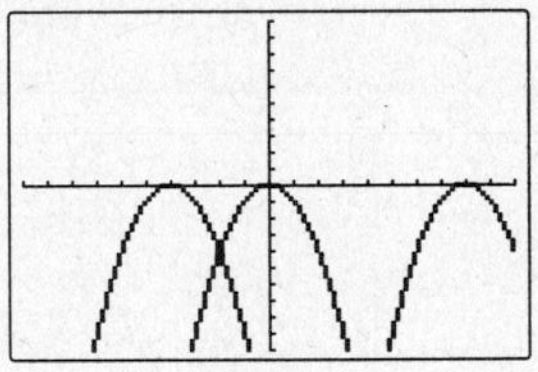

4. All open downward, have the same shape, and have vertices along the y-axis. However, each vertex is different.

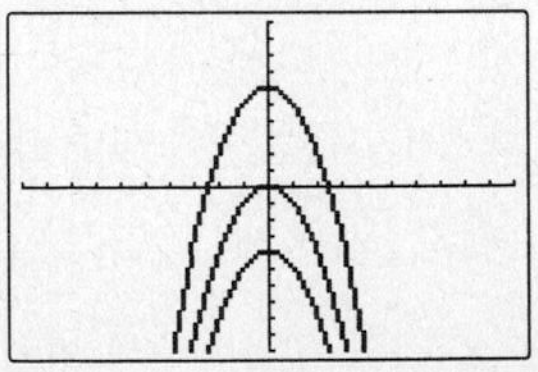

5. It will open upward, have a vertex at the origin, and be narrower than $y = x^2$.

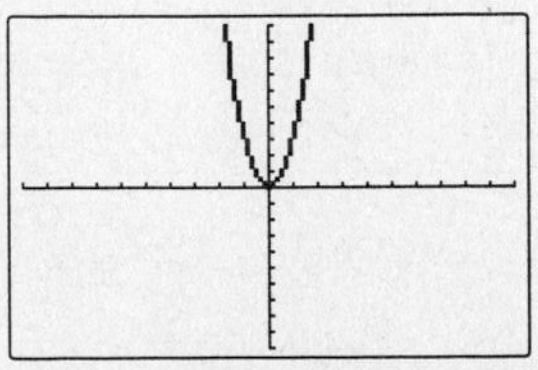

6. It will open upward and have the same shape as $y = x^2$, but its vertex will be at $(0, -6)$.

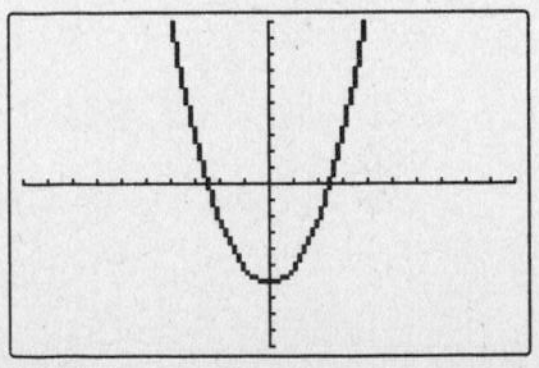

7. It will have a vertex at the origin, open downward, and be wider than $y = x^2$.

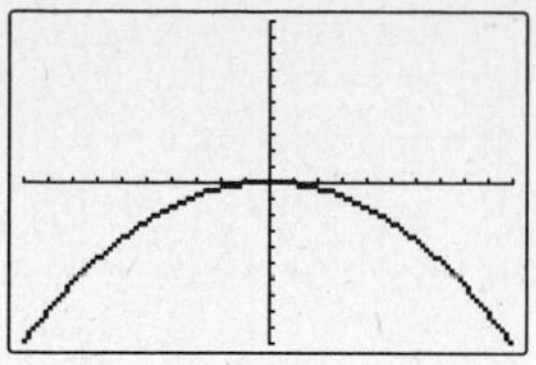

8. It will open upward and have the same shape as $y = x^2$, but its vertex will be at $(-1, 0)$.

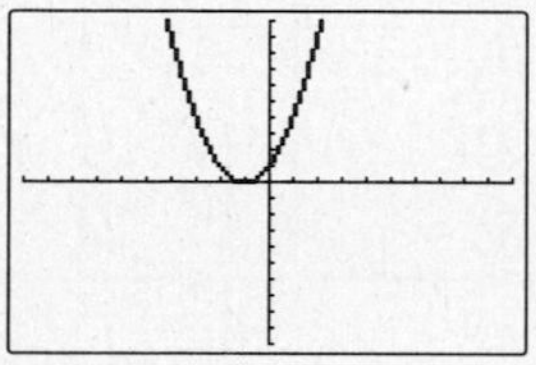

9a. If $|a| > 1$, the graph is narrower than the graph of $y = x^2$. If $0 < |a| < 1$, the graph is wider than the graph of $y = x^2$. If $a < 0$, it opens downward; if $a > 0$, it opens upward.

9b. The graph has the same shape as $y = x^2$, but is shifted a units (up if $a > 0$, down if $a < 0$).

9c. The graph has the same shape as $y = x^2$, but is shifted a units (left if $a > 0$, right if $a < 0$).

9d. The graph has the same shape as $y = x^2$, but is shifted a units left or right and b units up or down as prescribed in 9b and 9c.

11-2 Solving Quadratic Equations by Graphing

Pages 624–625 Check for Understanding

1. The x-intercept is where the function equals 0.
2. Hanna, because factoring only works when the polynomial making up the equation is factorable. Graphing will always give you an estimate of the solutions if they are real.
3. $x^2 + 9x + 2 = 3x - 4$
   $f(x) = x^2 + 6x + 6$
4. 500 employees
5. See students' work.
6. 1 distinct root
7. 2 real roots
8. no real roots ($\varnothing$)
9. $-1, 2$
10. $f(x) = x^2 - 7x + 6$

x	$f(x)$
1	0
2	−4
3	−6
4	−6
5	−4
6	0

roots: 1, 6

axis of symmetry: $x = \frac{7}{2}$

vertex: $\left(\frac{7}{2}, \frac{-25}{4}\right)$

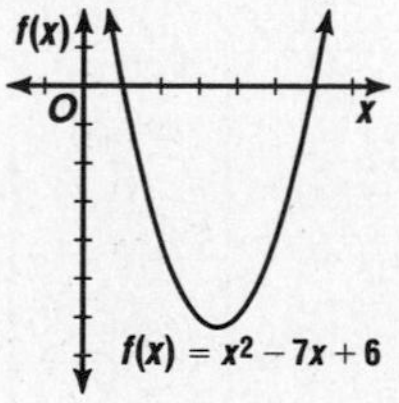

11. $f(c) = c^2 - 5c - 24$

axis of symmetry: $c = \frac{5}{2}$

vertex: $\left(\frac{5}{2}, -30\frac{1}{4}\right)$

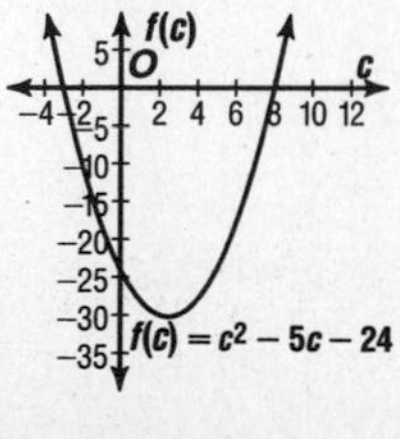

c	$f(c)$
−3	0
−2	−10
−1	−18
0	−24
1	−28
2	−30
3	−30
4	−28
5	−24
6	−18
7	−10
8	0

roots: −3, 8

12. $f(n) = 5n^2 + 2n + 6$

n	$f(n)$
−2	22
−1	9
0	6
1	13
2	30
3	57

$\varnothing$

axis of symmetry: $n = -\frac{1}{5}$

vertex: $\left(-\frac{1}{5}, 5.8\right)$

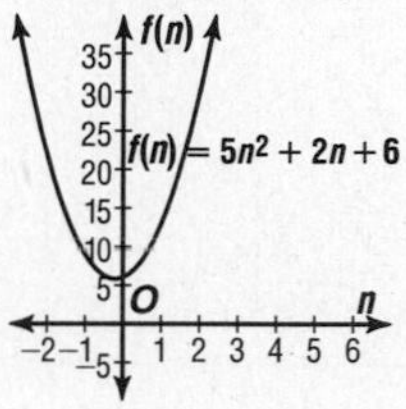

13. $w^2 - 3w = 5$
   $w^2 - 3w - 5 = 0$
   $f(w) = w^2 - 3w - 5$

w	$f(w)$
−2	5
−1	−1
0	−5
1	−7
2	−7
3	−5
4	−1
5	5

axis of symmetry: $w = \frac{3}{2}$

vertex: $\left(\frac{3}{2}, -7\frac{1}{4}\right)$

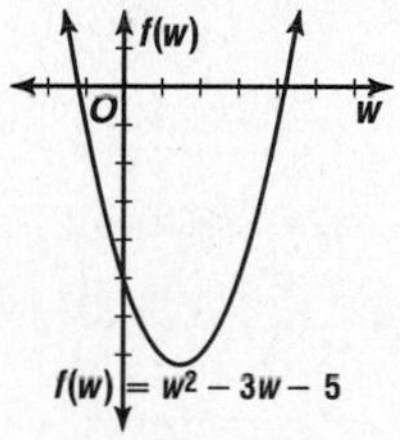

roots: $-2 < w < -1$, $4 < w < 5$

14. $f(b) = b^2 - b + 4$

b	$f(b)$
−2	10
−1	6
0	4
1	4
2	6
3	10

$\varnothing$

axis of symmetry: $b = \frac{1}{2}$

vertex: $\left(\frac{1}{2}, 3\frac{3}{4}\right)$

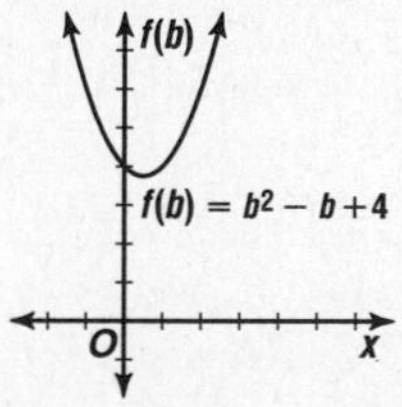

15. $a^2 - 10a = -25$
   $a^2 - 10a + 25 = 0$
   $f(a) = a^2 - 10a + 25$

a	$f(a)$
3	4
4	1
5	0
6	1
7	4

root: 5

axis of symmetry: $a = 5$

vertex: $(5, 0)$

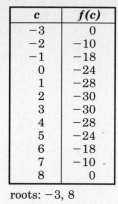

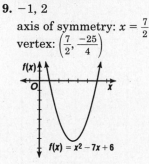

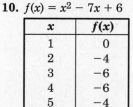

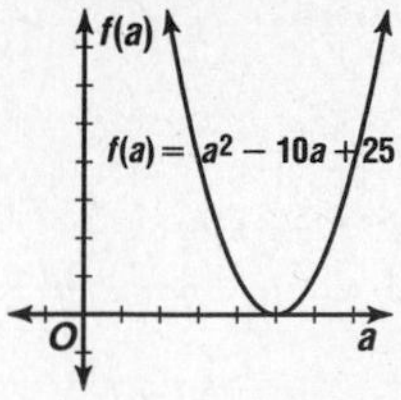

16. Let x represent one of the numbers. Then the other number is $5 - x$.
Solve $f(x) = x(5 - x)$ if $f(x) = -24$.

$$-24 = x(5 - x)$$
$$-24 = 5x - x^2$$
$$x^2 - 5x - 24 = 0$$
$$(x - 8)(x + 3) = 0$$
$$x - 8 = 0 \quad \text{or} \quad x + 3 = 0$$
$$x = 8 \qquad\qquad x = -3$$

8 and -3

Pages 625–627 Exercises

17. $-2, -6$ **18.** $-2, 2$ **19.** 2

20. $f(x) = x^2 + 7x + 12$

x	$f(x)$
-6	6
-5	2
-4	0
-3	0
-2	2
-1	6

axis of symmetry: $x = -\frac{7}{2}$
vertex: $\left(-\frac{7}{2}, -\frac{1}{4}\right)$

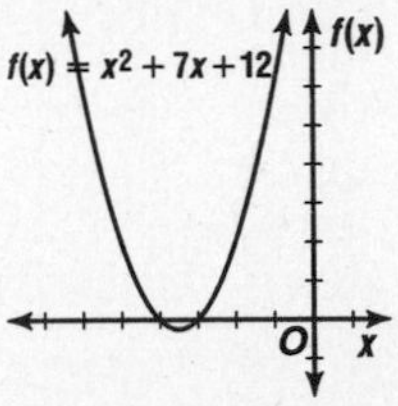

roots: $-3, -4$

21. $f(x) = x^2 - 16$

x	$f(x)$
-4	0
-3	-7
-2	-12
-1	-15
0	-16
1	-15
2	-12
3	-7
4	0

axis of symmetry: $x = 0$
vertex: $(0, -16)$

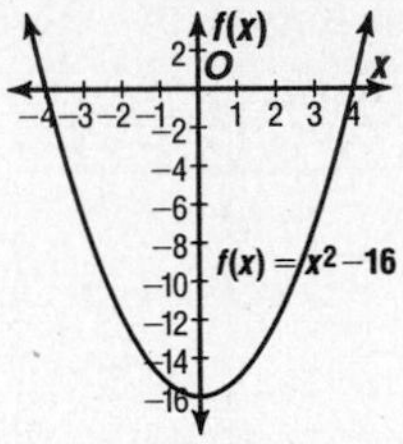

roots: $-4, 4$

22. $f(a) = a^2 + 6a + 7$

a	$f(a)$
-6	7
-5	2
-4	-1
-3	-2
-2	-1
-1	2
0	7

axis of symmetry: $a = -3$
vertex: $(-3, -2)$

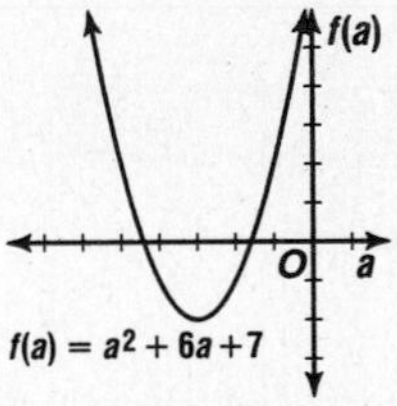

roots: $-5 < a < -4$,
$-2 < a < -1$

23. $f(x) = x^2 + 6x + 9$

x	$f(x)$
-5	4
-4	1
-3	0
-2	1
-1	4

axis of symmetry: $x = -3$
vertex: $(-3, 0)$

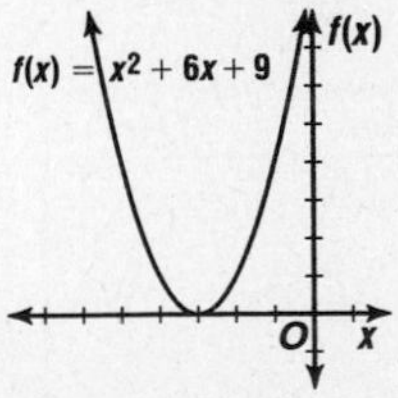

root: -3

24. $f(r) = r^2 + 4r - 12$

r	$f(r)$
-6	0
-5	-7
-4	-12
-3	-15
-2	-16
-1	-15
0	-12
1	-7
2	0

axis of symmetry: $r = -2$
vertex: $(-2, -16)$

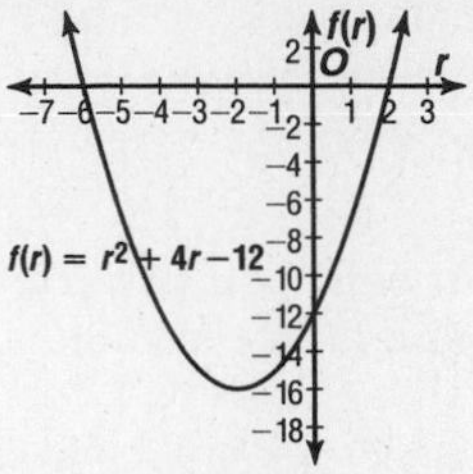

roots: $-6, 2$

25. $f(c) = c^2 + 3$

c	$f(c)$
-2	7
-1	4
0	3
1	4
2	7

$\varnothing$

axis of symmetry: $c = 0$
vertex: $(0, 3)$

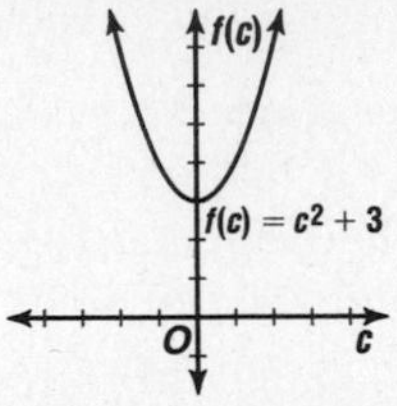

26. $f(c) = 2c^2 + 20c + 32$

c	$f(c)$
-8	0
-7	-10
-6	-16
-5	-18
-4	-16
-3	-10
-2	0

axis of symmetry: $c = -5$
vertex: $(-5, -18)$

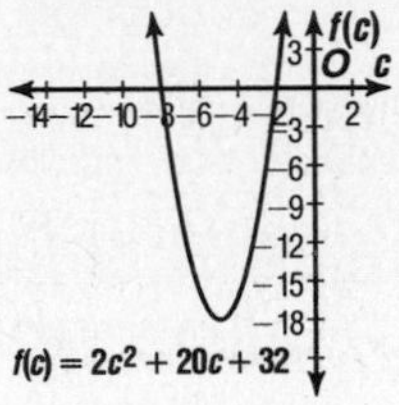

roots: $-8, -2$

27. $f(x) = 3x^2 + 9x - 12$

x	$f(x)$
-4	0
-3	-12
-2	-18
-1	-18
0	-12
1	0

axis of symmetry: $x = -\frac{3}{2}$
vertex: $\left(-\frac{3}{2}, -18\frac{3}{4}\right)$

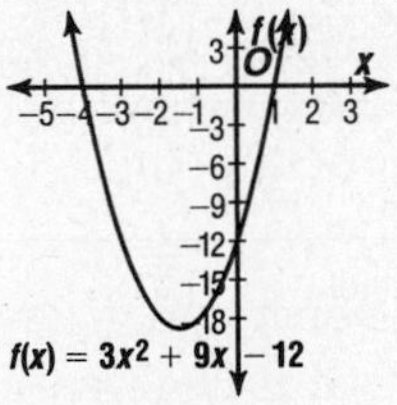

roots: $-4, 1$

28. $f(x) = 2x^2 - 18$

x	$f(x)$
-3	0
-2	-10
-1	-16
0	-18
1	-16
2	-10
3	0

axis of symmetry: $x = 0$
vertex: $(0, -18)$

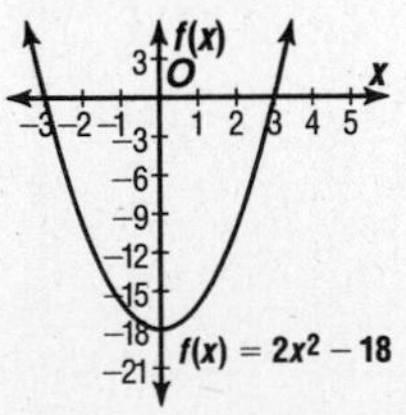

roots: $-3, 3$

29. $f(p) = p^2 - 8p + 16$

p	$f(p)$
2	4
3	1
4	0
5	1
6	4
7	9

axis of symmetry: $p = 4$
vertex: $(4, 0)$

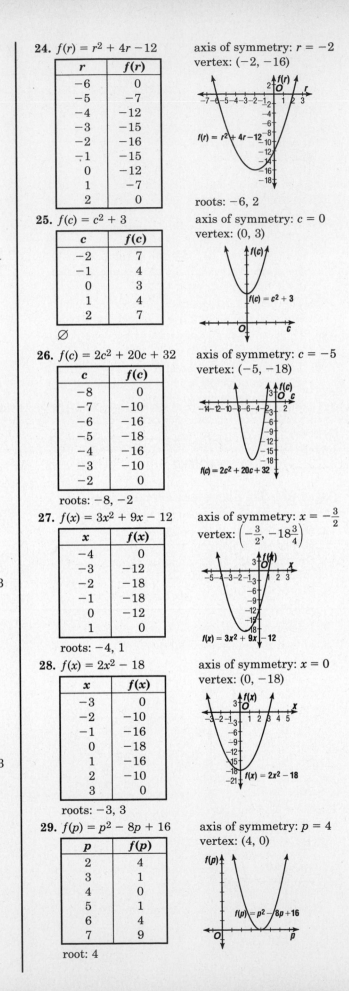

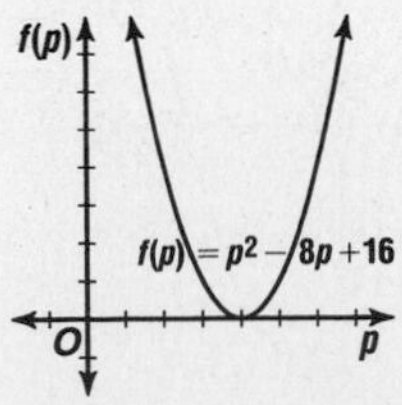

root: 4

30. $f(w) = w^2 - 10w + 21$

w	$f(w)$
2	5
3	0
4	−3
5	−4
6	−3
7	0
8	5

roots: 3, 7

axis of symmetry: $w = 5$
vertex: $(5, -4)$

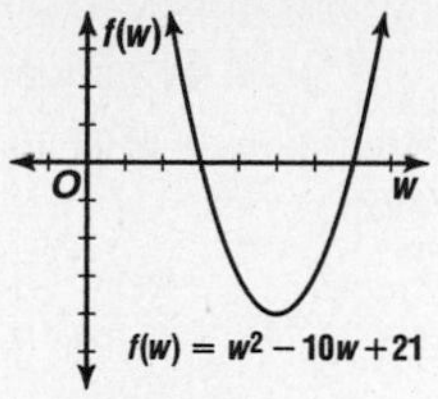

31. $f(a) = a^2 - 8a - 4$

a	$f(a)$
−1	5
0	−4
1	−11
2	−16
3	−19
4	−20
5	−19
6	−16
7	−11
8	−4
9	5

axis of symmetry: $a = 4$
vertex: $(4, -20)$

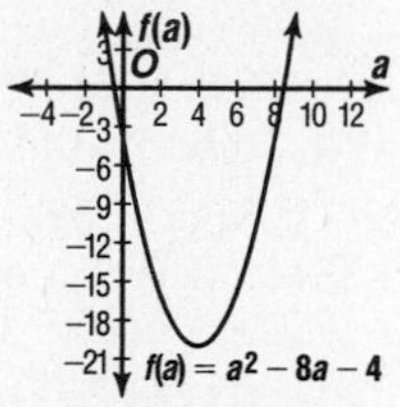

roots: $8 < a < 9$, $-1 < a < 0$

32. $f(m) = m^2 - 2m + 2$

m	$f(m)$
−1	5
0	2
1	1
2	2
3	5

$\varnothing$

axis of symmetry: $m = 1$
vertex: $(1, 1)$

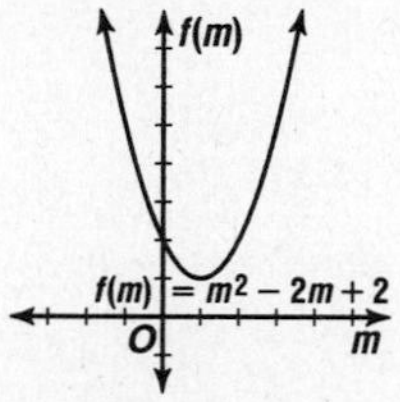

33. $f(n) = 12n^2 - 26n - 30$

n	$f(n)$
−1	8
0	−30
1	−44
2	−34
3	0
4	58

roots: 3, $-1 < n < 0$

axis of symmetry: $n = \frac{13}{12}$
vertex: $\left(\frac{13}{12}, -44\frac{1}{12}\right)$

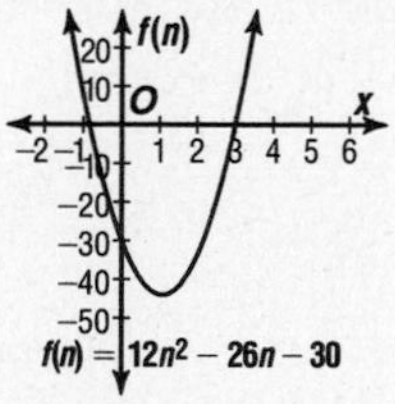

34. $f(x) = 4x^2 + 4x - 35$

x	$f(x)$
−4	13
−3	−11
−2	−27
−1	−35
0	−35
1	−27
2	−11
3	13

roots: $-4 < x < -3$, $2 < x < 3$

axis of symmetry: $x = -\frac{1}{2}$
vertex: $\left(-\frac{1}{2}, -36\right)$

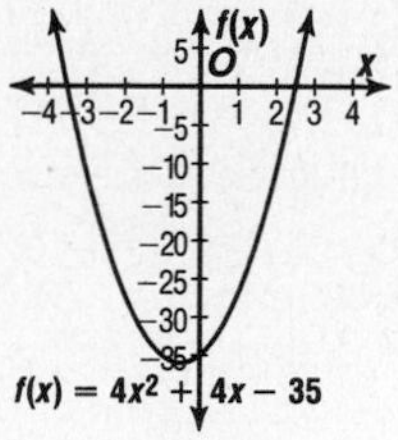

35.

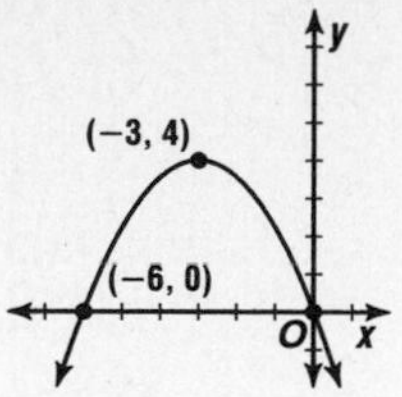

36.

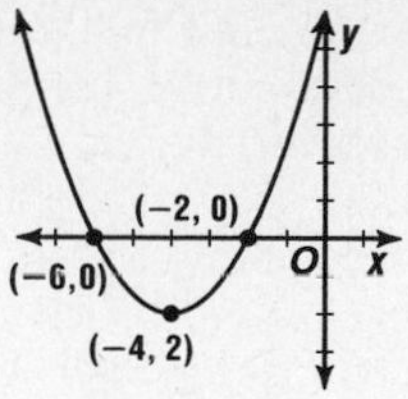

37.

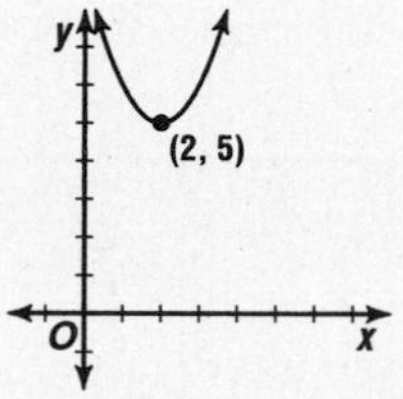

38.

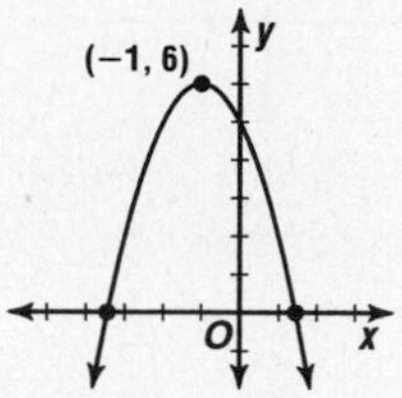

39. Let n represent one of the numbers. Then the other number is $n - 4$.

$n(n - 4) = 32$
$n^2 - 4n = 32$
$n^2 - 4n - 32 = 0$
$(n - 8)(n + 4) = 0$
$n - 8 = 0$ or $n + 4 = 0$
$n = 8$ $\quad n = -4$
$n - 4 = 8 - 4$ or 4 $\quad n - 4 = -4 - 4$ or -8
$-4, -8$ or 4, 8

40. Let n represent one of the numbers. Then the other number is $9 - n$.

$n(9 - n) = 20$
$9n - n^2 = 20$
$n^2 - 9n + 20 = 0$
$(n - 4)(n - 5) = 0$
$n - 4 = 0$ or $n - 5 = 0$
$n = 4$ $\quad n = 5$
4, 5

41. Let n represent one of the numbers. Then the other number is $4 - n$.

$n(4 - n) = 5$
$4n - n^2 = 5$
$0 = n^2 + 4n + 5$ not factorable
no solution

42. Let n represent one of the numbers. Then the other number is $n - 2$.

$130 = n^2 + (n - 2)^2$
$130 = n^2 + (n^2 - 4n + 4)$
$130 = 2n^2 - 4n + 4$
$0 = 2n^2 - 4n - 126$
$0 = n^2 - 2n - 63$
$0 = (n - 9)(n + 7)$
$n - 9 = 0$ or $n + 7 = 0$
$n = 9$ $\quad n = -7$
$n - 2 = 9 - 2$ or 7 $\quad n - 2 = -7 - 2$ or -9
9 and 7 or -9 and -7

43. $x = -0.75y^2 - 6y - 9$
axis of symmetry: $y = -4$
vertex: $(3, -4)$

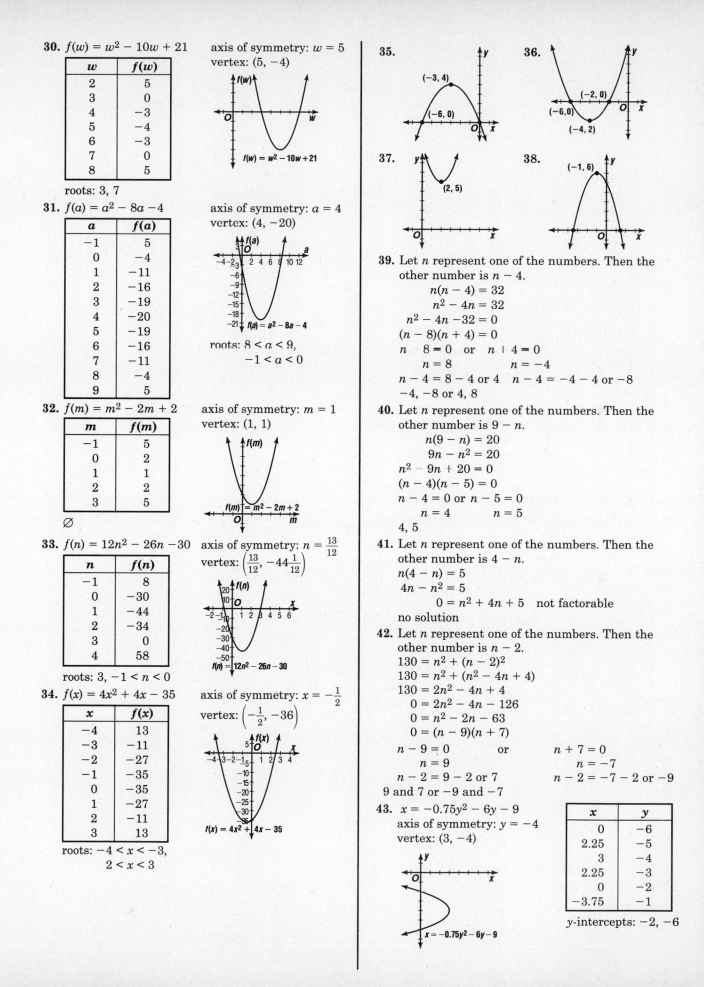

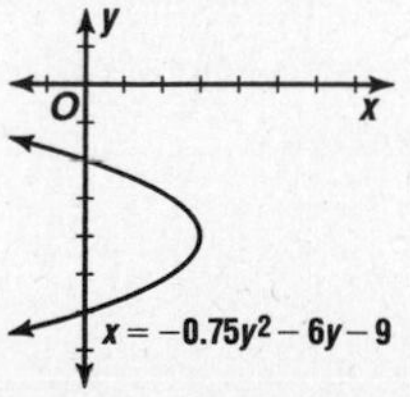

x	y
0	−6
2.25	−5
3	−4
2.25	−3
0	−2
−3.75	−1

y-intercepts: $-2, -6$

44. $x = y^2 - 4y + 1$
axis of symmetry: $y = 2$
vertex: $(-3, 2)$

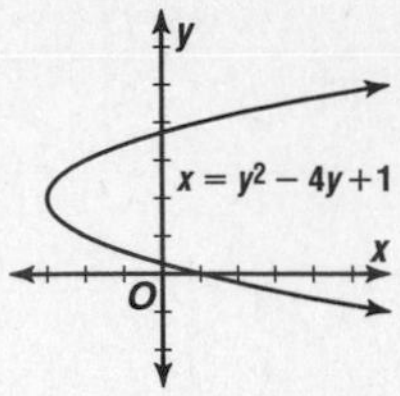

x	y
1	0
−2	1
−3	2
−2	3
1	4
6	5

y-intercepts: $0 < y < 1$, $3 < y < 4$

45. $x = 3y^2 + 2y + 4$
axis of symmetry: $y = -\frac{1}{3}$
vertex: $\left(-\frac{1}{3}, \frac{11}{3}\right)$

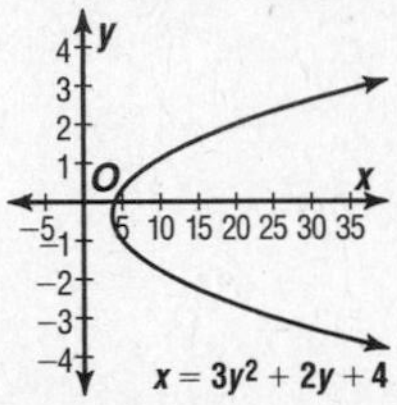

x	y
12	−2
5	−1
4	0
9	1
20	2
37	3

no y-intercepts

46. Graph $y = 4x^2 - 11$ in the standard viewing window. Use the ROOT feature; −1.66, 1.66.

47. Graph $y = -2x^2 - x - 3$ in the standard viewing window. Use the ROOT feature; no real roots.

48. Graph $y = x^2 + 22x + 121$ in the standard viewing window. Use the ROOT feature; −11.

49. Graph $y = 6x^2 - 12x + 3$ in the standard viewing window. Use the ROOT feature; 0.29, 1.71.

50. Graph $y = 5x^2 + 4x - 7$ in the standard viewing window. Use the ROOT feature; −1.6, 0.85.

51. Graph $y = -4x^2 + 7x + 8$ in the standard viewing window. Use the ROOT feature; −0.79, 2.54.

52(a). 2.25
52(b). $k < 2.25$
52(c). $k > 2.25$

53(a). −2
53(b). $k > -2$
53(c). $k < -2$

54. The value of the function changes from negative to positive as it moves from $x = 10$ to $x = 11$. In order to do this, it must cross the x-axis between 10 and 11. Therefore, an x-intercept occurs between 10 and 11. Thus, the root of the related equation lies between 10 and 11.

55a. $f(x) = -x^2 - 4x + 12$
axis of symmetry: $x = -2$
vertex: $(-2, 16)$

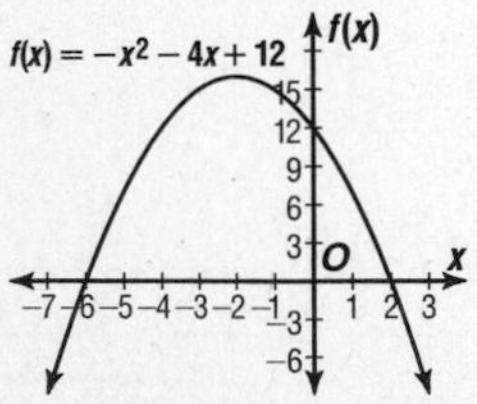

x	$f(x)$
−6	0
−5	7
−4	12
−3	15
−2	16
−1	15
0	12
1	7
2	0

x-intercepts: −6, 2

55b. $2 - (-6) = 8$ feet (distance between x-intercepts)

55c. $16 - 0 = 16$ feet (floor to vertex)

55d. $A = \frac{2}{3}bh$
$= \frac{2}{3}(8)(16)$
$= 85\frac{1}{3}$ ft^2

55e. $12\left(85\frac{1}{3}\right) = 1024$ ft^2
$(1024)(2) = 2048$ ft^2 *She applies 2 coats.*
$\frac{2048}{200} = 10.24$ gallons
She must buy 11 gallons at \$27/gallon for a cost of \$297.

56a.

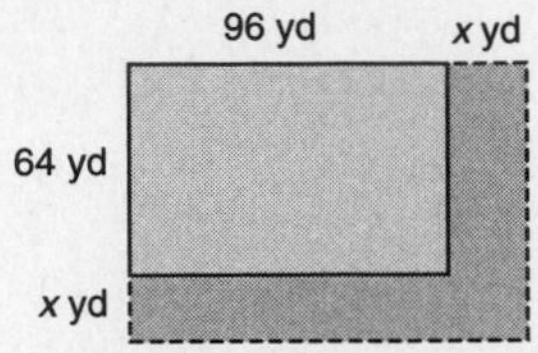

56b. $(64 + x)(96 + x) = 2(64)(96)$
$x^2 + 160x + 6144 = 12{,}288$
$x^2 + 160x - 6144 = 0$

56c. $(x + 192)(x - 32) = 0$
$x + 192 = 0$ or $x - 32 = 0$
$x = -192$ $x = 32$
32 yards

56d. $64 + 32 = 96$
$96 + 32 = 128$
96 yards × 128 yards

57. $y = -3x^2 + 4$, $a = -3$, $b = 0$
axis of symmetry: $x = -\frac{b}{2a} = -\frac{0}{2(-3)}$ or $x = 0$
$y = -3(0)^2 + 4$
$= 4$
The coordinates of the vertex are (0, 4).

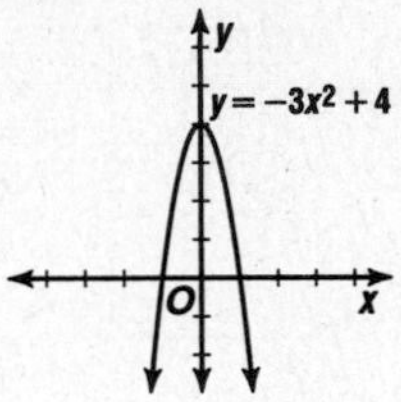

58. $81x^3 + 36x^2 = -4x$
$81x^3 + 36x^2 + 4x = 0$
$x(81x^2 + 36x + 4) = 0$
$x(9x + 2)(9x + 2) = 0$
$x = 0$ or $9x + 2 = 0$
$9x = -2$
$x = -\frac{2}{9}$
$\left\{0, -\frac{2}{9}\right\}$

59. $8x^2 - 10x + 3 = (4x - 3)(2x - 1)$
$(4x - 3)$ m by $(2x - 1)$ m

60. $(x - 2y)^3 = (x - 2y)(x - 2y)(x - 2y)$
$= (x - 2y)(x^2 - 4xy + 4y^2)$
$= x(x^2 - 4xy + 4y^2) - 2y(x^2 - 4xy + 4y^2)$
$= x^3 - 4x^2y + 4xy^2 - 2x^2y + 8xy^2 - 8y^3$
$= x^3 - 6x^2y + 12xy^2 - 8y^3$

61. The degree of $6x^2y$ is 3.
The degree of $5x^3y^2z$ is 6.
The degree of $-x$ is 1.
The degree of x^2y^2 is 4.
Thus, the degree of $6x^2y + 5x^3y^2z - x + x^2y^2$ is 6.

62. $x + y = 3$ Solve for y: $y = -x + 3$
$x + y = 4$ $y = -x + 4$

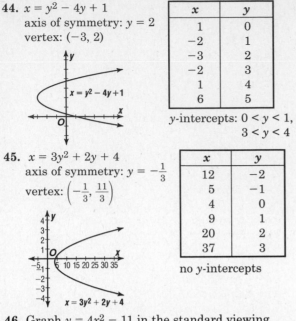

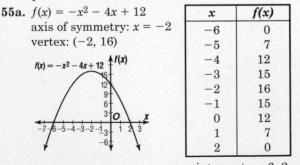

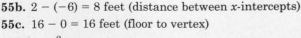

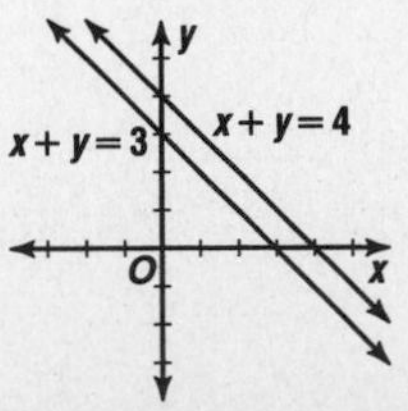

no solution

63. $|3x + 4| < 8$

$3x + 4 < 8$ and $3x + 4 > -8$

$3x < 4$ $\quad 3x > -12$

$x < \frac{4}{3}$ $\quad x > -4$

$-4 < x < \frac{4}{3}$

64. $y = -x + 6$

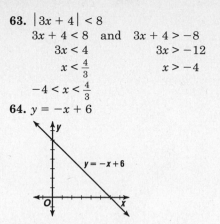

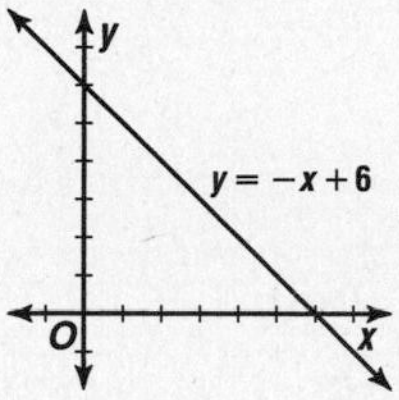

65. Discount is $0.25(33) = \$8.25$

$\$33 - \$8.25 = \$24.75$

66. $-4 + 6 + (-10) + 8 = 2 + (-10) + 8$

$= -8 + 8$

$= 0$

11-3 Solving Quadratic Equations by Using the Quadratic Formula

Page 631 Check for Understanding

1. Evaluate the formula using + for one root; then reevaluate using − for the other.

2. You get the square root of a negative number.

3a. $1992 - 1824 = 168$

$V(t) = 0.0046t^2 - 0.185t + 3.30$

$V(168) = 0.0046(168)^2 - 0.185(168) + 3.30$

$= 102.05$ million

3b. $2000 - 1824 = 176$

$V(t) = 0.0046t^2 - 0.185t + 3.30$

$V(176) = 0.0046(176)^2 - 0.185(176) + 3.30$

$= 113.23$ million

4. See students' work.

5. $a = 1, b = 3, c = -18$

$x = \frac{-3 \pm \sqrt{(3)^2 - 4(1)(-18)}}{2(1)}$

$= \frac{-3 \pm \sqrt{9 + 72}}{2}$

$= \frac{-3 \pm \sqrt{81}}{2}$

$= \frac{-3 \pm 9}{2}$

$x = \frac{-3 + 9}{2}$ or $x = \frac{-3 - 9}{2}$

$= \frac{6}{2}$ or 3 $\quad = \frac{-12}{2}$ or -6

$3, -6$

6. $14 = 12 - 5x - x^2$

$0 = -2 - 5x - x^2$

$a = -1, b = -5, c = -2$

$x = \frac{-(-5) + \sqrt{(-5)^2 - 4(-1)(-2)}}{2(-1)}$

$= \frac{5 \pm \sqrt{25 - 8}}{2}$

$= \frac{-5 \pm \sqrt{17}}{2}$

$x = \frac{-5 + \sqrt{17}}{2}$ or $x = \frac{-5 - \sqrt{17}}{2}$

≈ -0.44 $\quad \approx -4.56$

$-4.56, -0.44$

7. $4x^2 - 2x + 15 = 0$

$a = 4, b = -2, c = 15$

$x = \frac{-(-2) \pm \sqrt{(-2)^2 - 4(4)(15)}}{2(4)}$

$= \frac{2 \pm \sqrt{4 - 240}}{8}$

$= \frac{2 \pm \sqrt{-236}}{8}$

no real roots

8. $x^2 - 25 = 0$

$a = 1, b = 0, c = -25$

$x = \frac{-0 \pm \sqrt{(0)^2 - 4(1)(-25)}}{2(1)}$

$= \frac{\pm \sqrt{100}}{2}$

$= \frac{\pm 10}{2}$

$x = \frac{10}{2}$ or $x = -\frac{10}{2}$

$= 5$ $\quad = -5$

$5, -5$

9. $4x^2 + 2x - 17 = 0$

$a = 4, b = 2, c = -17$

$x = \frac{-2 \pm \sqrt{(2)^2 - 4(4)(-17)}}{2(4)}$

$= \frac{-2 \pm \sqrt{4 + 272}}{8}$

$= \frac{-2 \pm \sqrt{276}}{8}$

$x = \frac{-2 + \sqrt{276}}{8}$ or $x = \frac{-2 - \sqrt{276}}{8}$

≈ 1.83 $\quad \approx -2.33$

$1.83, -2.33$

10. $3b^2 + 5b + 11 = 0$

$a = 3, b = 5, c = 11$

$b = \frac{-5 \pm \sqrt{(5)^2 - 4(3)(11)}}{2(3)}$

$= \frac{-5 \pm \sqrt{25 - 132}}{6}$

$= \frac{-5 \pm \sqrt{-107}}{6}$

$\varnothing$

11. $x^2 + 7x + 6 = 0$

$a = 1, b = 7, c = 6$

$x = \frac{-7 \pm \sqrt{(7)^2 - 4(1)(6)}}{2(1)}$

$= \frac{-7 \pm \sqrt{49 - 24}}{2}$

$= \frac{-7 \pm \sqrt{25}}{2}$

$= \frac{-7 \pm 5}{2}$

$x = \frac{-7 + 5}{2}$ or $x = \frac{-7 - 5}{2}$

$= \frac{-2}{2}$ or -1 $\quad = \frac{-12}{2}$ or -6

$-1, -6$

12. $2^2 - 13z - 32 = 0$

$a = 1, b = -13, c = -32$

$z = \frac{-(-13) \pm \sqrt{(-13)^2 - 4(1)(-32)}}{2(1)}$

$= \frac{13 \pm \sqrt{169 + 128}}{2}$

$= \frac{13 \pm \sqrt{297}}{2}$

$z = \frac{13 + \sqrt{297}}{2}$ or $z = \frac{13 - \sqrt{297}}{2}$

$\approx \frac{30.23}{2}$ or 15.12 $\approx \frac{-4.23}{2}$ or $-$ 2.12

$-2.12, 15.12$

13. $4v^2 + 5v - 2 = \frac{1200Hn}{L}$

$4v^2 + 5v - 2 = \frac{1200(10)(6)}{20}$

$4v^2 + 5v - 2 = 3600$

$4v^2 + 5v - 3602 = 0$

$a = 4, b = 5, c = -3602$

$v = \frac{-5 \pm \sqrt{(5)^2 - 4(4)(-3602)}}{2(4)}$

$= \frac{-5 \pm 25 + \sqrt{57{,}632}}{8}$

$= \frac{-5 \pm \sqrt{57{,}657}}{8}$

$\approx \frac{-5 \pm 240.1}{8}$

$v \approx \frac{-5 + 240.1}{8} = 29.4$ or $v \approx \frac{-5 - 240.1}{8} = -30.64$

The water is flowing at about 29.4 ft/s

Pages 631–633 Exercises

14. $x^2 - 2x - 24 = 0$

$a = 1, b = -2, c = -24$

$x = \frac{-(-2) \pm \sqrt{(-2)^2 - 4(1)(-24)}}{2(1)}$

$= \frac{2 \pm \sqrt{4 + 96}}{2}$

$= \frac{2 \pm \sqrt{100}}{2}$

$= \frac{2 \pm 10}{2}$

$x = \frac{2 + 10}{2}$ or $x = \frac{2 - 10}{2}$

$= \frac{12}{2}$ or 6 $= -\frac{8}{2}$ or -4

$-4, 6$

15. $a^2 + 10a + 12 = 0$

$a = 1, b = 10, c = 12$

$a = \frac{-10 \pm \sqrt{(10)^2 - 4(1)(12)}}{2(1)}$

$= \frac{-10 \pm \sqrt{100 - 48}}{2}$

$= \frac{-10 \pm \sqrt{52}}{2}$

$a = \frac{-10 + \sqrt{52}}{2}$ or $a = \frac{-10 - \sqrt{52}}{2}$

≈ -1.39 ≈ -8.61

$-1.39, -8.61$

16. $c^2 + 12c + 20 = 0$

$a = 1, b = 12, c = 20$

$c = \frac{-12 \pm \sqrt{(12)^2 - 4(1)(20)}}{2(1)}$

$= \frac{-12 \pm \sqrt{144 - 80}}{2}$

$= \frac{-12 \pm \sqrt{64}}{2}$

$= \frac{-12 \pm 8}{2}$

$c = \frac{-12 + 8}{2}$ or $c = \frac{-12 - 8}{2}$

$= \frac{-4}{2}$ or -2 $= \frac{-20}{2}$ or -10

$-10, -2$

17. $5y^2 - y - 4 = 0$

$a = 5, b = -1, c = -4$

$y = \frac{-(-1) \pm \sqrt{(-1)^2 - 4(5)(-4)}}{2(5)}$

$= \frac{1 \pm \sqrt{1 + 80}}{10}$

$= \frac{1 \pm \sqrt{81}}{10}$

$= \frac{1 \pm 9}{10}$

$y = \frac{1 + 9}{10}$ or $y = \frac{1 - 9}{10}$

$= \frac{10}{10}$ or 1 $= -\frac{8}{10}$ or $-\frac{4}{5}$

$-\frac{4}{5}, 1$

18. $r^2 + 25 = 0$

$a = 1, b = 0, c = 25$

$r = \frac{-0 \pm \sqrt{(0)^2 - 4(1)(25)}}{2(1)}$

$= \frac{\pm \sqrt{-100}}{2}$

$\varnothing$

19. $3b^2 - 7b - 20 = 0$

$a = 3, b = -7, c = -20$

$b = \frac{-(-7) \pm \sqrt{(-7)^2 - 4(3)(-20)}}{2(3)}$

$= \frac{7 \pm \sqrt{49 + 240}}{6}$

$= \frac{7 \pm \sqrt{289}}{6}$

$= \frac{7 \pm 17}{6}$

$b = \frac{7 + 17}{6}$ or $b = \frac{7 - 17}{6}$

$= \frac{24}{6}$ or 4 $= \frac{-10}{6}$ or $-\frac{5}{3}$

$-\frac{5}{3}, 4$

20. $y^2 + 12y + 36 = 0$

$a = 1, b = 12, c = 36$

$y = \frac{-12 \pm \sqrt{(12)^2 - 4(1)(36)}}{2(1)}$

$= \frac{-12 \pm \sqrt{144 - 144}}{2}$

$= \frac{-12}{2}$ or -6

21. $2r^2 + r - 14 = 0$
$a = 2, b = 1, c = -14$
$r = \frac{-1 \pm \sqrt{(1)^2 - 4(2)(-14)}}{2(2)}$
$= \frac{-1 \pm \sqrt{1 + 112}}{4}$
$= \frac{-1 \pm \sqrt{113}}{4}$
$r = \frac{-1 + \sqrt{113}}{4}$ or $r = \frac{-1 - \sqrt{113}}{4}$
$\approx 2.41 \qquad \approx -2.91$
$-2.91, 2.41$

22. $2x^2 + 4x - 30 = 0$
$x^2 + 2x - 15 = 0$
$a = 1, b = 2, c = -15$
$x = \frac{-2 \pm \sqrt{(2)^2 - 4(1)(-15)}}{2(1)}$
$= \frac{-2 \pm \sqrt{4 + 60}}{2}$
$= \frac{-2 \pm \sqrt{64}}{2}$
$= \frac{2 \pm 8}{2}$
$x = \frac{-2 + 8}{2}$ or $x = \frac{-2 - 8}{2}$
$= \frac{6}{2}$ or $3 \qquad = -\frac{10}{2}$ or -5
$-5, 3$

23. $2x^2 - 28x + 98 = 0$
$x^2 - 14x + 49 = 0$
$a = 1, b = -14, c = 49$
$x = \frac{-(-14) \pm \sqrt{(-14)^2 - 4(1)(49)}}{2(1)}$
$= \frac{14 \pm \sqrt{196 - 196}}{2}$
$= \frac{14}{2}$ or 7

24. $24x^2 - 14x - 6 = 0$
$12x^2 - 7x - 3 = 0$
$a = 12, b = -7, c = -3$
$x = \frac{-(-7) \pm \sqrt{(-7)^2 - 4(12)(-3)}}{2(12)}$
$= \frac{7 \pm \sqrt{49 + 144}}{24}$
$= \frac{7 \pm \sqrt{193}}{24}$
$x = \frac{7 + \sqrt{193}}{24}$ or $x = \frac{7 - \sqrt{193}}{24}$
$\approx 0.87 \qquad \approx -0.29$
$-0.29, 0.87$

25. $6x^2 + 19x + 15 = 0$
$a = 6, b = 19, c = 15$
$x = \frac{-19 \pm \sqrt{(19)^2 - 4(6)(15)}}{2(6)}$
$= \frac{-19 \pm \sqrt{361 - 360}}{12}$
$= \frac{-19 \pm \sqrt{1}}{12}$
$= \frac{-19 \pm 1}{12}$
$x = \frac{-19 + 1}{12}$ or $x = \frac{-19 - 1}{12}$
$= \frac{-18}{12}$ or $-\frac{3}{2} \qquad = \frac{-20}{12}$ or $-\frac{5}{3}$
$-\frac{3}{2}, -\frac{5}{3}$

26. $12x^2 = 48$
$12x^2 - 48 = 0$
$x^2 - 4 = 0$
$a = 1, b = 0, c = -43$
$x = \frac{-0 \pm \sqrt{(0)^2 - 4(1)(-4)}}{2(1)}$
$= \frac{\pm \sqrt{16}}{2}$
$= \frac{\pm 4}{2}$
$x = \frac{4}{2}$ or $x = \frac{-4}{2}$
$= 2 \qquad = -2$
$-2, 2$

27. $x^2 + 6x = 3x + 6x$
$x^2 - 36 = 0$
$a = 1, b = 0, c = -36$
$x = \frac{-0 \pm \sqrt{(0)^2 - 4(1)(-36)}}{2(1)}$
$= \frac{0 \pm \sqrt{0 + 144}}{2}$
$= \frac{\pm 12}{2}$
$x = \frac{12}{2}$ or $x = \frac{-12}{2}$
$= 6 \qquad = -6$
$-6, 6$

28. $1.34a^2 - 1.1a + 1.02 = 0$
$a = 1.34, b = -1.1, c = 1.02$
$a = \frac{-(-1.1) \pm \sqrt{(-1.1)^2 - 4(1.34)(1.02)}}{2(1.34)}$
$= \frac{1.1 \pm \sqrt{1.21 - 5.4672}}{2.68}$
$= \frac{1.1 \pm \sqrt{-4.2572}}{2.68}$
$\varnothing$

29. $3m^2 - 2m - 1 = 0$
$a = 3, b = -2, c = -1$
$m = \frac{-(-2) \pm \sqrt{(-2)^2 - 4(3)(-1)}}{2(3)}$
$= \frac{2 \pm \sqrt{4 + 12}}{6}$
$= \frac{2 \pm \sqrt{16}}{6}$
$= \frac{2 \pm 4}{6}$
$m = \frac{2 + 4}{6}$ or $m = \frac{2 - 4}{6}$
$= \frac{6}{6}$ or $1 \qquad = \frac{-2}{6}$ or $-\frac{1}{3}$
$-\frac{1}{3}, 1$

30. $24a^2 - 2a - 15 = 0$
$a = 24, b = -2, c = -15$
$a = \frac{-(-2) \pm \sqrt{(-2)^2 - 4(24)(-15)}}{2(24)}$
$= \frac{2 \pm \sqrt{4 + 1440}}{48}$
$= \frac{2 \pm \sqrt{1444}}{48}$
$= \frac{2 \pm 38}{48}$
$a = \frac{2 + 38}{48}$ or $a = \frac{2 - 38}{48}$
$= \frac{40}{48}$ or $\frac{5}{6} \qquad = \frac{-36}{48}$ or $-\frac{3}{4}$
$-\frac{3}{4}, \frac{5}{6}$

31. $2w^2 = (7w + 3)$

$2w^2 = -7w - 3$

$2w^2 + 7w + 3 = 0$

$a = 2,\ b = 7,\ c = 3$

$a = \frac{-7 \pm \sqrt{(7)^2 - 4(2)(3)}}{2(2)}$

$= \frac{-7 \pm \sqrt{49 - 24}}{4}$

$= \frac{-7 \pm \sqrt{25}}{4}$

$= \frac{-7 \pm 5}{4}$

$a = \frac{-7 + 5}{4}$ or $a = \frac{-7 - 5}{4}$

$= \frac{-2}{4}$ or $-\frac{1}{2}$ $\quad = \frac{-12}{4}$ or -3

$-3, -\frac{1}{2}$

32. $a^2 - \frac{3}{5}a + \frac{2}{25} = 0$

$25a^2 - 15a + 2 = 0$

$a = 25,\ b = -15,\ c = 2$

$a = \frac{-(-15) \pm \sqrt{(-15)^2 - 4(25)(2)}}{2(25)}$

$= \frac{15 \pm \sqrt{225 - 200}}{50}$

$= \frac{15 \pm \sqrt{25}}{50}$

$= \frac{15 \pm 5}{50}$

$a = \frac{15 + 5}{50}$ or $a = \frac{15 - 5}{50}$

$= \frac{20}{50}$ or $\frac{2}{5}$ $\quad = \frac{10}{50}$ or $\frac{1}{5}$

$\frac{2}{5}, \frac{1}{5}$

33. $-2x^2 + 0.7x + 0.3 = 0$

$2x^2 - 0.7x - 0.3 = 0$

$a = 2,\ b = -0.7,\ c = -0.3$

$x = \frac{-(-0.7) \pm \sqrt{(-0.7)^2 - 4(2)(-0.3)}}{2(2)}$

$= \frac{0.7 \pm \sqrt{0.49 + 2.4}}{4}$

$= \frac{0.7 \pm \sqrt{2.89}}{4}$

$= \frac{0.7 \pm 1.7}{4}$

$x = \frac{0.7 + 1.7}{4}$ or $x = \frac{0.7 - 1.7}{4}$

$= \frac{2.4}{4}$ or 0.60 $\quad = \frac{-1.0}{4}$ or -0.25

$0.60, -0.25$

34. $2y^2 - \frac{5}{4}y - \frac{1}{2} = 0$

$8y^2 - 5y - 2 = 0$

$a = 8,\ b = -5,\ c = -2$

$y = \frac{-(-5) \pm \sqrt{(-5)^2 - 4(8)(-2)}}{2(8)}$

$= \frac{5 \pm \sqrt{25 + 64}}{16}$

$= \frac{5 \pm \sqrt{89}}{16}$

$y = \frac{5 + \sqrt{89}}{16}$ or $y = \frac{5 - \sqrt{89}}{16}$

≈ 0.90 $\quad \approx -0.28$

$-0.28, 0.90$

35. $f(x) = 2x^2 - 5x + 2$

$a = 2,\ b = -5,\ c = 2$

$x = \frac{-(-5) \pm \sqrt{(-5)^2 - 4(2)(2)}}{2(2)}$

$= \frac{5 \pm \sqrt{25 - 16}}{4}$

$= \frac{5 \pm \sqrt{9}}{4}$

$= \frac{5 \pm 3}{4}$

$y = \frac{5 + 3}{4}$ or $x = \frac{5 - 3}{4}$

$= \frac{8}{4}$ or 2 $\quad = \frac{2}{4}$ or 0.5

$0.5, 2$

36. $f(x) = 4x^2 - 9x + 4$

$a = 4,\ b = -9,\ c = 4$

$x = \frac{-(-9) \pm \sqrt{(-9)^2 - 4(4)(4)}}{2(4)}$

$= \frac{9 \pm \sqrt{81 - 64}}{8}$

$= \frac{9 \pm \sqrt{17}}{8}$

$x = \frac{9 + \sqrt{17}}{8}$ or $x = \frac{9 - \sqrt{17}}{8}$

≈ 1.6 $\quad \approx 0.6$

$0.6, 1.6$

37. $f(x) = 13x^2 - 16x - 4$

$a = 13,\ b = -16,\ c = -4$

$x = \frac{-(-16) \pm \sqrt{(-16)^2 - 4(13)(-4)}}{2(13)}$

$= \frac{16 \pm \sqrt{256 + 208}}{26}$

$= \frac{16 \pm \sqrt{464}}{26}$

$x = \frac{16 + \sqrt{464}}{26}$ or $x = \frac{16 - \sqrt{464}}{26}$

≈ 1.4 $\quad \approx -0.2$

$-0.2, 1.4$

38. Sample answer:

$[x - (-1 + \sqrt{3})][x - (-1 - \sqrt{3})]$

$= (x + 1 - \sqrt{3})(x + 1 + \sqrt{3})$

$= x^2 + x + \sqrt{3}x + x + 1 + \sqrt{3} - \sqrt{3}x - \sqrt{3} - 3$

$= x^2 + 2x - 2$

$a = 1,\ b = 2,\ c = -2;\ x^2 + 2x - 2 = 0$

39. Sample answer:

$\left[x - \left(\frac{-5 + \sqrt{2}}{2}\right)\right]\left[x - \left(\frac{-5 - \sqrt{2}}{2}\right)\right]$

$= \left(x + \frac{5 - \sqrt{2}}{2}\right)\left(x + \frac{5 + \sqrt{2}}{2}\right)$

$= x^2 + \frac{5 + \sqrt{2}}{2}x + \frac{5 - \sqrt{2}}{2}x + \left(\frac{5 - \sqrt{2}}{2}\right)\left(\frac{5 - \sqrt{2}}{2}\right)$

$= x^2 + \left(\frac{5}{2} + \frac{\sqrt{2}}{2}\right)x + \left(\frac{5}{2} - \frac{\sqrt{2}}{2}\right)x + \frac{25 + 5\sqrt{2} - 5\sqrt{2} - 2}{2}$

$= x^2 + \frac{5}{2}x + \frac{\sqrt{2}}{2}x + \frac{5}{2}x - \frac{\sqrt{2}}{2}x + \frac{23}{2}$

$= x^2 + \frac{5}{2}x + \frac{5}{2}x + \frac{25}{4} - \frac{2}{4}$

$= x^2 + 5x + \frac{23}{4}$

$= 4x^2 + 20x + 23$

$a = 4,\ b = 20,\ c = 23;\ 4x^2 + 20x + 23 = 0$

40. Sample answer:

$$\left(x - \frac{4+\sqrt{29}}{2}\right)\left(x - \frac{4-\sqrt{29}}{2}\right)$$
$$= x^2 - \frac{4-\sqrt{29}}{2}x - \frac{4+\sqrt{29}}{2}x + \left(\frac{4+\sqrt{29}}{2}\right)\left(\frac{4-\sqrt{29}}{2}\right)$$
$$= x^2 - \left(\frac{4}{2} + \frac{\sqrt{29}}{2}\right)x - \left(\frac{4}{2} - \frac{\sqrt{29}}{2}\right)x + \frac{16 - 4\sqrt{29} + 4\sqrt{29} - 29}{4}$$
$$= x^2 - \frac{4}{2}x - \frac{\sqrt{29}}{2}x - \frac{4}{2}x + \frac{\sqrt{29}}{2}x + \left(-\frac{13}{4}\right)$$
$$= x^2 - 4x - \frac{13}{4}$$
$$a = 1,\ b = -4,\ c = -\frac{13}{4};\ x^2 - 4x - \frac{13}{4} = 0$$

41a. 2 REAL ROOTS, 10, 1

41b. NO REAL ROOTS

41c. 1 DISTINCT ROOT: -0.5

41d. 2 REAL ROOTS, -1, 0.7142857143

42. See chart below.

43a. Discriminant is not a perfect square.

43b. Discriminant is a perfect square, but the expression is not an integer.

43c. Discriminant is a perfect square, and the equation can be factored.

43d. Discriminant is 0, and the equation is a perfect square.

44a. D: $0 \le t \le 13$: R: $511.4 \le I(t) \le 1205$

44b. $I(t) = 0.26t^2 + 49.94t + 511.4$
$I(13) = 0.26(13)^2 + 49.94(13) + 511.4$
$= \$1204.6$ billion

44c. $I(20) = 0.26(20)^2 + 49.94(20) + 511.4$
$= \$1614.2$ billion

44d. $1000 = 0.26t^2 + 49.94t + 511.4$
$0 = 0.26t^2 + 49.94t - 488.6$
$a = 0.26,\ b = 49.94,\ c = -488.6$
$$t = \frac{-49.94 \pm \sqrt{(49.94)^2 - 4(0.26)(-488.6)}}{2(0.26)}$$
$$= \frac{-49.94 \pm \sqrt{2494 + 508.14}}{0.52}$$
$$= \frac{-49.94 \pm \sqrt{3002.14}}{0.52}$$
$$\approx \frac{-49.94 \pm 54.79}{0.52}$$
$t \approx \frac{-49.94 + 54.79}{0.52} \approx \frac{4.85}{0.52}$ or about 9   or $t \approx \frac{-49.94 - 54.79}{0.52} \approx \frac{-104.73}{0.52}$ or -201

$1980 + 9 = 1989$

42.

Equation	$x^2 - 4x + 1 = 0$	$x^2 + 6x + 11 = 0$	$x^2 - 4x + 4 = 0$
Value of Discriminant	$(-4)^2 - 4(1)(1) = 12$	$(6)^2 - 4(1)(11) = -8$	$(-4)^2 - 4(1)(4) = 0$
Graph of the Equation	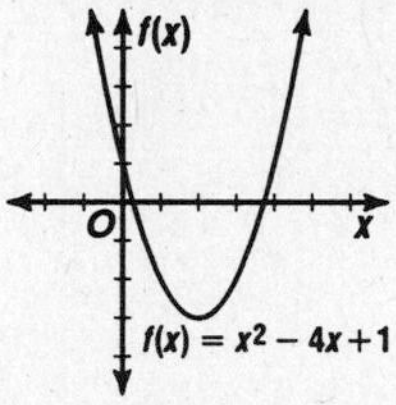	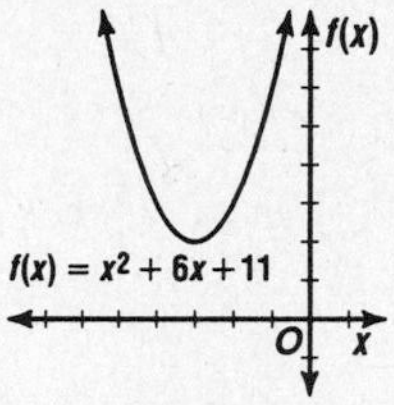	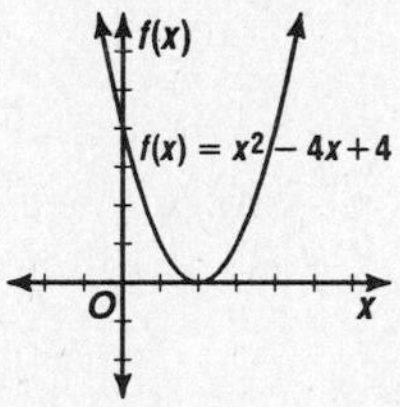
Number of x-intercepts	2	none	1
Number of Real Roots	2	none	1 distinct root

45a. $c = \frac{ad}{a + 12}$ $\qquad$ $c = \frac{(a+1)d}{24}$

$= \frac{6(30)}{6 + 12}$ $\qquad$ $= \frac{(6+1)30}{24}$

$= \frac{180}{18}$ or 10 mg $\qquad$ $= \frac{210}{24}$ or 8.75 mg

Y, 10 mg; C, 8.75 mg

45b. $\frac{ad}{a + 12} = \frac{(a+1)d}{24}$

$\frac{a}{a + 12} = \frac{a+1}{24}$

$24a = (a + 1)(a + 12)$

$24a = a^2 + 13a + 12$

$0 = a^2 - 11a + 12$

$a = 1,\ b = -11,\ c = 12$

$a = \frac{-(-11) \pm \sqrt{(-11)^2 - 4(1)(12)}}{2(1)}$

$= \frac{11 \pm \sqrt{121 - 48}}{2}$

$= \frac{11 \pm \sqrt{73}}{2}$

$a = \frac{11 + \sqrt{73}}{2}$ or $a = \frac{11 - \sqrt{73}}{2}$

≈ 9.8 $\qquad$ ≈ 1.2

$0 = a^2 - 11a + 12$; 1.2 yr, 9.8 yr

46. $x^2 + 10x + 21 = 0$

x	$f(x)$
−7	0
−6	−3
−5	−4
−4	−3
−3	0

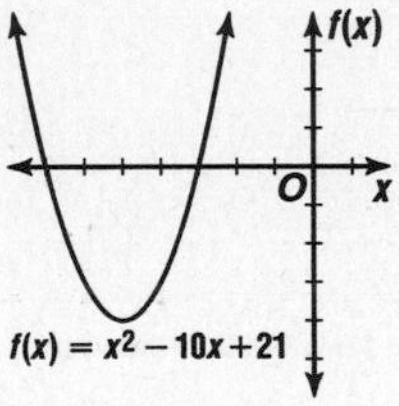

roots: −7, −3

47. $4s^2 = -36s$

$4s^2 + 36s = 0$

$4s(s + 9) = 0$

$4s = 0$ or $s + 9 = 0$

$s = 0$ $\qquad$ $s = -9$

$\{0, -9\}$

48. $3a^2(a - 4) + 6a(3a^2 + a - 7) - 4(a - 7)$

$= 3a^3 - 12a^2 + 18a^3 + 6a^2 - 42a - 4a + 28$

$= 21a^3 - 6a^2 - 46a + 28$

49. Let x = one number and let y = the other number.

$x + y = 42$ $\qquad$ $x + y = 42$ $\qquad$ $x + y = 42$

$x - y = 6$ $\qquad$ $(+)\ x - y = 6$ $\qquad$ $24 + y = 42$

$2x = 48$ $\qquad$ $y = 18$

$x = 24$

The numbers are 24 and 18.

50.

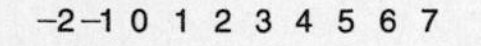

51. Each element of the domain is priced with exactly one element of the range; yes.

52. $3x + 8 = 2x - 4$

$3x - 2x + 8 = 2x - 2x - 4$

$x + 8 = -4$

$x + 8 - 8 = -4 - 8$

$x = -12$

53. $36 - 40 = 36 + (-40)$

$= -4°F$

Page 633 Self Test

1. $y = x^2 - x - 6,\ a = 1,\ b = -1$

axis of symmetry: $x = -\frac{b}{2a} = -\frac{(-1)}{2(1)}$ or $x = \frac{1}{2}$

$y = x^2 - x - 6$

$= \left(\frac{1}{2}\right)^2 - \left(\frac{1}{2}\right) - 6$

$= \frac{1}{4} - \frac{1}{2} - 6$

$= -\frac{25}{4}$

The coordinates of the vertex are $\left(\frac{1}{2}, -\frac{25}{4}\right)$.

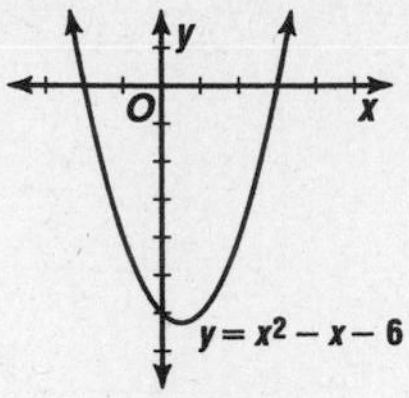

2. $y = 2x^2 + 3,\ a = 2,\ b = 0$

axis of symmetry: $x = -\frac{b}{2a} = -\frac{(0)}{2(2)}$ or $x = 0$

$y = 2x^2 + 3$

$= 2(0)^2 + 3$

$= 3$

The coordinates of the vertex are (0, 3).

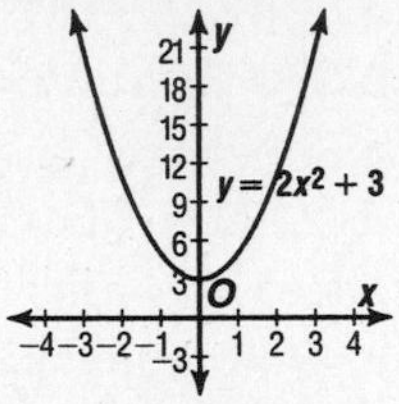

3. $y = -x^2 + 7,\ a = -1,\ b = 0$

axis of symmetry: $x = -\frac{b}{2a} = -\frac{(0)}{2(-1)}$ or $x = 0$

$y = -x^2 + 7$

$= -(0)^2 + 7$

$= 7$

The coordinates of the vertex are (0, 7).

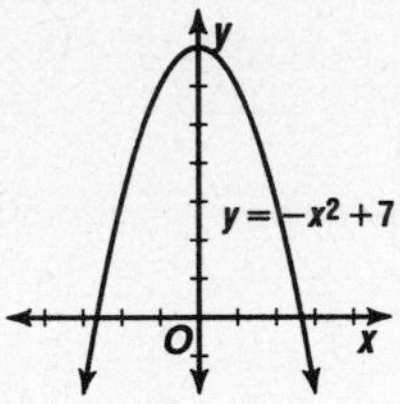

4a. $h = -16t^2 + 2320t + 125$

$84{,}225 = -16t^2 + 2320t + 125$

$0 = -16t^2 + 2320t + 125$

$a = -16,\ b = 2320$

$x = -\frac{b}{2a} = -\frac{(2320)}{2(-16)}$ or 72.5 s

4b. 0 seconds; this is the maximum height.

5. $f(x) = x^2 - 81$

axis of symmetry: $x = 0$

vertex: $(0, -81)$

x	$f(x)$
−9	0
−6	−45
−3	−72
0	−81
3	−72
6	−45
9	0

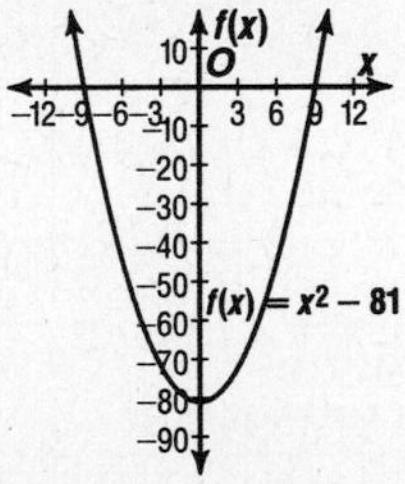

roots: −9, 9

6. $f(x) = 4x^2 + 4x - 35$

axis of symmetry: $x = -\frac{1}{2}$

vertex: $\left(-\frac{1}{2}, -36\right)$

x	$f(x)$
−4	13
−3	−11
−2	−27
−1	−35
0	−35
1	−27
2	−11
3	13
4	45

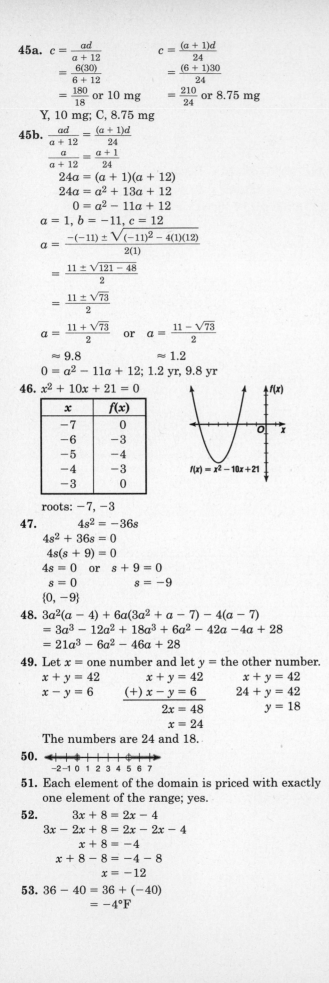

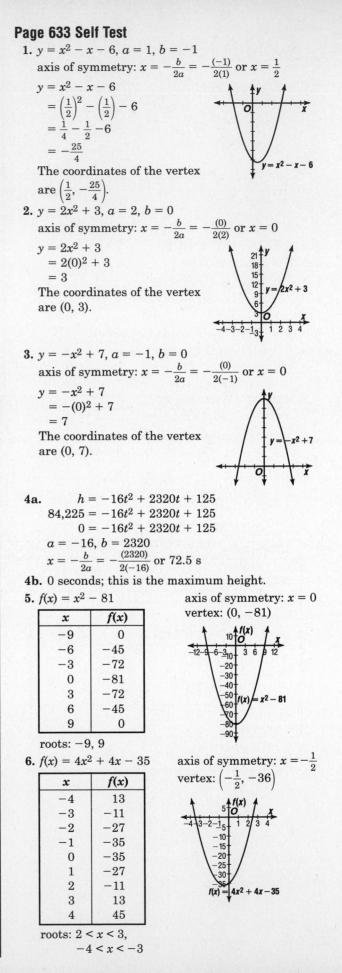

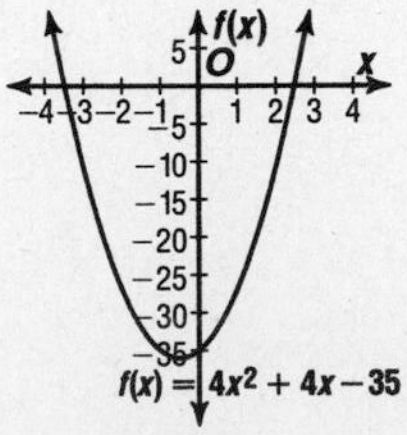

roots: $2 < x < 3$,

$-4 < x < -3$

7. $f(x) = 6x^2 + 36$

x	$f(x)$
−3	90
−2	60
−1	42
0	36
1	42
2	60

axis of symmetry: $x = 0$
vertex: (0, 36)

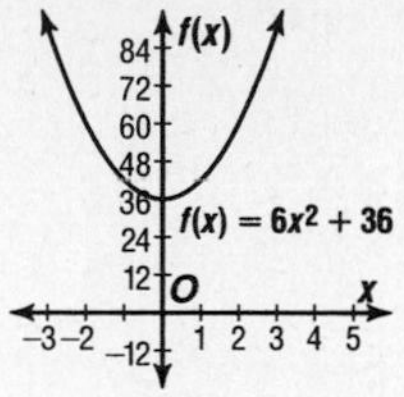

∅

8. $a^2 + 7a + 6 = 0$

$a = 1, b = 7, c = 6$

$$a = \frac{-7 \pm \sqrt{(7)^2 - 4(1)(6)}}{2(1)}$$
$$= \frac{-7 \pm \sqrt{49 - 24}}{2}$$
$$= \frac{-7 \pm \sqrt{25}}{2}$$
$$= \frac{-7 \pm 5}{2}$$
$$a = \frac{-7 + 5}{2} \quad \text{or} \quad a = \frac{-7 - 5}{2}$$
$$= \frac{-2}{2} \text{ or } -1 \qquad = \frac{-12}{2} \text{ or } -6$$

$-6, -1$

9. $y^2 + 6y + 10 = 0$

$a = 1, b = 6, c = 10$

$$y = \frac{-6 \pm \sqrt{(6)^2 - 4(1)(10)}}{2(1)}$$
$$= \frac{-6 \pm \sqrt{36 - 40}}{2}$$
$$= \frac{-6 \pm \sqrt{-4}}{2}$$

∅

10. $z^2 - 13z - 32 = 0$

$a = 1, b = -13, c = -32$

$$z = \frac{-(-13) \pm \sqrt{(-13)^2 - 4(1)(-32)}}{2(1)}$$
$$= \frac{13 \pm \sqrt{169 + 128}}{2}$$
$$= \frac{13 \pm \sqrt{297}}{2}$$
$$z = \frac{13 + \sqrt{297}}{2} \quad \text{or} \quad z = \frac{13 - \sqrt{297}}{2}$$
$$\approx 15.12 \qquad \approx -2.12$$

$-2.12, 15.12$

11-4A Graphing Technology Exponential Functions

Page 634 Exercises

1. Enter: [Y=] 2 [^] [X,T,θ] [ZOOM] 6

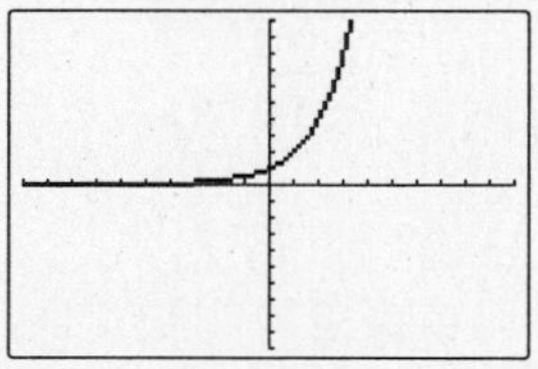

2. Enter: [Y=] 5 [^] [X,T,θ] [ZOOM] 6

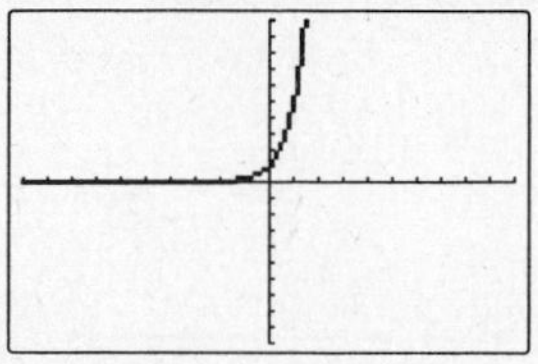

3. Enter: [Y=] .1 [^] [X,T,θ] [ZOOM] 6

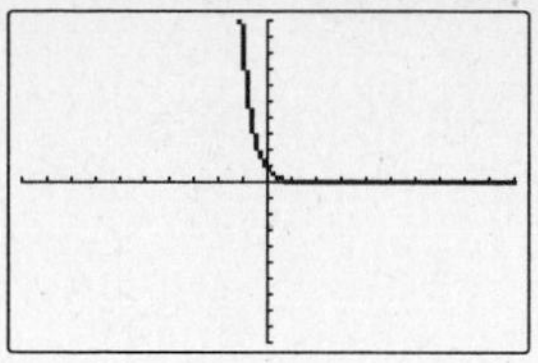

4. Enter: [Y=] = [(] 2 [÷] 3 [)] [^] [X,T,θ] [GRAPH]

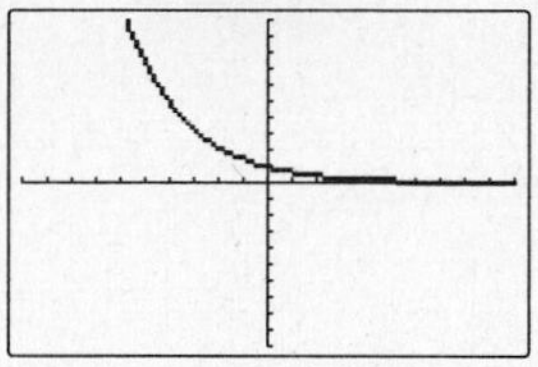

5. Enter: [Y=] .25 [^] [X,T,θ] [ZOOM] 6

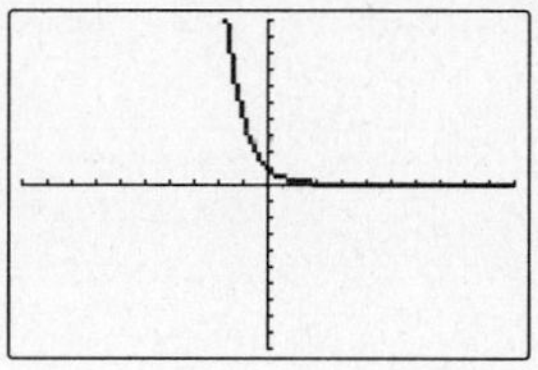

6. Enter: [Y=] 1.6 [^] [X,T,θ] [ZOOM] 6

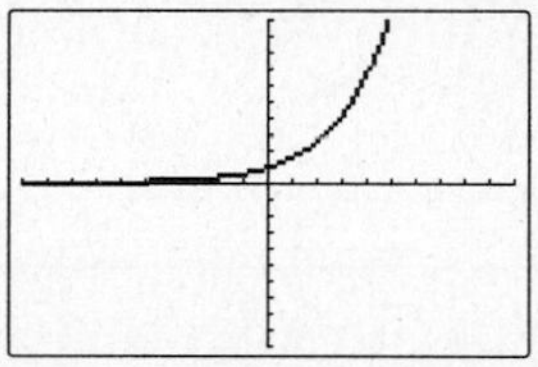

7. Enter: [Y=] .2 [^] [X,T,θ] [ZOOM] 6

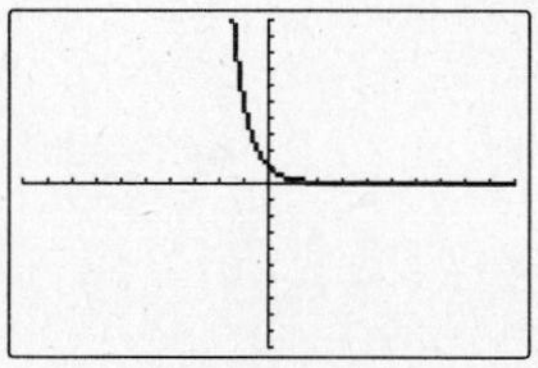

8. Enter: [Y=] .5 [^] [(−)] [X,T,θ] [ZOOM] 6

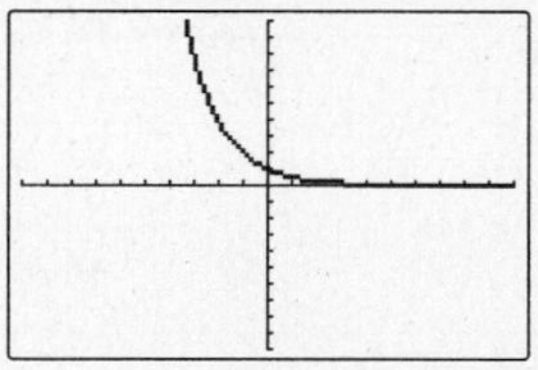

9. Enter [Y=] 10 [^] [X,T,θ] [ZOOM] 6

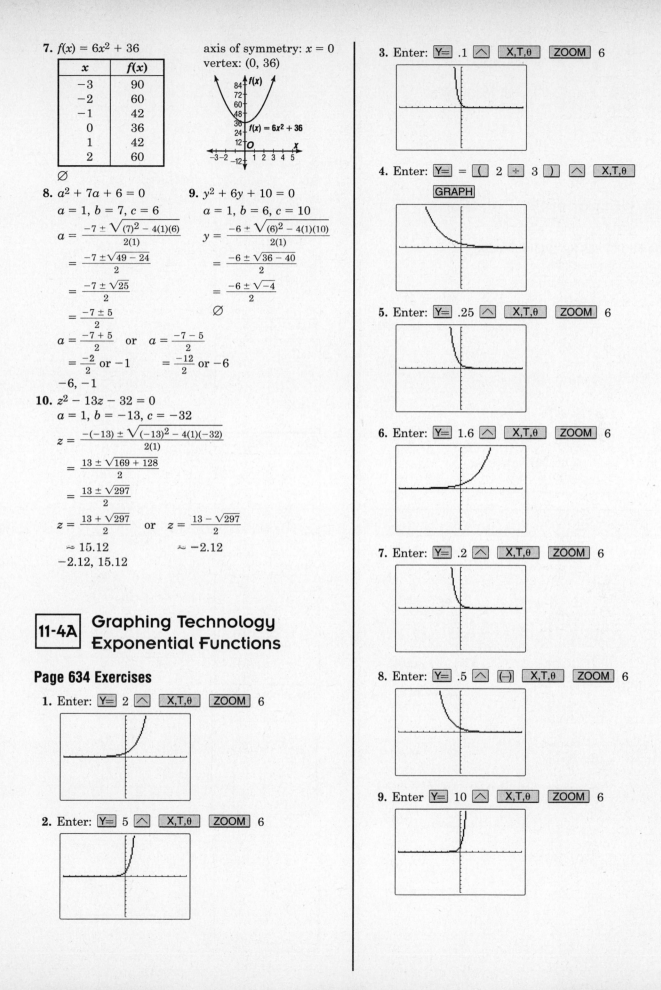

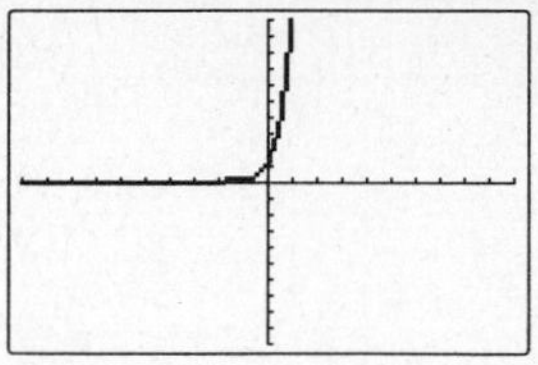

10. Sample answers:
(1) Graph $y = 1.2^x$ and $y = 10$ and find their intersection,
(2) Graph $y = 1.2^x - 10$ and find its zero,
(3) Graph $y = 1.2^x$ and use trace to find where $y = 10$.
12.63

11-4 Exponential Functions

Page 640 Check for Understanding

1a. $2^{64} = 1.844674407 \times 10^{19}$

1b. 24,000 grains $\approx$ 1 pound

$1.844674407 \times 10^{19}$ grains $\times \frac{1\ \text{pound}}{24,000\ \text{grains}} \times$

$\frac{1\ \text{ton}}{2000\ \text{pounds}} \approx 3.8 \times 10^{11}$ tons; over 3.8×10^{11} tons

2a. No, it does not.

2b. Sample answer: Use the graph of $y = 2^x$ and the TRACE feature on a graphing calculator to examine the y values.

2c. no; only those of the form $y = a^x$

3a. No, it does not. **3b.** See students' work.

3c. Yes.

4. If $a = 1$, $a^x = 1$ for any value of x.

5. See students' work.

6a.

Fold	1	2	3	4	5	6
Area	$\frac{1}{2}$	$\frac{1}{4}$	$\frac{1}{8}$	$\frac{1}{16}$	$\frac{1}{32}$	$\frac{1}{64}$

6b. Each fold makes a rectangle whose area is $\frac{1}{2^x}$, where x is the number of folds.

6c. $y = \left(\frac{1}{2}\right)^x$ or $y = 0.5^x$

7. 5.20   **8.** 0.37   **9.** 12.51

10.

x	y
-2	4
-1	2
0	1
1	$\frac{1}{2}$
2	$\frac{1}{4}$

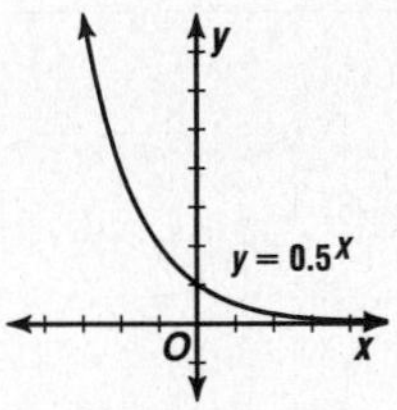

The y-intercept is 1.

11.

x	y
-2	$6\frac{1}{4}$
-1	$6\frac{1}{2}$
0	7
1	8
2	11

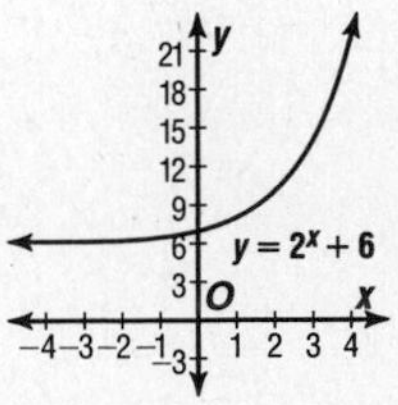

The y-intercept is 7.

12. Yes, increases by a factor of 6.

13. $5^{3y+4} = 5^y$
$3y + 4 = y$
$3y = y - 4$
$2y = -4$
$y = -2$

14. $2^5 = 2^{2x-1}$
$5 = 2x - 1$
$6 = 2x$
$3 = x$

15. $3^x = 9^{x+1}$
$3^x = (3^2)^{x+1}$
$3^x = 3^{2x+2}$
$x = 2x + 2$
$-x = 2$
$x = -2$

16. $B = 100 \cdot 2^t$
$1000 = 100 \cdot 2^t$
$10 = 2^t$
$2^{3.32} \approx 2^t$
$t \approx 3.32$ hours

Pages 640–642 Exercises

17. 10.56 **18.** 0.32 **19.** 1.63 **20.** 0.01
21. 25.86 **22.** 1.38 **23.** 0.86 **24.** 844.49

25.

x	y
-2	$4\frac{1}{4}$
-1	$4\frac{1}{2}$
0	5
1	6
2	8

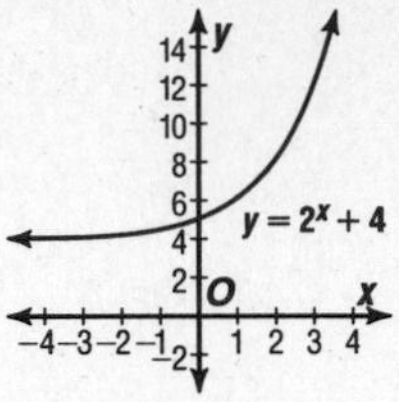

The y-intercept is 5.

26.

x	y
-2	4
-1	8
0	16
1	32
2	64

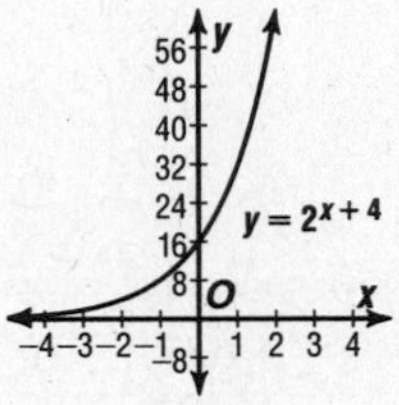

The y-intercept is 16.

27.

x	y
-2	27
-1	9
0	3
1	1
2	$\frac{1}{3}$

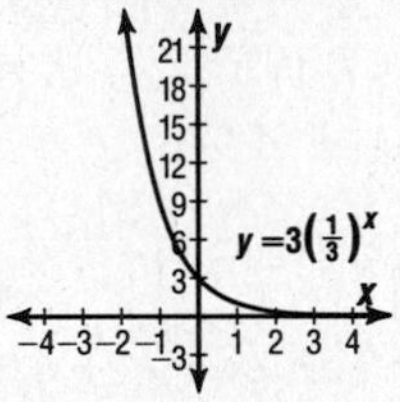

The y-intercept is 3.

28.

x	y
-2	$\frac{2}{9}$
-1	$\frac{2}{3}$
0	2
1	6
2	18

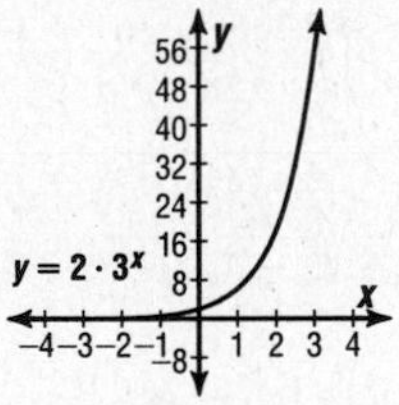

The y-intercept is 2.

29.

x	y
-2	$\frac{1}{16}$
-1	$\frac{1}{4}$
0	1
1	4
2	16

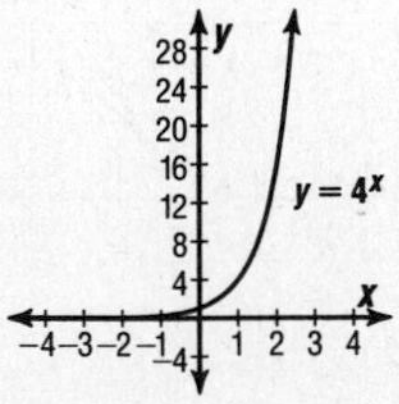

The y-intercept is 1.

30.

x	y
-2	16
-1	4
0	1
1	$\frac{1}{4}$
2	$\frac{1}{16}$

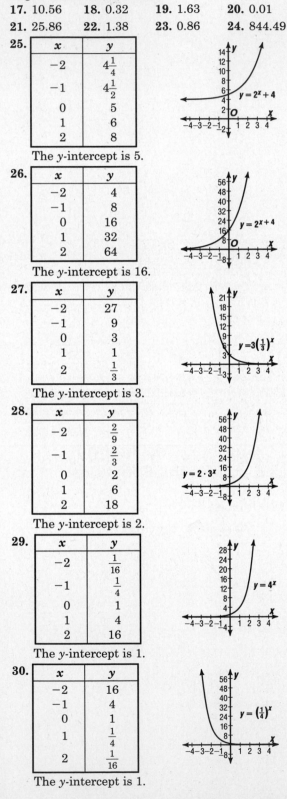

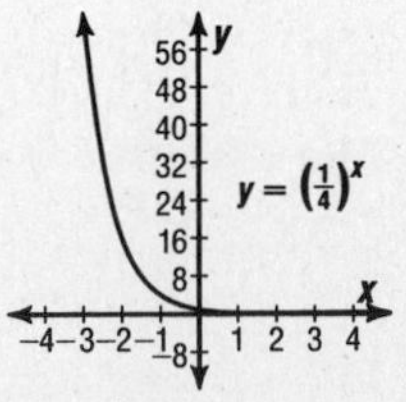

The y-intercept is 1.

31. $-5 + 3 = -2$, $-2 + 3 = 1$, $3 + 1 = 4$; no, linear

32. $1(0.5) = 0.5$, $(0.5)(0.5) = 0.25$; yes, constant factor

33. no, no pattern

34. $5^{3x} = 5^{-3}$
$3x = -3$
$x = -1$

35. $2^{x+3} = 2^{-4}$
$x + 3 = -4$
$x = -7$

36. $5^x = 5^{3x+1}$
$x = 3x + 1$
$-2x = 1$
$x = -\frac{1}{2}$ or -0.5

37. $10^x = 0.001$
$10^x = \frac{1}{1000}$
$10^x = 10^{-3}$
$x = -3$

38. $2^{2x} = \frac{1}{8}$
$2^{2x} = \frac{1}{2^3}$
$2^{2x} = 2^{-3}$
$2x = -3$
$x = -\frac{3}{2}$

39. $\left(\frac{1}{6}\right)^q = 6^{q-6}$
$(6^{-1})^q = 6^{q-6}$
$6^{-q} = 6^{q-6}$
$-q = q - 6$
$-2q = -6$
$q = 3$

40. $16^{x-1} = 64^x$
$(4^2)^{x-1} = (4^3)^x$
$4^{2x-2} = 4^{3x}$
$2x - 2 = 3x$
$-2 = x$

41. $81^x = 9^{x^2-3}$
$(9^2)^x = 9^{x^2-3}$
$9^{2x} = 9^{x^2-3}$
$2x = x^2 - 3$
$0 = x^2 - 2x - 3$
$0 = (x - 3)(x + 1)$
$x - 3 = 0$ or $x + 1 = 0$
$x = 3$ $\quad x = -1$
$3, -1$

42. $4^{x^2-2x} = 8^{x^2+1}$
$(2^2)^{x^2-2x} = (2^3)^{x^2+1}$
$2^{2x^2-4x} = 2^{3x^2+3}$
$2x^2 - 4x = 3x^2 + 3$
$0 = x^2 + 4x + 3$
$0 = (x + 1)(x + 3)$
$x + 1 = 0$ or $x + 3 = 0$
$x = -1$ $\quad x = -3$
$-1, -3$

43.

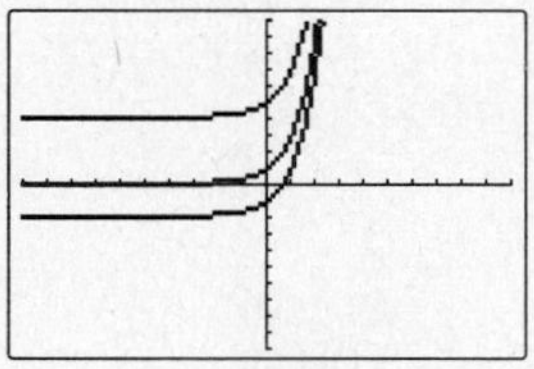

All have the same shape but different y-intercepts.

44.

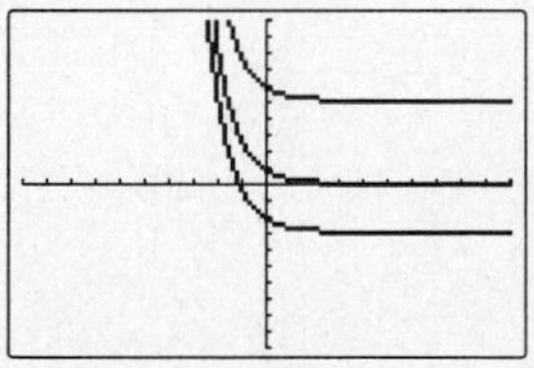

All have the same shape but different y-intercepts.

45.

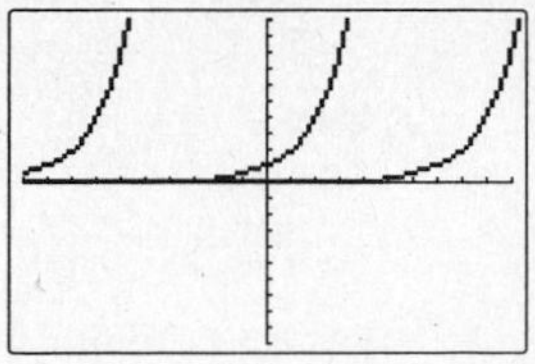

All have the same shape but are positioned at different places along the x-axis.

46.

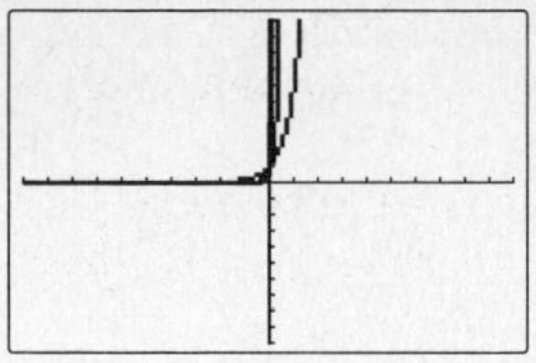

All have the same y-intercept, but each rises more steeply than the previous one.

47a. 2.51

47b. You cannot write 10 as a power of 2.5.

48a. 0 **48b.** 0 **48c.** -7

48d. c **48e.** c

49. Let x = the number of 15-minute intervals.
$B = 100 \cdot 2^x$
$= 100 \cdot 2^4$
$= 100 \cdot 16$
$= 1600$ bacteria

50a. $1920 - 1910 = 10$, $1950 = 1910 = 40$,
$1980 - 1910 = 70$, $2000 - 1910 = 90$

50b. $M(10) = 2.08(1.06)^{10} \approx \$3.72$ billion
$M(40) = 2.08(1.06)^{40} \approx \$21.39$ billion
$M(70) = 2.08(1.06)^{70} \approx \$122.88$ billion
$M(90) = 2.08(1.06)^{90} \approx \$394.09$ billion

51. $2x^2 + 3 = -7x$
$2x^2 + 7x + 3 = 0$
$a = 2, b = 7, c = 3$
$x = \frac{-7 \pm \sqrt{(7)^2 - 4(2)(3)}}{2(2)}$
$= \frac{-7 \pm \sqrt{49 - 24}}{4}$
$= \frac{-7 \pm \sqrt{25}}{4}$
$= \frac{-7 \pm 5}{4}$
$x = \frac{-7 + 5}{4}$ or $x = \frac{-7 - 5}{4}$
$= \frac{-2}{4}$ or $-\frac{1}{2}$ $\quad = \frac{-12}{4}$ or -3
$-3, -\frac{1}{2}$

52a. $16p^2 - 40pr + 25r^2 = (4p - 5r)(4p - 5r)$
$(4p - 5r)$ km by $(4p - 5r)$ km

52b.

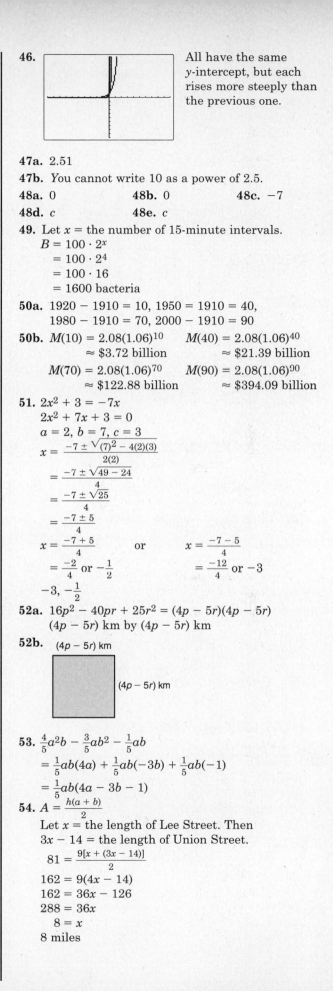

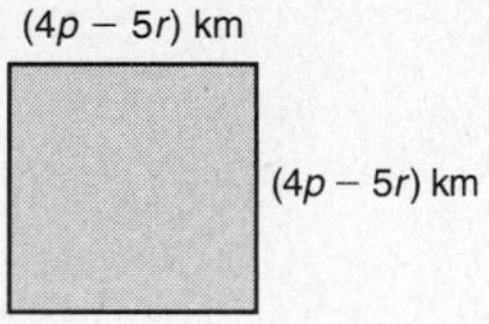

53. $\frac{4}{5}a^2b - \frac{3}{5}ab^2 - \frac{1}{5}ab$
$= \frac{1}{5}ab(4a) + \frac{1}{5}ab(-3b) + \frac{1}{5}ab(-1)$
$= \frac{1}{5}ab(4a - 3b - 1)$

54. $A = \frac{h(a + b)}{2}$
Let x = the length of Lee Street. Then
$3x - 14$ = the length of Union Street.
$81 = \frac{9[x + (3x - 14)]}{2}$
$162 = 9(4x - 14)$
$162 = 36x - 126$
$288 = 36x$
$8 = x$
8 miles

55. Let x = the number of points scored by the Pistons. Then $x - 2$ = the number of points scored by the Nuggets.

$x + (x - 2) = 370$
$2x - 2 = 370$
$2x = 372$
$x = 186$
$x - 2 = 186 - 2$ or 184

The Nuggets' final score was 184.

56. Test (0,0): $y \leq 2x + 2$
$0 \stackrel{?}{\leq} 2(0) + 2$
$0 \leq 2$ true

Test (0,0): $y \geq -x - 1$
$0 \stackrel{?}{\geq} -0 - 1$
$0 \geq -1$ true

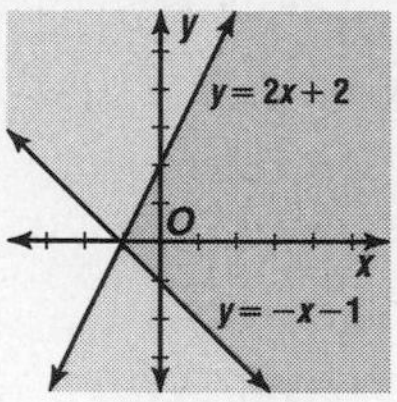

57a–b.

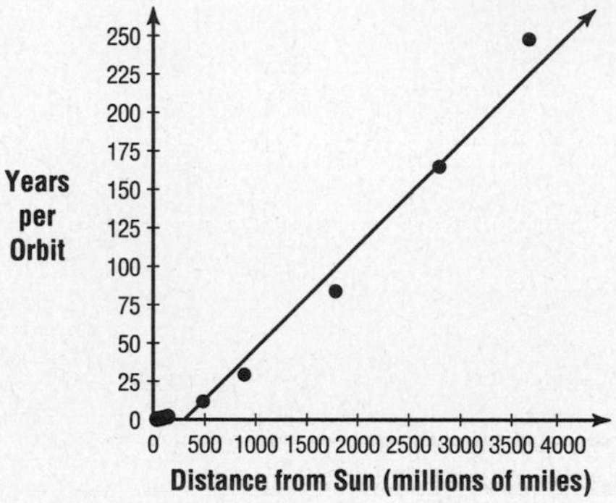

57b. Sample answer: $y = 0.07x - 12$

57c. 275 years

58. $\frac{s}{s + 150} = \frac{50}{150}$

$\frac{s}{s + 150} = \frac{1}{3}$

$3s = s + 150$
$2s = 150$
$s = 75$ m

59. $(-2)(3)(-10) = (-6)(-10)$
$= 60$

11-5 Growth and Decay

Pages 646–647 Check for Understanding

1a. California

1b. $t = 2000 - 1900 = 100$

California	Nebraska
$y = 1.77(1.03)^{100}$	$y = 1.14(1.004)^{100}$
≈ 34.02 million	≈ 1.70 million

CA: 34.02 million; NE: 1.70 million

2. The 7% graph would rise more steeply than the 0.7% graph when using the same scale.

3a. 1 **3b.** 2 **3c.** 4 **3d.** 365

4. $y = 10(1.03)^x$
$= 10(1 + 0.03)^x$
growth

5. $y = 10(0.50)^x$
$= 10(1 - 0.50)^x$
decay

6. $y = 10(0.75)^x$
$= 10(1 - 0.25)^x$
decay

7. $A = P\left(1 + \frac{r}{n}\right)^{nt}$, $P = \$24$, $r = 0.06$, $n = 1$, $t = 374$
$= 24\left(1 + \frac{0.06}{1}\right)^{1(374)}$
= about \$70,000,000,000

8. $A = C(1 - r)^t$

Years	Depreciated Value
1	$50,000(1 - 0.10)^1 = 45,000$
2	$50,000(1 - 0.10)^2 = 40,500$
3	$50,000(1 - 0.10)^3 = 36,450$
4	$50,000(1 - 0.10)^4 = 32,805$
5	$50,000(1 - 0.10)^5 = 29,524.50$
6	$50,000(1 - 0.10)^6 = 26,572.05$
7	$50,000(1 - 0.10)^7 \approx 23,914.85$

about 7 years

Pages 647–649 Exercises

9. $A = P\left(1 + \frac{r}{n}\right)^{nt}$
$= 400\left(1 + \frac{0.0725}{4}\right)^{4(7)}$
$\approx \$661.44$

10. $A = P\left(1 + \frac{r}{n}\right)^{nt}$
$= 500\left(1 + \frac{0.0575}{12}\right)^{12(25)}$
$\approx \$2097.86$

11. $A = P\left(1 + \frac{r}{n}\right)^{nt}$
$= 10,000\left(1 + \frac{0.06125}{365}\right)^{365(1.5)}$
$\approx \$10,962.19$

12. $A = P\left(1 + \frac{r}{n}\right)^{nt}$
$= 250\left(1 + \frac{0.103}{12}\right)^{12(40)}$
$\approx \$15,121.61$

13a. Each equation represents growth and t is the number of years since 1994.
Ethiopia: $y = 58.7(1.025)^t$
India: $y = 919.9(1.019)^t$
Colombia: $y = 35.6(1.021)^t$
Singapore: $y = 2.9(1.013)^t$

13b. Ethiopia: $y = 58.7(1.025)^6 \approx 68.1$ million
India: $y = 919.9(1.019)^6 \approx 1029.9$ million
Colombia: $y = 35.6(1.021)^6 \approx 40.3$ million
Singapore: $y = 2.9(1.013)^6 \approx 3.1$ million

13c.

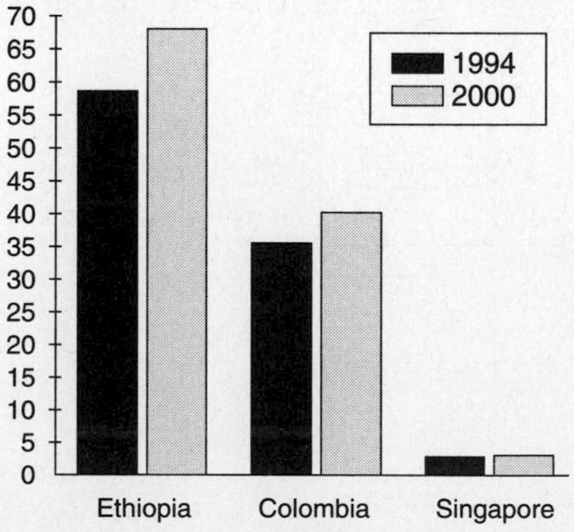

14a. $y = 114.6(0.934)^t$, t = years since 1950, decay

14b. It never reaches 0, but comes close in about 100 years.

15a. $y = 231.5(1.0963)^t$, t = years since 1950, growth

15b. $t = 2010 - 1950 = 60$
$y = 231.5(1.0963)^{60}$
$\approx \$57.6$ trillion

16a. $y = 1.2(0.932)^t$, t = number of years since 1980, decay

16b. $t = 1990 - 1980 = 10$
$y = 1.2(0.932)^{10}$
≈ 0.59 million
In the year 1990.

16c. preservation efforts, conservation of land, domestic reproduction in zoos, poaching

17a. $A = P\left(1 + \frac{r}{n}\right)^{nt}$

$A = 5000\left(1 + \frac{0.0825}{4}\right)^{4(4)}$ $\quad$ *P = 5000, r = 0.0825, n = 4, t = 4*
$= \$6931.53$

17b. $n = 365$
$A = 5000\left(1 + \frac{0.0825}{365}\right)^{365(4)}$
$\approx \$6954.58$

17c. $\$6954.58 - \$6931.53 = \$23.05$

17d. daily

18. $f(d) = 88(1.0137)^d$
$= 88(1.0137)^{7.5}$ $\quad$ $d = \frac{15}{2} = 7.5$
≈ 97.5 MHz

19a–c. See students' work.

20a. $y = Ne^{kt}$
$N = 250,\ y = 50,\ e \approx 2.72,\ k = -0.08042$
$50 \approx 250(2.72)^{0.08042t}$
$0.2 \approx 2.72^{0.08042t}$
$t \approx 20$ years

20b. $y = Ne^{kt}$
$y - 100,\ N = 200,\ e \approx 2.72,\ t = 10$
$100 \approx 200(2.72)^{k(10)}$
$0.5 \approx 2.72^{10k}$
$k \approx -0.0693$

21. $a > 1$, growth; $0 < a < 1$, decay; x represents time

22. The y-intercept is C.

23.
$$\begin{aligned} 3^y &= 3^{3y+1} \\ y &= 3y + 1 \\ -2y &= 1 \\ y &= -\frac{1}{2} \end{aligned}$$

24.
$$\begin{array}{rl} & (n^2 + 5n + 3) \\ (-) & \underline{(2n^2 + 8n + 8)} \end{array} \rightarrow \begin{array}{rl} & n^2 + 5n + 3 \\ (+) & \underline{-2n^2 - 8n - 8} \\ & -n^2 - 3n - 5 \end{array}$$

25.
$$\begin{aligned} \frac{-6r^3s^5}{18r^{-7}s^5t^{-2}} &= \frac{-6}{18}\left(\frac{r^3}{r^{-7}}\right)\left(\frac{s^5}{s^5}\right)\left(\frac{1}{t^{-2}}\right) \\ &= \frac{-1}{3}r^{3-(-7)}s^{5-5}t^2 \\ &= \frac{-1}{3}r^{10}t^2 \\ &= -\frac{r^{10}t^2}{3} \end{aligned}$$

26.
$$\begin{aligned} V &= s^3 \\ &= (yz^4)^3 \\ &= (y)^3(z^4)^3 \\ &= y^3z^{12} \end{aligned}$$

27.
$$\begin{aligned} 2x - 5y &= 3 \\ -5y &= -2x + 3 \\ y &= \frac{2}{5}x - \frac{3}{5} \end{aligned}$$
$m = -\frac{5}{2}$; $(-2, 7)$
$$\begin{aligned} y - y_1 &- m(x - x_1) \\ y - 7 &= -\frac{5}{2}[x - (-2)] \\ y - 7 &= -\frac{5}{2}(x + 2) \\ y - 7 &= -\frac{5}{2}x - 5 \\ y &= -\frac{5}{2}x + 2 \\ y &= -2.5x + 2 \end{aligned}$$

Page 649 Mathematics and Society

1. See students' work.
2. Sample answer: The methods used for rapid calculation in biological computers might be applied to similar problems in other real-world applications.
3. Sample answer: It could help to find the defective gene and perhaps eliminate the disease completely.

Chapter 11 Highlights

Page 651 Understanding and Using the Vocabulary

1. d exponential growth formula	**2.** g quadratic function
3. i symmetry	**4.** a equation of axis of symmetry
5. c exponential function	**6.** j vertex
7. b exponential decay formula	**8.** h roots
10. e parabola	**9.** f quadratic formula

Chapter 11 Study Guide and Assessment

Pages 652–654 Skills and Concepts

11. $y = -3x^2 + 4,\ a = -3,\ b = 0$

axis of symmetry: $x = -\frac{b}{2a} = -\frac{(0)}{2(-3)}$ or $x = 0$
$$\begin{aligned} y &= -3x^2 + 4 \\ &= -3(0)^2 + 4 \\ &= 0 + 4 \\ &= 4 \end{aligned}$$
The coordinates of the vertex are (0, 4).

12. $y = x^2 - 3x - 4,\ a = 1,\ b = -3$

axis of symmetry: $x = -\frac{b}{2a} = -\frac{(-3)}{2(1)}$ or $x = \frac{3}{2}$
$$\begin{aligned} y &= x^2 - 3x - 4 \\ &= \left(\frac{3}{2}\right)^2 - 3\left(\frac{3}{2}\right) - 4 \\ &= \frac{9}{4} - \frac{9}{2} - 4 \text{ or } -\frac{25}{4} \end{aligned}$$
The coordinates of the vertex are $\left(\frac{3}{2}, -\frac{25}{4}\right)$.

13. $y = 3x^2 + 6x - 17$, $a = 3$, $b = 6$

axis of symmetry: $x = -\frac{b}{2a} = -\frac{(6)}{2(3)}$ or $x = -1$

$y = 3x^2 + 6x - 17$

$= 3(-1)^2 + 6(-1) - 17$

$= 3 - 6 - 17$ or -20

The coordinates of the vertex are $(-1, -20)$.

14. $y = 3(x + 1)^2 - 20$

$= 3(x^2 + 2x + 1) - 20$

$= 3x^2 + 6x + 3 - 20$

$= 3x^2 + 6x - 17$, $a = 3$, $b = 6$

axis of symmetry: $x = -\frac{b}{2a} = -\frac{(6)}{2(3)}$ or $x = -1$

$y = 3x^2 + 6x - 17$

$= 3(-1 + 1)^2 - 20$

$= 0 - 20$

$= -20$

The coordinates of the vertex are $(-1, -20)$.

15. $y = x^2 + 2x$, $a = 1$, $b = 2$

axis of symmetry: $x = -\frac{b}{2a} = -\frac{2}{2(1)}$ or $x = -1$

$y = x^2 + 2x$

$= (-1)^2 + 2(-1)$

$= 1 - 2$ or -1

The coordinates of the vertex are $(-1, -1)$.

16.

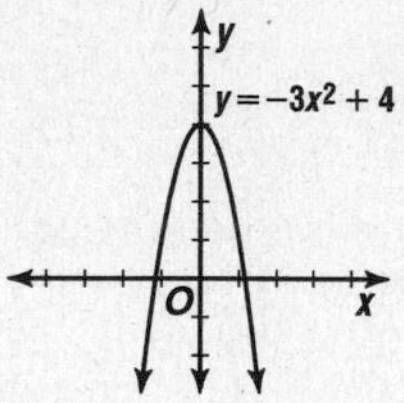

17.

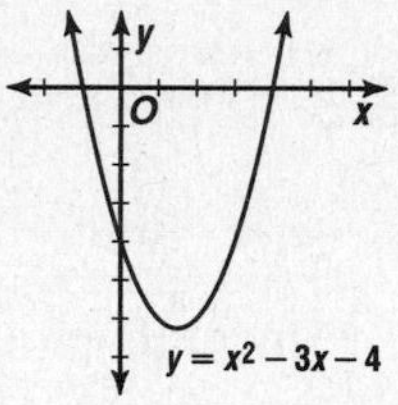

18.

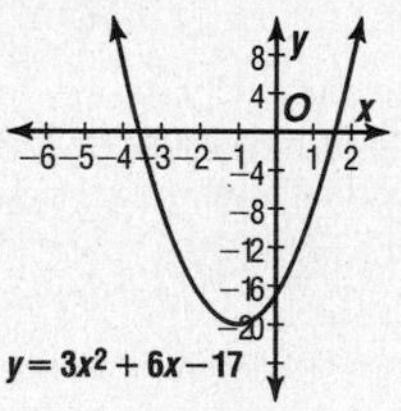

19.

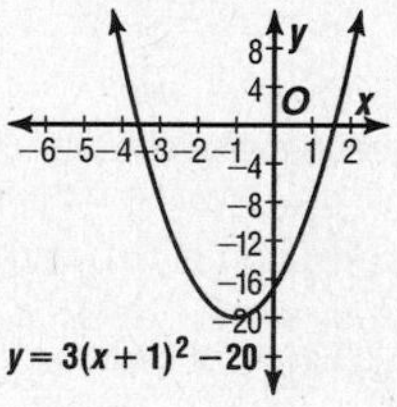

20.

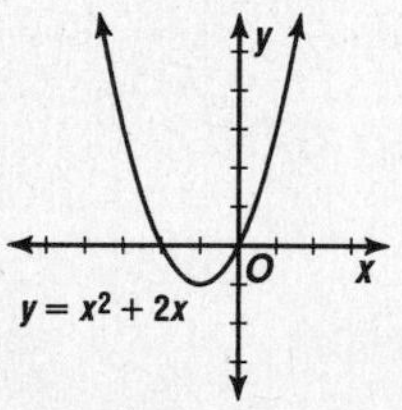

21. $y = x^2 - x - 12$

axis of symmetry: $x = \frac{1}{2}$

vertex: $\left(\frac{1}{2}, -\frac{49}{4}\right)$

x	y
−3	0
−2	−6
−1	−10
0	−12
1	−12
2	−10
3	−6
4	0

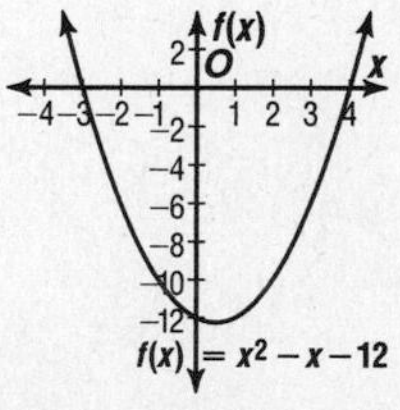

roots: $-3, 4$

22. $y = x^2 + 6x + 9$

axis of symmetry: $x = -3$

vertex: $(-3, 0)$

x	y
−6	9
−5	4
−4	1
−3	0
−2	1
−1	4
0	9

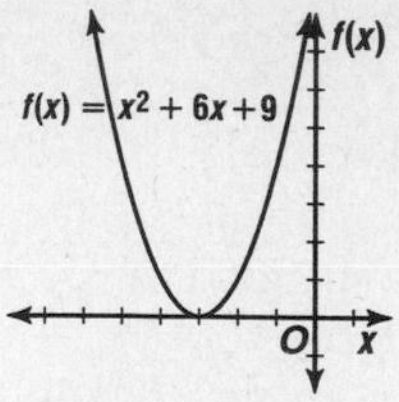

root: -3

23. $y = x^2 + 4x - 3$

axis of symmetry: $x = -2$

vertex: $(-2, -7)$

x	y
−6	9
−5	2
−4	−3
−3	−6
−2	−7
−1	−6
0	−3
1	2
2	9

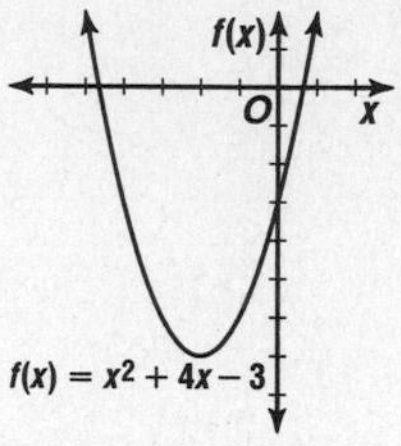

roots: $-5 < x < -4$,
$0 < x < 1$

24. $y = 2x^2 - 5x + 4$

axis of symmetry: $x = \frac{5}{4}$

vertex: $\left(\frac{5}{4}, \frac{7}{8}\right)$

x	y
−1	11
0	4
1	1
2	2
3	7
4	16

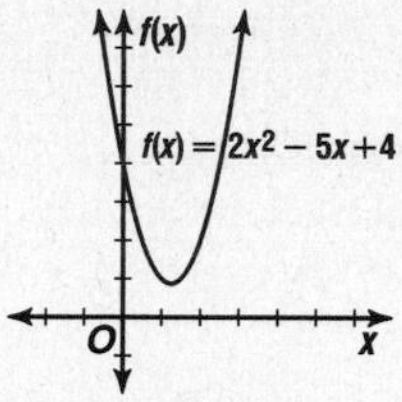

roots: $\varnothing$

25. $y = x^2 - 10x + 21$

axis of symmetry: $x = 5$

vertex: $(5, -4)$

x	y
3	0
4	−3
5	−4
6	−3
7	0

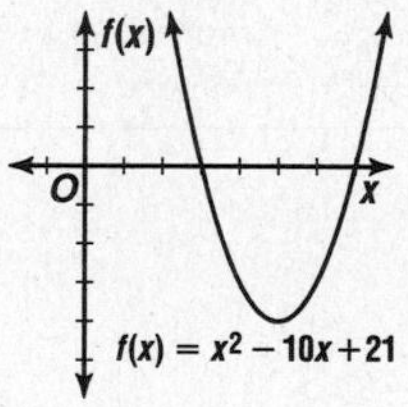

roots: $3, 7$

26. $y = 6x^2 - 13x - 15$

axis of symmetry: $\frac{13}{12}$

vertex: $\left(\frac{13}{12}, -22\frac{1}{24}\right)$

x	y
−2	35
−1	4
0	−5
1	−22
2	−17
3	0
4	29

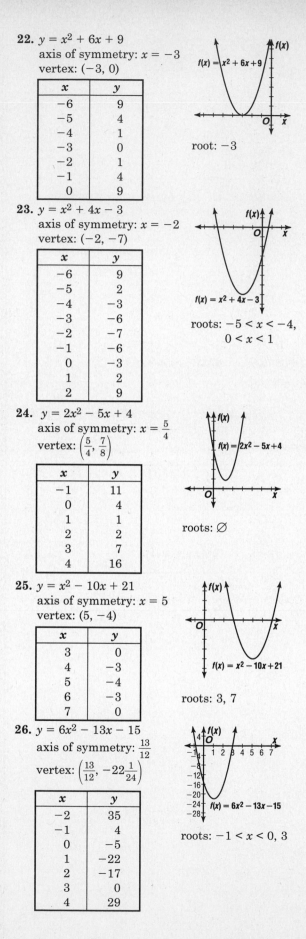

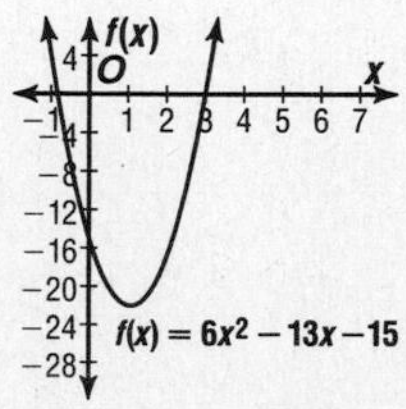

roots: $-1 < x < 0$, 3

27. $x^2 - 8x - 20 = 0$
$a = 1, b = -8, c = -20$
$x = \frac{-(-8) \pm \sqrt{(-8)^2 - 4(1)(-20)}}{2(1)}$
$= \frac{8 \pm \sqrt{64 + 80}}{2}$
$= \frac{8 \pm \sqrt{144}}{2}$
$= \frac{8 \pm 12}{2}$
$x = \frac{8 + 12}{2}$ or $x = \frac{8 - 12}{2}$
$= \frac{20}{2}$ or 10 $= \frac{-4}{2}$ or -2
$10, -2$

28. $r^2 + 10r + 9 = 0$
$a = 1, b = 10, c = 9$
$r = \frac{-10 \pm \sqrt{(10)^2 - 4(1)(9)}}{2(1)}$
$= \frac{-10 \pm \sqrt{100 - 36}}{2}$
$= \frac{-10 \pm \sqrt{64}}{2}$
$= \frac{-10 \pm 8}{2}$
$r = \frac{-10 + 8}{2}$ or $r = \frac{-10 - 8}{2}$
$= -\frac{2}{2}$ or -1 $= -\frac{18}{2}$ or -9
$-1, -9$

29. $4p^2 + 4p - 15 = 0$
$a = 4, b = 4, c = -15$
$p = \frac{-4 \pm \sqrt{(4)^2 - 4(4)(-15)}}{2(4)}$
$= \frac{-4 \pm \sqrt{16 + 240}}{8}$
$= \frac{-4 \pm \sqrt{256}}{8}$
$= \frac{-4 \pm 16}{8}$
$p = \frac{-4 + 16}{8}$ or $p = \frac{-4 - 16}{8}$
$= \frac{12}{8}$ or $\frac{3}{2}$ $= -\frac{20}{8}$ or $-\frac{5}{2}$
$\frac{3}{2}, -\frac{5}{2}$

30. $2y^2 + 8y + 3 = 0$
$a = 2, b = 8, c = 3$
$y = \frac{-8 \pm \sqrt{(8)^2 - 4(2)(3)}}{2(2)}$
$= \frac{-8 \pm \sqrt{64 - 24}}{4}$
$= \frac{-8 \pm \sqrt{40}}{4}$
$y = \frac{-8 + \sqrt{40}}{4}$ or $y = \frac{-8 - \sqrt{40}}{4}$
≈ -0.42 ≈ -3.58
$-0.42, -3.58$

31. $9k^2 - 13k + 4 = 0$
$a = 9, b = -13, c = 4$
$k = \frac{-(-13) \pm \sqrt{(-13)^2 - 4(9)(4)}}{2(9)}$
$= \frac{13 \pm \sqrt{169 - 144}}{18}$
$= \frac{13 \pm \sqrt{25}}{18}$
$= \frac{13 \pm 5}{18}$
$k = \frac{13 + 5}{18}$ or $k = \frac{13 - 5}{18}$
$= \frac{18}{18}$ or 1 $= \frac{8}{18}$ or $\frac{4}{9}$
$1, \frac{4}{9}$

32. $9a^2 - 30a + 25 = 0$
$a = 9, b = -30, c = 25$
$a = \frac{-(-30) \pm \sqrt{(-30)^2 - 4(9)(25)}}{2(9)}$
$= \frac{30 \pm \sqrt{900 - 900}}{18}$
$= \frac{30}{18}$
$a = \frac{5}{3}$

33. $-a^2 + 5a - 6 = 0$
$a^2 - 5a + 6 = 0$
$a = 1, b = -5, c = 6$
$a = \frac{-(-5) \pm \sqrt{(-5)^2 - 4(1)(6)}}{2(1)}$
$= \frac{5 \pm \sqrt{25 - 24}}{2}$
$= \frac{5 \pm \sqrt{1}}{2}$
$= \frac{5 \pm 1}{2}$
$a = \frac{5 + 1}{2}$ or $a = \frac{5 - 1}{2}$
$= \frac{6}{2}$ or 3 $= \frac{4}{2}$ or 2
$2, 3$

34. $-2d^2 + 8d + 3 = 3$
$2d^2 - 8d = 0$
$a = 2, b = -8, c = 0$
$d = \frac{-(-8) \pm \sqrt{(-8)^2 - 4(2)(0)}}{2(2)}$
$= \frac{8 \pm \sqrt{64}}{4}$
$= \frac{8 \pm 8}{4}$
$d = \frac{8 + 8}{4}$ or $d = \frac{8 - 8}{4}$
$= \frac{16}{4}$ or 4 $= 0$
$0, 4$

35. $21a^2 + 5a - 7 = 0$
$a = 21, b = 5, c = -7$
$a = \frac{-5 \pm \sqrt{(5)^2 - 4(21)(-7)}}{2(21)}$
$= \frac{-5 \pm \sqrt{25 + 588}}{42}$
$= \frac{-5 \pm \sqrt{613}}{42}$
$a = \frac{-5 + \sqrt{613}}{42}$ or $a = \frac{-5 - \sqrt{613}}{42}$
≈ 0.47 ≈ -0.71
$0.47, -0.71$

36. $2m^2 - \frac{17}{6}m + 1 = 0$
$12m^2 - 17m + 6 = 0$
$a = 12, b = -17, c = 6$
$m = \frac{-(-17) \pm \sqrt{(-17)^2 - 4(12)(6)}}{2(12)}$
$= \frac{17 \pm \sqrt{289 - 288}}{24}$
$= \frac{17 \pm \sqrt{1}}{24}$
$= \frac{17 \pm 1}{24}$
$m = \frac{17 + 1}{24}$ or $m = \frac{17 - 1}{24}$
$= \frac{18}{24}$ or $\frac{3}{4}$ $= \frac{16}{24}$ or $\frac{2}{3}$
$\frac{3}{4}, \frac{2}{3}$

37.

x	y
-2	$6\frac{1}{9}$
-1	$6\frac{1}{3}$
0	7
1	9
2	15

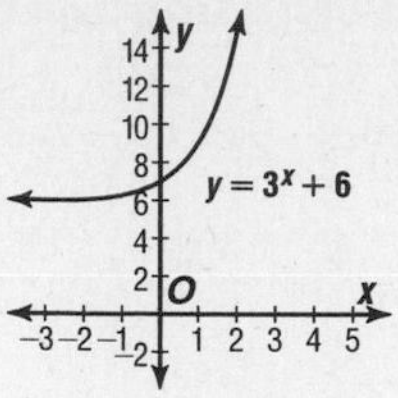

The y-intercept is 7.

38.

x	y
-2	1
-1	3
0	9
1	27
2	81

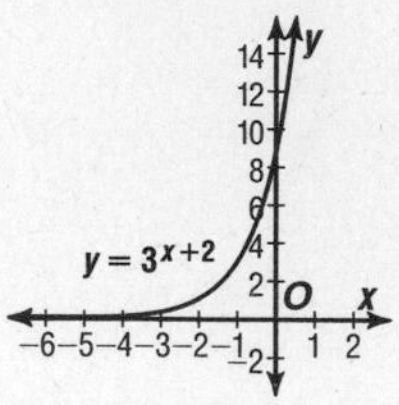

The y-intercept is 9.

39.

x	y
-2	$\frac{1}{4}$
-1	$\frac{1}{2}$
0	1
1	2
2	4

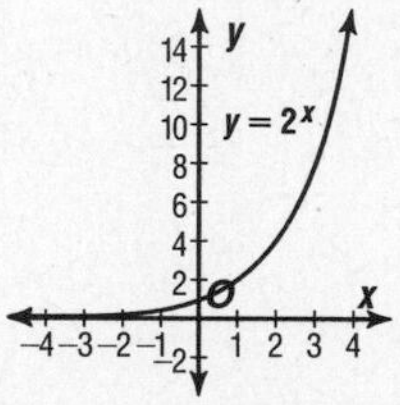

The y-intercept is 1.

40.

x	y
-2	8
-1	4
0	2
1	1
2	$\frac{1}{2}$

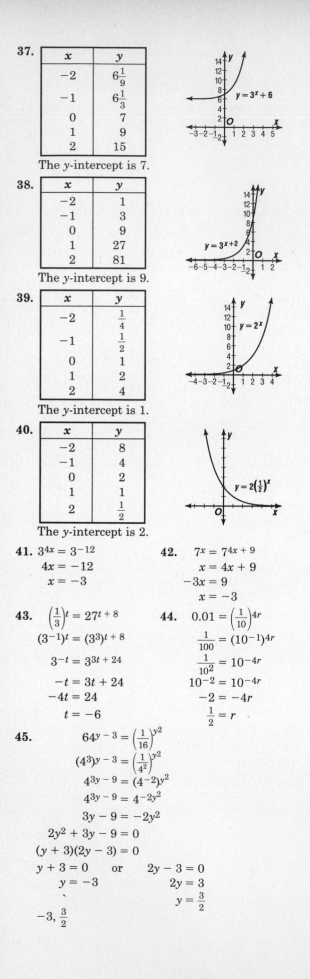

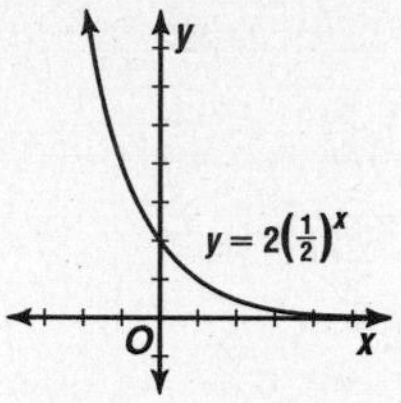

The y-intercept is 2.

41. $3^{4x} = 3^{-12}$

$4x = -12$

$x = -3$

42. $7^x = 7^{4x+9}$

$x = 4x + 9$

$-3x = 9$

$x = -3$

43. $\left(\frac{1}{3}\right)^t = 27^{t+8}$

$(3^{-1})^t = (3^3)^{t+8}$

$3^{-t} = 3^{3t+24}$

$-t = 3t + 24$

$-4t = 24$

$t = -6$

44. $0.01 = \left(\frac{1}{10}\right)^{4r}$

$\frac{1}{100} = (10^{-1})^{4r}$

$\frac{1}{10^2} = 10^{-4r}$

$10^{-2} = 10^{-4r}$

$-2 = -4r$

$\frac{1}{2} = r$

45. $64^{y-3} = \left(\frac{1}{16}\right)^{y^2}$

$(4^3)^{y-3} = \left(\frac{1}{4^2}\right)^{y^2}$

$4^{3y-9} = (4^{-2})^{y^2}$

$4^{3y-9} = 4^{-2y^2}$

$3y - 9 = -2y^2$

$2y^2 + 3y - 9 = 0$

$(y + 3)(2y - 3) = 0$

$y + 3 = 0$ or $2y - 3 = 0$

$y = -3$ $\quad 2y = 3$

$y = \frac{3}{2}$

$-3, \frac{3}{2}$

46. $A = P\left(1 + \frac{r}{n}\right)^{nt}$

$= 2000\left(1 + \frac{0.08}{4}\right)^{4(8)}$

$\approx \$3769.08$

47. $A = P\left(1 + \frac{r}{n}\right)^{nt}$

$= 5500\left(1 + \frac{0.0525}{12}\right)^{12(15)}$

$\approx \$12{,}067.68$

48. $A = P\left(1 + \frac{r}{n}\right)^{nt}$

$= 15{,}000\left(1 + \frac{0.075}{12}\right)^{12(25)}$

$\approx \$97{,}243.21$

49. $A = P\left(1 + \frac{r}{n}\right)^{nt}$

$= 500\left(1 + \frac{0.0975}{365}\right)^{365(40)}$

$\approx \$24{,}688.37$

Page 654 Applications and Problem Solving

50. $h = 112t - 16t^2$, $a = -16$, $b = 112$

$x = -\frac{b}{2a} = -\frac{112}{2(-16)} = 3.5$

$h = 112(3.5) - 16(3.5)^2$

$= 392 - 196$

$= 196$ ft

51. $96 = 96t - 16t^2$

$16t^2 - 96t + 96 = 0$

$t^2 - 6t + 6 = 0$

$a = 1, b = -6, c = 6$

$t = \frac{-(-6) \pm \sqrt{(-6)^2 - 4(1)(6)}}{2(1)}$

$= \frac{6 \pm \sqrt{36 - 24}}{2}$

$= \frac{6 \pm \sqrt{12}}{2}$

$t = \frac{6 + \sqrt{12}}{2}$ or $t = \frac{6 - \sqrt{12}}{2}$

≈ 4.7 $\quad \approx 1.3$

1.3 seconds and 4.7 seconds

52. $A = P\left(1 + \frac{r}{n}\right)^{nt}$

$P = 1400$, $r = 0.065$, $n = 4$, $t = 8$

$A = 1400\left(1 + \frac{0.065}{4}\right)^{4(8)}$

$\approx \$2345$

53. $h = -x^2 + 2x + 10$

$0 = -x^2 + 2x + 10$

axis of symmetry: $x = 1$

vertex: (1, 11)

x	h
2	10
3	7
4	2
5	-5

between 4 meters and 5 meters

54. Let x = the number.

$$x^2 = 168 + 2x$$
$$x^2 - 2x - 168 = 0$$
$$a = 1, b = -2, c = -168$$
$$x = \frac{-(-2) \pm \sqrt{(-2)^2 - 4(1)(-168)}}{2}$$
$$= \frac{2 \pm \sqrt{4 + 672}}{2}$$
$$= \frac{2 \pm \sqrt{676}}{2}$$
$$= \frac{2 \pm 26}{2}$$
$$x = \frac{2 + 26}{2} \quad \text{or} \quad x = \frac{2 - 26}{2}$$
$$= \frac{28}{2} \text{ or } 14 \qquad = \frac{-24}{2} \text{ or } -12$$

-12 or 14

55. $A = P\left(1 + \frac{r}{n}\right)^{nt}$

CD:
$P = 500$, $r = 0.08$, $n = 12$
$A = 500\left(1 + \frac{0.08}{12}\right)^{12(1)}$
$\approx \$541.50$

Savings:
$P = 500$, $r = 0.06$, $n = 365$
$A = 500\left(1 + \frac{0.06}{365}\right)^{365(1)}$
$\approx \$530.92$

CD, which yields \$541.50 vs. savings at \$530.92

Page 655 Alternative Assessment: Thinking Critically

- If the value of a function changes from negative to positive between the x values of 1 and 2, then there is a root between 1 and 2 because there would be an x-intercept between $x = 1$ and $x = 2$.
- If $ac < 0$, then $b^2 - 4ac > 0$ and the quadratic equation would have 2 real roots.

Chapter 12 Exploring Rational Expressions and Equations

12-1 Simplifying Rational Expressions

Page 663 Check for Understanding

1. When $x = 2$, the denominator becomes zero. Division by zero is undefined.
2. about 3
3. Factor the denominator, set each of its factors equal to zero, and solve for x. This will tell you that the restricted values are -5 and -1.
4. Sample answer: $\frac{x-2}{(x+2)(x-7)}$
5. The multiplication effect of using a tool or lever to carry out a task.
6. $\frac{13a}{14ay} = \frac{\cancel{(a)}^1(13)}{\cancel{(a)}_1(14y)}$
$= \frac{13}{14y}$
GCF: a; $\frac{13}{14y}$; $a \neq 0,\ y \neq 0$
7. $\frac{-7a^2b^3}{21a^5b} = \frac{\cancel{(7a^2b)}^1(-b^2)}{\cancel{(7a^2b)}_1(3a^3)}$
$= \frac{-b^2}{3a^3}$
GCF: $7a^2b$; $\frac{-b^2}{3a^3}$; $a \neq 0,\ b \neq 0$
8. $\frac{a(m+3)}{a(m-2)} = \frac{\cancel{a}^1(m+3)}{\cancel{a}_1(m-2)}$
$= \frac{m+3}{m-2}$
GCF: a; $\frac{m+3}{m-2}$; $m \neq 2,\ a \neq 0$
9. $\frac{3b}{b(b+5)} = \frac{\cancel{b}^1(3)}{\cancel{b}_1(b+5)}$
$= \frac{3}{b+5}$
GCF: b; $\frac{3}{b+5}$; $b \neq 0,\ b \neq -5$
10. $\frac{(r+s)(r-s)}{(r-s)(r-s)} = \frac{\cancel{(r-s)}^1(r+s)}{\cancel{(r-s)}_1(r-s)}$
$= \frac{r+s}{r-s}$
GCF: $r - s$; $\frac{r+s}{r-s}$; $r - s \neq 0$
11. $\frac{m-3}{m^2-9} = \frac{m-3}{(m-3)(m+3)}$
$= \frac{\cancel{m-3}^1}{\cancel{(m-3)}_1(m+3)}$
$= \frac{1}{m+3}$
Exclude the values for which $m^2 - 9 = 0$.
$m^2 - 9 = 0$
$(m-3)(m+3) = 0$
$m = 3$ or $m = -3$
GCF: $m - 3$; $\frac{1}{m+3}$; $m \neq \pm 3$
12. Enter: (2 x^2 + 7 X 2 + 12) ÷ (2 + 3) ENTER 6

13a. $MA = \frac{s-r}{r}$
$= \frac{6-(6-5)}{(6-5)}$
$= \frac{6-1}{1}$
$= 5$

13b. $5 \cdot 150 = 750$ lb

Pages 664–665 Exercises

14. $\frac{15a}{39a^2} = \frac{(3a)(5)}{(3a)(13a)}$
$= \frac{\cancel{(3a)}^1(5)}{\cancel{(3a)}_1(13a)}$
$= \frac{5}{13a}$; $a \neq 0$

15. $\frac{35y^2z}{14yz^2} = \frac{(7yz)(5y)}{(7yz)(2z)}$
$= \frac{\cancel{(7yz)}^1(5y)}{\cancel{(7yz)}_1(2z)}$
$= \frac{5y}{2z}$; $y \neq 0,\ z \neq 0$

16. $\frac{28a^2}{49ab} = \frac{(7a)(4a)}{(7a)(7b)}$
$= \frac{\cancel{(7a)}^1(4a)}{\cancel{(7a)}_1(7b)}$
$= \frac{4a}{7b}$; $a \neq 0,\ b \neq 0$

17. $\frac{56x^2y}{70x^3y} = \frac{(14x^2y)(4)}{(14x^2y)(5x)}$
$= \frac{\cancel{(14x^2y)}^1(4)}{\cancel{(14x^2y)}_1(5x)}$
$= \frac{4}{5x}$; $x \neq 0,\ y \neq 0$

18. $\frac{4a}{3a+a^2} = \frac{(a)(4)}{(a)(3+a)}$
$= \frac{\cancel{(a)}^1(4)}{\cancel{(a)}_1(3+a)}$
$= \frac{4}{3+a}$
Exclude the values for which $3a + a^2 = 0$.
$a(3+a) = 0$
$a \neq 0$ or -3

19. $\frac{y+3y^2}{3y+1} = \frac{(3y+1)(y)}{3y+1}$
$= \frac{\cancel{(3y+1)}^1(y)}{\cancel{3y+1}_1}$
$= y$; $y \neq -\frac{1}{3}$
Exclude the value for which $3y + 1 = 0$.
$3y = -1$
$y = -\frac{1}{3}$

20. $\frac{x^2-9}{2x+6} = \frac{(x+3)(x-3)}{2(x+3)}$
$= \frac{\cancel{(x+3)}^1(x-3)}{\cancel{(x+3)}_1(2)}$
$= \frac{x-3}{2}$; $x \neq -3$

21. $\frac{y^2-49x^2}{y-7x} = \frac{(y-7x)(y+7x)}{y-7x}$
$= \frac{\cancel{(y-7x)}^1(y+7x)}{\cancel{y-7x}_1}$
$= y + 7x$; $y \neq 7x$

22. $\frac{x+5}{x^2+x-20} = \frac{x+5}{(x+5)(x-4)}$
$= \frac{\cancel{(x+5)}^1}{\cancel{(x+5)}_1(x-4)}$
$= \frac{1}{x-4}$
Exclude the values for which $x^2 + x - 20 = 0$.
$(x+5)(x-4) = 0$
$x \neq -5$ or 4

23. $\frac{a-3}{a^2-7a+12} = \frac{a-3}{(a-3)(a-4)}$
$= \frac{\cancel{a-3}^1}{\cancel{(a-3)}_1(a-4)}$
$= \frac{1}{a-4}$
Exclude the values for which $a^2 - 7a + 12 = 0$.
$(a-3)(a-4) = 0$
$a \neq 3$ or 4

24. $\frac{3x-15}{x^2-7x+10} = \frac{(x-5)(3)}{(x-2)(x-5)}$
$= \frac{\cancel{(x-5)}^1(3)}{(x-2)\cancel{(x-5)}_1}$
$= \frac{3}{x-2}$
Exclude the values for which $x^2 - 7x + 10 = 0$.
$(x-2)(x-5) = 0$
$x \neq 2$ or 5

25. $\frac{x+4}{x^2+8x+16} = \frac{(x+4)}{(x+4)(x+4)}$
$= \frac{\overset{1}{\cancel{(x+4)}}}{\underset{1}{\cancel{(x+4)}}(x+4)}$
$= \frac{1}{x+4}$
Exclude the values for which $x^2 + 8x + 16 = 0$.
$(x + 4)(x + 4) = 0$
$x \neq -4$

26. $\frac{x^2-2x-15}{x^2-x-12} = \frac{(x+3)(x-5)}{(x+3)(x-4)}$
$= \frac{\overset{1}{\cancel{(x+3)}}(x-5)}{\underset{1}{\cancel{(x+3)}}(x-4)}$
$= \frac{x-5}{x-4}$
Exclude the values for which $x^2 - x - 12 = 0$.
$(x + 3)(x - 4) = 0$
$x \neq 4$ or -3

27. $\frac{a^2+4a-12}{a^2+2a-8} = \frac{(a-2)(a+6)}{(a-2)(a+4)}$
$= \frac{\overset{1}{\cancel{(a-2)}}(a+6)}{\underset{1}{\cancel{(a-2)}}(a+4)}$
$= \frac{a+6}{a+4}$
Exclude the values for which $a^2 + 2a - 8 = 0$.
$(a - 2)(a + 4) = 0$
$a \neq -4$ or 2

28. $\frac{x^2-36}{x^2+x-30} = \frac{(x+6)(x-6)}{(x+6)(x-5)}$
$= \frac{\overset{1}{\cancel{(x+6)}}(x-6)}{\underset{1}{\cancel{(x+6)}}(x-5)}$
$= \frac{x-6}{x-5}$
Exclude the values for which $x^2 + x - 30 = 0$.
$(x + 6)(x - 5) = 0$
$x \neq -6$ or 5

29. $\frac{b^2-3b-4}{b^2-13b+36} = \frac{(b-4)(b+1)}{(b-4)(b-9)}$
$= \frac{\overset{1}{\cancel{(b-4)}}(b+1)}{\underset{1}{\cancel{(b-4)}}(b-9)}$
$= \frac{b+1}{b-9}$
Exclude the values for which $b^2 - 13b + 36 = 0$.
$(b - 4)(b - 9) = 0$
$b \neq 9$ or 4

30. $\frac{14x^2+35x+21}{12x^2+30x+18} = \frac{7(2x^2+5x+3)}{6(2x^2+5x+3)}$
$= \frac{7\overset{1}{\cancel{(2x^2+5x+3)}}}{6\underset{1}{\cancel{(2x^2+5x+3)}}}$
$= \frac{7}{6}$
Exclude the values for which $12x^2 + 30x + 18 = 0$.
$6(2x + 3)(x + 1) = 0$
$x \neq -1.5$ or -1

31. $\frac{4x^2+8x+4}{5x^2+10x+5} = \frac{4(x^2+2x+1)}{5(x^2+2x+1)}$
$= \frac{4\overset{1}{\cancel{(x^2+2x+1)}}}{5\underset{1}{\cancel{(x^2+2x+1)}}}$
$= \frac{4}{5}$
Exclude the values for which $5x^2 + 10x + 5 = 0$.
$5(x + 1)(x + 1) = 0$
$x \neq -1$

32. Enter: [(] [(] [(-)] 3 [)] [x^2] [−] [(-)] 3 [)] [÷] [(] 3 [X] [(-)] 3 [)] [ENTER]
-1.333333333 or $-\frac{4}{3}$

33. Enter: [(] [(] [(-)] 1 [)] [^] 4 [−] 16 [)] [÷] [(] [(] [(-)] 1 [)] [^] 4 [−] 8 [X] [(] [(-)] 1 [)] [x^2] [+] 16 [)] [ENTER]
-1.666666667 or $-\frac{5}{3}$

34. Enter: [(] 3 [+] 2 [)] [÷] [(] 3 [x^2] [+] 2 [X] 3 [X] 2 [+] 2 [x^2] [)] [ENTER]
$.2$ or $\frac{1}{5}$

35. $\frac{x^3y^3+5x^3y^2+6x^3y}{xy^5+5xy^4+6xy^3} = \frac{x^3y(y^2+5y+6)}{xy^3(y^2+5y+6)}$
$= \frac{x^3y(y+2)(y+3)}{xy^3(y+2)(y+3)}$
excluded values: $x \neq 0$, $y \neq 0, -2, -3$; not possible, $y \neq -2$

36. Because $m \neq -4$ in the original expression.

37a. $MA = \frac{48}{\frac{1}{4}}$
$= 48(4)$ or 192

37b. $192 \cdot 20 = 3840$ lb

38a. $P = \frac{-9.05\left[\left(\frac{20{,}000}{1000}\right)^2 - \frac{65(20{,}000)}{1000}\right]}{\left(\frac{20{,}000}{1000}\right)^2 + 40\left(\frac{20{,}000}{1000}\right)}$
$= \frac{-9.05[(20)^2 - 65(20)]}{(20)^2 + 40(20)}$
$= 6.79$ lb/in^2

38b. $P = \frac{-9.05\left[\left(\frac{40{,}000}{1000}\right)^2 - \frac{65(40{,}000)}{1000}\right]}{\left(\frac{40{,}000}{1000}\right)^2 + 40\left(\frac{40{,}000}{1000}\right)}$
$= \frac{-9.05[(40)^2 - 65(40)]}{(40)^2 + 40(40)}$
$= 2.83$ lb/in^2

38c. no, $6.79 - 2.83 = 3.96$ lb/in^2

39a. $\frac{(212 - 159.8)°\text{F}}{29{,}002 \text{ ft}} \cdot \frac{5280 \text{ ft}}{1 \text{ mile}} = \frac{9.5°\text{F}}{\text{mile}}$ or 9.5°/mile

39b. $-\frac{9.5}{1} \cdot \frac{10}{10} = -\frac{95}{10} = -\frac{19}{2}$

39c.
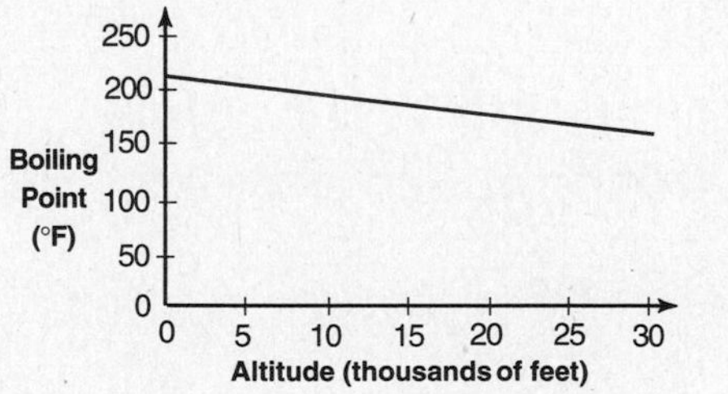

40. $A = P\left(1 + \frac{r}{n}\right)^{nt}$
$P = \$2500$, $r = 0.06$, $n = 4$, $t = 18$
$A = \$2500\left(1 + \frac{0.06}{4}\right)^{4(18)}$
$\approx \$7302.90$

41. Let x = the number.

$x^2 - 121 = 0$

$(x + 11)(x - 11) = 0$

$x + 11 = 0$ or $x - 11 = 0$

$x = -11$ $\quad x = 11$

± 11

42. $3x(-5x^2 - 2x + 7) = 3x(-5x^2) + 3x(-2x) + 3x(7)$

$= -15x^3 - 6x^2 + 21x$

43. $y \geq x - 2$ $\qquad y \leq 2x - 1$

Test (0, 0): $\qquad$ Test (2, 0):

$0 \geq 0 - 2$ $\qquad 0 \leq 2(2) - 1$

$0 \geq -2$ $\qquad 0 \leq 3$

True $\qquad$ True

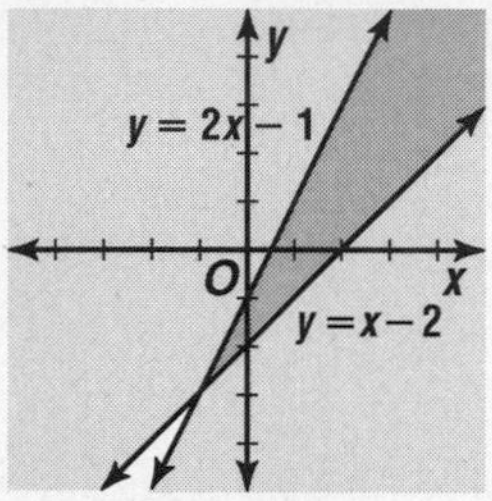

44. $4 + |x| = 12$

$|x| = 8$

$x = 8$ or $x = -8$

$\{8, -8\}$

45. $y = 3x + 2$

$m = 3$, y-intercept: 2

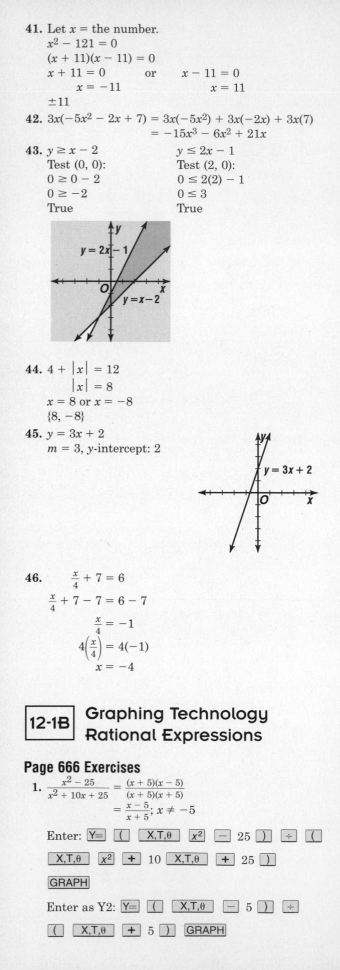

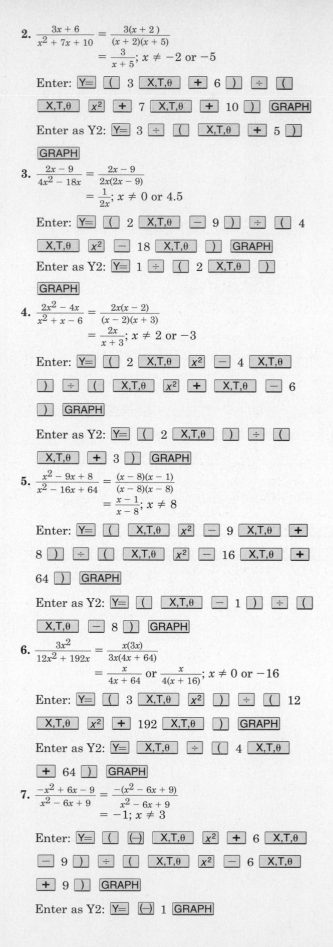

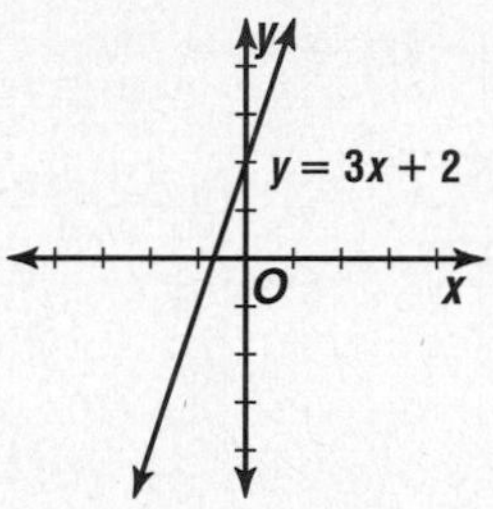

46. $\frac{x}{4} + 7 = 6$

$\frac{x}{4} + 7 - 7 = 6 - 7$

$\frac{x}{4} = -1$

$4\left(\frac{x}{4}\right) = 4(-1)$

$x = -4$

12-1B Graphing Technology Rational Expressions

Page 666 Exercises

1. $\frac{x^2 - 25}{x^2 + 10x + 25} = \frac{(x + 5)(x - 5)}{(x + 5)(x + 5)}$

$= \frac{x - 5}{x + 5}; x \neq -5$

Enter: [Y=] [(] [X,T,θ] [x^2] [−] 25 [)] [÷] [(] [X,T,θ] [x^2] [+] 10 [X,T,θ] [+] 25 [)] [GRAPH]

Enter as Y2: [Y=] [(] [X,T,θ] [−] 5 [)] [÷] [(] [X,T,θ] [+] 5 [)] [GRAPH]

2. $\frac{3x + 6}{x^2 + 7x + 10} = \frac{3(x + 2)}{(x + 2)(x + 5)}$

$= \frac{3}{x + 5}; x \neq -2$ or -5

Enter: [Y=] [(] 3 [X,T,θ] [+] 6 [)] [÷] [(] [X,T,θ] [x^2] [+] 7 [X,T,θ] [+] 10 [)] [GRAPH]

Enter as Y2: [Y=] 3 [÷] [(] [X,T,θ] [+] 5 [)] [GRAPH]

3. $\frac{2x - 9}{4x^2 - 18x} = \frac{2x - 9}{2x(2x - 9)}$

$= \frac{1}{2x}; x \neq 0$ or 4.5

Enter: [Y=] [(] 2 [X,T,θ] [−] 9 [)] [÷] [(] 4 [X,T,θ] [x^2] [−] 18 [X,T,θ] [)] [GRAPH]

Enter as Y2: [Y=] 1 [÷] [(] 2 [X,T,θ] [)] [GRAPH]

4. $\frac{2x^2 - 4x}{x^2 + x - 6} = \frac{2x(x - 2)}{(x - 2)(x + 3)}$

$= \frac{2x}{x + 3}; x \neq 2$ or -3

Enter: [Y=] [(] 2 [X,T,θ] [x^2] [−] 4 [X,T,θ] [)] [÷] [(] [X,T,θ] [x^2] [+] [X,T,θ] [−] 6 [)] [GRAPH]

Enter as Y2: [Y=] [(] 2 [X,T,θ] [)] [÷] [(] [X,T,θ] [+] 3 [)] [GRAPH]

5. $\frac{x^2 - 9x + 8}{x^2 - 16x + 64} = \frac{(x - 8)(x - 1)}{(x - 8)(x - 8)}$

$= \frac{x - 1}{x - 8}; x \neq 8$

Enter: [Y=] [(] [X,T,θ] [x^2] [−] 9 [X,T,θ] [+] 8 [)] [÷] [(] [X,T,θ] [x^2] [−] 16 [X,T,θ] [+] 64 [)] [GRAPH]

Enter as Y2: [Y=] [(] [X,T,θ] [−] 1 [)] [÷] [(] [X,T,θ] [−] 8 [)] [GRAPH]

6. $\frac{3x^2}{12x^2 + 192x} = \frac{x(3x)}{3x(4x + 64)}$

$= \frac{x}{4x + 64}$ or $\frac{x}{4(x + 16)}; x \neq 0$ or -16

Enter: [Y=] [(] 3 [X,T,θ] [x^2] [)] [÷] [(] 12 [X,T,θ] [x^2] [+] 192 [X,T,θ] [)] [GRAPH]

Enter as Y2: [Y=] [X,T,θ] [÷] [(] 4 [X,T,θ] [+] 64 [)] [GRAPH]

7. $\frac{-x^2 + 6x - 9}{x^2 - 6x + 9} = \frac{-(x^2 - 6x + 9)}{x^2 - 6x + 9}$

$= -1; x \neq 3$

Enter: [Y=] [(] [(−)] [X,T,θ] [x^2] [+] 6 [X,T,θ] [−] 9 [)] [÷] [(] [X,T,θ] [x^2] [−] 6 [X,T,θ] [+] 9 [)] [GRAPH]

Enter as Y2: [Y=] [(−)] 1 [GRAPH]

8. $\dfrac{5x^2 + 10x + 5}{3x^2 + 6x + 3} = \dfrac{5(x^2 + 2x + 1)}{3(x^2 + 2x + 1)}$
$\qquad\qquad = \dfrac{5}{3}; x \neq -1$

Enter: Y= (5 X,T,θ x^2 10 X,T,θ + 5

) ÷ (3 X,T,θ x^2 + 6 X,T,θ +

3) GRAPH

Enter as Y2: Y= 5 ÷ 3 GRAPH

9. $\dfrac{25 - x^2}{x^2 + x - 30} = \dfrac{-(x + 5)(x - 5)}{(x + 6)(x - 5)}$
$\qquad\qquad = -\dfrac{x + 5}{x + 6}; x \neq -6 \text{ or } 5$

Enter: Y= (25 − X,T,θ x^2) ÷ (

X,T,θ x^2 + X,T,θ − 30) GRAPH

Enter as Y2: Y= (−) (X,T,θ + 5) ÷

(X,T,θ + 6) GRAPH

12-2 Multiplying Rational Expressions

Pages 668–669 Check for Understanding

1. $\dfrac{x}{x - 4}, y$

2. Angie; she divided out the GCF.

3. See students' work.

4. $\dfrac{12m^2 y}{5r^2} \cdot \dfrac{r^2}{my} = \dfrac{12m^2 yr^2}{5myr^2}$
$\qquad\qquad = \dfrac{(\overset{1}{\cancel{myr^2}})(12m)}{(\underset{1}{\cancel{myr^2}})(5)}$
$\qquad\qquad = \dfrac{12m}{5}$

5. $\dfrac{16xy^2}{3m^2 p} \cdot \dfrac{27m^3 p}{32x^2 y^3} = \dfrac{432m^3 pxy^2}{96m^2 px^2 y^3}$
$\qquad\qquad = \dfrac{(\overset{1}{\cancel{48m^2 pxy^2}})(9m)}{(\underset{1}{\cancel{48m^2 pxy^2}})(2xy)}$
$\qquad\qquad = \dfrac{9m}{2xy}$

6. $\dfrac{x - 5}{r} \cdot \dfrac{r^2}{(x - 5)(y + 3)} = \dfrac{(x - 5)(r^2)}{(x - 5)(r)(y + 3)}$
$\qquad\qquad = \dfrac{(\overset{1}{\cancel{x - 5}})(\overset{r}{\cancel{r^2}})}{(\underset{1}{\cancel{x - 5}})(\underset{1}{\cancel{r}})(y + 3)}$
$\qquad\qquad = \dfrac{r}{y + 3}$

7. $\dfrac{x + 4}{4y} \cdot \dfrac{16y}{x^2 + 7x + 12} = \dfrac{16y(x + 4)}{4y(x^2 + 7x + 12)}$
$\qquad\qquad = \dfrac{16y(x + 4)}{4y(x + 3)(x + 4)}$
$\qquad\qquad = \dfrac{\overset{4}{\cancel{16}}\overset{1}{\cancel{y}}\overset{1}{\cancel{(x + 4)}}}{\underset{1}{\cancel{4y}}(x + 3)\underset{1}{\cancel{(x + 4)}}}$
$\qquad\qquad = \dfrac{4}{x + 3}$

8. $\dfrac{a^2 + 7a + 10}{a + 1} \cdot \dfrac{3a + 3}{a + 2} = \dfrac{(a + 5)(a + 2)}{a + 1} \cdot \dfrac{3(a + 1)}{a + 2}$
$\qquad\qquad = \dfrac{3(\overset{1}{\cancel{a + 1}})(\overset{1}{\cancel{a + 2}})(a + 5)}{(\underset{1}{\cancel{a + 1}})(\underset{1}{\cancel{a + 2}})}$
$\qquad\qquad = 3(a + 5)$

9. $\dfrac{4(x - 7)}{3(x^2 - 10x + 21)} \cdot (x - 3) = \dfrac{4(x - 7)(x - 3)}{3(x - 7)(x - 3)}$
$\qquad\qquad = \dfrac{4(\overset{1}{\cancel{x - 7}})(\overset{1}{\cancel{x - 3}})}{3(\underset{1}{\cancel{x - 7}})(\underset{1}{\cancel{x - 3}})}$
$\qquad\qquad = \dfrac{4}{3}$

10. $3(x + 6) \cdot \dfrac{x + 3}{9(x^2 + 7x + 6)} = \dfrac{3(x + 6)(x + 3)}{9(x + 6)(x + 1)}$
$\qquad\qquad = \dfrac{\overset{1}{\cancel{3}}(\overset{1}{\cancel{x + 6}})(x + 3)}{\underset{3}{\cancel{9}}(\underset{1}{\cancel{x + 6}})(x + 1)}$
$\qquad\qquad = \dfrac{x + 3}{3(x + 1)}$

11a. $\dfrac{2.54 \text{ cm}}{1 \text{ in.}} \cdot \dfrac{12 \text{ in.}}{1 \text{ ft}} \cdot \dfrac{3 \text{ ft}}{1 \text{ yd}} = 91.44 \text{ cm/yd}$

11b. changing centimeters to yards

12. yes; $\dfrac{20 \text{ mi}}{1 \text{ h}} \cdot \dfrac{5280 \text{ ft}}{1 \text{ mi}} \cdot \dfrac{1 \text{ h}}{60 \text{ min}} = 1760 \text{ ft/min}$

Pages 669–670 Exercises

13. $\dfrac{7a^2}{5} \cdot \dfrac{15}{14a} = \dfrac{105a^2}{70a}$
$\qquad\qquad = \dfrac{(\overset{1}{\cancel{35a}})(3a)}{(\underset{1}{\cancel{35a}})(2)}$
$\qquad\qquad = \dfrac{3a}{2}$

14. $\dfrac{3m^2}{2m} \cdot \dfrac{18m^2}{9m} = \dfrac{54m^4}{18m^2}$
$\qquad\qquad = \dfrac{(\overset{1}{\cancel{18m^2}})(3m^2)}{(\underset{1}{\cancel{18m^2}})}$
$\qquad\qquad = 3m^2$

15. $\dfrac{10r^3}{6x^3} \cdot \dfrac{42x^2}{35r^3} = \dfrac{420r^3 x^2}{210r^3 x^3}$
$\qquad\qquad = \dfrac{(\overset{1}{\cancel{210r^3 x^2}})(2)}{(\underset{1}{\cancel{210r^3 x^2}})(x)}$
$\qquad\qquad = \dfrac{2}{x}$

16. $\dfrac{7ab^3}{11r^2} \cdot \dfrac{44r^3}{21a^2 b} = \dfrac{308ab^3 r^3}{231a^2 br^2}$
$\qquad\qquad = \dfrac{(\overset{1}{\cancel{77abr^2}})(4b^2 r)}{(\underset{1}{\cancel{77abr^2}})(3a)}$
$\qquad\qquad = \dfrac{4b^2 r}{3a}$

17. $\dfrac{64y^2}{5y} \cdot \dfrac{5y}{8y} = \dfrac{320y^3}{40y^2}$
$\qquad\qquad = \dfrac{(\overset{1}{\cancel{40y^2}})(8y)}{(\underset{1}{\cancel{40y^2}})}$
$\qquad\qquad = 8y$

18. $\dfrac{2a^2}{b} \cdot \dfrac{5bc}{6a} = \dfrac{10a^2 bc}{6ab}$
$\qquad\qquad = \dfrac{(\overset{1}{\cancel{2ab}})(5ac)}{(\underset{1}{\cancel{2ab}})(3)}$
$\qquad\qquad = \dfrac{5ac}{3}$

19. $\dfrac{m + 4}{3m} \cdot \dfrac{4m^2}{m^2 + 9m + 20} = \dfrac{4m^2(m + 4)}{3m(m^2 + 9m + 20)}$
$\qquad\qquad = \dfrac{4m^2(m + 4)}{3m(m + 4)(m + 5)}$
$\qquad\qquad = \dfrac{4\overset{m}{\cancel{m^2}}\overset{1}{\cancel{(m + 4)}}}{3\underset{1}{\cancel{m}}\underset{1}{\cancel{(m + 4)}}(m + 5)}$
$\qquad\qquad = \dfrac{4m}{3(m + 5)}$

20. $\dfrac{m^2 + 8m + 15}{a + b} \cdot \dfrac{7a + 14b}{m + 3} = \dfrac{(m + 3)(m + 5)}{a + b} \cdot \dfrac{7(a + 2b)}{m + 3}$
$\qquad\qquad = \dfrac{7(a + 2b)(\overset{1}{\cancel{m + 3}})(m + 5)}{(a + b)(\underset{1}{\cancel{m + 3}})}$
$\qquad\qquad = \dfrac{7(a + 2b)(m + 5)}{a + b}$

21. $\dfrac{5a + 10}{10m^2} \cdot \dfrac{4m^3}{a^2 + 11a + 18} = \dfrac{5(a + 2)}{10m^2} \cdot \dfrac{4m^3}{(a + 2)(a + 9)}$
$\qquad\qquad = \dfrac{\overset{2}{\cancel{20}}\overset{m}{\cancel{m^3}}\overset{1}{\cancel{(a + 2)}}}{\underset{1}{\cancel{10}}\underset{1}{\cancel{m^2}}\underset{1}{\cancel{(a + 2)}}(a + 9)}$
$\qquad\qquad = \dfrac{2m}{a + 9}$

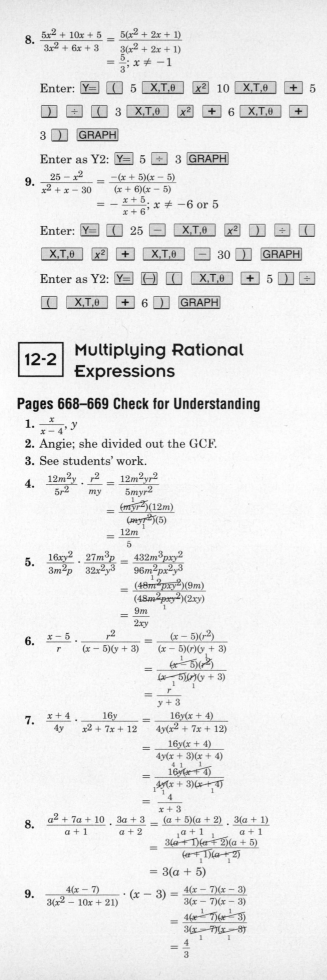

22. $\frac{6r+3}{r+6}\cdot\frac{r^2+9r+18}{2r+1} = \frac{3(2r+1)}{r+6}\cdot\frac{(r+6)(r+3)}{2r+1}$

$= \frac{3\cancel{(2r+1)}\cancel{(r+6)}(r+3)}{\cancel{(r+6)}\cancel{(2r+1)}}$

$= 3(r+3)$

23. $2(x+1)\cdot\frac{x+4}{x^2+5x+4} = 2(x+1)\cdot\frac{x+4}{(x+4)(x+1)}$

$= \frac{2\cancel{(x+1)}\cancel{(x+4)}}{\cancel{(x+4)}\cancel{(x+1)}}$

$= 2$

24. $4(a+7)\cdot\frac{12}{3(a^2+8a+7)} = 4(a+7)\cdot\frac{12}{3(a+7)(a+1)}$

$= \frac{\cancel{48}^{16}\cancel{(a+7)}}{\cancel{3}\cancel{(a+7)}(a+1)}$

$= \frac{16}{a+1}$

25. $\frac{x^2-y^2}{12}\cdot\frac{36}{x+y} = \frac{(x+y)(x-y)}{12}\cdot\frac{36}{x+y}$

$= \frac{\cancel{36}^{3}\cancel{(x+y)}(x-y)}{\cancel{12}\cancel{(x+y)}}$

$= 3(x-y)$

26. $\frac{3a+9}{a}\cdot\frac{a^2}{a^2-9} = \frac{3(a+3)}{a}\cdot\frac{a^2}{(a+3)(a-3)}$

$= \frac{3\cancel{a^2}^{a}\cancel{(a+3)}}{\cancel{a}\cancel{(a+3)}(a-3)}$

$= \frac{3a}{a-3}$

27. $\frac{9}{3+2x}\cdot(12+8x) = \frac{9}{3+2x}\cdot 4(3+2x)$

$= \frac{36\cancel{(3+2x)}}{\cancel{(3+2x)}}$

$= 36$

28. $(3x+3)\cdot\frac{x+4}{x^2+5x+4} = 3(x+1)\cdot\frac{x+4}{(x+1)(x+4)}$

$= \frac{3\cancel{(x+1)}\cancel{(x+4)}}{\cancel{(x+1)}\cancel{(x+4)}}$

$= 3$

29. $\frac{4x}{9x^2-25}\cdot(3x+5) = \frac{4x}{(3x+5)(3x-5)}\cdot(3x+5)$

$= \frac{4x\cancel{(3x+5)}}{\cancel{(3x+5)}(3x-5)}$

$= \frac{4x}{3x-5}$

30. $(b^2+12b+11)\cdot\frac{b+9}{b^2+20b+99}$

$= (b+11)(b+1)\cdot\frac{(b+9)}{(b+9)(b+11)}$

$= \frac{\cancel{(b+11)}(b+1)\cancel{(b+9)}}{\cancel{(b+9)}\cancel{(b+11)}}$

$= b+1$

31. $\frac{4x+8}{x^2-25}\cdot\frac{x-5}{5x+10} = \frac{4(x+2)}{(x+5)(x-5)}\cdot\frac{x-5}{5(x+2)}$

$= \frac{4\cancel{(x+2)}\cancel{(x-5)}}{5\cancel{(x-5)}(x+5)\cancel{(x+2)}}$

$= \frac{4}{5(x+5)}$

32. $\frac{a^2-a-6}{a^2-9}\cdot\frac{a^2+7a+12}{a^2+4a+4} = \frac{(a-3)(a+2)}{(a-3)(a+3)}\cdot\frac{(a+3)(a+4)}{(a+2)(a+2)}$

$= \frac{\cancel{(a-3)}\cancel{(a+2)}\cancel{(a+3)}(a+4)}{\cancel{(a-3)}\cancel{(a+3)}\cancel{(a+2)}(a+2)}$

$= \frac{a+4}{a+2}$

33. $\frac{32\text{ ft}}{1\text{ sec}}\cdot\frac{60\text{ sec}}{1\text{ min}}\cdot\frac{60\text{ min}}{1\text{ hr}}\cdot\frac{1\text{ mi}}{5280\text{ ft}}$

$= \frac{\cancel{32}^{4}\,\cancel{\text{ft}}}{1\,\cancel{\text{sec}}}\cdot\frac{\cancel{60}^{1}\,\cancel{\text{sec}}}{1\,\cancel{\text{min}}}\cdot\frac{60\,\cancel{\text{min}}}{1\text{ hr}}\cdot\frac{1\text{ mi}}{\cancel{5280}_{\cancel{88}\;11}\,\cancel{\text{ft}}}$

$= \frac{240}{11}\text{mi/hr}$

$= 21.8$ mph

converts ft/s to mph

34. $10\text{ ft}\cdot 18\text{ ft}\cdot 3\text{ ft}\cdot\frac{1\text{ yd}^3}{27\text{ ft}^3} = \cancel{10\text{ ft}}\cdot\cancel{18}^{2}\cancel{\text{ft}}\cdot\cancel{3}^{1}\cancel{\text{ft}}\cdot\frac{1\text{ yd}^3}{\cancel{27}_{\cancel{3}\;1}\cancel{\text{ft}^3}}$

$= 20\text{ yd}^3$

converts ft^3 to yd^3

35. $20\text{ grams}\cdot\frac{540\text{ Calories}}{1\text{ gram}} = 10{,}800$ Calories

36. $\frac{4.025\text{ grams}}{1\text{ amp-hr}}\cdot 2\text{ amps}\cdot 5\text{ hrs} = 40.25$ grams

37. Sample answer: $\frac{3(x+2)}{x+7}\cdot\frac{2(x-3)}{x-4}$;

$\frac{6}{x+7}\cdot\frac{x^2-x-1}{x-4}$

38a. $\frac{24\text{ s}}{1\text{ car}}\cdot\frac{6864\text{ cars}}{8\text{ collectors}}\cdot\frac{1\text{ min}}{60\text{ s}}\cdot\frac{1\text{ h}}{60\text{ min}}$

38b. $\frac{\cancel{24}^{1\,\cancel{8}}\,\cancel{\text{sec}}}{\cancel{1\text{ car}}}\cdot\frac{\cancel{6864}^{286\,\cancel{1144}}\,\cancel{\text{cars}}}{\cancel{8}_{1}\text{ collectors}}\cdot\frac{1\,\cancel{\text{min}}}{\cancel{60}_{\cancel{20}\;5}\,\cancel{\text{sec}}}\cdot\frac{1\text{ h}}{\cancel{60}_{10}\,\cancel{\text{min}}}$

$= \frac{286}{50}$ h/collector

$= 5.72$ h/collector

It would take all the collectors working 5.72 hours to collect the tolls.

39a. $\frac{1\text{ franc}}{0.1981\text{ dollars}}$; $\frac{0.1981\text{ dollars}}{1\text{ franc}}\cdot\frac{\frac{1}{0.1981\text{ dollar}}}{\frac{1}{0.1981\text{ dollar}}} \approx \frac{1}{5.05\,\frac{\text{francs}}{\text{dollar}}}$

$\approx \frac{1\text{ dollar}}{5.05\text{ francs}}$

39b. $12{,}500\text{ pesos}\cdot\frac{0.1597\text{ dollars}}{1\text{ peso}}\cdot\frac{1\text{ franc}}{0.1981\text{ dollars}}$

$\approx 10{,}077$ francs

39c. Convert to American dollars and then to Hong Kong's dollar.

40a. $\frac{4500}{1000} = 4.5$

40b. $a = \frac{3500}{1000} = 3.5$

$t = \frac{40[25+1.85(3.5)]}{50-1.85(3.5)}$

$= \frac{1259}{43{,}525}$

≈ 29 minutes

40c. $a = \frac{7000}{1000} = 7$

$t = \frac{40[25+1.85(7)]}{50-1.85(7)}$

$= \frac{1518}{37.05}$

≈ 41 minutes

40d. The times are not doubled; the difference is 12 minutes.

41. $y = 3^{2x}$

$= 3^{2(3)}$

$= 3^6$

$= 729$

42. $5x^2 + 30x + 45 = 0$

$5(x^2 + 6x + 9) = 0$

$5(x+3)(x+3) = 0$

$x + 3 = 0$

$x = -3$

43. degree of $6x^2yz$ is 4

degree of $5xyz$ is 3

degree of $-x^3$ is 3

The degree of $6x^2yz + 5xyz - x^3$ is 4.

44.
$$\begin{aligned} 5 &= 2x - 3y & \rightarrow \quad 2x - 3y &= 5 \\ -1 &= -4x + 3y & \rightarrow \quad (+)\ -4x + 3y &= -1 \\ & & -2x &= 4 \\ & & x &= -2 \end{aligned}$$

$$\begin{aligned} 2x - 3y &= 5 \\ 2(-2) - 3y &= 5 \\ -4 - 3y &= 5 \\ -3y &= 9 \\ y &= -3 \end{aligned}$$

$(-2, -3)$

45. $m = \frac{y_2 - y_1}{x_2 - x_1} = \frac{5 - 5}{-3 - 8} = \frac{0}{-11}$ or 0

46. 45% of $\$1567 = 0.45(1567)$
$= 705.15$

$\$705$

12-3 Dividing Rational Expressions

Pages 672–673 Check for Understanding

1. The wrong reciprocal was used.
2. $\frac{10}{d}, \frac{d}{r}$
3. See students' work.

4. $\frac{3}{m^2}$ **5.** $\frac{5}{x}$ **6.** $\frac{4y}{-9}$

7. $\frac{y+3}{x^2-9}$ **8.** $\frac{1}{m-3}$ **9.** $\frac{1}{x^2+2x+5}$

10. $\frac{x}{x+7} \div \frac{x-5}{x+7} = \frac{x}{x+7} \cdot \frac{x+7}{x-5}$
$= \frac{x}{\underset{1}{\cancel{x+7}}} \cdot \frac{\overset{1}{\cancel{x+7}}}{x-5}$
$= \frac{x}{x-5}$

11. $\frac{m^2+3m+2}{4} \div \frac{m+1}{m+2} = \frac{m^2+3m+2}{4} \cdot \frac{m+2}{m+1}$
$= \frac{(m+2)\overset{1}{\cancel{(m+1)}}}{4} \cdot \frac{m+2}{\underset{1}{\cancel{m+1}}}$
$= \frac{(m+2)^2}{4}$

12. $\frac{5a+10}{a+5} \div (a+2) = \frac{5a+10}{a+5} \cdot \frac{1}{a+2}$
$= \frac{5\overset{1}{\cancel{(a+2)}}}{a+5} \cdot \frac{1}{\underset{1}{\cancel{a+2}}}$
$= \frac{5}{a+5}$

13. $\frac{x^2+7x+12}{x+6} \div (x+3) = \frac{x^2+7x+12}{x+6} \cdot \frac{1}{x+3}$
$= \frac{\overset{1}{\cancel{(x+3)}}(x+4)}{x+6} \cdot \frac{1}{\underset{1}{\cancel{x+3}}}$
$= \frac{x+4}{x+6}$

14. $(8\text{ ft} \cdot 3\text{ ft} \cdot 12\text{ ft}) \div \frac{27\text{ ft}^3}{1\text{ yd}^3} = (8\text{ ft} \cdot 3\text{ ft} \cdot 12\text{ ft}) \cdot \frac{1\text{ yd}^3}{27\text{ ft}^3}$
$= (8\,\cancel{\text{ft}} \cdot \overset{1}{\cancel{3}}\,\cancel{\text{ft}} \cdot \overset{4}{\cancel{12}}\,\cancel{\text{ft}}) \cdot \frac{1\text{ yd}^3}{\underset{3}{\cancel{\underset{9}{\cancel{27}}}}\,\cancel{\text{ft}^3}}$
$= \frac{32}{3}\text{ yd}^3$
≈ 10.7 cubic yards

15. $(12\text{ in.} \cdot 18\text{ in.} \cdot 4\text{ in.}) \div \frac{1728\text{ in}^3}{1\text{ ft}^3}$
$= (12\text{ in.} \cdot 18\text{ in.} \cdot 4\text{ in.}) \cdot \frac{1\text{ ft}^3}{1728\text{ in}^3}$
$= (\overset{1}{\cancel{12}}\,\cancel{\text{in.}} \cdot \overset{1}{\cancel{18}}\,\cancel{\text{in.}} \cdot \overset{1}{\cancel{4}}\,\cancel{\text{in.}}) \cdot \frac{1\text{ ft}^3}{\underset{2}{\cancel{\underset{8}{\cancel{\underset{96}{\cancel{1728}}}}}}\,\cancel{\text{in}^3}}$
$= \frac{1}{2}\text{ ft}^3$
$= 0.5$ cubic feet

16a. $\frac{40\text{ mi}}{1\text{ h}} \cdot \frac{5280\text{ ft}}{1\text{ mi}} \cdot \frac{1\text{ h}}{60\text{ min}} \cdot \frac{1\text{ car}}{48\text{ ft}}$

16b. $\frac{\overset{2}{\cancel{40}}\,\cancel{\text{mi}}}{1\,\cancel{\text{h}}} \cdot \frac{\overset{110}{\cancel{5280}}\,\cancel{\text{ft}}}{1\,\cancel{\text{mi}}} \cdot \frac{1\,\cancel{\text{h}}}{\underset{3}{\cancel{60}}\text{ min}} \cdot \frac{1\text{ car}}{\underset{1}{\cancel{48}}\,\cancel{\text{ft}}} = \frac{220\text{ cars}}{3\text{ min}} = 73\frac{1}{3}$ cars

Pages 673–674 Exercises

17. $\frac{a}{a+3} \div \frac{a+11}{a+3} = \frac{a}{a+3} \cdot \frac{a+3}{a+11}$
$= \frac{a}{\underset{1}{\cancel{a+3}}} \cdot \frac{\overset{1}{\cancel{a+3}}}{a+11}$
$= \frac{a}{a+11}$

18. $\frac{m+7}{m} \div \frac{m+7}{m+3} = \frac{m+7}{m} \cdot \frac{m+3}{m+7}$
$= \frac{\overset{1}{\cancel{m+7}}}{m} \cdot \frac{m+3}{\underset{1}{\cancel{m+7}}}$
$= \frac{m+3}{m}$

19. $\frac{a^2b^3c}{m^2y^2} \div \frac{a^2bc^3}{m^3y^2} = \frac{a^2b^3c}{m^2y^2} \cdot \frac{m^3y^2}{a^2bc^3}$
$= \frac{\overset{1}{\cancel{a^2}}\overset{b^2}{\cancel{b^3}}\overset{1}{\cancel{c}}}{\underset{1}{\cancel{m^2}}\underset{1}{\cancel{y^2}}} \cdot \frac{\overset{m}{\cancel{m^3}}\overset{1}{\cancel{y^2}}}{\underset{1}{\cancel{a^2}}\underset{1}{\cancel{b}}\underset{c^2}{\cancel{c^3}}}$
$= \frac{b^2m}{c^2}$

20. $\frac{5x^2}{7} \div \frac{10x^3}{21} = \frac{5x^2}{7} \cdot \frac{21}{10x^3}$
$= \frac{\overset{1}{\cancel{5}}\overset{1}{\cancel{x^2}}}{\underset{1}{\cancel{7}}} \cdot \frac{\overset{3}{\cancel{21}}}{\underset{2}{\cancel{10}}\underset{x}{\cancel{x^3}}}$
$= \frac{3}{2x}$

21. $\frac{3m+15}{m+4} \div \frac{3m}{m+4} = \frac{3m+15}{m+4} \cdot \frac{m+4}{3m}$
$= \frac{\overset{1}{\cancel{3}}(m+5)}{\underset{1}{\cancel{m+4}}} \cdot \frac{\overset{1}{\cancel{m+4}}}{\underset{1}{\cancel{3}}m}$
$= \frac{m+5}{m}$

22. $\frac{3x}{x+2} \div (x-1) = \frac{3x}{x+2} \cdot \frac{1}{x-1}$
$= \frac{3x}{(x+2)(x-1)}$

23. $\frac{4z+8}{z+3} \div (z+2) = \frac{4z+8}{z+3} \cdot \frac{1}{(z+2)}$
$= \frac{4\overset{1}{\cancel{(z+2)}}}{z+3} \cdot \frac{1}{\underset{1}{\cancel{z+2}}}$
$= \frac{4}{z+3}$

24. $\frac{x+3}{x+1} \div (x^2+5x+6) = \frac{x+3}{x+1} \cdot \frac{1}{x^2+5x+6}$
$= \frac{\cancel{x+3}}{x+1} \cdot \frac{1}{(x+2)\underset{1}{\cancel{(x+3)}}}$
$= \frac{1}{(x+1)(x+2)}$

25. $\frac{2x+4}{x^2+11x+18} \div \frac{x+1}{x^2+14x+45}$
$= \frac{2x+4}{x^2+11x+18} \cdot \frac{x^2+14x+45}{x+1}$
$= \frac{2\overset{1}{\cancel{(x+2)}}}{\underset{1}{\cancel{(x+2)}}\underset{1}{\cancel{(x+9)}}} \cdot \frac{(x+5)\overset{1}{\cancel{(x+9)}}}{(x+1)}$
$= \frac{2(x+5)}{x+1}$

26. $\frac{k+3}{m^2+4m+4} \div \frac{2k+6}{m+2} = \frac{k+3}{m^2+4m+4} \cdot \frac{m+2}{2k+6}$
$= \frac{\overset{1}{\cancel{k+3}}}{(m+2)\underset{1}{\cancel{(m+2)}}} \cdot \frac{\overset{1}{\cancel{m+2}}}{2\underset{1}{\cancel{(k+3)}}}$
$= \frac{1}{2(m+2)}$

27. $\dfrac{2x+6}{x+5} \div \dfrac{2}{x+5} = \dfrac{2x+6}{x+5} \cdot \dfrac{x+5}{2}$

$\qquad = \dfrac{\overset{1}{\cancel{2}}(x+3)}{\cancel{x+5}} \cdot \dfrac{\cancel{x+5}}{\cancel{2}}$

$\qquad = x+3$

28. $\dfrac{m-8}{m+7} \div (m^2 - 7m - 8) = \dfrac{m-8}{m+7} \cdot \dfrac{1}{m^2 - 7m - 8}$

$\qquad = \dfrac{\overset{1}{\cancel{m-8}}}{m+7} \cdot \dfrac{1}{(m-8)(m+1)}$

$\qquad = \dfrac{1}{(m+7)(m+1)}$

29. $\dfrac{x^2+5x+6}{x^2-x-12} \div \dfrac{x+2}{x^2+x-20} = \dfrac{x^2+5x+6}{x^2-x-12} \cdot \dfrac{x^2+x-20}{x+2}$

$\qquad = \dfrac{\overset{1}{\cancel{(x+3)}}(x+2)}{\cancel{(x-4)}(x+3)} \cdot \dfrac{(x+5)(x-4)}{x+2}$

$\qquad = x+5$

30. $\dfrac{m^2+m-6}{m^2+8m+15} \div \dfrac{m^2-m-2}{m^2+9m+20}$

$\qquad = \dfrac{m^2+m-6}{m^2+8m+15} \cdot \dfrac{m^2+9m+20}{m^2-m-2}$

$\qquad = \dfrac{\overset{1}{\cancel{(m+3)}}(m-2)}{\cancel{(m+3)}(m+5)} \cdot \dfrac{\overset{1}{\cancel{(m+5)}}(m+4)}{(m-2)(m+1)}$

$\qquad = \dfrac{m+4}{m+1}$

31. $\dfrac{2x^2+7x-15}{x+2} \div \dfrac{2x-3}{x^2+5x+6} = \dfrac{2x^2+7x-15}{x+2} \cdot \dfrac{x^2+5x+6}{2x-3}$

$\qquad = \dfrac{\overset{1}{\cancel{(2x-3)}}(x+5)}{\cancel{(x+2)}} \cdot \dfrac{(x+3)\cancel{(x+2)}}{\cancel{(2x-3)}}$

$\qquad = (x+5)(x+3)$

32. $\dfrac{t^2-2t-8}{w-3} \div \dfrac{t-4}{w^2-7w+12} = \dfrac{t^2-2t-8}{w-3} \cdot \dfrac{w^2-7w+12}{t-4}$

$\qquad = \dfrac{\overset{1}{\cancel{(t-4)}}(t+2)}{\cancel{w-3}} \cdot \dfrac{\overset{1}{\cancel{(w-3)}}(w-4)}{\cancel{t-4}}$

$\qquad = (t+2)(w-4)$

33. $\left(\dfrac{60 \text{ mi}}{1 \text{ h}} \cdot \dfrac{5280 \text{ ft}}{1 \text{ mi}} \div \dfrac{60 \text{ mi}}{1 \text{ h}}\right) \div \dfrac{60 \text{ s}}{1 \text{ min}}$

$= \left(\dfrac{60 \text{ mi}}{1 \text{ h}} \cdot \dfrac{5280 \text{ ft}}{1 \text{ mi}} \cdot \dfrac{1 \text{ h}}{60 \text{ min}}\right) \cdot \dfrac{1 \text{ min}}{60 \text{ s}}$

$= \dfrac{\overset{1}{\cancel{60}} \text{ mi}}{\cancel{1 \text{ h}}} \cdot \dfrac{\overset{88}{\cancel{5280}} \text{ ft}}{1 \cancel{\text{ mi}}} \cdot \dfrac{\cancel{1 \text{ h}}}{\cancel{60} \text{ min}} \cdot \dfrac{1 \cancel{\text{ min}}}{\cancel{60} \text{ s}}$

$= 88 \text{ ft/s}$

Sample answer: changes 60 mph to ft/s

34. $\dfrac{23.75 \text{ in.}}{1 \text{ rev}} \cdot \dfrac{33\frac{1}{3} \text{ rev}}{1 \text{ min}} \cdot 16.5 \text{ min}$

$= \dfrac{23.75 \text{ in.}}{1 \cancel{\text{ rev}}} \cdot \dfrac{33\frac{1}{3} \cancel{\text{ rev}}}{1 \cancel{\text{ min}}} \cdot 16.5 \cancel{\text{ min}}$

$= 13{,}062.5 \text{ in.}$

Sample answer: calculates how far a needle travels on a record for a song 16.5 minutes long

35. $(5 \text{ ft} \cdot 16.5 \text{ ft} \cdot 9 \text{ ft}) \div \dfrac{27 \text{ ft}^3}{1 \text{ yd}^3} = (5 \text{ ft} \cdot 16.5 \text{ ft} \cdot 9 \text{ ft}) \cdot \dfrac{1 \text{ yd}^3}{27 \text{ ft}^3}$

$\qquad = 5 \cancel{\text{ ft}} \cdot \overset{5.5}{\cancel{16.5}} \cancel{\text{ ft}} \cdot \cancel{9} \cancel{\text{ ft}} \cdot \dfrac{1 \text{ yd}^3}{\cancel{27} \cancel{\text{ ft}^3}}$

$\qquad = 27.5 \text{ yd}^3$

Sample answer: changes cubic feet to cubic yards

36. $\left[\left(\dfrac{60 \text{ km}}{1 \text{ h}} \cdot \dfrac{1000 \text{ m}}{1 \text{ km}}\right) \div \dfrac{60 \text{ min}}{1 \text{ h}}\right] \div \dfrac{60 \text{ s}}{1 \text{ min}}$

$= \left(\dfrac{60 \text{ km}}{1 \text{ h}} \cdot \dfrac{1000 \text{ m}}{1 \text{ km}} \cdot \dfrac{1 \text{ h}}{60 \text{ min}}\right) \cdot \dfrac{1 \text{ min}}{60 \text{ s}}$

$= \dfrac{\overset{1}{\cancel{60}} \text{ km}}{\cancel{1 \text{ h}}} \cdot \dfrac{\overset{50}{\cancel{1000}} \text{ m}}{1 \cancel{\text{ km}}} \cdot \dfrac{\cancel{1 \text{ h}}}{\cancel{60} \text{ min}} \cdot \dfrac{1 \cancel{\text{ min}}}{\cancel{60}_{3} \text{ s}}$

$= \dfrac{50}{3} \text{ m/s}$

$\approx 16.7 \text{ meters/s}$

Sample answer: changes 60 km/h to m/s

37. $\text{A} = \ell w$

$\text{A} \div \ell = w$

$\left(\dfrac{x^2-y^2}{2}\right) \div (2x+2y) = \dfrac{x^2-y^2}{2} \cdot \dfrac{1}{(2x+2y)}$

$\qquad = \dfrac{\overset{1}{\cancel{(x+y)}}(x-y)}{2} \cdot \dfrac{1}{2\cancel{(x+y)}}$

$\qquad = \dfrac{x-y}{4}$

38a. $V = \dfrac{d(a+b)}{2} \cdot w$

$= \left[\dfrac{5 \text{ ft}(18 \text{ ft} + 15 \text{ ft})}{2} \cdot 9 \text{ ft}\right] \div \dfrac{27 \text{ ft}^3}{1 \text{ yd}^3}$

38b. $\left[\dfrac{5 \text{ ft}(18 \text{ ft} + 15 \text{ ft})}{2} \cdot 9 \text{ ft}\right] \div \dfrac{27 \text{ ft}^3}{1 \text{ yd}^3}$

$= \left[\dfrac{5(18+15)}{2} \cdot 9\right] \cdot \dfrac{1}{27}$

$= 27.5 \dfrac{\text{yd}^3}{\text{truckload}}$

$20{,}000 \text{ yd}^3 \div 27.5 \dfrac{\text{yd}^3}{\text{truckload}}$

$= 20{,}000 \text{ yd}^3 \cdot \dfrac{1 \text{ truckload}}{27.5 \text{ yd}^3}$

$= 727.\overline{27} \text{ truckloads}$

39a. $605{,}000 \text{ cars} \cdot \dfrac{48 \text{ ft}}{1 \text{ car}} \cdot \dfrac{1 \text{ mi}}{5280 \text{ ft}} = 5500 \text{ miles}$

39b. $227{,}000 \text{ miles} \div 5500 \dfrac{\text{miles}}{\text{train}} = 227{,}000 \text{ mi} \cdot \dfrac{1 \text{ train}}{5500 \text{ mi}}$

$\qquad \approx 41.3 \text{ trains}$

39c. $1{,}168{,}000 \cdot \dfrac{48 \text{ ft}}{1 \text{ car}} \cdot \dfrac{1 \text{ mi}}{5280 \text{ ft}} = 10{,}618.2 \text{ miles}$

$290{,}000 \text{ mi} \div 10{,}618.2 \dfrac{\text{mi}}{\text{train}} = 290{,}000 \text{ mi} \cdot \dfrac{1 \text{ train}}{10{,}618.2 \text{ mi}}$

$\qquad = 27.3 \text{ trains}$

40a. $\dfrac{2\pi\left(3\frac{3}{4} \text{ in.}\right)}{1 \text{ revolution}} \cdot \dfrac{33\frac{1}{3} \text{ revolutions}}{1 \text{ minute}} \cdot \dfrac{16.5 \text{ minutes}}{1}$

40b. $12{,}959.1 \text{ in. or } 12{,}959.1 \text{ in.} \times \dfrac{1 \text{ ft}}{12 \text{ in.}} \approx 1079.92 \text{ ft}$

41. $\dfrac{2m+3}{4} \cdot \dfrac{32}{(2m+3)(m-5)} = \dfrac{32(2m+3)}{4(2m+3)(m-5)}$

$\qquad = \dfrac{\overset{8}{\cancel{32}}\overset{1}{\cancel{(2m+3)}}}{\underset{1}{\cancel{4}}\underset{1}{\cancel{(2m+3)}}(m-5)}$

$\qquad = \dfrac{8}{m-5}$

42. $f(x) = x^2 + 6x + 8$

axis of symmetry: $x = -3$

vertex: $(-3, -1)$

x	$f(x)$
-5	3
-4	0
-3	-1
-2	0
-1	3

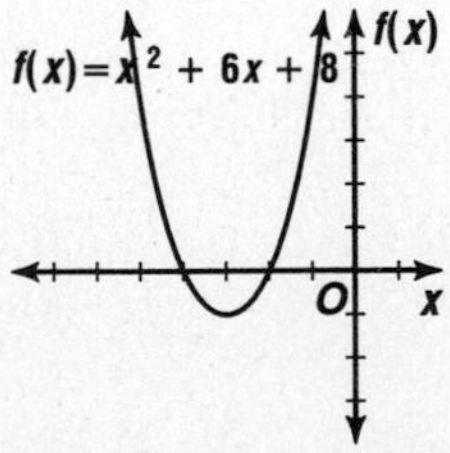

roots: $-4, -2$

43. $16a^2 - 24ab^2 + 9b^4 = (4a)^2 - 2(4a)(3b^2) + (3b^2)^2$

$\qquad = (4a - 3b^2)^2$

44. $2{,}460{,}000{,}000 = 2.46 \times 1{,}000{,}000{,}000$

$\qquad = 2.46 \times 10^9$

45. $-3x + 6 > 12$

$\qquad -3x > 6$

$\qquad x < -2$

46. $-3 + 4 - 10 = -3 + 4 + (-10)$
$= 1 + (-10)$
$= -9$

47. $7 + 2 = 2 + 7$

12-4 Dividing Polynomials

Pages 678–679 Check for Understanding

1. dividend, $2x^2 - 11x - 20$; divisor, $2x + 3$; quotient, $x - 7 + \frac{1}{2x + 3}$

2. It means the divisor goes evenly into the dividend or it is a factor of the dividend.

3. $\frac{52 \text{ ft} - 7 \text{ ft}}{3 \text{ ft/yd}} = 15$ yd; Three rolls are 15 yards, so Tomi should buy 3 rolls of border.

4a.

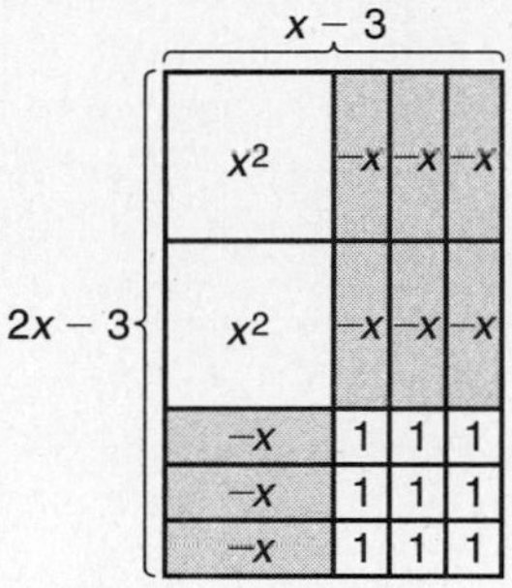

$2x^2 - 9x + 9 = (2x - 3)(x - 3)$

4b. $x - 3$; $2x - 3$

5. $(9b^2 - 15) \div 3 = \frac{9b^2 - 15}{3}$
$= \frac{9b^2}{3} - \frac{15}{3}$
$= \frac{\overset{3}{\cancel{9}}b^2}{\underset{1}{\cancel{3}}} - \frac{\overset{5}{\cancel{15}}}{\underset{1}{\cancel{3}}}$
$= 3b^2 - 5$

6. $(a^2 + 5a + 13) \div 5a = \frac{a^2 + 5a + 13}{5a}$
$= \frac{a^2}{5a} + \frac{5a}{5a} + \frac{13}{5a}$
$= \frac{\overset{a}{\cancel{a^2}}}{5\cancel{a}} + \frac{\overset{1}{\cancel{5a}}}{\underset{1}{\cancel{5a}}} + \frac{13}{5a}$
$= \frac{a}{5} + 1 + \frac{13}{5a}$

7. $(t^2 + 6t - 7) \div (t + 7) = \frac{\overset{1}{\cancel{(t + 7)}}(t - 1)}{\underset{1}{\cancel{(t + 7)}}}$
$= t - 1$

8. $(s^2 + 11s + 18) \div (s + 2) = \frac{(s + 9)\overset{1}{\cancel{(s + 2)}}}{\underset{1}{\cancel{(s + 2)}}}$
$= s + 9$

9.
$$\begin{array}{r} 2m + 3 \\ m + 2\overline{)2m^2 + 7m + 3} \\ \underline{(-)\ 2m^2 + 4m} \\ 3m + 3 \\ \underline{(-)\ 3m + 6} \\ -3 \end{array}$$

$2m + 3 + \frac{-3}{m + 2}$

10.
$$\begin{array}{r} 3r - 4 \\ r + 5\overline{)3r^2 + 11r + 7} \\ \underline{(-)\ 3r^2 + 15r} \\ -4r + 7 \\ \underline{(-)\ -4r - 20} \\ 27 \end{array}$$

$3r - 4 + \frac{27}{r + 5}$

11. $A = \ell w$
$\ell = \frac{A}{w}$
$\ell = \frac{10x^2 + 29x + 21}{5x + 7}$
$= \frac{\overset{1}{\cancel{(5x + 7)}}(2x + 3)}{\underset{1}{\cancel{5x + 7}}}$
$= (2x + 3)$ meters

Pages 679–680 Exercises

12. $(x^3 + 2x^2 - 5) \div 2x = \frac{x^3 + 2x^2 - 5}{2x}$
$= \frac{x^3}{2x} + \frac{2x^2}{2x} - \frac{5}{2x}$
$= \frac{\overset{x^2}{\cancel{x^3}}}{2\cancel{x}} + \frac{\overset{1\ x}{\cancel{2x^2}}}{\underset{1\ 1}{\cancel{2x}}} - \frac{5}{2x}$
$= \frac{x^2}{2} + x - \frac{5}{2x}$

13. $(b^2 + 9b - 7) \div 3b = \frac{b^2 + 9b - 7}{3b}$
$= \frac{b^2}{3b} + \frac{9b}{3b} - \frac{7}{3b}$
$= \frac{\overset{b}{\cancel{b^2}}}{3\underset{1}{\cancel{b}}} + \frac{\overset{3\ 1}{\cancel{9b}}}{\underset{1\ 1}{\cancel{3b}}} - \frac{7}{3b}$
$= \frac{b}{3} + 3 - \frac{7}{3b}$

14. $(3a^2 + 6a + 2) \div 3a = \frac{3a^2 + 6a + 2}{3a}$
$= \frac{3a^2}{3a} + \frac{6a}{3a} + \frac{2}{3a}$
$= \frac{\overset{1\ a}{\cancel{3a^2}}}{\underset{1\ 1}{\cancel{3a}}} + \frac{\overset{2\ 1}{\cancel{6a}}}{\underset{1\ 1}{\cancel{3a}}} + \frac{2}{3a}$
$= a + 2 + \frac{2}{3a}$

15. $(m^2 + 7m - 28) \div 7m = \frac{m^2 + 7m - 28}{7m}$
$= \frac{m^2}{7m} + \frac{7m}{7m} - \frac{28}{7m}$
$= \frac{\overset{m}{\cancel{m^2}}}{7\underset{1}{\cancel{m}}} + \frac{\overset{1}{\cancel{7m}}}{\underset{1}{\cancel{7m}}} - \frac{\overset{4}{\cancel{28}}}{\underset{1}{\cancel{7}}m}$
$= \frac{m}{7} + 1 - \frac{4}{m}$

16. $(9xy^2 - 15xy + 3) \div 3xy = \frac{9xy^2 - 15xy + 3}{3xy}$
$= \frac{9xy^2}{3xy} - \frac{15xy}{3xy} + \frac{3}{3xy}$
$= \frac{\overset{3\ \ y}{\cancel{9xy^2}}}{\cancel{3xy}} - \frac{\overset{5}{\cancel{15xy}}}{\cancel{3xy}} + \frac{\overset{1}{\cancel{3}}}{\underset{1}{\cancel{3}}xy}$
$= 3y - 5 + \frac{1}{xy}$

17.
$$\begin{array}{r} a^2 + 2a + 12 \\ a - 2\overline{)a^3 + 0a^2 + 8a - 21} \\ \underline{(-)\ a^3 - 2a^2} \\ 2a^2 + 8a \\ \underline{(-)\ 2a^2 - 4a} \\ 12a - 21 \\ \underline{(-)\ 12a - 24} \\ 3 \end{array}$$

$a^2 + 2a + 12 + \frac{3}{a - 2}$

18.
$$\begin{array}{r} b+2 \\ 2b-1\overline{)2b^2+3b-5} \\ \underline{(-)\,2b^2-b} \\ 4b-5 \\ \underline{(-)\,4b-2} \\ -3 \end{array}$$
$b+2-\frac{3}{2b-1}$

19.
$$\begin{array}{r} m-3 \\ m+7\overline{)m^2+4m-23} \\ \underline{(-)\,m^2+7m} \\ -3m-23 \\ \underline{(-)\,-3m-21} \\ -2 \end{array}$$
$m-3-\frac{2}{m+7}$

20.
$$\begin{array}{r} x-5 \\ 2x+3\overline{)2x^2-7x-16} \\ \underline{(-)\,2x^2+3x} \\ -10x-16 \\ \underline{(-)\,-10x-15} \\ -1 \end{array}$$
$x-5-\frac{1}{2x+3}$

21.
$$\begin{array}{r} 2x+6 \\ x-7\overline{)2x^2-8x-41} \\ \underline{(-)\,2x^2-14x} \\ 6x-41 \\ \underline{(-)\,6x-42} \\ 1 \end{array}$$
$2x+6+\frac{1}{x-7}$

22. $\frac{14a^2b^2+35ab^2+2a^2}{7a^2b^2} = \frac{14a^2b^2}{7a^2b^2}+\frac{35ab^2}{7a^2b^2}+\frac{2a^2}{7a^2b^2}$

$= \frac{\overset{2}{\cancel{14a^2b^2}}}{\cancel{7a^2b^2}}+\frac{\overset{5}{\cancel{35ab^2}}}{\cancel{7a^2b^2}_{a}}+\frac{\overset{1}{\cancel{2a^2}}}{7\cancel{a^2}_{1}b^2}$

$= 2+\frac{5}{a}+\frac{2}{7b^2}$

23. $\frac{12m^3k+16mk^3-8mk}{4mk} = \frac{12m^3k}{4mk}+\frac{16mk^3}{4mk}-\frac{8mk}{4mk}$

$= \frac{\overset{3\ m^2}{\cancel{12m^3k}}}{\underset{1}{\cancel{4mk}}}+\frac{\overset{4\ k^2}{\cancel{16mk^3}}}{\underset{1}{\cancel{4mk}}}-\frac{\overset{2}{\cancel{8mk}}}{\underset{1}{\cancel{4mk}}}$

$= 3m^2+4k^2-2$

24.
$$\begin{array}{r} 3r+2 \\ r+6\overline{)3r^2+20r+11} \\ \underline{(-)\,3r^2+18r} \\ 2r+11 \\ \underline{(-)\,2r+12} \\ -1 \end{array}$$
$3r+2-\frac{1}{r+6}$

25.
$$\begin{array}{r} a+7 \\ a+3\overline{)a^2+10a+20} \\ \underline{(-)\,a^2+3a} \\ 7a+20 \\ \underline{(-)\,7a+21} \\ -1 \end{array}$$
$a+7-\frac{1}{a+3}$

26.
$$\begin{array}{r} 2m-3 \\ 2m+7\overline{)4m^2+8m-19} \\ \underline{(-)\,4m^2+14m} \\ -6m-19 \\ \underline{(-)\,-6m-21} \\ 2 \end{array}$$
$2m-3+\frac{2}{2m+7}$

27.
$$\begin{array}{r} 3x-2 \\ 2x+3\overline{)6x^2+5x+15} \\ \underline{(-)\,6x^2+9x} \\ -4x+15 \\ \underline{(-)\,-4x-6} \\ 21 \end{array}$$
$3x-2+\frac{21}{2x+3}$

28.
$$\begin{array}{r} y-15 \\ y-4\overline{)y^2-19y+9} \\ \underline{(-)\,y^2-4y} \\ -15y+9 \\ \underline{(-)\,-15y+60} \\ -51 \end{array}$$
$y-15-\frac{51}{y-4}$

29.
$$\begin{array}{r} t+4 \\ 4t+1\overline{)4t^2+17t-1} \\ \underline{(-)\,4t^2+t} \\ 16t-1 \\ \underline{(-)\,16t+4} \\ -5 \end{array}$$
$t+4-\frac{5}{4t+1}$

30.
$$\begin{array}{r} x+6 \\ x+3\overline{)x^2+9x+15} \\ \underline{(-)\,x^2+3x} \\ 6x+15 \\ \underline{(-)\,6x+18} \\ -3 \end{array}$$
$x+6+\frac{-3}{x+3}$

31. $\frac{56x^3+32x^2-63x}{7x} = \frac{56x^3}{7x}+\frac{32x^2}{7x}-\frac{63x}{7x}$

$= \frac{\overset{8\ x^2}{\cancel{56x^3}}}{\cancel{7x}}+\frac{32\overset{x}{\cancel{x^2}}}{7\cancel{x}}-\frac{\overset{9}{\cancel{63x}}}{\underset{1}{\cancel{7x}}}$

$= 8x^2+\frac{32x}{7}-9$

32a. $7x-9+\frac{15}{x+2}$

32b. $\frac{1}{3}x-\frac{46}{9}-\frac{4\frac{5}{9}}{3x+4}$

33a. x^2+4x+4

33b. $5t^2-3t-2$

33c. $2a^2+3a-4$

```
PROGRAM: POLYDIV
:Disp "ENTER A, B, C, D"
:Input A: Input B:
 Input C: Input D:
:Disp "ENTER R"
:Input R
:Disp "COEFFICIENTS"
:Disp "OF QUOTIENT:"
:Disp A
:Disp B+A*R
:Disp "REMAINDER:"
:Disp C+B*R+A*R^2
:Disp D+C*R+B*R^2+A*
 R^3
```

34.
$$\begin{array}{r} x-9 \\ x+7\overline{)x^2-2x-k} \\ \underline{(-)\,x^2+7x} \\ -9x-k \\ \underline{(-)\,-9x-63} \\ -k+63=0 \\ k=63 \end{array}$$

35.
$$\begin{array}{r} m+5 \\ 2m-3\overline{)2m^2+7m+k} \\ \underline{(-)\,2m^2-3m} \\ 10m+k \\ \underline{(-)\,10m-15} \\ k+15=0 \\ k=-15 \end{array}$$

36.
$$\begin{array}{r} x^2-5x-6 \\ x-2\overline{)x^3-7x^2+4x+k} \\ \underline{(-)\,x^3-2x^2} \\ -5x^2+4x \\ \underline{(-)\,-5x^2+10x} \\ -6x+k \\ \underline{(-)\,-6x+12} \\ k-12=15 \\ k=27 \end{array}$$

37. $C=\frac{120{,}000p}{1-p}$

$=\frac{120{,}000(0.80)}{1-(0.80)}$

$=\$480{,}000$

38a.

Material	Density
aluminum	$\frac{4.15}{1.54} \approx 2.7$
gold	$\frac{2.32}{0.12} \approx 19.3$
silver	$\frac{6.30}{0.60} \approx 10.5$
steel	$\frac{7.80}{1.00} \approx 7.8$
iron	$\frac{15.20}{1.95} \approx 7.8$
copper	$\frac{2.48}{0.28} \approx 8.9$
blood	$\frac{4.35}{4.10} \approx 1.1$
lead	$\frac{11.30}{1.00} \approx 11.3$
brass	$\frac{17.90}{2.08} \approx 8.6$
concrete	$\frac{40.00}{20.00} \approx 2.0$

38b.

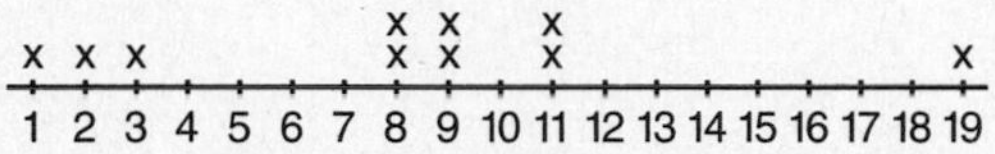

38c. The data's density is clustered around 9.

39. $\frac{x^2-16}{16-x^2} \div \frac{7}{x} = \frac{x^2-16}{16-x^2} \cdot \frac{x}{7}$

$= \frac{x^2-16}{-(x^2-16)} \cdot \frac{x}{7}$

$= \frac{\overset{1}{\cancel{x^2-16}}}{-\underset{1}{\cancel{(x^2-16)}}} \cdot \frac{x}{7}$

$= -\frac{x}{7}$

40. $y = -x^2 + 2x + 3$

axis of symmetry: $x = -\frac{b}{2a} = -\frac{2}{(-2)}$ or $x = 1$

vertex: (1, 4)

x	y
−1	0
0	3
1	4
2	3
3	0

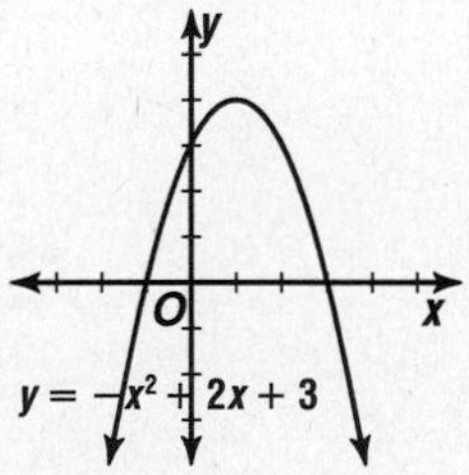

41. $3x^2 - 6x - 105 = 3(x^2 - 2x - 35)$

$= 3(x-7)(x+5)$

42. $A = \ell w$

$= (2x+y)(x+y)$

$= (2x^2 + 3xy + y^2)$ units^2

43. $y = 2x + 1$ $\qquad$ $y = -2x + 5$

$m = 2$; y-intercept: 1 $\qquad$ $m = -2$; y-intercept: 5

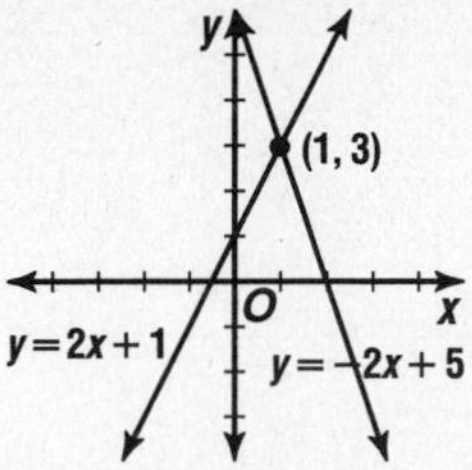

(1, 3)

44. $\frac{\text{change in range}}{\text{change in domain}} = \frac{6-4}{3-1}$ or $\frac{2}{1}$

$y = 2x$

45.

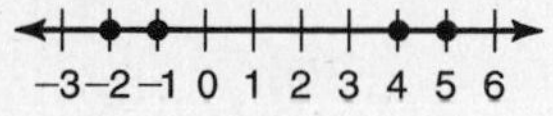

Page 680 Self Test

1. $\frac{25x^3y^4}{36x^2y^5} = \frac{x^2y^4(25x)}{x^2y^4(36y)}$

$= \frac{\overset{1}{\cancel{x^2y^4}}(25x)}{\underset{1}{\cancel{x^2y^4}}(36y)}$

$= \frac{25x}{36y}$

2. already simplified

3. $\frac{x^2-16}{x^2+5x+6} \cdot \frac{4x^2+2x-3}{x^2-5x+4} = \frac{(x+4)(x-4)}{(x+3)(x+2)} \cdot \frac{4x^2+2x-3}{(x-4)(x-1)}$

$= \frac{(x+4)\overset{1}{\cancel{(x-4)}}(4x^2+2x-3)}{(x+3)(x+2)\underset{1}{\cancel{(x-4)}}(x-1)}$

$= \frac{(x+4)(4x^2+2x-3)}{(x+3)(x+2)(x-1)}$

4. $\frac{2x^2-5x+2}{x^2-5x+6} \div \frac{2x^2+9x-5}{x^2-4x+3} = \frac{2x^2-5x+2}{x^2-5x+6} \cdot \frac{x^2-4x+3}{2x^2+9x-5}$

$= \frac{(2x-1)(x-2)}{(x-3)(x-2)} \cdot \frac{(x-3)(x-1)}{(2x-1)(x+5)}$

$= \frac{\overset{1}{\cancel{(2x-1)}}\overset{1}{\cancel{(x-2)}}\overset{1}{\cancel{(x-3)}}(x-1)}{\underset{1}{\cancel{(x-3)}}\underset{1}{\cancel{(x-2)}}\underset{1}{\cancel{(2x-1)}}(x+5)}$

$= \frac{x-1}{x+5}$

5. $(3x-2) \cdot \frac{x-5}{3x^2+10x-8} = 3x-2 \cdot \frac{x-5}{(3x-2)(x+4)}$

$= \frac{\overset{1}{\cancel{(3x-2)}}(x-5)}{\underset{1}{\cancel{(3x-2)}}(x+4)}$

$= \frac{x-5}{x+4}$

6. $\frac{7x^2+36x+5}{x-5} \div (7x+1) = \frac{7x^2+36x+5}{x-5} \cdot \frac{1}{(7x+1)}$

$= \frac{(7x+1)(x+5)}{(x-5)} \cdot \frac{1}{(7x+1)}$

$= \frac{\overset{1}{\cancel{(7x+1)}}(x+5)}{(x-5)\underset{1}{\cancel{(7x+1)}}}$

$= \frac{x+5}{x-5}$

7. $\frac{4x^2-18x+20}{2x-4} = \frac{\overset{1}{\cancel{(2x-4)}}(2x-5)}{\underset{1}{\cancel{(2x-4)}}}$

$= 2x - 5$

8.

$$\begin{array}{r} 3x \phantom{{}-4} \\ x-2\overline{)3x^2-6x-4} \\ (-)\ 3x^2-6x \phantom{{}-4} \\ \hline -4 \end{array}$$

$3x + \frac{-4}{x-2}$

9. $A = \ell w$

$\ell = \frac{A}{w}$

$= \frac{12x^2+20x-8}{x+2}$

$= \frac{4(3x-1)\overset{1}{\cancel{(x+2)}}}{\underset{1}{\cancel{(x+2)}}}$

$= 4(3x-1)$ units or $(12x-4)$ units

10. $d = rt$ $\qquad$ $d = rt$

$\frac{d}{t} = r$ $\qquad$ $d = (55)(6)$

$\frac{440}{8} = 55$ mph $\qquad$ $= 330$ miles

12-5 Rational Expressions with Like Denominators

Page 683 Check for Understanding

1. The two expressions whose sum is zero have opposite signs but equal absolute values, and the two expressions whose difference is zero are equal and have the same sign.
2. Combine the numerators, use their like denominator, and simplify.
3. She added the denominators.

4. $\frac{5x}{7} + \frac{2x}{7} = \frac{5x + 2x}{7}$
$= \frac{7x}{7}$
$= \frac{\overset{1}{\cancel{7}}x}{\underset{1}{\cancel{7}}}$
$= x$

5. $\frac{3}{x} + \frac{7}{x} = \frac{3 + 7}{x}$
$= \frac{10}{x}$

6. $\frac{7}{3m} - \frac{4}{3m} = \frac{7 - 4}{3m}$
$= \frac{3}{3m}$
$= \frac{\overset{1}{\cancel{3}}}{\underset{1}{\cancel{3}}m}$
$= \frac{1}{m}$

7. $\frac{3}{a + 2} + \frac{7}{a + 2} = \frac{3 + 7}{a + 2}$
$= \frac{10}{a + 2}$

8. $\frac{2m}{m + 3} - \frac{-6}{m + 3} = \frac{2m - (-6)}{m + 3}$
$= \frac{2m + 6}{m + 3}$
$= \frac{2(m + 3)}{m + 3}$
$= \frac{2\overset{1}{\cancel{(m + 3)}}}{\underset{1}{\cancel{(m + 3)}}}$
$= 2$

9. $\frac{3x}{x + 4} - \frac{-12}{x + 4} = \frac{3x - (-12)}{x + 4}$
$= \frac{3x + 12}{x + 4}$
$= \frac{3(x + 4)}{x + 4}$
$= \frac{3\overset{1}{\cancel{(x + 4)}}}{\underset{1}{\cancel{x + 4}}}$
$= 3$

10. $\frac{5x - 1}{3x + 2} - \frac{2x - 1}{3x + 2} = \frac{5x - 1 - (2x - 1)}{3x + 2}$
$= \frac{3x}{3x + 2}$

The numerator is $3x$.

Pages 683–684 Exercises

11. $\frac{m}{3} + \frac{2m}{3} = \frac{m + 2m}{3}$
$= \frac{\overset{1}{\cancel{3}}m}{\cancel{3}}$
$= \frac{3m}{3}$
$= m$

12. $\frac{3y}{11} - \frac{8y}{11} = \frac{3y - 8y}{11}$
$= -\frac{5y}{11}$

13. $\frac{5a}{12} - \frac{7a}{12} = \frac{5a - 7a}{12}$
$= \frac{-\overset{1}{\cancel{2}}a}{\cancel{12}}$
$= \frac{-\overset{1}{2}a}{12}$
$= -\frac{a}{6}$

14. $\frac{4}{3z} + \frac{-7}{3z} = \frac{4 + (-7)}{3z}$
$= \frac{\overset{-1}{\cancel{-3}}}{\cancel{3}z}$
$= \frac{\overset{1}{-}3}{3z}$
$= -\frac{1}{z}$

15. $\frac{x}{2} - \frac{x - 4}{2} = \frac{x - (x - 4)}{2}$
$= \frac{x - x + 4}{2}$
$= \frac{4}{2}$
$= 2$

16. $\frac{a + 3}{6} - \frac{a - 3}{6} = \frac{a + 3 - (a - 3)}{6}$
$= \frac{a + 3 - a + 3}{6}$
$= \frac{6}{6}$
$= 1$

17. $\frac{2}{x + 7} + \frac{5}{x + 7} = \frac{2 + 5}{x + 7}$
$= \frac{7}{x + 7}$

18. $\frac{2x}{x + 1} + \frac{2}{x + 1} = \frac{2x + 2}{x + 1}$
$= \frac{2(x + 1)}{x + 1}$
$= \frac{2\overset{1}{\cancel{(x + 1)}}}{\underset{1}{\cancel{x + 1}}}$
$= 2$

19. $\frac{y}{y - 2} + \frac{2}{2 - y} = \frac{y}{y - 2} - \frac{2}{y - 2}$
$= \frac{y - 2}{y - 2}$
$= 1$

20. $\frac{4m}{2m + 3} + \frac{5}{2m + 3} = \frac{4m + 5}{2m + 3}$

21. $\frac{-5}{3x - 5} + \frac{3x}{3x - 5} = \frac{-5 + 3x}{3x - 5}$
$= 1$

22. $\frac{3r}{r + 5} + \frac{15}{r + 5} = \frac{3r + 15}{r + 5}$
$= \frac{3(r + 5)}{r + 5}$
$= \frac{3\overset{1}{\cancel{(r + 5)}}}{\underset{1}{\cancel{(r + 5)}}}$
$= 3$

23. $\frac{2x}{x + 2} + \frac{2x}{x + 2} = \frac{2x + 2x}{x + 2}$
$= \frac{4x}{x + 2}$

24. $\frac{2m}{m - 9} + \frac{18}{9 - m} = \frac{2m}{m - 9} - \frac{18}{m - 9}$
$= \frac{2m - 18}{m - 9}$
$= \frac{2(m - 9)}{m - 9}$
$= \frac{2\overset{1}{\cancel{(m - 9)}}}{\underset{1}{\cancel{(m - 9)}}}$
$= 2$

25. $\frac{2y}{y + 3} + \frac{-6}{y + 3} = \frac{2y - 6}{y + 3}$

26. $\frac{3m}{m - 2} - \frac{5}{m - 2} = \frac{3m - 5}{m - 2}$

27. $\frac{4x}{2x + 3} - \frac{-6}{2x + 3} = \frac{4x - (-6)}{2x + 3}$
$= \frac{4x + 6}{2x + 3}$
$= \frac{2(2x + 3)}{2x + 3}$
$= \frac{2\overset{1}{\cancel{(2x + 3)}}}{\underset{1}{\cancel{2x + 3}}}$
$= 2$

28. $\frac{4t - 1}{1 - 4t} + \frac{2t + 3}{1 - 4t} = \frac{4t - 1 + (2t + 3)}{1 - 4t}$
$= \frac{6t + 2}{1 - 4t}$

29. $\frac{3x - 100}{2x + 5} + \left(\frac{11x - 5}{2x + 5} + \frac{11x + 12}{2x + 5}\right)$
$= \frac{3x - 100}{2x + 5} + \left(\frac{11x - 5 + 11x + 12}{2x + 5}\right)$
$= \frac{3x - 100}{2x + 5} + \frac{22x + 7}{2x + 5}$
$= \frac{3x - 100 + 22x + 7}{2x + 5}$
$= \frac{25x - 93}{2x + 5}$

30. $\left(\frac{b-15}{2b+12}+\frac{-3b+12}{2b+12}\right)-\frac{-3b+4}{2b+12}$

$= \frac{b-15+(-3b+12)}{2b+12}-\frac{-3b+4}{2b+12}$

$= \frac{-2b-3}{2b+12}-\frac{-3b+4}{2b+12}$

$= \frac{-2b-3-(-3b+4)}{2b+12}$

$= \frac{-2b-3+3b-4}{2b+12}$

$= \frac{b-7}{2b+12}$

31. $P = 2\ell + 2w$

$= 2\left(\frac{12x}{7x-2y}\right)+2\left(\frac{13y}{7x-2y}\right)$

$= \frac{2(12x)+2(13y)}{7x-2y}$

$= \frac{24x+26y}{7x-2y}$

32. $P = 2\ell + 2w$

$= 2\left(\frac{4a+5b}{3a+7b}\right)+2\left(\frac{2a+9b}{3a+7b}\right)$

$= \frac{2(4a+5b)+2(2a+9b)}{3a+7b}$

$= \frac{8a+10b+4a+18b}{3a+7b}$

$= \frac{12a+28b}{3a+7b}$

$= \frac{4(3a+7b)}{3a+7b}$

$= \frac{4\cancel{(3a+7b)}^{1}}{\cancel{3a+7b}_{1}}$

$= 4$

33. b

34a. $\frac{7.48 \text{ gal}}{1 \text{ ft}^3} \cdot 0.89 = 6.657$ gallons per cubic foot

34b. $1 \text{ mi} \cdot \frac{5280 \text{ ft}}{1 \text{ mi}} \cdot 2 \text{ mi} \cdot \frac{5280 \text{ ft}}{1 \text{ mi}} \cdot 800 \text{ ft} \cdot \frac{6.657 \text{ gal}}{1 \text{ ft}^3}$

$= 296{,}938{,}414{,}100$ gallons

35. $\frac{1 \text{ day}}{168 \text{ gal}} \cdot 0.75(296{,}947{,}335{,}168) \text{ gal} \cdot \frac{1}{3{,}000{,}000} =$ 442 days

36. $\pi d = 1$ mi

$\pi d = 5280$ ft

$d = \frac{5280}{\pi}$

≈ 1680.7 feet

37.

$25x^2 = 36$

$25x^2 - 36 = 0$

$(5x-6)(5x+6) = 0$

$5x - 6 = 0$ or $5x + 6 = 0$

$x = \frac{6}{5}$ $\quad x = -\frac{6}{5}$

$\pm\frac{6}{5}$

38. $P = (x^2 - y) + (2x + 4) + (x^2 + 5y) + (2x + 4y)$

$= 2x^2 + 8y + 4x + 4$

39. $x - 2y = -11$

$x = 2y - 11$

$x + 2y = 5$

$(2y - 11) + 2y = 5$

$4y - 11 = 5$

$4y = 16$

$y = 4$

$x = 2y - 11$

$x = 2(4) - 11$

$x = 8 - 11$

$x = -3$

$(-3, 4)$

40.

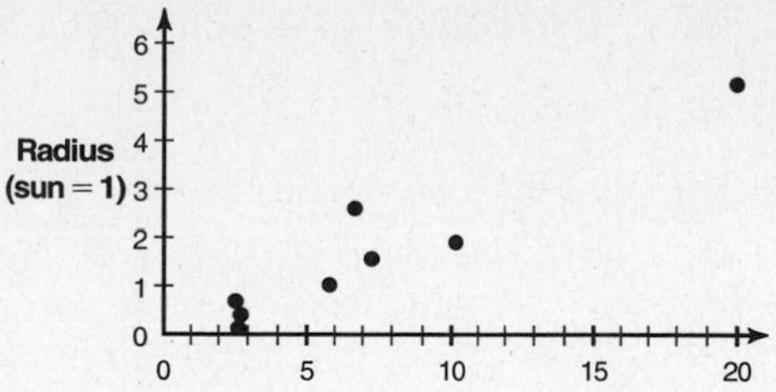

41. $\frac{1}{6} \cdot \frac{1}{6} \cdot \frac{1}{6} = \frac{1}{216}$

12-6 Rational Expressions with Unlike Denominators

Page 687 Check for Understanding

1. Yes; no; no common factors were divided.

2. $\frac{3x}{4} + \frac{7}{8x}$; $8x$ is the LCD.

3. x^2: $x \cdot x$

x: x

LCD $= x \cdot x$ or x^2

4. a^2b: $a \cdot a \cdot b$

ab^2: $a \cdot b \cdot b$

LCD $= a \cdot a \cdot b \cdot b$ or a^2b^2

5. $15m^2$: $3 \cdot 5 \cdot m \cdot m$

$18mb^2$: $2 \cdot 3 \cdot 3 \cdot m \cdot b \cdot b$

LCD: $2 \cdot 3 \cdot 3 \cdot 5 \cdot m \cdot m \cdot b \cdot b$ or $90m^2b^2$

6. LCD $= (a + 6)(a + 7)$ **7.** LCD $= (x - 3)(x + 3)$

8. $2x - 8$: $2(x - 4)$

$x - 4$: $x - 4$

LCD $= 2(x - 4)$

9. $15m^2$: $3 \cdot 5 \cdot m \cdot m$

$5m$: $5 \cdot m$

LCD $= 3 \cdot 5 \cdot m \cdot m$ or $15m^2$

$\frac{7}{15m^2} + \frac{3}{5m} = \frac{7}{15m^2} + \frac{3(3m)}{5m(3m)}$

$= \frac{7}{15m^2} + \frac{9m}{15m^2}$

$= \frac{9m + 7}{15m^2}$

10. LCD $= (x + 3)(x - 2)$

$\frac{2}{x+3} + \frac{3}{x-2} = \frac{2(x-2)}{(x+3)(x-2)} + \frac{3(x+3)}{(x+3)(x-2)}$

$= \frac{2x-4}{(x+3)(x-2)} + \frac{3x+9}{(x+3)(x-2)}$

$= \frac{2x-4+3x+9}{(x+3)(x-2)}$

$= \frac{5x+5}{(x+3)(x-2)}$

11. LCD $= x + 2$

$3x + 6 - \frac{9}{x+2} = \frac{3x(x+2)}{x+2} + \frac{6(x+2)}{x+2} - \frac{9}{x+2}$

$= \frac{3x^2+6x}{x+2} + \frac{6x+12}{x+2} - \frac{9}{x+2}$

$= \frac{3x^2+6x+6x+12-9}{x+2}$

$= \frac{3x^2+12x+3}{x+2}$

$= \frac{3(x^2+4x+1)}{x+2}$

12. $m^2 + 4m + 3$: $(m + 3)(m + 1)$
$m + 3$: $m + 3$
LCD: $(m + 3)(m + 1)$

$$\frac{m+2}{m^2+4m+3} - \frac{6}{m+3} = \frac{m+2}{(m+3)(m+1)} - \frac{6(m+1)}{(m+3)(m+1)}$$
$$= \frac{m+2-6(m+1)}{(m+3)(m+1)}$$
$$= \frac{m+2-6m-6}{(m+3)(m+1)}$$
$$= \frac{-5m-4}{(m+3)(m+1)}$$

13. $3y^2$: $3 \cdot y \cdot y$
$6y$: $2 \cdot 3 \cdot y$
LCD: $2 \cdot 3 \cdot y \cdot y$ or $6y^2$

$$\frac{11}{3y^2} - \frac{7}{6y} = \frac{11(2)}{3y^2(2)} - \frac{7(y)}{6y(y)}$$
$$= \frac{22}{6y^2} - \frac{7y}{6y^2}$$
$$= \frac{22-7y}{6y^2}$$

14. LCD: $(2g - 7)(3g + 1)$

$$\frac{4}{2g-7} + \frac{5}{3g+1} = \frac{4(3g+1)}{(2g-7)(3g+1)} + \frac{5(2g-7)}{(2g-7)(3g+1)}$$
$$= \frac{4(3g+1)+5(2g-7)}{(2g-7)(3g+1)}$$
$$= \frac{12g+4+10g-35}{(2g-7)(3g+1)}$$
$$= \frac{22g-31}{(2g-7)(3g+1)}$$

15. 6: $2 \cdot 3$
7: 7
8: $2 \cdot 2 \cdot 2$
LCD: $2 \cdot 2 \cdot 2 \cdot 3 \cdot 7$ or 168
168 members

Pages 687–689 Exercises

16. 4: $2 \cdot 2$
5: 5
LCD: $2 \cdot 2 \cdot 5$ or 20

$$\frac{m}{4} + \frac{3m}{5} = \frac{(m)(5)}{(4)(5)} + \frac{(3m)(4)}{(4)(5)}$$
$$= \frac{5m+12m}{20}$$
$$= \frac{17m}{20}$$

17. 7: 7
9: $3 \cdot 3$
LCD: $3 \cdot 3 \cdot 7$ or 63

$$\frac{x}{7} - \frac{2x}{9} = \frac{(x)(9)}{(7)(9)} - \frac{(2x)(7)}{(7)(9)}$$
$$= \frac{9x-14x}{63}$$
$$= \frac{-5x}{63}$$

18. m: m
$3m$: $3 \cdot m$
LCD: $3 \cdot m$ or $3m$

$$\frac{m+1}{m} + \frac{m-3}{3m} = \frac{(3)(m+1)}{(3)(m)} + \frac{m-3}{3m}$$
$$= \frac{3(m+1)+m-3}{3m}$$
$$= \frac{3m+3+m-3}{3m}$$
$$= \frac{4m}{3m}$$
$$= \frac{4}{3}$$

19. x: x
xyz: $x \cdot y \cdot z$
LCD: $x \cdot y \cdot z$ or xyz

$$\frac{7}{x} + \frac{3}{xyz} = \frac{7(yz)}{x(yz)} + \frac{3}{xyz}$$
$$= \frac{7yz+3}{xyz}$$

20. $6a^2$: $2 \cdot 3 \cdot a \cdot a$
$3a$: $3 \cdot a$
LCD: $2 \cdot 3 \cdot a \cdot a$ or $6a^2$

$$\frac{7}{6a^2} - \frac{5}{3a} = \frac{7}{6a^2} - \frac{5(2a)}{(3a)(2a)}$$
$$= \frac{7}{6a^2} - \frac{10a}{6a^2}$$
$$= \frac{7-10a}{6a^2}$$

21. st^2: $s \cdot t \cdot t$
s^2t: $s \cdot s \cdot t$
LCD: $s \cdot s \cdot t \cdot t$ or s^2t^2

$$\frac{2}{st^2} - \frac{3}{s^2t} = \frac{2(s)}{st^2(s)} - \frac{3(t)}{s^2t(t)}$$
$$= \frac{2s}{s^2t^2} - \frac{3t}{s^2t^2}$$
$$= \frac{2s-3t}{s^2t^2}$$

22. $7m$: $7 \cdot m$
$5m^2$: $5 \cdot m \cdot m$
LCD: $5 \cdot 7 \cdot m \cdot m$ or $35m^2$

$$\frac{3}{7m} + \frac{4}{5m^2} = \frac{3(5m)}{7m(5m)} + \frac{4(7)}{5m^2(7)}$$
$$= \frac{15m}{35m^2} + \frac{28}{35m^2}$$
$$= \frac{15m+28}{35m^2}$$

23. LCD: $(z + 5)(z - 4)$

$$\frac{3}{z+5} + \frac{4}{z-4} = \frac{3(z-4)}{(z+5)(z-4)} + \frac{4(z+5)}{(z+5)(z-4)}$$
$$= \frac{3z-12}{(z+5)(z-4)} + \frac{4z+20}{(z+5)(z-4)}$$
$$= \frac{3z-12+4z+20}{(z+5)(z-4)}$$
$$= \frac{7z+8}{(z+5)(z-4)}$$

24. LCD: $(d + 4)(d + 3)$

$$\frac{d}{d+4} + \frac{3}{d+3} = \frac{d(d+3)}{(d+4)(d+3)} + \frac{3(d+4)}{(d+4)(d+3)}$$
$$= \frac{d^2+3d}{(d+4)(d+3)} + \frac{3d+12}{(d+4)(d+3)}$$
$$= \frac{d^2+3d+3d+12}{(d+4)(d+3)}$$
$$= \frac{d^2+6d+12}{(d+4)(d+3)}$$

25. LCD: $(k + 5)(k - 3)$

$$\frac{k}{k+5} - \frac{2}{k+3} = \frac{k(k+3)}{(k+5)(k+3)} - \frac{2(k+5)}{(k+5)(k+3)}$$
$$= \frac{k^2+3k}{(k+5)(k+3)} - \frac{2k+10}{(k+5)(k+3)}$$
$$= \frac{(k^2+3k)-(2k+10)}{(k+5)(k+3)}$$
$$= \frac{k^2+k-10}{(k+5)(k+3)}$$

26. LCD: $(y - 3)(y + 4)$

$$\frac{3}{y-3} - \frac{y}{y+4} = \frac{3(y+4)}{(y-3)(y+4)} - \frac{y(y-3)}{(y-3)(y+4)}$$
$$= \frac{3y+12}{(y-3)(y+4)} - \frac{y^2-3y}{(y-3)(y+4)}$$
$$= \frac{(3y+12)-(y^2-3y)}{(y-3)(y+4)}$$
$$= \frac{-y^2+6y+12}{(y-3)(y+4)}$$

27. LCD: $(3r - 2)(r - 5)$

$$\frac{10}{3r-2} - \frac{9}{r-5} = \frac{10(r-5)}{(3r-2)(r-5)} - \frac{9(3r-2)}{(3r-2)(r-5)}$$
$$= \frac{10r-50}{(3r-2)(r-5)} - \frac{27r-18}{(3r-2)(r-5)}$$
$$= \frac{(10r-50)-(27r-18)}{(3r-2)(r-5)}$$
$$= \frac{-17r-32}{(3r-2)(r-5)}$$

28. $3a - 6: 3(a - 2)$
$a + 2: a + 2$
LCD: $3(a - 2)(a + 2)$

$$\frac{4}{3a-6} + \frac{a}{2+a} = \frac{4(a+2)}{3(a-2)(a+2)} + \frac{a(3)(a-2)}{3(a-2)(a+2)}$$
$$= \frac{4a+8}{3(a-2)(a+2)} + \frac{3a^2-6a}{3(a-2)(a+2)}$$
$$= \frac{4a+8+3a^2-6a}{3(a-2)(a+2)}$$
$$= \frac{3a^2-2a+8}{3(a-2)(a+2)}$$

29. $2m - 3: 2m - 3$
$6 - 4m: -2(2m - 3)$
LCD: $-2(2m - 3)$

$$\frac{5}{2m-3} - \frac{m}{6-4m} = \frac{5(-2)}{-2(2m-3)} - \frac{m}{-2(2m-3)}$$
$$= \frac{-10}{-2(2m-3)} - \frac{m}{-2(2m-3)}$$
$$= \frac{-10-m}{-2(2m-3)}$$
$$= \frac{-(10+m)}{-2(2m-3)}$$
$$= \frac{10+m}{2(2m-3)}$$

30. $3b + 2: 3b + 2$
$9b + 6: 3(3b + 2)$
LCD: $3(3b + 2)$

$$\frac{b}{3b+2} + \frac{2}{9b+6} = \frac{b(3)}{3(3b+2)} + \frac{2}{3(3b+2)}$$
$$= \frac{3b}{3(3b+2)} + \frac{2}{3(3b+2)}$$
$$= \frac{3b+2}{3(3b+2)}$$
$$= \frac{\overset{1}{\cancel{3b+2}}}{3(\underset{1}{\cancel{3b+2}})}$$
$$= \frac{1}{3}$$

31. $5w + 2: 5w + 2$
$15w + 6: 3(5w + 2)$
LCD: $3(5w + 2)$

$$\frac{w}{5w+2} - \frac{4}{15w+6} = \frac{w(3)}{3(5w+2)} - \frac{4}{3(5w+2)}$$
$$= \frac{3w}{3(5w+2)} - \frac{4}{3(5w+2)}$$
$$= \frac{3w-4}{3(5w+2)}$$

32. $h^2 + 4h + 4: (h + 2)(h + 2)$
$h + 2: h + 2$
LCD: $(h + 2)(h + 2)$ or $(h + 2)^2$

$$\frac{h-2}{h^2+4h+4} + \frac{h-2}{h+2} = \frac{h-2}{(h+2)^2} + \frac{(h-2)(h+2)}{(h+2)^2}$$
$$= \frac{h-2}{(h+2)^2} + \frac{(h^2-4)}{(h+2)^2}$$
$$= \frac{h-2+h^2-4}{(h+2)^2}$$
$$= \frac{h^2+h-6}{(h+2)^2}$$

33. $n + 3: n + 3$
$n^2 + 4n + 3: (n + 3)(n + 1)$
LCD: $(n + 3)(n + 1)$

$$\frac{n+2}{n^2+4n+3} - \frac{6}{n+3} = \frac{n+2}{(n+3)(n+1)} - \frac{6(n+1)}{(n+3)(n+1)}$$
$$= \frac{n+2}{(n+3)(n+1)} - \frac{6n+6}{(n+3)(n+1)}$$
$$= \frac{(n+2)-(6n+6)}{(n+3)(n+1)}$$
$$= \frac{-5n-4}{(n+3)(n+1)}$$

34. $5 - a: (-1)(a - 5)$
$a^2 - 25: (a + 5)(a - 5)$
LCD: $(-1)(a + 5)(a - 5)$

$$\frac{a}{5-a} - \frac{3}{a^2-25} = \frac{a(a+5)}{(-1)(a+5)(a-5)} - \frac{3(-1)}{(-1)(a+5)(a-5)}$$
$$= \frac{a^2+5a+3}{(-1)(a+5)(a-5)}$$
$$= \frac{(-1)(-a^2-5a-3)}{(-1)(a+5)(a-5)}$$
$$= \frac{-a^2-5a-3}{(a+5)(a-5)}$$

35. LCD: $(t + 3)(10t - 9)$

$$\frac{3}{10t-9} - \frac{2}{t+3} = \frac{3(t+3)}{(t+3)(10t-9)} - \frac{2(10t-9)}{(t+3)(10t-9)}$$
$$= \frac{3t+9}{(t+3)(10t-9)} - \frac{20t-18}{(t+3)(10t-9)}$$
$$= \frac{3t+9-(20t-18)}{(t+3)(10t-9)}$$
$$= \frac{-17t+27}{(t+3)(10t-9)}$$

36. $y^2 + 7y + 12: (y + 3)(y + 4)$
$y + 4: y + 4$
LCD: $(y + 3)(y + 4)$

$$\frac{2y}{y^2+7y+12} + \frac{y+2}{y+4} = \frac{2y}{(y+4)(y+3)} + \frac{(y+2)(y+3)}{(y+4)(y+3)}$$
$$= \frac{2y}{(y+4)(y+3)} + \frac{y^2+5y+6}{(y+4)(y+3)}$$
$$= \frac{2y+y^2+5y+6}{(y+4)(y+3)}$$
$$= \frac{y^2+7y+6}{(y+4)(y+3)}$$

37. $v + 4: v + 4$
$v - 1: v - 1$
$v^2 + 3v - 4: (v + 4)(v - 1)$
LCD: $(v + 4)(v - 1)$

$$\frac{2}{v+4} + \frac{v}{v-1} + \frac{5v}{v^2+3v-4}$$
$$= \frac{2(v-1)}{(v+4)(v-1)} + \frac{v(v+4)}{(v+4)(v-1)} + \frac{5v}{(v+4)(v-1)}$$
$$= \frac{2v-2}{(v+4)(v-1)} + \frac{v^2+4v}{(v+4)(v-1)} + \frac{5v}{(v+4)(v-1)}$$
$$= \frac{2v-2+v^2+4v+5v}{(v+4)(v-1)}$$
$$= \frac{v^2+11v-2}{(v+4)(v-1)}$$

38. LCD: $(a + 1)(a - 2)$

$$\frac{6}{a-2} - \frac{2}{a+1} = \frac{6(a+1)}{(a-2)(a+1)} - \frac{2(a-2)}{(a-2)(a+1)}$$
$$= \frac{6a+6}{(a-2)(a+1)} - \frac{2a-4}{(a-2)(a+1)}$$
$$= \frac{(6a+6)-(2a-4)}{(a-2)(a+1)}$$
$$= \frac{4a+10}{(a-2)(a+1)}$$
$$= \frac{2(2a+5)}{(a-2)(a+1)}$$

(Continued next page)

$$\frac{2}{a+1} - \frac{6}{a-2} = \frac{2(a-2)}{(a-2)(a+1)} - \frac{6(a+1)}{(a-2)(a+1)}$$
$$= \frac{2a-4}{(a-2)(a+1)} - \frac{6a+6}{(a-2)(a+1)}$$
$$= \frac{(2a-4)-(6a+6)}{(a-2)(a+1)}$$
$$= \frac{-4a-10}{(a-2)(a+1)}$$
$$= \frac{-2(2a+5)}{(a-2)(a+1)}$$

They are opposite.

39a. $5 \cdot 24 = 360$
GCF: 3
LCM: 120
GCF $\cdot$ LCM $= 3 \cdot 120$ or 360

39b. $18 \cdot 30 = 540$
GCF: 6
LCM: 90
GCF $\cdot$ LCM $= 6 \cdot 90$ or 540

39c. The GCF times the LCM of two numbers is equal to the product of the two numbers.

39d. Divide the GCF into the product of the two numbers to find the LCM.

40. 3: 3
6: $2 \cdot 3$
7: 7
LCD: $2 \cdot 3 \cdot 7$ or 42

41. 3 months $\cdot$ 5 = 15 months for 15,000 miles
15 months later or July 20, 1997

42. $45 - 12 = 33$ years; LCD of 2, 3, 6 and 33 is $2 \cdot 3 \cdot 11$ or 66. Jaheed lived 66 years.

43. $$\frac{8z+3}{3z+4} - \frac{2z-5}{3z+4} = \frac{(8z+3)-(2z-5)}{3z+4}$$
$$= \frac{6z+8}{3z+4}$$
$$= \frac{2(3z+4)}{3z+4}$$
$$= \frac{2\cancel{(3z+4)}^{1}}{\cancel{3z+4}_{1}}$$
$$= 2$$

44. $$\frac{x^2+7x+6}{3x^2+x-2} = \frac{(x+6)(x+1)}{(3x-2)(x+1)}$$
$$= \frac{(x+6)\cancel{(x+1)}^{1}}{(3x-2)\cancel{(x+1)}_{1}}$$
$$= \frac{x+6}{3x-2}$$

Excluded values:
$3x^2 + x - 2 = 0$
$(3x-2)(x+1) = 0$
$3x - 2 = 0$ or $x + 1 = 0$
$x = \frac{2}{3}$ $\quad$ $x = -1$

$\frac{x+6}{3x-2}$; $-1, \frac{2}{3}$

45. $2x^2 - 3x - 4 = 0$
$a = 2, b = -3, c = -4$
$$x = \frac{-(-3) \pm \sqrt{(-3)^2 - 4(2)(-4)}}{(2)2}$$
$$= \frac{3 \pm \sqrt{9+32}}{4}$$
$$= \frac{3 \pm \sqrt{41}}{4}$$
$$x = \frac{3+\sqrt{41}}{4} \approx 2.35 \text{ or } x = \frac{3-\sqrt{41}}{4} \approx -0.85$$
$\frac{3 \pm \sqrt{41}}{4}$ or about 2.35 and -0.85

46. $3x^2y + 6xy + 9y^2 = 3y(x^2) + 3y(2x) + 3y(3y)$
$= 3y(x^2 + 2x + 3y)$

47. $(3a^2b)(-5a^4b^2) = (3 \cdot -5)(a^2 \cdot a^4)(b \cdot b^2)$
$= -15a^{2+4}b^{1+2}$
$= -15a^6b^3$

48. $3x > -15$ and $2x \leq 6$
$x > -5$ $\quad$ $x \leq 3$

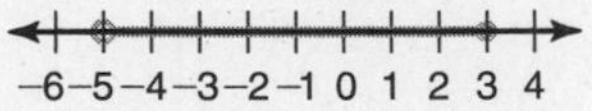

49.
$$3n - 12 = 5n - 20$$
$$3n - 3n - 12 = 5n - 3n - 20$$
$$-12 = 2n - 20$$
$$-12 + 20 = 2n - 20 + 20$$
$$8 = 2n$$
$$4 = n$$

50.

Stem	Leaf
0	3
1	0 3 8 9
2	0 0 1 2
3	9
4	5 7 9

0 | 3 = 30 thousand

Page 689 Mathematics and Society

1. 25, 17 and 4: 17, 4 and 33
2. Yes, because food intake is daily and per serving information better suits daily calculations.
3. See students' work.

12-7 Mixed Expressions and Complex Fractions

Page 693 Check for Understanding

1. $\frac{3}{4}$

2a. $2x(x-2)$

2b. $3 + \frac{x}{2} + \frac{4}{x} + \frac{x^2+3x+15}{x-2}$
$$= \frac{3(2x)(x-2)}{2x(x-2)} + \frac{x(x)(x-2)}{2x(x-2)} + \frac{4(2)(x-2)}{2x(x-2)} + \frac{(2x)(x^2+3x+15)}{2x(x-2)}$$
$$= \frac{3(2x)(x-2) + x(x)(x-2) + 4(2)(x-2) + 2x(x^2+3x+15)}{2x(x-2)}$$
$$= \frac{6x^2 - 12x + x^3 - 2x^2 + 8x - 16 + 2x^3 + 6x^2 + 30x}{2x(x-2)}$$
$$= \frac{3x^3 + 10x^2 + 26x - 16}{2x(x-2)}$$

3. LCD: x
$$8 + \frac{3}{x} = \frac{8(x)}{x} + \frac{3}{x}$$
$$= \frac{8(x)+3}{x}$$
$$= \frac{8x+3}{x}$$

4. LCD: $3m$
$$5 + \frac{8}{3m} = \frac{5(3m)}{3m} + \frac{8}{3m}$$
$$= \frac{5(3m)+8}{3m}$$
$$= \frac{15m+8}{3m}$$

5. LCD: $2m$
$$3m + \frac{m+1}{2m} = \frac{3m(2m)}{2m} + \frac{m+1}{2m}$$
$$= \frac{3m(2m)+m+1}{2m}$$
$$= \frac{6m^2+m+1}{2m}$$

6. $\dfrac{4\frac{1}{3}}{5\frac{4}{7}} = \dfrac{\frac{13}{3}}{\frac{39}{7}}$

$= \frac{13}{3} \div \frac{39}{7}$

$= \frac{13}{3} \cdot \frac{7}{39}$

$= \frac{7}{9}$

7. $\dfrac{6\frac{2}{5}}{3\frac{5}{9}} = \dfrac{\frac{32}{5}}{\frac{32}{9}}$

$= \frac{32}{5} \div \frac{32}{9}$

$= \frac{32}{5} \cdot \frac{9}{32}$

$= \frac{9}{5}$

8. $\dfrac{\frac{3}{x}}{\frac{x}{3}} = \frac{3}{x} \div \frac{x}{3}$

$= \frac{3}{x} \cdot \frac{3}{x}$

$= \frac{9}{x^2}$

9. $\dfrac{\frac{5}{y}}{\frac{10}{y^2}} = \frac{5}{y} \div \frac{10}{y^2}$

$= \frac{5}{y} \cdot \frac{y^2}{10}$

$= \frac{y}{2}$

10. $\dfrac{\frac{x+4}{x-2}}{\frac{x+5}{x-2}} = \frac{x+4}{x-2} \div \frac{x+5}{x-2}$

$= \frac{x+4}{x-2} \cdot \frac{x-2}{x+5}$

$= \frac{x+4}{x+5}$

11. $\dfrac{\frac{a-b}{a+b}}{\frac{3}{a+b}} = \frac{a-b}{a+b} \div \frac{3}{a+b}$

$= \frac{a-b}{a+b} \cdot \frac{a+b}{3}$

$= \frac{a-b}{3}$

12. Division; $\frac{x+2}{3x-1} \div \frac{2x^2-8}{3x-1} = \frac{x+2}{3x-1} \cdot \frac{3x-1}{2(x-2)(x+2)}$

$= \frac{1}{2(x-2)}$

Pages 693–695 Exercises

13. $3 + \frac{6}{x+3} = \frac{3(x+3)}{x+3} + \frac{6}{x+3}$

$= \frac{3(x+3)+6}{x+3}$

$= \frac{3x+9+6}{x+3}$

$= \frac{3x+15}{x+3}$

14. $11 + \frac{a-b}{a+b} = \frac{11(a+b)}{a+b} + \frac{a-b}{a+b}$

$= \frac{11(a+b)+a-b}{a+b}$

$= \frac{11a+11b+a-b}{a+b}$

$= \frac{12a+10b}{a+b}$

15. $3 - \frac{4}{2x+1} = \frac{3(2x+1)}{2x+1} - \frac{4}{2x+1}$

$= \frac{3(2x+1)-4}{2x+1}$

$= \frac{6x-1}{2x+1}$

16. $3 + \frac{x-4}{x+y} = \frac{3(x+y)}{x+y} + \frac{x-4}{x+y}$

$= \frac{3(x+y)+x-4}{x+y}$

$= \frac{3x+3y+x-4}{x+y}$

$= \frac{4x+3y-4}{x+y}$

17. $5 + \frac{r-3}{r^2-9} = \frac{5(r^2-9)}{r^2-9} + \frac{r-3}{r^2-9}$

$= \frac{5(r^2-9)+r-3}{r^2-9}$

$= \frac{5r^2-45+r-3}{r^2-9}$

$= \frac{5r^2+r-48}{r^2-9}$

18. $3 + \frac{x^2+y^2}{x^2-y^2} = \frac{3(x^2-y^2)}{x^2-y^2} + \frac{x^2+y^2}{x^2-y^2}$

$= \frac{3(x^2-y^2)+x^2+y^2}{x^2-y^2}$

$= \frac{3x^2-3y^2+x^2+y^2}{x^2-y^2}$

$= \frac{4x^2-2y^2}{x^2-y^2}$

19. $\dfrac{7\frac{2}{3}}{5\frac{3}{4}} = \dfrac{\frac{23}{3}}{\frac{23}{4}}$

$= \frac{23}{3} \div \frac{23}{4}$

$= \frac{23}{3} \cdot \frac{4}{23}$

$= \frac{4}{3}$

20. $\dfrac{6\frac{1}{7}}{8\frac{3}{5}} = \dfrac{\frac{43}{7}}{\frac{43}{5}}$

$= \frac{43}{7} \div \frac{43}{5}$

$= \frac{43}{7} \cdot \frac{5}{43}$

$= \frac{5}{7}$

21. $\dfrac{\frac{a^3}{b}}{\frac{a^2}{b^2}} = \frac{a^3}{b} \div \frac{a^2}{b^2}$

$= \frac{a^3}{b} \cdot \frac{b^2}{a^2}$

$= ab$

22. $\dfrac{\frac{x^2y^2}{a}}{\frac{x^2y}{a^3}} = \frac{x^2y^2}{a} \div \frac{x^2y}{a^3}$

$= \frac{x^2y^2}{a} \cdot \frac{a^3}{x^2y}$

$= a^2y$

23. $\dfrac{2+\frac{5}{x}}{\frac{x}{3}+\frac{5}{6}} = \dfrac{\frac{2(x)}{x}+\frac{5}{x}}{\frac{(x)(2)}{3(2)}+\frac{5}{6}}$

$= \dfrac{\frac{2x+5}{x}}{\frac{2x+5}{6}}$

$= \frac{2x+5}{x} \div \frac{2x+5}{6}$

$= \frac{2x+5}{x} \cdot \frac{6}{2x+5}$

$= \frac{6}{x}$

24. $\dfrac{4+\frac{3}{y}}{\frac{3}{8}+\frac{y}{2}} = \dfrac{\frac{4(y)}{y}+\frac{3}{y}}{\frac{3}{8}+\frac{4(4)}{2(4)}}$

$= \dfrac{\frac{4y+3}{y}}{\frac{3+4y}{8}}$

$= \frac{4y+3}{y} \div \frac{4y+3}{8}$

$= \frac{4y+3}{y} \cdot \frac{8}{4y+3}$

$= \frac{8}{y}$

25. $\dfrac{a-\frac{15}{a-2}}{a+3} = \dfrac{\frac{a(a-2)}{a-2}-\frac{15}{a-2}}{a+3}$

$= \dfrac{\frac{a(a-2)-15}{a-2}}{a+3}$

$= \dfrac{\frac{a^2-2a-15}{a-2}}{a+3}$

$= \frac{a^2-2a-15}{a-2} \div (a+3)$

$= \frac{(a+3)(a-5)}{a-2} \cdot \frac{1}{a+3}$

$= \frac{a-5}{a-2}$

26. $\dfrac{x + \dfrac{35}{x+12}}{x+7} = \dfrac{\dfrac{x(x+12)}{x+12} + \dfrac{35}{x+12}}{x+7}$

$= \dfrac{\dfrac{x^2 + 12x + 35}{x+12}}{x+7}$

$= \dfrac{x^2 + 12x + 35}{x+12} \div (x+7)$

$= \dfrac{(x+5)(x+7)}{x+12} \cdot \dfrac{1}{x+7}$

$= \dfrac{x+5}{x+12}$

27. $\dfrac{\dfrac{x^2-4}{x^2+5x+6}}{x-2} = \dfrac{x^2-4}{x^2+5x+6} \div (x-2)$

$= \dfrac{(x+2)(x-2)}{(x+3)(x+2)} \cdot \dfrac{1}{x-2}$

$= \dfrac{1}{x+3}$

28. $\dfrac{m + \dfrac{3m+7}{m+5}}{m+1} = \dfrac{\dfrac{m(m+5)}{m+5} + \dfrac{3m+7}{m+5}}{m+1}$

$= \dfrac{\dfrac{m^2 + 5m + 3m + 7}{m+5}}{m+1}$

$= \dfrac{\dfrac{m^2 + 8m + 7}{m+5}}{m+1}$

$= \dfrac{m^2 + 8m + 7}{m+5} \div (m+1)$

$= \dfrac{(m+7)(m+1)}{m+5} \cdot \dfrac{1}{m+1}$

$= \dfrac{m+7}{m+5}$

29. $\dfrac{m + 5 + \dfrac{2}{m+2}}{m + 1 + \dfrac{6}{m+6}} = \dfrac{\dfrac{(m+5)(m+2)}{m+2} + \dfrac{2}{m+2}}{\dfrac{(m+1)(m+6)}{m+6} + \dfrac{6}{m+6}}$

$= \dfrac{\dfrac{m^2 + 7m + 10 + 2}{m+2}}{\dfrac{m^2 + 7m + 6 + 6}{m+6}}$

$= \dfrac{\dfrac{m^2 + 7m + 12}{m+2}}{\dfrac{m^2 + 7m + 12}{m+6}}$

$= \dfrac{\dfrac{(m+3)(m+4)}{m+2}}{\dfrac{(m+3)(m+4)}{m+6}}$

$= \dfrac{(m+3)(m+4)}{m+2} \cdot \dfrac{m+6}{(m+3)(m+4)}$

$= \dfrac{m+6}{m+2}$

30. $\dfrac{a + 1 + \dfrac{3}{a+5}}{a + 1 + \dfrac{3}{a-1}} = \dfrac{\dfrac{(a+1)(a+5)}{a+5} + \dfrac{3}{a+5}}{\dfrac{(a+1)(a-1)}{a-1} + \dfrac{3}{a-1}}$

$= \dfrac{\dfrac{a^2 + 6a + 5 + 3}{a+5}}{\dfrac{a^2 - 1 + 3}{a-1}}$

$= \dfrac{\dfrac{a^2 + 6a + 8}{a+5}}{\dfrac{a^2 + 2}{a-1}}$

$= \dfrac{\dfrac{(a+4)(a+2)}{a+5}}{\dfrac{a^2 + 2}{a-1}}$

$= \dfrac{(a+4)(a+2)(a-1)}{(a+5)(a^2+2)}$

31. $\dfrac{y + 6 + \dfrac{3}{y+2}}{y + 11 + \dfrac{48}{y-3}} = \dfrac{\dfrac{(y+6)(y+2)}{y+2} + \dfrac{3}{y+2}}{\dfrac{(y+11)(y-3)}{y-3} + \dfrac{48}{y-3}}$

$= \dfrac{\dfrac{y^2 + 8y + 12 + 3}{y+2}}{\dfrac{y^2 + 8y - 33 + 48}{y-3}}$

$= \dfrac{\dfrac{y^2 + 8y + 15}{y+2}}{\dfrac{y^2 + 8y + 15}{y-3}}$

$= \dfrac{\dfrac{(y+5)(y+3)}{y+2}}{\dfrac{(y+5)(y+3)}{y-3}}$

$= \dfrac{(y+5)(y+3)}{y+2} \cdot \dfrac{y-3}{(y+5)(y+3)}$

$= \dfrac{y-3}{y+2}$

32. $\dfrac{x + 3 + \dfrac{4}{x-2}}{x - 1 - \dfrac{2}{x+3}} = \dfrac{\dfrac{(x+3)(x-2)}{x-2} + \dfrac{4}{x-2}}{\dfrac{(x-1)(x+3)}{x+3} - \dfrac{2}{x+3}}$

$= \dfrac{\dfrac{x^2 + x - 6 + 4}{x-2}}{\dfrac{x^2 + 2x - 3 - 2}{x+3}}$

$= \dfrac{\dfrac{x^2 + x - 2}{x-2}}{\dfrac{x^2 + 2x - 5}{x+3}}$

$= \dfrac{\dfrac{(x+2)(x-1)}{x-2}}{\dfrac{x^2 + 2x - 5}{x+3}}$

$= \dfrac{(x+2)(x-1)(x+3)}{(x-2)(x^2 + 2x - 5)}$

33. $$\frac{t+1+\frac{1}{t+1}}{1-t-\frac{1}{t+1}} = \frac{\frac{(t+1)(t+1)}{t+1}+\frac{1}{t+1}}{\frac{(1-t)(t+1)}{t+1}-\frac{1}{t+1}}$$
$$= \frac{\frac{t^2+2t+1+1}{t+1}}{\frac{1-t^2-1}{t+1}}$$
$$= \frac{\frac{t^2+2t+2}{t+1}}{\frac{-t^2}{t+1}}$$
$$= \frac{t^2+2t+2}{t+1}\cdot\frac{t+1}{-t^2}$$
$$= \frac{t^2+2t+2}{-t^2}$$

34. $$\frac{b+\frac{1}{b}}{a+\frac{1}{a}} = \frac{\frac{b(b)}{b}+\frac{1}{b}}{\frac{a(a)}{a}+\frac{1}{a}}$$
$$= \frac{\frac{b^2+1}{b}}{\frac{a^2+1}{a}}$$
$$= \frac{b^2+1}{b}\cdot\frac{a}{a^2+1}$$
$$= \frac{a(b^2+1)}{b(a^2+1)}$$

35. $$\frac{\frac{4b^3}{2c}}{\frac{7b^3}{8c^2}} = \frac{4b^3}{2c} \div \frac{7b^3}{8c^2}$$
$$= \frac{4b^3}{2c}\cdot\frac{8c^2}{7b^3}$$
$$= \frac{16c}{7}$$
$$\frac{2b^2}{5c}\cdot\frac{16c}{7} = \frac{32b^2c}{35c}$$
$$= \frac{32b^2}{35}$$

36. $$1+\frac{1}{1+\frac{1}{1+\frac{1}{1+\frac{1}{x}}}} = 1+\frac{1}{1+\frac{1}{1+\frac{1}{\frac{x}{x}+\frac{1}{x}}}}$$
$$= 1+\frac{1}{1+\frac{1}{1+\frac{1}{\frac{x+1}{x}}}}$$
$$= 1+\frac{1}{1+\frac{1}{1+\frac{x}{x+1}}}$$
$$= 1+\frac{1}{1+\frac{1}{\frac{x+1}{x+1}+\frac{x}{x+1}}}$$
$$= 1+\frac{1}{1+\frac{1}{\frac{2x+1}{x+1}}}$$
$$= 1+\frac{1}{1+\frac{x+1}{2x+1}}$$
$$= 1+\frac{1}{\frac{2x+1}{2x+1}+\frac{x+1}{2x+1}}$$
$$= 1+\frac{1}{\frac{3x+2}{2x+1}}$$
$$= 1+\frac{2x+1}{3x+2}$$
$$= \frac{3x+2}{3x+2}+\frac{2x+1}{3x+2}$$
$$= \frac{5x+3}{3x+2}$$

37a. $$y = \frac{\frac{x+3}{2x}}{\frac{3x+9}{4}}$$
$$= \frac{x+3}{2x} \div \frac{3x+9}{4}$$
$$= \frac{x+3}{2x}\cdot\frac{4}{3(x+3)}$$
$$= \frac{2}{3x}$$

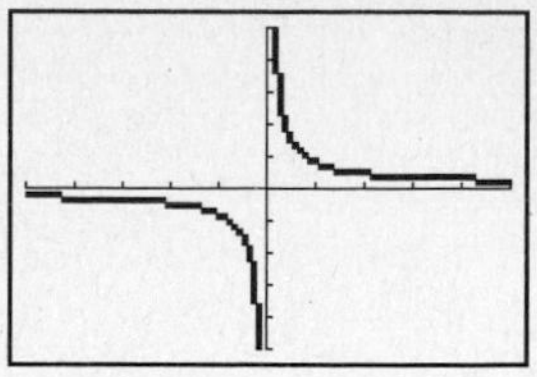

excluded values: $x \neq 0$, $x \neq -3$

37b. Graph is the same as in part a.
excluded values: $x \neq 0$, $x \neq -3$

37c. yes

38. $$\frac{3}{1-\frac{3}{3+y}} - \frac{3}{\frac{3}{3-y}-1} = \frac{3}{\frac{3+y}{3+y}-\frac{3}{3+y}} - \frac{3}{\frac{3}{3-y}-\frac{3-y}{3-y}}$$
$$= \frac{3}{\frac{3+y-3}{3+y}} - \frac{3}{\frac{3-(3-y)}{3-y}}$$
$$= \frac{3}{\frac{y}{3+y}} - \frac{3}{\frac{y}{3-y}}$$
$$= \frac{3(y+3)}{y} - \frac{3(3-y)}{y}$$
$$= \frac{3(y+3)-3(3-y)}{y}$$
$$= \frac{3y+9-9+3y}{y}$$
$$= \frac{6y}{y}$$
$$= 6$$

39a. $$h = \frac{f}{1-\frac{v}{s}}$$
$$= \frac{f}{\frac{s}{s}-\frac{v}{s}}$$
$$= \frac{f}{\frac{s-v}{s}}$$
$$= f\cdot\frac{s}{s-v}$$
$$= \frac{fs}{s-v}$$

39b. $$h = \frac{370(760)}{760-80}$$
$$= 413.5$$

39c. 415.3 is G#
It rose by approximately 2 notes.

39d. $$h = \frac{370(760)}{760-236}$$
$$= 536.6$$
523.2 is C
It rose by approximately 6 notes.

40. New Jersey $= \frac{7{,}879{,}000 \text{ people}}{7419 \text{ mi}^2}$
≈ 1062 people/mi^2

Alaska $= \frac{599{,}000 \text{ people}}{570{,}374 \text{ mi}^2}$
≈ 1.1 people/mi^2

$1062 - 1.1 = 1061$
approximately 1061 people/mi^2

41. $2x + 6$: $2(x + 3)$
$x + 3$: $x + 3$
LCD $= 2(x + 3)$
$$\frac{4x}{2x+6}+\frac{3}{x+3} = \frac{4x}{2(x+3)}+\frac{3(2)}{2(x+3)}$$
$$= \frac{4x+3(2)}{2(x+3)}$$
$$= \frac{4x+6}{2(x+3)}$$
$$= \frac{2(2x+3)}{2(x+3)}$$
$$= \frac{2x+3}{x+3}$$

42. $\frac{b-5}{b^2-7b+10} \cdot \frac{b-2}{3} = \frac{b-5}{(b-5)(b-2)} \cdot \frac{b-2}{3}$

$= \frac{\cancel{b-5}^{\,1}}{\cancel{(b-5)}_1\cancel{(b-2)}_1} \cdot \frac{\cancel{b-2}^{\,1}}{3}$

$= \frac{1}{3}$

43. $4x^2 - 1 = (2x)^2 - (1)^2$

$= (2x + 1)(2x - 1)$

44. $x^4y^5 \div xy^3 = \frac{x^4y^5}{xy^3}$

$= \left(\frac{x^4}{x}\right)\left(\frac{y^5}{y^3}\right)$

$= (x^{4-1})(y^{5-3})$

$= x^3y^2$

45. $3a + 4b = -25 \quad \rightarrow \quad 9a + 12b = -75$

$2a - 3b = 6 \quad \rightarrow \quad (+)\ 8a - 12b = 24$

$17a = -51$

$a = -3$

$3a + 4b = -25$

$3(-3) + 4b = -25$

$-9 + 4b = -25$

$4b = -16$

$b = -4$

$(-3, -4)$

46a.

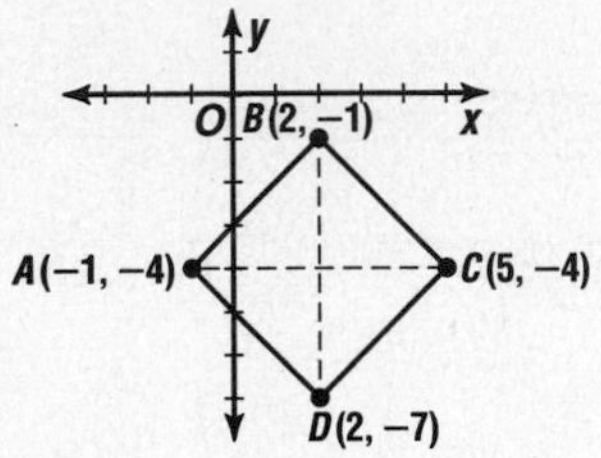

$\overline{AB}$: $m = \frac{-3}{-3}$ or 1 $\qquad$ $\overline{CD}$: $m = \frac{3}{3}$ or 1

$\overline{BC}$: $m = \frac{3}{-3}$ or -1 $\qquad$ $\overline{AC}$: $m = \frac{0}{-6}$ or 0

$\overline{AD}$: $m = \frac{3}{-3}$ or -1 $\qquad$ $\overline{BD}$: $m = \frac{-6}{0}$ or undefined

$\overline{AB}$ and $\overline{CD}$ have the same slope, 1;
$\overline{BC}$ and $\overline{AD}$ have the same slope, -1;
$\overline{AB}$ and $\overline{BC}$, $\overline{AB}$ and $\overline{AD}$, $\overline{BC}$ and $\overline{CD}$, $\overline{AD}$ and $\overline{CD}$ have opposite slopes;
$\overline{AC}$ and $\overline{BD}$ are perpendicular.

Opposite sides are parallel, adjacent sides are perpendicular, perpendicular diagonals.

46b. square

47. $P = 2\ell + 2w$

$P - 2\ell = 2w$

$\frac{P - 2\ell}{2} = \frac{2w}{2}$

$\frac{P - 2\ell}{2} = w$

48. $\sqrt{225} = 15$

12-8 Solving Rational Equations

Page 699 Check for Understanding

1. $\frac{t}{3} + \frac{t}{6} = 1$

$6\left(\frac{t}{3} + \frac{t}{6}\right) = 1(6)$

$2t + t = 6$

$3t = 6$

$t = 2$

2 hours

2. She correctly solved the equation, but $m = 1$ makes a denominator zero and it must therefore be discarded as a solution.

3. A rational equation contains rational expressions whereas a linear equation has integer coefficients.

4a–b. See students' work.

5. $\frac{1}{4} + \frac{4}{x} = \frac{1}{x}$ $\qquad$ LCD: $4x$

$4x\left(\frac{1}{4} + \frac{4}{x}\right) = 4x\left(\frac{1}{x}\right)$

$4x\left(\frac{1}{4}\right) + 4x\left(\frac{4}{x}\right) = 4x\left(\frac{1}{x}\right)$

$x + 16 = 4$

$x = -12$

6. $\frac{1}{5} + \frac{3}{2y} = \frac{3}{3y}$ $\qquad$ LCD: $30y$

$30y\left(\frac{1}{5} + \frac{3}{2y}\right) = \left(\frac{3}{3y}\right)(30y)$

$30y\left(\frac{1}{5}\right) + 30y\left(\frac{3}{2y}\right) = \left(\frac{3}{3y}\right)(30y)$

$6y + 45 = 30$

$6y = -15$

$y = \frac{-15}{6}$ or $-\frac{5}{2}$

7. $\frac{4}{x+5} = \frac{4}{3(x+2)}$

$4[3(x + 2)] = 4(x + 5)$

$12x + 24 = 4x + 20$

$8x + 24 = 20$

$8x = -4$

$x = -\frac{4}{8}$ or $-\frac{1}{2}$

8. $\frac{x}{2} = \frac{3}{x+1}$

$x(x + 1) = 3(2)$

$x^2 + x = 6$

$x^2 + x - 6 = 0$

$(x + 3)(x - 2) = 0$

$x + 3 = 0$ or $x - 2 = 0$

$x = -3 \qquad x = 2$

$-3, 2$

9. $\frac{a-1}{a+1} - \frac{2a}{a-1} = -1$

LCD: $(a + 1)(a - 1)$

$(a + 1)(a - 1)\left(\frac{a-1}{a+1} - \frac{2a}{a-1}\right) = -1(a + 1)(a - 1)$

$(a + 1)(a - 1)\left(\frac{a-1}{a+1}\right) + (a + 1)(a - 1)\left(\frac{-2a}{a-1}\right)$

$= -1(a + 1)(a - 1)$

$(a - 1)^2 - 2a(a + 1) = -(a^2 - 1)$

$a^2 - 2a + 1 - 2a^2 - 2a = -a^2 + 1$

$-a^2 - 4a + 1 = -a^2 + 1$

$-4a + 1 = 1$

$-4a = 0$

$a = 0$

10. $\frac{w-2}{w} - \frac{w-3}{w-6} = \frac{1}{w}$

LCD: $w(w-6)$

$$w(w-6)\left(\frac{w-2}{w} - \frac{w-3}{w-6}\right) = \frac{1}{w}[w(w-6)]$$
$$w(w-6)\left(\frac{w-2}{w}\right) + w(w-6)\left(\frac{-w-3}{w-6}\right) - \frac{1}{w}[w(w-6)]$$
$$(w-6)(w-2) + w[-(w-3)] = w-6$$
$$w^2 - 8w + 12 - w^2 + 3w = w - 6$$
$$-5w + 12 = w - 6$$
$$12 = 6w - 6$$
$$18 = 6w$$
$$3 = w$$

11a. $r \cdot t = w$
$\frac{1}{5} \cdot 1 = \frac{1}{5}$

11b. $r \cdot t = w$
$\frac{1}{5} \cdot 3 = \frac{3}{5}$

11c. $r \cdot t = w$
$\frac{1}{5} \cdot x = \frac{x}{5}$

12.

	d	r	$t = \frac{d}{r}$
downstream	9	$3 + c$	$\frac{9}{3+c}$
upstream	3	$3 - c$	$\frac{3}{3-c}$

12a. $\frac{9}{3+c} = \frac{3}{3-c}$

12b.
$$\frac{9}{3+c} = \frac{3}{3-c}$$
$$9(3-c) = 3(3+c)$$
$$27 - 9c = 9 + 3c$$
$$18 - 9c = 3c$$
$$18 = 12c$$
$$\frac{18}{12} = c$$
$\frac{18}{12}$ or 1.5 mph

13.
$$\frac{1}{R_T} = \frac{1}{R_1} + \frac{1}{R_2}$$
$$\frac{1}{R_T} = \frac{1}{8} + \frac{1}{6}$$
$$\frac{1}{R_T} = \frac{3}{24} + \frac{4}{24}$$
$$\frac{1}{R_T} = \frac{7}{24}$$
$$7R_T = 24$$
$R_T = \frac{24}{7}$ or 3.429 ohms

14.
$$\frac{1}{R_T} = \frac{1}{R_1} + \frac{1}{R_2}$$
$$\frac{1}{2.\overline{2}} = \frac{1}{R_1} + \frac{1}{5}$$
$$\frac{1}{2.\overline{2}} - \frac{1}{5} = \frac{1}{R_1}$$
$$\frac{9}{20} - \frac{1}{5} = \frac{1}{R_1}$$
$$\frac{9}{20} - \frac{4}{20} = \frac{1}{R_1}$$
$$\frac{5}{20} = \frac{1}{R_1}$$
$$5R_1 = 20$$
$R_1 = 4$ ohms

15.
$$\frac{1}{R_T} = \frac{1}{R_1} + \frac{1}{R_2}$$
$$\frac{1}{2.\overline{6}} = \frac{1}{2R_2} + \frac{1}{R_2}$$
$$\frac{1}{\frac{24}{9}} = \frac{1}{2R_2} + \frac{1(2)}{R_2(2)}$$
$$\frac{9}{24} = \frac{1+2}{2R_2}$$
$$\frac{9}{24} = \frac{3}{2R_2}$$
$$18R_2 = 72$$
$R_2 = 4$ ohms
$R_1 = 2(4)$ or 8 ohms
8 ohms, 4 ohms

Pages 700–702 Exercises

16. $\frac{1}{4} + \frac{3}{x} = \frac{1}{x}$ LCD: $4x$

$$4x\left(\frac{1}{4} + \frac{3}{x}\right) = \left(\frac{1}{x}\right)4x$$
$$4x\left(\frac{1}{4}\right) + 4x\left(\frac{3}{x}\right) = \left(\frac{1}{x}\right)4x$$
$$x + 12 = 4$$
$$x = -8$$

17. $\frac{1}{5} - \frac{4}{3m} = \frac{2}{m}$ LCD: $15m$

$$15m\left(\frac{1}{5} - \frac{4}{3m}\right) = \left(\frac{2}{m}\right)15m$$
$$15m\left(\frac{1}{5}\right) - 15m\left(\frac{4}{3m}\right) = \frac{2}{m}(15m)$$
$$3m - 20 = 30$$
$$3m = 50$$
$$m = \frac{50}{3}$$

18.
$$x + 3 = -\frac{2}{x}$$
$$x(x+3) = -2$$
$$x^2 + 3x = -2$$
$$x^2 + 3x + 2 = 0$$
$$(x+1)(x+2) = 0$$
$x + 1 = 0$ or $x + 2 = 0$
$x = -1$ $\quad x = -2$

19. $\frac{m+1}{m} + \frac{m+4}{m} = 6$ LCD: m

$$m\left(\frac{m+1}{m} + \frac{m+4}{m}\right) = 6(m)$$
$$m\left(\frac{m+1}{m}\right) + m\left(\frac{m+4}{m}\right) = 6(m)$$
$$m + 1 + m + 4 = 6m$$
$$2m + 5 = 6m$$
$$5 = 4m$$
$$\frac{5}{4} = m$$

20. $\frac{x}{x+1} + \frac{5}{x-1} = 1$ LCD: $(x+1)(x-1)$

$$(x+1)(x-1)\left(\frac{x}{x+1} + \frac{5}{x-1}\right) = 1(x+1)(x-1)$$
$$(x+1)(x-1)\left(\frac{x}{x+1}\right) + (x+1)(x-1)\left(\frac{5}{x-1}\right) = (x+1)(x-1)$$
$$x(x-1) + 5(x+1) = (x+1)(x-1)$$
$$x^2 - x + 5x + 5 = x^2 - 1$$
$$4x + 5 = -1$$
$$4x = -6$$
$$x = \frac{-6}{4} \text{ or } \frac{-3}{2}$$

21. $\frac{m-1}{m+1} - \frac{2m}{m-1} = -1$

LCD: $(m+1)(m-1)$

$$(m+1)(m-1)\left(\frac{m-1}{m+1} - \frac{2m}{m-1}\right) = -1(m+1)(m-1)$$
$$(m+1)(m-1)\left(\frac{m-1}{m+1}\right) + (m+1)(m-1)\left(\frac{-2m}{m-1}\right) = -1(m+1)(m-1)$$
$$(m-1)(m-1) + -2m(m+1) = -m^2 + 1$$
$$m^2 - 2m + 1 - 2m^2 - 2m = -m^2 + 1$$
$$-m^2 - 4m + 1 = -m^2 + 1$$
$$-4m = 0$$
$$m = 0$$

22. $\frac{-4}{a+1} + \frac{3}{a} = 1$ LCD: $a(a+1)$

$$a(a+1)\left(\frac{-4}{a+1} + \frac{3}{a}\right) = 1(a)(a+1)$$
$$a(a+1)\left(\frac{-4}{a+1}\right) + a(a+1)\left(\frac{3}{a}\right) = 1(a)(a+1)$$
$$-4a + 3(a+1) = a(a+1)$$
$$-4a + 3a + 3 = a^2 + a$$
$$-a + 3 = a^2 + a$$
$$0 = a^2 + 2a - 3$$
$$0 = (a-1)(a+3)$$
$a - 1 = 0$ or $a + 3 = 0$
$a = 1$ $\quad a = -3$
1 or -3

23. $\frac{3x}{10} - \frac{1}{5x} = \frac{1}{2}$ LCD: $10x$

$$10x\left(\frac{3x}{10} - \frac{1}{5x}\right) = \frac{1}{2}(10x)$$
$$10x\left(\frac{3x}{10}\right) + 10x\left(-\frac{1}{5x}\right) = \frac{1}{2}(10x)$$
$$3x^2 - 2 = 5x$$
$$3x^2 - 5x - 2 = 0$$
$$(x - 2)(3x + 1) = 0$$
$x - 2 = 0$ or $3x + 1 = 0$

$x = 2$ $\quad x = -\frac{1}{3}$

2 or $-\frac{1}{3}$

24. $\frac{b}{4} + \frac{1}{b} = \frac{-5}{3}$ LCD: $12b$

$$12b\left(\frac{b}{4} + \frac{1}{b}\right) = \left(\frac{-5}{3}\right)(12b)$$
$$12b\left(\frac{b}{4}\right) + 12b\left(\frac{1}{b}\right) = \left(\frac{-5}{3}\right)(12b)$$
$$3b^2 + 12 = -20b$$
$$3b^2 + 20b + 12 = 0$$
$$(b + 6)(3b + 2) = 0$$
$b + 6 = 0$ or $3b + 2 = 0$

$b = -6$ $\quad 3b = -2$

$b = -\frac{2}{3}$

-6 or $-\frac{2}{3}$

25. $\frac{-4}{n} = 11 - 3n$ LCD: n

$$n\left(\frac{-4}{n}\right) = (11 - 3n)n$$
$$-4 = 11n - 3n^2$$
$$3n^2 - 11n - 4 = 0$$
$$(n - 4)(3n + 1) = 0$$
$n - 4 = 0$ or $3n + 1 = 0$

$n = 4$ $\quad n = -\frac{1}{3}$

4 or $-\frac{1}{3}$

26. $\frac{x - 3}{x} = \frac{x - 3}{x - 6}$

$$(x - 3)(x - 6) = x(x - 3)$$
$$x^2 - 9x + 18 = x^2 - 3x$$
$$-9x + 18 = -3x$$
$$18 = 6x$$
$$3 = x$$

27. $\frac{7}{a - 1} = \frac{5}{a + 3}$

$$7(a + 3) = 5(a - 1)$$
$$7a + 21 = 5a - 5$$
$$2a + 21 = -5$$
$$2a = -26$$
$$a = -13$$

28. $\frac{3}{r + 4} - \frac{1}{r} = \frac{1}{r}$ LCD: $r(r + 4)$

$$r(r + 4)\left(\frac{3}{r + 4} - \frac{1}{r}\right) = \frac{1}{r}(r)(r + 4)$$
$$r(r + 4)\left(\frac{3}{r + 4}\right) + r(r + 4)\left(-\frac{1}{r}\right) = \frac{1}{r}(r)(r + 4)$$
$$3r - (r + 4) = r + 4$$
$$3r - r - 4 = r + 4$$
$$2r - 4 = r + 4$$
$$r - 4 = 4$$
$$r = 8$$

29. $\frac{3}{x} + \frac{4x}{x - 3} = 4$ LCD: $x(x - 3)$

$$x(x - 3)\left(\frac{3}{x} + \frac{4x}{x - 3}\right) = 4x(x - 3)$$
$$x(x - 3)\left(\frac{3}{x}\right) + x(x - 3)\left(\frac{4x}{x - 3}\right) = 4x(x - 3)$$
$$3(x - 3) + 4x(x) = 4x^2 - 12x$$
$$3x - 9 + 4x^2 = 4x^2 - 12x$$
$$3x - 9 = -12x$$
$$-9 = -15x$$
$$x = \frac{9}{15} \text{ or } \frac{3}{5}$$

30. $\frac{1}{4m} + \frac{2m}{m - 3} = 2$ LCD: $4m(m - 3)$

$$4m(m - 3)\left(\frac{1}{4m} + \frac{2m}{m - 3}\right) = 2(4m)(m - 3)$$
$$4m(m - 3)\left(\frac{1}{4m}\right) + 4m(m - 3)\left(\frac{2m}{m - 3}\right)$$
$$= 2(4m)(m - 3)$$
$$m - 3 + 4m(2m) = 8m^2 - 24m$$
$$m - 3 + 8m^2 = 8m^2 - 24m$$
$$m - 3 = -24m$$
$$-3 = -25m$$
$$\frac{3}{25} = m$$

31. $\frac{a - 2}{a} - \frac{a - 3}{a - 6} = \frac{1}{a}$ LCD: $a(a - 6)$

$$a(a - 6)\left(\frac{a - 2}{a} - \frac{a - 3}{a - 6}\right) = \frac{1}{a}(a)(a - 6)$$
$$a(a - 6)\left(\frac{a - 2}{a}\right) + a(a - 6)\left(-\frac{a - 3}{a - 6}\right) = \frac{1}{a}(a)(a - 6)$$
$$(a - 6)(a - 2) + a(-a + 3) = a - 6$$
$$a^2 - 8a + 12 - a^2 + 3a = a - 6$$
$$-5a + 12 = a - 6$$
$$-5a + 18 = a$$
$$18 = 6a$$
$$3 = a$$

32. $\frac{x + 3}{x + 5} + \frac{2}{x - 9} = \frac{-20}{x^2 - 4x - 45}$ LCD: $(x + 5)(x - 9)$

$$(x + 5)(x - 9)\left(\frac{x + 3}{x + 5} + \frac{2}{x - 9}\right) = \frac{-20}{(x + 5)(x - 9)}(x + 5)(x - 9)$$
$$(x + 5)(x - 9)\left(\frac{x + 3}{x + 5}\right) + (x + 5)(x - 9)\left(\frac{2}{x - 9}\right)$$
$$= -20$$
$$(x - 9)(x + 3) + 2(x + 5) = -20$$
$$x^2 - 6x - 27 + 2x + 10 = -20$$
$$x^2 - 4x - 17 = -20$$
$$x^2 - 4x + 3 = 0$$
$$(x - 3)(x - 1) = 0$$
$x - 3 = 0$ or $x - 1 = 0$

$x = 3$ $\quad x = 1$

33. $\frac{-1}{w + 2} = \frac{w^2 - 7w - 8}{3w^2 + 2w - 8}$

$$\frac{-1}{w + 2} = \frac{(w - 8)(w + 1)}{(3w - 4)(w + 2)}$$
$$-(3w - 4)(w + 2) = (w + 2)(w - 8)(w + 1)$$
$$-(3w - 4) = (w - 8)(w + 1)$$
$$-3w + 4 = w^2 - 7w - 8$$
$$0 = w^2 - 4w - 12$$
$$0 = (w - 6)(w + 2)$$
$w - 6 = 0$ or $w + 2 = 0$

$w = 6$ $\quad w = -2$

Since $w = -2$ is an excluded value, the only solution is $w = 6$.

34. $\frac{1}{R_T} = \frac{1}{R_1} + \frac{1}{R_2 + R_3}$

$\frac{1}{R_T} = \frac{1}{5} + \frac{1}{4+3}$

$\frac{1}{R_T} = \frac{1}{5} + \frac{1}{7}$

$\frac{1}{R_T} = \frac{7}{35} + \frac{5}{35}$

$\frac{1}{R_T} = \frac{12}{35}$

$35 = 12R_T$

$\frac{35}{12} = R_T$

$\frac{35}{12}$ or 2.92 ohms

35. $\frac{1}{R_T} = \frac{1}{R_1} + \frac{1}{R_2 + R_3}$

$\frac{1}{2\frac{10}{13}} = \frac{1}{R_1} + \frac{1}{3+6}$

$\frac{1}{\frac{36}{13}} = \frac{1}{R_1} + \frac{1}{9}$

$\frac{13}{36} = \frac{1}{R_1} + \frac{1}{9}$

$\frac{13}{36} - \frac{1}{9} = \frac{1}{R_1}$

$\frac{13}{36} - \frac{4}{36} = \frac{1}{R_1}$

$\frac{9}{36} = \frac{1}{R_1}$

$9R_1 = 36$

$R_1 = 4$ ohms

36. $\frac{1}{R_T} = \frac{1}{R_1} + \frac{1}{R_2 + R_3}$

$\frac{1}{3.5} = \frac{1}{5} + \frac{1}{R_2 + 4}$

$\frac{1}{3.5} - \frac{1}{5} = \frac{1}{R_2 + 4}$

$\frac{10}{35} - \frac{7}{35} = \frac{1}{R_2 + 4}$

$\frac{3}{35} = \frac{1}{R_2 + 4}$

$3(R_2 + 4) = 35$

$3R_2 + 12 = 35$

$3R_2 = 23$

$R_2 = \frac{23}{3}$ or $7.\overline{6}$ ohms

37. $\frac{1}{R_T} = \frac{1}{R_1} + \frac{1}{R_2}$ LCD: $R_1R_2R_T$

$R_1R_2R_T\left(\frac{1}{R_T}\right) = \left(\frac{1}{R_1} + \frac{1}{R_2}\right)(R_1R_2R_T)$

$R_1R_2R_T\left(\frac{1}{R_T}\right) = R_1R_2R_T\left(\frac{1}{R1}\right) + R_1R_2R_T\left(\frac{1}{R_2}\right)$

$R_1R_2 = R_2R_T + R_1R_T$

$R_1R_2 - R_1R_T = R_2R_T$

$R_1(R_2 - R_T) = R_2R_T$

$\frac{R_1(R_2 - R_T)}{R_2 - R_T} = \frac{R_2R_T}{R_2 - R_T}$

$R_1 = \frac{R_2R_T}{R_2 - R_T}$

38. $I = \frac{E}{r + R}$

$I(r + R) = E$

$Ir + IR = E$

$IR = E - Ir$

$\frac{IR}{I} = \frac{E - Ir}{I}$

$R = \frac{E - Ir}{I}$

39. $I = \frac{nE}{nr + R}$

$I(nr + R) = nE$

$Inr + IR = nE$

$IR = nE - Inr$

$IR = n(E - Ir)$

$\frac{IR}{E - Ir} = \frac{n(E - Ir)}{E - Ir}$

$\frac{IR}{E - Ir} = n$

40. $I = \frac{E}{\frac{r}{n} + R}$

$I\left(\frac{r}{n} + R\right) = E$

$\frac{Ir}{n} + IR = E$

$n\left(\frac{Ir}{n} + IR\right) = E(n)$

$n\left(\frac{Ir}{n}\right) + n(IR) = En$

$Ir + nIR = En$

$Ir = En - IRn$

$\frac{Ir}{I} = \frac{En - IRn}{I}$

$r = \frac{En - IRn}{I}$

41. Let x = the number.

$\frac{4 + x}{11 + x} = \frac{2}{3}$

$3(4 + x) = 2(11 + x)$

$12 + 3x = 22 + 2x$

$12 + x = 22$

$x = 10$

The number is 10.

42a. $\frac{1}{R_T} = \frac{1}{R_2} + \frac{1}{R_3}$ LCD: $R_2R_3R_T$

$R_2R_3R_T\left(\frac{1}{R_T}\right) = R_2R_3R_T\left(\frac{1}{R_2} + \frac{1}{R_3}\right)$

$R_2R_3 = R_2R_3R_T\left(\frac{1}{R_2}\right) + R_2R_3R_T\left(\frac{1}{R_3}\right)$

$R_2R_3 = R_3R_T + R_2R_T$

$R_2R_3 = R_T(R_3 + R_2)$

$\frac{R_2R_3}{R_3 + R_2} = R_T$

$R_T = R_1 + \frac{R_2R_3}{R_2 + R_3}$

42b. $R_T = 5 + \frac{4(6)}{4+6}$

$= 5 + \frac{24}{10}$

$= 5 + 2.4$

$= 7.4$ ohms

43. $R_T = 8(12)$

$= 96$ ohms

44. $\frac{1}{R_T} = \frac{1}{60} + \frac{1}{20} + \frac{1}{80}$ LCD: 240

$R_T = \frac{4}{240} + \frac{12}{240} + \frac{3}{240}$

$\frac{1}{R_T} = \frac{19}{240}$

$19R_T = 240$

$R_T = \frac{240}{19}$ or 12.63 ohms

45a. $rt = d$

$(520 - 120)t = 1000$

$400t = 1000$

$t = 2.5$ hours

45b. $rt = d$

$(520 + 120)t = 1400$

$640t = 1400$

$t = 2.19$ hours

45c. $t = \frac{d}{r}$: $\frac{d}{640} = \frac{2400 - d}{400}$

$400d = 640(2400 - d)$

$400d = 1{,}536{,}000 - 640d$

$1040d = 1{,}536{,}000$

$d \approx 1476.9$

$2400 - 1476.9 = 923.1$ miles

after 923 miles

46a.

	r	t	$d = rt$
Todd	20	t	$20t$
Kristie	16	t	$16t$

$20t + 16t = 24$

$36t = 24$

$t = \frac{2}{3}$ h or 40 min

$16\left(\frac{2}{3}\right) = 10\frac{2}{3}$ miles from one end or

$20\left(\frac{2}{3}\right) = 13\frac{1}{3}$ miles from the other end

46b.

	r	d	$t = \frac{d}{t}$
Todd	$20 - x$	12	$\frac{12}{20 - x}$
Kristie	$16 + x$	12	$\frac{12}{16 + x}$

$$\frac{12}{20 - x} = \frac{12}{16 + x}$$
$$12(16 + x) = 12(20 - x)$$
$$192 + 12x = 240 - 12x$$
$$24x = 48$$
$$x = 2 \text{ mph}$$

46c. $20t = 16t + 24$
$4t = 24$
$t = 6$ hours
Todd catches up to Kristie after 6 hours.

47a. $c = \frac{100w}{\ell}$
$c\ell = 100w$
$\frac{c\ell}{100} = \frac{100w}{100}$
$w = \frac{c\ell}{100}$

47b. $c = \frac{100w}{\ell}$
$c\ell = 100w$
$\frac{c\ell}{c} = \frac{100w}{c}$
$\ell = \frac{100w}{c}$

48a. $i = \frac{100m}{c}$
$ic = 100m$
$\frac{ic}{100} = \frac{100m}{100}$
$m = \frac{ic}{100}$

48b. $i = \frac{100m}{c}$
$ic = 100m$
$ic = \frac{100m}{i}$
$c = \frac{100m}{i}$

49. $\frac{32 + x}{128 + x} = 0.300$
$0.300(128 + x) = 32 + x$
$38.4 + 0.3x = 32 + x$
$6.4 + 0.3x = x$
$6.4 = 0.7x$
$9.14 = x$
10 consecutive hits

50. $$\frac{\frac{x^2 - 5x}{x^2 + x - 30}}{\frac{x^2 + 2x}{x^2 + 9x + 18}} = \frac{x^2 - 5x}{x^2 + x - 30} \div \frac{x^2 + 2x}{x^2 + 9x + 18}$$
$$= \frac{x^2 - 5x}{x^2 + x - 30} \cdot \frac{x^2 + 9x + 18}{x^2 + 2x}$$
$$= \frac{x(x - 5)}{(x - 5)(x + 6)} \cdot \frac{(x + 6)(x + 3)}{x(x + 2)}$$
$$= \frac{\overset{1}{\cancel{x}}\overset{1}{\cancel{(x - 5)}}}{\underset{1}{\cancel{(x - 5)}}\underset{1}{\cancel{(x + 6)}}} \cdot \frac{\overset{1}{\cancel{(x + 6)}}(x + 3)}{{}_1\cancel{x}(x + 2)}$$
$$= \frac{x + 3}{x + 2}$$

51. $$\frac{a + 2}{b^2 + 4b + 4} \div \frac{4a + 8}{b + 4} = \frac{a + 2}{b^2 + 4b + 4} \cdot \frac{b + 4}{4a + 8}$$
$$= \frac{a + 2}{(b + 2)^2} \cdot \frac{b + 4}{4(a + 2)}$$
$$= \frac{\overset{1}{\cancel{a + 2}}}{(b + 2)^2} \cdot \frac{b + 4}{4\underset{1}{\cancel{(a + 2)}}}$$
$$= \frac{b + 4}{4(b + 2)^2}$$

52. $(0.5a + 0.25b)^2$
$= (0.5a)^2 + 2(0.5a)(0.25b) + (0.25b)^2$
$= 0.25a^2 + 0.25ab + 0.0625b^2$

53.

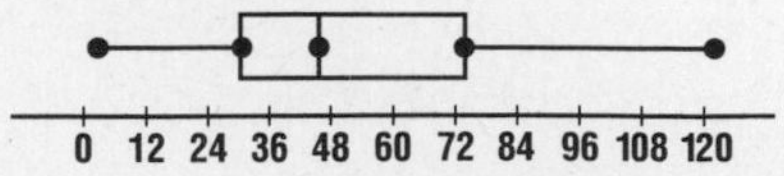

54. range: $122.30 - 1.99 = 120.31$
median: $\frac{45.76 + 46.03}{2} = 45.90$
Q_3: $\frac{60.82 + 88.12}{2} = 74.47$
Q_1: $\frac{29.15 + 32.18}{2} = 30.67$
IQR: $Q_3 - Q_1 = 74.47 - 30.67 = 43.80$
outliers:
$x \geq Q_3 + 1.5(\text{IQR})$ $\quad$ $x \leq Q_1 - 1.5(\text{IQR})$
$x \geq 74.47 + 1.5(43.80)$ $\quad$ $x \leq 30.67 - 65.70$
$x \geq 140.17$ $\quad$ $x \leq -35.03$
no outliers

55. $\frac{12 \text{ pounds}}{100 \text{ ounces}} \cdot \frac{16 \text{ ounces}}{1 \text{ pound}} = \frac{192}{100} = \frac{48}{25}$

56. $3x = -15$
$x = -5$

57. $(-2)(3)(-3) = -6(-3)$
$= 18$

58. $3(2 + x) = 6 + 3x$

Chapter 12 Highlights

Page 703 Understanding and Using the Vocabulary

1. false, rational
2. $\frac{\frac{4}{5}}{\frac{2}{3}} = \frac{4}{5} \div \frac{2}{3}$
$= \frac{4}{5} \cdot \frac{3}{2}$
$= \frac{6}{5}$ true
3. LCD: $x - 1$
$x - 1\left(\frac{x}{x - 1} + \frac{2x - 3}{x - 1}\right) = 2(x - 1)$
$x + 2x - 3 = 2x - 2$
$3x - 3 = 2x - 2$
$x = 1$ true
4. $6 - \frac{a - 2}{a + 3} = \frac{6(a + 3)}{a + 3} - \frac{a - 2}{a + 3}$
$= \frac{6a + 18 - (a - 2)}{a + 3}$
$= \frac{5a + 20}{a + 3}$
false, $\frac{5a + 20}{a + 3}$
5. $x^2 - 144$: $(x + 12)(x - 12)$
$x + 12$: $x + 12$
LCM: $(x + 12)(x - 12)$
false, $x^2 - 144$
6. $x^2 - x - 12 = 0$
$(x - 4)(x + 3) = 0$
$x - 4 = 0$ or $x + 3 = 0$
$x = 4$ $\quad$ $x = -3$
true
7. false, least common multiple

Chapter 12 Study Guide and Assessment

Pages 704–706 Skills and Concepts

8. $\dfrac{3x^2y}{12xy^3z} = \dfrac{3xy(x)}{3xy(4y^2z)}$

$= \dfrac{x}{4y^2z},\ x, y, z \neq 0$

9. $\dfrac{z^2 - 3z}{z - 3} = \dfrac{z(z - 3)}{z - 3}$

$= \dfrac{z\cancel{(z - 3)}}{\cancel{z - 3}}$

$= z,\ z \neq 3$

10. $\dfrac{a^2 - 25}{a^2 + 3a - 10} = \dfrac{(a + 5)(a - 5)}{(a + 5)(a - 2)}$

$= \dfrac{\cancel{(a + 5)}(a - 5)}{\cancel{(a + 5)}(a - 2)}$

$= \dfrac{a - 5}{a - 2}$

Excluded values:

$a^2 + 3a - 10 = 0$

$(a + 5)(a - 2)$

$a \neq -5, 2$

11. $\dfrac{3a^3}{3a^3 + 6a^2} = \dfrac{3a^2(a)}{3a^2(a + 2)}$

$= \dfrac{\cancel{3a^2}(a)}{\cancel{3a^2}(a + 2)}$

$= \dfrac{a}{a + 2}$

Excluded values:

$3a^3 + 6a^2 = 0$

$3a^2(a + 2) = 0$

$a \neq 0, -2$

12. $\dfrac{x^2 + 10x + 21}{x^3 + x^2 - 42x} = \dfrac{(x + 3)(x + 7)}{x(x + 7)(x - 6)}$

$= \dfrac{(x + 3)\cancel{(x + 7)}}{x\cancel{(x + 7)}(x - 6)}$

$= \dfrac{x + 3}{x(x - 6)}$

Excluded values:

$x^3 + x^2 - 42x = 0$

$x(x + 7)(x - 6) = 0$

$x \neq 0, -7, 6$

13. $\dfrac{b^2 - 5b + 6}{b^4 - 13b^2 + 36} = \dfrac{(b - 3)(b - 2)}{(b - 3)(b + 3)(b - 2)(b + 2)}$

$= \dfrac{\cancel{(b - 3)}\cancel{(b - 2)}}{\cancel{(b - 3)}(b + 3)\cancel{(b - 2)}(b + 2)}$

$= \dfrac{1}{(b + 3)(b + 2)}$

Excluded values:

$b^4 - 13b^2 + 36 = 0$

$(b + 3)(b - 3)(b + 2)(b - 2) = 0$

$b \neq \pm -2, \pm -3$

14. $\dfrac{7b^2}{9} \cdot \dfrac{6a^2}{b} = \dfrac{7b^{\cancel{2}}}{\cancel{9}_3} \cdot \dfrac{\cancel{6}^2a^2}{\cancel{b}}$

$= \dfrac{14a^2b}{3}$

15. $\dfrac{5x^2y}{8ab} \cdot \dfrac{12a^2b}{25x} = \dfrac{\cancel{5}^1\cancel{x^2}^x y}{\cancel{8}_2\cancel{a}\cancel{b}} \cdot \dfrac{\cancel{12}^3\cancel{a^2}^a\cancel{b}}{\cancel{25}_5\cancel{x}_1}$

$= \dfrac{3axy}{10}$

16. $(3x + 30) \cdot \dfrac{10}{x^2 - 100} = 3\cancel{(x + 10)} \cdot \dfrac{10}{\cancel{(x + 10)}(x - 10)}$

$= \dfrac{30}{x - 10}$

17. $\dfrac{3a - 6}{a^2 - 9} \cdot \dfrac{a + 3}{a^2 - 2a} = \dfrac{3\cancel{(a - 2)}}{\cancel{(a + 3)}(a - 3)} \cdot \dfrac{\cancel{a + 3}}{a\cancel{(a - 2)}}$

$= \dfrac{3}{a(a - 3)}$

$= \dfrac{3}{a^2 - 3a}$

18. $\dfrac{x^2 + x - 12}{x + 2} \cdot \dfrac{x + 4}{x^2 - x - 6} = \dfrac{(x + 4)\cancel{(x - 3)}}{x + 2} \cdot \dfrac{x + 4}{\cancel{(x - 3)}(x + 2)}$

$= \dfrac{(x + 4)^2}{(x + 2)^2}$

19. $\dfrac{b^2 + 19b + 84}{b - 3} \cdot \dfrac{b^2 - 9}{b^2 + 15b + 36}$

$= \dfrac{(b + 7)\cancel{(b + 12)}}{\cancel{b - 3}} \cdot \dfrac{\cancel{(b + 3)}\cancel{(b - 3)}}{\cancel{(b + 3)}\cancel{(b + 12)}}$

$= b + 7$

20. $\dfrac{p^3}{2q} \div \dfrac{p^2}{4q} = \dfrac{p^3}{2q} \cdot \dfrac{4q}{p^2}$

$= \dfrac{\cancel{p^3}^p}{\cancel{2q}} \cdot \dfrac{\cancel{4q}^2}{\cancel{p^2}}$

$= 2p$

21. $\dfrac{y^2}{y + 4} \div \dfrac{3y}{y^2 - 16} = \dfrac{y^2}{y + 4} \cdot \dfrac{y^2 - 16}{3y}$

$= \dfrac{\cancel{y^2}^y}{\cancel{y + 4}} \cdot \dfrac{\cancel{(y + 4)}(y - 4)}{3y}$

$= \dfrac{y(y - 4)}{3}$

$= \dfrac{y^2 - 4y}{3}$

22. $\dfrac{3y - 12}{y + 4} \div (y^2 - 6y + 8) = \dfrac{3y - 12}{y + 4} \cdot \dfrac{1}{y^2 - 6y + 8}$

$= \dfrac{3\cancel{(y - 4)}}{y + 4} \cdot \dfrac{1}{\cancel{(y - 4)}(y - 2)}$

$= \dfrac{3}{(y + 4)(y - 2)}$

$= \dfrac{3}{y^2 + 2y - 8}$

23. $\dfrac{2m^2 + 7m - 15}{m + 5} \div \dfrac{9m^2 - 4}{3m + 2}$

$= \dfrac{2m^2 + 7m - 15}{m + 5} \cdot \dfrac{3m + 2}{9m^2 - 4}$

$= \dfrac{(2m - 3)\cancel{(m + 5)}}{\cancel{m + 5}} \cdot \dfrac{\cancel{3m + 2}}{\cancel{(3m + 2)}(3m - 2)}$

$= \dfrac{2m - 3}{3m - 2}$

24. $(4a^2b^2c^2 - 8a^3b^2c + 6abc^2) \div (2ab^2)$

$= \dfrac{4a^2b^2c^2}{2ab^2} - \dfrac{8a^3b^2c}{2ab^2} + \dfrac{6abc^2}{2ab^2}$

$= 2ac^2 - 4a^2c + \dfrac{3c^2}{b}$

25.

$$\begin{array}{r}
x^2 + 4x - 2 \\
x + 3\ \overline{)\,x^3 + 7x^2 + 10x - 6} \\
\underline{(-)\ x^3 + 3x^2\qquad\qquad} \\
4x^2 + 10x\qquad \\
\underline{(-)\ 4x^2 + 12x\qquad} \\
-2x - 6 \\
\underline{-2x - 6} \\
0
\end{array}$$

26.
$$\begin{array}{r} x^2 + 2x - 3 \\ x - 2\,\overline{)\,x^3 + 0x^2 - 7x + 6} \\ \underline{(-)\ x^3 - 2x^2\qquad\qquad} \\ 2x^2 - 7x\quad\ \\ \underline{(-)\ 2x^2 - 4x\quad\ } \\ -3x + 6 \\ \underline{-3x + 6} \\ 0 \end{array}$$

27.
$$\begin{array}{r} x^3 + 5x^2 + 12x + 23 \\ x - 2\,\overline{)\,x^4 + 3x^3 + 2x^2 - x + 6} \\ \underline{(-)\ x^4 - 2x^3\qquad\qquad\qquad} \\ 5x^3 + 2x^2\qquad\quad \\ \underline{(-)\ 5x^3 - 10x^2\qquad\quad} \\ 12x^2 - x\quad\ \\ \underline{(-)\ 12x^2 - 24x\quad\ } \\ 23x + 6 \\ \underline{(-)\ 23x - 46} \\ 52 \end{array}$$

$x^3 + 5x^2 + 12x + 23 + \frac{52}{x-2}$

28.
$$\begin{array}{r} 4b + 1 \\ 12b - 1\,\overline{)\,48b^2 + 8b + 7} \\ \underline{(-)\ 48b^2 - 4b\quad\ } \\ 12b + 7 \\ \underline{(-)\ 12b - 1} \\ 8 \end{array}$$

$4b + 1 + \frac{8}{12b - 1}$

29. $\frac{7a}{m^2} - \frac{5a}{m^2} = \frac{7a - 5a}{m^2}$

$= \frac{2a}{m^2}$

30. $\frac{2x}{x-3} - \frac{6}{x-3} = \frac{2x - 6}{x - 3}$

$= \frac{2\cancel{(x-3)}^{1}}{\cancel{x-3}_{1}}$

$= 2$

31. $\frac{m+4}{5} + \frac{m-1}{5} = \frac{m + 4 + m - 1}{5} = \frac{2m + 3}{5}$

32. $\frac{-5}{2n-5} + \frac{2n}{2n-5} = \frac{2n-5}{2n-5}$

$= 1$

33. $\frac{a^2}{a-b} + \frac{-b^2}{a-b} = \frac{a^2 - b^2}{a - b}$

$= \frac{(a+b)\cancel{(a-b)}^{1}}{\cancel{a-b}_{1}}$

$= a + b$

34. $\frac{m^2}{m-n} - \frac{2mn - n^2}{m-n} = \frac{m^2 - (2mn - n^2)}{m - n}$

$= \frac{m^2 - 2mn + n^2}{m - n}$

$= \frac{(m-n)^{\cancel{2}}}{\cancel{m-n}}$

$= m - n$

35. $\frac{7n}{3} - \frac{9n}{7} = \frac{7n(7)}{3(7)} - \frac{9n(3)}{7(3)}$

$= \frac{49n}{21} - \frac{27n}{21}$

$= \frac{49n - 27n}{21}$

$= \frac{22n}{21}$

36. $\frac{7}{3a} - \frac{3}{6a^2} = \frac{7(2a)}{3a(2a)} - \frac{3}{6a^2}$

$= \frac{14a}{6a^2} - \frac{3}{6a^2}$

$= \frac{14a - 3}{6a^2}$

37. $\frac{2c}{3d^2} + \frac{3}{2cd} = \frac{2c(2c)}{3d^2(2c)} + \frac{3(3d)}{2cd(3d)}$

$= \frac{4c^2}{6cd^2} + \frac{9d}{6cd^2}$

$= \frac{4c^2 + 9d}{6cd^2}$

38. $\frac{2a}{2a+8} - \frac{4}{5a+20} = \frac{2a(5)}{2(a+4)(5)} - \frac{4(2)}{5(a+4)(2)}$

$= \frac{10a}{10(a+4)} - \frac{8}{10(a+4)}$

$= \frac{10a - 8}{10(a+4)}$

$= \frac{\cancel{2}(5a-4)}{\cancel{10}_{5}(a+4)}$

$= \frac{5a - 4}{5a + 20}$

39. $\frac{r^2 + 21r}{r^2 - 9} + \frac{3r}{r+3} = \frac{r^2 + 21r}{(r+3)(r-3)} + \frac{3r(r-3)}{(r+3)(r-3)}$

$= \frac{r^2 + 21r + 3r(r-3)}{(r+3)(r-3)}$

$= \frac{r^2 + 21r + 3r^2 - 9r}{(r+3)(r-3)}$

$= \frac{4r^2 + 12r}{(r+3)(r-3)}$

$= \frac{4r\cancel{(r+3)}^{1}}{\cancel{(r+3)}_{1}(r-3)}$

$= \frac{4r}{r-3}$

40. $\frac{3a}{a-2} + \frac{5a}{a+1} = \frac{3a(a+1)}{(a-2)(a+1)} + \frac{5a(a-2)}{(a-2)(a+1)}$

$= \frac{3a(a+1) + 5a(a-2)}{(a-2)(a+1)}$

$= \frac{3a^2 + 3a + 5a^2 - 10a}{(a-2)(a+1)}$

$= \frac{8a^2 - 7a}{(a-2)(a+1)}$

41. $4 + \frac{m}{m-2} = \frac{4(m-2)}{(m-2)} + \frac{m}{m-2}$

$= \frac{4(m-2) + m}{m-2}$

$= \frac{4m - 8 + m}{m-2}$

$= \frac{5m - 8}{m - 2}$

42. $2 - \frac{x+2}{x^2-4} = \frac{2(x^2-4)}{x^2-4} - \frac{x+2}{x^2-4}$

$= \frac{2(x^2-4) - (x+2)}{x^2-4}$

$= \frac{2x^2 - 8 - x - 2}{x^2 - 4}$

$= \frac{2x^2 - x - 10}{x^2 - 4}$

$= \frac{(2x-5)\cancel{(x+2)}^{1}}{\cancel{(x+2)}_{1}(x-2)}$

$= \frac{2x - 5}{x - 2}$

43. $\dfrac{\frac{x^2}{y^3}}{\frac{3x}{9y^2}} = \frac{x^2}{y^3} \div \frac{3x}{9y^2}$

$= \frac{x^2}{y^3} \cdot \frac{9y^2}{3x}$

$= \frac{\cancel{x^2}^{x}}{\cancel{y^3}_{y}} \cdot \frac{\cancel{9}^{3}\cancel{y^2}^{1}}{\cancel{3}_{1}\cancel{x}_{1}}$

$= \frac{3x}{y}$

44. $\dfrac{5+\frac{4}{a}}{\frac{a}{2}-\frac{3}{4}} = \dfrac{\frac{5(a)}{a}+\frac{4}{a}}{\frac{a(2)}{2(2)}-\frac{3}{4}}$

$= \dfrac{\frac{5a+4}{a}}{\frac{2a-3}{4}}$

$= \dfrac{5a+4}{a} \div \dfrac{2a-3}{4}$

$= \dfrac{5a+4}{a} \cdot \dfrac{4}{2a-3}$

$= \dfrac{4(5a+4)}{a(2a-3)}$

$= \dfrac{20a+16}{2a^2-3a}$

45. $\dfrac{x-\frac{35}{x+2}}{x+\frac{42}{x+13}} = \dfrac{\frac{x(x+2)}{x+2}-\frac{35}{x+2}}{\frac{x(x+13)}{x+13}+\frac{42}{x+13}}$

$= \dfrac{\frac{x(x+2)-35}{x+2}}{\frac{x(x+13)+42}{x+13}}$

$= \dfrac{\frac{x^2+2x-35}{x+2}}{\frac{x^2+13x+42}{x+13}}$

$= \dfrac{x^2+2x-35}{x+2} \div \dfrac{x^2+13x+42}{x+13}$

$= \dfrac{x^2+2x-35}{x+2} \cdot \dfrac{x+13}{x^2+13x+42}$

$= \dfrac{\overset{1}{\cancel{(x+7)}}(x-5)}{x+2} \cdot \dfrac{x+13}{\underset{1}{\cancel{(x+7)}}(x+6)}$

$= \dfrac{(x-5)(x+13)}{(x+2)(x+6)}$

$= \dfrac{x^2+8x-65}{x^2+8x+12}$

46. $\dfrac{y+9-\frac{6}{y+4}}{y+4+\frac{2}{y+1}} = \dfrac{\frac{(y+9)(y+4)}{y+4}-\frac{6}{y+4}}{\frac{(y+4)(y+1)}{y+1}+\frac{2}{y+1}}$

$= \dfrac{\frac{(y+9)(y+4)-6}{y+4}}{\frac{(y+4)(y+1)+2}{y+1}}$

$= \dfrac{\frac{y^2+13y+36-6}{y+4}}{\frac{y^2+5y+4+2}{y+1}}$

$= \dfrac{\frac{y^2+13y+30}{y+4}}{\frac{y^2+5y+6}{y+1}}$

$= \dfrac{y^2+13y+30}{y+4} \div \dfrac{y^2+5y+6}{y+1}$

$= \dfrac{y^2+13y+30}{y+4} \cdot \dfrac{y+1}{y^2+5y+6}$

$= \dfrac{(y+10)\overset{1}{\cancel{(y+3)}}}{y+4} \cdot \dfrac{y+1}{(y+2)\underset{1}{\cancel{(y+3)}}}$

$= \dfrac{(y+10)(y+1)}{(y+4)(y+2)}$

$= \dfrac{y^2+11y+10}{y^2+6y+8}$

47. $\frac{4y}{3}+\frac{7}{2}=\frac{7x}{12}-\frac{1}{4}$ LCD: 12

$12\left(\frac{4y}{3}+\frac{7}{2}\right)=\left(\frac{7x}{12}-\frac{1}{4}\right)(12)$

$12\left(\frac{4x}{3}\right)+12\left(\frac{7}{2}\right)=12\left(\frac{7x}{12}\right)+12\left(-\frac{1}{4}\right)$

$16x+42=7x-3$

$42=-9x-3$

$45=-9x$

$-5=x$

48. $\frac{11}{2x}-\frac{2}{3x}=\frac{1}{6}$ LCD: $6x$

$6x\left(\frac{11}{2x}-\frac{2}{3x}\right)=\left(\frac{1}{6}\right)6x$

$6x\left(\frac{11}{2x}\right)-6x\left(\frac{2}{3x}\right)=\left(\frac{1}{6}\right)6x$

$33-4=x$

$29=x$

49. $\frac{2}{3r}-\frac{3r}{r-2}=-3$ LCD: $3r(r-2)$

$3r(r-2)\left(\frac{2}{3r}-\frac{3r}{r-2}\right)=-3(3r)(r-2)$

$2(r-2)-3r(3r)=-9r^2+18r$

$2r-4-9r^2=-9r^2+18r$

$2r-4=18r$

$-4=16r$

$-\frac{4}{16}=r$

$-\frac{1}{4}=r$

50. $\frac{x-2}{x}-\frac{x-3}{x-6}=\frac{1}{x}$ LCD: $x(x-6)$

$x(x-6)\left(\frac{x-2}{x}-\frac{x-3}{x-6}\right)=\frac{1}{x}(x)(x-6)$

$(x-6)(x-2)+x(-x+3)=x-6$

$x^2-8x+12-x^2+3x=x-6$

$-5x+12=x-6$

$-6x=-18$

$x=3$

51. $-\frac{5}{m}=19-4m$

$-5=m(19-4m)$

$-5=19m-4m^2$

$4m^2-19m-5=0$

$(4m+1)(m-5)=0$

$4m+1=0$ or $m-5=0$

$m=-\frac{1}{4}$ $\quad m=5$

$5, -\frac{1}{4}$

52. $\frac{1}{h+1}+2=\frac{2h+3}{h-1}$ LCD: $(h+1)(h-1)$

$(h+1)(h-1)\left(\frac{1}{h+1}+2\right)=\left(\frac{2h+3}{h-1}\right)(h+1)(h-1)$

$h-1+2(h+1)(h-1)=(2h+3)(h+1)$

$h-1+2h^2-2=2h^2+5h+3$

$2h^2+h-3=2h^2+5h+3$

$h-3=5h+3$

$-6=4h$

$-\frac{6}{4}=h$

$-\frac{3}{2}=h$

Page 706 Applications and Problem Solving

53. Make a table to show the possibilities. Recall that wagons do not have pedals and bicycles and tricycles each have 2 pedals.

Bicycles (2 wheels)	10	20	18	10	8	6
Tricycles (3 wheels)	10	20	20	22	24	24
Wagons (4 Wheels)	10	20	21	22	24	24
Total Wheels	90	180	180	174	184	180
Total Pedals	40	80	76	64	64	60
Solution?	no	no	no	no	no	yes

So there are 6 bicycles, 24 tricycles, and 24 wagons in stock.

54a. $R_T = R_1 + R_2$
$= 4 + 6$
$= 10$ ohms

54b. $\frac{1}{R_T} = \frac{1}{R_1} + \frac{1}{R_2}$
$\frac{1}{R_T} = \frac{1}{4} + \frac{1}{6}$
$\frac{1}{R_T} = \frac{3}{12} + \frac{2}{12}$
$\frac{1}{R_T} = \frac{5}{12}$
$5R_T = 12$
$R_T = \frac{12}{5}$ or 2.4 ohms

55. $\frac{t}{5} + \frac{t}{3} = 1$ LCD: 15
$15\left(\frac{t}{5} + \frac{t}{3}\right) = 1(15)$
$3t + 5t = 15$
$8t = 15$
$t = \frac{15}{8}$ or $1\frac{7}{8}$ hours

Page 707 Alternative Assessment: Thinking Critically

- Sample answer: $\frac{2}{x-a} = \frac{4}{2x-2a}, \frac{3}{x-a} = \frac{6}{2x-2a}, \frac{5}{x-a} = \frac{10}{2x-2a}$
- $\frac{x}{x} = 1$ Sometimes true, because if $x = 0$, it is not true.

$\frac{ab^2}{b^2} = ab^3$
$a = ab^3$ Sometimes true, only when $b = 1$.

$\frac{x^2 + 6x - 5}{2x + 2} \stackrel{?}{=} \frac{x + 5}{2}$
$2(x^2 + 6x - 5) \stackrel{?}{=} (2x + 2)(x + 5)$
$2x^2 + 12x - 10 \stackrel{?}{=} 2x^2 + 10x + 2x + 10$
$2x^2 + 12x - 10 \neq 2x^2 + 12x + 10$ never true

Cumulative Review, Chapters 1–12

Pages 708–709

1. $A = s^2$
$129 = s^2$
$\sqrt{129} = s$
$11.36 \approx s$
C

$P = 4s$
$= 4\,(11.36)$
$= 45.43$ in.

2. D $\{(4, 3), (5, 2), (8, -1), (-6, 2)\}$

3. $\frac{x^2 + 3x - 10}{x^2 + 8x + 15} \cdot \frac{x^2 + 5x + 6}{x^2 + 4x + 4} = \frac{\overset{1}{\cancel{(x+5)}}(x-2)}{\underset{1}{\cancel{(x+5)}}\underset{1}{\cancel{(x+3)}}} \cdot \frac{\overset{1}{\cancel{(x+3)}}\overset{1}{\cancel{(x+2)}}}{\underset{x+2}{\cancel{(x+2)^2}}}$
$= \frac{x - 2}{x + 2}$ B

4. $\frac{40}{52} = \frac{10}{13}$ D

5. $H = -4.9t^2 + vt + b$
$0 = -4.9t + 15t + 10$
$a = -4.9,\ b = 15,\ c = 10$
$t = \frac{-15 \pm \sqrt{(15)^2 - 4(4.9)(10)}}{2(-4.9)}$
$= \frac{-15 \pm \sqrt{225 + 196}}{-9.8}$
$= \frac{-15 \pm \sqrt{421}}{-9.8}$
$\approx \frac{-15 \pm 20.5}{-9.8}$
$\approx \frac{-35.5}{-9.8}$
≈ 3.6 A

6. $\dfrac{\frac{x^2 + 8x + 15}{x^2 + x - 6}}{\frac{x^2 + 2x - 15}{x^2 - 2x - 3}} = \frac{x^2 + 8x + 15}{x^2 + x - 6} \div \frac{x^2 + 2x - 15}{x^2 - 2x - 3}$
$= \frac{x^2 + 8x + 15}{x^2 + x - 6} \cdot \frac{x^2 - 2x - 3}{x^2 + 2x - 15}$
$= \frac{\overset{1}{\cancel{(x+5)}}\overset{1}{\cancel{(x+3)}}}{\underset{1}{\cancel{(x+3)}}(x-2)} \cdot \frac{\overset{1}{\cancel{(x-3)}}(x+1)}{\underset{1}{\cancel{(x+5)}}\underset{1}{\cancel{(x-3)}}}$
$= \frac{x + 1}{x - 2}$ D

7. $P = 4s$
$60 = 4s$
$15 = s$
$A = s^2$
$4x^2 - 28x + 49 = 15^2$
$4x^2 - 28x + 49 = 225$
$4x^2 - 28x - 176 = 0$
$x^2 - 7x - 44 = 0$
$(x - 11)(x + 4) = 0$
$x - 11 = 0$ or $x + 4 = 0$
$x = 11$ $x = -4$
11 cm B

8. $\frac{a + 2}{a^2 - 9} - \frac{2a}{6a^2 - 17a - 3}$
$= \frac{a + 2}{(a - 3)(a + 3)} - \frac{2a}{(a - 3)(6a + 1)}$
$= \frac{(a + 2)(6a + 1)}{(a - 3)(a + 3)(6a + 1)} - \frac{2a(a + 3)}{(a - 3)(a + 3)(6a + 1)}$
$= \frac{6a^2 + 13a + 2 - 2a^2 - 6a}{(a - 3)(a + 3)(6a + 1)}$
$= \frac{4a^2 + 7a + 2}{(a - 3)(a + 3)(6a + 1)}$ A

9. $42 \div 7 - 1 - 5 + 8 \cdot 2 + 14 \div 2 - 8$
$= 6 - 1 - 5 + 16 + 7 - 8$
$= 15$

10. $(12 + x)(8 + x) = 2(8)(12)$
$96 + 20x + x^2 = 192$
$x^2 + 20x - 96 = 0$
$(x - 4)(x + 24) = 0$
$x - 4 = 0$ or $x + 24 = 0$
$x = 4$ $x = -24$
4 meters

11. $2x - 3y = 13$

$$-3y = -2x + 13$$
$$y = \frac{2}{3}x - \frac{13}{3}$$

$$y = \frac{2}{3}x - \frac{13}{3}$$
$$= \frac{2}{3}(0) - \frac{13}{3}$$
$$= -\frac{13}{3}$$

$$y = \frac{2}{3}x - \frac{13}{3}$$
$$0 = \frac{2}{3}x - \frac{13}{3}$$
$$\frac{13}{3} = \frac{2}{3}x$$
$$\frac{13}{2} = x$$

slope $= \frac{2}{3}$, y-intercept: $-\frac{13}{3}$, x-intercept: $\frac{13}{2}$

12.
$$\begin{array}{r} x^2 - 5x - 6 \\ x - 2\overline{)x^3 - 7x^2 + 4x + k} \\ \underline{(-)\ x^3 - 2x^2} \\ -5x^2 + 4x \\ \underline{(-)\ -5x^2 + 10x} \\ -6x + k \\ \underline{(-)\ -6x + 12} \\ k - 12 = 15 \\ k = 27 \end{array}$$

13. Let t = the tens digit and let u = the units digit.

$$t = 2u + 1$$
$$10u + t = 4 + 3(u + t)$$
$$10u + t = 4 + 3u + 3t$$
$$7u - 2t = 4$$
$$7u - 2(2u + 1) = 4$$
$$7u - 4u - 2 = 4$$
$$3u - 2 = 4$$
$$3u = 6$$
$$u = 2$$

$t = 2u + 1$
$t = 2(2) + 1$
$t = 5$

The number is 52.

14.

	r	d	$t = \frac{d}{r}$
with wind	$r + 3$	30	$\frac{30}{r+3}$
against wind	$r - 3$	18	$\frac{18}{r-3}$

$$\frac{30}{r+3} = \frac{18}{r-3}$$
$$30(r - 3) = 18(r + 3)$$
$$30r - 90 = 18r + 54$$
$$12r = 144$$
$$r = 12 \text{ mph}$$

15. $-2 \le 2x + 4 < 6$

$-2 \le 2x + 4$ and $2x + 4 < 6$
$-6 \le 2x$ $2x < 2$
$-3 \le x$ $x < 1$
$\{x \mid -3 \le x < 1\}$

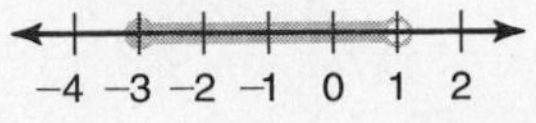

16. $\frac{40 \text{ times}}{1 \text{ sec}} \cdot 30 \text{ min} \cdot \frac{60 \text{ sec}}{1 \text{ min}}$ to $\frac{50 \text{ times}}{1 \text{ sec}} \cdot 30 \text{ min} \cdot \frac{60 \text{ sec}}{1 \text{ min}}$

72,000 to 90,000
$7.2 \times 10{,}000$ to $9.0 \times 10{,}000$
7.2×10^4 to 9.0×10^4

17.
$$P = 2x + y$$
$$120 = 2x + y$$
$$120 - 2x = y$$

$$A = xy$$
$$A = x(120 - 2x)$$
$$A = 120x - 2x^2$$
$$a = -2,\ b = 120$$
$$x = -\frac{b}{2a} = -\frac{120}{-4} = 30$$

$$120 - 2(30) = y$$
$$120 - 60 = y$$
$$60 = y$$
$$A = xy = (30)(60) = 1800 \text{ m}^2$$

18. Let x = the number of flats of impatiens and let y = the number of flats of petunias.

$$10x + 8.75y = 111.25$$
$$x = y - 2$$
$$10(y - 2) + 8.75y = 111.25$$
$$10y - 20 + 8.75y = 111.25$$
$$18.75y = 131.25$$
$$y = 7$$

$$x = y - 2$$
$$x = 7 - 2 \text{ or } 5$$

5 flats of impatiens; 7 flats of petunias

19. $y = -x^2 + 6x + 16$

axis of symmetry: $x = -\frac{b}{2a} = -\frac{6}{2(-1)}$ or $x = 3$

$$y = -x^2 + 6x + 16$$
$$= -(3)^2 + 6(3) + 16$$
$$= -9 + 18 + 16$$
$$= 25$$

The coordinates of the vertex are (3, 25).

x	y
-2	0
-1	9
0	16
1	21
2	24
3	25
4	24
5	21
6	16
7	9
8	0

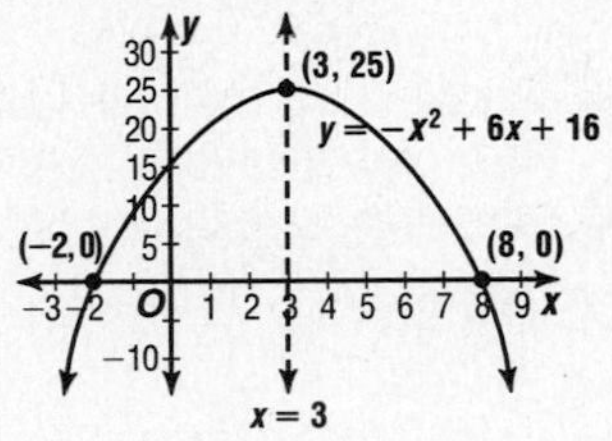

roots: -2, 8

20. $y \le x + 3$

$$2x - 2y < 8$$
$$-2y < -2x + 8$$
$$y > x - 4$$

$$2y + 3x > 4$$
$$2y > -3x + 4$$
$$y > \frac{-3}{2}x + 2$$

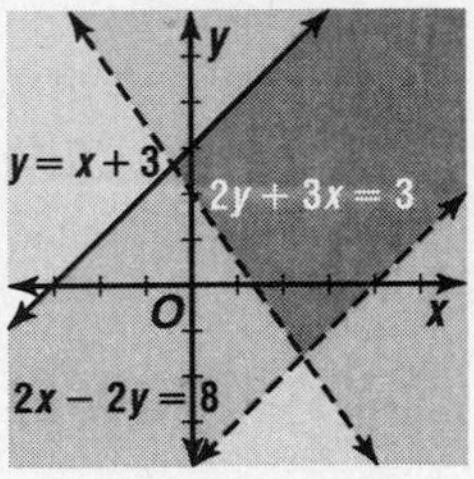

Sample answer: (2, 2), (4, 3), (6, 4)

Chapter 13 Exploring Radical Expressions and Equations

13-1A Modeling Mathematics: The Pythagorean Theorem

Page 712

1. $4 + 4 = 8$
2. $9 + 1 = 10$
3. $16 + 9 = 25$
4. 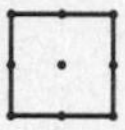
5. 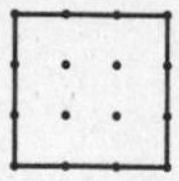
6. 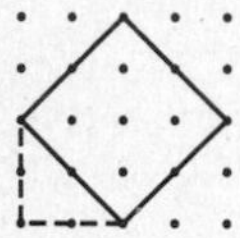
7. 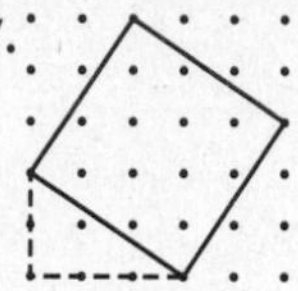
8. 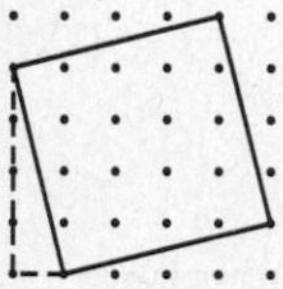
9. 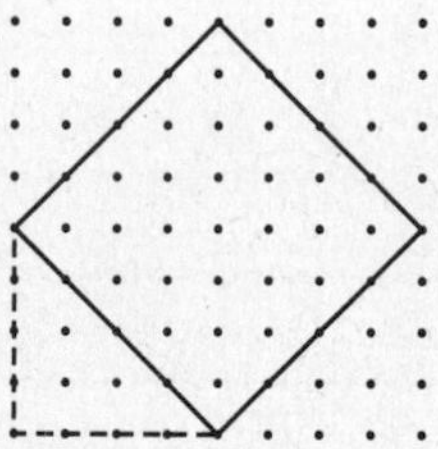
10. The total area of the 4 triangles equals the area of the large square minus the area of the triangle in each corner minus the area of the small square, $49 - 4(6) - 16$ or 9 square units.

13-1 Integration: Geometry The Pythagorean Theorem

Pages 715–716 Check for Understanding

1. 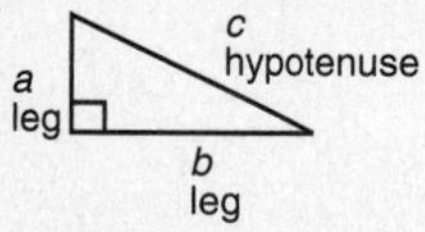

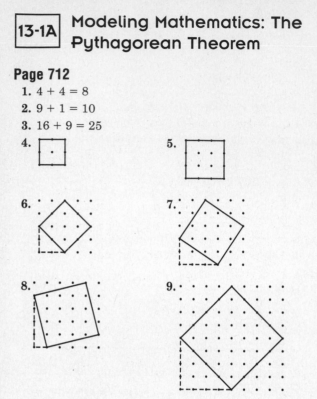

2. By squaring the two shorter sides and adding them; then, comparing their sum to the square of the third or longer side. If they are equal, it is a right triangle.

3a. 3, 4, 5

3b. $3^2 + 4^2 \stackrel{?}{=} 5^2$
$9 + 16 \stackrel{?}{=} 25$
$25 = 25$ ✔

4. Since the Pythagorean theorem finds the length of a side, it has to be positive. Distance is not negative.
5. $16 + 4 = 20$
6. $5^2 + 12^2 = c^2$
$25 + 144 = c^2$
$169 = c^2$
$\pm\sqrt{169} = c$
$13 = c$

7. $a^2 + 24^2 = 25^2$
$a^2 + 576 = 625$
$a^2 = 49$
$a = \pm\sqrt{49}$
$a = 7$

8. $16^2 + b^2 = 20^2$
$256 + b^2 = 400$
$b^2 = 144$
$b = \pm\sqrt{144}$
$b = 12$

9. $c^2 = a^2 + b^2$
$c^2 = 7^2 + 9^2$
$c^2 = 49 + 81$
$c^2 = 130$
$c = \pm\sqrt{130}$
$c \approx 11.40$

10. $c^2 = a^2 + b^2$
$15^2 = a^2 + 5^2$
$225 = a^2 + 25$
$200 = a^2$
$\pm\sqrt{200} = a$
$14.14 \approx a$

11. $c^2 = a^2 + b^2$
$c^2 = 9^2 + 12^2$
$c^2 = 81 + 144$
$c^2 = 225$
$c = \pm\sqrt{225}$
$c = 15$

12. $c^2 = a^2 + b^2$
$6^2 = (\sqrt{11})^2 + b^2$
$36 = 11 + b^2$
$25 = b^2$
$\pm\sqrt{25} = b$
$5 = b$

13. $c^2 = a^2 + b^2$
$(\sqrt{34})^2 = a^2 + (\sqrt{30})^2$
$34 = a^2 + 30$
$4 = a^2$
$\pm\sqrt{4} = a$
$2 = a$

14. $c^2 = a^2 + b^2$
$c^2 = 7^2 + 4^2$
$c^2 = 49 + 16$
$c^2 = 65$
$c = \pm\sqrt{65}$
$c = \sqrt{65} \approx 8.06$

15. $20^2 \stackrel{?}{=} 12^2 + 16^2$
$400 \stackrel{?}{=} 144 + 256$
$400 = 400$
yes

16. $8^2 \stackrel{?}{=} 2^2 + 8^2$
$64 \stackrel{?}{=} 4 + 64$
$64 \neq 68$
no; $2^2 + 8^2 \neq 8^2$

17. $c^2 = a^2 + b^2$
$c^2 = 90^2 + 90^2$
$c^2 = 8100 + 8100$
$c^2 = 16{,}200$
$c \approx 127.28$
The distance from home plate to second base is about 127.28 ft.

Pages 716–718 Exercises

18. $c^2 = a^2 + b^2$
$c^2 = 2^2 + 8^2$
$c^2 = 4 + 64$
$c^2 = 68$
$c = \pm\sqrt{68}$
$c \approx 8.25$

19. $c^2 = a^2 + b^2$
$19^2 = 13^2 + b^2$
$361 = 169 + b^2$
$192 = b^2$
$\pm\sqrt{192} = b$
$13.86 \approx b$

20. $c^2 = a^2 + b^2$
$16^2 = a^2 + 5^2$
$256 = a^2 + 25$
$231 = a^2$
$\pm\sqrt{231} = a$
$15.20 \approx a$

21. $c^2 = a^2 + b^2$
$14^2 = a^2 + 5^2$
$196 = a^2 + 25$
$171 \approx a^2$
$\pm\sqrt{171} = a$
$13.08 \approx a$

22. $c^2 = a^2 + b^2$
$c^2 = 6^2 + 11^2$
$c^2 = 36 + 121$
$c^2 = 157$
$c = \pm\sqrt{157}$
$c \approx 12.53$

23. $c^2 = a^2 + b^2$
$15^2 = 3^2 + b^2$
$225 = 9 + b^2$
$216 = b^2$
$\pm\sqrt{216} = b$
$14.70 \approx b$

24. $c^2 = a^2 + b^2$
$c^2 = 16^2 + 30^2$
$c^2 = 256 + 900$
$c^2 = 1156$
$c = \pm\sqrt{1156}$
$c = 34$

25. $c^2 = a^2 + b^2$
$61^2 = 11^2 + b^2$
$3721 = 121 + b^2$
$3600 = b^2$
$\pm\sqrt{3600} = b$
$60 = b$

26.
$$c^2 = a^2 + b^2$$
$$(\sqrt{233})^2 = a^2 + 13^2$$
$$233 = a^2 + 169$$
$$64 = a^2$$
$$\pm\sqrt{64} = a$$
$$8 = a$$

27.
$$c^2 = a^2 + b^2$$
$$c^2 = (\sqrt{7})^2 + (\sqrt{9})^2$$
$$c^2 = 7 + 9$$
$$c^2 = 16$$
$$c = \pm\sqrt{16}$$
$$c = 4$$

28.
$$c^2 = a^2 + b^2$$
$$c^2 = 6^2 + 3^2$$
$$c^2 = 36 + 9$$
$$c^2 = 45$$
$$c = \pm\sqrt{45}$$
$$c = \sqrt{45} \approx 6.71$$

29.
$$c^2 = a^2 + b^2$$
$$12^2 = a^2 + (\sqrt{77})^2$$
$$144 = a^2 + 77$$
$$67 = a^2$$
$$\pm\sqrt{67} = a$$
$$a = \sqrt{67} \approx 8.19$$

30.
$$c^2 = a^2 + b^2$$
$$11^2 = a^2 + 10^2$$
$$121 = a^2 + 100$$
$$21 = a^2$$
$$\pm\sqrt{21} = a$$
$$a = \sqrt{21} \approx 4.58$$

31.
$$c^2 = a^2 + b^2$$
$$c^2 = 4^2 + (\sqrt{11})^2$$
$$c^2 = 16 + 11$$
$$c^2 = 27$$
$$c = \pm\sqrt{27}$$
$$c = \sqrt{27} \approx 5.20$$

32.
$$c^2 = a^2 + b^2$$
$$c^2 = 15^2 + (\sqrt{28})^2$$
$$c^2 = 225 + 28$$
$$c^2 = 253$$
$$c = \pm\sqrt{253}$$
$$c = \sqrt{253} \approx 15.91$$

33.
$$c^2 = a^2 + b^2$$
$$17^2 = 12^2 + b^2$$
$$289 = 144 + b^2$$
$$145 = b^2$$
$$\pm\sqrt{145} = b$$
$$b = \sqrt{145} \approx 12.04$$

34.
$$12^2 \stackrel{?}{=} 6^2 + 9^2$$
$$144 \stackrel{?}{=} 36 + 81$$
$$144 \neq 117$$
no; $6^2 + 9^2 \neq 12^2$

35.
$$75^2 \stackrel{?}{=} 45^2 + 60^2$$
$$5625 \stackrel{?}{=} 2025 + 3600$$
$$5625 = 5625$$
yes

36.
$$50^2 \stackrel{?}{=} 30^2 + 40^2$$
$$2500 \stackrel{?}{=} 900 + 1600$$
$$2500 = 2500$$
yes

37.
$$15^2 \stackrel{?}{=} 11^2 + 12^2$$
$$225 \stackrel{?}{=} 121 + 144$$
$$225 \neq 265$$
no; $11^2 + 12^2 \neq 15^2$

38.
$$20^2 \stackrel{?}{=} 16^2 + (\sqrt{32})^2$$
$$400 \stackrel{?}{=} 256 + 32$$
$$400 \neq 288$$
no; $16^2 + (\sqrt{32})^2 \neq 20^2$

39.
$$16^2 \stackrel{?}{=} 15^2 + (\sqrt{31})^2$$
$$256 \stackrel{?}{=} 225 + 31$$
$$256 = 256$$
yes

40.
$$d^2 = s^2 + s^2$$
$$d^2 = 128 + 128$$
$$d^2 = 256$$
$$d = \pm\sqrt{256}$$
$$d = 16 \text{ cm}$$

41.
$$d^2 = s^2 + s^2$$
$$d^2 = 5^2 + 5^2$$
$$d^2 = 25 + 25$$
$$d^2 = 50$$

$$c^2 = d^2 + 5^2$$
$$c^2 = 50 + 5^2$$
$$c^2 = 50 + 25$$
$$c^2 = 75$$
$$c = \pm\sqrt{75}$$
$c = \sqrt{75}$ in. or about 8.66 in.

42a. $x^2 + (x + 6)^2 = (30)^2$

42b.
$$x^2 + x^2 + 12x + 36 = 900$$
$$2x^2 + 12x + 36 = 900$$
$$2x^2 + 12x - 864 = 0$$
$$x^2 + 6x - 432 = 0$$
$$(x + 24)(x - 18) = 0$$
$x + 24 = 0$ or $x - 18 = 0$

$x = -24$ $\quad$ $x = 18$

One leg is 18 cm, the other leg is 18 + 6 or 24 cm.

43a.

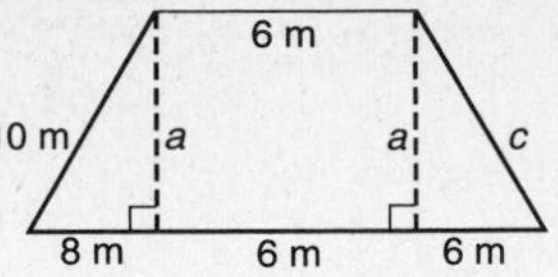

$$10^2 = 8^2 + a^2$$
$$100 = 64 + a^2$$
$$36 = a^2$$
$$6 = a$$

$$c^2 = 6^2 + 6^2$$
$$c^2 = 36 + 36$$
$$c^2 = 72$$
$$c \approx 8.49$$

$P = 10 + 6 + 8.49 + 12 + 8 = 44.49$ m

43b.
$$A = \frac{1}{2}h(b_1 + b_2)$$
$$A = \frac{1}{2}(6)(6 + 20)$$
$A = 3(26)$ or 78 m^2

44a. HYPOTENUSE IS 7.28

44b. HYPOTENUSE IS 15

44c. HYPOTENUSE IS 19.85

44d. HYPOTENUSE IS 10.82

44e. HYPOTENUSE IS 20

45.

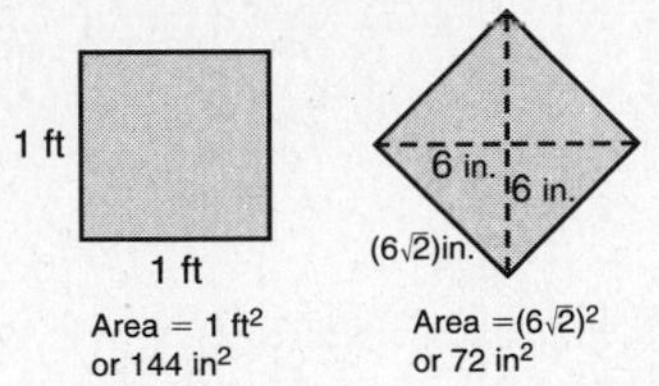

46.
$$c^2 = a^2 + b^2$$
$$c^2 = 60^2 + 100^2$$
$$c^2 = 3600 + 10{,}000$$
$$c^2 = 13{,}600$$
$$c \approx 116.62 \text{ ft}$$

47.
$$c^2 = a^2 + b^2$$
$$c^2 = 0.9^2 + 2.5^2$$
$$c^2 = 0.81 + 6.25$$
$$c^2 = 7.06$$
$$c \approx 2.66 \text{ m}$$

48.
$$36^2 = s^2 + s^2$$
$$1296 = 2s^2$$
$$648 = s^2$$
$$25.5 \approx s$$
A side of the dance floor is about 25.5 ft.

49.
$$\frac{a + 2}{a} + \frac{a + 5}{a} = 1$$
$$\frac{a + 2 + a + 5}{a} = 1$$
$$\frac{2a + 7}{a} = 1$$
$$2a + 7 = a$$
$$a = -7$$

50. $y = x^2 - 6x + 8$, $a = 1$, $b = -6$

axis of symmetry: $x = -\frac{b}{2a} = -\frac{(-6)}{2(1)}$ or $x = 3$

$$y = (3)^2 - 6(3) + 8$$
$= 9 - 18 + 8$ or -1

The coordinates of the vertex are $(3, -1)$.

x	y
0	8
1	3
2	0
3	−1
4	0
5	3

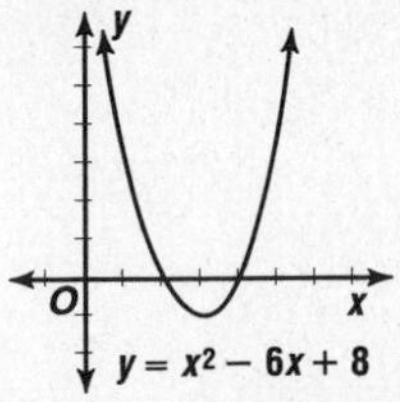

51.
$$(4r^5)(3r^2) = (4 \cdot 3)(r^5 \cdot r^2)$$
$$= 12r^7$$

52. Let x = one number and let y = the other number.

$$x + y = 38 \qquad \begin{array}{r} x + y = 38 \\ (+)\ x - y = 6 \\ \hline 2x = 44 \\ x = 22 \end{array} \qquad \begin{array}{r} x + y = 38 \\ 22 + y = 38 \\ y = 16 \end{array}$$
$$x - y = 6$$

The numbers are 16 and 22.

53. $5c - 2 \geq c$
$4c - 2 \geq 0$
$4c \geq 2$
$c \geq \frac{1}{2}$
$\left\{c \mid c \geq \frac{1}{2}\right\}$

54. (0, 3), (2, −1)
$m = \frac{y_2 - y_1}{x_2 - x_1} = \frac{-1 - 3}{2 - 0} = \frac{-4}{2}$ or -2
y-intercept: 3
$y = -2x + 3$

55. $f(x) = 2x^2 - 5x + 8$
$f(-3) = 2(-3)^2 - 5(-3) + 8$
$= 2(9) + 15 + 8$
$= 18 + 15 + 8$
$= 41$

56. $-\frac{5}{6}y = 15$
$\left(-\frac{6}{5}\right)\left(-\frac{5}{6}y\right) = 15\left(-\frac{6}{5}\right)$
$y = -18$

13-2 Simplifying Radical Expressions

Pages 723–724 Check for Understanding

1. to ensure nonnegative results
2. Multiply the numerator and denominator of a fraction by the same number so that a radical is not left in the denominator.
3. Melanie is correct. In step 4, the square root of a negative number was taken. This value is not defined in the set of real numbers.
4. Sample answer: You may have to take steps so that the radicand contains no perfect squares or fractions.
5. $5 - \sqrt{2}$
$(5 + \sqrt{2})(5 - \sqrt{2}) = (5)^2 - (\sqrt{2})^2$
$= 25 - 2$
$= 23$
6. $\sqrt{3} + \sqrt{7}$
$(\sqrt{3} - \sqrt{7})(\sqrt{3} + \sqrt{7}) = (\sqrt{3})^2 - (\sqrt{7})^2$
$= 3 - 7$
$= -4$
7. $\frac{\sqrt{7}}{\sqrt{7}}$
8. $\frac{4 + \sqrt{3}}{4 + \sqrt{3}}$
9. $\sqrt{18} = \sqrt{3 \cdot 3 \cdot 2}$
$= \sqrt{3^2} \cdot \sqrt{2}$
$= 3\sqrt{2}$
10. $\frac{\sqrt{20}}{\sqrt{5}} = \sqrt{\frac{20}{5}}$
$= \sqrt{4}$
$= 2$
11. $\sqrt{\frac{3}{7}} = \frac{\sqrt{3}}{\sqrt{7}} \cdot \frac{\sqrt{7}}{\sqrt{7}}$
$= \frac{\sqrt{21}}{7}$
12. $\sqrt{\frac{2}{3}} \cdot \sqrt{\frac{5}{2}} = \sqrt{\frac{2 \cdot 5}{3 \cdot 2}}$
$= \sqrt{\frac{5}{3}}$
$= \frac{\sqrt{5}}{\sqrt{3}} \cdot \frac{\sqrt{3}}{\sqrt{3}}$
$= \frac{\sqrt{15}}{3}$
13. $(\sqrt{2} + 4)(\sqrt{2} + 6) = 2 + 6\sqrt{2} + 4\sqrt{2} + 24$
$= 10\sqrt{2} + 26$
14. $(y - \sqrt{5})(y + \sqrt{5}) = (y)^2 - (\sqrt{5})^2$
$= y^2 - 5$
15. $\frac{6}{3 - \sqrt{2}} = \frac{6}{3 - \sqrt{2}} \cdot \frac{3 + \sqrt{2}}{3 \cdot \sqrt{2}}$
$= \frac{6(3) + 6\sqrt{2}}{3^2 - (\sqrt{2})^2}$
$= \frac{18 + 6\sqrt{2}}{9 - 2}$
$= \frac{18 + 6\sqrt{2}}{7}$
16. $\sqrt{80a^2b^3} = \sqrt{4^2 \cdot 5 \cdot a^2 \cdot b^3}$
$= \sqrt{4^2} \cdot \sqrt{5} \cdot \sqrt{a^2} \cdot \sqrt{b^2} \cdot \sqrt{b}$
$= 4|a|b\sqrt{5b}$
17. $4\sqrt{3} \cdot \sqrt{3} \ \underline{?}\ \sqrt{48} + \sqrt{8}$
$4(3) \ \underline{?}\ \sqrt{16 \cdot 3} + \sqrt{4 \cdot 2}$
$12 > 4\sqrt{3} + 2\sqrt{2}$
18. $\sqrt{\frac{12}{7}} \ ?\ \frac{\sqrt{18} \cdot \sqrt{2}}{\sqrt{21}}$
$\sqrt{\frac{12}{7}} \ ?\ \sqrt{\frac{36}{21}}$
$\sqrt{\frac{12}{7}} = \sqrt{\frac{12}{7}}$
19. $1020\sqrt{P}(1 - 0.01\sqrt{P}) = 1020\sqrt{55}(1 - 0.1\sqrt{55})$
≈ 7003.5 gal/min

Pages 724–725 Exercises

20. $\sqrt{75} = \sqrt{3 \cdot 5 \cdot 5}$
$= \sqrt{5^2} \cdot \sqrt{3}$
$= 5\sqrt{3}$
21. $\sqrt{80} = \sqrt{2^4 \cdot 5}$
$= \sqrt{2^4} \cdot \sqrt{5}$
$= 2^2 \cdot \sqrt{5}$
$= 4\sqrt{5}$
22. $\sqrt{280} = \sqrt{2^3 \cdot 5 \cdot 7}$
$= \sqrt{2^2} \cdot \sqrt{2 \cdot 5 \cdot 7}$
$= 2\sqrt{70}$
23. $\sqrt{500} = \sqrt{2^2 \cdot 5^3}$
$= \sqrt{2^2} \cdot \sqrt{5^2} \cdot \sqrt{5}$
$= 2 \cdot 5 \cdot \sqrt{5}$
$= 10\sqrt{5}$
24. $\frac{\sqrt{7}}{\sqrt{3}} = \frac{\sqrt{7}}{\sqrt{3}} \cdot \frac{\sqrt{3}}{\sqrt{3}}$
$= \frac{\sqrt{21}}{3}$
25. $\frac{\sqrt{5}}{\sqrt{10}} = \sqrt{\frac{5}{10}}$
$= \sqrt{\frac{1}{2}}$
$= \frac{\sqrt{1}}{\sqrt{2}} \cdot \frac{\sqrt{2}}{\sqrt{2}}$
$= \frac{\sqrt{2}}{2}$
26. $\sqrt{\frac{2}{7}} = \frac{\sqrt{2}}{\sqrt{7}} \cdot \frac{\sqrt{7}}{\sqrt{7}}$
$= \frac{\sqrt{14}}{7}$
27. $\sqrt{\frac{11}{32}} = \frac{\sqrt{11}}{\sqrt{2^5}} \cdot \frac{\sqrt{2}}{\sqrt{2}}$
$= \frac{\sqrt{22}}{\sqrt{2^6}}$
$= \frac{\sqrt{22}}{8}$

28. $5\sqrt{10} \cdot 3\sqrt{10} = (5 \cdot 3)(\sqrt{10})^2$
$= 15(10)$
$= 150$

29. $7\sqrt{30} \cdot 2\sqrt{6} = (7 \cdot 2)(\sqrt{5 \cdot 6} \cdot \sqrt{6})$
$= 14(\sqrt{6^2 \cdot 5})$
$= 14 \cdot \sqrt{6^2} \cdot \sqrt{5}$
$= 14 \cdot 6 \cdot \sqrt{5}$
$= 84\sqrt{5}$

30. $\sqrt{\frac{3}{5}} \cdot \sqrt{\frac{7}{3}} = \sqrt{\frac{3}{5} \cdot \frac{7}{3}}$
$= \sqrt{\frac{7}{5}}$
$= \frac{\sqrt{7}}{\sqrt{5}} \cdot \frac{\sqrt{5}}{\sqrt{5}}$
$= \frac{\sqrt{35}}{5}$

31. $\sqrt{\frac{1}{6}} \cdot \sqrt{\frac{6}{11}} = \sqrt{\frac{1}{6} \cdot \frac{6}{11}}$
$= \sqrt{\frac{1}{11}}$
$= \frac{\sqrt{1}}{\sqrt{11}} \cdot \frac{\sqrt{11}}{\sqrt{11}}$
$= \frac{\sqrt{11}}{11}$

32. $\sqrt{40b^4} = \sqrt{2^2 \cdot 5 \cdot b^4}$
$= \sqrt{2^3} \cdot \sqrt{5} \cdot \sqrt{b^4}$
$= 2\sqrt{2} \cdot \sqrt{5} \cdot b^2$
$= 2b^2\sqrt{10}$

33. $\sqrt{54a^2b^2} = \sqrt{2 \cdot 3^3 \cdot a^2 \cdot b^2}$
$= \sqrt{2} \cdot \sqrt{3^2} \cdot \sqrt{3} \cdot \sqrt{a^2} \cdot \sqrt{b^2}$
$= 3 \cdot |ab|\sqrt{2 \cdot 3}$
$= 3|ab|\sqrt{6}$

34. $\sqrt{60m^2y^4} = \sqrt{2^2 \cdot 3 \cdot 5 \cdot m^2 \cdot y^4}$
$= \sqrt{2^2} \cdot \sqrt{3 \cdot 5} \cdot \sqrt{m^2} \cdot \sqrt{y^4}$
$= 2|m|y^2\sqrt{15}$

35. $\sqrt{147x^5y^7} = \sqrt{3 \cdot 7^2 \cdot x^5 \cdot y^7}$
$= \sqrt{7^2} \cdot \sqrt{3} \cdot \sqrt{x^4} \cdot \sqrt{x} \cdot \sqrt{y^6} \cdot \sqrt{y}$
$= 7x^2y^3\sqrt{3xy}$

36. $\frac{\sqrt{t}}{\sqrt{8}} = \frac{\sqrt{t}}{\sqrt{2^3}} \cdot \frac{\sqrt{2}}{\sqrt{2}}$
$= \frac{\sqrt{2t}}{\sqrt{2^4}}$
$= \frac{\sqrt{2t}}{4}$

37. $\sqrt{\frac{27}{p^2}} = \frac{\sqrt{27}}{\sqrt{p^2}}$
$= \frac{\sqrt{3^3}}{|p|}$
$= \frac{\sqrt{3^2} \cdot \sqrt{3}}{|p|}$
$= \frac{3\sqrt{3}}{|p|}$

38. $\sqrt{\frac{5n^5}{4m^5}} = \frac{\sqrt{5n^5}}{\sqrt{4m^5}}$
$= \frac{\sqrt{5} \cdot \sqrt{n^4} \cdot \sqrt{n}}{\sqrt{4} \cdot \sqrt{n^4} \cdot \sqrt{m}}$
$= \frac{n^2\sqrt{5n}}{2m^2\sqrt{m}}$
$= \frac{n^2\sqrt{5n}}{2m^2\sqrt{m}} \cdot \frac{\sqrt{m}}{\sqrt{m}}$
$= \frac{n^2\sqrt{5mn}}{2|m^3|}$

39. $\frac{\sqrt{9x^5y}}{\sqrt{12x^2y^6}} = \frac{\sqrt{9} \cdot \sqrt{x^4} \cdot \sqrt{x} \cdot \sqrt{y}}{\sqrt{2 \cdot 2 \cdot 3} \cdot \sqrt{x^2} \cdot \sqrt{y^6}}$
$= \frac{3x^2\sqrt{xy}}{2xy^3\sqrt{3}}$
$= \frac{3x^2\sqrt{xy}}{2xy^3\sqrt{3}} \cdot \frac{\sqrt{3}}{\sqrt{3}}$
$= \frac{3x^2\sqrt{3xy}}{6xy^3}$
$= \frac{x\sqrt{3xy}}{2y^3}$

40. $(1 + 2\sqrt{5})^2 = (1)^2 + 2(1)(2\sqrt{5}) + (2\sqrt{5})^2$
$= 1 + 4\sqrt{5} + 20$
$= 21 + 4\sqrt{5}$

41. $(y - \sqrt{7})^2 = (y)^2 - 2(y)(\sqrt{7}) + (\sqrt{7})^2$
$= y^2 - 2y\sqrt{7} + 7$

42. $(\sqrt{m} + \sqrt{20})^2 = (\sqrt{m})^2 + 2(\sqrt{m})(\sqrt{20}) + (\sqrt{20})^2$
$= m + 2\sqrt{20m} + 20$
$= m + 2\sqrt{2^2 \cdot 5 \cdot m} + 20$
$= m + 2 \cdot 2\sqrt{5m} + 20$
$= m + 4\sqrt{5m} + 20$

43. $\frac{14}{\sqrt{8} - \sqrt{5}} = \frac{14}{\sqrt{8} - \sqrt{5}} \cdot \frac{\sqrt{8} + \sqrt{5}}{\sqrt{8} + \sqrt{5}}$
$= \frac{14\sqrt{8} + 14\sqrt{5}}{(\sqrt{8})^2 - (\sqrt{5})^2}$
$= \frac{14\sqrt{2^3} + 14\sqrt{5}}{8 - 5}$
$= \frac{14 \cdot 2\sqrt{2} + 14\sqrt{5}}{3}$
$= \frac{28\sqrt{2} + 14\sqrt{5}}{3}$

44. $\frac{9a}{6 + \sqrt{a}} = \frac{9a}{6 + \sqrt{a}} \cdot \frac{6 - \sqrt{a}}{6 - \sqrt{a}}$
$= \frac{54a - 9a\sqrt{a}}{(6)^2 - (\sqrt{a})^2}$
$= \frac{54a - 9a\sqrt{a}}{36 - a}$

45. $\frac{2\sqrt{5}}{-4 + \sqrt{8}} = \frac{2\sqrt{5}}{-4 + \sqrt{8}} \cdot \frac{-4 - \sqrt{8}}{-4 - \sqrt{8}}$
$= \frac{-8\sqrt{5} - 2\sqrt{40}}{(-4)^2 - (\sqrt{8})^2}$
$= \frac{-8\sqrt{5} - \sqrt{2^2 \cdot 10}}{16 - 8}$
$= \frac{-8\sqrt{5} - 4\sqrt{10}}{8}$
$= \frac{-2\sqrt{5} - \sqrt{10}}{2}$

46. $\frac{3\sqrt{7}}{5\sqrt{3} + 3\sqrt{5}} = \frac{3\sqrt{7}}{5\sqrt{3} + 3\sqrt{5}} \cdot \frac{5\sqrt{3} - 3\sqrt{5}}{5\sqrt{3} - 3\sqrt{5}}$
$= \frac{15\sqrt{21} - 9\sqrt{35}}{(5\sqrt{3})^2 - (3\sqrt{5})^2}$
$= \frac{15\sqrt{21} - 9\sqrt{35}}{25 \cdot 3 - 9 \cdot 5}$
$= \frac{15\sqrt{21} - 9\sqrt{35}}{75 - 45}$
$= \frac{15\sqrt{21} - 9\sqrt{35}}{30}$
$= \frac{5\sqrt{21} - 3\sqrt{35}}{10}$

47. $\frac{\sqrt{c} - \sqrt{d}}{\sqrt{c} + \sqrt{d}} = \frac{(\sqrt{c} - \sqrt{d})}{(\sqrt{c} + \sqrt{d})} \cdot \frac{(\sqrt{c} - \sqrt{d})}{(\sqrt{c} - \sqrt{d})}$
$= \frac{(\sqrt{c})^2 - 2\sqrt{c} \cdot \sqrt{d} + (\sqrt{d})^2}{(\sqrt{c})^2 - (\sqrt{d})^2}$
$= \frac{c - 2\sqrt{cd} + d}{c - d}$

48. $(\sqrt{2x}-\sqrt{6})(\sqrt{2x}+\sqrt{6}) = (\sqrt{2x})^2-(\sqrt{6})^2$
$= 2x-6$

49. $(x-4\sqrt{3})(x-\sqrt{3}) = x^2 - x\sqrt{3} - 4x\sqrt{3} + 12$
$= x^2 - 5x\sqrt{3} + 12$

50. $\sqrt{\frac{8}{9}}\cdot\frac{2}{\sqrt{8}} \stackrel{?}{=} \frac{2}{\sqrt{51}}\cdot\sqrt{\frac{17}{3}}$
$\frac{\sqrt{8}}{\sqrt{9}}\cdot\frac{2}{\sqrt{8}} \stackrel{?}{=} \frac{2}{\sqrt{17}\cdot\sqrt{3}}\cdot\frac{\sqrt{17}}{\sqrt{3}}$
$\frac{2}{3}=\frac{2}{3}$

51. $\sqrt{10}\cdot\sqrt{30} \stackrel{?}{=} \frac{10}{\sqrt{5}+9}$
$\sqrt{300} \stackrel{?}{=} \frac{10}{\sqrt{5}+9}\cdot\frac{\sqrt{5}-9}{\sqrt{5}-9}$
$\sqrt{10^2\cdot 3} \stackrel{?}{=} \frac{10\sqrt{5}-90}{5-81}$
$10\sqrt{3} > \frac{10\sqrt{5}-90}{-76}$

52. $\frac{2}{\sqrt{6}-\sqrt{5}} \stackrel{?}{=} \frac{20}{6+\sqrt{3}}$
$\frac{2}{\sqrt{6}-\sqrt{5}}\cdot\frac{\sqrt{6}+\sqrt{5}}{\sqrt{6}+\sqrt{5}} \stackrel{?}{=} \frac{20}{6+\sqrt{3}}\cdot\frac{6-\sqrt{3}}{6-\sqrt{3}}$
$\frac{2\sqrt{6}+2\sqrt{5}}{(\sqrt{6})^2-(5)^2} \stackrel{?}{=} \frac{120-20\sqrt{3}}{(6)^2-(\sqrt{3})^2}$
$\frac{2\sqrt{6}+2\sqrt{5}}{1} > \frac{120-20\sqrt{3}}{33}$

53. $\frac{3\sqrt{2}-\sqrt{7}}{2\sqrt{3}-5\sqrt{2}} \stackrel{?}{=} \frac{4\sqrt{5}-3\sqrt{7}}{\sqrt{6}}$
$\frac{3\sqrt{2}-\sqrt{7}}{2\sqrt{3}-5\sqrt{2}}\cdot\frac{2\sqrt{3}+5\sqrt{2}}{2\sqrt{3}+5\sqrt{2}} \stackrel{?}{=} \frac{4\sqrt{5}-3\sqrt{7}}{\sqrt{6}}\cdot\frac{\sqrt{6}}{\sqrt{6}}$
$\frac{6\sqrt{6}+15\sqrt{4}-2\sqrt{21}-5\sqrt{14}}{12-50} \stackrel{?}{=} \frac{4\sqrt{30}-3\sqrt{42}}{6}$
$\frac{6\sqrt{6}+30-2\sqrt{21}-5\sqrt{14}}{-38} < \frac{4\sqrt{30}-3\sqrt{42}}{6}$

54. No, because square roots of negative numbers are not defined in the set of real numbers; $\sqrt{(-2)\cdot(-3)} \neq \sqrt{-2}\cdot\sqrt{-3}$

55. $\frac{\sqrt{158}+17.5-2}{2.37} \approx \frac{28.07}{2.37}$
≈ 11.84
Yes, the result is about 11.84.

56. $V=\sqrt{PR}$
$V=\sqrt{75\cdot 110}$
$V=\sqrt{8250}$
$V\approx 90.83$
about 90.83 volts

57. $x^2 = 12^2+14^2$
$x^2 = 144+196$
$x^2 = 340$
$x = \pm\sqrt{340}$
$x \approx 18.44$ cm

58. $\frac{2a^2+11a-6}{a^2-2a-48} = \frac{(2a-1)(a+6)}{(a-8)(a+6)}$
$= \frac{(2a-1)(a+6)}{(a-8)(a+6)}$
$= \frac{2a-1}{a-8};\ a \neq 8, -6$
excluded values: $a^2-2a-48=0$
$(a-8)(a+6)=0$
$a-8=0$ or $a+6=0$
$a=8$ $\quad a=-6$

59. $3x^2-5x+2=0,\ a=3,\ b=-5,\ c=2$
$x = \frac{-(-5)\pm\sqrt{(-5)^2-4(3)(2)}}{2(3)}$
$= \frac{5\pm\sqrt{25-24}}{6}$
$x=\frac{5+1}{6}$ or $x=\frac{5-1}{6}$
$=1$ $\quad = \frac{2}{3}$
$1, \frac{2}{3}$

60. $12a^2b^2-28ab^2c^2 = 4ab^2(3ab)+4ab^2(-7c^2)$
$= 4ab^2(3ab-7c^2)$

61. $2{,}700{,}000{,}000 = 2.7\times 1{,}000{,}000{,}000$
$= 2.7\times 10^9$ acres

62. $4-2.3t<17.8$
$-2.3t<13.8$
$\frac{-2.3t}{-2.3} > \frac{13.8}{-2.3}$
$t>-6$
$\{t \mid t>-6\}$

63. $y=-5x+2;\ m=-5$
line perpendicular: $m=\frac{1}{5}$
y-intercept: (0, 6)
$y=mx+b$
$y=\frac{1}{5}x+6$

64. $\{(-1,3),(-1,4),(1,4),(1,-3),(3,5)\}$
Domain: $\{-1, 1, 3\}$
Range: $\{3, 4, -3, 5\}$

65. $6(x+3)=3x$
$6x+18=3x$
$18=-3x$
$-6=x$

66. $\frac{1}{4}x^2$

13-2B Graphing Technology Simplifying Radical Expressions

Page 726 Exercises

1. $\sqrt{1372} = \sqrt{2^2\cdot 7^3}$
$= \sqrt{2^2}\cdot\sqrt{7^2}\cdot\sqrt{7}$
$= 2\cdot 7\cdot\sqrt{7}$
$= 14\sqrt{7}\approx 37.04$
Verify with the calculator.
Enter: [2nd] [√] 1372 [ENTER] ≈ 37.04
14 [X] [2nd] [√] 7 [ENTER] ≈ 37.04

2. $\sqrt{32}\cdot\sqrt{12} = \sqrt{2^5}\cdot\sqrt{2^2\cdot 3}$
$= \sqrt{2^4\sqrt{2}\sqrt{2^2}\sqrt{3}}$
$= 4\cdot 2\sqrt{2\cdot 3}$
$= 8\sqrt{6}\approx 19.60$
Verify with the calculator.
Enter: [2nd] [√] 32 [X] [2nd] [√] 12 [ENTER] ≈ 19.60
8 [X] [2nd] [√] 6 [ENTER] ≈ 19.60

3. $\sqrt{2}(\sqrt{6}+3) = \sqrt{2}(\sqrt{6})+3\sqrt{2}$
$= \sqrt{12}+3\sqrt{2}$
$= \sqrt{2^2\cdot 3}+3\sqrt{2}$
$= 2\sqrt{3}+3\sqrt{2}\approx 7.71$
Verify with the calculator.
Enter: [2nd] [√] 2 [X] [(] [2nd] [√] 6 [+] 3 [)] [ENTER] ≈ 7.71
2 [X] [2nd] [√] 3 [+] 3 [X] [2nd] [√] 2 [ENTER] ≈ 7.71

4. $\sqrt{\frac{5}{6}} = \frac{\sqrt{5}}{\sqrt{6}} \cdot \frac{\sqrt{6}}{\sqrt{6}}$
$= \frac{\sqrt{30}}{6} \approx 0.91$

Verify with the calculator.

Enter: 2nd √ (5 ÷ 6) ENTER ≈ 0.91

2nd √ 30 ÷ 6 ENTER ≈ 0.91

5. $\frac{4}{\sqrt{7}} = \frac{4}{\sqrt{7}} \cdot \frac{\sqrt{7}}{\sqrt{7}}$
$= \frac{4\sqrt{7}}{7} \approx 1.51$

Verify with the calculator.

Enter: 4 ÷ 2nd √ 7 ENTER ≈ 1.51

(4 X 2nd √ 7) ÷ 7 ENTER ≈ 1.51

6. $\frac{2}{\sqrt{11}+8} = \frac{2}{(\sqrt{11}+8)} \frac{(\sqrt{11}-8)}{(\sqrt{11}-8)}$
$= \frac{2\sqrt{11}-2(8)}{(\sqrt{11})^2-(8)^2}$
$= \frac{2\sqrt{11}-16}{\sqrt{11}-64}$
$= -\frac{2\sqrt{11}-16}{53} \approx 0.18$

Verify with the calculator.

Enter 2 ÷ (2nd √ 11 + 8) ENTER

≈ 0.18

(2 X 2nd √ 11 − 16) ÷ (−) 53

ENTER ≈ 0.18

7. $\sqrt{12} + \sqrt{3} = \sqrt{2^2 \cdot 3} + \sqrt{3}$
$= 2\sqrt{3} + \sqrt{3}$
$= 3\sqrt{3} \approx 5.20$

Verify with the calculator.

Enter: 2nd √ 12 + 2nd √ 3 ENTER

≈ 5.20

3 X 2nd √ 3 ENTER ≈ 5.20

8. $\frac{4}{5}\sqrt{2} + \frac{3}{5}\sqrt{2} = \frac{7}{5}\sqrt{2} \approx 1.98$

Verify with the calculator.

Enter: (4 ÷ 5) X 2nd √ 2 +

(3 ÷ 5) X 2nd √ 2 ENTER ≈ 1.98

(7 ÷ 5) X 2nd √ 2 ENTER ≈ 1.98

9. $\frac{\sqrt{3}}{2} - \frac{\sqrt{5}}{3} + \sqrt{18} = \frac{\sqrt{3}}{2} - \frac{\sqrt{5}}{3} + \sqrt{2 \cdot 3^2}$
$= \frac{\sqrt{3}}{2} - \frac{\sqrt{5}}{3} + 3\sqrt{2}$
≈ 4.36

Verify with the calculator.

Enter: 2nd √ 3 ÷ 2 − 2nd √ 5 ÷

3 + 2nd √ 18 ENTER ≈ 4.36

2nd √ 3 ÷ 2 − 2nd √ 5 + 3 X

2nd √ 2 ENTER ≈ 4.36

10. $\sqrt{18} + \sqrt{108} + \sqrt{50}$
$= \sqrt{2 \cdot 3^2} + \sqrt{2^2 \cdot 3^3} + \sqrt{2 \cdot 5^2}$
$= 3\sqrt{2} + \sqrt{2^2} \cdot \sqrt{3^2}\sqrt{3} + 5\sqrt{2}$
$= 8\sqrt{2} + 2 \cdot 3\sqrt{3}$
$= 8\sqrt{2} + 6\sqrt{3}$
≈ 21.71

Verify with the calculator.

Enter: 2nd √ 18 + 2nd √ 108 + 2nd

√ 50 ENTER ≈ 21.71

8 X 2nd √ 2 + 6 X 2nd √ 3

ENTER ≈ 21.71

11. $\sqrt{\frac{2}{3}} + \frac{\sqrt{6}}{3} - 6\sqrt{6} = \frac{\sqrt{2}}{\sqrt{3}} \cdot \frac{\sqrt{3}}{\sqrt{3}} + \frac{\sqrt{6}}{3} - 6\sqrt{6}$
$= \frac{\sqrt{6}}{3} + \frac{\sqrt{6}}{3} - \frac{18\sqrt{6}}{3}$
$= \frac{\sqrt{6}+\sqrt{6}-18\sqrt{6}}{3}$
$= \frac{-16\sqrt{6}}{3} \approx -13.06$

Verify with the calculator.

Enter: 2nd √ (2 ÷ 3) + 2nd √

6 ÷ 3 − 6 X 2nd √ 6 ENTER ≈ −13.06

((−) 16 X 2nd √ 6) ÷ 3 ENTER

≈ −13.06

13-3 Operations with Radical Expressions

Page 729 Check for Understanding

1. Sample answer: $4\sqrt{3}, 2\sqrt{3}, 6\sqrt{3}$
2. to determine if there are any like radicands
3. Sample answer: $\sqrt{x} + \sqrt{y} \stackrel{?}{=} \sqrt{x+y}$
$\sqrt{3} + \sqrt{6} \stackrel{?}{=} \sqrt{9}$
$4.1815 \neq 3$
4. The distributive property allows you to add like terms. Radicals with like radicands can be added or subtracted.
5. $3\sqrt{5}, 3\sqrt{20} = 6\sqrt{5}$
6. $-5\sqrt{7}, 2\sqrt{28} = 4\sqrt{7}$ **7.** none
8. $9\sqrt{32} = 36\sqrt{2}, 2\sqrt{50} = 10\sqrt{2}, 3\sqrt{200} = 30\sqrt{2}$
9. $3\sqrt{6} + 10\sqrt{6} = (3+10)\sqrt{6}$
$= 13\sqrt{6}$
10. in simplest form
11. $8\sqrt{7x} + 4\sqrt{7x} = (8+4)\sqrt{7x}$
$= 12\sqrt{7x}$
12. $8\sqrt{5} + 3\sqrt{5} = (8+3)\sqrt{5}$
$= 11\sqrt{5} \approx 24.60$
13. $8\sqrt{3} - 2\sqrt{2} + 3\sqrt{2} + 5\sqrt{3}$
$= (8+5)\sqrt{3} + (3-2)\sqrt{2}$
$= 13\sqrt{3} + \sqrt{2} \approx 23.93$
14. $2\sqrt{3} + 12 = 2\sqrt{3} + \sqrt{2^2 \cdot 3}$
$= 2\sqrt{3} + \sqrt{2^2} \cdot \sqrt{3}$
$= 2\sqrt{3} + 2\sqrt{3}$
$= (2+2)\sqrt{3}$
$= 4\sqrt{3} \approx 6.93$

15. $\sqrt{7} + \sqrt{\frac{1}{7}} = \sqrt{7} + \frac{\sqrt{1}}{\sqrt{7}} \cdot \frac{\sqrt{7}}{\sqrt{7}}$
$= \sqrt{7} + \frac{\sqrt{7}}{7}$
$= \frac{7\sqrt{7}}{7} + \frac{\sqrt{7}}{7}$
$= \frac{7\sqrt{7} + \sqrt{7}}{7}$
$= \frac{(7 + 1)\sqrt{7}}{7}$
$= \frac{8}{7}\sqrt{7} \approx 3.02$

16. $\sqrt{2}(\sqrt{18} + 4\sqrt{3}) = \sqrt{2}(\sqrt{18}) + \sqrt{2}(4\sqrt{3})$
$= \sqrt{36} + 4\sqrt{6}$
$= 6 + 4\sqrt{6}$

17. $(4 + 5)(4 - 5) = (4)^2 - (5)^2$
$= 16 - 5$
$= 11$

18. $P = 2\ell + 2w$
$= 2(\sqrt{3}) + 2(4\sqrt{7} - 2\sqrt{12})$
$= 2\sqrt{3} + 2(4\sqrt{7}) + 2(-2\sqrt{12})$
$= 2\sqrt{3} + 8\sqrt{7} - 4\sqrt{12}$
$= 2\sqrt{3} + 8\sqrt{7} - 4(2\sqrt{3})$
$= 2\sqrt{3} + 8\sqrt{7} - 8\sqrt{3}$
$= 8\sqrt{7} - 6\sqrt{3}$

$A = \ell w$
$= \sqrt{3}(4\sqrt{7} - 2\sqrt{12})$
$= \sqrt{3}(4\sqrt{7}) + (\sqrt{3})(-2\sqrt{12})$
$= 4\sqrt{21} - 2\sqrt{36}$
$= 4\sqrt{21} - 2(6)$
$= 4\sqrt{21} - 12$

Pages 730–731 Exercises

19. $25\sqrt{13} + \sqrt{13} = (25 + 1)\sqrt{13}$
$= 26\sqrt{13}$

20. $7\sqrt{2} - 15\sqrt{2} + 8\sqrt{2} = (7 - 15 + 8)\sqrt{2}$
$= 0$

21. in simplest form

22. $2\sqrt{11} - 6\sqrt{11} - 3\sqrt{11} = (2 - 6 - 3)\sqrt{11}$
$= -7\sqrt{11}$

23. $18\sqrt{2x} + 3\sqrt{2x} = (18 + 3)\sqrt{2x}$
$= 21\sqrt{2x}$

24. $3\sqrt{5m} - 5\sqrt{5m} = (3 - 5)\sqrt{5m}$
$= -2\sqrt{5m}$

25. $4\sqrt{3} + 7\sqrt{3} - 2\sqrt{3} = (4 + 7 - 2)\sqrt{3}$
$= 9\sqrt{3} \approx 15.59$

26. $5\sqrt{5} + 3\sqrt{5} - 18\sqrt{5} = (5 + 3 - 18)\sqrt{5}$
$= -10\sqrt{5} \approx -22.36$

27. $\sqrt{6} + 2\sqrt{2} + \sqrt{10} \approx 8.44$

28. $4\sqrt{6} + \sqrt{7} - 6\sqrt{2} + 4\sqrt{7}$
$= 4\sqrt{6} - 6\sqrt{2} + (1 + 4)\sqrt{7}$
$= 4\sqrt{6} - 6\sqrt{2} + 5\sqrt{7} \approx 14.54$

29. $3\sqrt{7} - 2\sqrt{28} = 3\sqrt{7} - 2\sqrt{2^2 \cdot 7}$
$= 3\sqrt{7} - 2(2\sqrt{7})$
$= 3\sqrt{7} - 4\sqrt{7}$
$= (3 - 4)\sqrt{7}$
$= -\sqrt{7} \approx -2.65$

30. $2\sqrt{50} - 3\sqrt{32} = 2\sqrt{5^2 \cdot 2} - 3\sqrt{4^2 \cdot 2}$
$= 2(5\sqrt{2}) - 3(4\sqrt{2})$
$= 10\sqrt{2} - 12\sqrt{2}$
$= (10 - 12)\sqrt{2}$
$= -2\sqrt{2} \approx -2.83$

31. $3\sqrt{27} + 5\sqrt{48} = 3\sqrt{3^2 \cdot 3} + 5\sqrt{4^2 \cdot 3}$
$= 3(\sqrt{3^2} \cdot \sqrt{3}) + 5(\sqrt{4^2} \cdot \sqrt{3})$
$= 3(3\sqrt{3}) + 5(4\sqrt{3})$
$= 9\sqrt{3} + 20\sqrt{3}$
$= (9 + 20)\sqrt{3}$
$= 29\sqrt{3} \approx 50.23$

32. $2\sqrt{20} - 3\sqrt{24} - \sqrt{180}$
$= 2\sqrt{2^2 \cdot 5} - 3\sqrt{2^2 \cdot 6} - \sqrt{6^2 \cdot 5}$
$= 2(\sqrt{2^2} \cdot \sqrt{5}) - 3(\sqrt{2^2} \cdot \sqrt{6}) - (\sqrt{6^2} \cdot \sqrt{5})$
$= 2(2\sqrt{5}) - 3(2\sqrt{6}) - 6\sqrt{5}$
$= 4\sqrt{5} - 6\sqrt{6} - 6\sqrt{5}$
$= (4 - 6)\sqrt{5} - 6\sqrt{6}$
$= -2\sqrt{5} - 6\sqrt{6} \approx -19.17$

33. $\sqrt{80} + \sqrt{98} + \sqrt{128}$
$= \sqrt{4^2 \cdot 5} + \sqrt{7^2 \cdot 2} + \sqrt{8^2 \cdot 2}$
$= (\sqrt{4^2} \cdot \sqrt{5}) + (\sqrt{7^2} \cdot \sqrt{5}) + (\sqrt{8^2} \cdot \sqrt{5})$
$= 4\sqrt{5} + 7\sqrt{2} + 8\sqrt{2}$
$= 4\sqrt{5} + (7 + 8)\sqrt{2}$
$= 4\sqrt{5} + 15\sqrt{2} \approx 30.16$

34. $\sqrt{10} - \sqrt{\frac{2}{5}} = \sqrt{10} - \frac{\sqrt{2}}{\sqrt{5}} \cdot \frac{\sqrt{5}}{\sqrt{5}}$
$= \sqrt{10} - \frac{\sqrt{10}}{5}$
$= \frac{5\sqrt{10}}{5} - \frac{\sqrt{10}}{5}$
$= \frac{5\sqrt{10} - \sqrt{10}}{5}$
$= \frac{4}{5}\sqrt{10} \approx 2.53$

35. $3\sqrt{3} - \sqrt{45} + 3\sqrt{\frac{1}{3}}$
$= 3\sqrt{3} - \sqrt{3^2 \cdot 5} + 3\frac{\sqrt{1}}{\sqrt{3}} \cdot \frac{\sqrt{3}}{\sqrt{3}}$
$= 3\sqrt{3} - (\sqrt{3^2} \cdot \sqrt{5}) + 3\left(\frac{\sqrt{3}}{3}\right)$
$= 3\sqrt{3} - 3\sqrt{5} + \sqrt{3}$
$= (3 + 1)\sqrt{3} - 3\sqrt{5}$
$= 4\sqrt{3} - 3\sqrt{5} \approx 0.22$

36. $6\sqrt{\frac{7}{4}} + 3\sqrt{28} - 10\sqrt{\frac{1}{7}}$
$= 6\left(\frac{\sqrt{7}}{\sqrt{4}}\right) + 3\sqrt{2^2 \cdot 7} - 10\frac{\sqrt{1}}{\sqrt{7}} \cdot \frac{\sqrt{7}}{\sqrt{7}}$
$= \frac{6\sqrt{7}}{2} + 3(\sqrt{2^2} \cdot \sqrt{7}) - \frac{10\sqrt{7}}{7}$
$= 3\sqrt{7} + 3(2\sqrt{7}) - \frac{10\sqrt{7}}{7}$
$= 3\sqrt{7} + 6\sqrt{7} - \frac{10\sqrt{7}}{7}$
$= \frac{21\sqrt{7}}{7} + \frac{42\sqrt{7}}{7} - \frac{10\sqrt{7}}{7}$
$= \frac{21\sqrt{7} + 42\sqrt{7} - 10\sqrt{7}}{7}$
$= \frac{(21 + 42 - 10)\sqrt{7}}{7}$
$= \frac{53\sqrt{7}}{7} \approx 20.03$

37. $\sqrt{5}(2\sqrt{10} + 3\sqrt{2}) = \sqrt{5}(2\sqrt{10}) + \sqrt{5}(3\sqrt{2})$
$= 2\sqrt{50} + 3\sqrt{10}$
$= 2\sqrt{5^2 \cdot 2} + 3\sqrt{10}$
$= 2(5\sqrt{2}) + 3\sqrt{10}$
$= 10\sqrt{2} + 3\sqrt{10}$

38. $\sqrt{6}(\sqrt{3} + 5\sqrt{2}) = \sqrt{6}(\sqrt{3}) + \sqrt{6}(5\sqrt{2})$
$= \sqrt{18} + 5\sqrt{12}$
$= \sqrt{3^2 \cdot 2} + 5\sqrt{2^2 \cdot 3}$
$= 3\sqrt{2} + 5(2\sqrt{3})$
$= 3\sqrt{2} + 10\sqrt{3}$

39. $(2\sqrt{10} + 3\sqrt{15})(3\sqrt{3} - 2\sqrt{2})$
$= (2\sqrt{10})(3\sqrt{3}) + (2\sqrt{10})(-2\sqrt{2}) + (3\sqrt{15})(3\sqrt{3}) + (3\sqrt{15})(-2\sqrt{2})$
$= 6\sqrt{30} - 4\sqrt{20} + 9\sqrt{45} - 6\sqrt{30}$
$= 6\sqrt{30} - 4(2\sqrt{5}) + 9(3\sqrt{5}) - 6\sqrt{30}$
$= -8\sqrt{5} + 27\sqrt{5}$
$= (27 - 8)\sqrt{5}$
$= 19\sqrt{5}$

40. $(\sqrt{5} - \sqrt{2})(\sqrt{14} + \sqrt{35})$
$= (\sqrt{5})(\sqrt{14}) + (\sqrt{5})(\sqrt{35}) + (-\sqrt{2})(\sqrt{14}) + (-\sqrt{2})(\sqrt{35})$
$= \sqrt{70} + \sqrt{175} - \sqrt{28} - 70$
$= \sqrt{5^2 \cdot 7} - \sqrt{2^2 \cdot 7}$
$= 5\sqrt{7} - 2\sqrt{7}$
$= 3\sqrt{7}$

41. $(\sqrt{6} + \sqrt{8})(\sqrt{24} + \sqrt{2})$
$= (\sqrt{6})(\sqrt{24}) + (\sqrt{6})(\sqrt{2}) + (\sqrt{8})(\sqrt{24}) + (\sqrt{8})(\sqrt{2})$
$= \sqrt{144} + \sqrt{12} + \sqrt{192} + \sqrt{16}$
$= \sqrt{12^2} + \sqrt{2^2 \cdot 3} + \sqrt{8^2 \cdot 3} + \sqrt{4^2}$
$= 12 + 2\sqrt{3} + 8\sqrt{3} + 4$
$= 10\sqrt{3} + 16$

42. $(5\sqrt{2} + 3\sqrt{5})(2\sqrt{10} - 3)$
$= (5\sqrt{2})(2\sqrt{10}) + (5\sqrt{2})(-3) + (3\sqrt{5})(2\sqrt{10}) + (3\sqrt{5})(-3)$
$= 10\sqrt{20} - 15\sqrt{2} + 6\sqrt{50} - 9\sqrt{5}$
$= 10\sqrt{2^2 \cdot 5} - 15\sqrt{2} + 6\sqrt{5^2 \cdot 2} - 9\sqrt{5}$
$= 10(2\sqrt{5}) - 15\sqrt{2} + 6(5\sqrt{2}) - 9\sqrt{5}$
$= 20\sqrt{5} - 15\sqrt{2} + 30\sqrt{2} - 9\sqrt{5}$
$= 15\sqrt{2} + 11\sqrt{5}$

43. Both $(x - 5)^2$ and $(x - 5)^4$ must be nonnegative, but $x - 5$ may be negative.

44. $\sqrt{\frac{3(670)}{2}} - \sqrt{\frac{3(530)}{2}} = \sqrt{1005} - \sqrt{795}$
$\approx 31.70 - 28.19$
≈ 3.51 mi

45. $a + b = 20$ $\quad b^2 = a^2 + 12^2$
$a = 20 - b$ $\quad b^2 = (20 - b)^2 + 144$
$b^2 = 400 - 40b + b^2 + 144$
$b^2 = 544 - 40b + b^2$
$40b = 544$
$b = 13\frac{3}{5}$

$a = 20 - 13\frac{3}{5}$ or $6\frac{2}{5}$ ft

46. $\frac{\sqrt{3}}{\sqrt{6}} = \frac{\sqrt{3}}{\sqrt{6}} \cdot \frac{\sqrt{6}}{\sqrt{6}}$
$= \frac{\sqrt{18}}{6}$
$= \frac{\sqrt{2 \cdot 3^2}}{6}$
$= \frac{3\sqrt{2}}{6}$
$= \frac{\sqrt{2}}{2}$

47. $\frac{x^2 - y^2}{3} \cdot \frac{9}{x + y} = \frac{(x + y)(x - y)}{3} \cdot \frac{9}{x + y}$
$= \frac{\overset{1}{\cancel{(x + y)}}(x - y)}{\cancel{3}_1} \cdot \frac{\overset{3}{\cancel{9}}}{\underset{1}{\cancel{x + y}}}$
$= 3(x - y)$
$= 3x - 3y$

48. $3a^2 + 19a - 14 = 3a^2 + (21 - 2)a - 14$
$= 3a^2 + 21a - 2a - 14$
$= (3a^2 + 21a) + (-2a - 14)$
$= 3a(a + 7) - 2(a + 7)$
$= (3a - 2)(a + 7)$

49. degree of $16s^3t^2$: 5
degree of $3s^2t$: 3
degree of $7s^6t$: 7
The degree of $16s^3t^2 + 3s^2t + 7s^6t$ is 7.

50. $\frac{x + 47 + 45 + 48 + 45}{5} = 46$
$\frac{x + 185}{5} = 46$
$x + 185 = 230$
$x = 45$

He must receive at least 45 points.

51. $\frac{8}{12}$ or $\frac{2}{3}$

52. $\tan A = \frac{3}{8}$
$\tan A = 0.375$
$A \approx 21°$

53a. 1991; about 9 million

53b. $10 - 4 = 6$ million

Page 731 Self Test

1. $c^2 = a^2 + b^2$
$c^2 = 21^2 + 28^2$
$c^2 = 441 + 784$
$c^2 = 1225$
$c = \pm\sqrt{1225}$
$c = 35$

2. $c^2 = a^2 + b^2$
$8^2 = (\sqrt{41})^2 + b^2$
$64 = 41 + b^2$
$23 = b^2$
$\pm 23 = b$
$4.80 \approx b$

3. $c^2 = a^2 + b^2$
$54^2 = a^2 + 28^2$
$2916 = a^2 + 784$
$2132 = a^2$
$\pm\sqrt{2132} = a$
$46.17 \approx a$

4. $\sqrt{20} = \sqrt{2^2 \cdot 5}$
$= \sqrt{2^2} \cdot \sqrt{5}$
$= 2\sqrt{5}$

5. $2\sqrt{5} \cdot \sqrt{5} = 2 \cdot 5$
$= 10$

6. $\frac{\sqrt{42x^2}}{\sqrt{6y^3}} = \frac{|x|\sqrt{42}}{\sqrt{6} \cdot \sqrt{x^2}\sqrt{y}} \cdot \frac{\sqrt{y}}{\sqrt{y}}$
$= \frac{|x|42\sqrt{y}}{\sqrt{6}\, y^2}$
$= \frac{|x|}{y^2}\sqrt{\frac{42}{6}} \cdot \sqrt{y}$
$= \frac{|x|\sqrt{7y}}{y^2}$

7. $8\sqrt{6} + 3\sqrt{6} = (8 + 3)\sqrt{6}$
$= 11\sqrt{6}$

8. $10\sqrt{17} + 9\sqrt{7} - 8\sqrt{17} + 6\sqrt{7}$
$= (10 - 18)\sqrt{17} + (9 + 6)\sqrt{7}$
$= 2\sqrt{17} + 15\sqrt{7}$

9. $(6 + \sqrt{3})(2\sqrt{5} - \sqrt{3})$
$= 6(2\sqrt{5}) + 6(-\sqrt{3}) + (\sqrt{3})(2\sqrt{5}) + (\sqrt{3})(-\sqrt{3})$
$= 12\sqrt{5} - 6\sqrt{3} + 2\sqrt{15} - 3$

10. $c^2 = 3^2 + 12^2$
$c^2 = 9 + 144$
$c^2 = 153$
$c = \pm\sqrt{153}$
$c \approx 12.37$

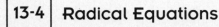

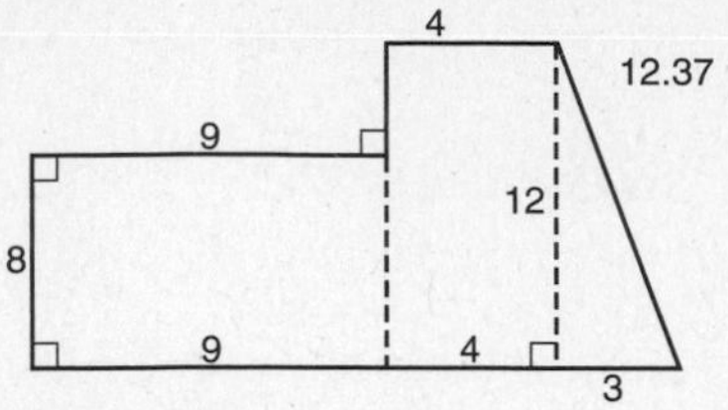

$P \approx 8 + 9 + 4 + 4 + 12.37 + 16$
≈ 53.37 cm
$A = 8(9) + 4(12) + \frac{1}{2}(12)(3)$
$= 72 + 48 + 18$
$= 138$ cm^2

13-4 Radical Equations

Pages 734–735 Check for Understanding

1. Isolate the radical.

2. $\frac{7}{x} = \frac{x}{y}$
$x^2 = 7y$
$x = \pm\sqrt{7y}$

3a. $s = 3.1\sqrt{d}$
$\frac{s}{3.1} = \sqrt{d}$
$\left(\frac{s}{3.1}\right)^2 = (\sqrt{d})^2$
$\left(\frac{s}{3.1}\right)^2 = d$

3b. $d = \left(\frac{400}{3.1}\right)^2$
$\approx 16{,}649$ m

4. Ellen is correct; for $\sqrt{x} = -4$, there is no real solution.

5a. Sample answer: Isolate the radical, square both sides of the equation, and simplify.

5b. The solution may not satisfy the original equation.

6. $\sqrt{x} = 6$
$(\sqrt{x})^2 = 6^2$
$x = 36$

7. $\sqrt{a + 3} = 2$
$(\sqrt{a + 3})^2 = 2^2$
$a + 3 = 4$

8. $13 = \sqrt{2y - 5}$
$13^2 = (\sqrt{2y - 5})^2$
$169 = 2y - 5$

9. $\sqrt{m} = 4$
$(\sqrt{m})^2 = 4^2$
$m = 16$

10. $\sqrt{b} = -3$
no real solution

11. $-\sqrt{x} = -6$
$\sqrt{x} = 6$
$(\sqrt{x})^2 = 6^2$
$x = 36$

12. $\sqrt{7x} = 7$
$(\sqrt{7x})^2 = 7^2$
$7x = 49$
$x = 7$

13. $\sqrt{-3a} = 6$
$(\sqrt{-3a})^2 = 6^2$
$-3a = 36$
$a = -12$

14. $\sqrt{y - 2} = 8$
$(\sqrt{y - 2})^2 = 8^2$
$y - 2 = 64$
$y \quad = 66$

15. $V = \sqrt{2.5h}$
$V = \sqrt{2.5(6)}$
$V = \sqrt{15}$
$V \approx 3.9$ mph

Pages 735–736 Exercises

16. $\sqrt{a} = 5\sqrt{2}$
$(\sqrt{a})^2 = (5\sqrt{2})^2$
$a = 50$

17. $3\sqrt{7} = \sqrt{-x}$
$(3\sqrt{7})^2 = (\sqrt{-x})^2$
$63 = -x$
$-63 = x$

18. $\sqrt{m} - 4 = 0$
$\sqrt{m} = 4$
$(\sqrt{m})^2 = 4^2$
$m = 16$

19. $\sqrt{2d} + 1 = 0$
$\sqrt{2d} = -1$
no real solution

20. $10 - \sqrt{3y} = 1$
$-\sqrt{3y} = -9$
$\sqrt{3y} = 9$
$(\sqrt{3y})^2 = 9^2$
$3y = 81$
$y = 27$

21. $3 + 5\sqrt{n} = 12$
$5\sqrt{n} = 9$
$\sqrt{n} = \frac{9}{5}$
$(\sqrt{n})^2 = \left(\frac{9}{5}\right)^2$
$n = \frac{81}{25}$

22. $\sqrt{8s + 1} = 5$
$(\sqrt{8s + 1})^2 = 5^2$
$8s + 1 = 25$
$8s = 24$
$s = 3$

23. $\sqrt{4b + 1} - 3 = 0$
$\sqrt{4b + 1} = 3$
$(\sqrt{4b + 1})^2 = 3^2$
$4b + 1 = 9$
$4b = 8$
$b = 2$

24. $\sqrt{3r - 5} + 7 = 3$
$\sqrt{3r - 5} = -4$
no real solution

25. $\sqrt{\frac{w}{6}} = 2$
$\left(\sqrt{\frac{w}{6}}\right)^2 = 2^2$
$\frac{w}{6} = 4$
$w = 24$

26. $\sqrt{\frac{4x}{5}} - 9 = 3$
$\sqrt{\frac{4x}{5}} = 12$
$\left(\sqrt{\frac{4x}{5}}\right)^2 = 12^2$
$\frac{4x}{5} = 144$
$4x = 540$
$x = 180$

27. $5\sqrt{\frac{4t}{3}} - 2 = 0$
$5\sqrt{\frac{4t}{3}} = 2$
$\sqrt{\frac{4t}{3}} = \frac{2}{5}$
$\left(\sqrt{\frac{4t}{3}}\right)^2 = \left(\frac{2}{5}\right)^2$
$\frac{4t}{3} = \frac{4}{25}$
$100t = 12$
$t = \frac{12}{100}$
$t = \frac{3}{25}$

28. $\sqrt{2x^2 - 121} = x$
$(\sqrt{2x^2 - 121})^2 = x^2$
$\sqrt{2x^2 - 121} = x^2$
$x^2 - 121 = 0$
$(x + 11)(x - 11) = 0$
$x + 11 = 0$ or $x - 11 = 0$
$x = -11 \qquad x = 11$
Since -11 does not satisfy the original equation, 11 is the only solution.

29. $7\sqrt{3z^2 - 15} = 7$

$\sqrt{3z^2 - 15} = 1$

$(\sqrt{3z^2 - 15})^2 = 1^2$

$3z^2 - 15 = 1$

$3z^2 = 16$

$z^2 = \frac{16}{3}$

$z = \pm\sqrt{\frac{16}{3}}$

$z = \pm\frac{4}{\sqrt{3}} \cdot \frac{\sqrt{3}}{\sqrt{3}}$

$z = \pm\frac{4}{3}\sqrt{3}$

30. $\sqrt{x + 2} = x - 4$

$(\sqrt{x + 2})^2 = (x - 4)^2$

$x + 2 = x^2 - 8x + 16$

$0 = x^2 - 9x + 14$

$0 = (x - 2)(x - 7)$

$x - 2 = 0$ or $x - 7 = 0$

$x = 2$ $\quad x = 7$

Since 2 does not satisfy the original equation, 7 is the only solution.

31. $\sqrt{5x^2 - 7} = 2x$

$(\sqrt{5x^2 - 7})^2 = (2x)^2$

$5x^2 - 7 = 4x^2$

$-7 = -x^2$

$7 = x^2$

$\pm\sqrt{7} = x$

Since $-\sqrt{7}$ does not satisfy the original equation, $\sqrt{7}$ is the only solution.

32. $\sqrt{1 - 2m} = 1 + \mathrm{m}$

$(\sqrt{1 - 2m})^2 = (1 + m)^2$

$1 - 2m = 1 + 2m + m^2$

$0 = m^2 + 4m$

$0 = m(m + 4)$

$m = 0$ or $m + 4 = 0$

$m = -4$

Since 4 does not satisfy the original equation, 0 is the only solution.

33. $4 + \sqrt{b - 2} = b$

$\sqrt{b - 2} = b - 4$

$(\sqrt{b - 2})^2 = (b - 4)^2$

$b - 2 = b^2 - 8b + 16$

$0 = b^2 - 9b + 18$

$(b - 6)(b - 3) = 0$

$b - 6 = 0$ or $b - 3 = 0$

$b = 6$ $\quad b = 3$

Since 3 does not satisfy the original equation, 6 is the only solution.

34. Let x = the number.

$\frac{24}{x} = \frac{6}{24}$

$6x = 576$

$x = 96$

The number is 96.

35. Let n represent the lesser number.
Let $n + 7$ represent the greater number.

$\frac{n}{\sqrt{30}} = \frac{\sqrt{30}}{n + 7}$

$n^2 + 7n = 30$

$n^2 + 7n - 30 = 0$

$(n + 10)(n - 3) = 0$

$n + 10 = 0$ or $n - 3 = 0$

$n = -10$ $\quad n = 3$

$n + 7 = -10 + 7$ $\quad n + 7 = 3 + 7$

$= -3$ $\quad = 10$

$-3, -10$ or $3, 10$

36. Let n represent one number.
Let $3n - 11$ represent the other number.

$\frac{n}{12} = \frac{12}{3n - 11}$

$3n^2 - 11n = 144$

$3n^2 - 11n - 144 = 0$

$(3n + 16)(n - 9) = 0$

$3n + 16 = 0$ or $n - 9 = 0$

$n = -\frac{16}{3}$ $\quad n = 9$

$3n - 11 = 3\left(-\frac{16}{3}\right) - 11$ $\quad 3n - 11 = 3(9) - 11$

$= -16 - 11$ $\quad = 27 - 11$

$= -27$ $\quad = 16$

$-\frac{16}{3}, -27$ or $9, 16$

37. $\sqrt{x - 12} = 6 - \sqrt{x}$

$(\sqrt{x - 12})^2 = (6 - \sqrt{x})^2$

$x - 12 = 36 - 12\sqrt{x} + x$

$-48 = -12\sqrt{x}$

$4 = \sqrt{x}$

$4^2 = (\sqrt{x})^2$

$16 = x$

38. $\sqrt{x} + 4 = \sqrt{x + 16}$

$(\sqrt{x} + 4)^2 = (\sqrt{x + 16})^2$

$x + 8\sqrt{x} + 16 = x + 16$

$8\sqrt{x} = 0$

$\sqrt{x} = 0$

$(\sqrt{x})^2 = 0$

$x = 0$

39. $\sqrt{x + 7} = 7 + \sqrt{x}$

$(\sqrt{x + 7})^2 = (7 + \sqrt{x})^2$

$x + 7 = 49 + 14\sqrt{x} + x$

$-42 = 14\sqrt{x}$

no real solution

40. $2\sqrt{a} + 5\sqrt{b} = 6$

$\underline{(+)3\sqrt{a} - 5\sqrt{b} = 9}$

$5\sqrt{a} = 15$

$\sqrt{a} = 3$

$(\sqrt{a})^2 = 3^2$

$a = 9$

$2\sqrt{a} + 5\sqrt{b} = 6$

$2\sqrt{9} + 5\sqrt{b} = 6$

$6 + 5\sqrt{b} = 6$

$5\sqrt{b} = 0$

$\sqrt{b} = 0$

$b = 0$

(9, 0)

41.

$$-3\sqrt{x} + 3\sqrt{y} = 1 \text{ (Multiply by } -2.) \quad 6\sqrt{x} - 6\sqrt{y} = -2$$
$$-4\sqrt{x} + 6\sqrt{y} = 3 \qquad \underline{-4\sqrt{x} + 6\sqrt{y} = \ \ 3}$$
$$2\sqrt{x} \qquad = 1$$
$$\sqrt{x} = \frac{1}{2}$$
$$(\sqrt{x})^2 = \left(\frac{1}{2}\right)^2$$
$$x = \frac{1}{4}$$

$$-3\sqrt{x} + 3\sqrt{y} = 1$$
$$-3\left(\sqrt{\frac{1}{4}}\right) + 3\sqrt{y} = 1$$
$$-3\left(\frac{1}{2}\right) + 3\sqrt{y} = 1$$
$$-\frac{3}{2} + 3\sqrt{y} = 1$$
$$3\sqrt{y} = \frac{5}{2}$$
$$\sqrt{y} = \frac{5}{6}$$
$$(\sqrt{y})^2 = \left(\frac{5}{6}\right)^2$$
$$y = \frac{25}{36}$$

$\left(\frac{1}{4}, \frac{25}{36}\right)$

42. $s = 4t$

$$\sqrt{s} - 5\sqrt{t} = -6$$
$$\sqrt{4t} - 5\sqrt{t} = -6$$
$$2\sqrt{t} - 5\sqrt{t} = -6$$
$$-3\sqrt{t} = -6$$
$$\sqrt{t} = 2$$
$$(\sqrt{t})^2 = 2^2$$
$$t = 4$$

$s = 4t$
$s = 4(4)$
$s = 16$
$(16, 4)$

43.

$$x + 2 = x\sqrt{3}$$
$$2 = x\sqrt{3} - x$$
$$2 = x(\sqrt{3} - 1)$$
$$\frac{2}{\sqrt{3} - 1} = x$$
$$\frac{2}{\sqrt{3} - 1} \cdot \frac{\sqrt{3} + 1}{\sqrt{3} + 1} = x$$
$$\frac{2\sqrt{3} + 2}{3 - 1} = x$$
$$\frac{2(\sqrt{3} + 1)}{2} = x$$
$$\sqrt{3} + 1 = x$$

44. Let x = one number.
Let y = the other number.

$$\sqrt{x + y} = 5 \qquad \sqrt{x + y} = 5$$
$$\sqrt{xy} = 12 \qquad (\sqrt{x + y})^2 = 5^2$$
$$x + y = 25$$
$$x = 25 - y$$

$$\sqrt{(25 - y)y} = 12$$
$$(\sqrt{(25 - y)y})^2 = 12^2$$
$$(25 - y)y = 144$$
$$25y - y^2 = 144$$
$$0 = y^2 - 25y + 144$$
$$0 = (y - 16)(y - 9)$$
$$y - 16 = 0 \qquad y - 9 = 0$$
$$y = 16 \qquad y = 9$$

The two numbers are 16 and 9.

45. $y^2 = x^2 + 10^2$

$$y = \sqrt{x^2 + 100}$$

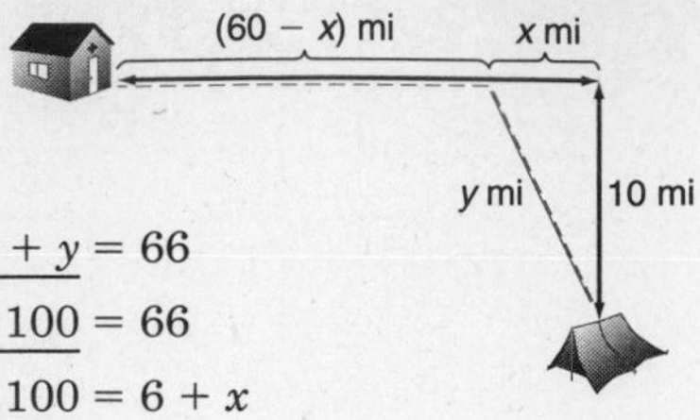

$$60 - x + y = 66$$
$$60 - x + \sqrt{x^2 + 100} = 66$$
$$\sqrt{x^2 + 100} = 6 + x$$
$$(\sqrt{x^2 + 100})^2 = (6 + x)^2$$
$$x^2 + 100 = 36 + 12x + x^2$$
$$64 = 12x$$
$$5\tfrac{1}{3} = x$$

$$60 - x = 60 - 5\tfrac{1}{3}$$
$$= 54\tfrac{2}{3} \text{ mi}$$

The jeep traveled $54\frac{2}{3}$ mi east.

46a.

$$V = 20\sqrt{t + 273}$$
$$356 = 20\sqrt{t + 273}$$
$$17.8 = \sqrt{t + 273}$$
$$17.8^2 = (\sqrt{t + 273})^2$$
$$316.84 = t + 273$$
$$43.84 = t$$

43.84°C

46b.

$$V = 20\sqrt{t + 273}$$
$$340 = 20\sqrt{t + 273}$$
$$17 = \sqrt{t + 273}$$
$$17^2 = (\sqrt{t + 273})^2$$
$$289 = t + 273$$
$$16 = t$$

16°C

47a.

$$s = \sqrt{30fd}$$
$$30 = \sqrt{30(0.4)(d)}$$
$$30^2 = (\sqrt{30(0.4)d})^2$$
$$900 = 12d$$
$$75 = d$$

No, at 30 mph, her car should have skidded 75 feet after the brakes were applied and not 110 feet.

47b.

$$s = \sqrt{30(0.4)d}$$
$$s = \sqrt{30(0.4)(110)}$$
$$s \approx 36 \text{ mph}$$

48. $5\sqrt{6} - 11\sqrt{3} - 8\sqrt{6} + \sqrt{27}$

$$= 5\sqrt{6} - 11\sqrt{3} - 8\sqrt{6} + \sqrt{3^2 \cdot 3}$$
$$= 5\sqrt{6} - 11\sqrt{3} - 8\sqrt{6} + 3\sqrt{3}$$
$$= (5 - 8)\sqrt{6} + (-11 + 3)\sqrt{3}$$
$$= -3\sqrt{6} - 8\sqrt{3}$$

49.

$$
\begin{array}{r}
6b - 26 \\
b + 5\overline{)6b^2 + \ \ 4b + 20} \\
\underline{(-)\ 6b^2 + 30b} \\
-26b + 20 \\
\underline{(-)\ -26b - 130} \\
150
\end{array}
$$

$$6b - 26 + \frac{150}{b + 5}$$

50.

x	y
−2	0
−1	−5
0	−8
1	−9
2	−8
3	−5
4	0

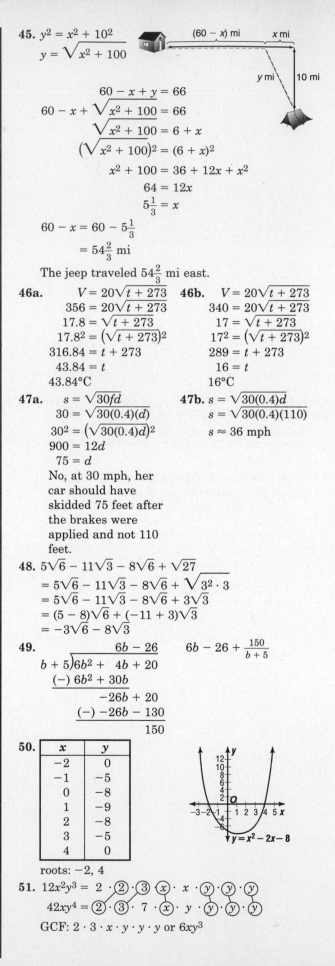

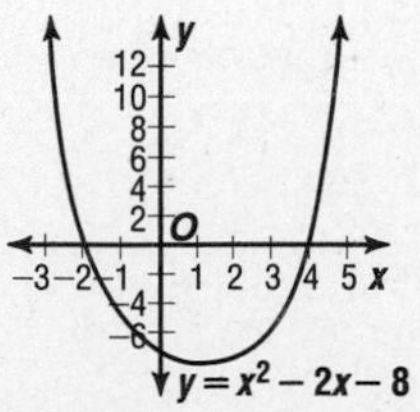

roots: −2, 4

51.

$$12x^2y^3 = 2 \cdot \textcircled{2} \cdot \textcircled{3} \cdot \textcircled{x} \cdot x \cdot \textcircled{y} \cdot \textcircled{y} \cdot \textcircled{y}$$
$$42xy^4 = \textcircled{2} \cdot \textcircled{3} \cdot 7 \cdot \textcircled{x} \cdot y \cdot \textcircled{y} \cdot \textcircled{y} \cdot \textcircled{y}$$

GCF: $2 \cdot 3 \cdot x \cdot y \cdot y \cdot y$ or $6xy^3$

52. $(6a - 2m) - (4a + 7m) = 6a - 2m - 4a - 7m$
$= 2a - 9m$

53. $x + 4y = 16$
$x = 16 - 4y$

$3x + 6y = 18$
$3(16 - 4y) + 6y = 18$
$48 - 12y + 6y = 18$
$48 - 6y = 18$
$-6y = -30$
$y = 5$

$x = 16 - 4y$
$x = 16 - 4(5)$
$x = -4$

$(-4, 5)$

54. $m = \frac{y_2 - y_1}{x_2 - x_1}$
$m = \frac{-1-2}{6-3} = \frac{-3}{3}$ or -1
$y - y_1 = m(x - x_1)$
$y - 2 = -(x - 3)$
$y - 2 = -x + 3$
$y = -x + 5$

55. $\frac{8}{8+5} = \frac{8}{13}$

56. $\frac{3}{7} + \left(-\frac{4}{9}\right) = \frac{3}{7}\left(\frac{9}{9}\right) + \left(-\frac{4}{9}\right)\left(\frac{7}{7}\right)$
$= \frac{27}{63} - \frac{28}{63}$
$= -\frac{1}{63}$

Page 736 Mathematics and Society

1. Sample answer: You need to enter all the possible variations. This could involve entering huge numbers of variables.
2. Sample answer: Advances in computing power and the widespread use of computers have enabled more organizations to solve nonlinear equations.

13-5 Integration: Geometry The Distance Formula

Pages 738–739 Check for Understanding

1. The values that are subtracted are squared before being added, the square of a negative is always positive, and distances are never negative numbers.

2a. See students' work. **2b.** See students' work.

3a. The distance between them is the absolute value of the difference of their x-coordinates, $|12 - 3|$ or 9 units.

3b. The distance between them is the absolute value of the difference of their y-coordinates, $|7 - (-5)|$ or 12 units.

4. See students' work.

5. $d = \sqrt{(6-3)^2 + (8-4)^2}$
$= \sqrt{3^2 + 4^2}$
$= \sqrt{9 + 16}$
$= \sqrt{25}$
$= 5$

6. $d = \sqrt{(-2-3)^2 + (-5-7)^2}$
$= \sqrt{(-5)^2 + (-12)^2}$
$= \sqrt{25 + 144}$
$= \sqrt{169}$
$= 13$

7. $d = \sqrt{(5-2)^2 + (-1-2)^2}$
$= \sqrt{3^2 + (-3)^2}$
$= \sqrt{9 + 9}$
$= \sqrt{18}$
$= 3\sqrt{2}$ or 4.24

8. $d = \sqrt{(10-2)^2 + (-4-7)^2}$
$= \sqrt{8^2 + (-11)^2}$
$= \sqrt{64 + 121}$
$= \sqrt{185}$ or 13.60

9. $d = \sqrt{(x_2 - x_1)^2 + (y_2 - y_1)^2}$
$5 = \sqrt{(a-4)^2 + (3-7)^2}$
$5 = \sqrt{(a-4)^2 + (-4)^2}$
$5 = \sqrt{a^2 - 8a + 16 + 16}$
$5 = \sqrt{a^2 - 8a + 32}$
$5^2 = (\sqrt{a^2 - 8a + 32})^2$
$25 = a^2 - 8a + 32$
$0 = a^2 - 8a + 7$
$0 = (a - 7)(a - 1)$
$a - 7 = 0$ or $a - 1 = 0$
$a = 7$ $\quad a = 1$

10. $d = \sqrt{(x_2 - x_1)^2 + (y_2 - y_1)^2}$
$\sqrt{10} = \sqrt{(5-6)^2 + (a-1)^2}$
$\sqrt{10} = \sqrt{(-1)^2 + (a-1)^2}$
$\sqrt{10} = \sqrt{1 + a^2 - 2a + 1}$
$\sqrt{10} = \sqrt{a^2 - 2a + 2}$
$(\sqrt{10})^2 = (\sqrt{a^2 - 2a + 2})^2$
$10 = a^2 - 2a + 2$
$0 = a^2 - 2a - 8$
$0 = (a + 2)(a - 4)$
$a + 2 = 0$ or $a - 4 = 0$
$a = -2$ $\quad a = 4$

11. $d = \sqrt{(x_2 - x_1)^2 + (y_2 - y_1)^2}$
$= \sqrt{(-5-4)^2 + (2-5)^2}$
$= \sqrt{(-9)^2 + (-3)^2}$
$= \sqrt{81 + 9}$
$= \sqrt{90}$
≈ 9.49 mi

Pages 739–741 Exercises

12. $d = \sqrt{(5-11)^2 + (-1-7)^2}$
$= \sqrt{(-6)^2 + (-8)^2}$
$= \sqrt{36 + 64}$
$= \sqrt{100}$
$= 10$

13. $d = \sqrt{(-4-4)^2 + (2-17)^2}$
$= \sqrt{(-8)^2 + (-15)^2}$
$= \sqrt{64 + 225}$
$= \sqrt{289}$
$= 17$

14. $d = \sqrt{(-3-5)^2 + (8-4)^2}$
$= \sqrt{(-8)^2 + 4^2}$
$= \sqrt{64 + 16}$
$= \sqrt{80}$
$= 4\sqrt{5}$ or 8.94

15. $d = \sqrt{[-8-(-3)]^2 + [-4-(-8)]^2}$
$= \sqrt{(-5)^2 + 4^2}$
$= \sqrt{25 + 16}$
$= \sqrt{41}$ or 6.40

16. $d = \sqrt{(9-3)^2 + [-2-(-6)]^2}$
$= \sqrt{6^2 + 4^2}$
$= \sqrt{36 + 16}$
$= \sqrt{52}$
$= 2\sqrt{13}$ or 7.21

17. $d = \sqrt{(4-6)^2 + \left[2 - \left(-\frac{2}{3}\right)\right]^2}$
$= \sqrt{(-2)^2 + \left(\frac{8}{3}\right)^2}$
$= \sqrt{4 + \frac{64}{9}}$
$= \sqrt{\frac{36}{9} + \frac{64}{9}}$
$= \sqrt{\frac{100}{9}}$
$= \frac{10}{3}$ or 3.33

18. $d = \sqrt{(4-3)^2 + \left(-\frac{2}{7} - \frac{3}{7}\right)^2}$
$= \sqrt{1^2 + \left(-\frac{5}{7}\right)^2}$
$= \sqrt{1 + \frac{25}{49}}$
$= \sqrt{\frac{49}{49} + \frac{25}{49}}$
$= \frac{\sqrt{74}}{7}$ or 1.23

19. $d = \sqrt{\left(\frac{4}{5} - 2\right)^2 + \left[(-1) - \left(-\frac{1}{2}\right)\right]^2}$
$= \sqrt{\left(-\frac{6}{5}\right)^2 + \left(-\frac{1}{2}\right)^2}$
$= \sqrt{\frac{36}{25} + \frac{1}{4}}$
$= \sqrt{\frac{144}{100} + \frac{25}{100}}$
$= \sqrt{\frac{169}{100}}$
$= \frac{13}{10}$ or 1.30

20. $d = \sqrt{(4\sqrt{5} - 6\sqrt{5})^2 + (7-1)^2}$
$= \sqrt{(-2\sqrt{5})^2 + 6^2}$
$= \sqrt{20 + 36}$
$= \sqrt{56}$
$= 2\sqrt{14}$ or 7.48

21. $d = \sqrt{(5\sqrt{2} - 7\sqrt{2})^2 + (8-10)^2}$
$= \sqrt{(-2\sqrt{2})^2 + (-2)^2}$
$= \sqrt{8 + 4}$
$= \sqrt{12}$
$= 2\sqrt{3}$ or 3.46

22. $d = \sqrt{(x_2 - x_1)^2 + (y_2 - y_1)^2}$
$10 = \sqrt{(a-3)^2 + [7-(-1)]^2}$
$10 = \sqrt{a^2 - 6a + 9 + 8^2}$
$10 = \sqrt{a^2 - 6a + 9 + 64}$
$10 = \sqrt{a^2 - 6a + 73}$
$10^2 = \left(\sqrt{a^2 - 6a + 73}\right)^2$
$100 = a^2 - 6a + 73$
$0 = a^2 - 6a - 27$
$0 = (a-9)(a+3)$
$a - 9 = 0$ or $a + 3 = 0$
$a = 9$ $\quad a = -3$

23. $d = \sqrt{(x_2 - x_1)^2 + (y_2 - y_1)^2}$
$17 = \sqrt{(-4-4)^2 + (a-2)^2}$
$17 = \sqrt{(-8)^2 + (a-2)^2}$
$17 = \sqrt{64 + a^2 - 4a + 4}$
$17 = \sqrt{a^2 - 4a + 68}$
$17^2 = \left(\sqrt{a^2 - 4a + 68}\right)^2$
$289 = a^2 - 4a + 68$
$0 = a^2 - 4a - 221$
$0 = (a-17)(a+13)$
$a - 17 = 0$ or $a + 13 = 0$
$a = 17$ $\quad a = -13$

24. $d = \sqrt{(x_2 - x_1)^2 + (y_2 - y_1)^2}$

$\sqrt{29} = \sqrt{[a - (-7)]^2 + (5 - 3)^2}$

$\sqrt{29} = \sqrt{(a + 7)^2 + 2^2}$

$\sqrt{29} = \sqrt{a^2 + 14a + 49 + 4}$

$\sqrt{29} = \sqrt{a^2 + 14a + 53}$

$(\sqrt{29})^2 = (\sqrt{a^2 + 14a + 53})^2$

$29 = a^2 + 14a + 53$

$0 = a^2 + 14a + 24$

$0 = (a + 2)(a + 12)$

$a + 2 = 0$ or $a + 12 = 0$

$a = -2$ $\quad$ $a = -12$

25. $d = \sqrt{(x_2 - x_1)^2 + (y_2 - y_1)^2}$

$\sqrt{130} = \sqrt{(-3 - 6)^2 + [a - (-3)]^2}$

$\sqrt{130} = \sqrt{(-9)^2 + (a + 3)^2}$

$\sqrt{130} = \sqrt{81 + a^2 + 6a + 9}$

$\sqrt{130} = \sqrt{a^2 + 6a + 90}$

$(\sqrt{130})^2 = (\sqrt{a^2 + 6a + 90})^2$

$130 = a^2 + 6a + 90$

$0 = a^2 + 6a - 40$

$0 = (a + 10)(a - 4)$

$a + 10 = 0$ or $a - 4 = 0$

$a = -10$ $\quad$ $a = 4$

26. $d = \sqrt{(x_2 - x_1)^2 + (y_2 - y_1)^2}$

$\sqrt{145} = \sqrt{(10 - 1)^2 + [a - (-6)]^2}$

$\sqrt{145} = \sqrt{9^2 + (a + 6)^2}$

$\sqrt{145} = \sqrt{81 + a^2 + 12a + 36}$

$\sqrt{145} = \sqrt{a^2 + 12a + 117}$

$(\sqrt{145})^2 = (\sqrt{a^2 + 12a + 117})^2$

$145 = a^2 + 12a + 117$

$0 = a^2 + 12a - 28$

$0 = (a - 2)(a + 14)$

$a - 2 = 0$ or $a + 14 = 0$

$a = 2$ $\quad$ $a = -14$

27. $d = \sqrt{(x_2 - x_1)^2 + (y_2 - y_1)^2}$

$\sqrt{340} = \sqrt{(a - 20)^2 + [9 - (-5)]^2}$

$\sqrt{340} = \sqrt{(a - 20)^2 + 14^2}$

$\sqrt{340} = \sqrt{a^2 - 40a + 400 + 196}$

$\sqrt{340} = \sqrt{a^2 - 40a + 596}$

$(\sqrt{340})^2 = (\sqrt{a^2 - 40a + 596})^2$

$340 = a^2 - 40a + 596$

$0 = a^2 - 40a + 256$

$0 = (a - 8)(a - 32)$

$a - 8 = 0$ or $a - 32 = 0$

$a = 8$ $\quad$ $a = 32$

28. $LM = \sqrt{(-1 - 7)^2 + [2 - (-4)]^2}$

$= \sqrt{(-8)^2 + 6^2}$

$= \sqrt{100}$ or 10

$MN = \sqrt{(-1 - 5)^2 + [2 - (-6)]^2}$

$= \sqrt{(-6)^2 + 8^2}$

$= \sqrt{100}$ or 10

$LN = \sqrt{(7 - 5)^2 + [-4 - (-6)]^2}$

$= \sqrt{2^2 + 2^2}$

$= \sqrt{8}$ or $2\sqrt{2}$

Yes; since $\overline{LM}$ and $\overline{MN}$ have the same length, 10, they are congruent. So ΔLMN is an isosceles triangle.

29. $TU = \sqrt{(1 - 3)^2 + (-8 - 5)^2}$

$= \sqrt{(-2)^2 + (-13)^2}$ or $\sqrt{173}$

$UV = \sqrt{(-1 - 3)^2 + (7 - 5)^2}$

$= \sqrt{(-4)^2 + 2^2}$ or $\sqrt{20}$

$TV = \sqrt{(-1 - 1)^2 + [7 - (-8)]^2}$

$= \sqrt{(-2)^2 + 15^2}$ or $\sqrt{229}$

No; since no two sides have the same length, ΔTUV is not isosceles.

30. $d = \sqrt{(x_2 - x_1)^2 + (y_2 - y_1)^2}$

$= \sqrt{(-3 - 6)^2 + (4 - 7)^2}$

$= \sqrt{(-9)^2 + (-3)^2}$

$= \sqrt{81 + 9}$

$= \sqrt{90}$

$= 3\sqrt{10}$

$P = 4(3\sqrt{10})$

$= 12\sqrt{10}$ or 37.9 units

31. $AC = \sqrt{(-2 - 9)^2 + (2 - 8)^2}$

$= \sqrt{(-11)^2 + (-6)^2}$ or $\sqrt{157}$

$BD = \sqrt{(10 - 0)^2 + (6 - 5)^2}$

$= \sqrt{(10)^2 + 1^2}$ or $\sqrt{101}$

$\sqrt{157} \neq \sqrt{101}$; Trapezoid is not isosceles.

32a. 10 **32b.** ≈ 16.55 **32c.** ≈ 13.88

33. The distance between (3, −2) and (−3, 7) is $3\sqrt{13}$ units. The distance between (−3, 7) and (−9, 3) is $2\sqrt{13}$ units. The distance between (3, −2) and (−9, 3) is 13 units. Since $(3\sqrt{13})^2 + (2\sqrt{13})^2 = 13^2$, the triangle is a right triangle.

34. (11, 4) (16, 16)

$d = \sqrt{(x_2 - x_1)^2 + (y_2 - y_1)^2}$

$= \sqrt{(16 - 11)^2 + (16 - 14)^2}$

$= \sqrt{5^2 + 2^2}$

$= \sqrt{25 + 4}$

$= \sqrt{29}$ or 5.4

3.3(5.4) = 18 in.

35. $d = \sqrt{(x_2 - x_1)^2 + (y_2 - y_1)^2}$
$= \sqrt{(254 - 132)^2 + (105 - 428)^2}$
$= \sqrt{122^2 + (-323)^2}$
$= \sqrt{14{,}884 + 104{,}329}$
$= \sqrt{119{,}213}$
≈ 345.27
$345.27(0.316) \approx 109$ miles

36. $4t = \sqrt{d}$
$(4t)^2 = (\sqrt{d})^2$
$16t^2 = d$
$16t^2 = 16(t - 1)^2 + 112$
$16t^2 = 16(t^2 - 2t + 1) + 112$
$16t^2 = 16t^2 - 32t + 128$
$32t = 128$
$t = 4$
It took her stone 4 seconds to hit the ground.

37. $\sqrt{\frac{8}{9}} = \frac{\sqrt{8}}{\sqrt{9}}$
$= \frac{\sqrt{2^2 \cdot 2}}{\sqrt{3^2}}$
$= \frac{\sqrt{2^2} \cdot \sqrt{2}}{3}$
$= \frac{2\sqrt{2}}{3}$

38. $\frac{4p^3}{p-1} \div \frac{p^2}{p-1} = \frac{4p^3}{p-1} \cdot \frac{p-1}{p^2}$
$= \frac{4p^3}{p-1} \cdot \frac{p-1}{p^2}$
$= 4p$

39. $4x - y = 2$
$y = 4x + 2$
$y - 4x = 4$
$y = 4x + 4$

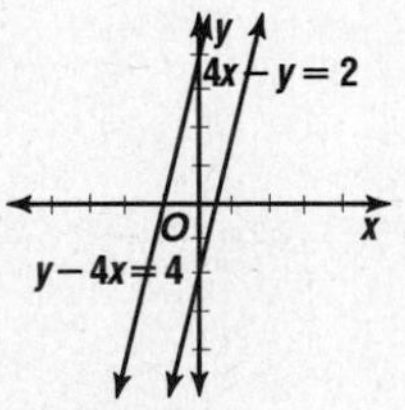

no solution

40. savings = 0.30(145)
= $43.50

41a. (22)(16)(20)(1.05) = 7392 BTU

41b. (13)(12)(25)(0.95) = 3705 BTU

41c. (17)(14)(25)(1.05) = 6247.5 BTU

41d. (26)(18)(30)(1.00) = 14,040 BTU

41e. (23.5)(15.3)(20)(0.95) = 6831.45 BTU

13-6A Modeling Mathematics: Completing the Square

Page 742

1.

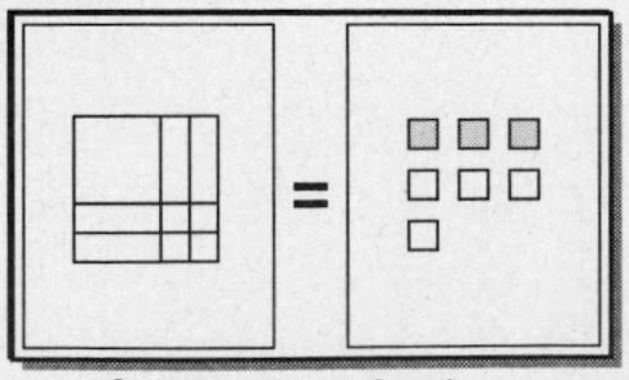

$x^2 + 4x + 4 = -3 + 4$
$(x + 2)^2 = 1$

2.

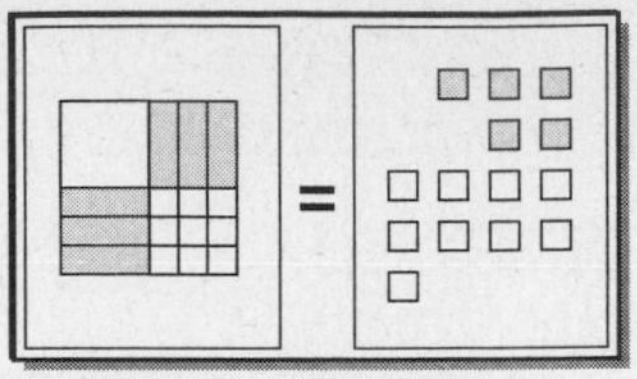

$x^2 - 6x + 9 = -5 + 9$
$(x - 3)^2 = 4$

3.

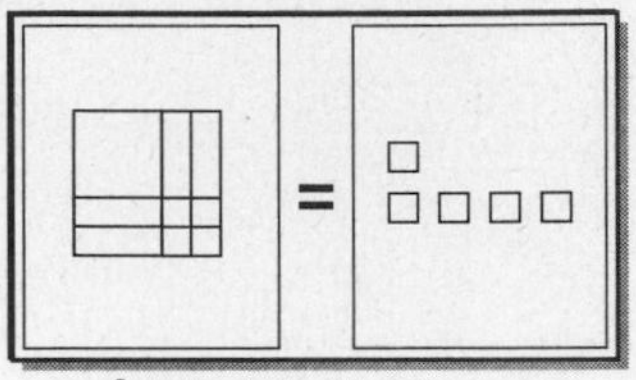

$x^2 + 4x + 4 = 1 + 4$
$(x + 2)^2 = 5$

4.

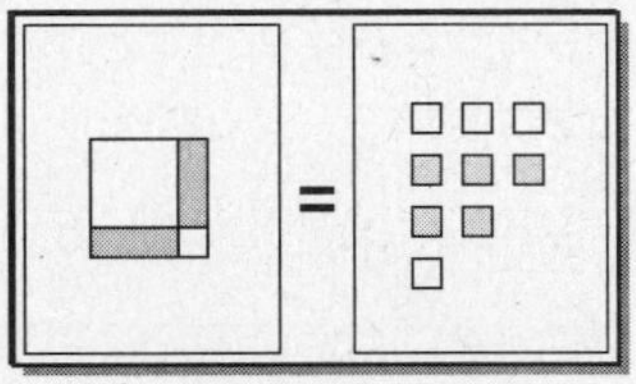

$x^2 - 2x + 1 = 3 - 5 + 1$
$(x - 1)^2 = -1$

5.

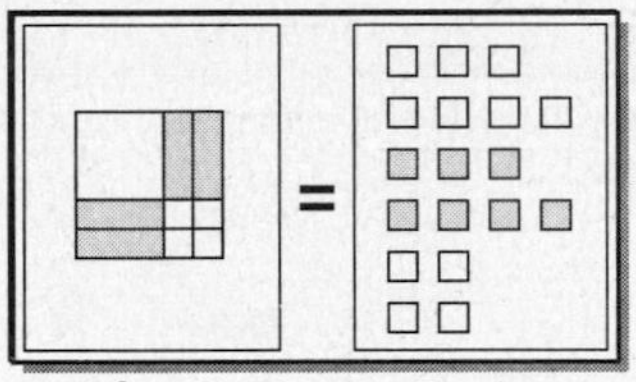

$x^2 - 4x + 4 = 8 - 7 + 4$
$(x - 2)^2 = 5$

6.

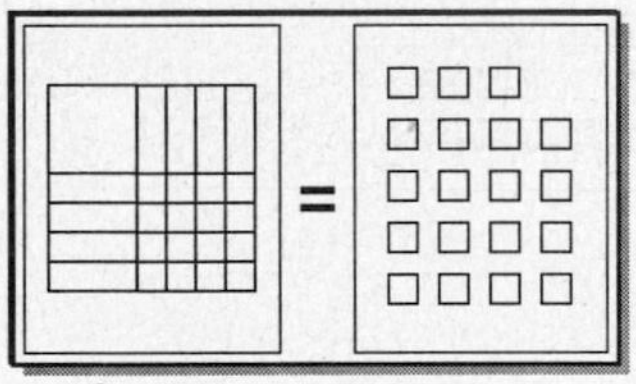

$x^2 + 8x + 16 = 3 + 16$
$(x + 4)^2 = 19$

7.

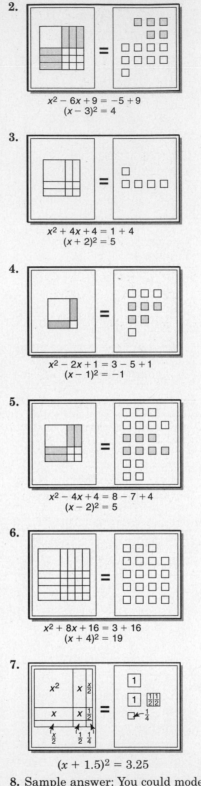

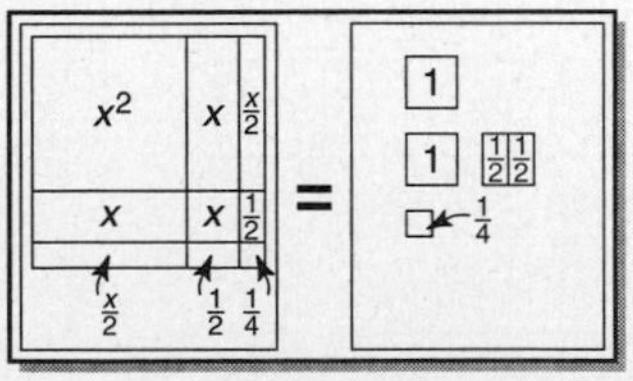

$(x + 1.5)^2 = 3.25$

8. Sample answer: You could model the expression on one side of the mat. Then add the appropriate 1-tiles needed to complete the square to each side of the mat.

13-6 Solving Quadratic Equations by Completing the Square

Pages 745–746 Check for Understanding

1. completing the square
2. Step 1: Find one-half of b.
   Step 2: Square the result of Step 1.
   Step 3: Add the result of Step 2 to $x^2 + bx$.
3. Sample answer: $x^2 + 4x + 12 = 0$, $(x + 2)^2 = -8$; Since the number on the right side is negative, there are no real roots.
4. 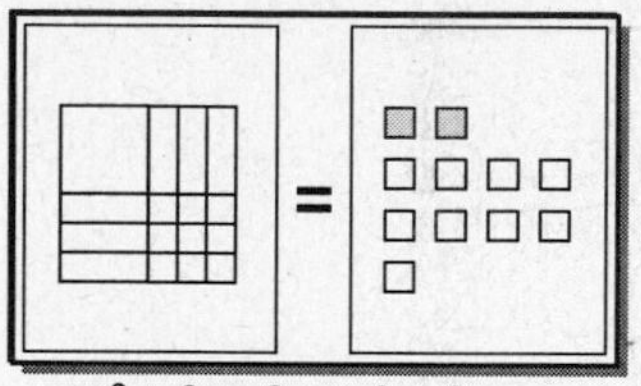

$x^2 + 6x + 9 = -2 + 9$
$(x + 3)^2 = 7$

5. Step 1: $\frac{16}{2} = 8$
   Step 2: $8^2 = 64$
   Step 3: $x^2 + 16x + 64$
   $c = 64$
6. Step 1: $\frac{-7}{2}$
   Step 2: $\left(-\frac{7}{2}\right)^2 = \frac{49}{4}$
   Step 3: $a^2 - 7a + \frac{49}{4}$
   $c = \frac{49}{4}$
7. $x^2 + 4x + 3 = 0$
   $x^2 + 4x = -3$
   $x^2 + 4x + 4 = -3 + 4$
   $(x + 2)^2 = 1$
   $x + 2 = \pm 1$
   $x = -2 \pm 1$
   $x = -2 + 1$ or $x = -2 - 1$
   $= -1$ $\quad = -3$
8. $d^2 - 8d + 7 = 0$
   $d^2 - 8d = -7$
   $d^2 - 8d + 16 = -7 + 16$
   $(d - 4)^2 = 9$
   $d - 4 = \pm 3$
   $d = 4 \pm 3$
   $d = 4 + 3$ or $d = 4 - 3$
   $= 7$ $\quad = 1$
9. $a^2 - 4a = 21$
   $a^2 - 4a + 4 = 21 + 4$
   $(a - 2)^2 = 25$
   $a - 2 = \pm 5$
   $a = 2 \pm 5$
   $a = 2 + 5$ or $a = 2 - 5$
   $= 7$ $\quad = -3$
10. $4x^2 - 20x + 25 = 0$
    $x^2 - 5x + \frac{25}{4} = 0$
    $x^2 - 5x = -\frac{25}{4}$
    $x^2 - 5x + \frac{25}{4} = -\frac{25}{4} + \frac{25}{4}$
    $\left(x - \frac{5}{2}\right)^2 = 0$
    $x - \frac{5}{2} = 0$
    $x = \frac{5}{2}$
11. $r^2 - 4r = 2$
    $r^2 - 4r + 4 = 2 + 4$
    $(r - 2)^2 = 6$
    $r - 2 = \pm\sqrt{6}$
    $r = 2 \pm \sqrt{6}$
12. $2t^2 + 3t - 20 = 0$
    $t^2 + \frac{3}{2}t - 10 = 0$
    $t^2 + \frac{3}{2}t = 10$
    $t^2 + \frac{3}{2}t + \frac{9}{16} = 10 + \frac{9}{16}$
    $\left(t + \frac{3}{4}\right)^2 = \frac{169}{16}$
    $t + \frac{3}{4} = \pm\frac{13}{4}$
    $t = -\frac{3}{4} \pm \frac{13}{4}$
    $t = -\frac{3}{4} + \frac{13}{4}$ or $t = -\frac{3}{4} - \frac{13}{4}$
    $= \frac{10}{4}$ $\quad = -4$
    $= \frac{5}{2}$
13. 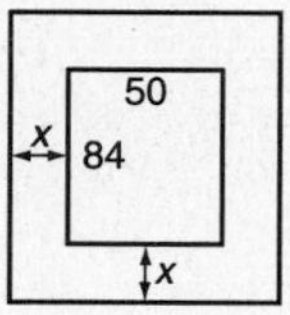

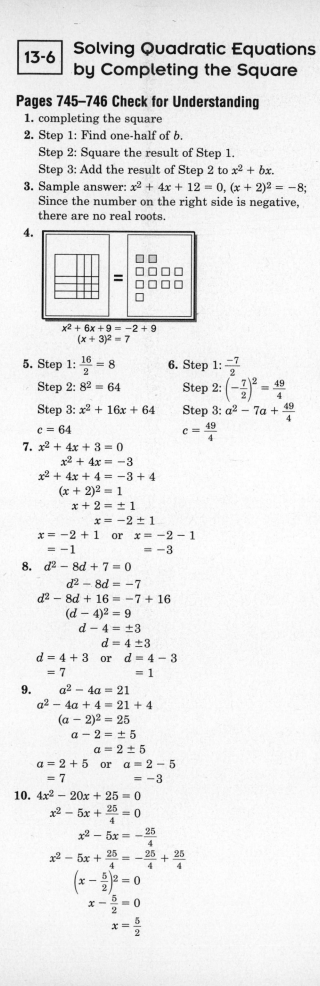

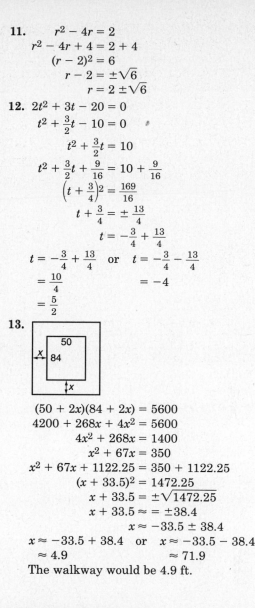

    $(50 + 2x)(84 + 2x) = 5600$
    $4200 + 268x + 4x^2 = 5600$
    $4x^2 + 268x = 1400$
    $x^2 + 67x = 350$
    $x^2 + 67x + 1122.25 = 350 + 1122.25$
    $(x + 33.5)^2 = 1472.25$
    $x + 33.5 = \pm\sqrt{1472.25}$
    $x + 33.5 \approx = \pm 38.4$
    $x \approx -33.5 \pm 38.4$
    $x \approx -33.5 + 38.4$ or $x \approx -33.5 - 38.4$
    ≈ 4.9 $\quad \approx 71.9$
    The walkway would be 4.9 ft.

Pages 746–747 Exercises

14. Step 1: $\frac{-6}{2} = -3$
    Step 2: $(-3)^2 = 9$
    Step 3: $x^2 - 6x + 9$
    $c = 9$
15. Step 1: $\frac{8}{2} = 4$
    Step 2: $4^2 = 16$
    Step 3: $b^2 + 8b + 16$
    $c = 16$
16. Step 1: $\frac{-5}{2}$
    Step 2: $\left(\frac{-5}{2}\right)^2 = \frac{25}{4}$
    Step 3: $m^2 - 5m + \frac{25}{4}$
    $c = \frac{25}{4}$
17. Step 1: $\frac{11}{2}$
    Step 2: $\left(\frac{11}{2}\right)^2 = \frac{121}{4}$
    Step 3: $a^2 + 11a + \frac{121}{4}$
    $c = \frac{121}{4}$
18. Step 1: $\frac{-2}{2} = -1$
    Step 2: $(-1)^2 = 1$
    Step 3: $9t^2 - 18t + 9$
    $c = 9$
19. Step 1: $\frac{-8}{2} = -4$
    Step 2: $(-4)^2 = 16$
    Step 3: $\frac{1}{2}x^2 - 4x + 8$
    $c = 8$

20. $x^2 + 7x + 10 = -2$

$x^2 + 7x = -12$

$x^2 + 7x + \frac{49}{4} = -12 + \frac{49}{4}$

$\left(x + \frac{7}{2}\right)^2 = \frac{1}{4}$

$x + \frac{7}{2} = \pm\sqrt{\frac{1}{4}}$

$x = -\frac{7}{2} \pm \frac{1}{2}$

$x = -\frac{7}{2} + \frac{1}{2}$ or $x = -\frac{7}{2} - \frac{1}{2}$

$x = -3$ $\quad$ $x = -4$

21. $a^2 - 5a + 2 = -2$

$a^2 - 5a = -4$

$a^2 - 5a + \frac{25}{4} = -4 + \frac{25}{4}$

$\left(a - \frac{5}{2}\right)^2 = \frac{9}{4}$

$a - \frac{5}{2} = \pm\sqrt{\frac{9}{4}}$

$a = \frac{5}{2} \pm \frac{3}{2}$

$a = \frac{5}{2} + \frac{3}{2}$ or $a = \frac{5}{2} - \frac{3}{2}$

$a = 4$ $\quad$ $a = 1$

22. $r^2 + 14r - 9 = 6$

$r^2 + 14r = 15$

$r^2 + 14r + 49 = 15 + 49$

$(r + 7)^2 = 64$

$r + 7 = \pm\sqrt{64}$

$r = -7 \pm 8$

$r = -7 + 8$ or $r = -7 - 8$

$r = 1$ $\quad$ $r = -15$

23. $9b^2 - 42b + 49 = 0$

$b^2 - \frac{14}{3}b + \frac{49}{9} = 0$

$b^2 - \frac{14}{3}b = -\frac{49}{9}$

$b^2 - \frac{14}{3}b + \frac{49}{9} = -\frac{49}{9} + \frac{49}{9}$

$\left(b - \frac{7}{3}\right)^2 = 0$

$b - \frac{7}{3} = 0$

$b = \frac{7}{3}$

24. $x^2 - 24x + 9 = 0$

$x^2 - 24x = -9$

$x^2 - 24x + 144 = -9 + 144$

$(x - 12)^2 = 135$

$x - 12 = \pm\sqrt{135}$

$x = 12 \pm 3\sqrt{15}$

25. $t^2 + 4 = 6t$

$t^2 - 6t = -4$

$t^2 - 6t + 9 = -4 + 9$

$(t - 3)^2 = 5$

$t - 3 = \pm\sqrt{5}$

$t = 3 \pm \sqrt{5}$

26. $m^2 - 8m = 4$

$m^2 - 8m + 16 = 4 + 16$

$(m - 4)^2 = 20$

$m - 4 = \pm\sqrt{20}$

$m = 4 \pm 2\sqrt{5}$

27. $p^2 - 10p = 23$

$p^2 - 10p + 25 = 23 + 25$

$(p - 5)^2 = 48$

$p - 5 = \pm\sqrt{48}$

$p = 5 \pm 4\sqrt{3}$

28. $x^2 - \frac{7}{2}x + \frac{3}{2} = 0$

$x^2 - \frac{7}{2}x = -\frac{3}{2}$

$x^2 - \frac{7}{2}x + \frac{49}{16} = -\frac{3}{2} + \frac{49}{16}$

$(x - \frac{7}{4})^2 = \frac{25}{16}$

$x - \frac{7}{4} = \pm\sqrt{\frac{25}{16}}$

$x = \frac{7}{4} \pm \frac{5}{4}$

$x = \frac{7}{4} + \frac{5}{4}$ or $x = \frac{7}{4} - \frac{5}{4}$

$x = 3$ $\quad$ $x = \frac{1}{2}$

29. $5x^2 + 10x - 7 = 0$

$5x^2 + 10x = 7$

$x^2 + 2x = \frac{7}{5}$

$x^2 + 2x + 1 = \frac{7}{5} + 1$

$(x + 1)^2 = \frac{12}{5}$

$x + 1 = \pm\sqrt{\frac{12}{5}}$

$x = -1 \pm \frac{2\sqrt{15}}{5}$

$x = \frac{-5 \pm 2\sqrt{15}}{5}$

30. $\frac{1}{2}d^2 - \frac{5}{4}d - 3 = 0$

$d^2 - \frac{5}{2}d - 6 = 0$

$d^2 - \frac{5}{2}d = 6$

$d^2 - \frac{5}{2}d + \frac{25}{16} = 6 + \frac{25}{16}$

$\left(d - \frac{5}{4}\right)^2 = \frac{121}{16}$

$d - \frac{5}{4} = \pm\sqrt{\frac{121}{16}}$

$d = \frac{5}{4} \pm \frac{11}{4}$

$d = \frac{5}{4} + \frac{11}{4}$ or $d = \frac{5}{4} - \frac{11}{4}$

$d = 4$ $\quad$ $d = -\frac{3}{2}$

31. $0.3t^2 + 0.1t = 0.2$

$t^2 + \frac{1}{3}t = \frac{2}{3}$

$t^2 + \frac{1}{3}t + \frac{1}{36} = \frac{2}{3} + \frac{1}{36}$

$\left(t + \frac{1}{6}\right)^2 = \frac{25}{36}$

$t + \frac{1}{6} = \pm\sqrt{\frac{25}{36}}$

$t = -\frac{1}{6} \pm \frac{5}{6}$

$t = -\frac{1}{6} + \frac{5}{6}$ or $t = -\frac{1}{6} - \frac{5}{6}$

$t = \frac{2}{3}$ $\quad$ $t = -1$

32. $b^2 + 0.25b = 0.5$

$b^2 + 0.25b + 0.015625 = 0.5 + 0.015625$

$(b + 0.125)^2 = 0.515625$

$b + 0.125 = \pm\sqrt{0.515625}$

$b = -0.125 \pm\sqrt{0.515625}$

33. $3p^2 - 7p - 3 = 0$

$p^2 - \frac{7}{3}p - 1 = 0$

$p^2 - \frac{7}{3}p = 1$

$p^2 - \frac{7}{3}p + \frac{49}{36} = 1 + \frac{49}{36}$

$\left(p - \frac{7}{6}\right)^2 = \frac{85}{36}$

$p - \frac{7}{6} = \pm\sqrt{\frac{85}{36}}$

$p = \frac{7}{6} \pm \frac{\sqrt{85}}{6}$

$p = \frac{7 \pm \sqrt{85}}{6}$

34. $2r^2 - 5r + 8 = 7$

$2r^2 - 5r = -1$

$r^2 - \frac{5}{2}r = -\frac{1}{2}$

$r^2 - \frac{5}{2}r + \frac{25}{16} = -\frac{1}{2} + \frac{25}{16}$

$\left(r - \frac{5}{4}\right)^2 = \frac{17}{16}$

$r - \frac{5}{4} = \pm\sqrt{\frac{17}{16}}$

$r = \frac{5}{4} \pm \frac{\sqrt{17}}{4}$

$r = \frac{5 \pm \sqrt{17}}{4}$

35. $(x + 9)^2 = x^2 + 18x + 81$

$(x - 9)^2 = x^2 - 18x + 81$

18, −18

36. $(2x + 15)^2 = 4x^2 + 60x + 225$

$(2x - 15)^2 = 4x^2 - 60x + 225$

60, −60

37. $3\left(\frac{c}{3}x^2 + 10x + 25\right)$

$\frac{c}{3} = 1$

$c = 3$

38. $\frac{4}{9}\left(\frac{c}{\frac{9}{4}}x^2 - 8x + 16\right)$

$\frac{c}{\frac{9}{4}} = 1$

$c = \frac{9}{4}$

39. $x^2 - 4x + c = 0$

$x^2 - 4x = -c$

$x^2 - 4x + 4 = 4 - c$

$(x - 2)^2 = 4 - c$

$x - 2 = \pm\sqrt{4 - c}$

$x = 2 \pm \sqrt{4 - c}$

40. $x^2 + bx + c = 0$

$x^2 + bx = -c$

$x^2 + bx + \frac{b^2}{4} = \frac{b^2}{4} - c$

$\left(x + \frac{b}{2}\right)^2 = \frac{b^2 - 4c}{4}$

$x + \frac{b}{2} = \pm\sqrt{\frac{b^2 - 4c}{4}}$

$x = \frac{-b \pm \sqrt{b^2 - 4c}}{2}$

41. $x^2 + 4bx + b^2 = 0$

$x^2 + 4bx = -b^2$

$x^2 + 4bx + 4b^2 = -b^2 + 4b^2$

$(x + 2b)^2 = 3b^2$

$x + 2b = \pm\sqrt{3b^2}$

$x = -2b \pm b\sqrt{3}$

$x = b(-2 \pm \sqrt{3})$

42a. $y = x^2 - 8x + 15$

$y = x^2 - 8x + 16 - 1$

$y = (x - 4)^2 - 1$

42b.

x	y
1	8
2	3
3	0
4	−1
5	0
6	3

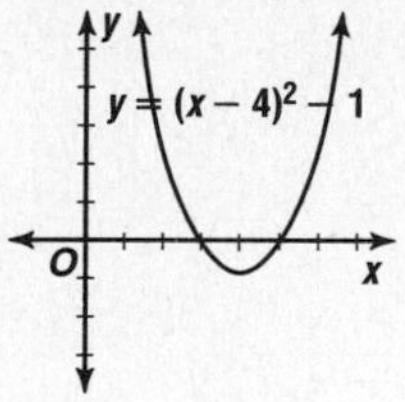

42c. It is the vertex of the graph.

43. Let r = the speed of the first train. Then $r + 10$ = the speed of the second train

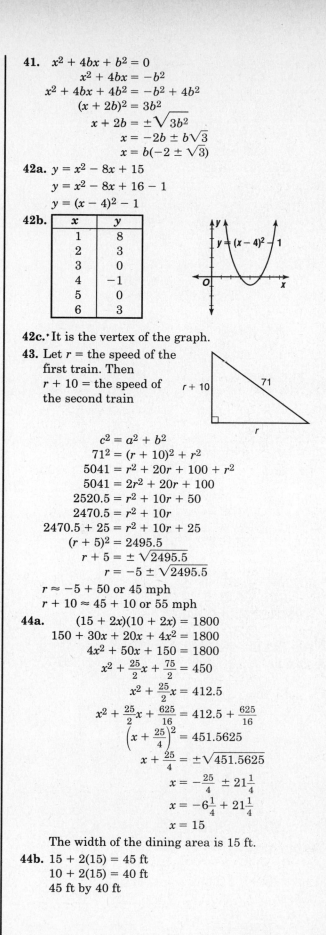

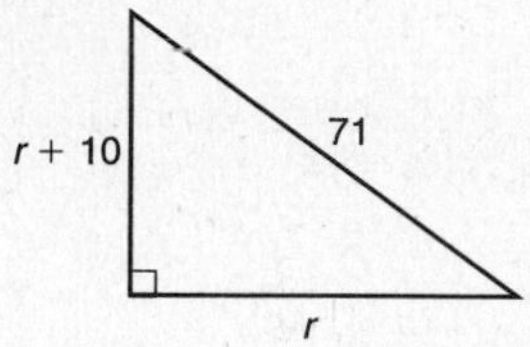

$c^2 = a^2 + b^2$

$71^2 = (r + 10)^2 + r^2$

$5041 = r^2 + 20r + 100 + r^2$

$5041 = 2r^2 + 20r + 100$

$2520.5 = r^2 + 10r + 50$

$2470.5 = r^2 + 10r$

$2470.5 + 25 = r^2 + 10r + 25$

$(r + 5)^2 = 2495.5$

$r + 5 = \pm\sqrt{2495.5}$

$r = -5 \pm \sqrt{2495.5}$

$r \approx -5 + 50$ or 45 mph

$r + 10 \approx 45 + 10$ or 55 mph

44a. $(15 + 2x)(10 + 2x) = 1800$

$150 + 30x + 20x + 4x^2 = 1800$

$4x^2 + 50x + 150 = 1800$

$x^2 + \frac{25}{2}x + \frac{75}{2} = 450$

$x^2 + \frac{25}{2}x = 412.5$

$x^2 + \frac{25}{2}x + \frac{625}{16} = 412.5 + \frac{625}{16}$

$\left(x + \frac{25}{4}\right)^2 = 451.5625$

$x + \frac{25}{4} = \pm\sqrt{451.5625}$

$x = -\frac{25}{4} \pm 21\frac{1}{4}$

$x = -6\frac{1}{4} + 21\frac{1}{4}$

$x = 15$

The width of the dining area is 15 ft.

44b. $15 + 2(15) = 45$ ft

$10 + 2(15) = 40$ ft

45 ft by 40 ft

45. $A(3, 6), B(-4, 2)$

$$d = \sqrt{(x_2 - x_1)^2 + (y_2 - y_1)^2}$$
$$\overline{AB} = \sqrt{(-4 - 3)^2 + (2 - 6)^2}$$
$$= \sqrt{(-7)^2 + (-4)^2}$$
$$= \sqrt{49 + 16}$$
$$= \sqrt{65} \approx 8.06$$

46. $c^2 = a^2 + b^2$
$9^2 \stackrel{?}{=} 5^2 + 7^2$
$81 \stackrel{?}{=} 25 + 49$
$81 \neq 74$
no

47. $12 = 2^2 \cdot 3$
$30 = 2 \cdot 3 \cdot 5$
LCM: $2^2 \cdot 3 \cdot 5 = 60$
$1982 + 60 = 2042$

48. $(5y - 3)(y + 2) = 5y(y) + 5y(2) + (-3)(y) + (-3)(2)$
$= 5y^2 + 10y - 3y - 6$
$= 5y^2 + 7y - 6$

49. $5y - 4x = 2$
$2y + x = 6 \quad \rightarrow$

$5y - 4x = 2$
$(+)\ 8y + 4x = 24$
$3y = 26$
$y = 2$

$2y + x = 6$
$2(2) + x = 6$
$4 + x = 6$
$x = 2$
$(2, 2)$

50a. IV **50b.** II **50c.** III

51a. mean $= \frac{180 + 220 + 230 + 270 + 223}{5} = \frac{1123}{5} = 224.6$

51b. mean $= \frac{140 + 180 + 160 + 200 + 180}{5} = \frac{860}{5} = 172$

52. $|a| + |4b| = |-3| + |4(-6)|$
$= 3 + |-24|$
$= 3 + 24$
$= 27$

Chapter 13 Highlights

Page 749 Understanding and Using the Vocabulary

1. false, $-3 - \sqrt{7}$ **2.** true
3. false, $-2 - 2\sqrt{3} - \sqrt{5} - \sqrt{15}$
4. false, $\frac{9}{4}$ **5.** true **6.** true
7. false, $3x + 19 = x^2 + 6x + 9$
8. true **9.** false, $\frac{x\sqrt{2xy}}{y}$
10. false, $25^2 = 15^2 + 20^2$

Chapter 13 Study Guide and Assessment

Pages 750–752 Skills and Concepts

11. $c^2 = a^2 + b^2$
$c^2 = 30^2 + 16^2$
$c^2 = 900 + 256$
$c^2 = 1156$
$c = 34$

12. $c^2 = a^2 + b^2$
$c^2 = 6^2 + 10^2$
$c^2 = 36 + 100$
$c^2 = 136$
$c = \sqrt{136}$
$c = 2\sqrt{34} \approx 11.66$

13. $c^2 = a^2 + b^2$
$15^2 = 10^2 + b^2$
$225 = 100 + b^2$
$125 = b^2$
$\sqrt{125} = b$
$b = 5\sqrt{5} \approx 11.18$

14. $c^2 = a^2 + b^2$
$56^2 = a^2 + 4^2$
$3136 = a^2 + 16$
$3120 = a^2$
$\sqrt{3120} = a$
$a = 4\sqrt{195} \approx 55.86$

15. $c^2 = a^2 + b^2$
$30^2 = 18^2 + b^2$
$900 = 324 + b^2$
$576 = b^2$
$24 = b$

16. $c^2 = a^2 + b^2$
$c^2 = 1.2^2 + 1.6^2$
$c^2 = 1.44 + 2.56$
$c^2 = 4$
$c = 2$

17. $c^2 = a^2 + b^2$
$20^2 \stackrel{?}{=} 9^2 + 16^2$
$400 \stackrel{?}{=} 81 + 256$
$400 \neq 337$
no; $9^2 + 16^2 \neq 20^2$

18. $c^2 = a^2 + b^2$
$29^2 \stackrel{?}{=} 20^2 + 21^2$
$841 \stackrel{?}{=} 400 + 441$
$841 = 841$
yes

19. $c^2 = a^2 + b^2$
$41^2 \stackrel{?}{=} 9^2 + 40^2$
$1681 \stackrel{?}{=} 81 + 1600$
$1681 = 1681$
yes

20. $c^2 = a^2 + b^2$
$30^2 \stackrel{?}{=} (\sqrt{24})^2 + 18^2$
$900 \stackrel{?}{=} 24 + 324$
$900 \neq 348$
no; $18^2 + (\sqrt{24})^2 \neq 30^2$

21. $\sqrt{480} = \sqrt{4^2 \cdot 2 \cdot 3 \cdot 5}$
$= \sqrt{4^2} \cdot \sqrt{2 \cdot 3 \cdot 5}$
$= 4\sqrt{30}$

22. $\sqrt{\frac{60}{y^2}} = \frac{\sqrt{60}}{\sqrt{y^2}}$
$= \frac{\sqrt{2^2 \cdot 3 \cdot 5}}{|y|}$
$= \frac{2\sqrt{15}}{|y|}$

23. $\sqrt{44a^2b^5} = \sqrt{2^2 \cdot 11 \cdot a^2 \cdot b^4 \cdot b}$
$= \sqrt{2^2} \cdot \sqrt{11} \cdot \sqrt{a^2} \cdot \sqrt{b^4} \cdot \sqrt{b}$
$= 2|a|b^2\sqrt{11b}$

24. $\sqrt{96x^4} = \sqrt{4^2 \cdot 6 \cdot x^4}$
$= \sqrt{4^2} \cdot \sqrt{6} \cdot \sqrt{x^4}$
$= 4x^2\sqrt{6}$

25. $(3 - 2\sqrt{12})^2 = (3)^2 - 2(3)(2\sqrt{12}) + (2\sqrt{12})^2$
$= 9 - 12\sqrt{12} + 48$
$= 57 - 12(2\sqrt{3})$
$= 57 - 24\sqrt{3}$

26. $\frac{9}{3 + \sqrt{2}} = \frac{9}{3 + \sqrt{2}} \cdot \frac{3 - \sqrt{2}}{3 - \sqrt{2}}$
$= \frac{9(3) - 9\sqrt{2}}{3^2 - (\sqrt{2})^2}$
$= \frac{27 - 9\sqrt{2}}{9 - 2}$
$= \frac{27 - 9\sqrt{2}}{7}$

27. $\frac{2\sqrt{7}}{3\sqrt{5} + 5\sqrt{3}} = \frac{2\sqrt{7}}{3\sqrt{5} + 5\sqrt{3}} \cdot \frac{3\sqrt{5} - 5\sqrt{3}}{3\sqrt{5} - 5\sqrt{3}}$
$= \frac{6\sqrt{35} - 10\sqrt{21}}{(3\sqrt{5})^2 - (5\sqrt{3})^2}$
$= \frac{6\sqrt{35} - 10\sqrt{21}}{9\sqrt{25} - 25\sqrt{9}}$
$= \frac{2(3\sqrt{35} - 5\sqrt{21})}{45 - 75}$
$= \frac{2(3\sqrt{35} - 5\sqrt{21})}{-30}$
$= \frac{3\sqrt{35} - 5\sqrt{21}}{-15}$

28. $\frac{\sqrt{3a^3b^4}}{\sqrt{8ab^{10}}} = \frac{\sqrt{3}}{\sqrt{8}} \cdot \sqrt{\frac{a^3}{a} \cdot \frac{b^4}{b^{10}}}$

$= \frac{\sqrt{3}}{2\sqrt{2}} \cdot \frac{\sqrt{a^2}}{\sqrt{b^6}}$

$= \frac{|a|\sqrt{3}}{2|b^3|\sqrt{2}} \cdot \frac{\sqrt{2}}{\sqrt{2}}$

$= \frac{|a|\sqrt{6}}{4|b^3|}$

29. $2\sqrt{6} - \sqrt{48} = 2\sqrt{6} - \sqrt{4^2 \cdot 3}$

$= 2\sqrt{6} - (\sqrt{4^2 \cdot 3})$

$= 2\sqrt{6} - 4\sqrt{3}$

30. $2\sqrt{13} + 8\sqrt{15} - 3\sqrt{15} + 3\sqrt{13}$

$= (2 + 3)\sqrt{13} + (8 - 3)\sqrt{15})$

$= 5\sqrt{13} + 5\sqrt{15}$

31. $4\sqrt{27} + 6\sqrt{48} = 4\sqrt{3 \cdot 3^2} + 6\sqrt{4^2 \cdot 3}$

$= 4(\sqrt{3^2 \cdot 3}) + 6(\sqrt{4^2} \cdot \sqrt{3})$

$= 4(3\sqrt{3}) + 6(4\sqrt{3})$

$= 12\sqrt{3} + 24\sqrt{3}$

$= (12 + 24)\sqrt{3}$

$= 36\sqrt{3}$

32. $5\sqrt{18} - 3\sqrt{112} - 3\sqrt{98}$

$= 5\sqrt{3^2 \cdot 2} - 3\sqrt{4^2 \cdot 7} - 3\sqrt{7^2 \cdot 2}$

$= 5(\sqrt{3^2} \cdot \sqrt{2}) - 3(\sqrt{4^2} \cdot \sqrt{7}) - 3(\sqrt{7^2} \cdot \sqrt{2})$

$= 5(3\sqrt{2}) - 3(4\sqrt{7}) - 3(7\sqrt{2})$

$= 15\sqrt{2} - 12\sqrt{7} - 21\sqrt{2}$

$= -6\sqrt{2} - 12\sqrt{7}$

33. $\sqrt{8} + \sqrt{\frac{1}{8}} = \sqrt{2^2 \cdot 2} + \frac{\sqrt{1}}{\sqrt{2^2 \cdot 2}}$

$= 2\sqrt{2} + \frac{1}{2\sqrt{2}}$

$= 2\sqrt{2} + \frac{1}{2\sqrt{2}} \cdot \frac{\sqrt{2}}{\sqrt{2}}$

$= 2\sqrt{2} + \frac{\sqrt{2}}{4}$

$= \frac{8\sqrt{2}}{4} + \frac{\sqrt{2}}{4}$

$= \frac{9\sqrt{2}}{4}$

34. $4\sqrt{7k} - 7\sqrt{7k} + 2\sqrt{7k} = (4 - 7 + 2)\sqrt{7k}$

$= -\sqrt{7k}$

35. $\sqrt{3x} = 6$

$(\sqrt{3x})^2 = 6^2$

$3x = 36$

$x = 12$

36. $\sqrt{t} = 2\sqrt{6}$

$(\sqrt{t})^2 = (2\sqrt{6})^2$

$t = 24$

37. $\sqrt{7x - 1} = 5$

$(\sqrt{7x - 1})^2 = 5^2$

$7x - 1 = 25$

$7x = 26$

$x = \frac{26}{7}$

38. $\sqrt{x + 4} = x - 8$

$(\sqrt{x + 4})^2 = (x - 8)^2$

$x + 4 = x^2 - 16x + 64$

$0 = x^2 - 17x + 60$

$0 = (x - 12)(x - 5)$

$x - 12 = 0$ or $x - 5 = 0$

$x = 12$ $\quad$ $x = 5$

Since 5 does not satisfy the original equation, 12 is the only solution.

39. $\sqrt{r} = 3\sqrt{5}$

$(\sqrt{r})^2 = (3\sqrt{5})^2$

$r = 45$

40. $\sqrt{3x - 14} + x = 6$

$\sqrt{3x - 14} = 6 - x$

$(\sqrt{3x - 14})^2 = (6 - x)^2$

$3x - 14 = 36 - 12x + x^2$

$0 = x^2 - 15x + 50$

$0 = (x - 5)(x - 10)$

$x - 5 = 0$ or $x - 10 = 0$

$x = 5$ $\quad$ $x = 10$

Since 10 does not satisfy the original equation, 5 is the only solution.

41. $\sqrt{\frac{4a}{3}} - 2 = 0$

$\sqrt{\frac{4a}{3}} = 2$

$\left(\sqrt{\frac{4a}{3}}\right)^2 = 2^2$

$\frac{4a}{3} = 4$

$4a = 12$

$a = 3$

42. $9 = \sqrt{\frac{5n}{4}} - 1$

$10 = \sqrt{\frac{5n}{4}}$

$10^2 = \left(\sqrt{\frac{5n}{4}}\right)^2$

$100 = \frac{5n}{4}$

$400 = 5n$

$80 = n$

43. $10 + 2\sqrt{b} = 0$

$2\sqrt{b} = -10$

$\sqrt{b} = -5$

no solution

44. $\sqrt{a + 4} = 6$

$(\sqrt{a + 4})^2 = 6^2$

$a + 4 = 36$

$a = 32$

45. $d = \sqrt{(x_2 - x_1)^2 + (y_2 - y_1)^2}$

$= \sqrt{(9 - 1)^2 + (-2 - 13)^2}$

$= \sqrt{8^2 + (-15)^2}$

$= \sqrt{64 + 225}$ or $\sqrt{289} = 17$

46. $d = \sqrt{(x_2 - x_1)^2 + (y_2 - y_1)^2}$

$= \sqrt{(7 - 4)^2 + (-9 - 2)^2}$

$= \sqrt{3^2 + (-11)^2}$

$= \sqrt{9 + 121}$ or $\sqrt{130} \approx 11.40$

47. $d = \sqrt{(x_2 - x_1)^2 + (y_2 - y_1)^2}$

$= \sqrt{[4 - (-2)]^2 + (-6 - 7)^2}$

$= \sqrt{6^2 + (-13)^2}$

$= \sqrt{36 + 169}$ or $\sqrt{205} \approx 14.32$

48. $d = \sqrt{(x_2 - x_1)^2 + (y_2 - y_1)^2}$

$= \sqrt{(2\sqrt{5} - 4\sqrt{5})^2 + (9 - 3)^2}$

$= \sqrt{(-2\sqrt{5})^2 + 6^2}$

$= \sqrt{20 + 36}$

$= \sqrt{56}$ or $2\sqrt{14} \approx 7.48$

49. $d = \sqrt{(x_2 - x_1)^2 + (y_2 - y_1)^2}$

$5 = \sqrt{(-3 - 1)^2 + (2 - a)^2}$

$5 = \sqrt{(-4)^2 + a^2 - 4a + 4}$

$5 = \sqrt{16 + a^2 - 4a + 4}$

$5 = \sqrt{a^2 - 4a + 20}$

$5^2 = (\sqrt{a^2 - 4a + 20})^2$

$25 = a^2 - 4a + 20$

$0 = a^2 - 4a - 5$

$0 = (a - 5)(a + 1)$

$a - 5 = 0$ or $a + 1 = 0$

$a = 5$ $\quad$ $a = -1$

50. $d = \sqrt{(x_2 - x_1)^2 + (y_2 - y_1)^2}$

$\sqrt{170} = \sqrt{(a - 5)^2 + [-3 - (-2)]^2}$

$\sqrt{170} = \sqrt{a^2 - 10a + 25 + (-1)^2}$

$\sqrt{170} = \sqrt{a^2 - 10a + 26}$

$(\sqrt{170})^2 = (\sqrt{a^2 - 10a + 26})^2$

$170 = a^2 - 10a + 26$

$0 = a^2 - 10a - 144$

$0 = (a - 18)(a + 8)$

$a - 18 = 0$ or $a + 8 = 0$

$a = 18$ $\quad a = -8$

51. $d = \sqrt{(x_2 - x_1)^2 + (y_2 - y_1)^2}$

$5 = \sqrt{(4 - 1)^2 + (a - 1)^2}$

$5 = \sqrt{3^2 + a^2 - 2a + 1}$

$5 = \sqrt{a^2 - 2a + 10}$

$5^2 = (\sqrt{a^2 - 2a + 10})^2$

$25 = a^2 - 2a + 10$

$0 = a^2 - 2a - 15$

$0 = (a - 5)(a + 3)$

$a - 5 = 0$ or $a + 3 = 0$

$a = 5$ $\quad a = -3$

52. Step 1: $\frac{-12}{2} = -6$

Step 2: $(-6)^2 = 36$

Step 3: $y^2 - 12y + 36$

$c = 36$

53. Step 1: $\frac{7}{2}$

Step 2: $\left(\frac{7}{2}\right)^2 = \frac{49}{4}$

Step 3: $m^2 + 7m + \frac{49}{4}$

$c = \frac{49}{4}$

54. Step 1: $\frac{18}{2} = 9$

Step 2: $(9)^2 = 81$

Step 3: $b^2 - 18b + 81$

$c = 81$

55. Step 1: $\frac{1}{2}\left(-\frac{2}{3}\right) = -\frac{1}{3}$

Step 2: $\left(-\frac{1}{3}\right)^2 = \frac{1}{9}$

Step 3: $p^2 - \frac{2}{3}p + \frac{1}{9}$

$c = \frac{1}{9}$

56. $x^2 - 16x + 32 = 0$

$x^2 - 16x = -32$

$x^2 - 16x + 64 = -32 + 64$

$(x - 8)^2 = 32$

$x - 8 = \pm\sqrt{32}$

$x = 8 \pm 4\sqrt{2}$

57. $m^2 - 7m = 5$

$m^2 - 7m + \frac{49}{4} = 5 + \frac{49}{4}$

$\left(m - \frac{7}{2}\right)^2 = \frac{69}{4}$

$m - \frac{7}{2} = \pm\sqrt{\frac{69}{4}}$

$m = \frac{7}{2} \pm \frac{\sqrt{69}}{2}$

$m = \frac{7 \pm \sqrt{69}}{2}$

58. $4a^2 + 16a + 15 = 0$

$a^2 + 4a + \frac{15}{4} = 0$

$a^2 + 4a = -\frac{15}{4}$

$a^2 + 4a + 4 = -\frac{15}{4} + 4$

$(a + 2)^2 = \frac{1}{4}$

$a + 2 = \pm\sqrt{\frac{1}{4}}$

$a = -2 \pm \frac{1}{2}$

$a = -2 + \frac{1}{2}$ or $a = -2 - \frac{1}{2}$

$a = -\frac{3}{2}$ $\quad a = -\frac{5}{2}$

59. $\frac{1}{2}y^2 + 2y - 1 = 0$

$y^2 + 4y - 2 = 0$

$y^2 + 4y = 2$

$y^2 + 4y + 4 = 2 + 4$

$(y + 2)^2 = 6$

$y + 2 = \pm\sqrt{6}$

$y = -2 \pm \sqrt{6}$

60. $n^2 - 3n + \frac{5}{4} = 0$

$n^2 - 3n = -\frac{5}{4}$

$n^2 - 3n + \frac{9}{4} = -\frac{5}{4} + \frac{9}{4}$

$\left(n - \frac{3}{2}\right)^2 = 1$

$n - \frac{3}{2} = \pm\sqrt{1}$

$n = \frac{3}{2} \pm 1$

$n = \frac{3}{2} + 1$ or $n = \frac{3}{2} - 1$

$n = \frac{5}{2}$ $\quad n = \frac{1}{2}$

Page 752 Applications and Problem Solving

61. $P = 4\sqrt{24} + 5\sqrt{6} + 3\sqrt{54}$

$= 4\sqrt{2^2 \cdot 6} + 5\sqrt{6} + 3\sqrt{3^2 \cdot 6}$

$= 4(2\sqrt{6}) + 5\sqrt{6} + 3(3\sqrt{6})$

$= 8\sqrt{6} + 5\sqrt{6} + 9\sqrt{6}$

$= 22\sqrt{6} \approx 53.9$ cm

62a. $V = 3.5\sqrt{h}$

$V = 3.5\sqrt{9}$

$V = 3.5(3)$

$V = 10.5$ km

62b. $V = 3.5\sqrt{h}$

$56 = 3.5\sqrt{h}$

$16 = \sqrt{h}$

$16^2 = (\sqrt{h})^2$

$h = 256$ m

63. $d = \sqrt{(x_2 - x_1)^2 + (y_2 - y_1)^2}$

$d = \sqrt{(-3 - 4)^2 + (1 - 2)^2}$
$= \sqrt{(-7)^2 + (-1)^2}$
$= \sqrt{49 + 1}$
$= \sqrt{50}$

$d = \sqrt{(-3 - 5)^2 + [1 - (-4)]^2}$
$= \sqrt{(-8)^2 + 5^2}$
$= \sqrt{64 + 25}$
$= \sqrt{89}$

$d = \sqrt{(5 - 4)^2 + (-4 - 2)^2}$
$= \sqrt{1^2 + (-6)^2}$
$= \sqrt{1 + 36}$
$= \sqrt{37}$

Scalene triangle

64. Let n = the number.
$10n - 6 = 4n^2$
$0 - 4n^2 - 10n + 6$
$0 = 2n^2 - 5n + 3$
$0 = (2n - 3)(n - 1)$
$2n - 3 = 0$ or $n - 1 = 0$
$n = 1.5$ $\quad n = 1$

The numbers are 1 and 1.5.

65.

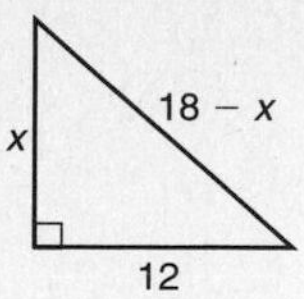

$c^2 = a^2 + b^2$
$(18 - x)^2 = x^2 + 12^2$
$324 - 36x + x^2 = x^2 + 144$
$-36x = -180$
$x = 5$

5 ft

66. $T = 2\pi\sqrt{\frac{L}{32}}$
$= 2\pi\sqrt{\frac{4}{32}}$
$= 2\pi\sqrt{\frac{2}{16}}$
$= \frac{2\pi\sqrt{2}}{4}$
$= \frac{\sqrt{2}}{2}\pi$ or about 2.22 s

67. $s = \sqrt{15d}$
$55 = \sqrt{15d}$
$55^2 = (\sqrt{15d})^2$
$3025 = 15d$
$201.7 = d$

No, it should skid about 201.7 ft.

Page 753 Alternative Assessment

- Yes, the radicals may be combined if the radicands are the same, but the expression would be irrational. If the radicands are different then you would have the sum of two irrational numbers.
- $\sqrt{n^t} = n^{\frac{t-1}{2}}\sqrt{n}$

EXTRA PRACTICE

Page 756 Lesson 1-1

1. $7x$
2. $\frac{r}{s}$
3. $b + 21$
4. $t - 6$
5. a^3
6. 16^2
7. n minus 7
8. the product of x and y
9. m to the fifth power
10. 8 to the fourth power
11. 6 times r squared
12. z to the seventh power plus 2
13. 5^3
14. $7a^4$
15. $2m^3$
16. 5^3x^2y
17. p^6
18. 4^3t^2
19. $2^4 = 2 \cdot 2 \cdot 2 \cdot 2 = 16$
20. $8^2 = 8 \cdot 8 = 64$
21. $7^3 = 7 \cdot 7 \cdot 7 = 343$
22. $10^4 = 10 \cdot 10 \cdot 10 \cdot 10$
    $= 10{,}000$
23. $3^6 = 3 \cdot 3 \cdot 3 \cdot 3 \cdot 3 \cdot 3$
    $= 729$
24. $4^5 = 4 \cdot 4 \cdot 4 \cdot 4 \cdot 4$
    $= 1024$

Page 756 Lesson 1-2

1.

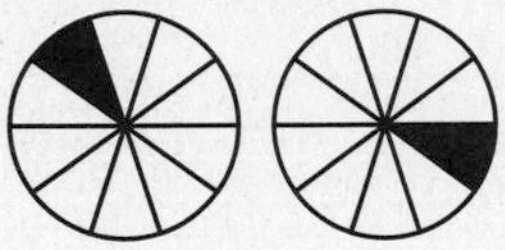

2.

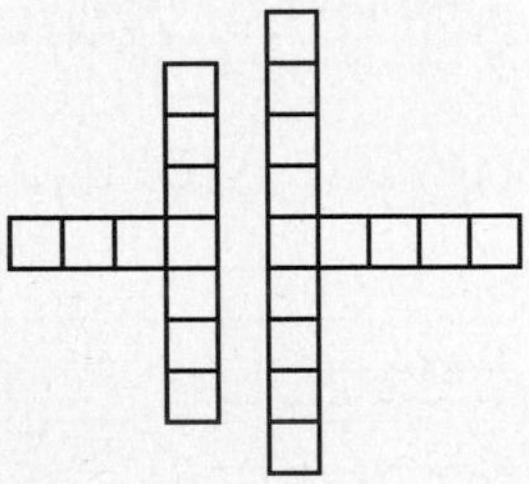

3. $45 + 11 = 56$
   $56 + 11 = 67$
   56, 67
4. $21 - 6 = 15$
   $15 - 6 = 9$
   15, 9
5. $9.6 + 1.2 = 10.8$
   $10.8 + 1.2 = 12$
   10.8, 12
6. $72.5 - 4.5 = 68$
   $68 - 4.5 = 63.5$
   68, 63.5
7. $32 \times 2 = 64$
   $64 \times 2 = 128$
   64, 128
8. $25 \div 5 = 5$
   $5 \div 5 = 1$
   5, 1
9. $30 + 6 = 36$
   $36 + 7 = 43$
   36, 43
10. $(w - 8) - 2 = w - 10$
    $(w - 10) - 2 = w - 12$
    $w - 10, w - 12$
11. $6 + 1 = 7$
    $7 - 3 = 4$
    7, 4

Page 756 Lesson 1-3

1. $3 + 8 \div 2 - 5 = 3 + 4 - 5$
   $= 7 - 5$
   $= 2$
2. $4 + 7.2 + 8 = 4 + 14 + 8$
   $= 18 + 8$
   $= 26$
3. $5(9 + 3) - 3.4 = 5(12) - 12$
   $= 60 - 12$
   $= 48$
4. $4(11 + 7) - 9.8 = 4(18) - 72$
   $= 72 - 72$
   $= 0$
5. $5^3 + 6^3 - 5^2 = 125 + 216 - 25$
   $= 341 - 25$
   $= 316$
6. $16 \div 2 \cdot 5 \cdot 3 \div 6 = 8 \cdot 5 \cdot 3 \div 6$
   $= 40 \cdot 3 \div 6 = 120 \div 6$
   $= 20$
7. $7(5^3 + 3^2) = 7(125 + 9)$
   $= 7(134)$
   $= 938$
8. $\frac{9.4 + 2.6}{7.7} = \frac{36 + 8}{49}$
   $= \frac{48}{49}$
9. $25 - \frac{1}{3}(18 + 9) = 25 - \frac{1}{3}(27)$
   $= 25 - 9$
   $= 16$
10. $8a + b = 8(2) + 5$
    $= 16 + 5$
    $= 21$
11. $12x + ab = 12(4) + (2)(5)$
    $= 48 + 10$
    $= 58$
12. $a(6 - 3n) = 2[6 - 3(10)]$
    $= 2(6 - 30)$
    $= 2(-24)$
    $= -48$
13. $bx + an = 5(4) + 2(10)$
    $= 20 + 20$
    $= 40$
14. $x^2 - 4n = (4)^2 - 4(10)$
    $= 16 - 40$
    $= -24$
15. $3b + 16a - 9n = 3(5) + 16(2) - 9(10)$
    $= 15 + 32 - 90$
    $= 47 - 90$
    $= -43$
16. $n^2 + 3(a + 4) = 10^2 + 3(2 + 4)$
    $= 100 + 3(6)$
    $= 100 + 18$
    $= 118$
17. $(2x)^2 + an - 5b = (2 \cdot 4)^2 + (2)(10) - 5(5)$
    $= 8^2 + 20 - 25$
    $= 64 + 20 - 25$
    $= 84 - 25$
    $= 59$
18. $[a + 8(b - 2)]^2 \div 4 = [2 + 8(5 - 2)]^2 \div 4$
    $= [2 + 8(3)]^2 \div 4$
    $= (2 + 24)^2 \div 4$
    $= (26)^2 \div 4$
    $= 679 \div 4$
    $= 169$

Page 757 Lesson 1-4

1. stem 24, leaf 6
2. stem 35, leaf 8
3. stem 4, leaf 2
4. stem 5, leaf 9
5. stem 0, leaf 6
6. stem 17, leaf 9

7a. \$740–\$749
7b. \$260–\$269
7c. 6
7d. weekly earnings of \$510 – \$519

Page 757 Lesson 1-5

1.
$$b + \frac{2}{3} = \frac{3}{4} + \frac{1}{3}$$
$$\frac{1}{2} + \frac{2}{3} \overset{?}{=} \frac{3}{4} + \frac{1}{3}$$
$$\frac{6}{12} + \frac{8}{12} \overset{?}{=} \frac{9}{12} + \frac{4}{12}$$
$$\frac{14}{12} \neq \frac{13}{12} \quad \text{false}$$

2.
$$\frac{2+13}{y} = \frac{3}{5}y$$
$$\frac{2+13}{5} \overset{?}{=} \frac{3}{5}(5)$$
$$\frac{15}{5} \overset{?}{=} 3$$
$$3 = 3 \quad \text{true}$$

3.
$$x^8 = 9^4$$
$$3^8 = 9^4$$
$$6561 = 6561$$
true

4.
$$4t^2 - 5(3) = 9$$
$$4(7)^2 - 5(3) \overset{?}{=} 9$$
$$4(49) - 5(3) \overset{?}{=} 9$$
$$196 - 15 \overset{?}{=} 9$$
$$181 \neq 9 \quad \text{false}$$

5.
$$\frac{3^2 - 5x}{3^2 - 1} \leq 2$$
$$\frac{9 - 5(4)}{9 - 1} \overset{?}{\leq} 2$$
$$\frac{9 - 20}{8} \overset{?}{\leq} 2$$
$$\frac{-11}{8} \leq 2$$
true

6.
$$a^6 \div 4 \div a^3 \div a < 3$$
$$2^6 \div 4 \div 2^3 \div 2 \overset{?}{<} 3$$
$$64 \div 4 \div 8 \div 2 \overset{?}{<} 3$$
$$16 \div 8 \div 2 \overset{?}{<} 3$$
$$2 \div 2 \overset{?}{<} 3$$
$$1 < 3 \quad \text{true}$$

7.

Replace x with:	$x + 2 > 7$	True or False?
4	$4 + 2 \overset{?}{>} 7 \to 6 \not> 7$	false
5	$5 + 2 \overset{?}{>} 7 \to 7 \not> 7$	false
6	$6 + 2 \overset{?}{>} 7 \to 8 > 7$	true
7	$7 + 2 \overset{?}{>} 7 \to 9 > 7$	true
8	$8 + 2 \overset{?}{>} 7 \to 10 > 7$	true

The solution set for $x + 2 > 7$ is {6, 7, 8}.

8.

Replace x with:	$x - 1 > 3$	True or False?
4	$4 - 1 \overset{?}{>} 3 \to 3 \not> 3$	false
5	$5 - 1 \overset{?}{>} 3 \to 4 > 3$	true
6	$6 - 1 \overset{?}{>} 3 \to 5 > 3$	true
7	$7 - 1 \overset{?}{>} 3 \to 6 > 3$	true
8	$8 - 1 \overset{?}{>} 3 \to 7 > 3$	true

The solution set for $x - 1 > 3$ is {5, 6, 7, 8}.

9.

Replace y with:	$2y - 15 \leq 17$	True or False?
10	$2(10) - 15 \overset{?}{\leq} 17 \to 5 \leq 17$	true
12	$2(12) - 15 \overset{?}{\leq} 17 \to 9 \leq 17$	true
14	$2(14) - 15 \overset{?}{\leq} 17 \to 13 \leq 17$	true
16	$2(16) - 15 \overset{?}{\leq} 17 \to 17 \leq 17$	true

The solution set for $2y - 15 \leq 17$ is {10, 12, 14, 16}.

10.

Replace y with:	$y + 12 < 25$	True or False?
10	$10 + 12 \overset{?}{\leq} 25 \to 22 < 25$	true
12	$12 + 12 \overset{?}{\leq} 25 \to 24 < 25$	true
14	$14 + 12 \overset{?}{\leq} 25 \to 26 \not< 25$	false
16	$16 + 12 \overset{?}{\leq} 25 \to 28 \not< 25$	false

The solution set for $y + 12 < 25$ is {10, 12}.

11.

Replace y with:	$\frac{y + 12}{7} \geq 4$	True or False?
10	$\frac{10 + 12}{7} \overset{?}{\geq} 4 \to \frac{22}{7} \ngeq 4$	false
12	$\frac{12 + 12}{7} \overset{?}{\geq} 4 \to \frac{24}{7} \ngeq 4$	false
14	$\frac{14 + 12}{7} \overset{?}{\geq} 4 \to \frac{26}{7} \ngeq 4$	false
16	$\frac{16 + 12}{7} \overset{?}{\geq} 4 \to 4 \geq 4$	true

The solution set of $\frac{y + 12}{7} \geq 4$ is {16}.

12.

Replace x with:	$\frac{2(x-2)}{3} < \frac{4}{7-5}$	True or False?
4	$\frac{2(4-2)}{3} \overset{?}{<} \frac{4}{7-5} \to \frac{4}{3} < 2$	true
5	$\frac{2(5-2)}{3} \overset{?}{<} \frac{4}{7-5} \to 2 \not< 2$	false
6	$\frac{2(6-2)}{3} \overset{?}{<} \frac{4}{7-5} \to \frac{8}{3} \not< 2$	false
7	$\frac{2(7-2)}{3} \overset{?}{<} \frac{4}{7-5} \to \frac{10}{3} \not< 2$	false
8	$\frac{2(8-2)}{3} \overset{?}{<} \frac{4}{7-5} \to \frac{12}{3} \not< 2$	false

The solution set of $\frac{2(x-2)}{3} < \frac{4}{7-5}$ is {4}.

13.

Replace x with:	$x - 4 > \frac{x+2}{3}$	True or False?
4	$4 - 4 \overset{?}{>} \frac{4+2}{3} \to 0 \not> 2$	false
5	$5 - 4 \overset{?}{>} \frac{5+2}{3} \to 1 \not> \frac{7}{3}$	false
6	$6 - 4 \overset{?}{>} \frac{6+2}{3} \to 2 \not> \frac{8}{3}$	false
7	$7 - 4 \overset{?}{>} \frac{7+2}{3} \to 3 \not> 3$	false
8	$8 - 4 \overset{?}{>} \frac{8+2}{3} \to 4 > \frac{10}{3}$	true

The solution set of $x - 4 > \frac{x+2}{3}$ is {8}.

14.

Replace y with:	$y^2 - 100 > 4y$	True or False?
10	$10^2 - 100 \overset{?}{>} 4(10) \to 0 \not> 40$	false
12	$12^2 - 100 \overset{?}{>} 4(12) \to 44 \not> 48$	false
14	$14^2 - 100 \overset{?}{>} 4(14) \to 69 > 56$	true
16	$16^2 - 100 \overset{?}{>} 4(16) \to 156 > 64$	true

The solution set of $y^2 - 100 > 4y$ is {14, 16}.

15.

Replace x with:	$9x - 20 \geq x^2$	True or False?
4	$9(4) - 20 \overset{?}{\geq} 4^2 \rightarrow 16 \geq 16$	true
5	$9(5) - 20 \overset{?}{\geq} 5^2 \rightarrow 25 \geq 25$	true
6	$9(6) - 20 \overset{?}{\geq} 6^2 \rightarrow 34 \not\geq 36$	false
7	$9(7) - 20 \overset{?}{\geq} 7^2 \rightarrow 43 \not\geq 49$	false
8	$9(8) - 20 \overset{?}{\geq} 8^2 \rightarrow 52 \not\geq 64$	false

The solution set of $9x - 20 \geq x^2$ is {4, 5}.

16.

Replace x with:	$0.3(x + 4) \leq 0.4(2x + 3)$	True or False?
4	$0.3(4 + 4) \overset{?}{\leq} 0.4[2(4) + 3] \rightarrow 2.4 \leq 4.4$	true
5	$0.3(5 + 4) \overset{?}{\leq} 0.4[2(5) + 3] \rightarrow 2.7 \leq 5.2$	true
6	$0.3(6 + 4) \overset{?}{\leq} 0.4[2(6) + 3] \rightarrow 3.0 \leq 6.0$	true
7	$0.3(7 + 4) \overset{?}{\leq} 0.4[2(7) + 3] \rightarrow 3.3 \leq 6.8$	true
8	$0.3(8 + 4) \overset{?}{\leq} 0.4[2(8) + 3] \rightarrow 3.6 \leq 7.4$	true

The solution set of $0.3(x + 4) \leq 0.4(2x + 3)$ is {4, 5, 6, 7, 8}.

17.

Replace x with:	$1.3x - 12 < 0.9x + 4$	True or False?
4	$1.3(4) - 12 \overset{?}{<} 0.9(4) + 4 \rightarrow -7.2 < 7.6$	true
5	$1.3(5) - 12 \overset{?}{<} 0.9(5) + 4 \rightarrow -5.5 < 8.5$	true
6	$1.3(6) - 12 \overset{?}{<} 0.9(6) + 4 \rightarrow -4.2 < 9.4$	true
7	$1.3(7) - 12 \overset{?}{<} 0.9(7) + 4 \rightarrow -2.9 < 10.3$	true
8	$1.3(8) - 12 \overset{?}{<} 0.9(8) + 4 \rightarrow -1.6 < 11.2$	true

The solution set of $1.3x - 12 < 0.9x + 4$ is {4, 5, 6, 7, 8}.

18.

Replace y with:	$1.2y - 8 \leq 0.7y - 3$	True or False?
10	$1.2(10) - 8 \overset{?}{\leq} 0.7(10) - 3 \rightarrow 4 \leq 4$	true
12	$1.2(12) - 8 \overset{?}{\leq} 0.7(12) - 3 \rightarrow 6.4 \not\leq 5.4$	false
14	$1.2(14) - 8 \overset{?}{\leq} 0.7(14) - 3 \rightarrow 8.8 \not\leq 6.8$	false
16	$1.2(16) - 8 \overset{?}{\leq} 0.7(16) - 3 \rightarrow 11.2 \not\leq 8.2$	false

The solution set of $1.2y - 8 \leq 0.7y - 3$ is {10}.

19. $x = \frac{17 + 9}{2}$
$= \frac{26}{2}$
$= 13$

20. $3(8) + 4 = b$
$24 + 4 = b$
$28 = b$

21. $\frac{18 - 7}{13 - 2} = y$
$\frac{11}{11} = y$
$1 = y$

22. $28 - (-14) = z$
$28 + 14 = z$
$42 = z$

23. $20.4 - 5.67 = t$
$20.4 + (-5.67) = t$
$14.73 = t$

24. $t = 91.8 \div 27$
$= 3.4$

25. $-\frac{5}{8}\left(-\frac{4}{5}\right) = c$
$\frac{20}{40} = c$
$\frac{1}{2} = c$

26. $8\frac{1}{12} - 5\frac{5}{12} = e$
$7\frac{13}{12} - 5\frac{5}{12} = e$
$2\frac{8}{12} = e$
$2\frac{2}{3} = e$

27. $\frac{3}{4} - \frac{9}{16} = s$
$\frac{12}{16} - \frac{9}{16} = s$
$\frac{3}{16} = s$

28. $\frac{5}{8} + \frac{1}{4} = y$
$\frac{5}{8} + \frac{2}{8} = y$
$\frac{7}{8} = y$

29. $n = \frac{84 \div 7}{18 \div 9}$
$= \frac{12}{2}$
$= 6$

30. $d = 3\frac{1}{2} \div 2$
$= \frac{7}{2} \cdot \frac{1}{2}$
$= \frac{7}{4}$

Page 757 Lesson 1-6

1. symmetric (=)
2. substitution (=)
3. substitution (=)
4. multiplicative identity
5. multiplicative inverse
6. multiplicative inverse, multiplicative identity
7. additive identity
8. symmetric (=)
9. multiplicative property of 0
10. reflexive (=)
11. multiplicative identity
12. additive identity
13. transitive (=)

Page 758 Lesson 1-7

1. $3(5 + w) = 3(5) + 3(w)$
$= 15 + 3w$

2. $(h - 8)7 = 7(h) - 7(8)$
$= 7h - 56$

3. $6(y + 4) = 6(y) + 6(4)$
$= 6y + 24$

4. $9(3n + 5) = 9(3n) + 9(5)$
$= 27n + 45$

5. $32\left(x - \frac{1}{8}\right) = 32(x) - 32\left(\frac{1}{8}\right)$
$= 32x - 4$

6. $c(7 - d) = 7(c) - c(d)$
$= 7c - cd$

7. $6 \cdot 55 = 6(50 + 5)$
$= 6(50) + 6(5)$
$= 300 + 30$
$= 330$

8. $4\frac{1}{18}(18) = \left(4 + \frac{1}{18}\right)18$
$= 4(18) + \frac{1}{18}(18)$
$= 72 + 1$
$= 73$

9. $15(108) = 15(100 + 8)$
$= 15(100) + 15(8)$
$= 1500 + 120 = 1620$

10. $14(3.7) = 14(3 + 0.7)$
$= 14(3) + 14(0.7)$
$= 42 + 9.8$
$= 51.8$

11. $689.5 = (690 - 1)5$
$= (690)5 - (1)5$
$= 3450 - 5$
$= 3445$

12. $7 \times 314 = 7(315 - 1)$
$= 7(315) - 7(1)$
$= 2205 - 7$
$= 2198$

13. $13a + 5a = (13 + 5)a$
$= 18a$

14. $21x - 10x = (21 - 10)x$
$= 11x$

15. $8(3x + 7) = 8(3x) + 8(7)$
$= 24x + 56$

16. in simplest form

17. $3(5am - 4) = 3(5am) - 3(4)$
$= 15am - 12$
18. $15x^2 + 7x^2 = (15 + 7)x^2$
$= 22x^2$
19. $9y^2 + 13y^2 + 3 = (9 + 13)y^2 + 3$
$= 22y^2 + 3$
20. $11a^2 - 11a^2 + 12a^2 = (11 - 11 + 12)a^2$
$= 12a^2$
21. $6a + 7a + 12b + 18b = (6 + 7)a + (12 + 8)b$
$= 13a + 20b$

Page 758 Lesson 1-8

1. multiplicative identity
2. commutative property (+)
3. commutative property (×)
4. additive identity 5. distributive property
6. commutative property (+)
7. associative property (×)
8. multiplicative property of zero
9. substitution (=) 10. associative property (+)
11. associative property (×)
12. associative property (+)
13. $5a + 6b + 7a = 5a + 7a + 6b$
$= (5 + 7)a + 6b$
$= 12a + 6b$
14. $8x + 4y + 9x = 8x + 9x + 4y$
$= (8 + 9)x + 4y$
$= 17x + 4y$
15. $3a + 5b + 2c + 8b = 3a + 5b + 8b + 2c$
$= 3a + (5 + 8)b + 2c$
$= 3a + 13b + 2c$
16. $\frac{2}{3}x^2 + 5x + x^2 = \frac{2}{3}x^2 + x^2 + 5x$
$= \left(\frac{2}{3} + 1\right)x^2 + 5x$
$= \frac{5}{3}x^2 + 5x$
17. $(4p - 7q) + (5q - 8p) = 4p - 8p - 7q + 5q$
$= (4 - 8)p + (-7 + 5)q$
$= -4p - 2q$
18. $8q + 5r - 7q - 6r = 8q - 7q + 5r - 6r$
$= (8 - 7)q + (5 - 6)r$
$= q - r$
19. $4(2x + y) + 5x = 4(2x) + 4(y) + 5x$
$= 8x + 4y + 5x$
$= 8x + 5x + 4y$
$= (8 + 5)x + 4y$
$= 13x + 4y$
20. $9r^5 + 2r^2 + r^5 = 9r^5 + r^5 + 2r^2$
$= (9 + 1)r^5 + 2r^2$
$= 10r^5 + 2r^2$
21. $12b^3 + 12 + 12b^3 = 12b^3 + 12b^3 + 12$
$= (12 + 12)b^3 + 12$
$= 24b^3 + 12$
22. $7 + 3(uv - 6) + u = 7 + 3(uv) + 3(-6) + u$
$= 7 + 3uv - 18 + u$
$= (7 - 18) + 3uv + u$
$= -11 + 3uv + u$
23. $3(x + 2y) + 4(3x + y) = 3(x) + 3(2y) + 4(3x) + 4(y)$
$= 3x + 6y + 12x + 4y$
$= 3x + 12x + 6y + 4y$
$= (3 + 12)x + (6 + 4)y$
$= 15x + 10y$
24. $6.2(a + b) + 2.6(a + b) + 3a$
$= 6.2a + 6.2b + 2.6a + 2.6b + 3a$
$= 6.2a + 2.6a + 3a + 6.2b + 2.6b$
$= (6.2 + 2.6 + 3)a + (6.2 + 2.6)b$
$= 11.8a + 8.8b$
25. $3 + 8(st + 3w) + 3st = 3 + 8(st) + 8(3w) + 3st$
$= 3 + 8st + 24w + 3st$
$= 3 + 8st + 3st + 24w$
$= 3 + (8 + 3)st + 24w$
$= 3 + 11st + 24w$
26. $5.4(s - 3t) + 3.6(s - 4)$
$= 5.4(s) + 5.4(-3t) + 3.6(s) + 3.6(-4)$
$= 5.4s - 16.2t + 3.6s - 14.4$
$= (5.4 + 3.6)s - 16.2t - 14.4$
$= 9s - 16.2t - 14.4$
27. $3[4 + 5(2x + 3y)] = 3[4 + 5(2x) + 5(3y)]$
$= 3(4 + 10x + 15y)$
$= 3(4) + 3(10x) + 3(15y)$
$= 12 + 30x + 45y$

Page 758 Lesson 1-9

1. Graph 3 2. Graph 1 3. Graph 4 4. Graph 2

Page 759 Lesson 2-1

1. $\{-3, -2, -1, 0, 1, 2, 3, 4\}$
2. $\{-2, 0, 2, 3, 6\}$ 3. $\{2, 3, 4\}$
4. $\{7, 8, 9, 10, 11, 12, 13\}$ 5. $\{-8, -6, -4, -2, 0\}$
6. $\{-2, -1, 0, 1, 2, 3, 4\}$

7.
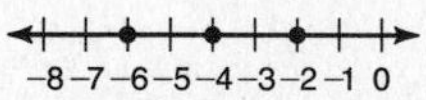

8.
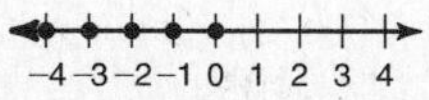

9.
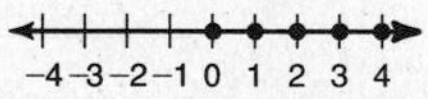

10.
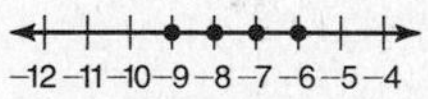

11.
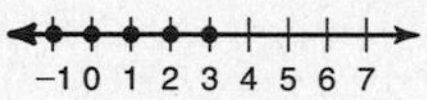

12.
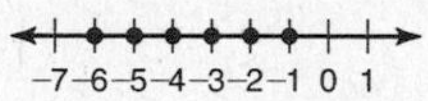

Page 759 Lesson 2-2

1. 50 2. 22 3. 31
4. 8 5. 26

6.
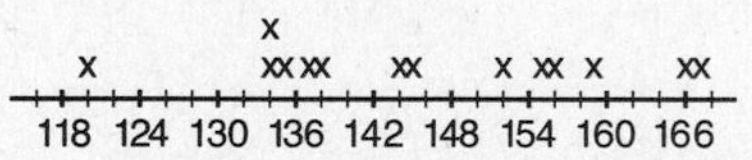

7.
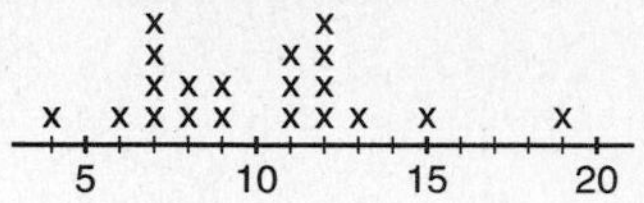

8.
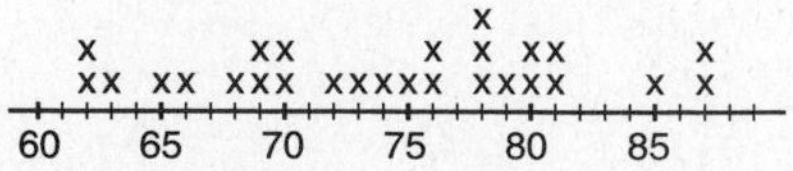

9.

Page 759 Lesson 2-3

1. 13

2. $27 - 19 = 27 + (-19) = 8$

3. $8 - 13 = 8 + (-13) = -5$

4. 5

5. -29

6. 22

7. $19m - 12m = (19 - 12)m = [19 + (-12)]m = 7m$

8. $8h - 23h = (8 - 23) = [8 + (-23)]h = -15h$

9. $24b - (-9b) = 24b + 9b = (24 + 9)b = 33b$

10. 18

11. $4 + (-12) + (-18) = (-8) + (-18) = -26$

12. $7 + (-11) + 32 = -4 + 32 = 28$

13. $|-28 + (-67)| = |-95| = 95$

14. $|-89 + 46| = |43| = 43$

15. $|-285 + (-641)| = |-926| = 926$

16. $-35 - (-12) = -35 + 12 = -23$

17. 9

18. -28

19. -28

20. $8 - 17 + (-3) = 8 + (-17) + (-3) = -9 + (-3) = -12$

21. $27 - 14 - (-19) = 27 + (-14) + 19 = 13 + 19 = 32$

22. $|-9 + 15| = |6| = 6$

23. $\begin{bmatrix} 5 + (-3) & -4 + 4 \\ 0 + (-2) & 3 + (-4) \end{bmatrix} = \begin{bmatrix} 2 & 0 \\ -2 & -1 \end{bmatrix}$

24. $\begin{bmatrix} 1 - 4 & -4 - (-3) \\ 5 - 7 & -6 - (-1) \end{bmatrix} = \begin{bmatrix} 1 + (-4) & -4 + 3 \\ 5 + (-7) & -6 + 1 \end{bmatrix} = \begin{bmatrix} -3 & -1 \\ -2 & -5 \end{bmatrix}$

Page 760 Lesson 2-4

1. >

2. >

3. >

4. <

5. <

6. $-5 + 2 \ \underline{?}\ -3 - 3$
$= -3$

7. $7 \ \underline{?}\ 13 - (-6)$
$7 \ \underline{?}\ 13 + 6$
$7 < 19$

8. $3.4 - 5.7 \ \underline{?}\ -2$
$3.4 + (-5.7) \ \underline{?}\ -2$
$-2.3 < -2$

9. $-\frac{18}{6} \ \underline{?}\ -3$
$-3 = -3$

10. $\frac{8}{13} \ \underline{?}\ \frac{9}{14}$
$8(14) \ \underline{?}\ 9(13)$
$112 < 117$
$\frac{8}{13} < \frac{9}{14}$

11. $-\frac{25}{8} \ \underline{?}\ -\frac{25}{7}$
$-25(7) \ \underline{?}\ -25(8)$
$-175 > -200$
$-\frac{25}{8} > -\frac{25}{7}$

12. $6\left(\frac{5}{3}\right) \ \underline{?}\ \frac{3}{2}(6)$
$10 > 9$

13. $\frac{0.6}{7} \ \underline{?}\ \frac{1.8}{12}$
$0.6(12) \ \underline{?}\ 7(1.8)$
$7.2 < 12.6$
$\frac{0.6}{7} < \frac{1.8}{12}$

14. $24.6 \ \underline{?}\ 13.8 - (-12.8)$
$24.6 \ \underline{?}\ 13.8 + 12.8$
$24.6 < 26.6$

15. $-54 + 26.5 \ \underline{?}\ 27.5$
$-27.5 < 27.5$

16. $\frac{5.4}{18} \ \underline{?}\ -4 + 1$
$0.3 > -3$

17. $(4.1)(0.2) \ \underline{?}\ 8.4$
$0.82 < 8.4$

18. $-\frac{12}{17} \ \underline{?}\ -\frac{9}{14}$
$-12(14) \ \underline{?}\ -9(17)$
$-168 < -153$

Page 760 Lesson 2-5

1. $-\frac{11}{9} + -\frac{7}{9} = -\frac{18}{9} = -2$

2. $\frac{5}{11} - \frac{6}{11} = \frac{5}{11} + \left(-\frac{6}{11}\right) = -\frac{1}{11}$

3. $\frac{2}{7} - \frac{3}{14} = \frac{4}{14} + \left(-\frac{3}{14}\right) = \frac{1}{14}$

4. -1.6

5. $-1.7 - 3.9 = -1.7 + (-3.9) = -5.6$

6. $-72.5 - 81.3 = -72.5 + (-81.3) = -153.8$

7. $-\frac{3}{5} + \frac{5}{6} = -\frac{18}{30} + \frac{25}{30} = \frac{7}{30}$

8. $\frac{3}{8} + \left(-\frac{7}{12}\right) = \frac{9}{24} + \left(-\frac{14}{24}\right) = -\frac{5}{24}$

9. $-\frac{7}{15} + \left(-\frac{5}{12}\right) = -\frac{28}{60} + \left(-\frac{25}{60}\right) = -\frac{53}{60}$

10. $-4.5 - 8.6 = -4.5 + (-8.6) = -13.1$

11. $89.3 - (-14.2) = 89.3 + 14.2 = 103.5$

12. 0.053

13. $-\frac{2}{7} + \frac{3}{14} + \frac{3}{7} = -\frac{4}{14} + \left(\frac{3}{14} + \frac{6}{14}\right) = -\frac{4}{14} + \frac{9}{14} = \frac{5}{14}$

14. $-\frac{3}{5} + \frac{6}{7} + \left(-\frac{2}{35}\right) = \left[-\frac{3}{5} + \left(-\frac{2}{35}\right)\right] + \frac{6}{7} = \left[-\frac{21}{35} + \left(-\frac{2}{35}\right)\right] + \frac{30}{35} = -\frac{23}{35} + \frac{30}{35} = \frac{7}{35} = \frac{1}{5}$

15. $\frac{7}{3} + \left(-\frac{5}{6}\right) + \left(-\frac{2}{3}\right) = \frac{7}{3} + \left[-\frac{5}{6} + \left(-\frac{2}{3}\right)\right] = \frac{14}{6} + \left[-\frac{5}{6} + \left(-\frac{4}{6}\right)\right] = \frac{14}{6} + \left(-\frac{9}{6}\right) = \frac{5}{6}$

16. $-4.13 + (-5.18) + 9.63 = -9.31 + 9.63 = 0.32$

17. $6.7 + (-8.1) + (-7.3) = 6.7 + (-15.4) = -8.7$

18. $\frac{3}{4} + \left(-\frac{5}{8}\right) + \frac{3}{32} = \left(\frac{24}{32} + \frac{3}{32}\right) - \frac{20}{32}$
$= \frac{27}{32} - \frac{20}{32}$
$= \frac{7}{32}$

19. $1.9 - (-7) = 1.9 + 7$
$= 8.9$

20. $-1.8 - 3.7 = -1.8 + (-3.7)$
$= -5.5$

21. $-18 - (-1.3) = -18 + 1.3$
$= -16.7$

Page 760 Lesson 2-6

1. 60 2. −66 3. 35 4. $\frac{7}{24}$

5. $(-5)\left(-\frac{2}{5}\right) = \frac{10}{5}$
$= 2$

6. $(-6)(4)(-3) = -24\,(-3)$
$= 72$

7. $(4)(-2)(-1)(-3) = -8(-1)(-3)$
$= (8)(-3)$
$= -24$

8. $(-6.8)(-5.415)(3.1) = (36.822)(3.1)$
$= 114.1482$

9. -17.088

10. $\left(\frac{3}{5}\right)\left(-\frac{5}{7}\right) = -\frac{15}{35}$
$= -\frac{3}{7}$

11. $\left(-\frac{7}{15}\right)\left(\frac{9}{14}\right) = -\frac{63}{210}$
$= -\frac{3}{10}$

12. $(4.2)(-5.1)(3.6) = (21.42)(3.6)$
$= -77.112$

13. $-6\left(\frac{5}{3}\right)\left(\frac{9}{10}\right) = -\frac{6}{1}\left(\frac{45}{30}\right)$
$= -\frac{270}{30}$
$= -9$

14. 0

15. $(-21)(-2)(-1) = 42(-1)$
$= -42$

Page 761 Lesson 2-7

1. −6 2. 7 3. −8

4. $-\frac{3}{4} - 9 = -\frac{3}{4} \cdot \frac{1}{9}$
$= -\frac{3}{36}$
$= -\frac{1}{12}$

5. $-9 \div \left(-\frac{10}{17}\right) = -9 \cdot \left(-\frac{17}{10}\right)$
$= \frac{153}{10}$
$= 15\frac{3}{10}$

6. $-45n$ 7. $6a$ 8. $-7a$

9. $8 \div \left(-\frac{5}{4}\right) = 8 \cdot -\frac{4}{5}$
$= -\frac{32}{5}$
$= -6\frac{2}{5}$

10. $\frac{\frac{7}{8}}{-10} = \frac{7}{8} \div -10$
$= \frac{7}{8} \cdot -\frac{1}{10}$
$= -\frac{7}{80}$

11. $\frac{12}{\frac{-8}{5}} = 12 \div \left(\frac{-8}{5}\right)$
$= 12 \cdot \frac{5}{-8}$
$= -\frac{60}{8}$
$= -\frac{15}{2} = -7\frac{1}{2}$

12. $\frac{6a + 24}{6} = \frac{6a}{6} + \frac{24}{6}$
$= a + 4$

13. $\frac{20a + 30b}{-2} = \frac{20a}{-2} + \frac{30b}{-2}$
$= -10a - 15b$

14. $\frac{\frac{11}{5}}{-6} = \frac{11}{5} \div (-6)$
$= \frac{11}{5} \cdot \left(-\frac{1}{6}\right)$
$= -\frac{11}{30}$

15. $\frac{70a - 42b}{-14} = \frac{70a}{-14} + \frac{(-42b)}{-14}$
$= -5a + 3b$

16. $\frac{-32x + 12y}{-4} = \frac{-32x}{-4} + \frac{12y}{-4}$
$= 8x - 3y$

17. $-\frac{7}{12} \div \frac{1}{18} = -\frac{7}{12} \cdot \frac{18}{1}$
$= -\frac{126}{12}$
$= -\frac{21}{2}$
$= -10\frac{1}{2}$

18. $\frac{\frac{5}{15}}{-7} = 5 \div \left(\frac{15}{-7}\right)$
$= 5 \cdot \left(\frac{-7}{15}\right)$
$= \frac{-35}{15}$
$= -\frac{7}{3}$
$= -2\frac{1}{3}$

Page 761 Lesson 2-8

1. −9 2. 0.04 3. ±14.35

4. $\pm\frac{9}{8}$ 5. 9.22 6. $-\frac{6}{14}$ or $-\frac{3}{7}$

7. −12.21 8. ±31 9. 3.2

10. $\sqrt{m} = \sqrt{529}$
$= 23$

11. $-\sqrt{c - d} = -\sqrt{1.097 - 1.0171}$
$= -\sqrt{0.0799}$
≈ -0.28

12. $-\sqrt{ab} = -\sqrt{(1.2)(2.7)}$
$= -\sqrt{3.24}$
≈ -1.8

13. $\pm\sqrt{\frac{x}{y}} = \pm\sqrt{\frac{144}{1521}}$
$\approx \pm 0.31$

Page 761 Lesson 2-9

1. $a^2 - b^3 = c$ 2. $29 - xy < z$

3. $P = 2(a + b)$ 4. $\frac{4}{5}(mnp^2) > 26$

5. $30 + \frac{s}{t} = v$ 6. $A = \frac{1}{2}h(a + b)$

Page 762 Lesson 3-1

1. $-2 + g = 7$
$-2 + 2 + g = 7 + 2$
$g = 9$

2. $9 + s = -5$
$9 - 9 + s = -5 - 9$
$s = -14$

3. $-4 + y = -9$
$-4 + 4 + y = -9 + 4$
$y = -5$

4. $m + 6 = 2$
$m + 6 - 6 = 2 - 6$
$m = -4$

5. $t + (-4) = 10$
$t + (-4) + 4 = 10 + 4$
$t = 14$

6. $v - 7 = -4$
$v - 7 + 7 = -4 + 7$
$v = 3$

7. $a - (-6) = -5$
$a + 6 = -5$
$a + 6 - 6 = -5 - 6$
$a = -11$

8. $-2 - x = -8$
$-2 - x + 2 = -8 + 2$
$-x = -6$
$x = 6$

9. $d + (-44) = -61$
$d + (-44) + 44 = -61 + 44$
$d = -17$

10. $e - (-26) = 41$
$e + 26 = 41$
$e + 26 - 26 = 41 - 26$
$e = 15$

11. $p - 47 = 22$
$p - 47 + 47 = 22 + 47$
$p = 69$

12. $-63 - t = -82$
$-63 - t + 63 = -82 + 63$
$-t = -19$
$t = 19$

13. $c + 5.4 = -11.33$
$c + 5.4 - 5.4 = -11.33 - 5.4$
$c = -16.73$

14. $-6.11 + b = 14.321$
$-6.11 + b + 6.11 = 14.321 + 6.11$
$b = 20.431$

15. $-5 = y - 22.7$
$-5 + 22.7 = y - 22.7 + 22.7$
$17.7 = y$

16. $-5 - q = 1.19$
$-5 - q + 5 = 1.19 + 5$
$-q = 6.19$
$q = -6.19$

17. $n + (-4.361) = 59.78$
$n + (-4.361) + 4.361 = 59.78 + 4.361$
$n = 64.141$

18. $t - (-46.1) = -3.673$
$t + 46.1 = -3.673$
$t + 46.1 - 46.1 = -3.673 - 46.1$
$t = -49.773$

19. $\frac{7}{10} - a = \frac{1}{2}$
$\frac{7}{10} - a - \frac{7}{10} = \frac{1}{2} - \frac{7}{10}$
$-a = \frac{5}{10} - \frac{7}{10}$
$-a = -\frac{2}{10}$
$a = \frac{2}{10}$ or $\frac{1}{5}$

20. $t - \left(-\frac{1}{8}\right) = \frac{3}{10}$
$t + \frac{1}{8} = \frac{3}{10}$
$t + \frac{1}{8} - \frac{1}{8} = \frac{3}{10} - \frac{1}{8}$
$t = \frac{12}{40} - \frac{5}{40}$
$t = \frac{7}{40}$

21. $-4\frac{5}{12} = t - \left(-10\frac{1}{36}\right)$
$-4\frac{5}{12} = t + 10\frac{1}{36}$
$-4\frac{5}{12} - 10\frac{1}{36} = t + 10\frac{1}{36} - 10\frac{1}{36}$
$-4\frac{15}{36} - 10\frac{1}{36} = t$
$-14\frac{16}{36} = t$
$-14\frac{4}{9} = t$

22. $x + \frac{3}{8} = \frac{1}{4}$
$x + \frac{3}{8} - \frac{3}{8} = \frac{1}{4} - \frac{3}{8}$
$x = \frac{2}{8} - \frac{3}{8}$
$x = -\frac{1}{8}$

23. $1\frac{7}{16} + s = \frac{9}{8}$
$1\frac{7}{16} + s - 1\frac{7}{16} = \frac{9}{8} - 1\frac{7}{16}$
$s = \frac{18}{16} + \left(-\frac{23}{16}\right)$
$s = -\frac{5}{16}$

24. $17\frac{8}{9} = d + \left(-2\frac{5}{6}\right)$
$17\frac{8}{9} + 2\frac{5}{6} = d + \left(-2\frac{5}{6}\right) + 2\frac{5}{6}$
$17\frac{16}{18} + 2\frac{15}{18} = d$
$19\frac{31}{18} = d$
$20\frac{13}{18} = d$

Page 762 Lesson 3-2

1. $-5p = 35$
$\frac{-5p}{-5} = \frac{35}{-5}$
$p = -7$

2. $-3x = -24$
$\frac{-3x}{-3} = \frac{-24}{-3}$
$x = 8$

3. $62y = -2356$
$\frac{62y}{62} = \frac{-2356}{62}$
$y = -38$

4. $\frac{a}{-6} = -2$
$(-6)\left(\frac{a}{-6}\right) = -2(-6)$
$a = 12$

5. $\frac{c}{-59} = -7$
$(-59)\left(\frac{c}{-59}\right) = -7(-59)$
$c = 413$

6. $\frac{t}{14} = -63$
$(14)\left(\frac{t}{14}\right) = -63(14)$
$t = -882$

7. $84 = \frac{x}{97}$
$97(84) = \frac{x}{97}(97)$
$8148 = x$

8. $\frac{w}{5} = 3$
$(5)\left(\frac{w}{5}\right) = 3(5)$
$w = 15$

9. $\frac{q}{9} = -3$
$9\left(\frac{q}{9}\right) = -3(9)$
$q = -27$

10. $\frac{2}{5}x = \frac{4}{7}$
$\left(\frac{5}{2}\right)\left(\frac{2}{5}x\right) = \frac{4}{7}\left(\frac{5}{2}\right)$
$x = \frac{20}{14}$
$x = \frac{10}{7}$ or $1\frac{3}{7}$

11. $\frac{z}{6} = -\frac{5}{12}$
$(6)\frac{z}{6} = -\frac{5}{12}(6)$
$z = -\frac{30}{12}$
$z = -\frac{5}{2}$

12. $-\frac{5}{9}r = 7\frac{1}{2}$
$-\frac{5}{9}r = \frac{15}{2}$
$\left(-\frac{9}{5}\right)\left(-\frac{5}{9}r\right) = \left(\frac{15}{2}\right)\left(-\frac{9}{5}\right)$
$r = -\frac{135}{10}$
or $-13\frac{1}{2}$

13. $2\frac{1}{6}j = 5\frac{1}{5}$
$\frac{13}{6}j = \frac{26}{5}$
$\left(\frac{6}{13}\right)\left(\frac{13}{6}j\right) = \left(\frac{26}{5}\right)\left(\frac{6}{13}\right)$
$j = \frac{156}{65}$
$j = \frac{12}{5}$ or $2\frac{2}{5}$

14. $3 = 1\frac{7}{11}q$

$3 = \frac{18}{11}q$

$\left(\frac{11}{18}\right)(3) = \left(\frac{18}{11}q\right)\left(\frac{11}{18}\right)$

$q = \frac{11}{6}$ or $1\frac{5}{6}$

15. $-1\frac{3}{4}p = -\frac{5}{8}$

$-\frac{7}{4}p = -\frac{5}{8}$

$\left(-\frac{4}{7}\right)\left(-\frac{7}{4}p\right) = \left(-\frac{5}{8}\right)\left(-\frac{4}{7}\right)$

$p = \frac{20}{56}$ or $\frac{5}{14}$

16. $57k = 0.1824$

$\frac{57k}{57} = \frac{0.1824}{57}$

$k = 0.0032$

17. $0.0022b = 0.1958$

$\frac{0.0022b}{0.0022} = \frac{0.1958}{0.0022}$

$b = 89$

18. $5j = -32.15$

$\frac{5j}{5} = -\frac{32.15}{5}$

$j = -6.43$

19. $\frac{w}{-2} = -2.48$

$(-2)\left(\frac{w}{-2}\right) = -2.48(-2)$

$w = 4.96$

20. $\frac{z}{2.8} = -6.2$

$(2.8)\left(\frac{z}{2.8}\right) = (-6.2)(2.8)$

$z = -17.36$

21. $\frac{x}{-0.063} = 0.015$

$(-0.0063)\left(\frac{x}{-0.063}\right) = (0.015)(-0.063)$

$x = -0.000945$

22. $15\frac{3}{8} = -5.125p$

$15.375 = -5.125p$

$\frac{15.375}{-5.125} = \frac{-5.125p}{-5.125}$

$-3 = p$

23. $-7.25 = -3\frac{5}{8}g$

$-7.25 = -3.625g$

$\frac{-7.25}{-3.625} = \frac{-3.625g}{-3.625}$

$2 = g$

24. $-18\frac{1}{4} = 2.50x$

$-18.25 = 2.50x$

$\frac{-18.25}{2.50} = \frac{2.50x}{2.50}$

$-7.3 = x$

Page 762 Lesson 3-3

1. $2x - 5 = 3$

$2x - 5 + 5 = 3 + 5$

$2x = 8$

$\frac{2x}{2} = \frac{8}{2}$

$x = 4$

2. $4t + 5 = 37$

$4t + 5 - 5 = 37 - 5$

$4t = 32$

$\frac{4t}{4} = \frac{32}{4}$

$t = 8$

3. $7a + 6 = -36$

$7a + 6 - 6 = -36 - 6$

$7a = -42$

$\frac{7a}{7} = \frac{-42}{7}$

$a = -6$

4. $47 = -8g + 7$

$47 - 7 = -8g + 7 - 7$

$40 = -8g$

$\frac{40}{-8} = \frac{-8g}{-8}$

$-5 = g$

5. $-3c - 9 = -24$

$-3c - 9 + 9 = -24 + 9$

$-3c = -15$

$\frac{-3c}{-3} = \frac{-15}{-3}$

$c = 5$

6. $5k - 7 = -52$

$5k - 7 + 7 = -52 + 7$

$5k = -45$

$\frac{5k}{5} = \frac{-45}{5}$

$k = -9$

7. $5s + 4s = -72$

$9s = -72$

$\frac{9s}{9} = \frac{-72}{9}$

$s = -8$

8. $3x - 7 = 2$

$3x - 7 + 7 = 2 + 7$

$3x = 9$

$\frac{3x}{3} = \frac{9}{3}$

$x = 3$

9. $8 + 3x = 5$

$8 + 3x - 8 = 5 - 8$

$3x = -3$

$\frac{3x}{3} = \frac{-3}{3}$

$x = -1$

10. $-3y + 7.569 = 24.069$

$-3y + 7.569 - 7.569 = 24.069 - 7.569$

$-3y = 16.5$

$\frac{-3y}{-3} = \frac{16.5}{-3}$

$y = -5.5$

11. $7 - 9.1f = 137.585$

$7 - 9.1f - 7 = 137.585 - 7$

$-9.1f = 130.585$

$\frac{-9.1f}{-9.1} = \frac{130.585}{-9.1}$

$f = -14.35$

12. $6.5 = 2.4m - 4.9$

$6.5 + 4.9 = 2.4m - 4.9 + 4.9$

$11.4 = 2.4m$

$\frac{11.4}{2.4} = \frac{2.4m}{2.4}$

$4.75 = m$

13. $\frac{e}{5} + 6 = -2$

$\frac{e}{5} + 6 - 6 = -2 - 6$

$\frac{e}{5} = -8$

$5\left(\frac{e}{5}\right) = -8(5)$

$e = -40$

14. $\frac{d}{4} - 8 = -5$

$\frac{d}{4} - 8 + 8 = -5 + 8$

$\frac{d}{4} = 3$

$4\left(\frac{d}{4}\right) = 3(4)$

$d = 12$

15. $-\frac{4}{13}y - 7 = 6$

$-\frac{4}{13}y - 7 + 7 = 6 + 7$

$-\frac{4}{13}y = 13$

$\left(-\frac{13}{4}\right)\left(-\frac{4}{13}y\right) = 13\left(-\frac{13}{4}\right)$

$y = -\frac{169}{4}$

$y = -42\frac{1}{4}$

16. $\frac{p + 10}{3} = 4$

$(3)\left(\frac{p + 10}{3}\right) = 4(3)$

$p + 10 = 12$

$p + 10 - 10 = 12 - 10$

$p = 2$

17. $\frac{h - 7}{6} = 1$

$6\left(\frac{h - 7}{6}\right) = 1(6)$

$h - 7 = 6$

$h - 7 + 7 = 6 + 7$

$h = 13$

18. $\frac{5f + 1}{8} = -3$

$8\left(\frac{5f + 1}{8}\right) = -3(8)$

$5f + 1 = -24$

$5f + 1 - 1 = -24 - 1$

$5f = -25$

$\frac{5f}{5} = \frac{-25}{5}$

$f = -5$

19. $\frac{4n - 8}{-2} = 12$

$(-2)\left(\frac{4n - 8}{-2}\right) = 12(-2)$

$4n - 8 = -24$

$4n - 8 + 8 = -24 + 8$

$4n = -16$

$\frac{4n}{4} = \frac{-16}{4}$

$n = -4$

20. $\frac{2a}{7} + 9 = 3$
$\frac{2a}{7} + 9 - 9 = 3 - 9$
$\frac{2a}{7} = -6$
$\left(\frac{7}{2}\right)\left(\frac{2}{7}a\right) = (-6)\left(\frac{7}{2}\right)$
$a = \frac{-42}{2}$
$a = -21$

21. $\frac{-3t - 4}{2} = 8$
$2\left(\frac{-3t - 4}{2}\right) = 8(2)$
$-3t - 4 = 16$
$-3t - 4 + 4 = 16 + 4$
$-3t = 20$
$\frac{-3t}{-3} = \frac{20}{-3}$
$t = -6\frac{2}{3}$

Page 763 Lesson 3-4

1. $90 - 15 = 75°$ **2.** $90 - 79 = 11°$
3. $90 - 88 = 2°$ **4.** $(90 - a)°$
5. $(90 - 3c)°$
6. $90 - (b - 15) = 90 - b + 15$
$= 90 + 15 - b$
$= (105 - b)°$
7. $180 - 156 = 24°$ **8.** $180 - 94 = 86°$
9. $180 - 21 = 159°$ **10.** $(180 - a)°$
11. $(180 - 3c)°$
12. $180 - (b - 15) = 180 - b + 15$
$= 180 + 15 - b$
$= (195 - b)°$
13. $180 - (90 + 2) = 180 - 92$
$= 88°$
14. $180 - (34 + 132) = 180 - 166$
$= 14°$
15. $180 - (111 + 28) = 180 - 139$
$= 41°$
16. $(180 - a - b)°$
17. $180 - (a + a - 15) = 180 - a - a + 15$
$= 180 + 15 - 2a$
$= (195 - 2a)°$
18. $180 - (b + 3b - 2) = 180 - b - 3b + 2$
$= 180 + 2 - b - 3b$
$= (182 - 4b)°$

Page 763 Lesson 3-5

1. $6(y - 5) = 18$
$6y - 30 = 18$
$6y - 30 + 30 = 18 + 30$
$6y = 48$
$\frac{6y}{6} = \frac{48}{6}$
$y = 8$

2. $-21 = 7(p - 10)$
$-21 = 7p - 70$
$-21 + 70 = 7p - 70 + 70$
$49 = 7p$
$\frac{49}{7} = \frac{7p}{7}$
$7 = p$

3. $3(h + 2) = 12$
$3h + 6 = 12$
$3h + 6 - 6 = 12 - 6$
$3h = 6$
$\frac{3h}{3} = \frac{6}{3}$
$h = 2$

4. $-3(x + 2) = -18$
$-3x - 6 = -18$
$-3x - 6 + 6 = 18 + 6$
$-3x = -12$
$\frac{-3x}{-3} = \frac{-12}{-3}$
$x = 4$

5. $11.2n + 6 = 5.2n$
$11.2n - 11.2n + 6 = 5.2n - 11.2n$
$6 = -6n$
$\frac{6}{-6} = \frac{-6n}{-6}$
$-1 = n$

6. $2m + 5 - 6m = 25$
$2m - 6m + 5 = 25$
$-4m + 5 = 25$
$-4m + 5 - 5 = 25 - 5$
$-4m = 20$
$\frac{-4m}{-4} = \frac{20}{-4}$
$m = -5$

7. $3z - 1 = 23 - 3z$
$3z + 3z - 1 = 23 - 3z + 3z$
$6z - 1 = 23$
$6z - 1 + 1 = 23 + 1$
$6z = 24$
$\frac{6z}{6} = \frac{24}{6}$
$z = 4$

8. $5a - 5 = 7a - 19$
$5a - 5a - 5 = 7a - 5a - 19$
$-5 = 2a - 19$
$-5 + 19 = 2a - 19 + 19$
$14 = 2a$
$\frac{14}{2} = \frac{2a}{2}$
$7 = a$

9. $5b + 12 = 3b - 6$
$5b - 3b + 12 = 3b - 3b - 6$
$2b + 12 = -6$
$2b + 12 - 12 = -6 - 12$
$2b = -18$
$\frac{2b}{2} = \frac{-18}{2}$
$b = -9$

10. $3x - 5 = 7x + 7$
$3x - 3x - 5 = 7x - 3x + 7$
$-5 = 4x + 7$
$-5 - 7 = 4x + 7 - 7$
$-12 = 4x$
$\frac{-12}{4} = \frac{4x}{4}$
$-3 = x$

11. $1.9s + 6 = 3.1 - s$
$1.9s + s + 6 = 3.1 - s + s$
$2.9s + 6 = 3.1$
$2.9s + 6 - 6 = 3.1 - 6$
$2.9s = -2.9$
$\frac{2.9s}{2.9} = \frac{-2.9}{2.9}$
$s = -1$

12. $2.85y - 7 = 12.85y - 2$
$2.85y - 2.85y - 7 = 12.85y - 2.85y - 2$
$-7 = 10y - 2$
$-7 + 2 = 10y - 2 + 2$
$-5 = 10y$
$\frac{-5}{10} = \frac{10y}{10}$
$-\frac{1}{2} = y$

13. $2.9m + 1.7 = 3.5 + 2.3m$
$2.9m - 2.3m + 1.7 = 3.5 + 2.3m - 2.3m$
$0.6m + 1.7 = 3.5$
$0.6m + 1.7 - 1.7 = 3.5 - 1.7$
$0.6m = 1.8$
$\frac{0.6m}{0.6} = \frac{1.8}{0.6}$
$m = 3$

14. $3(x + 1) - 5 = 3x - 2$
$3x + 3 - 5 = 3x - 2$
$3x - 2 = 3x - 2$
identity

15. $4(2y - 1) = -10(y - 5)$
$8y - 4 = -10y + 50$
$8y + 10y - 4 = -10y + 10y + 50$
$18y - 4 = 50$
$18y - 4 + 4 = 50 + 4$
$18y = 54$
$\frac{18y}{18} = \frac{54}{18}$
$y = 3$

16. $\frac{6v - 9}{3} = v$
$3\left(\frac{6v - 9}{3}\right) = 3(v)$
$6v - 9 = 3v$
$6v - 6v - 9 = 3v - 6v$
$-9 = -3v$
$\frac{-9}{-3} = \frac{-3v}{-3}$
$3 = v$

17. $\frac{3t + 1}{4} = \frac{3}{4}t - 5$
$4\left(\frac{3t + 1}{4}\right) = 4\left(\frac{3}{4}t - 5\right)$
$3t + 1 = 3t - 20$
$3t - 3t + 1 = 3t - 3t - 20$
$1 = -20$
no solution

18. $\frac{2}{5}y + \frac{y}{2} = 9$
$10\left(\frac{2}{5}y + \frac{y}{2}\right) = 9(10)$
$10\left(\frac{2}{5}y\right) + 10\left(\frac{y}{2}\right) = 90$
$4y + 5y = 90$
$9y = 90$
$\frac{9y}{9} = \frac{90}{9}$
$y = 10$

19. $3y - \frac{4}{5} = \frac{1}{3}y$
$15\left(3y - \frac{4}{5}\right) = 15\left(\frac{1}{3}y\right)$
$15(3y) + 15\left(-\frac{4}{5}\right) = 5y$
$45y - 12 = 5y$
$-45y + 45y - 12 = 5y - 45y$
$-12 = -40y$
$\frac{-12}{-40} = \frac{-40y}{-40}$
$\frac{3}{10} = y$

20. $\frac{3}{4}x - 4 = 7 + \frac{1}{2}x$
$4\left(\frac{3}{4}x - 4\right) = 4\left(7 + \frac{1}{2}x\right)$
$4\left(\frac{3}{4}x\right) + 4(-4) = 4(7) + 4\left(\frac{1}{2}x\right)$
$3x - 16 = 28 + 2x$
$3x - 16 + 16 = 28 + 16 + 2x$
$3x = 44 + 2x$
$3x - 2x = 44 + 2x - 2x$
$x = 44$

21. $\frac{x}{2} - \frac{1}{3} = \frac{x}{3} - \frac{1}{2}$
$6\left(\frac{x}{2} - \frac{1}{3}\right) = 6\left(\frac{x}{3} - \frac{1}{2}\right)$
$6\left(\frac{x}{2}\right) + 6\left(-\frac{1}{3}\right) = 6\left(\frac{x}{3}\right) + 6\left(-\frac{1}{2}\right)$
$3x - 2 = 2x - 3$
$3x - 2 + 2 = 2x - 3 + 2$
$3x = 2x - 1$
$3x - 2x = 2x - 2x - 1$
$x = -1$

Page 763 Lesson 3-6

1. $x + r = q$
$x + r - r = q - r$
$x = q - r$

2. $ax + 4 = 7$
$ax + 4 - 4 = 7 - 4$
$ax = 3$
$\frac{ax}{a} = \frac{3}{a}$
$x = \frac{3}{a}$

3. $2bx - b = -5$
$2bx - b + b = -5 + b$
$2bx = -5 + b$
$\frac{2bx}{2b} = \frac{-5 + b}{2b}$
$x = \frac{-5 + b}{2b}$

4. $\frac{x - c}{c + a} = a$
$(c + a)\left(\frac{x - c}{c + a}\right) = (c + a)a$
$x - c = c(a) + a(a)$
$x - c = ca + a^2$
$x - c + c = a^2 + ca + c$
$x = a^2 + ca + c$

5. $\frac{x + y}{c} = d$
$(c)\left(\frac{x + y}{c}\right) = c(d)$
$x + y = cd$
$x + y - y = cd - y$
$x = cd - y$

6. $\frac{ax + 1}{2} = b$
$(2)\left(\frac{ax + 1}{2}\right) = (2)(b)$
$ax + 1 = 2b$
$ax + 1 - 1 = 2b - 1$
$ax = 2b - 1$
$\frac{ax}{a} = \frac{2b - 1}{a}$
$x = \frac{2b - 1}{a}$

7. $\frac{x+t}{4} = d$

$(4)\left(\frac{x+t}{4}\right) = (4)(d)$

$x + t = 4d$

$x + t - t = 4d - t$

$x = 4d - t$

8. $6x - 7 = -r$

$6x - 7 + 7 = -r + 7$

$6x = 7 - r$

$\frac{6x}{6} = \frac{7-r}{6}$

$x = \frac{7-r}{6}$

9. $kx + 4y = 5z$

$kx + 4y - 4y = 5z - 4y$

$kx = 5z - 4y$

$\frac{kx}{k} = \frac{5z-4y}{k}$

$x = \frac{5z-4y}{k}$

10. $ax - 6 = t$

$ax - 6 + 6 = t + 6$

$ax = t + 6$

$\frac{ax}{a} = \frac{t+6}{a}$

$x = \frac{t+6}{a}$

11. $\frac{2}{3}x + a = b$

$\frac{2}{3}x + a - a = b - a$

$\frac{2}{3}x = b - a$

$\frac{3}{2}\left(\frac{2}{3}x\right) = (b-a)\left(\frac{3}{2}\right)$

$x = \frac{3}{2}(b - a)$

12. $q(x + 1) = 5$

$q(x) + q(1) = 5$

$qx + q = 5$

$qx + q - q = 5 - q$

$qx = 5 - q$

$\frac{qx}{q} = \frac{5-q}{q}$

$x = \frac{5}{q} - 1$

13. $\frac{x-y}{z} = 8$

$(z)\left(\frac{x-y}{z}\right) = 8(z)$

$x - y = 8z$

$x - y + y = 8z + y$

$x = 8z + y$

14. $\frac{7a+b}{x} = 1$

$x\left(\frac{7a+b}{x}\right) = (1)(x)$

$7a + b = x$

15. $\frac{4cx+t}{7} = 2$

$(7)\left(\frac{4cx+t}{7}\right) = (2)(7)$

$4cx + t = 14$

$4cx + t - t = 14 - t$

$4cx = 14 - t$

$\frac{4cx}{4c} = \frac{14-t}{4c}$

$x = \frac{14-t}{4c}$

16. $\frac{9x-4c}{z} = z$

$(z)\left(\frac{9x-4c}{z}\right) = (z)(z)$

$9x - 4c = z^2$

$9x - 4c + 4c = z^2 + 4c$

$9x = z^2 + 4c$

$\frac{9x}{9} = \frac{z^2+4c}{9}$

$x = \frac{z^2+4c}{9}$

17. $cx + a = bx$

$cx + a - a = bx - a$

$cx = bx - a$

$cx - bx = bx - bx - a$

$cx - bx = -a$

$x(c - b) = -a$

$\frac{x(c-b)}{(c-b)} = \frac{-a}{(c-b)}$

$x = \frac{-a}{c-b}$

18. $\frac{12q-x}{5} = t$

$(5)\left(\frac{12q-x}{5}\right) = (5)(t)$

$12q - x = 5t$

$12q - 12q - x = 5t - 12q$

$-x = 5t - 12q$

$\frac{-x}{-1} = \frac{5t-12q}{-1}$

$x = 12q - 5t$

Page 764 Lesson 3-7

1. mean $= \frac{103{,}332}{20} = 5166.6$

median $= \frac{458 + 625}{2} = \frac{1083}{2} = 541.5$

mode: none

2. mean $= \frac{178}{40} = 4.45$

median = 4

mode: 3, 5

3. new rushing average $= \frac{5(137.6) + 155}{6}$

$= \frac{843}{6}$

$= 140.5$

4. mean $= \frac{562.3}{14} = 40.164$

median $= \frac{40.2 + 40.1}{2} = \frac{80.3}{2} = 40.15$

mode: 40.2, 43.4

Page 764 Lesson 4-1

1. $\frac{4}{5} = \frac{x}{20}$

$4(20) = 5x$

$80 = 5x$

$\frac{80}{5} = \frac{5x}{5}$

$16 = x$

2. $\frac{b}{63} = \frac{3}{7}$

$7b = 3(63)$

$7b = 189$

$\frac{7b}{7} = \frac{189}{7}$

$b = 27$

3. $\frac{y}{5} = \frac{3}{4}$

$4y = 3(5)$

$4y = 15$

$\frac{4y}{4} = \frac{15}{4}$

$y = \frac{15}{4} = 3.75$

4. $\frac{7}{4} = \frac{3}{a}$

$7a = 3(4)$

$7a = 12$

$\frac{7a}{7} = \frac{12}{7}$

$a = \frac{12}{7} \approx 1.71$

5. $\frac{t-5}{4} = \frac{3}{2}$

$2(t - 5) = 4(3)$

$2(t) + 2(-5) = 12$

$2t - 10 = 12$

$2t - 10 + 10 = 12 + 10$

$2t = 22$

$\frac{2t}{2} = \frac{22}{2}$

$t = 11$

6. $\frac{x}{9} = \frac{0.24}{3}$

$3x = 9(0.24)$

$3x = 2.16$

$\frac{3x}{3} = \frac{2.16}{3}$

$x = 0.72$

7. $\frac{n}{3} = \frac{n+4}{7}$

$7n = 3(n + 4)$

$7n = 3(n) + 3(4)$

$7n = 3n + 12$

$7n - 3n = 3n - 3n + 12$

$4n = 12$

$\frac{4n}{4} = \frac{12}{4}$

$n = 3$

8.

$$\frac{12q}{-7} = \frac{30}{14}$$
$$14(12q) = -7(30)$$
$$168q = -210$$
$$\frac{168q}{168} = \frac{-210}{168}$$
$$q = -\frac{5}{4} = -1.25$$

9.

$$\frac{1}{y-3} = \frac{3}{y-5}$$
$$y - 5 = 3(y - 3)$$
$$y - 5 = 3(y) + 3(-3)$$
$$y - 5 = 3y - 9$$
$$y - y - 5 = 3y - y - 9$$
$$-5 = 2y - 9$$
$$-5 + 9 = 2y - 9 + 9$$
$$4 = 2y$$
$$\frac{4}{2} = \frac{2y}{2}$$
$$2 = y$$

10.

$$\frac{r-1}{r+1} = \frac{3}{5}$$
$$5(r - 1) = 3(r + 1)$$
$$5(r) + 5(-1) = 3(r) + 3(1)$$
$$5r - 5 = 3r + 3$$
$$5r - 3r - 5 = 3r - 3r + 3$$
$$2r - 5 = 3$$
$$2r - 5 + 5 = 3 + 5$$
$$2r = 8$$
$$\frac{2r}{2} = \frac{8}{2}$$
$$r = 4$$

11.

$$\frac{a-3}{8} = \frac{3}{4}$$
$$4(a - 3) = 8(3)$$
$$4(a) + 4(-3) = 24$$
$$4a - 12 = 24$$
$$4a - 12 + 12 = 24 + 12$$
$$4a = 36$$
$$\frac{4a}{4} = \frac{36}{4}$$
$$a = 9$$

12.

$$\frac{6p-2}{7} = \frac{5p+7}{8}$$
$$8(6p - 2) = 7(5p + 7)$$
$$8(6p) + 8(-2) = 7(5p) + 7(7)$$
$$48p - 16 = 35p + 49$$
$$48p - 35p - 16 = 35p - 35p + 49$$
$$13p - 16 = 49$$
$$13p - 16 + 16 = 49 + 16$$
$$13p = 65$$
$$\frac{13p}{13} = \frac{65}{13}$$
$$p = 5$$

13.

$$\frac{2}{9} = \frac{k+3}{2}$$
$$2(2) = 9(k + 3)$$
$$4 = 9(k) + 9(3)$$
$$4 = 9k + 27$$
$$4 - 27 = 9k + 27 - 27$$
$$-23 = 9k$$
$$-\frac{23}{9} = \frac{9k}{9}$$
$$k = -\frac{23}{9} \approx -2.56$$

14.

$$\frac{5m-3}{4} = \frac{5m+3}{6}$$
$$6(5m - 3) = 4(5m + 3)$$
$$6(5m) + 6(-3) = 4(5m) + 4(3)$$
$$30m - 18 = 20m + 12$$
$$30m - 18 + 18 = 20m + 12 + 18$$
$$30m - 20m = 20m - 20m + 30$$
$$10m = 30$$
$$\frac{10m}{10} = \frac{30}{10}$$
$$m = 3$$

15.

$$\frac{w-5}{4} = \frac{w+3}{3}$$
$$3(w - 5) = 4(w + 3)$$
$$3(w) + 3(-5) = 4(w) + 4(3)$$
$$3w - 15 = 4w + 12$$
$$3w - 3w - 15 = 4w - 3w + 12$$
$$-15 = w + 12$$
$$-15 - 12 = w + 12 - 12$$
$$-27 = w$$

16.

$$\frac{96.8}{t} = \frac{12.1}{7}$$
$$7(96.8) = 12.1t$$
$$677.6 = 12.1t$$
$$\frac{677.6}{12.1} = \frac{12.1t}{12.1}$$
$$56 = t$$

17.

$$\frac{x}{6.03} = \frac{4}{17.42}$$
$$17.42x = 4(6.03)$$
$$17.42x = 24.12$$
$$\frac{17.42x}{17.42} = \frac{24.12}{17.42}$$
$$x \approx 1.385$$

18.

$$\frac{4n+5}{5} = \frac{2n+7}{7}$$
$$7(4n + 5) = 5(2n + 7)$$
$$7(4n) + 7(5) = 5(2n) + 5(7)$$
$$28n + 35 = 10n + 35$$
$$28n + 35 - 35 = 10n + 35 - 35$$
$$28n = 10n$$
$$28n - 10n = 10n - 10n$$
$$18n = 0$$
$$n = 0$$

Page 764 Lesson 4-2

1. no
2. yes, corresponding angles have equal measures
3. no
4. no
5. yes, corresponding angles have equal measures
6. no

Page 765 Lesson 4-3

1. $\sin N = \frac{36}{39} \approx 0.923$

$\cos N = \frac{15}{39} \approx 0.385$

$\tan N = \frac{36}{15} = 2.400$

2. $\sin N = \frac{14}{50} = 0.280$

$\cos N = \frac{48}{50} = 0.960$

$\tan N = \frac{14}{48} \approx 0.292$

3. $\sin N = \frac{35}{37} \approx 0.946$

$\cos N = \frac{12}{37} \approx 0.324$

$\tan N = \frac{35}{12} \approx 2.917$

4. 0.9063 **5.** 0.6009 **6.** 0.9455 **7.** 0.4384
8. 0.1584 **9.** 0.0349 **10.** 28° **11.** 32°
12. 75° **13.** 69° **14.** 12° **15.** 44°

Page 765 Lesson 4-4

1. $\frac{1}{4} = \frac{n}{100}$
   $100 = 4n$
   $25 = n$
   $\frac{25}{100}$ or 25%, 0.25

2. $\frac{34}{100}$ or 34%, 0.34

3. $\frac{4}{25} = \frac{n}{100}$
   $400 = 25n$
   $16 = n$
   $\frac{16}{100}$ or 16%, 0.16

4. $\frac{3}{20} = \frac{n}{100}$
   $300 = 20n$
   $15 = n$
   $\frac{15}{100}$ or 15%, 0.15

5. $\frac{7}{8} = \frac{n}{100}$
   $700 = 8n$
   $87\frac{1}{2} = n$
   $\frac{87\frac{1}{2}}{100}$ or $87\frac{1}{2}$%, 0.875

6. $\frac{9}{10} = \frac{n}{100}$
   $900 = 10n$
   $90 = n$
   $\frac{90}{100}$ or 90%, 0.9

7. $\frac{24}{40} = \frac{n}{100}$
   $2400 = 40n$
   $60 = n$
   $\frac{60}{100}$ or 60%, 0.6

8. $\frac{4}{50} = \frac{n}{100}$
   $400 = 50n$
   $8 = n$
   $\frac{8}{100}$ or 8%, 0.08

9. $\frac{7}{15} = \frac{n}{100}$
   $700 = 15n$
   $46\frac{2}{3} = n$
   $\frac{46\frac{2}{3}}{100}$ or $46\frac{2}{3}$%, $0.4\overline{6}$

10. $\frac{4}{9} = \frac{n}{100}$
    $400 = 9n$
    $44\frac{4}{9} = n$
    $\frac{44\frac{4}{9}}{100}$ or $44\frac{4}{9}$%, $0.\overline{4}$

11. $\frac{36}{15} = \frac{n}{100}$
    $3600 = 15n$
    $240 = n$
    $\frac{240}{100}$ or 240%, 2.4

12. $\frac{18}{4} = \frac{n}{100}$
    $1800 = 4n$
    $450 = n$
    $\frac{450}{100}$ or 450%, 4.5

13. $\frac{24}{48} = \frac{n}{100}$
    $2400 = 48n$
    $50 = n$
    50%

14. $\frac{14}{70} = \frac{n}{100}$
    $1400 = 70n$
    $20 = n$
    20%

15. $\frac{9}{72} = \frac{n}{100}$
    $900 = 72n$
    $12\frac{1}{2} = n$
    $12\frac{1}{2}$%; 12.5%

16. $\frac{14}{n} = \frac{17.5}{100}$
    $17.5n = 1400$
    $n = 80$

17. $\frac{5.12}{16} = \frac{n}{100}$
    $512 = 16n$
    $32 = n$
    32%

18. $\frac{n}{64} = \frac{25}{100}$
    $100n = 1600$
    $n = 16$

19. $\frac{2}{80} = \frac{n}{100}$
    $200 = 80n$
    $2.5 = n$
    2.5%

20. $\frac{45}{112.5} = \frac{n}{100}$
    $4500 = 112.5n$
    $40 = n$
    40%

Page 765 Lesson 4-5

1. decrease; $\frac{100 - 67}{100} = \frac{33}{100} = 33\%$

2. increase; $\frac{98 - 62}{62} = \frac{36}{62} = \frac{r}{100}$
   $3600 = 62r$
   $58 = r$
   58%

3. decrease; $\frac{322 - 289}{322} = \frac{r}{100}$
   $\frac{33}{322} = \frac{r}{100}$
   $3300 = 322r$
   $10 = r$
   10%

4. decrease; $\frac{78 - 36}{78} = \frac{r}{100}$
   $\frac{42}{78} = \frac{r}{100}$
   $4200 = 78r$
   $54 = r$
   54%

5. increase; $\frac{230 - 212}{212} = \frac{r}{100}$
   $\frac{18}{212} = \frac{r}{100}$
   $1800 = 212r$
   $8 = r$
   8%

6. increase; $\frac{65 - 35}{35} = \frac{r}{100}$
   $\frac{30}{35} = \frac{r}{100}$
   $3000 = 35r$
   $86 = r$
   86%

7. sales tax: $0.045(299) \approx \$13.46$
   total price: $\$299 + \$13.46 = \$312.46$

8. discount: $0.15(49.99) \approx \$7.50$
   $\$49.99 - 7.50 = \$42.49$
   sales tax: $0.035(42.49) \approx \$1.49$
   total price: $\$42.49 + \$1.49 = \$43.98$

9. discount: $0.10(28.95) \approx \$2.90$
   $\$28.95 - \$2.90 = \$26.05$
   sales tax: $0.05(26.05) \approx \$1.30$
   total price: $\$26.05 + \$1.30 = \$27.35$

10. sales tax: $0.0625(36.99) = \$2.31$
    total price: $\$36.99 + \$2.31 = \$39.30$

11. discount: $0.30(65) = \$19.50$
    $\$65 - \$19.50 = \$45.50$
    sales tax: $0.04(45.50) = \$1.82$
    total price: $\$45.50 + \$1.82 = \$47.32$

12. sales tax: $0.07(15.95) = \$1.12$
    total price: $\$15.95 + \$1.12 = \$17.07$

Page 766 Lesson 4-6

1. $P(\text{tails}) = \frac{1}{2}$
2. $P(\text{December 1}) = 1$
3. $P(\text{girl}) = \frac{1}{2}$
4. $P(\text{400 days/year}) = 0$
5. $P(\text{algebra book}) = 1$
6. $P(\text{Wednesday}) = \frac{1}{7}$
7. $P(\text{e}) = \frac{1}{7}$
8. $P(\text{not c}) = \frac{5}{7}$
9. $P(\text{s}) = \frac{3}{7}$
10. $P(\text{b}) = \frac{0}{7} = 0$
11. $P(\text{vowel}) = \frac{2}{7}$
12. $P(\text{u or c}) = \frac{3}{7}$
13. 1:5
14. 3:3 or 1:1

15. 2:4 or 1:2
16. 4:2 or 2:1
17. 3:3 or 1:1
18. 5:1

Page 766 Lesson 4-7

1.

	Quarts	Amount of Orange Juice
10% juice	5	0.10(5)
pure juice	p	1.00p
40% juice	$p + 5$	$0.40(p + 5)$

$0.10(5) + 1.00p = 0.40(p + 5)$
$0.5 + 1.00p = 0.40p + 2$
$1.00p = 0.40p + 1.5$
$0.60p = 1.5$
$p = 2.5$
2.5 quarts of pure orange juice

2.

	Principal	Rate	Interest
4.5%	x	0.045	$0.045x$
6%	$6000 - x$	0.06	$0.06(6000 - x)$

$0.045x + 0.06(6000 - x) = 279$
$0.045x + 360 - 0.06x = 279$
$-0.015x + 360 = 279$
$-0.015x = -81$
$x = 5400$
$6000 - x = 6000 - 5400$
$= 600$
Jane deposited $5400 at 4.5% and $600 at 6%.

3.

	Number of Tickets	Cost per Ticket	Total Cost
adult	x	$5.50	$5.50x$
children	$21 - x$	$3.50	$3.50(21 - x)$

$5.50x + 3.50(21 - x) = 83.50$
$5.50x + 73.50 - 3.5x = 83.50$
$2x + 73.50 = 83.50$
$2x = 10$
$x = 5$

$21 - x = 21 - 5$
$= 16$

5 adults, 16 children

4.

	Amount of Solution (quarts)	Amount of Pure Antifreeze
20% antifreeze	$14 - x$	$0.2(14 - x)$
100% antifreeze	x	$1.0x$
40% antifreeze	14	0.4(14)

$0.2(14 - x) + 1.0x = 0.4(14)$
$2.8 - 0.2x + 1.0x = 5.6$
$2.8 + 0.8x = 5.6$
$0.8x = 2.8$
$x = 3.5$
3.5 quarts should be drained and replaced.

5.

	Liters	Amount of Butterfat
9.2% butterfat	1	0.092(1)
2% butterfat	x	$0.02x$
6.4% butterfat	$1 + x$	$0.064(1 + x)$

$0.092 + 0.02x = 0.064(1 + x)$
$0.092 + 0.02x = 0.064 + 0.064x$
$0.028 + 0.02x = 0.064x$
$0.028 = 0.044x$
$0.\overline{63} = x$
$0.\overline{63}$ L of 2% butterfat should be added.

Page 766 Lesson 4-8

1. inverse, 6
2. inverse, 50
3. direct, $\frac{1}{5}$
4. direct, 3
5. inverse, 14
6. direct, 2

7. $\frac{y_1}{y_2} = \frac{x_1}{x_2}$
$\frac{45}{y_2} = \frac{9}{7}$
$9y_2 = 45(7)$
$9y_2 = 315$
$y_2 = 35$
Thus, $y = 35$ when $x = 7$.

8. $\frac{y_1}{y_2} = \frac{x_1}{x_2}$
$\frac{18}{8} = \frac{27}{x_2}$
$18x_2 = 27(8)$
$18x_2 = 216$
$x_2 = 12$
Thus, $x = 12$ when $y = 8$.

9. $\frac{y_1}{y_2} = \frac{x_1}{x_2}$
$\frac{450}{y_2} = \frac{6}{10}$
$450(10) = 6y_2$
$4500 = 6y_2$
$750 = y_2$
Thus, $y = 750$ when $x = 10$.

10. $\frac{y_1}{y_2} = \frac{x_1}{x_2}$
$\frac{6}{y_2} = \frac{48}{20}$
$6(20) = 48y_2$
$120 = 48y_2$
$2.5 = y_2$
Thus, $y = 2.5$ when $x = 20$.

11. $\frac{y_1}{y_2} = \frac{x_1}{x_2}$
$\frac{25}{35} = \frac{20}{x_2}$
$25x_2 = 20(35)$
$25x_2 = 700$
$x_2 = 28$
Thus, $x = 28$ when $y = 35$.

12. $\frac{y_1}{y_2} = \frac{x_1}{x_2}$
$\frac{100}{y_2} = \frac{40}{16}$
$16(100) = 40y_2$
$1600 = 40y_2$
$40 = y_2$
Thus, $y = 40$ when $x = 16$.

13. $\frac{y_1}{y_2} = \frac{x_1}{x_2}$
$\frac{-7}{-84} = \frac{-1}{x_2}$
$-7x_2 = -1(-84)$
$-7x_2 = 84$
$x_2 = -12$
Thus, $x = -12$ when $y = -84$.

14. $\frac{y_1}{y_2} = \frac{x_1}{x_2}$
$\frac{5}{y_2} = \frac{-10}{50}$
$5(50) = -10y_2$
$250 = -10y_2$
$-25 = y_2$
Thus, $y = -25$ when $x = 50$.

15. $\frac{y_1}{y_2} = \frac{x_1}{x_2}$
$\frac{24}{y_2} = \frac{6}{14}$
$24(14) = 6y_2$
$336 = 6y_2$
$56 = y_2$
Thus, $y = 56$ when $x = 14$.

16. $\frac{y_1}{y_2} = \frac{x_1}{x_2}$
$\frac{-10}{-15} = \frac{-4}{x_2}$
$-10x_2 = -4(-15)$
$-10x_2 = 60$
$x_2 = -6$
Thus, $x = -6$ when $y = -15$.

17. $x_1y_1 = x_2y_2$
$4(54) = x_2(27)$
$216 = 27x_2$
$8 = x_2$
Thus, $x = 8$
when $y = 27$.

18. $x_1y_1 = x_2y_2$
$6(18) = x_2(12)$
$108 = 12x_2$
$9 = x_2$
Thus, $x = 9$
when $y = 12$.

19. $x_1y_1 = x_2y_2$
$2(26) = 4(y_2)$
$52 = 4y_2$
$13 = y_2$
Thus, $y = 13$
when $x = 4$.

20. $x_1y_1 = x_2y_2$
$8(3) = x_2(4)$
$24 = 4x_2$
$6 = x_2$
Thus, $x = 6$
when $y = 4$.

21. $x_1y_1 = x_2y_2$
$(24)(12) = x_2(9)$
$288 = 9x_2$
$32 = x_2$
Thus, $x = 32$
when $y = 9$.

22. $x_1y_1 = x_2y_2$
$-8(8) = (-16)y_2$
$-64 = -16y_2$
$4 = y_2$
Thus, $y = 4$
when $x = -16$.

23. $x_1y_1 = x_2y_2$
$-8(3) = (4)y_2$
$-24 = 4y_2$
$-6 = y_2$
Thus, $y = -6$
when $x = 4$.

24. $x_1y_1 = x_2y_2$
$\frac{1}{3}(27) = \left(\frac{3}{4}\right)y_2$
$9 = \frac{3}{4}y_2$
$12 = y_2$
Thus, $y = 12$
when $x = \frac{3}{4}$.

25. $x_1y_1 = x_2y_2$
$63(19.5) = x_2(10.5)$
$122.85 = 10.5x_2$
$11.7 = x_2$
Thus, $x = 11.7$
when $y = 10.5$.

26. $x_1y_1 = x_2y_2$
$10(4.8) = 19.2y_2$
$48 = 19.2y_2$
$2.5 = y_2$
Thus, $y = 2.5$
when $x = 19.2$.

Page 767 Lesson 5-1

1. (1, 2), I **2.** (−5, 0), none **3.** (6, −2), IV
4. (0, 6), none **5.** (−2, −2), III **6.** (4, 5), I
7. (2, −5), IV **8.** (4, 0), none **9.** (−3, 5), II
10. (7, 3), I **11.** (−7, −5), III **12.** (−6, 4), II

13-20.

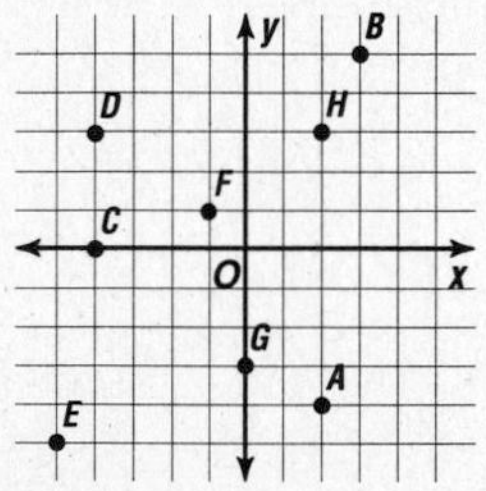

Page 767 Lesson 5-2

1. {5, 0, −9}; {2, 0, −1}
2. {−4, −2, 0, 2}; {2, 0, 4}
3. {7, −2, 4, 5, −9}; {5, −3, 0, −7, 2}
4. {3.1, −4.7, 2.4, −9}; {−1, 3.9, −3.6, 12.12}
5. {(1, 3), (2, 4), (3, 5), (4, 6), (5, 7)}; {1, 2, 3, 4, 5}; {3, 4, 5, 6, 7}; {(3, 1), (4, 2), (5, 3), (6, 4), (7, 5)}
6. {(−4, 1), (−2, 3), (0, 1), (2, 3), (4, 1)}; {−4, −2, 0, 2, 4}; {1, 3}; {(1, −4), (3, −2), (1, 0), (3, 2), (1, 4)}
7. {(−1, 5), (−2, 5), (−2, 4), (−2, 1), (−6, 1)}; {−1, −2, −6}; {5, 4, 1}; {(5, −1), (5, −2), (4, −2), (1, −2), (1, −6)}
8. {(3, 7), (5, 2), (9, 1), (−3, 2)}; {3, 5, 9, −3}; {7, 1, 2}; {(7, 3), (2, 5), (1, 9), (2, −3)}
9. { (0, 0), (1, 1), (2, 3), (2, −1), (−2, 2), (−2, −1), (−4, −3)}; {0, 1, 2, −2 −4}; {0, 1, 3, −1, 2, −3}; { (0, 0), (1, 1), (3, 2), (−1, 2), (2,−2), (−1, −2), (−3, −4)}
10. {(−3, 1), (−3, −3), (−2, 0), (−2, 2), (−1, 3), (−1, −1), (0, −2), (1, 3), (1, −1), (2, 0), (2, 2), (3, 1), (3, −3)}; {−3, −2, −1, 0, 1, 2, 3}; {−3, 1, 0, 2, −1, −2, 3}; {(1, −3), (−3, −3)(0, −2), (2, −2), (3, −1), (−1, −1), (−2, 0), (3, 1), (−1, 1), (0, 2), (2, 2), (1, 3), (−3, 3)}

Page 767 Lesson 5-3

1. $3r = 8s - 4$

a. $3\left(\frac{2}{3}\right) \stackrel{?}{=} 8\left(\frac{3}{4}\right) - 4$
$2 \stackrel{?}{=} 6 - 4$
$2 = 2$
true

b. $3(0) \stackrel{?}{=} 8\left(\frac{1}{2}\right) - 4$
$0 \stackrel{?}{=} 4 - 4$
$0 = 0$
true

c. $3(4) \stackrel{?}{=} 8(2) - 4$
$12 \stackrel{?}{=} 16 - 4$
$12 = 12$
true

d. $3(2) \stackrel{?}{=} 8(4) - 4$
$6 \stackrel{?}{=} 32 - 4$
$6 \neq 28$
false

a, b, c

2. $3y = x + 7$

a. $3(4) \stackrel{?}{=} 2 + 7$
$12 \neq 9$
false

b. $3(-1) \stackrel{?}{=} 2 + 7$
$-3 \neq 9$
false

c. $3(3) \stackrel{?}{=} 2 + 7$
$9 = 9$
true

d. $3(2) \stackrel{?}{=} -1 + 7$
$6 = 6$
true

c, d

3. $4x = 8 - 2y$

a. $4(2) \stackrel{?}{=} 8 - 2(0)$
$8 \stackrel{?}{=} 8 - 0$
$8 = 8$
true

b. $4(0) \stackrel{?}{=} 8 - 2(2)$
$0 \stackrel{?}{=} 8 - 4$
$0 \neq 4$
false

c. $4(0.5) \stackrel{?}{=} 8 - 2(-3)$
$2 \stackrel{?}{=} 8 + 6$
$2 \neq 14$
false

d. $4(1) \stackrel{?}{=} 8 - 2(-2)$
$4 \stackrel{?}{=} 8 + 4$
$4 \neq 12$
false

a

4. $3n = 10 - 4m$

a. $3(3) \stackrel{?}{=} 10 - 4(0)$
$9 \stackrel{?}{=} 10 - 0$
$9 \neq 10$
false

b. $3(6) \stackrel{?}{=} 10 - 4(-2)$
$18 \stackrel{?}{=} 10 + 8$
$18 = 18$
true

c. $3(2) \stackrel{?}{=} 10 - 4(1)$
$6 \stackrel{?}{=} 10 - 4$
$6 = 6$
true

d. $3(1) \stackrel{?}{=} 10 - 4(2)$
$3 \stackrel{?}{=} 10 - 8$
$3 \neq 2$
false

b, c

5. $y = 2x$

$\frac{y}{2} = x$

y	$\frac{y}{2}$	x	(x, y)
-3	$\frac{-3}{2}$	$-\frac{3}{2}$	$\left(-\frac{3}{2}, -3\right)$
-1	$\frac{-1}{2}$	$-\frac{1}{2}$	$\left(-\frac{1}{2}, -1\right)$
0	$\frac{0}{2}$	0	$(0, 0)$
2	$\frac{2}{2}$	1	$(1, 2)$
3	$\frac{3}{2}$	$\frac{3}{2}$	$\left(\frac{3}{2}, 3\right)$

$\left\{\left(-\frac{3}{2}, -3\right), \left(-\frac{1}{2}, -1\right), (0, 0), (1, 2), \left(\frac{3}{2}, 3\right)\right\}$

6. $y = 5x + 1$

$y - 1 = 5x$

$\frac{y-1}{5} = x$

y	$\frac{y-1}{5}$	x	(x, y)
-3	$\frac{-3-1}{5}$	$-\frac{4}{5}$	$\left(-\frac{4}{5}, -3\right)$
-1	$\frac{-1-1}{5}$	$-\frac{2}{5}$	$\left(-\frac{2}{5}, -1\right)$
0	$\frac{0-1}{5}$	$-\frac{1}{5}$	$\left(-\frac{1}{5}, 0\right)$
2	$\frac{2-1}{5}$	$\frac{1}{5}$	$\left(\frac{1}{5}, 2\right)$
3	$\frac{3-1}{5}$	$\frac{2}{5}$	$\left(\frac{2}{5}, 3\right)$

$\left\{\left(-\frac{4}{5}, -3\right), \left(-\frac{2}{5}, -1\right), \left(-\frac{1}{5}, 0\right), \left(\frac{1}{5}, 2\right), \left(\frac{2}{5}, 3\right)\right\}$

7. $2a + b = 4$

$2a = 4 - b$

$a = \frac{4-b}{2}$

b	$\frac{4-b}{2}$	a	(a, b)
-3	$\frac{4-(-3)}{2}$	$\frac{7}{2}$	$\left(\frac{7}{2}, -3\right)$
-1	$\frac{4-(-1)}{2}$	$\frac{5}{2}$	$\left(\frac{5}{2}, -1\right)$
0	$\frac{4-0}{2}$	2	$(2, 0)$
2	$\frac{4-2}{2}$	1	$(1, 2)$
3	$\frac{4-3}{2}$	$\frac{1}{2}$	$\left(\frac{1}{2}, 3\right)$

$\left\{\left(\frac{7}{2}, -3\right), \left(\frac{5}{2}, -1\right), (2, 0), (1, 2), \left(\frac{1}{2}, 3\right)\right\}$

8. $4r + 3s = 13$

$4r = 13 - 3s$

$r = \frac{13-3s}{4}$

s	$\frac{13-3s}{4}$	r	(r, s)
-3	$\frac{13-3(-3)}{4}$	$\frac{11}{2}$	$\left(\frac{11}{2}, -3\right)$
-1	$\frac{13-3(-1)}{4}$	4	$(4, -1)$
0	$\frac{13-3(0)}{4}$	$\frac{13}{4}$	$\left(\frac{13}{4}, 0\right)$
2	$\frac{13-3(2)}{4}$	$\frac{7}{4}$	$\left(\frac{7}{4}, 2\right)$
3	$\frac{13-3(3)}{4}$	1	$(1, 3)$

$\left\{\left(\frac{11}{2}, -3\right), (4, -1), \left(\frac{13}{4}, 0\right), \left(\frac{7}{4}, 2\right), (1, 3)\right\}$

9. $5b = 8 - 4a$

$5b - 8 = -4a$

$\frac{5b-8}{-4} = a$

b	$\frac{5b-8}{-4}$	a	(a, b)
-3	$\frac{5(-3)-8}{-4}$	$\frac{23}{4}$	$\left(\frac{23}{4}, -3\right)$
-1	$\frac{5(-1)-8}{-4}$	$\frac{13}{4}$	$\left(\frac{13}{4}, -1\right)$
0	$\frac{5(0)-8}{-4}$	2	$(2, 0)$
2	$\frac{5(2)-8}{-4}$	$-\frac{1}{2}$	$\left(-\frac{1}{2}, 2\right)$
3	$\frac{5(3)-8}{-4}$	$-\frac{7}{4}$	$\left(-\frac{7}{4}, 3\right)$

$\left\{\left(\frac{23}{4}, -3\right), \left(\frac{13}{4}, -1\right), (2, 0), \left(-\frac{1}{2}, 2\right), \left(-\frac{7}{4}, 3\right)\right\}$

10. $6m - n = -3$

$6m = -3 + n$

$m = \frac{-3+n}{6}$

n	$\frac{-3+n}{6}$	m	(m, n)
-3	$\frac{-3+(-3)}{6}$	-1	$(-1, -3)$
-1	$\frac{-3+(-1)}{6}$	$-\frac{2}{3}$	$\left(-\frac{2}{3}, -1\right)$
0	$\frac{-3+0}{6}$	$-\frac{1}{2}$	$\left(-\frac{1}{2}, 0\right)$
2	$\frac{-3+2}{6}$	$-\frac{1}{6}$	$\left(-\frac{1}{6}, 2\right)$
3	$\frac{-3+3}{6}$	0	$(0, 3)$

$\left\{(-1, -3), \left(-\frac{2}{3}, -1\right), \left(-\frac{1}{2}, 0\right), \left(-\frac{1}{6}, 2\right), (0, 3)\right\}$

Page 768 Lesson 5-4

1. yes; $3x - 2y = 0$
2. no
3. yes; $3x - 2y = 8$
4. yes; $5x - 7y = 2x - 7$
   $3x - 7y = -7$
5. yes; $2x + 5x = 7y$
   $7x - 7y = 0$
6. no

7. $3x + y = 4$
$y = 4 - 3x$

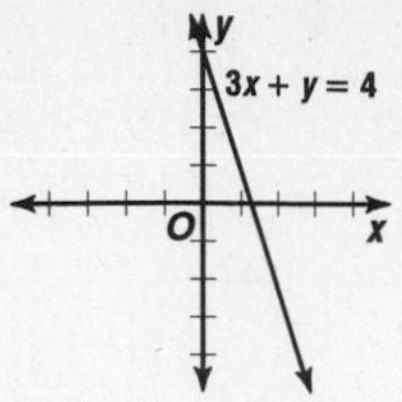

8. $y = 3x + 1$

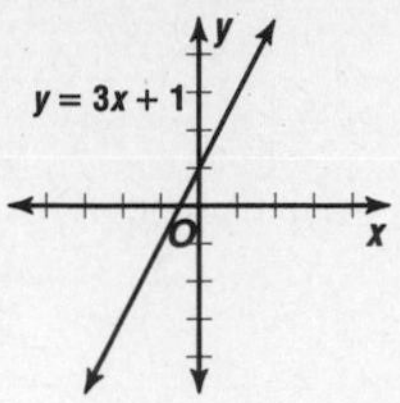

9. $3x - 2y = 12$
$-2y = -3x + 12$
$y = \frac{3}{2}x - 6$

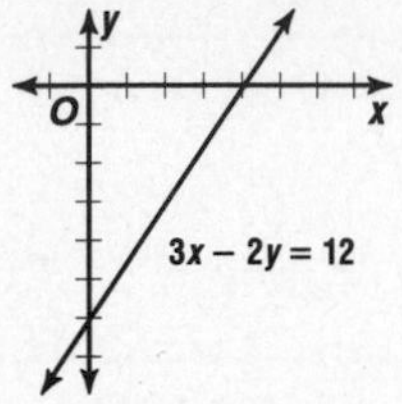

10. $2x - y = 6$
$-y = -2x + 6$
$y = 2x - 6$

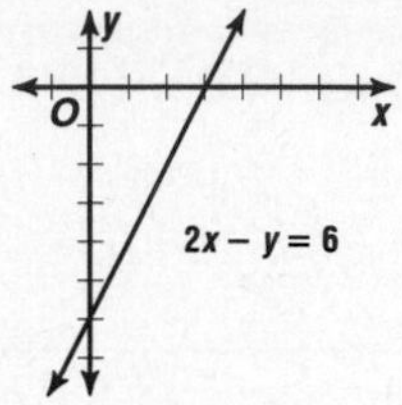

11. $3x - 2y = 8$
$-2y = -3x + 8$
$y = \frac{3}{2}x - 4$

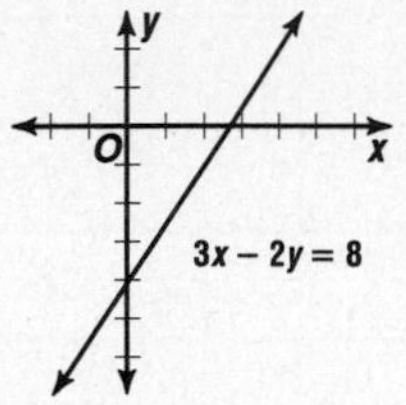

12. $y = \frac{3}{4}$

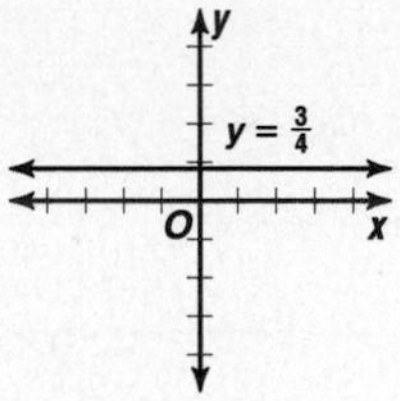

13. $y = 5x - 7$

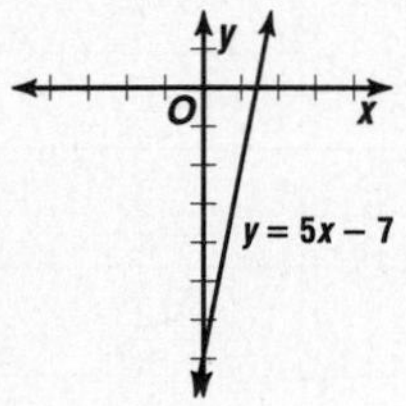

14. $x + \frac{1}{3}y = 6$
$\frac{1}{3}y = -x + 6$
$y = -3x + 18$

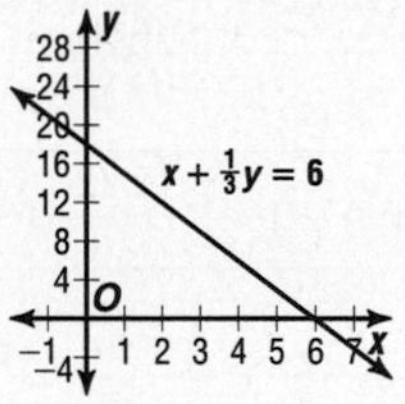

15. $x = -\frac{5}{2}$

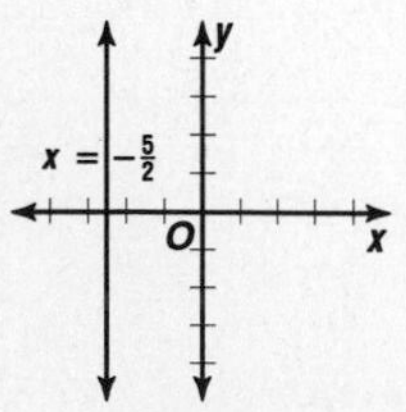

16. $5x - 2y = 8$
$-2y = -5x + 8$
$y = \frac{5}{2}x - 4$

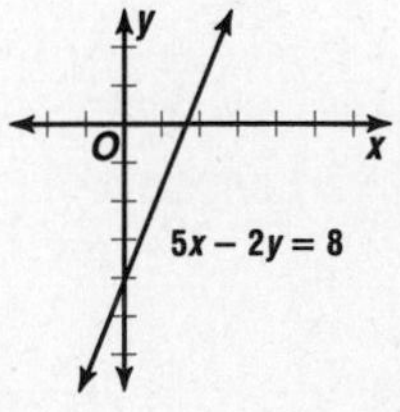

17. $4x + 2y = 9$
$2y = -4x + 9$
$y = -2x + \frac{9}{2}$

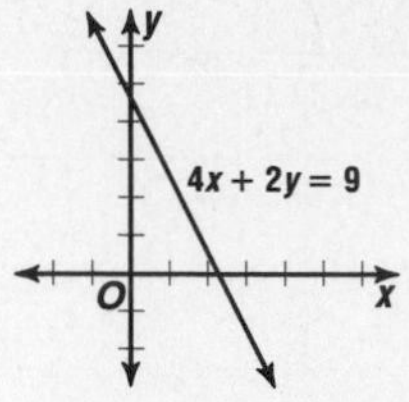

18. $4x + 3y = 12$
$3y = -4x + 12$
$y = -\frac{4}{3}x + 4$

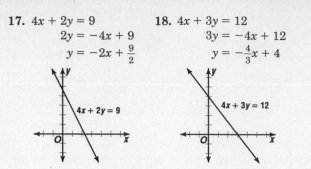

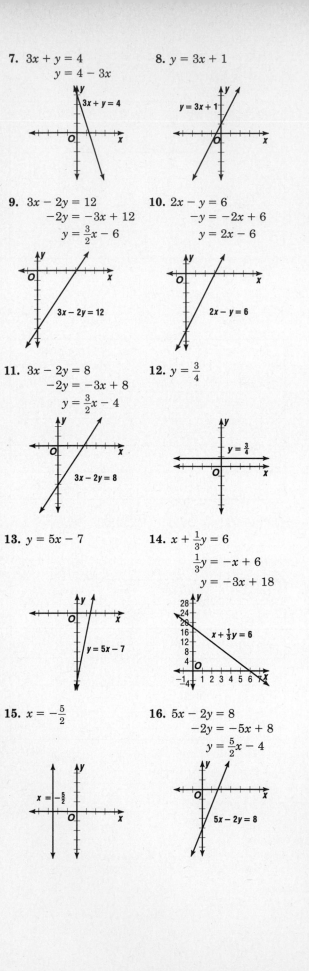

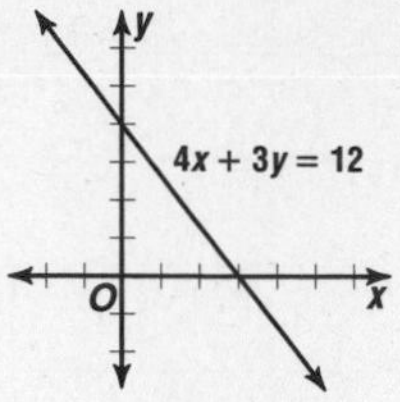

Page 768 Lesson 5-5

1. No; the element 1 in the domain is paired with both 3 and −7 in the range.
2. No; the element −2 in the domain is paired with both −4 and 2 in the range.
3. Yes; for any given value of *x*, there is only one value for *y*.
4. No; the *x* value of −1 is paired with *y* values of 0 and 2.
5. Yes; for any given value of *a*, there is only one value for *b*.
6. Yes; for each element of the domain, there is only one corresponding element in the range.
7. No; the element 1 in the domain is paired with both 3 and 4 in the range.
8. Yes; each element of the domain is paired with exactly one element in the range.
9. Yes; each element of the domain is paired with exactly one element in the range.
10. No; the element 4 in the domain is paired with both 7 and 5 in the range.
11. Yes; for any given value of *x*, there is only one value of *y* that will satisfy the equation.
12. Yes; for any given value of *x*, there is only one value of *y* that will satisfy the equation.

Page 768 Lesson 5-6

1. $\frac{\text{range differences}}{\text{domain differences}} = \frac{-3-(-4)}{4-2} = \frac{1}{2}$
$f(x) = \frac{1}{2}x - 5$

2. $f(x) = x^2 - 4$

3. $\frac{\text{range differences}}{\text{domain differences}} = \frac{11-7}{2-1} = \frac{4}{1}$ or 4
$f(x) = 4x + 3$

4. (0, 2), (3, 3)
$\frac{\text{range differences}}{\text{domain differences}} = \frac{3-2}{3-0} = \frac{1}{3}$
$y = \frac{1}{3}x + 2$

5. (0, 2), (2, −5)
$\frac{\text{range differences}}{\text{domain differences}} = \frac{-5-(-2)}{2-0} = \frac{-3}{2}$
$y = -\frac{3}{2}x - 2$

6. (−3, 0), (−4, −2)

$\frac{\text{range differences}}{\text{domain differences}} = \frac{-2-0}{-4-(-3)} = \frac{-2}{-1} = 2$

$y = 2x + 6$

7. $\frac{\text{range differences}}{\text{domain differences}} = \frac{14-12}{4-3} = \frac{2}{1}$

$y = 2x + 6$

8. $\frac{\text{range differences}}{\text{domain differences}} = \frac{8-4}{2-1} = \frac{4}{1}$

$y = 4x$

9. $\frac{\text{range differences}}{\text{domain differences}} = \frac{-6-(-8)}{-3-(-6)} = \frac{2}{3}$

$y = \frac{2}{3}x - 4$

10. $\frac{\text{range differences}}{\text{domain differences}} = \frac{7-9}{-2-(-3)} = \frac{-2}{1}$

$y = -2x + 3$

Page 769 Lesson 5-7

1. range: 56 − 10 = 46
median: $\frac{37+43}{2} = 40$
Q3: 45
Q1: 34
IQR: 45 − 34 = 11

2. range: 99 − 65 = 34
median: 78
Q3: 96
Q1: 68
IQR: 96 − 68 = 28

3. range: 100 − 30 = 70
median: $\frac{60+70}{2} = 65$
Q3: $\frac{80+90}{2} = 85$
Q1: $\frac{40+50}{5} = 45$
IQR: 85 − 45 = 40

4. range: 9 − 1 = 8
median: 4
Q3: 7.1
Q1: 2.4
IQR: 7.1 − 2.4 = 4.7

5. range: 73° − 0° = 73°
median: 31°
Q3: 56°
Q1: 13°
IQR: 56° − 13° = 43°

6. range: 775 − 112 = 663
median: 400
Q3: $\frac{527+648}{2} = 587.5$
Q1: $\frac{234+268}{2} = 251$
IQR: 587.5 − 251 = 336.5

7. range: 48 − 0 = 48
median: 26
Q3: 39
Q1: 17
IQR: 39 − 17 = 22

8. range: 11.9 − 7.3 = 4.6
median: 8.7
Q3: $\frac{10+10.1}{2} = 10.05$
Q1: $\frac{7.8+8.0}{2} = 7.9$
IQR: 10.05 − 7.9 = 2.15

9. range: 2990 − 2500 = 490
median: $\frac{2750-2760}{2} = 2755$
Q3: $\frac{2830-2850}{2} = 2840$
Q1: $\frac{2630+2640}{2} = 2635$
IQR: 2840 − 2635 = 205

Page 769 Lesson 6-1

1. $\frac{y\text{ change}}{x\text{ change}} = \frac{3}{1}$

$m = 3$

2. $\frac{y\text{ change}}{x\text{ change}} = \frac{-2}{2}$

$m = -1$

3. $\frac{y\text{ change}}{x\text{ change}} = \frac{3}{2}$

$m = \frac{3}{2}$

4. $\frac{y\text{ change}}{x\text{ change}} = 0$

$m = 0$

5. $\frac{y\text{ change}}{x\text{ change}} = \frac{5}{0}$

$m =$ undefined

6. $\frac{y\text{ change}}{x\text{ change}} = \frac{-1}{5}$

$m = -\frac{1}{5}$

7. $\frac{y\text{ change}}{x\text{ change}} = \frac{1}{3}$

$m = \frac{1}{3}$

8. $\frac{y\text{ change}}{x\text{ change}} = \frac{-2}{1}$

$m = -2$

9. $m = \frac{y_2 - y_1}{x_2 - x_1} = \frac{-3-2}{3-(-2)} = \frac{-5}{5} = -1$

10. $m = \frac{y_2 - y_1}{x_2 - x_1} = \frac{4-(-8)}{1-(-2)} = \frac{12}{3} = 4$

11. $m = \frac{y_2 - y_1}{x_2 - x_1} = \frac{6-4}{4-3} = \frac{2}{1} = 2$

12. $m = \frac{y_2 - y_1}{x_2 - x_1} = \frac{11-4}{-1-(-5)} = \frac{7}{4}$

13. $m = \frac{y_2 - y_1}{x_2 - x_1} = \frac{-10-(-4)}{6-18} = \frac{-6}{-12} = \frac{1}{2}$

14. $m = \frac{y_2 - y_1}{x_2 - x_1} = \frac{-8-(-6)}{-4-(-4)} = \frac{-2}{0}$

undefined

15.
$$m = \frac{y_2 - y_1}{x_2 - x_1}$$
$$-5 = \frac{-4-r}{1-(-1)}$$
$$-5 = \frac{-4-r}{2}$$
$$-10 = -4 - r$$
$$-6 = -r$$
$$6 = r$$

16.
$$m = \frac{y_2 - y_1}{x_2 - x_1}$$
$$\frac{3}{5} = \frac{4-1}{r-(-2)}$$
$$3(r+2) = 5(3)$$
$$3r + 6 = 15$$
$$3r = 9$$
$$r = 3$$

17.
$$m = \frac{y_2 - y_1}{x_2 - x_1}$$
$$-3 = \frac{r-3}{-3-(-1)}$$
$$-3 = \frac{r-3}{-2}$$
$$6 = r - 3$$
$$9 = r$$

18.
$$m = \frac{y_2 - y_1}{x_2 - x_1}$$
$$\frac{1}{2} = \frac{-2-r}{7-3}$$
$$\frac{1}{2} = \frac{-2-r}{4}$$
$$4 = 2(-2-r)$$
$$8 = -2r$$
$$-4 = r$$

19.
$$m = \frac{y_2 - y_1}{x_2 - x_1}$$
$$-\frac{1}{4} = \frac{-1-(-2)}{-7-r}$$
$$-\frac{1}{4} = \frac{1}{-7-r}$$
$$-1(-7-r) = 4$$
$$7 + r = 4$$
$$r = -3$$

20.
$$m = \frac{y_2 - y_1}{x_2 - x_1}$$
$$\frac{2}{3} = \frac{r-2}{7-(-3)}$$
$$\frac{2}{3} = \frac{r-2}{10}$$
$$20 = 3(r-2)$$
$$20 = 3r - 6$$
$$26 = 3r$$
$$\frac{26}{3} = r$$

Page 769 Lesson 6-2

1.
$$y - y_1 = m(x - x_1)$$
$$y - (-2) = 3(x - 5)$$
$$y + 2 = 3(x - 5)$$

2.
$$y - y_1 = m(x - x_1)$$
$$y - 4 = -5(x - 4)$$

3.
$$y - y_1 = m(x - x_1)$$
$$y - (-4) = \tfrac{3}{4}[x - (-2)]$$
$$y + 4 = \tfrac{3}{4}(x + 2)$$

4.
$$y - y_1 = m(x - x_1)$$
$$y - 1 = 0[x - (-3)]$$
$$y - 1 = 0$$

5. $y - y_1 = m(x - x_1)$
$y - 0 = \frac{2}{3}[x - (-1)]$
$y = \frac{2}{3}(x + 1)$

6. $y - y_1 = m(x - x_1)$
$y - 6 = -2(x - 0)$
$y - 6 = -2x$

7. $y - y_1 = m(x - x_1)$
$y - (-3) = -\frac{1}{2}[x - (-6)]$
$y + 3 = -\frac{1}{2}(x + 6)$
$-2(y + 3) = -2\left[-\frac{1}{2}(x + 6)\right]$
$-2y - 6 = x + 6$
$-12 = x + 2y$
$x + 2y = -12$

8. $y - y_1 = m(x - x_1)$
$y - (-3) = 2(x - 4)$
$y + 3 = 2x - 8$
$y + 11 = 2x$
$11 = 2x - y$
$2x - y = 11$

9. $y - y_1 = m(x - x_1)$
$y - 4 = -\frac{2}{3}(x - 5)$
$3(y - 4) = 3\left[-\frac{2}{3}(x - 5)\right]$
$3y - 12 = -2(x - 5)$
$3y - 12 = -2x + 10$
$2x + 3y = 22$

10. $x = 1$

11. $y - y_1 = m(x - x_1)$
$y - 6 = 0[x - (-2)]$
$y - 6 = 0$
$y = 6$

12. $y - y_1 = m(x - x_1)$
$y - (-2) = \frac{4}{3}(x - 6)$
$y + 2 = \frac{4}{3}(x - 6)$
$3(y + 2) = 3\left[\frac{4}{3}(x - 6)\right]$
$3y + 6 = 4(x - 6)$
$3y + 6 = 4x - 24$
$30 = 4x - 3y$
$4x - 3y = 30$

Page 770 Lesson 6-3

1. positive
2. negative
3. positive
4. positive
5. no correlation
6. negative

7a. It decreases.
7b. yes, negative

Page 770 Lesson 6-4

1. $3x + 2y = 6$
Let $y = 0$.
$3x + 2(0) = 6$
$3x = 6$
$x = 2$
Let $x = 0$.
$3(0) + 2y = 6$
$2y = 6$
$y = 3$
x-intercept: 2, y-intercept: 3

2. $5x + y = 10$
Let $y = 0$.
$5x + 0 = 10$
$5x = 10$
$x = 2$
Let $x = 0$.
$5(0) + y = 10$
$y = 10$
x-intercept: 2, y-intercept: 10

3. $2x + 5y = -11$
Let $y = 0$.
$2x + 5(0) = -11$
$2x = -11$
$x = -\frac{11}{2}$
Let $x = 0$.
$2(0) + 5y = -11$
$5y = -11$
$y = -\frac{11}{5}$
x-intercept: $-\frac{11}{2}$, y-intercept: $-\frac{11}{5}$

4. $3y = 12$
Let $y = 0$.
$3(0) = 12$
$0 \neq 12$
Let $x = 0$.
$3y = 12$
$y = 4$
x-intercept: none, y-intercept: 4

5. $y - 6x = 5$
Let $y = 0$.
$0 - 6x = 5$
$-6x = 5$
$x = -\frac{5}{6}$
Let $x = 0$.
$y - 6(0) = 5$
$y = 5$
x-intercept: $-\frac{5}{6}$, y-intercept: 5

6. $x = -2$
x-intercept: -2, y-intercept: none

7. $y = mx + b$
$y = -\frac{2}{5}x + 2$ slope-intercept
$5(y) = 5\left(-\frac{2}{5}x + 2\right)$
$5y = -2x + 10$
$2x + 5y = 10$ standard

8. $y = mx + b$
$y = 5x - 15$ slope-intercept
$y + 15 = 5x$
$-5x + y = -15$
$5x - y = 15$ standard

9. $y = mx + b$
$y = -\frac{7}{4}x + 2$ slope-intercept
$4(y) = 4\left(-\frac{7}{4}x + 2\right)$
$4y = -7x + 8$
$7x + 4y = 8$ standard

10. $y = mx + b$
$y = -\frac{4}{3}x + \frac{5}{3}$ slope-intercept
$3(y) = 3\left(-\frac{4}{3}x + \frac{5}{3}\right)$
$3y = -4x + 5$
$4x + 3y = 5$ standard

11. $y = mx + b$
$y = -6x + 15$ slope-intercept
$6x + y = 15$ standard

12. $y = mx + b$
$y = 12x - 24$ slope-intercept
$y + 24 = 12x$
$24x = 12x - y$
$12x - y = 24$ standard

13. $y - \frac{3}{5}x = -\frac{1}{4}$
$y = \frac{3}{5}x - \frac{1}{4}$
$m = \frac{3}{5}$, y-intercept: $-\frac{1}{4}$

14. $y = 3x - 7$
$m = 3$; y-intercept: -7

15. $\frac{2}{3}x + \frac{1}{6}y = 2$
$\frac{1}{6}y = -\frac{2}{3}x + 2$
$6\left(\frac{1}{6}y\right) = 6\left(-\frac{2}{3}x + 2\right)$
$y = -4x + 12$
$m = -4$; y-intercept: 12

16. $2x + 3y = 5$

$3y = -2x + 5$

$y = -\frac{2}{3}x + \frac{5}{3}$

$m = -\frac{2}{3}$; y-intercept: $\frac{5}{3}$

17. $3y = 8x + 2$

$y = \frac{8}{3}x + \frac{2}{3}$

$m = \frac{8}{3}$; y-intercept: $\frac{2}{3}$

18. $5y = -8x - 2$

$y = -\frac{8}{5}x - \frac{2}{5}$

$m = -\frac{8}{5}$; y-intercept: $-\frac{2}{5}$

19. $m = \frac{y_2 - y_1}{x_2 - x_1}$

$= \frac{-2 - 7}{8 - (-1)} = \frac{-9}{9} = -1$

$y - y_1 = m(x - x_1)$, using (8, 2)

$y - (-2) = -1(x - 8)$

$y + 2 = -x + 8$

$x + y = 6$

20. $m = \frac{y_2 - y_1}{x_2 - x_1}$

$= \frac{4 - 0}{0 - 6} = -\frac{4}{6} = -\frac{2}{3}$

$y - y_1 = m(x - x_1)$, using (0, 4)

$y - 4 = -\frac{2}{3}(x - 0)$

$3(y - 4) = 3\left(-\frac{2}{3}x\right)$

$3y - 12 = -2x$

$2x + 3y = 12$

21. $m = \frac{y_2 - y_1}{x_2 - x_1}$

$= \frac{-1 - (-1)}{8 - 7} = \frac{0}{1} = 0$

$y - y_1 = m(x - x_1)$, using (8, −1)

$y - (-1) = 0(x - 8)$

$y + 1 = 0$

$y = -1$

22. $m = \frac{y_2 - y_1}{x_2 - x_1}$

$= \frac{1 - 0}{0 - 1} = -1$

$y - y_1 = m(x - x_1)$, using (0, 1)

$y - 1 = -1(x - 0)$

$y - 1 = -x$

$x + y = 1$

23. $m = \frac{y_2 - y_1}{x_2 - x_1}$

$= \frac{7 - 6}{5 - (-1)} = \frac{1}{6}$

$y - y_1 = m(x - x_1)$, using (5, 7)

$y - 7 = \frac{1}{6}(x - 5)$

$6(y - 7) = 6\left[\frac{1}{6}(x - 5)\right]$

$6y - 42 = x - 5$

$x - 6y = -37$

24. $m = \frac{y_2 - y_1}{x_2 - x_1}$

$= \frac{-15 - (-5)}{3 - (-3)} = \frac{-10}{6} = -\frac{5}{3}$

$y - y_1 = m(x - x_1)$, using (3, −15)

$y - (-15) = -\frac{5}{3}(x - 3)$

$y + 15 = -\frac{5}{3}(x - 3)$

$3(y + 15) = 3\left[-\frac{5}{3}(x - 3)\right]$

$3y + 45 = -5(x - 3)$

$3y + 45 = -5x + 15$

$5x + 3y = -30$

Page 770 Lesson 6-5

1. $4x + y = 8$

$y = -4x + 8$

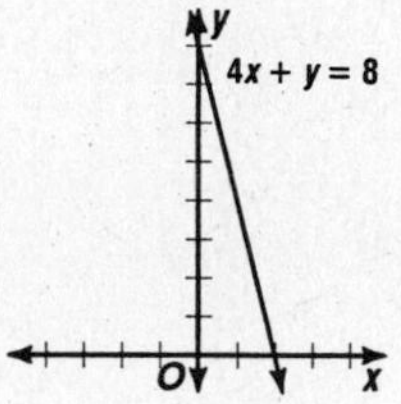

2. $2x - y = 8$

$-y = -2x + 8$

$y = 2x - 8$

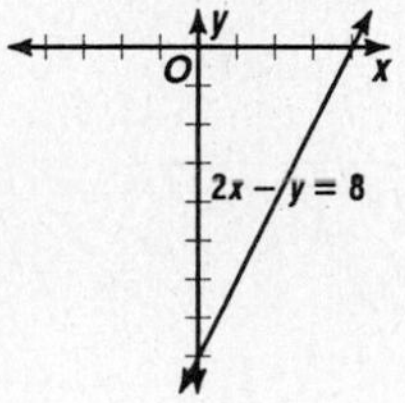

3. $3x - 2y = 6$

$-2y = -3x + 6$

$y = \frac{3}{2}x - 3$

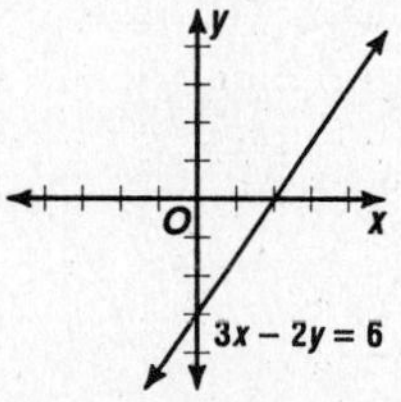

4. $6x - 3y = 6$

$-3y = -6x + 6$

$y = -2x - 2$

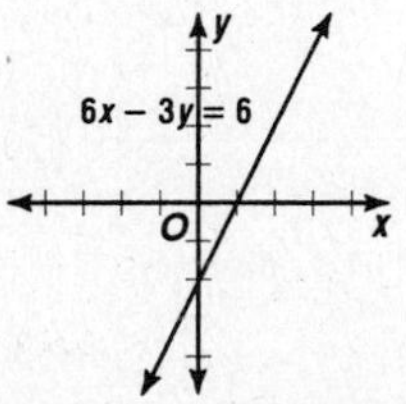

5. $x + \frac{1}{2}y = 4$

$\frac{1}{2}y = -x + 4$

$2\left(\frac{1}{2}y\right) = 2(-x + 4)$

$y = -2x + 8$

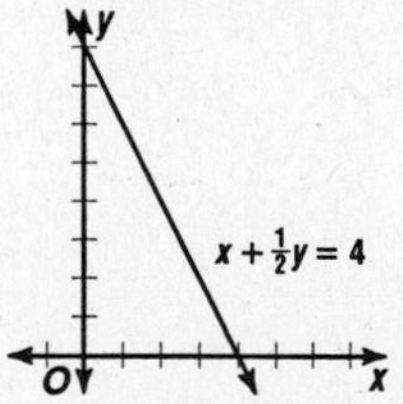

6. $4x + 5y = 20$

$5y = -4x + 20$

$y = -\frac{4}{5}x + 4$

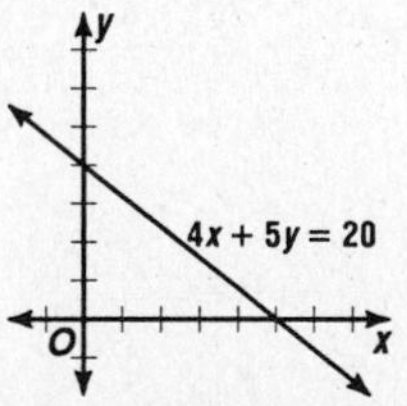

7. $y + 3 = -2(x + 4)$

$y + 3 = -2x - 8$

$y = -2x - 11$

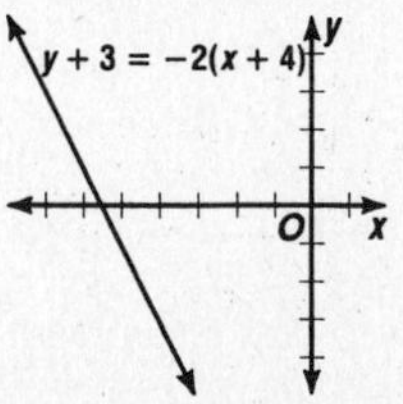

8. $y - 1 = 3(x - 5)$

$y - 1 = 3x - 15$

$y = 3x - 14$

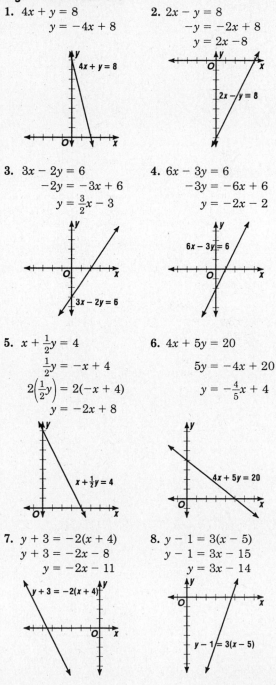

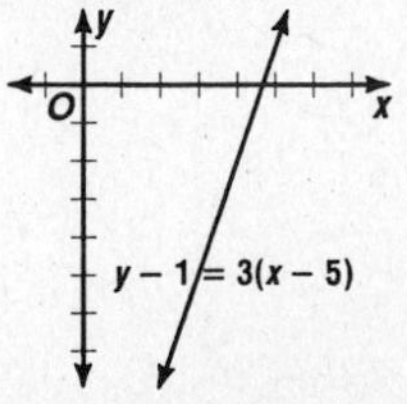

9. $y + 6 = -\frac{2}{3}(x + 1)$

$y + 6 = -\frac{2}{3}x - \frac{2}{3}$

$y = -\frac{2}{3}x - \frac{20}{3}$

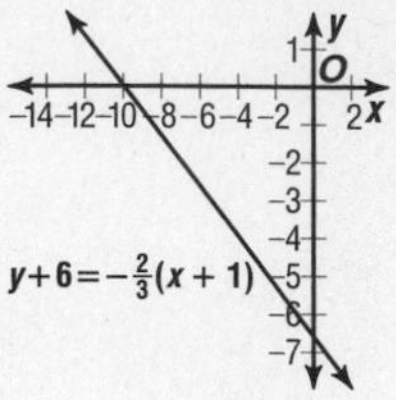

10. $y - 5 = 4(x + 6)$

$y - 5 = 4x + 24$

$y = 4x + 29$

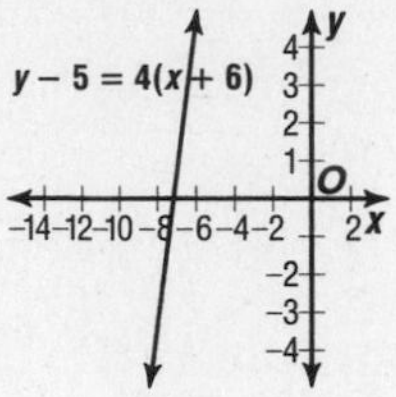

11. $y - 2 = (x + 7)$

$y = x + 9$

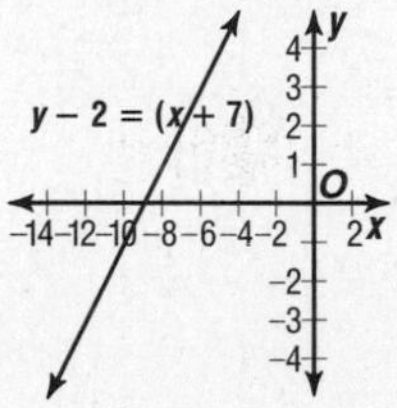

12. $3(x - 1) = y + \frac{4}{5}$

$3x - 3 = y + \frac{4}{5}$

$3x - \frac{19}{5} = y$

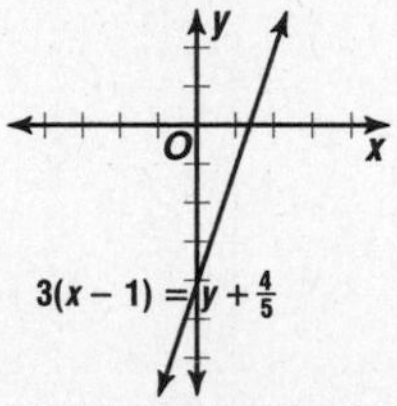

13. $y = \frac{3}{4}x + 4$

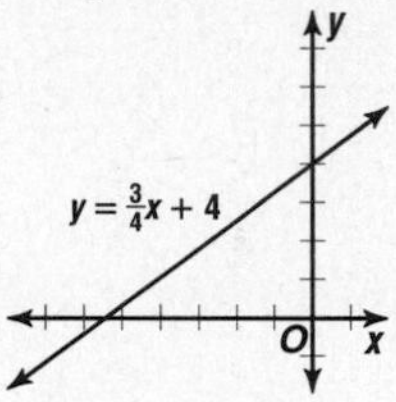

14. $y = 4x - 1$

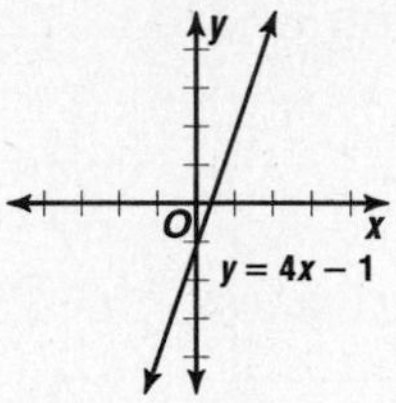

15. $-4x + y = 6$

$y = 4x + 6$

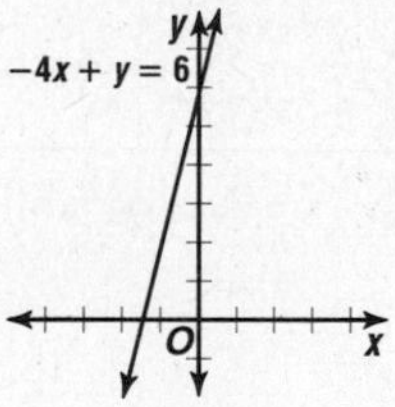

16. $-2x + y = 3$

$y = 2x + 3$

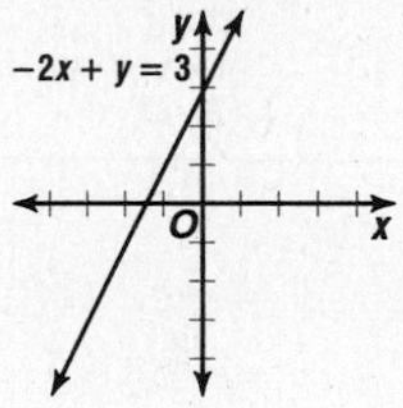

17. $5y - 6 = 3x$

$5y = 3x + 6$

$y = \frac{3}{5}x + \frac{6}{3}$

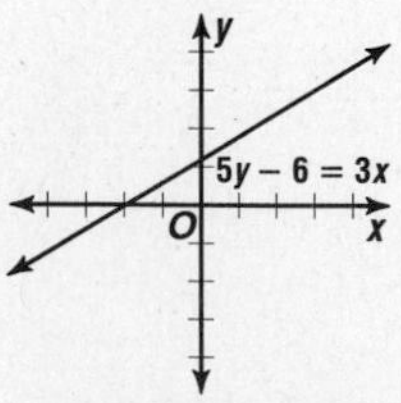

18. $y = \frac{3}{2}x - 5$

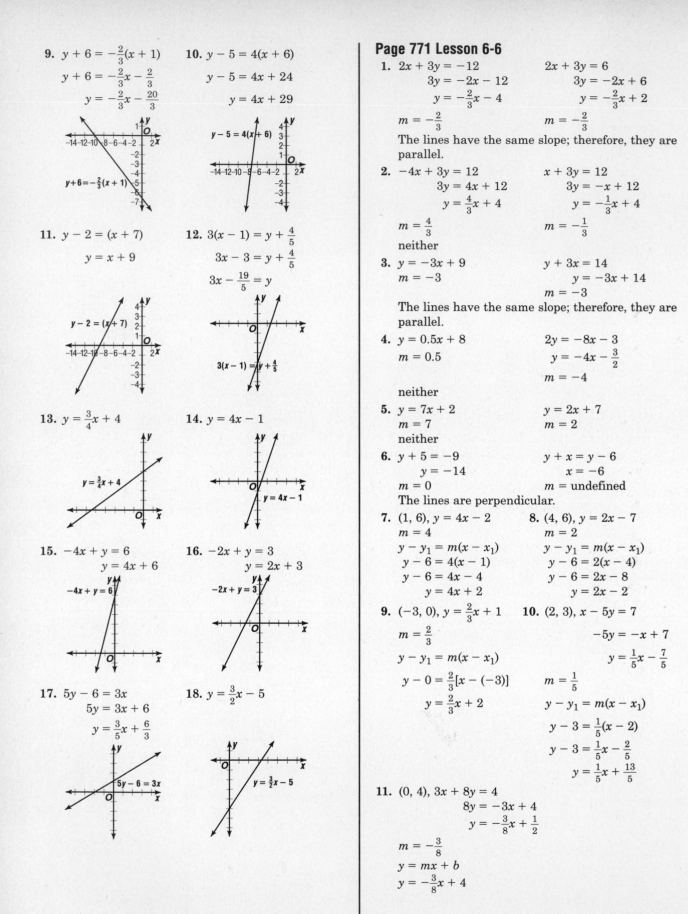

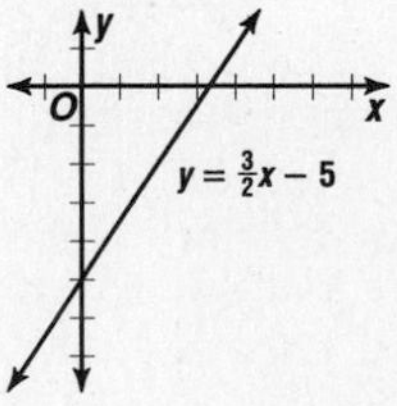

Page 771 Lesson 6-6

1. $2x + 3y = -12$; $3y = -2x - 12$; $y = -\frac{2}{3}x - 4$; $m = -\frac{2}{3}$

$2x + 3y = 6$; $3y = -2x + 6$; $y = -\frac{2}{3}x + 2$; $m = -\frac{2}{3}$

The lines have the same slope; therefore, they are parallel.

2. $-4x + 3y = 12$; $3y = 4x + 12$; $y = \frac{4}{3}x + 4$; $m = \frac{4}{3}$

$x + 3y = 12$; $3y = -x + 12$; $y = -\frac{1}{3}x + 4$; $m = -\frac{1}{3}$

neither

3. $y = -3x + 9$; $m = -3$

$y + 3x = 14$; $y = -3x + 14$; $m = -3$

The lines have the same slope; therefore, they are parallel.

4. $y = 0.5x + 8$; $m = 0.5$

$2y = -8x - 3$; $y = -4x - \frac{3}{2}$; $m = -4$

neither

5. $y = 7x + 2$; $m = 7$

$y = 2x + 7$; $m = 2$

neither

6. $y + 5 = -9$; $y = -14$; $m = 0$

$y + x = y - 6$; $x = -6$; $m =$ undefined

The lines are perpendicular.

7. $(1, 6)$, $y = 4x - 2$

$m = 4$

$y - y_1 = m(x - x_1)$

$y - 6 = 4(x - 1)$

$y - 6 = 4x - 4$

$y = 4x + 2$

8. $(4, 6)$, $y = 2x - 7$

$m = 2$

$y - y_1 = m(x - x_1)$

$y - 6 = 2(x - 4)$

$y - 6 = 2x - 8$

$y = 2x - 2$

9. $(-3, 0)$, $y = \frac{2}{3}x + 1$

$m = \frac{2}{3}$

$y - y_1 = m(x - x_1)$

$y - 0 = \frac{2}{3}[x - (-3)]$

$y = \frac{2}{3}x + 2$

10. $(2, 3)$, $x - 5y = 7$

$-5y = -x + 7$

$y = \frac{1}{5}x - \frac{7}{5}$

$m = \frac{1}{5}$

$y - y_1 = m(x - x_1)$

$y - 3 = \frac{1}{5}(x - 2)$

$y - 3 = \frac{1}{5}x - \frac{2}{5}$

$y = \frac{1}{5}x + \frac{13}{5}$

11. $(0, 4)$, $3x + 8y = 4$

$8y = -3x + 4$

$y = -\frac{3}{8}x + \frac{1}{2}$

$m = -\frac{3}{8}$

$y = mx + b$

$y = -\frac{3}{8}x + 4$

12. $(5, -2)$, $y = -3x - 7$
$$m = -3$$
$$y - y_1 = m(x - x_1)$$
$$y - (-2) = -3(x - 5)$$
$$y + 2 = -3x + 15$$
$$y = -3x + 13$$

13. $(0, -1)$, $y = -\frac{3}{5}x + 4$
$$m = \frac{5}{3}$$
$$y - y_1 = m(x - x_1)$$
$$y - (-1) = \frac{5}{3}(x - 0)$$
$$y + 1 = \frac{5}{3}x$$
$$y = \frac{5}{3}x - 1$$

14. $(-2, 3)$, $6x + y = 4$
$$y = -6x + 4$$
$$m = \frac{1}{6}$$
$$y - y_1 = m(x - x_1)$$
$$y - 3 = \frac{1}{6}[x - (-2)]$$
$$y - 3 = \frac{1}{6}x + \frac{1}{3}$$
$$y = \frac{1}{6}x + \frac{10}{3}$$

15. $(0, 0)$, $y = \frac{3}{4}x - 1$
$$m = -\frac{4}{3}$$
$$y = mx + b$$
$$y = -\frac{4}{3}x$$

16. $(4, 0)$, $4x - 3y = 2$
$$-3y = -4x + 2$$
$$y = \frac{4}{3}x - \frac{2}{3}$$
$$m = -\frac{3}{4}$$
$$y - y_1 = m(x - x_1)$$
$$y - 0 = -\frac{3}{4}(x - 4)$$
$$y = -\frac{3}{4}x + 3$$

17. $(6, 7)$, $3x - 5y = 1$
$$-5y = -3x + 1$$
$$y = \frac{3}{5}x - \frac{1}{5}$$
$$m = -\frac{5}{3}$$
$$y - y_1 = m(x - x_1)$$
$$y - 7 = \frac{5}{3}(x - 6)$$
$$y - 7 = -\frac{5}{3}x + 10$$
$$y = -\frac{5}{3}x + 17$$

18. $(5, -1)$, $8x + 4y = 15$
$$4y = -8x + 15$$
$$y = -2x + \frac{15}{4}$$
$$m = \frac{1}{2}$$
$$y - y_1 = m(x - x_1)$$
$$y - (-1) = \frac{1}{2}(x - 5)$$
$$y + 1 = \frac{1}{2}x - \frac{5}{2}$$
$$y = \frac{1}{2}x - \frac{7}{2}$$

Page 771 Lesson 6-7

1. midpoint of $\overline{LM} = \left(\frac{12 + 8}{2}, \frac{2 + 4}{2}\right)$
$$= \left(\frac{20}{2}, \frac{6}{2}\right)$$
$$= (10, 3)$$

2. midpoint of $\overline{ST} = \left(\frac{9 + 17}{2}, \frac{5 + 3}{2}\right)$
$$= \left(\frac{26}{2}, \frac{8}{2}\right)$$
$$= (13, 4)$$

3. midpoint of $\overline{DE} = \left(\frac{17 + 11}{2}, \frac{9 + (-3)}{2}\right)$
$$= \left(\frac{28}{2}, \frac{6}{2}\right)$$
$$= (14, 3)$$

4. midpoint of $\overline{FG} = \left(\frac{4 + 8}{2}, \frac{2 + (-6)}{2}\right)$
$$= \left(\frac{12}{2}, \frac{-4}{2}\right)$$
$$= (6, -2)$$

5. midpoint of $\overline{MN} = \left(\frac{19 + 11}{2}, \frac{-3 + 5}{2}\right)$
$$= \left(\frac{30}{2}, \frac{2}{2}\right)$$
$$= (15, 1)$$

6. midpoint of $\overline{BC} = \left(\frac{-6 + 8}{2}, \frac{5 + (-11)}{2}\right)$
$$= \left(\frac{2}{2}, \frac{-6}{2}\right)$$
$$= (1, -3)$$

7. midpoint of $\overline{TU} = \left(\frac{-11 + 12}{2}, \frac{6 + 4}{2}\right)$
$$= \left(\frac{2}{2}, \frac{10}{2}\right)$$
$$= (1, 5)$$

8. midpoint of $\overline{AB} = \left(\frac{-6 + 8}{2}, \frac{1 + 9}{2}\right)$
$$= \left(\frac{2}{2}, \frac{10}{2}\right)$$
$$= (1, 5)$$

9. midpoint of $\overline{JK} = \left(\frac{6.4 + 1.8}{2}, \frac{-3 + (-3)}{2}\right)$
$$= \left(\frac{8.2}{2}, \frac{-6}{2}\right)$$
$$= (4.1, -3)$$

10. midpoint of $\overline{RS} = \left(\frac{19 + 7}{2}, \frac{5 + 4}{2}\right)$
$$= \left(\frac{26}{2}, \frac{9}{2}\right)$$
$$= \left(13, \frac{9}{2}\right)$$

11. midpoint of $\overline{GH} = \left(\frac{8 + 16}{2}, \frac{10 + (-6)}{2}\right)$
$$= \left(\frac{24}{2}, \frac{4}{2}\right)$$
$$= (12, 2)$$

12. midpoint of $\overline{CD} = \left(\frac{7.6 + (-5)}{2}, \frac{8.3 + 6.1}{2}\right)$
$$= \left(\frac{2.6}{2}, \frac{14.4}{2}\right)$$
$$= (1.3, 7.2)$$

13. $1 = \frac{9 + x}{2}$ $\qquad$ $2 = \frac{3 + y}{2}$
$2 = 9 + x$ $\qquad$ $4 = 3 + y$
$-7 = x$ $\qquad$ $1 = y$
$(-7, 1)$

14. $5 = \frac{3+x}{2}$
$10 = 3 + x$
$7 = x$

$-7 = \frac{5+y}{2}$
$-14 = 5 + y$
$-19 = y$

$(7, -19)$

15. $8 = \frac{5+x}{2}$
$16 = 5 + x$
$11 = x$

$-\frac{15}{2} = \frac{-9+y}{2}$
$-30 = 2(-9 + y)$
$-30 = -18 + 2y$
$-12 = 2y$
$-6 = y$

$(11, -6)$

16. $-2 = \frac{4+x}{2}$
$-4 = 4 + x$
$-8 = x$

$-3 = \frac{-7+y}{2}$
$-6 = -7 + y$
$1 = y$

$(-8, 1)$

17. $3 = \frac{-3+x}{2}$
$6 = -3 + x$
$9 = x$

$-5 = \frac{8+y}{2}$
$-10 = 8 + y$
$-18 = y$

$(9, -18)$

18. $5 = \frac{x+5}{2}$
$10 = x + 5$
$5 = x$

$6 = \frac{7+y}{2}$
$12 = 7 + y$
$5 = y$

$(5, 5)$

19. $4 = \frac{-6+x}{2}$
$8 = -6 + x$
$14 = x$

$1 = \frac{12+y}{2}$
$2 = 12 + y$
$-10 = y$

$(14, -10)$

20. $-\frac{1}{2} = \frac{-8+x}{2}$
$-2 = 2(-8 + x)$
$-2 = -16 + 2x$
$14 = 2x$
$7 = x$

$2 = \frac{5+y}{2}$
$4 = 5 + y$
$-1 = y$

$(7, -1)$

21. $\frac{3}{2} = \frac{x+16}{2}$
$6 = 2(x + 16)$
$6 = 2x + 32$
$-26 = 2x$
$-13 = x$

$-\frac{13}{2} = \frac{y+(-9)}{2}$
$-26 = 2(y - 9)$
$-26 = 2y - 18$
$-8 = 2y$
$-4 = y$

$(-13, -4)$

22. $0 = \frac{-9+x}{2}$
$0 = -9 + x$
$9 = x$

$3 = \frac{y+14}{2}$
$6 = y + 14$
$-8 = y$

$(9, -8)$

23. $19 = \frac{x+21}{2}$
$38 = x + 21$
$17 = x$

$11 = \frac{18+y}{2}$
$22 = 18 + y$
$4 = y$

$(17, 4)$

24. $\frac{3}{16} = \frac{x+\frac{1}{4}}{2}$
$6 = 16\left(x + \frac{1}{4}\right)$
$6 = 16x + 4$
$2 = 16x$
$\frac{1}{8} = x$

$\frac{1}{3} = \frac{y+\frac{1}{3}}{2}$
$2 = 3\left(y + \frac{1}{3}\right)$
$2 = 3y + 1$
$1 = 3y$
$\frac{1}{3} = y$

$\left(\frac{1}{8}, \frac{1}{3}\right)$

Page 771 Lesson 7-1

1. $c + 9 \leq 3$
$c + 9 - 9 \leq 3 - 9$
$c \leq -6$
$\{c \mid c \leq -6\}$

2. $d - (-3) < 13$
$d + 3 < 13$
$d + 3 - 3 < 13 - 3$
$d < 10$
$\{d \mid d < 10\}$

3. $z - 4 > 20$
$z - 4 + 4 > 20 + 4$
$z > 24$
$\{z \mid z > 24\}$

4. $h - (-7) > -2$
$h + 7 > -2$
$h + 7 - 7 > -2 - 7$
$h > -9$
$\{h \mid h > -9\}$

5. $-11 > d - 4$
$-11 + 4 > d - 4 + 4$
$-7 > d$
$\{d \mid d < -7\}$

6. $2x > x - 3$
$2x - x > x - x - 3$
$x > -3$
$\{x \mid x > -3\}$

7. $2x - 3 \geq x$
$2x - x - 3 \geq x - x$
$x - 3 \geq 0$
$x - 3 + 3 \geq 0 + 3$
$x \geq 3$
$\{x \mid x \geq 3\}$

8. $16 + w < -20$
$16 - 16 + w < -20 - 16$
$w < -36$
$\{w \mid w < -36\}$

9. $14p > 5 + 13p$
$14p - 13p > 5 + 13p - 13p$
$p > 5$
$\{p \mid p > 5\}$

10. $-7 < 16 - z$
$-7 + z < 16 - z + z$
$-7 + z < 16$
$-7 + 7 + z < 16 + 7$
$z < 23$
$\{z \mid z < 23\}$

11. $-5 + 14b \leq -4 + 15b$
$-5 + 14b - 14b \leq -4 + 15b - 14b$
$-5 \leq -4 + b$
$-5 + 4 \leq -4 + 4 + b$
$-1 \leq b$
$\{b \mid b \geq -1\}$

12. $2s - 6.5 \geq -11.4 + s$
$2s - s - 6.5 \geq -11.4 + s - s$
$s - 6.5 \geq -11.4$
$s - 6.5 + 6.5 \geq -11.4 + 6.5$
$s \geq -4.9$
$\{s \mid s \geq -4.9\}$

13. $1.1v - 1 > 2.1v - 3$
$1.1v - 1.1v - 1 > 2.1v - 1.1v - 3$
$-1 > 1v - 3$
$-1 + 3 > v - 3 + 3$
$2 > v$
$\{v \mid v < 2\}$

14. $\frac{1}{2}t + \frac{1}{4} \geq \frac{3}{2}t - \frac{2}{3}$
$12\left(\frac{1}{2}t + \frac{1}{4}\right) \geq 12\left(\frac{3}{2}t - \frac{2}{3}\right)$
$6t + 3 \geq 18t - 8$
$6t - 6t + 3 \geq 18t - 6t - 8$
$3 \geq 12t - 8$
$3 + 8 \geq 12t - 8 + 8$
$11 \geq 12t$
$\frac{11}{12} \geq t$
$\left\{t \mid t \leq \frac{11}{2}\right\}$

15. $9x < 8x - 2$
$9x - 8x < 8x - 8x - 2$
$x < -2$
$\{x \mid x < -2\}$

16. $-2 + 9n \leq 10n$
$-2 + 9n - 9n \leq 10n - 9n$
$-2 \leq n$
$\{n \mid n \geq -2\}$

17. $a - 2.3 \geq -7.8$
$a - 2.3 + 2.3 \geq -7.8 + 2.3$
$a \geq -5.5$
$\{a \mid a \geq -5.5\}$

18. $5z - 6 > 4z$
$5z - 6 + 6 > 4z + 6$
$5z > 4z + 6$
$5z - 4z > 4z - 4z + 6$
$z > 6$
$\{z \mid z > 6\}$

Page 772 Lesson 7-2

1. $7b \geq -49$
$\frac{7b}{7} \geq -\frac{49}{7}$
$b \geq -7$
$\{b \mid b \geq -7\}$

2. $-5j < -60$
$\frac{-5j}{-5} > \frac{-60}{-5}$
$j > 12$
$\{j \mid j > 12\}$

3. $\frac{w}{3} > -12$
$3\left(\frac{w}{3}\right) > 3(-12)$
$w > -36$
$\{w \mid w > -36\}$

4. $\frac{p}{5} < 8$
$5\left(\frac{p}{5}\right) < 5(8)$
$p < 40$
$\{p \mid p < 40\}$

5. $-8f < 48$
$\frac{-8f}{-8} > \frac{48}{-8}$
$f > -6$
$\{f \mid f > -6\}$

6. $\frac{t}{-4} \geq -10$
$-4\left(\frac{t}{-4}\right) \leq -4(-10)$
$t \leq 40$
$\{t \mid t \leq 40\}$

7. $\frac{128}{-g} < 4$
$(g)\left(\frac{128}{-g}\right) < 4(g)$
$-128 < 4g$
$\frac{-128}{4} < \frac{4g}{4g}$
$-32 < g$
$\{g \mid g > -32\}$

8. $-4.3x < -2.58$
$\frac{-4.3x}{-4.3} > \frac{-2.58}{-4.3}$
$x > 0.6$
$\{x \mid x > 0.6\}$

9. $4c \geq -6$
$\frac{4c}{4} \geq \frac{-6}{4}$
$c \geq -\frac{3}{2}$
$\left\{c \mid c \geq -\frac{3}{2}\right\}$

10. $6 \leq 0.8n$
$\frac{6}{0.8} \leq \frac{0.8n}{0.8}$
$7.5 \leq n$
$\{n \mid n \geq 7.5\}$

11. $\frac{2}{3}m \geq -22$
$\left(\frac{3}{2}\right)\left(\frac{2}{3}m\right) \geq \left(\frac{3}{2}\right)(-22)$
$m \geq -33$
$\{m \mid m \geq -33\}$

12. $-25 > \frac{a}{-6}$
$(-6)(-25) < \left(\frac{a}{-6}\right)(-6)$
$150 < a$
$\{a \mid a > 150\}$

13. $-15a < -28$
$\frac{-15a}{-15} > \frac{-28}{-15}$
$a > \frac{28}{15}$
$\left\{a \mid a > \frac{28}{15}\right\}$

14. $-\frac{7}{9}x < 42$
$\left(-\frac{9}{7}\right)\left(-\frac{7}{9}\right) > (42)\left(-\frac{9}{7}\right)$
$x > -54$
$\{x \mid x > -54\}$

15. $\frac{3y}{8} \leq 32$
$\left(\frac{8}{3}\right)\left(\frac{3y}{8}\right) \leq (32)\left(\frac{8}{3}\right)$
$y \leq \frac{256}{3}$
$\left\{y \mid y \leq \frac{256}{3}\right\}$

16. $-7y \geq 91$
$\frac{-7y}{-7} \leq \frac{91}{-7}$
$y \leq -13$
$\{y \mid y \leq -13\}$

17. $0.8t > 0.96$
$\frac{0.8t}{0.8} > \frac{0.96}{0.8}$
$t > 1.2$
$\{t \mid t > 1.2\}$

18. $\frac{4}{7}z \leq -\frac{2}{5}$
$\left(\frac{7}{4}\right)\left(\frac{4}{7}z\right) \leq \left(-\frac{2}{5}\right)\left(\frac{7}{4}\right)$
$z \leq -\frac{7}{10}$
$\left\{z \mid z \leq -\frac{7}{10}\right\}$

Page 772 Lesson 7-3

1. $3y - 4 > -37$
$3y - 4 + 4 > -37 + 4$
$3y > -33$
$\frac{3y}{3} > \frac{-33}{3}$
$y > -11$
$\{y \mid y > -11\}$

2. $7s - 12 < 13$
$7s - 12 + 12 < 13 + 12$
$7s < 25$
$\frac{7s}{7} < \frac{25}{7}$
$s < \frac{25}{7}$
$\left\{s \mid s < \frac{25}{7}\right\}$

3. $-5e + 9 > 24$
$-5e + 9 - 9 > 24 - 9$
$-5e > 15$
$\frac{-5e}{-5} < \frac{15}{-5}$
$e < -3$
$\{e \mid e < -3\}$

4. $-6v - 3 \geq -33$
$-6v - 3 + 3 \geq -33 + 3$
$-6v \geq -30$
$\frac{-6v}{-6} \leq \frac{-30}{-6}$
$v \leq 5$
$\{v \mid v \leq 5\}$

5. $-2k + 12 < 30$
$-2k + 12 - 12 < 30 - 12$
$-2k < 18$
$\frac{-2k}{-2} > \frac{18}{-2}$
$k > -9$
$\{k \mid k > -9\}$

6. $-2x + 1 < 16 - x$
$-2x + 2x + 1 < 16 - x + 2x$
$1 < 16 + x$
$1 - 16 < 16 - 16 + x$
$-15 < x$
$\{x \mid x > -15\}$

7. $15t - 4 > 11t - 16$
$15t - 11t - 4 > 11t - 11t - 16$
$4t - 4 > -16$
$4t - 4 + 4 > -16 + 4$
$4t > -12$
$\frac{4t}{4} > \frac{-12}{4}$
$t > -3$
$\{t \mid t > -3\}$

8. $13 - y \leq 29 + 2y$
$13 - y + y \leq 29 + 2y + y$
$13 \leq 29 + 3y$
$13 - 29 \leq 29 - 29 + 3y$
$-16 \leq 3y$
$-\frac{16}{3} \leq \frac{3y}{3}$
$-\frac{16}{3} \leq y$
$\left\{y \mid y \geq -\frac{16}{3}\right\}$

9. $5q + 7 \leq 3(q + 1)$
$5q + 7 \leq 3q + 3$
$5q - 3q + 7 \leq 3q - 3q + 3$
$2q + 7 \leq 3$
$2q + 7 - 7 \leq 3 - 7$
$2q \leq -4$
$\frac{2q}{2} \leq \frac{-4}{2}$
$q \leq -2$
$\{q \mid q \leq -2\}$

10. $2(w + 4) \geq 7(w - 1)$
$2w + 8 \geq 7w - 7$
$2w - 2w + 8 \geq 7w - 2w - 7$
$8 \geq 5w - 7$
$8 + 7 \geq 5w - 7 + 7$
$15 \geq 5w$
$\frac{15}{5} \geq \frac{5w}{5}$
$3 \geq w$
$\{w \mid w \leq 3\}$

11. $-4t - 5 > 2t + 13$
$-4t + 4t - 5 > 2t + 4t + 13$
$-5 > 6t + 13$
$-5 - 13 > 6t + 13 - 13$
$-18 > 6t$
$\frac{-18}{6} > \frac{6t}{6}$
$-3 > t$
$\{t \mid t < -3\}$

12. $\frac{2t + 5}{3} < -9$
$3\left(\frac{2t + 5}{3}\right) < -9(3)$
$2t + 5 < -27$
$2t + 5 - 5 < -27 - 5$
$2t < -32$
$\frac{2t}{2} < \frac{-32}{2}$
$t < -16$
$\{t \mid t < -16\}$

13. $\frac{z}{4} + 7 \geq -5$
$\frac{z}{4} + 7 - 7 \geq -5 - 7$
$\frac{z}{4} \geq -12$
$4\left(\frac{z}{4}\right) \geq (-12)(4)$
$z \geq -48$
$\{z \mid z \geq -48\}$

14. $13r - 11 > 7r + 37$
$13r - 7r - 11 > 7r - 7r + 37$
$6r - 11 > 37$
$6r - 11 + 11 > 37 + 11$
$6r > 48$
$\frac{6r}{6} > \frac{48}{6}$
$r > 8$
$\{r \mid r > 8\}$

15. $8c - (c - 5) > c + 17$
$8c - c + 5 > c + 17$
$7c + 5 > c + 17$
$7c - c + 5 > c - c + 17$
$6c + 5 > 17$
$6c + 5 - 5 > 17 - 5$
$6c > 12$
$\frac{6c}{6} > \frac{12}{6}$
$c > 2$
$\{c \mid c > 2\}$

16. $-5(k + 4) \geq 3(k - 4)$
$-5k - 20 \geq 3k - 12$
$-5k + 5k - 20 \geq 3k + 5k - 12$
$-20 \geq 8k - 12$
$-20 + 12 \geq 8k - 12 + 12$
$-8 \geq 8k$
$-\frac{8}{8} \geq \frac{8k}{8}$
$-1 \geq k$
$\{k \mid k \leq -1\}$

17. $9m + 7 < 2(4m - 1)$
$9m + 7 < 8m - 2$
$9m - 8m + 7 < 8m - 8m - 2$
$m + 7 < -2$
$m + 7 - 7 < -2 - 7$
$m < -9$
$\{m \mid m < -9\}$

18. $3(3y + 1) < 13y - 8$
$9y + 3 < 13y - 8$
$9y - 9y + 3 < 13y - 9y - 8$
$3 < 4y - 8$
$3 + 8 < 4y - 8 + 8$
$11 < 4y$
$\frac{11}{4} < \frac{4y}{4}$
$\frac{11}{4} < y$
$\left\{y \mid y > \frac{11}{4}\right\}$

19. $5x \leq 10(3x + 4)$
$5x \leq 30x + 40$
$5x - 30x \leq 30x - 30x + 40$
$-25x \leq 40$
$\frac{-25x}{-25} \leq \frac{40}{-25}$
$x \geq -\frac{8}{5}$
$\left\{x \mid x \geq -\frac{8}{5}\right\}$

20.
$$3\left(a + \tfrac{2}{3}\right) \geq a - 1$$
$$3a + 2 \geq a - 1$$
$$3a - a + 2 \geq a - a - 1$$
$$2a + 2 \geq -1$$
$$2a + 2 - 2 \geq -1 - 2$$
$$2a \geq -3$$
$$\frac{2a}{2} \geq \frac{-3}{2}$$
$$a \geq -\frac{3}{2}$$
$$\left\{a \mid a \geq -\frac{3}{2}\right\}$$

21.
$$0.7(n - 3) \leq n - 0.6(n + 5)$$
$$0.7n - 2.1 \leq n - 0.6n - 3$$
$$0.7n - 2.1 \leq 0.4n - 3$$
$$0.7n - 0.4n - 2.1 \leq 0.4n - 0.4n - 3$$
$$0.3n - 2.1 \leq -3$$
$$0.3n - 2.1 + 2.1 \leq -3 + 2.1$$
$$0.3n \leq -0.9$$
$$\frac{0.3n}{0.3} \leq \frac{-0.9}{0.3}$$
$$n \leq -3$$
$$\{n \mid n \leq -3\}$$

Page 772 Lesson 7-4

1.
$$2 + x < -5 \quad \text{or} \quad 2 + x > 5$$
$$2 - 2 + x < -5 - 2 \quad\quad 2 + x - 2 > 5 - 2$$
$$x < -7 \quad\quad x > 3$$
$$\{x \mid x < -7 \text{ or } x > 3\}$$

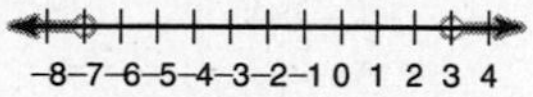

2.
$$-4 + t > -5 \quad \text{or} \quad -4 + t < 7$$
$$-4 + 4 + t > -5 + 4 \quad\quad -4 + 4 + t < 7 + 4$$
$$t > -1 \quad\quad t < 11$$
{all numbers}

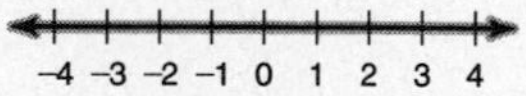

3.
$$3 \leq 2g + 7 \quad \text{and} \quad 2g + 7 \leq 15$$
$$3 - 7 \leq 2g + 7 - 7 \quad\quad 2g + 7 - 7 \leq 15 - 7$$
$$-4 \leq 2g \quad\quad 2g \leq 8$$
$$-\frac{4}{2} \leq \frac{2g}{2} \quad\quad \frac{2g}{2} \leq \frac{8}{2}$$
$$-2 \leq g \quad\quad g \leq 4$$
$$\{g \mid -2 \leq g \leq 4\}$$

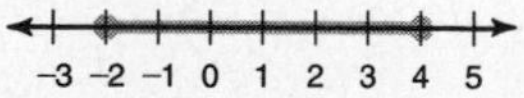

4.
$$2v - 2 \leq 3v \quad \text{and} \quad 4v - 1 \geq 3v$$
$$2v - 2v - 2 \leq 3v - 2v \quad\quad 4v - 3v - 1 \geq 3v - 3v$$
$$-2 \leq v \quad\quad v - 1 \geq 0$$
$$v - 1 + 1 \geq 0 + 1$$
$$v \geq 1$$
$$\{v \mid v \geq 1\}$$

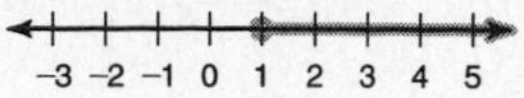

5.
$$3b - 4 \leq 7b + 12$$
$$3b - 3b - 4 \leq 7b - 3b + 12$$
$$-4 \leq 4b + 12$$
$$-4 - 12 \leq 4b + 12 - 12$$
$$-16 \leq 4b$$
$$\frac{-16}{4} \leq \frac{4b}{4}$$
$$-4 \leq b$$
and
$$8b - 7 \leq 25$$
$$8b - 7 + 7 \leq 25 + 7$$
$$8b \leq 32$$
$$\frac{8b}{8} \leq \frac{32}{8}$$
$$b \leq 4$$
$$\{b \mid -4 \leq b \leq 4\}$$

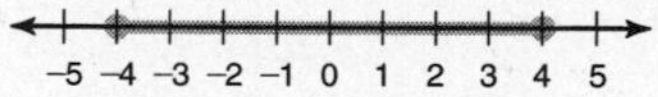

6.
$$-9 < 2z + 7 < 10$$
$$-9 < 2z + 7 \quad \text{and} \quad 2z + 7 < 10$$
$$-9 - 7 < 2z + 7 - 7 \quad\quad 2z + 7 - 7 < 10 - 7$$
$$-16 < 2z \quad\quad 2z < 3$$
$$\frac{-16}{2} < \frac{2z}{2} \quad\quad \frac{2z}{2} < \frac{3}{2}$$
$$-8 < z \quad\quad z < \frac{3}{2}$$
$$\left\{z \mid -8 < z < \frac{3}{2}\right\}$$

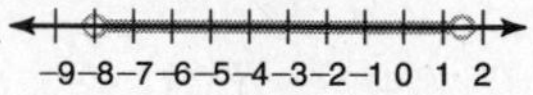

7.
$$5m - 8 \geq 10 - m$$
$$5m + m - 8 \geq 10 - m + m$$
$$6m - 8 \geq 10$$
$$6m - 8 + 8 \geq 10 + 8$$
$$6m \geq 18$$
$$\frac{6m}{6} \geq \frac{18}{6}$$
$$m \geq 3$$
or
$$5m + 11 < -9$$
$$5m + 11 - 11 < -9 - 11$$
$$5m < -20$$
$$\frac{5m}{5} < \frac{-20}{4}$$
$$m < -4$$
$$\{m \mid m \geq 3 \text{ or } m < -4\}$$

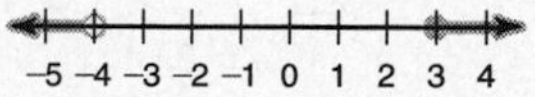

8.
$$12c - 4 < 5c + 10$$
$$12c - 5c - 4 < 5c - 5c + 10$$
$$7c - 4 < 10$$
$$7c - 4 + 4 < 10 + 4$$
$$7c < 14$$
$$\frac{7c}{7} < \frac{14}{7}$$
$$c < 2$$
or
$$-4c - 1 \leq c + 24$$
$$-4c - 1 + 4c \leq c + 4c + 24$$
$$-1 \leq 5c + 24$$
$$-1 - 24 \leq 5c + 24 - 24$$
$$-25 \leq 5c$$
$$\frac{-25}{5} \leq \frac{5c}{5}$$
$$-5 \leq c$$
{all numbers}

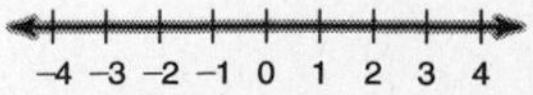

9. $2h - 2 \le 3h \le 4h - 1$

$2h - 2 \le 3h$

$2h - 2h - 2 \le 3h - 2h$

$-2 \le h$

and

$3h \le 4h - 1$

$-3h + 3h \le 4h - 3h - 1$

$0 \le h - 1$

$0 + 1 \le h - 1 + 1$

$1 \le h$

$\{h \mid h \ge 1\}$

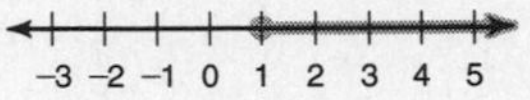

10. $3p + 6 < 8 - p$

$3p + 6 - 6 < 8 - 6 - p$

$3p < 2 - p$

$3p + p < 2 - p + p$

$4p < 2$

$\frac{4p}{4} < \frac{2}{4}$

$p < \frac{1}{2}$

and

$5p + 8 \ge p + 6$

$5p - p + 8 \ge p - p + 6$

$4p + 8 \ge 6$

$4p + 8 - 8 \ge 6 - 8$

$4p \ge -2$

$\frac{4p}{4} \ge \frac{-2}{4}$

$p \ge -\frac{1}{2}$

$\left\{p \mid -\frac{1}{2} < p < \frac{1}{2}\right\}$

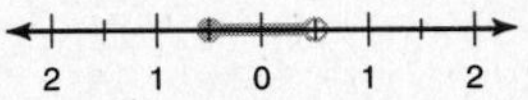

11. $2r + 8 > 16 - 2r$

$2r + 2r + 8 > 16 - 2r + 2r$

$4r + 8 > 16$

$4r + 8 - 8 > 16 - 8$

$4r > 8$

$\frac{4r}{4} > \frac{8}{4}$

$r > 2$

and

$7r + 21 < r - 9$

$7r - r + 21 < r - r + 9$

$6r + 21 < 9$

$6r + 21 - 21 < 9 - 21$

$6r < -12$

$\frac{6r}{6} < \frac{-12}{6}$

$r < -2$

$\varnothing$

12. $4j + 3 < j + 22$ and $j - 3 < 2j - 15$

$4j - j + 3 < j + 22 - j$ $\quad$ $j - 3 - j < 2j - j - 15$

$3j + 3 < 22$ $\quad$ $-3 < j - 15$

$3j + 3 - 3 < 22 - 3$ $\quad$ $-3 + 15 < j - 15 + 15$

$3j < 19$ $\quad$ $12 < j$

$j < \frac{19}{3}$

$\varnothing$

13. $2(q - 4) \le 3\,(q + 2)$

$2q - 8 \le 3q + 6$

$2q - 2q - 8 \le 3q - 2q + 6$

$-8 \le q + 6$

$-8 - 6 \le q + 6 - 6$

$-14 \le q$

or

$q - 8 \le 4 - q$

$q + q - 8 \le 4 - q + q$

$2q - 8 \le 4$

$2q - 8 + 8 \le 4 + 8$

$2q \le 12$

$\frac{2q}{2} \le \frac{12}{2}$

$q \le 6$

{all numbers}

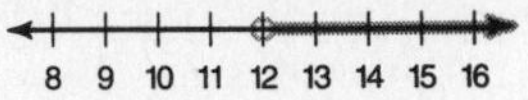

14. $\frac{1}{2}w + 5 \ge w + 2 \ge \frac{1}{2}w + 9$

$\frac{1}{2}w + 5 \ge w + 2$

$\frac{1}{2}w - \frac{1}{2}w + 5 \ge w - \frac{1}{2}w + 2$

$5 \ge \frac{1}{2}w + 2$

$5 - 2 \ge \frac{1}{2}w + 2 - 2$

$3 \ge \frac{1}{2}w$

$2(3) \ge \left(\frac{1}{2}w\right)(2)$

$6 \ge w$

and

$w + 2 \ge \frac{1}{2}w + 9$

$w - \frac{1}{2}w + 2 \ge \frac{1}{2}w - \frac{1}{2}w + 9$

$\frac{1}{2}w + 2 \ge 9$

$\frac{1}{2}w + 2 - 2 \ge 9 - 2$

$\frac{1}{2}w \ge 7$

$2\left(\frac{1}{2}w\right) \ge 7(2)$

$w \ge 14$

$\varnothing$

Page 773 Lesson 7-5

1a.

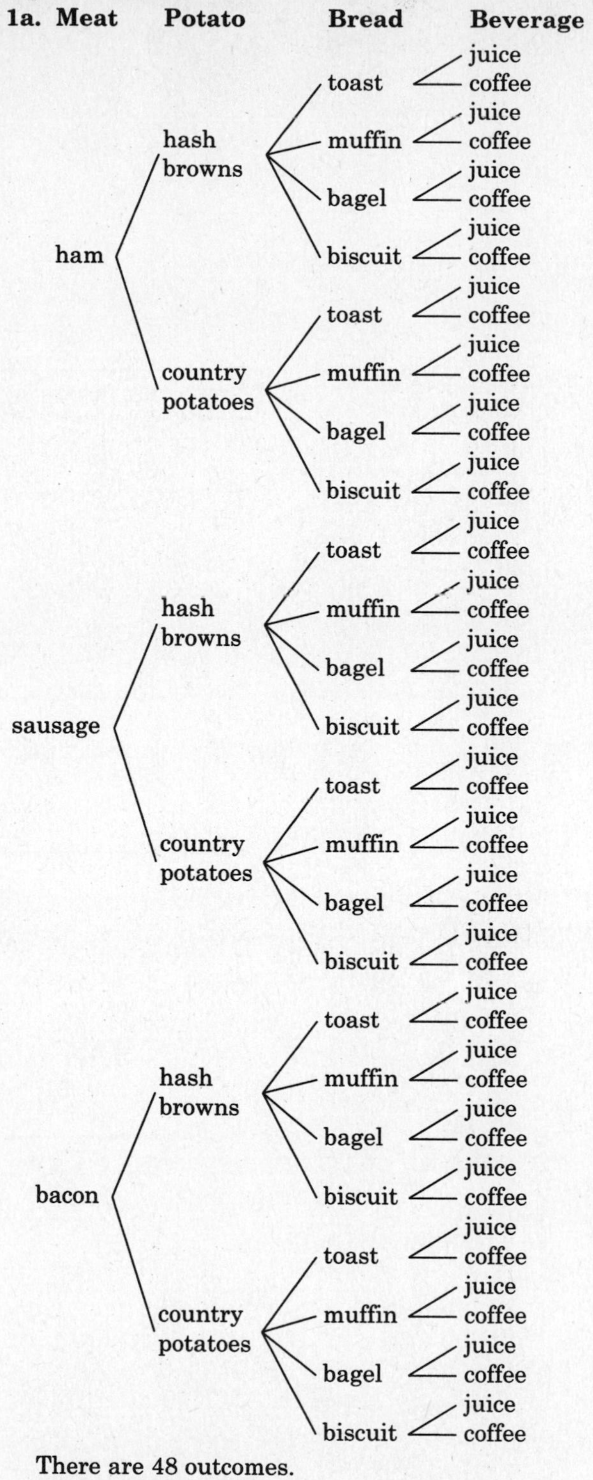

There are 48 outcomes.

$P(\text{ham}) = \frac{16}{48}$ or $\frac{1}{3}$

1b. $P(\text{biscuit and hash browns}) = \frac{6}{48}$ or $\frac{1}{8}$

1c. $P(\text{bagel, country potatoes, coffee}) = \frac{3}{48}$ or $\frac{1}{16}$

2.

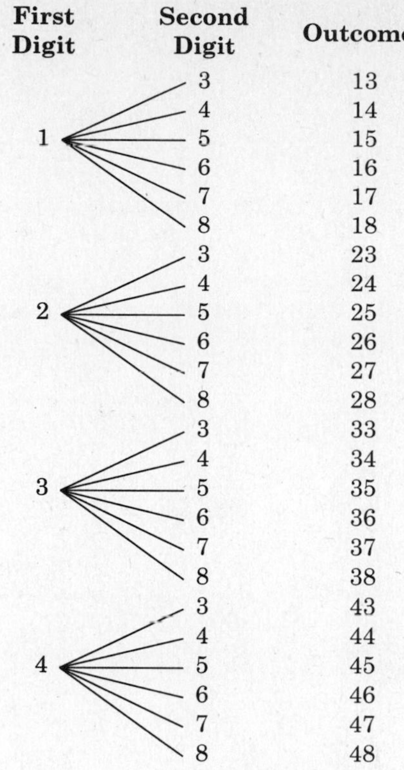

$P(\text{Trudy will win}) = \frac{\text{number of winners}}{\text{number of lottery numbers with 2 as the first digit}}$

$= \frac{1}{6} = 0.1\overline{6}$

3.

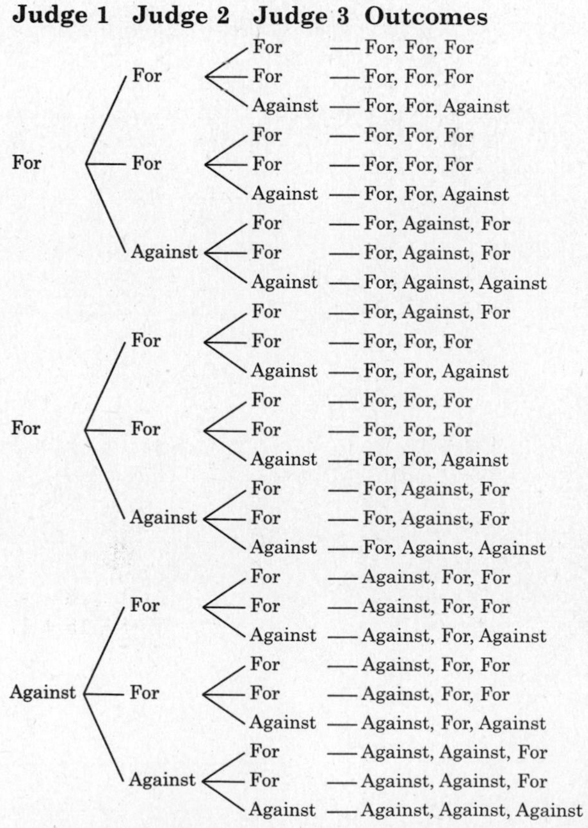

$P(\text{correct side will win}) = \frac{20}{27} \approx 0.741$

Page 773 Lesson 7-6

1. $\varnothing$

2. $|g + 6| > 8$

$g + 6 < -8$ or $g + 6 > 8$

$g + 6 - 6 < -8 - 6$ $\quad$ $g + 6 - 6 > 8 - 6$

$g < -14$ $\quad$ $g > 2$

$\{g \mid g < -14 \text{ or } g > 2\}$

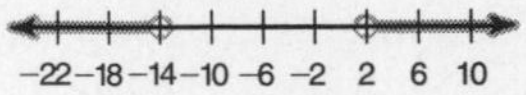

3. $|t - 5| \leq 3$

$t - 5 \leq 3$ and $t - 5 \geq -3$

$t - 5 + 5 \leq 3 + 5$ $\quad$ $t - 5 + 5 \geq -3 + 5$

$t \leq 8$ $\quad$ $t \geq 2$

$\{t \mid 2 \leq t \leq 8\}$

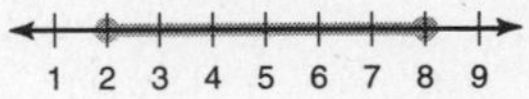

4. $|a + 5| \geq 0$

$a + 5 \geq 0$ and $a + 5 \leq 0$

$a + 5 - 5 \geq -5$ $\quad$ $a + 5 - 5 \leq -5$

$a \geq -5$ $\quad$ $a \leq -5$

{all numbers}

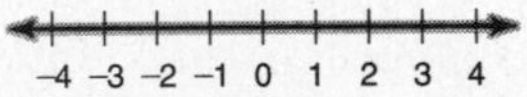

5. $|14 - 2z| = 16$

$14 - 2z = 16$

$14 - 14 - 2z = 16 - 14$

$-2z = 2$

$\frac{-2z}{-2} = \frac{2}{-2}$

$z = -1$

or

$14 - 2z = -16$

$14 - 14 - 2z = -16 - 14$

$-2z = -30$

$\frac{-2z}{-2} = \frac{-30}{-2}$

$z = 15$

$\{z \mid z = -1 \text{ or } z = 15\}$

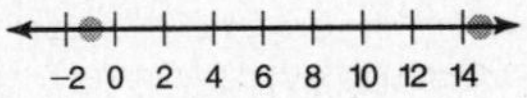

6. $|y - 9| < 19$

$y - 9 < 19$ and $y - 9 > -19$

$y - 9 + 9 < 19 + 9$ $\quad$ $y - 9 + 9 > -19 + 9$

$y < 28$ $\quad$ $y > -10$

$\{y \mid -10 < y < 28\}$

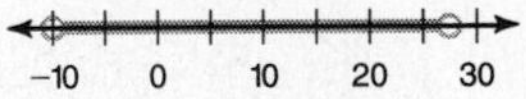

7. $|2m - 5| > 13$

$2m - 5 > 13$ or $2m - 5 < -13$

$2m - 5 + 5 > 3 + 5$ $\quad$ $2m - 5 + 5 < -13 + 5$

$2m > 18$ $\quad$ $2m < -8$

$\frac{2m}{2} > \frac{18}{2}$ $\quad$ $\frac{2m}{2} < \frac{-8}{2}$

$m > 9$ $\quad$ $m < -4$

$\{m \mid m < -4 \text{ or } m > 9\}$

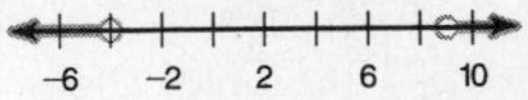

8. $|14 - w| \geq 20$

$14 - w \geq 20$

$14 - 14 - w \geq 20 - 14$

$-w \geq 6$

$\frac{-w}{-1} \leq \frac{6}{-1}$

$w \leq -6$

or

$14 - w \leq -20$

$14 - w - 14 \leq -20 - 14$

$-w \leq -34$

$\frac{-w}{-1} \leq \frac{-34}{-1}$

$w \geq 34$

$\{w \mid w \leq -6 \text{ or } w \geq 34\}$

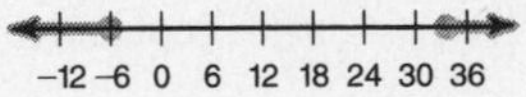

9. $|13 - 5y| = 8$

$13 - 5y = 8$

$13 - 13 - 5y = 8 - 13$

$-5y = -5$

$\frac{-5y}{-5} = \frac{-5}{-5}$

$y = 1$

or

$13 - 5y = -8$

$13 - 5y - 13 = -8 - 13$

$-5y = -21$

$\frac{-5y}{-5} = \frac{-21}{-5}$

$y = \frac{21}{5}$

$\left\{y \mid y = 1 \text{ or } y = \frac{21}{5}\right\}$

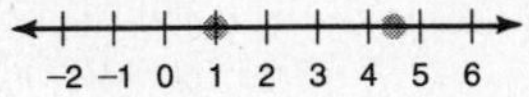

10. $|3p + 5| \leq 23$

$3p + 5 \leq 23$ and $3p + 5 \geq -23$

$3p + 5 - 5 \leq 23 - 5$ $\quad$ $3p + 5 - 5 \geq -23 - 5$

$3p \leq 18$ $\quad$ $3p \geq -28$

$\frac{3p}{3} \leq \frac{18}{3}$ $\quad$ $\frac{3p}{3} \geq \frac{-28}{3}$

$p \leq 6$ $\quad$ $p \geq -\frac{28}{3}$

$\left\{p \mid -\frac{28}{3} \leq p \leq 6\right\}$

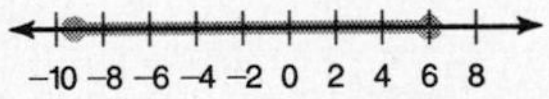

11. $|6b - 12| \leq 36$

$6b - 12 + 12 \leq 36 + 12$

$6b \leq 48$

$\frac{6b}{6} \leq \frac{48}{6}$

$b \leq 8$

and

$6b - 12 \geq -36$

$6b - 12 + 12 \geq -36 + 12$

$6b \geq -24$

$\frac{6b}{6} \geq \frac{-24}{6}$

$b \geq -4$

$\{b \mid -4 \leq b \leq 8\}$

12. $|25 - 3x| < 5$

$$25 - 3x < 5$$
$$25 - 25 - 3x < 5 - 25$$
$$-3x < -20$$
$$\frac{-3x}{-3} > \frac{-20}{-3}$$
$$x > \frac{20}{3}$$

and

$$25 - 3x > -5$$
$$25 - 3x - 25 > -5 - 25$$
$$-3x > -30$$
$$\frac{-3x}{-3} < \frac{-30}{-3}$$
$$x < 10$$

$\left\{x \mid \frac{20}{3} < x < 10\right\}$

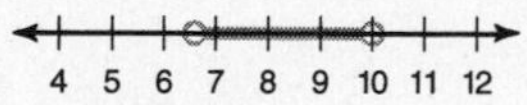

13. $|7 + 8x| > 39$

$$7 + 8x > 39$$
$$7 + 8x - 7 > 39 - 7$$
$$8x > 32$$
$$\frac{8x}{8} > \frac{32}{8}$$
$$x > 4$$

or

$$7 + 8x < -39$$
$$7 + 8x - 7 < -39 - 7$$
$$8x < -46$$
$$\frac{8x}{8} < \frac{-46}{8}$$
$$x < -\frac{23}{4}$$

$\left\{x \mid x > 4 \text{ or } x < -\frac{23}{4}\right\}$

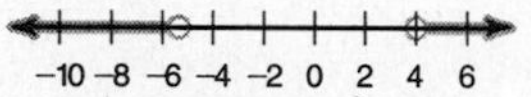

14. $|4c + 5| \geq 25$

$$4c + 5 \geq 25$$
$$4c + 5 - 5 \geq 25 - 5$$
$$4c \geq 20$$
$$\frac{4c}{4} \geq \frac{20}{4}$$
$$c \geq 5$$

or

$$4c + 5 \leq -25$$
$$4c + 5 - 5 \leq -25 - 5$$
$$4c \leq -30$$
$$\frac{4c}{4} \leq \frac{-30}{4}$$
$$c \leq -\frac{15}{2}$$

$\left\{c \mid c \leq -\frac{15}{2} \text{ or } c \geq 5\right\}$

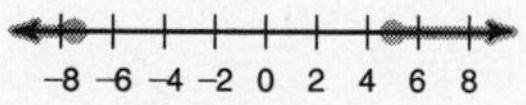

15. $|4 - 5s| > 46$

$4 - 5s > 46$	or	$4 - 5s < -46$
$4 - 4 - 5s > 46 - 4$		$4 - 4 - 5s < -46 - 4$
$-5s > 42$		$-5s < -50$
$\frac{-5s}{-5} < \frac{42}{-5}$		$\frac{-5s}{-5} > \frac{-50}{-5}$
$s < -\frac{42}{5}$		$s > 10$

$\left\{s \mid s < -\frac{42}{5} \text{ or } s > 10\right\}$

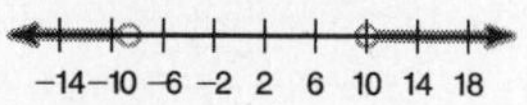

Page 773 Lesson 7-7

1. LV = 81.8

$Q_1 = \frac{83.1 + 83.2}{2} = 83.15$

$Q_2 = \frac{84.9 + 86.8}{2} = 85.85$

$Q_3 = \frac{89.3 + 90.8}{2} = \frac{180.1}{2} = 90.05$

GV = 95.0

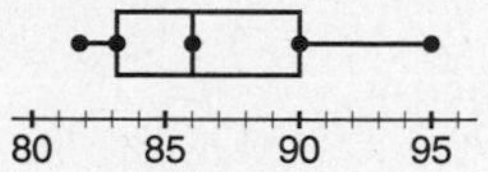

2. LV = 31.2

$Q_1 = \frac{32.9 + 33.1}{2} = 33.0$

$Q_2 = \frac{34.5 + 34.7}{2} = 34.6$

$Q_3 = \frac{36.5 + 37.1}{2} = 36.8$

GV = 50.4

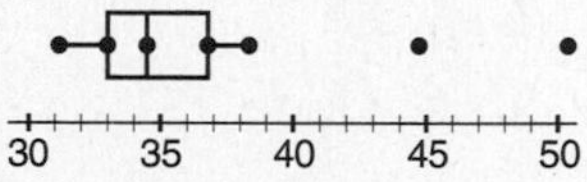

3a. median $= \frac{26 + 27}{2} = 26.5$

$Q_3 = \frac{32 + 33}{2} = 32.5$

$Q_1 = 24$

$IQR = Q_3 - Q_1 = 32.5 - 24 = 8.5$

3b. outliers:

$x \geq Q_3 + 1.5(IQR)$	$x \leq Q_1 - 1.5(IQR)$
$x \geq 32.5 + 1.5(8.5)$	$x \leq 24 - 1.5(8.5)$
$x \geq 45.25$	$x \leq 11.25$

none

3c.

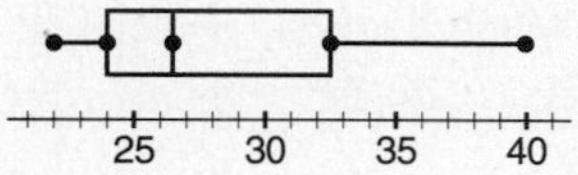

Page 774 Lesson 7-8

1.

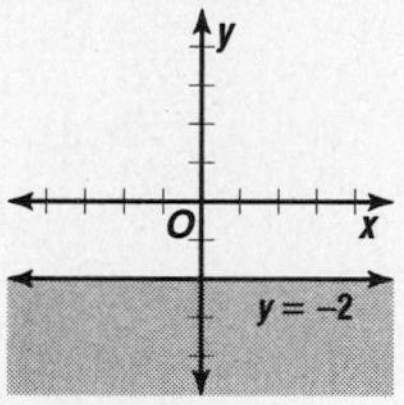

Test (0, −3).
$y \leq -2$
$-3 \leq -2$ true
Shade the half-plane containing (0, −3).

2.

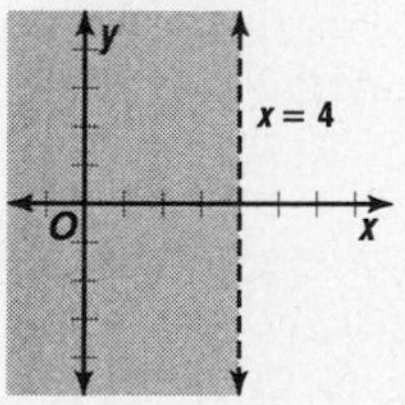

Test (0, 0).
$x < 4$
$0 < 4$ true
Shade the half-plane containing (0, 0).

3. Solve for y:

$$x + y < -2$$
$$y < -x - 2$$

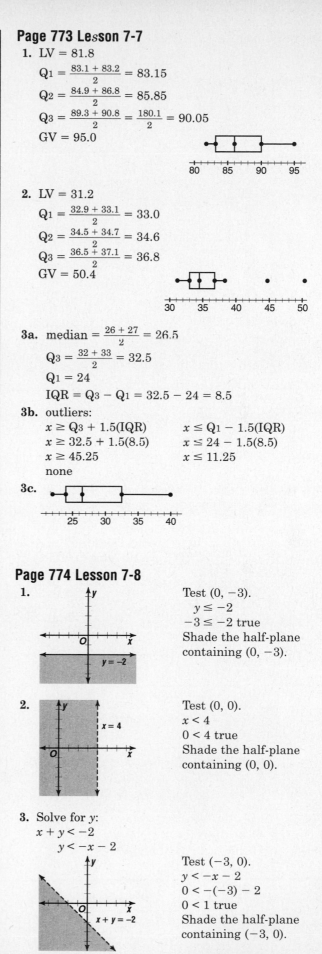

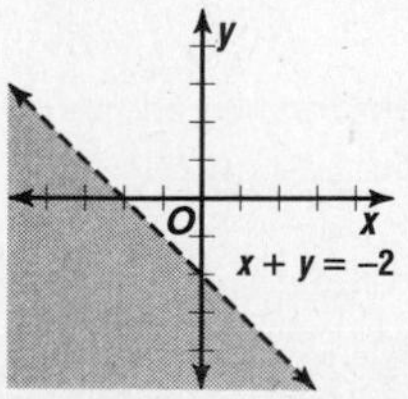

Test (−3, 0).
$y < -x - 2$
$0 < -(-3) - 2$
$0 < 1$ true
Shade the half-plane containing (−3, 0).

4. Solve for y:
$x + y > -4$
$y > -x - 4$

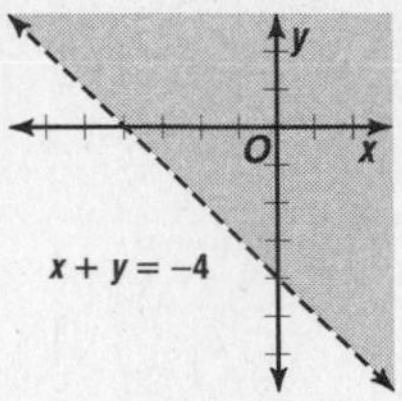

Test (0, 0).
$y > -x - 4$
$0 > -0 - 4$
$0 > -4$ true
Shade the half-plane containing (0, 0).

5. $y > 4x - 1$

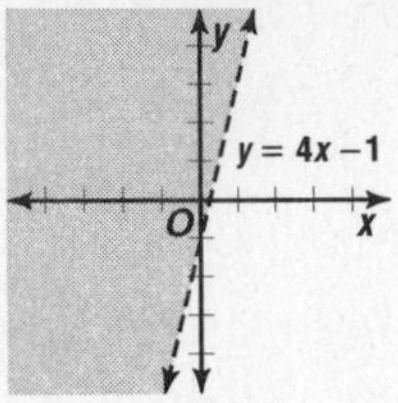

Test (0, 0).
$y > 4x - 1$
$0 > 4(0) - 1$
$0 > -1$ true
Shade the half-plane containing (0, 0).

6. Solve for y:
$3x + y > 1$
$y > -3x + 1$

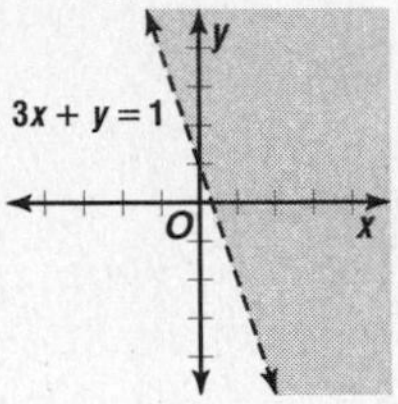

Test (1, 1).
$3x + y > 1$
$3(1) + 1 > 1$
$3 + 1 > 1$
$4 > 1$ true
Shade the half-plane containing (1, 1).

7. Solve for y:
$3y - 2x \le 2$
$3y \le 2x + 2$
$y \le \frac{2}{3}x + \frac{2}{3}$

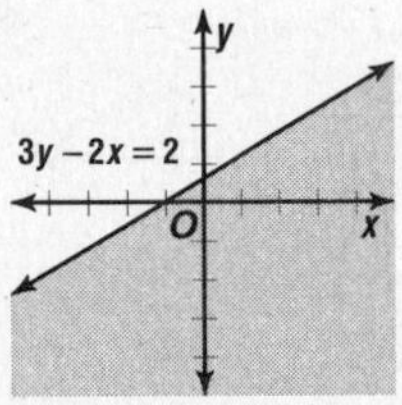

Test (0, 0).
$3y - 2x \le 2$
$3(0) - 2(0) \le 2$
$0 \le 2$ true
Shade the half-plane containing (0, 0).

8. Solve for y:
$x < y$
$y > x$

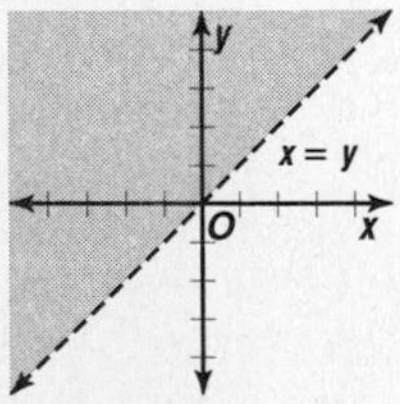

Test (0, 1).
$y > x$
$1 > 0$ true
Shade the half-plane containing (0, 1).

9. Solve for y:
$3x + y > 4$
$y > -3x + 4$

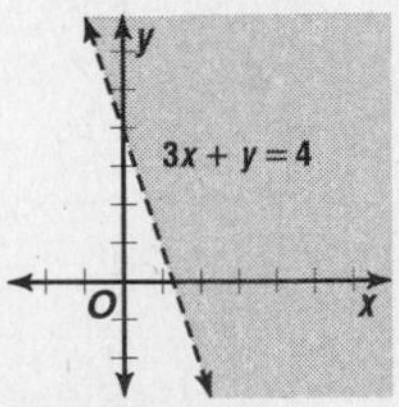

Test (2, 0).
$3x + y > 4$
$3(2) + 0 > 4$
$6 > 4$ true
Shade the half-plane containing (2, 0).

10. Solve for y:
$5x - y < 5$
$-y < -5x + 5$
$y > 5x - 5$

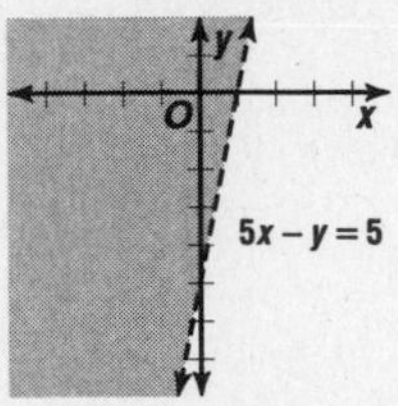

Test (0, 0).
$5x - y < 5$
$5(0) - 0 < 5$
$0 < 5$ true
Shade the half-plane containing (0, 0).

11. Solve for y:
$-4x + 3y \ge 12$
$3y \ge 4x + 12$
$y \ge \frac{4}{3}x + 4$

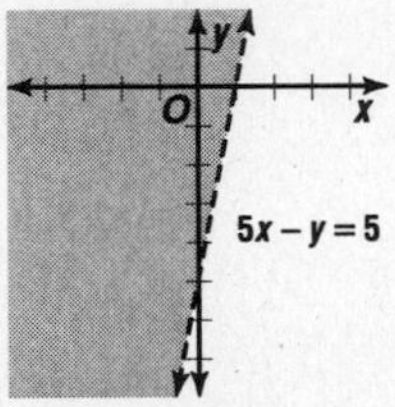

Test (−4, 0).
$-4x + 3y \ge 12$
$-4(-4) + 3(0) \ge 12$
$16 \ge 12$
true
Shade the half-plane containing (−4, 0).

12. Solve for y:
$-x + 3y \le 9$
$3y \le x + 9$
$y \le \frac{1}{3}x + 3$

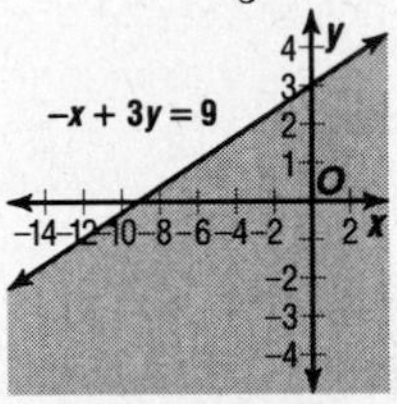

Test (0, 0).
$-x + 3y \le 9$
$0 + 3(0) \le 9$
$0 \le 9$ true
Shade the half-plane containing (0, 0).

13. $y > -3x + 7$

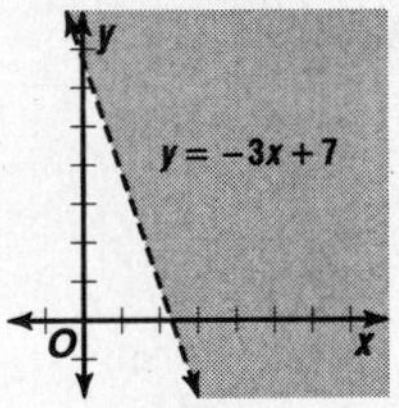

Test (3, 0).
$0 > -3(3) + 7$
$0 > -2$ true
Shade the half-plane containing (3, 0).

14. Solve for y:
$3x + 8y \le 4$
$8y \le -3x + 4$
$y \le -\frac{3}{8}x + \frac{1}{2}$

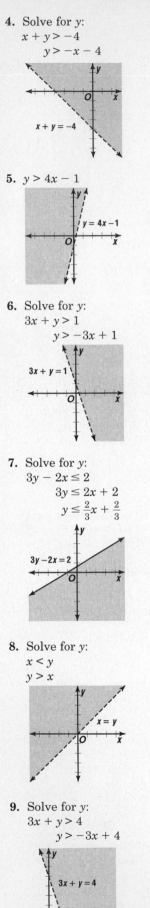

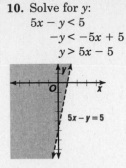

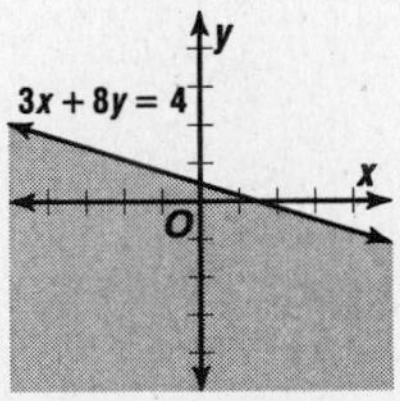

Test (0, 0).
$3x + 8y \le 4$
$3(0) + 8(0) \le 4$
$0 \le 4$ true
Shade the half-plane containing (0, 0).

15. Solve for y:

$5x - 2y \geq 6$

$-2y \geq -5x + 6$

$y \leq \frac{5}{2}x - 3$

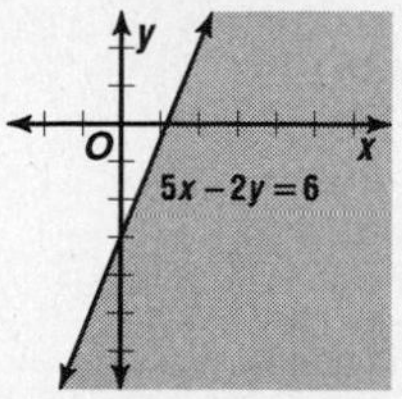

Test (2, 0).

$5x - 2y \geq 6$

$5(2) - 2(0) \geq 6$

$10 - 0 \geq 6$

$10 \geq 6$ true

Shade the half-plane containing (2, 0).

Page 774 Lesson 8-1

1. $y = 3x$

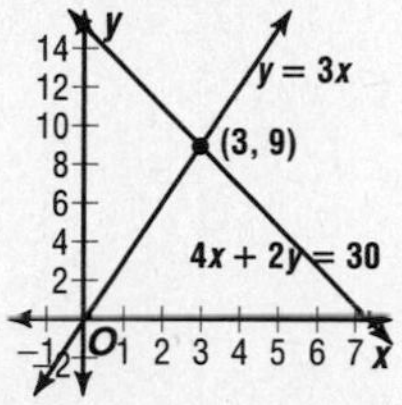

$4x + 2y = 30$

$2y = 30 - 4x$

$y = 15 - 2x$

one solution; (3, 9)

2. $x = -2y$

$-\frac{1}{2}x = y$

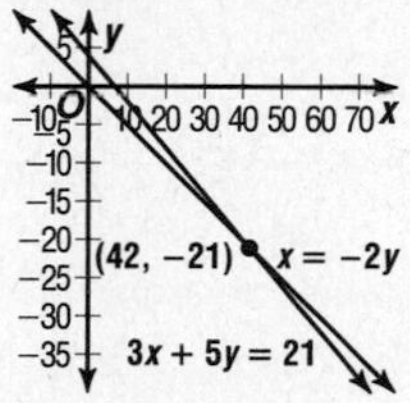

$3x + 5y = 21$

$5y = -3x + 21$

$y = -\frac{3}{5}x + \frac{21}{5}$

one solution; (42, −21)

3. $y = x + 4$

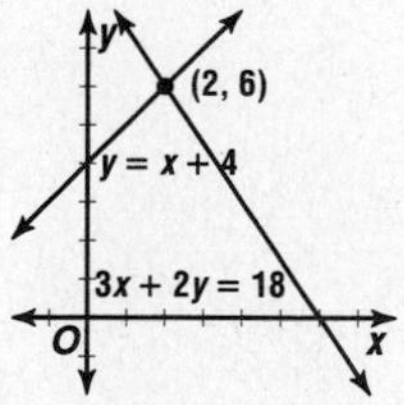

$3x + 2y = 18$

$2y = 18 - 3x$

$y = 9 - \frac{3}{2}x$

one solution; (2, 6)

4. $x + y = 6$

$y = 6 - x$

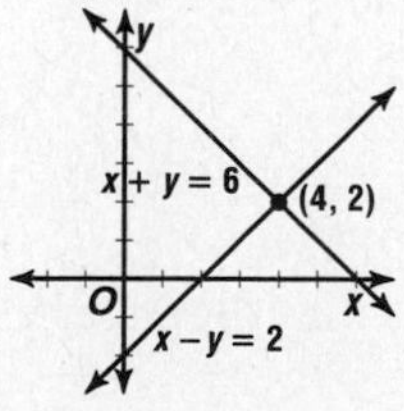

$x - y = 2$

$-y = 2 - x$

$y = x - 2$

one solution; (4, 2)

5. $x + y = 6$

$y = 6 - x$

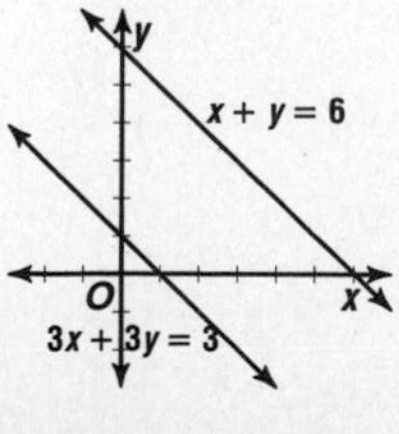

$3x + 3y = 3$

$3y = 3 - 3x$

$y = 1 - x$

no solution

6. $y = -3x$

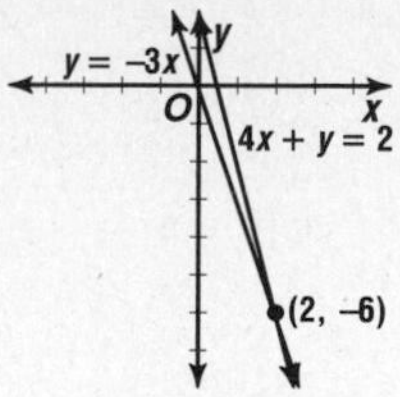

$4x + y = 2$

$y = -4x + 2$

one solution; (2, −6)

7. $x + y = 8$

$y = 8 - x$

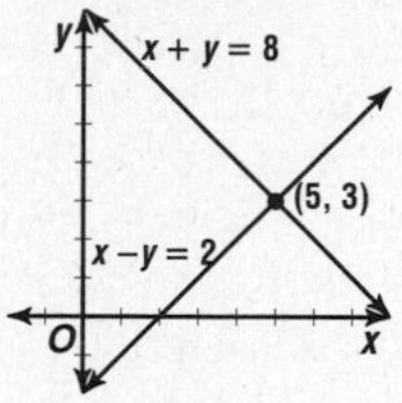

$x - y = 2$

$-y = 2 - x$

$y = x - 2$

one solution; (5, 3)

8. $\frac{1}{5}x - y = \frac{12}{5}$

$-y = -\frac{1}{5}x + \frac{12}{5}$

$y = \frac{1}{5}x - \frac{12}{5}$

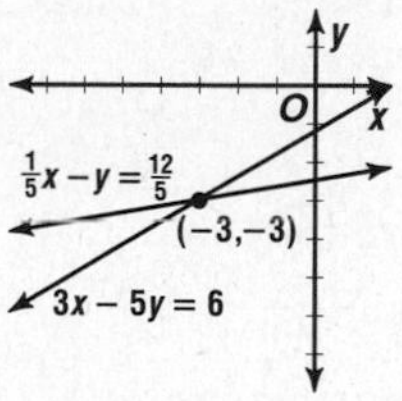

$3x - 5y = 6$

$-5y = 6 - 3x$

$y = \frac{3}{5}x - \frac{6}{5}$

one solution; (−3, −3)

9. $x + 2y = 0$

$2y = -x$

$y = -\frac{1}{2}x$

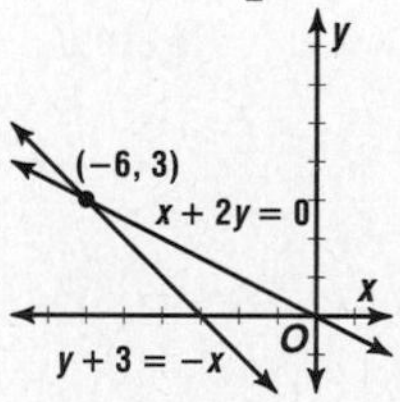

$y + 3 = -x$

$y = -x + 3$

one solution; (−6, 3)

10. $x + 2y = -9$

$2y = -x - 9$

$y = -\frac{1}{2}x - \frac{9}{2}$

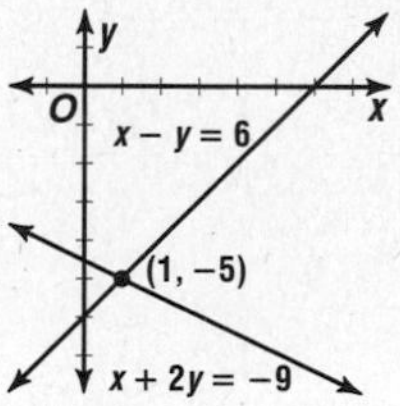

$x - y = 6$

$-y = 6 - x$

$y = x - 6$

one solution; (1, −5)

11. $x + \frac{1}{2}y = 3$

$\frac{1}{2}y = -x + 3$

$y = -2x + 6$

one solution; (2, 2)

$y = 3x - 4$

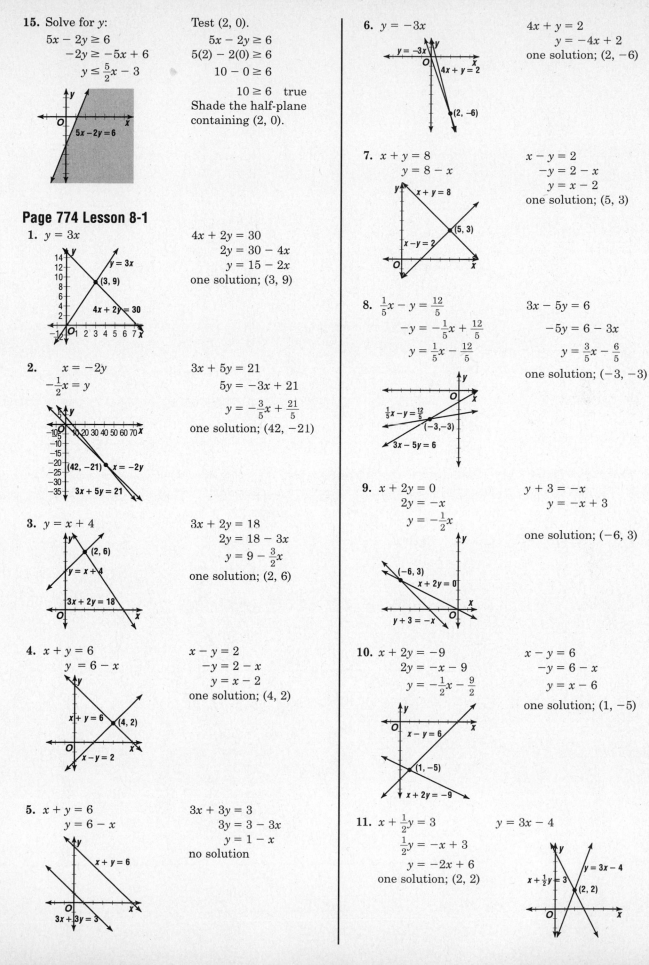

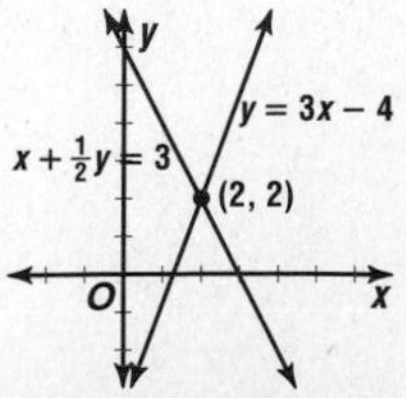

12. $\frac{2}{3}x + \frac{1}{2}y = 2$
$\frac{1}{2}y = -\frac{2}{3}x + 2$
$y = -\frac{4}{3}x + 4$

$4x + 3y = 12$
$3y = 12 - 4x$
$y = -\frac{4}{3}x + 4$
infinitely many

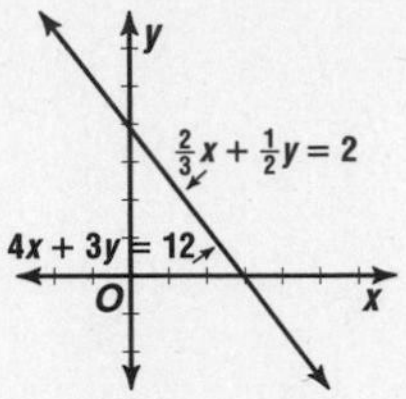

13. $x + \frac{1}{2}y = \frac{5}{2}$
$\frac{1}{2}y = -x + \frac{5}{2}$
$y = -2x + 5$

$y = x - 4$
one solution; $(3, -1)$

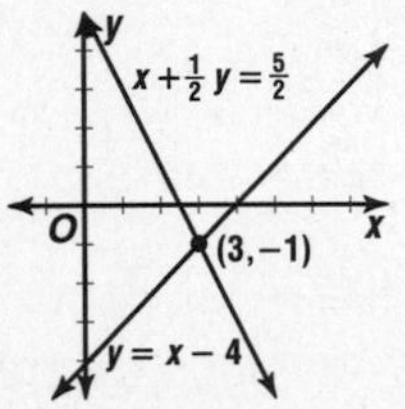

14. $2x + y = 3$
$y = -2x + 3$

$4x + 2y = 6$
$2y = -4x + 6$
$y = -2x + 3$
infinitely many

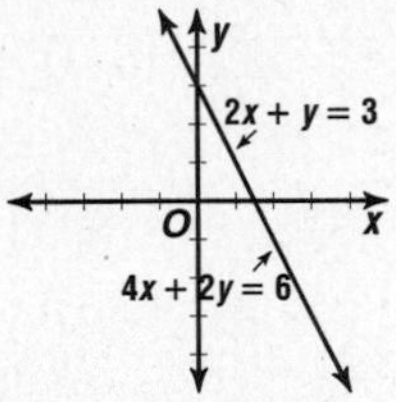

15. $12x - y = -21$
$-y = -12x - 21$
$y = 12x + 21$

$\frac{1}{2}x + \frac{2}{3}y = -3$
$\frac{2}{3}y = -3 - \frac{1}{2}x$
$y = -\frac{3}{4}x - \frac{9}{2}$
one solution; $(-2, -3)$

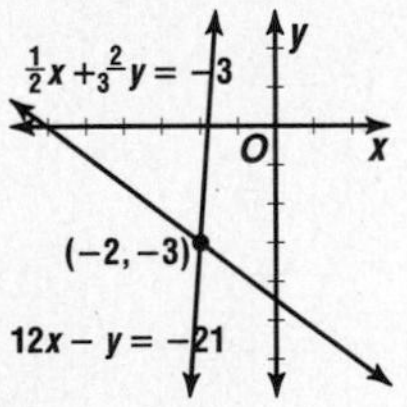

Page 774 Lesson 8-2

1. $5x = 12y$
$5x = 12x$
$0 = 7x$
$0 = x$
$(0, 0)$

$y = x$
$y = 0$

2. $2x - y = 8$
$2x - (7 - x) = 8$
$2x - 7 + x = 8$
$3x = 15$
$x = 5$
$(5, 2)$

$y = 7 - x$
$y = 7 - 5$
$y = 2$

3. $3y = 3x + 1$
$3y = 3(5 - y) + 1$
$3y = 15 - 3y + 1$
$6y = 16$
$y = \frac{16}{6}$ or $\frac{8}{3}$
$\left(\frac{7}{3}, \frac{8}{3}\right)$

$x = 5 - y$
$x = 5 - \frac{8}{3}$
$x = \frac{7}{3}$

4. $3x + y = 6$
$3(y + 2) + y = 6$
$3y + 6 + y = 6$
$4y = 0$
$y = 0$
$(2, 0)$

$y + 2 = x$
$0 + 2 = x$
$2 = x$

5. $x - 3y = 3$
$x = 3 + 3y$
$2x + 9y = 11$
$2(3 + 3y) + 9y = 11$
$6 + 6y + 9y = 11$
$15y = 5$
$y = \frac{1}{3}$
$\left(4, \frac{1}{3}\right)$

$x = 3 + 3y$
$x = 3 + 3\left(\frac{1}{3}\right)$
$x = 3 + 1$
$x = 4$

6. $x + 3y = 4$
$x = 4 - 3y$
$3x = -18 + 2y$
$3(4 - 3y) = -18 + 2y$
$12 - 9y = -18 + 2y$
$-11y = -30$
$y = \frac{30}{11}$
$\left(-\frac{46}{11}, \frac{30}{11}\right)$

$x = 4 - 3y$
$x = 4 - 3y\left(\frac{30}{11}\right)$
$x = -\frac{46}{11}$

7. $x + 2y = 10$
$x = 10 - 2y$
$-x + y = 2$
$-(10 - 2y) + y = 2$
$-10 + 2y + y = 2$
$-10 + 3y = 2$
$3y = 12$
$y = 4$
$(2, 4)$

$x = 10 - 2y$
$x = 10 - 2(4)$
$x = 10 - 8$
$x = 2$

8. $2x = 3 - y$
$2x - 3 = -y$
$-2x + 3 = y$
$2y = 12 - x$
$2(-2x + 3) = 12 - x$
$-4x + 6 = 12 - x$
$-3x = 6$
$x = -2$
$(-2, 7)$

$2x = 3 - y$
$2(-2) = 3 - y$
$-4 = 3 - y$
$-7 = -y$
$7 = y$

9. $6y - x = -36$
$6(-3x) - x = -36$
$-18x - x = -36$
$-19x = -36$
$x = \frac{36}{19}$
$\left(\frac{36}{19}, -\frac{108}{19}\right)$

$y = -3x$
$y = -3\left(\frac{36}{19}\right)$
$y = -\frac{108}{19}$

10. $x - y = 10$

$x = 10 + y$

$\frac{3}{4}x + \frac{1}{3}y = 1$

$\frac{3}{4}(10 + y) + 3y = 1$

$\frac{30}{4} + \frac{3}{4}y + \frac{1}{3}y = 12$

$90 + 9y + 4y = 12$

$13y = -78$

$y = -6$

$x = 10 + y$

$x = 10 + (-6)$

$x = 4$

$(4, -6)$

11. $x + 6y = 1$

$x = 1 - 6y$

$3x + 10y = 31$

$3(1 - 6y) - 10y = 31$

$3 - 18y - 10y = 31$

$-28y = 28$

$y = -1$

$x = 1 - 6y$

$x = 1 - 6(-1)$

$x = 1 + 6$

$x = 7$

$(7, -1)$

12. $\frac{3}{2}x - y = 3$

$\frac{3}{2}x - 3 = y$

$3x - 2y = 12$

$3x - 2\left(\frac{3}{2}x - 3\right) = 12$

$3x - 3x + 6 = 12$

$6 \neq 12$

no solution

13. $2x + 3y = 5$

$2x = 5 - 3y$

$x = \frac{5 - 3y}{2}$

$4x - 9y = 9$

$4\left(\frac{5 - 3y}{2}\right) - 9y = 9$

$2(5 - 3y) - 9y = 9$

$10 - 6y - 9y = 9$

$-15y = -1$

$y = \frac{1}{15}$

$2x + 3y = 5$

$2x + 3\left(\frac{1}{15}\right) = 5$

$2x + \frac{1}{5} = 5$

$2x = \frac{24}{5}$

$x = \frac{24}{10}$ or $\frac{12}{5}$

$\left(\frac{12}{5}, \frac{1}{15}\right)$

14. $x = 4 - 8y$

$3x + 24y = 12$

$3x + 24y = 12$

$3(4 - 8y) + 24y = 12$

$12 - 24y + 24y = 12$

$12 = 12$

infinitely many

15. $3x - 2y = 3$

$-2y = -3x - 3$

$y = \frac{3x + 3}{2}$

$25x + 10y = 215$

$25x + 10\left(\frac{3x + 3}{2}\right) = 215$

$25x + 5(3x + 3) = 215$

$25x + 15x + 15 = 215$

$40x = 200$

$x = 5$

$3x - 2y = -3$

$3(5) - 2y = -3$

$15 - 2y = -3$

$-2y = -18$

$y = 9$

$(5, 9)$

Page 775 Lesson 8-3

1. addition; $(8, -1)$

$x + y = 7$

$(+)\ x - y = 9$

$2x = 16$

$x = 8$

$x + y = 7$

$8 + y = 7$

$y = -1$

2. addition; $(23, 14)$

$2x - y = 32$

$(+)\ 2x + y = 60$

$4x = 92$

$x = 23$

$2x + y = 60$

$2(23) + y = 60$

$46 + y = 60$

$y = 14$

3. addition; $\left(\frac{11}{2}, -\frac{1}{2}\right)$

$-y + x = 6$

$(+)\ y + x = 5$

$2x = 11$

$x = \frac{11}{2}$

$y + x = 5$

$y + \frac{11}{2} = 5$

$y = -\frac{1}{2}$

4. addition; $(2, 2)$

$s + 2t = 6$

$(+)\ 3s - 2t = 2$

$4s = 8$

$s = 2$

$s + 2t = 6$

$2 + 2t - 6$

$2t = 4$

$t = 2$

5. substitution; $(-11, -4)$

$2x - 5y = -2$

$2(y - 7) - 5y = -2$

$2y - 14 - 5y = -2$

$-14 - 3y = -2$

$-3y = 12$

$y = -4$

$x = y - 7$

$x = -4 - 7$

$x = -11$

6. subtraction; $(-2, -2)$

$3x + 5y = -16$

$(-)\ 3x - 2y = -2$

$7y = -14$

$y = -2$

$3x + 5y = -16$

$3x + 5(-2) = -16$

$3x - 10 = -16$

$3x = -6$

$x = -2$

7. addition; $(3, 0)$

$x - y = 3$

$(+)\ x + y = 3$

$2x = 6$

$x = 3$

$x - y = 3$

$3 - y = 3$

$-y = 0$

$y = 0$

8. addition; $\left(\frac{14}{3}, \frac{10}{3}\right)$

$x + y = 8$

$(+)\ 2x - y = 6$

$3x = 14$

$x = \frac{14}{3}$

$x + y = 8$

$\frac{14}{3} + y = 8$

$y = \frac{10}{3}$

9. substition; $(1, 2)$

$2s - 3t = -4$

$s = 7 - 3t$

$2(7 - 3t) - 3t = -4$

$14 - 6t - 3t = -4$

$-9t = -18$

$t = 2$

$s = 7 - 3(2)$

$s = 7 - 6$

$s = 1$

10. addition; $\varnothing$

$-6x + 16y = -8$

$6x - 42 = 16y \quad \rightarrow$

$-6x + 16y = -8$

$(+)\ 6x - 16y = 42$

$0 \neq 34$

11. subtraction; (2, 5)

$$\begin{aligned} 3x + 0.2y &= 7 & 3x + 0.2y &= 7 \\ 3x &= 0.4y + 4 \rightarrow & (-)\ 3x - 0.4y &= 4 \\ & & 0.6y &= 3 \\ & & y &= 5 \end{aligned}$$

$$\begin{aligned} 3x + 0.2y &= 7 \\ 3x + 0.2(5) &= 7 \\ 3x + 1 &= 7 \\ 3x &= 6 \\ x &= 2 \end{aligned}$$

12. addition; $\left(\frac{26}{7}, -\frac{26}{7}\right)$

$$\begin{aligned} 9x + 2y &= 26 & 9x + 2y &= 26 \\ (+)\ 1.5x - 2y &= 13 & 9\left(\tfrac{26}{7}\right) + 2y &= 26 \\ 10.5x &= 39 & \tfrac{234}{7} + 2y &= 26 \\ x &= \tfrac{78}{21} \text{ or } \tfrac{26}{7} & 2y &= \tfrac{-52}{7} \\ & & y &= -\tfrac{26}{7} \end{aligned}$$

13. subtraction; (24, 4)

$$\begin{aligned} \tfrac{2}{3}x - \tfrac{1}{2}y &= 14 & \tfrac{2}{3}x - \tfrac{1}{2}y &= 14 \\ (-)\ \tfrac{5}{6}x - \tfrac{1}{2}y &= 18 & \tfrac{2}{3}(24) - \tfrac{1}{2}y &= 14 \\ -\tfrac{1}{6}x &= -4 & 16 - \tfrac{1}{2}y &= 14 \\ x &= 24 & -\tfrac{1}{2}y &= -2 \\ & & y &= 4 \end{aligned}$$

14. addition; $\left(\frac{14}{9}, -\frac{16}{3}\right)$

$$\begin{aligned} 4x - \tfrac{1}{3}y &= 8 & 4x - \tfrac{1}{3}y &= 8 \\ (+)\ 5x + \tfrac{1}{3}y &= 6 & 4\left(\tfrac{14}{9}\right) - \tfrac{1}{3}y &= 8 \\ 9x &= 14 & \tfrac{56}{9} - \tfrac{1}{3}y &= 8 \\ x &= \tfrac{14}{9} & -\tfrac{1}{3}y &= \tfrac{16}{9} \\ & & y &= -\tfrac{16}{3} \end{aligned}$$

15. subtraction; (3, 3)

$$\begin{aligned} 2x - y &= 3 & 2x - y &= 3 \\ (-)\ \tfrac{2}{3}x - y &= -1 & 2(3) - y &= 3 \\ \tfrac{4}{3}x &= 4 & 6 - y &= 3 \\ x &= 3 & -y &= -3 \\ & & y &= 3 \end{aligned}$$

Page 775 Lesson 8-4

1.

$$\begin{aligned} x + 8y &= 3 & x + 8y &= 3 \\ 4x - 2y &= 7 \rightarrow & (+)\ 16x - 8y &= 28 \\ & & 17x &= 31 \\ & & x &= \tfrac{31}{17} \end{aligned}$$

$$\begin{aligned} \tfrac{31}{17} + 8y &= 3 \\ 8y &= \tfrac{20}{17} \\ y &= \tfrac{5}{34} \end{aligned}$$

$\left(\frac{31}{17}, \frac{5}{34}\right)$

2.

$$\begin{aligned} 4x - y &= 4 \rightarrow & 8x - 2y &= 8 \\ x + 2y &= 3 & (+)\ x + 2y &= 3 \\ & & x + 2y &= 3 \\ & & 9x &= 11 \\ & & x &= \tfrac{11}{9} \end{aligned}$$

$$\begin{aligned} \tfrac{11}{9} + 2y &= 3 \\ 2y &= \tfrac{16}{9} \\ y &= \tfrac{8}{9} \end{aligned}$$

$\left(\frac{11}{9}, \frac{8}{9}\right)$

3.

$$\begin{aligned} 3y - 8x &= 9 & 3y - 8x &= 9 \\ y - x &= 2 \rightarrow & (+)\ -3y + 3x &= -6 \\ & & -5x &= 3 \\ & & x &= -\tfrac{3}{5} \end{aligned}$$

$$\begin{aligned} y - x &= 2 \\ y - \left(-\tfrac{3}{5}\right) &= 2 \\ y + \tfrac{3}{5} &= 2 \\ y &= \tfrac{7}{5} \end{aligned}$$

$\left(-\frac{3}{5}, \frac{7}{5}\right)$

4.

$$\begin{aligned} x + 4y &= 30 & x + 4y &= 30 \\ 2x - y &= -6 \rightarrow & (+)\ 8x - 4y &= -24 \\ & & 9x &= 6 \\ & & x &= \tfrac{2}{3} \end{aligned}$$

$$\begin{aligned} x + 4y &= 30 \\ \tfrac{2}{3} + 4y &= 30 \\ 4y &= \tfrac{88}{3} \\ y &= \tfrac{22}{3} \end{aligned}$$

$\left(\frac{2}{3}, \frac{22}{3}\right)$

5.

$$\begin{aligned} 3x - 2y &= 0 \rightarrow & 6x - 4y &= 0 \\ 4x + 4y &= 5 & (+)\ 4x + 4y &= 5 \\ & & 10x &= 5 \\ & & x &= \tfrac{1}{2} \end{aligned}$$

$$\begin{aligned} 4x + 4y &= 5 \\ 4\left(\tfrac{1}{2}\right) + 4y &= 5 \\ 2 + 4y &= 5 \\ 4y &= 3 \\ y &= \tfrac{3}{4} \end{aligned}$$

$\left(\frac{1}{2}, \frac{3}{4}\right)$

6.

$$\begin{aligned} 9x - 3y &= 5 & 9x - 3y &= 5 \\ x + y &= 1 \rightarrow & (+)\ 3x + 3y &= 3 \\ & & 12x &= 8 \\ & & x &= \tfrac{2}{3} \end{aligned}$$

$$\begin{aligned} x + y &= 1 \\ \tfrac{2}{3} + y &= 1 \\ y &= \tfrac{1}{3} \end{aligned}$$

$\left(\frac{2}{3}, \frac{1}{3}\right)$

7.

$$\begin{aligned} -3x + 2y &= 10 & -3x + 2y &= 10 \\ -2x - y &= -5 \rightarrow & (+)\ -4x - 2y &= -10 \\ & & -7x &= 0 \\ & & x &= 0 \end{aligned}$$

$$\begin{aligned} -2x - y &= -5 \\ -2(0) - y &= -5 \\ -y &= -5 \\ y &= 5 \end{aligned}$$

(0, 5)

8.

$$\begin{aligned} 2x + 5y &= 13 \rightarrow & -4x - 10y &= -26 \\ 4x - 3y &= -13 & (+)\ 4x - 3y &= -13 \\ & & -13y &= -39 \\ & & y &= 3 \end{aligned}$$

$$\begin{aligned} 2x + 5y &= 13 \\ 2x + 5(3) &= 13 \\ 2x + 15 &= 13 \\ 2x &= -2 \\ x &= -1 \end{aligned}$$

(−1, 3)

9. $5x + 3y = 4 \rightarrow 20x + 12y = 16$
$-4x + 5y = -18 \rightarrow (+)\ -20x + 25y = -90$
$37y = -74$
$y = -2$

$5x + 3y = 4$
$5x + 3(-2) = 4$
$5x - 6 = 4$
$5x = 10$
$x = 2$
$(2, -2)$

10. $2x - 7y = 9 \rightarrow 6x - 21y = 27$
$-3x + 4y = 6 \rightarrow (+)\ -6x + 8y = 12$
$-13y = 39$
$y = -3$

$2x - 7y = 9$
$2x - 7(-3) = 9$
$2x + 21 = 9$
$2x = -12$
$x = -6$
$(-6, -3)$

11. $2x - 6y = -16 \rightarrow 10x - 30y = -80$
$5x + 7y = -18 \rightarrow (+)\ -10x - 14y = 36$
$-44y = -44$
$y = 1$

$2x - 6y = -16$
$2x - 6(1) = -16$
$2x - 6 = -16$
$2x = -10$
$x = -5$
$(-5, 1)$

12. $6x - 3y = -9 \rightarrow 12x - 6y = -18$
$-8x + 2y = 4 \rightarrow (+)\ -24x + 6y = 12$
$-12x = -6$
$x = \frac{1}{2}$

$6x - 3y = -9$
$6\left(\frac{1}{2}\right) - 3y = -9$
$3 - 3y = -9$
$-3y = -12$
$y = 4$
$\left(\frac{1}{2}, 4\right)$

13. $\frac{1}{3}x - y = -1 \rightarrow -\frac{2}{15}x + \frac{2}{5}y = \frac{2}{5}$
$\frac{1}{5}x - \frac{2}{5}y = -1 \quad (+)\ \frac{1}{5}x - \frac{2}{5}y = -1$
$\frac{1}{15}x = -\frac{3}{5}$
$x = -9$

$\frac{1}{3}x - y = -1$
$\frac{1}{3}(-9) - y = -1$
$-3 - y = -1$
$-y = 2$
$y = -2$
$(-9, -2)$

14. $3x - 5y = 8 \rightarrow 12x - 20y = 32$
$4x - 7y = 10 \rightarrow (+)\ -12x + 21y = -30$
$y = 2$

$3x - 5y = 8$
$3x - 5(2) = 8$
$3x - 10 = 8$
$3x = 18$
$x = 6$
$(6, 2)$

15. $x - 0.5y = 1 \rightarrow 2x - y = 2$
$0.4x + y = -2 \quad (+)\ 0.4x + y = -2$
$2.4x = 0$
$x = 0$

$x - 0.5y = 1$
$0 - 0.5y = 1$
$y = -2$
$(0, -2)$

Page 775 Lesson 8-5

1. $x > 3$
$y < 6$

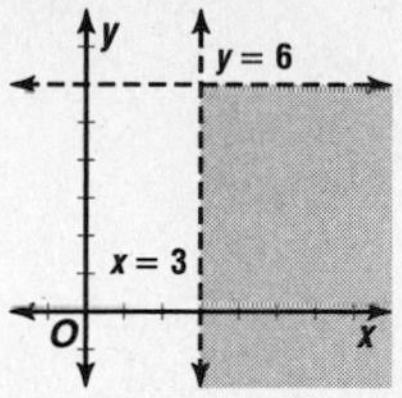

2. $y > 2$
$y > -x + 2$

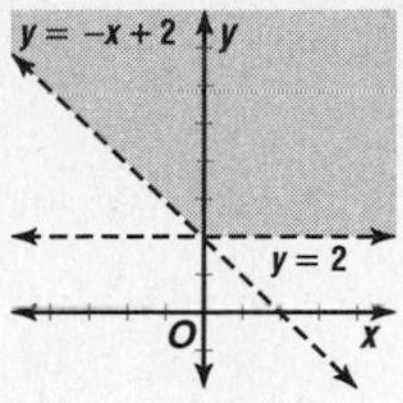

3. $x \leq 2$
$y - 3 \geq 5$
$y \geq 8$

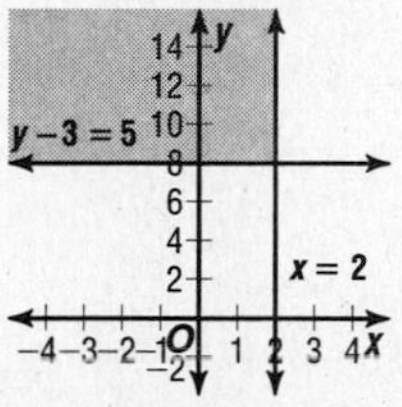

4. $x + y \leq -1$
$y \leq -x - 1$
$2x + y \leq 2$
$y \leq -2x + 2$

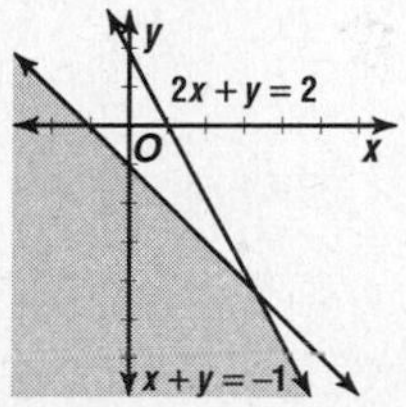

5. $y \geq 2x + 2$
$y \geq -x - 1$

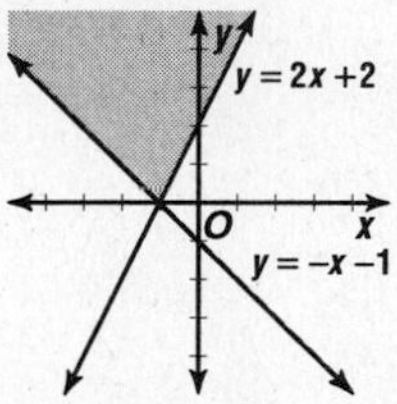

6. $y \leq x + 3$
$y \geq x + 2$

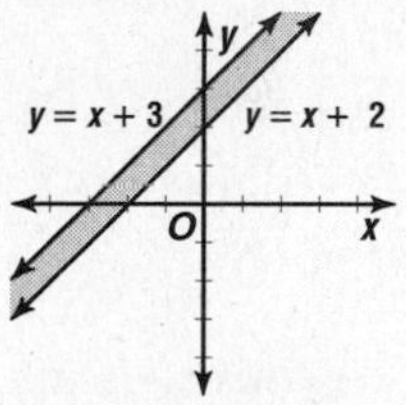

7. $x + 3y \geq 4$
$3y \geq -x + 4$
$y \geq -\frac{1}{3}x + \frac{4}{3}$
$2x - y < 5$
$-y < -2x + 5$
$y > 2x - 5$

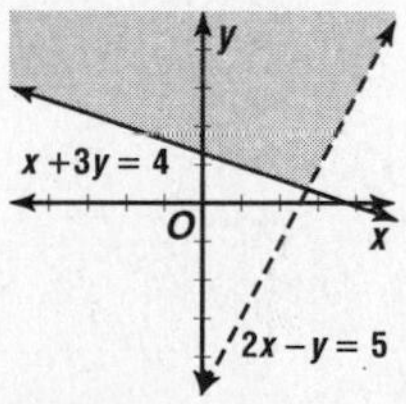

8. $y - x > 1$
$y > x + 1$
$y + 2x \leq 10$
$y \leq 10 - 2x$

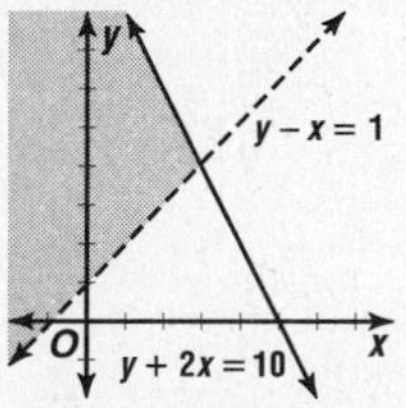

9. $5x - 2y > 15$
$-2y > -5x + 15$
$y < \frac{5}{2}x - \frac{15}{2}$
$2x - 3y < 6$
$-3y < 6 - 2y$
$y > -2 + \frac{2}{3}x$

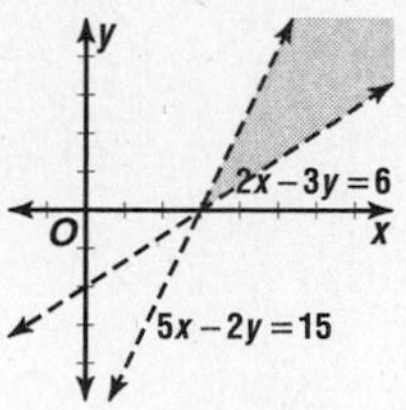

10. $4x + 3y > 4$
$3y > 4 - 4x$
$y > \frac{4}{3} - \frac{4}{3}x$
$2x - y < 0$
$-y < -2x$
$y > 2x$

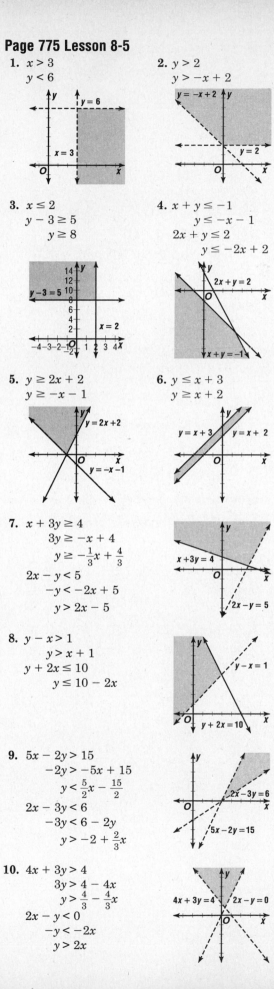

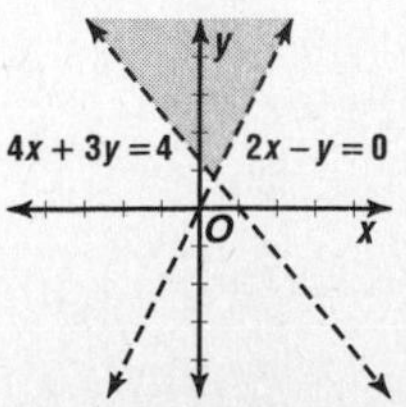

11. $4x + 5y \geq 20$
$$5y \geq -4x + 20$$
$$y \geq -\frac{4}{5}x + 4$$
$$y \geq x + 1$$

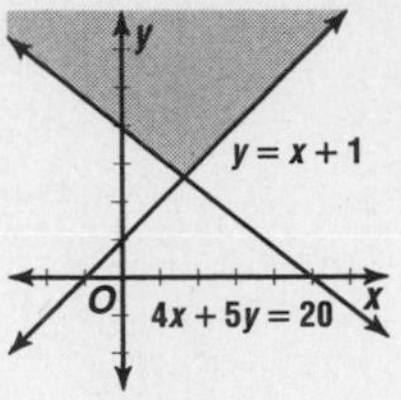

12. $-4x + 10y \leq 5$
$$10y \leq 5 + 4x$$
$$y \leq \frac{1}{2} + \frac{2}{5}x$$
$$-2x + 5y < -1$$
$$5y < 2x - 1$$
$$y < \frac{2}{5}x - \frac{1}{5}$$

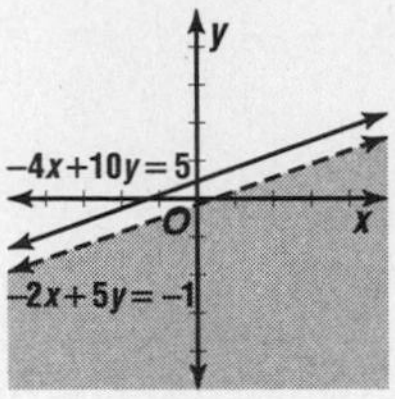

Page 776 Lesson 9-1

1. $(a^5)(a)(a^7) = a^{5+1+7}$
$= a^{13}$

2. $(r^3t^4)(r^4t^4) = (r^3 \cdot r^4)(t^4 \cdot t^4)$
$= (r^{3+4})(t^{4+4})$
$= r^7t^8$

3. $(x^3y^4)(xy^3) = (x^3 \cdot x)(y^4 \cdot y^3)$
$= (x^{3+1})(y^{4+3})$
$= x^4y^7$

4. $(bc^3)(b^4c^3) = (b \cdot b^4)(c^3 \cdot c^3)$
$= (b^{1+4})(c^{3+3})$
$= b^5c^6$

5. $(-3mn^2)(5m^3n^2) = (-3 \cdot 5)(m \cdot m^3)(n^2 \cdot n^2)$
$= -15m^{1+3}n^{2+2}$
$= -15m^4n^4$

6. $[(3^3)^2]^2 = (3^6)^2$
$= 3^{12}$
$= 531{,}441$

7. $(3s^3t^2)(-4s^3t^2) = (3 \cdot -4)(s^3 \cdot s^3)(t^2 \cdot t^2)$
$= -12s^{3+3}t^{2+2}$
$= -12s^6t^4$

8. $x^3(x^4y^3) = (x^3 \cdot x^4) \cdot y^3$
$= x^{3+4}y^3$
$= x^7y^3$

9. $(1.1g^2h^4)^3 = 1.1^3(g^2)^3(h^4)^3$
$= 1.331g^6h^{12}$

10. $-\frac{3}{4}a(a^2b^3c^4) = -\frac{3}{4}(a \cdot a^2)b^3c^4$
$= -\frac{3}{4}a^{1+2}b^3c^4$
$= -\frac{3}{4}a^3b^3c^4$

11. $\left(\frac{1}{2}w^3\right)^2(w^4)^2 = \left(\frac{1}{2}\right)^2(w^3)^2w^8$
$= \frac{1}{4}w^6 \cdot w^8$
$= \frac{1}{4}w^{6+8}$
$= \frac{1}{4}w^{14}$

12. $\left(\frac{2}{3}y^3\right)(3y^2)^3 = \frac{2}{3}y^3 \cdot 3^3(y^2)^3$
$= \frac{2}{3}y^3(27)(y^6)$
$= \left(\frac{2}{3} \cdot 27\right)(y^3 \cdot y^6)$
$= 18y^{3+6}$
$= 18y^9$

13. $[(-2^3)^3]^2 = [(-8)^3]^2$
$= (-8)^6$
$= 262{,}144$

14. $(10s^2t)(-2s^2t^2)^3 = (10s^3t)(-2)^3(s^2)^3(t^2)^3$
$= 10s^3t(-8)s^6t^6$
$= (10 \cdot -8)(s^3 \cdot s^6)(t \cdot t^6)$
$= -80s^{3+6}t^{1+6}$
$= -80s^9t^7$

15. $(-0.2w^3w^4)^3 = (-0.2)^3(u^3)^3(w^4)^3$
$= -0.008u^9w^{12}$

Page 776 Lesson 9-2

1. $\frac{b^6c^5}{b^3c^2} = \left(\frac{b^6}{b^3}\right)\left(\frac{c^5}{c^2}\right)$
$= b^{6-3}c^{5-2}$
$= b^3c^3$

2. $\frac{(-a)^4b^8}{a^4b^7} = \left(\frac{a^4}{a^4}\right)\left(\frac{b^8}{b^7}\right)$
$= a^{4-4}b^{8-7}$
$= a^0b$
$= b$

3. $\frac{(-x)^3y^3}{x^3y^6} = \left(\frac{-x^3}{x^3}\right)\left(\frac{y^3}{y^6}\right)$
$= -x^{3-3}y^{3-6}$
$= x^0y^{-3}$
$= -\frac{1}{y^3}$

4. $\frac{12ab^5}{4a^4b^3} = \left(\frac{12}{4}\right)\left(\frac{a}{a^4}\right)\left(\frac{b^5}{b^3}\right)$
$= 3a^{1-4}b^{5-3}$
$= 3a^{-3}b^2$
$= \frac{3b^2}{a^3}$

5. $\frac{24x^5}{-8x^2} = \left(\frac{24}{-8}\right)\left(\frac{x^5}{x^2}\right)$
$= -3x^{5-2}$
$= -3x^3$

6. $\frac{-9h^2k^4}{18h^5j^3k^4} = \left(\frac{-9}{18}\right)\left(\frac{h^2}{h^5}\right)\left(\frac{1}{j^3}\right)\left(\frac{k^4}{k^4}\right)$
$= \frac{-1h^{2-5}k^{4-4}}{2j^3}$
$= \frac{-h^{-3}k^0}{2j^3}$
$= \frac{-1}{2h^3j^3}$

7. $\frac{a^0}{2a^{-3}} = \frac{1}{2}\left(\frac{a^0}{a^{-3}}\right)$
$= \frac{1}{2}a^{0-(-3)}$
$= \frac{a^3}{2}$

8. $\frac{9a^2b^7c^3}{2a^5b^4c} = \left(\frac{a}{2}\right)\left(\frac{a^2}{a^5}\right)\left(\frac{b^7}{b^4}\right)\left(\frac{c^3}{c}\right)$
$= \frac{9}{2}a^{2-5}b^{7-4}c^{3-1}$
$= \frac{9}{2}a^{-3}b^3c^2$
$= \frac{9b^3c^2}{2a^3}$

9. $\frac{-15xy^5z^7}{-10x^4y^6z^4} = \left(\frac{-15}{-10}\right)\left(\frac{x}{x^4}\right)\left(\frac{y^5}{y^6}\right)\left(\frac{z^7}{z^4}\right)$
$= \frac{3}{2}x^{1-4}y^{5-6}z^{7-4}$
$= \frac{3}{2}x^{-3}y^{-1}z^3$
$= \frac{3z^3}{2x^3y}$

10. $\frac{(u^{-3}v^3)^2}{(u^3v)^{-3}} = \frac{(u^{-3})^2(v^3)^2}{(u^3)^{-3}(v)^{-3}}$
$= \frac{u^{-6}v^6}{u^{-9}v^{-3}}$
$= \left(\frac{u^{-6}}{u^{-9}}\right)\left(\frac{v^6}{v^{-3}}\right)$
$= u^{-6-(-9)}v^{6-(-3)}$
$= u^3v^9$

11. $\frac{(-r)s^5}{r^{-3}s^{-4}} = \left(\frac{-r}{r^{-3}}\right)\left(\frac{s^5}{s^{-4}}\right)$
$= -r^{1-(-3)}s^{5-(-4)}$
$= -r^4s^9$

12. $\frac{28a^{-4}b^0}{14a^3b^{-1}} = \left(\frac{28}{14}\right)\left(\frac{a^{-4}}{a^3}\right)\left(\frac{b^0}{b^{-1}}\right)$
$= 2a^{-4-3}b^{0-(-1)}$
$= 2a^{-7}b$
$= \frac{2b}{a^7}$

13. $\frac{(j^2k^3l)^4}{(jk^4)^{-1}} = \frac{(j^2)^4(k^3)^4(l)^4}{(j)^{-1}(k^4)^{-1}}$
$= \frac{j^8k^{12}l^4}{j^{-1}k^{-4}}$
$= \left(\frac{j^8}{j^{-1}}\right)\left(\frac{k^{12}}{k^{-4}}\right)l^4$
$= j^{8-(-1)}k^{12-(-4)}l^4$
$= j^9k^{16}l^4$

14. $\left(\frac{-2x^4y}{4y^2}\right)^0 = 1$

15. $\frac{3m^7n^2p^4}{9m^2np^3} = \left(\frac{3}{9}\right)\left(\frac{m^7}{m^2}\right)\left(\frac{n^2}{n}\right)\left(\frac{p^4}{p^3}\right)$
$= \frac{1}{3}m^{7-2}n^{2-1}p^{4-3}$
$= \frac{m^5np}{3}$

Page 776 Lesson 9-3

1. $6500 = 6.5 \times 1000$
$= 6.5 \times 10^3$

2. $953.56 = 9.5356 \times 100$
$= 9.5356 \times 10^2$

3. $0.697 = 6.97 \times 0.1$
$= 6.97 \times 10^{-1}$

4. $843.5 = 8.435 \times 100$
$= 8.435 \times 10^2$

5. $568{,}000 = 5.68 \times 100{,}000$
$= 5.68 \times 10^5$

6. $0.0000269 = 2.69 \times 0.00001$
$= 2.69 \times 10^{-5}$

7. $0.121212 = 1.21212 \times 0.1$
$= 1.21212 \times 10^{-1}$

8. $543 \times 10^4 = 5.43 \times 100 \times 10^4$
$= 5.43 \times 10^2 \times 10^4$
$= 5.43 \times {}^{2+4}$
$= 5.43 \times 10^6$

9. $739.9 = 7.399 \times 100 \times 10^{-5}$
$= 7.399 \times 10^2 \times 10^{-5}$
$= 7.399 \times 10^{2+(-5)}$
$= 7.399 \times 10^{-3}$

10. $6480 \times 10^{-2} = 6.48 \times 1000 \times 10^{-2}$
$= 6.48 \times 10^3 \times 10^{-2}$
$= 6.48 \times 10^{3+(-2)}$
$= 6.48 \times 10$

11. $0.336 \times 10^{-7} = 3.66 \times 0.1 \times 10^{-7}$
$= 3.66 \times 10^{-1} \times 10^{-7}$
$= 3.66 \times 10^{-1+(-7)}$
$= 3.66 \times 10^{-8}$

12. $167 \times 10^3 = 1.67 \times 100 \times 10^3$
$= 1.67 \times 10^2 \times 10^3$
$= 1.67 \times 10^{2+3}$
$= 1.67 \times 10^5$

13. $(2 \times 10^5)(3 \times 10^{-8}) = (2 \times 3)(10^5 \times 10^{-8})$
$= 6 \times 10^{-3}$; 0.006

14. $\frac{4.8 \times 10^3}{1.6 \times 10} = \left(\frac{4.8}{1.6}\right)\left(\frac{10^3}{10}\right)$
$= 3 \times 10^2$; 300

15. $(4 \times 10^2)(1.5 \times 10^6) = (4 \times 1.5)(10^2 \times 10^6)$
$= 6 \times 10^8$; 600,000,000

16. $\frac{8.1 \times 10^2}{2.7 \times 10^{-3}} = \left(\frac{8.1}{2.7}\right)\left(\frac{10^2}{10^{-3}}\right)$
$= 3 \times 10^5$; 300,000

17. $\frac{7.8 \times 10^{-5}}{1.3 \times 10^{-7}} = \left(\frac{7.8}{1.3}\right)\left(\frac{10^{-5}}{10^{-7}}\right)$
$= 6 \times 10^2$; 600

18. $(2.2 \times 10^{-2})(3.2 \times 10^5) = (2.2 \times 3.2)(10^{-2} \times 10^5)$
$= 7.04 \times 10^3$; 7040

19. $(3.1 \times 10^4)(4.2 \times 10^{-3}) = 13.02 \times 10^1$
$= 1.302 \times 10^1 \times 10^1$
$= 1.302 \times 10^2$; 130.2

20. $(78 \times 10^6)(0.01 \times 10^3) = (78 \times 0.01)(10^6 \times 10^3)$
$= 0.78 \times 10^9$
$= 7.8 \times 0.1 \times 10^9$
$= 7.8 \times 10^{-1} \times 10^9$
$= 7.8 \times 10^8$; 780,000,000

21. $\frac{2.31 \times 10^{-2}}{3.3 \times 10^{-3}} = \left(\frac{2.31}{3.3}\right)\left(\frac{10^{-2}}{10^{-3}}\right)$
$= 0.7 \times 10^1$
$= 7.0 \times 0.1 \times 10^1$
$= 7.0 \times 10^{-1} \times 10^1$
$= 7.0 \times 10^0$; 7

Page 777 Lesson 9-4

1. The degree of $5x^2y$ is 3.
The degree of $3xy$ is 2.
The degree of 7 is 0.
Thus, the degree of $5x^2 + 3xy + 7$ is 3.
yes, trinomial, 3

2. yes, monomial, 0

3. no

4. The degree of $3a^2x$ is 3.
The degree of $-5a$ is 1.
Thus, the degree of $3a^2x - 5a$ is 3.
yes, binomial, 3

5. no

6. The degree of $14abcd$ is 4.
The degree of $-6d^3$ is 3.
Thus, the degree of $14abcd - 6d^3$ is 4.
yes, binomial, 4

7. yes, monomial, 3

8. yes, monomial, 3

9. The degree of x^2 is 2.
The degree of $-\frac{x}{2}$ is 1.
The degree of $\frac{1}{3}$ is 0.
Thus, the degree of $x^2 - \frac{x}{2} + \frac{1}{3}$ is 2.
yes, trinomial, 2

10. $-3x^3 + 5x^2 + 2x + 7$

11. $x^5 + 4x^3 - 6x - 20$

12. $b^3x^2 + \frac{2}{3}bx + 5b$

13. $3px^3 + 21p^2x + p^4$

14. $-6a^2x^3 + 3ax^2 - 8x + 7a^3$

15. $4x^4 + \frac{1}{3}s^2x^3 - \frac{2}{5}s^4x^2 + \frac{1}{4}x$

Page 777 Lesson 9-5

1. $$\begin{array}{rrrr} & -7t^2 & + 4ts & - 6s^2 \\ (+) & -5t^2 & - 12ts & + 3s^2 \\ \hline & -12t^2 & - 8ts & - 3s^2 \end{array}$$

2. $$\begin{array}{rr} & 6a^2 - 7ab - 4b^2 \\ (-) & 2a^2 + 5ab + 6b^2 \\ \hline \end{array} \rightarrow \begin{array}{rr} & 6a^2 - 7ab - 4b^2 \\ (+) & -2a^2 - 5ab - 6b^2 \\ \hline & 4a^2 - 12ab - 10b^2 \end{array}$$

3. $$\begin{array}{rl} & 4a^2 - 10b^2 + 7c^2 \\ & -5a^2 \qquad\quad + 2c^2 \qquad + 2b \\ (+) & \qquad\quad 7b^2 - 7c^2 + 7a \\ \hline & -a^2 - 3b^2 + 2c^2 + 7a + 2b \end{array}$$

4. $$\begin{array}{rr} & z^2 + 6z - 8 \\ (-) & 4z^2 - 7z - 5 \\ \hline \end{array} \rightarrow \begin{array}{rr} & z^2 + 6z - 8 \\ (+) & -4z^2 + 7z + 5 \\ \hline & -3z^2 + 13z - 3 \end{array}$$

5. $$\begin{array}{rr} & 4d + 3e - 8f \\ (-) & -3d + 10e - 5f + 6 \\ \hline \end{array} \rightarrow \begin{array}{rr} & 4d + 3e - 8f \\ (+) & 3d - 10e + 5f - 6 \\ \hline & 7d - 7e - 3f - 6 \end{array}$$

6. $$\begin{array}{rl} & 7g + 8h \qquad - 9 \\ (+) & -g - 3h - 6k \\ \hline & 6g + 5h - 6k - 9 \end{array}$$

7. $$\begin{array}{rr} & 9x^2 - 11xy - 3y^2 \\ (-) & x^2 - 16xy + 12y^2 \\ \hline \end{array} \rightarrow \begin{array}{rr} & 9x^2 - 11xy - 3y^2 \\ (+) & -x^2 + 16xy - 12y^2 \\ \hline & 8x^2 + 5xy - 15y^2 \end{array}$$

8. $$\begin{array}{rr} & -3m + 9mn - 5n \\ (+) & 14m - 5mn - 2n \\ \hline & 11m + 4mn - 7n \end{array}$$

9. $$\begin{array}{rr} & 4x^2 - 8y^2 - 3z^2 \\ (-) & 7x^2 \qquad - 14z^2 - 12 \\ \hline \end{array} \rightarrow \begin{array}{rr} & 4x^2 - 8y^2 - 3z^2 \\ (+) & -7x^2 \qquad + 14z^2 + 12 \\ \hline & -3x^2 - 8y^2 + 11z^2 + 12 \end{array}$$

10. $$\begin{array}{rr} & 17z^4 \qquad - 5z^2 + 3z \\ (-) & 4z^4 + 2z^3 \qquad + 3z \\ \hline \end{array} \rightarrow \begin{array}{rr} & 17z^4 \qquad - 5z^2 + 3z \\ (+) & -4z^4 - 2z^3 \qquad - 3z \\ \hline & 13z^4 - 2z^3 - 5z^2 \end{array}$$

11. $$\begin{array}{rr} & 3y^2 - 7y + 6 \\ & -2y^2 - 5y + 3 \\ (+) & y^2 - 8y - 12 \\ \hline & 2y^2 - 20y - 3 \end{array}$$

12. $$\begin{array}{rr} & -3x^2 + 2x - 5 \\ & 2x - 6 \\ & 5x^2 \qquad + 3 \\ (+) & -9x^2 - 7x + 4 \\ \hline & -7x^2 - 3x - 4 \end{array}$$

Page 777 Lesson 9-6

1. $-3(8x + 5) = -3(8x) + (-3)(5)$
$= -24x - 15$

2. $3b(5b + 8) = 3b(5b) + (3b)(8)$
$= 15b^2 + 24b$

3. $1.1a(2a + 7) = 1.1a(2a) + 1.1a(7)$
$= 2.2a^2 + 7.7a$

4. $\frac{1}{2}x(8x - 6) = \frac{1}{2}x(8x) + \left(\frac{1}{2}x\right)(-6)$
$= 4x^2 - 3x$

5. $7xy(5x^2 - y^2) = 7xy(5x^2) + (7xy)(-y^2)$
$= 35x^3y - 7xy^3$

6. $5y(y^2 - 3y + 6) = 5y(y^2) + 5y(-3y) + 5y(6)$
$= 5y^3 - 15y^2 + 30y$

7. $-ab(3b^2 + 4ab - 6a^2)$
$= -ab(3b^2) + (-ab)(4ab) + (-ab)(-6a^2)$
$= -3ab^3 - 4a^2b^2 + 6a^3b$

8. $4m^2(9m^2n + mn - 5n^2)$
$= 4m^2(9m^2n) + (4m^2)(mn) + (4m^2)(-5n^2)$
$= 36m^4n + 4m^3n - 20m^2n^2$

9. $4st^2(-4s^2t^3 + 7s^5 - 3st^3)$
$= 4st^2(-4s^2t^3) + (4st^2)(7s^5) + (4st^2)(-3st^3)$
$= -16s^3t^5 + 28s^6t^2 - 12s^2t^5$

10. $-\frac{1}{3}x(9x^2 + x - 5)$
$= \left(-\frac{1}{3}x\right)(9x^2) + \left(-\frac{1}{3}x\right)(x) + \left(-\frac{1}{3}x\right)(-5)$
$= -3x^3 - \frac{1}{3}x^2 + \frac{5}{3}x$

11. $-2mn(8m^2 - 3mn + n^2)$
$= (-2mn)(8m^2) + (-2mn)(-3mn) + (-2mn)(n^2)$
$= -16m^3n + 6m^2n^2 - 2mn^3$

12. $-\frac{3}{4}ab^2\left(\frac{1}{3}b^2 - \frac{4}{9}b + 1\right)$
$= \left(-\frac{3}{4}ab^2\right)\left(\frac{1}{3}b^2\right) + \left(-\frac{3}{4}ab^2\right)\left(-\frac{4}{9}b\right) + \left(-\frac{3}{4}ab^2\right)(1)$
$= -\frac{1}{4}ab^4 + \frac{1}{3}ab^3 - \frac{3}{4}ab^2$

13. $-3(2a - 12) + 48 = 3a - 3$
$-6a + 36 + 48 = 3a - 3$
$-6a + 84 = 3a - 3$
$84 = 9a - 3$
$87 = 9a$
$a = \frac{87}{9}$ or $\frac{29}{3}$

14. $-6(12 - 2w) = 7(-2 - 3w)$
$-72 + 12w = -14 - 21w$
$-72 + 33w = -14$
$33w = 58$
$w = \frac{58}{33}$

15. $a(a - 6) + 2a = 3 + a(a - 2)$
$a^2 - 6a + 2a = 3 + a^2 - 2a$
$a^2 - 4a = 3 + a^2 - 2a$
$-4a = 3 - 2a$
$-2a = 3$
$a = -\frac{3}{2}$

16. $11(a - 3) + 5 = 2a + 44$
$11a - 33 + 5 = 2a + 44$
$11a - 28 = 2a + 44$
$9a - 28 = 44$
$9a = 72$
$a = 8$

17. $q(2q + 3) + 20 = 2q(q - 3)$
$2q^2 + 3q + 20 = 2q^2 - 6q$
$3q + 20 = -6q$
$20 = -9q$
$-\frac{20}{9} = q$

18. $w(w + 12) = w(w + 14) + 12$
$w^2 + 12w = w^2 + 14w + 12$
$12w = 14w + 12$
$-2w = 12$
$w = -6$

19. $x(x + 8) - x(x + 3) - 23 = 3x + 11$
$x^2 + 8x - x^2 - 3x - 23 = 3x + 11$
$5x - 23 = 3x + 11$
$2x - 23 = 11$
$2x = 34$
$x = 17$

20. $y(y - 12) + y(y + 2) + 25 = 2y(y + 5) - 15$
$y^2 - 12y + y^2 + 2y + 25 = 2y^2 + 10y - 15$
$2y^2 - 10y + 25 = 2y^2 + 10y - 15$
$-10y + 25 = 10y - 15$
$25 = 20y - 15$
$40 = 20y$
$2 = y$

21. $x(x - 3) + 4x - 3 = 8x + 4 + x(3 + x)$
$x^2 - 3x + 4x - 3 = 8x + 4 + 3x + x^2$
$x^2 + x - 3 = x^2 + 11x + 4$
$x - 3 = 11x + 4$
$-3 = 10x + 4$
$-7 = 10x$
$-\frac{7}{10} = x$

22. $c(c - 3) + 4(c - 2) = 12 - 2(4 + c) - c(1 - c)$
$c^2 - 3c + 4c - 8 = 12 - 8 - 2c - c + c^2$
$c^2 + c - 8 = c^2 - 3c + 4$
$c - 8 = -3c + 4$
$4c - 8 = 4$
$4c = 12$
$c = 3$

Page 778 Lesson 9-7

1. $(d + 2)(d + 3) = (d)(d) + (d)(3) + (2)(d) + (2)(3)$
$= d^2 + 3d + 2d + 6$
$= d^2 + 5d + 6$

2. $(z + 7)(z - 4) = (z)(z) + (z)(-4) + (7)(z) + (7)(-4)$
$= z^2 - 4z + 7z - 28$
$= z^2 + 3z - 28$

3. $(m - 8)(m - 5)$
$= (m)(m) + (m)(-5) + (-8)(m) + (-8)(-5)$
$= m^2 - 5m - 8m + 40$
$= m^2 - 13m + 40$

4. $(2x - 5)(x + 6)$
$= (2x)(x) + (2x)(6) + (-5)(x) + (-5)(x)$
$= 2x^2 + 12x - 5x - 30$
$= 2x^2 + 7x - 30$

5. $(7a - 4)(2a - 5)$
$= (7a)(2a) + (7a)(-5) + (-4)(2a) + (-4)(-5)$
$= 14a^2 - 35a - 8a + 20$
$= 14a^2 - 43a + 20$

6. $(4x + y)(2x - 3y)$
$= (4x)(2x) + (4x)(-3y) + (y)(2x) + (y)(-3y)$
$= 8x^2 - 12xy + 2xy - 3y^2$
$= 8x^2 - 10xy - 3y^2$

7. $(7v + 3)(v + 4) = (7v)(v) + (7v)(4) + (3)(v) + 3(4)$
$= 7v^2 + 28 + 3v + 12$
$= 7v^2 + 31v + 12$

8. $(7s - 8)(3s - 2)$
$= (7s)(3s) + (7s)(-2) + (-8)(3s) + (-8)(-2)$
$= 21s^2 - 14s - 24s + 16$
$= 21s^2 - 38s + 16$

9. $(4g + 3h)(2g - 5h)$
$= (4g)(2g) + (4g)(-5h) + (3h)(2g) + (3h)(-5h)$
$= 8g^2 - 20gh + 6gh - 15h^2$
$= 8g^2 - 14gh - 15h^2$

10. $(4a + 3)(2a - 1)$
$= (4a)(2a) + (4a)(-1) + (3)(2a) + (3)(-1)$
$= 8a^2 - 4a + 6a - 3$
$= 8a^2 + 2a - 3$

11. $(7y - 1)(2y - 3)$
$= (7y)(2y) + (7y)(-3) + (-1)(2y) + (-1)(-3)$
$= 14y^2 - 21y - 2y + 3$
$= 14y^2 - 23y + 3$

12. $(2x + 3y)(5x + 2y)$
$= (2x)(5x) + (2x)(2y) + (3y)(5x) + (3y)(2y)$
$= 10x^2 + 4xy + 15xy + 6y^2$
$= 10x^2 + 19xy + 6y^2$

13. $(12r - 4s)(5r + 8s)$
$= (12r)(5r) + (12r)(8s) + (-4s)(5r) + (-4s)(8s)$
$= 60r^2 + 96rs - 20rs - 32s^2$
$= 60r^2 + 76rs - 32s^2$

14. $(x - 2)(x^2 + 2x + 4)$
$= x(x^2 + 2x + 4) + (-2)(x^2 + 2x + 4)$
$= (x^3 + 2x^2 + 4x) + (-2x^2 - 4x - 8)$
$= x^3 + 2x^2 - 2x^2 + 4x - 4x - 8$
$= x^3 - 8$

15. $(3x + 5)(2x^2 - 5x + 11)$
$= 3x(2x^2 - 5x + 11) + 5(2x^2 - 5x + 11)$
$= (6x^3 - 15x^2 + 33x) + (10x^2 - 25x + 55)$
$= 6x^3 - 15x^2 + 10x^2 + 33x - 25x + 55$
$= 6x^3 - 5x^2 + 8x + 55$

16. $(4s + 5)(3s^2 + 8s - 9)$
$= 4s(3s^2 + 8s - 9) + 5(3s^2 + 8s - 9)$
$= (12s^3 + 32s^2 - 36s) + (15s^2 + 40s - 45)$
$= 12s^3 + 32s^2 + 15s^2 - 36s + 40s - 45$
$= 12s^3 + 47s^2 + 4s - 45$

17. $(3a + 5)(-8a^2 + 2a + 3)$
$= 3a(-8a^2 + 2a + 3) + 5(-8a^2 + 2a + 3)$
$= (-24a^3 + 6a^2 + 9a) + (-40a^2 + 10a + 15)$
$= -24a^3 + 6a^2 - 40a^2 + 9a + 10a + 15$
$= -24a^3 - 34a^2 + 19a + 15$

18. $(5x - 2)(-5x^2 + 2x + 7)$
$= 5x(-5x^2 + 2x + 7) + (-2)(-5x^2 + 2x + 7)$
$= (-25x^3 + 10x^2 + 35x) + (10x^2 - 4x - 14)$
$= -25x^3 + 10x^2 + 10x^2 + 35x - 4x - 14$
$= -25x^3 + 20x^2 + 31x - 14$

19. $(x^2 - 7x + 4)(2x^2 - 3x - 6)$
$= x^2(2x^2 - 3x - 6) + (-7x)(2x^2 - 3x - 6) +$
$4(2x^2 - 3x - 6)$
$= (2x^4 - 3x^3 - 6x^2) + (-14x^3 + 21x^2 + 42x) +$
$(8x^2 - 12x - 24)$
$= 2x^4 - 3x^3 - 14x^3 - 6x^2 + 21x^2 + 8x^2 + 42x -$
$12x - 24$
$= 2x^4 - 17x^3 + 23x^2 + 30x - 24$

20. $(a^2 + 2a + 5)(a^2 - 3a - 7)$
$= a^2(a^2 - 3a - 7) + (2a)(a^2 - 3a - 7) + (5)(a^2 - 3a - 7)$
$= (a^4 - 3a^3 - 7a^2) + (2a^3 - 6a^2 - 14a) + (5a^2 - 15a - 35)$
$= a^4 - 3a^3 + 2a^3 - 7a^2 - 6a^2 + 5a^2 - 14a - 15a - 35$
$= a^4 - a^3 - 8a^2 - 29a - 35$

21. $(5x^4 - 2x^2 + 1)(x^2 - 5x + 3)$
$= 5x^4(x^2 - 5x + 3) + (-2x^2)(x^2 - 5x + 3) + (1)(x^2 - 5x + 3)$
$= (5x^6 - 25x^5 + 15x^4) + (-2x^4 + 10x^3 - 6x^2) + (x^2 - 5x + 3)$
$= 5x^6 - 25x^5 + 15x^4 - 2x^4 + 10x^3 - 6x^2 + x^2 - 5x + 3$
$= 5x^6 - 25x^5 + 13x^4 + 10x^3 - 5x^2 - 5x + 3$

Page 778 Lesson 9-8

1. $(t + 7)^2 = t^2 + 2(t)(7) + 7^2$
$= t^2 + 14t + 49$

2. $(w - 12)(w + 12) = w^2 - (12)^2$
$= w^2 - 144$

3. $(q - 4h)^2 = q^2 - 2(q)(4h) + (4h)^2$
$= q^2 - 8qh + 16h^2$

4. $(10x + 11y)(10x - 11y) = (10x)^2 - (11y)^2$
$= 100x^2 - 121y^2$

5. $(4e + 3)^2 = (4e)^2 + 2(4e)(3) + (3)^2$
$= 16e^2 + 24e + 9$

6. $(2b - 4d)(2b + 4d) = (2b)^2 - (4d)^2$
$= 4b^2 - 16d^2$

7. $(a + 2b)^2 = (a)^2 + 2(a)(2b) + (2b)^2$
$= a^2 + 4ab + 4b^2$

8. $(4x + y)^2 = (4x)^2 + 2(4x)(y) + (y)^2$
$= 16x^2 + 8xy + y^2$

9. $(6m + 2n)^2 = (6m)^2 + 2(6m)(2n) + (2n)^2$
$= 36m^2 + 24mn + 4n^2$

10. $(5c - 2d)^2 = (5c)^2 - 2(5c)(2d) + (2d)^2$
$= 25c^2 - 20cd + 4d^2$

11. $(5b - 6)(5b + 6) = (5b)^2 - (6)^2$
$= 25b^2 - 36$

12. $(1 + x)^2 = (1)^2 + 2(1)(x) + (x)^2$
$= 1 + 2x + x^2$

13. $(4x - 9y)^2 = (4x)^2 - 2(4x)(9y) + (9y)^2$
$= 16x^2 - 72xy + 81y^2$

14. $(8a - 2b)(8a + 2b) = (8a)^2 - (2b)^2$
$= 64a^2 - 4b^2$

15. $\left(\frac{1}{2}a + b\right)^2 = \left(\frac{1}{2}a\right)^2 + 2\left(\frac{1}{2}a\right)(b) + (b)^2$
$= \frac{1}{4}a^2 + ab + b^2$

16. $(5a - 12b)^2 = (5a)^2 - 2(5a)(12b) + (12b)^2$
$= 25a^2 - 120ab + 144b^2$

17. $(a - 3b)^2 = (a)^2 - 2(a)(3b) + (3b)^2$
$= a^2 - 6ab + 9b^2$

18. $(7a^2 + b)(7a^2 - b) = (7a^2)^2 - (b)^2$
$= 49a^4 - b^2$

19. $(x + 2)(x - 2)(2x + 5) = [(x)^2 - (2)^2](2x + 5)$
$= (x^2 - 4)(2x + 5)$
$= (x^2)(2x) + (x^2)(5) + (-4)(2x) + (-4)(5)$
$= 2x^3 + 5x^2 - 8x - 20$

20. $(4x - 1)(4x + 1)(x - 4) = [(4x)^2 - (1)^2](x - 4)$
$= (16x^2 - 1)(x - 4)$
$= (16x^2)(x) + (16x^2)(-4) + (-1)(x) + (-1)(-4)$
$= 16x^3 - 64x^2 - x + 4$

21. $(x - 3)(x + 3)(x - 4)(x + 4)$
$= [(x)^2 - (3)^2][(x)^2 - (4)^2]$
$= (x^2 - 9)(x^2 - 16)$
$= (x^2)(x^2) + (x^2)(-16) + (-9)(x^2) + (-9)(-16)$
$= x^4 - 16x^2 - 9x^2 + 144$
$= x^4 - 25x^2 + 144$

Page 778 Lesson 10-1

1. 17: 1×17
factors: 1, 17

2. 21: 1×21
3×7
factors: 1, 3, 7, 21

3. 81: 1×81
3×27
9×9
factors: 1, 3, 9, 27, 81

4. 24: 1×24, 3×8
2×12, 4×6
factors: 1, 2, 3, 4, 6, 8, 12, 24

5. 18: 1×18
2×9
3×6
factors: 1, 2, 3, 6, 9, 18

6. 22: 1×22
2×11
factors: 1, 2, 11, 22

7. composite; $39 = 3 \cdot 13$

8. prime

9. composite;
$72 = 3 \cdot 24$
$= 3 \cdot 2 \cdot 12$
$= 3 \cdot 2 \cdot 2 \cdot 6$
$= 3 \cdot 2 \cdot 2 \cdot 2 \cdot 3$ or $2^3 \cdot 3^2$

10. prime

11. composite;
$57 = 3 \cdot 19$

12. composite;
$60 = 2 \cdot 30$
$= 2 \cdot 2 \cdot 15$
$= 2 \cdot 2 \cdot 3 \cdot 5$ or $2^2 \cdot 3 \cdot 5$

13. $-64 = -1 \cdot 64$
$= -1 \cdot 2 \cdot 32$
$= -1 \cdot 2 \cdot 2 \cdot 16$
$= -1 \cdot 2 \cdot 2 \cdot 2 \cdot 8$
$= -1 \cdot 2 \cdot 2 \cdot 2 \cdot 2 \cdot 4$
$= -1 \cdot 2 \cdot 2 \cdot 2 \cdot 2 \cdot 2 \cdot 2$

14. $-26 = -1 \cdot 26$
$= -1 \cdot 2 \cdot 13$

15. $-240 = -1 \cdot 240$
$= -1 \cdot 2 \cdot 120$
$= -1 \cdot 2 \cdot 2 \cdot 60$
$= -1 \cdot 2 \cdot 2 \cdot 2 \cdot 30$
$= -1 \cdot 2 \cdot 2 \cdot 2 \cdot 2 \cdot 15$
$= -1 \cdot 2 \cdot 2 \cdot 2 \cdot 2 \cdot 3 \cdot 5$

16. $-231 = -1 \cdot 231$
$= -1 \cdot 3 \cdot 77$
$= -1 \cdot 3 \cdot 7 \cdot 11$

17. $44rs^2t^3 = 2 \cdot 22 \cdot r \cdot s \cdot s \cdot t \cdot t \cdot t$
$= 2 \cdot 2 \cdot 11 \cdot r \cdot s \cdot s \cdot t \cdot t \cdot t$

18. $756(mn)^2 = 2 \cdot 378 \cdot m \cdot n \cdot m \cdot n$
$= 2 \cdot 2 \cdot 189 \cdot m \cdot m \cdot n \cdot n$
$= 2 \cdot 2 \cdot 3 \cdot 63 \cdot m \cdot m \cdot n \cdot n$
$= 2 \cdot 2 \cdot 3 \cdot 3 \cdot 21 \cdot m \cdot m \cdot n \cdot n$
$= 2 \cdot 2 \cdot 3 \cdot 3 \cdot 3 \cdot 7 \cdot m \cdot m \cdot n \cdot n$

19. $16 = 2 \cdot 2 \cdot 2 \cdot 2$
$60 = 2 \cdot 2 \cdot 3 \cdot 5$
GCF: $2 \cdot 2$ or 4

20. $15 = 3 \cdot 5$
$50 = 2 \cdot 5 \cdot 5$
GCF: 5

21. $-80 = -1 \cdot 2 \cdot 2 \cdot 2 \cdot 2 \cdot 5$
$45 = 3 \cdot 3 \cdot 5$
GCF: 5

22. $29 = 1 \cdot 29$
$-58 = -1 \cdot 2 \cdot 29$
GCF: 29

23. $305 = 5 \cdot 61$
$55 = 5 \cdot 11$
GCF: 5

24. $252 = 2 \cdot 2 \cdot 3 \cdot 3 \cdot 7$
$126 = 2 \cdot 3 \cdot 3 \cdot 7$
GCF: $2 \cdot 3 \cdot 3 \cdot 7$ or 126

25. $128 = 2 \cdot 2 \cdot 2 \cdot 2 \cdot 2 \cdot 2 \cdot 2$
$245 = 5 \cdot 7 \cdot 7$
GCF: 1

26. $7y^2 = 7 \cdot y \cdot y$
$14y^2 = 2 \cdot 7 \cdot y \cdot y$
GCF: $7 \cdot y \cdot y$ or $7y^2$

27. $4xy = 2 \cdot 2 \cdot x \cdot y$
$-6x = -1 \cdot 2 \cdot 3 \cdot x$
GCF: $2 \cdot x$ or $2x$

28. $35t^2 = 5 \cdot 7 \cdot t \cdot t$
$7t = 7 \cdot t$
GCF: $7 \cdot t$ or $7t$

29. $16pq^2 = 2 \cdot 2 \cdot 2 \cdot 2 \cdot p \cdot q \cdot q$
$12p^2q = 2 \cdot 2 \cdot 3 \cdot p \cdot p \cdot q$
GCF: $2 \cdot 2 \cdot p \cdot q$ or $4pq$

30. $5 = 1 \cdot 5$
$15 = 3 \cdot 5$
$10 = 2 \cdot 5$
GCF: 5

31. $12mn = 2 \cdot 2 \cdot 3 \cdot m \cdot n$
$10mn = 2 \cdot 5 \cdot m \cdot n$
$15mn = 3 \cdot 5 \cdot m \cdot n$
GCF: mn

32. $14 = 2 \cdot 7$
$12 = 2 \cdot 2 \cdot 3$
$20 = 2 \cdot 2 \cdot 5$
GCF: 2

33. $26jk^4 = 2 \cdot 13 \cdot j \cdot k \cdot k \cdot k \cdot k$
$16jk^3 = 2 \cdot 2 \cdot 2 \cdot 2 \cdot j \cdot k \cdot k \cdot k$
$8j^2 = 2 \cdot 2 \cdot 2 \cdot j \cdot j$
GCF: $2j$

Page 779 Lesson 10-2

1. $2x$ **2.** 1 **3.** $2ab$ **4.** r^2
5. $2x^2$ **6.** $12x$ **7.** $x + y$ **8.** $5x - 3$
9. $x^2 + 1$

10. $10a^2 = 2 \cdot 5 \cdot a \cdot a$
$40a = 2 \cdot 2 \cdot 2 \cdot 5 \cdot a$
GCF: $2 \cdot 5 \cdot a$ or $10a$
$10a^2 + 40a = 10a(a) + 10a(4)$
$= 10a(a + 4)$

11. $15wx = 3 \cdot 5 \cdot w \cdot x$
$-35wx^2 = -1 \cdot 5 \cdot 7 \cdot w \cdot x \cdot x$
GCF: $5wx$
$15wx - 35wx^2 = 5wx(3) + 5wx(-7x)$
$= 5wx(3 - 7x)$

12. $27a^2b = 3 \cdot 3 \cdot 3 \cdot a \cdot a \cdot b$
$9b^3 = 3 \cdot 3 \cdot b \cdot b \cdot b$
GCF: $3 \cdot 3 \cdot b$ or $9b$
$27a^2b + 9b^3 = 9b(3a^2) + 9b(b^2)$
$= 9b(3a^2 + b^2)$

13. $11x = 11 \cdot x$
$44x^2y = 2 \cdot 2 \cdot 11 \cdot x \cdot x \cdot y$
GCF: $11x$
$11x + 44x^2y = 11x(1) + 11x(4xy)$
$= 11x(1 + 4xy)$

14. $16y^2 = 2 \cdot 2 \cdot 2 \cdot 2 \cdot y \cdot y$
$8y = 2 \cdot 2 \cdot 2 \cdot y$
GCF: $2 \cdot 2 \cdot 2 \cdot y$ or $8y$
$16y^2 + 8y = 8y(2y) + 8y(1)$
$= 8y(2y + 1)$

15. $14mn^2 = 2 \cdot 7 \cdot m \cdot n \cdot n$
$2mn = 2 \cdot m \cdot n$
GCF: $2mn$
$14mn^2 + 2mn = 2mn(7n) + 2mn(1)$
$= 2mn(7n + 1)$

16. $25a^2b^2 = 5 \cdot 5 \cdot a \cdot a \cdot b \cdot b$
$30ab^3 = 2 \cdot 3 \cdot 5 \cdot a \cdot b \cdot b \cdot b$
GCF: $5 \cdot a \cdot b \cdot b$ or $5ab^2$
$25a^2b^2 + 30ab^3 = 5ab^2(5a) + 5ab^2(6b)$
$= 5ab^2(5a + 6b)$

17. $2m^3n^2 = 2 \cdot m \cdot m \cdot m \cdot n \cdot n$
$-16m^2n^3 = -1 \cdot 2 \cdot 2 \cdot 2 \cdot 2 \cdot m \cdot m \cdot n \cdot n \cdot n$
$8mn = 2 \cdot 2 \cdot 2 \cdot m \cdot n$
GCF: $2mn$
$2m^3n^2 - 16m^2n^3 + 8mn$
$= 2mn(m^2n) + 2mn(-8mn^2) + 2mn(4)$
$= 2mn(m^2n - 8mn^2 + 4)$

18. $2ax + 6xc + ba + 3bc = (2ax + 6xc) + (ba + 3bc)$
$= 2x(a + 3c) + b(a + 3c)$
$= (2x + b)(a + 3c)$

19. $6mx - 4m + 3rx - 2r = (6mx - 4m) + (3rx - 2r)$
$= 2m(3x - 2) + r(3x - 2)$
$= (2m + r)(3x - 2)$

20. $3ax - 6bx + 8b - 4a = (3ax - 6bx) + (8b - 4a)$
$= 3x(a - 2b) + 4(2b - a)$
$= 3x(a - 2b) - 4(a - 2b)$
$= (a - 2b)(3x - 4)$

21. $a^2 - 2ab + a - 2b = (a^2 - 2ab) + (a - 2b)$
$= a(a - 2b) + (1)(a - 2b)$
$= (a + 1)(a - 2b)$

22. $8ac - 2ad + 4bc - bd = (8ac - 2ad) + (4bc - bd)$
$= 2a(4c - d) + b(4c - d)$
$= (2a - b)(4c - d)$

23. $2e^2g + 2fg + 4e^2h + 4fh = 2(e^2g + fg + 2e^2h + 2fh)$
$= 2[(e^2g + fg) + (2e^2h + 2fh)]$
$= 2[g(e^2 + f) + 2h(e^2 + f)]$
$= 2(e^2 + f)(g + 2h)$

Page 779 Lesson 10-3

1. 10 2. 7 3. + 4. $4r$
5. 7 6. − 7. − 8. $4y$
9. $2z$ 10. 3

11. $5x^2 - 17x + 14 = 5x^2 + [-10 + (-7)]x + 14$
$= 5x^2 - 10x - 7x + 14$
$= (5x^2 - 10x) + (-7x + 14)$
$= 5x(x - 2) + (-7)(x - 2)$
$= (5x - 7)(x - 2)$

12. $a^2 - 9a - 36 = a^2[3 + (-12)]a - 36$
$= a^2 + 3a - 12a - 36$
$= (a^2 + 3a) + (-12a - 36)$
$= a(a + 3) + (-12)(a + 3)$
$= (a - 12)(a + 3)$

13. $x^2 + 2x - 15 = x^2 + (-3 + 5)x - 15$
$= x^2 - 3x + 5x - 15$
$= (x^2 - 3x) + (5x - 15)$
$= x(x - 3) + 5(x + 5)$
$= (x + 5)(x - 3)$

14. $n^2 - 8n + 15 = n^2 + [-5 + (-3)]n + 15$
$= n^2 - 5n - 3n + 15$
$= (n^2 - 5n) + (-3n + 15)$
$= n(n - 5) + (-3)(n - 5)$
$= (n - 3)(n - 5)$

15. $b^2 + 22b + 21 = b^2 + (1 + 21)b + 21$
$= b^2 + b + 21b + 21$
$= (b^2 + b) + (21b + 21)$
$= b(b + 1) + 21(b + 1)$
$= (b + 21)(b + 1)$

16. $c^2 + 2c - 3 = c^2 + (-1 + 3)c - 3$
$= c^2 - 1c + 3c - 3$
$= (c^2 - 1c) + (3c - 3)$
$= c(c - 1) + 3(c - 1)$
$= (c + 3)(c - 1)$

17. $x^2 - 5x - 24 = x^2 + [3 + (-8)]x - 24$
$= x^2 + 3x + (-8)x - 24$
$= (x^2 + 3x) + (-8x - 24)$
$= x(x + 3) + (-8)(x + 3)$
$= (x - 8)(x + 3)$

18. prime

19. $8m^2 - 10m + 3 = 8m^2 + [-4 + (-6)]m + 3$
$= 8m^2 - 4m - 6m + 3$
$= (8m^2 - 4m) + (-6m + 3)$
$= 4m(2m - 1) + (-3)(2m - 1)$
$= (4m - 3)(2m - 1)$

20. $z^2 + 15z + 36 = z^2 + (12 + 3)z + 36$
$= z^2 + 12z + 3z + 36$
$= (z^2 + 12z) + (3z + 36)$
$= z(z + 12) + 3(z + 12)$
$= (z + 3)(z + 12)$

21. $s^2 - 13st - 30t^2 = s^2 + (-15 + 2)st - 30t^2$
$= s^2 - 15st + 2st - 30t^2$
$= (s^2 - 15st) + (2st - 30t^2)$
$= s(s - 15t) + 2t(s - 15t)$
$= (s + 2t)(s - 15t)$

22. $6y^2 + 2y - 2 = 2(3y^2) + 2(y) + 2(-1)$
$= 2(3y^2 + y - 1)$

23. $2r^2 + 3r - 14 = 2r^2 + (-4 + 7)r - 14$
$= 2r^2 - 4r + 7r - 14$
$= (2r^2 - 4r) + (7r - 14)$
$= 2r(r - 2) + 7(r - 2)$
$= (2r + 7)(r - 2)$

24. $5x - 6 + x^2 = x^2 + 5x - 6$
$= x^2 + [6 + (-1)]x - 6$
$= x^2 + 6x - 1x - 6$
$= (x^2 + 6x) + (-1x - 6)$
$= x(x + 6) + (-1)(x + 6)$
$= (x - 1)(x + 6)$

25. $x^2 - 4xy - 5y^2 = x^2 + [1 + (-5)]xy - 5y^2$
$= x^2 + xy - 5xy - 5y^2$
$= (x^2 + xy) + (-5xy - 5y^2)$
$= x(x + y) + (-5y)(x + y)$
$= (x - 5y)(x + y)$

26. prime

27. $18v^2 + 42v + 12 = 6(3v^2 + 7v + 2)$
$= 6[3v^2 + (6 + 1)v + 2]$
$= 6(3v^2 + 6v + v + 2)$
$= 6(3v^2 + 6v) + (v + 2)$
$= 6[3v(v + 2) + (1)(v + 2)]$
$= 6(3v + 1)(v + 2)$

28. $4k^2 + 2k - 12 = 2(2k^2 + k - 6)$
$= 2\{2k^2 + [4 + (-3)]k - 6\}$
$= 2(2k^2 + 4k - 3k - 6)$
$= 2[(2k^2 + 4k) + (-3k - 6)]$
$= 2[2k(k + 2) + (-3)(k + 2)]$
$= 2(2k - 3)(k + 2)$

Page 779 10-4

1. $x^2 - 9 = (x)^2 - (3)^2$
$= (x - 3)(x + 3)$

2. $a^2 - 64 = (a)^2 - (8)^2$
$= (a - 8)(a + 8)$

3. $t^2 - 49 = (t)^2 - (7)^2$
$= (t - 7)(t + 7)$

4. $4x^2 - 9y^2 = (2x)^2 - (3y)^2$
$= (2x - 3y)(2x + 3y)$

5. $1 - 9z^2 = (1) - (3z)^2$
$= (1 - 3z)(1 + 3z)$

6. $16a^2 - 9b^2 = (4a)^2 - (3b)^2$
$= (4a - 3b)(4a + 3b)$

7. $8x^2 - 12y^2 = 4(2x^2) - (4)(3y^2)$
$= 4(2x^2 - 3y^2)$

8. $a^2 - 4b^2 = (a)^2 - (2b)^2$
$= (a - 2b)(a + 2b)$

9. $x^2 - y^2 = (x)^2 - (y)^2$
$= (x - y)(x + y)$

10. $75r^2 - 48 = 3(25r^2 - 16)$
$= 3[(5r)^2 - (4)^2]$
$= 3(5r + 4)(5r - 4)$

11. $x^2 - 36y^2 = (x)^2 - (6y)^2$
$= (x - 6y)(x + 6y)$

12. prime

13. $12t^2 - 75 = 3(4t^2 - 25)$
$= 3[(2t)^2 - (5)^2]$
$= 3(2t - 5)(2t + 5)$

14. $9x^2 - 100y^2 = (3x)^2 - (10y)^2$
$= (3x - 10y)(3x + 10y)$

15. $49 - a^2b^2 = (7)^2 - (ab)^2$
$= (7 - ab)(7 + ab)$

16. $12a^2 - 48 = 12(a^2 - 4)$
$= 12[(a)^2 - (2)^2]$
$= 12(a - 2)(a + 2)$

17. $169 - 16t^2 = (13)^2 - (4t)^2$
$= (13 - 4t)(13 + 4t)$

18. $8r^2 - 4 = 4(2r^2) + 4(-1)$
$= 4(2r^2 - 1)$

19. $-45m^2 + 5 = -5(9m^2 - 1)$
$= -5[(3m)^2 - (1)^2]$
$= -5(3m + 1)(3m - 1)$

20. $9x^4 - 16y^2 = (3x^2)^2 - (4y)^2$
$= (3x^2 - 4y)(3x^2 + 4y)$

21. $36b^2 - 64 = 4(9b^2 - 16)$
$= 4[(3b)^2 - (4)^2]$
$= 4(3b - 4)(3b + 4)$

22. $5g^2 - 20h^2 = 5(g^2 - 4h^2)$
$= 5[(g)^2 - (2h)^2]$
$= 5(g - 2h)(g + 2h)$

23. $\frac{1}{4}n^2 - 16 = \left(\frac{1}{2}n\right)^2 - (4)^2$
$= \left(\frac{1}{2}n - 4\right)\left(\frac{1}{2}n + 4\right)$

24. $\frac{1}{4}t^2 - \frac{4}{9}p^2 = \left(\frac{1}{2}t\right)^2 - \left(\frac{2}{3}p\right)^2$
$= \left(\frac{1}{2}t - \frac{2}{3}p\right)\left(\frac{1}{2}t + \frac{2}{3}p\right)$

25. prime

26. $12x^3 - 27xy^2 = 3x(4x^2 - 9y^2)$
$= 3x[(2x)^2 - (3y)^2]$
$= 3x(2x - 3y)(2x + 3y)$

27. $0.01n^2 - 1.69r^2 = (0.1n)^2 - (1.3r)^2$
$= (0.1n - 1.3r)(0.1n + 1.3r)$

28. $0.04m^2 - 0.09n^2 = (0.2m)^2 - (0.3n)^2$
$= (0.2m - 0.3n)(0.2m + 0.3n)$

29. $(x - y)^2 - y^2 = (x - y)^2 - (y)^2$
$= [(x - y) + y][(x - y) - y]$
$= x(x - 2y)$

30. $162m^4 - 32n^8 = 2(81m^4 - 16n^8)$
$= 2[(9m^2)^2 - (4n^4)^2]$
$= 2(9m^2 - 4n^4)(9m^2 + 4n^4)$
$= 2[(3m)^2 - (2n^2)^2](9m^2 + 4n^4)$
$= 2(3m - 2n^2)(3m + 2n^2)$
$(9m^2 + 4n^4)$

Page 780 Lesson 10-5

1. $x^2 + 12x + 36 = (x)^2 + 2(x)(6) + (6)^2$
$= (x + 6)^2$
yes; $(x + 6)^2$

2. $-13n \stackrel{?}{=} 2(n)(6)$
$-13n \neq -12n$ no

3. $a^2 + 4a + 4 = (a)^2 + (2)(a)(2) + (2)^2$
$= (a + 2)^2$
yes; $(a + 2)^2$

4. $b^2 - 14b + 49 = (b)^2 - 2(b)(7) + (7)^2$
$= (b - 7)^2$
yes; $(b - 7)^2$

5. -100 is not a perfect square; no

6. $-10y \stackrel{?}{=} -2(y)(10)$
$-10y \neq -20y$ no

7. $9b^2 - 6b + 1 = (3b)^2 - 2(3b)(1) + (1)^2$
$= (3b - 1)^2$
yes; $(3b - 1)^2$

8. $4x^2 + 4x + 1 = (2x)^2 + 2(2x)(1) + (1)^2$
$= (2x + 1)^2$
yes; $(2x + 1)^2$

9. 21 is not a perfect square; no

10. $-10x \stackrel{?}{=} -2(3x)(2)$
$-10x \neq -12x$ no

11. $8y \stackrel{?}{=} 2(3y)(4)$
$8y \neq 24y$ no

12. $4a^2 - 20a + 25 = (2a)^2 - 2(2a)(5) + (5)^2$
$= (2a + 5)^2$
yes; $(2a + 5)^2$

13. $n^2 - 8n + 16 = (n)^2 - 2(n)(4) + (4)^2$
$= (n - 4)^2$

14. $4k^2 - 4k + 1 = (2k)^2 - 2(2k)(1) + (1)^2$
$= (2k - 1)^2$

15. $x^2 + 16x + 64 = (x)^2 + 2(x)(8) + (8)^2$
$= (x + 8)^2$

16. prime

17. $x^2 + 22x + 121 = (x)^2 + 2(x)(11) + (11)^2$
$= (x + 11)^2$

18. $s^2 + 30s + 225 = (s)^2 + 2(s)(15) + (15)^2$
$= (s + 15)^2$

19. $1 - 10z + 25z^2 = (1)^2 - 2(z)(5) + (5z)^2$
$= (1 - 5z)^2$

20. prime

21. $9n^2 - 36nm + 36m^2 = 9(n^2 - 4nm + 4m^2)$
$= 9[(n)^2 - 2(n)(2m) + (2m)^2]$
$= 9(n - 2m)^2$

22. $16a^2 + 81 - 72a = 16a^2 - 72a + 81$
$= (4a)^2 - 2(4a)(9) + (9)^2$
$= (4a - 9)^2$

23. $9x^2 + 12xy + 4y^2 = (3x)^2 + 2(3x)(2y) + (2y)^2$
$= (3x + 2y)^2$

24. $m^2 + 16mn + 64n^2 = (m)^2 + 2(m)(8n) + (8n)^2$
$= (m + 8n)^2$

25. $8t^4 + 56t^3 + 98t^2 = 2t^2(4t^2 + 28t + 49)$
$= 2t^2[(2t)^2 + 2(2t)(7) + (7)^2]$
$= 2t^2(2t + 7)^2$

26. $4p^2 + 12pr + 9r^2 = (2p)^2 + 2(2p)(3r) + (3r)^2$
$= (2p + 3r)^2$

27. $16m^4 - 72m^2n^2 + 81n^4$
$= (4m^2)^2 - 2(4m^2)(9n^2) + (9n^2)^2$
$= (4m^2 - 9n^2)^2$
$= [(2m)^2 - (3n)^2]^2$
$= [(2m - 3n)(2m + 3n)]^2$
$= (2m - 3n)^2(2m + 3n)^2$

Page 780 Lesson 10-6

1. $y(y - 12) = 0$
$y = 0$ or $y - 12 = 0$
$y = 12$
$\{0, 12\}$

2. $2x(5x - 10) = 0$
$2x = 0$ or $5x - 10 = 0$
$x = 0$ $\quad 5x = 10$
$x = 2$
$\{0, 2\}$

3. $7a(a + 6) = 0$
$7a = 0$ or $a + 6 = 0$
$a = 0 \qquad a = -6$
$\{0, -6\}$

4. $(b - 3)(b - 5) = 0$
$b - 3 = 0$ or $b - 5 = 0$
$b = 3 \qquad b = 5$
$\{3, 5\}$

5. $(p - 5)(p + 5) = 0$
$p - 5 = 0$ or $p + 5 = 0$
$p = 5 \qquad p = -5$
$\{5, -5\}$

6. $(4t + 4)(2t + 6) = 0$
$4t + 4 = 0$ or $2t + 6 = 0$
$4t = -4 \qquad 2t = -6$
$t = -1 \qquad t = -3$
$\{-1, -3\}$

7. $(3x - 5)^2 = 0$
$(3x - 5)(3x - 5) = 0$
$3x - 5 = 0$
$3x = 5$
$x = \frac{5}{3}$
$\left\{\frac{5}{3}\right\}$

8. $x^2 - 6x = 0$
$x(x - 6) = 0$
$x = 0$ or $x - 6 = 0$
$x = 6$
$\{0, 6\}$

9. $n^2 + 36n = 0$
$n(n + 36) = 0$
$n = 0$ or $n + 36 = 0$
$n = -36$
$\{0, -36\}$

10. $2x^2 + 4x = 0$
$2x(x + 2) = 0$
$2x = 0$ or $x + 2 = 0$
$x = 0 \qquad x = -2$
$\{0, -2\}$

11. $2x^2 = x^2 - 8x$
$x^2 + 8x = 0$
$x(x + 8) = 0$
$x = 0$ or $x + 8 = 0$
$x = -8$
$\{0, -8\}$

12. $7y - 1 = -3y^2 + y - 1$
$3y^2 + 6y = 0$
$3y(y + 2) = 0$
$3y = 0$ or $y + 2 = 0$
$y = 0 \qquad y = -2$
$\{0, -2\}$

13. $\frac{1}{2}y^2 - \frac{1}{4}y = 0$
$\frac{1}{2}y\left(y - \frac{1}{2}\right) = 0$
$\frac{1}{2}y = 0$ or $y - \frac{1}{2} = 0$
$y = 0 \qquad y = \frac{1}{2}$
$\left\{0, \frac{1}{2}\right\}$

14. $\frac{5}{6}x^2 - \frac{1}{3}x = \frac{1}{3}x$
$\frac{5}{6}x^2 - \frac{2}{3}x = 0$
$\frac{1}{6}x(5x - 4) = 0$
$\frac{1}{6}x = 0$ or $5x - 4 = 0$
$x = 0 \qquad 5x = 4$
$x = \frac{4}{5}$
$\left\{0, \frac{4}{5}\right\}$

15. $\frac{2}{3}x = \frac{1}{3}x^2$
$0 = \frac{1}{3}x^2 - \frac{2}{3}x$
$0 = \frac{1}{3}x(x - 2)$
$\frac{1}{3}x = 0$ or $x - 2 = 0$
$x = 0 \qquad x = 2$
$\{0, 2\}$

16. $\frac{3}{4}a^2 + \frac{7}{8}a = a$
$\frac{3}{4}a^2 - \frac{1}{8}a = 0$
$8a(6a - 1) = 0$
$8a = 0 \qquad 6a - 1 = 0$
$a = 0 \qquad 6a = 1$
$a = \frac{1}{6}$
$\left\{0, \frac{1}{6}\right\}$

17. $n^2 - 3n = 0$
$n(n - 3) = 0$
$n = 0$ or $n - 3 = 0$
$n = 3$
$\{0, 3\}$

18. $3x^2 - \frac{3}{4}x = 0$
$3x\left(x - \frac{1}{4}\right) = 0$
$3x = 0$ or $x - \frac{1}{4} = 0$
$x = 0 \qquad x = \frac{1}{4}$
$\left\{0, \frac{1}{4}\right\}$

19. $8a^2 = -4a$
$8a^2 + 4a = 0$
$4a(2a + 1) = 0$
$4a = 0$ or $2a + 1 = 0$
$a = 0 \qquad 2a = -1$
$a = -\frac{1}{2}$
$\left\{-\frac{1}{2}, 0\right\}$

20. $(2y + 8)(3y + 24) = 0$
$2y + 8 = 0$ or $3y + 24 = 0$
$2y = -8 \qquad 3y = -24$
$y = -4 \qquad y = -8$
$\{-4, -8\}$

21. $(4x - 7)(3x + 5) = 0$
$4x - 7 = 0$ or $3x + 5 = 0$
$4x = 7 \qquad 3x = -5$
$x = \frac{7}{4} \qquad x = -\frac{5}{3}$
$\left\{\frac{7}{4}, -\frac{5}{3}\right\}$

Page 780 Lesson 11-1

1. $y = x^2 + 6x + 8$, $a = 1$, $b = 6$
axis of symmetry: $x = -\frac{b}{2a} = -\frac{(6)}{2(1)}$ or -3
$y = (-3)^2 + 6(-3) + 8$
$= 9 - 18 + 8$ or -1
The coordinates of the vertex are $(-3, -1)$, minimum.

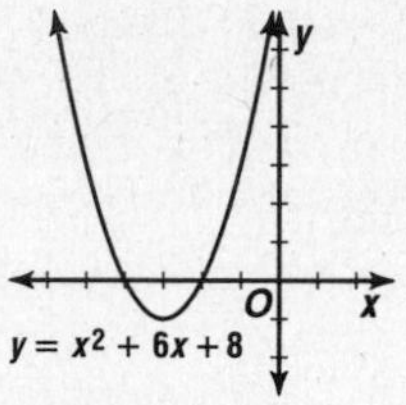

2. $y = -x^2 + 3x$, $a = -1$, $b = 3$
axis of symmetry: $x = -\frac{b}{2a} = -\frac{3}{2(-1)} = \frac{3}{2}$
$y = -\left(-\frac{3}{2}\right)^2 + 3\left(\frac{3}{2}\right)$
$= -\frac{9}{4} + \frac{9}{2}$ or $\frac{9}{4}$
The coordinates of the vertex are $\left(\frac{3}{2}, \frac{9}{4}\right)$, maximum.

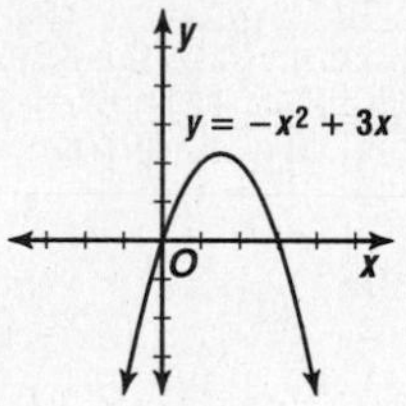

3. $y = -x^2 + 7$, $a = -1$, $b = 0$
axis of symmetry: $x = -\frac{b}{2a} = -\frac{0}{2(-1)}$ or 0
$y = -(0)^2 + 7$
$= 7$
The coordinates of the vertex are $(0, 7)$, maximum.

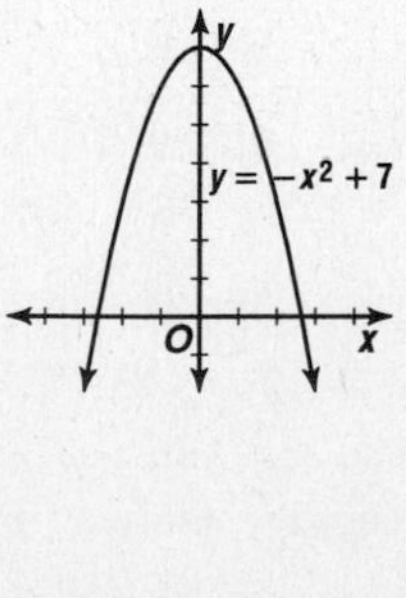

4. $y = x^2 + x + 3$, $a = 1$, $b = 1$

axis of symmetry: $x = -\frac{b}{2a} = -\frac{1}{2(1)}$ or $-\frac{1}{2}$

$y = \left(-\frac{1}{2}\right)^2 + \left(-\frac{1}{2}\right) + 3$

$= \frac{1}{4} - \frac{1}{2} + 3$ or $2\frac{3}{4}$

The coordinates of the vertex are $\left(-\frac{1}{2}, \frac{11}{4}\right)$, minimum.

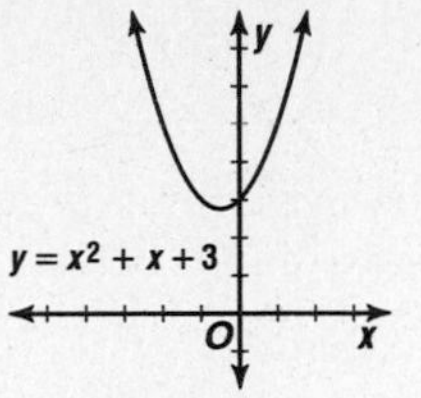

5. $y = -x^2 + 4x + 5$, $a = -1$, $b = 4$

axis of symmetry: $x = -\frac{b}{2a} = -\frac{4}{2(-1)}$ or 2

$y = -(2)^2 + 4(2) + 5$

$= -4 + 8 + 5$ or 9

The coordinates of the vertex are (2, 9), maximum.

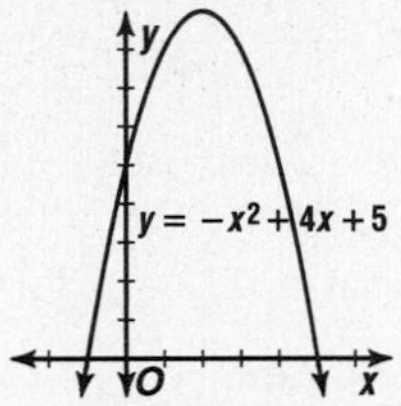

6. $y = 3x^2 + 6x + 16$, $a = 3$, $b = 6$

axis of symmetry: $x = -\frac{b}{2a} = -\frac{6}{2(3)}$ or -1

$y = 3(-1)^2 + 6(-1) + 16$

$= 3 - 6 + 16$ or 13

The coordinates of the vertex are $(-1, 13)$, minimum.

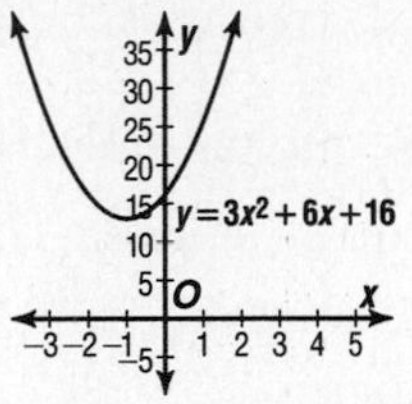

7. $y = -x^2 + 2x - 3$, $a = -1$ $b = 2$

axis of symmetry: $x = -\frac{b}{2a} = -\frac{(2)}{2(-1)}$ or 1

$y = -(1)^2 + 2(1) - 3$

$= -1 + 2 - 3$ or -2

The coordinates of the vertex are $(1, -2)$, maximum.

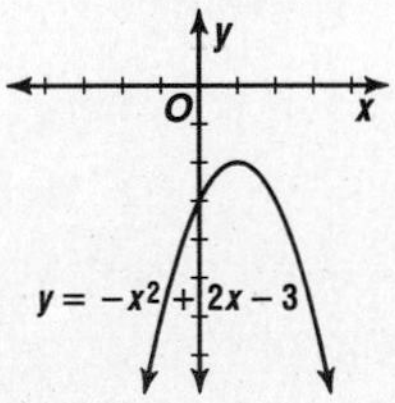

8. $y = 3x^2 + 24x + 80$, $a = 3$, $b = 24$

axis of symmetry: $x = -\frac{b}{2a} = -\frac{24}{2(3)}$ or -4

$y = 3(-4)^2 + 24(-4) + 80$

$= 48 - 96 + 80$ or 32

The coordinates of the vertex are $(-4, 32)$, minimum.

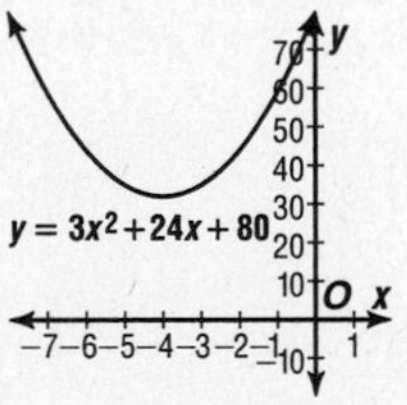

9. $y = x^2 - 4x - 4$, $a = 1$, $b = -4$

axis of symmetry: $x = -\frac{b}{2a} = -\frac{(-4)}{2(1)}$ or 2

$y = (2)^2 - 4(2) - 4$

$= 4 - 8 - 4$ or -8

The coordinates of the vertex are $(2, -8)$, minimum.

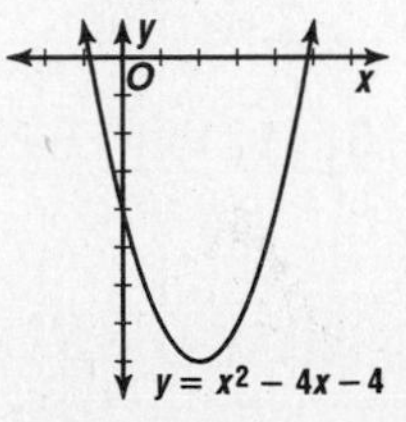

10. $y = 5x^2 - 20x + 37$, $a = 5$, $b = -20$

axis of symmetry: $x = -\frac{b}{2a} = -\frac{(-20)}{2(5)} = 2$

$y = 5(2)^2 - 20(2) + 37$

$= 5(4) - 40 + 37$ or 17

The coordinates of the vertex are (2, 17), minimum.

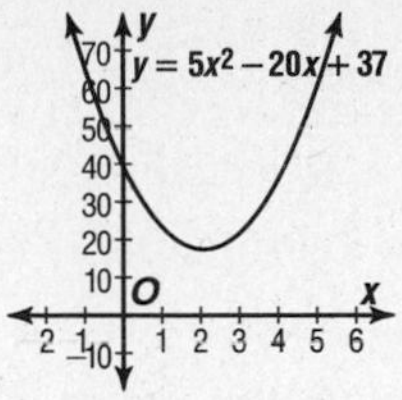

11. $y = 3x^2 + 6x + 3$, $a = 3$, $b = 6$

axis of symmetry: $x = -\frac{b}{2a} = -\frac{6}{2(3)}$ or -1

$y = 3(-1)^2 + 6(-1) + 3$

$= 3 - 6 + 3$ or 0

The coordinates of the vertex are $(-1, 0)$, minimum.

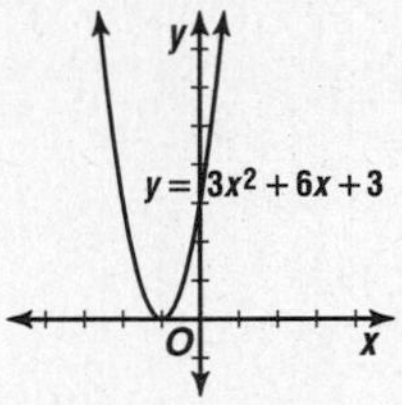

12. $y = 2x^2 + 12x$, $a = 2$, $b = 12$

axis of symmetry: $x = -\frac{b}{2a} = -\frac{12}{2(2)}$ or -3

$y = 2(-3)^2 + 12(-3)$

$= 18 - 36$ or -18

The coordinates of the vertex are $(-3, -18)$, minimum.

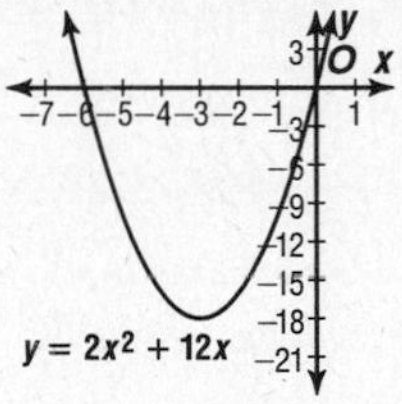

13. $y = x^2 - 6x + 5$, $a = 1$, $b = -6$

axis of symmetry: $x = -\frac{b}{2a} = -\frac{(-6)}{2(1)}$ or 3

$y = (3)^2 - 6(3) + 5$

$= 9 - 18 + 5$ or -4

The coordinates of the vertex are $(3, -4)$, minimum.

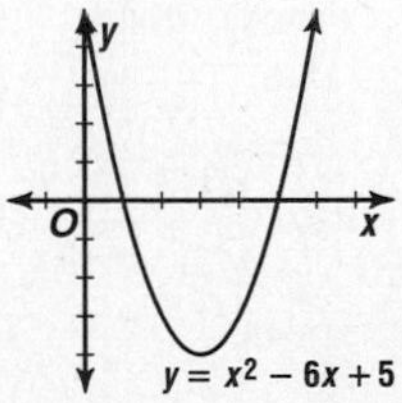

14. $y = \frac{1}{2}x^2 + 3x + \frac{9}{2}$, $a = \frac{1}{2}$, $b = 3$

axis of symmetry: $x = -\frac{b}{2a} = -\frac{3}{2\left(\frac{1}{2}\right)}$ or -3

$y = \frac{1}{2}(-3)^2 + 3(-3) + \frac{9}{2}$

$= \frac{9}{2} - 9 + \frac{9}{2}$ or 0

The coordinates of the vertex are $(-3, 0)$, minimum.

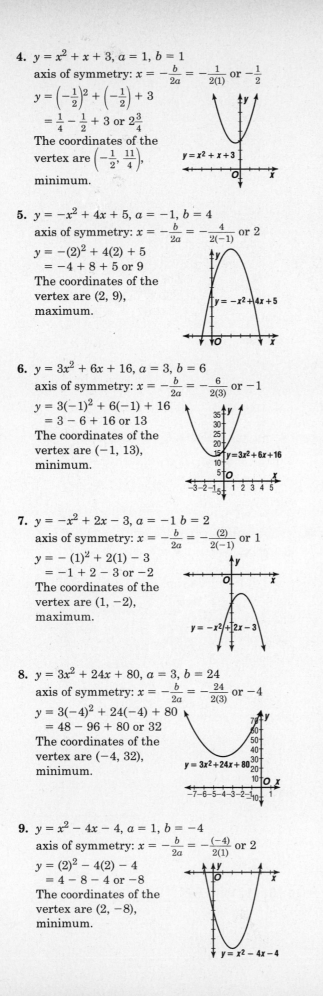

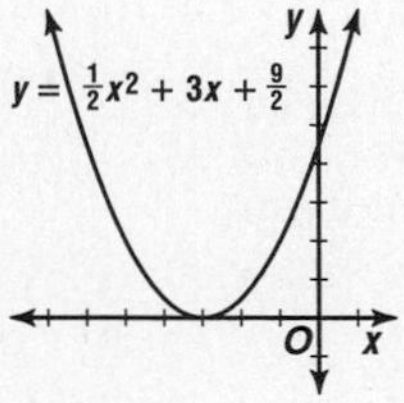

15. $y = \frac{1}{4}x^2 - 4x + \frac{15}{4}$, $a = \frac{1}{4}$, $b = -4$

axis of symmetry: $x = -\frac{b}{2a} = -\frac{(-4)}{2\left(\frac{1}{4}\right)}$ or 8

$y = \frac{1}{4}(8)^2 - 4(8) + \frac{15}{4}$

$= 16 - 32 + \frac{15}{4}$ or $-\frac{49}{4}$

The coordinates of the vertex are $\left(8, -\frac{49}{4}\right)$, minimum.

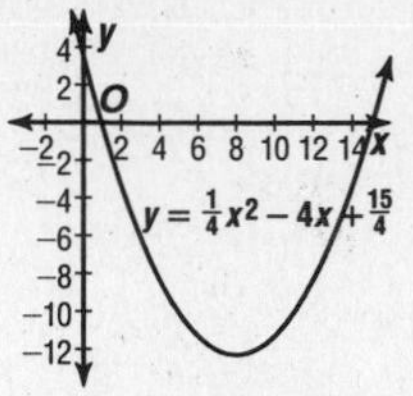

16. $y = 4x^2 - 1$, $a = 4$, $b = 0$

axis of symmetry: $x = -\frac{b}{2a} = -\frac{0}{2(4)}$ or 0

$y = 4(0)^2 - 1$

$= 0 - 1$ or -1

The coordinates of the vertex are $(0, -1)$, minimum.

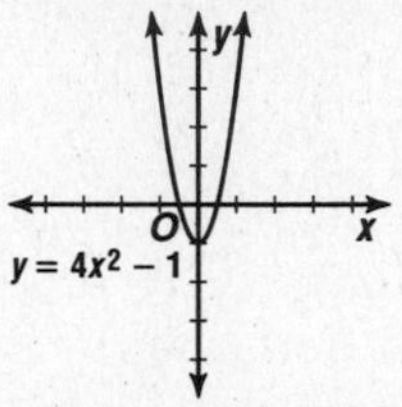

17. $y = -2x^2 - 2x + 4$, $a = -2$, $b = -2$

axis of symmetry: $x = -\frac{b}{2a} = -\frac{(-2)}{2(-2)}$ or $-\frac{1}{2}$

$y = -2\left(-\frac{1}{2}\right)^2 - 2\left(-\frac{1}{2}\right) + 4$

$= -\frac{1}{2} + 1 + 5$ or $\frac{11}{2}$

The coordinates of the vertex are $\left(-\frac{1}{2}, \frac{11}{2}\right)$, maximum.

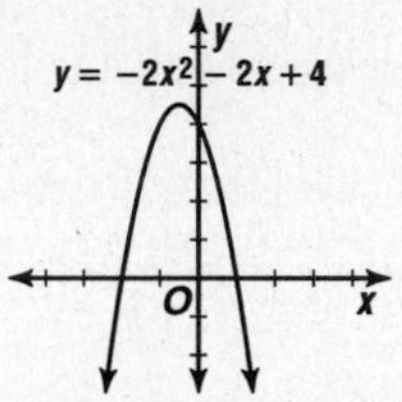

18. $y = 6x^2 - 12x - 4$, $a = 6$, $b = -12$

axis of symmetry: $x = -\frac{b}{2a} = -\frac{(-12)}{2(6)}$ or 1

$y = 6(1)^2 - 12(1) - 4$

$= 6 - 12 - 4$ or -10

The coordinates of the vertex are $(1, -10)$, minimum.

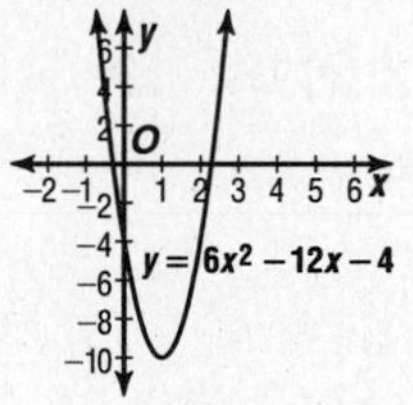

19. $y = x^2 - 1$, $a = 1$, $b = 0$

axis of symmetry: $x = -\frac{b}{2a} = -\frac{0}{2(1)}$ or 0

$y = 0 - 1$ or -1

The coordinates of the vertex are $(0, -1)$, minimum.

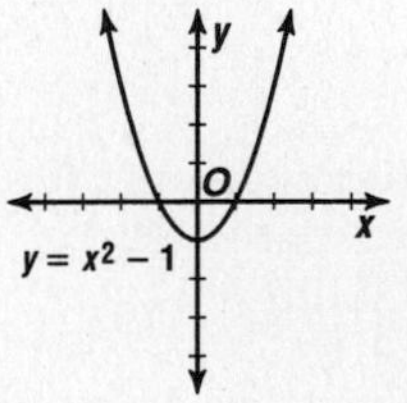

20. $y = -x^2 + x + 1$

axis of symmetry: $x = -\frac{b}{2a} = -\frac{1}{2(-1)}$ or $\frac{1}{2}$

$y = -\left(\frac{1}{2}\right)^2 + \frac{1}{2} + 1$

$= -\frac{1}{4} + \frac{1}{2} + 1$ or $\frac{5}{4}$

The coordinates of the vertex are $\left(\frac{1}{2}, \frac{5}{4}\right)$, maximum.

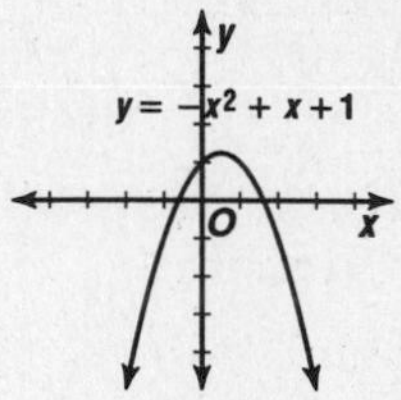

21. $y = -5x^2 - 3x + 2$, $a = -5$, $b = -3$

axis of symmetry: $x = -\frac{b}{2a} = -\frac{(-3)}{2(-5)} = -\frac{3}{10}$

$y = -5\left(-\frac{3}{10}\right)^2 - 3\left(-\frac{3}{10}\right) + 2$

$= -5\left(\frac{9}{100}\right) + \frac{9}{10} + 2$ or $2\frac{9}{20}$

The coordinates of the vertex are $\left(-\frac{3}{10}, 2\frac{9}{20}\right)$, maximum.

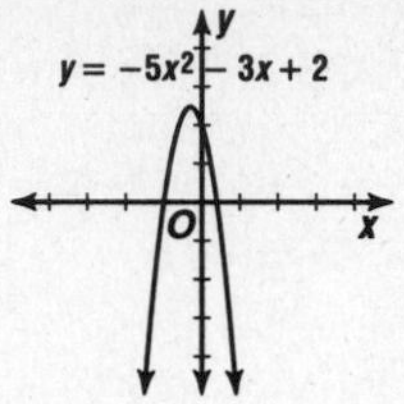

22. $y = x^2 - x - 6$, $a = 1$, $b = -1$

axis of symmetry: $x = -\frac{b}{2a} = -\frac{(-1)}{2(1)}$ or $\frac{1}{2}$

$y = \left(\frac{1}{2}\right)^2 - \frac{1}{2} - 6$

$= \frac{1}{4} - \frac{1}{2} - 6$ or $-\frac{25}{4}$

The coordinates of the vertex are $\left(\frac{1}{2}, -\frac{25}{4}\right)$, minimum.

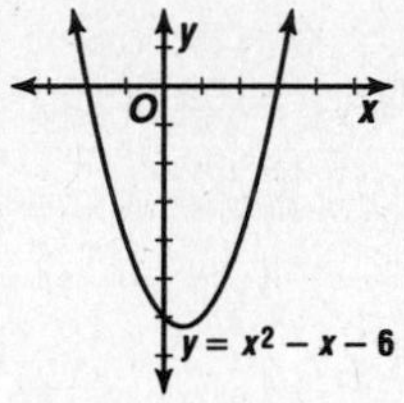

23. $y = 2x^2 + 5x - 2$, $a = 2$, $b = 5$

axis of symmetry: $x = -\frac{b}{2a} = -\frac{5}{2(2)}$ or $-\frac{5}{4}$

$y = 2\left(-\frac{5}{4}\right)^2 + 5\left(-\frac{5}{4}\right) - 2$

$= \frac{25}{8} - \frac{25}{4} - 2$ or $-\frac{41}{8}$

The coordinates of the vertex are $\left(-\frac{5}{4}, -\frac{41}{8}\right)$, minimum.

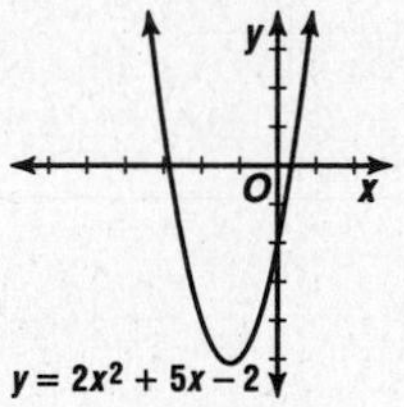

24. $y = -3x^2 - 18x - 15$, $a = -3$, $b = -18$

axis of symmetry: $x = -\frac{b}{2a} = -\frac{(-18)}{2(-3)}$ or -3

$y = -3(-3)^2 - 18(-3) - 15$

$= -27 + 54 - 15$ or 12

The coordinates of the vertex are $(-3, 12)$, maximum.

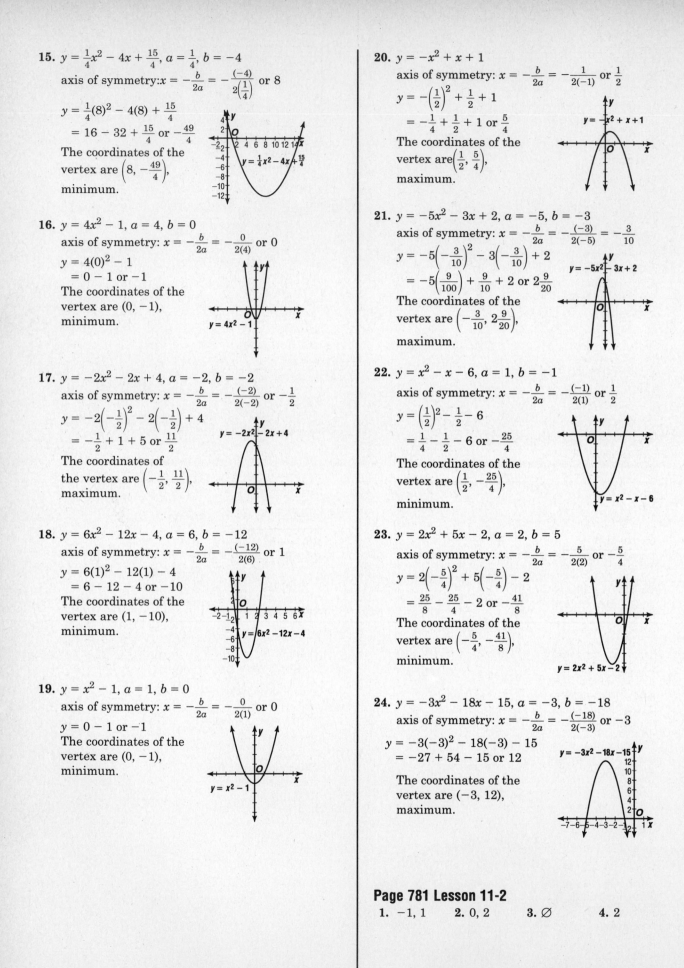

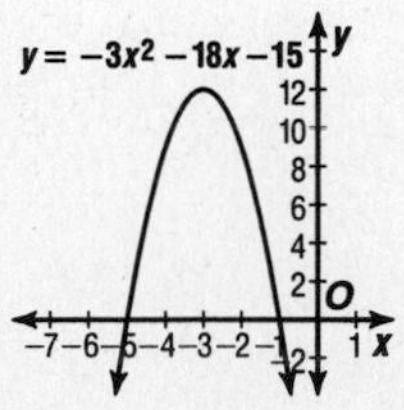

Page 781 Lesson 11-2

1. $-1, 1$ **2.** $0, 2$ **3.** $\varnothing$ **4.** 2

5.

x	$f(x)$
−3	0
−2	−3
−1	−4
0	−3
1	0

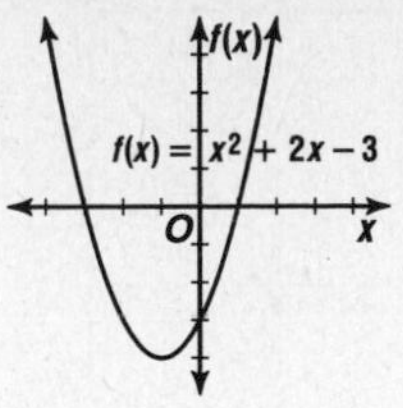

$f(x) = x^2 + 2x - 3$
axis of symmetry: $x = -1$
vertex: $(-1, -4)$
roots: $-3, 1$

6.

x	$f(x)$
1	0
2	3
3	4
4	3
5	0

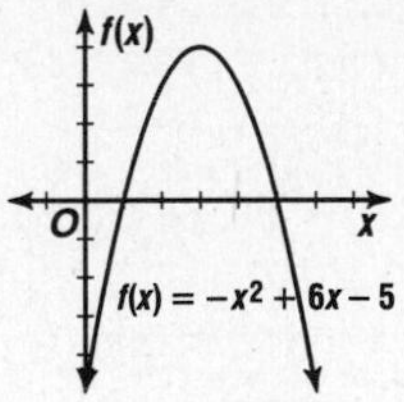

$f(x) = -x^2 + 6x - 5$
axis of symmetry: $x = 3$
vertex: $(3, 4)$
roots: $1, 5$

7.

a	$f(a)$
−3	0
−2	3
−1	4
0	3
1	0

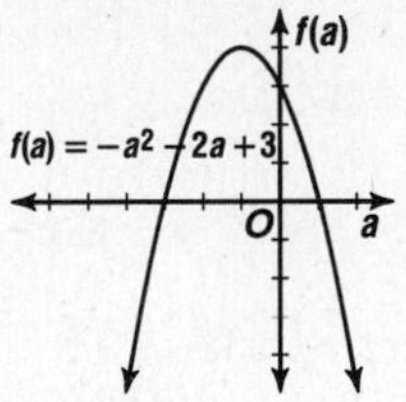

$f(a) = -a^2 - 2a + 3$
axis of symmetry: $a = -1$
vertex: $(-1, 4)$
roots: $-3, 1$

8.

r	$f(r)$
0	5
1	−1
2	−3
3	−1
4	5
5	15

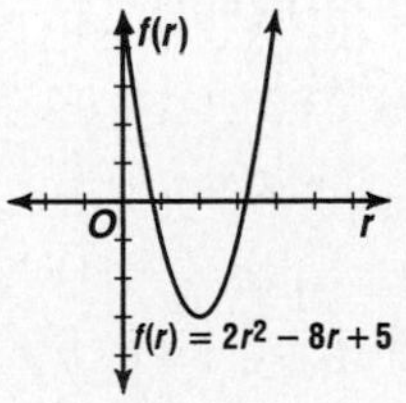

$f(r) = 2r^2 - 8r + 5$
axis of symmetry: $r = 2$
vertex: $(2, -3)$
roots: $0 < r < 1$, $3 < r < 4$

9.

x	$f(x)$
−1	−18
0	−9
1	−6
2	−9
3	−18
4	−33

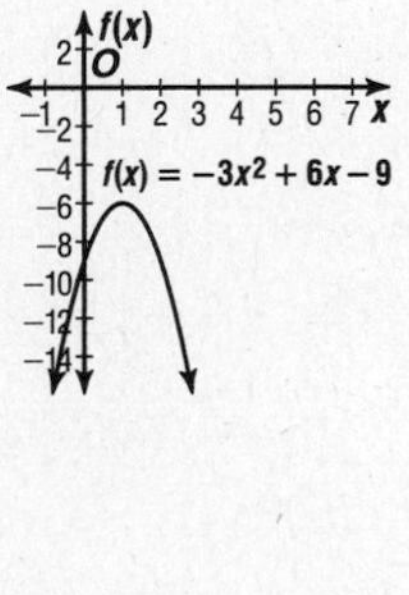

$f(x) = -3x^2 + 6x - 9$
axis of symmetry: $x = 1$
vertex: $(1, -6)$
roots: $\varnothing$

10.

c	$f(c)$
−2	2
−1	0
0	0
1	2

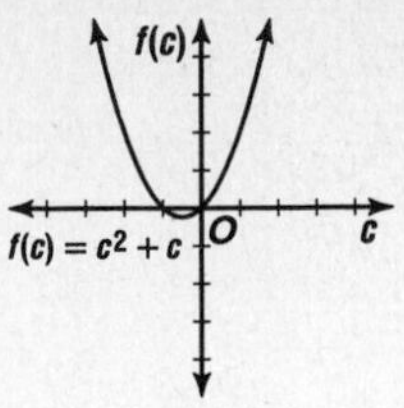

$f(c) = c^2 + c$
axis of symmetry: $c = -\frac{1}{2}$
vertex: $\left(-\frac{1}{2}, -\frac{1}{4}\right)$
roots: $-1, 0$

11.

t	$f(t)$
−2	14
−1	5
0	2
1	5

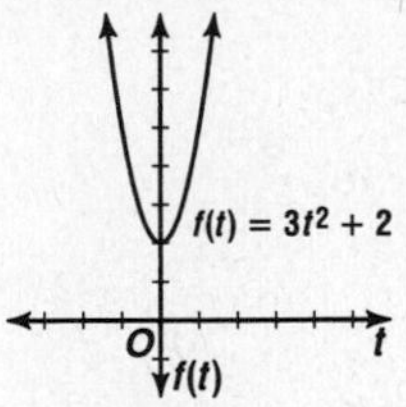

$f(t) = 3t^2 + 2$
axis of symmetry: $t = 0$
vertex: $(0, 2)$
roots: $\varnothing$

12.

b	$f(b)$
−1	−4
0	2
1	6
2	8
3	8
4	6
5	2
6	−4

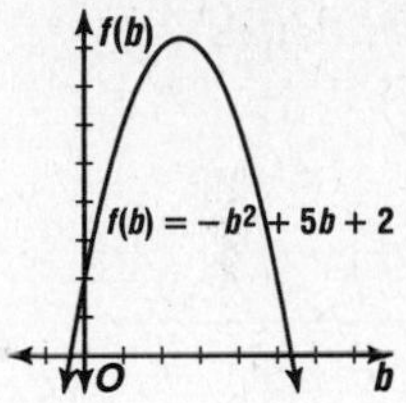

$f(b) = -b^2 + 5b + 2$
axis of symmetry: $b = \frac{5}{2}$
vertex: $\left(\frac{5}{2}, \frac{33}{4}\right)$
roots: $-1 < b < 0$, $5 < b < 6$

13.

x	$f(x)$
−3	5
−2	−3
−1	−5
0	−1
1	9
2	25

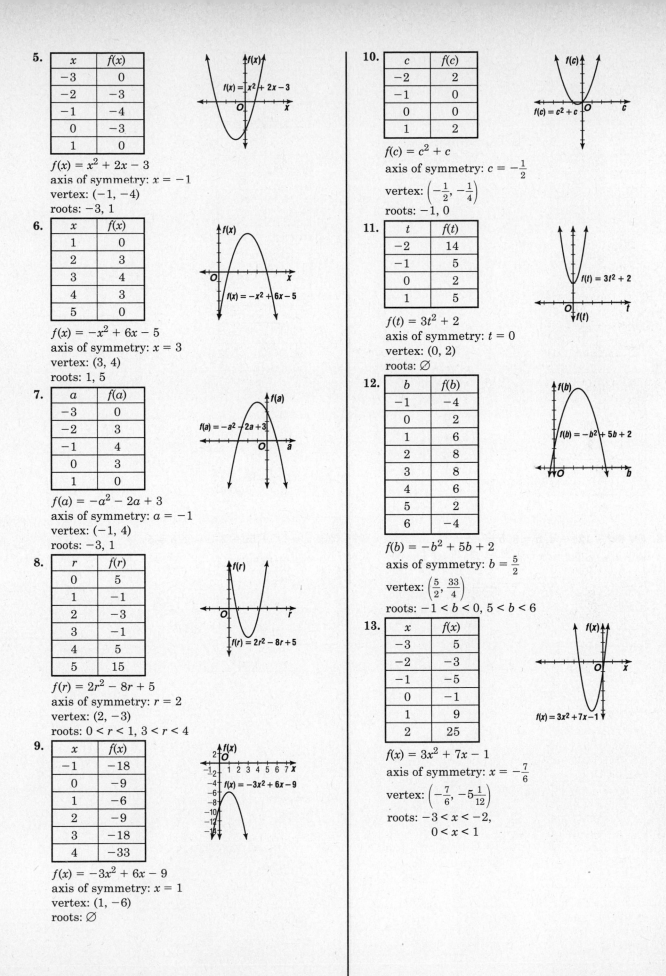

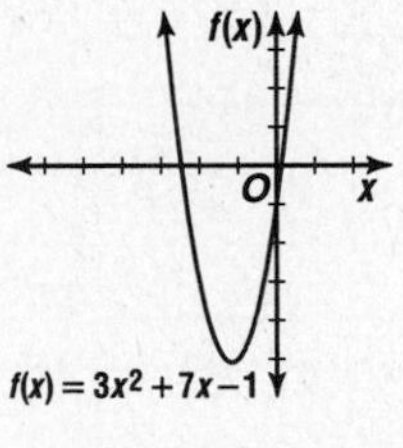

$f(x) = 3x^2 + 7x - 1$
axis of symmetry: $x = -\frac{7}{6}$
vertex: $\left(-\frac{7}{6}, -5\frac{1}{12}\right)$
roots: $-3 < x < -2$,
$0 < x < 1$

14.

x	$f(x)$
−8	0
−7	−10
−6	−18
−5	−24
−4	−28
−3	−30
−2	−30
−1	−28
0	−24
1	−18
2	−10
3	0

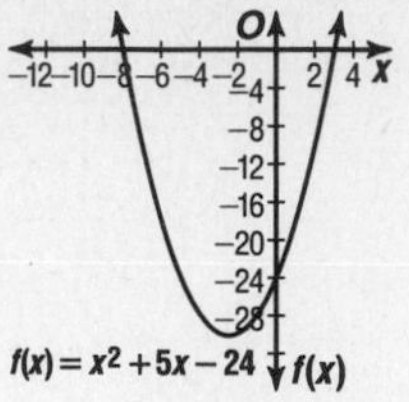

$f(x) = x^2 + 5x - 24$
axis of symmetry: $x = -\frac{5}{2}$
vertex: $\left(-\frac{5}{2}, -41\frac{1}{2}\right)$
roots: −8, 3

15.

k	$f(k)$
−3	−1
−2	4
−1	7
0	8
1	7
2	4
3	−1

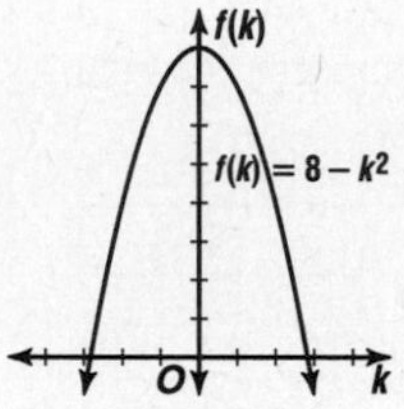

$f(k) = 8 - k^2$
axis of symmetry: $k = 0$
vertex: (0, 8)
roots: $-3 < k < -2$, $2 < k < 3$

16.

x	$f(x)$
−2	0
0	−18
2	−28
4	−30
6	−24
8	−10
9	0

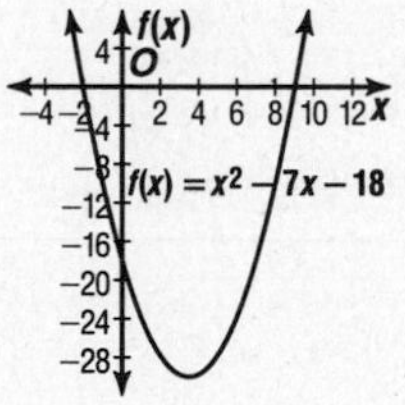

$f(x) = x^2 - 7x - 18$
axis of symmetry: $x = -\frac{7}{2}$
vertex: $\left(-\frac{7}{2}, 18\frac{3}{4}\right)$
roots: −2, 9

17.

a	$f(a)$
−8	4
−7	1
−6	0
−5	1
−4	4

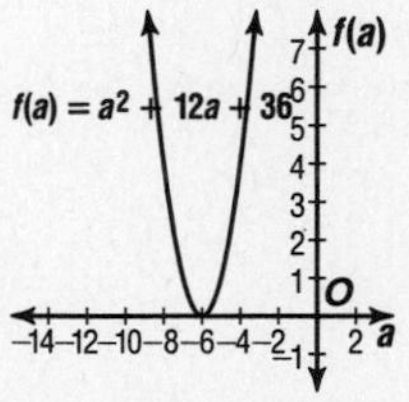

$f(a) = a^2 + 12a + 36$
axis of symmetry: $a = -6$
vertex: (−6, 0)
root: −6

18.

x	$f(x)$
−8	0
−6	28
−4	48
−2	60
0	64
2	60
4	48
6	28
8	0

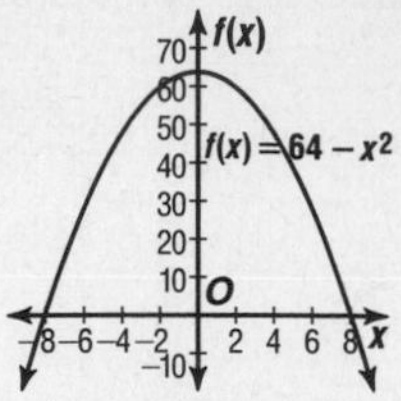

$f(x) = 64 - x^2$
axis of symmetry: $x = 0$
vertex: (0, 64)
roots: −8, 8

19.

x	$f(x)$
−2	−19
−1	−5
0	1
1	−1
2	−11

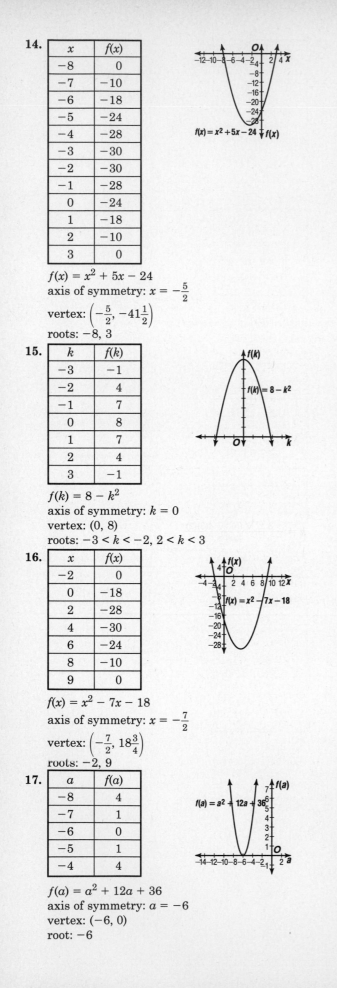

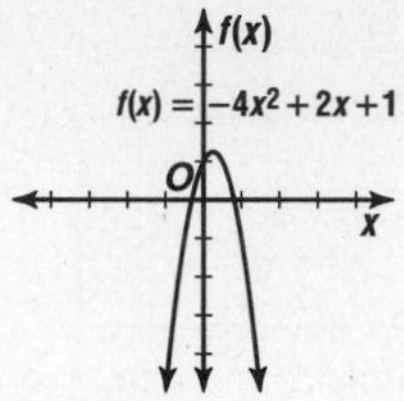

$f(x) = -4x^2 + 2x + 1$
axis of symmetry: $x = \frac{1}{4}$
vertex: $\left(\frac{1}{4}, \frac{5}{4}\right)$
roots: $-1 < x < 0$,
$0 < x < 1$

Page 781 Lesson 11-3

1. $x^2 - 8x - 4 = 0$, $a = 1$, $b = -8$, $c = -4$

$$x = \frac{-(-8) \pm \sqrt{(-8)^2 - 4(1)(-4)}}{2(1)}$$
$$= \frac{8 \pm \sqrt{64 + 16}}{2}$$
$$= \frac{8 \pm \sqrt{80}}{2}$$
$$= \frac{8 \pm 4\sqrt{5}}{2}$$
$$x = \frac{8 + 4\sqrt{5}}{2} \text{ or } x = \frac{-8 - 4\sqrt{5}}{2}$$
$$\approx -0.47 \qquad \approx 8.47$$

2. $x^2 + 7x + 6 = 0$, $a = 1$, $b = 7$, $c = 6$

$$x = \frac{-7 \pm \sqrt{(7)^2 - 4(1)(6)}}{2(1)}$$
$$= \frac{-7 \pm \sqrt{49 - 24}}{2}$$
$$= \frac{-7 \pm \sqrt{25}}{2}$$
$$= \frac{-7 \pm 5}{2}$$
$$x = \frac{-7 + 5}{2} \text{ or } x = \frac{-7 - 5}{2}$$
$$= -1 \qquad = -6$$

3. $x^2 + 5x - 6 = 0$, $a = 1$, $b = 5$, $c = -6$

$$x = \frac{-5 \pm \sqrt{(5)^2 - 4(1)(-6)}}{2(1)}$$
$$= \frac{-5 \pm \sqrt{25 + 24}}{2}$$
$$= \frac{-5 \pm \sqrt{49}}{2}$$
$$= \frac{-5 \pm 7}{2}$$
$$x = \frac{-5 + 7}{2} \text{ or } x = \frac{-5 - 7}{2}$$
$$= 1 \qquad = -6$$

4. $y^2 - 7y - 8 = 0$, $a = 1$, $b = -7$, $c = -8$

$$y = \frac{-(-7) \pm \sqrt{(-7)^2 - 4(1)(-8)}}{2(1)}$$
$$= \frac{7 \pm \sqrt{49 + 32}}{2}$$
$$= \frac{7 \pm \sqrt{81}}{2}$$
$$= \frac{7 \pm 9}{2}$$
$$y = \frac{7 + 9}{2} \text{ or } y = \frac{7 - 9}{2}$$
$$= 8 \qquad = -1$$

5. $m^2 - 2m = 35$

$m^2 - 2m - 35 = 0$, $a = 1$, $b = -2$, $c = -35$

$$m = \frac{-(-2) \pm \sqrt{(-2)^2 - 4(1)(-35)}}{2(1)}$$
$$= \frac{2 \pm \sqrt{4 + 140}}{2}$$
$$= \frac{2 \pm \sqrt{144}}{2}$$
$$= \frac{2 \pm 12}{2}$$
$$m = \frac{2 + 12}{2} \text{ or } m = \frac{2 - 12}{2}$$
$$= 7 \qquad = -5$$

6. $4n^2 - 20n = 0$, $a = 4$, $b = -20$, $c = 0$

$$n = \frac{-(-20) \pm \sqrt{(-20)^2 - 4(4)(0)}}{2(4)}$$
$$= \frac{20 \pm \sqrt{400}}{8}$$
$$= \frac{20 \pm 20}{8}$$
$$n = \frac{20 + 20}{8} \text{ or } n = \frac{20 - 20}{8}$$
$$= 5 \qquad = 0$$

7. $m^2 + 4m + 2 = 0$, $a = 1$, $b = 4$, $c = 2$

$$m = \frac{-4 \pm \sqrt{(4)^2 - 4(1)(2)}}{2(1)}$$
$$= \frac{-4 \pm \sqrt{16 - 8}}{2}$$
$$= \frac{-4 \pm \sqrt{8}}{2}$$
$$= \frac{-4 \pm 2\sqrt{2}}{2}$$
$$m = \frac{-4 + 2\sqrt{2}}{2} \text{ or } m = \frac{-4 - 2\sqrt{2}}{2}$$
$$\approx -0.59 \qquad \approx -3.41$$

8. $2t^2 - t - 15 = 0$, $a = 2$, $b = -1$, $c = -15$

$$t = \frac{-(-1) \pm \sqrt{(-1)^2 - 4(2)(-15)}}{2(2)}$$
$$= \frac{1 \pm \sqrt{1 + 120}}{4}$$
$$= \frac{1 \pm \sqrt{121}}{4}$$
$$= \frac{1 \pm 11}{4}$$
$$t = \frac{1 + 11}{4} \text{ or } t = \frac{1 - 11}{4}$$
$$= 3 \qquad = -\frac{5}{2} \text{ or } -2.5$$

9. $5t^2 = 125$

$5t^2 - 125 = 0$, $a = 5$, $b = 0$, $c = -125$

$$t = \frac{-0 \pm \sqrt{(0)^2 - 4(5)(-125)}}{2(5)}$$
$$= \frac{\pm 2500}{10}$$
$$= \pm \frac{50}{10}$$
$$t = \frac{50}{10} \text{ or } t = -\frac{50}{10}$$
$$= 5 \qquad = -5$$

10. $t^2 + 16 = 0$, $a = 1$, $b = 0$, $c = 16$

$$t = \frac{-0 \pm \sqrt{(0)^2 - 4(1)(16)}}{2(1)}$$
$$= \frac{0 \pm \sqrt{-64}}{2} \text{ not a real number}$$

$\varnothing$

11. $-4x^2 + 8x = -3$

$-4x^2 + 8x + 3 = 0$, $a = -4$, $b = 8$, $c = 3$

$$x = \frac{-8 \pm \sqrt{(8)^2 - 4(-4)(3)}}{2(-4)}$$
$$= \frac{-8 \pm \sqrt{64 + 48}}{-8}$$
$$= \frac{-8 \pm \sqrt{112}}{-8}$$
$$= \frac{-8 \pm 4\sqrt{7}}{-8}$$
$$x = \frac{-8 + 4\sqrt{7}}{-8} \text{ or } x = \frac{-8 - 4\sqrt{7}}{-8}$$
$$\approx -0.32 \qquad \approx 2.32$$

12. $3k^2 + 2 = -8k$

$3k^2 + 8k + 2 = 0$, $a = 3$, $b = 8$, $c = 2$

$$k = \frac{-8 \pm \sqrt{(8)^2 - 4(3)(2)}}{2(3)}$$
$$= \frac{-8 \pm \sqrt{64 - 24}}{6}$$
$$= \frac{-8 \pm \sqrt{40}}{6}$$
$$= \frac{-8 \pm 2\sqrt{10}}{6}$$
$$k = \frac{-8 + 2\sqrt{10}}{6} \text{ or } k = \frac{-8 - 2\sqrt{10}}{6}$$
$$\approx -0.28 \qquad \approx -2.39$$

13. $8t^2 + 10t + 3 = 0$, $a = 8$, $b = 10$, $c = 3$

$$t = \frac{-10 \pm \sqrt{(10)^2 - 4(8)(3)}}{2(8)}$$
$$= \frac{-10 \pm \sqrt{100 - 96}}{16}$$
$$= \frac{-10 \pm \sqrt{4}}{16}$$
$$= \frac{-10 \pm 2}{16}$$
$$t = \frac{-10 + 2}{10} \text{ or } t = \frac{-10 - 2}{16}$$
$$= -\frac{1}{2} \qquad = -\frac{3}{4}$$

14. $3x^2 - \frac{5}{4}x - \frac{1}{2} = 0$

$12x^2 - 5x - 2 = 0,\ a = 12,\ b = -5,\ c = -2$

$x = \frac{-(-5) \pm \sqrt{(-5)^2 - 4(12)(-2)}}{2(12)}$

$= \frac{5 \pm \sqrt{25 + 96}}{24}$

$= \frac{5 \pm \sqrt{121}}{24}$

$= \frac{5 \pm 11}{24}$

$x = \frac{5 + 11}{24}$ or $x = \frac{5 - 11}{24}$

$= \frac{2}{3}$ $\quad = -\frac{1}{4}$

15. $-5b^2 + 3b - 1 = 0,\ a = -5,\ b = 3,\ c = -1$

$b = \frac{-3 \pm \sqrt{(3)^2 - 4(-5)(-1)}}{2(-5)}$

$= \frac{-3 \pm \sqrt{9 - 20}}{-10}$

$= \frac{-3 \pm \sqrt{-11}}{-10}$ not a real number

$\varnothing$

16. $s^2 + 8s + 7 = 0,\ a = 1,\ b = 8,\ c = 7$

$s = \frac{-8 \pm \sqrt{(8)^2 - 4(1)(7)}}{2(1)}$

$= \frac{-8 \pm \sqrt{64 - 28}}{2}$

$= \frac{-8 \pm \sqrt{36}}{2}$

$= \frac{-8 \pm 6}{2}$

$s = \frac{-8 + 6}{2}$ or $s = \frac{-8 - 6}{2}$

$= -1$ $\quad = -7$

17. $d^2 - 14d + 24 = 0,\ a = 1,\ b = -14,\ c = 24$

$d = \frac{-(-14) \pm \sqrt{(-14)^2 - 4(1)(24)}}{2(1)}$

$= \frac{14 \pm \sqrt{196 - 96}}{2}$

$= \frac{14 \pm \sqrt{100}}{2}$

$= \frac{14 \pm 10}{2}$

$d = \frac{14 + 10}{2}$ or $d = \frac{14 - 10}{2}$

$= 12$ $\quad = 2$

18. $3k^2 + 11k = 4$

$3k^2 + 11k - 4 = 0,\ a = 3,\ b = 11,\ c = -4$

$k = \frac{-11 \pm \sqrt{(11)^2 - 4(3)(-4)}}{2(3)}$

$= \frac{-11 \pm \sqrt{121 + 48}}{6}$

$= \frac{-11 \pm \sqrt{169}}{6}$

$= \frac{-11 \pm 13}{6}$

$k = \frac{-11 + 13}{6}$ or $k = \frac{-11 - 13}{6}$

$= \frac{1}{3}$ $\quad = -4$

19. $n^2 - 3n + 1 = 0,\ a = 1,\ b = -3,\ c = 1$

$n = \frac{-(-3) \pm \sqrt{(-3)^2 - 4(1)(1)}}{2(1)}$

$= \frac{3 \pm \sqrt{9 - 4}}{2}$

$= \frac{3 \pm \sqrt{5}}{2}$

$n = \frac{3 + \sqrt{5}}{2}$ or $n = \frac{3 - \sqrt{5}}{2}$

≈ 2.62 $\quad \approx 0.38$

20. $2z^2 + 5z - 1 = 0,\ a = 2,\ b = 5,\ c = -1$

$z = \frac{-5 \pm \sqrt{(5)^2 - 4(2)(-1)}}{2(2)}$

$= \frac{-5 \pm \sqrt{25 + 8}}{4}$

$= \frac{-5 \pm \sqrt{33}}{4}$

$z = \frac{-5 + \sqrt{33}}{4}$ or $z = \frac{-5 - \sqrt{33}}{4}$

≈ 0.19 $\quad \approx -2.69$

21. $3h^2 = 27$

$3h^2 - 27 = 0,\ a = 3,\ b = 0,\ c = -27$

$h = \frac{-0 \pm \sqrt{(0)^2 - 4(3)(-27)}}{2(3)}$

$= \frac{\pm \sqrt{324}}{6}$

$= \frac{\pm 18}{6}$

$h = \frac{18}{6}$ or $h = -\frac{18}{6}$

$= 3$ $\quad = -3$

22. $3f^2 + 2f = 6$

$3f^2 + 2f - 6 = 0,\ a = 3,\ b = 2,\ c = -6$

$f = \frac{-2 \pm \sqrt{(2)^2 - 4(3)(-6)}}{2(3)}$

$= \frac{-2 \pm \sqrt{4 + 72}}{6}$

$= \frac{-2 \pm \sqrt{76}}{6}$

$= \frac{-2 \pm 2\sqrt{19}}{6}$

$f = \frac{-2 + 2\sqrt{19}}{6}$ or $f = \frac{-2 - 2\sqrt{19}}{6}$

≈ 1.12 $\quad \approx -1.79$

23. $2x^2 = 0.7x + 0.3$

$2x^2 - 0.7x - 0.3 = 0,\ a = 2,\ b = -0.7,\ c = -0.3$

$x = \frac{-(-0.7) \pm \sqrt{(-0.7)^2 - 4(2)(-0.3)}}{2(2)}$

$= \frac{0.7 \pm \sqrt{0.49 + 2.4}}{4}$

$= \frac{0.7 \pm \sqrt{2.89}}{4}$

$= \frac{0.7 \pm 1.7}{4}$

$x = \frac{0.7 + 1.7}{4}$ or $x = \frac{0.7 - 1.7}{4}$

$= 0.6$ $\quad = -0.25$

24. $3w^2 - 8w + 2 = 0$, $a = 3$, $b = -8$, $c = 2$

$$w = \frac{-(-8) \pm \sqrt{(-8)^2 - 4(3)(2)}}{2(3)}$$
$$= \frac{8 \pm \sqrt{64 - 24}}{6}$$
$$= \frac{8 \pm \sqrt{40}}{6}$$
$$= \frac{8 \pm 2\sqrt{10}}{6}$$
$$w = \frac{8 + 2\sqrt{10}}{6} \text{ or } w = \frac{8 - 2\sqrt{10}}{6}$$
$$\approx 2.39 \qquad \approx 0.28$$

25. $2r^2 - r - 3 = 0$, $a = 2$, $b = -1$, $c = -3$

$$r = \frac{-(-1) \pm \sqrt{(-1)^2 - 4(2)(-3)}}{2(2)}$$
$$= \frac{1 \pm \sqrt{1 + 24}}{4}$$
$$= \frac{1 \pm \sqrt{25}}{4}$$
$$= \frac{1 \pm 5}{4}$$
$$r = \frac{1 + 5}{4} \text{ or } r = \frac{1 - 5}{4}$$
$$= \frac{3}{2} \qquad = -1$$

26. $x^2 - 9x = 5$

$x^2 - 9x - 5 = 0$, $a = 1$, $b = -9$, $c = -5$

$$x = \frac{-(-9) \pm \sqrt{(-9)^2 - 4(1)(-5)}}{2(1)}$$
$$= \frac{9 \pm \sqrt{81 + 20}}{2}$$
$$= \frac{9 \pm \sqrt{101}}{2}$$
$$x = \frac{9 + \sqrt{101}}{2} \text{ or } x = \frac{9 - \sqrt{101}}{2}$$
$$\approx 9.52 \qquad \approx -0.52$$

27. $6t^2 - 4t - 9 = 0$, $a = 6$, $b = -4$, $c = -9$

$$t = \frac{-(-4) \pm \sqrt{(-4)^2 - 4(6)(-9)}}{2(6)}$$
$$= \frac{4 \pm \sqrt{16 + 216}}{12}$$
$$= \frac{4 \pm \sqrt{232}}{12}$$
$$= \frac{4 \pm 2\sqrt{58}}{12}$$
$$t = \frac{4 + 2\ 58}{12} \text{ or } t = \frac{4 - 2\sqrt{58}}{12}$$
$$\approx 1.60 \qquad \approx -0.94$$

Page 781 Lesson 11-4

1. 5.80 **2.** 0.63 **3.** 4.66 **4.** 0.13
5. 28.28 **6.** 3.30 **7.** 0.91 **8.** 84.51
9. 16.72

10. $y = 3^x + 1$

x	y
-3	$1\frac{1}{27}$
-2	$1\frac{1}{9}$
-1	$1\frac{1}{3}$
0	2
1	4
2	10

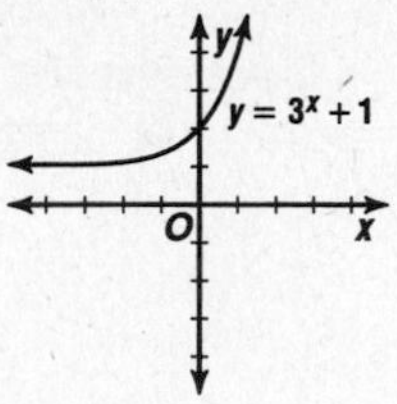

The y-intercept is 2.

11. $y = 2^x - 5$

x	y
-3	$-4\frac{7}{8}$
-2	$-4\frac{3}{4}$
-1	$-4\frac{1}{2}$
0	-5
1	-3
2	-1

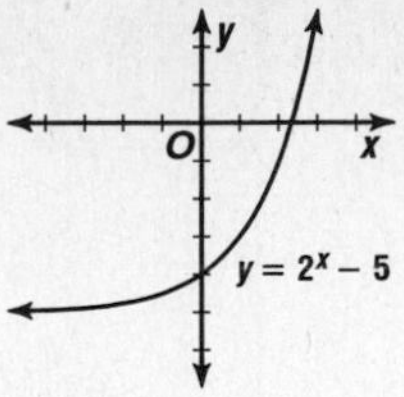

The y-intercept is -4.

12. $y = 2^{x+3}$

x	y
-3	1
-2	2
-1	4
0	8
1	16
2	32

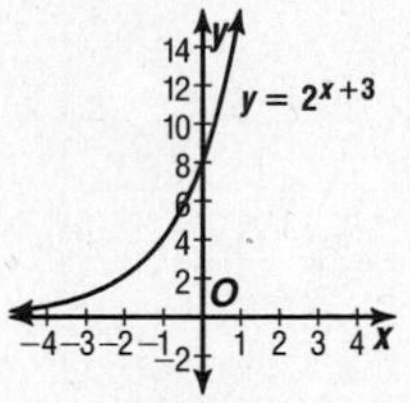

The y-intercept is 8.

13. $y = 3^{x+1}$

x	y
-3	$\frac{1}{9}$
-2	$\frac{1}{3}$
-1	1
0	3
1	9
2	27

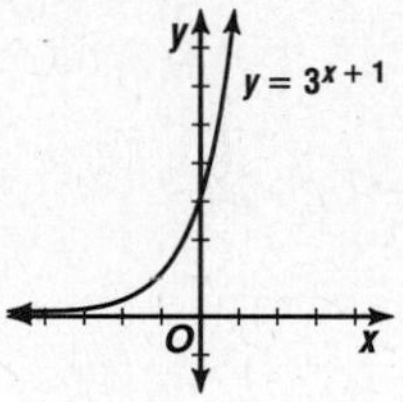

The y-intercept is 3.

14. $y = \left(\frac{1}{4}\right)^x$

x	y
-3	64
-2	16
-1	4
0	1
1	$\frac{1}{4}$
2	$\frac{1}{16}$

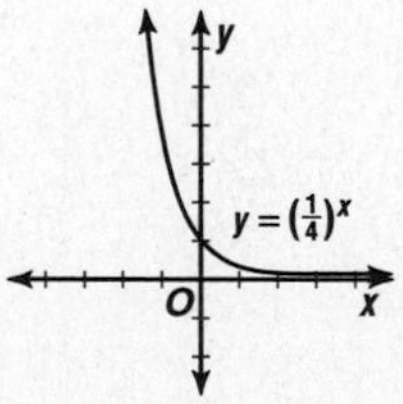

The y-intercept is 1.

15. $y = 5\left(\frac{2}{5}\right)^x$

x	y
-2	31.25
-1	12.5
0	5
1	2
2	0.8
3	0.32

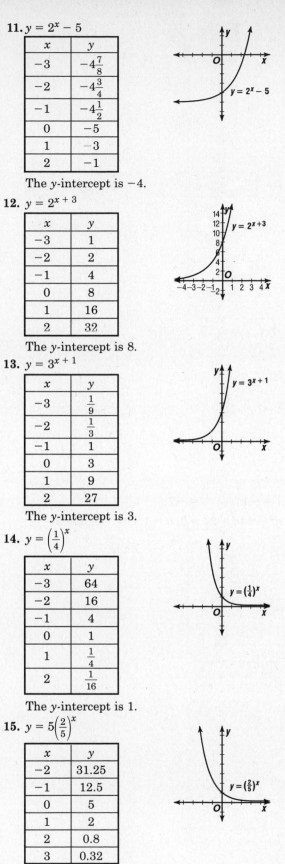

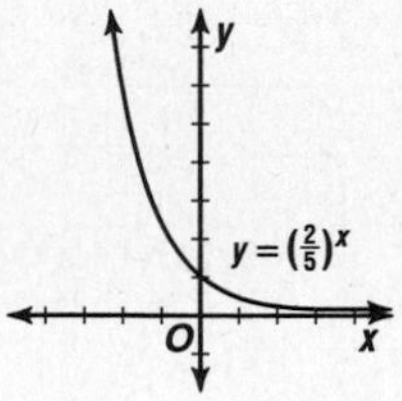

The y-intercept is 5.

16. $y = 3 \cdot 2^x$

x	y
−2	0.75
−1	1.5
0	3
1	6
2	12
3	24

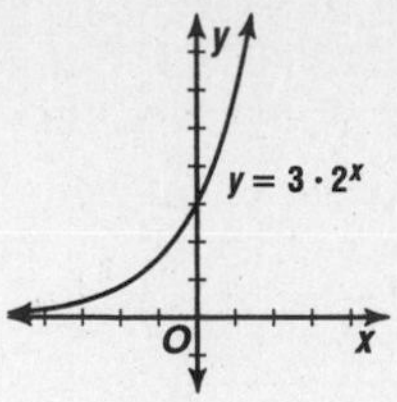

The y-intercept is 3.

17. $y = 4 \cdot 5^x$

x	y
−2	0.16
−1	0.8
0	4
1	20
2	100
3	500

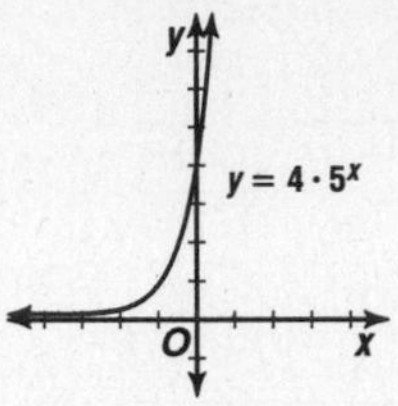

The y-intercept is 4.

18. $y = 6^x$

x	y
−2	$\frac{1}{36}$
−1	$\frac{1}{6}$
0	1
1	6
2	36
3	216

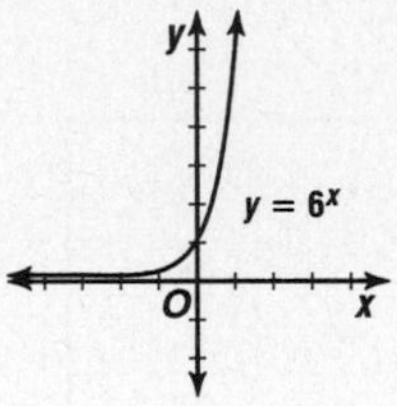

The y-intercept is 1.

19. $y = 3^x$

x	y
−2	$\frac{1}{9}$
−1	$\frac{1}{3}$
0	1
1	3
2	9
3	27

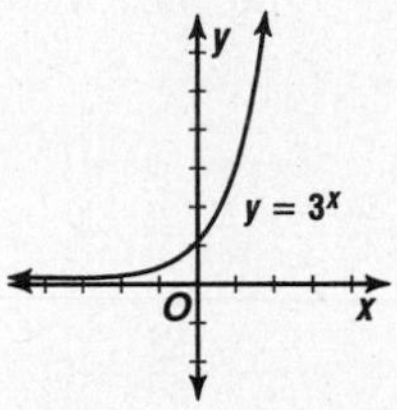

The y-intercept is 1.

20. $y = \left(\frac{1}{8}\right)^x$

x	y
−2	64
−1	8
0	1
1	$\frac{1}{8}$
2	$\frac{1}{64}$

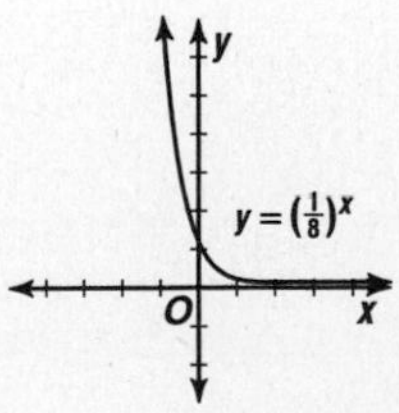

The y-intercept is 1.

21. $y = \left(\frac{3}{4}\right)^x$

x	y
−2	$\frac{16}{9}$
−1	$\frac{4}{3}$
0	1
1	$\frac{3}{4}$
2	$\frac{9}{16}$

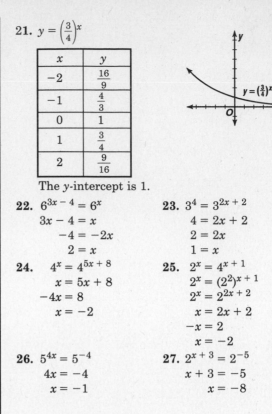

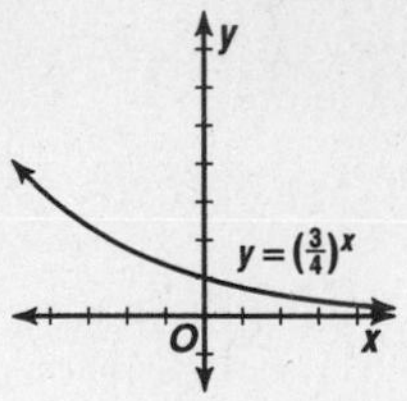

The y-intercept is 1.

22. $6^{3x-4} = 6^x$
$3x - 4 = x$
$-4 = -2x$
$2 = x$

23. $3^4 = 3^{2x+2}$
$4 = 2x + 2$
$2 = 2x$
$1 = x$

24. $4^x = 4^{5x+8}$
$x = 5x + 8$
$-4x = 8$
$x = -2$

25. $2^x = 4^{x+1}$
$2^x = (2^2)^{x+1}$
$2^x = 2^{2x+2}$
$x = 2x + 2$
$-x = 2$
$x = -2$

26. $5^{4x} = 5^{-4}$
$4x = -4$
$x = -1$

27. $2^{x+3} = 2^{-5}$
$x + 3 = -5$
$x = -8$

Page 781 Lesson 11-5

1. growth **2.** decay **3.** decay
4. growth **5.** growth **6.** decay

7a. $A = P\left(1 + \frac{r}{n}\right)^{nt}$ $\quad A = 2500, P = 1250, r = 0.12, n = 12$
$2500 = 1250\left(1 + \frac{0.12}{12}\right)^{12t}$
$2 = (1 + 0.01)^{12t}$
$2 = (1.01)^{12t}$
$5.8 \approx t$ *Use a calculator to estimate.*
t = about 5 years, 10 months ago

7b. $A = P\left(1 + \frac{r}{n}\right)^{nt}$ $\quad A = 2500, P = 1500, r = 0.12, n = 12$
$2500 = 1500\left(1 + \frac{0.12}{12}\right)^{12t}$
$\frac{5}{3} = (1.01)^{12t}$
$4.27 \approx t$ *Use a calculator to estimate.*
t = about 4 years, 3 months ago

8. $A = P\left(1 + \frac{r}{n}\right)^{nt}$ $\quad A = 800, P = 500, r = 0.0875, n = 12$
$800 = 500\left(1 + \frac{0.0875}{12}\right)^{12t}$
$1.6 \approx (1.0073)^{12t}$
$t \approx 5.38$ *Use a calculator to estimate.*
t = about 5 years, 5 months

9a. $y = 371{,}000(1.077)^t$

9b. $t = 2000 - 1994 = 6$
$y = 371{,}000(1.077)^6$
$= 578{,}986$

Page 782 Lesson 12-1

1. $\frac{13a}{39a^2} = \frac{(13a)(1)}{(13a)(3a)} = \frac{\cancel{(13a)}^1(1)}{\cancel{(13a)}_1(3a)} = \frac{1}{3a};\ a \neq 0$

2. $\frac{38x^2}{42xy} = \frac{(2x)(19x)}{(2x)(21y)} = \frac{\cancel{(2x)}^1(19x)}{\cancel{(2x)}_1(21y)} = \frac{19x}{21y};\ x, y \neq 0$

3. $\frac{14x^2z}{49yz^3} = \frac{(7yz)(2y)}{(7yz)(7z^2)} = \frac{\cancel{(7yz)}^1(2y)}{\cancel{(7yz)}_1(7z^2)} = \frac{2y}{7z^2};\ y, z \neq 0$

4. $\frac{p+5}{2(p+5)} = \frac{\cancel{p+5}^1}{2\cancel{(p+5)}_1} = \frac{1}{2};\ p \neq -5$

5. $\frac{79a^2b}{158a^3bc} = \frac{(79a^2b)(1)}{(79a^2b)(2ac)} = \frac{\cancel{(79a^2b)}^1(1)}{\cancel{(79a^2b)}_1(2ac)} = \frac{1}{2ac};\ a, b, c \neq 0$

6. $\frac{a+b}{a^2-b^2} = \frac{a+b}{(a+b)(a-b)} = \frac{\cancel{a+b}^1}{\cancel{(a+b)}_1(a-b)} = \frac{1}{a-b}$

excluded values:

$a^2 - b^2 = 0$

$(a-b)(a+b) = 0$

$a - b = 0$ or $a + b = 0$

$a = b \qquad a = -b$

$a \neq \pm b$

7. $\frac{y+4}{(y-4)(y+4)} = \frac{\cancel{y+4}^1}{(y-4)\cancel{(y+4)}_1} = \frac{1}{y-4}$

excluded values:

$(y-4)(y+4) = 0$

$y - 4 = 0$ or $y + 4 = 0$

$y = 4 \qquad y = -4$

$y \neq 4, -4$

8. $\frac{c^2-4}{(c+2)^2} = \frac{(c+2)(c-2)}{(c+2)^2} = \frac{\cancel{(c+2)}^1(c-2)}{\cancel{(c+2)^2}_{c+2}} = \frac{c-2}{c+2}$

excluded values:

$(c+2)^2 = 0$

$(c+2)(c+2) = 0$

$c + 2 = 0$

$c = -2$

$c \neq -2$

9. $\frac{a^2-a}{a-1} = \frac{a(a-1)}{a-1} = \frac{a\cancel{(a-1)}^1}{\cancel{(a-1)}_1} = a$

excluded values:

$a - 1 = 0$

$a = 1$

$a \neq 1$

10. $\frac{(w-4)(w+4)}{(w-2)(w-4)} = \frac{\cancel{(w-4)}^1(w+4)}{(w-2)\cancel{(w-4)}_1} = \frac{w+4}{w-2}$

excluded values:

$(w-2)(w-4) = 0$

$w - 2 = 0$ or $w - 4 = 0$

$w = 2 \qquad w = 4$

$w \neq 2, 4$

11. $\frac{m^2-2m}{m-2} = \frac{m(m-2)}{m-2} = \frac{m\cancel{(m-2)}^1}{\cancel{m-2}_1} = m$

excluded values:

$m - 2 = 0$

$m = 2$

$m \neq 2$

12. $\frac{x^2+4}{x^4-16} = \frac{x^2+4}{(x^2+4)(x^2-4)} = \frac{\cancel{x^2+4}^1}{\cancel{(x^2+4)}_1(x^2-4)} = \frac{1}{x^2-4}$

excluded values:

$x^4 - 16 = 0$

$(x^2+4)(x^2-4) = 0$

$(x^2+4)(x+2)(x-2) = 0$

$x^2 + 4 = 0 \qquad x + 2 = 0 \qquad x - 2 = 0$

$x^2 = -4 \qquad x = -2 \qquad x = 2$

no solution

$x \neq \pm 2$

13. $\frac{r^3-r^2}{r-1} = \frac{r^2(r-1)}{r-1} = \frac{r^2\cancel{(r-1)}^1}{\cancel{r-1}_1} = r^2$

excluded values:

$r - 1 = 0$

$r = 1$

$r \neq 1$

14. $\frac{3m^3}{6m^2-3m} = \frac{3m^3}{3m(2m-1)} = \frac{\cancel{3m^3}^{m^2}}{\cancel{3m}(2m-1)} = \frac{m^2}{2m-1}$

excluded values:

$6m^2 - 3m = 0$

$3m(2m-1) = 0$

$3m = 0$ or $2m - 1 = 0$

$m = 0 \qquad 2m = \frac{1}{2}$

$m \neq 0, \frac{1}{2}$

15. $\frac{4t^2-8}{4t-4} = \frac{4(t^2-2)}{4(t-1)} = \frac{\cancel{4}^1(t^2-2)}{\cancel{4}_1(t-1)} = \frac{t^2-2}{t-1}$

excluded values:

$4t - 4 = 0$

$4(t-1) = 0$

$t - 1 = 0$

$t = 1$

$t \neq 1$

16. $\frac{6y^3-12y^2}{12y^2-18} = \frac{6y^2(y-2)}{6(2y^2-3)} = \frac{\cancel{6}^1y^2(y-2)}{\cancel{6}_1(2y^2-3)} = \frac{y^2(y-2)}{2y^2-3}$

excluded values:

$12y^2 - 18 = 0$

$6(2y^2-3) = 0$

$2y^2 - 3 = 0$

$2y^2 = 3$

$y^2 = \frac{3}{2}$

$y = \pm\sqrt{\frac{3}{2}}\frac{(\sqrt{2})}{(\sqrt{2})}$

$y = \pm\frac{\sqrt{6}}{2}$

$y \neq \pm\frac{\sqrt{6}}{2}$

17. $\frac{x-3}{x^2+x-12} = \frac{x-3}{(x-3)(x+4)}$

$= \frac{\cancel{x-3}}{\cancel{(x-3)}(x+4)}$

$= \frac{1}{x+4}$

excluded values:

$x^2 + x - 12 = 0$

$(x-3)(x+4) = 0$

$x - 3 = 0$ or $x + 4 = 0$

$x = 3 \qquad x = -4$

$x \neq -4, 3$

18. $\frac{5x^2+10x+5}{3x^2+6x+3} = \frac{5\cancel{(x^2+2x+1)}}{3\cancel{(x^2+2x+1)}}$

$= \frac{5(x^2+2x+1)}{3(x^2+2x+1)}$

$= \frac{5}{3}$

excluded values:

$3x^2 + 6x + 3 = 0$

$3(x+1)^2 = 0$

$x + 1 = 0$

$x = -1$

$x \neq -1$

Page 782 Lesson 12-2

1. $\frac{a^2b}{b^2c} \cdot \frac{c}{d} = \frac{a^2bc}{b^2cd}$

$= \frac{a^2\cancel{bc}}{\cancel{b^2c}d}$

$= \frac{a^2}{bd}$

2. $\frac{6a^2n}{8n^2} \cdot \frac{12n}{9a} = \frac{72a^2n^2}{72an^2}$

$= \frac{\cancel{72a^2n^2}}{\cancel{72an^2}}$

$= a$

3. $\frac{2a^2d}{3bc} \cdot \frac{9b^2c}{16ad^2} = \frac{18a^2b^2cd}{48abcd^2}$

$= \frac{\cancel{18a^2b^2cd}}{\cancel{48abcd^2}}$

$= \frac{3ab}{8d}$

4. $\frac{10n^3}{6x^3} \cdot \frac{12n^2x^4}{25n^2x^2} = \frac{120n^5x^4}{150n^2x^5}$

$= \frac{\cancel{120n^5x^4}}{\cancel{150n^2x^5}}$

$= \frac{4n^3}{5x}$

5. $\left(\frac{2a}{b}\right)^2 \frac{5c}{6a} = \frac{4a^2}{b^2} \cdot \frac{5c}{6a}$

$= \frac{20a^2c}{6ab^2}$

$= \frac{\cancel{20a^2c}}{\cancel{6ab^2}}$

$= \frac{10ac}{3b^2}$

6. $\frac{6m^3n}{10a^2} \cdot \frac{4a^2m}{9n^3} = \frac{24a^2m^4n}{90a^2n^3}$

$= \frac{\cancel{24a^2m^4n}}{\cancel{90a^2n^3}}$

$= \frac{4m^4}{15n^2}$

7. $\frac{5n-5}{3} \cdot \frac{9}{n-1} = \frac{5(n-1)}{3} \cdot \frac{9}{n-1}$

$= \frac{5\cancel{(n-1)}}{\cancel{3}} \cdot \frac{\cancel{9}}{\cancel{n-1}}$

$= 15$

8. $\frac{a^2}{a-b} \cdot \frac{3a-3b}{a} = \frac{a^2}{a-b} \cdot \frac{3(a-b)}{a}$

$= \frac{\cancel{a^2}}{\cancel{a-b}} \cdot \frac{3\cancel{(a-b)}}{\cancel{a}}$

$= 3a$

9. $\frac{2a+4b}{5} \cdot \frac{25}{6a+8b} = \frac{2(a+2b)}{5} \cdot \frac{25}{2(3a+4b)}$

$= \frac{\cancel{2}(a+2b)}{\cancel{5}} \cdot \frac{\cancel{25}}{\cancel{2}(3a+4b)}$

$= \frac{5(a+2b)}{3a+4b}$

$= \frac{5a+10b}{3a+4b}$

10. $\frac{4t}{4t+40} \cdot \frac{3t+30}{2t} = \frac{4t}{4(t+10)} \cdot \frac{3(t+10)}{2t}$

$= \frac{\cancel{4t}}{\cancel{4(t+10)}} \cdot \frac{3\cancel{(t+10)}}{2\cancel{t}}$

$= \frac{3}{2}$

11. $\frac{3k+9}{k} \cdot \frac{k^2}{k^2-9} = \frac{3(k+3)}{k} \cdot \frac{k^2}{(k+3)(k-3)}$

$= \frac{3\cancel{(k+3)}}{\cancel{k}} \cdot \frac{\cancel{k^2}}{\cancel{(k+3)}(k-3)}$

$= \frac{3k}{k-3}$

12. $\frac{7xy^3}{11z^2} \cdot \frac{44z^3}{21x^2y} = \frac{\cancel{7xy^3}}{\cancel{11z^2}} \cdot \frac{\cancel{44z^3}}{\cancel{21x^2y}}$

$= \frac{4y^2z}{3x}$

13. $\frac{3}{x-y} \cdot \frac{(x-y)^2}{6} = \frac{\cancel{3}}{\cancel{x-y}} \cdot \frac{\cancel{(x-y)^2}}{\cancel{6}}$

$= \frac{x-y}{2}$

14. $\frac{x+5}{3x} \cdot \frac{12x^2}{x^2+7x+10} = \frac{x+5}{3x} \cdot \frac{12x^2}{(x+5)(x+2)}$

$= \frac{\cancel{x+5}}{\cancel{3x}} \cdot \frac{\cancel{12x^2}}{\cancel{(x+5)}(x+2)}$

$= \frac{4x}{x+2}$

15. $\frac{a^2-b^2}{4} \cdot \frac{16}{a+b} = \frac{(a+b)(a-b)}{4} \cdot \frac{16}{a+b}$

$= \frac{\cancel{(a+b)}(a-b)}{\cancel{4}} \cdot \frac{\cancel{16}}{\cancel{a+b}}$

$= 4(a-b)$

$= 4a - 4b$

16. $\frac{4a+8}{a^2-25} \cdot \frac{a-5}{5a+10} = \frac{4(a+2)}{(a+5)(a-5)} \cdot \frac{a-5}{5(a+2)}$

$= \frac{4\cancel{(a+2)}}{(a+5)\cancel{(a-5)}} \cdot \frac{\cancel{a-5}}{5\cancel{(a+2)}}$

$= \frac{4}{5(a+5)}$

$= \frac{4}{5a+25}$

17. $\frac{r^2}{r-s} \cdot \frac{r^2-s^2}{s^2} = \frac{r^2}{r-s} \cdot \frac{(r+s)(r-s)}{s^2}$

$= \frac{r^2}{\cancel{r-s}} \cdot \frac{(r+s)\cancel{(r-s)}}{s^2}$

$= \frac{r^2(r+s)}{s^2}$

$= \frac{r^3+r^2s}{s^2}$

18. $\frac{a^2-b^2}{a-b} \cdot \frac{7}{a+b} = \frac{(a+b)(a-b)}{a-b} \cdot \frac{7}{a+b}$

$= \frac{\cancel{(a+b)}\cancel{(a-b)}}{\cancel{a-b}} \cdot \frac{7}{\cancel{a+b}}$

$= 7$

Page 783 Lesson 12-3

1. $\frac{5m^2n}{12a^2} \div \frac{30m^4}{18an} = \frac{5m^2n}{12a^2} \cdot \frac{18an}{30m^4}$

$= \frac{90am^2n^2}{360a^2m^4}$

$= \frac{\cancel{90am^2}n^2}{\cancel{360a^2m^4}}$

$= \frac{n^2}{4am^2}$

2. $\frac{25g^7h}{28t^3} \div \frac{5g^5h^2}{42s^2t^3} = \frac{25g^7h}{28t^3} \cdot \frac{42s^2t^3}{5g^5h^2}$

$= \frac{\cancel{25g^7h}}{28\cancel{t^3}} \cdot \frac{\cancel{42s^2t^3}}{\cancel{5g^5h^2}}$

$= \frac{15g^2s^2}{2h}$

3. $\frac{6a+3b}{36} \div \frac{3a+2b}{45} = \frac{6a+3b}{36} \cdot \frac{45}{3a+2b}$

$= \frac{2(3a+2b)}{36} \cdot \frac{45}{3a+2b}$

$= \frac{2(\cancel{3a+2b})}{\cancel{36}_2} \cdot \frac{\cancel{45}^5}{\cancel{3a+2b}_1}$

$= \frac{5}{2}$

4. $\frac{x^2y}{18z} \div \frac{2yz}{3x^2} = \frac{x^2y}{18z} \cdot \frac{3x^2}{2yz}$

$= \frac{3x^4y}{36yz^2}$

$= \frac{\cancel{3}x^4\cancel{y}}{\cancel{36}\cancel{y}z^2}$

$= \frac{x^4}{12z^2}$

5. $\frac{p^2}{14qr^3} \div \frac{2r^2p}{7q} = \frac{p^2}{14qr^3} \cdot \frac{7q}{2r^2p}$

$= \frac{7p^2q}{28pqr^5}$

$= \frac{\cancel{7}p^{\cancel{2}}\cancel{q}}{\cancel{28}\cancel{p}\cancel{q}r^5}$

$= \frac{p}{4r^5}$

6. $\frac{5e-f}{5e+f} \div (25e^2-f^2) = \frac{5e-f}{5e+f} \cdot \frac{1}{(25e^2-f^2)}$

$= \frac{\cancel{5e-f}}{5e+f} \cdot \frac{1}{(5e+f)(\cancel{5e-f})}$

$= \frac{1}{(5e+f)^2}$

7. $\frac{t^2-2t-15}{t-5} \div \frac{t+3}{t+3} = \frac{t^2-2t-15}{t-5} \cdot \frac{t+5}{t+3}$

$= \frac{(\cancel{t-5})(\cancel{t+3})}{\cancel{t-5}} \cdot \frac{t+5}{\cancel{t+3}}$

$= t+5$

8. $\frac{5x+10}{x+2} \div (x+2) = \frac{5x+10}{x+2} \cdot \frac{1}{x+2}$

$= \frac{5(\cancel{x+2})}{\cancel{x+2}} \cdot \frac{1}{x+2}$

$= \frac{5}{x+2}$

9. $\frac{3d}{2d^2-3d} \div \frac{9}{2d-3} = \frac{3d}{2d^2-3d} \cdot \frac{2d-3}{9}$

$= \frac{\cancel{3d}}{\cancel{d}(\cancel{2d-3})} \cdot \frac{\cancel{2d-3}}{\cancel{9}_3}$

$= \frac{1}{3}$

10. $\frac{3v^2-27}{15v} \div \frac{v+3}{v^2} = \frac{3v^2-27}{15v} \cdot \frac{v^2}{v+3}$

$= \frac{\cancel{3}(\cancel{v+3})(v-3)}{\cancel{15v}_5} \cdot \frac{v^2}{\cancel{v+3}}$

$= \frac{v(v-3)}{5}$

11. $\frac{3g^2+15g}{4} \div \frac{g+5}{g^2} = \frac{3g^2+15g}{4} \cdot \frac{g^2}{g+5}$

$= \frac{3g(\cancel{g+5})}{4} \cdot \frac{g^2}{\cancel{g+5}}$

$= \frac{3g^3}{4}$

12. $\frac{b^2-9}{4b} \div (b-3) = \frac{b^2-9}{4b} \cdot \frac{1}{b-3}$

$= \frac{(b+3)(\cancel{b-3})}{4b} \cdot \frac{1}{\cancel{b-3}}$

$= \frac{b+3}{4b}$

13. $\frac{p^2}{y^2-4} \div \frac{p}{2-y} = \frac{p^2}{(y^2-4)} \cdot \frac{2-y}{p}$

$= \frac{\cancel{p^2}\,p}{(y+2)(\cancel{y-2})} \cdot -\frac{(\cancel{y-2})}{\cancel{p}}$

$= -\frac{p}{y+2}$

14. $\frac{k^2-81}{k^2-36} \div \frac{k-9}{k+6} = \frac{k^2-81}{k^2-36} \cdot \frac{k+6}{k-9}$

$= \frac{(k+9)(\cancel{k-9})}{(\cancel{k+6})(k-6)} \cdot \frac{\cancel{k+6}}{\cancel{k-9}}$

$= \frac{k+9}{k-6}$

15. $\frac{2a^3}{a+1} \div \frac{a^2}{a+1} = \frac{2a^3}{a+1} \cdot \frac{a+1}{a^2}$

$= \frac{2\cancel{a^3}}{\cancel{a+1}} \cdot \frac{\cancel{a+1}}{\cancel{a^2}}$

$= 2a$

16. $\frac{x^2-16}{16-x^2} \div \frac{7}{x} = \frac{x^2-16}{16-x^2} \cdot \frac{x}{7}$

$= \frac{\cancel{x^2-16}}{-(\cancel{x^2-16})} \cdot \frac{x}{7}$

$= -\frac{x}{7}$

17. $\frac{y}{5} \div \frac{y^2-25}{5-y} = \frac{y}{5} \cdot \frac{5-y}{y^2}-25$

$= \frac{y}{5} \cdot \frac{-(\cancel{y-5})}{(y+5)(\cancel{y-5})}$

$= \frac{-y}{5(y+5)}$

$= \frac{-y}{5y+25}$

18. $\frac{3m}{m+1} \div (m-2) = \frac{3m}{m+1} \cdot \frac{1}{m-2}$

$= \frac{3m}{(m+1)(m-2)}$

$= \frac{3m}{m^2-m-2}$

Page 783 Lesson 12-4

1.
$$\begin{array}{rr} & x-7 \\ 2x+3 & \overline{)\,2x^2-11x-20} \\ (-) & \underline{2x^2+3x} \\ & -14x-20 \\ (-) & \underline{-14x-21} \\ & 1 \end{array}$$

$x-7+\frac{1}{2x+3}$

2.
$$\begin{array}{rr} & a+4 \\ a+3 & \overline{)\,a^2+7a+12} \\ (-) & \underline{a^2+3a} \\ & 4a+12 \\ (-) & \underline{4a+12} \\ & 0 \end{array}$$

$a+4$

3.
$$\begin{array}{rr} & m+4 \\ m+5 & \overline{)\,m^2+9m+20} \\ (-) & \underline{m^2+5m} \\ & 4m+20 \\ (-) & \underline{4m+20} \\ & 0 \end{array}$$

$m+4$

4.
$$\begin{array}{rr} & x+5 \\ x-7 & \overline{)\,x^2-2x-35} \\ (-) & \underline{x^2-7x} \\ & 5x-35 \\ (-) & \underline{5x-35} \\ & 0 \end{array}$$

$x+5$

5.
$$\begin{array}{rr} & c+3 \\ c+9 & \overline{)\,c^2+12c+36} \\ (-) & \underline{c^2+9c} \\ & 3c+36 \\ (-) & \underline{3c+27} \\ & 9 \end{array}$$

$c+3+\frac{9}{c+9}$

6.
$$\begin{array}{rr} & y-9 \\ y+7 & \overline{)\,y^2-2y-30} \\ (-) & \underline{y^2+7y} \\ & -9y-30 \\ (-) & \underline{-9y-63} \\ & 33 \end{array}$$

$y-9+\frac{33}{y+7}$

7.
$$\begin{array}{rr} & t-6 \\ 3t+4 & \overline{)\,3t^2-14t-24} \\ (-) & \underline{3t^2+4t} \\ & -18t-24 \\ (-) & \underline{-18t-24} \\ & 0 \end{array}$$

$t-6$

8.
$$\begin{array}{rr} & r-5 \\ 2r+7 & \overline{)\,2r^2-3r-35} \\ (-) & \underline{2r^2+7r} \\ & -10r-35 \\ (-) & \underline{-10r-35} \\ & 0 \end{array}$$

$r-5$

9.
$$\begin{array}{r} 2n+\ \ 5 \\ 6n+3\overline{)12n^2+36n+15} \\ (-)\ 12n^2+\ \ 6n\qquad \\ \hline 30n+15 \\ (-)\qquad 30n+15 \\ \hline 0 \end{array}$$
$2n + 5$

10.
$$\begin{array}{r} 2x+\ \ 3 \\ 5x+7\overline{)10x^2+29x+21} \\ (-)\ 10x^2+14x\qquad \\ \hline 15x+21 \\ (-)\qquad 15x+21 \\ \hline 0 \end{array}$$
$2x + 3$

11.
$$\begin{array}{r} t^2+4t-1 \\ 4t+1\overline{)4t^3+17t^2+0t-1} \\ (-)\ 4t^3+\quad t^2\qquad\qquad \\ \hline 16t^2+0t \\ (-)\qquad 16t^2+4t \\ \hline -4t-1 \\ (-)\qquad -4t-1 \\ \hline 0 \end{array}$$
$t^2 + 4t - 1$

12.
$$\begin{array}{r} 2a^2+3a-\ \ 4 \\ a+3\overline{)2a^3+9a^2+5a-12} \\ (-)\ 2a^3+6a^2\qquad\qquad \\ \hline 3a^2+5a \\ (-)\qquad 3a^2+9a \\ \hline -4a-12 \\ (-)\qquad -4a-12 \\ \hline 0 \end{array}$$
$2a^2 + 3a - 4$

13.
$$\begin{array}{r} 2m^2+3m+\ \ 7 \\ 2m-3\overline{)4m^3+0m^2+5m-21} \\ (-)\ 4m^3-6m^2\qquad\qquad \\ \hline 6m^2+5m \\ (-)\qquad 6m^2-9m \\ \hline 14m-21 \\ (-)\qquad 14m-21 \\ \hline 0 \end{array}$$
$2m^2 + 3m + 7$

14.
$$\begin{array}{r} 3t^2-2t+\ \ 3 \\ 2t+3\overline{)6t^3+5t^2+0t+12} \\ (-)\ 6t^3+9t^2\qquad\qquad \\ \hline -4t^2+0t \\ (-)\qquad -4t^2-6t \\ \hline 6t+12 \\ (-)\qquad 6t+\ \ 9 \\ \hline 3 \end{array}$$
$3t^3 - 2t + 3 + \frac{3}{2t+3}$

15.
$$\begin{array}{r} 3c-2 \\ 9c-2\overline{)27c^2-24c+8} \\ (-)\ 27c^2-\ \ 6c\qquad \\ \hline -18c+4 \\ (-)\qquad -18c+4 \\ \hline 4 \end{array}$$
$3c - 2 + \frac{4}{9c-2}$

16.
$$\begin{array}{r} 3b^2+2b-3 \\ b+2\overline{)3b^3+8b^2+\ \ b-7} \\ (-)\ 3b^3+6b^2\qquad\qquad \\ \hline 2b^2+\ \ b \\ (-)\qquad 2b^2+4b \\ \hline -3b-7 \\ (-)\qquad -3b-6 \\ \hline -1 \end{array}$$
$3b^2 + 2b - 3 - \frac{1}{b+2}$

17.
$$\begin{array}{r} t^2+\ \ 4t-\ \ 3 \\ t-4\overline{)t^3+0t^2-19t+\ \ 9} \\ (-)\ t^3-4t^2\qquad\qquad \\ \hline 4t^2-19t \\ (-)\qquad 4t^2-16t \\ \hline -3t+\ \ 9 \\ (-)\qquad -3t+12 \\ \hline -3 \end{array}$$
$t^2 + 4t - 3 - \frac{3}{t-4}$

18.
$$\begin{array}{r} 3d^2+2d+3 \\ 3d-2\overline{)9d^3+0d^2+5d-8} \\ (-)\ 9d^3-6d^2\qquad\qquad \\ \hline 6d^2+5d \\ (-)\qquad 6d^2-4d \\ \hline 9d-8 \\ (-)\qquad 9d-6 \\ \hline -2 \end{array}$$
$3d^2 + 2d + 3 - \frac{2}{3d-2}$

Page 783 Lesson 12-5

1. $\frac{4}{z} + \frac{3}{z} = \frac{4+3}{z}$
$= \frac{7}{z}$

2. $\frac{a}{12} + \frac{2a}{12} = \frac{a+2a}{12}$
$= \frac{3a}{12}$
$= \frac{a}{4}$

3. $\frac{5}{2t} + \frac{-7}{2t} = \frac{5-7}{2t}$
$= \frac{-2}{2t}$
$= -\frac{1}{t}$

4. $\frac{y}{2} + \frac{y}{2} = \frac{y+y}{2}$
$= \frac{2y}{2}$
$= y$

5. $\frac{b}{x} + \frac{2}{x} = \frac{b+2}{x}$

6. $\frac{5x}{24} - \frac{3x}{24} = \frac{5x-3x}{24}$
$= \frac{2x}{24}$
$= \frac{x}{12}$

7. $\frac{7p}{p} - \frac{8p}{p} = \frac{7p-8p}{p}$
$= \frac{-p}{p}$
$= -1$

8. $\frac{8k}{5m} - \frac{3k}{5m} = \frac{8k - 3k}{5m}$

$= \frac{5k}{5m}$

$= \frac{k}{m}$

9. $\frac{y}{2} + \frac{y-6}{2} = \frac{y + (y-6)}{2}$

$= \frac{2y - 6}{2}$

$= \frac{\overset{1}{\cancel{2}}(y-3)}{\cancel{2}_1}$

$= y - 3$

10. $\frac{a+2}{6} - \frac{a+3}{6} = \frac{a + 2 - (a+3)}{6}$

$= -\frac{1}{6}$

11. $\frac{8}{m-2} - \frac{6}{m-2} = \frac{8-6}{m-2}$

$= \frac{2}{m-2}$

12. $\frac{x}{x+1} + \frac{1}{x+1} = \frac{x+1}{x+1}$

$= 1$

13. $\frac{2n}{2n-5} + \frac{5}{5-2n} = \frac{2n}{2n-5} - \frac{5}{2n-5}$

$= \frac{2n-5}{2n-5}$

$= 1$

14. $\frac{y}{b+6} - \frac{2y}{b+6} = \frac{y - 2y}{b+6}$

$= \frac{-y}{b+6}$

15. $\frac{x-y}{2-y} + \frac{x+y}{y-2} = \frac{-(x-y)}{y-2} + \frac{x+y}{y-2}$

$= \frac{-x + y + x + y}{y-2}$

$= \frac{2y}{y-2}$

16. $\frac{r^2}{r-s} + \frac{s^2}{r-s} = \frac{r^2 + s^2}{r-s}$

17. $\frac{12n}{3n+2} + \frac{8}{3n+2} = \frac{12n+8}{3n+2}$

$= \frac{4\overset{1}{\cancel{(3n+2)}}}{\cancel{3n+2}_1}$

$= 4$

18. $\frac{6x}{x+y} + \frac{6y}{x+y} = \frac{6x+6y}{x+y}$

$= \frac{6\overset{1}{\cancel{(x+y)}}}{\cancel{x+y}_1}$

$= 6$

Page 784 Lesson 12-6

1. $\frac{s}{3} + \frac{2s}{7} = \frac{s(7)}{3(7)} + \frac{2s(3)}{7(3)}$

$= \frac{7s}{21} + \frac{6s}{21}$

$= \frac{7s + 6s}{21}$

$= \frac{13s}{21}$

2. $\frac{5}{2a} + \frac{-3}{6a} = \frac{5(3)}{2a(3)} + \frac{-3}{6a}$

$= \frac{15}{6a} + \frac{-3}{6a}$

$= \frac{15-3}{6a}$

$= \frac{12}{6a} = \frac{2}{a}$

3. $\frac{2n}{5} - \frac{3m}{4} = \frac{2n(4)}{5(4)} - \frac{3m(5)}{4(5)}$

$= \frac{8n}{20} - \frac{15m}{20}$

$= \frac{8n - 15m}{20}$

4. $\frac{6}{5x} + \frac{7}{10x^2} = \frac{6(2x)}{5x(2x)} + \frac{7}{10x^2}$

$= \frac{12x}{10x^2} + \frac{7}{10x^2}$

$= \frac{12x + 7}{10x^2}$

5. $\frac{3z}{7w^2} - \frac{2z}{w} = \frac{3z}{7w^2} - \frac{2z(7w)}{w(7w)}$

$= \frac{3z}{7w^2} - \frac{2z(7w)}{7w^2}$

$= \frac{3z - 14wz}{7w^2}$

6. $\frac{s}{t^2} - \frac{r}{3t} = \frac{s(3)}{t^2(3)} - \frac{r(t)}{3t(t)}$

$= \frac{3s}{3t^2} - \frac{rt}{3t^2}$

$= \frac{3s - rt}{3t^2}$

7. $\frac{5}{xy} + \frac{6}{yz} = \frac{5(z)}{xy(z)} + \frac{6(x)}{yz(x)}$

$= \frac{5z}{xyz} + \frac{6x}{xyz}$

$= \frac{5z + 6x}{xyz}$

8. $\frac{2}{t} + \frac{t+3}{s} = \frac{2(s)}{t(s)} + \frac{(t+3)(t)}{(s)(t)}$

$= \frac{2s}{st} + \frac{t(t+3)}{st}$

$= \frac{2s + t(t+3)}{st}$

$= \frac{2s + t^2 + 3t}{st}$

9. $\frac{a}{a-b} + \frac{b}{2b+3a} = \frac{a(2b+3a)}{(a-b)(2b+3a)} + \frac{b(a-b)}{(a-b)(2b+3a)}$

$= \frac{a(2b+3) + b(a-b)}{(a-b)(3a+2b)}$

$= \frac{2ab + 3a^2 + ab - b^2}{3a^2 - ab - 2b^2}$

$= \frac{3a^2 + 3ab - b^2}{3a^2 - ab - 2b^2}$

10. $\frac{a}{a^2-4} - \frac{4}{a+2} = \frac{a}{(a+2)(a-2)} - \frac{4(a-2)}{(a+2)(a-2)}$

$= \frac{a - 4(a-2)}{(a+2)(a-2)}$

$= \frac{a - 4a + 8}{a^2 - 4} = \frac{-3a + 8}{a^2 - 4}$

11. $\frac{4a}{2a+6} + \frac{3}{a+3} = \frac{4a}{2(a+3)} + \frac{3}{a+3}$

$= \frac{2a}{a+3} + \frac{3}{a+3}$

$= \frac{2a+3}{a+3}$

12. $\frac{m}{(m-n)} - \frac{5}{m} = \frac{m(m)}{(m-n)(m)} - \frac{5(m-n)}{m(m-n)}$

$= \frac{m(m) - 5(m-n)}{m(m-n)}$

$= \frac{m^2 - 5m + 5n}{m(m-n)}$

13. $\frac{-3}{a-5} + \frac{-6}{a^2-5a} = \frac{-3(a)}{(a-5)(a)} + \frac{-6}{(a-5)(a)}$

$= \frac{-3a - 6}{a(a-5)}$

$= \frac{-3a - 6}{a^2 - 5a}$

14. $\frac{3t+2}{3t-6} - \frac{t+2}{t^2-4} = \frac{(3t+2)(t+2)}{3(t-2)(t+2)} - \frac{(t+2)(3)}{(t+2)(t-2)(3)}$

$= \frac{(3t+2)(t+2) - (t+2)(3)}{3(t-2)(t+2)}$

$= \frac{3t^2 + 8t + 4 - 3t - 6}{3(t-2)(t+2)}$

$= \frac{3t^2 + 5t - 2}{3(t-2)(t+2)}$

$= \frac{(3t-1)(t+2)}{3(t-2)(t+2)}$

$= \frac{3t-1}{3(t-2)}$

$= \frac{3t-1}{3t-6}$

15. $\frac{y+5}{y-5} + \frac{2y}{y^2-25} = \frac{(y+5)(y+5)}{(y-5)(y+5)} + \frac{2y}{(y+5)(y-5)}$

$= \frac{(y+5)^2 + 2y}{(y-5)(y+5)}$

$= \frac{y^2 + 10y + 25 + 2y}{(y-5)(y+5)}$

$= \frac{y^2 + 12y + 25}{y^2 - 25}$

16. $\frac{-18}{y^2-9} + \frac{7}{3-y} = \frac{-18}{(y+3)(y-3)} + \frac{-7(y+3)}{(y-3)(y+3)}$

$= \frac{-18 + -7(y+3)}{(y+3)(y-3)}$

$= \frac{-18 - 7y - 21}{(y+3)(y-3)}$

$= \frac{-7y - 39}{y^2 - 9}$

17. $\frac{c}{c^2 - 4c} - \frac{5c}{c-4} = \frac{c}{c(c-4)} - \frac{5c(c)}{c(c-4)}$

$= \frac{c - 5c(c)}{c(c-4)}$

$= \frac{c - 5c^2}{c(c-4)}$

$= \frac{c(1-5c)}{c(c-4)}$

$= \frac{1-5c}{c-4}$

18. $\frac{t+10}{t^2-100} + \frac{1}{t-10} = \frac{t+10}{(t+10)(t-10)} + \frac{1}{t-10}$

$= \frac{1}{t-10} + \frac{1}{t-10}$

$= \frac{1+1}{t-10}$

$= \frac{2}{t-10}$

Page 784 Lesson 12-7

1. $4 + \frac{2}{x} = \frac{4(x)}{(x)} + \frac{2}{x}$

$= \frac{4x+2}{x}$

2. $8 + \frac{5}{3t} = \frac{8(3t)}{3t} + \frac{5}{3t}$

$= \frac{24t+5}{3t}$

3. $3b + \frac{b+1}{2b} = \frac{3b(2b)}{2b} + \frac{b+1}{2b}$

$= \frac{3b(2b) + b + 1}{2b}$

$= \frac{6b^2 + b + 1}{2b}$

4. $2n + \frac{4+n}{n} = \frac{2n(n)}{n} + \frac{4+n}{n}$

$= \frac{2n(n) + 4 + n}{n}$

$= \frac{2n^2 + n + 4}{n}$

5. $a^2 + \frac{2}{a-2} = \frac{a^2(a-2)}{a-2} + \frac{2}{a-2}$

$= \frac{a^2(a-2) + 2}{a-2}$

$= \frac{a^3 - 2a^2 + 2}{a-2}$

6. $3r^2 + \frac{4}{2r+1} = \frac{3r^2(2r+1)}{2r+1} + \frac{4}{2r+1}$

$= \frac{3r^2(2r+1) + 4}{2r+1}$

$= \frac{6r^3 + 3r^2 + 4}{2r+1}$

7. $\frac{3\frac{1}{2}}{4\frac{3}{4}} = \frac{\frac{7}{2}}{\frac{19}{4}}$

$= \frac{7}{2} \div \frac{19}{4}$

$= \frac{7}{{}_1\cancel{2}} \cdot \frac{\cancel{4}^{2}}{19}$

$= \frac{14}{19}$

8. $\frac{\frac{x^2}{y}}{\frac{y}{x^3}} = \frac{x^2}{y} \div \frac{y}{x^3}$

$= \frac{x^2}{y} \cdot \frac{x^3}{y}$

$= \frac{x^5}{y^2}$

9. $\frac{\frac{t^4}{u}}{\frac{t^3}{u^2}} = \frac{t^4}{u} \div \frac{t^3}{u^2}$

$= \frac{\cancel{t^4}^{t}}{\cancel{u}_1} \cdot \frac{\cancel{u^2}^{u}}{\cancel{t^3}_1}$

$= tu$

10. $\frac{\frac{x^3}{y^2}}{\frac{x+y}{x-y}} = \frac{x^3}{y^2} \div \frac{x+y}{x-y}$

$= \frac{x^3}{y^2} \cdot \frac{x-y}{x+y}$

$= \frac{x^3(x-y)}{y^2(x+y)}$

11. $\frac{\frac{y}{3} + \frac{5}{6}}{2 + \frac{5}{y}} = \frac{\frac{y(2)}{3(2)} + \frac{5}{6}}{\frac{2(y)}{(y)} + \frac{5}{y}}$

$= \frac{\frac{2y}{6} + \frac{5}{6}}{\frac{2y}{y} + \frac{5}{y}}$

$= \frac{\frac{2y+5}{6}}{\frac{2y+5}{y}}$

$= \frac{\cancel{2y+5}^{1}}{6} \cdot \frac{y}{\cancel{2y+5}_1} = \frac{y}{6}$

12. $\frac{\frac{1}{x} + \frac{1}{y}}{\frac{1}{y} - \frac{1}{x}} = \frac{\frac{1(y)}{x(y)} + \frac{1(x)}{y(x)}}{\frac{1(x)}{y(x)} - \frac{1(y)}{x(y)}}$

$= \frac{\frac{y+x}{xy}}{\frac{x-y}{xy}}$

$= \frac{y+x}{xy} \div \frac{x-y}{xy}$

$= \frac{y+x}{\cancel{xy}_1} \cdot \frac{\cancel{xy}^{1}}{x-y}$

$= \frac{y+x}{x-y}$ or $\frac{x+y}{x-y}$

13. $\frac{t-2}{\frac{t^2-4}{t^2+5t+6}} = (t-2) \div \frac{t^2-4}{t^2+5t+6}$

$= (t-2) \cdot \frac{t^2+5t+6}{t^2-4}$

$= (\cancel{t-2}^{1}) \cdot \frac{(t+3)\cancel{(t+2)}}{\cancel{(t+2)}_1\cancel{(t-2)}_1}$

$= t + 3$

14. $\frac{\frac{y^2-1}{y^2+3y-4}}{y+1} = \frac{y^2-1}{y^2+3y-4} \div (y+1)$

$= \frac{y^2-1}{y^2+3y-4} \cdot \frac{1}{y+1}$

$= \frac{\cancel{(y+1)}\cancel{(y-1)}}{(y+4)\cancel{(y-1)}_1} \cdot \frac{1}{\cancel{y+1}_1}$

$= \frac{1}{y+4}$

Page 784 Lesson 12-8

1. $\frac{k}{6} + \frac{2k}{3} = -\frac{5}{2}$ LCD: 6

$6\left(\frac{k}{6} + \frac{2k}{3}\right) = \left(-\frac{5}{2}\right)6$

$k + 2(2k) = (-5)(3)$

$k + 4k = -15$

$5k = -15$

$k = -3$

2. $\frac{3x}{5} + \frac{3}{2} = \frac{7x}{10}$ LCD: 10

$10\left(\frac{3x}{5} + \frac{3}{2}\right) = \left(\frac{7x}{10}\right)10$

$2(3x) + 5(3) = 7x$

$6x + 15 = 7x$

$15 = x$

3. $\frac{18}{b} = \frac{3}{b} + 3$ LCD: b

$$b\left(\frac{18}{b}\right) = \left(\frac{3}{b} + 3\right)b$$
$$18 = 3 + 3b$$
$$15 = 3b$$
$$5 = b$$

4. $\frac{3}{5x} + \frac{7}{2x} = 1$ LCD: $10x$

$$10x\left(\frac{3}{5x} + \frac{7}{2x}\right) = 1(10x)$$
$$2(3) + 5(7) = 10x$$
$$6 + 35 = 10x$$
$$41 = 10x$$
$$\frac{41}{10} = x$$

5. $\frac{2a-3}{6} = \frac{2a}{3} + \frac{1}{2}$ LCD: 6

$$6\left(\frac{2a-3}{6}\right) = \left(\frac{2a}{3} + \frac{1}{2}\right)6$$
$$2a - 3 = 2(2a) + 3$$
$$2a - 3 = 4a + 3$$
$$-6 = 2a$$
$$-3 = a$$

6. $\frac{x+1}{x} + \frac{x+4}{x} = 6$ LCD: x

$$x\left(\frac{x+1}{x} + \frac{x+4}{x}\right) = 6(x)$$
$$x + 1 + x + 4 = 6x$$
$$2x + 5 = 6x$$
$$5 = 4x$$
$$\frac{5}{4} = x$$

7. $\frac{2b-3}{7} - \frac{b}{2} = \frac{b+3}{14}$ LCD: 14

$$14\left(\frac{2b-3}{7} - \frac{b}{2}\right) = \left(\frac{b+3}{14}\right)14$$
$$2(2b-3) - 7b = b + 3$$
$$4b - 6 - 7b = b + 3$$
$$-3b - 6 = b + 3$$
$$-4b = 9$$
$$b = -\frac{9}{4}$$

8. $\frac{2y}{y-4} - \frac{3}{5} = 3$ LCD: $5(y-4)$

$$5(y-4)\left(\frac{2y}{y-4} - \frac{3}{5}\right) = 3(5)(y-4)$$
$$5(2y) + (-3)(y-4) = 15(y-4)$$
$$10y - 3y + 12 = 15y - 60$$
$$7y + 12 = 15y - 60$$
$$72 = 8y$$
$$9 = y$$

9. $\frac{2t}{t+3} + \frac{3}{t} = 2$ LCD: $t(t+3)$

$$t(t+3)\left(\frac{2t}{t+3} + \frac{3}{t}\right) = 2(t)(t+3)$$
$$t(2t) + 3(t+3) = 2t(t+3)$$
$$2t^2 + 3t + 9 = 2t^2 + 6t$$
$$3t + 9 = 6t$$
$$9 = 3t$$
$$3 = t$$

10. $\frac{5x}{x+1} + \frac{1}{x} = 5$ LCD: $x(x+1)$

$$x(x+1)\left(\frac{5x}{x+1} + \frac{1}{x}\right) = 5(x)(x+1)$$
$$x(5x) + x + 1 = 5x(x+1)$$
$$5x^2 + x + 1 = 5x^2 + 5x$$
$$x + 1 = 5x$$
$$1 = 4x$$
$$\frac{1}{4} = x$$

11. $\frac{r-1}{r+1} - \frac{2r}{r-1} = -1$ LCD: $(r+1)(r-1)$

$$(r+1)(r-1)\left(\frac{r-1}{r+1} - \frac{2r}{r-1}\right) = -1(r+1)(r-1)$$
$$(r-1)(r-1) - 2r(r+1) = -(r+1)(r-1)$$
$$r^2 - 2r + 1 - 2r^2 - 2r = -r^2 + 1$$
$$-4r - r^2 + 1 = -r^2 + 1$$
$$-4r = 0$$
$$r = 0$$

12. $\frac{m}{m+1} + \frac{5}{m-1} = 1$

LCD: $(m+1)(m-1)$

$$(m+1)(m-1)\left(\frac{m}{m+1} + \frac{5}{m-1}\right) = 1(m+1)(m-1)$$
$$(m-1)(m) + 5(m+1) = (m+1)(m-1)$$
$$m^2 - m + 5m + 5 = m^2 - 1$$
$$m^2 + 4m + 5 = m^2 - 1$$
$$4m + 5 = -1$$
$$4m = -6$$
$$m = -\frac{3}{2}$$

13. $\frac{5}{5-p} - \frac{p^2}{5-p} = -2$ LCD: $5 - p$

$$(5-p)\left(\frac{5}{5-p} - \frac{p^2}{5-p}\right) = -2(5-p)$$
$$5 - p^2 = -10 + 2p$$
$$0 = p^2 + 2p - 15$$
$$0 = (p+5)(p-3)$$

$p + 5 = 0$ or $p - 3 = 0$

$p = -5$ $\quad p = 3$

14. $\frac{14}{b-6} = \frac{1}{2} + \frac{6}{b-8}$

LCD: $2(b-6)(b-8)$

$$2(b-6)(b-8)\left(\frac{14}{b-6}\right) = \left(\frac{1}{2} + \frac{6}{b-8}\right)(2)(b-6)(b-8)$$
$$2(b-8)(14) = (b-6)(b-8) + 6(2)(b-6)$$
$$28b - 224 = b^2 - 14b + 48 + 12b - 72$$
$$28b - 224 = b^2 - 2b - 24$$
$$0 = b^2 - 30b - 200$$
$$0 = (b-10)(b-20)$$

$b - 10 = 0$ or $b - 20 = 0$

$b = 10$ $\quad b = 20$

15. $\frac{r}{3r+6} - \frac{r}{5r+10} = \frac{2}{5}$ LCD: $15(r+2)$

$$15(r+2)\left(\frac{r}{3(r+2)} - \frac{r}{5(r+2)}\right) = \frac{2}{5}(15)(r+2)$$
$$5r - 3r = 2(3)(r+2)$$
$$2r = 6r + 12$$
$$-4r = 12$$
$$r = -3$$

16. $\frac{4x}{2x+3} - \frac{2x}{2x-3} = 1$

LCD: $(2x+3)(2x-3)$

$$(2x+3)(2x-3)\left(\frac{4x}{2x+3} - \frac{2x}{2x-3}\right) = 1(2x+3)(2x-3)$$
$$4x(2x-3) - 2x(2x+3) = 4x^2 - 9$$
$$8x^2 - 12x - 4x^2 - 6x = 4x^2 - 9$$
$$4x^2 - 18x = 4x^2 - 9$$
$$-18x = -9$$
$$x = \frac{1}{2}$$

17.
$$\frac{2a-3}{a-3} - 2 = \frac{12}{a+2}$$
LCD: $(a-3)(a+2)$
$$\begin{aligned}
(a-3)(a+2)\left(\frac{2a-3}{a-3} - 2\right) &= \frac{12}{a+2}(a-3)(a+2) \\
(a+2)(2a-3) - 2(a-3)(a+2) &= 12\,(a-3) \\
2a^2 + a - 6 - 2(a^2 - a - 6) &= 12a - 36 \\
2a^2 + a - 6 - 2a^2 + 2a + 12 &= 12a - 36 \\
3a + 6 &= 12a - 36 \\
42 &= 9a \\
\frac{42}{9} &= a \\
a &= \frac{14}{3}
\end{aligned}$$

18.
$$\frac{z+3}{a-1} + \frac{z+1}{z-3} = 2$$
LCD: $(z-1)(z-3)$
$$\begin{aligned}
(z-1)(z-3)\left(\frac{z+3}{z-1} + \frac{z+1}{z-3}\right) &= 2(z-1)(z-3) \\
(z-3)(z+3) + (z-1)(z+1) &= 2(z^2 - 4z + 3) \\
z^2 - 9 + z^2 - 1 &= 2z^2 - 8z + 6 \\
2z^2 - 10 &= 2z^2 - 8z + 6 \\
-16 &= -8z \\
z &= 2
\end{aligned}$$

Page 785 Lesson 13-1

1. $$\begin{aligned} c^2 &= a^2 + b^2 \\ 29^2 &= a^2 + 20^2 \\ 841 &= a^2 + 400 \\ 441 &= a^2 \\ \sqrt{441} &= a \\ 21 &= a \end{aligned}$$

2. $$\begin{aligned} c^2 &= a^2 + b^2 \\ c^2 &= 7^2 + 24^2 \\ c^2 &= 49 + 576 \\ c^2 &= 625 \\ c &= \sqrt{625} \\ c &= 25 \end{aligned}$$

3. $$\begin{aligned} c^2 &= a^2 + b^2 \\ c^2 &= 2^2 + 6^2 \\ c^2 &= 4 + 36 \\ c^2 &= 40 \\ c &= \sqrt{40} \approx 6.32 \end{aligned}$$

4. $$\begin{aligned} c^2 &= a^2 + b^2 \\ (\sqrt{200})^2 &= a^2 + 10^2 \\ 200 &= a^2 + 100 \\ 100 &= a^2 \\ \sqrt{100} &= a \\ 10 &= a \end{aligned}$$

5. $$\begin{aligned} c^2 &= a^2 + b^2 \\ (3\sqrt{2})^2 &= 3^2 + b^2 \\ 18 &= 9 + b^2 \\ 9 &= b^2 \\ \sqrt{9} &= b \\ 3 &= b \end{aligned}$$

6. $$\begin{aligned} c^2 &= a^2 + b^2 \\ 14^2 &= 6^2 + b^2 \\ 196 &= 36 + b^2 \\ 160 &= b^2 \\ b &= \sqrt{160} \approx 12.65 \end{aligned}$$

7. $$\begin{aligned} c^2 &= a^2 + b^2 \\ (\sqrt{47})^2 &= (\sqrt{11})^2 + b^2 \\ 47 &= 11 + b^2 \\ 36 &= b^2 \\ \sqrt{36} &= b \\ 6 &= b \end{aligned}$$

8. $$\begin{aligned} c^2 &= a^2 + b^2 \\ c^2 &= (\sqrt{13})^2 + b^2 \\ c^2 &= 13 + 36 \\ c^2 &= 49 \\ c &= \sqrt{49} \\ c &= 7 \end{aligned}$$

9. $$\begin{aligned} c^2 &= a^2 + b^2 \\ c^2 &= (\sqrt{6})^2 + 3^2 \\ c^2 &= 6 + 9 \\ c^2 &= 15 \\ c &= \sqrt{15} \approx 3.87 \end{aligned}$$

10. $$\begin{aligned} c^2 &= a^2 + b^2 \\ 10^2 &= a^2 + (\sqrt{75})^2 \\ 100 &= a^2 + 75 \\ 25 &= a^2 \\ \sqrt{25} &= a \\ 5 &= a \end{aligned}$$

11. $$\begin{aligned} c^2 &= a^2 + b^2 \\ (\sqrt{130})^2 &= a^2 + 9^2 \\ 130 &= a^2 + 81 \\ 49 &= a^2 \\ \sqrt{49} &= a \\ 7 &= a \end{aligned}$$

12. $$\begin{aligned} c^2 &= a^2 + b^2 \\ 15^2 &= 9^2 + b^2 \\ 225 &= 81 + b^2 \\ 144 &= b^2 \\ \sqrt{144} &= b \\ 12 &= b \end{aligned}$$

13. $$\begin{aligned} c^2 &= a^2 + b^2 \\ 11^2 &= a^2 + 5^2 \\ 121 &= a^2 + 25 \\ 96 &= a^2 \\ a &= \sqrt{96} \approx 9.80 \end{aligned}$$

14. $$\begin{aligned} c^2 &= a^2 + b^2 \\ c^2 &= (\sqrt{33})^2 + 4^2 \\ c^2 &= 33 + 16 \\ c^2 &= 49 \\ c &= \sqrt{49} \\ c &= 7 \end{aligned}$$

15. $$\begin{aligned} c^2 &= a^2 + b^2 \\ 50^2 &\stackrel{?}{=} 14^2 + 48^2 \\ 2500 &\stackrel{?}{=} 196 + 2300 \\ 2500 &= 2500 \end{aligned}$$
yes

16. $$\begin{aligned} c^2 &= a^2 + b^2 \\ 40^2 &\stackrel{?}{=} 20^2 + 30^2 \\ 1600 &\stackrel{?}{=} 400 + 900 \\ 1600 &\neq 1300 \end{aligned}$$
no

17. $$\begin{aligned} c^2 &= a^2 + b^2 \\ 75^2 &\stackrel{?}{=} 21^2 + 72^2 \\ 5625 &\stackrel{?}{=} 441 + 5184 \\ 5625 &= 5625 \end{aligned}$$
yes

18. $$\begin{aligned} c^2 &= a^2 + b^2 \\ 12^2 &\stackrel{?}{=} 5^2 + (\sqrt{119})^2 \\ 144 &\stackrel{?}{=} 25 + 119 \\ 144 &= 144 \end{aligned}$$
yes

19. $$\begin{aligned} c^2 &= a^2 + b^2 \\ 39^2 &\stackrel{?}{=} 15^2 + 36^2 \\ 1521 &\stackrel{?}{=} 225 + 1296 \\ 1521 &= 1521 \end{aligned}$$
yes

20. $$\begin{aligned} c^2 &= a^2 + b^2 \\ 13^2 &\stackrel{?}{=} (\sqrt{5})^2 + 12^2 \\ 169 &\stackrel{?}{=} 5 + 144 \\ 169 &\neq 149 \end{aligned}$$
no

21. $$\begin{aligned} c^2 &= a^2 + b^2 \\ 12^2 &\stackrel{?}{=} (\sqrt{22})^2 + 10^2 \\ 144 &\stackrel{?}{=} 22 + 100 \\ 144 &\neq 122 \end{aligned}$$
no

22. $$\begin{aligned} c^2 &= a^2 + b^2 \\ 4^2 &\stackrel{?}{=} 2^2 + 3^2 \\ 16 &\stackrel{?}{=} 4 + 9 \\ 16 &\neq 13 \end{aligned}$$
no

23. $$\begin{aligned} c^2 &= a^2 + b^2 \\ (\sqrt{71})^2 &\stackrel{?}{=} (\sqrt{7})^2 + 8^2 \\ 71 &\stackrel{?}{=} 7 + 64 \\ 71 &= 71 \end{aligned}$$
yes

Page 785 Lesson 13-2

1. $$\begin{aligned} \sqrt{50} &= \sqrt{5^2 \cdot 2} \\ &= \sqrt{5^2} \cdot \sqrt{2} \\ &= 5\sqrt{2} \end{aligned}$$

2. $$\begin{aligned} \sqrt{20} &= \sqrt{2^2 \cdot 5} \\ &= \sqrt{2^2} \cdot \sqrt{5} \\ &= 2\sqrt{5} \end{aligned}$$

3. $$\begin{aligned} \sqrt{162} &= \sqrt{9^2 \cdot 2} \\ &= \sqrt{9^2} \cdot \sqrt{2} \\ &= 9\sqrt{2} \end{aligned}$$

4. $$\begin{aligned} \sqrt{700} &= \sqrt{10^2 \cdot 7} \\ &= \sqrt{10^2} \cdot \sqrt{7} \\ &= 10\sqrt{7} \end{aligned}$$

5. $$\begin{aligned} \frac{\sqrt{3}}{\sqrt{5}} &= \frac{\sqrt{3}}{\sqrt{5}} \cdot \frac{\sqrt{5}}{\sqrt{5}} \\ &= \frac{\sqrt{15}}{5} \end{aligned}$$

6. $$\begin{aligned} \frac{\sqrt{72}}{\sqrt{6}} &= \sqrt{\frac{72}{6}} \\ &= \sqrt{12} \\ &= \sqrt{2^2 \cdot 3} \\ &= 2\sqrt{3} \end{aligned}$$

7. $$\begin{aligned} \sqrt{\frac{8}{7}} &= \frac{\sqrt{8}}{\sqrt{7}} \cdot \frac{\sqrt{7}}{\sqrt{7}} \\ &= \frac{\sqrt{56}}{7} \\ &= \frac{\sqrt{2^2 \cdot 2 \cdot 7}}{7} \\ &= \frac{2\sqrt{14}}{7} \end{aligned}$$

8. $$\sqrt{\frac{7}{32}} = \frac{\sqrt{7}}{\sqrt{32}} \cdot \frac{\sqrt{2}}{\sqrt{2}} = \frac{\sqrt{14}}{8}$$

9. $$\begin{aligned} \sqrt{10} \cdot \sqrt{20} &= \sqrt{200} \\ &= \sqrt{10^2 \cdot 2} \\ &= 10\sqrt{2} \end{aligned}$$

10. $\sqrt{7} \cdot \sqrt{3} = \sqrt{21}$

11. $6\sqrt{2} \cdot \sqrt{3} = 6\sqrt{6}$

12. $$\begin{aligned} 5\sqrt{6} \cdot 2\sqrt{3} &= 10\sqrt{18} \\ &= 10\sqrt{3^2 \cdot 2} \\ &= 10(3\sqrt{2}) \\ &= 30\sqrt{2} \end{aligned}$$

13. $\sqrt{4x^2y^3} = \sqrt{4 \cdot x^4 \cdot y^2 \cdot y}$
$= \sqrt{2^2} \cdot \sqrt{x^4} \cdot \sqrt{y^2} \cdot \sqrt{y}$
$= 2x^2y\sqrt{y}$

14. $\sqrt{200m^2y^3} = \sqrt{10^2 \cdot 2 \cdot m^2 \cdot y^2 \cdot y}$
$= \sqrt{10^2} \cdot \sqrt{m^2} \cdot \sqrt{y^2} \cdot \sqrt{2y}$
$= 10|m|y\sqrt{2y}$

15. $\sqrt{12ts^3} = \sqrt{2^2 \cdot 3 \cdot t \cdot s^2 \cdot s}$
$= \sqrt{2^2} \cdot \sqrt{3ts} \cdot \sqrt{s^2}$
$= 2s\sqrt{3ts}$

16. $\sqrt{175a^4b^6} = \sqrt{5^2 \cdot 7 \cdot a^4 \cdot b^6}$
$= \sqrt{5^2} \cdot \sqrt{a^4} \cdot \sqrt{b^6} \cdot \sqrt{7}$
$= 5a^2|b^3|\sqrt{7}$

17. $\sqrt{\frac{54}{g^2}} = \frac{\sqrt{54}}{\sqrt{g^2}}$
$= \frac{\sqrt{3^2 \cdot 6}}{|g|}$
$= \frac{3\sqrt{6}}{|g|}$

18. $\sqrt{99x^3y^7} = \sqrt{3^2 \cdot 11 \cdot x^2 \cdot x \cdot y^6 \cdot y}$
$= \sqrt{3^2} \cdot \sqrt{x^2} \cdot \sqrt{y^2} \cdot \sqrt{11xy}$
$= 3xy^3\sqrt{11xy}$

19. $\sqrt{\frac{32c^5}{9d^2}} = \frac{\sqrt{4^2 \cdot 2c^4 \cdot c}}{\sqrt{3^2d^2}}$
$= \frac{4c^2\sqrt{2c}}{3|d|}$

20. $\sqrt{\frac{27p^4}{3p^2}} = \sqrt{9p^2} = 3|p|$

21. $\frac{1}{3+\sqrt{5}} = \frac{1}{3+\sqrt{5}} \cdot \frac{3-\sqrt{5}}{3-\sqrt{5}}$
$= \frac{3-\sqrt{5}}{3^2-(\sqrt{5})^2}$
$= \frac{3-\sqrt{5}}{9-5} = \frac{3-\sqrt{5}}{4}$

22. $\frac{2}{\sqrt{3}-5} = \frac{2}{\sqrt{3}-5} \cdot \frac{\sqrt{3}+5}{\sqrt{3}+5}$
$= \frac{2\sqrt{3}+2(5)}{(\sqrt{3})^2-5^2}$
$= \frac{2\sqrt{3}+10}{3-25}$
$= \frac{2(\sqrt{3}+5)}{-22}$
$= \frac{\sqrt{3}+5}{-11}$

23. $\frac{\sqrt{3}}{\sqrt{3}-5} = \frac{\sqrt{3}}{\sqrt{3}-5} \cdot \frac{\sqrt{3}+5}{\sqrt{3}+5}$
$= \frac{(\sqrt{3})^2+5\sqrt{3}}{(\sqrt{3})^2-5^2}$
$= \frac{3+5\sqrt{3}}{3-25}$
$= \frac{3+5\sqrt{3}}{-22}$

24. $\frac{\sqrt{6}}{7-2\sqrt{3}} = \frac{\sqrt{6}}{7-2\sqrt{3}} \cdot \frac{7+2\sqrt{3}}{7+2\sqrt{3}}$
$= \frac{7\sqrt{6}+2\sqrt{3}(\sqrt{6})}{7^2-(2\sqrt{3})^2}$
$= \frac{7\sqrt{6}+2\sqrt{18}}{49-12}$
$= \frac{7\sqrt{6}+2\sqrt{3^2 \cdot 2}}{37}$
$= \frac{7\sqrt{6}+2(3\sqrt{2})}{37} = \frac{7\sqrt{6}+6\sqrt{2}}{37}$

25. $(\sqrt{p}+\sqrt{10})^2 = (\sqrt{p})^2 + 2\sqrt{p}\sqrt{10} + (\sqrt{10})^2$
$= p + 2\sqrt{10p} + 10$

26. $(2\sqrt{5}+\sqrt{7})(2\sqrt{5}-\sqrt{7}) = (2\sqrt{5})^2 - (\sqrt{7})^2$
$= 20 - 7 = 13$

27. $(t-2\sqrt{3})(t-\sqrt{3}) = t^2 - t\sqrt{3} - 2t\sqrt{3} + 2(\sqrt{3})^2$
$= t^2 - 3t\sqrt{3} + 6$

Page 785 Lesson 13-3

1. $3\sqrt{11} + 6\sqrt{11} - 2\sqrt{11} = (3+6-2)\sqrt{11}$
$= 7\sqrt{11}$

2. $6\sqrt{13} + 7\sqrt{13} = (6+7)\sqrt{13}$
$= 13\sqrt{13}$

3. $2\sqrt{12} + 5\sqrt{3} = 2\sqrt{2^2 \cdot 3} + 5\sqrt{3}$
$= 2(2\sqrt{3}) + 5\sqrt{3}$
$= 4\sqrt{3} + 5\sqrt{3}$
$= (4+5)\sqrt{3}$
$= 9\sqrt{3}$

4. $9\sqrt{7} - 4\sqrt{2} + 3\sqrt{2} + 5\sqrt{7}$
$= (9+5)\sqrt{7} + (-4+3)\sqrt{2}$
$= 14\sqrt{7} - \sqrt{2}$

5. in simplest form

6. $4\sqrt{8} - 3\sqrt{5} = 4\sqrt{2^2 \cdot 2} - 3\sqrt{5}$
$= 4(2\sqrt{2}) - 3\sqrt{5}$
$= 8\sqrt{2} - 3\sqrt{5}$

7. $2\sqrt{27} - 4\sqrt{12} = 2\sqrt{3^2 \cdot 3} - 4\sqrt{2^2 \cdot 3}$
$= 2(3\sqrt{3}) - 4(2\sqrt{3})$
$= 6\sqrt{3} - 8\sqrt{3}$
$= (6-8)\sqrt{3}$
$= -2\sqrt{3}$

8. $8\sqrt{32} + 4\sqrt{50} = 8\sqrt{4^2 \cdot 2} + 4\sqrt{5^2 \cdot 2}$
$= 8(4\sqrt{2}) + 4(5\sqrt{2})$
$= 32\sqrt{2} + 20\sqrt{2}$
$= (32+20)\sqrt{2}$
$= 52\sqrt{2}$

9. $\sqrt{45} + 6\sqrt{20} = \sqrt{3^2 \cdot 5} + 6\sqrt{2^2 \cdot 5}$
$= 3\sqrt{5} + 6(2\sqrt{5})$
$= 3\sqrt{5} + 12\sqrt{5}$
$= (3+12)\sqrt{5}$
$= 15\sqrt{5}$

10. $2\sqrt{63} - 6\sqrt{28} + 8\sqrt{45}$
$= 2\sqrt{3^2 \cdot 7} - 6\sqrt{2^2 \cdot 7} + 8\sqrt{3^2 \cdot 5}$
$= 2(3\sqrt{7}) - 6(2\sqrt{7}) + 8(3\sqrt{5})$
$= 6\sqrt{7} - 12\sqrt{7} + 24\sqrt{5}$
$= -6\sqrt{7} + 24\sqrt{5}$

11. $14\sqrt{3t} + \sqrt{3t} = (4+8)\sqrt{3t}$
$= 12\sqrt{3t}$

12. $7\sqrt{6x} - 12\sqrt{6x} = (7-12)\sqrt{6x}$
$= -5\sqrt{6x}$

13. $5\sqrt{7} - 3\sqrt{28} = 5\sqrt{7} - 3\sqrt{2^2 \cdot 7}$
$= 5\sqrt{7} - 3(2\sqrt{7})$
$= 5\sqrt{7} - 6\sqrt{7}$
$= (5-6)\sqrt{7}$
$= -\sqrt{7}$

14. $7\sqrt{8} - \sqrt{18} = 7\sqrt{2^2 \cdot 2} - \sqrt{3^2 \cdot 2}$
$= 7(2\sqrt{2}) - 3\sqrt{2}$
$= 14\sqrt{2} - 3\sqrt{2}$
$= (14-3)\sqrt{2}$
$= 11\sqrt{2}$

15. $7\sqrt{98} + 5\sqrt{32} - 2\sqrt{75}$
$= 7\sqrt{7^2 \cdot 2} + 5\sqrt{4^2 \cdot 2} - 2\sqrt{5^2 \cdot 3}$
$= 7(7\sqrt{2}) + 5(4\sqrt{2}) - 2(5\sqrt{3})$
$= 49\sqrt{2} + 20\sqrt{2} - 10\sqrt{3}$
$= 69\sqrt{2} - 10\sqrt{3}$

16. in simplest form

17. $-3\sqrt{20} + 2\sqrt{45} - \sqrt{7}$
$= -3\sqrt{2^2 \cdot 5} + 2\sqrt{3^2 \cdot 5} - \sqrt{7}$
$= -3(2\sqrt{5}) + 2(3\sqrt{5}) - \sqrt{7}$
$= -6\sqrt{5} + 6\sqrt{5} - \sqrt{7}$
$= -\sqrt{7}$

18. $4\sqrt{75} + 6\sqrt{27}$
$= 4\sqrt{5^2 \cdot 3} + 6\sqrt{3^2 \cdot 3}$
$= 4(5\sqrt{3}) + 6(3\sqrt{3})$
$= 20\sqrt{3} + 18\sqrt{3}$
$= (20 + 18)\sqrt{3}$
$= 38\sqrt{3}$

19. $10\sqrt{\frac{1}{5}} - \sqrt{45} - 12\sqrt{\frac{5}{9}}$
$= 10\frac{\sqrt{1}}{\sqrt{5}} \cdot \frac{\sqrt{5}}{\sqrt{5}} - \sqrt{3^2 \cdot 5} - 12\frac{\sqrt{5}}{\sqrt{9}}$
$= 10\left(\frac{\sqrt{5}}{5}\right) - 3\sqrt{5} - 12\left(\frac{\sqrt{5}}{3}\right)$
$= 2\sqrt{5} - 3\sqrt{5} - 4\sqrt{5}$
$= (2 - 3 - 4)\sqrt{5}$
$= -5\sqrt{5}$

20. $\sqrt{15} - \sqrt{\frac{3}{5}} = \sqrt{15} - \frac{\sqrt{3}}{\sqrt{5}} \cdot \frac{\sqrt{5}}{\sqrt{5}}$
$= \sqrt{15} - \frac{\sqrt{15}}{5}$
$= \frac{5\sqrt{15}}{5} - \frac{\sqrt{15}}{5}$
$= \frac{4\sqrt{15}}{5}$

21. $3\sqrt{\frac{1}{3}} - 9\sqrt{\frac{1}{12}} + \sqrt{243}$
$= 3\left(\frac{\sqrt{1}}{\sqrt{3}} \cdot \frac{\sqrt{3}}{\sqrt{3}}\right) - 9\left(\frac{\sqrt{1}}{\sqrt{12}} \cdot \frac{\sqrt{3}}{\sqrt{3}}\right) + \sqrt{9^2 \cdot 3}$
$= 3\left(\frac{\sqrt{3}}{3}\right) - 9\left(\frac{\sqrt{3}}{6}\right) + 9\sqrt{3}$
$= \sqrt{3} - \frac{3}{2}\sqrt{3} + 9\sqrt{3}$
$= \frac{2\sqrt{3}}{2} - \frac{3\sqrt{3}}{2} + \frac{18\sqrt{3}}{2}$
$= \frac{17\sqrt{3}}{2}$

Page 786 Lesson 13-4

1. $\sqrt{5x} = 5$
$(\sqrt{5x})^2 = 5^2$
$5x = 25$
$x = 5$

2. $4\sqrt{7} = \sqrt{-m}$
$(4\sqrt{7})^2 - (\sqrt{-m})^2$
$112 = -m$
$-112 = m$

3. $\sqrt{t} - 5 = 0$
$\sqrt{t} = 5$
$(\sqrt{t})^2 = 5^2$
$t = 25$

4. $\sqrt{3b} + 2 = 0$
$\sqrt{3b} = -2$
no real solution

5. $\sqrt{x - 3} = 6$
$(\sqrt{x - 3})^2 = 6^2$
$x - 3 = 36$
$x = 39$

6. $5 - \sqrt{3x} = 1$
$-\sqrt{3x} = -4$
$\sqrt{3x} = 4$
$(\sqrt{3x})^2 = 4^2$
$3x = 16$
$x = \frac{16}{3}$

7. $2 + 3\sqrt{y} = 13$
$3\sqrt{y} = 11$
$\sqrt{y} = \frac{11}{3}$
$(\sqrt{y})^2 = \left(\frac{11}{3}\right)^2$
$y = \frac{121}{9}$

8. $\sqrt{3g} = 6$
$(\sqrt{3g})^2 = 6^2$
$3g = 36$
$g = 12$

9. $\sqrt{a} - 2 = 0$
$\sqrt{a} = 2$
$(\sqrt{a})^2 = 2^2$
$a = 4$

10. $\sqrt{2j} - 4 = 8$
$\sqrt{2j} = 12$
$(\sqrt{2j})^2 = 12^2$
$2j = 44$
$j = 72$

11. $5 + \sqrt{x} = 9$
$\sqrt{x} = 4$
$(\sqrt{x})^2 = 4^2$
$x = 16$

12. $\sqrt{5y + 4} = 7$
$(\sqrt{5y + 4})^2 = 7^2$
$5y + 4 = 49$
$5y = 49$
$y = 9$

13. $7 + \sqrt{5c} = 9$
$\sqrt{5c} = 2$
$(\sqrt{5c})^2 = 2^2$
$5c = 4$
$c = \frac{4}{5}$

14. $2\sqrt{5t} = 10$
$\sqrt{5t} = 5$
$(\sqrt{5t})^2 = 5^2$
$5t = 25$
$t = 5$

15. $\sqrt{44} = 2\sqrt{p}$
$2\sqrt{11} = 2\sqrt{p}$
$\sqrt{11} = \sqrt{p}$
$(\sqrt{11})^2 = (\sqrt{p})^2$
$11 = p$

16. $4\sqrt{x - 5} = 15$
$\sqrt{x - 5} = \frac{15}{4}$
$(\sqrt{x - 5})^2 = \left(\frac{15}{4}\right)^2$
$x - 5 = \frac{225}{16}$
$x = \frac{305}{16}$

17. $4 - \sqrt{x - 3} = 9$
$-\sqrt{x - 3} = 5$
$\sqrt{x - 3} = -5$
no real solution

18. $\sqrt{10x^2 - 5} = 3x$
$(\sqrt{10x^2 - 5})^2 = (3x)^2$
$10x^2 - 5 = 9x^2$
$-5 = -x^2$
$5 = x^2$
$\pm\sqrt{5} = x$
Since $-\sqrt{5}$ does not satisfy the original equation, $\sqrt{5}$ is the only solution.

19. $\sqrt{2a^2 - 144} = a$
$(\sqrt{2a^2 - 144})^2 = a^2$
$2a^2 - 144 = a^2$
$-144 = -a^2$
$144 = a^2$
$\pm 12 = a$
Since -12 does not satisfy the original equation, 12 is the only solution.

20. $\sqrt{3y + 1} = y - 3$
$(\sqrt{3y + 1})^2 = (y - 3)^2$
$3y + 1 = y^2 - 6y + 9$
$0 = y^2 - 9y + 8$
$0 = (y - 8)(y - 1)$
$y - 8 = 0$ or $y - 1 = 0$
$y = 8 \quad y = 1$
Since 1 does not satisfy the original equation, 8 is the only solution.

21. $\sqrt{2x^2 - 12} = x$
$(\sqrt{2x^2 - 12})^2 = x^2$
$2x^2 - 12 = x^2$
$-12 = -x^2$
$12 = x^2$
$\pm\sqrt{12} = x$
$\pm 2\sqrt{3} = x$
Since $-2\sqrt{3}$ does not satisfy the original equation, $2\sqrt{3}$ is the only solution.

22. $\sqrt{b^2 + 16} + 2b = 5b$
$\sqrt{b^2 + 16} = 3b$
$(\sqrt{b^2 + 16})^2 = (3b)^2$
$b^2 + 16 = 9b^2$
$16 = 8b^2$
$2 = b^2$
$\pm\sqrt{2} = b$
Since $-\sqrt{2}$ does not satisfy the original equation, $\sqrt{2}$ is the only solution.

23. $\sqrt{m + 2} + m = 4$
$\sqrt{m + 2} = 4 - m$
$(\sqrt{m + 2})^2 = (4 - m)^2$
$m + 2 = 16 - 8m + m^2$
$0 = m^2 - 9m + 14$
$0 = (m - 7)(m - 2)$
$m - 7 = 0$ or $m - 2 = 0$
$m = 7$ $\quad m = 2$
Since 7 does not satisfy the original equation, 2 is the only solution.

24. $\sqrt{3 - 2c} + 3 = 2c$
$\sqrt{3 - 2c} = 2c - 3$
$(\sqrt{3 - 2c})^2 = (2c - 3)^2$
$3 - 2c = 4c^2 - 12c + 9$
$0 = 4c^2 - 10c + 6$
$0 = 2c^2 - 5c + 3$
$0 = (2c - 3)(c - 1)$
$2c - 3 = 0$ or $c - 1 = 0$
$c = \frac{3}{2}$ $\quad c = 1$
Since 1 does not satisfy the original equation, $\frac{3}{2}$ is the only solution.

Page 786 Lesson 13-5

1. $d = \sqrt{(x_2 - x_1)^2 + (y_2 - y_1)^2}$
$= \sqrt{(-2 - 4)^2 + (10 - 2)^2}$
$= \sqrt{(-6)^2 + 8^2}$
$= \sqrt{36 + 64}$
$= \sqrt{100}$
$= 10$

2. $d = \sqrt{(x_2 - x_1)^2 + (y_2 - y_1)^2}$
$= \sqrt{(-5 - 7)^2 + (1 - 6)^2}$
$= \sqrt{(-12)^2 + (-5)^2}$
$= \sqrt{144 + 25}$
$= \sqrt{169}$
$= 13$

3. $d = \sqrt{(x_2 - x_1)^2 + (y_2 - y_1)^2}$
$= \sqrt{(4 - 1)^2 + (-2 - 2)^2}$
$= \sqrt{3^2 + (-4)^2}$
$= \sqrt{9 + 16}$
$= \sqrt{25}$
$= 5$

4. $d = \sqrt{(x_2 - x_1)^2 + (y_2 - y_1)^2}$
$= \sqrt{(-2 - 4)^2 + [4 - (-2)]^2}$
$= \sqrt{(-6)^2 + 6^2}$
$= \sqrt{36 + 36}$
$= \sqrt{72}$
$= 6\sqrt{2}$ or 8.49

5. $d = \sqrt{(x_2 - x_1)^2 + (y_2 - y_1)^2}$
$= \sqrt{(-2 - 3)^2 + (-1 - 1)^2}$
$= \sqrt{(-5)^2 + (-2)^2}$
$= \sqrt{25 + 4}$
$= \sqrt{29}$ or 5.39

6. $d = \sqrt{(x_2 - x_1)^2 + (y_2 - y_1)^2}$
$= \sqrt{(-2 - 7)^2 + [4 - (-8)]^2}$
$= \sqrt{(-9)^2 + (12)^2}$
$= \sqrt{81 + 144}$
$= \sqrt{225}$
$= 15$

7. $d = \sqrt{(x_2 - x_1)^2 + (y_2 - y_1)^2}$
$= \sqrt{[-5 - (-9)]^2 + (0 - 6)^2}$
$= \sqrt{4^2 + (-6)^2}$
$= \sqrt{16 + 36}$
$= \sqrt{52}$
$= 2\sqrt{13}$ or 7.21

8. $d = \sqrt{(x_2 - x_1)^2 + (y_2 - y_1)^2}$
$= \sqrt{(5 - 5)^2 + (-1 - 13)^2}$
$= \sqrt{0^2 + (-14)^2}$
$= \sqrt{196}$
$= 14$

9. $d = \sqrt{(x_2 - x_1)^2 + (y_2 - y_1)^2}$
$= \sqrt{(2 - 10)^2 + (-3 - 8)^2}$
$= \sqrt{(-8)^2 + (-11)^2}$
$= \sqrt{64 + 121}$
$= \sqrt{185}$ or 13.60

10. $d = \sqrt{(x_2 - x_1)^2 + (y_2 - y_1)^2}$
$= \sqrt{(-7 - 2)^2 + [5 - (-7)]^2}$
$= \sqrt{(-9)^2 + 12^2}$
$= \sqrt{81 + 144}$
$= \sqrt{225}$
$= 15$

11. $d = \sqrt{(x_2 - x_1)^2 + (y_2 - y_1)^2}$
$= \sqrt{[-6 - (-5)]^2 + (-2 - 4)^2}$
$= \sqrt{(-1)^2 + (-6)^2}$
$= \sqrt{1 + 36}$
$= \sqrt{37}$ or 6.08

12. $d = \sqrt{(x_2 - x_1)^2 + (y_2 - y_1)^2}$
$= \sqrt{(8 - 3)^2 + (-10 - 2)^2}$
$= \sqrt{5^2 + (-12)^2}$
$= \sqrt{25 + 144}$
$= \sqrt{169}$
$= 13$

13. $d = \sqrt{(x_2 - x_1)^2 + (y_2 - y_1)^2}$
$= \sqrt{(4 - 7)^2 + [3 - (-9)^2}$
$= \sqrt{(-3)^2 + 6^2}$
$= \sqrt{9 + 36}$
$= \sqrt{45}$
$= 3\sqrt{5}$ or 6.71

14. $d = \sqrt{(x_2 - x_1)^2 + (y_2 - y_1)^2}$
$= \sqrt{(6 - 9)^2 + (3 - 7)^2}$
$= \sqrt{(-3)^2 + (-4)^2}$
$= \sqrt{9 + 16}$
$= \sqrt{25}$
$= 5$

15. $d = \sqrt{(x_2 - x_1)^2 + (y_2 - y_1)^2}$
$= \sqrt{(10 - 9)^2 + (0 - 7)^2}$
$= \sqrt{12 + (-7)^2}$
$= \sqrt{1 + 49}$
$= \sqrt{50}$
$= 5\sqrt{2}$ or 7.07

16. $d = \sqrt{(x_2 - x_1)^2 + (y_2 - y_1)^2}$
$= \sqrt{[2 - (-3)]^2 + (-1 - 3)^2}$
$= \sqrt{5^2 + (-4)^2}$
$= \sqrt{25 + 16}$
$= \sqrt{41}$ or 6.40

17. $d = \sqrt{(x_2 - x_1)^2 + (y_2 - y_1)^2}$
$= \sqrt{(-5 - 3)^2 + [4 - (-2)]^2}$
$= \sqrt{(-8)^2 + 6^2}$
$= \sqrt{64 + 36}$
$= \sqrt{100}$
$= 10$

18. $d = \sqrt{(x_2 - x_1)^2 + (y_2 - y_1)^2}$
$= \sqrt{(0 - 0)^2 + (-9 - 7)^2}$
$= \sqrt{0^2 + (-16)^2}$
$= \sqrt{256}$
$= 16$

19. $d = \sqrt{(x_2 - x_1)^2 + (y_2 - y_1)^2}$
$= \sqrt{(-1 - 8)^2 + (7 - 4)^2}$
$= \sqrt{(-9)^2 + 3^2}$
$= \sqrt{81 + 9}$
$= \sqrt{90}$
$= 3\sqrt{10}$ or 9.49

20. $d = \sqrt{(x_2 - x_1)^2 + (y_2 - y_1)^2}$
$= \sqrt{(9 - 3)^2 + [2 - (-3)^2}$
$= \sqrt{(-12)^2 + 5^2}$
$= \sqrt{144 + 25}$
$= \sqrt{169}$
$= 13$

21. $d = \sqrt{(x_2 - x_1)^2 + (y_2 - y_1)^2}$
$= \sqrt{(3\sqrt{2} - 5\sqrt{2})^2 + (7 - 9)^2}$
$= \sqrt{(-2\sqrt{2})^2 + (-2)^2}$
$= \sqrt{8 + 4}$
$= \sqrt{12}$
$= 2\sqrt{3}$ or 3.46

22. $d = \sqrt{(x_2 - x_1)^2 + (y_2 - y_1)^2}$
$= \sqrt{(6 - 10)^2 + (3 - 0)^2}$
$= \sqrt{(-4)^2 + 3^2}$
$= \sqrt{16 + 9}$
$= \sqrt{25}$
$= 5$

23. $d = \sqrt{(x_2 - x_1)^2 + (y_2 - y_1)^2}$
$= \sqrt{(5 - 3)^2 + (-5 - 6)^2}$
$= \sqrt{2^2 + (-11)^2}$
$= \sqrt{4 + 121}$
$= \sqrt{125}$
$= 5\sqrt{5}$ or 11.18

24. $d = \sqrt{(x_2 - x_1)^2 + (y_2 - y_1)^2}$
$= \sqrt{(-4 - 5)^2 + (2 - 4)^2}$
$= \sqrt{(-9)^2 + (-2)^2}$
$= \sqrt{81 + 4}$
$= \sqrt{85}$ or 9.22

Page 786 Lesson 13-6

1. Step 1: $\frac{6}{2} = 3$
Step 2: $3^2 = 9$
Step 3: $a^2 + 6a + 9$
$c = 9$

2. Step 1: $\frac{10}{2} = 5$
Step 2: $5^2 = 25$
Step 3: $x^2 + 10x + 25$
$c = 25$

3. Step 1: $\frac{12}{2} = 6$
Step 2: $6^2 = 36$
Step 3: $t^2 + 12t + 36$
$c = 36$

4. Step 1: $\frac{9}{2}$
Step 2: $\left(\frac{9}{2}\right)^2 = \frac{81}{4}$
Step 3: $y^2 - 9y + \frac{81}{4}$
$c = \frac{81}{4}$

5. Step 1: $\frac{14}{2} = 7$

Step 2: $7^2 = 49$

Step 3: $p^2 - 14p + 49$

$c = 49$

6. Step 1: $\frac{5}{2}$

Step 2: $\left(\frac{5}{2}\right)^2 = \frac{25}{4}$

Step 3: $b^2 + 5b + \frac{25}{4}$

$c = \frac{25}{4}$

7.
$$\begin{aligned} x^2 - 4x &= 5 \\ x^2 - 4x + 4 &= 5 + 4 \\ (x - 2)^2 &= 9 \\ x - 2 &= \pm 3 \\ x &= 2 \pm 3 \end{aligned}$$
$x = 2 + 3$ or $x = 2 - 3$

$x = 5$ $\quad$ $x = -1$

8.
$$\begin{aligned} t^2 + 12t - 45 &= 0 \\ t^2 + 12t &= 45 \\ t^2 + 12t + 36 &= 45 + 36 \\ (t + 6)^2 &= 81 \\ t + 6 &= \pm 9 \\ t &= -6 \pm 9 \end{aligned}$$
$t = -6 + 9$ or $t = -6 - 9$

$t = 3$ $\quad$ $t = -15$

9.
$$\begin{aligned} b^2 + 4b - 12 &= 0 \\ b^2 + 4b &= 12 \\ b^2 + 4b + 4 &= 12 + 4 \\ (b + 2)^2 &= 16 \\ b + 2 &= \pm 4 \\ b &= -2 \pm 4 \end{aligned}$$
$b = -2 + 4$ or $b = -2 - 4$

$b = 2$ $\quad$ $b = -6$

10.
$$\begin{aligned} a^2 - 8a - 84 &= 0 \\ a^2 - 8a &= 84 \\ a^2 - 8a + 16 &= 84 + 16 \\ (a - 4)^2 &= 100 \\ a - 4 &= \pm 10 \\ a &= 4 \pm 10 \end{aligned}$$
$a = 4 + 10$ or $a = 4 - 10$

$a = 14$ $\quad$ $a = -6$

11.
$$\begin{aligned} c^2 + 6 &= -5c \\ c^2 + 5c &= -6 \\ c^2 + 5c + \frac{25}{4} &= -6 + \frac{25}{4} \\ \left(c + \frac{5}{2}\right)^2 &= \frac{1}{4} \\ c + \frac{5}{2} &= \pm\frac{1}{2} \\ c &= -\frac{5}{2} \pm \frac{1}{2} \end{aligned}$$
$c = -\frac{5}{2} + \frac{1}{2}$ or $c = -\frac{5}{2} - \frac{1}{2}$

$c = -2$ $\quad$ $c = -3$

12.
$$\begin{aligned} t^2 - 7t &= -10 \\ t^2 - 7t + \frac{49}{4} &= -10 + \frac{49}{4} \\ \left(t - \frac{7}{2}\right)^2 &= \frac{9}{4} \\ t - \frac{7}{2} &= \pm \frac{3}{2} \\ t &= \frac{7}{2} \pm \frac{3}{2} \end{aligned}$$
$t = \frac{7}{2} + \frac{3}{2}$ or $t = \frac{7}{2} - \frac{3}{2}$

$t = 5$ $\quad$ $t = 2$

13.
$$\begin{aligned} p^2 - 8p + 5 &= 0 \\ p^2 - 8p &= -5 \\ p^2 - 8p + 16 &= -5 + 16 \\ (p - 4)^2 &= 11 \\ p - 4 &= \pm\sqrt{11} \\ p &= 4 \pm\sqrt{11} \end{aligned}$$

14.
$$\begin{aligned} a^2 + 4a + 2 &= 0 \\ a^2 + 4a &= -2 \\ a^2 + 4a + 4 &= -2 + 4 \\ (a + 2)^2 &= 2 \\ a + 2 &= \pm\sqrt{2} \\ a &= -2 \pm\sqrt{2} \end{aligned}$$

15.
$$\begin{aligned} 2y^2 + 7y - 4 &= 0 \\ y^2 + \frac{7}{2}y - 2 &= 0 \\ y^2 + \frac{7}{2}y &= 2 \\ y^2 + \frac{7}{2}y + \frac{49}{16} &= 2 + \frac{49}{16} \\ \left(y + \frac{7}{4}\right)^2 &= \frac{81}{16} \\ y + \frac{7}{4} &= \pm\frac{9}{4} \\ y &= -\frac{7}{4} \pm \frac{9}{4} \end{aligned}$$
$y = -\frac{7}{4} + \frac{9}{4}$ or $y = -\frac{7}{4} - \frac{9}{4}$

$y = \frac{1}{2}$ $\quad$ $y = -4$

16.
$$\begin{aligned} t^2 + 3t &= 40 \\ t^2 + 3t + \frac{9}{4} &= 40 + \frac{9}{4} \\ \left(t + \frac{3}{2}\right)^2 &= \frac{169}{4} \\ t + \frac{3}{2} &= \pm\frac{13}{2} \\ t &= -\frac{3}{2} \pm \frac{13}{2} \end{aligned}$$
$t = -\frac{3}{2} + \frac{13}{2}$ or $t = -\frac{3}{2} - \frac{13}{2}$

$t = 5$ $\quad$ $t = -8$

17.
$$\begin{aligned} x^2 + 8x - 9 &= 0 \\ x^2 + 8x &= 9 \\ x^2 + 8x + 16 &= 9 + 16 \\ (x + 4)^2 &= 25 \\ x + 4 &= \pm 5 \\ x &= -4 \pm 5 \end{aligned}$$
$x = -4 + 5$ or $x = -4 - 5$

$x = 1$ $\quad$ $x = -9$

18.
$$\begin{aligned} y^2 + 5y - 84 &= 0 \\ y^2 + 5y &= 84 \\ y^2 + 5y + \frac{25}{4} &= 84 + \frac{25}{4} \\ \left(y + \frac{5}{2}\right)^2 &= \frac{361}{4} \\ y + \frac{5}{2} &= \pm\frac{19}{2} \\ y &= -\frac{5}{2} \pm \frac{19}{2} \end{aligned}$$
$y = -\frac{5}{2} + \frac{19}{2}$ or $y = -\frac{5}{2} - \frac{19}{2}$

$y = 7$ $\quad$ $y = -12$

19.
$$\begin{aligned} x^2 + 2x - 6 &= 0 \\ x^2 + 2x &= 6 \\ x^2 + 2x + 1 &= 6 + 1 \\ (x + 1)^2 &= 7 \\ x + 1 &= \pm\sqrt{7} \\ x &= -1 \pm\sqrt{7} \end{aligned}$$

20. $t^2 + 12t + 32 = 0$

$$t^2 + 12t = -32$$
$$t^2 + 12t + 36 = -32 + 36$$
$$(t + 6)^2 = 4$$
$$t + 6 = \pm 2$$
$$t = -6 \pm 2$$
$$t = -6 + 2 \quad \text{or} \quad t = -6 - 2$$
$$t = -4 \qquad\qquad t = -8$$

21. $2x - 3x^2 = -8$

$$-3x^2 + 2x = -8$$
$$x^2 - \frac{2}{3}x = \frac{8}{3}$$
$$x^2 - \frac{2}{3}x + \frac{1}{9} = \frac{8}{3} + \frac{1}{9}$$
$$\left(x - \frac{1}{3}\right)^2 = \frac{25}{9}$$
$$x - \frac{1}{3} = \pm\frac{5}{3}$$
$$x = \frac{1}{3} \pm \frac{5}{3}$$
$$x = \frac{1}{3} + \frac{5}{3} \quad \text{or} \quad x = \frac{1}{3} - \frac{5}{3}$$
$$x = 2 \qquad\qquad x = -\frac{4}{3}$$

22. $2y^2 - y - 9 = 0$

$$y^2 - \frac{1}{2}y - \frac{9}{2} = 0$$
$$y^2 - \frac{1}{2}y = \frac{9}{2}$$
$$y^2 - \frac{1}{2}y + \frac{1}{16} = \frac{9}{2} + \frac{1}{16}$$
$$\left(y - \frac{1}{4}\right)^2 = \frac{73}{16}$$
$$y - \frac{1}{4} = \pm\frac{\sqrt{73}}{4}$$
$$y = \frac{1}{4} \pm \frac{\sqrt{73}}{4}$$
$$= \frac{1 + \sqrt{73}}{4}$$

23. $2z^2 - 5z - 4 = 0$

$$z^2 - \frac{5}{2}z - 2 = 0$$
$$z^2 - \frac{5}{2}z = 2$$
$$z^2 - \frac{5}{2}z + \frac{25}{16} = 2 + \frac{25}{16}$$
$$\left(z - \frac{5}{4}\right)^2 = \frac{57}{16}$$
$$z - \frac{5}{4} = \pm\frac{\sqrt{57}}{4}$$
$$z = \frac{5}{4} \pm \frac{\sqrt{57}}{4}$$
$$z = \frac{5 \pm \sqrt{57}}{4}$$

24. $4t^2 - 6t - \frac{1}{2} = 0$

$$t^2 - \frac{3}{2}t - \frac{1}{8} = 0$$
$$t^2 - \frac{3}{2}t = \frac{1}{8}$$
$$t^2 - \frac{3}{2}t + \frac{9}{16} = \frac{1}{8} + \frac{9}{16}$$
$$\left(t - \frac{3}{4}\right)^2 = \frac{11}{16}$$
$$t - \frac{3}{4} = \pm\frac{\sqrt{11}}{4}$$
$$t = \frac{3}{4} \pm \frac{\sqrt{11}}{4}$$
$$t = \frac{3 \pm \sqrt{11}}{4}$$

Chapter Tests

Page 787 Chapter 1 Test

1. $x + 13$ **2.** $\frac{1}{x^2}$ **3.** $x^3 - 7$ **4.** $5x^2$

5. 

6. $13 + 3 = 16$
$16 + 3 = 19$
16, 19

7. $17 + 9 = 26$
$26 + 11 = 37$
26, 37

8. $5^2 - 12 = 25 - 12$
$= 13$

9. $(0.5)^3 + 2.7 = 0.125 + 2 \cdot 7$
$= 0.125 + 14$
$= 14.125$

10. $\frac{2}{5}(16 - 9) = \frac{2}{5}(7)$
$= \frac{14}{5}$
$= 2\frac{4}{5}$

11. $a^2b + c = (2)^2(0.5) + 3$
$= 4(0.5) + 3$
$= 2 + 3$
$= 5$

12. $(cd)^3 = \left(3 \cdot \frac{4}{3}\right)^3$
$= 4^3$
$= 64$

13. $(a + d)c = \left(2 + \frac{4}{3}\right)(3)$
$= \left(\frac{6}{3} + \frac{4}{3}\right)(3)$
$= \left(\frac{10}{3}\right)(3)$
$= \frac{30}{3}$
$= 10$

14. $y = (4.5 + 0.8) - 3.2$
$= 5.3 - 3.2$
$= 2.1$

15. $4^2 - 3(4 - 2) = y$
$16 - 3(2) = y$
$16 - 6 = y$
$10 = y$

16. $\frac{2^3 - 1^3}{2 + 1} = y$
$\frac{8 - 1}{2 + 1} = y$
$\frac{7}{3} = y$

17. additive identity **18.** multiplicative inverse

19. transitive **20.** associative (×)

21. commutative (×) **22.** commutative (+)

23. $2m + 3m = (2 + 3)m$
$= 5m$

24. $4x + 2y - 2x + y = 4x - 2x + 2y + y$
$= (4 - 2)x + (2 + 1)y$
$= 2x + 3y$

25. $3(2a + b) - 1.5a - 1.5b$
$= 3(2a) + 3(b) - 1.5a - 1.5b$
$= 6a + 3b - 1.5a - 1.5b$
$= 6a - 1.5a + 3b - 1.5b$
$= (6 - 1.5)a + (3 - 1.5)b$
$= 4.5a + 1.5b$

26. 11, 14, 16, 18, 18, 20, 23, 23, 23, 25, 27, 29, 30, 30, 32, 36

27. 23

28. 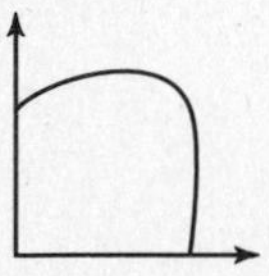

29. 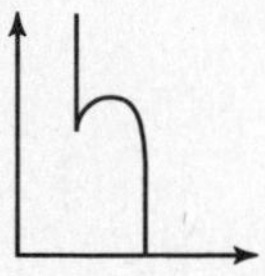

30. 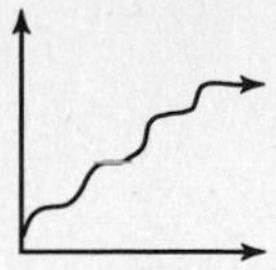

31. $d = rt$
$d = 50 \cdot 5$
$= 250$ miles

32. $A = \pi r^2$
$= 3.14(4)^2$
$= 3.14(16)$
$= 50.24 \text{ in}^2$

33. $P = 2l + 2w$
$= 2(11) + 2(14)$
$= 22 + 28$
$= 50$ yd

Page 788 Chapter 2 Test

1. $12 - 19 = 12 + (-19)$
$= -7$

2. $-21 + (-34) = -55$

3. $1.654 + (-2.367) = -0.713$

4. $-\frac{7}{16} - \frac{3}{8} = -\frac{7}{16} - \frac{3(2)}{8(2)}$
$= -\frac{7}{16} - \frac{3(2)}{16}$
$= \frac{-7 - 6}{16}$
$= -\frac{13}{16}$

5. $18b + 13xy - 46b = 18b - 46b + 13xy$
$= (18 - 46)b + 13xy$
$= -28b + 13xy$

6. $6.32 - (-7.41) = 6.32 + 7.41$
$= 13.73$

7. $\frac{5}{8} + \left(-\frac{3}{16}\right) + \left(-\frac{3}{4}\right) = \frac{5(2)}{8(2)} + \left(-\frac{3}{16}\right) + \frac{-3(4)}{4(4)}$
$= \frac{5(2)}{16} + \left(\frac{3}{16}\right) + \frac{-3(4)}{16}$
$= \frac{10 - 3 - 12}{16}$
$= -\frac{5}{16}$

8. $32y + (-73y) = (32 - 73)y$
$= -41y$

9. $|-28 + (-13)| = |-41|$
$= 41$

10. $\begin{bmatrix} -8 & 5 \\ 2 & -3 \end{bmatrix} + \begin{bmatrix} 3 & 6 \\ -4 & -7 \end{bmatrix} = \begin{bmatrix} -8 + 3 & 5 + 6 \\ 2 + (-4) & -3 + (-7) \end{bmatrix}$
$= \begin{bmatrix} -5 & 11 \\ -2 & -10 \end{bmatrix}$

11. $\begin{bmatrix} 1 & 0 \\ -9 & 3 \end{bmatrix} - \begin{bmatrix} 5 & 8 \\ -4 & 2 \end{bmatrix} = \begin{bmatrix} 1 - 5 & 0 - 8 \\ -9 - (-4) & 3 - 2 \end{bmatrix}$
$= \begin{bmatrix} -4 & -8 \\ -5 & 1 \end{bmatrix}$

12. $-x - 38 = -(-2) - 38$
$= 2 - 38$
$= -36$

13. $\left|-\frac{1}{2} + z\right| = \left|-\frac{1}{2} + \frac{1}{4}\right|$
$= \left|-\frac{2}{4} + \frac{1}{4}\right|$
$= \left|-\frac{1}{4}\right|$
$= \frac{1}{4}$

14. $mp - k = (-12)(1.5) - (-8)$
$= -18 + 8$
$= -10$

15. $w^2 - 15 = (5)^2 - 15$
$= 25 - 15$
$= 10$

16. $>$

17. $\frac{9}{20} \underline{?} \frac{7}{15}$
$9(15) \underline{?} 20(7)$
$135 < 140$
$\frac{9}{20} < \frac{7}{15}$

18. $<$

19. Sample answer: $-\frac{2}{3} = -\frac{56}{84}, -\frac{9}{14} = -\frac{54}{84}; -\frac{55}{84}$

20. Sample answer: $\frac{4}{7} = \frac{32}{56}, \frac{9}{4} = \frac{126}{56}; \frac{79}{56}$

21. Sample answer: $\frac{12}{7} = \frac{96}{56}, \frac{15}{8} = \frac{105}{56}; \frac{99}{56}$

22. $\frac{8(-3)}{2} = \frac{-24}{2}$
$= -12$

23. $(-5)(-2)(-2) - (-6)(-3) = -20 - 18$
$= -38$

24. $\frac{2}{3}\left(\frac{1}{2}\right) - \left(-\frac{3}{2}\right)\left(-\frac{2}{3}\right) = \frac{1}{3} - 1$
$= \frac{1}{3} - \frac{3}{3}$
$= -\frac{2}{3}$

25. $\frac{70x - 30y}{-5} = \frac{70x}{-5} - \frac{30y}{-5}$
$= -14x + 6y$

26. $\frac{7}{-\frac{2}{5}} = 7 \div -\frac{2}{5}$
$= 7 \cdot -\frac{5}{2}$
$= -\frac{35}{2}$

27. $\frac{3}{4}(8x + 12y) - \frac{5}{7}(21x - 35y)$
$= \frac{3}{4}(8x) + \frac{3}{4}(12y) + \left(-\frac{5}{7}\right)(21x) + \left(-\frac{5}{7}\right)(-35y)$
$= 6x + 9y - 15x + 25y$
$= 6x - 15x + 9y + 25y$
$= -9x + 34y$

28. $\pm\frac{4}{9} \approx 0.44$

29. 6.32

30. 1.7

31a.

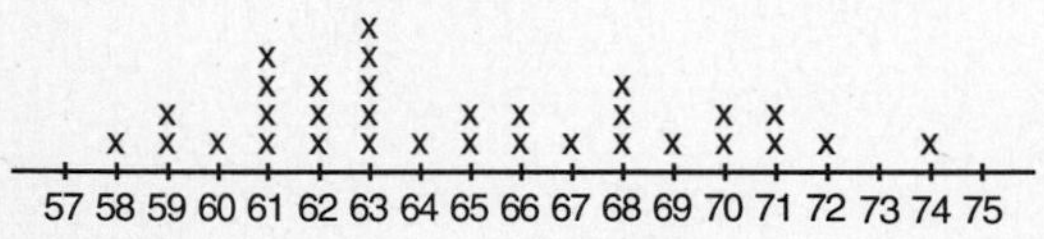

31b. 63

32. Let w = number of weeks on sale;
$380.25 - 18.25w = 252.50$.

33. The number r equals the cube of the difference of a and b.

Page 789 Chapter 3 Test

1. $-15 - k = 8$
$-15 - k + 15 = 8 + 15$
$-k = 23$
$-1(-k) = -1(23)$
$k = -23$

2. $-1.2x = 7.2$
$\frac{-1.2x}{-1.2} = \frac{7.2}{-1.2}$
$x = -6$

3. $\frac{3}{4}y = -27$
$\frac{4}{3}\left(\frac{3}{4}y\right) = \frac{4}{3}(-27)$
$y = -36$

4. $\frac{t - 7}{4} = 11$
$4\left(\frac{t - 7}{4}\right) = 4(11)$
$t - 7 = 44$
$t - 7 + 7 = 44 + 7$
$t = 51$

5. $-12 = 7 - \frac{y}{3}$
$-12 - 7 = 7 - \frac{y}{3} - 7$
$-19 = -\frac{y}{3}$
$-3(-19) = -3\left(-\frac{y}{3}\right)$
$57 = y$

6. $k - 16 = -21$
$k - 16 + 16 = -21 + 16$
$k = -5$

7. $t - (-3.4) = -5.3$
$t + 3.4 = -5.3$
$t + 3.4 - 3.4 = -5.3 - 3.4$
$t = -8.7$

8. $-3(x + 5) = 8x + 18$
$-3x - 15 = 8x + 18$
$-3x - 15 + 3x = 8x + 18 + 3x$
$-15 = 11x + 18$
$-15 - 18 = 11x + 18 - 18$
$-33 = 11x$
$-\frac{33}{11} = \frac{11x}{11}$
$-3 = x$

9. $2 - \frac{1}{4}(b - 12) = 9$
$2 - \frac{1}{4}b + 3 = 9$
$-\frac{1}{4}b + 5 = 9$
$-\frac{1}{4}b + 5 - 5 = 9 - 5$
$-\frac{1}{4}b = 4$
$-4\left(-\frac{1}{4}b\right) = -4(4)$
$b = -16$

10. $\frac{r}{5} - 3 = \frac{2r}{5} + 16$
$\frac{r}{5} - \frac{r}{5} - 3 = \frac{2r}{5} - \frac{r}{5} + 16$
$-3 = \frac{r}{5} + 16$
$-3 - 16 = \frac{r}{5} + 16 - 16$
$-19 = \frac{r}{5}$
$5(-19) = 5\left(\frac{r}{5}\right)$
$-95 = r$

11. $25 - 7w = 46$
$25 - 7w - 25 = 46 - 25$
$-7w = 21$
$\frac{-7w}{-7} = \frac{21}{-7}$
$w = -3$

12. $-w + 11 = 4.6$
$-w + 11 - 11 = 4.6 - 11$
$-w = -6.4$
$-1(-w) = -1(-6.4)$
$w = 6.4$

13. mean $= \frac{67 + 31 + 15 + 49 + 31 + 35 + 42 + 27}{8} = \frac{297}{8}$
$= 37.125$
15 27 31 (31 35) 42 49 67
median $= \frac{31 + 35}{2} = \frac{66}{2} = 33$
mode: 31

14. mean $= \frac{3030}{15} = 202$
median: 208
mode: 215

15. Let x = the other integer.
$-84 + x = -23$
$-84 + 84 + x = -23 + 84$
$x = 61$

16. Let x = the number.
$-\frac{2}{3}x = \frac{8}{5}$
$-\frac{3}{2}\left(-\frac{2}{3}x\right) = -\frac{3}{2}\left(\frac{8}{5}\right)$
$x = -\frac{12}{5}$

17. Let x = the number.
$x - 37 = -65$
$x - 37 + 37 = -65 + 37$
$x = -28$

18. Let x = the measure of the third angle.
$180 = 23 + 121 + x$
$180 = 144 + x$
$180 - 144 = 144 + x - 144$
$36° = x$

19. Let x = the first consecutive odd integer.
Then $x + 2$ = the second consecutive odd integer.
$x + (x + 2) = 172$
$2x + 2 = 172$
$2x + 2 - 2 = 172 - 2$
$2x = 170$
$x = 85$
$x + 2 = 85 + 2$
$= 87$

20. $h = at - 0.25vt^2$
$h + 0.25vt^2 = at - 0.25vt^2 + 0.25vt^2$
$h + 0.25vt^2 = at$
$\frac{h + 0.25vt^2}{t} = \frac{at}{t}$
$\frac{h + 0.25vt^2}{t} = a$

21. $A = \frac{1}{2}(b + B)h$
$2A = 2\left(\frac{1}{2}\right)(b + B)h$
$2A = (b + B)h$
$\frac{2A}{b + B} = \frac{(b + B)h}{(b + B)}$
$\frac{2A}{b + B} = h$

22. Let x = one of the angles;
let $4x - 37$ = the other angle.
$x + 4x - 37 = 180$
$5x - 37 = 180$
$5x - 37 + 37 = 180 + 37$
$5x = 217$
$x = 43.4°$
$4x - 37 = 4(43.4) - 37$ or $136.6°$

23. Let x = the score on his next test.
$\frac{338 + x}{5} = 82$
$5\left(\frac{338 + x}{5}\right) = 5(82)$
$338 + x = 410$
$338 + x - 338 = 410 - 338$
$x = 72$
He would need a 72%.

24. Let x = the number of flavored cartons.
Then $6x$ = the number of plain cartons.
$x + 6x = 49$
$7x = 49$
$\frac{7x}{7} = \frac{49}{7}$
$x = 7$
$6(7) = 42$
There are 42 cartons of plain yogurt.

25. Let x = the cost of a can of orange juice.
$2(0.99) + 2.59 + 3x - 0.50 = 8.51$
$3x + 4.07 = 8.51$
$3x + 4.07 - 4.07 = 8.51 - 4.07$
$3x = 4.44$
$x = 1.48$
Each can of orange juice costs $1.48.

Page 790 Chapter 4 Test

1. $\frac{2}{5} = \frac{x - 3}{-2}$
$2(-2) = 5(x - 3)$
$-4 = 5x - 15$
$-4 + 15 = 5x + 15$
$11 = 5x$
$\frac{11}{5} = x$

2. $\frac{n}{4} = \frac{3.25}{52}$
$52n = 4(3.25)$
$52n = 13$
$n = \frac{13}{52}$ or $\frac{1}{4}$

3. $\frac{x - 3}{x + 5} = \frac{9}{11}$
$11(x - 3) = 9(x + 5)$
$11x - 33 = 9x + 45$
$2x - 33 = 45$
$2x = 78$
$x = 39$

4. $\frac{x + 1}{-3} = \frac{x - 4}{5}$
$5(x + 1) = -3(x - 4)$
$5x + 5 = -3x + 12$
$8x + 5 = 12$
$8x = 7$
$x = \frac{7}{8}$

5. $x = \frac{6.5}{100} \cdot 80$
$= \frac{520}{100}$
$= 5.2$
6.5% of 80 is 5.2.

6. $\frac{42}{126} = \frac{r}{100}$
$42(100) = 126r$
$4200 = 126r$
42 is $33\frac{1}{3}$% of 126.

7. $84 = \frac{60}{100} \cdot x$
$\left(\frac{100}{60}\right)(84) = \left(\frac{60}{100}x\right)\left(\frac{100}{60}\right)$
$140 = x$
84 is 60% of 140.

8. $x - 0.20x = 16$
$0.80x = 16$
$x = \frac{16}{0.80}$
$x = 20$
20 decreased by 20% is 16.

9. $\frac{24}{8} = \frac{r}{100}$
$24(100) = 8r$
$2400 = 8r$
$300 = r$
24 is 300% of 8.

10. $54 = 0.20x + x$
$54 = 1.20x$
$45 = x$
54 is 20% more than 45.

11. $\frac{60-45}{60} = \frac{15}{60} = \frac{r}{100}$

$15(100) = 60r$

$1500 = 60r$

$25 = r$

Percent of decrease is 25%.

12. $p - 0.15p = 3.40$

$0.85p = 3.40$

$p = \$4$

13. $\frac{c}{h} = \frac{a}{j}$

$\frac{20}{15} = \frac{a}{12}$

$20(12) = 15a$

$240 = 15a$

$16 = a$

$\frac{c}{h} = \frac{b}{k}$

$\frac{20}{15} = \frac{b}{16}$

$20(16) = 15b$

$320 = 15b$

$\frac{64}{3} = b$

14. $\frac{c}{h} = \frac{a}{j}$

$\frac{12}{10} = \frac{6}{j}$

$12j = 6(10)$

$12j = 60$

$j = 5$

$\frac{c}{h} = \frac{b}{k}$

$\frac{12}{10} = \frac{13}{k}$

$12k = 13(10)$

$12k = 130$

$k = \frac{65}{6}$

15. $\frac{c}{h} = \frac{b}{k}$

$\frac{6.5}{h} = \frac{7.5}{5}$

$6.5(5) = 7.5h$

$32.5 = 7.5h$

$\frac{13}{3} = h$

$h = 4.\overline{3}$

$\frac{b}{k} = \frac{a}{j}$

$\frac{7.5}{5} = \frac{4.5}{j}$

$7.5j = 4.5(5)$

$7.5j = 22.5$

$j = 3$

16. $\frac{c}{h} = \frac{b}{k}$

$\frac{4\frac{1}{2}}{1\frac{1}{2}} = \frac{b}{2\frac{1}{4}}$

$4\frac{1}{2}\left(2\frac{1}{4}\right) = 1\frac{1}{2}b$

$\frac{9}{2}\left(\frac{9}{4}\right) = \frac{3}{2}b$

$\frac{81}{8} = \frac{3}{2}b$

$\frac{27}{4} = b$

$6\frac{3}{4} = b$

$\frac{c}{h} = \frac{a}{j}$

$\frac{4\frac{1}{2}}{1\frac{1}{2}} = \frac{3}{j}$

$4\frac{1}{2}j = 3\left(1\frac{1}{2}\right)$

$\frac{9}{2}j = 3\left(\frac{3}{2}\right)$

$\frac{9}{2}j = \frac{9}{2}$

$j = 1$

17. $m\angle A = 90 - 42$

$= 48°$

$\cos 42° = \frac{a}{10}$

$0.743 = \frac{a}{10}$

$7.4 \approx a$

$\sin 42° = \frac{b}{10}$

$0.6691 = \frac{b}{10}$

$6.7 \approx b$

18. $\tan A = \frac{15}{21}$

$\tan A \approx 0.7143$

$m\angle A \approx 36°$

$\sin 36° = \frac{15}{c}$

$0.5878c \approx 15$

$c \approx 25.5$

$m\angle B \approx 90 - 36$

$\approx 54°$

19. $\cos A = \frac{21}{29}$

$\cos A \approx 0.7241$

$m\angle A \approx 44°$

$\sin 44° = \frac{a}{29}$

$0.6947 \approx \frac{a}{29}$

$20 \approx a$

$m\angle B = 90 - 44$

$= 46°$

20. $\tan 15° = \frac{8}{a}$

$0.2679 \approx \frac{8}{a}$

$0.2679a \approx 8$

$a \approx 29.9$

$m\angle A = 90 - 15$

$= 75°$

$\sin 15° = \frac{8}{c}$

$0.2588 \approx \frac{8}{c}$

$0.2588c \approx 8$

$c \approx 30.9$

21a. $\frac{7}{20}$ **21b.** 5:15 or 1:3 **21c.** $\frac{8+7}{20} = \frac{15}{20}$ or $\frac{3}{4}$

22.

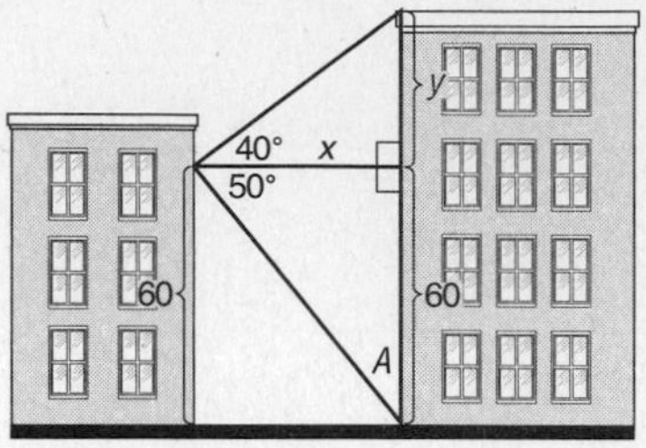

$\angle A = 90° - 50° = 40°$

$\tan A = \tan 40°$

$= \frac{x}{60}$

$x = 60(\tan 40°)$

≈ 50.3

$\tan 40° = \frac{y}{x}$

$= \frac{y}{50.3}$

$y = 50.3(\tan 40°)$

≈ 42.2

The second building is 60 + 42.2 or about 102 feet high.

23. $I = prt$

$7.80 = p(0.065)\left(\frac{6}{12}\right)$

$7.80 = 0.0325p$

$\$240 = p$

24. Discount: $0.15(399) = 59.85$

$399 - 59.85 = 339.15$

Tax: $0.06(339.15) = 20.35$

Total cost $= 339.15 + 20.35$

$= \$359.50$

25.

	r	t	d
Kris	r	6	$6r$
Amy	$5 + r$	6	$6(5 + r)$

$6r + 6(5 + r) = 510$

$6r + 30 + 6r = 510$

$12r + 30 = 510$

$12r = 480$

$r = 40$

Kris's average speed is 40 mph.

Page 791 Chapter 5 Test

1.

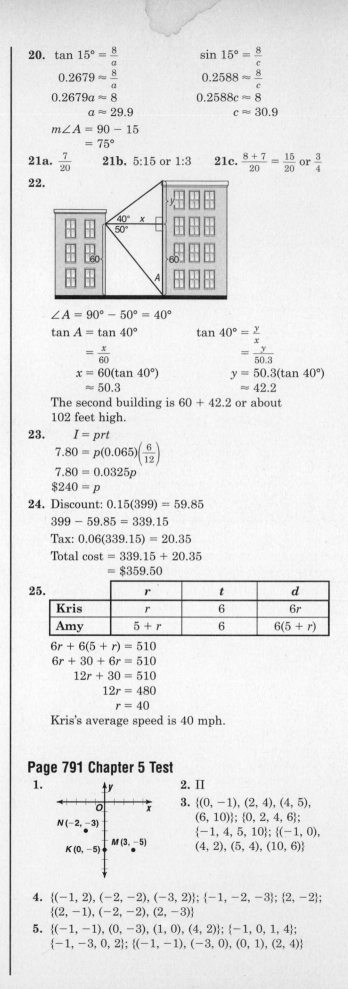

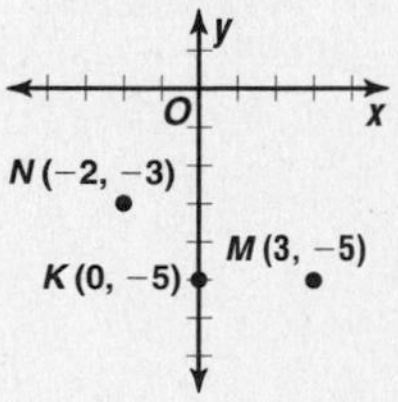

2. II

3. {(0, −1), (2, 4), (4, 5), (6, 10)}; {0, 2, 4, 6}; {−1, 4, 5, 10}; {(−1, 0), (4, 2), (5, 4), (10, 6)}

4. {(−1, 2), (−2, −2), (−3, 2)}; {−1, −2, −3}; {2, −2}; {(2, −1), (−2, −2), (2, −3)}

5. {(−1, −1), (0, −3), (1, 0), (4, 2)}; {−1, 0, 1, 4}; {−1, −3, 0, 2}; {(−1, −1), (−3, 0), (0, 1), (2, 4)}

6.

x	$-4x + 10$	y	(x, y)
-2	$-4(-2) + 10$	18	$(-2, 18)$
-1	$-4(-1) + 10$	14	$(-1, 14)$
0	$-4(0) + 10$	10	$(0, 10)$
2	$-4(2) + 10$	2	$(2, 2)$
4	$-4(4) + 10$	-6	$(4, -6)$

$\{(-2, 18), (-1, 14), (0, 10), (2, 2), (4, -6)\}$

7. $4 - 2x = 5y$

$\frac{4 - 2x}{5} = y$

x	$\frac{4-2x}{5}$	y	(x, y)
-2	$\frac{4-2(-2)}{5}$	$\frac{8}{5}$	$\left(-2, \frac{8}{5}\right)$
-1	$\frac{4-2(-1)}{5}$	$\frac{6}{5}$	$\left(-1, \frac{6}{5}\right)$
0	$\frac{4-2(0)}{5}$	$\frac{4}{5}$	$\left(0, \frac{4}{5}\right)$
2	$\frac{4-2(2)}{5}$	0	$(2, 0)$
4	$\frac{4-2(4)}{5}$	$-\frac{4}{5}$	$\left(4, -\frac{4}{5}\right)$

$\left\{\left(-2, \frac{8}{5}\right), \left(-1, \frac{6}{5}\right), \left(0, \frac{4}{5}\right), (2, 0), \left(4, -\frac{4}{5}\right)\right\}$

8. $-x + 3y = 1$

$3y = 1 + x$

$y = \frac{1 + x}{3}$

x	$\frac{1+x}{3}$	y	(x, y)
-2	$\frac{1+(-2)}{3}$	$-\frac{1}{3}$	$\left(-2, -\frac{1}{3}\right)$
-1	$\frac{1+(-1)}{3}$	0	$(-1, 0)$
0	$\frac{1+0}{3}$	$\frac{1}{3}$	$\left(0, \frac{1}{3}\right)$
2	$\frac{1+2}{3}$	1	$(2, 1)$
4	$\frac{1+4}{3}$	$\frac{5}{3}$	$\left(4, \frac{5}{3}\right)$

$\left\{\left(-2, -\frac{1}{3}\right), (-1, 0), \left(0, \frac{1}{3}\right), (2, 1), \left(4, \frac{5}{3}\right)\right\}$

9. $x + 2y = -1$

$2y = -1 - x$

$y = \frac{-1 - x}{2}$

x	$\frac{-1-x}{2}$	y	(x, y)
-1	$\frac{-1-(-1)}{2}$	0	$(-1, 0)$
0	$\frac{-1-0}{2}$	$-\frac{1}{2}$	$\left(0, -\frac{1}{2}\right)$
1	$\frac{-1-1}{2}$	-1	$(1, -1)$

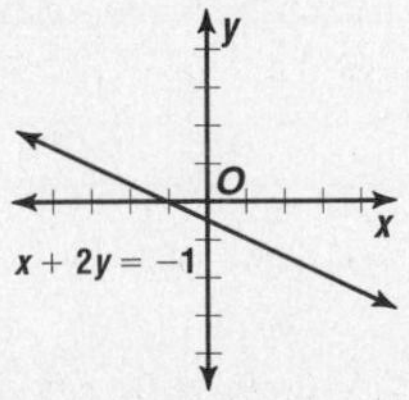

10. $-3x = 5 - y$

$y - 3x = 5$

$y = 3x + 5$

x	$3x + 5$	y	(x, y)
-1	$3(-1) + 5$	2	$(-1, 2)$
0	$3(0) + 5$	5	$(0, 5)$
1	$3(1) + 5$	8	$(1, 8)$

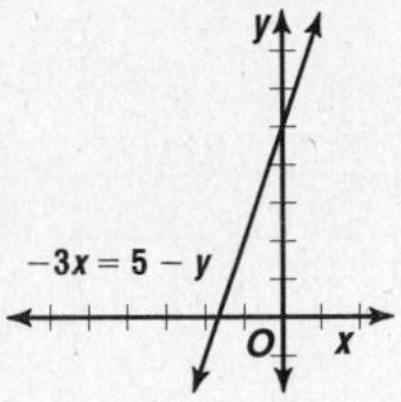

11. $-4 = x - \frac{1}{2}y$

$\frac{1}{2}y - 4 = x$

$\frac{1}{2}y = x + 4$

$y = 2x + 8$

x	$2x + 8$	y	(x, y)
-4	$2(-4) + 8$	0	$(-4, 0)$
-2	$2(-2) + 8$	4	$(-2, 4)$
0	$2(0) + 8$	8	$(0, 8)$
2	$2(2) + 8$	12	$(2, 12)$

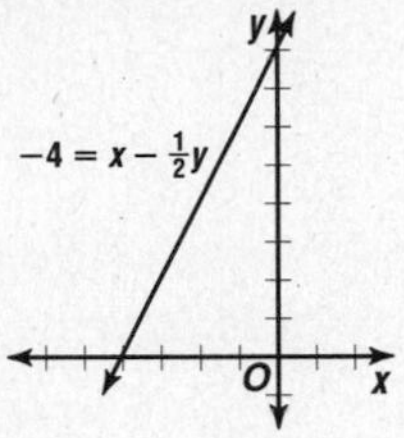

12. yes

13. yes

14. $f(x) = -2x + 5$

$f\left(\frac{1}{2}\right) = -2\left(\frac{1}{2}\right) + 5$

$= -1 + 5$

$= 4$

15. $g(x) = x^2 - 4x + 1$

$g(-2) = (-2)^2 - 4(-2) + 1$

$= 4 + 8 + 1$

$= 13$

16. $-2g(x) = -2(x^2 - 4x + 1)$

$-2g(3) = -2[(3)^2 - 4(3) + 1]$

$= -2(9 - 12 + 1)$

$= -2(-2)$

$= 4$

17. $\frac{\text{difference in } y}{\text{difference in } x} = \frac{5}{1} = 5$

$y = 5x - 2$

18. $\frac{\text{difference in } y}{\text{difference in } x} = \frac{12}{2}$ or 6

$y = 6x - 1$

19a. **Art:**

range: $97 - 54 = 43$

Q1: $\frac{66 + 68}{2} = 67$

Q3: 82

IQR $= 82 - 67 = 15$

Gina:

range: $100 - 57 = 43$

Q1: $\frac{69 + 70}{2} = 69.5$

Q3: $\frac{77 + 80}{2} = 78.5$

IQR: 9

19b. outliers:

Art: $x \geq Q_3 + 1.5(\text{IQR})$ or $x \leq Q_1 - 1.5(\text{IQR})$

$x \geq 82 + 1.5(15)$ $\quad x \leq 67 - 1.5(15)$

$x \geq 104.5$ $\quad x \leq 44.5$

no outliers

Gina: $x \geq Q_3 + 1.5(\text{IQR})$ or $x \leq Q_1 - 1.5(\text{IQR})$

$x \geq 78.5 + 1.5(9)$ $\quad x \leq 69.5 - 1.5(9)$

$x \geq 92$ $\quad x \leq 56$

outlier: 100

19c. Gina had more consistent scores since she had the smaller interquartile range.

20.

distance in miles	2	5	10
cost	6.30	11.25	19.50

$\frac{\text{difference in cost}}{\text{difference in miles}} = \frac{11.25 - 6.30}{5 - 2} = \frac{4.95}{3} = 1.65$

$y = 1.65x + 3$
$= 1.65(1) + 3$
$= 1.65 + 3$
$= \$4.65$

Page 792 Chapter 6 Test

1. $m = \frac{y_2 - y_1}{x_2 - x_1}$
$= \frac{7 - 8}{-3 - 5}$
$= \frac{-1}{-8}$ or $\frac{1}{8}$

2. $m = \frac{y_2 - y_1}{x_2 - x_1}$
$= \frac{9 - 5}{2 - (-2)}$
$= \frac{4}{4}$ or 1

3. $x - 8y = 3$
$-8y = -x + 3$
$y = \frac{1}{8}x - \frac{3}{8}$ $\quad m = \frac{1}{8}$

Let $y = 0$.
$x - 8(0) = 3$
$x = 3$
x-intercept: 3

Let $x = 0$.
$0 - 8y = 3$
$y = -\frac{3}{8}$
y-intercept: $-\frac{3}{8}$

4. $3x - 2y = 9$
$-2y = -3x + 9$
$y = \frac{3}{2}x - \frac{9}{2}$ $\quad m = \frac{3}{2}$

Let $y = 0$.
$3x - 2(0) = 9$
$x = 3$
x-intercept: 3

Let $x = 0$.
$3(0) - 2y = 9$
$-2y = 9$
$y = -\frac{9}{2}$
y-intercept: $-\frac{9}{2}$

5. $y = 7$
$m = 0$
x-intercept: none
y-intercept: 7

6. $4x - 3y = 24$
$-3y = -4x + 24$
$y = \frac{4}{3}x - 8$
$m = \frac{4}{3}$, y-intercept: -8

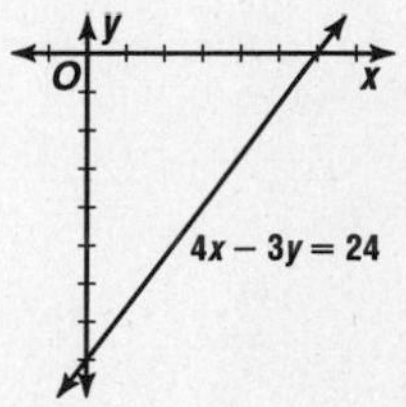

7. $2x + 7y = 16$
$7y = -2x + 16$
$y = -\frac{2}{7} + \frac{16}{7}$
$m = -\frac{2}{7}$, y-intercept: $\frac{16}{7}$

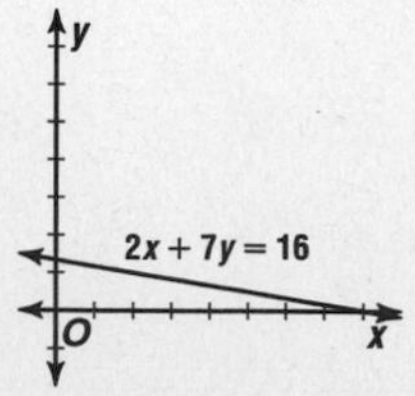

8. $y = \frac{2}{3}x + 3$
$m = \frac{2}{3}$, y-intercept: 3

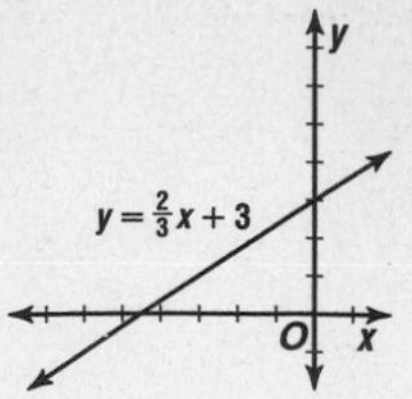

9. $y = 4x - 11$
$m = 4$

$2y = 1 + 8x$
$y = 4x + \frac{1}{2}$
$m = 4$

The lines are parallel.

10. $-7y = 4x + 14$
$y = -\frac{4}{7}x - 2$
$m = -\frac{4}{7}$

$7x - 4y = -12$
$-4y = -7x - 12$
$y = \frac{7}{4}x + 3$
$m = \frac{7}{4}$

The lines are perpendicular.

11. (2, 5), (8, −3)
$m = \frac{-3 - 5}{8 - 2} = -\frac{8}{6}$ or $-\frac{4}{3}$
$y - y_1 = m(x - x_1)$
$y - 5 = -\frac{4}{3}(x - 2)$
$3(y - 5) = 3\left(-\frac{4}{3}\right)(x - 2)$
$3y - 15 = -4(x - 2)$
$3y - 15 = -4x + 8$
$4x + 3y = 23$

12. (−2, −1), (6, −4)
$m = \frac{-4 - (-1)}{6 - (-2)} = \frac{-3}{8}$
$y - y_1 = m(x - x_1)$
$y - (-1) = -\frac{3}{8}[x - (-2)]$
$y + 1 = -\frac{3}{8}(x + 2)$
$8(y + 1) = 8\left(-\frac{3}{8}\right)(x + 2)$
$8y + 8 = -3(x + 2)$
$8y + 8 = -3x - 6$
$3x + 8y = -14$

13. $m = 2$, y-intercept $= 3$
$y = mx + b$
$y = 2x + 3$
$-3 = 2x - y$
$2x - y = -3$

14. y-intercept $= -4$, (5, −3)
(0, −4)
$m = \frac{-4 - (-3)}{0 - 5} = \frac{-1}{-5}$ or $\frac{1}{5}$
$y = mx + b$
$y = \frac{1}{5}x - 4$
$5y = x - 20$ or $x - 5y = 20$

15. $m = \frac{3}{4}$, (6, −2)
$y - y_1 = m(x - x_1)$
$y - (-2) = \frac{3}{4}(x - 6)$
$y + 2 = \frac{3}{4}(x - 6)$
$4(y + 2) = 4\left(\frac{3}{4}\right)(x - 6)$
$4y + 8 = 3(x - 6)$
$4y + 8 = 3x - 18$
$26 = 3x - 4y$
$3x - 4y = 26$

16. parallel to $6x - y = 7$

$$6x - 7 = y$$

$m = 6$, $(-2, 8)$

$y - y_1 = m(x - x_1)$

$y - 8 = 6[x - (-2)]$

$y - 8 = 6(x + 2)$

$y - 8 = 6x + 12$

$-20 = 6x - y$ or $6x - y = -20$

17. $(4, -2)$, $(0, 0)$

$m = \frac{-2 - 0}{4 - 0} = \frac{-2}{4}$ or $-\frac{1}{2}$

$y - y_1 = m(x - x_1)$

$y - 0 = -\frac{1}{2}(x - 0)$

$y = -\frac{1}{2}x$

18. $(-2, -5)$, $(8, -3)$

$m = \frac{-5 - (-3)}{-2 - 8} = \frac{-2}{-10}$ or $\frac{1}{5}$

$y - y_1 = m(x - x_1)$

$y - (-3) = \frac{1}{5}(x - 8)$

$y + 3 = \frac{1}{5}x - \frac{8}{5}$

$y = \frac{1}{5}x - \frac{23}{5}$

19. $(6, 4)$, y-intercept $= -2$

$(6, 4)$, $(0, -2)$

$m = \frac{-2 - 4}{0 - 6} = \frac{-6}{-6}$ or 1

$y - y_1 = m(x - x_1)$

$y - (-2) = 1(x - 0)$

$y + 2 = x$

$y = x - 2$

20. $m = -\frac{2}{3}$, y-intercept: 5

$y = -\frac{2}{3}x + 5$

21. $m = 6$, $(-3, -4)$

$y - y_1 = m(x - x_1)$

$y - (-4) = 6[x - (-3)]$

$y + 4 = 6(x + 3)$

$y + 4 = 6x + 18$

$y = 6x + 14$

22. perpendicular to $5x - 3y = 9$

$$-3y = -5x + 9$$

$$y = \frac{5}{3}x - 3$$

$m = -\frac{3}{5}$, $(0, 0)$

$y - y_1 = m(x - x_1)$

$y - 0 = -\frac{3}{5}(x - 0)$

$y = -\frac{3}{5}x$

23. parallel to $3x + 7y = 4$

$$7y = -3x + 4$$

$$y = -\frac{3}{7}x + \frac{4}{7}$$

$m = -\frac{3}{7}$, $(5, -2)$

$y - y_1 = m(x - x_1)$

$y - (-2) = -\frac{3}{7}(x - 5)$

$y + 2 = -\frac{3}{7}x + \frac{15}{7}$

$y = -\frac{3}{7}x + \frac{1}{7}$

24. perpendicular to $x + 3y = 7$

$$3y = -x + 7$$

$$y = -\frac{1}{3}x + \frac{7}{3}$$

$m = 3$, $(5, 2)$

$y - y_1 = 3(x - x_1)$

$y - 2 = 3(x - 5)$

$y - 2 = 3x - 15$

$y = 3x - 13$

25. $6 = \frac{-2 + x}{2}$ $\quad$ $-5 = \frac{-7 + y}{2}$

$12 = -2 + x$ $\quad$ $-10 = -7 + y$

$14 = x$ $\quad$ $-3 = y$

$B(14, -3)$

26a.

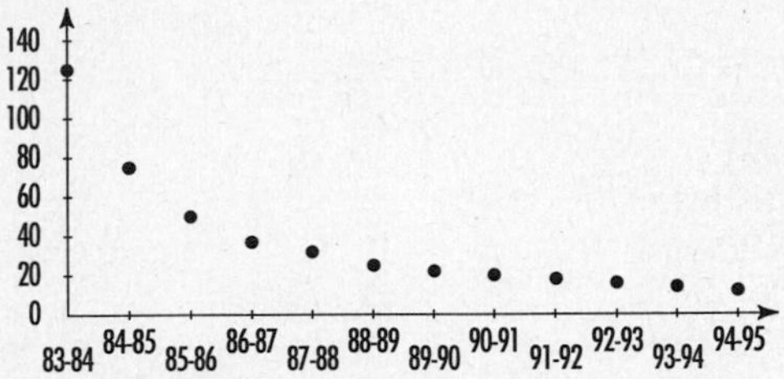

26b. negative

26c. No, they are not linear.

Page 793 Chapter 7 Test

1.
$-12 \leq d + 7$

$-12 - 7 \leq d + 7 - 7$

$-19 \leq d$

$\{d \mid d \geq -19\}$

2.
$7x < 6x - 11$

$7x - 6x < 6x - 6x - 11$

$x < -11$

$\{x \mid x < -11\}$

3.
$z - 1 \geq 2z - 3$

$z - 1 - z \geq 2z - z - 3$

$-1 \geq z - 3$

$-1 + 3 \geq z - 3 + 3$

$2 \geq z$

$\{z \mid z \leq 2\}$

4.
$5 - 4b > -23$

$5 - 5 - 4b > -23 - 5$

$-4b > -28$

$\frac{-4b}{-4} < \frac{-28}{-4}$

$b < 7$

$\{b \mid b < 7\}$

5.
$-\frac{2}{3}r \leq \frac{7}{12}$

$\left(-\frac{3}{2}\right)\left(-\frac{2}{3}r\right) \geq \frac{7}{12}\left(-\frac{3}{2}\right)$

$r \geq -\frac{7}{8}$

$\left\{r \mid r \geq -\frac{7}{8}\right\}$

6.
$8y + 3 < 13y - 9$

$8y + 3 - 8y < 13y - 9 - 8y$

$3 < 5y - 9$

$3 + 9 < 5y + 9$

$12 < 5y$

$\frac{12}{5} < \frac{5y}{5}$

$\frac{12}{5} < y$

$\left\{y \mid y > \frac{12}{5}\right\}$

7.
$8(1 - 2z) \leq 25 + z$

$8 - 16z \leq 25 + z$

$8 - 16z + 16z \leq 25 + z + 16z$

$8 \leq 25 + 17z$

$8 - 25 \leq 25 - 25 + 17z$

$-17 \leq 17z$

$-\frac{17}{17} \leq \frac{17z}{17}$

$-1 \leq z$

$\{z \mid z \geq -1\}$

8. $0.3(m + 4) > 0.5(m - 4)$
$0.3m + 1.2 > 0.5m - 2$
$0.3m + 1.2 - 0.3m > 0.5m - 2 - 0.3m$
$1.2 > 0.2m - 2$
$1.2 + 2 > 0.2m - 2 + 2$
$3.2 > 0.2m$
$16 > m$
$\{m \mid m < 16\}$

9. $\frac{2n-3}{-7} \leq 5$
$-7\left(\frac{2n-3}{-7}\right) \geq (5)(-7)$
$2n - 3 \geq -35$
$2n - 3 + 3 \geq -35 + 3$
$2n \geq -32$
$n \geq -16$
$\{n \mid n \geq -16\}$

10. $y + \frac{5}{8} > \frac{11}{24}$
$y + \frac{5}{8} - \frac{5}{8} > \frac{11}{24} - \frac{5}{8}$
$y > -\frac{4}{24}$ or $-\frac{1}{6}$
$\left\{y \middle| y > -\frac{1}{6}\right\}$

11. $x + 1 > -2$ and $3x < 6$
$x + 1 - 1 > -2 - 1$ $\quad$ $x < 2$
$x > -3$
$\{x \mid -3 < x < 2\}$

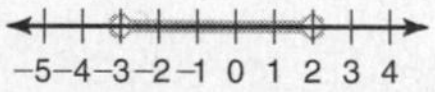

12. $2n + 1 \geq 15$ or $2n + 1 \leq -1$
$2n + 1 - 1 \geq 15 - 1$ $\quad$ $2n + 1 - 1 \leq -1 - 1$
$2n \geq 14$ $\quad$ $2n \leq -2$
$n \geq 7$ $\quad$ $n \leq -1$
$\{n \mid n \geq 7 \text{ or } n \leq -1\}$

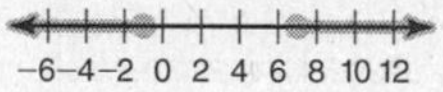

13. $8 + 3t > 2$ and $-12 > 11t - 1$
$8 + 3t - 8 > 2 - 8$ $\quad$ $-12 + 1 > 11t - 1 + 1$
$3t > -6$ $\quad$ $-11 > 11t$
$t > -2$ $\quad$ $-1 > t$
$\{t \mid -2 < t < -1\}$

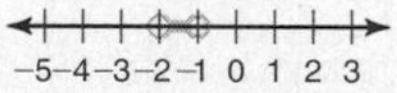

14. $|2x - 1| < 5$
$2x - 1 < 5$ and $2x - 1 > -5$
$2x - 1 + 1 < 5 + 1$ $\quad$ $2x - 1 + 1 > -5 + 1$
$2x < 6$ $\quad$ $2x > -4$
$x < 3$ $\quad$ $x > -2$
$\{x \mid -2 < x < 3\}$

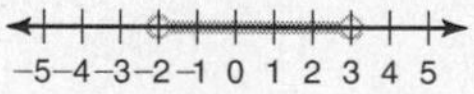

15. $|5 - 3b| \geq 1$
$5 - 3b \geq 1$ or $5 - 3b \leq -1$
$5 - 3b - 5 \geq 1 - 5$ $\quad$ $5 - 3b - 5 \leq -1 - 5$
$-3b \geq -4$ $\quad$ $-3b \leq -6$
$\frac{-3b}{-3} \leq \frac{-4}{-3}$ $\quad$ $\frac{-3b}{-3} \geq \frac{-6}{-3}$
$b \leq \frac{4}{3}$ $\quad$ $b \geq 2$
$\left\{b \middle| b \geq 2 \text{ or } b \leq \frac{4}{3}\right\}$

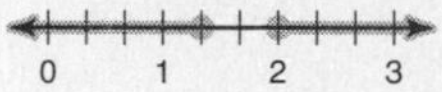

16. $|3 - 5y| < 8$
$3 - 5y < 8$ and $3 - 5y > -8$
$3 - 5y - 3 < 8 - 3$ $\quad$ $3 - 5y - 3 > -8 - 3$
$-5y < 5$ $\quad$ $-5y > -11$
$\frac{-5y}{-5} > \frac{5}{-5}$ $\quad$ $\frac{-5y}{-5} < \frac{-11}{-5}$
$y > -1$ $\quad$ $y < \frac{11}{5}$
$\left\{y \middle| -1 < y < \frac{11}{5}\right\}$

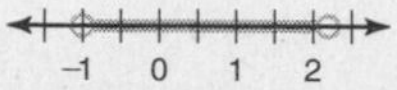

17. Let n = the number.
$12 - 2n \geq n + 27$
$12 - 2n + 2n \geq n + 27 + 2n$
$12 \geq 3n + 27$
$12 - 27 \geq 3n + 27 - 27$
$-15 \geq 3n$
$-5 \geq n$
$\{n \mid n \leq -5\}$

18. Let n = the number.
$71 < 2n - 7 < 83$
$71 < 2n - 7$ and $2n - 7 < 83$
$71 + 7 < 2n - 7 + 7$ $\quad$ $2n - 7 + 7 < 83 + 7$
$78 < 2n$ $\quad$ $2n < 90$
$39 < n$ $\quad$ $n < 45$
$\{n \mid 39 < n < 45\}$

19. Let n = the other integer.
$6n \geq 30$
$n \geq 5$
5 or more

20. Let x = the first of the consecutive odd integers; then $x + 2$ = the second integer, $x + 4$ = the third integer, and $x + 6$ = the greatest of the integers.

$\frac{x + (x + 2) + (x + 4) + (x + 6)}{4} < 20$
$\frac{4x + 12}{4} < 20$
$4x + 12 < 80$
$4x + 12 - 12 < 80 - 12$
$4x < 68$
$x < 17$

$x = 15$
$x + 2 = 15 + 2 = 17$
$x + 4 = 15 + 4 = 19$
$x + 6 = 15 + 6 = 21$
15, 17, 19, 21

21. $y \geq 5x + 1$
Test $(-1, 0)$.
$0 \overset{?}{\geq} 5(-1) + 1$
$0 \geq -4$ true

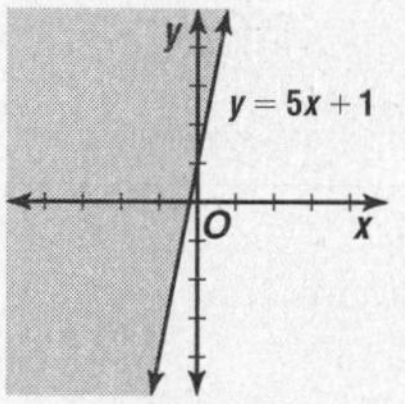

22. $x - 2y > 8$
$-2y > -x + 8$
$y < \frac{1}{2}x - 4$
Test $(0, -5)$.
$0 - 2(-5) \overset{?}{>} 8$
$10 > 8$ true

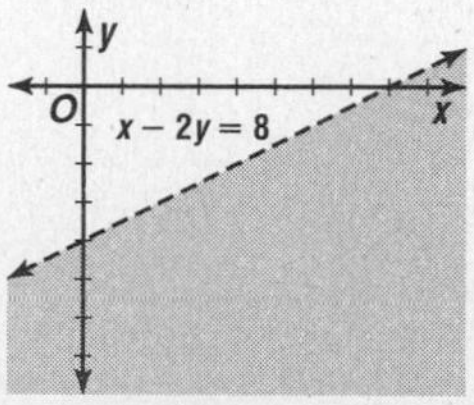

23. $3x - 2y < 6$
$-2y < -3x + 6$
$y > \frac{3}{2}x - 3$
Test $(0, 0)$.
$3(0) - 2(0) \overset{?}{<} 6$
$0 < 6$ true

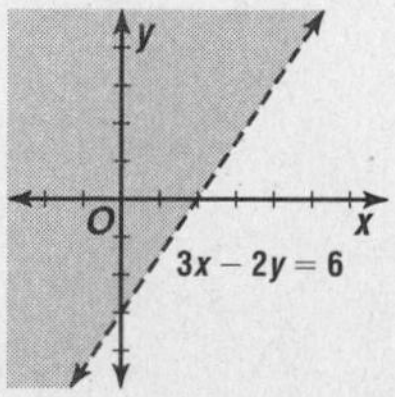

24a.

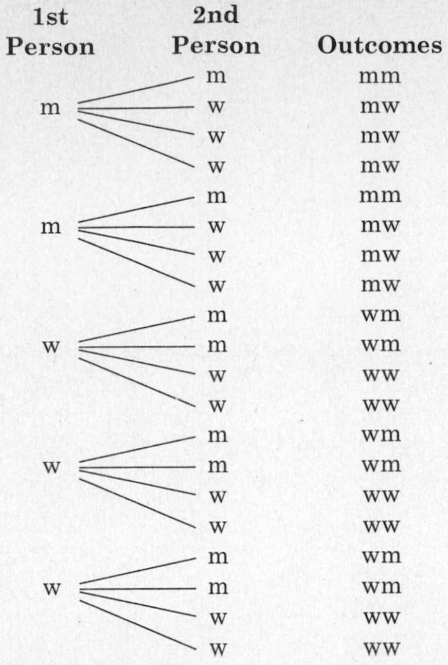

1st Person	2nd Person	Outcomes

$$\frac{6}{20} = \frac{3}{10} \text{ or } 0.3$$

24b. $\frac{18}{20} = \frac{9}{10}$ or 0.9   **24c.** man and woman

25a. LV = 1   median: 3
   GV = 10 $Q_3 = 6$
   $Q_1 = 1$

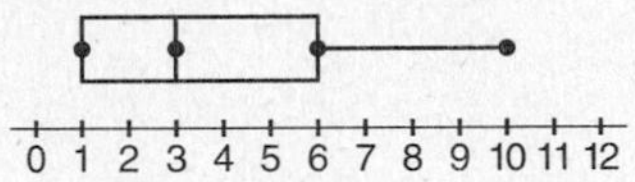

25b. 1 and 6

Page 794 Chapter 8 Test

1.

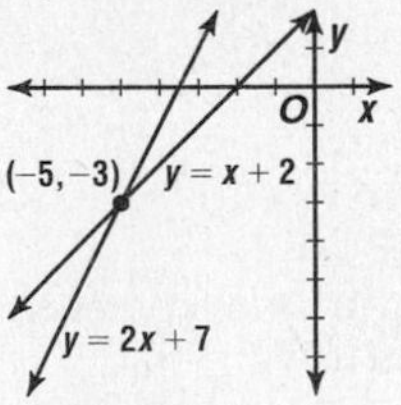

(−5, −3) $y = x + 2$
$y = 2x + 7$

one; (−5, −3)

2.

$x + 2y = 11$
$x = 14 − 2y$

no solution

3.

(3, 2) $2x + 5y = 16$
$5x − 2y = 11$

one; (3, 2)

4.

$2y − 10 = −6y$
$3x + y = 5$

infinitely many

5.

$y + 2x = −1$
$y − 4 = −2x$

no solution

6.

(−6, 8)
$5x + 3y = −6$
$2x + y = −4$

one; (−6, 8)

7.
$$x - y = -3 \qquad y = 7 - x$$
$$x - (7 - x) = -3 \qquad y = 7 - 2$$
$$x - 7 + x = -3 \qquad y = 5$$
$$2x - 7 = -3$$
$$2x = 4$$
$$x = 2$$
(2, 5)

8.
$$y - 3x = -9 \qquad x = 2y - 7$$
$$y - 3(2y - 7) = -9 \qquad x = 2(6) - 7$$
$$y - 6y + 21 = -9 \qquad x = 12 - 7$$
$$-5y + 21 = -9 \qquad x = 5$$
$$-5y = -30$$
$$y = 6$$
(5, 6)

9.
$$x + y = 8 \qquad x + y = 8$$
$$\underline{(+) \ x - y = 2} \qquad 5 + y = 8$$
$$2x \quad = 10 \qquad y = 3$$
$$x = 5$$
(5, 3)

10.
$$3x - y = 11 \qquad \rightarrow \qquad 6x - 2y = 22$$
$$x + 2y = -36 \qquad \qquad \underline{(+) \ x + 2y = -36}$$
$$\qquad \qquad \qquad \qquad 7x \quad = -14$$
$$x + 2y = -36 \qquad \qquad x = -2$$
$$(-2) + 2y = -36$$
$$2y = -34$$
$$y = -17$$
(−2, −17)

11.
$$3x \ + y = 10 \qquad 3x + y = 10$$
$$\underline{(-) \ 3x - 2y = 16} \qquad 3x + (-2) = 10$$
$$3y = -6 \qquad 3x = 12$$
$$y = -2 \qquad x = 4$$
(4, −2)

12.
$$5x - 3y = 12 \qquad 5x - 3y = 12$$
$$\underline{(+) \ -2x + 3y = -3} \qquad 5(3) - 3y = 12$$
$$3x = 9 \qquad 15 - 3y = 12$$
$$x = 3 \qquad -3y = -3$$
$$\qquad \qquad \qquad y = 1$$
(3, 1)

13. $2x + 5y = 12$
$$x - 6y = -11 \qquad \rightarrow \qquad \begin{array}{r} 2x + 5y = 12 \\ \underline{(+) \ -2x + 12y = 22} \\ 17y = 34 \\ y = 2 \end{array}$$

$$x - 6y = -11$$
$$x - 6(2) = -11$$
$$x - 12 = -11$$
$$x = 11$$
(1, 2)

14. $x + y = 6$
$$3x - 3y = 13 \qquad \rightarrow \qquad \begin{array}{r} 3x + 3y = 18 \\ \underline{(+) \ 3x - 3y = 13} \\ 6x \quad = 31 \\ x = \frac{31}{6} \end{array}$$

$$x + y = 6$$
$$\frac{31}{6} + y = 6$$
$$y = \frac{5}{6}$$
$$\left(\frac{31}{6}, \frac{5}{6}\right)$$

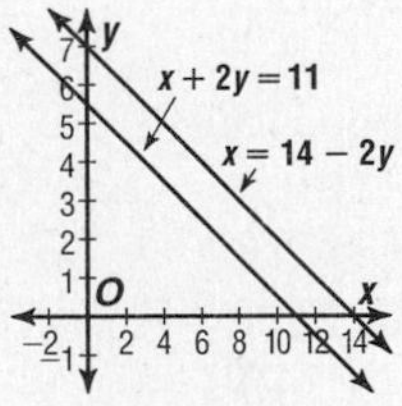

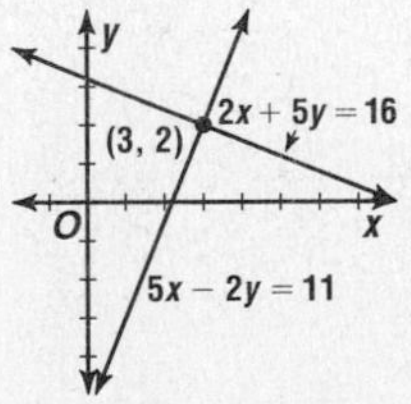

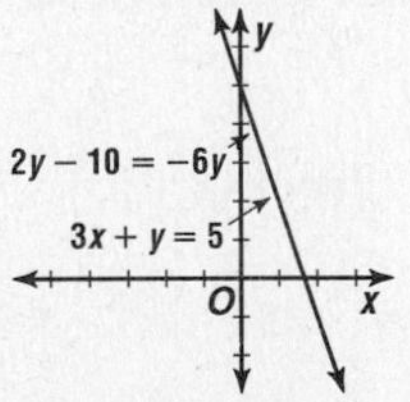

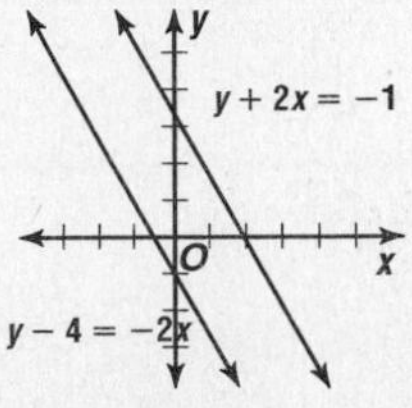

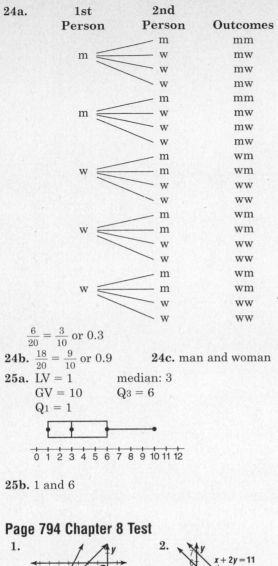

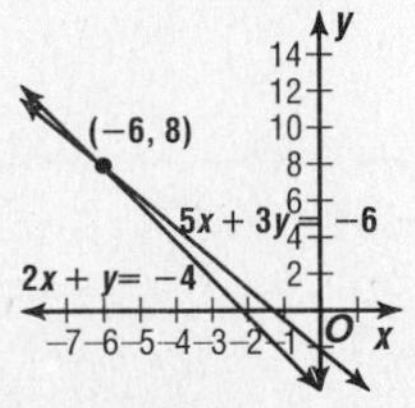

15. $3x + \frac{1}{3}y = 10 \rightarrow 45x + 5y = 150$

$2x - \frac{5}{3}y = 35 \rightarrow \underline{6x - 5y = 105}$

$51x = 225$

$x = 5$

$3x + \frac{1}{3}y = 10$

$3(5) + \frac{1}{3}y = 10$

$15 + \frac{1}{3}y = 10$

$\frac{1}{3}y = -5$

$y = -15$

$(5, -15)$

16. $8x - 6y = 14 \rightarrow 24x - 18y = 42$

$6x - 9y = 15 \rightarrow \underline{(+) -24x + 36y = -60}$

$18y = -18$

$y = -1$

$8x - 6y = 14$

$8x - 6(-1) = 14$

$8x + 6 = 14$

$8x = 8$

$x = 1$

$(1, -1)$

17. $5x - y = 1$ $\quad y = -3x + 1$

$5x - (-3x + 1) = 1$ $\quad y = -3\left(\frac{1}{4}\right) + 1$

$5x + 3x - 1 = 1$ $\quad y = -\frac{3}{4} + 1$

$8x - 1 = 1$ $\quad y = \frac{1}{4}$

$8x = 2$

$x = \frac{1}{4}$

$\left(\frac{1}{4}, \frac{1}{4}\right)$

18. $7x + 3y = 13 \rightarrow 14x + 6y = 26$

$3x - 2y = -1 \rightarrow \underline{(+) 9x - 6y = -3}$

$23x = 23$

$x = 1$

$7x + 3y = 13$

$7(1) + 3y = 13$

$7 + 3y = 13$

$3y = 6$

$y = 2$

$(1, 2)$

19.

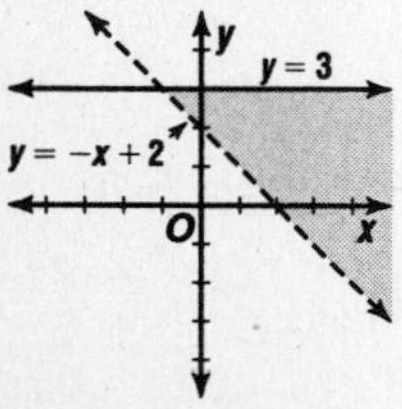

20.

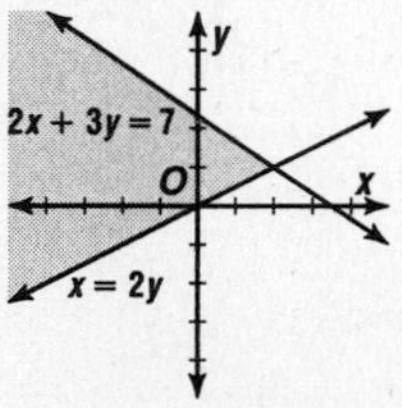

21.

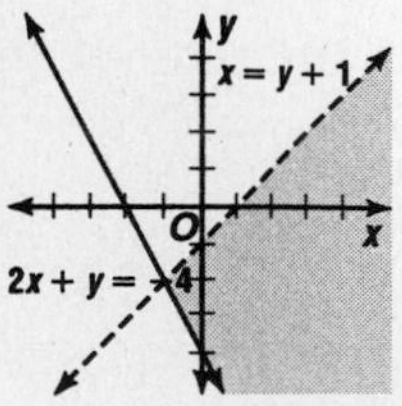

22. Let u = the units digit and let t = the tens digit.

$u = 2t + 1$ $\quad u + t = 10$

$u + t = 10$ $\quad (2t + 1) + t = 10$

$3t + 1 = 10$

$3t = 9$

$t = 3$

$u = 2t + 1$

$u = 2(3) + 1$

$u = 6 + 1$

$u = 7$

The number is 37.

23. Let ℓ = the length and let w = the width.

$\ell - w = 7$ $\quad \ell - w = 7$

$P = 2\ell + 2w$ $\quad \underline{(+)\ \ell + w = 25}$

$50 = 2\ell + 2w$ $\quad 2\ell = 32$

$25 = \ell + w$ $\quad \ell = 16$

$\ell - w = 7$

$16 - w = 7$

$-w = -9$

$w = 9$

The dimensions are 16 cm by 9 cm.

24. Let x = the amount invested at 6% and let y = the amount invested at 8%.

$x + y = 10{,}000 \rightarrow -0.06x - 0.06y = -600$

$0.06x + 0.08y = 760 \rightarrow \underline{(+)\ 0.06x + 0.08y = 760}$

$0.02y = 160$

$y = 8000$

$x + y = 10{,}000$

$x + 8000 = 10{,}000$

$x = 2000$

She invested $2000 at 6% and $8000 at 8%.

25. Let s = the number of small peaches and let ℓ = the number of large peaches.

$s + \ell = 30 \rightarrow -0.20s - 0.20\ell = -6.00$

$0.20s + 0.35\ell = 7.50 \rightarrow \underline{(+)\ 0.20s + 0.35\ell = 7.50}$

$0.15\ell = 1.50$

$\ell = 10$

$s + \ell = 30$

$s + 10 = 30$

$s = 20$

Joey sold 20 small peaches and 10 large peaches.

Page 795 Chapter 9 Test

1. $(a^2b^4)(a^3b^5) = (a^2 \cdot a^3)(b^4 \cdot b^5)$
$= a^5b^9$

2. $(-12abc)(4a^2b^4) = (-12 \cdot 4)(a \cdot a^2)(b \cdot b^4)(c)$
$= -48a^3b^5c$

3. $\left(\frac{3}{5}m\right)^2 = \left(\frac{3}{5}\right)^2 m^2$
$= \frac{9}{25}m^2$

4. $(-3a)^4(a^5b)^2 = (-3)^4a^4(a^5)^2(b^2)$
$= 81a^4(a^{10})(b^2)$
$= 81(a^4 \cdot a^{10})(b^2)$
$= 81a^{14}b^2$

5. $(-5a^2)(-6b^3)^2 = (-5a^2)(-6)^2(b^3)^2$
$= -5a^2(36)(b^6)$
$= (-5 \cdot 36)a^2b^6$
$= -180a^2b^6$

6. $(5a)^2b + 7a^2b = (5)^2a^2b + 7a^2b$
$= 25a^2b + 7a^2b$
$= 32a^2b$

7. $\frac{y^{11}}{y^6} = y^{11-6}$
$= y^5$

8. $\frac{mn^4}{m^3n^2} = \frac{m}{m^3} \cdot \frac{n^4}{n^2}$
$= m^{1-3} \cdot n^{4-2}$
$= m^{-2}n^2$
$= \frac{n^2}{m^2}$

9. $\frac{9a^2bc^2}{63a^4bc} = \frac{9}{63} \cdot \frac{a^2}{a^4} \cdot \frac{b}{b} \cdot \frac{c^2}{c}$
$= \frac{1}{7} \cdot a^{2-4} \cdot c^{2-1}$
$= \frac{1}{7}a^{-2}c$
$= \frac{c}{7a^2}$

10. $\frac{48a^2bc^5}{(3ab^3c^2)^2} = \frac{48a^2bc^5}{3^2a^2(b^3)^2(c^2)^2}$
$= \frac{48a^2bc^5}{9a^2b^6c^4}$
$= \frac{48}{9} \cdot \frac{a^2}{a^2} \cdot \frac{b}{b^6} \cdot \frac{c^5}{c^4}$
$= \frac{16}{3}b^{1-6}c^{5-4}$
$= \frac{16}{3}b^{-5}c^1$
$= \frac{16c}{3b^5}$

11. $\frac{14ab^{-3}}{21a^2b^{-5}} = \frac{14}{21} \cdot \frac{a}{a^2} \cdot \frac{b^{-3}}{b^{-5}}$
$= \frac{2}{3}a^{1-2}b^{-3-(-5)}$
$= \frac{2}{3}a^{-1}b^2$
$= \frac{2b^2}{3a}$

12. $\frac{(10a^2bc^4)^{-2}}{(5^{-1}a^{-1}b^{-5})^2} = \frac{10^{-2}(a^2)^{-2}b^{-2}(c^4)^{-2}}{(5^{-1})^2(a^{-1})^2(b^{-5})^2}$
$= \frac{10^{-2}a^{-4}b^{-2}c^{-8}}{5^{-2}a^{-2}b^{-10}}$
$= \frac{5^2}{10^2} \cdot \frac{a^{-4}}{a^{-2}} \cdot \frac{b^{-2}}{b^{-10}} \cdot c^{-8}$
$= \frac{25}{100} \cdot a^{-4-(-2)} \cdot b^{-2-(-10)} \cdot c^{-8}$
$= \frac{1}{4}a^{-2}b^8c^{-8}$
$= \frac{b^8}{4a^2c^8}$

13. $46{,}300 = 4.63 \times 10{,}000$
$= 4.63 \times 10^4$

14. $0.003892 = 3.892 \times 0.001$
$= 3.892 \times 10^{-3}$

15. $284 \times 10^3 = 2.84 \times 100 \times 10^3$
$= 2.84 \times 10^2 \times 10^3$
$= 2.84 \times 10^5$

16. $0.0031 \times 10^4 = 3.1 \times 0.001 \times 10^4$
$= 3.1 \times 10^{-3} \times 10^4$
$= 3.1 \times 10$

17. $(3 \times 10^3)(2 \times 10^4) = (3 \times 2)(10^3 \times 10^4)$
$= 6 \times 10^7$

18. $\frac{2.5 \times 10^3}{5 \times 10^{-3}} = \frac{2.5}{5} \times \frac{10^3}{10^{-3}}$
$= 0.5 \times 10^6$
$= 5 \times 0.1 \times 10^6$
$= 5 \times 10^{-1} \times 10^6$
$= 5 \times 10^5$

19. $\frac{14.72 \times 10^{-4}}{3.2 \times 10^{-3}} = \frac{14.7^2}{3.2} \times \frac{10^{-4}}{10^{-3}}$
$= 4.6 \times 10^{-1}$

20. $(15 \times 10^{-7})(3.1 \times 10^4) = (15 \times 3.1)(10^{-7} \times 10^4)$
$= 46.5 \times 10^{-3}$
$= 4.65 \times 10 \times 10^{-3}$
$= 4.65 \times 10^{-2}$

21. degree of $5ya^3$: 4
degree of -7: 0
degree of $-y^2a^2$: 4
degree of $2y^3a$: 4
degree of $5ya^3 - 7 - y^2a^2 + 2y^3a$: 4
$2y^3a - y^2a^2 + 5ya^3 - 7$

22.
$$\begin{array}{rl} & 5ax^2 + 3a^2x - 7a^3 \\ (+) & 2ax^2 - 8a^2x \qquad\quad + 4 \\ \hline & 7ax^2 - 5a^2x - 7a^3 + 4 \end{array}$$

23.
$$\begin{array}{rl} & x^3 - 3x^2y + 4xy^2 + y^3 \\ (-) & 7x^3 + x^2y - 9xy^2 + y^3 \\ \hline \end{array} \rightarrow$$
$$\begin{array}{rl} & x^3 - 3x^2y + 4xy^2 + y^3 \\ (+) & -7x^3 - x^2y + 9xy^2 - y^3 \\ \hline & -6x^3 - 4x^2y + 13xy^2 \end{array}$$

24. $(n^2 - 5n + 4) - (5n^2 + 3n - 1)$
$= n^2 - 5n + 4 - 5n^2 - 3n + 1$
$= (n^2 - 5n^2) + (-5n - 3n) + (4 + 1)$
$= -4n^2 - 8n + 5$

25. $(ab^3 - 4a^2b^2 + ab - 7) + (-2ab^3 + 4ab^2 + 3ab + 2)$
$= (ab^3 - 2ab^3) + (-4a^2b^2) + 4ab^2 + (ab + 3ab) +$
$(-7 + 2)$
$= -ab^3 - 4a^2b^2 + 4ab^2 + 4ab - 5$

26. $(h - 5)^2 = h^2 - 2(h)(5) + (5)^2$
$= h^2 - 10h + 25$

27. $(2x - 5)(7x + 3)$
$= (2x)(7x) + (2x)(3) + (-5)(7x) + (-5)(3)$
$= 14x^2 + 6x - 35x - 15$
$= 14x^2 - 29x - 15$

28. $(4x - y)(4x + y) = (4x)^2 - (y)^2$
$= 16x^2 - y^2$

29. $(2a^2b + b^2)^2 = (2a^2b)^2 + 2(2a^2b)(b^2) + (b^2)^2$
$= 4a^4b^2 + 4a^2b^3 + b^4$

30. $3x^2y^3(2x - xy^2) = 6x^3y^3 - 3x^3y^5$

31. $(4m + 3n)(2m - 5n)$
$= (4m)(2m) + (4m)(-5n) + (3n)(2m) + (3n)(-5n)$
$= 8m^2 - 20mn + 6mn - 15n^2$
$= 8m^2 - 14mn - 15n^2$

32. $x^2(x - 8) - 3x(x^2 - 7x + 3) + 5(x^3 - 6x^2)$
$= x^3 - 8x^2 - 3x^3 + 21x^2 - 9x + 5x^3 - 30x^2$
$= (x^3 - 3x^3 + 5x^3 + (-8x^2 + 21x^2 - 30x^2) - 9x$
$= 3x^3 - 17x^2 - 9x$

33. $(x - 6)(x^2 - 4x + 5)$
$= x(x^2 - 4x + 5) - 6(x^2 - 4x + 5)$
$= (x^3 - 4x^2 + 5x) - (6x^2 - 24x + 30)$
$= x^3 - 4x^2 + 5x - 6x^2 + 24x - 30$
$= x^3 - 10x^2 + 29x - 30$

Page 796 Chapter 10 Test

1. $48 = 2 \cdot 2 \cdot 2 \cdot 2 \cdot 3$
   $64 = 2 \cdot 2 \cdot 2 \cdot 2 \cdot 2 \cdot 2$
   GCF: $2 \cdot 2 \cdot 2 \cdot 2$ or 16
2. $18a^2b = 2 \cdot 3 \cdot 3 \cdot a \cdot a \cdot b$
   $28a^3b^2 = 2 \cdot 2 \cdot 7 \cdot a \cdot a \cdot a \cdot b \cdot b$
   GCF: $2 \cdot a \cdot a \cdot b$ or $2a^2b$
3. $6x^2y^3 = 2 \cdot 3 \cdot x \cdot x \cdot y \cdot y \cdot y$
   $12x^2y^2z = 2 \cdot 2 \cdot 3 \cdot x \cdot x \cdot y \cdot y \cdot z$
   $15x^2y = 3 \cdot 5 \cdot x \cdot x \cdot y$
   GCF: $3 \cdot x \cdot x \cdot y$ or $3x^2y$
4. $25y^2 - 49w^2 = (5y)^2 - (7w)^2$
   $= (5y - 7w)(5y + 7w)$
5. $t^2 - 16t + 64 = (t)^2 - 2(t)(8) + (8)^2$
   $= (t - 8)^2$
6. $x^2 + 14x + 24 = (x + 12)(x + 2)$
7. $28m^2 + 18m = 2m(14m) + 2m(9)$
   $= 2m(14m + 9)$
8. $a^2 - 11ab + 18b^2 = (a - 2b)(a - 9b)$
9. $12x^2 + 23x - 24 = 12x^2 + (-9 + 32)x - 24$
   $= 12x^2 - 9x + 32x - 24$
   $= (12x^2 - 9x) + (32x - 24)$
   $= 3x(4x - 3) + 8(4x - 3)$
   $= (3x + 8)(4x - 3)$
10. prime
11. $6x^3 + 15x^2 - 9x = (2x^2)(3x) + (5x)(3x) - 3(3x)$
    $= 3x(2x^2 + 5x - 3)$
    $= 3x[2x^2 + (-1 + 6)x - 3]$
    $= 3x(2x^2 - x + 6x - 3)$
    $= 3x[(2x^2 - x) + (6x - 3)]$
    $= 3x[x(2x - 1) + 3(2x - 1)]$
    $= 3x(x + 3)(2x - 1)$
12. $4my - 20m + 3py - 15p$
    $= (4my - 20m) + (3py - 15p)$
    $= 4m(y - 5) + 3p(y - 5)$
    $= (4m + 3p)(y - 5)$
13. $x^3 - 4x^2 - 9x + 36 = (x^3 - 4x^2) + (-9x + 36)$
    $= x^2(x - 4) + (-9)(x - 4)$
    $= (x^2 - 9)(x - 4)$
    $= [(x)^2 - (3)^2]\,(x - 4)$
    $= (x - 3)(x + 3)(x - 4)$
14. $36a^2b^3 - 45ab^4 = 4a(9ab^3) + (-5b)(9ab^3)$
    $= 9ab^3(4a - 5b)$
15. $36m^2 + 60mm + 25n^2$
    $= (6m)^2 + 2(6m)(5n) + (5n)^2$
    $= (6m + 5n)^2$
16. $\frac{1}{4}a^2 - \frac{4}{9} = \left(\frac{1}{2}a\right)^2 - \left(\frac{2}{3}\right)^2$
    $= \left(\frac{1}{2}a - \frac{2}{3}\right)\left(\frac{1}{2}a + \frac{2}{3}\right)$
17. prime
18. $15a^2b + 5a^2 - 10a = 3ab(5a) + a(5a) + (-2)(5a)$
    $= 5a(3ab + a - 2)$
19. $6y^2 - 5y - 6 = 6y^2 + (4 - 9)y - 6$
    $= 6y^2 + 4y - 9y - 6$
    $= (6y^2 + 4y) + (-9y - 6)$
    $= 2y(3y + 2) + (-3)(3y - 2)$
    $= (2y - 3)(3y + 2)$
20. $4s^2 - 100t^2 = 4(s^2) - 4(25t^2)$
    $= 4(s^2 - 25t^2)$
    $= 4[(s)^2 - (5t)^2]$
    $= 4(s - 5t)(s + 5t)$
21. $2d^2 + d - 1 = 2d^2 + (2 - 1)d - 1$
    $= 2d^2 + 2d - d - 1$
    $= (2d^2 + 2d) + (-d - 1)$
    $= 2d(d + 1) + (-1)(d + 1)$
    $= (2d - 1)(d + 1)$
22. prime
23. $2xz + 2yz - x - y = (2xz + 2yz) + (-x - y)$
    $= 2z(x + y) + (-1)(x + y)$
    $= (2z - 1)(x + y)$
24. $(4x - 3)(3x + 2) = 0$
    $4x - 3 = 0$ or $3x + 2 = 0$
    $4x = 3$ $\quad 3x = -2$
    $x = \frac{3}{4}$ $\quad x = -\frac{2}{3}$
    $\left\{\frac{3}{4}, -\frac{2}{3}\right\}$
25. $18s^2 + 72s = 0$
    $(18s)s + (18s)(4) = 0$
    $18s(s + 4) = 0$
    $18s = 0$ or $s + 4 = 0$
    $s = 0$ $\quad s = -4$
    $\{0, -4\}$
26. $4x^2 = 36$
    $4x^2 - 36 = 0$
    $4(x^2 - 9) = 0$
    $4[(x)^2 - (3)^2] = 0$
    $4(x + 3)(x - 3) = 0$
    $x + 3 = 0$ or $x - 3 = 0$
    $x = -3$ $\quad x = 3$
    $\{-3, 3\}$
27. $t^2 + 25 = 10t$
    $t^2 - 10t + 25 = 0$
    $(t)^2 - 2(t)(5) + (5)^2 = 0$
    $(t - 5)^2 = 0$
    $t - 5 = 0$
    $t = 5$
    $\{5\}$
28. $a^2 - 9a - 52 = 0$
    $(a + 4)(a - 13) = 0$
    $a + 4 = 0$ or $a - 13 = 0$
    $a = -4$ $\quad a = 13$
    $\{-4, 13\}$
29. $x^3 - 5x^2 - 66x = 0$
    $x(x^2 - 5x - 66) = 0$
    $x(x - 11)(x + 6) = 0$
    $x = 0$ or $x - 11 = 0$ or $x + 6 = 0$
    $x = 11$ $\quad x = -6$
    $\{-6, 0, 11\}$
30. $2x^2 = 9x + 5$
    $2x^2 - 9x - 5 = 0$
    $(2x + 1)(x - 5) = 0$
    $2x + 1 = 0$ or $x - 5 = 0$
    $2x = -1$ $\quad x = 5$
    $x = -\frac{1}{2}$
    $\left\{-\frac{1}{2}, 5\right\}$

31. $3b^2 + 6 = 11b$

$3b^2 - 11b + 6 = 0$

$(3b - 2)(b - 3) = 0$

$3b - 2 = 0$ or $b - 3 = 0$

$b = \frac{2}{3}$ $\qquad$ $b = 3$

$\left\{\frac{2}{3}, 3\right\}$

32. Let x = the amount of increase.

$(4 + x)(7 + x) = 4(7) + 26$

$x^2 + 4x + 7x + 28 = 28 + 26$

$x^2 + 11x + 28 = 54$

$x^2 + 11x - 26 = 0$

$(x - 2)(x + 13) = 0$

$x - 2 = 0$ or $x + 13 = 0$

$x = 2$ $\qquad$ $x = -13$

$4 + x = 4 + 2$ or 6 in.

$7 + x = 7 + 2$ or 9 in.

6 in. by 9 in.

33.

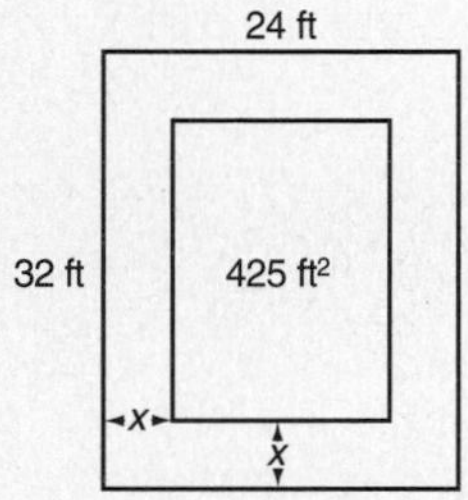

Let x = the width of the walk.

$(32 - 2x)(24 - 2x) = 425$

$768 - 64x - 48x + 4x^2 = 425$

$4x^2 - 112x + 768 = 425$

$4x^2 - 112x + 343 = 0$

$(2x - 7)(2x - 49) = 0$

$2x - 7 = 0$ or $2x - 49 = 0$

$x = \frac{7}{2}$ $\qquad$ $x = \frac{49}{2}$

The width of the walk will be $\frac{7}{2}$ or 3.5 ft.

Page 797 Chapter 11 Test

1. $y = x^2 - 4x + 13$, $a = 1$, $b = -4$

axis of symmetry: $x = -\frac{b}{2a} = -\frac{(-4)}{2(1)}$ or $x = 2$

$y = x^2 - 4x + 13$

$= (2)^2 - 4(2) + 13$

$= 4 - 8 + 13$ or 9

The coordinates of the vertex are (2, 9), minimum.

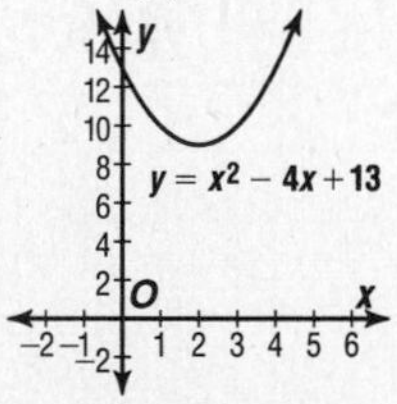

2. $y = -3x^2 - 6x + 4$, $a = -3$, $b = -6$

axis of symmetry: $x = -\frac{b}{2a} = -\frac{(-6)}{2(-3)}$ or $x = -1$

$y = -3x^2 - 6x + 4$

$= -3(-1)^2 - 6(-1) + 4$

$= -3 + 6 + 4$ or 7

The coordinates of the vertex are (−1, 7), maximum.

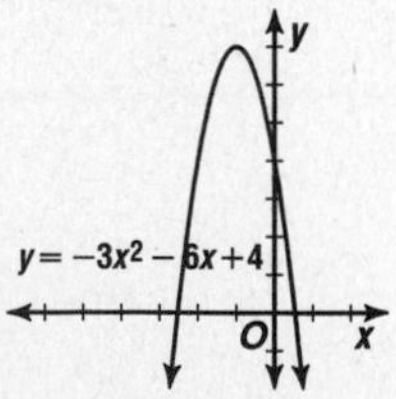

3. $y = 2x^2 + 3$, $a = 2$, $b = 0$

axis of symmetry: $x = -\frac{b}{2a} = -\frac{0}{2(2)}$ or $x = 0$

$y = 2x^2 + 3$

$= 2(0)^2 + 3$

$= 3$

The coordinates of the vertex are (0, 3), minimum.

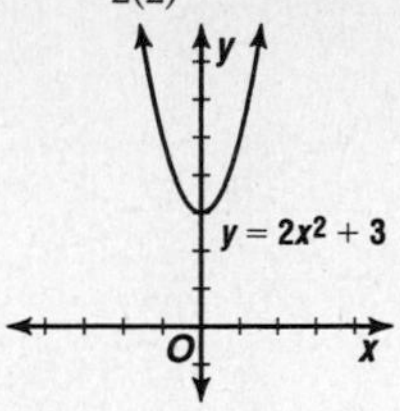

4. $y = -1(x - 2)^2 + 1$

$= -1(x^2 - 4x + 4) + 1$

$= -x^2 + 4x - 4 + 1$

$= -x^2 + 4x - 3$; $a = -1$, $b = 4$

axis of symmetry: $x = -\frac{b}{2a} = -\frac{4}{2(-1)}$ or $x = 2$

$y = -1(x - 2)^2 + 1$

$= -1(2 - 2)^2 + 1$

$= 1$

The coordinates of the vertex are (2, 1) maximum.

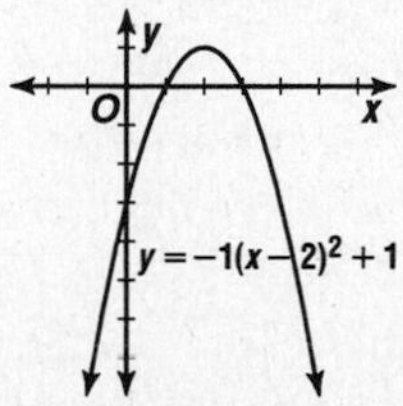

5.

x	$f(x)$
−1	5
0	2
1	1
2	2

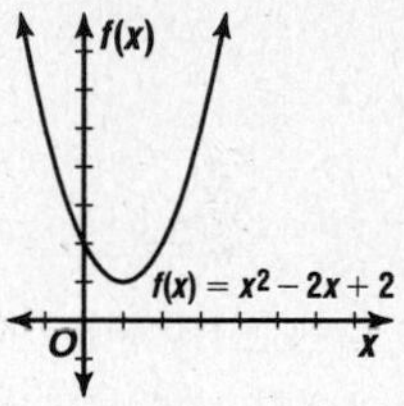

roots: ∅

$f(x) = x^2 - 2x + 2$

axis of symmetry: $x = -\frac{b}{2a} = -\frac{(-2)}{2(1)}$ or $x = 1$

vertex: (1, 1)

6.

x	$f(x)$
−5	2
−4	−1
−3	−2
−2	−1
−1	2

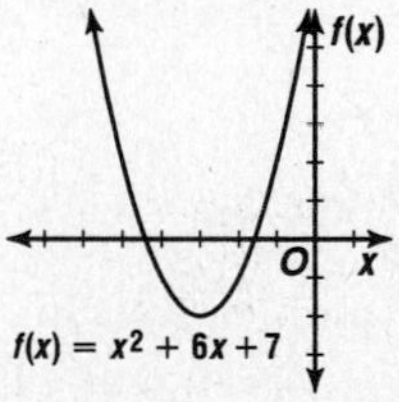

roots: $-5 < x < -4$

$-2 < x < -1$

$f(x) = x^2 + 6x + 7$

axis of symmetry: $x = -\frac{b}{2a} = -\frac{6}{2(1)}$ or $x = -3$

vertex: (−3, −2)

7.

x	$f(x)$
−14	4
−13	1
−12	0
−11	1
−10	4

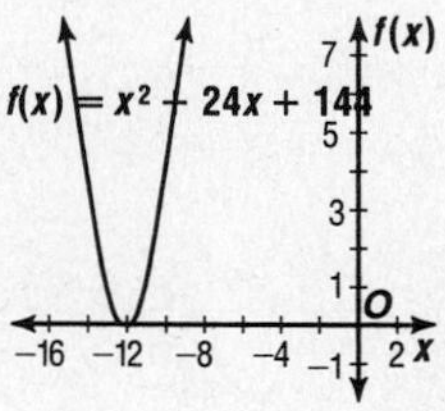

root: −12

$f(x) = x^2 + 24x + 144$

axis of symmetry: $x = -\frac{b}{2a} = -\frac{24}{2(1)}$ or $x = -12$

vertex: (−12, 0)

8.

x	$f(x)$
−3	0
−2	−18
−1	−32
0	−42
1	−48
2	−50
3	−48
4	−42
5	−32
6	−18
7	0

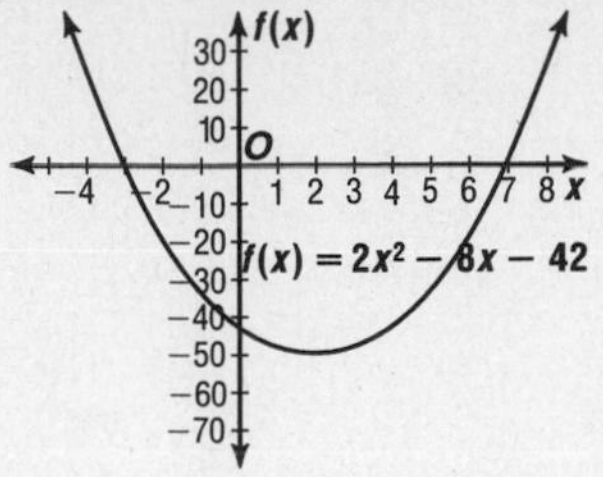

roots: −3, 7

$f(x) = 2x^2 - 8x - 42$

axis of symmetry: $x = -\frac{b}{2a} = -\frac{(-8)}{2(2)}$ or $x = 2$

vertex: (2, −50)

9. $x^2 + 7x + 6 = 0$

$a = 1, b = 7, c = 6$

$x = \frac{-7 \pm \sqrt{(7)^2 - 4(1)(6)}}{2(1)}$

$= \frac{-7 \pm \sqrt{25}}{2}$

$x = \frac{-7 + 5}{2}$ or $x = \frac{-7 - 5}{2}$

$= -1$ $\quad$ $= -6$

10. $2x^2 - 5x - 12 = 0$

$a = 2, b = -5, c = -12$

$x = \frac{-(-5) \pm \sqrt{(-5)^2 - 4(2)(-12)}}{2(2)}$

$= \frac{5 \pm \sqrt{121}}{4}$

$x = \frac{5 + 11}{4}$ or $x = \frac{5 - 11}{4}$

$= 4$ $\quad$ $= -\frac{3}{2}$

11. $6n^2 + 7n = 20$

$6n^2 + 7n - 20 = 0$

$a = 6, b = 7, c = -20$

$n = \frac{-7 \pm \sqrt{(7)^2 - 4(6)(-20)}}{2(6)}$

$= \frac{-7 \pm \sqrt{529}}{12}$

$n = \frac{-7 + 23}{12}$ or $n = \frac{-7 - 23}{12}$

$= \frac{4}{3}$ $\quad$ $= -\frac{5}{2}$

12. $3k^2 + 2k = 5$

$3k^2 + 2k - 5 = 0$

$a = 3, b = 2, c = -5$

$k = \frac{-2 \pm \sqrt{(2)^2 - 4(3)(-5)}}{2(3)}$

$= \frac{-2 \pm \sqrt{64}}{6}$

$k = \frac{-2 + 8}{6}$ or $k = \frac{-2 - 8}{6}$

$= 1$ $\quad$ $= -\frac{5}{3}$

13. $y^2 - \frac{3y}{5} + \frac{2}{25} = 0$

$25y^2 - 15y + 2 = 0$

$a = 25, b = -15, c = 2$

$y = \frac{-(-15) \pm \sqrt{(-15)^2 - 4(25)(2)}}{2(25)}$

$= \frac{15 \pm 5}{50}$

$y = \frac{15 + 5}{50}$ or $y = \frac{15 - 5}{50}$

$= \frac{2}{5}$ $\quad$ $= \frac{1}{5}$

14. $-3x^2 + 5 = 14x$

$3x^2 + 14x - 5 = 0$

$a = 3, b = 14, c = -5$

$x = \frac{-14 \pm \sqrt{(14)^2 - 4(3)(-5)}}{2(3)}$

$= \frac{-14 \pm \sqrt{256}}{6}$

$x = \frac{-14 + 16}{6}$ or $x = \frac{-14 - 16}{6}$

$= \frac{1}{3}$ $\quad$ $= -5$

15. $4^{x-2} = 16^{2x+5}$

$4^{x-2} = (4^2)^{2x+5}$

$4^{x-2} = 4^{4x+10}$

$x - 2 = 4x + 10$

$-12 = 3x$

$-4 = x$

16. $1000^x = 10{,}000^{6x+4}$

$10^{3x} = (10^4)^{6x+4}$

$10^{3x} = 10^{24x+16}$

$3x = 24x + 16$

$-21x = 16$

$x = -\frac{16}{21}$

17. $5^{x^2} = 5^{15-2x}$

$x^2 = 15 - 2x$

$x^2 + 2x - 15 = 0$

$(x + 5)(x - 3) = 0$

$x + 5 = 0$ or $x - 3 = 0$

$x = -5$ $\quad$ $x = 3$

18. $\left(\frac{1}{2}\right)^{x-2} = 4^{5x}$

$(2^{-1})^{x-2} = (2^2)^{5x}$

$2^{-x+2} = 2^{10x}$

$-x + 2 = 10x$

$2 = 11x$

$\frac{2}{11} = x$

19.

x	$f(x)$
−2	4
−1	2
0	1
1	0.5
2	0.25

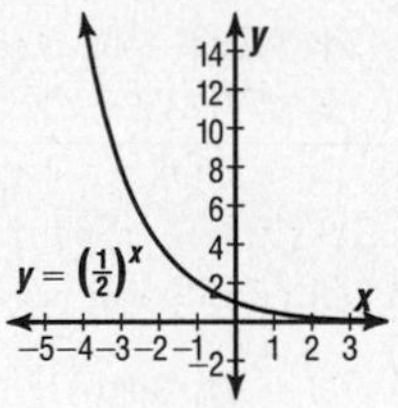

The y-intercept is 1.

20. $y = 4 \cdot 2^x$

x	$f(x)$
−2	1
−1	2
0	4
1	8
2	16

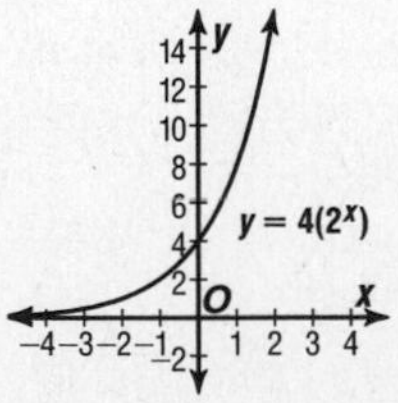

The y-intercept is 4.

21. $y = \left(\frac{1}{3}\right)^x - 3$

x	y
-2	6
-1	0
0	-2
1	$-2\frac{2}{3}$
2	$-2\frac{8}{9}$

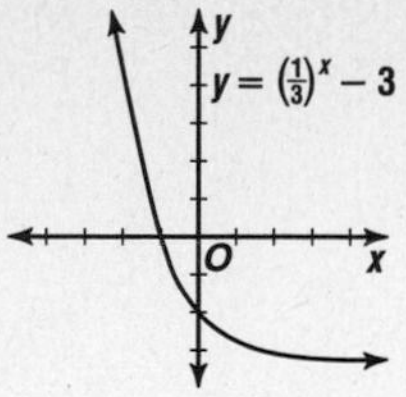

The y-intercept is -2.

22. $A = C(1 - r)^t$

$C = 17{,}369,\ r = 0.16,\ t = 2$

Depreciated price $= 17{,}369(0.84)^2$

$= \$12{,}255$

$\$14{,}458 - \$12{,}255 = \$2202$

The depreciated value is \$2202 less than the buyout price.

23. Let x = the side of a square.

$$x^2 = \frac{1}{2}(x + 2)(x + 3)$$
$$2x^2 = (x + 2)(x + 3)$$
$$2x^2 = x^2 + 5x + 6$$
$$x^2 - 5x - 6 = 0$$
$$(x - 6)(x + 1) = 0$$

$x - 6 = 0$ or $x + 1 = 0$

$x = 6$ $\quad$ $x = -1$

The dimensions are 6 cm by 6 cm.

24. Let x = one integer; then $21 - x$ = the other integer.

$$x(21 - x) = 90$$
$$21x - x^2 = 90$$
$$x^2 - 21x + 90 = 0$$
$$(x - 6)(x - 15) = 0$$

$x - 6 = 0$ or $x - 15 = 0$

$x = 6$ $\quad$ $x = 15$

The two integers are 6 and 15.

25. $A = P\left(1 + \frac{r}{n}\right)^{nt}$

$A = 8479,\ r = 0.09,\ t = 6,\ n = 2$

$$8479 = P\left(1 + \frac{0.09}{2}\right)^{2(6)}$$
$$8479 = P(1.045)^{12}$$
$$\$5000 \approx P$$

The original amount was \$5000.

Page 798 Chapter 12 Test

1. $\frac{5 - 2m}{6m - 15} = \frac{-1(2m - 5)}{3(2m - 5)}$

$= \frac{-1(\cancel{2m - 5})^{1}}{3(\cancel{2m - 5})_{1}}$

$= -\frac{1}{3};\ m \neq \frac{5}{2}$

excluded values:

$6m - 15 = 0$

$m = \frac{5}{2}$

2. $\frac{3 + x}{2x^2 + 5x - 3} = \frac{3 + x}{(3 + x)(2x - 1)}$

$= \frac{\cancel{3 + x}^{1}}{(\cancel{3 + x})_{1}(2x - 1)}$

$= \frac{1}{2x - 1}$

excluded values:

$2x^2 + 5x - 3 = 0$

$(3 + x)(2x - 1) = 0$

$3 + x = 0$ or $2x - 1 = 0$

$x = -3$ $\quad$ $x = \frac{1}{2}$

$x \neq \frac{1}{2}, -3$

3. $\frac{4c^2 + 12c + 9}{2c^2 - 11c - 21} = \frac{\cancel{(2c + 3)^2}^{(2c + 3)}}{(\cancel{2c + 3})_{1}(c - 7)}$

$= \frac{2c + 3}{c - 7}$

excluded values:

$2c^2 - 11c - 21 = 0$

$(2c + 3)(c - 7) = 0$

$2c + 3 = 0$ or $c - 7 = 0$

$c = -\frac{3}{2}$ $\quad$ $c - 7$

$c \neq -\frac{3}{2}, 7$

4. $\frac{1 - \frac{9}{t}}{1 - \frac{81}{t^2}} = \frac{\frac{t}{t} - \frac{9}{t}}{\frac{t^2}{t^2} - \frac{81}{t^2}}$

$= \frac{\frac{t - 9}{t}}{\frac{t^2 - 81}{t^2}}$

$= \frac{t - 9}{t} \div \frac{t^2 - 81}{t^2}$

$= \frac{t - 9}{t} \cdot \frac{t^2}{t^2 - 81}$

$= \frac{\cancel{t - 9}^{1}}{\cancel{t}_{1}} \cdot \frac{\cancel{t^2}^{t}}{(t + 9)(\cancel{t - 9})_{1}}$

$= \frac{t}{t + 9}$

5. $\frac{\frac{5}{6} + \frac{u}{t}}{\frac{2u}{t} - 3} = \frac{\frac{5(t)}{6(t)} + \frac{u(6)}{t(6)}}{\frac{2u}{t} - \frac{3t}{t}}$

$= \frac{\frac{5t + 6u}{6t}}{\frac{2u - 3t}{t}}$

$= \frac{5t + 6u}{6t} \div \frac{2u - 3t}{t}$

$= \frac{5t + 6u}{6\cancel{t}_{1}} \cdot \frac{\cancel{t}^{1}}{2u - 3t}$

$= \frac{6u + 5t}{6(2u - 3t)}$

$= \frac{6u + 5t}{12u - 18t}$

6. $\dfrac{x + 4 + \dfrac{5}{x-2}}{x + 6 + \dfrac{15}{x-2}} = \dfrac{\dfrac{(x+4)(x-2)}{(x-2)} + \dfrac{5}{x-2}}{\dfrac{(x+6)(x-2)}{(x-2)} + \dfrac{15}{x-2}}$

$= \dfrac{\dfrac{(x+4)(x-2) + 5}{x-2}}{\dfrac{(x+6)(x-2) + 15}{x-2}}$

$= \dfrac{x^2 + 2x - 3}{x - 2} \div \dfrac{x^2 + 4x + 3}{x - 2}$

$= \dfrac{x^2 + 2x - 3}{x - 2} \cdot \dfrac{x - 2}{x^2 + 4x + 3}$

$= \dfrac{\overset{1}{\cancel{(x + 3)}}(x - 1)}{\underset{1}{\cancel{x - 2}}} \cdot \dfrac{\overset{1}{\cancel{x - 2}}}{\underset{1}{\cancel{(x + 3)}}(x + 1)}$

$= \dfrac{x - 1}{x + 1}$

7. $\dfrac{2x}{x - 7} - \dfrac{14}{x - 7} = \dfrac{2x - 14}{x - 7}$

$= \dfrac{2(x - 7)}{x - 7}$

$= \dfrac{2\overset{1}{\cancel{(x - 7)}}}{\underset{1}{\cancel{x - 7}}}$

$= 2$

8. $\dfrac{n + 3}{2n - 8} \cdot \dfrac{6n - 24}{2n + 1} = \dfrac{n + 3}{\underset{1}{\cancel{2(n - 4)}}} \cdot \dfrac{\overset{3}{\cancel{6}}\overset{1}{\cancel{(n - 4)}}}{2n + 1}$

$= \dfrac{3(n + 3)}{2n + 1}$

$= \dfrac{3n + 9}{2n + 1}$

9.
$$\begin{array}{r}
5m + 12 \\
2m - 3 \overline{)10m^2 + 9m - 36} \\
\underline{(-)10m^2 - 15m} \\
24m - 36 \\
\underline{(-)24m - 36} \\
0
\end{array}$$

10. $\dfrac{x^2 + 4x - 32}{x + 5} \cdot \dfrac{x - 3}{x^2 - 7x + 12} = \dfrac{(x + 8)(x - 4)}{x + 5} \cdot \dfrac{x - 3}{(x - 3)(x - 4)}$

$= \dfrac{(x + 8)\overset{1}{\cancel{(x - 4)}}}{x + 5} \cdot \dfrac{\overset{1}{\cancel{x - 3}}}{\underset{1}{\cancel{(x - 3)}}\underset{1}{\cancel{(x - 4)}}}$

$= \dfrac{x + 8}{x + 5}$

11. $\dfrac{z^2 + 2z - 15}{z^2 + 9z + 20} \div (z - 3) = \dfrac{(z + 5)(z - 3)}{(z + 5)(z + 4)} \cdot \dfrac{1}{z - 3}$

$= \dfrac{\overset{1}{\cancel{(z + 5)}}\overset{1}{\cancel{(z - 3)}}}{\underset{1}{\cancel{(z + 5)}}(z + 4)} \cdot \dfrac{1}{\underset{1}{\cancel{z - 3}}}$

$= \dfrac{1}{z + 4}$

12. $\dfrac{4x^2 + 11x + 6}{x^2 - x - 6} \div \dfrac{x^2 + 8x + 16}{x^2 + x - 12}$

$= \dfrac{4x^2 + 11x + 6}{x^2 - x - 6} \cdot \dfrac{x^2 + x - 12}{x^2 + 8x + 16}$

$= \dfrac{(4x + 3)(x + 2)}{(x - 3)(x + 2)} \cdot \dfrac{(x + 4)(x - 3)}{(x + 4)^2}$

$= \dfrac{(4x + 3)\overset{1}{\cancel{(x + 2)}}}{\underset{1}{\cancel{(x - 3)}}\underset{1}{\cancel{(x + 2)}}} \cdot \dfrac{\overset{1}{\cancel{(x + 4)}}\overset{1}{\cancel{(x - 3)}}}{\underset{(x + 4)}{\cancel{(x + 4)^2}}}$

$= \dfrac{4x + 3}{x + 4}$

13. $(10z^4 + 5z^3 - z^2) \div 5z^3 = \dfrac{10z^4}{5z^3} + \dfrac{5z^3}{5z^3} - \dfrac{z^2}{5z^3}$

$= 2z + 1 - \dfrac{1}{5z}$

14. $\dfrac{y}{7y + 14} + \dfrac{6}{3y + 6} = \dfrac{y(3)}{7(y + 2)(3)} + \dfrac{6(7)}{3(y + 2)(7)}$ LCD: $21(y + 2)$

$= \dfrac{y(3) + 6(7)}{21(y + 2)}$

$= \dfrac{3y + 42}{21(y + 2)}$

$= \dfrac{\overset{1}{\cancel{3}}(y + 14)}{\underset{7}{\cancel{21}}(y + 2)}$

$= \dfrac{y + 14}{7y + 14}$

15. $\dfrac{x + 5}{x + 2} + 6 = \dfrac{x + 5}{x + 2} + \dfrac{6(x + 2)}{x + 2}$

$= \dfrac{x + 5 + 6(x + 2)}{x + 2}$

$= \dfrac{7x + 17}{x + 2}$

16. $\dfrac{x^2 - 1}{x + 1} - \dfrac{x^2 + 1}{x - 1} = \dfrac{\overset{1}{\cancel{(x + 1)}}(x - 1)}{\underset{}{\cancel{x + 1}}} - \dfrac{x^2 + 1}{x - 1}$ LCD: $x - 1$

$= x - 1 - \dfrac{x^2 + 1}{x - 1}$

$= \dfrac{(x - 1)(x - 1)}{(x - 1)} - \dfrac{x^2 + 1}{x - 1}$

$= \dfrac{(x - 1)(x - 1) - (x^2 + 1)}{x - 1}$

$= \dfrac{x^2 - 2x + 1 - x^2 - 1}{x - 1}$

$= \dfrac{-2x}{x - 1}$

17. $\dfrac{-3}{a - 5} + \dfrac{15}{a^2 - 5a} = \dfrac{-3(a)}{(a - 5)(a)} + \dfrac{15}{a(a - 5)}$ LCD: $a(a - 5)$

$= \dfrac{-3a + 15}{a(a - 5)}$

$= \dfrac{-3(a - 5)}{a(a - 5)}$

$= \dfrac{-3\overset{1}{\cancel{(a - 5)}}}{a\underset{1}{\cancel{(a - 5)}}}$

$= \dfrac{-3}{a}$

18. $\dfrac{8}{m^2} \cdot \left(\dfrac{m^2}{2c}\right)^2 = \dfrac{8}{m^2} \cdot \dfrac{m^4}{4c^2}$

$= \dfrac{8m^4}{4c^2m^2}$

$= \dfrac{\overset{2}{\cancel{8}}m^{\overset{2}{\cancel{4}}}}{\underset{1}{\cancel{4}}c^2m^{\underset{1}{\cancel{2}}}}$

$= \dfrac{2m^2}{c^2}$

19. $\dfrac{2}{3t} + \dfrac{1}{2} = \dfrac{3}{4t}$ LCD: $12t$

$12t\left(\dfrac{2}{3t} + \dfrac{1}{2}\right) = \left(\dfrac{3}{4t}\right)12t$

$4(2) + 6t(1) = 3(3)$

$8 + 6t = 9$

$6t = 1$

$t = \dfrac{1}{6}$

20. LCD: $(e - 4)(e + 5)$

$\dfrac{2e}{e - 4} - 2 = \dfrac{4}{e + 5}$

$(e - 4)(e + 5)\left(\dfrac{2e}{e - 4} - 2\right) = \left(\dfrac{4}{e + 5}\right)(e - 4)(e + 5)$

$2e(e + 5) - 2(e - 4)(e + 5) = 4(e - 4)$

$2e^2 + 10e - 2(e^2 + e - 20) = 4e - 16$

$2e^2 + 10e - 2e^2 - 2e + 40 = 4e - 16$

$8e + 40 = 4e - 16$

$4e = -56$

$e = -14$

21. $\frac{4}{h-4} = \frac{3h}{h+3}$
$4(h+3) = 3h(h-4)$
$4h + 12 = 3h^2 - 12h$
$0 = 3h^2 - 16h - 12$
$0 = (h-6)(3h+2)$
$h - 6 = 0$ or $3h + 2 = 0$
$h = 6$ $h = -\frac{2}{3}$

22. $F = G\left(\frac{Mm}{d^2}\right)$
$\left(\frac{d^2}{Mm}\right)F = G\left(\frac{Mm}{d^2}\right)\left(\frac{d^2}{Mm}\right)$
$\frac{Fd^2}{Mm} = G$
$G = \frac{Fd^2}{Mm}$

23. $\frac{1}{R_T} = \frac{1}{R_1} + \frac{1}{R_2}$
$R_TR_1R_2\left(\frac{1}{R_T}\right) = \left(\frac{1}{R_1} + \frac{1}{R_2}\right)R_TR_1R_2$
$R_1R_2 = R_TR_2 + R_TR_1$
$R_1R_2 - R_TR_2 = R_TR_1$
$R_2(R_1 - R_T) = R_TR_1$
$\frac{R_2(R_1 - R_T)}{(R_1 - R_T)} = \frac{R_TR_1}{(R_1 - R_T)}$
$R_2 = \frac{R_TR_1}{R_1 - R_T}$

24. $\frac{1}{6} + \frac{1}{4.5} = \frac{1}{x}$
$27x\left(\frac{1}{6} + \frac{1}{4.5}\right) = \frac{1}{x}(27x)$
$4.5x + 6x = 27$
$10.5x = 27$
$105x = 270$
$x = 2\frac{4}{7}$ hours

25. $\frac{1}{R_T} = \frac{1}{R_1} + \frac{1}{R_2} + \frac{1}{R_3}$
$\frac{1}{R_T} = \frac{1}{120} + \frac{1}{20} + \frac{1}{12}$
$\frac{1}{R_T} = \frac{2}{240} + \frac{12}{240} + \frac{20}{240}$
$\frac{1}{R_T} = \frac{34}{240}$
$34R_T = 240$
$R_T = 7\frac{1}{17}$ ohms

Page 799 Chapter 13 Test

1. $\sqrt{480} = \sqrt{4^2 \cdot 2 \cdot 3 \cdot 5}$
$= \sqrt{4^2} \cdot \sqrt{2 \cdot 3 \cdot 5}$
$= 4\sqrt{30}$

2. $\sqrt{72} \cdot \sqrt{48} = \sqrt{6^2 \cdot 2 \cdot 4^2 \cdot 3}$
$= \sqrt{6^2} \cdot \sqrt{4^2} \cdot \sqrt{2 \cdot 3}$
$= 6 \cdot 4 \cdot \sqrt{6}$
$= 24\sqrt{6}$

3. $\sqrt{54x^4y} = \sqrt{3^2 \cdot 6 \cdot x^4 \cdot y}$
$= \sqrt{3^2} \cdot \sqrt{x^4} \cdot \sqrt{6 \cdot y}$
$= 3x^2\sqrt{6y}$

4. $\sqrt{\frac{32}{25}} = \frac{\sqrt{32}}{\sqrt{25}}$
$= \frac{\sqrt{4^2 \cdot 2}}{5}$
$= \frac{4\sqrt{2}}{5}$

5. $\sqrt{\frac{3x^2}{4n^3}} = \frac{\sqrt{3x^2}}{\sqrt{4n^3}}$
$= \frac{\sqrt{x^2} \cdot \sqrt{3}}{\sqrt{4} \cdot \sqrt{n^2} \cdot \sqrt{n}}$
$= \frac{|x|\sqrt{3n}}{2n\sqrt{n}} \cdot \frac{\sqrt{n}}{\sqrt{n}}$
$= \frac{|x|\sqrt{3n}}{2n^2}$

6. $\sqrt{6} + \sqrt{\frac{2}{3}} = \sqrt{6} + \frac{\sqrt{2}}{\sqrt{3}} \cdot \frac{\sqrt{3}}{\sqrt{3}}$
$= \sqrt{6} + \frac{\sqrt{6}}{3}$
$= \frac{3\sqrt{6}}{3} + \frac{\sqrt{6}}{3}$
$= \frac{4\sqrt{6}}{3}$

7. $(x + \sqrt{3})^2 = x^2 + 2(x)(\sqrt{3}) + (\sqrt{3})^2$
$= x^2 + 2x\sqrt{3} + 3$

8. $\frac{7}{7+\sqrt{5}} = \frac{7}{7+\sqrt{5}} \cdot \frac{7-\sqrt{5}}{7-\sqrt{5}}$
$= \frac{7(7) - 7\sqrt{5}}{7^2 - (\sqrt{5})^2}$
$= \frac{49 - 7\sqrt{5}}{49 - 5}$
$= \frac{49 - 7\sqrt{5}}{44}$

9. $3\sqrt{50} - 2\sqrt{8} = 3\sqrt{5^2 \cdot 2} - 2\sqrt{2^2 \cdot 2}$
$= 3(\sqrt{5^2} \cdot \sqrt{2}) - 2(\sqrt{2^2} \cdot \sqrt{2})$
$= 3(5\sqrt{2}) - 2(2\sqrt{2})$
$= 15\sqrt{2} - 4\sqrt{2}$
$= 11\sqrt{2}$

10. $\sqrt{\frac{10}{3}} \cdot \sqrt{\frac{4}{30}} = \sqrt{\frac{40}{90}}$
$= \sqrt{\frac{4}{9}}$
$= \frac{2}{3}$

11. $2\sqrt{27} + \sqrt{63} - 4\sqrt{3}$
$= 2\sqrt{3^2 \cdot 3} + \sqrt{3^2 \cdot 7} - 4\sqrt{3}$
$= 2(\sqrt{3^2} \cdot \sqrt{3}) + \sqrt{3^2} \cdot \sqrt{7} - 4\sqrt{3}$
$= 2(3\sqrt{3}) + 3\sqrt{7} - 4\sqrt{3}$
$= 6\sqrt{3} - 4\sqrt{3} + 3\sqrt{7}$
$= 2\sqrt{3} + 3\sqrt{7}$

12. $(1 - \sqrt{3})(3 + \sqrt{2})$
$= 1(3) + 1(\sqrt{2}) + (-\sqrt{3})(3) + (-\sqrt{3})(\sqrt{2})$
$= 3 + \sqrt{2} - 3\sqrt{3} - \sqrt{6}$

13. $d = \sqrt{(x_2 - x_1)^2 + (y_2 - y_1)^2}$
$= \sqrt{(4-4)^2 + (-2-7)^2}$
$= \sqrt{0^2 + (-9)^2}$
$= \sqrt{81}$
$= 9$

14. $d = \sqrt{(x_2 - x_1)^2 + (y_2 - y_1)^2}$

$= \sqrt{\left(-9 - \frac{2}{3}\right)^2 + \left(2 - \frac{1}{2}\right)^2}$

$= \sqrt{\left(-\frac{29}{3}\right)^2 + \left(\frac{3}{2}\right)^2}$

$= \sqrt{\frac{841}{9} + \frac{9}{4}}$

$= \sqrt{\frac{3445}{36}} = \frac{\sqrt{3445}}{6}$

15. $d = \sqrt{(x_2 - x_1)^2 + (y_2 - y_1)^2}$

$= \sqrt{(-1 - 1)^2 + [1 - (-5)]^2}$

$= \sqrt{(-2)^2 + 6^2}$

$= \sqrt{4 + 36}$

$= \sqrt{40}$ or $2\sqrt{10}$

16. $c^2 = a^2 + b^2$

$c^2 = 8^2 + 10^2$

$c^2 = 64 + 100$

$c^2 = 164$

$c = \sqrt{164}$

$c = 2\sqrt{41} \approx 12.81$

17. $c^2 = a^2 + b^2$

$20^2 = 12^2 + b^2$

$400 = 144 + b^2$

$256 = b^2$

$\sqrt{256} = b$

$16 = b$

18. $c^2 = a^2 + b^2$

$12^2 = (6\sqrt{2})^2 + b^2$

$144 = 72 + b^2$

$72 = b^2$

$\sqrt{72} = b$

$b = 6\sqrt{2} \approx 8.49$

19. $c^2 = a^2 + b^2$

$17^2 = a^2 + 13^2$

$289 = a^2 + 169$

$120 = a^2$

$a = \sqrt{120}$

$a = 2\sqrt{30} \approx 10.95$

20. $\sqrt{4x + 1} = 5$

$(\sqrt{4x + 1})^2 = 5^2$

$4x + 1 = 25$

$4x = 24$

$x = 6$

21. $\sqrt{4x - 3} = 6 - x$

$(\sqrt{4x - 3})^2 = (6 - x)^2$

$4x - 3 = 36 - 12x + x^2$

$0 = x^2 - 16x + 39$

$0 = (x - 3)(x - 13)$

$x - 3 = 0$ or $x - 13 = 0$

$x = 3$ $\quad$ $x = 13$

Since 13 does not satisfy the original equation, the only solution is 3.

22. $y^2 - 5 = -8y$

$y^2 + 8y = 5$

$y^2 + 8y + 16 = 5 + 16$

$(y + 4)^2 = 21$

$y + 4 = \pm\sqrt{21}$

$y = -4 \pm \sqrt{21}$

23. $2x^2 - 10x - 3 = 0$

$x^2 - 5x - \frac{3}{2} = 0$

$x^2 - 5x = \frac{3}{2}$

$x^2 - 5x + \frac{25}{4} = \frac{3}{2} + \frac{25}{4}$

$\left(x - \frac{5}{2}\right)^2 = \frac{31}{4}$

$x - \frac{5}{2} = \pm\sqrt{\frac{31}{4}}$

$x = \frac{5}{2} \pm \frac{\sqrt{31}}{2}$

24. $P = 2l + 2w$

$= 2(2\sqrt{32} - 3\sqrt{6}) + 2(\sqrt{6})$

$= 4\sqrt{32} - 6\sqrt{6} + 2\sqrt{6}$

$= 4\sqrt{4^2 \cdot 2} - 6\sqrt{6} + 2\sqrt{6}$

$= 4(4\sqrt{2}) - 6\sqrt{6} + 2\sqrt{6}$

$= 16\sqrt{2} - 4\sqrt{6}$

$A = lw$

$= \sqrt{6}(2\sqrt{32} - 3\sqrt{6})$

$= 2\sqrt{192} - 18$

$= 2\sqrt{8^2 \cdot 3} - 18$

$= 2(8\sqrt{3}) - 18$

$= 16\sqrt{3} - 18$

25. $c^2 = a^2 + b^2$

$c^2 = 9^2 + 12^2$

$c^2 = 81 + 144$

$c^2 = 225$

$c = \sqrt{225} = 15$ miles

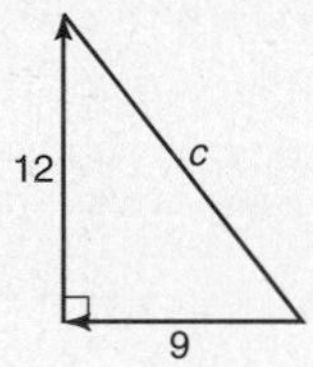